Praise for Werner & Jones!

"I felt that the author was talking to me. The writing style is clear and effective and supports effective teaching. The use of well-known companies throughout gives more credibility to the reading. **I have used many introductory texts and I feel that this is one of the best presentations."**

— A. J. Potts, Uni

"I believe there are two topics that present the greatest difficulty for ... cash versus accrual bases of accounting. The second is the process of ... via debits and credits, normalization, and posting the ledger. **The We ... both of these issues better than my current text."**

— Marshall Pitman, University of Texas–San Antonio

"Chapter F11 is excellent! It gives a very good description of where to look for information of a nonfinancial nature. This is an unusual asset in a beginning accounting text, and the authors should be congratulated. **This one chapter is enough to justify buying the book."**

— Harold Wyman, Florida International University

"This is my favorite Management Accounting text today.... I find that the Werner/Jones text is perfect for my class—it provides all the material we need in a text that is easy (and almost fun!) to read."

— Mark Bettini, University of California–Berkeley

"Chapter M8 includes the best discussion of Capital Budgeting I have ever seen. I particularly like the explanation of the source and calculation of the cost of capital."

— Michael Palma, Gwinett Technical College, Lawrenceville, GA

"It is my personal belief that the 'Analyzing of Financial Statements' chapter is the most important chapter in the course. After all, what's it all about if a student doesn't know how to use the financial statements to make important business decisions about a company?... Trying to be objective, **I must tell you that Werner and Jones have done an excellent job in this chapter."**

— Ken Couvillion, San Joaquin Delta College

"I enjoyed reading the chapter [on relevant costing]. It takes a step-by-step approach for each example, and the authors did a good job teaching the material."

— Cheryl Mitchem, Virginia State University

"The authors have explained the complex subject of ABC overhead allocation with clear and concise examples (Chapter M4)."

— Sally J. Nelson, Northeast Iowa Community College

"The authors have done an excellent job of taking complex concepts (Chapter M5, Cost Behavior) and making them very easy to understand. The explanation of relevant range is very good. By using a step-by-step approach in the explanations, the text makes it unnecessary to spend large amounts of class time going through examples and frees up more time to work on discussion of concepts."

— Ann Selk, University of Wisconsin–Green Bay

Introduction to Accounting

A User Perspective

Introduction to Accounting

A User Perspective

SECOND EDITION

Michael L. Werner

University of Miami

Kumen H. Jones

Arizona State University, Retired

PEARSON

Prentice Hall

Upper Saddle River, NJ 07458

Library of Congress Cataloging-in-Publication Data
Werner, Michael L.
    Introduction to accounting : a user perspective / Michael L. Werner, Kumen
H. Jones.—2nd ed.
        p. cm.
    Rev. ed. of: Introduction to accounting / Kumen H. Jones . . . [et al.]. c2000.
    Includes bibliographical references and index.
    ISBN 0-13-032758-1
        1. Accounting 2. Accounting—United States. I. Jones, Kumen H. II. Introduction to accounting.
    III. Title.
HF5635.I654 2003
657—dc21

                                                                    2003049850

Executive Editor: Mac Mendelsohn
Editor-in-Chief: P. J. Boardman
Assistant Editor: Sam Goffinet
Senior Editorial Assistant: Jane Avery
Development Editor: Amy Whitaker
Senior Media Project Manager: Nancy Welcher
Executive Marketing Manager: Beth Toland
Marketing Assistant: Patrick Danzuso
Managing Editor (Production): John Roberts
Production Editor: Kelly Warsak

Production Assistant: Joe DeProspero
Permissions Supervisor: Suzanne Grappi
Manufacturing Buyer: Michelle Klein
Art Director: Jayne Conte
Cover Illustration: Getty Images, Inc.
Composition/Full-Service Project Management:
Linda Begley/Rainbow Graphics

Credits and acknowledgments borrowed from other sources and reproduced, with permission, in this textbook appear on appropriate page within text.

Pearson Prentice Hall™ is a trademark of Pearson Education, Inc.
Pearson® is a registered trademark of Pearson plc
Prentice Hall® is a registered trademark of Pearson Education, Inc.

Pearson Education LTD.
Pearson Education Singapore, Pte. Ltd
Pearson Education, Canada, Ltd
Pearson Education—Japan

Pearson Education Australia PTY, Limited
Pearson Education North Asia Ltd
Pearson Educación de Mexico, S.A. de C.V.
Pearson Education Malaysia, Pte. Ltd

ISBN 0-13-032758-1

Dedication

To the younger generation of my family—Suzanne Elsea, Lauren Elsea, Jessica Werner, Amanda Werner, Jason Hinds, and Ashley Hinds.

—Michael Werner

To Mary Ann.

—Kumen Jones

Contents

INTRODUCTION TO MANAGEMENT ACCOUNTING: A USER PERSPECTIVE

M–1

Preface

The world is changing, accounting education is changing, and so are accounting textbooks. Our book is no exception. In this edition, we have incorporated a number of changes that we believe will make this book an even better teaching resource than previous editions. In addition to rewriting much of the material for improved clarity, we have integrated coverage of the statement of cash flows and key financial ratios throughout the text. We've also consolidated the two balance sheet chapters into one. We've added significantly to the assignment material and improved its alignment with the topics covered in each chapter. We've revised the chapter opening vignettes to increase student interest and to suggest the need for the accounting applications covered in the chapters. We are sure you will find that these changes, along with many others, help make this text an easy-to-use tool to teach beginning accounting students.

◆ BASIC PHILOSOPHY

Businesspeople must be prepared to perform tasks that only people can perform; in particular, they must be able to communicate, to think, and to make solid, well-informed decisions. Decision making is the critical skill in today's business world, and *Introduction to Accounting: A User Perspective*. Second Edition, helps students to better use accounting information to improve their decision making skills.

This text provides an introduction to accounting within the context of business and business decisions. Readers will explore accounting information's role in the decision making process and learn how to use the accounting information found in financial statements and annual reports. Seeing how accounting information can be used to make better business decisions will benefit all students, regardless of their major course of study or chosen career.

We agree with the recommendations made by the Accounting Education Change Commission in its Position Statement No. Two: The First Course in Accounting. We believe the course should be a broad introduction to accounting, rather than introductory accounting as it has traditionally been taught. It should emphasize what accounting information is, why it is important, and how it is used by economic decision makers.

This text is purposely written so students will find it easy to read and understand. In this edition, many passages have been rewritten to further enhance readability and student understanding. In addition, we've included the exhibits necessary to get important points across, but we very intentionally have not included the array of glitz and graphics that can break up the flow and distract student attention. Generally, we have not segregated material into special presentation boxes that might be skipped by students attempting to focus on the most relevant points. All of the points of interest and examples we present are woven into the body of the text.

◆ SUPPORT FOR THE INTERACTIVE CLASSROOM

We believe this text provides tools to actively involve students in their learning processes. The conversational tone of the text, its user perspective, and the logical presentation of topics all contribute to the ability of this text to meet that goal. However, several features are particularly important in developing a classroom atmosphere in which students share ideas, ask questions, and relate their learning to the world around them.

Throughout each chapter of the text, you will find Discussion Questions (DQs) that challenge students to reach beyond the surface of the written text to determine answers. Far from typical review questions, for which the students can scan a few pages of the text to locate an answer, many of the DQs provide relevant learning by relating students' personal experiences to the knowledge they gain through the text. The DQs provide a variety of classroom experiences:

- Many DQs provide the basis for lively classroom discussions, requiring students to think about issues and formulate or defend their opinions.
- Some DQs are springboards for group assignments (in or out of the classroom) to put cooperative learning into practice.
- DQs may be assigned as individual writing assignments to allow students to practice and develop their writing skills.
- Combining individually written DQ responses with follow-up group discussions can spark lively debate!
- Having students keep a journal of their responses to all DQs (regardless of whether they are used in another way) encourages contemplation of accounting concepts.

The DQs comprise an important part of the text's pedagogy. They are designed to emphasize important points that students may skim across in their initial reading. Even if they are not formally part of the required work for your course, students will gain a greater understanding of the concepts discussed when they take time to consider each question as part of the text.

Students get enthused about accounting when working with real companies. Chapter F1 and its appendix provide students with the knowledge they need to use library and Internet resources to research real companies. The chapter also introduces students to the annual report and Form 10-K. We have included the 2002 *Pier 1 Imports, Inc.,* annual report with our text with the hope that instructors will find it a helpful resource for class examples. We've also used *Pier 1*'s annual report for selected assignment material and to demonstrate financial analysis in Chapter F11. Although companies generally do not publish their management accounting information, we've attempted to include a reasonable number of real-world examples in the management accounting chapters as well.

Aside from its support for the interactive classroom, a major distinction of this text is its total separation of the use of accounting information and its preparation.

◆ SEPARATION OF ACCOUNTING AND BOOKKEEPING

Coverage of recording procedures differs from school to school. Some schools choose to have all students learn basic accounting procedures; others require only accounting majors to acquire these skills. Our text offers institutions the flexibility to cover accounting procedures to a significant degree, to cover just the basics, or to omit the coverage of accounting procedures entirely. In this text, we do not use debits and credits or journal entries to demonstrate or explain characteristics and uses of accounting information. In fact, except in the accounting procedures chapter itself (Chapter F6), no references are made to the recording process except in chapter appendices. To facilitate the separation of accounting and bookkeeping, we introduce the accounting cycle in Chapter F6 and complete its coverage in appendices to Chapters F7, F8, F9, M2, M3, and M10.

We hold off coverage of accounting procedures until Chapter F6 to give students the chance to acquire the basic accounting background that will help make accounting procedures easier to comprehend and learn.

Institutions that choose not to teach recording procedures would simply omit Chapter F6 and these appendices from their course coverage.

For those institutions that would like to include accounting procedures in their introductory accounting curriculum, Chapter F6 and the appendices in the remainder of the book cover the complete accounting cycle from analyzing transactions through post-closing trial balance. Coverage includes debits and credits, journal entries, adjusting entries, posting to the general ledger, trial balance preparation, the worksheet, and financial statement preparation. Chapter F6 assignment material includes short, medium, and long accounting procedure problems. In addition, the chapter includes three substantial mini practice sets that take a student from the beginnings of a company all the way through the preparation of financial statements.

◆ IMPROVED AND EXPANDED ASSIGNMENT MATERIAL

In this edition, for the financial accounting chapters we added significantly to the assignment material and improved its alignment with the topics coved in each chapter. The assignment material includes:

- *Discussion Questions.* As we have already mentioned, throughout each chapter of the text, you will find Discussion Questions (DQs) that challenge students to reach beyond the surface of the written text to determine answers.
- *Review the Facts.* Students can use these basic, definitional questions to review the key points of each chapter. The questions are in a sequence reflecting the coverage of topics in the chapter.
- *Annual Report Project.* The text includes a completely revised annual report project that begins in Chapter F1 and continues throughout the financial accounting chapters (F1–F11). Adventures into real information about real companies always raise student interest! In addition, it can foster an open, interactive environment in the classroom. In Chapter F1, the annual report project assignment requires students to select a publicly traded company and to obtain the company's Form 10-K and annual report. Instructors should not be concerned that they will need to spend valuable class time to tell students how to accomplish the assignment. The text and the material included in the assignment itself provide enough guidance so that students should be able to obtain the Form 10-K and annual report by themselves. The annual report project requirements in later chapters are similarly supported by the text. In Chapter F3, students use key financial ratios to analyze their company, and in Chapter F6, students select a peer company to use as a comparison throughout the remainder of the project. Instructors should note that even if they omit coverage of Chapter F6, the annual report project for Chapter F6 should be assigned, as it is vital to the continuity of the project.
- *Apply What You Have Learned.* Many of these assignment materials can be used as the basis for classroom discussions; they will also work well as group assignments. There are three versions of most problems—one to use as an example in class, one for homework, and one extra.
- *Financial Reporting Exercises.* Financial Reporting Exercises included in the assignment material for each of the financial accounting chapter encourage students to use the Internet including the SEC's EDGAR system.

◆ TOPICS COVERED

We have carefully considered the inclusion or exclusion of topics and feel that our coverage has resulted in a balanced text consistent with our pedagogical goals of building a foundation that supports effective student learning. As we considered individual topics, we continually explored whether their inclusion would enhance a student's ability to interpret and use accounting information throughout his or her personal and professional life. The result is that *Introduction to Accounting: A User Perspective*, Second Edition, covers those topics that every accounting student should leave the course understanding well.

For example, in the financial accounting chapters we cover the calculations of only two depreciation methods—straight line and double declining balance. By limiting the coverage of detailed depreciation calculations, we have the opportunity to focus on the concepts of cost allocation, expense recognition, financial statement differences between the two methods, and the distinction between gains and revenues and losses and expenses. Students will not only know how to calculate depreciation expense, but will also understand why they are calculating it and how to use those calculations in making business decisions. In the chapter, students learn how to properly interpret gains and losses. Most of them are surprised to find out that two companies buying identical assets for the same price can sell them later for the same amount and have different results—one company can have a gain and the other experience a loss.

Similarly, in the management accounting chapters we demonstrate how to use *Microsoft* Excel to prepare cost behavior charts and insert trend lines but do not demonstrate the calculations for regression analysis. This allows us to focus on the usefulness of cost behavior rather than on tedious number crunching, which, in practice, is generally done by a computer.

We've carefully chosen the sequence of coverage so the material flows from one topic to the next. Not only does this make accounting easier to teach, but it is more understandable as well. To effectively present the user perspective, we've developed a logical flow of topics so that each chapter builds on what the student has already learned. Students can easily understand how the topics fit together logically and how they are used together to make good decisions. Moreover, students can see that accounting and the information it provides is not merely something that exists unto itself, but rather it is something developed in response to the needs of economic decision makers.

If you could read the entire text before using it in your classroom, you would have a very clear picture of the experience awaiting your students. However, even a short tour through the material covered in each chapter will show you how we have structured our presentation of the topics to maximize student learning.

◆ FINANCIAL ACCOUNTING CHAPTER HIGHLIGHTS

Chapter F1 provides a brief overview of business and the role of accounting in the business world, setting the stage for the introduction of accounting information. Without the world of business, there would be no need for accounting information or the accounting profession. We also introduce the balance sheet, the income statement, the statement of owners' equity, and the statement of cash flows. The standard-setting process and outside assurance is also covered including the roles of the SEC, the FASB, and the external auditor. In the appendix, we provide students with information they can use to access accounting and other information for publicly traded companies.

Chapter F2 presents an introduction to economic decision making. Because the purpose of financial accounting information is to provide information to be used in making decisions, we believe an understanding of the decision making process is essential. In today's business environment, an understanding of ethics is essential. We cover ethics and personal values and discuss how they impact business decisions. We explore the qualitative characteristics crucial to making accounting information useful in that process.

Chapter F3 covers the balance sheet. In this chapter, we focus on how equity and debt financing affects businesses and how its results are reflected on balance sheets. We also cover using cash to acquire assets, the statement of cash flows and how it is impacted by the financing and investing activities covered in the chapter, and key financial ratios that relate to the balance sheet.

Chapter F4 covers the income statement and statement of owners' equity. The chapter also covers financial statement articulation and how the financial statements relate to one another. We also cover the statement of cash flows and how it is affected by the operating activities covered in the chapter, and seven key financial ratios that relate profitability.

Chapter F5 compares the cash basis and accrual basis of accounting. The coverage helps students understand that accrual accounting is *one* basis of measurement and not *the* measurement basis. The material in this chapter helps students understand the weaknesses of cash basis accounting and makes the logic of accrual accounting much easier to grasp.

Chapter F6 is an optional chapter covering the accounting system and recording process. As we mentioned earlier, we hold off coverage of accounting procedures until Chapter F6 to give students the chance to acquire the basic accounting background that will help make accounting procedures easier to grasp. To afford maximum teaching flexibility and to make the material easier to understand, we present the chapter in two parts.

Part I introduces students to the accounting bookkeeping system and the accounting cycle. This part of the chapter introduces and describes the concept of analyzing transactions, journal entries, posting to the general ledger, the trial balance, adjusting entries, preparing financial statements from the adjusted trial balance or worksheet, and closing entries and the post-closing trial balance.

Part II covers the details of the application of accounting procedures. This part of the chapter begins with a presentation to help students learn and remember how debits and credits work. Then, each part of the accounting cycle is explained and demonstrated in a step-by-step fashion. We cover everything from analyzing transactions and preparing journal entries to preparing a bank reconciliation and adjusting entries, through preparing trial balances, the worksheet, and financial statements. Finally, Part II concludes with a step-by-step procedure to prepare closing entries and the post-closing trial balance.

We understand that some schools will choose to omit this chapter entirely while others will cover only Part I, and still others will include the entire chapter in their curriculum.

Chapter F7 explores issues surrounding the acquisition, depreciation, and disposal of long-lived assets under accrual accounting. This chapter examines the effects of depreciation method choice, using straight line and double declining balance as examples. We also show students how to properly interpret gains and losses and depreciation's impact on cash. The appendix demonstrates how to record the acquisition, depreciation, and disposal of assets.

Chapter F8 explores accounting for inventory. The periodic and perpetual inventory systems are introduced. Students learn how to calculate amounts under LIFO, FIFO, and average cost methods for the perpetual inventory system. They also learn how the choice of cost flow method affects the accounting information that income statements and balance sheets provide. The chapter also covers the impact of inventory transactions on the statement of cash flows and financial ratios dealing with inventory turnover. This chapter has two appendices. The first appendix covers some inventory purchasing issues and presents a discussion of freight terms and cash discounts and how they alter the cost of inventory. The second appendix presents the recording procedures for inventory using the perpetual inventory system.

Chapter F9 takes a closer look at the way the balance sheet and income statement are organized. We explore each of the balance sheet's classifications. In addition, we explore the income statement in detail including nonrecurring items (discontinued operations, extraordinary items, and changes in accounting principles). Income tax disclosure relative to nonrecurring items and an introduction to basic and diluted earnings per share are included. The chapter concludes with coverage of several key financial ratios.

Chapter F10 takes an up-close look at the statement of cash flows. The chapter reviews operating, investing, and financing activities and provides step-by-step coverage of the statement's preparation using the indirect method. Students also learn how to read and interpret the information provided on the statement of cash flows and how to use two key financial ratios relating to cash flows. The appendix to this chapter provides step-by-step coverage of preparing the operating section of the statement using the direct method.

Chapter F11 covers financial statement analysis. The chapter reviews the 17 ratios presented throughout the earlier chapters of the text. The chapter covers industry classification codes and peer company and industry comparisons. In addition, the chapter discusses general economic conditions, political events and political climate, and the industry outlook. For each of the 17 ratios, the chapter presents charts comparing *Pier 1 Imports, Inc.,* to two peer companies and discusses *Pier 1*'s ratios relative to its peers and to industry averages.

◆ MANAGEMENT ACCOUNTING CHAPTER HIGHLIGHTS

Chapter M1 explores management accounting, its environment and future. The chapter introduces management accounting and contrasts it with financial accounting. It discusses where management accounting fits in a company as well as the origin and evolution of management accounting and the challenges and trends that lie ahead.

Chapter M2 explores various cost classifications and concepts. The chapter covers product costs and period costs for merchandisers and manufacturers as well as cost of services and period costs for service firms. The chapter discusses direct material, direct labor, manufacturing overhead as well as the various manufacturing inventories (raw materials, work-in-process, finished goods). The chapter also provides a comparison of merchandising, manufacturing, and service costs. The chapter appendix covers the accounting procedures (journal entries) for simple manufacturing environments where manufacturing overhead is recorded directly in work-in-process inventory. (Overhead allocation techniques and journal entries are covered in Chapter M3.)

Chapter M3 describes how companies determine the cost of their products. The chapter covers job order costing and introduces overhead allocation. The chapter also covers process costing in a simplified presentation that makes process costing basics very understandable. (Only the average cost flow method is presented and the presentation assumes that the percentage complete for direct materials, direct labor, and manufacturing overhead is the same.) The chapter appendix covers accounting procedures including journal entries for manufacturing overhead allocation.

Chapter M4 covers cost allocation and the use of activity-based costing (ABC). The chapter takes a closer look at overhead allocation by further examining traditional overhead allocation and introducing ABC. Basic concepts of ABC are explored, including its implementation, ABC calculations, and benefits and drawbacks of using ABC.

Chapter M5 covers cost behavior, including fixed costs, variable costs, and the relevant range. The chapter also introduces the concept of mixed cost and includes an easy-to-understand presentation of techniques to separate mixed costs into fixed and variable components. Step-by-step calculations are presented for the scatter graph and high–low methods. Regression analysis is discussed, and the chapter includes a step-by-step presentation of scatter graphing using *Microsoft* Excel's Chart Wizard.

Chapter M6 explores business decisions using cost behavior. The contribution income statement and cost–volume–profit (CVP) analysis for single-product and multiple-product situations are introduced and explored. The chapter includes step-by-step presentations of breakeven and the calculations to determine sales needed to meet target profit. The chapter also introduces a CVP graph and sensitivity analysis.

Chapter M7 explores the use of relevant information for decision making. The chapter describes relevant information, costs and benefits and their characteristics. Qualitative and quantitative considerations are discussed. The chapter demonstrates the importance of relevant information with a series of examples including equipment replacement, special orders, and outsourcing—the make or buy decision.

Chapter M8 introduces various aspects of business planning and explores capital budget and evaluating capital expenditures. The chapter introduces the business planning process and setting company goals, strategic plan, the capital budget, and the operating budget. Then, it explores the capital budget, the cost of capital and the evaluation of potential capital projects. The chapter demonstrates discounted cash flow capital budgeting decision methods such as net present value and internal rate of return using both financial tables and a financial calculator. The chapter supports instructors demonstrating concepts using financial tables, or a financial calculator, or both. The chapter also demonstrates nondiscounted cash flow capital budgeting decision methods including payback period and accounting rate of return. Appendix A to this chapter demonstrates detailed future value and present value calculations using financial tables. Appendix B demonstrates using a financial calculator for future and present value calculation.

Chapter M9 explores the operating budget. The chapter is presented in two parts. Part I presents an overview of the operating budget including the benefits of budgeting, the contents of the operating budget (it also introduces various operating budgets), and approaches to budgeting. Part II covers preparing and using the operating budget. It includes step-by-step presentation of preparation of 8 budgets from the sales budget to budgeted financial statements.

Chapter M10 explores standard costing. The chapter explains why standard costing is used, discusses ideal versus practical standards, and describes some of the problems with standard costing. The chapter demonstrates basic standard costing for a manufacturer using an easy-to-understand example based on a small student-owned company manufacturing wood mailboxes in a rented garage. Calculations are shown for the direct material variances, direct labor variances, variable manufacturing overhead variances, and fixed manufacturing overhead variances. The chapter concludes with a look at variance analysis and using variances to manage by exception and includes an appendix that demonstrates the journal entries used in standard costing.

Chapter M11 covers various aspects of evaluating performance. Business segments and the segmented income statement are presented and the pitfalls of allocating common fixed costs are discussed. The chapter discusses the basics of service department cost allocation and activity-based service department cost allocation. The chapter discusses revenue centers, cost centers, profit centers, and investment centers. Return on investment, residual income, and economic value added (EVA™) are discussed and demonstrated. The Balanced Scorecard and nonfinancial performance measures and just-in-time (JIT) are also covered.

◆ OTHER IMPORTANT FEATURES OF THIS TEXT

In addition to the Discussion Questions and the inclusion of the ***Pier 1 Imports, Inc.*** annual report, our text offers other features that will enhance the learning process:

- *Learning Objectives.* Previewing each chapter with these objectives allows students to see what direction the chapter is taking, which makes the journey through the material a bit easier.
- *Marginal Glossary.* Students often find the process of learning accounting terminology to be a challenge. As each new key word is introduced in the text, it is shown in bold and also defined in the margin. This feature offers students an easy way to review the key terms and locate their introduction in the text.
- *Summary.* This concise summary of each chapter provides an overview of the main points, but is in no way a substitute for reading the chapter.
- *Key Terms.* At the end of each chapter, a list of the new key words directs students to the page on which the key word or phrase was introduced.
- *Review the Facts.* Students can use these basic, definitional questions to review the key points of each chapter. The questions are in a sequence reflecting the coverage of topics in the chapter.
- *Apply What You Have Learned.* Our end-of-chapter assignment materials include a mix of traditional types of homework problems and innovative assignments requiring critical thinking and writing. Many of the requirements can be used as the basis for classroom discussions. You will find matching problems, short essay questions, and calculations. Assignments dealing directly with the use of financial statements are also included. Many of these applications also work well as group

assignments. There are three versions of most problems—one to use as an example in class, one for homework, and one extra.
- *Glossary of Accounting Terms.* An alphabetical listing of important accounting terms, including all of the key terms plus additional terms.
- *Company Index.* A listing of the companies used in the text as examples or in assignment material.

◆ SUPPLEMENTS FOR USE BY THE INSTRUCTOR

Additional support for your efforts in the classroom is provided by our group of supplements.

Instructor's Resource Manual, Connie Groer (Frostburg State University)

Substantially revised, this resource manual provides insightful and useful tips on how to best manage course content when using Werner/Jones in class. Chapter-by-chapter explanations and pedagogical philosophies are clearly delineated and oriented to greatly aid the teaching process. Also included are chapter outlines organized by objectives, lecture suggestions, teaching tips, group activities, and suggested readings, as well as suggested solutions to text discussion questions. Available online at *www.prenhall.com/werner.*

Solutions Manual, Stacy Sexton, Mike Werner, and Seth Levine (University of Miami), with accuracy checking by Bob Bauman (Allan Hancock College)

Solutions for all end-of-chapter material. Available online at *www.prenhall.com/ werner.*

Test Item File, Tim Carse (CPA)

A ready-to-use bank of testing material. Each chapter includes a variety of types of questions, including true/false, multiple choice, essay, and critical thinking problems. Intended for ease of use, each question is linked to chapter objectives, and also provides suggested difficulty level and reference to text pages where answers can be found. Available online at *www.prenhall.com/werner.*

PowerPoint Presentations, Olga Quintana (University of Miami)

Complete PowerPoint presentations for each chapter. Instructors may download and use each presentation as is or customize the slides to create a tailor-made slide show. Each presentation allows instructors to offer a more interactive experience using colorful graphics, outlines of chapter material, and graphical explanations of difficult topics. Available online at *www.prenhall.com/werner.*

Instructor's Resource CD-ROM

The IRCD is a powerful teaching and learning tool. It first serves as a roadmap through the chapters to identify key concepts and then guides instructors to the CD-ROM where they can further develop their skills. The IRCD contains all print and technology (e.g., TestGen, PowerPoints) supplements on a single CD-ROM. Enjoy the freedom to transport the entire package from office, to home, to classroom. This enables you to customize any of the ancillaries, print only the chapters or materials you wish to use, or access any item from the package within the classroom!

Course Web site at *www.prenhall.com/werner*

A complete online resource that offers a variety of Internet-based teaching and learning support. Our Web site provides a wealth of resources for students and faculty. These resources include:

- An online study guide
- Downloadable supplements, including PowerPoint Presentations
- Downloadable General Ledger Software for student use

Introduction to Financial Accounting

A User Perspective

- Learning assessment sections
- Practice tests with immediate feedback for self-study use

◆ ACKNOWLEDGMENTS

This project would not have been possible without support and encouragement from a number of people, the faith in the concept's value from Prentice Hall, and the suggestions for improvements from our colleagues.

In particular, we thank executive editor Debbie Hoffman for her patience, determination, and faith in the project. She was always there for us. We also express our debt of gratitude to Amy Whitaker, our development editor, for her significant contributions to this edition. We appreciate the support of Prentice Hall team members P. J. Boardman, Stephen Deitmer, Mac Mendelsohn, Alana Bradley, Jane Avery, Beth Toland, Kelly Warsak, and Elena Picinic for their help and contributions. We also appreciate Bob Bauman (Allan Hancock College) for his contributions to this project. He accuracy checked each and every end-of-chapter problem and solution.

We are also grateful to Annie Todd, Katherene P. Terrell, and Robert L. Terrell for all their support in the past and for truly making this project possible. We also thank Linda Begley and the rest of the staff at Rainbow Graphics for their help in transforming our manuscript into a book. Sincere thanks, too, to Thomas R. Robinson and Oscar J. Holzmann, both of the University of Miami, for their help with the financial statement analysis material. We are grateful for the inspiration and encouragement of Sherry Shu Zhang and Tom and Cathy Norris. We also thank Thomas Greco, Manta Racing; Bruce Perlmuter, The Perlmuter Printing Company; Cam Matheis and Steve Speace, who gave us valuable editorial help and guidance, and Stacy Sexton, who contributed editorial help and assignment material.

We thank our colleagues for their intellectual contributions and friendship that have helped to enrich this book. Martha Doran, San Diego State University, good friend and teacher, shared her wisdom with us about learning and teaching, and our students are better off because of it. Connie Groer, Frostburg State University, reviewed the first six chapters with extraordinary care. Thank you. Many other colleagues tested our ideas, were brave enough to offer constructive criticism, and gave us friendship through the difficult times. They include: Gary J. Weber and Kay C. Cames, Gonzaga University; Connie D. Weaver, University of Texas–Austin; Thomas R. Robinson, Oscar J. Holzmann, Paul Munter, Frank Collins, Mark Friedman, Seth Levine, Kay Tatum, Larry Phillips, Juan M. Rodriguez, Carlos Garcia, Guillermo Arguello, Teresita Miglio, Ray Placid, Sergio Varona, Manny Sicre, and Diane Clifford, University of Miami; Richard E. Flaherty, Harriet MacCracken, Patrick B. McKenzie, and Karen Gieger, Arizona State University; Charles R. Pursifull, Mary F. Sheets, Thomas K. Miller, Ura Lee Denson, David J. Harris, Joan Stone, Karen Price, and Jane Calvert, University of Central Oklahoma; Aileen Ormiston and Charles Lewis, Mesa Community College; Allison L. Drews-Bryan, Clemson University; and Tim Carse.

We would also like to thank the following second edition reviewers for their recommendations:

Mark E. Bettini, University of California–Berkeley
Joseph H. Bylinski, University of North Carolina at Chapel Hill
David F. Caslan, Bethune-Cookman College
Kenneth P. Couvillion, San Joaquin Delta College
Cherie Francisco, Simpson College
Connie J. Groer, Frostburg State University
Cheryl Mitchem, Virginia State University
Sally J. Nelson, Northeast Iowa Community College
Michael R. Palma, Gwinnett Technical Institute
Marshall K. Pitman, University of Texas–San Antonio
A. J. Potts, University of Southern Maine
S.E.C. Purvis, California State University–San Bernardino

Olga Quintana, University of Miami
Suzanne S. Roe, University of Wyoming
Robert W. Rouse, College of Charleston
Nanette Sanders-Cobb, Craven Community College
Ann E. Selk, University of Wisconsin–Green Bay
Jerry D. Siebel, University of South Florida
Judith Walery, Grossmont College
Michael G. Welker, Drexel University
Harold E. Wyman, Florida International University

Other colleagues who have provided suggestions as adopters, as focus group members, or as reviewers of previous editions:

Jeffrey J. Archambault, Clarkson University
Gerald Ashley, Grossmont College
Lorren H. Beavers, University of Central Oklahoma
Sheila Bradford, Tulsa Community College
Carol E. Buehl, Northern Michigan University
Roger K. Doost, Clemson University
Suzanne Elsea, Anheuser–Busch Corporation
Jessica J. Frazier, Eastern Kentucky University
Edward S. Goodhart, Shippensburg University
Bambi A. Hora, University of Central Oklahoma
Steven D. Hunter, Western Baptist College
Thomas A. Jones
Raymond L. Larson, Appalachian State University
Mary D. Maury, St. John's University
Alfonso R. Oddo, Niagara University
Charles J. Pineno, Clarion University
Mary Ann M. Prater, Clemson University
John C. Robison, California Polytechnic State University–San Luis Obispo
Joanne Sheridan, Montana State University–Billings
Sheldon R. Smith, Brigham Young University–Hawaii
Patricia M. Sommerville, Saint Mary's University
Carolyn Streuly
George R. Violette, University of Southern Maine
Marilyn T. Zarzeski, University of Central Florida

We believe the approach we have taken will help students see how accounting fits into the "big picture of business." We hope students will find that what they learn from this text and in their introductory accounting class relates directly to them, regardless of their career path.

Please feel free to contact us at *mwerner@miami.edu* with your comments or suggestions.

Michael L. Werner
Kumen H. Jones

CHAPTER 1

Introduction to Business in the United States

People make decisions every day. Information makes decisions easier to make. For example, let's say you are in the market for a new cellular phone and service. First, you must choose a phone. Many companies—**Nokia, Ericsson,** and **Motorola**—manufacture cell phones with various and often different features. In addition, you must select a service plan from the assortment that **Sprint PCS, AT&T, Verizon, Nextel,** and other cell phone service providers offer. You have a myriad of choices. How will you decide? Well, you could just buy the first phone you find, but you may be disappointed if you later determine that the phone doesn't have all the features you like and the service plan does not suit your needs. In contrast, you could begin your quest for a phone by gathering information about cellular phones and cellular service plans. Once you had the information, your decision would become much easier to make. The information wouldn't make the decision for you—you would still have to weigh various factors—but it would help you make a better decision. Whether you are making a personal decision such as which cellular phone to buy or a business decision such as which investment to make, useful information won't make the decision for you, but it sure makes it easier to make better choices.

So, we make decisions, and solid information makes decisions easier to make. But what does all this have to do with accounting? The purpose of accounting is to provide useful economic information to decision makers. Accounting is simply a mechanism to provide useful information by recording, classifying, and reporting economic activities. Company managers use accounting information to help them make decisions about how to operate their business. People outside a company such as investors, creditors, and customers also use accounting information to help make decisions concerning the company. Often, the decisions made in business have a ripple effect throughout society. Because these business decisions are based on accounting information, accounting impacts each of us even though most of us have little or no direct contact with it. Accounting is often called the language of business. To help you better understand this language, we begin by exploring business in its many different forms.

The business of America is business.

—CALVIN COOLIDGE
30th President of the United States

The word *business* means different things to different people. For some, the word conjures up a dream of excitement and opportunity; for others, it represents a nightmare of greed and exploitation. *Webster's New World Dictionary* gives several definitions of business:

Busi-ness (biz'nis) n. **1:** One's work or occupation. **2:** A special task or duty. **3:** A matter or affair. **4:** Commerce or trade. **5:** A commercial or industrial establishment.[1]

---

[1]*Webster's New World Dictionary* (New York: Prentice Hall, 1939), 59.

As you can see, not only do people have different impressions of business, but the word itself has different meanings in different contexts. The last two definitions are particularly relevant for this book. It is important to understand that at times *business* is used to describe the entirety of commerce and trade and at other times it is used to describe an individual company. In fact, in the economic world, and in books about the world of business (including this one), the words *company* and *business* are often used interchangeably. So whenever you see the word *business,* make sure you understand the context in which it is used.

Accounting information is one of the key ingredients for making wise business decisions. This chapter will provide you with the background necessary to put the accounting concepts presented throughout this text into the proper business context.

Learning Objectives

After completing your work on this chapter, you should be able to do the following:

1. Describe the four factors of production.
2. Explain the basic concepts of capitalism and how they relate to the profit motive.
3. Distinguish between gross and net income. Be able to calculate each.
4. Distinguish among the three basic forms of business organization—the proprietorship, the partnership, and the corporation—and describe the advantages and disadvantages of each.
5. Distinguish among the three major types of business activities and define hybrid-type businesses.
6. Explain the basic need for international business trade and the complications involved in this activity.
7. Describe what is shown in each of the four financial statements.
8. Discuss the SEC's and FASB's authority over accounting reporting standards and describe the current standard-setting process in the United States.
9. Describe the basic objectives of financial reporting.
10. Explain the purpose of an independent financial audit and describe the four basic types of audit opinions.
11. Gather information about a company and obtain an annual report. (Appendix)
12. Describe the information found in a typical annual report and Form 10-K. (Appendix)

◆ WHAT IS BUSINESS?

business Depending on the context, the area of commerce or trade, an individual company, or the process of producing and distributing goods and services.

Essentially, **business** is the process of producing goods (manufacturing) and providing services and then distributing them (selling) to those who want or need them. This process sounds simple enough, but it is actually quite complex.

Although we cannot present an in-depth study of all of the aspects of business, we must talk about a few basics at the outset to present accounting in its proper context. We begin with the factors of production.

FACTORS OF PRODUCTION

factors of production The four major items needed to support economic activity: natural resources, labor, capital, and entrepreneurship.

The **factors of production** are the key ingredients needed to support economic activity (see Exhibit 1–1). Economists classify the factors of production into four categories:

1. **Natural resources**—land and the materials that come from the land, such as timber, mineral deposits, oil deposits, and water.
2. **Labor**—the mental and physical efforts of all workers, regardless of their skill or education, who perform the tasks required to produce and sell goods and services. Labor is sometimes called the human resource factor.

natural resources
Land and the materials that come from the land, such as timber, mineral deposits, oil deposits, and water. One of the factors of production.

labor   The mental and physical efforts of all workers performing tasks required to produce and sell goods and services. This factor of production is also called the human resource factor.

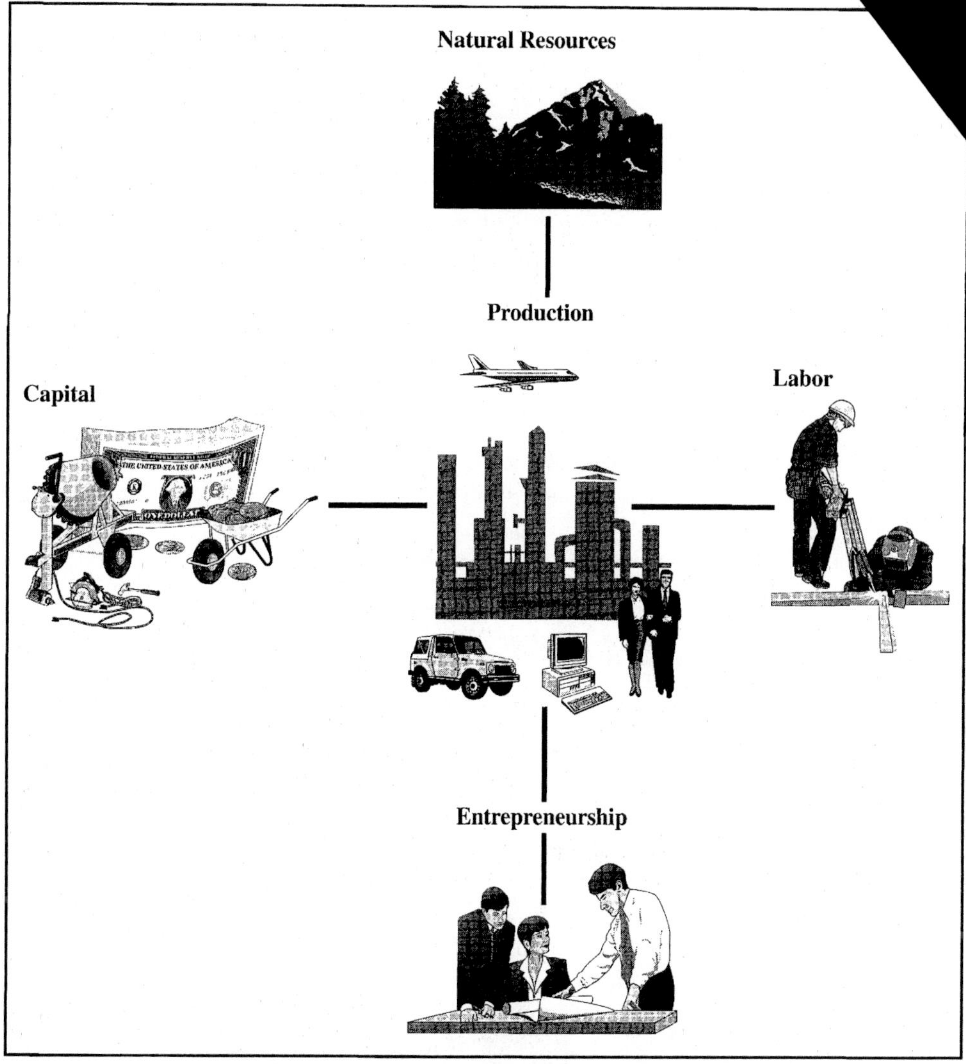

EXHIBIT 1-1   Factors of Production

capital   A factor of production that includes the buildings, machinery, and tools used to produce goods and services. Also, sometimes used to refer to the money used to buy those items.

entrepreneurship   The factor of production that brings the other three factors—natural resources, labor, and capital—together to form a business.

communism   An example of a planned economy. A *planned economy* is one with a strong centralized government that controls all or most of the natural resources, labor, and capital used to produce goods and services.

capitalism   An example of a market economy. A *market economy* is one that relies on competition to determine the most efficient way to allocate the economy's resources.

3. **Capital**—the buildings, machinery, and tools used to produce goods and services. The word *capital* has many meanings. Sometimes it refers to the *money* that buys the buildings, machinery, and tools used in production. Because this double usage can be confusing, be careful to note the context in which the word *capital* is being used.

4. **Entrepreneurship**—the activity that brings the first three factors together to form a business. *Entrepreneurs* are the people willing to accept the opportunities and risks of starting and running businesses. They provide or acquire the capital, assemble the labor force, and utilize available natural resources to produce and sell goods and services.

The way these four factors of production combine to produce goods and services depends on the type of economic system that organizes a society.

In a *planned economy*, a strong centralized government controls all or most of the natural resources, labor, and capital used to produce goods and services, replacing the entrepreneur. **Communism** is an example of a planned economy. In contrast, a *market economy* relies on competition in the marketplace to determine the most efficient way to allocate the economy's resources. **Capitalism** is an example of a market economy. Capitalism, also known as the *free enterprise, free market,* or *private enterprise system,* is the economic system used to conduct business in the United States.

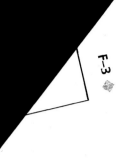

THE PROFIT MOTIVE

The *profit motive* stimulates a person to do something when the *benefit* derived from doing it is greater than the *sacrifice* required to do it. A rational person desires the greatest benefit with the least amount of sacrifice. When this natural desire in one person is pitted against the same desire in another person, competition results.

To illustrate the profit motive, let's say that Steve needs a new pair of pants. Because he is a rational person, Steve desires the best pair of pants he can buy for the lowest possible price. Tanner owns a clothing store. Being a rational person, Tanner desires to sell his clothes for the highest price he can. Steve goes to Tanner's clothing store and looks at a pair of pants Tanner has priced at $50. Assuming he likes the pants and can afford to pay $50, Steve will buy them if he feels they provide him with the most benefit for the least sacrifice.

Now, let's add one other ingredient to the situation—competition. Enter Chelsea, who also owns a clothing store. She sells pants identical to the pair Steve is considering buying at Tanner's. The difference is that she is selling them for $45.

Discussion Questions ••

1–1. What do you think caused Tanner and Chelsea to establish different selling prices for an identical pair of pants?

1–2. Assuming Steve decides to buy the pants, what do you think will determine where he buys them?

In this example, Steve's self-interest pits the self-interests of Tanner and Chelsea against each other because Steve's desire to pay the lowest price possible for the pants will make Tanner and Chelsea compete for his business. If Tanner loses enough sales to Chelsea because she is selling pants for less than he is, he will be forced to lower his selling price. In fact, he may want to lower his price for the pants Steve likes to $40 in order to attract sales away from Chelsea. She will then be forced to lower her selling price. No one forces Tanner and Chelsea to reduce their prices; the force comes from competition in the market. Adam Smith (1723–1790), the great Scottish philosopher and economist, called this phenomenon *the invisible hand*.

If competitors lower their selling prices too much, losses will occur. For example, if Tanner and Chelsea pay $30 for the pants, they obviously don't want to resell those pants for less than that. **Profit** is the excess of benefit over sacrifice. Steve decides to buy the pants from Tanner for $50, so Tanner's gross profit can be calculated as:

profit The excess of benefit over sacrifice. A less formal name for net income or net profit.

Amount received from Steve (BENEFIT)	$ 50
Less what Tanner paid for the pants (SACRIFICE)	− 30
Equals GROSS PROFIT on the sale of pants	$ 20

The $20 profit that Tanner earned on the pair of pants is called *gross profit* or *gross margin*. However, it does not represent his actual profit from operating the clothing store. In addition to the cost of the merchandise he buys to sell, he has other costs such as rent on the store, utilities, and wages paid to employees. All these items must be taken into account before he can calculate his real profit, which businesspeople generally call **net income** or **net profit.**

net income The amount of profit that remains after all costs have been considered. The net reward of doing business for a specific time period.

If Tanner does not earn a sufficient profit in the clothing store business, he will be forced to close it and go into another line of work. The same, of course, holds true for Chelsea. In a capitalistic economy, businesses (except for charities and other not-for-profit organizations) that do not earn profits eventually cease to exist.

net profit Same as net income.

PROFITS VERSUS SOCIAL RESPONSIBILITY

People feel many ways about business. Some believe that "profit" is a dirty word and that society would be better off if companies were motivated by something other than the "Almighty Dollar." These people think that business should strike a balance between profit and social responsibility. On the other side of the spectrum are those who believe that businesses have no obligation beyond earning profits and contend that companies have no social responsibility at all.

We live in a society that often measures success by whether someone "beats" someone else. It is what has been described as a zero-sum game, meaning that for every winner, there must be a loser. The following quotation from Vince Lombardi, legendary coach of the Green Bay Packers, seems to more accurately capture the workings of our economy than the quotation by sportswriter Grantland Rice:

> *Winning is not everything, it is the only thing!*
>
> —VINCE LOMBARDI

> *It matters not whether you win or lose, but how you play the game.*
>
> —GRANTLAND RICE

Recently, however, society is renewing its concern over how the game of business is played. An increasing number of investors, creditors, and other economic decision makers are interested not only in "the bottom line" (making money), but also in the way companies conduct themselves as citizens in the community. In other words, there is a movement in business toward a win–win rather than a win–lose situation.

A growing number of people refuse to invest in or do business with companies they believe are insensitive to social and environmental concerns. For example, many investors, both individuals and companies, refuse to invest in alcohol or tobacco companies, or in firms known to pollute the environment. In response to this trend, many companies are now committed to responsible and ethical business practices and make a point of communicating that commitment to their stakeholders. A **stakeholder** is anyone to whom a company owes a responsibility; anyone who has a *stake* in the way a company is run.

stakeholder Anyone who is affected by the way a company conducts its business.

One of the great challenges facing any business today is determining exactly who its stakeholders are and just what responsibility it has to each of them. Stakeholders include present and potential investors, customers, employees, the community at large, and governmental bodies. To improve stakeholder confidence in the company's good citizenship, many companies now include a section in their annual report about social responsibility. For example, ***Wendy's International*** lists community involvement as one of its eight core values. It appears that the era of conducting business without regard to anything but making a profit is very likely gone forever.

Discussion Questions ●●●●●●●●●●●●●●●●●●●●●●●●●●●●●●●●●●●●●●●

1-3. Make a list of those to whom you think a chemical manufacturing company owes responsibility. What are the specific responsibilities it has to each of these stakeholders? How do you think the company could best go about fulfilling each of those responsibilities?

1-4. Make a list of those to whom you think a retail clothing company owes a responsibility. What are the stakes that each group has? How can the company fulfill each responsibility?

1-5. Can you think of any companies that have fulfilled the responsibilities you outlined in your answers to question 1–3 or 1–4 and yet managed to remain profitable?

◆ FORMS OF BUSINESS ORGANIZATION

Generally, there are three forms of business organization in the United States: sole proprietorships, partnerships, and corporations. Each has certain advantages and disadvantages in relation to the others.

SOLE PROPRIETORSHIPS

sole proprietorship An unincorporated business that is owned by one person. Also called a proprietorship.

proprietorship Same thing as a sole proprietorship.

A **sole proprietorship,** or **proprietorship,** is a business that is owned by one individual. A common misconception about this form of business is that it is always small. While the majority of sole proprietorships *are* small, the classification suggests nothing about the size of the business, only that it has a single owner.

ADVANTAGES OF SOLE PROPRIETORSHIPS

1. *Easy and inexpensive to establish.* There are no special legal requirements associated with starting a sole proprietorship. All a person must do is decide what kind of business he or she wants to establish, obtain the necessary licenses and permits, and that person may begin doing business.
2. *Total control.* This is probably the number one reason people start their own companies. Virtually everyone who works for someone else sometimes feels stifled by having to "answer to the boss." A sole proprietor answers to no one when making decisions about how to run the business (as long as it's legal).
3. *Independence.* This is closely related to having total control, but it has a broader meaning than simply being in control of how the company is run. Think of independence as the freedom to choose one's lifestyle. There is no set number of "vacation days" for sole proprietors. Rather, the proprietor is free to take days off whenever he wants to, if he feels he can spare the time from the business. A proprietor can work his own hours.
4. *No sharing of profits.* A single owner shares profits only with the government in the form of taxes. Whatever the business earns after taxes belongs solely to the owner.
5. *No separate income taxes.* From a legal standpoint, a sole proprietorship is simply an extension of its owner. Therefore, a proprietorship pays no separate income tax. The earnings of the company are considered the earnings of the owner and become a part of his or her personal taxable income.
6. *Few government regulations.* There are no special government requirements that must be satisfied to form a proprietorship. Once formed, as long as the company conforms to business regulations and the owner pays his or her taxes, a proprietorship is reasonably free of government intervention.
7. *Easy and inexpensive to dissolve.* Sole proprietorships are about as easy to end as they are to start. If the owner decides to shut the company down, all he or she must do is notify the state and local government agencies and pay off remaining debts.

DISADVANTAGES OF SOLE PROPRIETORSHIPS

1. *Unlimited liability.* Because from a legal standpoint a sole proprietorship is simply an extension of its owner, all business obligations become the owner's legal obligations. Therefore, if the company fails to pay its debts, the creditors can sue the owner for the owner's personal property, including his or her investments, house, car, boat, or other holdings.
2. *Limited access to capital.* All businesses must have money and other assets to operate. Economists refer to these assets as *capital.* The amount of capital available to a sole proprietorship is limited to the amount of personal assets the owner can contribute to the business or the amount he or she can borrow on a personal loan. Legally, a proprietorship is not distinguished from its owner; therefore, when the business borrows money, it is the owner who is actually borrowing.
3. *Limited management expertise.* No one is an expert in everything (although we're sure you know people who think they are), and a sole proprietorship is limited to whatever management expertise the proprietor possesses. Many proprietorships fail because the owner lacks skills or expertise in areas critical to the survival of the company. Even though a proprietorship can hire individuals who possess the needed talents, the hired employees may lack the drive and motivation to employ these talents as enthusiastically as an owner would.
4. *Personal time commitment.* Running a business is hard work, and most sole proprietors work very long hours—probably longer hours than if they worked for someone else. Most sole proprietors, however, consider the time well spent because it benefits them personally. But make no mistake about it, it takes a tremendous amount of time to run your own business.
5. *Limited life.* Unless the company is sold to another entity or is passed on to the owner's heirs, the life of the business cannot exceed the life of the owner.

Notwithstanding the disadvantages of proprietorships, many people dream of owning their own business, and nearly 72 percent of companies in the United States are sole proprietorships. Because most of them are small businesses, only about five percent of all business revenues come from this form of business.

PARTNERSHIPS

partnership A business form similar to a proprietorship, but having two or more owners.

Think of a **partnership** as a proprietorship with two or more owners sharing in the risks and rewards of the business. A common misconception is that all partnerships are small businesses. In fact, some partnerships are quite large. For example, ***Pricewaterhouse-Coopers,*** a large public accounting firm, has 9,000 partners and 160,000 partners and staff.

ADVANTAGES OF PARTNERSHIPS
1. *Easy to establish.* From a legal standpoint, partnerships are about as easy to form as proprietorships. Once the partners obtain the appropriate licenses and permits, a partnership is in business. Although not required by law, partners are wise to commit the ownership and profit-sharing structure of the partnership to a formal written partnership agreement, signed by each partner, to clarify their understanding of these issues. A well-written partnership agreement anticipates future problems and helps to resolve conflicts before they arise.
2. *Increased management expertise.* Partnerships are often formed because each partner has skills in a critical area of business that complement the skills of the others. Combining those areas of expertise into a partnership enhances the business's chances of success.
3. *Access to more capital.* Having more than one person involved in the ownership of the business usually increases access to capital (money and other assets). In fact, many partnerships are formed for this very reason.
4. *Few government regulations.* Like proprietorships, partnerships are subject to fewer government regulations than corporations. There are no special government requirements that must be satisfied to form a partnership. Once formed, as long as the partnership conforms to business regulations, and each partner pays his or her individual taxes, there is little government intervention.
5. *No separate income taxes.* A partnership is not legally separate from its owners and therefore does not pay separate income taxes. Rather, the partnership tax return is an information report that allocates the partnership profits among the partners according to the partnership profit-sharing agreement. Each partner pays personal income tax on his or her share of the partnership profits, regardless of whether or not these profits are withdrawn from the business.
6. *Greater business continuity.* Because more people are involved, partnerships are more likely to have longer lives than are sole proprietorships. When a partner dies or withdraws from the partnership, the legal life of the partnership ends. The heirs do not inherit the right to be partners in the firm. For all practical purposes, however, the business generally need not stop its operations. The partnership agreement may allow the remaining partner or partners to either continue with one less partner or admit another partner to the firm.

DISADVANTAGES OF PARTNERSHIPS
1. *Unlimited liability.* Because partnerships are not legally separate from their owners, the partners are personally liable for all obligations of the business. In fact, in most instances, each partner is personally liable for the *total* obligations of the partnership. Therefore, if any partner makes a decision that obligates the partnership, all the other partners become responsible, even if they knew nothing about the decision.
2. *Sharing of profits.* When a partnership is formed, the partners should prepare an agreement that outlines how to divide company profits. The profit-sharing arrangement usually takes into account the amount of capital each partner invests in the partnership, how much time each partner commits on a regular basis, and

any special expertise a partner may contribute. Regardless of whether the agreement is fair and equitable, once a partnership has been formed, partners will share profits with each other.

3. *Potential conflicts between partners.* Suppose one partner wants the company to begin selling a new product and another partner disagrees. If the two partners have equal power, a gridlock may result. The bases for conflicts among partners range from personal habits to overall business philosophy. Most conflicts are minor, but there may be no other way to resolve severe conflicts than to dissolve the partnership.

4. *Difficulty in dissolving.* Ending a partnership can often be a devastating emotional experience; it may result in conflicts that sever personal and professional ties. If individuals forming a partnership are wise, they will include specific provisions for dissolution in the original partnership agreement when all the partners have positive attitudes toward one another. Think of this as the business version of a prenuptial agreement: The parties forming the business agree on how the business "marriage" will end.

While there are advantages to the partnership form of business, many people believe the disadvantages outweigh them. Only about 6 percent of all businesses in the United States are partnerships, and they account for just about 7 percent of all business revenues.

SEPARATE ENTITY ASSUMPTION

In our discussion of the proprietorship and partnership forms of business, we stressed that in both cases there is no legal distinction between a company and its owner or owners. Only in the corporate form is a company considered a separate legal entity from its owners. From a record-keeping and accounting standpoint, however, proprietorships, partnerships, and corporations are considered to be completely separate from their owners. This is called the **separate entity assumption,** and reflects the notion that economic activity can be identified with a particular economic entity whether it is an individual, proprietorship, corporation, or even a division of a business.

separate entity assumption The assumption that economic activity can be identified with a particular economic entity and that the results of activities for each entity will be recorded separately.

CORPORATIONS

In 1819, Chief Justice John Marshall of the United States Supreme Court made this statement:

> *A corporation is an artificial being, invisible, intangible, and existing only in contemplation of law.*

This ruling changed the course of business in the United States forever. As a separate legal entity, a **corporation** has many of the rights and obligations of a person, including the right to enter into contracts and the right to buy, own, and sell property. The law requires a corporation to discharge its obligations lawfully, and creditors can sue the corporation itself for recovery if it does not. A corporation can be taken to court if it breaks the law, and it is obligated to pay taxes like an individual. In addition to the legal obligations of corporations, the moral obligation of corporations to be socially responsible is currently a topic of widespread discussion. Virtually all of the large publicly traded companies like *Target, Texaco, Intel,* and *Walt Disney,* for example, are corporations. For various reasons, not the least of which is that corporations are separate legal entities, there are several distinct advantages and disadvantages to the corporate form.

corporation A business that is a separate legal entity from its stockholders (owners).

ADVANTAGES OF CORPORATIONS

1. *Limited liability.* Because a corporation is a separate legal entity from its stockholders (owners), the owners are not personally liable for the corporation's obligations. The maximum amount a stockholder can lose is the amount of his or her investment. However, the limited liability feature of corporations is not a universal truth. Many owners of small corporations sometimes forfeit their limited liability rights by signing a *personal guarantee* to obtain business credit. When an owner signs a personal guarantee, she or he agrees to be personally liable if the corporation fails to pay.

2. *Greater access to capital.* By dividing the ownership of the firm into relatively low-cost shares of stock, corporations can often attract a great number of investors. Although a corporation can be owned by just one individual, some corporations in the United States have more than a million stockholders.

3. *Greater management expertise.* Corporations generally have a more formal management structure than proprietorships and partnerships. Corporate stockholders elect a board of directors who have the ultimate responsibility of managing the firm. The board of directors, in turn, hires professional managers to run the company. These managers then staff the organization with people possessing the skills and expertise required to run the day-to-day operations of the business.

4. *Easy transferability of ownership.* Because shares of ownership in corporations are usually relatively low in cost, they can be purchased or sold by individual investors much more easily than can an ownership interest in either of the other two forms of business. Additionally, in contrast to the approval required to accept a new partner into a partnership, generally no approval or permission is required for buying and selling corporate stock.

5. *Continuity of life.* Because a corporation is legally separate and distinct from its owner or owners, it continues to exist even when a complete change in ownership occurs. For example, **DuPont** has been in existence since the early 1900s, and although the company continues to thrive, virtually none of its original owners are still alive.

DISADVANTAGES OF CORPORATIONS

1. *Greater tax burden.* All businesses, regardless of form, must pay property taxes and payroll taxes. In addition to these taxes, corporations must pay a federal income tax, and in many states must also pay state and local income taxes on the profits they earn. Corporations often distribute at least part of the firm's after-tax profit to their shareholders as dividends. The stockholders then must consider these dividends as personal income and pay personal income taxes on them. This situation is referred to as double taxation, and it has been the subject of fierce debate for many years in the United States. We should mention here that double taxation does not exist for all corporations. Small, privately held corporations (usually with 75 or fewer stockholders) may elect a special tax classification, called an *S Corporation*, so they are treated very much like partnerships for federal income tax purposes. In this case, the corporation itself does not pay income tax. Rather, the individual stockholders include their proportional share of the company's profits as part of their personal taxable income, thus avoiding double taxation.

2. *Greater government regulation.* Corporations are subject to significantly more government control than either sole proprietorships or partnerships. Many corporations, especially publicly traded ones like **Hewlett Packard, Gap,** and **Union Carbide,** must file reports with both federal and state regulatory bodies.

3. *Absentee ownership.* In almost all proprietorships and in most partnerships, the owners manage their business themselves. In many corporations, especially those that are publicly traded, few of the stockholders participate in the day-to-day operations of the business. The board of directors hires professional managers to operate the company on behalf of the owners. Professional managers sometimes operate the company in their own best interest, rather than in the owners' best interest.

Although corporations represent a small percentage of the total number of businesses in the United States, they transact approximately six times as much business as all proprietorships and partnerships combined. Corporations also control the majority of business resources in the United States. Exhibit 1–2 summarizes the advantages and disadvantages of the three forms of business.

OTHER BUSINESS FORMS

Evolutionary changes in business have prompted the creation of new forms of business organizations that combine characteristics of partnerships and corporations. A

	Advantages	Disadvantages
Proprietorship	Easy and inexpensive to form No sharing of profits Owner has total control Independence Few government regulations No separate income taxes Easy and inexpensive to dissolve	Unlimited liability Limited access to capital Limited management expertise Personal time commitment Limited life
Partnership	Easy to form Increased management expertise Access to more capital Few government regulations No separate income taxes Greater business continuity	Unlimited liability Sharing of profits Potential conflicts between partners Difficulty in dissolving
Corporation	Limited liability Greater access to capital Easy transferability of ownership Continuity of life Greater management expertise	Greater tax burden Greater government regulation Absentee ownership

EXHIBIT 1-2 Advantages and Disadvantages of the Three Forms of Business Organization

limited partnership (LP) consists of at least one general partner and one or more limited partners. The general partners have unlimited liability and operate the partnership. The limited partners enjoy limited liability (like corporate stockholders), but are precluded from a decision making role in the organization. In a *limited liability partnership (LLP)*, the liability of a general partner is limited to his or her own negligence or misconduct, or the conduct of persons he or she controls. In a regular partnership, each partner is liable for all partnership debts and the conduct of all partners and employees. In a *limited liability corporation (LLC)*, stockholders enjoy the limited liability status of a corporation but are taxed as partners in a partnership, thus avoiding double taxation.

Discussion Question ◦

1-6. If you had the opportunity to start your own company, would you prefer to own (or be part owner) of a proprietorship, partnership, or corporation? Give specific reasons for your choice.

◆ TYPES OF BUSINESS ACTIVITIES

Companies in the United States are classified not only according to organizational form (proprietorship, partnership, or corporation), but also according to the type of business activity in which they engage. The three broad classifications are *manufacturing, merchandising*, and *service*. Although a single company can be involved in all three of these business activities, usually one of the three constitutes the company's major area of business.

MANUFACTURING COMPANIES

manufacturing The business activity that converts purchased raw materials into some tangible, physical product.

A **manufacturing** company purchases raw materials and converts them into some tangible, physical product. Raw materials consist of both unprocessed natural resources (one of the factors of production) and completely finished products manufactured by others. For example, **Boeing** purchases many items, such as electronics from **Honeywell** and tires from **Goodyear,** which it uses to produce its jetliners. The electronics and tires—raw materials to **Boeing**—are manufactured finished products of **Honeywell** and **Goodyear.**

MERCHANDISING COMPANIES

merchandising   The business activity involving the selling of finished goods produced by other businesses.

Like a manufacturer, a **merchandising** company sells tangible, physical products, called *merchandise*, as its major business activity. Instead of manufacturing the product it sells, a merchandising company buys it in a finished form. There are two kinds of merchandisers:

- *Wholesale merchandiser.* A wholesaler buys its product from the manufacturer (or another wholesaler) and then sells that product to another business that eventually sells it to the final consumer. Examples of wholesale merchandisers are ***Brandess-Kalt-Aetna Corporation,*** a photo equipment wholesaler, and ***W. W. Grainger,*** a major wholesale merchandiser of electric motors and small tools. These names may be unfamiliar to you because, as a consumer, you most often deal directly with a retailer rather than with a wholesaler. Wholesalers provide a valuable service to manufacturers by creating more efficient channels of distribution, and to retailers by making the retailers' purchasing convenient and cost effective.
- *Retail merchandiser.* A retailer buys its product from a wholesaler or manufacturer and sells the product to the final consumer. Examples of major national retailers are ***Home Depot, Banana Republic, Pier 1 Imports,*** and ***Gap.*** Other retail chains focus on specific regions of the country. Still other successful retailers have one location, such as gift shops and specialty stores.

SERVICE COMPANIES

service company   A business that performs a service as its major business activity.

A **service company** does not sell tangible products, but performs a service as its major business activity. For example, doctors, lawyers, accountants, plumbers, and auto mechanics provide services instead of tangible products. Examples of service companies are ***Bank of America*** and ***FedEx.***

HYBRID COMPANIES

hybrid companies   Those companies involved in more than one type of activity (manufacturing, merchandising, service).

As we said earlier, some businesses participate in more than one type of activity. These are known as **hybrid companies.** For example, ***General Motors Corporation*** (GM) manufactures automobiles and trucks and is therefore classified as a manufacturer. Recently, however, ***GM*** became involved in activities that are classified as services. ***GM*** created ***General Motors Acceptance Corporation*** (GMAC) to provide financing for customers purchasing ***GM*** cars and trucks. Even more recently, it began to issue credit cards (***Visa*** and ***MasterCard***).

We can expect the distinction among manufacturing, merchandising, and service companies to become even more blurred. As the struggle for survival in the global marketplace becomes more intense, many companies find it beneficial to become involved in a wide variety of business activities.

Discussion Question

1-7. In what type of business activity (manufacturing, merchandising, or service) would you like to be involved? Describe the type of operation that most interests you. What characteristics of this type of business do you find appealing?

◆ GLOBAL NATURE OF BUSINESS IN THE 21ST CENTURY

U.S. businesses simply cannot produce all the goods and services demanded in the U.S. marketplace. On the other hand, certain items produced in the United States either have no U.S. market or are produced in greater quantities than can be sold here. These factors are the forces that drive international business. ***Ford Motor Company*** sold an average of 7.1 million cars per year during the five-year period between 1997 and 2001. Of these cars, 41.4 percent were sold outside the United States. Clearly, international trade is important to the financial health of ***Ford,*** as it is to many other firms.

imports Foreign products brought into a country.

exports Goods produced in a country but sold outside that country.

Foreign products brought into a country are called **imports.** Goods produced in a country but sold outside that country are called **exports.** Most countries' economic health depends on the importing and exporting of goods; however, conducting business across national borders causes economic and political complications.

ECONOMIC COMPLICATIONS

Complications can arise when a firm from a country with a market economy does business with a firm from a country with a planned economy, because the aims of these two types of economic systems are so different. Complications are also caused by countries using different currencies. For example, the United States uses the dollar, Europe uses the euro, and Japan uses the yen. When companies in different countries transact business, their contract establishes the currency they will use. One or both companies then must translate its funds into the specified currency. In business, *translation* means converting or exchanging the currency of one country (e.g., yen) into its equivalent in another country's currency (e.g., dollar).

POLITICAL COMPLICATIONS

Politics plays an important role in international trade. Even countries with the same economic system experience difficulties in economic dealings with each other. Because each country seeks to protect its own self-interest, it wants to export a larger quantity of products than it imports. When a product is exported, money comes into the country's economy. When a product is imported, money leaves the country's economy (it goes to the country where the product was manufactured). As an extreme example, assume that all of France's merchandisers decide to import all the products they sell in France, because the imported merchandise costs less than French-produced products. Before long, all the French manufacturing companies would close, the French manufacturing jobs would disappear, and an essential part of France's economic base would cease to exist. To provide protection for their own economic bases and to prevent this kind of scenario, countries create trade agreements.

quotas A limit on the quantities of particular items that can be imported.

tariffs Taxes that raise the price of imported products to about the same as similar domestic products.

Trade agreements are formal treaties between two or more countries that are designed to control imports and exports. These agreements generally establish quotas and/or tariffs on imported products. **Quotas** limit the quantities of particular items that can be imported. For example, a limit may be placed on the number of Japanese cars brought into and sold in the United States. **Tariffs** are taxes that raise the price of imported products to about the same as similar domestic products. Several years ago, for example, the U.S. government became concerned about the number of inexpensive Japanese automobiles being sold in the United States. Because these imported cars were less expensive than cars produced in the United States, American auto makers were losing sales. In an effort to make the domestically produced cars more attractive to consumers, the U.S. government imposed a tariff on the Japanese cars. This raised the consumer's price of these imported cars to about the same price as the domestically produced cars.

Trade agreements are an important aspect of world politics because of the enormous economic impact they can have on the countries involved. Shortly after World War II, for example, 92 countries signed the General Agreement on Tariffs and Trade (GATT). President Clinton renegotiated this agreement in 1994. Other recent treaties are the United States–Canada Free Trade Pact of 1989, which eliminated most trade barriers between the two countries, and the North American Free Trade Agreement (NAFTA) signed by the United States, Canada, and Mexico in 1993.

The problem with all these international trade agreements is the same as the problem with all treaties—getting the parties involved to abide by them. Even after the agreements have been formally ratified, there is no effective way to enforce them, so compliance essentially depends on the good faith of the treaty members.

◆ BUSINESS AND ACCOUNTING

Business is about making decisions—decisions about what business form to take (proprietorship, partnership, corporation), decisions about what type of business activity to engage in (manufacturing, merchandising, service), and decisions about whether to engage in international business, to name just a few. Accounting information, in one form or another, plays a significant role in these decisions and in many other business decisions as well.

This is an accounting text. Its emphasis, however, is not so much on how accounting information is *prepared* as on how accounting information is *used*. To illustrate the relationship between accounting and business decisions, let's return to the example involving Tanner, Steve, and Chelsea. Remember that Tanner paid $30 for the pair of pants he later sold to Steve for $50. We calculated the gross profit on the sale of these pants as:

Amount received from Steve (BENEFIT)	$ 50
Less what Tanner paid for the pants (SACRIFICE)	− 30
Equals GROSS PROFIT on the sale of pants	$ 20

We pointed out that the $20 does not represent Tanner's real profit because he has other costs associated with his clothing store that must be taken into account before he can calculate his real profit. Think about the phrase "taken into account": This is accounting. The function of accounting is to provide information to Tanner, Chelsea, and the clothing manufacturers so they can make sound business decisions. Every day, literally millions of business decisions are made around the world. Every one of those decisions has an economic impact on someone, and few of those decisions are made without considering some kind of accounting information.

Discussion Questions

1–8. If rent and other costs associated with his clothing store amount to $3,000 a month, how many pairs of pants must Tanner sell at $50 a pair before he earns a profit?

1–9. What should Tanner do if his competitor, Chelsea, begins to take sales away by selling identical pairs of pants for $45?

1–10. What if Tanner finds out he can buy the identical pair of pants from a manufacturer in Mexico for only $25 instead of the $30 he is paying the U.S. manufacturer?

1–11. What should the U.S. clothing manufacturer do if it begins to lose sales to the Mexican clothing manufacturer that is selling these identical pants at the cheaper price?

We live in the information age. Advances in technology give us almost instant access to information on almost any subject. Every advance, however, has its price. We sometimes find ourselves in "information overload." Trying to find the optimal amount of information specific to your needs sometimes feels like trying to empty the ocean with a teaspoon to get to the treasure you seek on the sea floor.

The purpose of this book is to provide you with the tools, knowledge, and skills you need to sift through and use the accounting information available to you.

◆ INTRODUCTION TO FINANCIAL ACCOUNTING REPORTS

internal decision makers
Economic decision makers within a company who make decisions for the company. They have access to much or all of the accounting information generated within the company.

We can classify economic decision makers broadly as either *internal* or *external*. **Internal decision makers** are individuals within a company who make decisions for the company, while **external decision makers** are individuals or organizations outside a company who make decisions about that company. The accounting information internal decision makers use is called **management accounting,** while the information external decision makers use is called **financial accounting.** Our coverage here focuses primarily on financial accounting information and the accounting reports prepared from that information. There are four of them: the *Balance Sheet,* the *Income Statement,* the *Statement of Owners' Equity,* and the *Statement of Cash Flows.* We will introduce them briefly here and in much greater detail throughout the remainder of the text.

external decision makers
Economic decision makers outside a company who make
decisions about the company.
The accounting information
they use to make those decisions is limited to what the
company provides them.

management accounting
The branch of accounting
developed to meet the informational needs of internal
decision makers.

financial accounting   The
branch of accounting developed to meet the informa-
tional needs of external decision makers.

THE BALANCE SHEET

The balance sheet presents the present condition of a business by showing the valu-
ables the business has, the debts the business owes, and the owners' holdings in the
company. The statement is based on the following equation:

$$\text{Assets} = \text{Liabilities} + \text{Owners' equity}$$

Basically, *assets* are the things of value a company owns or controls. Examples
include cash, equipment, land, buildings, and merchandise. *Liabilities* are debts and
obligations a company has. Examples include amounts owed for purchases made on
charge accounts and for loans from the bank. Most commonly, these obligations must
be paid in money. Sometimes, however, the transfer of an asset other than money will
settle the indebtedness, or in some cases, it is an obligation to provide services. *Owners'
Equity* represents the owners' holdings in the company. The formal name of the balance sheet is the *Statement of Financial Position*. It is a financial snapshot of a company
at a specific date in time. Like any other snapshot, it shows only what existed on the
day it was taken. It does not show what existed on the day before it was taken or what
might exist on the day after. For example, Exhibit 1–3 shows a very condensed balance
sheet for **Microsoft** as of June 30, 2001. The balance sheet will be covered in much more
detail later in the text beginning with Chapter 3.

THE INCOME STATEMENT

The income statement presents the past performance of a business by showing the
amount the company charged to its customers (revenues) and the costs that were
required to earn that revenue (expenses). The statement is based on the following
equation:

$$\text{Revenue} - \text{Expenses} = \text{Net income}$$

The income statement is prepared for some specific period of time. Although the statement can be prepared for any period of time, most commonly it is prepared for a
month, a quarter, or a year. Basically, *revenues* are what a business charges for its goods
and services during the time period covered by the income statement from selling
whatever it is the company sells. *Expenses* are the economic sacrifices that were
required to generate the revenue during that same time period. Exhibit 1–4 shows a
very condensed income statement for **Microsoft** for the year ended June 30, 2001. The
formal name of the income statement is the *Statement of Results of Operations* and will
be the subject of extensive coverage beginning with Chapter 4.

THE STATEMENT OF OWNERS' EQUITY

The statement of owners' equity traces the ownership interest in the company from the
beginning of a specific time period to the end of the period. The time period is the same
as the period covered by the income statement we just talked about. The statement is
based on the following equation:

Beginning equity + Investments by owners + Net income – Distributions to owners = Ending equity

EXHIBIT 1–3 *Microsoft* Condensed Balance Sheet as of June 30, 2001			
	Microsoft Balance Sheet June 30, 2001 (In millions)		
Assets	$59,257	Liabilities	$11,968
		Stockholders' equity	47,289
		Total liabilities and stockholders' equity	$59,257

Microsoft
Income Statement
For the Year Ended June 30, 2001
(In millions)

Revenue	$25,296
Expenses	(17,950)
Net income	$ 7,346

EXHIBIT 1-4   *Microsoft* Condensed Income Statement

The main components of owners' equity are investments by owners, net income for the period (from the income statement), and distributions to owners. The statement of owners' equity begins with the initial amount of owners' equity for the accounting period. Next, additional investments by owners that were made during the period are added. Then net income from the income statement for the period is added (or a net loss is subtracted), and, finally, distributions or payments to owners are subtracted to arrive at owners' equity as of the end of the period. We will discuss this statement in greater detail beginning in Chapter 4.

THE STATEMENT OF CASH FLOWS

The statement of cash flows depicts the sources and uses of cash in a company during a particular period of time. The time period is the same as that of the income statement. The statement is based on the following equation:

$$\text{Cash inflow} - \text{Cash outflow} + \text{Beginning cash} = \text{Ending cash}$$

The statement of cash flows is organized around three principal business activities: operating, investing, and financing. The operating activities section of the statements shows the inflows and outflows of cash that relate to a company's primary business activity. The investing activities section shows cash flows for investments in property, plant, and equipment used in the business, as well as in investments in stocks, bonds, or other securities. The financing activities section shows the company's cash flows associated with obtaining and repaying the funds it needs to conduct business as well as distributions to owners. Exhibit 1–5 shows a condensed statement of cash flows for *Microsoft* for the year ended June 30, 2001.

Many businesspeople consider the statement of cash flows to be the most important of the four financial statements. Therefore, in addition to devoting a full chapter to this financial statement, we will explore facets of the statement of cash flows as we examine the other three financial statements beginning in Chapter 3.

EXHIBIT 1-5   *Microsoft* Condensed Statement of Cash Flows

Microsoft
Statement of Cash Flows
For the Year Ended June 30, 2001
(In millions)

Cash from operating activities	$13,422
Cash used for investing activities	(8,734)
Cash used for financing activities	(5,612)
Net change in cash	(924)
Cash, beginning of year	4,846
Cash, end of year	$ 3,922

FINANCIAL STATEMENT ANALYSIS

If you look at the financial statements of the ***Pier 1 Imports, Inc.*** annual report accompanying this text, you will get an idea of what we meant by "information overload." To be truly useful to decision makers, the statements must be analyzed. For example, many financial statement users consider the relationship between assets and liabilities on a balance sheet to be extremely important. This relationship is called the *debt ratio,* and it reveals the proportion of assets financed by debt. The debt ratio is one of many financial ratios developed over time to help financial statement users analyze the reports they receive.

Chapter 11 of this text is devoted entirely to financial statement analysis. In addition, where appropriate in earlier chapters we will present a section on the use of financial statements including some pertinent facets of financial statement analysis.

AUTHORITY OVER ACCOUNTING REPORTS

generally accepted accounting principles (GAAP) Guidelines for presentation of financial accounting information designed to serve external decision makers' need for consistent and comparable information.

Over time, the accounting profession has developed a set of standards to be used for financial reporting. These standards are known as **generally accepted accounting principles (GAAP).** GAAP provides assurance to outsiders (external decision makers) that the information available in a given decision situation was prepared in accordance with a well-defined set of rules and guidelines.

THE SECURITIES AND EXCHANGE COMMISSION (SEC)

Securities and Exchange Commission (SEC) The government agency empowered to regulate the buying and selling of stocks and bonds and to establish accounting rules, standards, and procedures, and the form and content of published financial reporting.

Prior to the stock market crash of 1929 and the resulting Great Depression, there was not a set of accounting standards to be used in preparing financial reports. In fact, a great many people believe that the absence of such standards was at least partially responsible for the crash. Be that as it may, not long after the stock market crash, the U.S. Congress, in an attempt to protect investors and financial statement users, created the **Securities and Exchange Commission (SEC)** and gave it explicit authority to mandate for publicly traded companies:

> . . . the items or details to be shown in the balance sheet and earning statement, and the methods to be followed in the preparation of accounts, in the appraisal or valuation of assets and liabilities, in the determination of depreciation and depletion . . . and in the preparation . . . of consolidated balance sheets or income accounts.[2]

The SEC was given the authority to establish (1) the rules, standards, and procedures used to account for transactions and events and (2) the form and content of published financial reporting.

Many thought the creation of the SEC meant that the government would establish accounting rules and standards. In 1938, however, the SEC decided to allow the accounting profession to establish standards of accounting, as long as there was "substantial authoritative support" for those standards (ASR 4, subparagraph 101). The SEC viewed its principal objective as overseeing adequate disclosure in financial reporting.

The decision to leave the setting of accounting standards to the accounting profession was a profoundly important one. Had the SEC decided differently, U.S. accounting rules today would likely be established by the federal government. Instead, for over 60 years, a series of professional committees and boards, currently the **Financial Accounting Standards Board (FASB),** has determined the accounting standards.

Financial Accounting Standards Board (FASB) The organization that is principally responsible for establishing accounting guidelines and rules in the United States at the present time.

Recently, the relationship among business, the accounting profession, and the SEC is being closely scrutinized. The collapse of ***Enron*** and the serious problems at ***Global Crossing*** and ***WorldCom*** have caused the U.S. Congress to reevaluate the role of the federal government in the standard-setting and enforcement processes.

---

[2]Securities Act of 1933, Section 19.

Discussion Questions

1-12. What are the pros and cons of having accounting rules established by the federal government?

1-13. What are the pros and cons of having accounting rules established by the accounting profession?

1-14. If the choice were yours, would you prefer to have accounting standards determined by a government agency or by the accounting profession? Explain your decision.

FINANCIAL ACCOUNTING STANDARDS BOARD (FASB)

The express mission of the Financial Accounting Standards Board (FASB) is

> *. . . to establish and improve standards of financial accounting and reporting for the guidance and education of the public, including issuers, auditors, and users of financial information.*[3]

Because of the FASB's structure and operating methods, it has wide acceptance in both the accounting profession and the business community. The FASB is an independent body composed of seven full-time members, who are required to resign from any other employment during their FASB service. Not all members are accountants. Members come from diverse backgrounds, though they must know accounting, finance, and business in general. This diversity gives the FASB a broad perspective of the public interest in matters of financial accounting and reporting.

Discussion Question

1-15. If FASB members are not required to be accountants, from what other professional backgrounds are members likely to be drawn?

One of the first things the FASB did after it was established was to assess the state of the standard-setting process. They discovered that nobody had ever formally decided what the accounting standards were attempting to accomplish. That may sound odd to you, but it can be readily explained. Accounting standards always have been, and remain, responses to specific needs. By that we mean that a situation arises and a standard is established to deal with that situation. What this can lead to, over time, is a labyrinth of standards, often confusing, and often conflicting.

Early on, the FASB developed a **Conceptual Framework of Accounting** from which to approach the process of setting standards. We will refer to this often throughout the remaining chapters of this text; from here on we will usually refer to it simply as the *Conceptual Framework*. The *Conceptual Framework* is contained in six *Statements of Financial Accounting Concepts*. These six statements establish the objectives of financial reporting and the qualitative characteristics of useful accounting information, and they define the accounting elements, assumptions, principles, and constraints. Think of the *Conceptual Framework* as an arch (see Exhibit 1–6). The top of the arch (objectives) is what accounting information attempts to provide. The base of the arch (assumptions, principles, and constraints) outlines the environment in which accounting operates. On the base, supporting the top of the arch, are columns containing the qualitative characteristics accounting information must possess to be useful, and the accounting elements used to produce accounting information. We will discuss the qualitative characteristics in Chapter 2. Our discussion of the 10 accounting elements begins in Chapter 3 and continues throughout the remainder of the text. Because all of the assumptions, principles, and constraints relate to the qualitative characteristics and the accounting elements, we will discuss them as we present the characteristics and elements in later chapters. Our discussion of the *Conceptual Framework* in this chapter will focus on the objectives of financial reporting. As we discuss each of these items, we will give the actual FASB wording in italics followed by a brief explanation of certain terms.

Conceptual Framework of Accounting A framework created by the FASB to establish the objectives of financial reporting and the qualitative characteristics of useful accounting information, and to define the accounting elements, assumptions, principles, and constraints.

---

[3]Robert S. Kay and D. Gerald Searfoss (eds.), *Handbook of Accounting and Auditing*, 2nd ed. (Boston: Warren, Gorham & Lamont, 1989), 46–48.

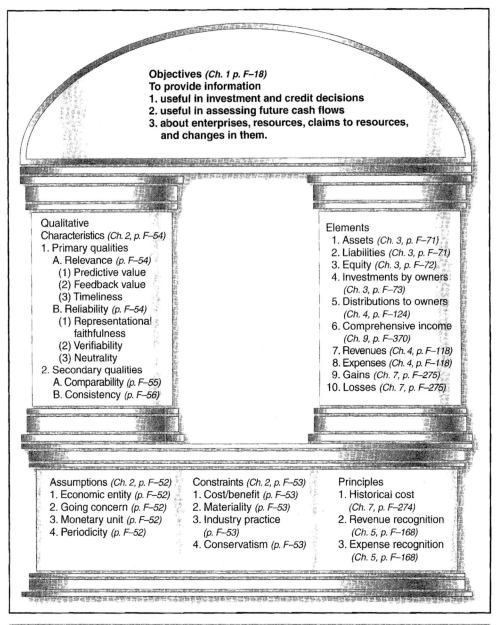

Objectives *(Ch. 1 p. F–18)*
To provide information
1. **useful in investment and credit decisions**
2. **useful in assessing future cash flows**
3. **about enterprises, resources, claims to resources, and changes in them.**

Qualitative
Characteristics *(Ch. 2, p. F–54)*
1. Primary qualities
  A. Relevance *(p. F–54)*
    (1) Predictive value
    (2) Feedback value
    (3) Timeliness
  B. Reliability *(p. F–54)*
    (1) Representational
       faithfulness
    (2) Verifiability
    (3) Neutrality
2. Secondary qualities
  A. Comparability *(p. F–55)*
  B. Consistency *(p. F–56)*

Elements
1. Assets *(Ch. 3, p. F–71)*
2. Liabilities *(Ch. 3, p. F–71)*
3. Equity *(Ch. 3, p. F–72)*
4. Investments by owners
  (Ch. 3, p. F–73)
5. Distributions to owners
  (Ch. 4, p. F–124)
6. Comprehensive income
  (Ch. 9, p. F–370)
7. Revenues *(Ch. 4, p. F–118)*
8. Expenses *(Ch. 4, p. F–118)*
9. Gains *(Ch. 7, p. F–275)*
10. Losses *(Ch. 7, p. F–275)*

Assumptions *(Ch. 2, p. F–52)*
1. Economic entity *(p. F–52)*
2. Going concern *(p. F–52)*
3. Monetary unit *(p. F–52)*
4. Periodicity *(p. F–52)*

Constraints *(Ch. 2, p. F–53)*
1. Cost/benefit *(p. F–53)*
2. Materiality *(p. F–53)*
3. Industry practice
  (p. F–53)
4. Conservatism *(p. F–53)*

Principles
1. Historical cost
  (Ch. 7, p. F–274)
2. Revenue recognition
  (Ch. 5, p. F–168)
3. Expense recognition
  (Ch. 5, p. F–168)

EXHIBIT 1–6 The Conceptual Framework of Accounting

OBJECTIVES OF FINANCIAL REPORTING

1. Information useful in investment and credit decisions — *Financial reporting should provide information that is useful to present and potential investors and creditors and other users in making rational investment, credit, and similar decisions. The information should be comprehensible to those who have a reasonable understanding of business and economic activities and are willing to study the information with reasonable diligence.* (Statement of Financial Accounting Concepts No. 1, paragraph 34) In the first sentence, *investors* include both those who buy a company's equity securities (stock) and those who buy a company's debt securities (bonds). *Creditors* include suppliers of goods and services, customers, and lending institutions. The *other users* include security analysts, brokers, lawyers, and regulatory agencies. The second sentence of this quotation describes responsibilities for both the users and the accounting profession. In order to use accounting information effectively, the various users must have a reasonable understanding of business *and* they must be willing to study the information with reasonable diligence. Users must fulfill their responsibility, and accountants are responsible to give them information that is comprehensible to them.

2.   **Information useful in assessing cash flows**—*Financial reporting should provide information that is useful to present and potential investors and creditors and other users in assessing the amounts, timing, and uncertainty of prospective cash receipts from dividends or interest and the proceeds from the sale, redemption, or maturity of securities or loans.* (Statement of Financial Accounting Concepts No. 1, paragraph 37) Think back to the first objective for just a minute. Why do investors invest or creditors lend money? They do it primarily to ultimately increase their own cash resources. These investors and creditors need information to help them form rational expectations about whether the prospective receipt of cash is sufficient to warrant the investment or loan. We will discuss this concept in greater detail in Chapter 2 when we cover economic decision making.

3.   **Information about enterprise resources, claims to resources, and changes in them**—*Financial reporting should provide information about the economic resources of an enterprise, the claims to those resources (obligations of the enterprise to transfer resources to other entities and owners' equity), and the effects of transactions, events, and circumstances that change resources and claims to those resources.* (Statement of Financial Accounting Concepts No. 1, paragraph 40) The term *economic resources* refers to assets owned or controlled by the enterprise. *Claims to resources* means debts owed by the company. These debts will be paid by transferring assets (usually cash) to whoever has the claim.

THE STANDARD-SETTING PROCESS TODAY

From its beginning, the FASB has employed a due process approach to setting standards. A due process approach focuses on the protection of individual rights. From the time the FASB identifies an issue that may require a new (or revised) standard to the time a standard is set, interested parties have an opportunity to express their opinions on the matter to FASB. Under the guidance of the FASB, setting standards follows a 10-step circular process emphasizing due process:

1. **Identifying issues.**   The FASB, the American Institute of Certified Public Accountants (AICPA), public accounting firms, business organizations, and the U.S. Congress identify accounting issues and problems. The FASB attempts to treat seriously all issues these parties raise.
2. **Setting an agenda.**   The FASB selects issues it will consider in the standard-setting process. In selecting an issue, the FASB takes account of its own resources, the perceived urgency of the matter, and any interrelationship with other projects already under consideration.
3. **Appointing a task force.**   Once it places an item on the agenda, the FASB appoints a task force to see the project through to its conclusion—either the creation of a new standard or the elimination of the project. Task forces usually include FASB members and outside experts in related areas with diverse views to obtain as many different perspectives as possible.
4. **Creating a discussion memorandum.**   The appointed task force prepares a discussion memorandum, which defines the problem, explains the issues, describes the scope of the project, and includes several alternative solutions. All interested parties may respond to the memorandum.
5. **Holding public hearings.**   The FASB holds public hearings on major projects under consideration and announces the hearings in the financial press, inviting interested parties to make an oral presentation of their views.
6. **Inviting comment letters.**   Those unable to attend the public hearings may write comment letters. The FASB considers every letter.
7. **Deliberating.**   After considering the comments from the public hearings, comment letters, FASB's technical staff, and the task force, the FASB decides whether to issue an exposure draft or drop the issue.
8. **Writing an exposure draft.**   The FASB prepares a draft version of the proposed standard and exposes it to public comment for at least 60 days. Comments received at this stage often bring about significant changes in the exposure draft.

9. **Issuing a Statement of Financial Accounting Standards.**   After a proposed standard goes through the first eight steps of the process, FASB members vote on whether to issue a new standard. When a majority of the seven members approves the new rule, a new *Statement of Financial Accounting Standards (SFAS)* becomes part of GAAP.

10. **Conducting a post-enactment review.**   Because financial accounting and reporting are dynamic areas, the FASB constantly reconsiders, refines, or amends the standards.

The FASB has issued well over 100 official pronouncements establishing standards that constitute GAAP. If a company is required to conform to GAAP, these standards are applied in preparing its financial statements and related financial information.

Only companies whose stocks or bonds are traded on an organized exchange are legally required to follow GAAP because they are regulated by the SEC. Companies not subject to SEC regulation may use whatever accounting principles they desire, unless external financial statement users demand that GAAP be followed. For instance, banks and other lending institutions often require financial information that conforms to GAAP from its borrowers. Also, any company a certified public accountant (CPA) firm audits will likely need to follow GAAP in the preparation of its financial statements whether it is regulated by the SEC or not. We will discuss the importance of independent audits in the next section.

Discussion Question ●

1–16. Why do you think a company might be opposed to adopting GAAP?

◆ OUTSIDE ASSURANCE ON FINANCIAL STATEMENTS

Common sense dictates that external decision makers cannot rely solely on the integrity of a company's management, because it is usually in management's best interests to present financial statements that reflect as favorably as possible on the company's performance. There is a need for some assurance from outside the company as to the fairness of its financial statement presentation. That outside assurance is provided by independent audits.

WHAT EXACTLY IS AN AUDIT?

Financial statement users rely on an independent auditor's opinion to assure them that they can trust what they read in the financial statements. The auditor must be independent. That is, the auditor must not have a real or perceived vested interest in the success or failure of the company being audited. Accordingly, the auditor cannot be an employee of the company being audited. He or she must be an independent contractor hired in accordance with a strict set of state legislated rules of conduct. The *independence* of an independent audit is the principal source of the audit's value. What was obviously a lack of independence between **Enron** and **Andersen** (the company's auditor) contributed significantly to **Enron** top management's ability to get away with fraudulent practices for as long as it did. This and other examples, like **WorldCom** (**Andersen** was its auditor, as well), points out the importance of the need for independence. We should note here, however, that thousands of audits are conducted in the United States every year by thousands of auditors that maintain the independence required to provide an audit opinion external parties can rely on.

The auditor examines the client's financial statements and supporting documentation to determine whether the financial statements present a fair picture of the client's financial condition and results of its operations, and to ensure that the financial statements have been presented in accordance with GAAP. It is not feasible for the auditor to examine all the client's records because to do so would make the audits so expensive that companies would not be able to afford them. Auditors examine enough of the records to satisfy themselves as to the fairness of the financial statement numbers. An

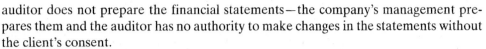

auditor does not prepare the financial statements—the company's management prepares them and the auditor has no authority to make changes in the statements without the client's consent.

In addition to examining financial records, auditors also evaluate the policies and procedures that are in place to safeguard company assets. This safeguarding of company assets is called internal control.

Generally accepted accounting principles were developed to improve the usefulness of financial accounting. The independent audit is a mechanism to provide assurance to external parties that the financial statements they use have been prepared in accordance with established standards.

Discussion Questions

1-17. How would you decide which and how many records to examine to determine whether your social club's treasurer's report portrays a fair picture of the club's financial activity for the past year?

1-18. How might your answer to question 1–17 change if you were to look at your local Wal-Mart's records for the year?

Auditing standards require auditors to have an extensive knowledge of the economy, the relevant industry, and the client's business. Auditors make inquiries of company personnel, review company financial records, and conduct numerous audit procedures to achieve reasonable assurance that there are no material misstatements in the financial statements. "Reasonable assurance" is what a rational person would consider sufficient. In an accounting context, something is *material* when it would influence the judgment of a reasonable person. A "material misstatement" is one that is significant enough that it could possibly change a reasonable person's decision about a company's financial condition.

WHO PERFORMS AUDITS?

In the United States, only licensed CPAs are permitted to perform independent audits, but not all CPAs are auditors. Auditing is a highly specialized accounting function governed by a set of standards called *generally accepted auditing standards (GAAS)*. The American Institute of Certified Public Accountants (AICPA) details the procedures that CPAs must follow during audits through pronouncements called *Statements on Auditing Standards (SAS)*.

Auditors walk a curious tightrope in our society. Lawyers have one responsibility: to represent their clients who pay them to fulfill that responsibility. Doctors have one responsibility: to care for their patients who pay them to fulfill that responsibility. Auditors, on the other hand, have a dual responsibility: They are responsible to the clients who pay them, but they also have a responsibility to all the users of audited financial statements. Auditors must be independent of the entity they are auditing and objective in their assessment of the financial statements' fairness. It is a difficult balancing act, and auditors face a rising level of litigation from statement users who relied on financial statements and then suffered losses.

Discussion Question

1-19. What potential problems do you think can arise from the auditor's dual responsibility?

THE AUDIT OPINION

At the conclusion of an audit, the auditor issues an *opinion* as to the fairness of the financial statement presentation. GAAS allows the CPA to issue one of several different opinions, depending on the findings of the audit. Most firms receive an *unqualified* opinion, in which the CPA attests that the financial statements "present fairly, in all material respects, the financial position . . . and the results of operations and its cash flows . . . in conformity with generally accepted accounting principles." Also commonly called a *clean* opinion, all firms seek to have this opinion rendered on their financial

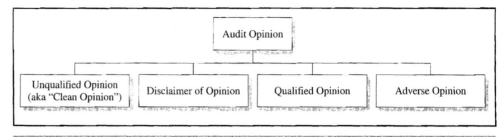

	Audit Opinion		
Unqualified Opinion (aka "Clean Opinion")	Disclaimer of Opinion	Qualified Opinion	Adverse Opinion

EXHIBIT 1-7 Four Possible Audit Opinions

statements. A financial statement user should be concerned about financial statements that do not receive an unqualified opinion.

Auditors may issue several other opinions. If an auditor is unable to achieve reasonable assurance because the company has not provided enough evidence or has not allowed the auditor to perform enough audit tests, the auditor may be unable to achieve reasonable assurance and will therefore issue a *disclaimer of opinion.* The financial statement user has no assurance from the auditor of fairness or conformity with GAAP when the auditor issues a disclaimer of opinion. Auditors have the option of issuing a *qualified* opinion in which they state an exception to the general fairness of presentation of the financial statements or to their lack of conformity with GAAP. Obviously, financial statement users should carefully consider the exception(s) the auditor raises. The most devastating opinion an auditor can render is the *adverse* opinion, in which the auditor states that the financial statements are not fairly presented or that they do not conform to GAAP. Readers should not rely on such financial statements. A financial statement user should examine the audit opinion to determine the auditor's level of assurance before reading the financial statements. Exhibit 1–7 illustrates the four possible audit opinions.

Discussion Question

1–20. Find the audit opinion in the annual report of Pier 1 Imports, Inc. contained in the company's 2002 annual report. Who are the auditors? What type of opinion did the auditors issue?

Earlier in this chapter we said that external decision makers use financial accounting information. There are two major sources of financial accounting information available to external decision makers, the *annual report,* and the *Form 10-K.* See the appendix to this chapter for a discussion of these two important financial reports.

Summary

The word business has several different meanings, but in the context of this book, it means either commerce or trade as a whole or a specific company involved in commerce or trade. All economic activity revolves around the four factors of production: natural resources, labor, capital, and entrepreneurship. In a planned economy, a strong centralized government controls most or all of the factors. In a market economy, most of the factors are privately owned.

Capitalism, like the market economy in the United States, relies on a profit motive that spurs competition, drives the allocation of resources, and forces business to operate efficiently. Modern U.S. business practice balances companies' profit motive with their social responsibilities to various stakeholders.

The three basic forms of business organizations are the proprietorship (one owner), the partnership (two or more owners), and the corporation (a legal entity separate from its owner or owners). Most business activity can be categorized as manufacturing, merchandising, or service. Hybrid businesses are those that conduct more than one of these types of activities.

Economic decision makers are classified broadly as either internal or external to an entity. The information designed for use by external parties is called financial accounting information and is contained in four general-purpose financial statements: the balance sheet, the income statement, the statement of owners' equity, and the statement of cash flows.

In response to the users' need for relevant, reliable financial information, accountants developed standards called generally accepted accounting principles (GAAP). The Securities and Exchange Commission (SEC) has the legal authority to regulate the accounting profession. However, under the SEC's watchful eye, the Financial Accounting Standards Board (FASB), a private body created in 1973, establishes most of the GAAP in the United States. The FASB uses a due process approach, whereby anyone who wishes to express his or her opinion has an opportunity to do so as the FASB creates new accounting standards. Early on, the FASB created the *Conceptual Framework of Accounting* and works to ensure that new accounting standards are consistent with this framework.

External users of financial statements need some form of assurance that the financial statements are fairly presented and are prepared according to GAAP. In large part, this assurance is achieved through independent audits, whereby independent CPAs examine enough of a company's records to determine whether the company's financial statements fairly present the company's economic position and that they are prepared in accordance with GAAP. The auditor then issues an audit opinion to express his or her findings.

Corporate Reporting and the Annual Report

annual report A corporate document that provides interested parties with a variety of information including financial statements and a host of general information about the company and its management.

Form 10-K Less glamorous than the annual report, this corporate document includes additional financial and nonfinancial details that are invaluable to external decision makers.

Every publicly traded corporation has various stakeholders and potential stakeholders. These include shareholders and potential shareholders, creditors, customers, and employees and potential employees. To make sound decisions, these stakeholders must have access to financial information about the company. Two major sources of financial information in the United States are the corporate *annual report* and the SEC's *Form 10-K*. The **annual report** includes a variety of information including financial statements and a host of general information about the company and its management. The **Form 10-K,** which is required by the SEC, is much less glamorous than the annual report, but it includes financial and nonfinancial details that are not included in the annual report. Both documents provide invaluable information to external decision makers.

HOW TO GET AN ANNUAL REPORT

The SEC requires that each publicly traded firm prepare an annual report to communicate important information about the company. As part of the SEC requirement, if you own shares of stock in a corporation, you will automatically receive a copy of its annual report. But how should you go about getting an annual report if you are not a shareholder? There are several ways to get a copy of an annual report. In addition to calling the company directly to request a copy, you can find annual report information on the Internet, in the *Wall Street Journal* Annual Report Service, and at most libraries.

- Almost all companies maintain a Web site on the Internet. Company Web sites often include a cyber version of the annual report or at least financial statements and other information taken directly from the annual report. You can download or print the annual report or, if you would rather, you can make an online request for a copy of the annual report itself.

  It may take some trial and error to find a particular company's Web site, but as the following examples show, in almost all cases the Web site address is just a modified form of the company name.

Company Name	Internet Address
Gap Inc.	*www.gap.com*
Sears	*www.sears.com*
Hallmark	*www.hallmark.com*
JCPenney	*www.jcpenney.com*

- The *Wall Street Journal* provides an Annual Report Service for selected companies. The *Wall Street Journal* listing for some companies includes a small cloverleaf. This cloverleaf signifies that the *Journal's* annual report service can provide a copy of the company's annual report. Call 1-800-654-2582 to request an annual report.

- Many libraries provide computers and access to various CD-ROM sources for company information. Some of the most popular are:
  - *Infotrac.* Infotrac contains company profiles, investment reports, and article citations.
  - *Proquest.* Proquest is the CD-ROM version of ABI/Inform, the premier source of business articles. Proquest contains citations and the full text of articles, including photos and graphical images.
  - *Mergent's* (formerly *Moody's*). Mergent's provides full-text annual reports of U.S. and international operations.

  Online systems that search databases provide access to extensive information. Among the most widely used databases for company information are:
  - *DIALOG.* DIALOG provides access to over 400 databases covering a wide range of topics, not all of which are business related. Available information includes annual reports and articles (both full text and citations).
  - *LEXIS/NEXIS.* LEXIS/NEXIS provides full text of all SEC-required filings (such as the Form 10-K) and various business articles and newsletters.

  In addition to the annual report sources listed already, you can always contact the company directly. Do not hesitate to ask a company for its annual report. Corporations know that public image is a critical factor in a company's success or failure so they are generally happy to provide a copy of their annual report upon request. To order an annual report directly from a company, first locate the corporate headquarters address, phone number, or fax number on their Web site, in telephone listings, or in some other library reference source, then simply phone, write, or fax your request to the company's public relations or investor relations department.

INFORMATION PROVIDED IN ANNUAL REPORTS

Annual reports from various companies contain much the same categories of information, mainly because the SEC requires that most of it be included. The table of contents for ***Pier 1 Imports, Inc.***'s 2002 annual report shown below represents the type of information found in most corporate annual reports. An asterisk indicates that the SEC requires the information.

Financial Highlights
Letter to Stockholders
Key Financial Statistics
*Five-Year Selected Financial Data
*Management Discussion and Analysis
*Independent Auditors' Report
*Report of Management
*Consolidated Statements of Operations
*Consolidated Balance Sheets
*Consolidated Statements of Cash Flows
*Consolidated Statements of Shareholders' Equity
*Notes to Consolidated Financial Statements
*Shareholder Information
*Directors and Officers

Discussion Question ○

1–21. What other information would you want to know about Pier 1 Imports? Would you feel comfortable enough to call, e-mail, or write to the company with a specific question? Where can you find the address and phone number for Pier 1 in the annual report?

FORM 10-K

A Form 10-K looks very different from an annual report. The annual report is an expensive public relations brochure with high-quality glossy pages, color photos, and eye-catching graphics. The 10-K is printed on thin paper with no pictures and no color graphics. It contains a wealth of information about the company, much of which is also included in the annual report. This is not surprising because the SEC regulates disclosure requirements for both documents. That said, the annual report may be "included by reference" in the Form 10-K to avoid duplication of various required items. Exhibit 1–8 lists the required contents of the 10-K.

EXHIBIT 1–8 Outline of the Contents of Form 10-K

Part I
Item 1. Business
Item 2. Properties
Item 3. Legal Proceedings
Item 4. Submission of Matters to a Vote of Security Holders
Part II
Item 5. Market for the Company's Common Equity and Related Stockholder Matters
Item 6. Selected Financial Data
Item 7. Management's Discussion and Analysis of Financial Condition and Results of Operations
Item 8. Financial Statements and Supplementary Data
Item 9. Changes in and Disagreements with Accountants on Accounting and Financial Disclosure
Part III
Item 10. Directors and Executive Officers of the Company
Item 11. Executive Compensation
Item 12. Security Ownership of Certain Beneficial Owners and Management
Item 13. Certain Relationships and Related Transactions
Part IV
Item 14. Exhibits, Financial Statements, and Schedules and Reports on Form 8-K

Electronic Data Gathering, Analysis. and Retrieval (EDGAR)
A system operated by the SEC to facilitate the collection, and more importantly, the dissemination of corporate information to all interested parties. Access to EDGAR is available over the Internet at www.sec.gov.

The SEC prescribes the contents of Form 10-K in Regulation S-X and Regulation S-K, as revised in 1982. Those revisions created the SEC's Integrated Disclosure System, which simplified and improved the quality of disclosures and reduced its cost, in part by eliminating duplicate reports. The SEC's **Electronic Data Gathering, Analysis, and Retrieval (EDGAR)** system is an important component of the integrated disclosure system. Each publicly traded domestic company reporting to the SEC is required to file its Form 10-K and many other disclosure documents and schedules on EDGAR. So what does this mean to you? Well, EDGAR was specifically designed to help collect, and more importantly to disseminate, corporate information to interested parties (that is, to anyone who wants it). This means that if a document is filed on EDGAR, you have easy access to that document via the Internet. For example, all you have to do to get a Form 10-K for any publicly traded company is to log on to the SEC's Web site at www.sec.gov and click on the EDGAR link. What's more, EDGAR puts a wealth of other information about the company at your fingertips. Whether you want to obtain general information about a company, a company's financial information, or information about a particular company's industry, EDGAR at www.sec.gov can help you get it. Remember that you can log on to the EDGAR system Web site to obtain a copy of a Form 10-K for virtually any publicly traded company.

GATHERING ADDITIONAL INFORMATION ABOUT A COMPANY

If you would like more information about a company than its annual report and Form 10-K provides, try the following sources:

- The company's Web site usually contains current press releases about company accomplishments, problems, financial results, and other important news.
- You can conduct a search for news about the company with any of the Web search engines.
- Libraries generally have a wide variety of resources available, including handbooks and periodicals. Examples are:
  - *Hoover's Handbook of American Business* offers information about each of the companies it profiles. Exhibit 1–9 shows the Hoover's profile for *Pier 1 Imports, Inc.* Most of the information it provides about a company is not available in the company's annual report, and background details provided in the sections titled "Overview" and "History" are particularly relevant to potential employees. Visit: www.hoovers.com.
  - *Standard and Poor's Stock Reports* details recent news about companies. This loose-leaf publication is updated monthly and contains various types of information. Visit: www2.standardandpoors.com.
  - *Mergent's Industrial Manual* (formerly *Moody's Industrial Manual*) offers extensive company histories and more detailed financial information than can be found in *Hoover's Handbook of American Business* and *Standard and Poor's Stock Reports*. Visit: www.mergent.com.
  - *Investor's Business Daily* provides critical information previously available only to institutional investors (pension and mutual funds, banks, insurance companies, and government organizations). Features include corporate ratings that provide fundamental and technical evaluations on stocks traded on the NASDAQ and the American and New York exchanges. Visit: www.investors.com.
  - Periodical indexes help you find articles about the company. Usually available in hardback or CD-ROM, the Business Periodicals Index or the *Wall Street Journal* Index can be helpful in locating information about a particular company. The most trustworthy sources for information in the press are the *Wall Street Journal, BusinessWeek, Fortune,* and *Forbes.*

SUMMARY OF APPENDIX

The most comprehensive presentation of financial reporting to stockholders is the annual report. The SEC has specific disclosure requirements for information provided in the annual report and the Form 10-K, required annually for publicly traded companies. The SEC prescribes the rules for the form and content of the financial statements and other information included in the 10-K under Regulations S-X and S-K. The SEC's Integrated Disclosure System encourages companies to eliminate duplication between the annual report and Form 10-K through "incorporation by reference."

You can gather additional information about publicly traded companies on the Internet, in the library, or from news sources.

PIER 1 IMPORTS, INC.

Overview

Wicker World? Rattans 'R' Us? How about Pier 1 Imports? The Fort Worth, Texas-based company sells about 5,000 home furnishings items imported from more than 50 countries—mostly Asia—in almost 800 US stores. In addition to its growing US operations, Pier 1 has about 35 stores in Canada, and it also operates about 25 The Pier stores in the UK.

Pier 1 gradually has changed its merchandise from the exotic knickknacks the baby boomers used to decorate their dorm rooms to the more upscale, but still exotic, household furnishings they buy today. The product line favors natural materials (rattan, wood) and handcrafted goods. Furniture accounts for more than a third of sales, and decorative items such as lamps, vases, and baskets account for another quarter. The stores also sell bed and bath products, housewares, and seasonal items. With more than a million active holders, Pier 1's private-label credit card is used to charge almost 30% of sales.

Pier 1 started selling online in 2000 and has hinted that it might create or buy high-end and low-end home furnishings chains (a la The Gap's upscale Banana Republic and lower-priced Old Navy chains). In 2001 it acquired the Cargo Furniture chain from home furnishings manufacturer Tandycrafts.

History

Attracted by a Fisherman's Wharf import outlet called Cost Plus, marketing guru Charles Tandy (founder of RadioShack) made a loan to its owner and obtained the right to open other Cost Plus stores. Opening his first Cost Plus store in 1962 in San Francisco, Tandy leveraged the strength of the US dollar against weaker foreign currencies. He bought inexpensive wicker furniture, brass candlesticks, and other items from countries like India, Mexico, and Thailand and gave them healthy markups, yet still managed to price them attractively for US customers.

The store was a hit with the peace and free-love generation of the 1960s, who dug its beads, incense, and wicker furniture. In 1965, with 16 locations, the company changed its name to Pier 1 Imports. Pressed by RadioShack, Tandy sold Pier 1 the next year. In 1969, with 42 stores, including its first store in Canada, the company went public on the American Stock Exchange.

By 1971 Pier 1 had 123 stores and was celebrating 100% sales gains for four consecutive years. It expanded its international presence, adding locations in Australia and Europe, and moved to the NYSE the next year. The chain experimented with alternative retail formats, including art supply, rug outlets, and fabric stores, but had abandoned them, as well as its foreign stores, by the mid-1970s. Pier 1 boasted nearly 270 locations by 1975.

Baby boomers, key to the chain's success, grew up and acquired different tastes, however. The dollar had also weakened, increasing costs. Performance faltered, and in 1980 the company brought in Robert Camp, who had successfully operated his own Pier 1 stores in Canada, to give it a makeover. Camp closed poorly performing stores, opened larger stores in more profitable areas, and began changing the merchandise mix from novelties to higher-quality goods.

In 1983 investment group Intermark bought more than a third of the company. The next year Pier 1 acquired 36 Nurseryland Garden Centers from Intermark (boosting Intermark's stake in Pier 1 to about 50%) and merged the stores with its Wolfe's Nursery to form Sunbelt Nursery Group, which was spun off in 1985. That year Pier 1 named Clark Johnson its CEO. At the time it operated nearly 265 locations, showing little growth in store count in a decade.

Johnson initiated an ambitious plan to double the number of Pier 1 stores, which reached 500 in early 1989. With Intermark struggling, Pier 1 bought back Sunbelt (including a 50% stake in Sunbelt from Intermark) in 1990. The following year Intermark sold its stake in Pier 1 to pay back debt. That year Pier 1 took Sunbelt public, keeping a 57% stake (Sunbelt has since been dissolved). In 1993 the company launched The Pier, a chain of stores in the UK, and opened boutiques in Sears stores in Mexico.

Having spruced up stores, the chain continued to adjust the merchandise mix, dumping apparel in 1997 in favor of higher-margin goods. Also in 1997 Pier 1 purchased a national bank charter from Texaco to standardize the interest rates and fees on its private-label credit card. Marvin Girouard replaced Johnson as CEO in 1998 and as chairman in 1999. Pier 1 began selling online with the launch of its Web site in June 2000.

In February 2001 the company acquired the 21-store Cargo Furniture chain from home furnishings manufacturer Tandycrafts.

Officers

Chairman and CEO: Marvin J. Girouard, age 61, $2,132,000 pay
SVP of Finance, CFO, and Treasurer: Charles H. Turner, age 44, $580,250 pay
SVP of Stores: Robert A. Arlauskas, age 46
SVP of Merchandising: Jay R. Jacobs, age 46, $580,250 pay
SVP of Legal Affairs: J. Rodney Lawrence, age 55, $424,000 pay
SVP of Marketing: Phil E. Schneider, age 49
SVP of Logistics and Allocations: David A. Walker, age 50
SVP of Human Resources: E. Mitchell Weatherly, age 53, $404,000 pay
Auditors: Ernst & Young LLP

Locations

HQ: 301 Commerce St., Ste. 600, Fort Worth, TX 76102
Phone: 817-252-8000   **Fax:** 817-252-8028
Web: www.pier1.com

Pier 1 Imports has about 800 stores in 48 states, plus 35 in Canada. It also owns 23 The Pier stores in the UK and 21 Cargo Furniture stores in the US. It also owns or franchises about 30 stores in Japan, Mexico, and Puerto Rico.

Products/Operations

2001 North American Sales

	% of sales
Furniture	40
Decorative accessories	22
Bed & bath	17
Housewares	12
Seasonal	9
Total	100

Selected Merchandise
Baskets
Bed and bath accessories
Candles
Ceramics
Dinnerware
Dried and silk flowers
Fragrance products
Furniture
Lamps
Seasonal products
Vases
Wall decor

EXHIBIT 1-9 *Pier 1 Imports, Inc.* Entry in Hoover's Handbook of American Business

EXHIBIT 1–9   *Pier 1 Imports, Inc.* Entry in *Hoover's Handbook of American Business (Continued)*

Competitors

Bed Bath & Beyond	Lechters
Bombay Company	Linens 'n Things
Container Store	Michaels Stores
Cost Plus	MJDesigns
Euromarket Designs	Spiegel
Garden Ridge	Williams-Sonoma
IKEA	

Historical Financials & Employees

NYSE: PSR FYE: Sat. nearest last day in Feb.	Annual Growth	2/92	2/93	2/94	2/95	2/96	2/97	2/98	2/99	2/00	2/01
Sales ($ mil.)	10.2%	587	629	685	712	811	947	1,075	1,139	1,231	1,412
Net income ($ mil.)	15.3%	26	23	6	25	10	44	78	80	75	95
Income as % of sales	—	4.5%	3.7%	0.9%	3.5%	1.2%	4.7%	7.3%	7.1%	6.1%	6.7%
Earnings per share ($)	13.9%	0.30	0.26	0.07	0.27	0.11	0.43	0.72	0.77	0.75	0.97
Stock price - FY high ($)	—	5.14	5.56	5.19	4.29	5.95	8.31	18.84	20.76	12.38	14.50
Stock price - FY low ($)	—	1.91	2.81	3.49	3.02	3.45	5.28	7.23	6.06	5.25	7.94
Stock price - FY close ($)	13.3%	4.24	4.92	3.71	4.18	5.84	7.73	17.84	8.63	8.75	13.00
P/E - high	—	17	21	74	16	54	17	24	25	16	15
P/E - low	—	6	11	50	11	31	11	9	7	7	8
Dividends per share ($)	—	0.00	0.03	0.05	0.05	0.06	0.07	0.07	0.12	0.12	0.15
Book value per share ($)	11.7%	2.04	2.27	2.27	2.53	2.56	3.19	3.87	4.14	4.70	5.53
Employees	7.5%	7,600	7,500	7,850	8,671	9,399	11,255	12,571	12,600	13,600	14,600

Stock Price History

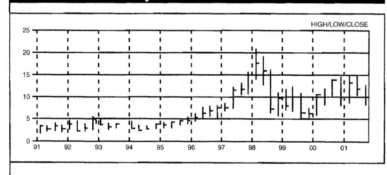

2001 Fiscal Year-End

Debt ratio: 4.5%
Return on equity: 19.5%
Cash ($ mil.): 47
Current ratio: 3.31
Long-term debt (5 mil.): 23
No. of shares (mil.): 96
Dividends
   Yield: 1.2%
   Payout: 15.5%
Market value ($ mil.): 1.250

Courtesy of *Hoover's Online* (www.hoovers.com)

Key Terms

- annual report, F–24
- business, F–2
- capital, F–3
- capitalism, F–3
- communism, F–3
- Conceptual Framework of Accounting, F–17
- corporation, F–8
- Electronic Data Gathering, Analysis, and Retrieval (EDGAR), F–26
- entrepreneurship, F–3
- exports, F–12
- external decision makers, F–14
- factors of production, F–2
- financial accounting, F–14
- Financial Accounting Standards Board (FASB), F–16
- Form 10-K, F–24
- generally accepted accounting principles (GAAP), F–16
- hybrid companies, F–11
- imports, F–12
- internal decision makers, F–13
- labor, F–3
- management accounting, F–14
- manufacturing, F–10
- merchandising, F–11
- natural resources, F–3
- net income, F–4
- net profit, F–4
- partnership, F–7
- profit, F–4
- proprietorship, F–5
- quotas, F–12
- Securities and Exchange Commission (SEC), F–16
- separate entity assumption, F–8
- service company, F–11
- sole proprietorship, F–5
- stakeholder, F–5
- tariffs, F–12

Review the Facts

A. What are the four factors of production? Define each.
B. Describe the primary difference between a planned economy and a market economy.
C. Explain what is meant by the profit motive.
D. What is gross profit?
E. How does net income differ from gross profit?
F. Explain the meaning of stakeholder.
G. Name the three basic forms of business organization and describe the advantages and disadvantages of each.
H. Describe the separate entity assumption.
I. Name and describe the three major types of businesses.
J. In the context of business activity, what is a hybrid company?
K. Define quotas and tariffs. Explain the purpose of each.
L. Describe the relationship between business and accounting.
M. What information does a balance sheet provide?
N. What information does an income statement provide?
O. What are the three business activities listed on the statement of cash flows?
P. Broadly define GAAP.
Q. Explain the role of the SEC in the regulation of accounting practice.
R. What is the FASB, and what does the acronym FASB stand for?
S. Briefly describe the purpose of the *Conceptual Framework of Accounting.*
T. What are the main objectives of financial reporting?
U. List the 10 steps of the FASB's due process for standard setting.
V. What is the purpose of an independent audit, and who can perform one?
W. What is an audit opinion?
X. Name and describe the four types of audit report an auditor can issue.
Y. Identify the two major financial reports that publicly traded corporations must prepare annually.
Z. *What is the primary purpose of the SEC's EDGAR system?
AA. *Why are corporations generally cooperative when individuals request their annual reports?
BB. What are the required sections of a company's annual report? Briefly describe each.

Apply What You Have Learned

LO 1 & 2: TERMINOLOGY

1–22. Below are items relating to some of the concepts in this chapter, followed by the definitions of those items in scrambled order.

a. Entrepreneurship
b. Labor
c. Planned economy
d. Capitalism
e. Factors of production
f. Natural resources
g. Capital
h. Profit motive

1. _____ The human resource factor
2. _____ Land and materials that come from land
3. _____ The factor of production that brings all the other factors of production together
4. _____ The motivation to do something when the benefits exceed the sacrifice of doing it
5. _____ A type of market economy
6. _____ The four major items needed to support economic activity
7. _____ Buildings, machinery, tools, and money used to produce goods and services
8. _____ A strong, centralized government controls all or most of the factors of production

Required: Match the letter next to each item on the list with the appropriate definition. Use each letter only once.

*Based on material in the Appendix.

LO 2, 4, & 5: BUSINESS TERMINOLOGY

1–23. Below are items relating to some of the concepts in this chapter, followed by the definitions of those items in scrambled order.

a. Hybrid company   f. Manufacturing company
b. Wholesaler   g. Merchandising company
c. Imports   h. Retailer
d. Exports   i. Translation
e. Tariffs   j. Quota

1. _____ Goods sold outside the country in which they were produced
2. _____ A business that converts purchased raw materials into some tangible, physical product
3. _____ A company involved in more than one type of business activity
4. _____ A type of business operated by either a wholesaler or a retailer
5. _____ A quantity limitation placed on imported goods
6. _____ A business known as a middleman
7. _____ The conversion of the currency of one country into its equivalent in another country's currency
8. _____ Taxes that raise the price of imported products
9. _____ A business that sells products to the final consumer
10. _____ Goods brought into a country that were produced in another country

Required: Match the letter next to each item on the list with the appropriate definition. Use each letter only once.

LO 3: COMPUTATION OF GROSS PROFIT AND NET INCOME

1–24. Larry Melman owns and operates a retail clothing store. Last month clothing sales totaled $5,200. Melman paid $2,800 for the clothing sold last month. He also paid rent of $300 and wages to employees totaling $900.

Required:

a. Calculate the gross profit on sales for last month.
b. Identify the expenses incurred during the month and explain whether they should be used to compute gross profit or net income.
c. Calculate the net income for last month.

LO 3: COMPUTATION OF GROSS PROFIT AND NET INCOME

1–25. James Marks sells fine imported cigars. During the month of December, James sold 3,000 cigars at a total price of $15,000. James paid $9,000 for the cigars that he sold in December.

Required: Determine the gross profit for James in December.

LO 3: COMPUTATION OF GROSS PROFIT AND NET INCOME

1–26. Carol Levine owns and operates a retail hardware store. In June her sales were $18,000. The items sold cost Ms. Levine $12,600. Ms. Levine spent $1,000 for store rent, $300 for utilities expense, and $1,500 for employee wages.

Required:

a. Calculate the gross profit on sales for June.
b. Identify the expenses incurred during the month and explain whether they should be used to compute gross profit or net income.
c. Calculate the net income for June.

LO 3: COMPUTATION OF GROSS PROFIT AND NET INCOME

1–27. In August, Mary bought 24 quilts for $100 each.

Required:

a. If Mary sells the quilts for $150 each, what is her gross profit for each quilt?
b. If she sells all of the quilts in August, what is her total gross profit?
c. If Mary rents an office for $200 and pays utilities expense of $75, advertising expense of $150, and bank charges of $15, calculate her net income for August.

LO 3 & 4: COMPUTATION OF GROSS PROFIT AND NET INCOME FOR DIFFERENT BUSINESS TYPES

1–28. The Computer Center of America manufactures and sells computers. During the month of October the center produced and sold 1,000 computers. The sale of the computers generated $1,000,000. The cost of the computers sold included $300,000 for the parts to build the computers, $200,000 for the labor to assemble the computers, and $100,000 for all other costs (overhead) necessary to make the computers. Aside from the cost of the computers themselves, the Computer Center spent $50,000 on selling and administrative expenses.

Required:

a. What type of business does the Computer Center operate (i.e., manufacturing, merchandising, service, or hybrid)?

b. Calculate the gross profit for the month of October.

c. Calculate the net income for the month of October.

LO 4: STOCKHOLDER VERSUS STAKEHOLDER

1–29. Explain the concept behind the term *stakeholder,* and contrast it with the definition of the term *stockholder.*

LO 4: FORMS OF BUSINESS ORGANIZATION

1–30. Below are the three basic forms of business in the United States, followed by some of the advantages relating to those forms of business:

a. Proprietorship   b. Partnership   c. Corporation

1. _____ Owner has total control
2. _____ Greater business continuity
3. _____ Easy transfer of ownership
4. _____ Limited liability
5. _____ Greater access to capital
6. _____ Easy and inexpensive to establish
7. _____ Few government regulations
8. _____ Easy to dissolve
9. _____ No special income taxes
10. _____ No sharing of profits
11. _____ Greater management expertise

Required: Match the letter next to each form of business with the appropriate advantage. Each letter will be used more than once and it is possible that a particular advantage applies to more than one of the business forms.

LO 4: FORMS OF BUSINESS ORGANIZATION

1–31. Below are the three basic forms of business in the United States, followed by some of the disadvantages relating to those forms of business:

a. Proprietorship   b. Partnership   c. Corporation

1. _____ Usually has less access to capital than the other two forms
2. _____ Greater tax burden
3. _____ Limited management expertise
4. _____ Unlimited liability
5. _____ Absentee ownership
6. _____ Must share profits
7. _____ Greater government regulation
8. _____ Often difficult to dissolve
9. _____ Potential ownership conflicts

Required: Match the letter (or letters) next to each form of business with the appropriate disadvantage. Each letter will be used more than once and it is possible that a particular disadvantage applies to more than one of the business forms.

LO 4: FORMS OF BUSINESSES

1–32. Professor Seth Levine is opening the Levine Publishing Company to publish and distribute travel books throughout the United States. Levine has invited all his friends to invest in his new business. He is offering shares of stock for a mere $10 each.

Required:

    a. What form of business is Professor Levine opening?

    b. Briefly explain four advantages of doing business in this form.

LO 5: DISTINGUISHING AMONG TYPES OF BUSINESSES ACTIVITIES

1–33. Phil Jackson owns and operates a jewelry store. During the past month, he sold a necklace to a customer for $2,500. Phil had purchased the necklace for $1,800.

Required:

    a. What type of business does Phil own (manufacturer, wholesaler, retailer, etc.)? Explain how you determined your response.

    b. Calculate Phil's gross margin on the sale of the necklace.

    c. Identify four costs besides the $1,800 cost of the necklace that Phil might incur in the operation of his jewelry store.

    d. If Phil's operating costs are $900 per month, what is his net income (or loss) for the month?

LO 5: TYPES OF BUSINESS ACTIVITIES

1–34. This chapter discusses five types of business in the United States, namely:

    1. Manufacturing
    2. Wholesale merchandising
    3. Retail merchandising
    4. Service
    5. Hybrid

Required:

    a. In your own words, describe the characteristics of each type of business.

    b. Discuss how each of these five types of business is different from the other four.

    c. Without citing any of the examples from the chapter, provide two examples of each type of business and explain how you determined your answers.

LO 8: REPORTING STANDARDS

1–35. Following are the 10 steps in the standard-setting process used by the Financial Accounting Standards Board:

    1. Identifying issues
    2. Placing the issue on the FASB's agenda
    3. Appointing a task force
    4. Creating a discussion memorandum
    5. Holding public hearings
    6. Inviting comment letters
    7. Deliberating
    8. Writing an exposure draft
    9. Issuing a Statement of Financial Accounting Standards
    10. Conducting a post-enactment review

Required:

    a. In your own words, explain what happens in each of the 10 steps of the standard-setting process.

    b. What is meant by a "due process approach" to setting accounting standards?

LO 8: REPORTING STANDARDS

1–36. Generally accepted accounting principles have been developed over time to aid in comparability among the financial statements of different companies. They are also intended to maintain consistency in the way a firm accounts for transactions and events from period to period.

An audit is intended to provide some assurance to external parties that the financial statements examined are reasonably presented.

Required:

a. What determines whether a company in the United States is required to prepare its financial statements according to GAAP?

b. Why are some companies forced to adhere to GAAP even though they are not required by law to do so?

LO 11 & 12: REPORTING STANDARDS (APPENDIX)

1–37. Below are some of the items discussed in this chapter's appendix, followed by the definitions of those items in scrambled order.

a. Financial reporting
b. Financial statements
c. SEC Integrated Disclosure System
d. Annual report
e. SEC Form 10-K
f. Notes to financial statements

1. _____ One of its objectives is to simplify and improve the quality of disclosures provided to investors and other users of financial information.
2. _____ Disclosures provided to economic decision makers that include not only quantitative information but also descriptive information.
3. _____ Intended to provide important information that should be considered by financial statement users when reading financial statements.
4. _____ Its content is prescribed by the SEC.
5. _____ The balance sheets for two years and statements of income, cash flows, and stockholders' equity for three years are presented as a part of the annual report.
6. _____ Originally intended to be used only by stockholders but now is broadly used by a variety of other economic decision makers.

Required: Match the letter next to each item on the list with the appropriate definition. Use each letter only once.

LO 10: FINANCIAL REPORTING

1–38. Below are some items related to the issue of outside assurance discussed in this chapter, followed by the definitions of those items in scrambled order.

a. Audit
b. Unqualified opinion
c. Adverse opinion
d. Qualified opinion
e. Disclaimer

1. _____ Caused by a material uncertainty the auditor does not feel can be adequately communicated, or by the placing of a significant restriction on the auditor as to what records may be examined.
2. _____ The process of examining a company's records to determine whether the financial statements have been prepared in accordance with GAAP standards.
3. _____ Rendered when there are departures from GAAP so pervasive that a reasonable person cannot rely on the financial statements.
4. _____ Unofficially referred to as a "clean" opinion.
5. _____ An auditor states an exception in the audit report.

Required: Match the letter next to each item with the appropriate definition. Use each letter only once.

LO 10: FINANCIAL REPORTING

1–39. Your uncle, who owns a small business, knows that you are taking a course in accounting. He tells you that his banker is requiring him to provide an audited set of financial statements for the last fiscal year. He does not understand why the bank is making this request and he asks you why they would want an audit of his financial statements. How do you respond to his question?

LO 12: ANNUAL REPORTS (APPENDIX)

1–40. Listed below are the items required by the SEC to be included in the annual report, along with some items not required but normally included:

1. _____ Audited financial statements
2. _____ The principal market in which the securities of the firm are traded
3. _____ Industry segment disclosures for the last three fiscal years
4. _____ The management report
5. _____ Offer to provide a free copy of Form 10-K to shareholders upon written request, unless the annual report complies with Form 10-K disclosure requirements
6. _____ Report on corporate citizenship
7. _____ Management's discussion and analysis of financial condition and results of operations
8. _____ Five-year selected financial data
9. _____ Brief description of the business
10. _____ Letter to the stockholders
11. _____ Identification of directors and executive officers, with the principal occupation and employer of each
12. _____ High and low market prices of the company's common stock for each quarter of the two most recent fiscal years and dividends paid on common stock during those years

Required: Identify each of the items as either required (R) or optional (O).

Financial Reporting Exercises ●

LO 11 & 12: ANNUAL REPORTS (APPENDIX)

1–41. Use the information contained in the 2002 annual report of *Pier 1 Imports* on page F–503 to answer the following:

Required:

a. What is the name of the CPA firm who audited the financial statements?
b. What type of opinion was rendered by the audit firm?
c. Which paragraph of the audit report identifies the party responsible for the financial statements?
d. Which paragraph of the audit report identifies who is responsible for the audit of the financial statements?
e. Which paragraph of the audit report actually reports the expression of an opinion?

LO 12: ANNUAL REPORTS (APPENDIX)

1–42. Use the information contained in the 2002 annual report of *Pier 1 Imports* on page F–503 to answer the following:

Required:

a. List the title and the time period covered by each financial statement included in the annual report.
b. The assets, liabilities, and stockholders' equity are listed in which of the financial statements?
c. The sales, cost of goods sold, and the operating expenses are reported in which financial statement?

LO 12: ANNUAL REPORTS (APPENDIX)

1–43. Use the information contained in the 2002 annual report of *Pier 1 Imports* on page F–503 to answer the following:

Required:

a. Who wrote the letter to the stockholders? In your opinion, what were the three most important messages in the letter?
b. What are the divisions of Pier 1? For each division, list the following information:

(1) Name
(2) Major markets

(3) Distinction in the marketplace

(4) Goals for the current year

c. How does the information in parts a and b help a potential investor, creditor, or employee?

LO 12: ANNUAL REPORTS (APPENDIX)

1–44. The following is the 2001 letter to the stockholders from Craig R. Barrett, CEO of *Intel Corporation.*

Education is a critical focus for Intel and for our employees around the world. In 2001 Intel Corporation and the Intel Foundation contributed over $103 million to help improve education. Through our Intel® Innovation in Education Initiative, teachers developed the skills to integrate technology into their classrooms and young people in underserved communities gained access to technology to develop new skills through neighborhood centers. In addition, we continued to reward and encourage our future scientists and engineers both at the high school and university level with scholarships, research opportunities, and curriculum support. Finally, we explored new ways to use the Internet as a means of providing content and resources for educators.

As a global community, we have witnessed some terrible events this past year. In February, India was hit with a devastating earthquake. Intel employees and the Intel Foundation responded with a donation of over $1.6 million to relief efforts. In response to the events of September 11th, the Intel Foundation immediately donated $1 million to the American Red Cross and promised to match employee donations, which eventually reached $1.2 million—for a total Intel contribution of $3.4 million from the Intel Foundation and Intel employees to help victims of the disaster. Through Operation Unity, Intel employees responded to meet immediate needs in New York by providing humanitarian aid and assistance to emergency services agencies, small businesses, and non-profit organizations.

Each of our Intel locations is actively involved in a variety of efforts that directly support their local communities with both funding and volunteer efforts. With all of our programs, our strength lies in our employees. In 2001, employees volunteered hundreds of thousands of hours at schools, community projects, and relief efforts around the world. These Intel employee "ambassadors" ensure that Intel can play a positive role in our communities—and truly make Intel a Great Place to Work.

As we all know, 2001 was a difficult year for our industry and for the economy in general. Intel will continue to support our education efforts and our communities for the same reason we continue to spend on our research and development programs—they are long-term investments in our future and the future of our world.

CR Barrett

Craig R. Barrett

Chief Executive Officer

Intel Corporation

Required:

a. In what types of community projects does *Intel Corporation* participate?

b. What does this tell you about the culture of this company?

c. Is this the type of company in which you would seek a career? Why?

d. Suppose there was a company equal to *Intel Corporation* in every way except they didn't have any community service. Would you think any less of the company? Would you be less likely to invest in or seek a career in that company?

LO 12: ANNUAL REPORTS (APPENDIX)

1–45. The following is an excerpt from the 2001 Annual Report of *UPS.*

SERVING THE COMMUNITY

UPS serves more than its customers; we also serve our communities. Because we drive through neighborhoods and knock on the doors of homes and businesses around the world, we see first-hand the problems facing today's society. At UPS, we are committed to providing both our time and money to help strengthen the communities where our employees and customers live and work.

THE UPS FOUNDATION/CORPORATE RELATIONS

Celebrating its 50th anniversary, The UPS Foundation has a long history of enriching lives and strengthening communities through its various initiatives and programs. The Foundation supports major initiatives in the fields of volunteerism, literacy, and hunger relief, but offers its time, money, and expertise to other causes as well.

In 2001 alone, The UPS Foundation contributed $40.3 million to charitable organizations addressing education and urgent human needs through grants, scholarships, employee gift-matching, and support of United Way.

Through its Corporate Relations programs, UPS manages to match its financial resources to its human resources. UPS has long partnered with other national organizations committed to equal justice, equal opportunity, and building stronger communities. The synergy between Corporate Relations and The UPS Foundation extends the reach of UPS's philanthropy and strengthens the impact of its social investments.

UNITED WAY

Since UPS's first United Way campaign in 1982, the company and its employees have contributed more than $500 million to support a broad range of human care services. UPS is the first company in United Way's history to exceed $50 million in annual giving, and in 2001, it was the largest corporate contributor for the second consecutive year.

THE UPS COMMUNITY INTERNSHIP PROGRAM

The UPS Community Internship Program is a unique executive training program designed to attune UPS managers to the increasingly complex needs of a diverse workforce and customer base. Each year, a select group of managers immerse themselves in community service for one month at one of four internship sites, which helps create awareness, promotes understanding, heightens sensitivity, and encourages involvement.

Such community service builds better managers and more well rounded individuals. It also bridges the gap between corporations and communities. Since 1968, UPS has dedicated more than $12 million to its Community Internship Program, with more than 1,100 senior level managers having participated in the training experience.

EMPLOYMENT INITIATIVES

UPS also helps the community through its various employment initiatives, which include:

Earn & Learn Program, which offers education assistance at participating UPS locations to part-time employees who are attending a college, university, or approved trade or technical school.

School to Work Program, which provides high school students aged 17 and older with the opportunity to earn college credit while gaining work experience with UPS. The program is available in several large cities such as Chicago, Dallas, Louisville, Philadelphia, and Washington, DC.

Supplier Diversity Process, which offers minority- and women-owned businesses the opportunity to compete equally with other UPS suppliers. More than 25,000 small, minority- and women-owned businesses across America are partners in the UPS supplier network.

Welfare to Work Partnership, which works with government agencies, faith-based groups, and nonprofit organizations to develop, train, and mentor qualified candidates for positions at UPS and other area businesses.

ENVIRONMENTAL INITIATIVES

At UPS, environmental stewardship has long been recognized both as a responsibility and as a good business practice. Some significant initiatives include:

- UPS's industry-leading research into alternative fuels, designed to reduce emissions and maximize fuel economy.
- UPS's re-engineered express packaging, which eliminates bleach and reduces production waste by up to 50 percent. The Reusable Next Day Air Letter is made of 100 percent recycled fiber, saving more than 12,000 trees per year and more than $1 million in production costs.
- UPS's Electronic Equipment Recycling Program, through which the company recycled almost 3 million pounds of outdated electronic equipment in 2001.

- UPS's Automatic Return Service (ARS), through which the company assists customers in returning their used toner cartridges, automotive parts, computer and medical equipment, etc. These products are disassembled for reuse or disposed of in a responsible manner.
- UPS's delivery notices are made from recycled paper, saving more than 1,500 trees annually. To learn more about UPS's community involvement, visit www.community.ups.com.

Required:

a. In what types of community projects does *UPS* participate?
b. What does this tell you about the culture of this company?
c. Is this the type of company in which you would seek a career? Why?
d. Which company (UPS or Intel) seems to be more involved in the community? Which seems to involve more of its employees in its program? Would this make you more or less interested in becoming a part of these companies?

LO 12: ANNUAL REPORTS (APPENDIX)

1–46. The following is the opening section of the 2001 letter to shareholders from Kenneth I. Chenault, Chairman and Chief Executive Officer of *American Express Company*:

> 2001 was a year unlike any other in American Express Company's history. The nature and magnitude of the challenges we faced were unprecedented. As we have throughout our history, we are resolving these challenges with resilience and strength. We did not meet our long-term financial objectives. We did, however, make a number of fundamental changes in our businesses that will enable us to emerge from this extraordinary period a far stronger, more focused company.

Required:

a. Summarize the main points of the CEO's message.
b. How do you believe that a CEO should give bad news to stockholders? Why?
c. Do you think the way Chenault gives bad news is effective? Why or why not? Do you think he instills confidence in the future?

ANNUAL REPORT PROJECT

1–47. General Information

The purpose of this project is to introduce you to the financial reporting information published by publicly traded companies. The assignment in this chapter is the first of a continuing 11-part project. Our hope is that you will learn about the various sources and uses of the valuable information available to you via a company's Form 10K, its annual report, the Internet, the financial press, and through stock market reports.

By the time you have completed the project, you should be in a position to draw conclusions and form an opinion regarding whether the company you selected to analyze is a good investment candidate. You may also form an opinion regarding the employment prospect with the company.

When it is complete, your annual report project will include the following sections (unless modified by your instructor):

Section   1—Selecting a Company and Obtaining an Annual Report
Section   2—General Information
Section   3—Basic Balance Sheet Information
Section   4—Basic Income Statement and Statement of Stockholders' Equity
Section   5—Strengths, Weaknesses, Opportunities and Threats (SWOT)
Section   6—Finding a Peer Company and Peer Company Comparisons
Section   7—Long-Lived Assets
Section   8—Inventories and Cost of Goods Sold
Section   9—Financial Statements—A Closer Look
Section 10—The Statement of Cash Flows
Section 11—Summary, Conclusions, and Recommendations

Organize your annual report project. Use a pocket folder to hold your company's annual report and other documents, and a binder to accommodate the three-hole punched pages you will generate to fulfill the requirements of each assignment.

Section 1—Selecting a Company and Obtaining an Annual Report

In this section, you will select a company for your project and obtain its Form 10-K and Annual Report.

Required:

a. List several publicly traded companies that interest you. They might interest you as investment candidates or employment prospects, or simply because you are familiar with their products.

b. From your list of companies, select a publicly traded United States company that sells a tangible product. It can be either a manufacturer or a merchandiser, but for purposes of this annual report project, do not select an insurance company, a stock brokerage firm, a bank, a utility company or another type of service company.

c. Once you select a company, download a copy of its Form 10-K through the SEC's EDGAR system. If you are working in a group, each member of the group should secure his or her own copy of the Form 10-K. The Form 10-K will provide you with a wealth of information about the company you have selected.

   Below are the step-by-step instructions to help you find and obtain a copy of your company's Form 10-K by using the SEC's EDGAR system.

   1. Go to the SEC's home page at www.sec.gov.
   2. Click on *Search for Company Filings* (listed under "Filings & Forms (EDGAR)").
   3. Click on *Search Companies and Filings*.
   4. Enter your company's name in the appropriate place and click *Find Companies*.
   5. Find the latest version of your company's Form 10-K. (All publicly traded companies must file a Form 10-K annually so you will want to be sure you select the latest one.) Click on the appropriate place next to the latest Form 10-K. The "text" version loads more quickly and is easier to save and print than the HTML version.

d. Obtain a copy of the company's annual report. In most cases, you can download the annual report from the company's Web site. If you are unable to obtain an annual report for your company this way, you can contact the company and ask that one be sent to you. If you are working in a group, each member of the group should secure his or her own copy of the report.

e. If you are using a downloaded copy of the company's annual report, contact your company to request an actual hardcopy of the company's printed annual report in addition to the copy you downloaded. It may take some time to receive it, so make your request as soon as possible.

CHAPTER 2

Economic Decision Making

S uppose you and some friends decide to go on a spring break vacation. Where will you go? Lots of places come to mind—Cancun, the Bahamas, Daytona Beach—but which destination will you choose? Will you just blindly pick one? Of course not. Before making a final selection, you'll gather information about each vacation spot from various sources. You'll want to know about the destination city itself, airline fares and schedules, car rentals, and hotels. Then, based on that information, you and your friends will compare the various destinations before making a final selection.

This spring break "decision" is quite complex because it is really a series of decisions. What's more, some of the decisions will be group decisions, while others will be made individually. Once all the decisions and reservations are made, the vacation's outcome is still uncertain. This uncertainty adds a dimension of adventure to the whole experience.

Life entails making thousands of decisions, some very complex and others relatively simple. Because we cannot know the future, the outcomes of the decisions we make are uncertain. While in our spring break example we were able to tolerate a bit of uncertainty because it added intrigue, uncertainty in business is something we strive to reduce. By collecting and using as much relevant, reliable information as possible, we can work to reduce the uncertainty that threatens the outcome of the decisions we make.

Regardless of the form of organization or the business activity, success—and sometimes even survival—in the world of business depends on making wise economic decisions. A key ingredient is an understanding of the decision making process itself. We designed this chapter to help you learn a logical decision making process.

Learning Objectives

After completing your work on this chapter, you should be able to do the following:

1. Explain the concepts of extrinsic and intrinsic rewards, sacrifices, and opportunity costs as they pertain to routine and nonroutine decision situations.

2. Use a cognitive problem-solving model to make decisions.

3. Explain how information processing styles affect decision making and be able to identify examples of systematic and intuitive styles.

4. Explain the importance of creativity and the role of values and ethics in the decision making process.

5. Describe the advantages and disadvantages of individual and group decision making.

6. Explain the basic differences between management accounting and financial accounting.

7. List the three questions all economic decision makers attempt to answer and explain why these questions are so important.

8. Describe the importance of cash as a measure of business success or failure.

9. Describe the basic assumptions and constraints underlying accounting information and distinguish accounting information from accounting data.

10. Describe the qualitative characteristics of useful accounting information and apply them in decision making situations.

11. Identify, discuss, and contrast information found in typical annual reports.

◆ WHAT IS DECISION MAKING?

Decision making is the process of identifying alternative courses of action and selecting an appropriate alternative in a given decision situation. This definition presents two important parts:

1. *Identifying alternative courses of action.* This does not mean that an ideal solution exists or can be identified.

2. *Selecting an appropriate alternative.* This implies that there may be a number of appropriate alternatives and that inappropriate alternatives are to be evaluated and rejected. Thus, judgment is fundamental to decision making.

Choice is implicit in our definition of decision making. We may not like the alternatives available to us, but we are seldom left without choices.

REWARDS AND SACRIFICES: THE TRADE-OFF

In general, the aim of all decisions is to obtain some type of reward, either economic or personal. Reward requires sacrifice. When you made the decision to attend college, for example, you certainly desired a reward. What was the sacrifice?

Discussion Questions ●●●●●●●●●●●●●●●●●●●●●●●●●●●●●●●

2–1. What rewards do you hope to obtain by attending college?

2–2. What sacrifices are you personally making to attend college?

Think of some things that you can't do because you are attending college. Some sacrifices cannot be measured in dollars, for example, the loss of leisure time while you do homework for your accounting class. Some, however, can be measured in dollars. Suppose that instead of attending college you could work full time and earn $25,000 a year. In a very real sense, then, attending college costs you that $25,000 in addition to what you pay for tuition and books. We call the $25,000 an **opportunity cost** of making the decision to attend college. An opportunity cost is the reward we give up because we choose a particular alternative instead of another. It is the amount of benefit we *would* have received if we had made a different choice. Most decisions include opportunity costs.

opportunity cost The benefit or benefits forgone by not selecting a particular alternative. Once an alternative is selected in a decision situation, the benefits of all rejected alternatives become part of the opportunity cost of the alternative selected.

Decision makers strive to maximize the rewards or benefits from a decision and to minimize the sacrifice or cost required (see Exhibit 2–1). Examining the relationship between rewards and sacrifices is known as *cost/benefit analysis*. In a condition of absolute certainty, where we know the outcome of a decision without doubt, determining the cost/benefit is no problem. Unfortunately, absolute certainty rarely, if ever, exists.

In the examples we use to describe the trade-off between rewards and sacrifices, money is usually the reward. Money is an example of what we call an *extrinsic reward*, meaning that it comes from outside ourselves. An *intrinsic reward* is one that comes from inside us. When you accomplish a difficult task, the intrinsic reward comes from the sense of satisfaction you feel. An old adage says, "The best things in life are free." Not necessarily so! Many things worth having require sacrifice.

Discussion Questions ●●●●●●●●●●●●●●●●●●●●●●●●●●●●●●●

2–3. What is the one thing you desire most from life? What sacrifices must you make to obtain it?

2–4. What sacrifices do you make when you buy a graphing calculator for your math class?

2–5. What benefit do you derive from purchasing the calculator?

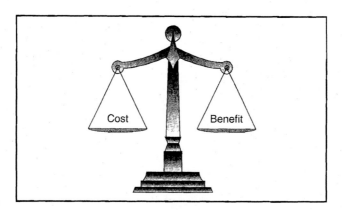

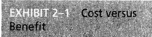

EXHIBIT 2–1   Cost versus Benefit

COPING WITH UNCERTAINTY AND RISK

Uncertainty in any given decision situation increases the chances of making the wrong choice. The higher the degree of uncertainty, the greater the risk. In decision making, we can't eliminate uncertainty completely, so we must learn to cope with it. The relationship between uncertainty and reward is called the **risk/reward trade-off.** Financial decision makers recognize the relationship in the risk/reward trade-off and therefore demand greater rewards when the risk is high. For example, banks such as *First Union* and *Bank of America* set interest rates based on the credit risk of each borrower. The higher the risk of default on a loan, the higher the interest rate charged by the bank.

So how do you cope with uncertainty, knowing that it can never be entirely eliminated? You gather as much relevant information as you can and use it to gain insight into the decision alternatives. Knowing more about each alternative helps reduce the amount of risk involved and increases your level of comfort in making the decision. This is a valuable strategy no matter what type of decision you are making.

risk/reward trade-off
The relationship between uncertainty and reward. It indicates that the higher the risk, the higher the reward required to induce the risk taking.

Discussion Question ●

2–6. How would you judge the risk of loaning a friend the graphing calculator you bought for your math class?

ROUTINE AND NONROUTINE DECISIONS

We make some decisions so frequently that our choice is automatic or routine. We need to solve such recurring problems only once, and our decision then becomes a rule or standard. Whenever the situation recurs, such as choosing the route to drive from home to work, we implement the rule.

Not all *routine decisions* arise in simple situations. Landing a jet aircraft at a busy airport with 300 people on board may be routine, but it is still complex. Whether a decision is routine depends not on its complexity, but rather on whether the situation recurs.

When a decision we make concerns a new and unfamiliar circumstance, we are making a *nonroutine decision.* Whether intricate or simple, an unfamiliar problem is considered nonroutine by its infrequency—not by its complexity. The decision to attend college certainly is a nonroutine decision. Another example is the vacation scenario we presented in the opening vignette to this chapter.

It is important that we identify the decisions we make as routine or nonroutine, because routine problems have rule-based solutions while nonroutine decisions do not. If we apply routine decision rules to nonroutine situations, we can worsen the situation by applying a solution that doesn't fit the problem.

Discussion Questions ●

2–7. Think of a decision you consider routine. Can you remember the first time you had to make that particular decision? How did you go about making it?

2–8. Can you think of a nonroutine decision you faced? How did you go about making that decision?

2–9. Describe a situation in which you or someone else applied a decision rule developed for a routine decision to a nonroutine situation and experienced unexpected results.

◆ HOW WE MAKE DECISIONS

We think constantly, yet we rarely stop to analyze our thinking in a methodical, orderly way. It may sound silly, but we really should spend some time thinking about the way we think, because the way we process information relates directly to the quality of our decisions.

INFORMATION PROCESSING STYLES

There has been a great deal of research into how people use their brains to process information. Psychological researchers have identified two general information processing styles—the *intuitive style* and the *systematic style* (see Exhibit 2–2).[1]

Intuitive thinkers prefer to solve problems by looking at the overall situation, exploring many possible solutions, and making a decision based on their hunches or gut reaction. Intuitive thinkers tend to prefer nonroutine situations. They enjoy rapidly changing environments, dealing with broad issues, and general policy options; they are "big-picture" people.

Conversely, systematic thinkers prefer to solve problems by careful analysis, breaking the problem into component parts. They prefer working in an environment that allows them to think methodically; they are "detail" people.

Everyone uses both styles to some degree, but all of us prefer to employ one style over the other. Each style has advantages and disadvantages and each can be effective. For example, some investment analysts use primarily an intuitive style and others tend to use a systematic style. The job of a Wall Street investment analyst at **Lehman**

EXHIBIT 2–2　Information Processing Styles

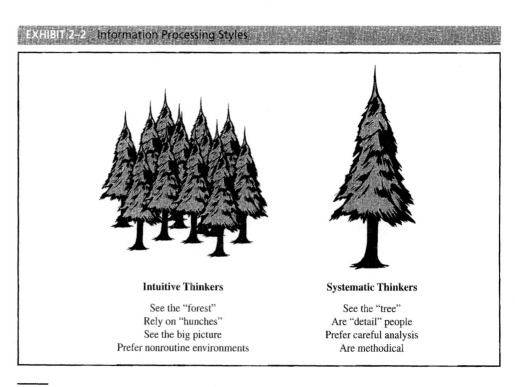

Intuitive Thinkers	Systematic Thinkers
See the "forest"	See the "tree"
Rely on "hunches"	Are "detail" people
See the big picture	Prefer careful analysis
Prefer nonroutine environments	Are methodical

---

[1]Weston H. Agor, "Managing Brain Skills: The Last Frontier," *Personnel Administrator* (October 1987): 55–56.

Brothers or **Merrill Lynch** is to pick stocks that will earn dividends and go up in price rather than down. Some analysts systematically study an extensive amount of information about a company, carefully sifting the numbers through a computer and analyzing statistics before making a decision. Other analysts do a little analysis but mainly rely on their intuition. Some of the most successful investors on Wall Street claim to "feel" what is going to happen to the price of a particular stock. Although it is difficult if not impossible to learn to be more intuitive, one can learn to be a more systematic thinker.

Discussion Questions

2–10. To which careers do you think intuitive people are most attracted?

2–11. To which careers do you think systematic people are most attracted?

2–12. Which of the two information-processing styles do you believe you use more often?

2–13. What problems and benefits could arise when you work with someone using an information-processing style that differs from your own?

REASONED DECISION MAKING

Reasoned decision making, also called *cognitive* or *rational* decision making, involves considering various aspects of a situation before deciding on a course of action. This approach to decision making can be used with both intuitive and systematic information processing. Systematic thinkers will feel comfortable with this approach, and intuitive thinkers will become more disciplined thinkers, which may improve their intuitive skills. Reasoned decision making can be described as a seven-step process (see Exhibit 2–3).

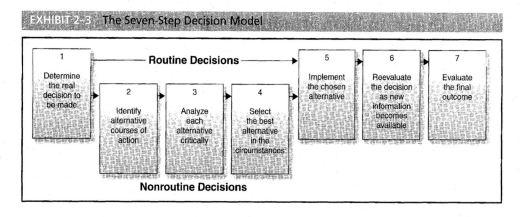

EXHIBIT 2–3   The Seven-Step Decision Model

Step 1: *Determine the real decision to be made.*
The key to successful reasoned decision making is identifying the real problem. This is frequently the most difficult task in the decision process. Too often, we concentrate on a symptom of the problem and not on the problem itself. This step is so important that firms sometimes hire consultants to identify the real problems and to determine the decisions to be made.

Step 2: *Identify alternative courses of action.*
Before identifying alternative courses of action, we should first determine whether the decision we are making is routine or nonroutine. If the decision is routine, we simply apply the appropriate decision rule and skip steps 2, 3, and 4 of this decision model. For nonroutine decisions, we must work to identify alternatives. Some alternatives will emerge quickly, but these often treat symptoms, not problems. We may be comfortable choosing an obvious course of action, but the obvious course may not be the best.

In order to make sound nonroutine decisions, you must think creatively to uncover as many decision alternatives as possible. Eliminate only impossible potential solutions and consider everything else, however improbable. Sherlock Holmes, the great master sleuth, offered this explanation as to why Dr. Watson had been unable to unravel a particular mystery:

Once again, Watson, you have confused the impossible with the improbable.
—SIR ARTHUR CONAN DOYLE

Fictional characters like Sherlock Holmes can always make correct decisions, but real-life decision making is more difficult. Because it is an important topic, following this presentation of the seven-step decision making process, we will discuss creative decision making in greater detail.

Step 3: *Analyze each alternative critically.*
Critical analysis of each decision alternative requires us to trace the alternatives into the future and consider the possible outcomes of each. In most cases, a completely accurate assessment is impossible because there are too many variables. We often must select a few critical factors, such as cost, completion time, and risk, and evaluate the strengths and weaknesses of each alternative relative to those factors.

Step 4: *Select the best alternative in the circumstances.*
Russell Ackoff, a noted scholar in the field of problem solving, identified three types of alternatives that occur in any decision situation:

Those that will resolve the problem,
Those that will solve the problem, and
Those that will dissolve the problem.[2]

Resolving a problem means finding an acceptable alternative. *Solving* a problem means finding the absolute best solution. *Dissolving* a problem means changing the circumstances that caused the problem, thereby not only eliminating the problem but also ensuring that it will not happen again. Ideally, the results of a decision making process will produce an alternative that dissolves the problem, but realistically, this occurs only occasionally. In fact, Ackoff suggests that most decisions merely resolve problems by finding acceptable, stopgap solutions. For this reason, one decision may create the need to make other decisions.

Step 5: *Implement the chosen alternative.*
On the surface, this appears to be the easiest of all the steps in this process. Not so! Regardless of how methodical and analytical our approach to making the decision, we know we have not considered everything, and we hesitate. This hesitation is called *cognitive dissonance*,[3] or "second thoughts." When cognitive dissonance sets in, all the alternatives you have rejected begin to look better and better. There is no easy remedy for this hesitation except to understand that second thoughts are a part of life and that there comes a point when we must find the courage to implement the chosen alternative.

Step 6: *Reevaluate the decision as new information becomes available.*
After overcoming second thoughts, decision makers become very committed to their decision. In fact, most of us will go out of our way to avoid new information after implementing a decision. Why? Because it puts us back in the position of questioning the soundness of our decision, which can make us extremely uncomfortable. It may sound odd, but to become good at making tough decisions, you must become comfortable with being uncomfortable. You should not be afraid to revisit a decision in light of new and better information, even after you implement the decision.

---

[2]Russell L. Ackoff, "The Art and Science of Mess Management," *Interfaces* 11, No. 1 (February 1981): 20–21.
[3]Leon Festinger, *A Theory of Cognitive Dissonance* (Stanford, CA: Stanford University Press, 1975).

Step 7: *Evaluate the final outcome.*

It may be a long time before we can determine whether our decision was a good one, and factors outside our control may influence the outcome. Nevertheless, evaluation is an important step in the process if we are to continue refining our decision making skills.

This basic decision model, in one form or another, is found in numerous textbooks for various courses. The one we presented here is not the only correct way to make decisions; however, it does offer you a reasoned, cognitive approach to decision making.

Discussion Questions

2–14. If you had used the seven-step decision model when you were selecting your university, would you have made the same choice? Explain.

2–15. Think again about your decision to attend your particular college. At what point will you be able to apply step 7 to your decision making process?

CREATIVE DECISION MAKING

The second step of the decision making model stresses the importance of being creative in identifying possible courses of action. Going beyond the obvious alternatives reduces your chances of overlooking the best possible solution.

Anyone can become a more creative decision maker. Sidney J. Parnes, a professor of creative studies at Buffalo State University, states that creativity increases when the problem solver progresses from "what is" (awareness of the facts surrounding the present situation), to "what might be" (free-thinking consideration of many possible alternatives), to "what can be" (elimination of impossible and unacceptable alternatives), to "what will be" (choice of the best alternative in the circumstances), and finally to an action that creates a new "what is."[4] For example, sales representatives used to go door-to-door selling sets of *World Book Encyclopedias.* Today, you can simply log on to *www.worldbookonline.com* and subscribe to **World Book**'s encyclopedia service!

Discussion Questions

2–16. Think of a daily irritation that you currently endure. Use Professor Parnes's creative process to create at least three feasible alternatives under "what might be."

2–17. If you could change one other "what is" into a new "what is," what would it be? How would you do it?

◆ PERSONAL VALUES AND DECISION MAKING

The most important influence on the decisions we make is the set of personal values we hold. *Personal values* are just that—personal. Yours are different, even if only slightly, from those of every other person. What is important in relation to personal values and decision making is that each of us examines critically what is truly important to us.

ETHICS AND PERSONAL VALUES

There are two very different approaches to ethics (see Exhibit 2–4). The first approach is *virtues ethics,* or *character ethics.* This approach to ethics, called classical ethics because it is derived from the teachings of Socrates, Plato, and Aristotle, comes from within a person. It requires you to contemplate what kind of person you want to be. Once you have identified the virtues and character traits required to be that kind of person, they determine your reaction to any situation. Virtues ethics presumes that the virtues and character traits the individual identifies as desirable will include respect for others.

---

[4]Sidney J. Parnes, "Learning Creative Behavior," *The Futurist* (August 1984): 30.

Virtues Ethics =
Character or Classical Ethics

Rules Ethics =
Quandary or Modern Ethics

EXHIBIT 2-4 Two Approaches to Ethics

The second approach is *rules ethics*, or *quandary ethics*. This approach, also called modern ethics, traces its roots to organized religion and law. It imposes rules that dictate how to react to given problems. Successful application of rules ethics depends on the individual's ability to apply the appropriate rule in a given situation and on society's acceptance of the rules and those who establish them. An inability to apply the appropriate rule or a loss of respect for the rules or rule makers leads to moral confusion and uncertainty.

Most businesspeople have discovered that "good ethics is good business." Historically, ethical companies that hire ethical management eventually rise above less ethical firms. Businesspeople constantly face ethical dilemmas. For example, should a U.S. shoe manufacturer open a plant in Southeast Asia, where workers are paid only 50 cents an hour? We might argue that the company is exploiting those workers. On the other hand, 50 cents hour might be double the going wage in that country, providing employment for those who otherwise have no jobs. It's a tough decision, without any clear-cut "right" answer.

Discussion Questions ●

2–18. Do you agree with the statement, "Good ethics is good business?" Explain your position.

2–19. Do U.S. companies exploit workers in other countries when they pay them less than the U.S. minimum wage?

2–20. Should U.S. companies follow U.S. labor laws for their foreign operations or the less stringent local labor laws?

2–21. Do you believe it is ethical to buy products manufactured by a U.S. company in a foreign country with less restrictive labor laws than the United States?

2–22. What is your responsibility as a consumer to determine whether products are made under fair labor practices?

◆ INDIVIDUAL VERSUS GROUP DECISION MAKING

Thus far, we have discussed the challenges in decision making caused by uncertainty and different information-processing styles. We've also looked at routine versus non-routine decision situations, the need for creativity in decision making, and the influence of personal values on the decision making process. We now consider *individual decision making* versus *group decision making*. If the old saying that two heads are better than one is true, does involving more people in the decision process improve the chances of making the right decision? Not always.

Individual decision making has some distinct advantages over group decision making. First, you do not spend a lot of time organizing meetings. Second, you do not have to consider others' comments and suggestions that you know for a fact are no good. Finally, compromise is unnecessary because you are a committee of one. However, your decision will be only as good as your individual judgment and grasp of the circumstances. This becomes the most significant drawback to making decisions on your own. This limitation is the reason that when we make important, nonroutine decisions by ourselves, most of us need to bounce the decision off someone else. We know, or at least fear, that we may have failed to consider all of the important factors.

Groups bring a greater knowledge base to the decision making process simply because more people are involved. Viewing the problem from various perspectives usually generates more alternative solutions. Groups take the pressure of responsibility for decisions off individuals. Also, groups tend to be confident that the decision alternative chosen to solve the problem is a reasonable solution.

On the surface, it would seem that group decision making is superior to individual decision making; however, some serious problems are associated with working in groups. Some of these have to do with the actual functioning of groups, and others with the quality of decisions made by groups.

At one time or another, each of us is called on to work as part of a group. Knowing about and being able to recognize the classic problems associated with working in groups will not only reduce your level of frustration, but it will also make your work in groups more effective and rewarding.

PROBLEMS WITH GROUP DECISIONS

- *Information-processing styles.* If all members of the group are intuitive types, the group may have many grandiose ideas but wind up short on specifics. If all members are systematic types, the group may never get past deciding on a seating arrangement at the first meeting. Ideally, the group should be a mix of the two types, but working together will be a challenge. The group must be able to utilize the best aspects of each style, or the group can become paralyzed.
- *Domineering members.* In any group situation, there will be members that are more domineering than others. This is a natural occurrence. The quality of group decision making usually suffers when some members of the group cave in to other members simply because those other members talk louder and longer. Now that you know this, don't allow yourself to steamroll over other group members and don't let others roll over you. Keep in mind that just because a person has an ability to be persuasive does not mean they know more and are more capable than the other members of the group.
- *Social pressure.* The pressure to conform to the views of other members of the group, coupled with the natural desire to not look foolish, can stifle an individual's creative contributions. Group members should work to keep this from happening.
- *Goal replacement.* The goal of the group should always be to accomplish the purpose for which it was formed. Secondary considerations, such as winning an argument, proving a point, or taking revenge on a fellow group member, sometimes become more important to some members of the group.
- *Differing personal values.* Each member of the group will bring a different set of personal values to the process. From time to time, those values may conflict, making resolution difficult or impossible.
- *Unequal effort.* This phenomenon occurs in virtually all groups. And, with the vast differences in personalities, drive, abilities, and interests of group members, it is completely understandable that the problem of unequal effort occurs so often. Groups are certainly more effective when all members do their share of the work. It is best to somehow even the workload because, in addition to negatively affecting the morale of the other group members, underperformers also tend to reduce the overall effectiveness of the group.
- *Groupthink.* Many people consider groupthink to be the most dangerous threat to good group decision making. Group members may ignore their own sound judg-

ments in evaluating alternatives to allow the group to achieve consensus. A group member may not feel good about the decision being made but *thinks* everyone else in the group does, and so he or she goes along with the decision. Disaster occurs when several group members go along with an apparent consensus only to find later that few, if any, in the group actually agreed with the decision. Have you ever heard one friend say to another, "What do you mean you didn't even want to come here? I only agreed to come here because I thought you wanted to come here." In such a case, both parties *agree* to something, each erroneously thinking she or he is going along with the wishes of the other person.

Discussion Questions

2–23. Which of the group decision making problems have you encountered at work or in school? Was the problem resolved? If so, how?

2–24. If you were an instructor in a course that required students to work in groups, what policies would you institute to avoid the classic problems associated with group work?

◆ ECONOMIC DECISION MAKING

The term *economic decision making,* as used in this book, refers to the process of making business decisions involving money. All economic decisions of any consequence require the use of some sort of accounting information, often in the form of financial reports. Anyone using accounting information to make economic decisions must understand the business and economic environment in which accounting information is generated, and they must also be willing to devote the necessary time and energy to make sense of the accounting reports.

Economic decision makers are either internal or external. **Internal decision makers** are individuals within a company who make decisions on behalf of the company, while **external decision makers** are individuals or organizations outside a company who make decisions that affect the company. For example, people that work for *General Mills,* such as company managers, supervisors, and other employees, are internal decision makers. Those that do not work for *General Mills,* such as bankers, investors and potential investors, and customers, are external decision makers even if they have a close relationship with the company.

INTERNAL DECISION MAKERS

Internal decision makers decide such things as whether the company should sell a particular product, whether it should enter a new market, or whether it should hire or fire employees. Note that in all these matters, the internal decision maker makes the decision not for himself or herself, but rather *for* the company.

Depending on their position within the company, internal decision makers may have access to much, or even all, of the company's financial information. Even so, they do not have complete information, because all decisions relate to the future and the future always involves unknowns.

EXTERNAL DECISION MAKERS

External decision makers make decisions *about* a company. External decision makers decide such things as whether to invest in the company, whether to sell to or buy from the company, and whether to lend money to the company.

Unlike internal decision makers, external decision makers have limited financial information on which to base their decisions about the company. In fact, they have only the information the company gives them—which is never all the information the company possesses. Exhibit 2–5 lists examples of external and internal decision makers.

internal decision makers Economic decision makers within a company who make decisions for the company. They have access to much or all of the accounting information generated within the company.

external decision makers Economic decision makers outside a company who make decisions about the company. The accounting information they use to make those decisions is limited to what the company provides them.

External Decision Makers	Internal Decision Makers
Make decisions *about* the company	**Make decisions *for* the company**
Use Financial Accounting	**Use Managerial Accounting**
Available information is limited to what the company supplies to external users	Available information is limited only by time and the user's position within the company
• Stockholders (Present and Potential) • Bankers and Other Lending Institutions • Bondholders (Present and Potential) • Suppliers • Customers	• Marketing Managers • Salespersons • Production Managers • Strategic Planners • Company President • Engineers • Financial Officers

EXHIBIT 2–5 Economic Decision Makers

Discussion Questions

2–25. Why would a company withhold certain financial information from external parties?

2–26. Do you think it is entirely ethical for company managers to limit the information available to their own internal decision makers?

2–27. Is it ethical for a company to limit the information it provides to external decision makers?

The decisions made by internal and external decision makers are similar in some ways but very different in others—so different, in fact, that over time, two separate branches of accounting evolved to meet the needs of the two categories of users. **Management accounting** generates information for use by internal decision makers, whereas **financial accounting** generates information for use by external parties. Exhibit 2–6 contrasts financial accounting and management accounting.

management accounting The branch of accounting developed to meet the informational needs of internal decision makers.

financial accounting The branch of accounting developed to meet the informational needs of external decision makers.

EXHIBIT 2–6 Contrast of Financial and Management Accounting

Feature	Financial Accounting	Management Accounting
Principal users	External parties for decisions *about* firm	Internal parties for decisions *for* firm
Rules and regulations	Governed by GAAP	Company policy. Need not conform to GAAP
Level of detail	Little detail. Deals with the company as a whole	Quite detailed. Deals with various parts of the company
Timeliness	Quarterly and annually	As needed by users
Future/past orientation	Depicts the present condition and past results. Does not generally include future projections	Includes future projections in addition to present condition and past results

WHAT ALL ECONOMIC DECISION MAKERS WANT TO KNOW

Virtually all economic decision makers, whether internal or external, are trying to make decisions in light of what might happen in the future. Specifically, economic decision makers attempt to predict future cash flow—the movement of cash in and out of a company. These decision makers need information that can help them predict what future cash flows will be. Accordingly, one of the major objectives of financial reporting is to provide helpful information to those trying to predict cash flows.

> Thus, financial reporting should provide information to help investors, creditors, and others assess the amounts, timing, and uncertainty of prospective net cash inflows to the related enterprise.[5]

net cash flow
The difference between cash inflows and cash outflows; it can be either positive or negative.

The mathematical difference between cash inflows and cash outflows is: **net cash flow.** Positive net cash flow occurs when the amount of cash flowing into the company exceeds the amount flowing out of the company during a particular period. For example, a company that collects $1 million during a period when it pays out $950,000 has a positive cash flow of $50,000. Negative net cash flow occurs when the amount of cash flowing out of the company exceeds the amount flowing into the company during a particular period (see Exhibit 2–7).

EXHIBIT 2–7 Cash Flow

	Positive	Negative
Cash Inflow	1,000,000	500,000
Cash Outflow	950,000	575,000
Net Cash Flow	50,000	(75,000)

All economic decisions involve attempts to predict the future of cash flows by searching for the answers to the following three questions:

1. Will I be paid?
   This question refers to the *uncertainty* of cash flows.
2. When will I be paid?
   This question refers to the *timing* of cash flows.
3. How much will I be paid?
   This question refers to the *amounts* of cash flows.

The answer to each question contains two parts: return *on* investment and return *of* investment. *Return on investment* consists of the earnings and profits an investment returns to the investor. *Return of investment* is the ultimate return of the principal invested. Exhibit 2–8 shows the conceptual link between the three major questions posed by economic decision makers and the resulting cash flows using the following example. Assume you wish to invest in a $1,000 certificate of deposit (CD) at your bank, which will earn 10 percent interest per year, payable every three months, over the course of two years. If you invest in this CD, you must hold it for two years, after which the bank will return your $1,000.

---

[5]Statement of Financial Accounting Concepts No. 1, paragraph 39.

	Concepts	Return on Investment	Return of Investment
1. Will I be paid?	Uncertainty	Interest	CD Maturity
2. When will I be paid?	Timing	Every quarter	At the end of two years
3. How much will I be paid?	Amount	$25 per quarter; Total of $200	$1,000

EXHIBIT 2–8   Three Big Questions for Economic Decision Makers

Before you make this economic decision, you must attempt to answer the three questions:

1. *Will you be paid?* Because it is impossible to know the future, making an economic decision always involves risk. However, assuming the economy does not collapse and the bank stays in business, you will be paid both your return on investment and your return of investment.

2. *When will you be paid?* You will receive an interest payment every three months for two years (return on investment), and then at the end of two years, you will receive your initial $1,000 investment back (return of investment).

3. *How much will you be paid?* The return on your investment is the interest you receive quarterly $25 ($1,000 × 10 percent × 3/12), and the return of your investment is the $1,000 the bank gives you back. The total received in interest in two years is $200 (8 × $25).

Interest: Return on Investment	$ 200
Principal: Return of Investment	1,000
Total Return	1,200
Less: Initial Investment	1,000
Profit on Investment	$ 200

We can answer these questions easily for a government-insured certificate of deposit. In the vast majority of economic decision situations, however, the answers to the three questions are much less certain. We will show you how to use accounting information to answer them in various economic decision situations throughout this text.

Discussion Questions ⊙

2–28. Describe how you would apply the seven-step decision model in deciding whether to invest in a certificate of deposit.

2–29. Assume that you have $10,000 you will lend to only one of three loan applicants. What information would you require of each applicant to help you answer the three questions?

CASH IS THE "BALL" OF BUSINESS

In games such as baseball, football, or soccer, players must keep their eye on the ball if they want to win. Well, in the game of business, cash is the ball. Because the business game is so complex, businesspeople can easily become distracted and lose sight of the ball—cash. Various measures of performance such as gross profit, net income, net worth, and equity help those in business to make economic decisions. These are important measures of financial performance, *but they are not cash*! Never allow yourself to become so focused on any of them that you lose sight of cash, because when a company runs out of cash, it dies. Remember that the three questions we talked about in the previous section—Will I be paid? When will I be paid? How much will I be paid?—are all centered on cash. The secret to becoming a street-smart user of accounting information is learning to balance the complexity of business with the simple rule of keeping your eye on cash flow.

◆ ACCOUNTING INFORMATION

accounting A service activity that has the function of providing quantitative information, primarily financial in nature, about economic entities that is intended to be useful in making economic decisions.

accounting information Raw data concerning transactions that have been transformed into financial numbers that can be used by economic decision makers.

data The raw results of transactions. Facts and figures that are not organized enough to be useful to decision makers.

information Facts and figures that are sorted, arranged, and summarized and otherwise put into a form that is useful to decision makers.

economic entity The assumption that economic activities can be identified with a particular enterprise.

going concern The assumption that unless there is persuasive evidence otherwise, a particular business enterprise will stay in business indefinitely.

monetary unit The assumption that all economic transactions and events can be measured by some monetary unit. In the United States, for example, the dollar is used.

periodicity The assumption that the economic activities of an entity can be traced to some specific time period and results of those activities can be reported for any arbitrary time period chosen.

The dictionary defines **accounting** as a reckoning of financial matters, and *information* as knowledge or news. Putting the two together, we see that **accounting information** is knowledge or news about a reckoning of financial matters. The accounting profession's definition of accounting is as follows:

> Accounting is a service activity. Its function is to provide quantitative information, primarily financial in nature, about economic entities that is intended to be useful in making economic decisions.[6]

A company or a person generates accounting data with every business transaction. You generate a number of transactions each month when you pay your rent, buy groceries, make car payments, lend money to a friend, and so on. In business, the volume of accounting data can be staggering.

DATA VERSUS INFORMATION

Accounting data and *accounting information* are not interchangeable terms. **Data** are the raw results of transactions: Data become **information** only when they are put into some useful form. Clearly, the correct data items must be gathered and converted into useful information before they are of any help to economic decision makers. Suppose you are the credit manager for a major electronics supplier and you are trying to decide whether to extend credit to a particular customer. You have learned that the customer's sales are $15 million annually and that it just paid various suppliers $800,000 for goods and services. Do you extend the credit? Although you know two bits of data, they provide insufficient information on which to base a credit decision. You need to know more facts and figures than the two already presented, and they must be organized so that they are useful.

USEFUL ACCOUNTING INFORMATION

In Chapter 1, we introduced you to the Financial Accounting Standards Board's (FASB's) *Conceptual Framework of Accounting*. Recall that we described the framework as an arch, which we have reproduced as Exhibit 2–9.

The top of the arch outlines the objective of financial reporting, which we discussed in Chapter 1. In this chapter, we will discuss the qualitative characteristics accounting information must possess to be useful to economic decision makers (the left pillar of the arch). Before we do that, however, we need to talk about the base of the arch. As we stated in Chapter 1, these assumptions, constraints, and accounting principles make up the environment in which accounting information is produced. Our treatment here will focus on the assumptions and constraints. We will wait to cover the accounting principles in later chapters when we discuss the accounting elements to which they relate.

Assumptions Underlying Accounting Information

1. **Economic entity**—All economic activities can be identified with a particular enterprise. This means that the accounting information produced for a particular company is associated with that company and no other company or individual.
2. **Going concern**—Unless there is persuasive evidence otherwise, a particular business enterprise will stay in business indefinitely. This means that unless there is persuasive evidence to the contrary, a company will be around to continue its business and to fulfill its obligations and commitments in the future.
3. **Monetary unit**—All economic transactions and events can be measured by some monetary unit. This means that companies in the United States use the dollar, in Europe they use the euro, in Japan they use the yen, and so on.
4. **Periodicity**—An entity's economic activities can be reasonably divided into specific time periods. This means that when a company produces accounting reports for a specific time period (month, quarter, year, etc.), those reports contain information related to that specific time period.

---

[6]Statement of the Accounting Principles Board #4, 1970, p. 6.

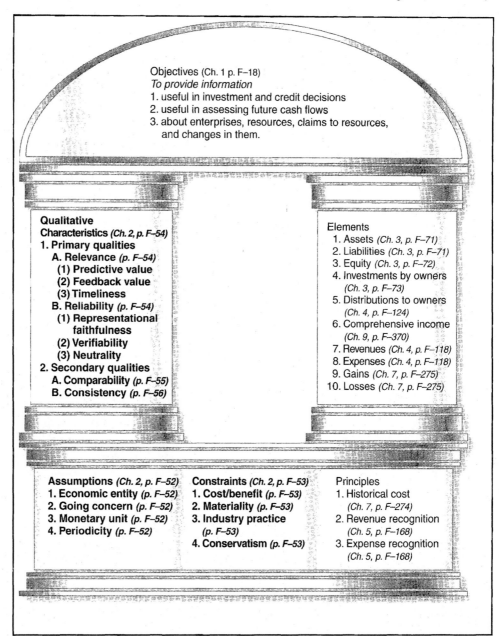

EXHIBIT 2–9   The Conceptual Framework

cost/benefit   Deals with the trade-off between the rewards of selecting a given alternative and the sacrifices required to obtain those rewards.

materiality   Something that will influence the judgment of a reasonable person.

industry practice   The notion that the peculiar nature of some industries actually causes adherence to GAAP to have misleading results, and therefore, these industries have developed accounting treatments for certain items that depart from GAAP.

conservatism   Provides a guideline in difficult valuation or measurement situations. Accountants should guard against accounting treatments that unjustly overstate financial position or earnings.

Constraints to Consider in Generating Accounting Information

1. **Cost/benefit**—The trade-off between the benefit received and the cost to obtain that benefit. For example, a certain level of detail in accounting information costs a certain amount. The benefit received from that level of detail should outweigh the cost. If that level of detail makes little or no difference, then the detail may not be worth its cost. We referred to this constraint earlier in this chapter when we discussed decision making.
2. **Materiality**—Relates to whether particular information is significant enough to influence the judgment of a reasonably prudent person. If it is, it is material. If not, it is immaterial.
3. **Industry practice**—The peculiar nature of some industries actually causes adherence to generally accepted accounting principles (GAAP) to have misleading results. Therefore, these industries have developed accounting treatments for certain items that depart from GAAP. Because all companies in the industry account for these items the same way, however, their accounting treatment is permissible.
4. **Conservatism**—Provides a guideline in difficult valuation or measurement situations. Accountants should guard against accounting treatments that unjustly overstate financial position or earnings.

Now that we have considered the assumptions and constraints under which accounting information is produced, we can proceed to our discussion of the qualitative characteristics of useful accounting information. As we did in Chapter 1, we will give the actual FASB wording in italics followed by a brief explanation of certain terms.

◆ QUALITATIVE CHARACTERISTICS OF USEFUL ACCOUNTING INFORMATION

In the *Conceptual Framework*'s discussion of the characteristics of useful accounting information, the FASB made it plain that the interrelationship among the various characteristics makes consideration of them individually extremely difficult. As a consequence, the FASB treatment of the characteristics is quite complex, and in fact covers 66 pages. As the arch in Exhibit 2–8 shows, however, the characteristics can be boiled down to two major categories: primary and secondary.

PRIMARY CHARACTERISTICS

The qualities that distinguish "better" (more useful) information from "inferior" (less useful) information are primarily the qualities of relevance and reliability, with some other characteristics that those qualities imply (Statement of Financial Accounting Concepts No. 2, paragraph 15). The *other characteristics* to which the FASB refers are timeliness, predictive or feedback value, verifiability, representational faithfulness, and neutrality. If accounting information lacks relevance or reliability (with the other related qualities), it is not useful.

Relevance

To be relevant to investors, creditors, and others for investment, credit, and similar decisions, accounting information must be capable of making a difference in a decision by helping users to form predictions about the outcomes of past, present, and future events or to confirm or correct expectations (Statement of Financial Accounting Concepts No. 2, paragraph 47). To be considered **relevant,** then, accounting information must have a bearing on the particular decision situation. That is, it must make a difference to decision makers. The accuracy of the information does not matter if its content does not pertain to the decision being made. To be relevant, accounting information possesses at least two characteristics:

relevance Pertinent to the decision at hand. The capability of making a difference in a decision by helping users to form predictions or to adjust their expectations.

predictive value A primary characteristic of relevance. To be useful, accounting must provide information to decision makers that can be used to predict the future and timing of cash flows.

feedback value A primary characteristic of relevance. To be useful, accounting must provide decision makers with information that allows them to assess the progress of an investment.

1. **Predictive value and/or feedback value.** Before economic decision makers commit resources to one alternative instead of another, they must be satisfied that a reasonable expectation of a return *on* investment and a return *of* investment exists. Accounting information that helps reduce the uncertainty of that expectation has predictive value. This is not to say that financial accounting information itself is a prediction. Rather, by meaningfully reflecting past and present events, accounting helps the information user to predict future outcomes. Just as information about someone's past driving record is useful in helping to predict future driving tendencies, information about a company's present condition and past financial performance can be an excellent indicator of the company's financial future.

   After making an investment decision, the decision maker must have information to assess the progress of that investment. Recall the seven-step decision model. Step 6 is a reevaluation of the decision as new information becomes available, and step 7 is an evaluation of the final outcome of the decision. If accounting information provides input for those evaluations, it has feedback value.

timeliness A primary characteristic of relevance. To be useful, accounting information must be provided in time to influence a particular decision.

2. **Timeliness.** Predictive value and/or feedback value alone do not make information relevant. If information providers delay making information available until every number is perfectly accurate, it may be too late to be of any value. That is, it becomes irrelevant. This does not mean that accuracy does not matter. But if accounting information is not timely, it has no value.

Reliability

That information should be reliable as well as relevant is a notion that is central to accounting. It is, therefore, important to be clear about the nature of the claim that is being made for an accounting number that is described as reliable.

The reliability of a measure rests on the faithfulness with which it represents what it purports to represent, coupled with an assurance for the user, which comes through verification, that it has that representational quality (Statement of Financial Accounting Concepts No. 2, paragraphs 58 and 59). This statement says, then, that to be **reliable,** accounting information must possess the qualities of representational faithfulness and verifiability. Not mentioned in the quotation, but implicit, is the characteristic of neutrality.

reliability A characteristic of information whereby decision makers can depend on information actually depicting the reality of a given situation.

representational faithfulness A primary characteristic of reliability. To be useful, accounting information must reasonably report what actually happened.

verifiability A primary characteristic of reliability. Information is considered verifiable if several individuals, working independently, would arrive at similar conclusions using the same data.

neutrality A primary characteristic of reliability. To be useful, accounting information must be free of bias.

1. **Representational faithfulness.** There must be agreement between what the accounting information says and what really happened. If a company's accounting information reports sales revenue of $1,000 and the company really had sales revenue of $1,000, the accounting information is representationally faithful. However, if a company's accounting information reports sales revenue of $1,000 and the company really had sales revenue of only $800, then the accounting information lacks representational faithfulness.
2. **Verifiability.** We consider accounting information verifiable if several qualified persons, working independently of one another, would arrive at similar conclusions using the same data. For example, if we asked two people to independently determine the amount of an employee's wages last year, they should come to the same conclusion; using the canceled paychecks and other payroll documents for that employee, each should arrive at the same annual wage. If however, payroll documents were unavailable or incomplete, the employee's wages may not be verifiable.
3. **Neutrality.** To be useful, accounting information must be free of bias, which means accountants should not omit details simply because the information is unpleasant. We have stressed how difficult it is to make good decisions. Good decision making is even more difficult when information is suppressed or slanted, either positively or negatively. Accounting information should not unduly glorify or downplay the transactions and events it depicts. The need to remain neutral is one of the most difficult challenges facing the accounting profession.

Discussion Questions

2–30. How would the absence of relevance and reliability affect steps 3 and 4 of the seven-step decision model?
2–31. Do you think these qualities should apply to nonaccounting information? Explain.

Besides the primary qualities of relevance and reliability, the *Conceptual Framework* also discussed two secondary qualities of useful accounting information: comparability and consistency.

SECONDARY CHARACTERISTICS

Information about an enterprise gains greatly in usefulness if it can be compared with similar information about other enterprises and with similar information about the same enterprise for some other period or some other point in time (Statement of Financial Accounting Concepts No. 2, paragraph 111).

Comparability

Economic decision makers evaluate alternatives. Accounting information for one alternative must therefore be *comparable* to accounting information for the others. For example, assume you intend to make an investment in one of two companies. If each company used completely different accounting methods, you would find it very difficult to make a useful comparison.

To achieve **comparability,** accounting rules require that every company provide accounting information that conforms to a fairly uniform structure. This is useful when an accounting information user is comparing one company to another. Under GAAP, every company uses the same basic classification and valuation structure and issues the same basic set of financial reports. That said, companies may choose from alternative accounting techniques and formats so the information from one company will not be exactly the same as that of the next, but it will be close enough to be comparable.

comparability A quality needed to meaningfully assess the relative performance on *two different entities.* The requirement that every company provide accounting information in conformity with a fairly uniform structure enables decision makers to compare one company to another.

Consistency

consistency A quality that is needed to meaningfully assess the performance of a *single entity* over time. Consistent application of accounting rules enables us to track a single company's performance over time.

To achieve **consistency,** accounting rules require that once a company chooses an accounting technique, it should continue to use the technique. This is helpful when an accounting information user is trying to track the financial progress of a particular entity over time. We said in the preceding paragraph that companies may choose from alternative accounting techniques and formats, but once they decide, they should continue to use the chosen accounting treatment. Otherwise, information users who are trying to plot the financial progress of a company may be confused or distracted by changes in accounting information that are due solely to a change in the accounting methods the company uses rather than due to a change in the company's situation.

Accounting students often confuse comparability and consistency. Comparability is a quality needed to meaningfully assess the relative performance on *two different entities.* Comparability enables us to compare one company to another. On the other hand, consistency is a quality that is needed to meaningfully assess the performance of a *single entity.* Consistent application of accounting rules enables us to track a single company's performance over time.

Discussion Question ●

2–32. How would the absence of comparability and consistency affect steps 4 and 6 of the seven-step decision model?

◆ DECISION MAKERS AND UNDERSTANDABILITY

Now that you understand the qualities required to make accounting information useful, you can appreciate the fact that, as a decision maker and user of accounting information, you must evaluate financial information to assess its usefulness. You must also recognize that the information presented in the financial statements you receive from accountants constitutes only a part of the information you need to make sound economic decisions. It is an important part, to be sure, but only a part. As various financial statements are introduced and discussed throughout the rest of this text, keep in mind that each has its limitations and imperfections. After working with the material provided here and the remainder of the text, however, you should be able to use the information contained in each of the financial statements to its fullest potential.

Summary ●

In general, the aim of all decisions is to obtain some type of reward, either extrinsic or intrinsic. To obtain that reward, some sacrifice must be made. Good decisions are those that result in situations where the rewards outweigh the sacrifice even in the context of uncertainty.

Decisions can be classified as either routine (recurring) or nonroutine (those that must be made in new and unfamiliar circumstances). A key to good decision making is the ability to distinguish between routine and nonroutine decision situations. Neither style is necessarily better than the other; each is useful in certain decision situations.

However, another key to good decision making is establishing a cognitive approach to the decision process, such as the seven-step model presented in this chapter.

A third key to good decision making is to develop a more creative approach to the process. A creative thinker has the ability to consider alternatives that are not readily apparent.

Economic decisions are those involving money. For our purposes, they are decisions within the context of business transactions. These decisions are made by internal decision makers (individuals within a company) or external decision makers (individuals or organizations outside a company). Management accounting information is prepared for use by internal parties, and financial accounting information is prepared for use by external parties (but is also used by internal parties).

Both internal and external parties attempt to predict the future and timing of cash flows. Essentially, they are all trying to determine whether they will be paid, when they will be paid, and how much they will be paid. Cash flow, then, is an important criterion to evaluate business success or failure, along with other accounting measures of performance.

Accounting information is a key ingredient of good decision making. Business activity produces data. These data are of no value to decision makers until they are put into a useful form and become information. Accounting information must possess certain qualitative characteristics: (1) relevance, including timeliness and either predictive value or feedback value; and (2) reliability, including verifiability, representational faithfulness, and neutrality. Useful accounting information should also possess comparability and consistency and be understandable to economic decision makers.

Key Terms

- accounting, F–52
- accounting information, F–52
- comparability, F–55
- conservatism, F–53
- consistency, F–56
- cost/benefit, F–53
- data, F–52
- economic entity, F–52
- external decision makers, F–48
- feedback value, F–54

- financial accounting, F–49
- going concern, F–52
- industry practice, F–53
- information, F–52
- internal decision makers, F–48
- management accounting, F–49
- materiality, F–53
- monetary unit, F–52
- net cash flow, F–50
- neutrality, F–55

- opportunity cost, F–40
- periodicity, F–52
- predictive value, F–54
- relevance, F–54
- reliability, F–55
- representational faithfulness, F–55
- risk/reward trade-off, F–41
- timeliness, F–54
- verifiability, F–55

Review the Facts

A. Define cost/benefit analysis.
B. Describe the difference between an extrinsic reward and an intrinsic reward.
C. What is the relationship between risk and reward?
D. What is the difference between routine and nonroutine decisions?
E. Describe the two major information-processing styles.
F. Explain the term *reasoned decision making*.
G. Describe the seven steps of the decision model presented in this chapter.
H. What is creative decision making and why is it important?
I. What is the role of personal values in the decision making process?
J. Name and describe the two different approaches to ethics.
K. Describe the advantages and disadvantages of both individual and group decision making.
L. What is economic decision making?
M. Name the two broad categories of economic decision makers, and explain the differences between them.
N. List the two major branches of accounting mentioned in the chapter and describe how they differ from one another.
O. List the three major questions asked by economic decision makers.
P. What is accounting information?
Q. Explain the difference between data and information.
R. List and define the four accounting assumptions.
S. List and define the four accounting constraints.
T. Name the two primary qualitative characteristics of useful accounting information.
U. What characteristics are necessary for accounting information to be relevant?
V. List the characteristics necessary for accounting information to be reliable.
W. Name and describe the secondary qualities of useful accounting information.

Apply What You Have Learned

LO 1: INTRINSIC VS. EXTRINSIC REWARDS

2–33. Fred Payne, a college senior, has just gotten a part-time job working with developmentally challenged children making $10 per hour. Fred has always wanted to work with such children and thinks he may pursue this work as a career.

Required:

    a. From the facts given in the problem, what would you consider to be the extrinsic and intrinsic rewards Fred will receive from his new job?

    b. Which do you think will be more valuable to Fred, the extrinsic rewards or the intrinsic rewards? Explain your reasoning.

LO 1: ROUTINE VS. NONROUTINE DECISIONS

2–34. Some situations occur routinely in business, and management has standard operating procedures to apply when they happen. Below are a number of situations.

    1. _____ An employee calls in sick.
    2. _____ An employee makes a mistake in adding his travel claim.
    3. _____ Five dollars is missing from the petty cash fund.
    4. _____ The petty cash fund and the petty cashier are missing.
    5. _____ A vendor bills the company for 25 items and only 24 are received.
    6. _____ A vendor bills the company for 25 items that are neither ordered nor received.
    7. _____ The company's delivery person taps the bumper of a car while parking.
    8. _____ The company's driver totals the delivery van in a one-vehicle accident.
    9. _____ The building loses its roof in a tornado.
    10. _____ The building suffers extensive hail damage in a storm.
    11. _____ An employee fails to return from lunch.

Required: Identify whether these situations should invoke a routine (R) or nonroutine (N) decision.

LO 3: INTUITIVE VS. SYSTEMATIC INFORMATION PROCESSING

2–35. Briefly describe the intuitive and the systematic information-processing styles. Include in your answer ways in which these two styles are similar and ways in which they differ.

LO 3: INTUITIVE VS. SYSTEMATIC INFORMATION PROCESSING

2–36. Most people have a predominate style of processing information that is either systematic or intuitive. In a given situation, you may prefer to have one style of thinker over another.

    1. _____ You need a designer for your dream home.
    2. _____ You need a contractor to build a warehouse.
    3. _____ You need an engineer to plan a highway system in a wilderness area.
    4. _____ You need an engineer to design a five-mile expansion bridge.
    5. _____ Two employees have a serious, ongoing conflict. You need to refer them to a mediator.
    6. _____ Your business has serious financial problems that must be solved within one week. You need to hire a consultant.
    7. _____ You are a systematic thinker and you need a partner.
    8. _____ You need an advertising consultant to promote a new product.

Required: Identify whether you prefer to have an intuitive (I) thinker or a systematic (S) thinker in each of these situations and state your reasons why.

LO 2: APPLICATION OF SEVEN-STEP DECISION MODEL

2–37. Kathy Stumpe is in trouble! She has been in Paris on business for the past week. This morning, she was supposed to fly to New York for a very important dinner meeting. Unfortunately, Kathy overslept and missed her flight. As she hurries to shower and get dressed, she is trying to decide what to do next. "If only I had not slept through my alarm," she says to herself over and over. "That's the real problem."

Required:

    a. Do you think Kathy has determined her real problem? If not, help her identify it.

    b. Now that the real problem has been determined, identify two alternative courses of action Kathy might take to solve her problem. Then analyze each of them critically.

LO 2: APPLICATION OF SEVEN-STEP DECISION MODEL

2–38. You are presented with the responsibility of choosing the new copy machine for your office. Using the seven-step decision model, describe how you would approach this decision.

LO 2: APPLICATION OF SEVEN-STEP DECISION MODEL

2–39. Upon graduation from college, you receive three different job offers. Identify the various factors that you might consider to make your decision and illustrate how you would apply the seven-step decision model.

LO 2: APPLICATION OF SEVEN-STEP DECISION MODEL

2–40. Your employer offers two different types of retirement plans to all eligible employees. You may select only one of the plans. Plan A requires you to contribute 10 percent of your monthly salary, which your employer matches equally. You may not withdraw or borrow from the plan until you reach age 60. Plan B requires you to contribute 10 percent of your salary but is matched by your employer with an additional 5 percent. This plan allows you to borrow against the balance at any time without penalty.

Required: Using the seven-step decision model, discuss how you would choose between the plans assuming:

a. You are a single individual 23 years of age.
b. You are a married individual 40 years of age with two teenage children.

LO 2: APPLICATION OF SEVEN-STEP DECISION MODEL

2–41. As the chief lending officer for the bank, you received loan requests from three different clients for $150,000 each. Assume you may only make one of the loans. The following information is available to you:

1. The first applicant is 21 years old and needs the loan for four years of Harvard Medical School.
2. The second applicant is a 45-year-old businessman who wants to start his own manufacturing business. He needs the loan for equipment and start-up expenses.
3. The third applicant is a 30-year-old dental school graduate who wishes to start her own practice. She needs the loan for equipment and to cover some operating expenses.

Required:

a. Use the seven-step decision model to decide who should receive the loan.
b. Now assume that you can make the loan to all three candidates and that the interest rates you can assess range between 3 percent and 12 percent. Using the concepts of risk and uncertainty, discuss the factors that would influence the interest rate you would select for each loan candidate.

LO 2: APPLICATION OF SEVEN-STEP DECISION MODEL

2–42. Let's say that you would like to begin investing in the stock market. After your preliminary research, you have decided that you will invest in pharmaceutical companies, airlines, and computer technology companies.

Required:

a. List 10 pieces of information that you would like to have for each company in each of the three industries. Be specific and make sure the information that you request is relevant to your decision. Remember that the 10 pieces of information should allow you to make comparisons of each company within the industries.
b. Now that you have your list of 10 pieces of relevant information, where do you think you might look to find this information?

LO 2: APPLICATION OF SEVEN-STEP DECISION MODEL

2–43. Compare and contrast the seven-step decision model presented in this chapter with the process outlined in Chapter 1 that demonstrates how the Financial Accounting Standards Board approaches the problem of standard setting. Do you think that the FASB follows the seven-step decision model?

LO 2 & 3: APPLICATION OF SEVEN-STEP DECISION MODEL

2–44. The semester break is approaching and Seth Levine, a college student, is trying to decide how he will spend the week. He has narrowed his options to these three:

Option 1: He could go to Vail, Colorado, and ski for the week (he is an avid skier). He estimates the total cost of the trip—airfare, lodging, food, and lift tickets—to be $1,700. If he selects this option, he will have to cut the last day of classes before the break. He will also have to take time off from his part-time restaurant job. He earns $10 per hour and could work as many as 60 hours over the break.

Option 2: He could drive to his parents' home for the week. They live only 140 miles from Seth's school, so he would not have to leave until after his last class. This option requires no out-of-pocket cost because he will be staying with his parents and his father has offered to pay for the gas. He would, however, have to take time off from work, just as in Option 1.

Option 3: He can remain at school for the week and devote his time to studying and working at the restaurant.

The final decision, of course, is Seth's. However, he has come to you for advice because he believes you are a person of sound judgment.

Required:

a. Tell Seth what you think are the most important factors he needs to consider when making his decision. Some of these factors may involve money, others will not. Identify the factor you consider to be most important, and explain why you think it is crucial.

b. Prepare an analysis for Seth of what you perceive to be the potential benefits and costs of each of his three alternatives. Although economic benefits and costs are always important, do not restrict yourself to the financial considerations for either benefits or costs.

c. Assume that about a month before semester break, Seth decides to go skiing in Vail (Option 1). Identify three relevant pieces of new information Seth might receive before he leaves on his ski trip and explain how each of them might cause him to rethink his decision.

LO 4: PERSONAL VALUES AND ETHICS

2–45. The chapter states that the most important influences on the decisions we make are the personal values we hold.

Required:

a. Explain in your own words the relationship between personal values and ethics.

b. How do you think that a person's values and ethics change over time? What will cause a person's values and ethics to change?

LO 5: PERSONAL VALUES AND ETHICS

2–46. Charles Rickman, an employee of Failsafe, Inc., has been away on business in Bedford Falls, Pennsylvania, for the past two weeks. Bedford Falls happens to be his hometown, and Charles stayed the entire two weeks with his mother. Wilbur Parker, Charles's boyhood pal, owns the local motel and offered to provide Charles with receipts for a two-week stay at the motel. Charles could submit the receipts and be reimbursed by his company. Failsafe generally expects to reimburse its employees for out-of-town lodging, so the company would not be out of any unexpected costs.

Required:

a. Explain how Charles would approach this decision situation using virtues ethics.

b. Explain how Charles would approach this decision situation using rules ethics.

c. Which approach do you think would serve Charles better in all such decision situations? Explain your reasoning.

LO 5: PERSONAL VALUES AND ETHICS

2–47. Assume that you have been working as a staff accountant for Fox Manufacturing Company for the past six months. Your boss needs you to increase the current year's profit by $25,000 and has asked for your help. He tells you of certain accounting entries and how you could make them to make it seem like the company earned the additional profit. Even though he is the boss, based on your knowledge, you believe what he is asking you to do is not really proper.

Required:

a. Using the concept of virtues ethics, how would you respond in this situation?
b. How would you apply rules ethics in this situation, and would that change your overall response?
c. Assuming that the method your boss wishes you to use to increase profits is technically legal, how do you reconcile his request with your personal values?

LO 5: GROUP DECISION MAKING

2–48. Listed below are the disadvantages of group decision making presented in the chapter, followed by the definitions of those disadvantages in scrambled order:

a. Different information-processing styles
b. Domineering members of the group
c. Social pressure
d. Goal replacement
e. Differing personal values
f. Unequal effort
g. Groupthink

1. _____ Some members of the group may not work as hard as others.
2. _____ Not everyone believes the same way.
3. _____ The group may contain both intuitive types and systematic types.
4. _____ The natural desire to not look foolish may stifle a group member's creative contribution.
5. _____ Group members are often tempted to ignore their own judgment to achieve consensus.
6. _____ Winning an argument, proving a point, or taking revenge can become more important than accomplishing the task at hand.
7. _____ The work of the group suffers simply because some members can talk louder and longer than others.

Required: Match the letter next to each disadvantage with the appropriate definition. Use each letter only once.

LO 5: GROUP DECISION MAKING

2–49. Explain in your own words the advantages and disadvantages of group decision making in relation to individual decision making.

LO 7 & 8: ECONOMIC DECISION MAKING

2–50. Tommy Hoag is a commercial artist and sign painter by trade. He received a $15,000 order from Bill Bates, Inc. for *1,500* signs to be displayed in Bates's retail outlets. This is a very large job for Tommy's new business. He has concerns because he estimates it will take him a month working full time to complete the signs and Bates proposes to pay him the full contract amount 30 days after he delivers the signs. These are Bates's standard payment terms. Tommy did a small job for Bates last year ($1,500) and received payment 50 days after completing the work.

Tommy estimates the materials (sign board, paint, brushes, etc.) will cost $9,500, which he can buy on 30-day terms from Long's Art Supply Company.

Tommy remembers from his first accounting course that any economic decision entails attempting to answer the following three questions:

• Will I be paid?
• When will I be paid?
• How much will I be paid?

Required:

    a. If Tommy can satisfy himself as to the first question (Will I be paid?), what are the answers to the other two questions? Remember the last question (How much?) has two parts.

    b. The problem states that Tommy has concerns. What do you think is troubling him about the order from Bill Bates, Inc.?

    c. Based on your answer to the previous requirement, identify three things Tommy could do to solve his dilemma.

LO 7 & 8: ECONOMIC DECISION MAKING

2–51. Jon Smythe is a trained automobile engine mechanic. He has received a $25,000 contract from David Watts and Company to replace 25 automobile engines for Watts' taxi cabs. Jon has concerns about the terms of the contract. He estimates it will take him a month working full time to complete the engine changes and Watts has agreed to pay him 30 days after he completes the work. These are Watts's standard payment terms, and Watts has paid Jon on average after 40 days in the past.

    Jon estimates the parts will cost $13,000, which he can buy on a 30-day charge account from Sam's Auto Supply Company. Jon has the typical questions that any economic decision maker has:

- Will I be paid?
- When will I be paid?
- How much will I be paid?

Required:

    a. Jon believes that Watts will pay him based on their prior dealings. What are the answers to the other two questions? Remember the last question (How much?) has two parts.

    b. The problem states that Jon is concerned about the contract terms. Why do you think he is concerned?

    c. Based on your answer to the previous requirement, identify three things Jon could do to lessen his concerns.

LO 7 & 8: ECONOMIC DECISION MAKING

2–52. Rob Schwinn is a furniture manufacturer who specializes in high-quality wooden tables and chairs. He received a $50,000 contract from Dillon Corporation to build 100 upholstered sofas, to be sold in Dillon's stores. Rob believes he needs two months to complete the sofas. He must purchase an industrial sewing machine for the fabric work on the sofas at a cost of $10,000 for the machine and training, which will equal the profit that he will make on this contract. Dillon has agreed to pay Rob Schwinn 30 days after delivery of the sofas.

    Rob knows that he can buy the sewing machine on a 90-day plan from Dan's Sewing Machine Company. Rob knows that any economic decision entails attempting to answer the following three questions:

- Will I be paid?
- When will I be paid?
- How much will I be paid?

Required:

    a. Assuming Rob can be satisfied as to the first question (Will I be paid?), what are the answers to the other two questions? Remember the last question (How much?) has two parts.

    b. List the pros and cons of Rob's accepting this contract.

LO 8: CASH CONCEPTS

2–53. In sports, you often hear the expressions, "keep your eye on the ball." Interpret the following statement: "cash is the 'ball' of business."

LO 9 & 10: QUALITATIVE CHARACTERISTICS OF ACCOUNTING INFORMATION

2–54. Below are the qualitative characteristics of useful accounting information as discussed in the chapter, followed by definitions of those items in scrambled order:

a. Relevance
b. Timeliness
c. Predictive value
d. Feedback value
e. Reliability
f. Verifiability
g. Representational faithfulness
h. Neutrality
i. Comparability
j. Consistency

1. _____ The same measurement application methods are used over time.
2. _____ The accounting information is free of bias.
3. _____ The information provides input to evaluate a previously made decision.
4. _____ The information allows the evaluation of one alternative against another alternative.
5. _____ In assessing the information, qualified persons working independently would arrive at similar conclusions.
6. _____ The information helps reduce the uncertainty of the future.
7. _____ The information has a bearing on a particular decision situation.
8. _____ The information is available soon enough to be of value.
9. _____ The information is dependable.
10. _____ There must be agreement between what the information says and what really happened.

Required: Match the letter next to each item with the appropriate definition. Each letter will be used only once.

LO 9 & 10: CHAPTER TERMS AND CONCEPTS

2–55. Presented below are items relating to the concepts discussed in this chapter, followed by the definitions of those items in scrambled order:

a. Cash flow
b. Comparability
c. Data
d. Financial accounting
e. Information
f. Management accounting
g. Net cash flow
h. Economic decision making

1. _____ The raw results of transactions and events
2. _____ A branch of accounting developed to meet the information needs of internal decision makers
3. _____ Data transformed so they are useful in the decision making process
4. _____ The movement of cash in and out of a company
5. _____ Any decisions involving money
6. _____ Reports generated for one entity may be compared with reports generated for other entities
7. _____ The difference between the cash coming into a company and the cash going out of a company
8. _____ A branch of accounting developed to meet the information needs of external decision makers

Required: Match the letter next to each item with the appropriate definition. Use each letter only once.

LO 10: QUALITATIVE CHARACTERISTICS OF ACCOUNTING INFORMATION

2–56. Emma Peel is the chief accountant of Venture Company. She is trying to decide whether to extend credit to Freed Company, a new customer. Venture does most of its business on credit but is very strict in granting credit terms. Frank Freed, the owner and president of Freed Company, has sent the following items for Emma to examine as she performs her evaluation.

1. All company bank statements for the past seven years (a total of 84 bank statements)
2. A detailed analysis showing the amount of sales the company expects to have in the coming year and its estimated profit
3. Another, less detailed analysis outlining projected company growth over the next 20 years

4. A biographical sketch of each of the company's officers and a description of the function each performs in the company
5. Ten letters of reference from close friends and relatives of the company's officers
6. A report of the company's credit history prepared by company employees on Freed Company letterhead
7. A letter signed by all company officers expressing their willingness to personally guarantee the credit Venture extends to Freed. (Assume this is a legally binding document.)

Required:

a. As she evaluates Freed Company's application for credit, is Emma Peel an internal decision maker or an external decision maker? Explain your reasoning.
b. Analyze each item Freed sent in light of the primary qualitative characteristics of relevance (including timeliness, predictive value, and feedback value) and reliability (including verifiability, representational faithfulness, and neutrality). Explain how each item either possesses or does not possess these characteristics.

LO 10: QUALITATIVE CHARACTERISTICS OF ACCOUNTING INFORMATION

2–57. You are in the market for a used car. You notice a promising advertisement in the local newspaper and make an appointment to meet with the seller, whose name is Chet. During your meeting, you obtain the following information:

- The car is a 1996 model.
- Chet said he has used the car only for commuting to and from work.
- You notice the car has out-of-state license tags.
- The odometer reading is 65,319 miles.
- Chet reports that he has had the oil changed every 3,000 miles since he bought the car new.
- Chet says this is the greatest car he has ever owned.
- The glove box contains a maintenance record prepared by a licensed mechanic.

Required:

a. Evaluate each item from the list above in terms of its relevance (specifically, predictive value and timeliness) to your decision about whether to buy Chet's car.
b. Evaluate each item from the list above in terms of its reliability (verifiability, representational faithfulness, and neutrality) for deciding whether to buy Chet's car.

LO 10: QUALITATIVE CHARACTERISTICS OF ACCOUNTING INFORMATION

2–58. The chapter states that to be useful, accounting information must possess the primary qualitative characteristics of relevance (timeliness and predictive value or feedback value) and reliability (verifiability, representational faithfulness, and neutrality). These characteristics are also applicable to other types of information.

Suppose that prior to taking your midterm exam in this course, your instructor gives you two options:

Option 1: One week before the midterm exam, you will be given a rough idea of what is going to be on the exam.

or

Option 2: On the day following the exam, you will be given a copy of the actual midterm exam with an answer key.

Assume further that you have two goals:

Goal 1: To prepare for the midterm exam.
Goal 2: To evaluate your performance on the midterm exam.

Required: Within the context of each of your two goals, evaluate both options using the primary qualitative characteristics. Be sure to explain how the primary characteristics are present or absent and how such presence or absence affects you as a rational decision maker.

LO 10: QUALITATIVE CHARACTERISTICS OF ACCOUNTING INFORMATION

2–59. Suppose you are about to buy a new car. The car you want is a *Nissan* Maxima. You have enough money in the bank, ready to spend on the new car. You obtain the following items of information:

1. On your first visit to *Quality Nissan,* a salesperson casually tells you that the price of a new *Nissan* Maxima is about $25,500.
2. A friend tells you he heard that someone was selling a three-year-old Maxima for $17,000.
3. Another friend just bought a new *Chevy* pickup truck for $23,500.
4. The sticker price of a Maxima with the options you want is $27,188.
5. A *Nissan* dealer in the area is advertising a new Maxima with the options you want for $25,000.
6. A friend tells you she heard that someone bought a new Maxima a couple months ago for around $24,000.

Assume that you are about to visit another *Nissan* dealership and your goal is to buy a new Maxima for the best price. You intend to use the previous information to evaluate whether or not the price you get is a good deal.

Required:
  a. Evaluate each item from the list above in terms of its relevance (feedback value, predictive value, and timeliness). Explain how the presence or absence of the characteristics affects your ability to use the information to determine if you are getting a good deal.
  b. Evaluate each item from the list above in terms of its reliability (verifiability, representational faithfulness, and neutrality). Explain how the presence or absence of these characteristics affects your ability to use the information to determine if you are getting a good deal.

LO 10: QUALITATIVE CHARACTERISTICS OF ACCOUNTING INFORMATION

2–60. Your accounting midterm exam is in about two weeks. You can't figure out exactly how you should prepare for the exam. As you are walking across campus, you see the following notice pinned to a bulletin board:

Worried About the Accounting Mid-Term???
I CAN HELP!
WILL TUTOR FOR $15 PER HOUR

I GUARANTEE AN "A" OR "B"

Qualifications:

1. Got an "A" in the course myself.
2. Have outlines of all chapters of the text.
3. Have over 120 satisfied customers from previous semesters.
4. Know the professor personally.
5. Know the authors of the text personally.
6. Working on a graduate degree in Biology.

CALL BILL AUSTIN AT 555-5555

Required: Evaluate each of Bill's claimed qualifications in relation to the primary characteristics of:
  a. Relevance (including timeliness and predictive value or feedback value).
  b. Reliability (including verifiability, representational faithfulness, and neutrality).

Financial Reporting Exercises ●

LO 9 & 10: QUALITATIVE CHARACTERISTICS OF ACCOUNTING INFORMATION

2–61. Presented below are the qualitative characteristics of useful accounting information.

a. Relevance	f. Verifiability
b. Timeliness	g. Representational faithfulness
c. Predictive value	h. Neutrality
d. Feedback value	i. Comparability
e. Reliability	j. Consistency

In 2001, **WorldCom** allegedly published misleading financial statements that made it appear as though the company had billions of dollars more in profits and billions of dollars more in assets than the company really had.

Required:

    a. Which four of the qualitative characteristics of accounting information listed above were most directly violated by **WorldCom**'s actions?

    b. What impact does such a major misrepresentation have on the credibility of **WorldCom**'s published financial information?

    c. What impact does this particular misrepresentation have on the credibility of all financial information?

LO 11: IDENTIFY SPECIFIC ANNUAL REPORT INFORMATION

2–62. Look at **Pier 1**'s annual report and answer the following questions.

    a. List the three divisions of stores that **Pier 1 Imports** accounts for in their annual reports.

    b. Name five cities in North America where **Pier 1** opened a new store in the fiscal year.

    c. List the five types of products **Pier 1** sells.

    d. Name and briefly describe the relationships of **Pier 1** with all of its subsidiaries.

    e. Which of the subsidiaries is an example of a situation that resulted in the closing of that part of the company? Explain why. What is another way in which this might happen with another one of the subsidiaries?

LO 11: IDENTIFY AND CONTRAST INFORMATION FROM ANNUAL REPORTS

2–63. **Williams Sonoma Inc.** is a competitor of **Pier 1 Imports.** Visit its Web site by clicking on **Williams Sonoma**'s link at the PHLIP Web site to find its annual report information.

Required:

    a. What are the two reportable segments that **Williams Sonoma** uses?

    b. List some of the types of products that **Williams Sonoma** sells.

    c. How many stores did **Williams Sonoma** open in 2001? How many did it close?

    d. List the subsidiaries of **Williams Sonoma.** Which of these names has the most stores?

    e. Did you know that **Williams Sonoma** owned all these subsidiaries? Why do you think the corporation keeps all of these names separate?

    f. Which company (**Williams Sonoma** or **Pier 1 Imports**) do you consider to be involved in more types of business? Do you consider this to be more of an asset or a liability to this company?

LO 11: IDENTIFY AND DISCUSS SPECIFIC ANNUAL REPORT INFORMATION

2–64. **JCPenney** operated the **Thrift Drug** store chain profitably for 28 years. **Penney's** purchased **Kerr Drug** in 1995 and **Fay's** in 1996. In February 1997, **Penney's** completed the purchase of **Eckerd Drug** to have the fourth-largest drug store chain in the United States. (For more information on **JCPenney**, visit the PHLIP Web site and click on the **JCPenney** link.)

Required:

    a. Why would a mall-centered retail department store acquire large chains of pharmacies?

    b. Why do you think **JCPenney** operates all of the drug stores under the **Eckerd** name instead of the **JCPenney** name?

    c. Name a couple of the services other than clothes, shoes, and the like that **JCPenney's** has within their stores. Why would they want to provide these services under their own name as opposed to opening new stores under different names to provide them?

ANNUAL REPORT PROJECT

2–65. Section 2— General Information

By now, you should have a copy of the annual report for the company you selected for your annual report project. In this assignment, you will prepare a report based on general information found in your company's annual report.

Required: Prepare a report that includes the following information:

a. A listing of the contents of the company's annual report. Preparing this list will help you become familiar with the annual report. If you are working in a group, it would be best if each member made his or her own list of the report's contents. Your list should include each major section of the report and its page number. Among other things, your list should include the following:

Five-Year Selected Financial Data	Page ?
Management Discussion and Analysis	Page ?
Independent Auditor's Report	Page ?
Report of Management	Page ?
Consolidated Statements of Operations	Page ?
Consolidated Balance Sheets	Page ?
Consolidated Statements of Cash Flows	Page ?
Consolidated Statements of Shareholders' Equity	Page ?
Notes to Consolidated Financial Statements	Page ?
Shareholder Information	Page ?
Directors and Officers Information	Page ?

b. The name of your company's auditing firm. You can find this in the auditor's report, which usually follows the financial statements in the company's annual report.

c. Your company's Standard Industry Code (SIC) or North American Industry Classification System (NAICS) code and a description of that industry. You can find one or both of these codes in several ways. We have listed step-by-step instructions to help you find your company's SIC code using the Securities and Exchange Commission's (SEC's) Electronic Data Gathering, Analysis, and Retrieval (EDGAR) system.

Step-by-step instructions to find a company's SIC using the SEC's Web site:

a. Go to the SEC's home page at *www.sec.gov.*
b. Click on *Search for Company Filings* (listed under *"Filings and Form (EDGAR)"*).
c. Click on *Search Companies and Filings*.

d. Enter your company's name in the appropriate place and click *Find Companies*.
e. The company's SIC code and a description of the company's industry will appear just under the company's name in the upper left area of the page. For example, for ***Pier 1 Imports, Inc.,*** the following information appears on the Web page just under the SEC's logo and seal:

```
PIER 1 IMPORTS INC
SIC: 5700-Retail-Home Furniture, Furnishings & Equipment
Stores
```

Company SIC codes are also available on the front page of the company's Form 10Q SEC filings. You can find this form and many other filings by logging on to the SEC's EDGAR system.

f. A statement regarding how you feel the description of the industry pertaining to your company's SIC code compares to the company's actual business as described in its annual report.

g. A brief summary of the president's (or CEO's) message included in your company's annual report.

h. A brief summary of the general information and promotional material included in your company's annual report. Your summary should include a general description of your company's business and a summary of the firm's views on social responsibility, marketing strategy, direction for the future, environmental issues, and so forth.

i. An outline of the major points covered in the letter to stockholders.

j. With respect to the report of the independent auditors:

1. What does the opinion say about the division of responsibility between the auditor and management?
2. What does it mean when the auditor's report says something similar to "present

fairly, in all material respects"?

3. What does it mean when the auditor's report says something similar to "in accordance with generally accepted accounting principles"?

4. What does the audit report say about auditing standards?

5. In the context of the auditor's report, what does "on a test basis" mean?

k. Following the presentation of the company's financial statements, there is a series of notes. The first note presents information about significant accounting policies. Summarize the kind of information the note includes. Explain how the information in this note would help a decision maker understand the company's financial statements.

CHAPTER 3

The Balance Sheet and External Financing

Last night you woke up at 2:30 A.M. and simply could not get back to sleep, so you turned on the TV and began surfing through the channels. As is typical for middle-of-the-night broadcasting, nearly every channel was showing an infomercial of one kind or another. Most of them had to do with either making a fortune in real estate with no money down or losing weight by eating more. Neither topic held much interest for you. Then you stumbled on a channel that was showing *The New Yankee Workshop*. Norm, the host of this popular woodworking show, can build just about anything you can imagine and makes even the most intricate project look easy. In this episode, Norm was crafting a bedroom dresser. What luck! You've needed a dresser for quite some time. You tune in, thinking you may get some tips about what to look for in a dresser. The longer you watch, the more excited you get. Although you've never built a piece of furniture before and don't even own any tools, you find yourself thinking, "I could build that dresser," and indeed this is what you decided to do.

This morning, you set off for **Home Depot** to buy the supplies you'll need to build your dresser. You haven't made a list of the tools Norm used, as you're sure you'll recognize them when you see them on the shelves. But when you reach the tool department, you're shocked to realize it covers about 30 acres and brims with tools of all types and description. In the area displaying saws, for example, you see hand saws (crosscut and rip), power circular saws, table saws, jigsaws, miter saws, and coping saws, to name just a few. "What in the world?", you ask yourself. "Isn't there just one saw I can buy that will do everything I need to do to build my dresser?"

The answer, unfortunately, is no. No single saw will serve every need. And what's true for saws is true for every other tool, as well. Tools are developed to solve specific problems; they are responses to specific needs. Well-developed tools, properly used, produce satisfactory results. Inadequate or improperly used tools result in difficulties at best and disaster at worst. Consider the following parable:

> *The Problem* developed. So, somebody analyzed *The Problem* and, having figured out what needed to be done to solve it, invented *The Tool*. Soon, people began using *The Tool* to solve *The Problem*. Eventually, no one would even consider using anything else.
>
> For many years *The Tool* was used with great success. There came a time, however, when it no longer solved *The Problem*, but nobody realized it. Whenever confronted with *The Problem*, folks instinctively reached for *The Tool*. Even when results were devastating, no one ever questioned the use of *The Tool*.

There are at least three possible explanations for what happened in the situation described above:

1. The nature of *The Problem* had changed. If this were the case, it's no wonder *The Tool* would no longer solve the problem.
2. Those using *The Tool* thought they were applying it to *The Problem*, when in fact they were attempting to use it to solve *Another Problem*, which, on the surface, looked like *The Problem*.

3. *The Tool* never really did solve *The Problem*, but merely appeared to, and reality finally caught up with it.

Think of financial information as a tool developed to solve economic problems. People have been using financial tools for hundreds of years, but their use has not always met with favorable results. In fact, the inadequacy of financial tools in the late 1920s was at least partially responsible for the stock market crash of 1929 and the resulting Great Depression. Fortunately, since then, the Securities and Exchange Commission (SEC), the Financial Accounting Standards Board (FASB), and other organizations have worked to improve the quality of the financial tools available to us. But it is our responsibility to know what tools are available, what those tools can do, and what they cannot do. In the words of the FASB's *Conceptual Framework*:

> *Financial information is a tool and, like most tools, cannot be of much direct help to those who are unable or unwilling to use it or who misuse it. Its use can be learned, however, and financial reporting should provide information that can be used by all—nonprofessionals as well as professionals—who are willing to learn to use it properly.*[1]

We must update the financial tools we use so they keep up with changing circumstances. We must bear in mind that a financial tool that addresses a particular financial problem may not necessarily help solve other financial problems. And, before reaching for a tool to solve a financial problem, we must be sure we have properly identified the problem. Then, we can select the appropriate tool for that problem.

Although there is a substantial number of financial schedules and reports, many of them are used only by company managers and are not available to company outsiders. Financial accounting, the focus of this book, deals with the financial tools that are available to these outsiders (external parties). General purpose financial statements—and the related financial information that accompanies them—are the primary tools available to external parties. Like all tools, these statements were developed in response to specific needs.

In this chapter, we will focus primarily on one of these financial statements—the balance sheet. Near the end of the chapter, we will also show the effects of certain investing and financing transactions on another financial statement—the statement of cash flows. We will discuss the other financial statements in the chapters that follow.

No matter which organizational form companies take (proprietorship, partnership, or corporation) or which type of business (service, merchandising, or manufacturing), all companies have one thing in common: They must obtain capital (money) to support their operations. In the long run, a company must finance its activities with the profits it generates. We call this **internal financing.** However, when either starting out or in a time of expansion, companies must obtain capital from sources other than the profits. This is called **external financing.**

The two external sources of capital are equity financing and debt financing. **Equity financing** exchanges an ownership interest in the company for the needed cash. Virtually every business begins its life using cash invested by its owner or owners. In many cases, however, the company needs more cash than can be raised from investments by owners. Consequently, almost all companies at one time or another need to obtain financing by borrowing money. Borrowing funds to support a business is called **debt financing.** In this chapter, we will discuss external financing and illustrate its impact on the balance sheets of proprietorships, partnerships, and corporations.

Learning Objectives

After completing your work on this chapter, you should be able to do the following:

1. Identify and explain the meaning of the accounting elements shown on the balance sheet.

2. Prepare a basic balance sheet for a proprietorship, a partnership, and a corporation and demonstrate how the balance sheet provides information about the financial position of a business.

---

[1]Statement of Financial Accounting Concepts No. 1, paragraph 36.

internal financing Providing funds for the operation of a company through the earnings process of that company.

external financing Acquiring funds from outside the company. Equity and debt financing are the two major types of external financing.

equity financing Acquiring funds for business operations by giving up ownership interest in the company. For a corporation, this means issuing capital stock. Equity financing is one type of external financing.

debt financing Acquiring funds for business operations by borrowing. Debt financing is one type of external financing.

3. Describe how a corporation is formed and how the equity of a corporate balance sheet is structured.

4. Describe various forms of debt and equity financing and their effects on the balance sheet.

5. Perform basic interest calculations.

6. Compare and contrast two investment alternatives—equity investments and debt investments, including return on and return of investments for each alternative.

7. Read and understand a basic statement of cash flows and describe the information it includes.

8. Perform basic financial analysis relating to financing activities.

◆ INTRODUCTION TO THE BALANCE SHEET

In Chapter 2, we said decision makers must evaluate alternative investment opportunities to determine whether they will be paid and, if so, when the payments will occur and how much the payments will be. This evaluation begins by assessing an investment's present condition and its past performance. Remember, however, that the present and the past are useful only if they have predictive value or feedback value. Over time, accountants developed financial tools to convey information about the present condition and past performance of an entity. The **balance sheet** is the financial tool that focuses on the present condition of a business.

balance sheet The financial tool that focuses on the present condition of a business.

Discussion Questions ●

3–1. Assume you are locked in a room that has no windows and only one door. To get out of the room, you must request one tool and explain how you will use it to get out. You may not request a key or any lock-picking equipment. Choose the one tool you request and describe its features. Then explain in detail how you will use it to get out of the room.

3–2. Assume your uncle's will stipulates that you and your cousin (with whom you have always competed) will each inherit one of his two businesses. You get first choice, and you may ask 10 questions to determine the present condition of each company. Lawyers for the estate will provide the answers. List your 10 questions.

THE ACCOUNTING ELEMENTS

As you recall from Chapter 1, the FASB's *Conceptual Framework of Accounting* includes 10 accounting elements. (See Exhibit 3–1.) These accounting elements are really nothing more than broad classifications. We can use these elements, or classifications, to categorize the results of every economic transaction or event a company has. In this chapter, we will discuss the elements associated with the balance sheet.

The main accounting elements that make up the balance sheet are assets, liabilities, and equity. As we discuss each of these elements, we will give the actual FASB definition in italics followed by a less technical explanation.

assets An accounting element that is one of the three components of a balance sheet. Assets are probable future economic benefits controlled by an entity as a result of previous transactions or events—that is, what a company has.

- **Assets**—*Probable future economic benefits obtained or controlled by a particular entity as a result of past transactions or events* (Statement of Financial Accounting Concepts No. 6, paragraph 25). Assets are the things of value a company owns or controls. Generally, companies *own* their assets, but technically, a company would include certain assets it *controls* by virtue of long-term leases. The key here is that, to be an asset, the item must have probable future value. Examples of assets include cash, land, buildings, equipment, vehicles, and stocks of merchandise or supplies. Assets listed on **Office Depot**'s balance sheet for example include cash, short-term investments, receivables, merchandise inventories, and property, plant, and equipment.

liabilities An accounting element that is one of the three components of a balance sheet. Liabilities are probable future sacrifices of assets arising from present obligations of an entity as a result of past transactions or events—that is, what a company owes.

- **Liabilities**—*Probable future sacrifices of economic benefits arising from present obligations of a particular entity to transfer assets or provide services to other entities in the future as a result of past transactions or events* (Statement of Financial Accounting Concepts No. 6, paragraph 35). Liabilities are the debts a company

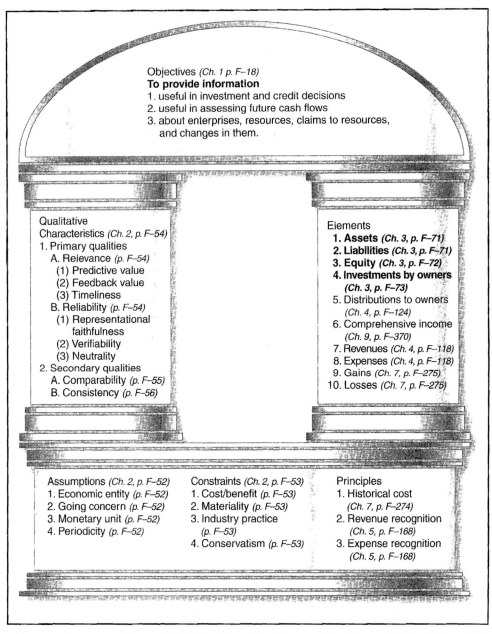

Objectives *(Ch. 1 p. F–18)*
To provide information
1. useful in investment and credit decisions
2. useful in assessing future cash flows
3. about enterprises, resources, claims to resources, and changes in them.

Qualitative
Characteristics *(Ch. 2, p. F–54)*
1. Primary qualities
   A. Relevance *(p. F–54)*
     (1) Predictive value
     (2) Feedback value
     (3) Timeliness
   B. Reliability *(p. F–54)*
     (1) Representational
        faithfulness
     (2) Verifiability
     (3) Neutrality
2. Secondary qualities
   A. Comparability *(p. F–55)*
   B. Consistency *(p. F–56)*

Elements
  1. Assets *(Ch. 3, p. F–71)*
  2. Liabilities *(Ch. 3, p. F–71)*
  3. Equity *(Ch. 3, p. F–72)*
  4. Investments by owners
     (Ch. 3, p. F–73)*
  5. Distributions to owners
     (Ch. 4, p. F–124)
  6. Comprehensive income
     (Ch. 9, p. F–370)
  7. Revenues *(Ch. 4, p. F–118)*
  8. Expenses *(Ch. 4, p. F–118)*
  9. Gains *(Ch. 7, p. F–275)*
10. Losses *(Ch. 7, p. F–275)*

Assumptions *(Ch. 2, p. F–52)*
1. Economic entity *(p. F–52)*
2. Going concern *(p. F–52)*
3. Monetary unit *(p. F–52)*
4. Periodicity *(p. F–52)*

Constraints *(Ch. 2, p. F–53)*
1. Cost/benefit *(p. F–53)*
2. Materiality *(p. F–53)*
3. Industry practice
   (p. F–53)
4. Conservatism *(p. F–53)*

Principles
1. Historical cost
   (Ch. 7, p. F–274)
2. Revenue recognition
   (Ch. 5, p. F–168)
3. Expense recognition
   (Ch. 5, p. F–168)

EXHIBIT 3–1 The Conceptual Framework of Accounting—Accounting Elements Highlighted

owes. Liabilities include obligations to transfer cash or other assets to pay off debt, as well as obligations to provide goods or services when the company receives payment in advance. The key consideration is that the company must owe something for a liability to exist. Liabilities arise from past transactions; they are debts that an entity must settle (pay) some time in the future. Liabilities listed on **Coca-Cola**'s balance sheet, for example, include accounts payable, notes payable, payables for income taxes, and long-term debt. The word *payable* is used to describe many liabilities because they are amounts to be paid.

- **Equity**—*The residual interest in the assets of an entity that remains after deducting its liabilities* (Statement of Financial Accounting Concepts No. 6, paragraph 44). Equity is the ownership interest in a company. It is the difference between the company's assets and its liabilities on those assets. The result represents the portion of the assets that the owner(s) owns free and clear. Consequently, the FASB also refers to equity as *net assets*. In practice, this element is usually referred to as *owners' equity*, and by some as *net worth*.

equity An accounting element that is one of the three components of a balance sheet. Equity is the residual interest in the assets of an entity that remains after deducting liabilities. Also called net assets.

Discussion Questions

3–3. Assume you are applying for a car loan. As part of the loan application, you are required to prepare a list of your assets. What assets would you list?

3–4. Assume that as part of the loan application you are required to prepare a list of your liabilities. What liabilities would you list?

Although we said the balance sheet shows three main accounting elements, one of these elements—equity—consists of two parts. As we will soon learn, one of these parts is itself an accounting element, according to the FASB. The two parts or sources of equity are:

investments by owners
That part of owners' equity generated by the receipt of cash (or other assets) from the owners.

- **Investments by owners.** The *Conceptual Framework* lists investments by owners as a separate element, but it really is a subset of equity. The FASB defines investments by owners as *increases in equity of a particular business enterprise resulting from transfers to it from other entities of something valuable to obtain or increase ownership interests (or equity) in it* (Statement of Financial Accounting Concepts No. 6, paragraph 66). Investment by owners is the amount the owners have contributed to the company in exchange for their ownership interest. Think of it as the amount of "seed money" the owners put into the company to get it started or to finance its expansion.

earned equity The total amount a company has earned since its beginning, less any amounts distributed to the owner(s). In a corporation, this amount is called retained earnings.

- **Earned equity.** This is the total amount a company has earned since it was first started, less the earnings the company has distributed to its owners. Earned equity comes from the profitable operation of the company over time. Think of it as the portion of income that the company keeps to plow back into the business. While earned equity is not itself considered an accounting element according to the FASB, it is composed of the remaining six elements (distributions to owners, comprehensive income, revenues, expenses, gains, and losses). Earned equity is our major focus in Chapter 4.

ORGANIZATION OF THE BALANCE SHEET

A constant relationship exists among the three main elements on the balance sheet (assets, liabilities, and equity). Logically, what a company has (assets) will be equal to the claims that are made on those assets: the creditors' claims (liabilities) or the owners' claims (equity). The following equation expresses this relationship mathematically:

$$\text{Assets} = \text{Liabilities} + \text{Owners' Equity}$$

This equation is called the *accounting equation*. We might also call it the *business equation* because it sums up an important reality of business. Accounting uses this equation to measure that reality. The rules of mathematics allow us to rearrange the accounting equation as follows:

$$\text{Assets} - \text{Liabilities} = \text{Owners' Equity}$$

This presentation of the equation shows the reality of equity as the owners' residual interest in the company. In most cases, both creditors and owners share claims to the assets (see Exhibit 3–2).

EXHIBIT 3–2 Accounting Equation

If you were to buy an automobile for $8,000, paying $3,000 in cash and borrowing $5,000 from the bank, both you and the bank would have a claim against the car.

Assets	=	Liabilities	+	Equity
Car	=	Bank Loan	+	Your Ownership Interest
$8,000	=	$5,000	+	$3,000

By rearranging the equation in the following way, you can more clearly see that in this example you would have a car valued at $8,000, the bank would have a $5,000 claim against the car, and your equity in the car would be $3,000.

Assets	–	Liabilities	=	Equity
$8,000	–	$5,000	=	$3,000

To understand the balance sheet, you must understand the accounting equation. The term *balance sheet* comes from the need to keep the two sides of the equation in balance. The financial statement's formal name is the *statement of financial position* or *statement of financial condition*, both of which are more descriptive of the true purpose of the statement than balance sheet. Common usage in the business world, however, remains the balance sheet, so we will use it throughout our discussions of the statement. Exhibit 3–3 shows ***Best Buy***'s 2001 balance sheet.

At this point, don't get caught up in trying to understand each and every asset, liability, and equity ***Best Buy*** lists. That will come later. But you should take note of the general format of the balance sheet and the fact that ***Best Buy***'s total assets are equal

EXHIBIT 3–3   Balance Sheet for ***Best Buy***

Best Buy Co., Inc.
Consolidated Balance Sheets
$ in thousands, except per share amounts

Assets	March 3 2001	Feb. 26 2000
Current Assets		
Cash and cash equivalents	$ 746,879	$ 750,723
Receivables	209,031	189,301
Recoverable costs from developed properties	103,846	72,770
Merchandise inventories	1,766,934	1,183,681
Other current assets	101,973	41,985
Total current assets	2,928,663	2,238,460
Property and Equipment		
Land and buildings	170,978	76,228
Leasehold improvements	556,534	254,767
Fixtures and equipment	1,259,880	762,476
	1,987,392	1,093,471
Less accumulated depreciation and amortization	543,220	395,387
Net property and equipment	1,444,172	698,084
Goodwill, Net	385,355	—
Other Assets	81,397	58,798
Total Assets	$4,839,587	$2,995,342

Liabilities and Shareholders' Equity	2001	2000
Current Liabilities		
Accounts payable	$1,772,722	$1,313,940
Accrued compensation and related expenses	154,159	102,065
Accrued liabilities	545,590	287,888
Accrued income taxes	127,287	65,366
Current portion of long-term debt	114,940	5,790
Total current liabilities	2,714,698	1,785,049
Long-Term Liabilities	121,952	99,448
Long-Term Debt	181,009	14,860
Shareholders' Equity		
Preferred stock, $1.00 par value: Authorized – 400,000 shares; Issued and outstanding – none	—	—
Common stock, $.10 par value: Authorized – 1,000,000,000 shares; Issued and outstanding – 208,138,000 and 200,379,000 shares, respectively	20,814	20,038
Additional paid-in capital	576,818	247,490
Retained earnings	1,224,296	828,457
Total shareholders' equity	1,821,928	1,095,985
Total Liabilities and Shareholders' Equity	$ 4,839,587	$2,995,342

to its total liabilities and equity. In other words, ***Best Buy***'s accounting equation balances as we show below.

$$\text{Assets} = \text{Liabilities} + \text{Equity}$$
$$\$4{,}839{,}587 = \$3{,}017{,}659 + \$1{,}821{,}928$$

$$\$4{,}839{,}587 = \qquad \$4{,}839{,}587$$

Companies present their balance sheets in either of two acceptable formats: the account form or the report form. As you can see in Exhibit 3–4, the account form balance sheet places assets on the left side of the page and the liabilities and owners' equity on the right.

EXHIBIT 3–4   Account Form Balance Sheet

The Toland Company
Balance Sheet
December 31, 2003

Assets:		Liabilities:	
Asset one	$$$	Liability one	$$$
Asset two	$$$	Liability two	$$$
Asset three	$$	Total liabilities	$$$$
Asset four	$$		
Asset five	$$	Owners' equity	$$$
Total assets	$$$$$	Total liabilities and owners' equity	$$$$$

THESE AMOUNTS MUST BE EQUAL

The report form, shown in Exhibit 3–5, depicts the same information in a vertical format. Although the report form of the balance sheet presents the statement's balancing feature less graphically, it is more popular than the account form, simply because it is easier to fit the balance sheet on a single page using the report form.

EXHIBIT 3–5   Report Form Balance Sheet

The Toland Company
Balance Sheet
December 31, 2003

Assets:	
Asset one	$$$
Asset two	$$$
Asset three	$$
Asset four	$$
Asset five	$$
Total assets	$$$$$
Liabilities:	
Liability one	$$$
Liability two	$$
Total liabilities	$$$$
Owners' equity	$$$
Total liabilities and owners' equity	$$$$$

THESE TWO AMOUNTS MUST BE EQUAL

Discussion Question ●

3–5. Prepare a personal balance sheet for yourself in accounting and report formats using the assets and liabilities you listed for Discussion Questions 3–3 and 3–4.

The balance sheet is a financial "snapshot" of a company. It represents the assets the company possessed and who had claim to those assets on the day the snapshot was taken. Now we will explore the balance sheets of proprietorships, partnerships, and corporations.

◆ STARTING A PROPRIETORSHIP OR PARTNERSHIP: INVESTMENTS BY OWNERS

Jessica Lynne has worked in the cosmetics industry for several years and would like to start a business distributing health and beauty aids to retail outlets. What does she need to do? Well, she will have to establish relationships with suppliers and carve out a market for the products she will sell. And, she will also need to buy the desks, computers, and the other business equipment she needs to begin her business, even if she works out of her house. If she wants to start bigger, she may need to rent office space and hire employees, among other things.

Even the smallest company has start-up costs. Therefore, Jessica's new operation needs cash! The business will need cash to buy equipment, merchandise, and to cover other costs. Any entrepreneur's first task in starting a new company is to get cash into the business so the business can get under way, and the initial funding almost always comes directly from the owner. In Jessica's case, she will have to transfer funds from her personal holdings to the business. Writing a personal check to the business and using it to open a business bank account under the company name most easily accomplishes this. Let's assume Jessica writes a personal check for $10,000 and deposits it into a business bank account for Jessica's Beauty Supply. Now, *the company's* records should reflect an increase in cash of $10,000 and an increase in owner's equity of $10,000, and the accounting equation would look like this:

$$\text{Assets} = \text{Liabilities} + \text{Owners' Equity}$$

$$\$10,000 = \$0 + \$10,000$$

BALANCE SHEET FOR A PROPRIETORSHIP

If we assume that Jessica's Beauty Supply began operations on January 1, 2003, with a $10,000 cash investment from Jessica, the company's first balance sheet would look like the one in Exhibit 3–6.

EXHIBIT 3–6   Balance Sheet for a Proprietorship

Jessica's Beauty Supply
Balance Sheet
January 1, 2003

Assets:		Liabilities:	$ 0
Cash	$10,000		
		Owners' equity:	
		Jessica, capital	**10,000**
Total assets	$10,000	Total liabilities and	
		owners' equity	$10,000

We use the word *capital* to represent the owner's claim to the assets held by a sole proprietorship. Since the capital in our simple example company includes no earned equity yet, capital in this case is made up entirely of investments by the owner. In a proprietorship, there is only one owner so there will be only one capital amount.

If we now assume that Jessica had started the business with another individual, the business would be a partnership instead of a proprietorship. The balance sheet for a partnership is slightly different from that of a proprietorship because the equity section reflects more than one owner and perhaps a different company name.

BALANCE SHEET FOR A PARTNERSHIP

Partnerships, you recall from Chapter 1, are similar to proprietorships, except that they have more than one owner. If we assume that Jessica invests $6,000 and a partner, Stephanie Meadows, invests $4,000, the first balance sheet for the company would look like the one in Exhibit 3–7.

EXHIBIT 3–7   Balance Sheet for a Partnership

Jessica and Stephanie's Beauty Supply
Balance Sheet
January 1, 2003

Assets:		Liabilities:	$ 0
Cash	$10,000		
		Owners' equity:	
		Jessica, capital	**$ 6,000**
		Stephanie, capital	**4,000**
		Total liabilities and	
Total assets	$10,000	owners' equity	$10,000

When we compare the balance sheet for this partnership with that for the proprietorship (Exhibit 3–6), we notice that they are very similar except that the company names are different and equity section of the partnership's balance sheet shows a separate capital amount for each partner.

◆ STARTING A CORPORATION

Unlike proprietorships and partnerships, corporations are legal entities, separate from their owners. With very few exceptions, such as national banks that must be incorporated under federal law, incorporators obtain a corporate charter from one of the 50 states to create a corporation. This charter is a legal agreement between the corporation and the state allowing the company to conduct business as a distinct, separate legal entity with many of the same rights as individuals.

CORPORATE ORGANIZATIONAL STRUCTURE

To form a corporation, the *incorporators* must submit a formal application for a *corporate charter* to an appropriate state agency. The application, called the *articles of incorporation*, generally must include (1) basic information about the corporation and its purpose; (2) details concerning the types of stock the corporation will issue; and (3) the names and addresses of the individuals responsible for the corporation.

If the state agency approves the application, it issues a *charter* that entitles the corporation to begin operations. The incorporators then meet to formulate the *corporate bylaws*. These bylaws serve as basic rules for management to use in conducting the corporation's business. Next, the corporation raises capital by issuing stock, thereby exchanging ownership interests in the corporation for cash or other assets. Once the stock has been issued, the stockholders elect a *board of directors* that will be responsible for overall policy and strategic direction. The directors meet and appoint a *president*, who will be responsible for day-to-day operations and management, and other *officers*, as they deem necessary to manage the company.

CORPORATE CAPITAL STRUCTURE

As part of the formal application to create a corporation, the incorporators must include information regarding their plans to sell shares of stock. They request the authority to issue (sell) a certain number of shares of stock, called **authorized shares.** Authorized shares are the maximum number of shares a corporation can legally issue under its corporate charter. These authorized shares do not really exist until they are issued, however, and ownership of the corporation is based on issued, not authorized, shares. For example, even though **Best Buy** has 1 billion authorized shares, as of March 2001, only about one fifth of those shares have been issued. **Issued shares** are the shares of stock a corporation has already distributed to stockholders in exchange for cash or other assets. **Outstanding shares** are the shares of stock currently being held by stockholders. In many instances, the number of shares issued will equal the number of shares outstanding, but not always. Occasionally, a corporation reacquires shares of stock it has previously issued by purchasing them in the open market. This reacquired stock, called **treasury stock,** will cause the numbers of shares outstanding to be fewer than the number of shares issued. For example, assume a corporation has issued 100,000 shares of its stock and then later reacquires 2,000 of those shares. The company still has 100,000 shares issued but now has only 98,000 outstanding shares. The cash paid to reacquire the treasury stock is deducted from both cash and total stockholders' equity, which keeps the accounting equation in balance. In most instances, the number of shares companies reacquire as treasury stock is comparatively small relative to the number of shares issued. In the late 1990s, however, **Honeywell, Inc.** reacquired 60 million of its 180 million issued shares.

Discussion Question ✦

3–6. What do you think would motivate a company to reacquire shares of its own stock in the open market?

For corporations, owners' equity is called *stockholders' equity* (sometimes *shareholders'* or *shareowners' equity*) and it is the excess of assets over liabilities, just as it is for proprietorships and partnerships. There are, however, some differences in the way equity items are classified on the balance sheet of a corporation.

On a corporation's balance sheet, common stock replaces the owners' capital designation. By law, most states require stockholders' equity to be divided into the portion invested by the owners and the portion of earnings the company retains. The amount the corporation receives in exchange for shares of stock is called **paid-in capital** or **contributed capital,** and a classification called **retained earnings** is used to reflect earnings kept in the company rather than distributed to the owners. When the corporate earnings are distributed to the owners, such a distribution is called **dividends.** Although not generally used in practice, a more descriptive term for retained earnings would be *reinvested earnings.* Total stockholders' equity is a combination of contributed capital and retained earnings.

Because corporations often have many stockholders, some into the thousands or even millions, the individual ownership interest of each stockholder is not disclosed on the face of the balance sheet. Instead, only totals of the ownership interests represented by each class of stock are shown. The two basic classes of stock are *common stock* and *preferred stock.*

Common Stock

Generally, **common stock** is the voting stock of the corporation, because each share of common stock represents a share of the corporation's ownership. If a company has 10,000 shares of common stock outstanding, for example, each of those shares represents 1/10,000th ownership of the company. If you own 1,500 of those shares, you own 15 percent of the company. Regularly (usually at least annually), all those who own shares of common stock—the owners—are invited to a shareholders meeting where they vote on matters of importance to the company. These matters might include approving the amount of dividends the company plans to give to the stockholders or approving plans to expand into new markets. The point is, common stockholders are the owners of the company, and (theoretically, at least) company management must

---

authorized shares The maximum number of shares of stock a corporation has been given permission to issue under its corporate charter.

issued shares Stock that has been distributed to the owners of the corporation in exchange for cash or other assets.

outstanding shares Shares of stock actually held by shareholders. The number may be different than that for issued shares because a corporation may reacquire its own stock (treasury stock).

treasury stock Corporate stock that has been issued and then reacquired by the corporation.

paid-in capital Total amount invested in a corporation by its shareholders.

contributed capital Another name for paid-in capital.

retained earnings The sum of all earnings of a corporation minus the amount of dividends declared.

dividends A distribution of earnings from a corporation to its owners. Dividends are most commonly distributed in the form of cash.

common stock A share of ownership in a corporation. Each share represents one vote in the election of the board of directors and other pertinent corporate matters.

obtain approval from those stockholders before it can take significant steps involving the owners' investment. The stockholders' equity section of a corporate balance sheet shows information about common stock, such as the number of shares authorized, the number of shares issued (and the dollar amount the company received from the sale of those shares), and any shares that have been repurchased (treasury stock), including the dollar amount paid for those shares.

par value (stock)   An arbitrary amount assigned to each share of stock by the incorporators at the time of incorporation.

Common stock may or may not have a par value. **Par value** is an arbitrary dollar amount assigned to the stock by the incorporators at the time they apply for the corporate charter. It has nothing to do with the market value of the stock, which is determined by the stock market. The legal reasons for having a par value no longer exist, and all 50 states have removed the par value requirement. So why do we discuss par value if it is no longer required? Because most of the large corporations in the United States were formed before the requirement was eliminated, so their stocks carry a par value. Also, for reasons that defy understanding, many incorporators elect to issue par value stock in newly formed corporations even though there is no longer any requirement to do so.

Discussion Question

3–7. If you were setting up a new corporation, would you establish a par value for your common stock? Why or why not?

Most corporations set the par value of their stock considerably below its actual value because, historically, most states did not allow stock to be sold for less than its par. It is not unusual to see par values of $1 per share or even lower. **Pfizer Inc.,** for example, has a par value on its stock of five cents per share and some have even lower par. Exhibit 3–8 shows a comparison of par and market values for some major corporate common stock.

EXHIBIT 3-8   Examples of Par Value Versus Market Value of Common Stock (August 18, 2002)

Company	Par Value	Market Value (August 18, 2002)
GM	1 2/3¢	$25.00
IBM	20¢	79.35
GE	6¢	31.55
Philip Morris	33 1/3¢	50.95
Chevron	75¢	76.92
Boeing	$5.00	37.50
PepsiCo	.01 2/3¢	44.39

Instead of a par value, some companies have a *stated value* for their common stock, which for all practical purposes is the same thing as a par value. For example, **Wendy's** common stock has a stated value of $.10 per share.

Preferred Stock

preferred stock   A share of ownership in a corporation that has preference over common stock as to dividends and as to assets upon liquidation of the corporation. Usually nonvoting stock.

Preferred stock, also called *preference stock*, is another type of stock some companies issue. It has different features than common stock. Preferred stockholders do not have voting rights (and are therefore not owners of the corporation), but they receive a variety of other benefits. Although these benefits differ somewhat from one preferred stock issue to another, two ownership benefits normally found in preferred stock agreements are:

- Preferred stockholders must receive their dividend before any dividend can be paid to common stockholders.
- In the event of a corporation's liquidation, preferred stockholders receive their distribution of assets before any assets can be distributed to common stockholders. Liquidation refers to the process of going out of business.

The stockholders' equity section of a corporate balance sheet shows information about preferred stock, such as the number of shares authorized and the number of shares issued (including the dollar amount the company received from the sale of those shares). Usually, preferred stock precedes common in the balance sheet presentation.

Preferred stock may have a par value. Although par value has little meaning for common stock, the par value of preferred stock may be important because dividends are often stated as a percentage of the stock's par value. For example, if a corporation issued 8 percent preferred stock with a par value of $100 per share, the annual dividend would be $8 per share ($100 × 8% = $8). Among other things, corporations must offer a reasonable dividend to encourage investors to buy their preferred stock. When the dividends are stated as a percentage of par, preferred stock usually has a par value of $50 to $100. Investors in preferred stock tend to be conservative investors, and they frequently buy preferred stock to earn a guaranteed rate of return through the stated dividend.

Sometimes preferred stock dividends are not expressed as a percentage of par, but rather as a specific dollar amount per share. In such a case, the stock is described by the dollar amount of the dividend per share. For example, *Colgate* designates a dividend of $4.25 per share for its preferred stock. In its annual report, *Colgate* describes this stock as its $4.25 Preferred Stock.

CONSTRUCTING THE CORPORATE BALANCE SHEET

To demonstrate how to construct a corporate balance sheet, let's return to Jessica and her beauty supply company, and assume that Jessica selects the corporate form organization for her new company. Further assume that Jessica, acting as the incorporator, has received a corporate charter from the State of Florida for her new business, aptly named Jessica's Beauty Supply, Inc.

To provide the initial financing for the operation, Jessica intends to invest $40,000 in the new venture and would like to maintain complete control of the company. Stephanie, Jessica's lifelong friend, does not want to participate actively in the company but has great faith in Jessica's abilities and wants to invest about $20,000 in the corporation.

After hours of discussion, Jessica and Stephanie agree that Jessica will purchase 4,000 shares of the company's one-dollar par common stock for $40,000 and Stephanie will purchase 200 shares of the company's 8 percent, $100 par preferred stock for $105 per share or $21,000.

As we prepare the new company's balance sheet, we must keep in mind that we are looking at this situation from the corporation's point of view, not the point of view of the stockholders. The corporation receives a total of $61,000 in cash from Jessica and Stephanie so the corporation's assets, cash in this case, increase by that amount. The transaction also affects the stockholders' equity because the corporation must show that Jessica has a $40,000 common stock ownership interest and Stephanie has a $21,000 preferred stock ownership interest in the corporation.

additional paid-in capital The amount in excess of the stock's par value received by the corporation when par value stock is issued.

paid-in capital in excess of par Same thing as additional paid-in capital.

If a stock carries a par value, only the par value of the stock multiplied by the number of shares issued is classified as stock. Any amount received in excess of the stock's par value is classified on the balance sheet as **additional paid-in capital,** sometimes called **paid-in capital in excess of par** or a similarly descriptive title. At one time, the laws governing corporations in all states required this accounting treatment, and even though this requirement no longer exists in most states, companies still show stock this way on the balance sheet. What this means in our example is that of the $40,000 the company received from Jessica in exchange for the $1 par value common stock, $4,000 (4,000 shares × $1 par value) is classified as Common Stock and the remaining $36,000 is classified as Additional Paid-In Capital—Common. For the sale of the $100 par preferred stock to Stephanie, $20,000 (200 shares × $100 par value) is classified as preferred stock and the remaining $1,000 is classified as Additional Paid-In Capital—Preferred. Exhibit 3–9 shows a balance sheet for Jessica's Beauty Supply, Inc., immediately following the sale of the preferred and common stock.

Jessica's Beauty Supply, Inc.
Balance Sheet
January 1, 2003

Assets:		Liabilities:	
Cash	$61,000		$ 0
		Stockholders' equity:	
		Preferred stock	**$20,000**
		Additional paid-in capital—preferred	**1,000**
		Common stock	**4,000**
		Additional paid-in capital—common	**36,000**
		Total stockholders' equity	61,000
Total assets	$61,000	Total liabilities and stockholders' equity	$61,000

EXHIBIT 3–9 Corporate Balance Sheet with Preferred and Common Stock

The total dollar amount the balance sheet shows for the preferred and common stock is simply the amounts the company received for the stock. As time goes on, the value of these stocks will likely fluctuate as conditions in the company and in the economy change. To use a balance sheet effectively, you must understand what it *can* and *cannot* tell you. A company's balance sheet does not keep track of a stock's current value because it does not reflect the changes in a stock's market value. It can only tell you the amount the company received when it originally sold the stock. In other words, the balance sheet tells you how much the company sold the stock for, but it does not tell you how much the stock is currently worth. Although this practice makes the balance sheet less relevant, it prevents manipulation so the balance sheet amounts are more reliable.

Discussion Question ◦

3–8. If you were to look at the balance sheet for **Harley-Davidson, Inc.,** it would not show the current market value of its shares of stock. Where can an investor find this information?

We should mention that if Jessica had been wise enough not to have a par value for her corporation's common stock, the company would have classified the entire $40,000 received from issuing the stock as common stock. There would be no need for a classification for additional paid-in capital—common.

We mentioned at the beginning of this chapter that businesses obtain external financing from two sources, equity financing and debt financing. We have illustrated the impact of equity financing on the balance sheet and will now turn our attention to debt financing.

◆ DEBT FINANCING

Neither a borrower nor a lender be!

—WILLIAM SHAKESPEARE

Although Shakespeare's advice may serve you well in your personal life, most companies could not survive without borrowing. Borrowing and lending have become an integral part of today's business world. It is truly a win–win situation. The borrower is happy to get the needed cash and the lender is happy to put cash to work earning interest.

Companies borrow funds for various reasons, and the need for external funding is *not* necessarily a sign of weakness. For example, some very strong companies, including **Goodyear, Dow Chemical,** and **Coca-Cola,** regularly finance their operations by borrowing. In fact, many very successful companies need to borrow cash because they are growing so fast that the cash provided from their business operations just can't keep up. In this section, you will learn about two debt-financing options: borrowing from financial institutions and borrowing by issuing bonds.

BORROWING FROM FINANCIAL INSTITUTIONS—PROMISSORY NOTES

For most of us, there will come a time when we want something but we just don't have enough money to pay for it, such as when we want to buy a house or a car. We don't want to wait until we have saved enough money to pay for it; we want it now. Lucky for us, we can borrow the money we need from a financial institution, such as a bank. By borrowing the money we need to buy a house, a car, or some other asset, we have the benefit of using the asset while we pay for it. Companies do much the same thing, except as they use the asset, they actually use it to earn a profit that will meet or exceed the amount they need for the loan payments.

Banks and other financial institutions must meet the borrowing needs of both individuals and businesses. If the purpose of a loan is personal, that is to say that the loan is for a nonbusiness purpose, the loan is called **consumer borrowing.** When a loan is to a business for a business purpose, the loan is called **commercial borrowing.**

Several distinct types of financial institutions serve the needs of consumer and commercial borrowers. Some, such as *savings and loan associations (S&Ls), mutual savings banks (MSBs),* and *credit unions (CUs),* originated to satisfy the need for consumer loans but have since begun to branch into commercial lending. Others, most notably *commercial banks,* were established specifically to meet the financing needs of businesses.

As the name implies, commercial banks are heavily involved in commercial lending, although they also offer consumer financing. At *Citibank,* the earnings from its consumer banking are about equal to that from its commercial banking services.

Whenever a company borrows money, most lenders require it to sign a promissory note. A **promissory note** is a written agreement or debt instrument between a lender and a borrower that sets forth the terms of the liability and the stipulations for the borrower to repay both principal and interest. Borrowers reflect the debt associated with a promissory note as a *note payable* in the liabilities section of their balance sheets. The reason it is called a note payable is that, after all, it is a promissory *note,* and it is an amount *payable* by the company. Borrowing cash by signing a promissory note adds to the assets of the company (cash), but at the same time creates a liability.

In addition to signing a promissory note, the lender may require the borrower to put up collateral to secure the loan. Such a loan is called a *secured loan,* whereas if no collateral is pledged to secure the loan, the loan is called an *unsecured loan.* **Collateral** is something of value that the borrower would forfeit to the lender if the borrower fails to make payments as agreed. For example, when a company borrows money from *Citibank* to buy real estate, the bank may require that the real estate serve as collateral for the loan. If the company fails to make the payments, *Citibank* will repossess the real estate and sell it to get its money back. Although it is very common for small and medium-sized companies to secure their borrowing with collateral, most of the borrowing by large companies is unsecured.

When the loan is backed by collateral, the lender has less risk, so companies can borrow more money for a greater length of time at a lower interest rate. The loan document that identifies the collateral and specifies other legal aspects of the loan agreement is called a **mortgage.** When a company uses a mortgage to borrow, the loan appears on the balance sheet as a *mortgage payable.* The difference between a notes payable and a mortgage payable is the absence or presence of collateral, respectively.

consumer borrowing
Loans obtained by individuals to buy homes, cars, or other personal property.

commercial borrowing
The process that businesses go through to obtain financing.

promissory note   A written promise to repay a loan.

collateral   Something of value that will be forfeited if a borrower fails to make payments as agreed.

mortgage   A document that states the agreement between a lender and a borrower who has secured the loan by offering something of value as collateral.

THE COST OF BORROWING

You can't use someone else's money for free. There is a cost, and that cost is called interest. The difference between the amount one borrows and the amount one repays is the cost of borrowing, or interest. The cost of borrowing can be determined once we know three things — the amount borrowed, the interest rate, and the loan period. Consider the following example:

> *Boston Brothers borrowed $5,000 on January 2, 2003, by signing an 8 percent, three-month note.*

Because interest rates are almost always stated as an annual percentage, the 8 percent refers to the amount of interest the lender would require for one full year, regardless of the length of time of the loan. Interest is based on the amount borrowed, called the **principal.** The formula to determine the interest amount is:

principal In the case of notes and mortgages, the amount of funds actually borrowed.

$$\text{Principal} \times \text{Rate} \times \text{Time} = \text{Interest}$$
$$P \quad \times \quad R \quad \times \quad T \quad = \quad I$$

In the above equation, *principal* refers to the outstanding balance of the loan, *rate* refers to the annual interest percentage, and *time* refers to the period of time for which we are calculating interest. If the interest period is for less than a whole year, as it is in our example, time is expressed as the fractional part of a year. For example, if we are calculating interest for one month, the fraction would be 1/12. In our example, the loan is for three months, so the time period equals 3/12. If the interest calculation is for a whole year, the time period is equal to one, so it is generally not even shown in the equation. As we have said, in our example, since the funds are borrowed for three months, time is represented by 3/12, indicating three of the 12 months in a year. The amount of interest due at the end of the three-month period for our example is:

$$P \quad \times \quad R \times \quad T \quad = \quad I$$
$$\$5{,}000 \times .08 \times 3/12 = \$100$$

(Notice that for purposes of calculations, we converted the percentage rates to decimals.)

If the loan had been for an entire year, the interest would be calculated as follows:

$$P \quad \times R \times T = \quad I$$
$$\$5{,}000 \times .08 \times 1 = \$400$$

Or simply:

$$P \quad \times R \quad = \quad I$$
$$\$5{,}000 \times .08 = \$400$$

Remember that the difference between the amount borrowed and the amount paid back represents the cost of borrowing. For the one-year example, the cost of borrowing is $400. It is calculated as follows:

Amount repaid over the life of a loan:

Interest (**$5,000 × 8%**)	$ 400
Principal	5,000
Total cash outflow to pay lender	$ 5,400
Less: Original amount borrowed	(5,000)
Cost of borrowing (interest)	$ 400

Discussion Questions ●

3–9. In the example of the Boston Brothers' three-month loan, what is the lender's return of investment and what is their return on investment?

The next two Discussion Questions require that you look up the current interest rates in the business section of your local newspaper.

3–10. List the different rates a local bank is paying on various certificates of deposit (CDs). Explain why the bank is offering these various rates.

3–11. What are the current rates banks are charging for mortgages in your area? What are the current credit card rates? Why are there differences between these two rates?

BORROWING BY ISSUING BONDS

bond An interest-bearing debt instrument that allows corporations to borrow large amounts of funds for long periods of time and creates a liability for the borrower.

debenture bond An unsecured bond payable.

par value (bonds) The amount that must be paid back upon maturity of a bond. Also called face value or maturity value.

indenture The legal agreement made between a bond issuer and a bondholder that states repayment terms and other details.

A **bond** is a type of promissory note, usually a $1,000 interest-bearing debt instrument. The main differences between borrowing with bonds and borrowing with other promissory notes are the length of the loan and the amount of money borrowed and the number of lenders involved. Other promissory notes are usually up to 10 years in duration and are often limited to the amount of money a single lender feels it can lend to one customer. Bonds can have very long terms, say, 40 years or more. By selling bonds to many different investors, the total amount the company borrows can exceed what one bank could (or would) lend. Most often, bonds are sold without a pledge of collateral. These bonds are called **debenture bonds.**

Bonds are issued in set denominations, generally $1,000 for each bond. That set denomination is printed right on the face of the bond and is called the bond's **par value,** also called the *face value* or the *maturity value.* What this means is that when the par value is $1,000, the borrower repays $1,000 when the bond matures. Companies must provide information in their annual report for each bond issue including its par value, its interest rate, the timing of interest payments, and the bond's maturity date. The legal document that details the bond agreement and all the pertinent details is called an **indenture.** See Exhibit 3–10 for examples of corporate bonds.

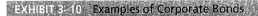
EXHIBIT 3–10 Examples of Corporate Bonds

Source: The Bond Market Association

nominal interest rate The interest rate set by the issuers of bonds, stated as a percentage of the par value of the bonds. Also called the contract rate.

effective interest rate The rate of interest actually earned by a lender. This amount will be different from the nominal interest rate if a bond is bought at a discount or premium, or a note is discounted. Also called yield rate or market interest rate.

market price (of bonds) The amount that investors are actually willing to pay for a bond. A bond's selling price.

premium If a bond's selling price is above its par value, the bond is being sold at a premium.

The **nominal interest rate** is the interest rate printed on the bond and used to calculate the bond's interest payments. It is always stated as a percentage of the par value of the bond. In other words, it is the interest rate the issuing company (the borrower) has agreed to pay on the face value of the bond. The nominal rate is also called the *contract rate, coupon rate,* or *stated rate,* and these terms are used interchangeably.

In contrast to the nominal interest rate, which is printed right on the bond and therefore remains constant, the effective interest rate fluctuates with market conditions. The **effective interest rate** is the actual interest rate the bondholder will earn over the life of the bond. Unlike the nominal rate, which is determined by the issuing company, the effective rate is determined by the financial markets and may cause a bond to sell for more or less than its par value. That's right, the rate printed on the bond cannot be changed, and so to *effectively* change the rate of interest the bondholder will earn, the *selling price* of the bond is adjusted. The effective rate is also called the *yield rate* or *market interest rate,* and these terms are used interchangeably.

A bond's **market price,** also called the bond's *selling price,* is the amount that investors are actually willing to pay for the bond. The effective interest rate that investors demand for a particular bond determines its selling price. Bond prices are stated in terms of their par value. A bond selling "at 100" means that it is selling at 100 percent of its par value. Likewise, a bond selling "at 102" is selling for 102 percent of its par value and a bond selling "at 97" is selling at 97 percent of its par value. If the bond is selling for more than its par value, it is selling at a **premium;** if it is selling for less than its par value, it is

discount If a bond's selling price is below its par value, the bond is being sold at a discount.

selling at a **discount.** Now, as we said, the effective interest rate that investors demand for a particular bond will determine whether the bond sells at par, at a premium, or at a discount. If the effective interest rate and the nominal interest rate are the same, the bond will sell at par or at 100. If the effective interest rate that investors demand is higher than the bond's nominal interest rate, investors will not buy the bonds at par. If you think about it, you will realize why bonds sell for more or less than their par values. Imagine that you are trying to sell a bond at its face value when the bond has a nominal interest rate of 8 percent, in a market where investors are getting 9 percent on similar bonds. Would anyone buy your bond? Probably not, unless you do what any department store does when its merchandise is not selling. You reduce the selling price. In other words, you discount the price of the bond until it sells. At that magical selling price, the effective interest rate on the bond will equal the rate the market demands for such an investment.

For example, assume Yoko Industries issues 1,000, 12 percent, 10-year, $1,000 bonds at 95. The bonds sell below par because investors in the market require a higher rate of return than the bond's 12 percent nominal rate. The total cost of borrowing is calculated as follows:

Interest (**$1,000,000 × 12% × 10 years**)	$1,200,000
Principal (**1,000 bonds × $1,000 face**)	1,000,000
Total cash outflow from issuer of bonds	$2,200,000
Less: Original bond proceeds from investors (**$1,000,000 × 95%**)	(950,000)
Net cost to the issuer and return on investment to the investors	$1,250,000

As you can see, the total cost of borrowing ($1,250,000) for 10 years exceeds the cash payments for interest ($1,200,000). This $50,000 difference is due to the lower selling price of the bond and is technically considered part of interest cost. Therefore, the effective interest rate is higher than the 12 percent nominal interest rate. Because bond terms exceed one year, the effective interest rate must be computed using present value techniques. These calculations are beyond the scope of this text.

As we have mentioned, bonds may also sell at a premium, or for more than their par value. This happens when a bond's stated interest rate is more than the market interest rate. For instance, assume that Matson Industries is trying to sell its bond issue of 1,000, 12 percent, 10-year, $1,000 bonds. Assume further that the market interest rate for similar securities is less than 12 percent. If Matson sells the bonds at par, investors would clamor to buy them because they pay 12 percent when other bonds in the market pay less than that. With such an outpouring of demand, Matson would soon realize that it can increase the selling price of the bonds to a point that they still sell, but at a normal pace. Let's say that this would occur when the company prices the bonds at 104. Although the calculations to determine this exact selling price for the bonds are beyond the scope of this course, we can see by the calculations below that if the bonds sell at 104, the total cost of borrowing is less than 12 percent interest.

Interest (**$1,000,000 × 12% × 10 years**)	$1,200,000
Principal (**1,000 bonds × $1,000 face**)	1,000,000
Total cash outflow from issuer of bonds	$2,200,000
Less: Original bond proceeds from investors (**$1,000,000 × 104%**)	(1,040,000)
Net cost to the issuer and return on investment to the investors	$1,160,000

The total cost of borrowing for 10 years is less than the cash interest paid, indicating that the bonds yield less than the cash interest paid, and therefore, the market interest rate required is less than the nominal interest rate.

CONSTRUCTING THE BALANCE SHEET REFLECTING DEBT

Building upon the example of Jessica's Beauty Supply, Inc., introduced earlier, assume that on January 1, 2003, the corporation borrowed $50,000 on a 9 percent, one-year promissory note and has issued 200, $1,000 ,10-year, 8 percent bonds at par ($200,000). The company's cash would increase by the amount of the borrowing ($250,000), and the two debts would be listed in the liability section of the balance sheet. Exhibit 3–11

```
                    Jessica's Beauty Supply, Inc.
                          Balance Sheet
                         January 1, 2003

Assets:                        Liabilities:
  Cash        $311,000           Notes payable                          $ 50,000
                                 Bonds payable                           200,000
                                 Total liabilities                       250,000
                                 Stockholders' equity:
                                   Preferred stock                        20,000
                                   Additional paid-in capital—preferred    1,000
                                   Common stock                            4,000
                                   Additional paid-in capital—common      36,000
                                 Total stockholders' equity               61,000
  Total assets  $311,000         Total liabilities and stockholders' equity $311,000
```

EXHIBIT 3–11   Corporate Balance Sheet with Notes and Bonds Payable

shows the balance sheet for Jessica's Beauty Supply, Inc., immediately after the company borrowed the $250,000.

The balance sheet information indicates that the company has borrowed $50,000 on a promissory note and $200,000 by issuing bonds. The borrowing provided the company with $250,000 additional cash, so total assets rose to $311,000. Jessica's Beauty Supply, Inc., now owes the bank $50,000 and bondholders $200,000. Notice that even with this change, the business equation still holds true:

```
                        Assets    =   Liabilities   +  Owners' Equity

Sale of stock:
  Common              $ 40,000    =      00         +    $40,000
  Preferred           $ 21,000    =      00         +    $21,000
Borrowing:
  Promissory note     $ 50,000    =   $ 50,000      +       00
  Bond issue          $200,000    =   $200,000      +       00
  Totals              $311,000    =   $250,000      +    $61,000
```

We should point out that in real life it would be highly unlikely for a fledgling company such as the one in our example to actually issue $200,000 in bonds to the general public. It would be difficult, if not impossible, for the company to meet the SEC requirements for such a bond issue, and further, it is very unlikely that anyone in the investing public would buy the bonds of a new, unknown company.

◆ USING CASH TO ACQUIRE ASSETS

Once a company secures the financing it needs, it can use the cash to purchase the various assets it will need for its business operation. Let's assume, for example, that Jessica's Beauty Supply, Inc., uses the cash it has obtained to purchase land for $50,000, a building for $120,000, computer equipment for $35,000, and a small truck for $25,000. Even after these assets have been purchased, the following presentation shows that the accounting equation still holds true.

```
                      Assets   = Liabilities +  Owners' Equity
Sale of stock:
  Common            $ 40,000   =     00    +    $40,000
  Preferred           21,000   =     00    +     21,000
Borrowing:
  Promissory note     50,000   =   50,000  +       00
  Bond issue         200,000   =  200,000  +       00
```

Purchase of assets

Cash	(230,000)
Land	50,000
Building	120,000
Computer equipment	35,000
Truck	25,000

Total $311,000 = $250,000 + $61,000

Exhibit 3–12 shows the balance sheet for Jessica's Beauty Supply, Inc., immediately following the acquisition of these assets.

EXHIBIT 3-12   Corporate Balance Sheet with Various Assets

Jessica's Beauty Supply, Inc.
Balance Sheet
January 1, 2003

Assets:		Liabilities:	
Cash	$ 81,000	Notes payable	$ 50,000
Land	50,000	Bonds payable	200,000
Building	120,000	Total liabilities	250,000
Computer equipment	35,000	Stockholders' equity:	
Truck	25,000	Preferred stock	$ 20,000
		Additional paid-in capital—preferred	1,000
		Common stock	4,000
		Additional paid-in capital—common	36,000
		Total stockholders' equity	61,000
Total assets	$311,000	Total liabilities and stockholders' equity	$311,000

EQUITY AND DEBT INVESTMENTS COMPARED

We presented equity and debt financing in this chapter from the standpoint of the company receiving the proceeds from the sale of stocks and bonds. We will now look at the same subject from the standpoint of the investor. Let's say you were trying to decide where to invest your money. Does it make more sense for you to buy stock (an equity investment) or to buy bonds (a debt investment)? Before you can decide, you need to ask how the two investment alternatives answer the three questions that should be posed by all economic decision makers:

1. Will I be paid?
2. When will I be paid?
3. How much will I be paid?

Remember that these three questions inherently consider a return *on* the investment and a return *of* the investment.

EQUITY INVESTMENTS

Question 1: *Will I Be Paid?* With equity investments, there is no way we can answer this question with absolute certainty; it is dependent on the present condition and future financial performance of the company in question. If it is a solid company with a good market for its products, if the economy is (and stays) strong, and if the industry is (and stays) healthy, you will probably receive both a return on and a return of your investment.

Question 2: When Will I Be Paid? We cannot answer this question with absolute certainty either. Payments on a stock investment are of two types. First, you may receive a periodic dividend on each share of stock you own. Remember, however, that corporations are not *required* to pay dividends. The company in which you invest may or may not pay dividends to its stockholders. Second, you can sell your stock, if other investors are willing to buy it. In any event, the company itself is under no obligation to return your investment. When you buy stock, you have contributed an amount to the company and must find a third party to buy your shares if you desire to sell them.

Question 3: How Much Will I Be Paid? Like the first two questions, we cannot answer this with absolute certainty. To answer it at all, we need to fully understand the two components of return on investment for an equity investment.

a. *Dividends.* The dividend component is easy to understand. A company may pay no dividend, or if, for example, the company pays a $2.00 dividend, all we would have to do is to multiply the number of shares you own, say 1,000, by the $2.00 per share and we are able to readily determine that the dividend you would receive is $2,000. The dividend, if one is paid at all, would constitute a part of the return on your investment.

b. *Stock Appreciation.* In most instances, stock appreciation represents the greater part of return on an equity investment. If the company performs well in the future, the price of each share of its common stock should increase. The stock appreciates in value because as the company earns profits, more and more investors will desire to own shares of its stock. They will, in effect, bid up the price. For example, suppose you purchased 1,000 shares of a particular stock for $22 per share. Assume further the company earns record profits and the stock's price rises to $34 per share. If you sell your 1,000 shares, you will have earned a return on investment of $12 per share, or a total of $12,000, calculated as follows:

	Per Share	Total
What you sold the stock for	$34	$34,000
What you paid for the stock	22	22,000
Your return on investment	$12	$12,000

Note that when you sell the stock, you received not only a return *on* your investment, but also a return *of* your investment as well.

In the final analysis, the equity investment alternative yields rather vague answers to the three questions. Now let us see how the debt investment alternative answers the same three questions.

DEBT INVESTMENTS

Question 1: Will I Be Paid? The answer to this first question is essentially the same for the debt investment alternative as it was for the equity investment alternative. That is, it is dependent on how the company in which you invest performs in the future. If it is a solid company with a good market for its products and/or services, if the economy is (and stays) strong, and if the industry is (and stays) healthy, you will probably receive both a return on and a return of your investment.

As a creditor of the company rather than a stockholder, you will have absolutely no voice in how the company conducts its business, as long as it makes the periodic interest payments on the bonds and accumulates a sufficient amount of cash to retire the bonds when they mature. If the company *does not* service the debt as it has agreed, it is technically in *default*, and if you and the other bondholders choose (the bondholders vote on this), you can actually take over the company. We might also note that, by law, companies must make their periodic interest payments before they can pay any dividends to shareholders.

Question 2: When Will I Be Paid? Assuming the company performs well enough to make the interest payments on the bonds and to retire them upon maturity, the answer to this question would be absolutely certain. The company would make interest payments and would pay off the bond in accordance with the terms of the bond.

Question 3: *How Much Will I Be Paid?* The answer to this question, too, is absolutely certain assuming the company performs well enough to meet the financial obligations created by issuing the bonds. Over the life of the bonds, you would earn a return on your investment in the form of interest adjusted for any bond premium or discount and, upon maturity of the bond, you would receive the return of your investment.

In the final analysis, if we can satisfy ourselves as to the answer to Question 1, the answers to the last two questions are very certain for the debt investment alternative.

WHICH IS BETTER, EQUITY INVESTMENTS OR DEBT INVESTMENTS?

Take a few minutes to ponder the way the two investment alternatives answered the three questions. Which investment would you rather make? On the surface, it appears to be no contest. Although the answer to Question 1 was essentially the same for both alternatives, the debt investment alternative is much more certain in its answers to Questions 2 and 3 than is the equity investment alternative. So why would anyone even consider the equity investment as an alternative? The one-word answer to that question is POTENTIAL!

Although risk is associated with any investment, equity investments are inherently riskier than debt investments. Oddly enough, the thing that provides bondholders with the answers to our Questions 2 and 3 in large part limits the potential return the bondholders will receive. This is because the return the bondholders will receive is stipulated in the terms of the bond. No such limitation accompanies common stock investments. The return that equity investors can potentially receive is dependent on the success of the company, not the stipulations in an agreement with the company. So with the additional risk associated with equity investments, comes the potential for greater reward. In other words, the potential associated with the equity investment alternative is theoretically unlimited.

Thus far, we have discussed equity and debt financing and how they affect the balance sheet. The balance sheet provides information about the assets of a company and the claims to those assets. Another financial statement, the statement of cash flows, serves a different purpose but is just as important. The statement of cash flows focuses on just one asset, cash, and it presents information about the changes in cash over time. Regardless of how much potential a business may have, without cash, it will never be able to realize that potential.

◆ STATEMENT OF CASH FLOWS

statement of cash flows
A financial statement that provides information about the causes of a change in the company's cash balance from the beginning to the end of a specific period.

The **statement of cash flows** shows a company's sources and uses of cash during a particular period of time. Unlike the balance sheet, which shows a particular point in time, the statement organizes cash flows based on three principal business activities: operating, investing, and financing. The statement of cash flows for *Best Buy* appears in Exhibit 3–13 on page F–90.

At this point, don't try to understand each and every item on the statement, just take note of the statement of cash flow's general format and use it as a reference as we describe it below.

OPERATING ACTIVITIES

operating activities
Activities that result in cash inflows and outflows generated from the normal course of business.

The **operating activities** section of the statement of cash flows includes cash inflows and outflows for revenues and expenses associated with a company's ongoing business operations. As we said at the beginning of this chapter, over the long term, the primary source of financing for a business should come from internal sources. Operating activities *are* those internal sources. We will discuss cash flows from operating activities in Chapter 4.

	Best Buy Co., Inc. Consolidated Statements of Cash Flows $ in thousands		
For the Fiscal Years Ended	March 3 2001	Feb. 26 2000	Feb. 27 1999
Operating Activities			
Net earnings	$ 395,839	$ 347,070	$ 216,282
Adjustments to reconcile net earnings to net cash provided by operating activities:			
Depreciation	167,369	103,709	73,627
Deferred income taxes	42,793	29,233	(749)
Other	20,609	5,832	4,740
Changes in operating assets and liabilities, net of acquired assets and liabilities:			
Receivables	(7,434)	(56,900)	(36,699)
Merchandise inventories	(143,969)	(137,315)	14,422
Other assets	(16,018)	(6,904)	(19,090)
Accounts payable	16,186	302,194	249,094
Other liabilities	198,721	91,715	89,639
Accrued income taxes	134,108	97,814	62,672
Total cash provided by operating activities	808,204	776,448	653,938
Investing Activities			
Additions to property and equipment	(657,706)	(361,024)	(165,698)
Acquisitions of businesses, net of cash acquired	(326,077)	—	—
Increase in recoverable costs from developed properties	(31,076)	(21,009)	(65,741)
Increase in other assets	(14,943)	(34,301)	(9,635)
Total cash used in investing activities	(1,029,802)	(416,334)	(241,074)
Financing Activities			
Long-term debt payments	(17,625)	(29,946)	(165,396)
Issuance of common stock	235,379	32,229	20,644
Repurchase of common stock	—	(397,451)	(2,462)
Total cash provided by (used in) financing activities	217,754	(395,168)	(147,214)
(Decrease) Increase in Cash and Cash Equivalents	(3,844)	(35,054)	265,650
Cash and Cash Equivalents at Beginning of Period	750,723	785,777	520,127
Cash and Cash Equivalents at End of Period	$ 746,879	$ 750,723	$ 785,777

EXHIBIT 3–13 *Best Buy*'s Statement of Cash Flows

INVESTING ACTIVITIES

investing activities
Business activities related to long-term assets. Examples are the purchase and sale of property, plant, and equipment.

The **investing activities** section of the statement of cash flows shows cash inflows and outflows for investments purchased or sold. In this context, *investments* include not only investments in securities such as stocks and bonds, but also investments in land, buildings, equipment, and other assets purchased for use by the business. In fact, if you look at recent statements of cash flows of such companies as *Wal-Mart, Royal Caribbean Cruises,* and *Best Buy,* the overwhelming majority of their cash outflow from investing activities was to purchase property, plant, and equipment.

Recall that our example company in this chapter, Jessica's Beauty Supply, Inc., used cash to purchase land, buildings, computer equipment, and a truck. All of these transactions are cash flows for investing activities.

FINANCING ACTIVITIES

financing activities
Business activities, such as the issuance of debt or equity and the payment of dividends, that focus on the external financing of the company.

The **financing activities** section of the statement of cash flows shows a firm's cash inflows and outflows from *external* financing. It includes cash inflows from borrowing and amounts received from the sale of company stock. Cash outflows from financing activities include debt repayments, distributions to owners to reduce (or eliminate) their investment, and profit distributions to owners. In the financing activities section of its most recent statement of cash flows, for example, **Best Buy** shows cash inflow from the sale of common stock and cash outflow for debt repayments. For example, Jessica's Beauty Supply, Inc., financed its operation by selling stock for $61,000, borrowing $50,000 on a promissory note, and issuing bonds totaling $200,000.

To prepare the statement of cash flows, the operating activities, investing activities, and financing activities cash flows are listed and totaled and then added to the beginning cash balance to arrive at the ending cash balance. A statement of cash flows for Jessica's Beauty Supply, Inc., showing both the investing activities and financing activities section is illustrated in Exhibit 3–14.

EXHIBIT 3–14   Statement of Cash Flows for Jessica's Beauty Supply, Inc.

Jessica's Beauty Supply, Inc.
Statement of Cash Flows
For the Month Ended January 31, 2003

Cash flows from operating activities:		
None	$ 0	
Net cash flows from operating activities		$ 0
Cash flows from investing activities:		
Purchase of land	$ (50,000)	
Purchase of building	(120,000)	
Purchase of computer equipment	(35,000)	
Purchase of truck	(25,000)	
Net cash flows from investing activities		$(230,000)
Cash flows from financing activities:		
Sale of common stock	40,000	
Sale of preferred stock	21,000	
Borrowing on note payable	50,000	
Sale of bonds	200,000	
Net cash flows from financing activities		311,000
Net change in cash		81,000
Cash at the beginning of the period		0
Cash at the end of the period		$ 81,000

As we said in Chapter 1, many people in business feel that the statement of cash flows is the most important financial statement. In addition to the extensive coverage of the statement in Chapter 10, we will further explore the facets of the statement of cash flows as we examine the income statement in Chapter 4.

◆ USING FINANCIAL INFORMATION

Charlene's Aunt Tillie recently passed away and left Charlene $1 million. After all the inheritance taxes were paid, Charlene received $750,000. Upon mature reflection, she decides to blow $250,000 on cars, world cruises, and other such extravagant items. She plans to invest the remaining $500,000. How should Charlene invest the $500,000?

Charlene should evaluate investment opportunities carefully, but how can she determine whether she will be paid at all, not to mention how much she will be paid and when she will be paid? The key to evaluating any investment alternative is reducing the uncertainty surrounding the prospects for receiving cash in the future. So, how can she accomplish this? You already know the answer. She can reduce uncertainty by using information—in this case financial information—to gain insight into the present condition and past performance of potential investments to help her form an opinion about the potential for future success of each investment.

To fully benefit from the financial information companies provide, decision makers should be able to analyze the information and draw conclusions that are relevant to the decisions that they are making. For example, the balance sheet and statement of cash flows for Jessica's Beauty Supply, Inc., seem to paint a bright picture with lots of cash coming in and a host of new assets for the company to use. With all the money in the bank, assets for its operation, the company is off to a good start, right? Well probably, but it is difficult to tell just by looking at individual items and amounts on the financial statements. Instead we need to analyze the financial statements.

financial statement analysis The process of looking beyond the face of the financial statements to gather more information.

Financial statement analysis entails looking closely at financial statements to scrutinize how the various financial statement items and amounts relate to one another and how they relate to those of other companies and industry averages. For example, we would probably all agree that it is a good thing to have assets totaling $311,000, but we would probably also all agree that it is not such a good thing if nearly all of the assets are financed by debt. In Jessica's case, the debt is $250,000. Is this too much? Well, for a major corporation, $250,000 in debt is nothing, but for an start-up company like Jessica's, it could be too much.

In the following section, we will look at the financial ratios that relate to the portion of the balance sheet we have covered thus far.

RATIO ANALYSIS

ratio analysis A technique for analyzing the relationship between two items from a company's financial statements for a given period.

The key concept of **ratio analysis** is that the *relationship* of one number to another may be just as important as the absolute dollar amounts of those numbers. For example, liabilities for Jessica's Beauty Supply, Inc., are only $250,000, a relatively small amount for a typical business. But when the amount is viewed in proportion to equity, $61,000, the amount for liabilities may seem disproportionately large by comparison.

Ratio analysis uses a series of calculations (ratios) to depict the relationships among financial statement amounts. Over the years, financial analysts have developed (invented) more and more ratios to accommodate their need for information. This has resulted in a myriad of ratios, many of which address the same or very similar areas of analysis. In this book, we will limit our calculations to 17 popular ratios. Lending institutions use financial ratios not only to evaluate potential loan candidates, but also as performance benchmarks. For example, the terms of ***The Wet Seal, Inc.***'s borrowing require the company to maintain certain financial ratios and to achieve certain levels of annual income.

Keep in mind that the ratios in this text are not intended to be an all-inclusive list of ratios or even a list of what everyone believes are the best ratios. Our selection of ratios is intended to give adequate basic coverage of four main concerns—profitability, efficiency, liquidity, and solvency. Profitability has to do with a company's ability to generate income. Efficiency has to do with the amount of business a company conducts relative to its investment in assets. Liquidity has to do with a company's cash position and its ability to pay its near-term bills. We will discuss these topics in later chapters. Solvency has to do with how a company is financed and the company's prospects for making payments to creditors and owners over the long term. The two solvency ratios we will cover in this chapter are debt ratio and the total liabilities to net worth ratio.

Debt Ratio

debt ratio A solvency ratio that indicates what proportion of a company's assets is financed by debt.

The **debt ratio** measures the proportion of a company's assets financed by debt. Remember, either its creditors or its owners have claim to a company's assets. The debt ratio indicates the proportion of assets claimed by creditors. Like most ratios, the specifics for calculating the debt ratio vary somewhat, but generally the calculation looks something like this:

$$\text{Debt ratio} = \frac{\text{Total liabilities}}{\text{Total assets}}$$

Based on the balance sheet for Jessica's Beauty Supply, Inc., in Exhibit 3–12, the debt ratio is calculated as follows:

$$\frac{\$250,000}{\$311,000} = 0.80386 \text{ or } 80.4\%$$

The debt ratio for Jessica's Beauty Supply, Inc., indicates that 80.4 percent of the company's assets are financed by debt. By extension then, 19.6 percent of the company's assets are financed by equity. There is no consensus regarding how much of a company's assets should be financed by debt, and acceptable levels of debt may vary significantly among different industries. Generally, however, creditors feel more secure when debt financing is relatively light compared to financing from equity. The creditors feel more secure when the owners' risk of loss in the company is substantial enough that the owners will do what it takes to keep the company successful. From the owners' point of view, although a high debt ratio may help them avoid the risk of a substantial loss, they may want to keep debt to a minimum for another reason. For every dollar borrowed, the company must pay some amount of interest. The more interest the company must pay, the more the company is required to earn. Equity investors may want to keep debt to a minimum to avoid the risk of the company being unable to earn enough profits to make its interest payments.

Debt-to-Equity Ratio

debt-to-equity ratio A financial ratio that expresses the proportional relationship between liabilities and equity.

The **debt-to-equity ratio** expresses the proportional relationship between liabilities and equity. Many financial publications call this ratio the *total liabilities to net worth* ratio. You must remember this, because many of these publications do not include a ratio called the debt-to-equity ratio. They have the ratio but call it something else. The formula for this ratio is:

$$\text{Debt-to-equity ratio} = \frac{\text{Total liabilities}}{\text{Total equity}}$$

Both the items necessary to calculate the debt-to-equity ratio come from the balance sheet. As you can see, the numerator, total liabilities, is the same as it is for the debt ratio, and for the denominator, we use total equity. Based on the balance sheet for Jessica's Beauty Supply, Inc., in Exhibit 3–12, the debt-to-equity ratio is calculated as follows:

$$\frac{\$250,000}{\$61,000} = 4.1 \text{ to } 1$$

This ratio reveals essentially the same information as the debt ratio but presents it slightly differently. The lower the debt-to-equity ratio, the lower total debt is relative to total equity.

The debt-to-equity ratio for Jessica's Beauty Supply, Inc., indicates the total liabilities are a whopping 4.1 times larger than equity. That is, there is $4.10 of debt for every $1 of equity. As was the case with the debt ratio, there is no consensus regarding how much a company's liabilities should be relative to equity. Even so, the debt-to-equity ratio for Jessica's Beauty Supply, Inc., seems excessive. What do you think?

In this chapter, we began our look at the financial tools available to economic decision makers. Our focus was on the balance sheet, and we also began our discussion of the statement of cash flows. Chapter 4 will introduce you to two additional financial tools—the income statement and the statement of owners' equity.

Summary ❦

In many ways, *financial statements* are the primary tools available to company outsiders for solving economic problems. Like all tools, financial statements were developed in response to a specific need—the need for useful information for economic decision makers.

All companies must obtain capital (money) to support their operations. In the long run, companies must finance their activities with the profits they generate. This is called internal financing. However, at times, all companies must also obtain capital from sources other than the profits. This is called external financing. The two external sources of capital are equity financing and debt financing. Equity financing offers an ownership interest in the company in exchange for needed cash. Companies can also obtain additional financing through borrowing, called debt financing.

The balance sheet, which focuses on the present condition of a business, shows a financial snapshot of the company and the relationship of three accounting elements: assets, liabilities, and owners' equity. ASSETS = LIABILITIES + OWNERS' EQUITY. Assets are the things of value a company owns or controls. Liabilities are the debts a company owes. Equity is the ownership interest in a company. It is the difference between the company's assets and its liabilities on those assets. Corporate equity is comprised of paid-in capital and earned equity.

Stockholders provide cash or other assets to the corporation in exchange for ownership shares—shares of stock—in the company. Amounts received by the corporation in exchange for shares of stock are called contributed capital or paid-in capital. There are two basic classes of stock. Common stock is the voting stock of the corporation. Preferred stock, also called preference stock, does not vote but has certain preference features that common stock does not.

Another major source of external financing is debt financing, or borrowing. Whenever a company borrows funds from a bank, the bank requires it to sign a promissory note. Borrowing adds to the company's assets but also creates a liability. Interest is the "rent" lenders charge borrowers for the use of money.

Bonds are interest-bearing securities companies sell to borrow large amounts of money from many lenders. A bond's nominal interest rate is the interest rate printed on the bond, and it is used to calculate the bond's interest payments. A bond's effective interest rate is the actual interest rate the bondholder will earn over the life of the bond based on the selling price of the bond. Bond selling prices are stated in relation to their par value. A bond selling at a price above its par value is selling at a premium, and a bond selling for less than its par value is selling at a discount. The effective interest rate that investors demand and other market conditions determine bond selling prices.

When comparing investment opportunities, investors need the answers to three important questions: (1) Will I be paid? (2) When will I be paid? and (3) How much will I be paid? In large part, the trade-off between risks and potential rewards will determine the type of investments a person chooses. The key to evaluating investment alternatives is reducing the uncertainty surrounding the question: Will I be paid?

The statement of cash flows shows cash flows from operating, investing, and financing activities. The operating activities section of the statement shows cash flows for revenues and expenses and a company's ongoing business operations. The investing activities section of the statement shows cash flows for the purchase and sale of securities and certain other assets used in the company's operations. The financing activities section of the statement shows the cash flows associated with a firm's external financing activities.

Financial statement analysis entails looking closely at a financial statement to scrutinize how the various financial statement items and amounts relate to one another and how they relate to those of other companies and industry averages. Ratio analysis uses a series of calculations (ratios) to depict the relationship between two amounts from a company's financial statements of a given period. Ratio analysis focuses on four main areas—profitability, efficiency, liquidity, and solvency. Profitability has to do with a company's ability to generate income. Liquidity has to do with a company's cash position and its ability to pay its near-term bills. Solvency has to do with a company's financial well-being and its prospects for making payments to its owners and creditors over the long term. The debt ratio measures the proportion of company assets financed by debt. The debt-to-equity ratio indicates the relative size of liabilities, stated in terms of a proportion to equity.

Key Terms

- additional paid-in capital, F–80
- assets, F–71
- authorized shares, F–78
- balance sheet, F–71
- bond, F–84
- collateral, F–82
- commercial borrowing, F–82
- common stock, F–78
- consumer borrowing, F–82
- contract rate. *See* nominal interest rate
- contributed capital, F–78
- coupon rate. *See* nominal interest rate
- debenture bond, F–84
- debt financing, F–70
- debt ratio, F–92
- debt-to-equity ratio, F–93
- discount, F–85
- dividends, F–78

- earned equity, F–73
- effective interest rate, F–84
- equity, F–72
- equity financing, F–70
- external financing, F–70
- financial statement analysis, F–92
- financing activities, F–90
- indenture, F–84
- internal financing, F–70
- investing activities, F–90
- investments by owners, F–73
- issued shares, F–78
- liabilities, F–71
- market interest rate. *See* effective interest rate
- market price (of bonds), F–84
- mortgage, F–82
- net assets. *See* equity
- net worth. *See* equity

- nominal interest rate, F–84
- operating activities, F–89
- outstanding shares, F–78
- paid-in capital, F–78
- paid-in capital in excess of par, F–80
- par value (bonds), F–84
- par value (stock), F–79
- preferred stock, F–79
- premium, F–84
- principal, F–83
- promissory note, F–82
- ratio analysis, F–92
- retained earnings, F–78
- selling price (of bonds). *See* market price (of bonds)
- stated rate. *See* nominal interest rate
- statement of cash flows, F–89
- treasury stock, F–78
- yield rate. *See* effective interest rate

Review the Facts

A. Explain the difference between internal and external financing.

B. What are the two major sources of external financing?

C. List and define the three main balance sheet accounting elements.

D. Describe the two components of equity.

E. State the accounting equation.

F. Name and describe the two formats of the balance sheet.

G. How do the balance sheets of proprietorships differ from those of partnerships?

H. Explain the differences among authorized, issued, and outstanding shares of stock.

I. Define the term *treasury stock*.

J. What are the two major classes of corporate stock and how do they differ?

K. What is meant by the par value of stock and what significance does it have?

L. What is interest on debt?

M. What is collateral? How can it help a borrower?

N. Explain the formula used to determine the amount of interest owed for a particular time period.

O. Why are bonds sometimes necessary to meet the borrowing needs of businesses?

P. Explain the terms *par value* and *stated rate* as they pertain to bonds.

Q. How do the nominal rate and the market rate of bonds differ?

R. Explain what causes a bond to sell for a premium or a discount.

S. Describe the effects of borrowing on the balance sheet of a business.

T. How does the statement of cash flows differ from the balance sheet?

U. Describe the purpose of operating, investing, and financing activities sections of the statement of cash flows.

V. What is financial statement analysis?

W. What is the key concept of ratio analysis?

X. What does the debt ratio measure?

Y. What does the debt-to-equity ratio indicate?

Apply What You Have Learned ●

LO 1: ACCOUNTING ELEMENTS

3–12. Below is a list of three accounting elements, followed by partial definitions of those items in scrambled order:

a. Assets   b. Liabilities   c. Equity

1. _____ Debts of the company
2. _____ Probable future economic benefits
3. _____ "Things" of value a company has
4. _____ The residual interest in the assets of an entity that remains after deducting its liabilities
5. _____ Probable future sacrifices of economic benefits
6. _____ What the company owes
7. _____ What the company has less what it owes
8. _____ The owner's interest in the company

Required: For each partial definition, identify the element (a, b, or c) to which it refers. Each letter will be used more than once.

LO 1: ACCOUNTING ELEMENTS

3–13. Below is a list of three accounting elements, followed by list of items in scrambled order:

a. Assets   b. Liabilities   c. Equity

1. _____ Cash
2. _____ Additional paid-in capital
3. _____ Bonds payable
4. _____ Land
5. _____ Common stock
6. _____ Retained earnings
7. _____ Notes payable
8. _____ Withdrawals
9. _____ Partners' capital
10. _____ Preferred stock

Required: For each item in the list, identify the element (a, b, or c) to which it refers. Each letter will be used more than once.

LO 1: ACCOUNTING EQUATION

3–14. a. Write the basic accounting equation.
   b. Define each element of the equation in your own words.
   c. Provide examples of each element of the basic accounting equation.

LO 3: TERMINOLOGY OF THE CORPORATE BUSINESS FORM

3–15. Below is a list of items relating to the corporate form of business, followed by definitions of those items in scrambled order:

a. Incorporators   f. Board of directors
b. Charter   g. Corporate officers
c. Bylaws   h. Par value
d. Stockholders   i. Additional paid-in capital
e. Stock certificate   j. Market value

1. _____ An arbitrary value placed on either common stock or preferred stock at the time a corporation is formed
2. _____ The group of men and women who have the ultimate responsibility for managing a corporation
3. _____ The owners of a corporation
4. _____ Any amount received by a corporation when it issues stock that is greater than the par value of the stock issued

5. _____ The formal document that legally allows a corporation to begin operations
6. _____ The group of men and women who manage the day-to-day operations of a corporation
7. _____ The person or persons who submit a formal application with the appropriate government agencies to form a corporation
8. _____ A legal document providing evidence of ownership in a corporation
9. _____ Rules established to conduct the business of a corporation
10. _____ The amount at which common stock sells

Required: Match the letter next to each item on the list with the appropriate definition. Use each letter only once.

LO 3: TERMINOLOGY OF THE CORPORATE FORM OF ORGANIZATION

3–16. a. Identify the various officers of a corporation and describe their individual duties.
  b. Explain the difference between authorized shares, issued shares, outstanding shares, and treasury stock.

LO 3: DIFFERENCES BETWEEN COMMON AND PREFERRED STOCK

3–17. A corporation is going out of business and has liquidated all of its assets and is about to distribute the limited proceeds to its preferred and common stockholders. Some of the preferred shareholders are worried that once a distribution is made to common shareholders, there won't be enough left for them. Are the preferred shareholders' concerns valid? Explain your answer.

LO 3: DIFFERENCES BETWEEN COMMON AND PREFERRED STOCK

3–18. Assume you have $20,000 to invest and you are trying to decide between investing in either the preferred stock or the common stock of Alpha Company.

Required:

  a. List and briefly explain at least two reasons why you would invest in the preferred stock rather than the common stock of Alpha Company.
  b. List and briefly explain at least two reasons why you would invest in the common stock rather than the preferred stock of Alpha Company.

LO 3: DIFFERENCES BETWEEN COMMON AND PREFERRED STOCK

3–19. For each characteristic listed below, determine if the characteristic applies to common stock (C), preferred stock (P), both (B), or neither (N).

  _____ Often has a par value
  _____ Must have a par value
  _____ Usually has voting rights
  _____ Usually does not have voting rights
  _____ Has preference in dividends
  _____ Has preference in liquidation
  _____ Is preferred by all investors

LO 3: DIFFERENCES BETWEEN COMMON AND PREFERRED STOCK

3–20. Discuss the characteristics of investors who invest in:

  a. Common stock
  b. Preferred stock

  Include in your discussion willingness to take risk, desire for current income, and desire for capital appreciation in addition to other factors.

LO 4: EFFECT OF INTEREST ON BANKS

3–21. Explain in your own words how banks make a profit when you borrow money to buy a new car.

LO 4: TERMINOLOGY

3–22. Below are some items related to notes payable and bonds payable, followed by definitions of those items in scrambled order.

a. Interest   f. Premium
b. Nominal interest rate   g. Principal
c. Effective interest rate   h. Defaulting
d. Maturity value   i. Notes payable
e. Discount   j. Bonds payable

1. _____ The amount above par value for which a bond is sold
2. _____ The amount of funds actually borrowed
3. _____ The rate of interest actually earned by a bondholder
4. _____ Failing to repay a loan as agreed
5. _____ Liabilities that allow corporations to borrow large amounts of money for long periods of time
6. _____ The cost of using someone else's money
7. _____ The amount below par value for which a bond is sold
8. _____ An agreement between a lender (usually a bank) and borrower that creates a liability for the borrower
9. _____ The interest rate set by the issuers of bonds, stated as a percentage of the par value of the bonds
10. _____ The amount that is payable at the end of a borrowing arrangement

Required: Match the letter next to each item on the list with the appropriate definition. Use each letter only once.

LO 4: TERMINOLOGY

3–23. Below are two definitions of items related to interest on bonds payable, followed by a list of terms used to describe bond interest.

a. The rate of interest actually earned by the bondholder
b. The interest rate set by the issuer of the bond, printed on the bond, and stated as a percentage of the par value of the bond

1. _____ Nominal interest rate
2. _____ Effective interest rate
3. _____ Stated interest rate
4. _____ Coupon rate
5. _____ The interest rate printed on the actual bond
6. _____ Market interest rate
7. _____ Contract rate
8. _____ Yield rate

Required: For each of the eight items above, indicate to which definition ("a" or "b") it refers. Each will be used more than once.

LO 2: CORPORATE BALANCE SHEET PREPARATION—STOCK ISSUANCES ONLY

3–24. Gaylord Corporation began operations on July 10, 2002, by issuing 10,000 shares of $5 par value common stock and 2,000 shares of $100 par value preferred stock. The common stock sold for $10 per share and the preferred stock sold for $130 per share.

Required: Prepare a balance sheet for Gaylord Corporation at July 10, 2002, immediately after the common stock and preferred stock were issued.

LO 2: CORPORATE BALANCE SHEET PREPARATION—STOCK ISSUANCES ONLY

3–25. Sheets Corporation began operations on May 5, 2003, by issuing 150,000 shares of $2 par value common stock and 25,000 shares of $100 par value preferred stock. The common stock sold for $10 per share and the preferred stock sold for $150 per share.

Required: Prepare a balance sheet for Sheets Corporation at May 5, 2003, immediately after the common stock and preferred stock were issued.

LO 2: CORPORATE BALANCE SHEET PREPARATION—STOCK ISSUANCES ONLY

3–26. Mayes Corporation began operations on April 15, 2003, by issuing 200,000 shares of no-par value common stock and 20,000 shares of $50 par value preferred stock. The common stock sold for $25 per share and the preferred stock sold for $125 per share.

Required: Prepare a balance sheet for Mayes Corporation at April 15, 2003, immediately after the common stock and preferred stock were issued.

LO 2: BALANCE SHEET PREPARATION WITH COMMON STOCK AND BORROWING ONLY

3–27. John Kenyon formed Offshore Racing Engines, Inc., on January 2, 2003. The company was established when it sold 1,200 shares of Offshore Racing Engines, Inc., common stock to John for $24,000. The common stock has a par value of $1 per share.

   On January 3, 2003, the company borrowed $12,000 from APBA National Bank by signing a one-year, 9 percent note. The principal and interest on the note must be paid to the bank on January 2, 2004.

Required:

   a. Prepare a balance sheet as of January 2, 2003, immediately following the $24,000 stock sale to John Kenyon, that is, before the company borrowed money.
   b. Prepare a balance sheet as of January 3, 2003, that reflects both the $24,000 stock sale to John Kenyon and the $12,000 borrowed from the bank.
   c. Calculate the amount of interest Offshore Racing Engines, Inc,. must pay on January 3, 2004.
   d. Assume that the note was for six months rather than one year, so it must be repaid on July 3, 2003. Calculate the amount of interest Offshore Racing Engines, Inc., must pay on July 3, 2003.

LO 2 & 4: BALANCE SHEET PREPARATION WITH COMMON STOCK AND BOND FINANCING ONLY

3–28. Bobbye Miller formed Offshore Public Relations, Inc., on January 2, 2003. The company was established when it sold 3,000 shares of Offshore Public Relations, Inc., common stock to Bobbye for $30,000 cash. The common stock has a par value of $5 per share.

   On January 3, 2003, Offshore Public Relations, Inc,. sold 100 of its $1,000, five-year, 9 percent bonds at par. Interest is to be paid semiannually on July 2 and January 2. The bonds must be repaid when they mature on January 2, 2008.

Required:

   a. Prepare a balance sheet for Offshore Public Relations, Inc., as of January 2, 2003, to reflect the $30,000 stock sale to Bobbye Miller.
   b. Prepare a balance sheet for Offshore Public Relations, Inc., as of January 3, 2003, to reflect both the $30,000 stock sale to Bobbye Miller and the sale of the bonds, assuming the bonds sold at their par value.
   c. Calculate the amount of interest Offshore Public Relations, Inc., must pay each July 2 and January 2.
   d. How much would Offshore Public Relations, Inc., have received from the sale of the bonds on January 3, 2003, if the bonds had sold at 99 (a discount)?
   e. How much would Offshore Public Relations, Inc., have received from the sale of the bonds on January 3, 2003, if they had sold at 105 (a premium)?

LO 2: CORPORATE BALANCE SHEET PREPARATION

3–29. The following information is taken from accounting records of Seth Industries, Inc., as of December 31, 2003:

Cash	$ 33,000
Land	120,000
Building	580,000
Office equipment	15,000
Notes payable	650,000
Common stock (no par)	98,000

Required:

    a. Classify each item as follows:

        A = Asset
        L = Liability
        EQ = Equity

    b. Prepare a balance sheet for the company as of December 31, 2003.

LO 2: CORPORATE BALANCE SHEET PREPARATION

3–30. The following information is taken from accounting records of Zhang Corporation as of December 31, 2003:

Cash	$ 28,000
Inventory	92,000
Store equipment	5,000
Notes payable	35,000
Common stock (no par)	90,000

Required:

    a. Classify each item as follows:

        A = Asset
        L = Liability
        EQ = Equity

    b. Prepare a balance sheet for the company as of December 31, 2003.

LO 2: CORPORATE BALANCE SHEET PREPARATION

3–31. The following information is taken from accounting records of Amanda's Cooking Supplies as of December 31, 2003:

Cash	$ 53,000
Notes payable	118,000
Land	100,000
Building	120,000
Equipment	18,000
Common stock, $1 par	10,000
Additional paid-in capital	163,000

Required: Prepare a balance sheet for the company as of December 31, 2003.

LO 2: CORPORATE BALANCE SHEET PREPARATION

3–32. The following information is taken from accounting records of Bill Hudik's Photo Shop as of December 31, 2003:

Cash	$ 18,000
Inventory	81,000
Supplies inventory	3,000
Delivery truck	18,000
Notes payable	24,000
Bonds payable	51,000
Common stock, $2 par	1,500
Additional paid-in capital	43,500

Required:

    a. Classify each item as follows:

        A = Asset
        L = Liability
        EQ = Equity

    b. Prepare a balance sheet as of December 31, 2003.

LO 2: CORPORATE BALANCE SHEET PREPARATION

3–33. The following information is taken from accounting records of Levine Company as of December 31, 2003:

Cash	$ 89,000
Merchandise inventory	320,000
Store supplies inventory	4,000
Delivery truck	21,000
Notes payable	20,000
Bonds payable	125,000
Common stock, $3 par	15,000
Additional paid-in capital	274,000

Required: Prepare a balance sheet as of December 31, 2003.

LO 2: CORPORATE BALANCE SHEET PREPARATION

3–34. The following information is taken from accounting records of Stacy's Giftware, Inc., as of December 31, 2003:

Cash	$ 13,000
Supplies inventory	3,000
Land	242,000
Building	378,000
Delivery truck	15,000
Notes payable	24,000
Bonds payable	30,000
Common stock, $5 par	55,000
Additional paid-in capital—common	439,000
Preferred stock, $100 par	100,000
Additional paid-in capital—preferred	3,000

Required: Prepare a balance sheet for the company as of December 31, 2003.

LO 2: CORPORATE BALANCE SHEET PREPARATION

3–35. The following information is taken from accounting records of Sherry's Frame Shop as of December 31, 2003:

Preferred stock, $50 par	$ 75,000
Additional paid-in capital—preferred	2,000
Common stock, $1 par	62,000
Additional paid-in capital—common	188,000
Cash	55,000
Land	380,000
Buildings	698,000
Equipment	35,000
Notes payable	41,000
Bonds payable	800,000

Required: Prepare a balance sheet as of December 31, 2003.

LO 2: CORPORATE BALANCE SHEET PREPARATION

3–36. The following information is taken from accounting records of Sexton Sales Corporation as of December 31, 2003:

Common stock (no par)	$ 76,000
Preferred stock, $75 par	90,000
Additional paid-in capital—preferred	4,000
Inventory	40,000
Cash	11,000
Supplies inventory	1,000
Land	35,000
Building	87,000
Store equipment	23,000
Notes payable	27,000

Required: Prepare a balance sheet for the company as of December 31, 2003.

LO 2: CORPORATE BALANCE SHEET PREPARATION

3–37. The following information is taken from accounting records of Maupin Promotion Company as of December 31, 2003:

Cash	$ 11,000
Office equipment	65,000
Notes payable	8,000
Common stock, $1 par	500
Additional paid-in capital—common	14,500
Preferred stock, $50 par	50,000
Additional paid-in capital—preferred	3,000

Required: Prepare a balance sheet as of December 31, 2003.

LO 2: CORRECTION AND PREPARATION OF SIMPLE CORPORATE BALANCE SHEET

3–38. Examine the following balance sheet:

Karen Bean Enterprises
Balance Sheet
December 31, 2003

Assets:		Liabilities and owner's equity:	
Land	$100,000	Cash	$ 20,000
Less: Notes payable	20,000	Common stock, $10 par value	40,000
		Additional paid-in capital	50,000
		Retained earnings	10,000
Total assets	$120,000	Total liabilities and owner's equity	$120,000

Required:

a. List the errors in the balance sheet.
b. Prepare a corrected balance sheet.

LO 2: CORRECTION AND PREPARATION OF SIMPLE CORPORATE BALANCE SHEET

3–39. Examine the following balance sheet:

L. Stallworth, Inc.
Balance Sheet
December 31, 2003

Assets:		Liabilities and owner's equity:	
Cash	$50,000	Notes payable	$10,000
Retained earnings	10,000	Stallworth, capital, $10 par value	40,000
		Equipment	10,000
Total assets	$60,000	Total liabilities and owner's equity	$60,000

Required:

a. List the errors in the balance sheet.
b. Prepare a corrected balance sheet.

LO 2: CORRECTION AND PREPARATION OF SIMPLE CORPORATE BALANCE SHEET

3–40. Examine the following balance sheet:

Sweet Corporation
Balance Sheet
For the Year Ended December 31, 2003

Assets:		Liabilities and owner's equity:	
Cash	$120,000	Notes payable	$30,000
		Common stock, $1 par value	20,000
Additional paid-in capital	40,000	Retained earnings	30,000
Total assets	$160,000	Total liabilities and owner's equity	$80,000

Required:

    a. List the errors in the balance sheet.

    b. Prepare a corrected balance sheet.

LO 2 & 3: BALANCE SHEET PREPARATION—PROPRIETORSHIP, PARTNERSHIP, AND CORPORATION

3–41. On January 2, 2003, Randy Peoples started an appliance repair business.

Required:

    a. Prepare a balance sheet as of January 2, 2003, assuming Randy's company is a proprietorship named Randy Peoples Enterprises and that he invested $5,000 cash in the operation.

    b. Now assume that the business organized on January 2, 2003, was a partnership started by Randy and his brother Sandy, which they have named R&S Enterprises. Randy invested $2,000 and Sandy invested $3,000. Prepare a balance sheet as of January 2, 2003, for the partnership to reflect the partners' investment.

    c. Now assume that the business organized on January 2, 2003, was a corporation started by Randy and his brother Sandy, which they have named R&S Enterprises, Inc. Randy invested $2,000 and received 200 shares of common stock. Sandy invested $3,000 and received 300 shares of common stock. The common stock has a par value of $2 per share. Prepare a balance sheet as of January 2, 2003, for the company to reflect the stockholders' investment.

    d. Assume the same facts as in requirement c, except that the common stock is no-par stock. Prepare a balance sheet as of January 2, 2003, for the company to reflect the stockholders' investment.

LO 2 & 3: BALANCE SHEET PREPARATION—PROPRIETORSHIP, PARTNERSHIP, AND CORPORATION

3–42. On June 2, 2003, Arthur Johnson started a manufacturing business.

Required:

    a. Prepare a balance sheet as of June 2, 2003, assuming Arthur's company is a proprietorship named Arthur Johnson Enterprises and that he invested $50,000 cash in the operation.

    b. Now assume that the business organized on June 2, 2003, was a partnership started by Arthur and his friend Charles Smith, which they have named A&C Enterprises. Arthur invested $50,000 and Charles invested $30,000. Prepare a balance sheet as of June 2, 2003, for the partnership to reflect the partners' investment.

    c. Now assume that the business organized on June 2, 2003, was a corporation started by Arthur and his friend Charles, which they have named A&C Enterprises, Inc. Arthur invested $50,000 and received 5,000 shares of common stock. Charles invested $30,000 and received 3,000 shares of common stock. The common stock has a par value of $1 per share. Prepare a balance sheet as of June 2, 2003, for the company to reflect the stockholders' investment.

    d. Assume the same facts as in requirement c, except that the common stock is no-par stock. Prepare a balance sheet as of June 2, 2003, for the company to reflect the stockholders' investment.

LO 2 & 3: BALANCE SHEET PREPARATION—PROPRIETORSHIP, PARTNERSHIP, AND CORPORATION

3–43. On July 1, 2003, Fred Berfel started a retail business.

Required:

    a. Prepare a balance sheet as of July 1, 2003, assuming Fred's company is a proprietorship named Fred Berfel Enterprises and that he invested $90,000 cash in the operation.

    b. Now assume that the business organized on July 1, 2003, was a partnership started by Fred and his father Dan, which they have named F&D Enterprises. Fred invested $40,000 and Dan invested $50,000. Prepare a balance sheet as of July 1, 2003, for the partnership to reflect the partners' investment.

c. Now assume that the business organized on July 1, 2003, was a corporation started by Fred and his father Dan, which they have named F&D Enterprises, Inc. Fred invested $40,000 and received 4,000 shares of common stock. Dan invested $50,000 and received 5,000 shares of common stock. The common stock has a par value of $2 per share. Prepare a balance sheet as of July 1, 2003, for the company to reflect the stockholders' investment.

    d. Assume the same facts as in requirement c, except that the common stock is no-par stock. Prepare a balance sheet as of July 1, 2003, for the company to reflect the stockholders' investment.

LO 2 & 3: BALANCE SHEET PREPARATION—PROPRIETORSHIP, PARTNERSHIP, AND CORPORATION

3–44. On March 1, 2003, Sandy Sanders started a business.

Required:

    a. Prepare a balance sheet as of March 1, 2003, assuming Sandy's company is a sole proprietorship named Sandy Sanders Enterprises and that he invested $40,000 cash in the operation and a piece of land valued at $5,000.

    b. Now assume that the business organized on March 1, 2003, was a partnership started by Sandy and his brother Darryl, which they have named S&D Enterprises. Sandy invested $40,000 cash and a piece of land valued at $10,000, and Darryl invested $30,000 cash. Prepare a balance sheet as of March 1, 2003, for the partnership to reflect the partners' investment.

    c. Now assume that the business organized on March 1, 2003, was a corporation started by Sandy and his brother Darryl, which they have named S&D Enterprises, Inc. Sandy invested $40,000 cash and the piece of land valued at $10,000 and received 5,000 shares of common stock. Darryl invested $30,000 cash and received 3,000 shares of common stock. The common stock has a par value of $1 per share. Prepare a balance sheet as of March 1, 2003, for the company to reflect the stockholders' investment.

    d. Assume the same facts as in requirement c, except that the common stock is no-par stock. Prepare a balance sheet as of March 1, 2003, for the company to reflect the stockholders' investment.

LO 2: COMPARE, CONTRAST BALANCE SHEETS OF THREE TYPES OF BUSINESS ORGANIZATIONS

3–45. The chapter discusses the balance sheet presentations for each of the three forms of business organization. Discuss the similarities and differences in the balance sheets of proprietorships, partnerships, and corporations.

LO 2 & 3: INTERPRETING STOCKHOLDERS' EQUITY

3–46. The balance sheet of Ramona Rahill, Inc., contains the following information in its equity section:

Stockholders' equity:

Common stock, $5 par value, 1,000,000 shares authorized, 800,000 shares issued and outstanding	$ 4,000,000
Additional paid-in capital	4,800,000
Retained earnings	2,000,000
Total stockholders' equity	$10,800,000

Required:

    a. What is the maximum number of shares of stock that Rahill could issue if the board of directors desired to do so?

    b. When the corporation sold its stock, what was the average selling price per share?

    c. If the board of directors declared a $1.25 per share dividend, how much cash would be required to pay the dividend?

    d. If Rahill has distributed $3,500,000 to shareholders since its formation, how much profit has the corporation earned since its formation?

LO 3: INTERPRETING STOCKHOLDERS' EQUITY

3–47. The balance sheet of Juliette Richard Corporation contains the following information in its equity section:

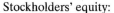

Stockholders' equity:
Common stock, $10 par value, 1,000,000 shares authorized,
800,000 shares issued and outstanding .... $ 8,000,000
Additional paid-in capital 8,000,000
Retained earnings 9,500,000
Total stockholders' equity $25,500,000

Required:

a. What is the maximum number of shares of stock that Richard Corporation could sell if the board of directors desired to do so?
b. When the corporation sold its stock, what was the average selling price per share?
c. If the board of directors declared a $2 per share dividend, how much cash would be required to issue the dividend?
d. If Richard has distributed $5,500,000 to shareholders since its formation, how much profit has the corporation earned since its formation?
e. If the board of directors wished to raise $5,000,000, how much would the average price per share need to be if all available shares were sold?

LO 2 & 3: INTERPRETING STOCKHOLDERS' EQUITY

3–48. The balance sheet of David Luza Corporation contains the following information in its equity section:

Stockholders' equity:
Common stock, $10 par value, 1,000,000 shares
authorized and issued and outstanding $10,000,000
Additional paid-in capital 8,000,000
Retained earnings 9,500,000
Total stockholders' equity $27,500,000

Required:

a. What is the maximum number of shares of stock that the corporation could sell if the board of directors desired to do so?
b. When the corporation sold its stock, what was the average selling price per share?
c. If the board of directors declared a $1.50 per share dividend, how much cash would be required to issue the dividend?
d. If Luza has earned $9,500,000 since its formation, how much profit has the corporation distributed to stockholders in the form of dividends since its formation?
e. If the current market price of the stock is $60 per share, how much cash could the board of directors raise if it sold all available shares?

LO 4 & 6: NOTES VS. BONDS

3–49. Miller Company needs to borrow funds to modernize its plant. Miller decided to issue $50 million worth of 30-year bonds in the bond market. Explain why Miller Company might issue bonds rather than borrowing from a bank.

LO 4: CALCULATING BOND PROCEEDS, BOND INTEREST, AND TOTAL BOND PAYMENTS

3–50. Assume that Zhang Company sells 6,500 of its five-year, $1,000 bonds paying 8 percent interest at 96.

Required:

a. How much cash will the company receive from the bond sale?
b. How much cash will the company pay to all the bondholders each year as interest?
c. Determine the total cash payments the company must make for each $1,000 bond to pay the bondholders their return on investment (interest) and the return of their investment.
d. Is the effective (market) interest rate less than, equal to, or greater than 8 percent? How can you determine this?

LO 4: CALCULATING BOND PROCEEDS, BOND INTEREST, AND TOTAL BOND PAYMENTS

3–51. Assume Sherry Company sells 2,500 of its five-year, $1,000 bonds paying 12 percent interest at 103.

Required:

    a. How much cash will the company receive from the bond sale?

    b. How much cash will the company pay to all the bondholders each year as interest?

    c. Determine the total cash payments the company must make for each $1,000 bond to pay the bondholders their return on investment (interest) and the return of their investment.

    d. Is the effective (market) interest rate less than, equal to, or greater than 12 percent? How can you determine this?

LO 4: BOND INTEREST AND PAYMENT CALCULATIONS

3–52. Assume that Phil Handley pays $950 for a five-year, $1,000, 9 percent bond.

Required:

    a. How much cash will Handley receive each year as interest?

    b. Calculate the amount of cash the bondholder will receive for his return on investment and the return of his investment for the $1,000 bond.

    c. Is the effective (market) interest rate less than, equal to, or greater than 9 percent? How can you determine this?

LO 4 & 5: BOND INTEREST AND PAYMENT CALCULATIONS

3–53. Assume Suzanne Weiser pays $1,040 for a five-year, $1,000 bond paying 8 percent interest.

Required:

    a. How much cash will Suzanne receive each year as interest?

    b. Calculate the amount of cash the bondholder will receive for her return on investment and the return of her investment for the $1,000 bond.

    c. Is the effective (market) interest rate less than, equal to, or greater than 8 percent? How can you determine this?

LO 5: COMPUTATION OF INTEREST

3–54. July 1, 2003, Alto, Inc., borrowed $10,000 from National Bank. Alto signed a 10 percent promissory note due on December 31, 2003.

Required:

    a. Determine the total amount Alto will have to pay (principal and interest) on December 31, 2003.

    b. How much interest will National Bank earn on this note?

    c. How would your answer to part b differ if the company borrowed the money on October 1, 2003?

LO 5: COMPUTATION OF INTEREST AND PRINCIPAL

3–55. The Leverett Company borrowed $20,000 to finance its business operation. The loan is due on December 31, 2004.

Required: Calculate the interest and principal Leverett Company would have to pay the bank on December 31, 2004, under each of the following assumptions:

    a. The loan is at 12 percent, borrowed on January 2, 2004.

    b. The loan is at 10 percent, borrowed on January 2, 2004.

    c. The loan is at 12 percent, borrowed on April 1, 2004.

    d. The loan is at 9 percent, borrowed on September 1, 2004.

LO 5: COMPUTATION OF INTEREST AND PRINCIPAL

3–56. The Habiger Company borrowed $100,000 due on December 31, 2004.

Required: Calculate the interest Habiger would have pay to the bank on December 31, 2004, under each of the following assumptions:

    a. The loan is at 6 percent interest, borrowed on January 2, 2004.
    b. The loan is at 8 percent interest, borrowed on January 2, 2004.
    c. The loan is at 6 percent interest, borrowed on May 1, 2004.
    d. The loan is at 8 percent interest, borrowed on August 1, 2004.

LO 4: EFFECT OF MARKET INTEREST ON BOND SELLING PRICES

3–57. Assume a company is selling 6 percent bonds. Explain how an increase in the market rate of interest will impact the selling price of the company's 6 percent bonds.

LO 4: EFFECT OF MARKET INTEREST ON BOND SELLING PRICES

3–58. Assume a company is selling 6 percent bonds. Explain how a decrease in the market rate of interest will impact the selling price of the 6 percent bonds.

LO 4: EFFECT OF MARKET INTEREST ON BOND SELLING PRICES

3–59. King Corporation is prepared to issue 5,000 of its 6 percent, $1,000 par value bonds. If the market rate of interest for such bonds is currently 6½ percent, would you expect the bonds to sell at par value, at a premium, or at a discount? Explain your answer.

LO 4: EFFECT OF MARKET INTEREST ON BOND SELLING PRICES

3–60. Tamara Corporation has decided to issue 9,000 of the company's 7 percent bonds, each with a par value of $1,000. If the market rate of interest for such securities is currently 6¾ percent, would you expect the bonds to sell at par value, at a premium, or at a discount? Explain your answer.

LO 4: EFFECT OF MARKET INTEREST ON BOND SELLING PRICES

3–61. Stacy Corporation has decided to sell 7,000 of its 5 percent bonds, each with a par value of $1,000. If the market rate of interest is currently 5¼ percent, would you expect the bonds to sell at par value, at a premium, or at a discount? Explain your answer.

LO 5: STOCK ISSUANCES

3–62. Klauss Corporation began operations in 1972 by issuing 20,000 shares of its no-par common stock for $5 per share. The following details provide information about the company's stock in the years since that time.

    1. In 1992, the company issued an additional 50,000 shares of common stock for $15 per share.
    2. Klauss Corporation stock is traded on the ***New York Stock Exchange (NYSE).*** During an average year, about 25,000 shares of its common stock are sold by one set of investors to another.
    3. On December 31, 2002, Klauss Corporation common stock was quoted on the ***NYSE*** at $38 per share.
    4. On December 31, 2003, Klauss Corporation common stock was quoted on the ***NYSE*** at $55 per share.

Required:

    a. How much money has Klauss Corporation received in total from the sales of its common stock since it was incorporated in 1972?
    b. When Klauss Corporation prepares its balance sheet as of December 31, 2003, what dollar amount will it show in the owners' equity section for common stock?
    c. What, if anything, can you infer about Klauss Corporation's performance during 2003 from the price of its common stock on December 31, 2002, and December 31, 2003?

LO 5: STOCK ISSUANCES

3–63. Shiner Corporation began operations in 1988 by issuing 35,000 shares of its $2 par value common stock for $10 per share. The following details provide information about the company's stock in the years since that time.

1. In 1998, the company issued an additional 80,000 shares of common stock for $15 per share.
2. Shiner Corporation stock is traded on the ***American Stock Exchange (AMEX).*** During an average year, about 40,000 shares of its common stock are sold by one set of investors to another.
3. On December 31, 2002, Shiner Corporation common stock was quoted on the ***AMEX*** at $79 per share.
4. On December 31, 2003, Shiner Corporation common stock was quoted on the ***AMEX*** at $45 per share.

Required:

a. How much money has Shiner Corporation received in total from the sales of its common stock since it was incorporated in 1988?
b. When Shiner Corporation prepares its balance sheet as of December 31, 2003, what dollar amount will it show in the owners' equity section for common stock?
c. What, if anything, can you infer about Shiner Corporation's performance during 2003 from the price of its common stock on December 31, 2002, and December 31, 2003?

LO 5: STOCK ISSUANCES

3–64. La Forge Corporation began operations in January, 1992, by issuing 90,000 shares of its no-par common stock for $25 per share and 10,000 shares of its $100 par value, 6 percent preferred stock for $100 per share. The following details provide information about the company's stock in the years since that time.

1. In January 1999, the company issued an additional 50,000 shares of common stock for $35 per share and 5,000 shares of preferred stock for $150 per share.
2. La Forge Corporation stock is traded on the ***New York Stock Exchange (NYSE).*** During an average year, about 100,000 shares of its common stock and 6,000 shares of preferred stock are sold by one set of investors to another.
3. On December 31, 2002, La Forge Corporation common stock was quoted on the ***NYSE*** at $55 per share. The preferred stock was quoted at $135 per share.
4. On December 31, 2003, La Forge Corporation common stock was quoted on the ***NYSE*** at $65 per share. The preferred stock was quoted at $150 per share.

Required:

a. How much money has La Forge Corporation received in total from the sales of its stock since it was incorporated in 1992?
b. When La Forge Corporation prepares its balance sheet as of December 31, 2003, what dollar amount will it show in the owners' equity section for common stock and for preferred stock?
c. What is the market value of La Forge's stock on December 31, 2002, and December 31, 2003?

LO 5: STOCK ISSUANCES

3–65. Bennett Corporation began operations in 1979 by issuing 40,000 shares of its no-par common stock for $10 per share. The following details provide information about the company's stock in the years since that time.

1. In 1998, the company issued an additional 70,000 shares of common stock for $15 per share.
2. Bennett Corporation stock is traded on the ***New York Stock Exchange (NYSE).*** During an average year, about 50,000 shares of its common stock are sold by one set of investors to another.
3. On December 31, 2002, Bennett Corporation common stock was quoted on the ***NYSE*** at $56 per share.
4. On December 31, 2003, Bennett Corporation common stock was quoted on the ***NYSE*** at $35 per share.

Required:

a. How much money has Bennett Corporation received in total from the sales of its common stock since it was incorporated in 1979?

b. When Bennett Corporation prepares its balance sheet as of December 31, 2003, what dollar amount will it show in the owners' equity section for common stock?

c. What, if anything, can you infer about Bennett Corporation's performance during 2003 from the price of its common stock on December 31, 2002, and December 31, 2003?

LO 6: EQUITY VS. DEBT

3–66. This chapter discussed two very different forms of financing available to corporations: debt and equity.

Required:

a. Explain why a corporation might prefer to issue bonds rather than shares of common stock.

b. Explain why an investor might prefer to purchase shares of a company's common stock rather than a company's corporate bonds.

LO 6: EQUITY VS. DEBT

3–67. Define *nominal interest rate* and *market interest rate* relative to bonds, and briefly explain how these rates affect a bond's selling price.

LO 6: DEBT VS. EQUITY INVESTMENTS

3–68. Ed Furgol has $20,000 to invest. His options are as follows:

Option 1: Big Company's five-year, $1,000 par value, 8 percent bonds, which are selling for 98 on the bond market. (Exactly three years remaining to maturity.)

Option 2: Little Company's initial offering of no-par common stock, which is selling for $20 per share. Although there is no formal requirement to pay dividends, it is anticipated that Little Company will pay an annual dividend of $0.80 per share on its common stock.

Required:

a. How many of the Big Company bonds can Ed buy with the $20,000 he has to invest?

b. How much cash will Ed receive from Big Company each year if he buys the bonds?

c. What will Ed's return on investment and return of investment be for the bonds if he holds them until maturity?

d. How many shares of Little Company's common stock can Ed purchase with the $20,000 he has to invest?

e. Assuming Little Company does pay the anticipated annual dividend on its common stock, how much will Ed receive each year if he invests his $20,000 in the stock?

LO 6: EQUITY VS. DEBT

3–69. Joshua Pak has $50,000 to invest. His options are as follows:

Option 1: Grand Oil Company's five-year, $1,000 par value, 12 percent bonds, which are selling for 103 on the bond market. (Exactly five years remaining to maturity.)

Option 2: Little Giant Oil Company's initial offering of no-par common stock, which is selling for $75 per share. Although there is no formal requirement to pay dividends, it is anticipated that Little Giant will pay an annual dividend of $2 per share on its common stock.

Required:

a. How many of the Grand Oil bonds can Joshua buy with the $50,000 he has to invest?

b. How much cash will Joshua receive from Grand Oil each year if he buys the bonds?

c. What will Joshua's return on investment and return of investment be for the bonds if he holds them until maturity?

d. How many shares of Little Giant's common stock can Joshua purchase with the $50,000 he has to invest?

e. Assuming Little Giant does pay the anticipated annual dividend on its common stock, how much will Joshua receive each year if he invests his $50,000 in the stock?

LO 7: STATEMENT OF CASH FLOWS PREPARATION—SIMPLE INVESTING AND FINANCING ACTIVITIES ONLY

3–70. The following information is from the records of the Elsea Corporation for the year ended December 31, 2003.

    1. Sold Elsea Corporation common stock for cash of $95,500
    2. Purchased equipment for cash $28,000
    3. Borrowed $7,000 from Miami National Bank
    4. Cash balance at December 31, 2003, was $30,000

Required: Prepare a statement of cash flows for Elsea Corporation for the year ended December 31, 2003.

LO 7: STATEMENT OF CASH FLOWS PREPARATION—SIMPLE INVESTING AND FINANCING ACTIVITIES ONLY

3–71. The following information is from the records of the Steinmann Industries for the year ended December 31, 2003.

    1. Sold Steinmann Industries common stock for cash of $30,000
    2. Borrowed $120,000 by selling bonds
    3. Purchased land for $40,000 cash
    4. Purchased a building for $60,000 cash
    5. Cash balance at December 31, 2002, was $20,000

Required: Prepare a statement of cash flows for Steinmann Industries for the year ended December 31, 2003.

LO 7: STATEMENT OF CASH FLOWS PREPARATION—SIMPLE INVESTING AND FINANCING ACTIVITIES ONLY

3–72. The following information is from the records of the Shandra Industries for the year ended December 31, 2003.

    1. Sold Shandra Industries common stock for cash of $73,000
    2. Sold Shandra bonds for $200,000 cash
    3. Borrowed $70,000 from XYZ Bank
    4. Purchased equipment for cash $240,000
    5. Purchased land for $35,000 cash
    6. Cash balance at December 31, 2002, was $20,000

Required: Prepare a statement of cash flows for Shandra Industries for the year ended December 31, 2003.

LO 7: STATEMENT OF CASH FLOWS PREPARATION—SIMPLE INVESTING AND FINANCING ACTIVITIES ONLY

3–73. The following information is from the records of the Jessie Lynne Company for the year ended December 31, 2003.

    1. Sold Jessie Lynne Company common stock for cash of $55,000
    2. Sold Jessie Lynne Company preferred stock for cash of $25,000
    3. Borrowed $100,000 from XYZ Bank
    4. Sold Jessie Lynne bonds for $120,000 cash
    5. Purchased equipment for cash $60,000
    6. Sold equipment for cash $1,500
    7. Cash balance at December 31, 2002, was $20,000

Required: Prepare a statement of cash flows for Jessie Lynne Company for the year ended December 31, 2003.

LO 7: STATEMENT OF CASH FLOWS PREPARATION—SIMPLE INVESTING AND FINANCING ACTIVITIES ONLY

3–74. The following information is from the records of the Alto Corporation for the year ended December 31, 2003.

1. Sold Alto Corporation common stock for cash of $65,000
2. Sold Alto Corporation preferred stock for cash of $50,000
3. Purchased equipment for cash $60,000
4. Sold Alto bonds for $300,000 cash
5. Sold equipment for cash $12,000
6. Paid $500 cash dividend
7. Borrowed $70,000 from Miami National Bank
8. Purchased IBM stock $15,000
9. Purchased land for $120,000 cash
10. Purchased building for $150,000 cash
11. Cash balance at December 31, 2002, was $30,000

Required: Prepare a statement of cash flows for Alto Corporation for the year ended December 31, 2003.

LO 7: STATEMENT OF CASH FLOWS PREPARATION—SIMPLE INVESTING AND FINANCING ACTIVITIES ONLY

3–75. The following information is from the records of the Foxmore Company for the year ended December 31, 2003.

1. Sold Foxmore Company common stock for cash of $195,000
2. Sold Foxmore Company preferred stock for cash of $75,000
3. Purchased equipment for cash $9,000
4. Sold equipment for cash $3,000
5. Borrowed $170,000 from **Bank of America,** signing a promissory note
6. Sold Foxmore bonds for $250,000 cash
7. Purchased land for $30,000 cash
8. Purchased building for $50,000 cash
9. Purchased machinery to use in the business for 180,000 cash
10. Paid cash dividend of $2,000
11. Cash balance at December 31, 2002, was $30,000

Required: Prepare a statement of cash flows for Foxmore Company for the year ended December 31, 2003.

LO 7: STATEMENT OF CASH FLOWS PREPARATION—SIMPLE INVESTING AND FINANCING ACTIVITIES ONLY

3–76. During the year ended December 31, 2003, Dale's Computer Center sold some of its common stock for cash of $90,000. In addition, the company purchased equipment for cash of $68,000 and borrowed $25,000 from **Bank of America.** The company's cash balance at December 31, 2002, was $22,000.

Required: Prepare a statement of cash flows for the company for the year ended December 31, 2003.

LO 7: STATEMENT OF CASH FLOWS PREPARATION—SIMPLE INVESTING AND FINANCING ACTIVITIES ONLY

3–77. During the year ended December 31, 2003, Ace Corporation sold some of its common stock for cash of $86,000. In addition, the company purchased land for cash of $33,000 and sold Ace bonds for $55,000 cash. The company's cash balance at December 31, 2002, was $12,000.

Required: Prepare a statement of cash flows for the company for the year ended December 31, 2003.

LO 7: STATEMENT OF CASH FLOWS PREPARATION—SIMPLE INVESTING AND FINANCING ACTIVITIES ONLY

3–78. During the year ended December 31, 2003, Ventura Corporation sold some of its common stock for cash of $180,000. In addition, the company borrowed $120,000 by selling bonds and $50,000 by signing a promissory note to the Bank of Key Largo. The company purchased land for $40,000 and a building for $60,000 cash. The company's cash balance at December 31, 2002, was $22,000.

Required: Prepare a statement of cash flows for the company for the year ended
December 31, 2003.

LO 7: STATEMENT OF CASH FLOWS PREPARATION—SIMPLE INVESTING AND FINANCING ACTIVITIES ONLY

3–79. During the year ended December 31, 2003, Mini-Me Corporation sold some of its common stock for cash of $400,000. In addition, the company borrowed $150,000 by selling bonds and $150,000 by signing a promissory note to the Bank of Brevard. The company purchased land for $210,000 and a building for $360,000 cash. The company's cash balance at December 31, 2002, was $88,000.

Required: Prepare a statement of cash flows for the company for the year ended
December 31, 2003.

LO 8: FINANCIAL RATIO CALCULATIONS—PROPRIETORSHIP

3–80. The following balance sheet of Gerner Enterprises was compiled shortly after Edward Gerner started his business:

Gerner Enterprises
Balance Sheet
October 1, 2003

Assets		Liabilities and owner's equity:	
Cash	$100,000	Notes payable — Union Bank	$ 50,000
Land	50,000	Graham Gerner, capital	100,000
Total assets	$150,000	Total liabilities and owner's equity	$150,000

Required:

    a. Based on the information provided in Gerner's balance sheet, write a brief paragraph that describes what Edward Gerner did financially to start his business.
    b. What type of business organization is Gerner Enterprises?
    c. Calculate the debt ratio for the company.
    d. Calculate the debt-to-equity ratio for the company.
    e. What do the ratios in parts c and d tell you about the company?

LO 8: FINANCIAL RATIO CALCULATIONS—PARTNERSHIP

3–81. The following balance sheet of Susan Drake and Associates was compiled at the end of its first year of operations:

Susan Drake and Associates
Balance Sheet
December 31, 2003

Assets:		Liabilities and owners' equity:	
Cash	$40,000	Notes payable — Central Bank	$10,000
Land	20,000	Susan Drake, capital	25,000
		Julie Pham, capital	25,000
Total assets	$60,000	Total liabilities and owners' equity	$60,000

Required:

    a. Write a paragraph that describes what this balance sheet tells you about the financial position of the company.
    b. What type of business organization is Susan Drake and Associates?
    c. Calculate the debt ratio for the company.
    d. Calculate the debt-to-equity ratio for the company.
    e. What do the ratios in parts c and d tell you about the company?

LO 8: FINANCIAL RATIO CALCULATIONS—CORPORATION

3–82. The following balance sheet was compiled for Quynh Vu Enterprises at the end of its first year of operations:

Quynh Vu Enterprises
Balance Sheet
December 31, 2003

Assets:		Liabilities and stockholders' equity:	
Cash	$120,000	Notes payable—Sooner Bank	$ 20,000
		Common stock, $10 par value	40,000
		Additional paid-in capital	50,000
		Retained earnings	10,000
		Total liabilities and stockholders'	
Total assets	$120,000	equity	$120,000

Required:

    a. Write a paragraph that describes what this balance sheet tells you about the financial position of the company.

    b. Assuming the company did not distribute any of its earnings to its owners, from the information provided, can you determine how much profit the company made in its first year?

    c. Can you tell how many stockholders Quynh Vu Enterprises has? Explain your answer.

    d. How many shares of stock did Quynh Vu Enterprises sell and what was the stock's average selling price per share?

    e. Calculate the debt ratio for the company.

    f. Calculate the debt-to-equity ratio for the company.

    g. What do the ratios in parts e and f tell you about the company?

LO 8: FINANCIAL RATIO CALCULATIONS—CORPORATION

3–83. The balance sheet below was compiled for Lauren Elsea Tour Enterprises, Inc.

Lauren Elsea Tour Enterprises, Inc.
Balance Sheet
December 31, 2003

Assets:		Liabilities:	
Cash	$15,000	Notes payable	$144,000
Land	120,000	Bonds payable	441,000
Building	215,000	Total liabilities	585,000
Office equipment	28,000	Stockholders' equity:	
Tour trolleys	149,000	Common stock	$ 57,000
Charter boat	205,000	Additional paid-in capital—common	90,000
		Total stockholders' equity	147,000
		Total liabilities and stockholders'	
Total assets	$732,000	equity	$732,000

Required:

    a. Calculate the debt ratio for the company.

    b. Calculate the debt-to-equity ratio for the company.

    c. What do the ratios in parts a and b tell you about the company?

LO 8: FINANCIAL RATIO CALCULATIONS—CORPORATION

3–84. The balance sheet below was compiled for South Beach Dive Center, Inc.

South Beach Dive Center, Inc.
Balance Sheet
November 30, 2003

Assets:		Liabilities:	
Cash	$11,000	Accounts payable	$ 62,000
Merchandise inventory	96,000	Notes payable	77,000
Computer system	6,000	Total liabilities	139,000
Office equipment	8,000	Stockholders' equity:	
Dive boat	188,000	Common stock	$68,000
		Additional paid-in capital—common	102,000
		Total stockholders' equity	170,000
		Total liabilities and stockholders'	
Total assets	$309,000	equity	$309,000

Required:

  a. Calculate the debt ratio for the company.
  b. Calculate the debt-to-equity ratio for the company.
  c. What do the ratios in parts a and b tell you about the company?

LO 6: FINANCIAL RATIO CALCULATIONS—CORPORATION

3–85. The balance sheet below was compiled for Panama City Charters, Inc.

Panama City Charters, Inc.
Balance Sheet
June 30, 2003

Assets:		Liabilities:	
Cash	$ 7,000	Accounts payable	$ 12,000
Office furniture inventory	15,000	Notes payable	52,000
Office equipment	8,000	Total liabilities	64,000
Computer equipment	18,000	Stockholders' equity:	
Tour buses	377,000	Common stock	$ 92,000
		Additional paid-in capital—common	269,000
		Total stockholders' equity	361,000
		Total liabilities and stockholders'	
Total assets	$425,000	equity	$425,000

Required:

  a. Calculate the debt ratio for the company.
  b. Calculate the debt-to-equity ratio for the company.
  c. What do the ratios in parts a and b tell you about the company?

LO 8: FINANCIAL RATIO CALCULATIONS—CORPORATION

3–86. Refer to the balance sheets presented in problems 3–83, 3–84, and 3–85.

Required:

  a. What industry would you say each of the three companies is in?
  b. Do they seem to be in the same industry?
  c. Calculate the debt ratios for each company.
  d. Calculate the debt-to-equity ratios for each company.
  e. Create a well-organized table that shows each of the company's names and their debt and debt-to-equity ratios.
  f. Assume each company has applied for a loan and you are the loan office evaluating their applications. Rank the companies according to their loan risk based on the information in the table you prepared for requirement e. Explain your ranking.

Financial Reporting Exercises ⦿⦿⦿⦿⦿⦿⦿⦿⦿⦿⦿⦿⦿⦿⦿⦿⦿⦿⦿⦿⦿⦿⦿⦿⦿⦿⦿

LO 1, 2, & 6: GATHERING EQUITY INFORMATION FROM PUBLISHED ANNUAL REPORT

3–87. Refer to *Pier 1 Imports* annual report on page F–503 to answer the following questions.

Required:

  a. What types of stock are reported on the company's balance sheet?
  b. For each type of stock listed, identify the number of shares authorized, the number issued, and the number outstanding for each year presented on the balance sheet.
  c. Why might *Pier 1* issue preferred stock?
  d. Present the accounting equation with dollar amounts for *Pier 1* for each of its balance sheets presented in the company's annual report.

LO 1, 2, & 6: GATHERING EQUITY INFORMATION FROM PUBLISHED ANNUAL REPORT

3–88. Go to the PHLIP Web site for this book to find the link to *Barnes & Noble Inc.* Refer to the information listed under February 2, 2002, and answer the following questions.

Required:

    a. What types of stock are reported on the balance sheet?

    b. If there is common and/or preferred stock, identify the number of shares authorized, the number issued, and the number outstanding. If there is treasury stock, list the number of shares.

    c. What is the total cost of the shares held in the treasury? What was the cost of these per share to the company?

    d. Write the accounting equation for ***Barnes & Noble Inc.,*** as of February 2, 2002.

LO 1, 2, 4, & 6: VARIOUS. GATHERING DEBT AND EQUITY INFORMATION FROM PUBLISHED ANNUAL REPORT

3–89. Go to the PHLIP Web site for this book to find the link to ***Emerson Radio Corporation.*** Refer to the information listed under January 31, 2002, and answer the following questions.

Required:

    a. What types of stock are reported on the balance sheet?

    b. If there is common and/or preferred stock, identify the number of shares authorized, the number issued, and the number outstanding. If there is treasury stock, list the number of shares.

    c. What is the total cost of the shares held in the treasury? What was the original cost per share to the company?

    d. Write the accounting equation for ***Emerson Radio Corp.,*** as of January 31, 2002.

LO — VARIOUS. INTERPRETING DEBT INFORMATION FROM PUBLISHED ANNUAL REPORT

3–90. In its 2002 10-K Report, ***Dell Computer Corporation*** reported total long-term liabilities of $520,000,000. Of that amount, $300,000,000 represented 4.87% debentures due in 2028.

Required:

    a. What is a debenture?

    b. Why might there be a difference in the current value of the bonds and the amount the company has listed?

    c. What percentage of the company's long-term liabilities are bonds?

    d. Assuming the bonds were issued in 2002, how much total interest will ***Dell Computer Corporation*** pay on them? Is this number dependent on the market?

LO — VARIOUS. INTERPRETING DEBT INFORMATION FROM PUBLISHED ANNUAL REPORT

3–91. ***Procter & Gamble Co.,*** multinational producer and marketer of such products as *Tide* laundry detergent, *Charmin* toilet paper, and *Pampers* diapers, included the following in its 2001 10-K Notes to Consolidated Financial Statements:

    Long-term debt maturities during the next five years are as follows: 2002 — $622,000,000; 2003 — $1,117,000,000; 2004 — $1,040,000,000; 2005 — $1,912,000,000 and 2006 — $32,000,000.

Required:

    a. Why would ***Procter & Gamble Co.*** include this information in the annual report?

    b. What information does this provide the annual report readers?

    c. If you were making a loan to ***Procter & Gamble Co.,*** in which one of the five years would you prefer to schedule the company's loan repayment to you?

LO 1, 2, 6, & 8: VARIOUS. INTERPRETING DEBT AND EQUITY INFORMATION, CALCULATING FINANCIAL RATIOS

3–92. Go to the PHLIP Web site for the link to look up the total liabilities and total stockholders' equity for ***Blockbuster, Inc.,*** from the 10-K Report's balance sheet under the listing for December 31, 2001.

Required:

    a. How much are the company's total assets?

    b. Calculate the debt ratio for the company.

c. Calculate the debt-to-equity ratio for the company.

d. What do these ratios tell you about ***Blockbuster, Inc?*** Do they tell you anything relative to the risk of investing in the company?

3–93. Go to the PHLIP Web site for the link to look up the total liabilities and total stockholders' equity for ***Elizabeth Arden, Inc.,*** from the 10-K Report's balance sheet under the listing for January 31, 2002.

Required:

a. How much are the company's total assets?

b. Calculate the debt ratio for the company.

c. Calculate the debt-to-equity ratio for the company.

d. What do these ratios tell you about ***Elizabeth Arden, Inc?*** Do they tell you anything relative to the risk of investing in the company?

ANNUAL REPORT PROJECT

3–94. Section 3—Basic Balance Sheet Information

In this assignment, you will prepare a report based on your company's balance sheet and other information.

Required: Prepare a report that includes the following information:

a. Describe your company's balance sheet presentation and the important information it includes. For example, how many years of balance sheet information does your company present? Does your company use the report form or the account form for its balance sheet presentation? Does it matter to you which format your company uses? Explain your reasoning.

b. Discuss the important items and amounts that appear on the balance sheet. What is the company's most significant asset? Which is the least significant? Is there any reason for this?

c. If your company has long-term debt, summarize the pertinent facts relating to the debt. Information for this requirement can be found in the notes to the financial statements.

d. Go to the notes to the financial statements and find the note regarding contingencies. Does your company have any contingent liabilities? If it does, provide a brief description of each. Describe why this information is important.

e. Does the balance sheet include categories called something similar to "other assets"? If it does, use information from the notes to the financial statement to describe the items in this category.

f. Does the balance sheet include categories called something similar to "other liabilities"? If it does, use information from the notes to the financial statement to describe the items in this category.

g. Prepare a schedule for your company that presents the following financial ratios:

- Debt ratio for two years
- Debt-to-equity ratio for two years

h. Comment in your report on the information that each ratio provides. Include comments regarding the changes in the amounts of ratios over time. Is the proportion of debt financing increasing or decreasing? Comment on your company's external financing including the relative proportions of liabilities and equity.

i. Your report should conclude with a summary of what you think of the company in light of what you discovered as you completed this assignment.

CHAPTER 4

Income Statement and Statement of Owners' Equity

Imagine for a moment that you are a fairly new commercial loan officer at **Bank of America** and you are evaluating the risk of lending $150,000 to a particular corporate customer. (Management considers you a rising star, so they have entrusted you with this evaluation even though you have never done one before.) Your job as a loan officer is to lend as much money as possible, but only to those corporations that will pay it back. It's quite a responsibility and you are naturally a bit nervous. If you fail to lend to a credit-worthy customer, the bank could lose interest revenue. Worse, the bank could lose the entire $150,000 if you approve a loan to a company that cannot repay it. The company applying for the loan has provided you with a set of financial statements—a balance sheet, an income statement, a statement of owners' equity, and a statement of cash flows.

As you sit in your office gazing at all these numbers, you remember a phrase from your accounting text in college: Sometimes trying to sift through all this information is like trying to empty the ocean with a teaspoon to get to the treasure on the sea floor. Well, the amount of material in these financial statements certainly seems to reflect that situation.

Unsure of exactly how to proceed, you seek the advice of Barney Barnes, an experienced loan officer who has been acting as a mentor to you. When you ask him what financial information is really important in helping you make sound lending decisions, he responds with a long list of things to consider, such as gross profit on sales (percentage and dollars), net profit margin (percentage and dollars), the amount of debt compared to equity, retained earnings, capital structure, the ability to generate cash through operations, dividends paid in the past, and, of course, how the financial statements articulate.

Your head is swimming as you return to your office. Some of these items you know come from the balance sheet, others from the income statement, and still others from the statement of owners' equity and the statement of cash flows. It's obvious to you that you need a solid understanding of all the financial statements and the information they provide as you assess whether to make the loan. You already know about the balance sheet and the information it provides. Certainly, this information is helpful, but it is not sufficient. Even though the balance sheet shows the present financial position of a company, it is only one of the pieces of information you should assemble before you make a final decision. For example, you also need to assess whether the company's business activities result in profits that are adequate enough for the company to remain viable.

In this chapter, you will learn how the income statement depicts this type of information. The income statement provides information about a company's economic performance over a specific period of time.

This chapter will also introduce you to the statement of owners' equity. This financial statement provides a bridge between the information the income statement provides and the information the balance sheet provides. It does this by tracing the changes in owners' equity (of which net income from the income statement is a part) from the beginning to the end of the accounting period.

The activity reflected by the income statement has a profound impact on cash flow, specifically cash flow from operating activities. Because so many decision makers look toward cash as their ultimate reward in business, information about cash and how it increases or decreases over time is critically important to them. In this chapter, we will show how the statement of cash flows reflects the sources and uses of cash from operating activities.

Financial statements provide so much information that it can become difficult to ascertain the relationships of the various financial statement amounts. As we learned in prior chapters, financial statement analysis is the process of evaluating financial statements and the relationships among the amounts they contain. In this chapter, we will discuss financial statement analysis associated with the income statement.

By the time you've finished this chapter, you will have explored four financial statements—the balance sheet, the income statement, the statement of owners' equity, and the statement of cash flows. Bear in mind that these are financial information tools for economic decision makers. Their importance lies in their usefulness and their contribution to the decision making process.

Learning Objectives

After completing your work on this chapter, you should be able to do the following:

1. Prepare a basic income statement and describe the information it provides.
2. Distinguish between single-step and multiple-step income statements.
3. Explain the impact of net income or net loss on owners' equity.
4. Prepare a basic statement of owners' equity for a proprietorship, a partnership, and a corporation and describe the information the statement provides.
5. Define drawings and dividends and discuss the circumstances under which they are paid.
6. Describe the articulation of income statements, statements of owners' equity, and balance sheets.
7. Explain the content and purpose of the operating activities section of the statement of cash flows.
8. Use financial ratios to evaluate business profits.

◆ INTRODUCTION TO THE INCOME STATEMENT

income statement A financial statement providing information about an entity's past performance. Its purpose is to measure the results of the entity's operations for some specific time period.

The **income statement** is a financial tool that provides information about a company's past performance. Recall that in our presentation of the balance sheet in Chapter 3 we discussed assets, liabilities, and owners' equity (including investments by owners)—four of the accounting elements described by the Financial Accounting Standards Board (FASB) in the *Conceptual Framework of Accounting*. The income statement also includes accounting elements (see Exhibit 4–1). The italicized definitions in the following discussion are provided by the FASB. A less formal definition of each element follows the words of the FASB.

revenue An accounting element representing the inflows of assets as a result of an entity's ongoing major or central operations. These are the rewards of doing business.

expense An accounting element representing the outflow of assets resulting from an entity's ongoing major or central operations. These are the sacrifices required to attain the rewards (revenues) of doing business.

- **Revenues**—*Inflows or other enhancements of assets to an entity . . . from delivering or producing goods, rendering services, or other activities that constitute the entity's ongoing major or central operations* (Statement of Financial Accounting Concepts No. 6, paragraph 78). Revenue represents what a company charges its customers for the goods and services it provides. If a company deposits money in a bank, the interest the company earns on that money is also revenue. Revenues are the reward of doing business.
- **Expenses**—*Outflows or other using up of assets . . . from delivering or producing goods, rendering services, or carrying out other activities that constitute the entity's major or central operations* (Statement of Financial Accounting Concepts No. 6, paragraph 80). Expenses are the sacrifices required to generate revenues. Unlike assets, which have future value, expenses are the costs of doing business that no longer have future value.

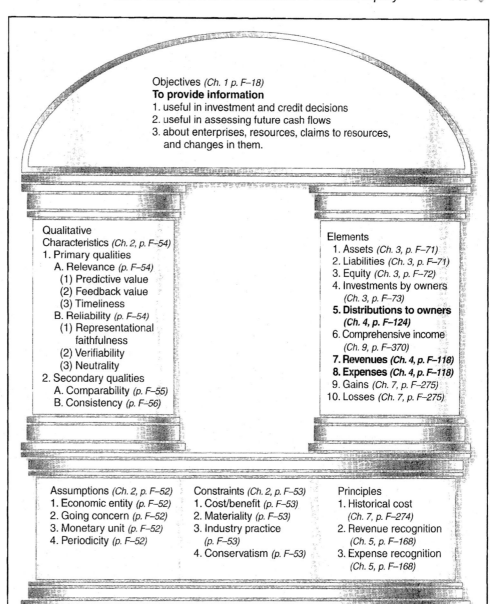

Objectives *(Ch. 1 p. F–18)*
To provide information
1. useful in investment and credit decisions
2. useful in assessing future cash flows
3. about enterprises, resources, claims to resources, and changes in them.

Qualitative
Characteristics *(Ch. 2, p. F–54)*
1. Primary qualities
  A. Relevance *(p. F–54)*
    (1) Predictive value
    (2) Feedback value
    (3) Timeliness
  B. Reliability *(p. F–54)*
    (1) Representational
      faithfulness
    (2) Verifiability
    (3) Neutrality
2. Secondary qualities
  A. Comparability *(p. F–55)*
  B. Consistency *(p. F–56)*

Elements
1. Assets *(Ch. 3, p. F–71)*
2. Liabilities *(Ch. 3, p. F–71)*
3. Equity *(Ch. 3, p. F–72)*
4. Investments by owners
  (Ch. 3, p. F–73)
5. **Distributions to owners**
  (Ch. 4, p. F–124)
6. Comprehensive income
  (Ch. 9, p. F–370)
7. **Revenues (Ch. 4, p. F–118)**
8. **Expenses (Ch. 4, p. F–118)**
9. Gains *(Ch. 7, p. F–275)*
10. Losses *(Ch. 7, p. F–275)*

Assumptions *(Ch. 2, p. F–52)*
1. Economic entity *(p. F–52)*
2. Going concern *(p. F–52)*
3. Monetary unit *(p. F–52)*
4. Periodicity *(p. F–52)*

Constraints *(Ch. 2, p. F–53)*
1. Cost/benefit *(p. F–53)*
2. Materiality *(p. F–53)*
3. Industry practice
  (p. F–53)
4. Conservatism *(p. F–53)*

Principles
1. Historical cost
  (Ch. 7, p. F–274)
2. Revenue recognition
  (Ch. 5, p. F–168)
3. Expense recognition
  (Ch. 5, p. F–168)

EXHIBIT 4-1   Accounting Elements

net income   The amount of profit that remains after all costs have been considered. The net reward of doing business for a specific time period.

net loss   The difference between revenues and expenses of a period in which expenses are greater than revenues.

    The excess of the rewards (revenues) over the sacrifices (expenses) for a given time period is the net reward of doing business, which we call **net income.** Accountants also call net income *earnings, net earnings,* or *net profit.* If the expenses for the period are greater than the revenues for the period, the result is a **net loss.** The relationship between revenues, expenses, and either net income or net loss can be represented by the following equation:

$$\text{Revenues} - \text{Expenses} = \text{Net Income (or Net Loss)}$$

This income statement equation forms the basis for the income statement itself. As we study the income statement, we will deal with the equation again and again, so fix its meaning in your mind!

Discussion Questions

4–1.   Of the transactions in your personal finances during the last month, which would you describe as revenues? Which would you describe as expenses?

4–2.   Use the income statement equation and your responses to Discussion Question 4–1 to determine whether you had a net income or a net loss for the month.

BUILDING THE INCOME STATEMENT

As an example of the basic format, the income statement of **Tiffany & Co.** is shown in Exhibit 4–2. Note that the heading includes the name of the business, the name of the statement, and the time period the statement depicts. As you recall, the heading for the balance sheet includes the precise date for which the information is being presented. While the balance sheet is a "snapshot" of a business at a particular point in time, the income statement is something like a "home video" of a company for a period of time (usually a month, quarter, or year). For this reason, the income statement heading identifies a period of time—not just a single date. The income statement indicates that during this specific time period, the company earned so much revenue, incurred so much expense, and produced either a net income or a net loss. Companies prepare income statements for external users annually and quarterly. Additionally, for internal decision makers, accountants prepare income statements monthly, or for any other time interval that would provide information managers need.

EXHIBIT 4–2   *Tiffany & Co.* Income Statement

Tiffany & Co.	
Income Statement	
For the Year Ended January 31, 2001	
(In thousands)	
Net Sales	$1,668,056
Cost of sales	719,642
Gross profit	948,414
Selling, general and administrative expense	621,018
Earnings from operations	327,396
Interest expense and financing cost	(16,207)
Other income, net	6,452
Earnings before income taxes	317,641
Provision for income taxes	127,057
Net earnings	$ 190,584

The income statement's formal name is the *statement of results of operations*, which is a far better description of its function than *income statement*. However, most companies use the informal title, "Income Statement." The authors of *Accounting Trends and Techniques*[1] report that of 600 companies surveyed in 2001, 284 used *income* as a key word in the headings of their 2000 financial statements, 198 used *operations*, and 108 used *earnings*.

A company may have more than one type of revenue. Revenues comprise earned inflows of the company arising from both primary operations and secondary company activities. A service firm's primary operation is providing service, and merchandising and manufacturing firms obtain and sell tangible products. In addition to revenues from its primary operations, a company may generate revenues through other activities. For example, a company may earn rent revenue by renting out extra space in its office building or it may earn interest revenue from investing some of its cash in certificates of deposit.

Discussion Question

4-3. For each of the following, determine whether the company's primary revenue comes from obtaining and selling products or providing services.

  a. **General Motors**
  b. **ExxonMobil**
  c. **Starbucks**
  d. **Prudential Insurance**
  e. **B. Dalton Bookstores**
  f. **AOL**

---

[1]*Accounting Trends and Techniques* (AICPA, 2001), 289.

Income statements show various expenses. Expenses take many different forms, such as salaries and wages expense for employees, rent expense for land and buildings occupied by the business, electricity expense for the electricity used by the company, fuel expense, and maintenance expense for vehicles the business owns. These are just a few examples of the numerous expenses a company may have.

The cost of the products that merchandisers and manufacturers sell make up an expense called the **cost of goods sold,** sometimes called *cost of sales*, or *cost of products sold*. For many companies, cost of goods sold comprises the major expense of doing business. For example, in its 2001 income statement, ***Best Buy*** reported total expenses (in thousands) of $14,722,244. Of this total, $12,267,459, or 83 percent, was cost of goods sold.

cost of goods sold   The cost of the product sold as the primary business activity of a company.

In the United States, companies must pay **income tax,** which is a tax based on the amount of income a company has earned. The specifics for calculating the amount of income tax a company should pay or the amount it should report as income tax expense is beyond the scope of this course. But basically, the way it works is that the amount of taxable income is multiplied by the company's tax rate.

income tax   A tax based on the amount of income a company has earned.

$$\text{Taxable Income} \times \text{Tax Rate} = \text{Income Tax Expense}$$

If you were to compare the tax rates of various companies, you would notice that each one has a somewhat different tax rate from the next. This is because of several factors including the fact that tax rates increase as income increases. The more income a company generates, the more income tax expense it will have.

INCOME STATEMENT FORMATS

There are two commonly used income statement formats: the single-step and the multiple-step formats. Of the 600 companies surveyed in 2001, the authors of *Accounting Trends and Techniques* reported that 134 companies used the single-step format and 466 used the multiple-step format for their 2000 income statements.

Although the presentation of the information differs between the single-step and the multiple-step income statements, the bottom line, or net income, would be the same regardless of the format used. However, there are some subtle but important differences between the two formats, so let's take a look at them.

SINGLE-STEP FORMAT OF THE INCOME STATEMENT

single-step income statement   A format of the income statement that gathers all revenues into "total revenues" and all expenses into "total expenses." Net income is calculated as a subtraction of total expenses from total revenues.

In the **single-step income statement** format, all revenues are grouped together and then totaled. Similarly, all expenses are grouped together and totaled. This format is called the single-step income statement because in one step, total expenses are subtracted from total revenues to determine net income or net loss. In actual practice, one exception to grouping *all* expenses together when the single-step format is used stands out. Of the 134 companies that used the single-step format in 2000, *Accounting Trends and Techniques* reported that every one of them showed income tax as a separate item and listed it just above net income. Accordingly, this is the format we will use for our presentations for the single-step format.

To illustrate the single-step format of the income statement, let's return to Jessica's Beauty Supply, Inc., the company we used in Chapter 3 to introduce the balance sheet. Assume that the company had $3,230 in sales revenue during January 2003 from selling hair care supplies to beauty shops. Additionally, the business earned $990 in rent revenue by renting some spare space in the back of its building during January. Also assume that expenses during the period were $955 for cost of goods sold, $675 for wages, $310 for utilities, and $120 for interest payments. Exhibit 4–3 on page F–122 shows a single-step income statement for Jessica's Beauty Supply, Inc., for the month ended January 31, 2003.

Income statements for proprietorships, partnerships, and corporations are quite similar to one another. The main difference between them is that corporations pay income tax, while proprietorships and partnerships do not. Therefore, if we were to prepare an income statement for our example company assuming it was organized as

---

Jessica's Beauty Supply, Inc.
Income Statement
For the Month Ended January 31, 2003

Revenues:		
Sales	$3,230	
Rent revenue	990	
Total revenues		$4,220
Expenses:		
Cost of goods sold	955	
Wages expense	675	
Utilities expense	310	
Interest expense	120	
Total expenses		(2,060)
Income before income tax		2,160
Income tax expense		540
Net income		$1,620

EXHIBIT 4–3   Single-Step Income Statement Format

---

either a proprietorship or a partnership, the only differences would be the company names and the absence of income tax. Accordingly, if Jessica's business was organized under the proprietorship form or the partnership form, the company's net income in either case would be the $2,160 instead of the after-tax amount of $1,620.

MULTIPLE-STEP FORMAT OF THE INCOME STATEMENT

multiple-step income statement   An income statement format that highlights gross margin and operating income.

gross margin   An item shown on a multiple-step income statement, calculated as: Sales – Cost of goods sold.

operating income   Income produced by the major business activity of the company. An item shown on the multiple-step income statement.

sales revenue   The revenue generated from the sale of a tangible product as a major business activity.

The **multiple-step income statement** provides two items of information not presented in a single-step income statement: (1) **gross margin** or *gross profit* and (2) **operating income** or *income from operations*. The single-step income statement format simply sums all revenues and all expenses. No special consideration is given to any specific revenue or expense. In contrast, the multiple-step format arranges revenue and expense items to highlight their relationship to one another. Exhibit 4–4 shows a multiple-step income statement for Jessica's Beauty Supply, Inc., for the month ended January 31, 2003. As you can see, the net income using the multiple-step format is the same as that shown on the single-step income statement in Exhibit 4–3. Notice, though, that the multiple-step format makes two important stops before arriving at the bottom line: gross margin and operating income (thus the term *multiple-step*).

Gross margin is an important piece of information shown on a multiple-step income statement. This item highlights the relationship between sales revenue and cost of goods sold. Recall that **sales revenue,** sometimes simply called *sales*, is the revenue generated from the sale of tangible products. Cost of goods sold is the cost of the products that have been sold. Sales revenue minus cost of goods sold equals gross margin, or gross profit as it is sometimes called. For example, *Nike* sells running shoes and other products to generate sales revenue. *Nike*'s cost of goods sold is the cost of all the products it actually sells during a particular period. The difference between these amounts represents *Nike*'s gross margin. For 2001, *Nike* reported sales of $9.49 billion and cost of goods sold totaling $5.78 billion. The company's 2001 gross margin, therefore, was $3.71 billion.

Discussion Question ●

4-4. Identify two manufacturing or merchandising companies and describe their source of sales revenue and the components of their cost of goods sold.

A merchandiser or manufacturer cannot be profitable unless it sells its products for more than it pays for them. Gross margin represents how much more a company

---

Jessica's Beauty Supply, Inc.
Income Statement
For the Month Ended January 31, 2003

Sales		$3,230
Less: Cost of goods sold		955
Gross margin		2,275
Operating expenses:		
Wages expense	$675	
Utilities expense	310	
Total operating expenses		(985)
Operating income		1,290
Other revenues:		
Rent revenue		990
Other expenses:		
Interest expense		(120)
Income before income tax		2,160
Income tax expense		(540)
Net income		$1,620

EXHIBIT 4-4   Multiple-Step Income Statement Format

received from the sale of its products than what the products cost the company. It also represents the amount available from sales to cover all other expenses the company incurs. For example, assume Kay Carnes Merchandising Company sells its product for $30 per unit. Assume further that each unit costs Carnes $24. If the company sold 5,000 units of product in January, it would have a gross margin of $30,000, calculated as follows:

Sales (5,000 × $30)	$150,000
LESS: Cost of goods sold (5,000 × $24)	120,000
Gross margin	$ 30,000

This $30,000 represents the amount Carnes has to cover all the company's other expenses for January. Assuming the company had no revenues other than sales, if those other expenses were less than $30,000, the company would have a net income for the month; if the other expenses were greater than $30,000, the company would experience a net loss.

Economic decision makers use gross margin as one measure to evaluate the performance of a manufacturing or merchandising company. Examining gross margin allows financial statement readers to quickly see the relationship among revenue produced by selling a product, the cost of the product, and all the other expenses the company incurs.

Discussion Question   ●

4-5. Consider the following simplified multiple-step income statement:

Kanaly Company
Income Statement
For the Year Ended December 31, 2003

Sales (1,000 units)	$375,000
LESS: Cost of goods sold	380,000
Gross margin	$ (5,000)
LESS: Operating expenses	(32,000)
Net income (loss)	$(37,000)

a. What can you learn about Kanaly Company from its gross margin?
b. If the selling price per unit remains constant, how many units must the company sell to earn a net income of $2,000?
c. If the company sells 1,000 units, at what selling price per unit would Kanaly earn a $5,000 net income?

In addition to highlighting the relationship between sales and cost of goods sold, the multiple-step income statement separates income generated by a firm's ongoing major business activity from revenues and expenses generated by secondary or incidental sources. Operating income or income from operations denotes the results associated with a company's primary business activity. For example, for a merchandiser, operating income would include all revenue and expenses related to the sale of products but would exclude revenues and expenses associated with incidental activities such as interest revenue, rent revenue, and interest expense. A quick look back at Exhibit 4–4 demonstrates this for Jessica's Beauty Supply, Inc. By separating the revenue and expenses in this way, a financial statement user learns not only the amount of the company's net income, but also the sources of that net income. When economic decision makers are attempting to use the past performance of a company as presented on the income statement to predict the future, operating income may be more useful than net income as an indicator of future performance. Therefore, multiple-step income statements may prove more useful than single-step statements.

NET INCOME AS AN INCREASE IN OWNERS' EQUITY

Net income increases the owners' equity in the business. Recall from our discussion of the elements found in a balance sheet, one of the two sources of owners' equity is earned equity. In this context, when we talk about a company's "earnings," we are really talking about its net income. Each revenue increases earned equity and each expense decreases earned equity. A net income, therefore, increases earned equity, while a net loss decreases earned equity.

A company's equity will change by the amount of its net income or loss. This means that the amounts reflected on the income statement have a direct effect on the amounts that appear on the balance sheet. A company that has income on its income statement will have a greater amount of retained earnings. This link is very logical when you realize that the past performance of a company is at least partially responsible for its present condition.

◆ DISTRIBUTIONS TO OWNERS

distributions to owners
Decreases in equity resulting from transferring assets to the owners of an enterprise.

In time, if the operations of a company are profitable, owners' equity will increase. Eventually, the owners will expect the company to distribute at least some of the earned equity to them. **Distributions to owners** is another accounting element shown in Exhibit 4–1. The FASB's *Conceptual Framework* defines distributions to owners as *decreases in equity of a particular business enterprise resulting from transferring assets, rendering services, or incurring liabilities by the enterprise to owners. Distributions to owners decrease ownership interest (or equity) in an enterprise* (Statement of Financial Accounting Concepts No. 6, paragraph 67). Just as net income increases owners' equity, distributions to owners decrease owners' equity.

Don't think of these distributions as salaries or wages paid to the owners. Distributions to owners are a distribution of income, *not* part of the expenses deducted from revenue to calculate income. Thus, they are not shown on the income statement. Distributions to owners represent a return on the investment they made. Regardless of the organizational form of the company, distributions to owners reduce total owners' equity.

PROPRIETORSHIPS AND PARTNERSHIPS—DRAWINGS

In the case of a proprietorship or partnership, little beyond common sense restricts the owners from taking money out of the company. If the cash is available and is not

drawings   Distributions to the owners of proprietorships and partnerships. Also called withdrawals.

needed by the business, the owner or owners may take it for their personal use. The distributions to the owners of proprietorships and partnerships are called **drawings** or *withdrawals*.

Partnership agreements may state explicitly when and in what amounts partners may take withdrawals, or they may leave it to the discretion of the partners. Clearly, the partnership must have sufficient cash to support the actions of its owners. When thinking of making a withdrawal of cash from the company, a partner must consider the impact of this action on his or her capital in the partnership. Partners may take withdrawals that are disproportionate to the profit-sharing arrangement. Frequently, partners agree to allow one partner to take larger withdrawals because of an unusual personal need. Another partner may decide to not take normal withdrawals but to leave the capital in the business. The timing and amount of partners' withdrawals are a common source of partnership conflict and, in severe cases, can lead to the dissolution of a partnership.

CORPORATIONS—DIVIDENDS

dividends   A distribution of earnings from a corporation to its owners. Dividends are most commonly distributed in the form of cash.

Owners of corporations (stockholders) may have much less control over when and in what amount they receive a distribution than do owners of proprietorships or partnerships. This is particularly true in large corporations. As we have already mentioned, distributions to owners of a corporation are called **dividends.** By law, unless there are contractual arrangements to the contrary, dividend distributions to shareholders must be proportionate to the number of shares they own. Although not legally required to do so, virtually all corporations pay dividends at some point in their existence.

Why do corporations pay dividends if they are not legally required to do so? In the long run, corporate investors demand this distribution. A number of factors cause a company's stock to either increase or decrease in value, but probably the most important factor is whether or not the company is profitable. Profitability is vital because investors know that profits lead to future dividends. A profitable corporation is more likely to pay dividends, and more profit ultimately means more dividends. On the other hand, if a corporation sustains losses or lacks the free cash to pay dividends, investors react and the demand for the company's stock declines. This decline in demand will result in falling stock prices. When this situation occurs, the corporation may find it difficult to obtain funds necessary to support its operations. Opportunities for both major types of external funding—issuing stock and borrowing funds—may disappear. Eventually, if enough people lose faith in the company, it will run out of cash and cease to exist. This explains why corporate executives are so interested in investor perception.

Some successful companies resist the pressure to pay dividends in order to reinvest profits to build the company for a better future, and they clearly communicate this strategy to the stockholders. *Microsoft* is one such company. Investors have accepted *Microsoft*'s reinvestment policy as a wise business strategy, and the company's stock price has not suffered.

The board of directors makes all decisions associated with the corporation's dividend policy. The policy includes whether or not to pay a dividend, the type of dividend to be paid, and when the dividend will be paid. The board of directors can also choose to distribute additional shares of the firm's stock as a dividend, called a stock dividend. It is, however, much more common for companies to distribute cash dividends. Of the 600 companies surveyed in 2001 by *Accounting Trends and Techniques*, 403 paid a cash dividend in 2000.[2]

CASH DIVIDENDS ON COMMON STOCK

A cash payment is what comes to mind when we hear the word *dividend*. To be able to pay a cash dividend, a corporation must have two things: sufficient retained earnings and sufficient cash.

---

[2]*Accounting Trends and Techniques* (AICPA, 2001), 433.

1. *Sufficient Retained Earnings.* Dividends are distributions of earnings; however, corporations are not restricted to the current year's earnings to cover the distribution. Although it may be desirable for a company to declare dividends from the current year's earnings, dividends are actually declared from retained earnings. Remember, net income is only this period's addition to retained earnings; thus, it is not necessary that current net income be greater than the dividend amount. The legal requirement is that the retained earnings balance exceeds the amount of the dividend. Exhibit 4–5 shows how retained earnings increase over time and how net income, net losses, and dividends affect them.

EXHIBIT 4–5   Effect of Net Income, Net Losses, and Dividends on Retained Earnings

Year	2001	2002	2003	2004	2005
Beginning retained Earnings balance	$ -0-	$ 800	$1,300	$ 700	$1,150
Net income (loss)	800	1,000	(100)	950	400
	800	1,800	1,200	1,650	1,550
Dividends	-0-	(500)	(500)	(500)	(500)
Ending retained Earnings balance	$ 800	$1,300	$ 700	$1,150	$1,050

Note two things as you look at Exhibit 4–5. First, the ending balance of one period (in this case, a year) becomes the beginning balance of the next period. This is something you should know and understand because, in addition to its applicability to retained earnings, it is a very common phenomenon in accounting in general. Second, the payment of dividends is not directly related to the profits of a given period. In 2003, for example, this company paid dividends even though it experienced a net loss for the year, and in 2005, it paid out more in dividends than it earned for the year. This company appears to have adopted a policy of paying $500 per year in total dividends, regardless of its net income or loss for a particular year. This policy is perfectly acceptable, as long as the company has both sufficient retained earnings and sufficient cash each year to cover the dividend amount.

2. *Sufficient Cash.* Bear in mind that retained earnings is not cash. The only item on the balance sheet that represents cash is the cash amount. Basically, retained earnings is the sum of all profits earned by the corporation since its inception minus all dividends. Except by extraordinary coincidence, the amount of retained earnings and the amount of cash on hand will differ. (In Chapter 5, we explore the reasons for the difference between cash and retained earnings.) A corporation must make certain it has, or can get, sufficient cash to pay the dividend. A company may feel so compelled to pay its regular cash dividend that it will borrow the cash it needs if the company's cash balance is insufficient.

Dividend Dates

The shares of stock of most large corporations are owned by thousands of investors and these shares change hands constantly. It is impossible for these publicly traded corporations to know exactly who owns their stock at a given moment because the stock is bought and sold every day and it takes time for the corporations to obtain and record the stock transaction information. For this reason, corporations do not declare and pay a dividend on the same day.

Three important dates are associated with the payment of a cash dividend:

date of declaration The date upon which a corporation announces plans to distribute a dividend. At this point, the corporation becomes legally obligated to make the distribution: A liability is created.

1. Date of Declaration. As stated earlier, the board of directors decides whether and when to pay a cash dividend. The day the board votes to pay a dividend is the date of declaration. The date of declaration marks the creation of the corporation's legal liability to pay the dividend.

date of record Owners of the shares of stock on this day are the ones who will receive the dividend announced on the date of declaration.

date of payment The date a corporate dividend is actually paid. The payment date is generally announced on the date of declaration.

2. **Date of Record.** Whoever owns shares of stock on the date of record will receive the dividend. Every time a company's stock changes hands, the company is notified, although that notification may take several days or even weeks, especially in large corporations. Accordingly, the date of record may follow the date of declaration by several weeks.
3. **Date of Payment.** The date the dividend is actually paid is the date of payment. The corporation pays the dividend to whoever owned shares of stock on the date of record, even though some of those people may have sold their shares of stock between the date of record and the date of payment. The payment of the cash dividend satisfies the company's liability for the dividend.

Generally, on the date the board of directors declares a dividend, the date of record and the date of payment are publicly announced as shown in Exhibit 4–6.

EXHIBIT 4-6   Examples of Dividends Reported in 2002

Company	Per.	Amount	Declaration Date	Record Date	Payment Date
IBM	Q	$.15	Apr. 30, 2002	May 10, 2002	June 10, 2002
Boeing	Q	.17	June 24, 2002	Aug. 16, 2002	Sept. 6, 2002
Southwest Airlines	Q	.045	July 18, 2002	Sept. 4, 2002	Sept. 25, 2002
ExxonMobil	Q	.23	Aug. 9, 2002	Aug. 13, 2002	Sept. 10, 2002
Wendy's Intl. Inc.	Q	.06	July 25, 2002	Aug. 5, 2002	Aug. 19, 2002

Discussion Questions

Let's say today is August 15, 2002. Use the information in Exhibit 4–6 to answer Discussion Questions 4–6 through 4–9.

4–6. You own 100 shares of ***ExxonMobil*** stock. How much is the next dividend you expect to receive and when do you expect to receive it?
4–7. How would the information in Exhibit 4–6 affect you if you were going to sell your shares of ***Southwest Airlines*** stock in the next few days?
4–8. You own 200 shares of ***Wendy's International.*** About how much would you expect to receive in dividends during the next year?
4–9. Which of the stocks listed has a dividend rate per share nearest to that of ***Boeing?***
4–10. An outspoken investor advocate, Ms. Nadera Ralphino, has just criticized Mega-Millions because the company paid only a $.60 per share dividend even though it has retained earnings of $6 billion. Why might Ms. Ralphino's criticism be unjustified?

CASH DIVIDENDS ON PREFERRED STOCK

The procedures associated with the payment of dividends on preferred stock are exactly the same as those for common stock. As with dividends on common stock, the board of directors declares preferred dividends and the dividends are paid in accordance with the three dividend dates outlined previously. The distinctions between common and preferred dividends are based on the preference features of preferred stocks. If a corporation has preferred stock and it elects to pay dividends, the preferred stockholders receive their dividend before the common stockholders can be paid.

◆ INTRODUCTION TO THE STATEMENT OF OWNERS' EQUITY

The **statement of owners' equity** is a bridge between the income statement and the balance sheet. The statement of owners' equity shows the changes to owners' equity from the beginning of the income statement period to the end of that period. The ending bal-

statement of owners' equity The financial statement that reports activity in the capital accounts of proprietorships and partnerships and in the stockholders' equity accounts of corporations. The statement of owners' equity serves as a bridge between the income statement and the balance sheet.

ance shown on the statement of owners' equity is equal to the amount shown for owners' equity on the balance sheet.

Owners' equity has three basic components: *contributions by owners, earned equity*, and *distributions to owners*. The earned equity, of course, is a culmination of all the revenues and expenses, netted to arrive at net income or net loss. For the remainder of our discussion here, we will use net income or net loss in place of earnings or revenues and expenses. The basic idea of the statement of owners' equity is expressed in the following equation:

$$
\begin{aligned}
&\text{Beginning Owners' Equity}\\
+\ &\text{Contributions by Owners}\\
+\ &\text{Net Income}\\
-\ &\underline{\text{Distributions to Owners}}\\
=\ &\text{Ending Owners' Equity}
\end{aligned}
$$

Although the specifics of the statement vary according to the organizational form of the company, all statements include a beginning equity balance, the changes in equity caused by the three components of equity, and an ending balance.

PROPRIETORSHIPS—STATEMENT OF CAPITAL

statement of capital A statement of owner's equity for a proprietorship.

Earned equity goes by various names, depending on the form of the business. Proprietorships and partnerships usually make no distinction between the equity from owner investments and earned equity. Because both forms of business are legally considered mere extensions of their owner or owners, the contributed equity and earned equity are combined and shown as one amount under the title "owners' equity" or "owners' capital." The statement of owner's equity for a sole proprietorship is generally called the **statement of capital.** In this context, the word *capital* refers to owner's equity. Exhibit 4–7 shows the format of a proprietorship's statement of capital using Jessica's Beauty Supply as an example. Note that the statement shows the changes in capital arising from the three components of equity and that the heading indicates the particular time period the statement reflects. This time period is usually the same one used in preparation of the income statement. Remember that, generally speaking, the ending balance of one period becomes the beginning balance for the next. Since this is Jessica's first month of operation, there was no beginning balance. The $10,000 contribution by owner is the investment Jessica made to start her business, as we discussed in Chapter 3. Remember, because a proprietorship pays no income tax, the company's net income would be $2,160, as we mentioned earlier in this chapter. We can also see that Jessica took a draw of $500, shown as a reduction of capital on the statement. The ending balance is calculated by combining the beginning balance of owner's capital, the contribution by owner, and the net income for the month. Then the distribution to Jessica is deducted to arrive at the ending balance of capital. It is important to note that this ending balance appears not only on the statement of capital but also in the owner's equity section of the balance sheet. Earlier, we said that the statement of owners' equity acts as a bridge between the income statement and the balance sheet. Now you

EXHIBIT 4–7 Statement of Capital for a Proprietorship	
Jessica's Beauty Supply Statement of Capital For the Month Ended January 31, 2003	
Jessica, capital, January 1, 2003	$ 0
ADD: Contributions by owner	10,000
Net income	2,160
	12,160
DEDUCT: Drawings (distributions to owner)	(500)
Jessica, capital, January 31, 2003	$11,660

can see that it bridges the statements by using the net income figure from the income statement to help calculate the ending owners' equity that appears on the balance sheet.

PARTNERSHIPS—STATEMENT OF CAPITAL

statement of partners' capital   A statement of owners' equity for a partnership.

A statement of capital for a partnership would follow the same general outline as that for a proprietorship but might be designated a **statement of partners' capital.** As we mentioned earlier in this chapter, because a partnership pays no income tax, the company's net income would be $2,160. Of course, there would be a capital balance for each partner, and the partners would share the net income of $2,160 according to their partnership agreement. Using Jessica and Stephanie's partnership as an example, Exhibit 4–8 shows a statement of capital for this type of business form assuming Jessica's drawings were $400 and Stephanie's drawings were $100.

Exhibit 4–8 assumes that the partners, Jessica and Stephanie, have agreed to share the net income in the same proportion as their initial investments. Thus, Jessica is entitled to a capital increase of 60 percent of the total net income for the period, and Stephanie is entitled to an increase of 40 percent of the net income.

EXHIBIT 4–8   Statement of Partners' Capital for a Partnership

Jessica and Stephanie's Beauty Supply
Statement of Partners' Capital
For the Month Ended January 31, 2003

Jessica, capital, January 1, 2003	$ 0	
ADD: Jessica's contribution	6,000	
Net income	1,296	
LESS: Drawings (distributions to owners)	(400)	
Jessica, capital, January 31, 2003		$ 6,896
Stephanie, capital, January 1, 2003	0	
ADD: Stephanie's contribution	4,000	
Net income	864	
LESS: Drawings (distributions to owners)	(100)	
Stephanie, capital, January 31, 2003		4,764
Total partners' capital, January 31, 2003		$11,660

As you can see from the exhibit, this statement of capital shows the impact of a withdrawal made by the partners. Jessica has taken a withdrawal of $400 while Stephanie took a withdrawal of only $100. This action reduces the amount of their capital accounts and the total amount of partners' equity.

CORPORATIONS—STATEMENT OF STOCKHOLDERS' EQUITY

statement of stockholders' equity   The financial statement that shows the changes in owners' equity for a corporation for a given time period.

The statement that shows the changes in owners' equity for a corporation is called the **statement of stockholders' equity.** Corporations are legally required to keep the equity from owners' investment and the earned equity separate. In corporations, you will recall, the investment by owners is called *contributed capital* and earned equity is called *retained earnings.*

The format of the statement of stockholders' equity varies somewhat from company to company, but the main idea is to trace the balances in stock, additional paid-in capital, and retained earnings from the beginning of the period to the end. The statement of stockholders' equity for Jessica's Beauty Supply, Inc., in Exhibit 4–9 on page F–130 traces common and preferred stock, additional paid-in capital, and retained earnings from their balances on January 1 to their balances on January 31, 2003.

The beginning balances on the statement of stockholders' equity are the previous period's ending balances. All the beginning balances are zero in this statement because

<table>
<tr><td colspan="7" align="center">Jessica's Beauty Supply, Inc.
Statement of Stockholders' Equity
For the Month Ended January 31, 2003</td></tr>
<tr><th></th><th>Preferred
Stock</th><th>Additional
Paid-in
Capital
Preferred</th><th>Common
Stock</th><th>Additional
Paid-in
Capital
Common</th><th>Retained
Earnings</th><th>Total
Stockholders'
Equity</th></tr>
<tr><td>Balance, January 1, 2003</td><td>$ 0</td><td>$ 0</td><td>$ 0</td><td>$ 0</td><td>$ 0</td><td>$ 0</td></tr>
<tr><td>Common stock issued</td><td></td><td></td><td>4,000</td><td>36,000</td><td></td><td>40,000</td></tr>
<tr><td>Preferred stock issued</td><td>20,000</td><td>1,000</td><td></td><td></td><td></td><td>21,000</td></tr>
<tr><td>Net income</td><td></td><td></td><td></td><td></td><td>1,620</td><td>1,620</td></tr>
<tr><td>Preferred dividends</td><td></td><td></td><td></td><td></td><td>(100)</td><td>(100)</td></tr>
<tr><td>Common dividends</td><td></td><td></td><td></td><td></td><td>(400)</td><td>(400)</td></tr>
<tr><td>Balance, January 31</td><td>$20,000</td><td>$1,000</td><td>$4,000</td><td>$36,000</td><td>$1,120</td><td>$62,120</td></tr>
</table>

EXHIBIT 4–9   Statement of Stockholders' Equity for Jessica's Beauty Supply, Inc.

this is the company's first month of operation. Notice that the statement of stockholders' equity reflects activity in both types of owners' equity—contributed capital and earned equity. Common and preferred stock and additional paid-in capital are components of contributed capital, and retained earnings represents the earned equity portion of stockholders' equity. The amount of retained earnings is increased by net income each period or decreased by net loss and decreased by dividend distributions to stockholders. The net income figure comes directly from the income statement. The dividend of $500 is comprised of $400 for common stock (4,000 × $.10 per share) and $100 for preferred stock (200 × $.50 per share), and it reduces retained earnings. Notice that the income and dividends affect only the retained earnings section. Both net income and dividends change the balance in retained earnings, but neither affects any part of contributed capital. We use the totals at the bottom of the statement of stockholders' equity to prepare the stockholders' equity section of the balance sheet.

Exhibit 4–10 outlines the differences among owners' equity for the three business forms we examined for Jessica's beauty supply company.

EXHIBIT 4–10   Owners' Equity by Business Organizational Form

	Proprietorship	*Partnership*	*Corporation*
Name of Statement	Statement of capital	Statement of partners' capital	• Statement of stockholders' equity
Statement Sections	Capital	Partner's capital	• Contributed capital • Retained earnings
Equity Account Titles	Jessica, capital	Jessica, capital Stephanie, capital	• Common stock • Preferred stock • Additional paid-in capital • Retained earnings

Discussion Question

4–11. How would it be possible for Jessica's Beauty Supply, Inc., to have a zero balance in retained earnings on January 1, 2003, even if January 2003 was not the company's first month of business? Is there any other financial statement information that might confirm that this was the first month of operations?

statement of retained earnings A corporate financial statement that shows the changes in retained earnings during a particular period.

STATEMENT OF RETAINED EARNINGS

If a corporation has not issued stock or engaged in any other activity that would affect contributed capital, it may issue a **statement of retained earnings** instead of the more comprehensive statement of stockholders' equity. A statement of retained earnings is similar in form to the statement of capital for proprietorships and partnerships. Exhibit 4–11 presents a statement of retained earnings for Jessica's Beauty Supply, Inc.

EXHIBIT 4–11   Statement of Retained Earnings for Jessica's Beauty Supply, Inc.

Jessica's Beauty Supply, Inc.
Statement of Retained Earnings
For the Month Ended January 31, 2003

Retained earnings, January 1, 2003		$ 0
ADD: Net income		1,620
		$1,620
DEDUCT: Preferred dividends	(100)	
Common dividends	(400)	(500)
Retained earnings, January 31, 2003		$1,120

This simpler statement is an acceptable substitute for the statement of stockholders' equity only if no changes have been made in a corporation's contributed capital. However, because most corporations are frequently involved in activities affecting their stock or other parts of their contributed capital, corporations use the statement of stockholders' equity more often than the statement of retained earnings. Of the 600 companies surveyed in 2001 by *Accounting Trends and Techniques*, 577 used the statement of stockholders' equity in 2000.[3] Only seven of the corporations presented a statement of retained earnings. The remaining group did not present either form of this "bridge statement," but rather placed a schedule in the notes to their financial statements.

◆ ARTICULATION

articulation   The links among the financial statements.

Earlier in this chapter, we referred to the link between income and owners' equity. We call this link the **articulation** (or connection) of the financial statements. When preparing financial statements, accountants prepare the income statement first, the statement of owners' equity second, and the balance sheet last. This is because the net income amount must be taken from the income statement and placed on the statement of owners' equity. Further, the ending balances from the statement of owners' equity are used to prepare the balance sheet. Amounts from one statement are needed to complete the next statement. While we will demonstrate articulation using only the corporate form, the concept is the same for proprietorships and partnerships. The blue lines on the financial statements in Exhibit 4–12 on page F–132 depict the articulation among the statements for Jessica's Beauty Supply, Inc.

As Exhibit 4–12 demonstrates, we prepare the income statement first to calculate net income. Then, we use net income from the income statement to prepare the statement of stockholders' equity. Finally, we use the ending balances shown on the statement of stockholders' equity to prepare the balance sheet. And after all this, the accounting equation shows that this important relationship still holds true.

Assets   = Liabilities + Owners' Equity

$312,120 = $250,000 + $62,120

Discussion Question   ◦◦◦◦◦◦◦◦◦◦◦◦◦◦◦◦◦◦◦◦◦◦◦◦◦◦◦◦◦

4–12. If a clerk in Jessica's Beauty Supply, Inc., decided to slip the cash from a sale into his pocket and not record the sale, how would each of the statements in Exhibit 4–12 be affected?

---

[3]*Accounting Trends and Techniques* (AICPA, 2001), 43.

Jessica's Beauty Supply, Inc.
Income Statement
For the Month Ended January 31, 2003

Sales		$3,230
Less cost of goods sold		955
Gross margin		2,275
Operating expenses:		
Wages expense	$675	
Utilities expense	310	
Total operating expenses		(985)
Operating income		1,290
Other revenues:		
Rent revenue		990
Other expenses:		
Interest expense		(120)
Income before income tax		2,160
Income tax expense		(540)
Net income		$1,620

Statement of Stockholders' Equity
For the Month Ended January 31, 2003

	Preferred Stock	Additional Paid-in Capital Preferred	Common Stock	Additional Paid-in Capital Common	Retained Earnings	Total Stockholders' Equity
Balance, January 1, 2003	$ 0	$ 0	$ 0	$ 0	$ 0	$ 0
Common stock issued			4,000	36,000		40,000
Preferred stock issued	20,000	1,000				21,000
Net income					1,620	1,620
Preferred dividends					(100)	(100)
Common dividends					(400)	(400)
Balance, January 31	$20,000	$1,000	$4,000	$36,000	$1,120	$62,120

Balance Sheet
January 31, 2003

Assets:		Liabilities:	
Cash	$ 82,120	Notes payable	$ 50,000
Land	50,000	Bonds payable	200,000
Building	120,000	Total liabilites	250,000
Computer equipment	35,000	Stockholders' equity:	
Truck	25,000	Preferred stock	$ 20,000
		Additional paid-in capital—preferred	1,000
		Common stock	4,000
		Additional paid-in capital—common	36,000
		Total contributed capital	61,000
		Retained earnings	1,120
		Total stockholders' equity	62,120
Total Assets	$312,120	Total liabilities and stockholders' equity	$312,120

EXHIBIT 4–12 Articulation Among Financial Statements for Jessica's Beauty Supply, Inc.

◆ STATEMENT OF CASH FLOWS

operating activities
Activities that result in cash inflows and outflows generated from the normal course of business.

As we mentioned in Chapter 3, the **operating activities** section of the statement of cash flows includes cash inflows and outflows for revenues and expenses associated with a company's ongoing business operations. Basically, these activities are related to the items found on the income statement. To simplify our introduction to the operating activities section of the statement of cash flows, we will assume that all of Jessica's Beauty Supply, Inc.'s revenues and expenses are received and paid in cash. Exhibit 4–13 shows the statement of cash flows for Jessica's Beauty Supply, Inc., for the month ended January 31, 2003.

Except for adding the $500 cash paid for dividends, we used the cash flow from investing and financing activities prepared in Chapter 3 for Jessica's Beauty Supply, Inc. As you can see, the statement of cash flows provides a wealth of important information. Not only does the statement show the ending cash balance, but it also tells us about the sources and uses of cash.

Discussion Questions

4–13. Where did Jessica's Beauty Supply, Inc., get most of its cash?

4–14. Where did Jessica's Beauty Supply, Inc., use the most cash?

4–15. The cash balance for Jessica's Beauty Supply, Inc., grew to $82,120 during its first month of business. Based on the statement of cash flows in Exhibit 4–13, do you think there are any problems with the company's cash situation?

EXHIBIT 4-13   Statement of Cash Flows for Jessica's Beauty Supply, Inc.

Jessica's Beauty Supply, Inc.
Statement of Cash Flows
For the Month Ended January 31, 2003

Cash flows from operating activities:		
Cash collections from customers	$ 3,230	
Cash received for rent	990	
Cash paid for merchandise	(955)	
Cash paid for wages	(675)	
Cash paid for utilities	(310)	
Cash paid for interest	(120)	
Cash paid for income tax	(540)	
Net cash flows from operating activities		$ 1,620
Cash flows from investing activities:		
Purchase of land	(50,000)	
Purchase of building	(120,000)	
Purchase of computer equipment	(35,000)	
Purchase of truck	(25,000)	
Net cash flows from investing activities		(230,000)
Cash flows from financing activities:		
Sale of common stock	40,000	
Sale of preferred stock	21,000	
Borrowing on notes payable	50,000	
Sale of bonds	200,000	
Cash paid for preferred dividends	(100)	
Cash paid for common dividends	(400)	
Net cash flows from financing activities		310,500
Increase in cash		82,120
Cash at the beginning of the period		0
Cash at the end of the period		$ 82,120

Now that we have a complete set of financial statements for Jessica's Beauty Supply, Inc., the question is, how is the company doing? Would it be a good investment? Would it be a good credit risk?

At the beginning of the chapter, we posed the hypothetical situation in which you were a loan officer evaluating the credit risk of a particular customer. Let's assume that Jessica's Beauty Supply, Inc., is that customer. Should you lend the $150,000 to Jessica's Beauty Supply, Inc.? It may be difficult to tell without additional information and without analyzing Jessica's financial statements.

PROFITABILITY RATIOS

In this chapter, we will present seven ratios used to evaluate profitability: gross profit margin ratio, net profit margin ratio, rate of return on assets ratio, rate of return on common equity ratio, dividend payout ratio, earnings per share, and the price-to-earnings ratio.

Gross Profit Margin Ratio

gross profit margin ratio
A financial ratio that expresses a company's gross profit (often called gross margin on the financial statements) as a percentage of sales revenue.

The **gross profit margin ratio** expresses a company's gross profit (often called gross margin on the financial statements) as a percentage of sales revenue. The formula for this ratio is:

$$\text{Gross Profit Margin Ratio} = \frac{\text{Gross Profit}}{\text{Net Sales}}$$

Using the information from the financial statements for Jessica's Beauty Supply, Inc., in Exhibit 4–12, the calculation is as follows:

$$\frac{\$2,275}{\$3,230} = .704 \text{ or } 70.4\%$$

The gross profit margin ratio for Jessica's company indicates that gross profit is 70.4 percent of sales.

This ratio calculation tells us that after covering the cost of products sold during the month, Jessica had 70.4 percent of each sales dollar remaining to cover all the company's operating expenses, interest cost, and income taxes. You can also look at it this way: For every one dollar of sales, the company had about 70.4 cents remaining after it paid for the merchandise it sold. This 70.4 cents is what Jessica's Beauty Supply, Inc., has left to pay all its other costs. Gross profit margin ratios vary from industry to industry, but clearly, the higher the gross profit margin percentage, the better.

Net Profit Margin Ratio

net profit margin ratio
A financial ratio that expresses a company's net profit (almost always called either net income or net earnings on the financial statements) as a percentage of sales revenue. It indicates the amount of net income generated by a dollar of sales.

The **net profit margin ratio** expresses a company's net profit (almost always called either net income or net earnings on the financial statements) as a percentage of sales revenue. It indicates the amount of net income generated by a dollar of sales. The formula for this ratio is:

$$\text{Net Profit Margin Ratio} = \frac{\text{Net Profit}}{\text{Net Sales}}$$

Using the information from the financial statements for Jessica's Beauty Supply, Inc., in Exhibit 4–12, the calculation is as follows:

$$\frac{\$1,620}{\$3,230} = .502 \text{ or } 50.2\%$$

This ratio tells us that during the month, Jessica's Beauty Supply, Inc., had 50.2 percent of each sales dollar remaining as profit after covering the cost of products sold, all operating expenses, interest cost, and income taxes. In other words, it reveals the percentage of each sales dollar remaining after *all* the costs of running the business for the year. So for every one dollar of sales, Jessica's had about 50.2 cents (of each sales dollar) remaining after it paid its costs for the year. Net profit margin ratios vary from industry to industry, but clearly, the higher the net profit margin percentage, the better.

Rate of Return on Assets Ratio

rate of return on assets ratio   A financial ratio that shows the amount of profit (net income) produced for a given level of assets.

The **rate of return on assets ratio** shows the amount of profit (net income) produced for a given level of assets. This is an important ratio because it indicates how effectively the company uses its total assets to generate net income. The formula for this ratio is:

$$\text{Rate of Return on Assets Ratio} = \frac{\text{Net Income}}{\text{Average Total Assets}}$$

The net income amount we use in the numerator of this ratio comes directly from the income statement. The amount we use as the denominator requires a bit of explanation. Since the net income in the numerator was earned throughout the month of January 2003 (some in the first week, some in the second, etc.), we want to know the amount of assets employed throughout the month. We determine this by calculating the average of the total assets. This is done by adding the beginning balance of total assets to the ending balance of total assets and then dividing that number by two. Since January 2003 is the first month of operation for Jessica's Beauty Supply, Inc., the beginning balance of total assets is $0. The ending balance comes from the January 31, 2003, balance sheet ($312,120). The average total assets for the month of January is $156,060 ($0 + $312,120 = $312,120/2 = $156,060). We calculate Jessica's rate of return on assets for January 2003 as:

$$\frac{\$1,620}{\$156,060} = .0104 \text{ or } 1.04\%$$

The return on assets for Jessica's Beauty Supply, Inc., indicates the company earned a return of only 1 percent on average total assets during January 2003. Even though the return on assets will vary depending on the industry and company, this return seems particularly low. What do you think?

Rate of Return on Common Equity Ratio

rate of return on common equity ratio   A financial ratio that shows the amount of profit (net income) in relation to the amount of investment by the company's owners.

The **rate of return on common equity ratio** shows the amount of profit (net income) in relation to the amount of investment by the company's owners. The purpose of this ratio is similar to that of the rate of return on assets ratio except that it focuses on the owners' investment (represented by the equity), rather than total assets. The formula for this ratio is:

$$\text{Rate of Return on Common Equity Ratio} = \frac{\text{Net Income} - \text{Total Preferred Dividends}}{\text{Average Common Stockholders' Equity}}$$

The net income used in the numerator of this ratio comes from the income statement, but it must be adjusted for any preferred stock dividend requirement, because that amount is not available to common stockholders. As Jessica's Beauty Supply, Inc.'s statement of stockholders' equity shows, the company paid a preferred dividend totaling $100 to Stephanie ($0.50 × 200 shares).

We use an average amount for the denominator in this calculation for the same reason we did in the rate of return on assets ratio. Since the net income in the numerator was earned throughout the month of January, we want to know the amount of common equity throughout the month. We determine this by calculating the average of the common stockholders' equity. This is done by adding the beginning balance of common stockholders' equity to the ending balance of common stockholders' equity and then dividing that number by two. Since January 2003 is the first month of operation for Jessica's Beauty Supply, Inc., the beginning balance of common stockholders' equity is $0. The ending balance comes from the January 31, 2003, balance sheet ($62,120 − $21,000 preferred stock = $41,120). The average common stockholders' equity for the month of January is $20,560 ($0 + $41,120 = $41,120/2 = $20,560). We calculate Jessica's rate of return on common equity for January 2003 as:

$$\frac{\$1,620 - \$100}{\$20,560} = .074 \text{ or } 7.4\%$$

This ratio tells us that during January 2003, Jessica's Beauty Supply, Inc.'s earned a 7.4 percent return on the owners' holdings in the company. Do not confuse this with what the owners themselves earned on their investment. The owners' return is a combination of the dividends they receive and appreciation of the stock's price in the marketplace. The company's rate of return on common equity does, however, greatly influence the market price of the company's stock and, therefore, the stockholders' return on their investment.

Dividend Payout Ratio

dividend payout ratio
A financial ratio that shows what portion of a company's net income for a given year was paid to its owners as cash dividends during that year.

The **dividend payout ratio** shows what portion of a company's net income for a given year was paid to its owners as cash dividends during that year. The formula for this ratio is:

$$\text{Dividend Payout Ratio} = \frac{\text{Total Cash Dividends}}{\text{Net Income}}$$

We can determine the amount of cash dividends to use in the numerator by examining the statement of stockholders' equity in Exhibit 4–12. The denominator is simply net income from the income statement. We calculate Jessica's Beauty Supply, Inc.'s dividend payout ratio for January 2003 as:

$$\frac{\$500}{\$1,620} = .309 \text{ or } 30.9\%$$

This ratio tells us that during January 2003, Jessica's paid out 30.9 percent of its net income to its stockholders as dividends. On the surface, it might seem that a high-dividend payout ratio is better than a low one, and for some investors this is true (those who count on dividends as a significant portion of their yearly income). Many investors and analysts, however, believe a low-dividend payout ratio is superior to a high one. The reason is actually pretty simple. Remember that a company can do only two things with the profits it earns: It can either distribute them to the stockholders as dividends, or it can reinvest them in the business in the form of property, plant, and equipment or new products and processes. A high-dividend payout ratio may indicate that a company is not investing sufficiently for the future.

Earnings per Share

earnings per share A calculation indicating how much of a company's total earnings is attributable to each share of common stock.

Earnings per share expresses the net income of a company as a per share amount on common stock. The formula for this ratio is:

$$\text{Earnings per Share} = \frac{\text{Net Income} - \text{Total Preferred Dividend}}{\text{Average Common Shares Outstanding}}$$

As you can see, preferred stock dividends have been deducted from net income in the numerator of this ratio. This is because the part of net income distributed to the preferred shareholders is not available to the common shareholders. The denominator of the ratio uses an average amount for the same reason earlier ratios did. Since the profit was earned throughout the period, we want to know the average number of shares outstanding for the period covered by the calculation of earnings per share. In this case, we use 4,000 common shares because the number of shares has been constant throughout the company's entire existence. Most companies must calculate a weighted average number of common shares because the number of shares outstanding changes. Earnings per share calculations, including the calculations for the number of weighted average common shares outstanding, is covered in more detail in Chapter 9.

Earnings per share is never calculated for preferred stock, so the number of preferred shares is never used in the calculation. The calculations for earnings per share for large publicly traded companies is quite complicated due to the ever-changing number of common shares outstanding and other factors that may be present that could dilute (lessen) the earnings per share amount. Using the information from the financial statements for Jessica's Beauty Supply, Inc., in Exhibit 4–12, we present the calculation for earnings per share in its most basic form as follows:

$$\frac{\$1,620 - \$100}{4,000 \text{ Shares}} = \$.38 \text{ per Share}$$

The earnings per share for Jessica's Beauty Supply, Inc., indicates the company earned 38 cents per share. Notice that the preferred dividends were deducted from net income before it was divided by common shares. Earnings per share is not an indication of how much the common stockholders received from the company. It reflects the amount earned, of which only a part is typically distributed to shareholders. In this case, the common shareholder, Jessica, only received $400 of the $1,620 available to common shareholders so she did not get 38 cents per share in dividends. Generally, the greater the earnings per share, the better. In fact, earnings per share has a huge impact on the value of publicly traded stocks.

Price-to-Earnings Ratio

price-to-earnings ratio
A financial ratio that is often called simply the PE ratio that expresses the relationship between a company's earnings per share and the market value of the company's stock.

The **price-to-earnings ratio** (often referred to as simply the PE ratio) expresses the relationship between a company's earnings per share and the market value of the company's stock. Financial analysts use this measure to decide whether a company's stock is *under*valued or *over*valued. This ratio is considered so valuable that it is published daily in stock market reports along with a stock's high and low prices and the volume of shares traded. The formula for this ratio is:

$$\text{Price-to-Earnings Ratio} = \frac{\text{Average Market Price per Share of Stock}}{\text{Earnings per Share}}$$

The numerator for this ratio is not found in any of a company's financial statements. Rather, it is the average price of the stock in the stock market. This is a subject we will discuss in much greater detail in Chapter 11. For now, let's assume that Jessica's Beauty Supply, Inc., has an average market price of $6.00 per share. The denominator is earnings per share from the income statement. We calculate Jessica's price to earnings ratio for January 2003 as:

$$\frac{\$6.00}{\$.38} = 15.79 \text{ times}$$

This ratio calculation tells us that Jessica's stock was selling for 15.79 times its earnings per share in January 2003. This is a difficult ratio to interpret because it means different things to different analysts. A high PE ratio may indicate that the stock is overvalued (and may be an unwise investment), whereas a low PE ratio may indicate that it is undervalued (and may be a wise investment). Since the market value of a stock is not directly related to earnings per share, smart analysts evaluate this ratio in conjunction with many other factors.

ANALYSIS OF THE STATEMENT OF CASH FLOWS

The statement of cash flows itself presents the results of an analysis of cash flows. Company accountants have done most of the analytical calculations so financial statement users are able to do more interpreting with less calculating. You already know that the statement of cash flows presents sources and uses of cash for operating, investing, and financing activities. As a financial statement user, you should evaluate not only the appropriateness of the uses of cash, but also the appropriateness of the sources of cash as well.

Cash Flow from Operating Activities
Net cash inflow from operating activities is a healthy sign. This is because a net cash inflow from operating activities constitutes cash that the company has generated internally instead of from additional investments by owners, borrowing, or selling off investments. In the long run, businesses must generate cash from operating activities to pay for investments and to pay a return to its owners and to pay its creditors. In evaluating a business's cash flow, you should examine the proportion of cash that comes from operating activities versus the amount that comes from investing and financing activities. Also compare net cash inflow from operations with net income to evaluate how much of the net income is actually being realized in cash.

Cash Flow from Investing Activities

Net cash *inflow* from investing activities may be an indication that the company is not investing in the land, buildings, equipment, and other assets it will need for the future, and in fact, it is selling off assets. You can just about count on a net cash *outflow* from investing activities in such companies as **Starbucks, Wal-Mart, McDonalds,** and other successful companies because they are constantly expanding by investing in new stores. Generally speaking, investments pay off in the future. If the company does not invest, there will be no payoff. Substantial, sustained cash outflows for investing in securities may indicate that the company is retaining cash that it really doesn't need for business operations. In such a case, perhaps some of the excess funds would be better used to pay down debt or to pay dividends to stockholders.

Cash Flow from Financing Activities

Unless the business is just beginning or expanding, net cash inflow from financing activities is not necessarily a positive indication. Any business can have a sizable stream of cash inflows from borrowing, at least for a while. But when a substantial portion of a company's cash routinely comes from borrowing, this ultimately spells trouble. Increased borrowing entails higher interest cost, and the loan must be repaid at some point. Within reason, it is generally better to see net cash outflow in the financing section of the statement of cash flows unless the company is in the start-up or expansion mode.

By now you should have a basic understanding of financial statements and how they relate to one another. The more you know about financial statements, the better you can utilize them for economic decisions. In the next chapter, we will introduce two bases of economic measurement: the cash basis and the accrual basis.

Summary ●

The income statement is a financial tool that provides information about a company's past performance. Like the balance sheet, the income statement is made up of accounting elements. The two elements included in the income statement are revenues and expenses, and the statement can be expressed by the following equation:

$$\text{Revenues} - \text{Expenses} = \text{Net Income (or Net Loss)}$$

The income statement equation forms the basis for the income statement itself. The income statement indicates that during this specific time period, the company earned so much revenue, incurred so much expense, and produced either a net income or a net loss. Publicly traded companies are required to prepare income statements for external users annually and quarterly. The income statement's formal name is the statement of results of operations.

There are two commonly used income statement formats: the single-step and the multiple-step formats. In the single-step income statement format, all revenues are grouped together and then totaled. This format is called the single-step income statement because in one step, total expenses are subtracted from total revenues to determine net income or net loss. The multiple-step income statement provides two items of information not presented in a single-step income statement: (1) gross margin (gross profit) and (2) operating income (income from operations).

A company's equity changes by the amount of its net income or loss. Net income increases the owners' equity in the business. Each revenue increases earned equity and each expense decreases earned equity. A net income, therefore, increases earned equity, while a net loss decreases earned equity.

Just as net income increases owners' equity, distributions to owners—another accounting element—decrease owners' equity. In the case of proprietorships and partnerships, distributions to owners are called drawings or withdrawals. Distributions to owners of a corporation are called dividends. To be able to pay a cash dividend, a corporation must have two things: sufficient retained earnings and sufficient cash.

The statement of owners' equity is a bridge between the income statement and the balance sheet. This statement shows the changes to owners' equity from the beginning of the income statement period to the end of that period. The ending balance shown on the statement of owners' equity is equal to the amount shown for owners' equity on the balance sheet. The statement of owners' equity for a sole proprietorship is generally called the statement of capital, and for a partnership, it is usually called the statement of partners' capital. Corporations generally call this statement the statement of stockholders' equity, although if there have been no changes in contributed capital during the period, the company may prepare a statement of retained earnings, which is similar in form to the statement of capital for proprietorships and partnerships.

The income statement, the statement of owners' equity, and the balance sheet have a special relationship of interdependence to one another called articulation. Articulation means that the net income shown on the income statement causes an increase in equity on the statement of owners' equity. Then, the ending balances from the statement of owners' equity are included in the equity section of the balance sheet. The ending balance of cash on the statement of cash flows should be the same as the balance of cash on the balance sheet. The operating activities section of the statement of cash flows includes cash inflows and outflows for revenues and expenses associated with a company's ongoing business operations.

Over time, financial analysts have developed several ratios to evaluate a company's profitability performance. In this chapter, we presented seven of them: the gross profit margin ratio, the net profit margin ratio, the rate of return on assets ratio, the rate of return on common equity ratio, the dividend payout ratio, earnings per share, and the price-to-earnings ratio.

Key Terms

- articulation, F–131
- cost of goods sold, F–121
- cost of products sold. *See* cost of goods sold
- cost of sales. *See* cost of goods sold
- date of declaration, F–126
- date of payment, F–127
- date of record, F–127
- distributions to owners, F–124
- dividend payout ratio, F–136
- dividends, F–125
- drawings, F–125
- earnings per share, F–136
- expense, F–118
- gross margin, F–122

- gross profit. *See* gross margin
- gross profit margin ratio, F–134
- income from operations. *See* operating income
- income statement, F–118
- income tax, F–121
- multiple-step income statement, F–122
- net earnings. *See* net income
- net income, F–119
- net loss, F–119
- net profit. *See* net income
- net profit margin ratio, F–134
- operating activities, F–133
- operating income, F–122
- price-to-earnings ratio, F–137

- rate of return on assets ratio, F–135
- rate of return on common equity ratio, F–135
- revenue, F–118
- sales revenue, F–122
- single-step income statement, F–121
- statement of capital, F–128
- statement of owners' equity, F–128
- statement of partners' capital, F–129
- statement of results of operations. *See* income statement
- statement of retained earnings, F–130
- statement of stockholders' equity, F–129
- withdrawals. *See* drawings

Review the Facts

A. Name and define in your own words the accounting elements used to determine net income.
B. What is the major expense of merchandisers and manufacturers?
C. Name the two formats of the income statement, and describe the differences between them.
D. What item is responsible for the primary increase in the capital account?
E. What is the difference between a statement of stockholders' equity and a statement of retained earnings?
F. What is the effect of owners' drawings and on what financial statement is this information reported?
G. Under what circumstances is a corporation unable to pay a dividend?
H. How is a corporation's financial position affected by the payment of a dividend?
I. Explain the following terms: *date of declaration, date of record*, and *date of payment*.
J. Describe the meaning of articulation as it is used in accounting.
K. Describe the operating activities sections of the statement of cash flows.
L. List and describe each of the seven profitability ratios.
M. Describe what you would prefer to see in a company's net cash inflows/outflows for each section of the statement of cash flows.

Apply What You Have Learned ●●●●●●●●●●●●●●●●●●●●●●●●

LO 1: TERMINOLOGY

4–16. Below is a list of items relating to the concepts discussed in this chapter, followed by definitions and examples of those items in scrambled order:

a. Assets   d. Revenues
b. Liabilities   e. Expenses
c. Equity

1. _____ Debts of the company
2. _____ Sales
3. _____ Probable future economic benefits
4. _____ Inflows of assets from delivering or producing goods, rendering services, or other activities
5. _____ "Things" of value a company has
6. _____ The residual interest in the assets of an entity that remains after deducting its liabilities
7. _____ Probable future sacrifices of economic benefits
8. _____ Outflows or other using up of assets from delivering or producing goods, rendering services, or carrying out other activities
9. _____ Costs that have no future value
10. _____ What the company owes
11. _____ What the company has less what it owes
12. _____ The owner's interest in the company

Required: Match the letter next to each item on the list with the appropriate definition. Letters may be used more than once.

LO 1: INCOME STATEMENT TERMINOLOGY

4–17. Define the following terms in your own words:

a. Revenue   d. Net loss
b. Expense   e. Profit
c. Net income   f. Earnings

LO 1, 5, & 6: TERMINOLOGY

4–18. Below is a list of items relating to the concepts discussed in this chapter, followed by definitions of those items in scrambled order:

a. Revenues   f. Drawings
b. Expenses   g. Date of declaration
c. Income statement   h. Date of record
d. Statement of owners' equity   i. Date of payment
e. Dividends   j. Articulation

1. _____ The date distributions of earnings to owners of a corporation are actually paid
2. _____ Inflows of assets from delivering or producing goods, rendering services, or other activities
3. _____ Distribution of earnings to the owners of a corporation
4. _____ The link between the income statement and the balance sheet
5. _____ A bridge statement showing how the income statement and balance sheet are related
6. _____ Distribution of earnings to the owners of proprietorships and partnerships
7. _____ Outflows or other using up of assets from delivering or producing goods, rendering services, or carrying out other activities
8. _____ The date a corporation announces it will make a distribution of earnings to its owners
9. _____ A financial tool providing information about an entity's past performance
10. _____ Whoever owns shares of stock on this date will receive the distribution of earnings previously declared

Required: Match the letter next to each item on the list with the appropriate definition. Use each letter only once.

LO 1 & 2: SIMPLE INCOME STATEMENT PREPARATION—NO INCOME TAXES

4–19. Phil Brock and Company had $75,985 in sales revenue during 2004. In addition to the regular sales revenue, Brock rented out a small building it owned and received $4,800 for the year. Cost of goods sold for the year totaled $31,812. Other expenses for the year were as follows:

Rent	$10,500
Utilities	2,195
Advertising	4,265
Wages	12,619
Interest	996

Required:

    a. Prepare a 2004 income statement for Phil Brock and Company using a single-step format.

    b. Prepare a 2004 income statement for Phil Brock and Company using a multiple-step format.

LO 1 & 2: SIMPLE INCOME STATEMENT PREPARATION—NO INCOME TAXES

4–20. Sam Sosa and Company had $245,000 in sales revenue during 2004. In addition, Sosa had interest revenue of $7,600 for the year. Cost of goods sold for the year totaled $102,000. Other expenses for the year were:

Rent	$24,000
Wages	13,500
Advertising	2,200
Utilities	2,900

Required:

    a. Prepare a 2004 income statement for Sam Sosa and Company using a single-step format.

    b. Prepare a 2004 income statement for Sam Sosa and Company using a multiple-step format.

LO 1 & 2: SIMPLE INCOME STATEMENT PREPARATION—CORPORATE

4–21. Pipkin's Camera and Video, Inc., had sales revenue of $770,000 during 2003. Expenses for the year were:

Wages	$ 72,000
Rent	64,000
Advertising	16,400
Cost of goods sold	550,000
Utilities	13,600
Income tax expense	16,200

Required:

    a. Prepare a 2003 income statement for Pipkin's Camera and Video, Inc., using a single-step format.

    b. Prepare a 2003 income statement for Pipkin's Camera and Video, Inc., using a multiple-step format.

LO 1 & 2: INCOME STATEMENT PREPARATION—CORPORATE

4–22. The following information is taken from the accounting records of Alex's Baseball Card Shop, Inc., for 2004:

Sales	$650,000
Wages	120,000
Store rent	39,000
Interest expense	42,000
Advertising	28,200

Electricity	6,800
Telephone	1,400
Cost of goods sold	420,000
Rent revenue	18,000
Income tax expense	2,120

Required:

a. Prepare a 2004 income statement for Alex's Baseball Card Shop, Inc., using a single-step format.

b. Prepare a 2004 income statement for Alex's Baseball Card Shop, Inc., using a multiple-step format.

c. If you were the owner of the company, which format of income statement would you prefer to use? Why?

LO 1 & 2: CORPORATE INCOME STATEMENT PREPARATION

4–23. The following information is taken from accounting records of Nancy's Chocolate Factory for the year ended December 31, 2003:

Sales	$356,000
Cost of goods sold	275,000
Wages and salaries	30,000
Rent	20,000
Electricity	9,000
Telephone	7,000
Advertising	5,000
Maintenance	1,000
Interest expense	4,000
Income tax	2,000

Required:

a. Prepare a 2003 income statement for the company using the single-step format.

b. Prepare a 2003 income statement for the company using a multiple-step format.

LO 1 & 2: CORPORATE INCOME STATEMENT PREPARATION

4–24. The following information is taken from accounting records of Al's Boating Supplies, Inc., for the year ended December 31, 2003:

Sales	$1,343,000
Cost of goods sold	1,100,000
Wages and salaries	80,000
Rent	70,000
Electricity	25,000
Telephone	23,000
Advertising	14,000
Maintenance	4,000
Interest revenue	9,000
Interest expense	12,000
Income tax	6,000

Required:

a. Prepare a 2003 income statement for the company using the single-step format.

b. Prepare a 2003 income statement for the company using a multiple-step format.

LO 1, 2, 4, & 6: CORPORATE INCOME STATEMENT AND RETAINED EARNINGS STATEMENT PREPARATION

4–25. The following information is taken from accounting records of Gina's Nail Salon for the year ended December 31, 2003:

Sales	$123,000
Cost of goods sold	75,000
Operating expenses	40,280
Interest revenue	1,200

Interest expense	6,240
Income tax	536
Beginning retained earnings balance	10,650
Dividends	500

Required:

    a. Prepare a 2003 income statement for the company using the single-step format.

    b. Prepare a 2003 income statement for the company using a multiple-step format.

    c. Prepare a 2003 retained earnings statement for the company.

LO 1, 2, 4, & 6: CORPORATE INCOME STATEMENT AND RETAINED EARNINGS STATEMENT PREPARATION

4–26. The following information is taken from accounting records of Michelle's Catering Co. for the year ended December 31, 2003:

Sales	$350,000
Cost of goods sold	265,400
Operating expenses	56,300
Rent revenue	2,400
Interest expense	9,850
Income tax	4,170
Beginning retained earnings balance	45,800
Dividends	1,500

Required:

    a. Prepare a 2003 income statement for the company using the single-step format.

    b. Prepare a 2003 income statement for the company using a multiple-step format.

    c. Prepare a 2003 retained earnings statement for the company.

LO 1, 2, 4, & 6: CORPORATE INCOME STATEMENT AND RETAINED EARNINGS STATEMENT PREPARATION

4–27. The following information is taken from accounting records of Jerry's Hunting & Fishing Supplies for the year ended December 31, 2003:

Sales	$538,400
Cost of goods sold	318,520
Operating expenses	198,560
Rent revenue	4,260
Interest expense	12,500
Income tax	3,270
Beginning retained earnings balance	36,800
Dividends	1,000

Required:

    a. Prepare a 2003 income statement for the company using the single-step format.

    b. Prepare a 2003 income statement for the company using a multiple-step format.

    c. Prepare a 2003 retained earnings statement for the company.

LO 1, 2, 4, & 6: CORPORATE INCOME STATEMENT AND RETAINED EARNINGS STATEMENT PREPARATION

4–28. The following information is taken from accounting records of Martha's Books for Kids for the year ended December 31, 2003:

Sales	$126,500
Cost of goods sold	80,520
Wages and salaries	22,000
Rent	12,000
Electricity	2,400
Telephone	1,200
Interest revenue	600
Interest expense	2,000

Income tax	1,745
Beginning retained earnings balance	21,000
Dividends	500

Required:

    a. Prepare a 2003 income statement for the company using the single-step format.
    b. Prepare a 2003 income statement for the company using a multiple-step format.
    c. Prepare a 2003 retained earnings statement for the company.

LO 1 & 2: INCOME STATEMENT PREPARATION–INCOME TAX DISREGARDED

4–29. The following information is taken from the accounting records of Bea's Pet Shop, Inc., for 2003:

Sales	$830,000
Cost of goods sold	440,000
Wages	280,000
Utilities	34,000
Rent	28,000
Advertising	22,000
Interest revenue	5,000

Required:

    a. Prepare a 2003 income statement for Bea's Pet Shop, Inc., using a single-step format.
    b. Prepare a 2003 income statement for Bea's Pet Shop, Inc., using a multiple-step format.

LO 3 & 4: IMPACT OF NET INCOME ON OWNERS' EQUITY

4–30. Refer to Bea's Pet Shop, Inc., in 4–29.

Required:

    a. Prepare the statement of capital for Bea's Pet Shop, Inc., for 2003 assuming that it operates as the sole proprietorship of Beatrice Wilson who had a beginning capital balance of $10,000 and withdrew $20,000 during 2003.
    b. Now assuming the company is a corporation, prepare the statement of retained earnings for Bea's Pet Shop, Inc., for 2003 assuming that Bea is the sole stockholder, the beginning retained earnings balance is $21,000, and Bea paid a dividend of $12,000.

LO 2 & 3: IMPACT OF NET INCOME ON OWNERS' EQUITY—PROPRIETORSHIP

4–31. The Alvin Smith Company reported the following information in the records for 2003:

Sales	$250,000
Cost of goods sold	120,000
Salaries	70,000
Utilities	4,000
Rent	3,000
Advertising	1,000
Interest expense	2,000

Required:

    a. Prepare the income statement for the Alvin Smith Company for the year of 2003 using the multiple-step format.
    b. Explain how the result determined in part a will affect the owner's equity for the year assuming that the company is a sole proprietorship.

LO 3 & 4: IMPACT OF NET INCOME ON OWNERS' EQUITY— PROPRIETORSHIP, PARTNERSHIP

4–32. Refer to the Alvin Smith Company in 4–31.

Required:

    a. Prepare the statement of capital for Alvin Smith Company assuming it operates as the sole proprietorship of Alvin Smith, Sr., who had a beginning capital balance of $50,000.

b. Prepare the statement of partners' capital for Alvin Smith Company assuming it operates as a partnership between Alvin Smith, Sr., and Alvin Smith, Jr.

	Smith, Sr.	Smith, Jr.
Partners' share of profits	60%	40%
Beginning capital balance	$50,000	$ 5,000
Withdrawals	$20,000	$20,000

LO 2 & 3: IMPACT OF NET INCOME ON OWNERS' EQUITY—PROPRIETORSHIP, CORPORATION, TAX DISREGARDED

4–33. The Ben Jones Company, Inc., reported the following information in the records for 2003:

Sales	$530,000
Cost of goods sold	220,000
Wages	160,000
Utilities	74,000
Rent	8,000
Advertising	11,000
Interest revenue	3,000

Required:

a. Prepare the income statement for the Ben Jones Company, Inc., for the year 2003 using the single-step format.
b. Explain how the result determined in part a will affect the owner's equity for the year assuming that the company is a sole proprietorship.
c. Explain how the result determined in part a will affect the equity of the corporation.

LO 3 & 4: IMPACT OF NET INCOME ON OWNERS' EQUITY—PROPRIETORSHIP, PARTNERSHIP, AND CORPORATION

4–34. Refer to the Ben Jones Company, Inc., in 4–33.

Required:

a. Prepare the statement of capital for Ben Jones Company, Inc., assuming it operates as the sole proprietorship of Ben Jones who had a beginning capital balance of $50,000.
b. Prepare the statement of partners' capital for Ben Jones Company, Inc., assuming it operates as a partnership between Ben Jones and Kathy Jones.

	Ben Jones	Kathy Jones
Partners' share of profits	35%	65%
Beginning capital balance	$15,000	$45,000
Withdrawals	$12,000	$25,000
Additional capital contributions	$ 5,000	$ 0

LO 3 & 4: IMPACT OF NET INCOME ON RETAINED EARNINGS

4–35. The Carl Smythe Company reported the following information in its records for the year ended December 31, 2004:

Sales	$85,000
Beginning balance—retained earnings	26,000
Cost of sales	55,000
Expenses	35,000
Dividends	2,000

Required:

a. Prepare a single-step income statement for 2004.
b. Prepare the statement of retained earnings for 2004.
c. What is the balance of retained earnings at the end of 2004?

LO 4, 5, & 6: PREPARATION OF A STATEMENT OF EQUITY—PROPRIETORSHIP, PARTNERSHIP, AND CORPORATION

4–36. Pfister Company was organized on January 3, 2003, and had modest net income of $9,500 in its first year.

Required:

a. Prepare a statement of capital for Pfister Company for the year ended December 31, 2003, assuming Ken Pfister began the company as a sole proprietorship by investing $20,000 of his own money. Also assume Ken took no drawings from the company.

b. Prepare a statement of partners' capital for Pfister Company for the year ended December 31, 2003, assuming Ken Pfister, Stephanie Winters, and Harriet Higgins began the company as a partnership. Assume the three partners have taken no drawings from the company and have agreed to share any income or loss in the same proportion as their initial investments, which were as follows:

Name	Investment
Pfister	$ 6,000
Winters	4,000
Higgins	2,000
Total	$12,000

c. Prepare a statement of stockholders' equity for Pfister Company for the year ended December 31, 2003. Assume Ken Pfister, Stephanie Winters, and Harriet Higgins organized the company as a corporation and that the company did not pay a dividend in 2003. The corporate charter authorized 50,000 shares of $2 par value common stock. The following shares were issued on January 3, 2003 (all at $10 per share):

500 shares to Pfister	$ 5,000
300 shares to Winters	3,000
200 shares to Higgins	2,000
Total	$10,000

LO 4, 5, & 6: PREPARATION OF STATEMENT OF EQUITY—SECOND YEAR, PROPRIETORSHIP, PARTNERSHIP, AND CORPORATION

4–37. This problem is a continuation of problem 4–36 for Pfister Company. Now assume it is the end of the company's second year, that is, December 31, 2004, and it is time to prepare the statement of owners' equity for Pfister Company. Net income for the year ended December 31, 2004, was $18,000, and there were no additional owners' investments during the year.

Required:

a. Prepare a statement of capital for Pfister Company for the year ended December 31, 2004, assuming the business was a proprietorship and that Pfister took drawings totaling $8,000 during 2004.

b. Prepare a statement of partners' capital for Pfister Company for the year ended December 31, 2004, assuming the partnership form. Recall from the previous problem that the partners share income in the same proportion as their initial investment. Drawings by the three partners during 2004 were as follows:

Name	Drawings
Pfister	$4,000
Winters	2,500
Higgins	1,500
Total	$8,000

c. Prepare a statement of stockholders' equity for Pfister Company for the year ended December 31, 2004, assuming the corporate form. Recall from the previous problem that 1,000 shares of common stock were issued at the time of incorporation. Dividends paid during the year were $6 per share.

d. Prepare a statement of retained earnings for Pfister Company assuming the same information given in part c.

LO 4, 5, & 6: PREPARATION OF A STATEMENT OF EQUITY—PROPRIETORSHIP, PARTNERSHIP, AND CORPORATION

4–38. Modell Company was organized on January 3, 2003, and the company experienced a modest net loss of $4,500 in 2003.

Required:

a. Prepare a statement of capital for Modell Company for the year ended December 31, 2003, assuming Art Modell began the company as a sole proprietorship by investing $50,000 of his own money. During 2003, Modell took no drawings.

b. Prepare a statement of partners' capital for Modell Company for the year ended December 31, 2003, assuming Art Modell, Sally Weber, and Hillary Hager began the company as a partnership. During 2003, the partners took no drawings. The three partners have agreed to share any income or loss in the same proportion as their initial investments, which were as follows:

Name	Investment
Modell	$ 5,000
Weber	4,000
Hager	1,000
Total	$10,000

c. Prepare a statement of stockholders' equity for Modell Company for the year ended December 31, 2003, assuming Modell, Weber, and Hager organized the company as a corporation. The corporate charter authorized 100,000 shares of $5 par value common stock. During 2003, the company paid no dividends. The following shares were issued on January 3, 2003 (all at $10 per share):

500 shares to Modell	$ 5,000
400 shares to Weber	4,000
100 shares to Hager	1,000
Total	$10,000

LO 4, 5, & 6: PREPARATION OF A STATEMENT OF EQUITY—SECOND YEAR, PROPRIETORSHIP, PARTNERSHIP, AND CORPORATION

4–39. This problem is a continuation of problem 4–38 for Modell Company. Now assume it is the end of the company's second year of business, December 31, 2004. Net income for the year ended December 31, 2004, was $54,000 and there were no additional owners' investments during the year.

Required:

a. Prepare a statement of capital for Modell Company for the year ended December 31, 2004, assuming the business was a proprietorship and that Modell took drawings totaling $18,000 during 2004.

b. Prepare a statement of partners' capital for Modell Company for the year ended December 31, 2004, assuming the partnership form. Recall from the previous problem that the partners share income in the same proportion as their initial investment. Drawings by the three partners during 2004 were as follows:

Name	Drawings
Modell	$ 8,000
Weber	5,000
Hager	5,000
Total	$18,000

c. Prepare a statement of stockholders' equity for Modell Company for the year ended December 31, 2004, assuming Modell Company took the corporate form. Recall from the previous problem that 1,000 shares of common stock were issued at the time of incorporation. Dividends paid during the year were $3 per share.

d. Prepare a statement of retained earnings for Modell Company assuming the same information given in part c.

LO 4, 5, & 6: PREPARE STATEMENT OF STOCKHOLDERS' EQUITY AND STATEMENT OF RETAINED EARNINGS

4–40. The Wynn Corporation had the following information available for 2004:

Common stock ($1 par value, 100,000 shares issued and outstanding)	$100,000
Net income for 2004	10,000
Dividends for 2004	5,000
Retained earnings at January 1, 2004	250,000
Additional paid-in capital	50,000

Required:

   a. Prepare a statement of stockholders' equity for 2004 for the Wynn Corporation. No stock transactions occurred during 2004.
   b. Prepare a statement of retained earnings for 2004 for the Wynn Corporation.
   c. Explain the difference between the two statements.

LO 4, 5, & 6: PREPARE STATEMENT OF STOCKHOLDERS' EQUITY AND STATEMENT OF RETAINED EARNINGS

4–41. The Bishop Corporation had the following information available at the end of 2004:

Common stock, January 1, 2004 ($5 par value, 50,000 shares authorized, 25,000 issued and outstanding)	$125,000
Net income for 2004	20,000
Dividends for 2004	10,000
Retained earnings at January 1, 2004	70,000
Additional paid-in capital, January 1, 2004	150,000
Sale of additional 5,000 shares of stock	75,000

Required:

   a. Prepare a statement of stockholders' equity for 2004 for the Bishop Corporation.
   b. Prepare a statement of retained earnings for 2004 for the Bishop Corporation.
   c. Explain the difference between the two statements. Considering the transactions that occurred this year, which statement would be most informative to the user?

LO 4, 5, & 6: PREPARE STATEMENT OF STOCKHOLDERS' EQUITY AND STATEMENT OF RETAINED EARNINGS

4–42. The Rook Corporation had the following information available for 2003:

Common stock, January 1, 2003 (no par value, 50,000 shares authorized, 25,000 shares issued and outstanding)	$175,000
Net loss for 2003	35,000
Dividends for 2003	10,000
Retained earnings at January 1, 2003	197,000
Sale of 10,000 shares of no-par stock during 2003	100,000

Required:

   a. Prepare a statement of stockholders' equity for 2003 for the Rook Corporation.
   b. Prepare a statement of retained earnings for 2003 for the Rook Corporation.
   c. Explain the difference between the two statements. Considering the transactions that occurred this year, which statement would be most informative to the user?

LO 4, 5, & 6: SHAREHOLDERS' EQUITY VS. RETAINED EARNINGS STATEMENTS—WITH TREASURY STOCK

4–43. The Einstein Corporation had the following information available for 2004:

Common stock, January 1, 2004 ($10 par value, 150,000 shares authorized, 25,000 shares issued and outstanding)	$250,000
Net income for 2004	55,000
Dividends for 2004	25,000
Retained earnings at January 1, 2004	160,000
Additional paid-in capital, January 1, 2004	75,000
Sale of 10,000 shares on March 10	150,000

Required: Prepare a statement of stockholders' equity for 2004 for the Einstein Corporation.

LO 5: DIVIDEND TERMINOLOGY

4–44. The Simpson Company decided to pay a cash dividend to its stockholders. This dividend is the first that has ever been paid and the board of directors questions the proper procedure.

Required: With respect to corporate dividend payments, there are three important dates to consider. Explain what happens on each of these important dates and how they help facilitate the payment of dividends.

LO 5: DIVIDENDS

4–45. The board of directors of McCormick Corporation is trying to decide whether or not to declare a cash dividend for the current year.

Required: Identify and discuss the various business and legal issues that the board of directors must consider as they contemplate whether or not to pay a dividend.

LO 1, 2, 4, 5, & 6: CORPORATE INCOME STATEMENT, RETAINED EARNINGS STATEMENT, AND BALANCE SHEET PREPARATION

4–46. The following information is taken from accounting records of Christie's Cheerleading Supplies for the year ended December 31, 2003:

Sales	$100,000
Cost of goods sold	60,000
Operating expenses	30,000
Income tax	2,500
Beginning retained earnings balance	12,000
Dividends	1,000
Cash	3,500
Inventory	12,000
Equipment	9,000
Notes payable	2,000
Common stock	500
Additional paid-in capital—common	3,500

Required:

a. Classify each item as follows:

   Asset = A
   Liability = L
   Equity = EQ
   Revenue = R
   Expense = EX

b. Prepare a 2003 income statement for the company using the single-step format.
c. Prepare a 2003 income statement for the company using a multiple-step format.
d. Prepare a 2003 retained earnings statement for the company.
e. Prepare a balance sheet for the company as of the end of the accounting period.

LO 1, 2, 4, 5, & 6: CORPORATE INCOME STATEMENT, RETAINED EARNINGS STATEMENT, AND BALANCE SHEET PREPARATION

4–47. The following information is taken from accounting records of Salon of Dadeland for the year ended December 31, 2003:

Sales	$129,850
Operating expenses	86,540
Rent revenue	2,000
Interest expense	280
Income tax	13,509
Beginning retained earnings balance	27,680
Dividends	20,000
Cash	12,680
Supplies	860

Equipment	27,500
Office equipment	1,685
Computer system	3,480
Notes payable	2,400
Common stock	1,200
Additional paid-in capital—common	3,404

Required:

a. Classify each item as follows:

Asset = A
Liability = L
Equity = EQ
Revenue = R
Expense = EX

b. Prepare a 2003 income statement for the company using the single-step format.
c. Prepare a 2003 income statement for the company using a multiple-step format.
d. Prepare a 2003 retained earnings statement for the company.
e. Prepare a balance sheet for the company as of the end of the accounting period.

LO 1, 2, 4, 5, & 6: CORPORATE INCOME STATEMENT, RETAINED EARNINGS STATEMENT, AND BALANCE SHEET PREPARATION

4–48. The following information is taken from accounting records of Manny's Auto Parts for the year ended December 31, 2003:

Sales	$34,620
Cost of goods sold	22,860
Operating expenses	7,680
Interest expense	600
Income tax	870
Beginning retained earnings balance	10,840
Dividends	250
Cash	1,980
Inventory	8,540
Equipment	13,850
Notes payable	7,000
Common stock	1,350
Additional paid-in capital—common	2,820

Required:

a. Prepare a 2003 income statement for the company using the single-step format.
b. Prepare a 2003 income statement for the company using a multiple-step format.
c. Prepare a 2003 retained earnings statement for the company.
d. Prepare a balance sheet for the company as of the end of the accounting period.

LO 1, 2, 4, 5, & 6: CORPORATE INCOME STATEMENT, RETAINED EARNINGS STATEMENT, AND BALANCE SHEET PREPARATION

4–49. The following information is taken from accounting records of the Hurricane Restaurant for the year ended December 31, 2003:

Sales	$864,200
Operating expenses	743,860
Interest expense	42,640
Income tax	24,864
Beginning retained earnings balance	254,630
Dividends	30,000
Cash	4,268
Land	120,680
Building	587,960

Equipment	128,520
Accounts payable	3,840
Notes payable	278,640
Bonds payable	200,000
Common stock	17,000
Additional paid-in capital—Common	64,482

Required:

a. Classify each item as follows:

   Asset = A
   Liability = L
   Equity = EQ
   Revenue = R
   Expense = EX

b. Prepare a 2003 income statement for the company using the single-step format.
c. Prepare a 2003 income statement for the company using a multiple-step format.
d. Prepare a 2003 retained earnings statement for the company.
e. Prepare a balance sheet for the company as of the end of the accounting period.

LO 1, 2, 4, 5, & 6: CORPORATE INCOME STATEMENT, RETAINED EARNINGS STATEMENT, AND BALANCE SHEET PREPARATION

4–50. The following information is taken from accounting records of Roger's Bike Sales for the year ended December 31, 2003:

Sales	$260,500
Cost of goods sold	182,530
Operating expenses	53,000
Rent revenue	2,100
Interest expense	4,570
Income tax	5,625
Beginning retained earnings balance	64,580
Dividends	2,900
Cash	5,800
Accounts receivable	12,300
Inventory	26,800
Supplies	575
Land	40,650
Building	68,450
Equipment	3,850
Computer system	1,550
Delivery truck	26,960
Accounts payable	6,860
Notes payable	5,000
Common stock	1,000
Additional paid-in capital—common	95,520

Required:

a. Classify each item as follows:

   Asset = A
   Liability = L
   Equity = EQ
   Revenue = R
   Expense = EX

b. Prepare a 2003 income statement for the company using the single-step format.
c. Prepare a 2003 income statement for the company using a multiple-step format.
d. Prepare a 2003 retained earnings statement for the company.
e. Prepare a balance sheet for the company as of the end of the accounting period.

LO 1, 2, 4, 5, & 6: CORPORATE INCOME STATEMENT, RETAINED EARNINGS STATEMENT, AND BALANCE SHEET PREPARATION

4–51. The following information is taken from accounting records of Tressa's Treasures for the year ended December 31, 2003:

Sales	$120,000
Cost of goods sold	80,000
Operating expenses	22,000
Interest revenue	2,000
Interest expense	5,000
Income tax	6,000
Beginning retained earnings balance	42,670
Dividends	3,000
Cash	11,000
Accounts receivable	22,000
Inventory	37,000
Land	35,800
Building	59,750
Equipment	13,000
Accounts payable	18,000
Notes payable	16,000
Common stock	7,000
Additional paid-in capital—common	88,880

Required:

  a. Prepare a 2003 income statement for the company using the single-step format.
  b. Prepare a 2003 income statement for the company using a multiple-step format.
  c. Prepare a 2003 retained earnings statement for the company.
  d. Prepare a balance sheet for the company as of the end of the accounting period.

LO 1, 2, 4, 5, & 6: CORPORATE INCOME STATEMENT, RETAINED EARNINGS STATEMENT, AND BALANCE SHEET PREPARATION

4–52. The following information is taken from accounting records of Home Pet Supplies, Inc., for the year ended December 31, 2003:

Sales	$56,250
Cost of goods sold	24,630
Wages and salaries	22,800
Rent	2,400
Electricity	1,260
Telephone	625
Interest expense	900
Income tax	727
Beginning retained earnings balance	12,850
Dividends	500
Cash	2,680
Inventory	8,880
Equipment	9,640
Computer system	3,750
Delivery truck	12,600
Accounts payable	5,480
Notes payable	4,500
Common stock	2,000
Additional paid-in capital—common	10,312

Required:

  a. Prepare a 2003 income statement for the company using the single-step format.
  b. Prepare a 2003 income statement for the company using a multiple-step format.
  c. Prepare a 2003 retained earnings statement for the company.
  d. Prepare a balance sheet for the company as of the end of the accounting period.

LO 1, 2, 4, 5, & 6: CORPORATE INCOME STATEMENT, RETAINED EARNINGS STATEMENT, AND BALANCE SHEET PREPARATION

4–53. The following information is taken from accounting records of Mendelsohn Electronics for the year ended December 31, 2003:

Sales	$12,856,850
Cost of goods sold	9,458,560
Operating expenses	3,128,950
Rent revenue	36,000
Interest expense	13,340
Income tax	99,280
Beginning retained earnings balance	2,460,350
Dividends	25,000
Cash	1,920,650
Accounts receivable	263,520
Inventory	2,462,250
Supplies	1,200
Land	750,520
Building	1,385,520
Equipment	265,220
Accounts payable	1,985,640
Notes payable	736,580
Bonds payable	500,000
Preferred stock	200,000
Common stock	998,590

Required:

a. Classify each item as follows:

   Asset = A
   Liability = L
   Equity = EQ
   Revenue = R
   Expense = EX

b. Prepare a 2003 income statement for the company using the single-step format.
c. Prepare a 2003 income statement for the company using a multiple-step format.
d. Prepare a 2003 retained earnings statement for the company.
e. Prepare a balance sheet for the company as of the end of the accounting period.

LO 1, 2, 4, 5, & 6: CORPORATE INCOME STATEMENT, RETAINED EARNINGS STATEMENT, AND BALANCE SHEET PREPARATION

4–54. The following information is taken from accounting records of Louie's Landscaping Co. for the year ended December 31, 2003:

Sales	$2,650,500
Cost of goods sold	1,825,000
Wages and salaries	420,000
Rent	108,000
Electricity	10,200
Telephone	4,200
Interest revenue	1,600
Interest expense	36,000
Income tax	79,584
Beginning retained earnings balance	43,116
Dividends	20,000
Cash	34,500
Accounts receivable	152,500
Inventory	231,232
Supplies	2,500
Delivery truck	20,300
Accounts payable	155,300

Notes payable	5,000
Bonds payable	31,000
Common stock	2,500
Additional paid-in capital—common	55,000

Required:

a. Classify each item as follows:

  Asset = A
  Liability = L
  Equity = EQ
  Revenue = R
  Expense = EX

b. Prepare a 2003 income statement for the company using the single-step format.
c. Prepare a 2003 income statement for the company using a multiple-step format.
d. Prepare a 2003 retained earnings statement for the company.
e. Prepare a balance sheet for the company as of the end of the accounting period.

LO 1, 2, 4, 5, & 6: CORPORATE INCOME STATEMENT, RETAINED EARNINGS STATEMENT, AND BALANCE SHEET PREPARATION

4–55. The following information is taken from accounting records of Cupcake's Specialty Bakery for the year ended December 31, 2003:

Sales	$1,265,300
Cost of goods sold	862,150
Operating expenses	345,890
Interest revenue	1,280
Interest expense	3,690
Income tax	16,455
Beginning retained earnings balance	225,950
Cash	37,560
Inventory	195,850
Supplies	2,000
Land	105,750
Building	225,500
Office equipment	26,800
Computer equipment	4,850
Delivery truck	23,800
Accounts payable	51,280
Notes payable	9,500
Bonds payable	27,000
Preferred stock	80,000
Additional paid-in capital—preferred	2,000
Common stock	32,000
Additional paid-in capital—common	155,985

Required:

a. Prepare a 2003 income statement for the company using the single-step format.
b. Prepare a 2003 income statement for the company using a multiple-step format.
c. Prepare a 2003 retained earnings statement for the company.
d. Prepare a balance sheet for the company as of the end of the accounting period.

LO 1, 2, 4, 5, & 6: CORPORATE SERVICE BUSINESS INCOME STATEMENT, RETAINED EARNINGS STATEMENT, AND BALANCE SHEET PREPARATION

4–56. The following information is taken from accounting records of Medical Service, Inc., for the year ended December 31, 2003:

Sales	$1,162,530
Operating expenses	485,600
Wages and salaries	485,600
Rent	36,000
Electricity	4,800

Telephone	1,250
Advertising	19,860
Maintenance	2,200
Rent revenue	2,400
Interest expense	6,200
Income tax	37,026
Beginning retained earnings balance	182,600
Dividends	40,000
Cash	125,800
Accounts receivable	98,560
Supplies	22,000
Equipment	295,000
Office equipment	3,600
Computer system	2,600
Computer equipment	2,560
Accounts payable	12,350
Notes payable	65,740
Preferred stock	28,000
Additional paid-in capital—preferred	400
Common stock	54,000
Additional paid-in capital—common	160,636

Required:

a. Prepare a 2003 income statement for the company using the single-step format.
b. Prepare a 2003 income statement for the company using a multiple-step format.
c. Prepare a 2003 retained earnings statement for the company.
d. Prepare a balance sheet for the company as of the end of the accounting period.

LO 1, 2, 4, 5, & 6: CORPORATE INCOME STATEMENT, RETAINED EARNINGS STATEMENT, AND BALANCE SHEET PREPARATION

4–57. The following information is taken from accounting records of Oxy's Toy Store for the year ended December 31, 2003:

Sales	$985,570
Cost of goods sold	654,340
Wages and salaries	195,820
Rent	24,000
Electricity	6,200
Telephone	2,460
Advertising	3,640
Maintenance	690
Interest revenue	520
Rent revenue	600
Interest expense	1,840
Income tax	31,264
Beginning retained earnings balance	235,860
Dividends	5,400
Cash	56,250
Accounts receivable	96,230
Inventory	275,860
Supplies	1,330
Equipment	13,590
Office equipment	35,980
Computer system	26,850
Delivery truck	28,460
Accounts payable	135,870
Notes payable	9,450
Bonds payable	10,000
Preferred stock	20,000
Additional paid-in capital—preferred	100
Common stock	3,200
Additional paid-in capital—common	59,034

Required:

    a. Prepare a 2003 income statement for the company using the single-step format.
    b. Prepare a 2003 income statement for the company using a multiple-step format.
    c. Prepare a 2003 retained earnings statement for the company.
    d. Prepare a balance sheet for the company as of the end of the accounting period.

LO 7: PREPARE A SIMPLE STATEMENT OF CASH FLOWS

4–58. The following information is from the records of the Super 211 Company for the year ended December 31, 2003.

    1. Cash sales to customers, $50,000
    2. Sold Super 211 Company stock for cash, $3,000
    3. Paid cash for merchandise, $24,000
    4. Paid cash dividend, $200
    5. Purchased **IBM** stock, $1,000
    6. Received cash dividend from **IBM,** $100
    7. Loaned $500 to ABC Company
    8. Paid cash for operating expenses, $4,000
    9. Paid income tax, $5,500
    10. Cash balance at December 31, 2002, was $20,000

Required: Prepare a statement of cash flows for Super 211 Company for the year ended December 31, 2003.

LO 7: PREPARE A SIMPLE STATEMENT OF CASH FLOWS

4–59. The following information is from the records of the Fox Company for the year ended December 31, 2003.

    1. Sold Fox Company stock for cash, $5,500
    2. Purchased equipment for cash, $8,000
    3. Cash sales to customers, $60,000
    4. Paid cash for merchandise, $25,000
    5. Paid $500 cash dividend
    6. Borrowed $7,000 from Miami National Bank
    7. Purchased **Dow Chemical** stock, $3,000
    8. Paid cash for operating expenses, $4,000
    9. Paid income tax, $7,500
    10. Cash balance at December 31, 2002, was $30,000

Required: Prepare a statement of cash flows for Fox Company for the year ended December 31, 2003.

LO 7: PREPARE A SIMPLE STATEMENT OF CASH FLOWS

4–60. The following information is from the records of the McCarthy Company for the year ended December 31, 2003.

    1. Cash sales to customers, $50,000
    2. Borrowed $7,000 from XYZ Bank
    3. Purchased equipment for cash, $10,000
    4. Sold equipment for cash, $1,500
    5. Sold McCarthy Company stock for cash, $3,000
    6. Made a loan payment to XYZ Bank for $1,090, which included $90 interest
    7. Paid cash for merchandise, $24,000
    8. Paid cash dividend, $200
    9. Purchased **IBM** stock, $1,000
    10. Received cash dividend from **IBM,** $100
    11. Paid cash to employees for wages, $6,000
    12. Loaned $500 to ABC Company
    13. Paid cash for other expenses, $4,000
    14. Paid income tax, $4,000
    15. Cash balance at December 31, 2002, was $20,000

Required: Prepare a statement of cash flows for McCarthy Company for the year ended December 31, 2003.

LO 7: PREPARE A SIMPLE STATEMENT OF CASH FLOWS

4–61. The following information is from the records of the Jaspers Computer, Inc., for the year ended December 31, 2003.

1. Cash sales to customers, $75,000
2. Borrowed from XYZ Bank, $9,000
3. Purchased equipment for cash, $12,000
4. Sold equipment for cash, $3,000
5. Sold Jaspers Computer, Inc., stock for cash of $3,000
6. Made a loan payment to XYZ Bank for $1,200, which included $150 interest
7. Paid cash for merchandise, $38,000
8. Paid $300 cash dividend
9. Purchased *IBM* stock, $1,300
10. Received cash dividend from *IBM,* $120
11. Paid cash to employees for wages, $8,000
12. Loaned $500 to ABC Company
13. Paid cash for other expenses, $10,000
14. Paid income tax, $2,500
15. Cash balance at December 31, 2002, was $25,000

Required: Prepare a statement of cash flows for Jaspers Computer, Inc., for the year ended December 31, 2003.

LO 7: PREPARE A SIMPLE STATEMENT OF CASH FLOWS

4–62. The following information is from the records of the Thomas Wholesale Company for the year ended December 31, 2003.

1. Loaned $1,500 to Smith Company
2. Sold Thomas Wholesale Company stock for cash, $6,000
3. Purchased equipment for cash, $11,000
4. Cash sales to customers totaled $70,000
5. Sold equipment for cash, $2,000
6. Paid cash to employees for wages, $5,000
7. Paid cash for merchandise, $35,000
8. Paid $500 cash dividend
9. Borrowed $5,000 from Miami National Bank
10. Purchased *Dow Chemical* stock, $3,000
11. Received cash dividend from *Dow Chemical,* $100
12. Paid cash for other expenses, $6,000
13. Paid income tax, $3,000
14. Made a loan payment to Miami National Bank for $1,100, which included $100 interest
15. Cash balance at December 31, 2002, was $40,000

Required: Prepare a statement of cash flows for Thomas Wholesale Company for the year ended December 31, 2003.

LO 7: PREPARE A SIMPLE STATEMENT OF CASH FLOWS

4–63. The following information is from the records of the Smith & Daughters Company for the year ended December 31, 2003.

1. Loaned $2,000 to Lynne Company
2. Sold Smith & Daughters Company stock for cash, $8,500
3. Purchased equipment for cash, $35,000
4. Cash sales to customers, $90,000
5. Sold equipment for cash, $2,000
6. Paid cash to employees for wages, $12,000
7. Paid cash for merchandise, $50,000
8. Paid $200 cash dividend
9. Borrowed $20,000 from Miami National Bank
10. Purchased *Dow Chemical* stock, $5,000
11. Received cash dividend from *Dow Chemical,* $500
12. Paid cash for other expenses, $14,000
13. Made a loan payment to Miami National Bank for $2,300, which included $300 interest.

14. Paid income tax, $6,000
15. Cash balance at December 31, 2002, was $9,000

Required: Prepare a statement of cash flows for Smith & Daughters Company for the year ended December 31, 2003.

LO 8: PROFITABILITY RATIO CALCULATIONS

4–64. The following information is available for the Matheis Company for the year ended December 31, 2003:

- Net sales were $13,552,000.
- Gross profit for 2003 was $3,132,200.
- Net income for the year was $709,500.
- Interest expense for the year totaled $103,400.
- The company's assets totaled $5,067,800 at December 31, 2002, and $5,520,200 at December 31, 2003.
- The company paid preferred dividends for the year totaling $26,000.
- The company paid common dividends for the year totaling $64,000.
- Common stockholders' equity totaled $3,156,800 at December 31, 2002, and $3,776,300 at December 31, 2003.
- Average number of common shares outstanding during the year was 825,000 shares.
- The company's common stock had an average market price of $16.50 per share.

Required:

a. Calculate the following profitability ratios for the company:

1. The gross profit margin ratio
2. The net profit margin ratio
3. The rate of return on assets ratio
4. The rate of return on common equity ratio
5. The dividend payout ratio
6. The company's earnings per share
7. The price-to-earnings ratio

b. Explain what the ratios tell you about the company

LO 8: PROFITABILITY RATIO CALCULATIONS

4–65. The following information is available for Rex International, Inc., for the year ended December 31, 2003:

- Net sales were $544,000.
- Gross profit for 2003 was $106,080.
- Net income for the year was $40,800.
- Interest expense for the year totaled $10,400.
- The company's assets totaled $1,300,000 at December 31, 2002, and $1,360,000 at December 31, 2003.
- The company paid preferred dividends for the year totaling $2,000.
- The company paid common dividends for the year totaling $4,000.
- Common stockholders' equity totaled $1,120,000 at December 31, 2002, and $1,154,800 at December 31, 2003.
- Average number of common shares outstanding during the year was 76,500 shares.
- The company's common stock had an average market price of $2.85 per share.

Required:

a. Calculate the following profitability ratios for the company:

1. The gross profit margin ratio
2. The net profit margin ratio
3. The rate of return on assets ratio
4. The rate of return on common equity ratio
5. The dividend payout ratio
6. The company's earnings per share
7. The price-to-earnings ratio

b. Explain what the ratios tell you about the company.

LO 8: PROFITABILITY RATIO CALCULATIONS

4–66. The following information is available for SOBE Entertainment, Inc., for the year ended December 31, 2003:

- Net sales were $846,000.
- Gross profit for 2003 was $448,500.
- Net income for the year was $80,900.
- Interest expense for the year totaled $20,500.
- The company's assets totaled $725,600 at December 31, 2002, and $795,400 at December 31, 2003.
- The company paid preferred dividends for the year totaling $12,000.
- The company paid common dividends for the year totaling $6,900.
- Common stockholders' equity totaled $345,000 at December 31, 2002, and $407,000 at December 31, 2003.
- Average number of common shares outstanding during the year was 110,250 shares.
- The company's common stock had an average market price of $12.59 per share.

Required:

a. Calculate the following profitability ratios for the company:

1. The gross profit margin ratio
2. The net profit margin ratio
3. The rate of return on assets ratio
4. The rate of return on common equity ratio
5. The dividend payout ratio
6. The company's earnings per share
7. The price-to-earnings ratio

b. Explain what the ratios tell you about the company.

LO 8: PROFITABILITY RATIO CALCULATIONS

4–67. The following information is available for Tom Robinson Industries, Inc.

Tom Robinson Industries, Inc.
Income Statement
For the Year Ended December 31, 2004
(In thousands)

Sales	$88,230
Less cost of goods sold	36,120
Gross margin	52,110
Operating expenses	(43,930)
Operating income	8,180
Other revenues:	
Rent revenue	80
Other expenses:	
Interest expense	(110)
Income before income tax	8,150
Income tax expense	2,771
Net income	$ 5,379

Statement of Stockholders' Equity
For the Year Ended December 31, 2004
(In thousands)

	Preferred Stock	Additional Paid-in Capital Preferred	Common Stock	Additional Paid-in Capital Common	Retained Earnings	Total Stockholders' Equity
Balance, January 1, 2004	$5,500	$ 250	$3,581	$22,872	$18,676	$50,879
Common stock issued						
Preferred stock issued						
Net income					5,379	5,379
Preferred dividend					(385)	(385)
Common dividends					(550)	(550)
Balance, December 31, 2004	$5,500	$ 250	$3,581	$22,872	$23,120	$55,323

Balance Sheet
December 31, 2004
(In thousands)

Assets:		Liabilities:	
Cash	$ 8,820	Current payable	$ 7,860
Land	27,548	Bonds payable	10,390
Building	33,750	Total liabilities	18,250
Other assets	3,455	Stockholders' equity:	
		Preferred stock, $50 par, 110 shares	
		issued and outstanding	$ 5,500
		Additional paid-in capital—preferred	250
		Common stock, $1 par, 3,581 shares	
		issued and outstanding	3,581
		Additional paid-in capital—common	22,872
		Total contributed capital	32,203
		Retained earnings	23,120
		Total stockholders' equity	55,323
Total assets	$73,573	Total liabilities and stockholders' equity	$73,573

Required: Assume the company's assets totaled $68,450 at December 31, 2003. Assume the company's common stock had an average market price of $12.90 per share as of December 31, 2004. Calculate the following profitability ratios for the company:

a. The gross profit margin ratio
b. The net profit margin ratio
c. The rate of return on assets ratio
d. The rate of return on common equity ratio
e. The dividend payout ratio
f. The company's earnings per share
g. The price-to-earnings ratio

LO 8: PROFITABILITY RATIO CALCULATIONS

4–68. The president of Wayne Industries, Inc., cannot understand why his company is having trouble obtaining additional external financing. "After all," he says, "the company earned a net income of over $1.7 million in 2004." The following information is also available:

Wayne Industries, Inc.
Income Statement
For the Year Ended December 31, 2004
(In thousands)

Sales	$144,230
Less cost of goods sold	110,090
Gross margin	34,140
Operating expenses	(30,710)
Operating income	3,430
Other revenues—rent revenue	30
Other expenses—interest expense	(990)
Income before income tax	2,470
Income tax expense	741
Net income	$ 1,729

Statement of Stockholders' Equity
For the Year Ended December 31, 2004
(In thousands)

	Preferred Stock	Additional Paid-in Capital Preferred	Common Stock	Additional Paid-in Capital Common	Retained Earnings	Total Stockholders' Equity
Balance, January 1, 2004	$5,000	$ 50	$9,320	$122,442	$11,801	$148,613
Common stock issued						
Preferred stock issued						
Net income					1,729	1,729
Preferred dividend					(400)	(400)
Common dividends					0	0
Balance, December 31, 2004	$5,000	$ 250	$9,320	$122,442	$13,130	$149,942

Balance Sheet
December 31, 2004
(In thousands)

Assets:			Liabilities:	
Cash	$ 1,820		Current payable	$ 44,560
Land	100,448		Bonds payable	12,375
Building	83,750		Total liabilities	56,935
Other assets	20,859		Stockholders' equity:	
			Preferred stock, $100 par, 50 shares	
			issued and outstanding	$ 5,000
			Additional paid-in capital—preferred	50
			Common stock, $.25 par, 37,280 shares	
			issued and outstanding	9,320
			Additional paid-in capital—common	122,442
			Total contributed capital	136,812
			Retained earnings	13,130
			Total stockholders' equity	149,942
Total assets	$206,877		Total liabilities and stockholders' equity	$206,877

Required:

a. Assume the company's assets totaled $201,443 at December 31, 2003. Note that the company had no common stock transactions during 2004, so the amount for common stock and additional paid-in capital for common did not change during the year. The average market price for the company's stock is $0.27 per share. Calculate the following profitability ratios for the company:

1. The gross profit margin ratio
2. The net profit margin ratio
3. The rate of return on assets ratio
4. The rate of return on common equity ratio
5. The dividend payout ratio
6. The company's earnings per share
7. The price-to-earnings ratio

b. Based on the ratios you calculated, discuss the reasons that the company may be having difficulty securing additional external financing.

LO 8: PROFITABILITY RATIO CALCULATIONS

4–69. The president of Stacy Sexton Industries, Inc., is expanding and would like to obtain additional external financing. The following information is also available:

Stacy Sexton Industries, Inc.
Income Statement
For the Year Ended December 31, 2004

Sales	$12,188,720
Less cost of goods sold	7,910,050
Gross margin	4,278,670
Operating expenses	(2,158,080)
Operating income	2,120,590
Other expenses—interest expense	(32,690)
Income before income tax	2,087,900
Income tax expense	751,644
Net income	$ 1,336,256

Balance Sheet
December 31, 2004

Total assets	$ 9,518,822
Total liabilities	408,625
Stockholders' equity:	
Preferred stock, no par, 8,000 shares	
issued and outstanding	800,000
Common stock, no par, 750,000 shares	
issued and outstanding	2,150,327
Retained earnings	6,159,870
Total stockholders' equity	9,110,197
Total liabilities and stockholders' equity	$ 9,518,822

Required: Assume the following:

- The company's common stock had an average market price of $34.29 per share.
- The company paid preferred dividends for the year totaling $56,000.
- The company paid common dividends for the year totaling $130,000.
- The company's assets totaled $8,947,877 at December 31, 2003.
- Retained earnings totaled $5,009,614 at December 31, 2003.
- No common stock transactions occurred during the year.

a. Calculate the following profitability ratios for the company:

1. The gross profit margin ratio
2. The net profit margin ratio
3. The rate of return on assets ratio
4. The rate of return on common equity ratio
5. The dividend payout ratio
6. The company's earnings per share
7. The price-to-earnings ratio

b. Based on the ratios you calculated, do you feel the company will have difficulty securing additional external financing? Explain your answer.

LO: COMPREHENSIVE

4–70. The Cronin Corporation has been a profitable company for many years and has paid a quarterly dividend for each of the past 45 quarters. The company's board of directors is meeting and will discuss the quarterly dividend declaration. The current quarter incurred a $150,000 net loss, which is not unusual for a second quarter of the year. Unfortunately, Cronin does not have enough cash to pay the dividend and to support its operation during the next 45 days.

Required:

a. Assuming the company could get the cash somehow, would the current quarter's loss preclude the company from paying a cash dividend? Explain your answer.
b. The problem indicates the company does not have enough cash to pay the dividend. What could the company do to get the cash it needs to pay the dividend?
c. Are there any reasons the company's board of directors would want to pay the cur-

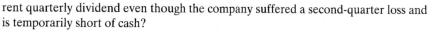

rent quarterly dividend even though the company suffered a second-quarter loss and is temporarily short of cash?

d. What do you think the board of directors should do?

LO 1, 2, & 4: INCOME STATEMENT, CAPITAL STATEMENT—PROPRIETORSHIP

4–71. The Michelle Miller Company began on January 15, 2003, when Ms. Miller contributed $10,000 to a business account. During 2003, she contributed another $10,000 on June 1 and $15,000 on September 30. Ms. Miller withdrew $5,000 on December 20. The following is a summary of the remaining receipts and expenditures for the year of 2003:

Receipts:	
Sales	$235,000
Inventory loan from bank	50,000
Expenditures:	
Inventory purchased and sold	140,000
Repayment of loan	40,000
Interest expense	2,000
Operating expenses:	
Selling expenses	37,000
Administrative expenses	39,000

Required:

a. Prepare a multiple-step income statement for 2003 for Michelle Miller Company.

b. Prepare a statement of capital for Michelle Miller Company for the year of 2003.

LO 1 & 4: STATEMENT OF STOCKHOLDERS' EQUITY—CORPORATION

4–72. Pezant, Inc., began operations during 2004. During that year, the corporation issued 30,000 shares of $10 par value stock on the following dates for the indicated amounts:

Date	Number of Shares	Price per Share
March 19	10,000	$15
May 16	15,000	$16
November 6	5,000	$20

The corporation earned a net income of $5,600 during 2004 and declared a modest $0.10 per share dividend on December 1 to shareholders of record on December 15, and paid the dividend on December 30.

Required: Prepare a statement of stockholders' equity for 2004.

Financial Reporting Exercises

LO 8: PROFITABILITY RATIOS

4–73. Using the **SEC**'s **EDGAR** system, obtain a copy of the **Office Depot, Inc.,** income statement, balance sheet, and statement of retained earnings from the company's Form 10K from 2001.

Required: Calculate the following profitability ratios for the company for 2001:

1. The gross profit margin ratio
2. The net profit margin ratio
3. The rate of return on assets ratio
4. The rate of return on common equity ratio
5. Why does this company not have a dividend payout ratio? What is their reasoning for this?
6. The company's earnings per share
7. The price-to-earnings ratio given that the average market price per share is $29.83

LO 8: PROFITABILITY RATIOS

4–74. Using the **SEC**'s **EDGAR** system, obtain a copy of the **OfficeMax, Inc.,** income statement, balance sheet, and statement of retained earnings from the company's 2001 Form 10K.

Required:

    a. Calculate the following profitability ratios for the company for each year presented:

        1. The gross profit margin ratio
        2. The net profit margin ratio
        3. The rate of return on assets ratio
        4. The rate of return on common equity ratio
        5. Why does this company not have a dividend payout ratio? What is their reasoning for this?
        6. The company's earnings per share
        7. Why doesn't this company have a price-to-earnings ratio?

    b. Look at the ratios for ***OfficeMax, Inc.,*** compared to ***Office Depot, Inc.*** For each ratio, circle which company has a more favorable ratio and why you think it is better. In which company would you rather invest? Why?

LO 8: PROFITABILITY RATIOS

4–75. Using the ***SEC***'s ***EDGAR*** system, obtain a copy of ***Staples, Inc.,*** income statement, balance sheet, and statement of retained earnings from the company's 2001 Form 10K.

Required:

    a. Calculate the following solvency ratios for the company for 2001:

        1. The debt ratio
        2. The debt-to-equity ratio

    b. Calculate the following profitability ratios for the company for 2001:

        1. The gross profit margin ratio
        2. The net profit margin ratio
        3. The rate of return on assets ratio
        4. The rate of return on common equity ratio
        5. Why does this company not have a dividend payout ratio? What is their reasoning for this?
        6. The company's earnings per share
        7. The price-to-earnings ratio given that the average market price per share of common stock is $16.32

    c. List for each ratio which of the three companies (***Office Depot, OfficeMax,*** or ***Staples***) is the most favorable.
    d. Which of the three companies would you be most likely to invest in and why?

LO 8: PROFITABILITY RATIOS

4–76. Select a publicly traded company that has positive earnings, preferred stock, pays dividends, and any other guidelines established by your instructor. Using the ***SEC***'s ***EDGAR*** system, obtain a copy of the company's income statement, its balance sheet, and its statement of retained earnings from the company's latest Form 10K.

Required:

    a. Calculate the following solvency ratios for the company for the most recent year:

        1. The debt ratio
        2. The debt-to-equity ratio

    b. Calculate the following profitability ratios for the company for the most recent year:

        1. The gross profit margin ratio
        2. The net profit margin ratio
        3. The rate of return on assets ratio
        4. The rate of return on common equity ratio
        5. The dividend payout ratio
        6. The company's earnings per share
        7. The price-to-earnings ratio

    c. What do the ratios tell you about the company? Would you rather invest in this company or a company from one of the previous three problems? Why?

ANNUAL REPORT PROJECT

4–77. Section 4—Basic Income Statement and Statement of Stockholders' Equity

In this assignment, you will prepare a report based on your company's income statement, its balance sheet, and other information.

Required: Prepare a report for your company that includes the following:

a. Companies are required to provide information on the various segments of their businesses. Describe your company's business segments. Describe the types of information your company's annual report includes for its various business segments. Indicate which segment you think contributes the most toward the success of your company. Explain your reasoning. Indicate which segment you think contributes the least. Explain your reasoning. Does the business segment information hint that the company should consider changing its business strategy or focus? Explain your reasoning.

b. Describe your company's income statement presentation and the important information it includes. For example, how many years of income statement information does your company present? Does your company use the single-step or multiple-step income statement format? Do you think there is any reason your company might use one format rather than the other? Which format would you prefer your company to use? Explain your reasoning. Discuss the important items and amounts that appear on the income statement. Is there a category on the income statement called something similar to "other income"? If so, use information from the notes to the financial statement to describe the items this category includes.

c. Describe your company's statement of stockholders' equity presentation. For example, how many years does your company present? Did your company issue stock during the year? Provide an explanation. What item seems to cause the most significant changes in stockholders equity? Your report should mention the number of common shares of stock authorized and the number outstanding, the number of preferred shares of stock authorized (if any) and the number outstanding. If your company has treasury stock, list the number of treasury shares presented and describe why you think the company reacquired its own stock. *Hint:* Check the managements' discussion and analysis and look in the note to the financial statements for this information.

d. Prepare a schedule that presents the following financial ratios:

- Gross profit margin ratios for three years
- Net profit margin ratios for three years
- Return on assets ratio for the latest year
- Return on common equity ratio for the latest year
- Dividend payout ratio for three years
- Earnings per share for three years
- Price-to-earnings ratio for the latest year

e. Comment in your report on the information that each one of the ratios provides. Where applicable, comment on the changes in the amounts of ratios over time.

f. Your report should conclude with a summary of your impressions of the company in light of what you discovered as you completed this assignment.

CHAPTER 5

Keeping Score: Bases of Economic Measurement

At the end of your sophomore year, you decide to start a small business to help with your college expenses. You spot an advertisement in the campus newspaper—"Used Delivery Truck for Sale." After some investigation into the potential services you could provide with it, you decide to buy the truck for $12,000 cash and begin to offer delivery services of furniture and mattresses around town. During your first month of business, you receive cash in the amount of $1,300 from Mattress City and bill Furniture Giant $2,100 for the delivery services you provided for them. In addition, you charge $225 for gasoline on your *Citibank VISA* card.

Your best friend is intrigued by your venture and asks what your company's income was for its first month of business. How do you respond? Do you say that the company earned $1,300 because you received that much cash and you really didn't pay out any cash for expenses? Or, since you paid cash for the truck, do you deduct the $12,000 from the $1,300 and say your business lost $10,700 in its first month? What about the $2,100 invoice to Furniture Giant that you won't collect on until next month? And how do you account for the gasoline you charged on the *VISA* card? Even though no cash changed hands, should you include those amounts in your income calculation?

What *was* your company's profit for its first month? Which amount is correct? Well, depending how you base your measurement, they are all correct, but the real question is this: Which figure best represents what actually happened in your business?

In the preceding two chapters, we explored the development of three financial tools—the balance sheet, the income statement, and the statement of owners' equity. We also showed how items on the balance sheet and income statement affect the statement of cash flows. Each of these statements measures economic activity. However, before decision makers can use these measurements with confidence, they must know the answer to one basic question: *From what perspective have the measurements been made?* Unless decision makers know what basis of economic measurement was used to prepare the financial statements, the information provided will be of little value to them.

There are two general bases of economic measurement—the cash basis and the accrual basis. In this chapter, we will consider these two approaches to measuring revenue and expense for a particular time period and explore in detail the distinctions between them.

Learning Objectives

After completing your work on this chapter, you should be able to do the following:

1. Explain the difference between reality and the measurement of reality.

2. Apply the criteria for revenue and expense recognition under the cash basis of accounting to determine periodic net income.

3. Apply the criteria for revenue and expense recognition under the accrual basis of accounting to determine periodic net income.

4. Explain the concept of matching and describe how it relates to depreciation.

5. Describe the difference between accruals and deferrals and identify examples of each.

6. Contrast the cash basis and accrual basis of economic measurement, describing the relative strengths and weaknesses of each.

◆ REALITY VERSUS THE MEASUREMENT OF REALITY

Every company performs a variety of functions. Some of the more common are purchasing inventory, selling goods, providing services, investing resources, and paying employees. These activities make up the actual events—the reality—of being in business and doing business. Every company must also measure these activities. As events occur, their effects are recorded in an attempt to measure the reality of the business. But remember this: *No matter how accurately the measurement of reality reflects reality, it is not reality.*

As an example of what we're talking about, assume a company purchased some office supplies and wrote a check for $480. In recording the check in the check register, the bookkeeper read the amount of the check incorrectly and entered $48. After deducting the $48, the check register indicated a balance of $1,127. The fact that the bookkeeper entered the wrong amount for the check in no way changes the reality of how much money the company spent and how much actually remains in the company's checking account.

Discussion Questions ⦁

5–1. Assuming there are no other errors in the check register, what is the actual cash balance in the company's checking account?

5–2. In what ways could this incorrect measurement of reality have an effect on reality? Explain.

THE PROBLEMS OF PERIODIC MEASUREMENT

Errors are one cause of differences between reality and the measurement of reality. However, there are also legitimate reasons for discrepancies between reality and its measure. An example is best demonstrated in the measurement of the revenues and expenses reported in a company's income statement for a particular period.

Most differences between reality and its measure occur when earnings activities are measured for a specific period of time. Regardless of the time period being measured (month, quarter, year, etc.), it is not always obvious which revenues and which expenses should be included in determining the earnings (net income) of that period.

Discussion Question ⦁

5–3. Checker Business Systems sells computer equipment to small businesses. During 2004, the sales activity was as follows:

February: Sold $6,000 of equipment to credit card or charge account customers (on account). The customers paid in full on March 15.

March: Sold $4,500 of equipment on account. Customers paid in full on April 15.

What activity would be included in each period if the business activity were measured

a. each month?

b. each quarter?

c. each year?

The only true measure of net income for a company is a comparison between revenues and expenses over the entire life of that company. In the fifteenth century, determining true net income was easier and more precise than it is today. In the era of Christopher Columbus, if an entrepreneur sailed to the New World and brought back goods to sell, the net income for that particular venture could be measured accurately. The entrepreneur began with a pile of money. With that, he bought a ship and supplies and hired men to help with the expedition. The group set sail, gathered up treasures and commodities from the New World, returned, and sold the goods. Then the workers were paid off, the ship was sold, and the entrepreneur ended up, once again, with a pile of money. If the pile of money he had at the end of his venture was greater than the pile of money he began with, the difference was a net income. If the amount of money he ended up with was smaller than the amount he started with, the entrepreneur suffered a net loss on the venture.

In today's world, it is unrealistic to expect companies to stop operations periodically and sell off all their assets so they can determine their "true" net income. So although lifetime net income is the only truly precise measurement of an operation's success or failure, users of accounting information demand current information every year, or quarter, or month. It is this need to artificially break the company's operations into time periods that requires us to make decisions about when revenues and expenses should be reported.

REVENUE AND EXPENSE RECOGNITION

In the base of the arch we have used to depict the Financial Accounting Standards Board's (FASB's) *Conceptual Framework of Accounting* (see Exhibit 5–1), certain accounting principles are listed. Revenue recognition and expense recognition are the two we will discuss in this chapter. As in previous chapters, the italicized definitions in the following discussion are provided by the FASB. A less formal discussion of certain items follows the words of the FASB.

In the *Conceptual Framework*, the FASB defined recognition in accounting as . . . *the process of formally recording or incorporating an item into the financial statements of an entity as an asset, liability, revenue, expense, or the like. Recognition includes depiction of an item in both words and numbers, with the amount included in the totals of the financial statements* (Statement of Financial Accounting Concepts No. 5, paragraph 6). **Recognition** in accounting, then, is the process of (1) recording in the books and (2) reporting on the financial statements.

recognition The process of recording an event in accounting records and reporting it in your financial statements.

The problem of when to recognize an item applies to all of the accounting elements we have discussed so far, as well as to the ones we have yet to discuss. The greatest difficulties, however, concern when to recognize revenues and expenses.

When should revenue be recognized? When should an expense be recognized? These are two very difficult questions, for which there are no clear-cut "right" answers. For financial statements of different companies to be comparable, there must be a consistently applied set of criteria to determine when accounting elements, particularly revenues and expenses, are recognized. Those of you who have taken another accounting class may have been taught a particular set of criteria for revenue and expense recognition and we are not asking you to forget what you learned. What we are asking you to do is slide those criteria to the back of your mind, because what you learned in the other accounting class is *a* set of criteria, not *the* set of criteria.

Discussion Questions ◦ ◦ ◦ ◦ ● ◦ ● ◦ ◦ ◦ ● ◦ ● ◦ ◦ ◦ ◦ ◦ ◦ ● ◦ ● ◦ ◦ ● ◦ ● ◦ ◦

5–4. If revenue is defined as the reward of doing business, at what point do you think it should be recognized? Explain.

5–5. If an expense is defined as the sacrifice necessary to obtain a revenue, at what point do you think it should be recognized? Explain.

BASES OF ECONOMIC MEASUREMENT

There are two basic approaches to recording economic activity—the *cash basis* of economic measurement and the *accrual basis* of economic measurement. As they are discussed, you will see that each has certain advantages over the other. Neither of them is "correct" in the sense of being in accordance with some natural law of finance and accounting. They are simply different approaches to the measurement of revenues, expenses, assets, liabilities, and owners' equity.

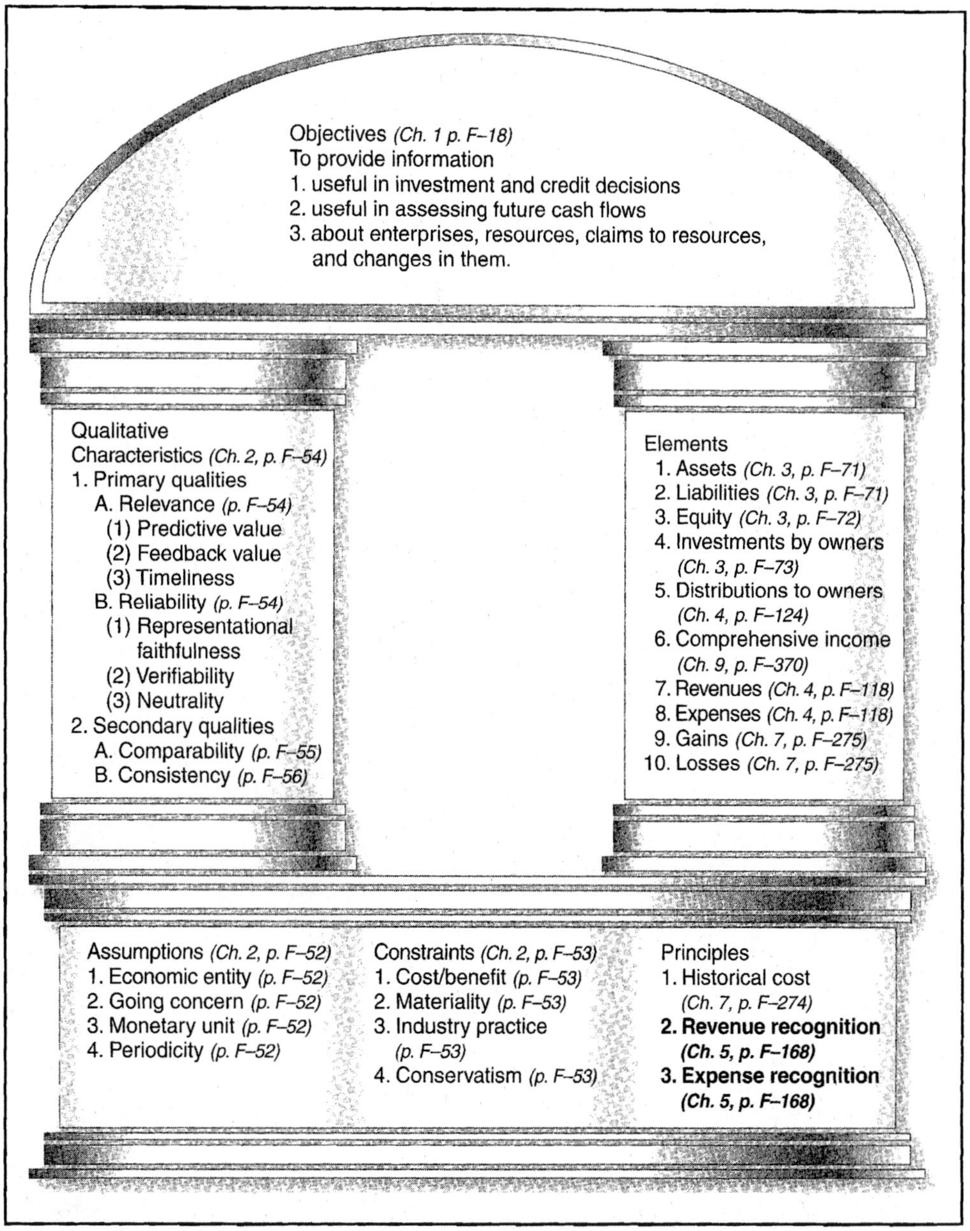

Objectives *(Ch. 1 p. F–18)*
To provide information
1. useful in investment and credit decisions
2. useful in assessing future cash flows
3. about enterprises, resources, claims to resources, and changes in them.

Qualitative
Characteristics *(Ch. 2, p. F–54)*
1. Primary qualities
   A. Relevance *(p. F–54)*
      (1) Predictive value
      (2) Feedback value
      (3) Timeliness
   B. Reliability *(p. F–54)*
      (1) Representational
          faithfulness
      (2) Verifiability
      (3) Neutrality
2. Secondary qualities
   A. Comparability *(p. F–55)*
   B. Consistency *(p. F–56)*

Elements
1. Assets *(Ch. 3, p. F–71)*
2. Liabilities *(Ch. 3, p. F–71)*
3. Equity *(Ch. 3, p. F–72)*
4. Investments by owners
   (Ch. 3, p. F–73)
5. Distributions to owners
   (Ch. 4, p. F–124)
6. Comprehensive income
   (Ch. 9, p. F–370)
7. Revenues *(Ch. 4, p. F–118)*
8. Expenses *(Ch. 4, p. F–118)*
9. Gains *(Ch. 7, p. F–275)*
10. Losses *(Ch. 7, p. F–275)*

Assumptions *(Ch. 2, p. F–52)*
1. Economic entity *(p. F–52)*
2. Going concern *(p. F–52)*
3. Monetary unit *(p. F–52)*
4. Periodicity *(p. F–52)*

Constraints *(Ch. 2, p. F–53)*
1. Cost/benefit *(p. F–53)*
2. Materiality *(p. F–53)*
3. Industry practice
   (p. F–53)
4. Conservatism *(p. F–53)*

Principles
1. Historical cost
   (Ch. 7, p. F–274)
2. **Revenue recognition**
   (Ch. 5, p. F–168)
3. **Expense recognition**
   (Ch. 5, p. F–168)

EXHIBIT 5–1   The Conceptual Framework of Accounting

We will use a single set of data to illustrate the two bases of measurement. Consider the following information concerning Corkel Incorporated, a dealer of sophisticated exercise equipment with a target market of movie stars and eccentric millionaires:

1. Max Corkel started the company on January 2, 2003, by incorporating and immediately purchasing 2,000 shares of the company's no-par common stock for $200,000.

2. Corkel Incorporated borrowed $100,000 from ***Citibank*** on January 2, by signing a one-year, 12 percent note payable. Although the $100,000 does not have to be repaid until January 2, 2004, the interest charge must be paid each month, beginning on February 2, 2003.

3. The company purchased a vehicle on January 2 for $14,000 cash. Max's best guess is that the vehicle will fill the company's needs for four years, after which he estimates the vehicle can be sold for $2,000.

4. The company paid cash for $75,000 of merchandise inventory on January 8.
5. On January 15, the company sold $42,000 of the merchandise inventory for a total selling price of $78,000 and collected cash the same day.
6. On January 22, the company sold $15,000 of the merchandise inventory for a total selling price of $32,000 on account (a credit sale). The terms of the sale were 30 days, meaning Corkel can expect to receive payment by February 22.
7. Cash payments for operating expenses in January totaled $22,500.
8. At the end of the month, the company owed $2,000 to employees of the company for work performed in January. They will be paid on February 3.
9. The company owed $700 at the end of the month for a utility bill that was received on January 26 and will be paid on February 15.

The above information is the reality of what happened in Corkel Incorporated during the month of January 2003. The measurement of that reality will be different, depending on whether you use the cash basis of accounting or the accrual basis of accounting. Remember, both treatments are based on exactly the same reality. They are simply different methods of measuring reality.

◆ CASH BASIS OF ECONOMIC MEASUREMENT

cash basis accounting
A basis of accounting in which cash is the major criterion used in measuring revenue and expense for a given income statement period. Revenue is recognized when the associated cash is received, and expense is recognized when the associated cash is paid.

The first approach we'll look at to measure economic activity is **cash basis accounting.** It is the simpler of the two bases, because everyone understands what cash is and can therefore readily grasp the measurement criterion of this method. Its greatest strength lies in the fact that it keeps the user's eye on the ball. As its name implies, the cash basis has only one measurement criterion: *CASH*!

As you recall, one of the three objectives of accounting information outlined by the FASB in the *Conceptual Framework* dealt specifically with cash. That objective says that to be useful, the information should help users assess a company's ability to generate sufficient cash to meet its obligations, support its operations, and to pay dividends. To do this, the FASB states that . . . *financial reporting should provide information to help investors, creditors, and others assess the amounts, timing, and uncertainty of prospective net cash inflows to the related enterprise* (Statement of Financial Accounting Concepts No. 1, paragraph 37). The underlying theoretical justification for the cash basis of accounting is that it keeps the users focused on cash flow. Under cash basis accounting, we recognize economic activity only when we receive or pay cash.

CASH BASIS REVENUE RECOGNITION

There are two things to keep in mind when considering cash basis revenue recognition. First, a company recognizes revenue only when it receives the associated cash. Second, cash basis accounting considers only cash received as a result of the earnings process to be revenue. For example, the cash a business receives from its owners is an investment by those owners rather than revenue. Also, the business considers the cash it receives when it borrows as a liability rather than revenue. Transactions such as these, which involve cash but are not considered revenues, are reported on the statement of owners' equity and/or on the balance sheet, but not on the income statement.

CASH BASIS EXPENSE RECOGNITION

A company recognizes an expense only when it pays the associated cash. As with revenues, under cash basis accounting, not all cash a company pays out is an expense. If a company pays a dividend to its owners, for example, the cash paid out is not an expense to the company. Such a payment is a distribution of profits or a return on the owners' original investment. Transactions such as these, which involve cash but are not considered expenses, are reported on the statement of owners' equity and/or on the balance sheet, but not on the income statement.

CASH BASIS FINANCIAL STATEMENTS

There are two keys, then, to revenue and expense recognition under the cash basis. First, cash must be involved in the transaction. Second, the receipt or disbursement must relate to delivering or producing goods, rendering services, or other profit-related activities. If a transaction meets both of these requirements, it is a revenue or expense transaction (depending on whether the cash is received or paid) and will be reported on the income statement.

In preparing the income statement, the statement of owners' equity, and the balance sheet using the cash basis, you must first isolate the events and transactions involving cash. For our example of Corkel Incorporated, of the nine transactions and events we listed earlier, only the following events and transactions involve cash:

1. Max Corkel started the company on January 2, 2003, by incorporating and immediately purchasing 2,000 shares of the company's no-par common stock for $200,000.
2. Corkel Incorporated borrowed $100,000 from **Citibank** on January 2, by signing a one-year, 12 percent note payable. Although the $100,000 does not have to be repaid until January 2, 2004, the interest charge must be paid each month, beginning on February 2, 2003.
3. The company purchased a vehicle on January 2 for $14,000 cash. Max's best guess is that the vehicle will fill the company's needs for four years, after which he estimates the vehicle can be sold for $2,000.
4. The company paid cash for $75,000 of merchandise inventory on January 8.
5. On January 15, the company sold $42,000 of the merchandise inventory for a total selling price of $78,000 and collected cash the same day.
7. Cash payments for operating expenses in January totaled $22,500.

Corkel records these transactions in its books and reports the results on one or more of the financial statements: the income statement, the statement of owners' equity, or the balance sheet.

In order to determine which of the transactions should be reported on the income statement, we must determine which relate directly to Corkel's major or central operation, which is the buying and selling of sophisticated exercise equipment. Transactions 3, 4, 5, and 7 meet that criterion. Exhibit 5–2 shows a multiple-step income statement for the month of January 2003 using the cash basis of accounting.

- *Sales revenue.* Because the company received $78,000 in cash from sales in the month of January, that is the amount it shows as revenue.
- *Cost of goods sold.* Corkel paid $75,000 in cash for merchandise inventory during January. Thus, that is the amount recognized as cost of goods sold.
- *Expenses.* The cash expenses of $22,500 plus the entire $14,000 for the vehicle the company purchased were recognized as expenses in January. The company will recognize the remaining expenses as it pays the cash.

EXHIBIT 5–2 Cash Basis Income Statement

Corkel Incorporated
Income Statement
For the Month Ended January 31, 2003

Sales revenue		$ 78,000
Cost of goods sold		(75,000)
Gross margin		$ 3,000
Expenses:		
Cost of vehicle	$14,000	
Cash operating expenses	22,500	
Total operating expenses		(36,500)
Net loss		($ 33,500)

Transaction 1, Max Corkel's investment of $200,000, reflects an inflow of cash, so the cash basis of measurement requires that it be recognized. This investment by the owner increases the company's capital, while the net loss determined in Exhibit 5–2 decreases capital. Exhibit 5–3 shows the statement of owners' equity prepared using the cash basis of accounting.

EXHIBIT 5–3   Cash Basis Statement of Owners' Equity

Corkel Incorporated
Statement of Stockholders' Equity
For the Month Ended January 31, 2003

	Common Stock	Retained Earnings	Total
Balances as of January 1, 2003	$ 0	$ 0	$ 0
Sale of common stock	200,000		200,000
Net loss		(33,500)	(33,500)
Balances as of January 31, 2003	$200,000	($33,500)	$166,500

The remaining cash transaction of Corkel Incorporated during January 2003 is Transaction 2, the $100,000 bank loan. Borrowing money creates a liability that appears on the balance sheet. Exhibit 5–4 shows Corkel Incorporated's balance sheet at January 31, 2003, under cash basis accounting.

EXHIBIT 5–4   Cash Basis Balance Sheet

Corkel Incorporated
Balance Sheet
January 31, 2003

Assets:		Liabilities:	
Cash	$266,500	Note payable	$100,000
		Stockholders' equity:	
		Common stock	200,000
		Retained earnings	(33,500)
		Total stockholders' equity	166,500
Total assets	$266,500	Total liabilities and stockholders' equity	$266,500

Notice the articulation of the financial statements for Corkel Incorporated. The net loss from the income statement is shown on the statement of owners' equity, and the ending balances from the statement of owners' equity are used on the balance sheet. The cash amount showing on the balance sheet is simply the $200,000 the owner invested in the company plus the $100,000 borrowed from the bank less the $33,500 net loss for the month of January.

Discussion Questions ●

5–6. Assume for a moment that you are Corkel's loan officer at the bank. How would you evaluate the income statement and balance sheet presented in Exhibits 5–2 and 5–4 in terms of the primary qualitative characteristic of relevance, including predictive value and feedback value? (*Hint*: See Chapter 2.)

5–7. If your response to Question 5–6 led you to the conclusion that there is a problem in terms of predictive value and feedback value, what item or items do you feel caused the problem? How do you think the company could account for the item or items to better relate costs to the revenues they generate?

STRENGTHS AND WEAKNESSES OF CASH BASIS ACCOUNTING

The greatest strength of cash basis accounting is that it keeps the focus on cash flow, and because of that, it is relatively simple to use. Further, it is relatively objective. Because cash is the only measurement criterion, the cash basis requires less subjective judgment than the accrual basis measurement, which we will discuss next. This is not to say that cash basis accounting is totally objective. For example, a company can manipulate the expenses it reports in a particular income statement period simply by delaying the payment of amounts owed. The greatest weakness of the cash basis is that it makes no attempt to recognize expenses in the same period as the revenues they helped generate. This makes the cash basis income statement very difficult to use either for predicting future profitability or for assessing past performance in cases in which cash is not immediately received when it is earned or paid when it is owed.

Discussion Question ⋅

5-8. The cash basis of accounting is very similar to maintaining a checking account balance. Provide two examples of situations in which your checkbook balance did not provide relevant information.

◆ ACCRUAL BASIS OF ECONOMIC MEASUREMENT

accrual basis accounting A method of accounting in which revenues are recognized when they are earned, regardless of when the associated cash is collected. The expenses incurred in generating the revenue are recognized when the benefit is derived rather than when the associated cash is paid.

accrue As used in accounting, to come into being as a legally enforceable claim.

The second basis of economic measurement we will discuss is **accrual basis accounting.** The key to understanding accrual basis accounting is to understand what the word **accrue** means, which is *to come into being as a legally enforceable claim.* This system does not rely on the receipt or payment of cash to determine when revenues and expenses should be recognized.

Essentially, in accrual basis accounting, a company recognizes sales, purchases, and all other business transactions whenever a legally enforceable claim to the associated cash is established. A legally enforceable claim to cash means that if somebody owes you money and they don't pay, you can legally force them to pay (or vice versa). The main focus of accrual accounting is determining when a legally enforceable claim to cash or other assets or services has been established between the parties involved in the transaction.

The legal considerations just discussed are all well and good, but more importantly from a practical standpoint, at least, is what accrual accounting and the resultant financial information is attempting to capture. Essentially, accrual accounting focuses on the earnings process rather than the cash flows resulting from that process. This is important because what it means is that accrual accounting takes the user's eye off the ball (cash). The FASB, in the *Conceptual Framework,* had this to say about accrual accounting:

> *Accrual accounting attempts to record the financial effects on an entity of transactions and other events and circumstances that have cash consequences for the entity in the periods in which those transactions, events, and circumstances occur rather than only in the periods in which cash is received or paid by the entity. Accrual accounting is concerned with an entity's acquiring of goods and services and using them to produce and distribute other goods or services. It is concerned with the process by which cash expended on resources and activities is returned as more (or perhaps less) cash to the entity, not just with the beginning and end of that process. It recognizes that the buying, producing, selling, distributing, and other operations of an entity during a period, as well as other events that affect entity performance, often do not coincide with the cash receipts and payments of the period* (Statement of Financial Accounting Concepts No. 6, paragraph 139).

Included in the concept of accrual accounting are the revenue and expense recognition principles the FASB discussed in the *Conceptual Framework.* Following the FASB's italicized words, we will explain how the principles are applied.

ACCRUAL BASIS REVENUE RECOGNITION

The FASB said this about accrual basis revenue recognition:

> *Revenues and gains of an enterprise during a period are generally measured by the exchange values of assets (goods or services) or liabilities involved, and recognition involves consideration of two factors (A) being realized or realizable and (B) being earned, with sometimes one and sometimes the other being the more important consideration* (Statement of Financial Accounting Concepts No. 5, paragraph 83).

First, let's address the FASB's reference to *revenues* and *gains*. While revenues and gains are similar, revenues result from a company's primary or central operations and gains result from what we call incidental or peripheral transactions. *Gains* are one of the 10 accounting elements listed on the arch, and we will discuss this topic in Chapter 7. For now we will focus on revenues that result from a company's primary operations.

If we are using accrual accounting then, we recognize revenue when it is *realized* or *realizable* or when we consider it *earned*. Revenues are realized when a company exchanges goods or services for cash or claims to cash. They are realizable when a company receives assets other than cash or claims to cash, when those assets can be exchanged for known amounts of cash or claims to cash. If you think this all sounds pretty confusing, you're not alone. Even practicing accountants with years of experience sometimes disagree about precisely what the concept of realized or realizable means and how it applies to day-to-day business transactions and events. For this reason, our focus will be on recognizing revenue when we consider it earned.

Under accrual accounting, we recognize revenue when it is deemed to be earned—that is, a company recognizes revenue when it has a legally enforceable claim to the cash associated with that revenue. Since in many instances the cash is collected some time other than when the revenue is earned, under accrual accounting, revenue recognition is completely unrelated to when the cash is received.

There are three possible relationships between when a company receives cash and when it recognizes revenue:

1. Cash is received at the time the revenue is earned. An example of this is when you buy a pair of jeans at *Gap* and pay cash. *Gap* receives cash at the same time as the store recognizes revenue from the sale.
2. Cash is received after the revenue has been earned. An example of this is a sale of merchandise on account (a credit sale). ***NAPA Auto Parts*** records revenue for sales made to its credit card customers in January but does not collect the cash until February.
3. Cash is received before the revenue has been earned. An example of this is when ***Time*** magazine receives the payment in advance from a customer for a year's subscription.

Remember that under accrual accounting, the trigger mechanism for determining when revenue should be recognized is the earning process, not when the cash is received. In Examples 1 and 2, the revenue is recorded in the books and shown on the financial statements at the time the sale is made. The fact that in Example 2 the company did not receive cash at that time does not affect recognition of the revenue. In Example 3, the receipt of cash does not cause revenue to be recognized because, under accrual accounting, the revenue is not recognized until it is earned (when the magazines have been sent to the customer).

Identifying the point in time when revenue is earned is not always a simple matter. There are three questions accountants try to answer to determine when revenue has been earned and should therefore be recognized:

title Legal ownership of something.

1. Has **title** (legal ownership) to whatever was sold been transferred to the customer? If the answer to this question is yes, the seller should definitely recognize the revenue.
2. Has an exchange taken place? In other words, has the customer received whatever he or she purchased? If the answer to this question is yes, the seller will likely recognize the revenue.

3. Is the earnings process virtually complete? This is the toughest of the three questions to answer. Let's say, for example, that you have contracted with Joe Dokes to remodel your kitchen. It's a two-week job, and midway through the second week, Joe decides that he doesn't want to be a remodeler anymore. Are you obligated to pay him for removing your old cabinets, stripping the wallpaper, and making a hole in the wall for the new window? Probably not. He cannot recognize revenue until the job is "virtually" complete.

The answer to all three questions need not be "yes" for a business to recognize revenue. In most cases, a positive answer to any one question is persuasive evidence that revenue has been earned and should be recognized.

Discussion Questions

5–9. On Saturday morning, you decide to buy a computer at Carl's Computer Mart. The salesperson has agreed to have all the software you need installed and have the machine delivered to you by Tuesday afternoon. Because you purchased your last computer at Carl's, the store has agreed to extend credit to you as an established customer. You have 30 days to pay for your new computer. As of Monday,

    a. has title passed?

    b. has an exchange taken place?

    c. is the earnings process complete?

5–10. When should Carl's Computer Mart recognize revenue:

    a. under the cash basis?

    b. under the accrual basis?

ACCRUAL BASIS EXPENSE RECOGNITION

The FASB said this about accrual basis expense recognition:

> *Expenses and losses are generally recognized when an entity's economic benefits are used up in delivering or producing goods, rendering services, or other activities that constitute its ongoing major or central operations or when previously recognized assets are expected to provide reduced or no further benefits* (Statement of Financial Accounting Concepts No. 5, paragraph 85).

First, let's address the FASB's reference to *expenses* and *losses*. Expenses and losses are similar, and in the reference just cited, the FASB states that both expenses and losses result from a company's ongoing or central operations. While it is true that some losses do result from a company's day-to-day operations, you should think of expenses as resulting from a company's primary or central operations, and consider losses as resulting from incidental or peripheral transactions. *Losses* are one of the 10 accounting elements in the arch, and we will discuss them in Chapter 7. For now, we will focus on expenses that result from a company's day-to-day operations.

According to the FASB, then, an entity should recognize expenses when its *economic benefits* are used up in delivering or producing goods or rendering services. Economic benefits, as you recall from Chapter 3, are assets. So expenses are assets used up in delivering or producing goods or rendering services. As with revenue recognition, expense recognition under accrual accounting is completely unrelated to the movement of cash.

Again, there are three possible relationships between when a company pays cash and when it recognizes an expense:

1. Cash is paid at the time the expense is incurred. An example of this is a check the manager of a *Gap* store writes to the catering company for food served at the store Christmas party held that same day.

2. Cash is paid after the expense has been incurred. An example of this is *NAPA Auto Parts*' payment of a utility bill in February that was for electricity used in January.

3. Cash is paid before the expense has been incurred. An example of this is insurance. *Time* magazine buys insurance coverage for a full year and pays the entire premium when the policy is purchased.

The key to expense recognition under accrual accounting is revenue recognition. That's right—*revenue recognition.* Remember that to be useful in predicting future profitability and cash flow, an income statement should measure revenues for a specific period of time *and* the expenses required to obtain those revenues. Thus, accrual accounting attempts to establish a relationship between revenues and expenses. This relationship is referred to as **matching.**

matching   Accounting principle that relates the expenses to the revenues of a particular income statement period. Once it is determined in which period a revenue should be recognized, the expenses that helped to generate the revenue are matched to that same period.

THE CONCEPT OF MATCHING

In the *Conceptual Framework*, the FASB stated:

> *Accrual accounting uses accrual, deferral, and allocation procedures whose goal is to relate revenues, expenses, gains, and losses to periods to reflect an entity's performance during a period instead of merely listing its cash receipts and outlays. Thus, recognition of revenues, expenses, gains, and losses and the related increments and decrements in assets and liabilities—including matching of costs and revenues, allocation, and amortization—is the essence of using accrual accounting to measure performance of entities* (Statement of Financial Accounting Concepts No. 6, paragraph 145).

The first step in the accrual matching process is to determine in which income statement period a company should recognize a particular revenue. The second step is to determine which expenses helped to generate that revenue. The company then recognizes those expenses in that same financial statement period. This approach makes the income statement for that time period more reflective of true earnings results and, therefore, more relevant for predicting future potential. It is important to note that it can be very difficult to determine which expenses generated which revenue, so a significant amount of judgment is required in recognizing expenses under the accrual basis of accounting. There are two possible relationships between revenues and expenses, and these determine when expenses are recognized: (1) direct cause and effect and (2) no direct cause and effect.

1. *Direct cause and effect.* This situation, in which a direct link can be found between an expense and the revenue it helped generate, is the more desirable of the two relationships. An example is sales commissions. If **Prudential Insurance Company** pays a 10 percent sales commission to its salespersons, and a sales representative makes a sale of $1,000, the company incurs a $100 expense. Once the company determines in which income statement period it should recognize the $1,000 revenue, it recognizes the $100 expense in that same period. Unfortunately, relatively few expenses can be linked directly to the revenues they help generate.
2. *No direct cause and effect.* This is the more common relationship. In this case, there are two possible treatments: (a) allocation to the periods benefited and (b) immediate recognition.
    a. *Allocation to the periods benefited.* If a purchased item has discernible benefit to future income statement periods and the periods can be reasonably estimated, a company records the item as an asset when purchased. The cost of that item is then systematically converted to expense in the periods benefited. An example of this is insurance. If a company pays a premium for two years of insurance coverage, there is no question that a benefit to future periods exists. Further, the estimate of those periods is clear—benefits will be derived for two years. As time passes during the two years, the company converts the cost of the insurance coverage to expense. This allows each of the two years covered by the insurance to show an equal amount of expense.
    b. *Immediate recognition.* There are two situations in which recording the expense immediately is the most appropriate action. First, if a purchased item has no dis-

cernible future benefit, or the periods benefited cannot be reasonably estimated, a company should recognize the cost of the item as an expense immediately. A good example of an expense requiring immediate recognition is **Ford Motor Company**'s television advertising to promote the sale of its cars and trucks. The future benefit of this type of advertising is not discernible. Television ads purchased and presented to the public in one period almost certainly benefit future periods, but how many periods and how much in each of those periods cannot be reasonably estimated. Thus, companies usually recognize the cost of television advertising as an expense in the periods when the ads are purchased.

The second situation requiring the immediate recognition of an expense is when allocation of the cost of a purchased item provides no additional useful information. An example of this situation is the purchase of a $10 item such as a stapler. Even if the stapler will be used in the office for five years, allocation of the $10 cost over the five-year period serves no useful purpose. Remember, the purpose of accounting is to provide information useful to decision makers. Will allocating this minor cost over a five-year period provide useful accounting information? Since most decision makers would be unaffected by the treatment of a $10 item, the answer is no. The record-keeping cost of recording the stapler as an asset on the balance sheet and then converting a portion of that cost per year as an expense on each of the next five year's income statements far outweighs the benefit of doing so. Recognizing the $10 cost as an immediate expense makes more sense. This is a perfect example of the materiality and cost/benefit constraints we discussed in Chapter 2.

The concept of "allocation to the periods benefited" has a more widely used application than the one just described. When assets that will benefit the company for several periods (often many years) are acquired, the cost is recorded as an asset on the balance sheet. As time passes, the cost is transferred to expense on the income statement. This form of "allocation to the periods benefited" is a process known as depreciation. Depreciation is applied to a variety of long-lived assets such as machinery, buildings, and equipment. One asset that has a long life, but is not depreciated, is land.

DEPRECIATION—WHAT IT IS *AND* WHAT IT IS NOT

depreciation The systematic and rational conversion of a long-lived asset's cost from asset to expense in the income statement periods benefited.

Depreciation is a systematic (methodical) and rational (reasoned) allocation of the cost of a long-lived item from asset to expense. You should recall that under cash basis accounting, Corkel Incorporated recognized the purchase of a $14,000 vehicle as a $14,000 expense because that amount of cash was spent. The real question is whether this asset has been "used up" (has the company received the total benefit from the vehicle?) or does the asset still have a future benefit? The answer is clearly that the asset (vehicle) has not been used up; the company has not received all the benefit from it. The accrual basis of measurement takes the position that the company should not recognize this cash payment of $14,000 as an expense at the time the cash is paid. Rather than recognize the cost of the vehicle as an expense immediately, under the accrual basis, it is recorded as an asset because it has probable future benefit. Over time, the cost of the vehicle will be converted from asset to expense as the benefit is derived from the use of the vehicle. The resulting expense is called depreciation expense.

There is probably nothing in all of accounting as misunderstood as the concept of depreciation. The confusion is caused by the difference between the meaning of *depreciation* in accounting and in ordinary speech. In virtually every context except accounting, depreciation means the lowering of value. In accounting, it simply means the allocation of cost to the periods benefited. This allocation requires two highly subjective estimates: (1) the useful life of the asset and (2) the residual value of the asset.

The useful life of an asset is the length of time that the asset will be of use to the company, not the length of time the asset will exist. Notice that in the case of Corkel Incorporated, Max Corkel feels that the vehicle will fill the company's needs for four years. This is not the same thing as saying the vehicle will last four years. This is an important distinction.

If the estimated useful life of an asset is less than the physical life of that asset, it follows that the asset will probably be sold at the end of its useful life. The estimated amount for which the asset can be sold at the end of its useful life is known as its residual value (sometimes called *salvage value* or *scrap value*).

In calculating depreciation, we subtract any estimated residual value from the cost of an asset to arrive at what is called the *depreciable base* or *depreciable amount*. In the case of Corkel Incorporated, the cost of the vehicle was $14,000, and the company estimated that at the end of its useful life, the vehicle could be sold for $2,000. The depreciable amount, therefore, is $12,000 ($14,000 − $2,000). In one sense, then, the true cost of the vehicle to Corkel is $12,000, because the company expects to recoup $2,000 of the purchase price when the vehicle is sold.

Once we have estimated the useful life and residual value of the asset, we must select a method of depreciation. Several have been developed over the years. The simplest method is straight-line depreciation, and we will use it to demonstrate how depreciation expense is calculated.

The straight-line approach allocates an equal amount of depreciation expense to each period of the asset's estimated useful life. The amount of expense is calculated by dividing the estimated useful life of the asset into the depreciable amount of the asset. In the case of Corkel's vehicle, which cost $14,000 and has a four-year estimated useful life and a $2,000 residual value, the amount of expense works out to $3,000 per year calculated as follows:

$$\frac{\text{Cost} - \text{Residual Value}}{\text{Useful Life}} = \frac{\$14,000 - \$2,000}{4} = \frac{\$12,000}{4} = \$3,000$$

Each year of the four-year estimated useful life, Corkel will transfer $3,000 of the asset "vehicle" on the balance sheet into the expense "depreciation" on the income statement. At the end of the four years, the company will have recognized the entire cost of the vehicle (except the $2,000 residual value) as expense.

Depreciation is an important process that is based on accrual accounting's attempt to recognize expenses in the periods in which they help to generate revenue. Even though all of the $14,000 in cash was spent during January 2003 for Corkel Incorporated's vehicle, the entire benefit expected from the asset has not been received at that time. Because the company expects the asset to help generate revenues in future periods, it will allocate part of the cost to depreciation expense in each of those periods. The depreciation process is just one result of accrual accounting's attempt to match expenses and revenues. We'll explore others next.

Discussion Question

5–11. Recall the scenario, introduced in Discussion Question 5–9, involving your purchase of a computer from Carl's Computer Mart. If the computer is to be used in the business you operate from your home, how should the purchase be treated:

   a. under the cash basis?
   b. under the accrual basis?

ACCRUALS AND DEFERRALS

adjustments Changes made in recorded amounts of revenues and expenses in order to follow the guidelines of accrual accounting.

Because accrual accounting attempts to recognize revenues in the income statement period they are earned, and attempts to match the expenses that generated that revenue to the same income statement period, **adjustments** must be made each period to ensure that these guidelines have been followed. The adjustment process takes place at the end of the financial statement period before the financial statements are prepared. This process involves reviewing the financial records to be sure that all items that should be recognized in the current period have been recorded. In addition, during the adjustment process, it is ascertained that no items that should be recognized in future periods appear in the current period's records. The two basic types of adjustments that are necessary are accruals and deferrals.

accruals Adjustments made to record items that should be included on the income statement but have not yet been recorded.

accrued revenues Revenues appropriately recognized under accrual accounting in one income statement period although the associated cash will be received in a later income statement period.

accrued expenses Expenses appropriately recognized under accrual accounting in one income statement period although the associated cash will be paid in a later income statement period.

deferrals Situations in which cash is either received or paid, but the income statement effect is delayed until some later period. Deferred revenues are recorded as liabilities, and deferred expenses are recorded as assets.

deferred revenues Revenues created when cash is received before the revenue is earned. Because the cash received has not yet been earned, an obligation is created and a liability is recorded. Later, when the cash is deemed to have been earned, it will be recognized as a revenue.

deferred expenses Expenses created when cash is paid before any benefit is received. Because the benefit to be derived is in the future, the item is recorded as an asset. Later, when the benefit is received from the item, it will be recognized as an expense.

1. **Accruals.** These adjustments are made to recognize items that should be included in the income statement period but have not yet been recorded. Accrual adjustments recognize revenue or expense *before* the associated cash is received or paid. In other words, this type of adjustment comes before the cash flow takes place. There are two types of accruals:

   a. **Accrued revenues.** These are revenues considered earned during the financial statement period because they met the criteria (answers to questions 1, 2, and 3 on pages F–174–F–175 were "yes"), but which have not yet been recognized. Consider Warner Management Consulting Services, Inc. For the clients that use its services on an ongoing basis, the company sends bills on the 2nd of each month for work done during the previous month. Warner has a legal claim at the end of December to what was earned in that month. Revenues recognized (recorded) should reflect the amount earned in December, even though the clients will not be billed until January 2 of the next year.

   b. **Accrued expenses.** These are expenses deemed to have been incurred during the financial statement period, but which have not yet been recognized. An example of this is accrued wages for employees. Assume Pellum Company pays its employees every two weeks for work performed in the previous two weeks. If part of the two-week pay period is in 2004 and part is in 2005, Pellum must make an adjustment at the end of 2004 to recognize the portion of wages expense incurred during that period. Even though the company will not spend any money until payday in January of 2005, part of that pay period's wages are 2004 expenses.

2. **Deferrals.** These are postponements of the recognition of revenue or expense even though the cash has been received or paid. Deferrals are the adjustment of revenues for which the cash has been collected but not yet earned, and of expenses for which cash has been paid but no benefit has yet been received. In other words, this type of adjustment comes after the cash flow has already taken place. There are two types of deferrals: (a) deferred revenues and (b) deferred expenses.

   a. **Deferred revenues.** These are created when cash is received before it is earned. For example, Larry's Lawn Service provides lawn care to many wealthy Miami families. On June 1, the Weatherby family sends Larry's Lawn Service $450 for the cost of lawn service for June, July, and August. As of June 1, Larry's Lawn Service has not earned any revenue, even though it has received cash. In fact, at that point, a liability has been created. The company owes the Weatherby family either three months of lawn service or their money back. The key here is who has legal claim to the cash. Because Larry's Lawn Service has no legal claim to the cash, it cannot rightly account for it as earned. By the time financial statements are prepared at the end of June, however, one month's worth of lawn service was performed, and $150 should be recognized as revenue. The remaining $300, representing two months of service, is deferred revenue. This amount represents a liability for Larry's Lawn Service and will remain so until the company either performs the services required to attain a legal claim to the cash or returns the cash to the Weatherby family.

   b. **Deferred expenses.** These are created when cash is paid before an expense has been incurred. On January 2, 2004, Crockett Cookie Company purchased a three-year insurance policy for $2,175. By December 31, 2004, one third of the insurance coverage has expired (one third of the benefit has been received). Financial statements prepared for 2004 should reflect the fact that one third of the cost of the policy ($725) is an expense for that year. The remaining portion of the policy, two years' worth of coverage, is an asset providing future benefits to the company. Even though the entire $2,175 was spent in 2004, two thirds of the cost is a deferred expense, an asset that will be recognized as an expense in future periods.

Accruals and deferrals are adjustments made to be sure that the financial statements reflect the guidelines of accrual accounting. Accruals occur in situations where the cash flow has not yet taken place, but the revenue or expense should be recognized.

Deferrals are necessary in cases when the cash flow has already taken place, but the associated revenue or expense should not be recognized yet. Understand, too, that the original transaction (the receipt or payment of cash) is not an adjustment, but rather creates a situation where an adjustment will be necessary later.

Whether they reflect expenses or revenues, accruals and deferrals will always possess the following three characteristics:

1. *A revenue item or an expense item will always be affected.* This is logical because the whole purpose of the adjustment process is to make certain that revenues and expenses associated with a given financial statement period are recognized in that period. Clearly, adjustments will always affect the income statement.
2. *An asset item or a liability item will always be affected.* This means the balance sheet will also be affected by the adjustment process.
3. *Cash is never affected by accruals or deferrals.* Remember, adjustments are made to properly recognize accounting elements. It is assumed that inflows and outflows of cash were properly recorded at the time they occurred.

ACCRUAL BASIS FINANCIAL STATEMENTS

Let us once again turn to the transactions of Corkel Incorporated for the month of January 2003. Again, here are the descriptions of the company's transactions:

1. Max Corkel started Corkel Incorporated on January 2, 2003, by incorporating and immediately purchasing 2,000 shares of the company's no-par common stock for $200,000.
2. Corkel Incorporated borrowed $100,000 from **Citibank** on January 2, by signing a one-year, 12 percent note payable. Although the $100,000 does not have to be repaid until January 2, 2004, the interest charge must be paid each month, beginning on February 2, 2003.
3. The company purchased a vehicle on January 2 for $14,000 cash. Max's best guess is that the vehicle will fill the company's needs for four years, after which he estimates the vehicle can be sold for $2,000.
4. The company paid cash for $75,000 of merchandise inventory on January 8.
5. On January 15, the company sold $42,000 of the merchandise inventory for a total selling price of $78,000 and collected cash the same day.
6. On January 22, the company sold $15,000 of the merchandise inventory for a total selling price of $32,000 on account (a credit sale). The terms of the sale were 30 days, meaning Corkel can expect to receive payment by February 22.
7. Cash payments for operating expenses in January totaled $22,500.
8. At the end of the month, the company owed $2,000 to employees of the company for work performed in January. They will be paid on February 3.
9. The company owed $700 at the end of the month for a utility bill that was received on January 26 and will be paid on February 15.

All nine transactions will affect the income statement and/or the balance sheet and the statement of owners' equity under the accrual basis of accounting. The income statement for January 2003 is presented in Exhibit 5–5.

Most of the items on this income statement differ from those on the income statement prepared under the cash basis (Exhibit 5–2). Let's discuss each item:

- *Sales revenue.* Under the accrual basis, a company recognizes revenue when it is earned, regardless of when the associated cash is received. Transaction 6 says the company made a $32,000 sale on January 22. The fact that the cash is not expected to be received until February 22 is irrelevant. Therefore, total sales revenue for the month using accrual accounting is $110,000 ($78,000 cash sale + $32,000 credit sale).
- *Cost of goods sold.* Under accrual accounting, we attempt to match all expenses to the same income statement period as the revenues they help generate. In the case of merchandise inventory, it is relatively easy to establish a direct cause and effect

Corkel Incorporated
Income Statement
For the Month Ended January 31, 2003

Sales revenue		$110,000
Cost of goods sold		57,000
Gross margin		$ 53,000
Expenses:		
Cash operating expenses	$22,500	
Wages expense	2,000	
Utilities expense	700	
Depreciation expense	250	
Total operating expenses		(25,450)
Operating income		27,550
Other expenses—interest		(1,000)
Net income		$ 26,550

EXHIBIT 5–5   Accrual Basis Income Statement

between the revenue (sale of the inventory) and the expense (cost of the inventory sold). Transaction 5 says $42,000 of merchandise inventory was sold on January 15, and transaction 6 says $15,000 of merchandise inventory was sold on January 22. The total cost of this merchandise is $57,000, so this is the amount shown on the accrual basis income statement as cost of goods sold. This means, of course, that there is $18,000 of merchandise inventory not yet accounted for ($75,000 purchased − $57,000 sold). We will discuss this remaining inventory when we talk about the balance sheet.

- *Cash operating expenses.* This is the clearest and most understandable expense figure on Corkel Incorporated's income statement. Under both cash basis and accrual basis measurement, expenses paid in cash this period to support operations during this period are considered to be expenses for this period.

- *Wages expense of $2,000.* Because these wages were earned by employees during January, Corkel has a legal liability at January 31 for this amount. Further, since the benefit derived from the employees' work was in January, the expense should be recognized in January regardless of when the employees will actually be paid.

- *Utilities expense of $700.* Since the bill was received in January, let us assume that it was for utilities purchased and used during January. In that case, the expense should be recognized in January.

- *Depreciation expense of $250.* Under cash accounting, the cost of the vehicle was considered an expense the day it was paid for. But as explained earlier, under accrual accounting, only a portion of the cost is recognized as expense each period. Using straight-line depreciation, the amount of depreciation is calculated as ($14,000 − $2,000)/4 = $3,000. This $3,000 represents the amount of depreciation expense that should be recognized during each year of the asset's useful life. Because the financial statements we are using in the Corkel Incorporated example are for only the month of January 2003, the amount of depreciation expense would be only $250 ($3,000/12) for the month.

- *Interest expense of $1,000.* The cost of the $100,000 loan is the interest Corkel must pay. Because the company had the $100,000 throughout the month of January, the interest cost for the month should be recognized as an expense even though it will not be paid until February 2. The amount is calculated using the formula explained in Chapter 3:

$$\text{Principal} \times \text{Rate} \times \text{Time} = \text{Interest Expense}$$
$$\$100,000 \times 12\% \times 1/12 = \$1,000 \text{ Interest Expense for January}$$

Discussion Questions •

5–12. Reexamine each item on Corkel Incorporated's accrual basis income statement and identify the items that are a result of the adjustment process.

5–13. Consider the following statement as it relates to the accrual basis of economic measurement: "Net income is an opinion; cash is a fact." What do you think this means?

Now that we have discussed the effect of accrual accounting on the income statement, we can look at what effects this system has on the statement of owners' equity. The owner's investment of $200,000 is treated just as it was under the cash basis. However, the results presented on the income statement under accrual accounting will be different, so the statement of owners' equity (Exhibit 5–6) will also be different under the accrual basis of measurement.

EXHIBIT 5–6   Accrual Basis Statement of Owners' (Stockholders') Equity

Corkel Incorporated
Statement of Stockholders' Equity
For the Month Ended January 31, 2003

	Common Stock	Retained Earnings	Total
Balances as of January 1, 2003	$ 0	$ 0	$ 0
Sale of common stock	200,000		200,000
Net income		26,550	26,550
Balances as of January 31, 2003	$200,000	$26,550	$226,550

The balance sheet for Corkel Incorporated at January 31, 2003, using the accrual basis of accounting is presented in Exhibit 5–7. Note that the items we discussed for the income statement have had an effect on the balance sheet as well.

EXHIBIT 5–7   Accrual Basis Balance Sheet

Corkel Incorporated
Balance Sheet
January 31, 2003

Assets:		Liabilities:	
Cash	$266,500	Accounts payable	$ 700
Accounts receivable	32,000	Wages payable	2,000
Inventory	18,000	Interest payable	1,000
Vehicle	14,000	Note payable	100,000
Less accumulated depreciation	(250)	Total liabilities	103,700
Vehicle, net	13,750	Stockholders' equity:	
		Common stock	200,000
		Retained earnings	26,550
		Total stockholders' equity	226,550
Total assets	$330,250	Total liabilities and stockholders' equity	$330,250

Again, many items on this balance sheet differ from those on the balance sheet prepared under the cash basis (Exhibit 5–4). Each item on the statement will be discussed in turn.

- *Cash of $266,500.* The amount of cash is counted and reported. Regardless of the basis of economic measurement, the amount of cash on hand cannot be changed. Note, however, that under the accrual basis, several items not directly related to cash affect net income. Therefore, net income is not equal to the increase in cash.
- *Accounts receivable of $32,000.* Transaction 6 created this asset. Corkel recognized the sale because an exchange had taken place and title to the merchandise inventory had passed to the customer. When that transaction occurred, Corkel had a legal claim to the $32,000. This is certainly an item that has probable future benefit to the business; it is therefore shown as an asset. It will remain classified as an asset until such time as the customer pays Corkel the cash.
- *Inventory of $18,000.* This is the remaining amount of merchandise inventory not recognized as cost of goods sold on the income statement. It is classified on the balance sheet as an asset because Corkel has not yet sacrificed it to generate revenue (it has probable future benefit). It will remain classified as an asset until such time as it is sold.
- *Vehicle of $14,000.* The original cost of the vehicle still shows on the balance sheet.
- *Accumulated depreciation of $250.* To show that a portion of the original cost of the vehicle has been converted to expense, an amount called accumulated depreciation has been deducted to arrive at what is called the net amount of the asset. This amount, $13,750, is also called the *book value* of the vehicle. In future periods, as more depreciation expense is recorded, the total amount recorded since the asset was acquired is shown as **accumulated depreciation.** Therefore, as time passes, accumulated depreciation increases and the book value of the asset decreases. This method of presentation tells decision makers the original cost of the asset and the amount not yet converted to expense (depreciated).
- *Accounts payable of $700.* This is for the utilities; the liability was created when Corkel recorded receiving the bill. Corkel has recognized the utilities expense, but the bill has not yet been paid. It is properly classified as a liability because it is an amount owed by the company and will require the sacrifice of assets (in this case, cash) in the future. It will remain classified as a liability until such time as Corkel pays the bill.
- *Wages payable of $2,000.* This is the amount Corkel owes its employees at the balance sheet date; the liability was created in the adjustment process.
- *Interest payable of $1,000.* This is the amount of interest Corkel owes the bank at the balance sheet date. Again, this liability was created in the adjustment process.
- *Note payable of $100,000.* This is a liability representing the amount Corkel Incorporated owes to **Citibank.**
- *Equity of $226,550.* This is the ending balance shown on the accrual basis statement of stockholders' equity. This amount is different from the equity balance shown on the cash basis balance sheet because of the difference in net income.

accumulated depreciation The total amount of cost that has been systematically converted to expense since a long-lived asset was first purchased.

STRENGTHS AND WEAKNESSES OF ACCRUAL BASIS ACCOUNTING

The strength of the accrual basis is that it establishes a relationship between revenues and the expenses incurred to generate the revenue. This is helpful to economic decision makers as they assess the past performance of a company and as they attempt to predict a company's future profitability.

Accrual accounting's most glaring weakness is that it takes the user's eye off cash. Accrual basis income statements do not provide information about inflows or outflows of cash. Because revenue and expense recognition under the accrual basis are totally unrelated to the receipt or payment of cash, net income does not represent an increase in cash for the period covered by the income statement. Neither does a net loss represent a decrease in cash.

Discussion Question

5-14. What complications can you see if revenue is recognized in December 2004, but the cash is not collected until January 2005?

Exhibits 5–8 and 5–9 depict two sets of financial statements for Corkel Incorporated. The first set is cash basis statements and the second set is accrual basis statements.

Each set illustrates the articulation of financial statements. The net loss presented on the cash basis income statement results in a reduction of owners' equity presented on the statement of stockholders' equity. The accrual basis income statement shows a net income of $26,550, which acts to increase owners' equity presented on the statement of stockholders' equity. In both sets of statements, the ending balance shown on the statement of owners' equity is used on the balance sheet.

Remember that both sets of statements are based on exactly the same transactions and events. The measurement criteria for the cash basis of accounting versus the measurement criteria for the accrual basis of accounting caused the differences, not the reality of what happened in Corkel Incorporated during the month.

Discussion Questions

5–15. Which of the two sets of financial statements do you think more closely relates the measurement of reality to reality? In other words, which set do you think is

EXHIBIT 5–8   Set of Cash Basis Financial Statements

Corkel Incorporated
Income Statement
For the Month Ended January 31, 2003

Sales revenue		$78,000
Cost of goods sold		75,000
Gross margin		$ 3,000
Expenses:		
Cost of vehicle	$14,000	
Cash operating expenses	22,500	
Total operating expenses		(36,500)
Net loss		($33,500)

Corkel Incorporated
Statement of Stockholders' Equity
For the Month Ended January 31, 2003

	Common Stock	Retained Earnings	Total
Balance as of January 1, 2003	$ 0	$ 0	$ 0
Sale of common stock	200,000		200,000
Net loss		(33,500)	(33,500)
Balance as of January 1, 2003	$200,000	($33,500)	$166,500

Corkel Incorporated
Balance Sheet
January 31, 2003

Assets:		Liabilites:	
Cash	$266,500	Notes payable	$100,000
		Stockholders' equity:	
		Common stock	200,000
		Retained earnings	(33,500)
		Total stockholders' equity	166,500
Total assets	$266,500	Total liabilities and stockholders' equity	$266,500

the better presentation of what actually happened during January 2003? Explain.

5–16. Which of the two sets of financial statements do you think better reflects Corkel Incorporated's future profit potential? Explain.

5–17. Are you coming to the conclusion that accounting lacks the exactness you once thought it possessed? Explain.

So, which of the bases is better? Well, that's not an easy question to answer. Each has strengths and weaknesses in relation to the other, and each is appropriate for certain entities in certain situations. However, having two valid bases of economic measurement does present a problem to economic decision makers, who often evaluate

---

EXHIBIT 5-9   Set of Accrual Basis Financial Statements

Corkel Incorporated
Income Statement
For the Month Ended January 31, 2003

Sales revenue		$110,000
Cost of goods sold		57,000
Gross margin		$ 53,000
Expenses:		
Cash operating expenses	$22,500	
Wages expense	2,000	
Utilities expense	700	
Depreciation expense	250	
Total operating expenses		(25,450)
Operating income		27,550
Other expenses—interest		1,000
Net income		$ 26,550

Corkel Incorporated
Statement of Stockholders' Equity
For the Month Ended January 31, 2003

	Common Stock	Retained Earnings	Total
Balance as of January 1, 2003	$ 0	$ 0	$ 0
Sale of common stock	200,000		200,000
Net income		26,550	26,550
Balance as of January 31, 2003	$200,000	$26,550	$226,550

Corkel Incorporated
Balance Sheet
January 31, 2003

Assets:		Liabilities:	
Cash	$266,500	Accounts payable	$ 700
Accounts receivable	32,000	Wages payable	2,000
Inventory	18,000	Interest payable	1,000
Vehicle	14,000	Note payable	100,000
Less accumulated depreciation	(250)	Total liabilites	103,700
Vehicle, net	13,750	Stockholders' equity:	
		Common stock	200,000
		Retained earnings	26,550
		Total stockholders' equity	226,550
Total assets	$330,250	Total liabilities and stockholders' equity	$330,250

choices among various companies. If one company uses cash basis accounting and another uses accrual accounting, what are decision makers to do? We have seen the different outcomes when we use the two different measurement bases to measure the same reality. Imagine how difficult it would be to evaluate two sets of financial statements with different measurement bases and different business activities!

Because the accounting profession has deemed that accrual accounting provides more useful information to economic decision makers than does cash accounting, accrual accounting has been adopted as the method used by those companies required to follow generally accepted accounting principles (GAAP). According to the FASB in the *Conceptual Framework*:

> *The information measured by accrual accounting generally provides a better indication of an organization's performance than does information about cash receipts and payments. Accrual accounting attempts to record the financial effects of transactions, events, and circumstances that have cash consequences for an organization in the periods in which those transactions, events, and circumstances occur rather than in only the periods in which cash is received or paid by the organization. Accrual accounting is concerned with the process by which cash is obtained and used, not with just the beginning and end of that process. It recognizes that the acquisition of resources needed to provide services and the rendering of services by an organization during a period often do not coincide with the cash receipts and payments of the period* (Statement of Financial Accounting Concepts No. 4, paragraph 50).

With that said, using accrual accounting does not, in and of itself, provide comparability. Even if the companies we are comparing both use the accrual basis of measurement, a number of factors could complicate the comparison. Chapters 7 and 8 explore areas in accounting that permit flexibility in the recognition of revenues and expenses. These variations reduce comparability of financial statement information between companies. In order to make the best use of accounting information, be aware of the variations. There is also the problem that accrual accounting takes the focus off cash flow. This problem has been addressed by the development of the statement of cash flows, which we have discussed briefly in previous chapters, and which we will discuss in much greater detail in Chapter 10.

Summary ❖

There are two things going on in business. First, there is the reality of business transactions and events. Second, there is the attempt to measure that reality in the accounting records and reports. For a number of reasons, the measurement of reality may not precisely reflect reality. Some of the differences between reality and the measurement of reality are a result of the basis selected to recognize revenues and expenses in a particular time period. This chapter presented two distinct bases: the cash basis and the accrual basis.

Under cash basis accounting, economic activity is recognized only when cash is paid or received. Under this basis, a company recognizes revenue only when it receives the associated cash. Remember, however, that cash basis accounting considers revenue only the cash that is received as a result of the earnings process.

Under cash basis accounting, a company recognizes an expense only when it pays the associated cash. However, under cash basis accounting, not all cash a company pays out is an expense. If a company pays a dividend to its owners, or pays the principal on a debt, the cash paid out is not an expense to the company. Because cash is the only measurement criterion, cash basis accounting requires less subjective judgment than the accrual basis measurement, but it has a weakness in that it makes no attempt to recognize expenses in the same period as the revenues they helped generate.

Under accrual basis accounting, a company recognizes sales, purchases, and all other business transactions whenever a legally enforceable claim to the associated cash is established. Essentially, accrual accounting focuses on the earnings process rather than the cash flows resulting from that process.

Under accrual accounting, revenue is recognized when it is deemed to be earned — that is, a company recognizes revenue when it has a legally enforceable claim to the cash associated with that revenue. Since in many instances the cash is collected some time other than when the revenue is earned, under accrual accounting, revenue recognition is completely unrelated to when the cash is received.

There are three possible relationships between when a company receives cash and when it recognizes a revenue: Cash is received at the time the revenue is earned, cash is received after the revenue has been earned, or cash is received before the revenue has been earned.

Under accrual accounting, we recognize expenses when their benefit is received (i.e., they produce revenues), regardless of when the associated cash is paid. As with revenue recognition, expense recognition under accrual accounting is completely unrelated to the movement of cash.

Accrual accounting attempts to establish a relationship between revenues and expenses. The first step in the accrual matching process is to determine in which income statement period a company should recognize a particular revenue. The company then recognizes those expenses in that same financial statement period.

Accrual accounting's most glaring weakness is that it takes the user's eye off cash. Accrual basis income statements do not provide information about inflows or outflows of cash. Because revenue and expense recognition under the accrual basis are totally unrelated to the receipt or payment of cash, net income does not represent an increase in cash for the period covered by the income statement.

If one company uses cash basis accounting and another uses accrual accounting, what are decision makers to do? Because the accounting profession has deemed that accrual accounting provides more useful information to economic decision makers than does cash accounting, accrual accounting has been adopted as the method used by those companies required to follow generally accepted accounting principles.

Key Terms

- accrual basis accounting, F–173
- accruals, F–179
- accrue, F–173
- accrued expenses, F–179
- accrued revenues, F–179

- accumulated depreciation, F–183
- adjustments, F–178
- cash basis accounting, F–170
- deferrals, F–179
- deferred expenses, F–179

- deferred revenues, F–179
- depreciation, F–177
- matching, F–176
- recognition, F–168
- title, F–174

Review the Facts

A. Explain the difference between reality and the measurement of reality, and provide an example of each.
B. In accounting, what does it mean for an item to be "recognized"?
C. Under the cash basis of measurement, when does revenue recognition occur?
D. Under the cash basis, when are expenses recognized?
E. What is the greatest strength of the cash basis?
F. What is the greatest weakness of the cash basis?
G. Under the accrual basis of measurement, when does revenue recognition occur?
H. Under the accrual basis, when are expenses recognized?
I. Explain the concept of matching.
J. What is depreciation and why is it necessary in accrual accounting?
K. What are accruals?
L. What are deferrals?
M. What is the greatest strength of the accrual basis?
N. What is the greatest weakness of the accrual basis?

Apply What You Have Learned ·

LO 1, 2, 3, & 4: TERMINOLOGY

5–18. Below is a list of items relating to the concepts discussed in this chapter, followed by definitions of those items in scrambled order:

a. Cash basis revenues
b. Accrual basis expenses
c. Immediate recognition
d. Matching principle
e. Title passes to customer

f. Depreciation
g. No direct cause and effect between costs and revenues
h. Cash basis expenses
i. Accrual basis revenues

1. _____ Recognized when cash associated with a sale is received
2. _____ The situation that causes costs to be either recognized immediately as an expense or allocated to the income statement periods supposed benefited
3. _____ One of three evidences that revenue has been earned under accrual accounting
4. _____ Recognized when the cash associated with a cost is paid
5. _____ Recognized when there is a legal claim to the cash associated with a sale
6. _____ An attempt to recognize expenses in the same income statement period as the revenues they generate
7. _____ Recognized when the benefit is received rather than when the cash is paid
8. _____ The process of converting the cost of a long-lived item from asset to expense
9. _____ The treatment for costs when no future benefit can be determined or allocation to future periods serves no useful purpose

Required: Match the letter next to each item on the list with the appropriate definition. Use each letter only once.

LO 1 & 2: CASH BASIS MEASUREMENT

5–19. Linda VanHook Company began operation on January 2, 2004. During its first month of operation, the company had the following transactions:

- Purchased $35,000 of merchandise inventory on January 2. The amount due is payable on February 2.
- Paid January office rent of $3,000 on January 3.
- Purchased $10,000 of merchandise inventory on January 5. Paid cash at the time of purchase.
- Sold inventory that cost $18,000 for $30,000 to a customer on January 10 and received the cash on that date.
- Sold inventory that cost $5,000 for $9,000 to a customer on January 20. The sale was on account and the customer has until February 20 to pay.
- Paid cash expenses during January of $7,500.
- Received bills for utilities, advertising, and phone service totaling $1,500. All these bills were for services received in January. They will all be paid the first week in February.

Required:

a. Prepare a January 2004 multiple-step income statement for Linda VanHook Company using the cash basis of accounting.
b. Do you think the income statement you prepared for the previous requirement provides a good measure of the reality of the company's performance during January? Explain your reasoning.

LO 3: ACCRUAL BASIS MEASUREMENT

5–20. Linda VanHook Company began operation on January 2, 2004. During its first month of operation, the company had the same seven transactions as noted in problem 5–19.

Required:

a. Prepare a January 2004 multiple-step income statement for Linda VanHook Company using the accrual basis of accounting.
b. Do you think the income statement you prepared for the previous requirement provides a good measure of the reality of the company's performance during January? Explain your reasoning.

LO 1 & 2: CASH BASIS MEASUREMENT

5–21. Snow and Ice Company began operation on June 1, 2004. During its first month of operation, the company had the following transactions:

- Purchased $40,000 of merchandise inventory on June 1. The amount due is payable on August 1.
- Paid June office rent of $2,000 on June 3.
- Purchased $20,000 of merchandise inventory on June 4. Paid cash at the time of purchase.
- Sold inventory that cost $30,000 for $42,000 to a customer on June 10 and received the cash on that date.
- Sold inventory that cost $10,000 for $14,000 to a customer on June 20. The sale was on account and the customer has until July 20 to pay.
- Paid cash expenses during June of $9,500.
- Received bills for utilities, advertising, and phone service totaling $3,500. All these bills were for services received in June. They will all be paid the first week in July.

Required:

    a. Prepare a June 2004 multiple-step income statement for Snow and Ice Company using the cash basis of accounting.

    b. Do you think the income statement you prepared for the previous requirement provides a good measure of the reality of the company's performance during June? Explain your reasoning.

LO 3: ACCRUAL BASIS MEASUREMENT

5–22. Snow and Ice Company began operation on June 1, 2004. During its first month of operation, the company had the same seven transactions as noted in problem 5–21.

Required:

    a. Prepare a June 2004 multiple-step income statement for Snow and Ice Company using the accrual basis of accounting.

    b. Do you think the income statement you prepared for the previous requirement provides a good measure of the reality of the company's performance during June? Explain your reasoning.

LO 2 & 3: CASH VS. ACCRUAL

5–23. Bob Franks and Company began operation on January 2, 2004. During its first month of operation, the company had the following transactions:

- Paid January office rent of $2,000 on January 2.
- Purchased $25,000 of merchandise inventory on January 5. The amount due is payable on February 5.
- Purchased $15,000 of merchandise inventory on January 8. Paid cash at the time of purchase.
- Sold merchandise that cost $12,000 for $18,000 to a customer on January 16 and received the cash on that date.
- Sold merchandise that cost $9,000 for $13,500 to a customer on January 26. The sale was on account and the customer has until February 26 to pay.
- Paid February office rent of $2,000 on January 31.

Required:

    a. Prepare a January 2004 multiple-step income statement for Bob Franks and Company using the cash basis of accounting.

    b. Prepare a January 2004 multiple-step income statement for Bob Franks and Company using the accrual basis of accounting.

    c. Explain what caused the differences between the income statement prepared under the cash basis and the one prepared under the accrual basis.

    d. Which of the two income statement presentations do you think:

        1. Provides better information as to cash flow for the month of January?

        2. Provides better information as to what Franks earned during the month of January?

        3. Better reflects Franks' ability to generate future earnings and cash flow?

LO 2, 3, & 4: CONTINUATION CASH VS. ACCRUAL—SECOND MONTH

5–24. This is a continuation of the Bob Franks and Company problem begun in 5–23. During its second month of business, that's February 2004, the company had the following transactions:

- Sold the entire merchandise inventory it had on hand at the beginning of February for $28,500 cash on February 2.
- On February 5, the company paid the $25,000 it owed for the merchandise inventory it purchased on January 5.
- Purchased $20,000 of merchandise inventory on February 11. Paid cash at the time of purchase.
- Sold the merchandise that cost $20,000 it had purchased on February 11 for $30,000 to a customer on February 21 and received the cash on that date.
- On February 26, Franks collected the $13,500 from the sale of January 26.

Required:

a. Prepare a February 2004 multiple-step income statement for Bob Franks and Company using the cash basis of accounting.
b. Prepare a February 2004 multiple-step income statement for Bob Franks and Company using the accrual basis of accounting.
c. Explain what caused the differences between the income statement prepared under the cash basis and the one prepared under the accrual basis.
d. Which of the two income statement presentations do you think:

1. Provides better information as to cash flow for the month of February?
2. Provides better information as to what Franks earned during the month of February?
3. Better reflects Franks' ability to generate future earnings and cash flow?

e. What is the total net income for January and February combined using the cash basis?
f. What is the total net income for January and February combined using the accrual basis?
g. What does the results of requirements e and f tell you?

LO 2, 3, & 4: CASH VS. ACCRUAL

5–25. Tom Dunn and Company began operation on August 2, 2004. During its first month of operation, the company had the following transactions:

- Paid August office rent of $3,000 on August 2.
- Purchased $35,000 of merchandise inventory on August 5. The amount due is payable on September 5.
- Purchased $25,000 of merchandise inventory on August 8. Paid cash at the time of purchase.
- Sold merchandise that cost $22,000 for $33,000 to a customer on August 16 and received the cash on that date.
- Sold merchandise that cost $10,000 for $15,000 to a customer on August 26. The sale was on account and the customer has until September 26 to pay.
- Paid September office rent of $3,000 on August 31.

Required:

a. Prepare an August 2004 multiple-step income statement for Tom Dunn and Company using the cash basis of accounting.
b. Prepare an August 2004 multiple-step income statement for Tom Dunn and Company using the accrual basis of accounting.
c. Explain in your own words what caused the differences between the income statement prepared under the cash basis and the one prepared under the accrual basis.
d. Which of the two income statement presentations do you think:

1. Provides better information as to cash flow for the month of August?
2. Provides better information as to what Tom Dunn earned during the month of August?
3. Better reflects Tom Dunn's ability to generate future earnings and cash flow?

LO 2, 3, & 4: CONTINUATION CASH VS. ACCRUAL—SECOND MONTH

5–26. This is a continuation of the Tom Dunn and Company problem begun in 5–25. During the company's second month of business, September 2004, the company had the following transactions:

- Sold all merchandise inventory it had on hand at the beginning of September for $42,000 cash on September 2.
- On September 5, the company paid the $35,000 it owed for the merchandise inventory it purchased on August 5.
- Purchased $30,000 of merchandise inventory on September 11. Paid cash at the time of purchase.
- Sold merchandise that cost $30,000 it had purchased on September 11 for $45,000 to a customer on September 21 and received the cash on that date.
- On September 26, Tom Dunn and Company collected the $15,000 from the sale of August 26.

Required:

a. Prepare a September 2004 multiple-step income statement for Tom Dunn and Company using the cash basis of accounting.

b. Prepare a September 2004 multiple-step income statement for Tom Dunn and Company using the accrual basis of accounting.

c. Explain in your own words what caused the differences between the income statement prepared under the cash basis and the one prepared under the accrual basis.

d. Which of the two income statement presentations do you think:

    1. Provides better information as to cash flow for the month of September?

    2. Provides better information as to what Tom Dunn and Company earned during the month of September?

    3. Better reflects Tom Dunn and Company's ability to generate future earnings and cash flow?

e. What is the total net income for August and September combined using the cash basis?

f. What is the total net income for August and September combined using the accrual basis?

g. What do the results of requirements e and f tell you?

LO 4: THE MATCHING PRINCIPLE

5–27. Maria Giudici, Inc., purchased $65,000 worth of inventory for cash in December 2003. The company sold $25,000 worth of the inventory in December and the remaining inventory of $40,000 in January 2004.

Required:

a. Calculate how much of the $65,000 of merchandise would appear in Cost of Goods Sold on the December 2003 income statement and how much would appear in Cost of Goods Sold on the January 2004 income statement if Giudici uses the cash basis of accounting.

b. Calculate how much of the $65,000 of merchandise would appear in Cost of Goods Sold on the December 2003 income statement and how much would appear in Cost of Goods Sold on the January 2004 income statement if Giudici uses the accrual basis of accounting.

LO 4: THE MATCHING PRINCIPLE

5–28. Alberto Pons Inc., purchased $100,000 of merchandise inventory on December 15, 2004, on a 30-day account. It sold merchandise that cost $35,000 in December and the remainder in January 2005.

Required:

a. On what date should Pons pay for the merchandise?

b. Calculate how much of the $100,000 of merchandise appears in Cost of Goods Sold on the December 2004 income statement and how much appears on the balance sheet in Merchandise Inventory on December 31, 2004, if Pons uses the cash basis of accounting.

c. Calculate how much of the $100,000 of merchandise appears in Cost of Goods Sold on the December 2004 income statement and how much appears on the balance sheet in Merchandise Inventory on December 31, 2004, if Pons uses the accrual basis of accounting.

LO 4: THE MATCHING PRINCIPLE

5–29. On December 5, 2004, Phil Handley, Inc., purchased $150,000 of merchandise inventory on account. The $150,000 is due in 90 days. It sold merchandise that cost $55,000 in December and $70,000 in January 2005.

Required:

 a. On what date should Handley pay for the merchandise?

 b. Calculate how much of the $150,000 of merchandise appears in Cost of Goods Sold on the December 2004 income statement and how much appears on the balance sheet in Merchandise Inventory on December 31, 2004, if Handley uses the cash basis of accounting.

 c. Calculate how much of the $150,000 of merchandise appears in Cost of Goods Sold on the January 2005 income statement and how much appears on the balance sheet in Merchandise Inventory on January 31, 2005, if Handley uses the cash basis of accounting.

 d. Calculate how much of the $150,000 of merchandise appears in Cost of Goods Sold on the December 2004 income statement and how much appears on the balance sheet in Merchandise Inventory on December 31, 2004, if Handley uses the accrual basis of accounting.

 e. Calculate how much of the $150,000 of merchandise appears in Cost of Goods Sold on the January 2005 income statement and how much appears on the balance sheet in Merchandise Inventory on January 31, 2005, if Handley uses the accrual basis of accounting.

LO 4: THE MATCHING PRINCIPLE

5–30. Davenport Corporation purchased a two-year insurance policy on May 1, 2004, by paying $4,800 on that date.

Required:

 a. Indicate how Davenport will list information concerning this policy on its 2004 income statement and its December 31, 2004, balance sheet under the cash basis.

 b. Indicate how Davenport will list information concerning this policy on its 2004 income statement and its December 31, 2004, balance sheet under the accrual basis.

 c. Indicate how Davenport will list information concerning this policy on its 2005 income statement and its December 31, 2005, balance sheet under the cash basis.

 d. Indicate how Davenport will list information concerning this policy on its 2005 income statement and its December 31, 2005, balance sheet under the accrual basis.

LO 4: THE MATCHING PRINCIPLE

5–31. Belski & Miglio paid their landlord $10,000 for five months' rent paid in advance on November 1, 2004. The partnership has a calendar year end.

Required:

 a. Indicate how Belski & Miglio will list information concerning this rental on its 2004 income statement and its December 31, 2004, balance sheet under the cash basis.

 b. Indicate how Belski & Miglio will list information concerning this rental on its 2004 income statement and its December 31, 2004, balance sheet under the accrual basis.

 c. Indicate how Belski & Miglio will list information concerning this rental on its 2005 income statement and its December 31, 2005, balance sheet under the cash basis.

 d. Indicate how Belski & Miglio will list information concerning this rental on its 2005 income statement and its December 31, 2005, balance sheet under the accrual basis.

LO 4: THE MATCHING PRINCIPLE

5–32. Avonia's Clothes paid its landlord $1,600 for the first and last months' rent on March 1, 2004, when Avonia opened her business. The lease on her shop is for one year.

Required:

 a. Indicate how Avonia's Clothes will list information concerning this rental on its March 2004 income statement and its March 31, 2004, balance sheet under the cash basis.

 b. Indicate how Avonia's Clothes will list information concerning this rental on its March 2004 income statement and its March 31, 2004, balance sheet under the accrual basis.

LO 4: THE MATCHING PRINCIPLE

5–33. Flemming Real Estate Company collected $10,000 from Phillips & Arguello for five months' rent paid in advance on November 1, 2004. Flemming operates on a February 28 year end.

Required:

a. How much rental revenue will Flemming recognize in its income statement for the year ended February 28, 2005, under the cash basis? How will this affect the February 28, 2005, balance sheet?

b. How much rental revenue will Flemming recognize in its income statement for the year ended February 28, 2005, under the accrual basis? How will this affect the February 28, 2005, balance sheet?

c. How much rental revenue will Flemming recognize in its income statement for the year ended February 28, 2006, under the cash basis? How will this affect the February 28, 2006, balance sheet?

d. How much rental revenue will Flemming recognize in its income statement for the year ended February 28, 2006, under the accrual basis? How will this affect the February 28, 2006, balance sheet?

LO 4: THE MATCHING PRINCIPLE

5–34. On December 1, 2004, Jeanette Park paid her accountant, Diane Clifford, $675 for three months' services. The services are to be performed evenly over December, January, and February. By the end of December, Clifford had completed the December services.

Required:

a. How much should Clifford report as revenue for the year ended December 31, 2004, under the cash basis? How will this affect Clifford's December 31, 2004, balance sheet?

b. How much should Clifford report as revenue for the year ended December 31, 2004, under the accrual basis? How will this affect Clifford's December 31, 2004, balance sheet?

c. How should Park report this payment on her income statement and balance sheet for December 31, 2004, under the cash basis?

d. How should Park report this payment on her income statement and balance sheet for December 31, 2004, under the accrual basis?

LO 4: THE MATCHING PRINCIPLE

5–35. Mike Fisher borrowed $15,000 for his business, Fisher Inc., at 9 percent interest from the Nations Bank on June 1, 2004; principal and interest are due on May 31, 2005.

Required:

a. How much interest will Fisher owe the bank when he pays the note on May 31, 2005?

b. How will Fisher report the interest on his income statement and balance sheet for calendar year 2004 if he uses the cash basis of accounting?

c. How will Fisher report the interest on his income statement and balance sheet for calendar year 2004 if he uses the accrual basis of accounting?

LO 4: THE MATCHING PRINCIPLE AND DEPRECIATION

5–36. Todd's Toppers bought a commercial stitching machine on July 1, 2004, for $25,000. Todd estimates this machine will be useful for five years and will have no residual value because there is little market for used stitching machines.

Required:

a. Assuming Todd uses the cash basis of accounting, how much will he recognize as expense for the stitching machine on his income statements for each of 2004, 2005, and 2006?

b. Assuming Todd uses the accrual basis of accounting, how much will he recognize as expense for the stitching machine on his income statements for each of 2004, 2005, and 2006?

c. Assuming Todd uses the cash basis of accounting, how will he report this on his ending balance sheets for 2004, 2005, and 2006?

d. Assuming Todd uses the accrual basis of accounting, how will he report this on his ending balance sheets for 2004, 2005, and 2006?

LO 4: THE MATCHING PRINCIPLE AND DEPRECIATION

5–37. Carole's Delivery Service purchased a van on October 1, 2003, to deliver parcels for local merchants. Carole estimates that the van will last four years and can be sold for $2,000 at the end of the fourth year.

Required:

a. For accrual basis accounting, how much will Carole recognize as depreciation expense for each of the calendar years 2003, 2005, and 2007 if the cost of the van was

   1. $26,000?
   2. $34,000?

b. What will be the balance of Accumulated Depreciation on December 31, 2003, 2005, and 2007, if the cost of the van was

   1. $26,000?
   2. $34,000?

LO 5: ACCRUALS AND DEFERRALS

5–38. Explain the difference between a deferred expense and an accrued expense and include at least one example of each in your answer.

LO 5: ACCRUALS AND DEFERRALS

5–39. Explain why accruals and deferrals are necessary under accrual basis accounting but not under cash basis accounting. In your answer, include an explanation of accruals and deferrals as they apply to both revenues and expenses.

LO 5: ACCRUALS AND DEFERRALS

5–40. The Fowks Company reported sales of $200,000 for the year ended December 31, 2005. Sales were reported on the accrual basis. The accounts receivable at December 31, 2004, were $25,000, and at December 31, 2005, the receivables were $12,000.

Required: Calculate the amount Fowks collected from customers for 2005.

LO 6: IMPACT OF THEFT ON FINANCIAL STATEMENTS

5–41. Reynolds, Inc., sold some merchandise inventory for cash during the current month. Unfortunately, the company's accounting clerk simply slipped the cash from the sale into his pocket and did not record the sale. Reynolds uses accrual accounting.

Required:

a. Explain how each of the following financial statements would be affected by the accounting clerk's behavior. Avoid using one-word responses such as understated and overstated. You should approach this requirement as if you were explaining the effects to someone with no knowledge of accounting or financial statements.

   1. Income statement
   2. Statement of stockholders' equity
   3. Balance sheet

b. Briefly explain how your answer would differ if Reynolds used the cash basis of accounting.

LO 6: IMPACT OF ACCOUNTING ERROR ON FINANCIAL STATEMENTS

5–42. The bookkeeper for Sunny Corporation mistakenly recorded a disbursement for equipment as if the payment had been for repairs and maintenance expense.

Required:

a. Explain how each of the following financial statements would be affected by the bookkeeper's error. Avoid using one-word responses such as understated and overstated. You should approach this requirement as if you were explaining the effects to someone with no knowledge of accounting or financial statements.

  1. Income statement
  2. Statement of stockholders' equity
  3. Balance sheet

 b. Briefly explain how your answer would differ if Sunny used the cash basis of accounting.

LO 6: IMPACT OF ACCOUNTING ERROR ON FINANCIAL STATEMENTS

5–43. The bookkeeper for Joan Rodgers Corporation mistakenly recorded a disbursement for advertising expense as if the payment had been for office furniture.

Required:

 a. Explain how each of the following financial statements would be affected by the bookkeeper's error. Avoid using one-word responses such as understated and overstated. You should approach this requirement as if you were explaining the effects to someone with no knowledge of accounting or financial statements.

  1. Income statement
  2. Statement of stockholders' equity
  3. Balance sheet

 b. Briefly explain how your answer would differ if Rodgers used the cash basis of accounting.

LO 6: IMPACT OF ACCOUNTING ERROR ON FINANCIAL STATEMENTS

5–44. The bookkeeper for Heart Corporation mistakenly recorded a disbursement for rent expense as if the payment had been for an insurance expense.

Required:

 a. Explain how each of the following financial statements would be affected by the bookkeeper's error. Avoid using one-word responses such as understated and overstated. You should approach this requirement as if you were explaining the effects to someone with no knowledge of accounting or financial statements.

  1. Income statement
  2. Statement of stockholders' equity
  3. Balance sheet

 b. Briefly explain how your answer would differ if Heart used the cash basis of accounting.

LO 6: CASH VS. ACCRUAL REVENUE RECOGNITION

5–45. Simon Corporation uses the accrual basis of accounting. Simon recognizes revenue at the time it delivers product or provides a service. The entity engages in the following activities during August:

 1. Collects $5,000 from customers for the sale of merchandise in the month of August.
 2. Collects $10,000 from customers for the sale of merchandise in the month of July.
 3. Collects $4,000 from customers for merchandise to be delivered in September.

Required:

 a. Calculate the amount of revenue Simon should recognize in August.
 b. Calculate the amount of revenue Simon should recognize in August if the company were on a cash basis.

LO 6: CASH VS. ACCRUAL REVENUE RECOGNITION

5–46. Knowles Corporation uses the accrual basis of accounting. Knowles recognizes revenue at the time it delivers product or provides a service. The entity engages in the following activities during November:

 1. Collects $10,000 from customers for the sale of merchandise in the month of October.
 2. Collects $18,000 from customers for the sale of merchandise in the month of November.
 3. Collects $12,000 from customers for merchandise to be delivered in December and January.

Required:

    a. Calculate the amount of revenue Knowles should recognize in November.

    b. Calculate the amount of revenue Knowles should recognize in November if the company were on a cash basis.

LO 4 & 6: CASH VS. ACCRUAL EXPENSE RECOGNITION

5–47. Green Corporation uses the accrual basis of accounting. Green recognizes expenses in accordance with the matching principle. The entity engaged in the following activities during July:

    1. Paid $20,000 to suppliers for office supplies used in the month of July.

    2. Paid $22,000 for radio and television advertising that aired in June.

    3. Paid $6,000 for insurance that covers the months of July, August, and September.

Required:

    a. Calculate the amount of expense Green should recognize in the month of July.

    b. Calculate the amount of expense Green should recognize in July if the company were on a cash basis.

LO 4 & 6: CASH VS. ACCRUAL EXPENSE RECOGNITION

5–48. Glenna Corporation uses the accrual basis of accounting. Glenna recognizes expenses in accordance with the matching principle. The entity engaged in the following activities during December:

    1. Paid $8,000 in December for December's office equipment rental.

    2. Paid $32,000 in December for radio and television advertising that aired in November.

    3. Paid $8,000 in December for insurance expense that covers the months of December through March.

Required:

    a. Calculate the amount of expense Glenna should recognize in December.

    b. Calculate the amount of expense Glenna should recognize in December if the company were on a cash basis.

LO 6: CASH VS. ACCRUAL DETERMINATION OF NET INCOME

5–49. The following list pertains to the Searcy Company for the month of January 2004:

    1. Purchased $10,000 of merchandise for resale paying cash.

    2. Paid $2,000 for office rent for January and February.

    3. Ordered $15,000 worth of merchandise to sell.

    4. Paid $3,000 for a piece of office furniture that will last five years with no residual value.

    5. Received and paid for merchandise ordered in transaction 3.

    6. Sold merchandise that cost $2,000 for $6,000 cash.

    7. Paid one month's salary of $3,500.

    8. Sold merchandise on credit for $20,000 that cost $7,000. Payment was received in February.

    9. Purchased advertising for January on credit for $2,000 agreeing to pay for it in February.

Required:

    a. Determine the net income or net loss for the month of January on a cash basis.

    b. Determine the net income or net loss for the month of January on the accrual basis.

LO 6: CASH VS. ACCRUAL DETERMINATION OF NET INCOME

5–50. The Friedman Corporation entered into the following transactions during February 2004:

    1. Purchased $56,000 of merchandise for cash.

    2. Paid $3,600 for office rent for January and February.

    3. Ordered $45,000 worth of merchandise to sell.

    4. Paid $5,400 for a computer for the accounting department. The computer should last three years with no residual value.

5. Received the merchandise ordered in transaction 3. Payment is due to the vendor on March 10.
6. Sold merchandise that cost $24,000 for $38,000 cash.
7. Paid weekly salaries of $4,500 for the first three weeks. The last week's salary will be paid March 1.
8. Sold merchandise on credit for $80,000 that cost $45,000. Payment was received in February.
9. Paid for advertising for January of $12,000. February's ads were $8,000 and will be paid by March 15.

Required:

    a. Determine February's net income or net loss on a cash basis.
    b. Determine February's net income or net loss on the accrual basis.

LO 6: CASH VS. ACCRUAL DETERMINATION OF NET INCOME

5–51. Nancy Jackson Enterprises completed the following transactions in November 2004:

1. Paid cash for purchase of $100,000 worth of merchandise for resale.
2. Paid $12,000 for office rent. The $12,000 covers rent for 12 months.
3. Ordered $85,000 worth of merchandise for resale.
4. Purchased a delivery van for $25,000 that should last five years.
5. Received the merchandise ordered in transaction 3. Payment is due in 30 days.
6. Sold merchandise that cost $72,000 for $106,000 cash.
7. Paid one month's salaries of $13,500.
8. Sold merchandise on credit for $72,000 that cost $54,000. Payment was received in December.
9. Purchased advertising for November on credit for $9,000 agreeing to pay for it in December.

Required:

    a. Determine the net income or net loss for the month of November on a cash basis.
    b. Determine the net income or net loss for the month of November on the accrual basis.

Financial Reporting Exercises

LO 3: ACCRUAL BASIS IN FINANCIAL REPORTS

5–52. Obtain *Carnival Cruise Lines'* balance sheet by using the Securities and Exchange Commission's (SEC's) Electronic Data Gathering, Analysis, and Retrieval (EDGAR) system. On the SEC site, locate *Carnival Cruise Lines* and select their 2001 Form 10-K. The Form 10K will include the company's balance sheet.

    Once you have *Carnival*'s balance sheet, find the liability *Carnival* calls *Customer Deposits*. This item represents payments *Carnival* has received from customers for future travel.

Required:

    a. How much does *Carnival* report for Customer Deposits? How significant is the amount relative to the various other liabilities the company lists?
    b. Like all companies that conform to GAAP, *Carnival* uses the accrual basis of accounting. If, however, *Carnival* used the cash basis instead of the accrual basis, how would the company report these deposits received from customers for future travel?

LO 3: ACCRUAL BASIS IN FINANCIAL REPORTS

5–53. Obtain the 10-K of *Readers Digest Association, Inc.,* through the SEC's EDGAR system. Use the balance sheet to classify the following.

Required:

    a. Does the company have deferred expenses? If so, what are they and what is the amount?
    b. Does the company have deferred revenues? If so, what are they and what is the amount?

c. Does the company have accrued expenses? If so, what are they and what is the amount?

d. Does the company have accrued revenues? If so, what are they and what is the amount?

e. Comparing the amounts above, do any of them seem significant? Are any substantially larger or smaller than the others? If so, can you think of a reason why?

f. For the one above that doesn't apply to ***Readers Digest Association, Inc.,*** why do you think that it doesn't? Name three companies that would and why.

LO: COMPREHENSIVE

5–54. Visit the ***Walt Disney Corporation*** Web site by finding the link on the PHLIP Web site for this book at *www.prenhall.com/werner.* Look up the current annual report and go to the footnotes section. Footnote 1 should describe the business and summarize the significant accounting policies.

Required: Does Disney use the cash or accrual basis of accounting? Write a one-page summary of the important issues discussed in the first footnote.

ANNUAL REPORT PROJECT

5–55. Section 5—Strengths, Weaknesses, Opportunities, and Threats (SWOT)

This section of the annual report project involves SWOT analysis for your selected company. The acronym SWOT stands for strengths, weaknesses, opportunities, and threats. This part of your project should be very interesting and informative. It should improve your ability to come to an overall conclusion about your company at the end of the project.

The strengths and weaknesses of the company should be viewed from an internal perspective, and the opportunities and threats are viewed from an external perspective.

Press releases and articles published about your company and its industry will be helpful in finding the necessary information you will need to complete this assignment. Another major source of information for this part of the project is the management's discussion and analysis section of your company's annual report.

Let's focus on the strengths and weaknesses first.

Required:

a. Prepare a schedule that specifies your company's strengths and weaknesses in the following areas:

A. Corporate Structure

1. Does the company seem to have a strong corporate structure?
2. Does the structure seem to fit the current business environment?

B. Corporate Culture

1. Can you readily determine the company's overall goals, beliefs, and values?
2. Is the corporate mission clear to employees, customers, and the community?
3. Is the corporate mission consistent with the corporate beliefs and values?
4. Is the mission carried out well?

C. Corporate Resources—How strong or weak are the following resources?

1. Human resources
2. Financial resources
3. Management information system
4. Manufacturing
5. Research and development
6. Marketing
7. Distinctive competencies (something this company is known for doing very well)

b. Prepare a summary of your thoughts regarding the strengths and weaknesses of your company's internal environment.

Next, let's focus on the opportunities and threats facing your company. The opportunities and threats are viewed from an external perspective.

c. Prepare a schedule that specifies your company's opportunities and threats in the following areas:

  A. Industry Environment—What specific problems or opportunities exist for your company with the following groups?

    1. Customers
    2. Suppliers
    3. Competitors
    4. Substitute products or services

  B. Macro-environment—What specific problems or opportunities exist for your company in the following areas?

    1. Economic
    2. Social (changes in societal trends and attitudes)
    3. Political/Legal
    4. Technology
    5. Globalization
    6. Demographics

d. Prepare a summary of your thoughts regarding the opportunities and threats for your company's external environment.
e. Prepare a summary that summarizes your overall feelings regarding the SWOT analysis for your company.

CHAPTER 6

The Accounting System

Let's assume for a moment that you are a division manager for a major software corporation. You are trying to determine why the amount you owe your vendors and suppliers (accounts payable) is so high, so you call your company's general accounting department. You complain that your accounts payable balance has *increased* by $150,000 even after they had told you that it would be *credited* for this amount. After listening to your inquiry, an accounting clerk explains to you that a credit to accounts payable actually increases the account, it does not decrease it.

Hmm. Without at least a basic understanding of how accounting works, you'd have difficulty comprehending the logic of what the accounting clerk has told you. In a very real way, you'd be at the mercy of the accounting clerk—you'd need to rely on her to explain the situation to you in terms that you could understand. This is why everyone in business, not just accountants, needs to have at least a rudimentary understanding of how accountants transform economic facts and figures into useful information.

Although financial statement users are not generally concerned with the mechanics of how accounting gathers data and converts them to useful information, the better a user understands the accounting process, the better he or she can appreciate how business events and transactions will affect financial statements. Knowledgeable users do not blindly accept the information accountants provide. Instead, they understand where it comes from and how it finds its way into financial statements and other accounting reports and schedules.

This chapter is divided into two sections, Part I and Part II. Part I introduces the accounting system. It describes the accounting cycle and the documents accountants use to help them convert facts and figures into useful accounting information. Part II covers the application of accounting procedures. This section includes the application of debit and credit entries, adjusting entries, closing entries, as well as the use of T-accounts, journals, ledgers, the trial balance, and the worksheet.

Part I: Introduction to the Accounting System

Every business has hundreds if not thousands of transactions and economic events each year. In Part I of this chapter, we describe the procedures accountants use to analyze, classify, and record these economic events and transactions. We will explore how an accounting system transforms basic facts and figures into the valuable economic information that decision makers need.

Learning Objectives

After you complete your work on Part I of this chapter, you should be able to do the following:

1. Describe the basic classification structure accounting uses.
2. Describe the nine steps of the accounting cycle.

3. Describe and use journals and ledgers.
4. Explain the purpose of preparing a trial balance.
5. Explain why accountants make adjusting entries and what these entries accomplish.
6. Explain the closing process and the reason for it.

◆ ACCOUNTING'S BASIC CLASSIFICATION STRUCTURE

To convert raw data into useful information, an accounting system needs some means of classifying economic events and transactions. As we have seen in previous chapters, accounting elements such as assets, liabilities, and equity are some basic classifications, but they are too broad to render the level of detail that is needed for the resulting information to be useful to decision makers. Therefore, accountants use subclassifications of these accounting elements. For example, some subclassifications that may be found under assets are accounts receivable, office supplies, and property, plant, and equipment. Under expenses, we may find wages, rent, and advertising.

accounts Subclassifications used to classify and record economic events and transactions. For example, some accounts that may be found under assets are accounts receivable, office supplies, and property, plant, and equipment. Under expenses, we may find wages, rent, and advertising.

general ledger accounts The same thing as accounts.

general ledger A book of final entry that contains a page for each account listed in the chart of accounts.

These subclassifications are called **accounts** or **general ledger accounts.** The reason accounts are sometimes called *general ledger accounts* is that historically they were kept in a ledger book. Today, although most accounting systems are computerized, all the accounts together are called the **general ledger.** The term *account* used in this context may be confusing. Just remember this: Generally, in accounting and certainly in this chapter, when we use the word *account*, we mean a general ledger account unless we state otherwise.

Each account in the general ledger is assigned a title. These account titles are not dictated by generally accepted accounting principles (GAAP) or by any other accounting rules. Rather, companies choose their own account titles based on the needs and desires of the firm. The only real requirement is that account titles adequately describe the items they represent.

Accounts are almost always also assigned account numbers. Again, accounting rules do not establish the numbering scheme; businesses are free to choose their own numbering system. Companies generally develop a numbering system that groups similar types of accounts together. For example, assets might be assigned account numbers in a particular numerical range, say 1000 to 1999, and liabilities might be assigned account numbers in the next range, say 2000 to 2999, and so forth.

The number of accounts a company uses depends on the diversity of its business activity and the level of detail the company needs. Some companies have hundreds of accounts, others have only a few.

chart of accounts A list of all the accounts used by a business entity. The list usually contains the name of the account and the account number.

A reference document that lists all of the company's accounts and their account numbers is called a **chart of accounts.** Companies can add accounts to their chart of accounts as needed to record new and different transactions. Each business entity tailors its chart of accounts to its business activities. Exhibit 6–1 on page F–202 shows the chart of accounts for Collins Container Corporation, a wholesaler that sells boxes, barrels, and ash urns to crematoriums.

The chart of accounts normally lists accounts by account number. Most companies design their numbering system so that the accounts are listed in the order they will appear on the balance sheet and then the income statement. Now that you are familiar with the basic accounting classifications, we can turn our attention to the accounting cycle.

◆ THE ACCOUNTING CYCLE

In the previous chapters, we were able to prepare financial statements without a formal accounting system because there were so few transactions, and we were easily able to keep track of how they affected the financial statements. But when a business has thousands of transactions, such a simplistic approach just doesn't work. In such cases, we need a formal accounting system to gather, record, and classify transactions data. In a

Collins Container Corporation
Chart of Accounts

Assets:
  101 Cash
  110 Accounts receivable
  120 Merchandise inventory
  130 Office supplies
  140 Prepaid insurance
  150 Delivery truck
  155 Accumulated depreciation on delivery truck

Liabilities:
  200 Accounts payable
  210 Wages payable
  220 Interest payable
  240 Accrued expenses
  245 Unearned revenue
  250 Notes payable

Stockholders' Equity:
  300 Common stock
  310 Additional paid-in capital
  320 Retained earnings
  325 Dividends

Revenues:
  400 Sales
  410 Delivery service revenue
  420 Interest revenue

Expenses:
  500 Cost of goods sold
  620 Wages expense
  630 Rent expense
  640 Electricity expense
  645 Supplies expense
  650 Gasoline expense
  655 Insurance expense
  660 Depreciation expense
  670 Bank service charge expense
  680 Interest expense

EXHIBIT 6–1 Chart of Accounts for Collins Container Corporation

formal accounting system, some events occur daily, some monthly, and some occur annually. As one year ends and another begins, the process begins anew. That is why the steps that accountants take to transform data into meaningful information are called the accounting cycle. The steps in the accounting cycle are as follows:

Step 1: Analyze economic events and transactions
Step 2: Journalize transactions
Step 3: Post transactions to the general ledger
Step 4: Prepare a trial balance
Step 5: Prepare, journalize, and post adjusting entries
Step 6: Prepare an adjusted trial balance
Step 7: Prepare financial statements
Step 8: Prepare, journalize, and post closing entries
Step 9: Prepare the post-closing trial balance

Before we delve into the specifics of accounting entries and procedures, let's look at the accounting cycle by presenting a general overview of each of its nine steps.

STEP 1: ANALYZING ECONOMIC EVENTS AND TRANSACTIONS

Analyzing transactions, the most important step in the accounting cycle, consists of two parts. The first part is determining if and when an economic event or transaction should be recorded in the accounting system. We record an economic event or transaction when it affects one or more accounting elements or accounts. For example, if a company buys merchandise on account, inventory increases as does accounts payable. In such a case, both assets and liabilities are affected. But what if the company had merely ordered the merchandise for delivery at a later time instead of purchasing it? Should we record this event in the company's accounting system? No, because the event has not affected assets, liabilities, equity, or any other accounting element. We do not record the event until title to the merchandise passes from the vendor to the buyer and the seller has the cash or a legally enforceable claim to cash. At that moment, the company has a new asset and a new liability.

The second part of analyzing transactions is identifying the nature of the transaction in terms of how the company's accounts are affected. All economic events and transactions that are recorded by accountants affect at least two areas and therefore at least two general ledger accounts. In a way, this makes sense because if every accounting entry affects the accounting equation, a change in one element of the equation would require a change in another to keep the equation in balance. This concept is the origin of the term *double-entry bookkeeping.* For example, if you use your credit card to buy a new television for $500, the transaction affects two things. First, you now have a new asset, a $500 television. Second, you now have a new $500 liability. When you pay the credit card company for the television, two things are affected as well. First, an asset (cash) decreases by $500, and second, liabilities decrease by $500.

When analyzing transactions, you should take a common sense look at the situation to figure out what has happened. Then, you can select and use accounts that will appropriately reflect the reality of the situation.

Discussion Question ● ◎

6–1. Why do you think it takes common sense and not just an accounting background to analyze economic events and transactions?

STEP 2. JOURNALIZING TRANSACTIONS

journal A book of original entry used to record the economic events and transactions that affect the accounts of a company.

book of original entry The same thing as a journal.

manual accounting system An accounting system in which the accountants and bookkeepers write all of the entries by hand in pen and ink.

computerized accounting system An accounting system in which the accountants and bookkeepers make entries in a computer system where the journals and ledgers consist of listings of transactions on computer printouts or in files in the computer's memory.

Journalizing transactions is the act of recording accounting transactions in a journal. Many people keep a daily personal journal—a chronological record of the things that happen in their life. Each day's entry includes the date and all the pertinent facts associated with the events they enter. An accounting **journal** is quite similar. It is a chronological record of the economic events and transactions that affect the accounting elements (the accounts) of a company. Each entry is dated, it indicates the accounts that were increased or decreased and the dollar amount of the change, and it may also include a description of the entry to provide additional detail. The first place an economic event or transaction is recorded is in a journal. For this reason, journals are sometimes called **books of original entry.**

In a **manual accounting system,** the accountants and bookkeepers write all of the entries by hand in pen and ink. In this case, the journals are nothing more than books with pages and pages of journal entries. In a **computerized accounting system,** the accountants and bookkeepers make entries in a computer system, and the journals are more likely to consist of a listing of transactions on a computer printout or a file in the computer's memory.

Regardless of its form, a journal lists transactions in the order of occurrence. Employees, managers, and auditors frequently use the journal's chronological listing of transactions to trace events and answer inquiries. For this reason, we record transactions formally into journals daily, weekly, or sometimes monthly for small businesses. Large companies use online, real-time processing techniques that make the journal entries as the transactions occur. Sophisticated cash register systems often create journal entries as the cashier scans the items sold.

Typically, a business will use not one, but several journals. Each journal is designed to record a particular type of transaction. For example, a cash receipts journal is used to record all cash collections, a cash payments journal is used to record all cash payments, and a sales journal is used to record all sales on account. A journal that is created to record a particular type of transaction is called a **special journal.** Special journals help to streamline the accounting process and greatly enhance accounting efficiency. In addition to special journals, every company has a **general journal** to record any transactions for which there is no special journal. If a company has no special journals, all transactions are recorded in the general journal. If a company has a full complement of special journals, very few transactions are recorded in the general journal.

special journal A book of original entry designed to record a specific type of transaction.

general journal A book of original entry in which is recorded all transactions not otherwise recorded in special journals.

STEP 3. POSTING TRANSACTIONS TO THE GENERAL LEDGER

Journals provide a wealth of valuable information about each transaction, but, when hundreds of transactions are involved, journals do not work well to provide information account by account. For example, if we wanted to know how much cash the company had received, how much it had paid out, and how much it had left, a journal would not be very much help. Even if the company's journal is 50 pages long and there were hundreds of transactions that affected cash, the only way to determine the balance in the cash account would be to page through the journal and find all the entries that impacted cash. Then, you would have to add them up to gain insight into what happened to cash. For this reason, a ledger page is prepared for each account. As we mentioned earlier, all these ledger pages are kept in a book called the general ledger. This is why accounts are sometimes called general ledger accounts. In computerized accounting systems, the general ledger consists of computer files and printouts.

posting The process of transcribing information from journals to the ledger.

The entries made in the journal are transcribed to the ledger in a process called **posting.** Posting is a fairly simple process of copying information from the journal to the appropriate ledger. What this means is that all the journal entries that affect cash are posted to the cash account, all the entries that affect supplies are posted to the supplies account, and so forth. See Exhibit 6–2 for an illustration of posting. Generally, the

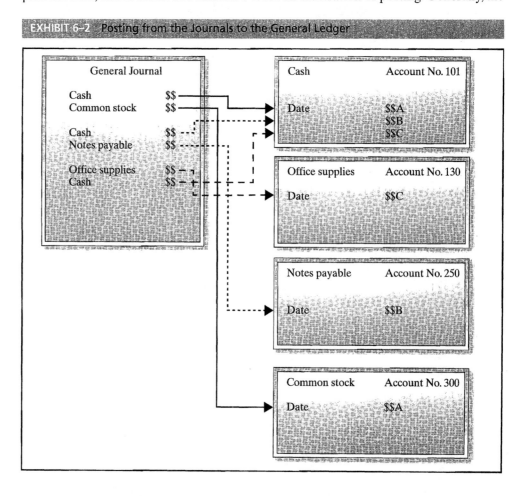

EXHIBIT 6–2 Posting from the Journals to the General Ledger

journal entries are posted to the general ledger at least monthly. Computers can perform this function in seconds.

Once all the journal entries have been posted to the general ledger, we add all increases and subtract all decreases to the previous balance of the account to arrive at a new account balance. We use the general ledger account balances to prepare financial statements after two additional steps in the accounting cycle.

Discussion Question ●

6–2. Why would a company need journals and a general ledger? Why wouldn't just one or the other be good enough?

STEP 4. PREPARING A TRIAL BALANCE

trial balance The listing of the general ledger account balances, which proves that the general ledger and therefore the accounting equation is in balance.

From time to time, we need to know the balances in the general ledger accounts to make sure that the accounting equation is in balance, or to review the general ledger balances as we prepare to make financial statements. To get these balances, instead of looking at each page of the general ledger, we prepare a trial balance. A **trial balance** is simply a listing of all the general ledger accounts and their balances. In manual accounting systems, preparing a trial balance is just a matter of accounting personnel paging through the general ledger and listing the account names and their balances. In a computerized system, accounting personnel select the appropriate menu option and the accounting software package creates the trial balance automatically. See Exhibit 6–3 for an illustration of a trial balance.

STEP 5. ADJUSTING THE GENERAL LEDGER ACCOUNTS

You might think that accountants are able to keep general ledger account balances up to date moment by moment. Unfortunately, this is not the case. Even when every member of the accounting staff has done his or her job perfectly, there are differences between what accounting records show and the reality of the situation. Why does this

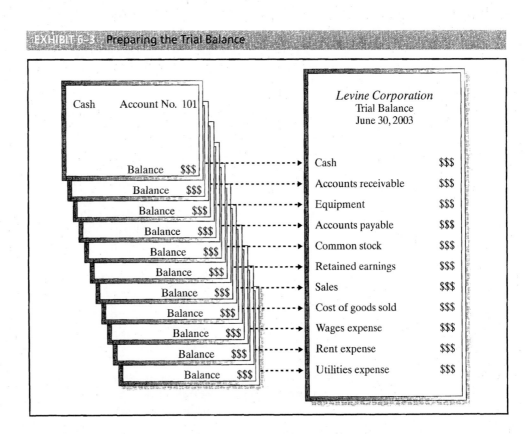

EXHIBIT 6-3 Preparing the Trial Balance

happen? Well, there are a number of reasons, but often it's simply a matter of timing. For example, there is almost always a difference between when economic events actually occur and when the accounting staff records the events. Sometimes, the events are recorded too soon (so what is recorded is not totally accurate), but more often, they are not recorded soon enough (so the accounting system doesn't provide timely information). Also, business situations can change over time. In those cases, the account balances that resulted when the accounting staff originally recorded the transaction fail to capture the essence of the new situation. So, accountants must review and update account balances before they prepare financial statements. Making entries to bring account balances up to date in order to prepare the most up-to-the-minute financial statements is part of the adjusting process.

adjusting entries The entries to modify account balances so that all revenue earned and all expenses incurred are recorded and all asset, liability, and equity accounts are properly stated as of the balance sheet date.

Prior to preparing financial statements, accountants review each general ledger account to determine whether the account balances reflect the company's situation as of the end of the accounting period. Then, they make **adjusting entries** as necessary so that all revenue earned is reported, but no more; that all expenses incurred are reported, but no more; and that asset, liability, and equity accounts are properly stated as of the balance sheet date. The adjustment process may involve entries to defer or accrue revenues or expenses, as we discussed in Chapter 5. During the adjusting process, accountants follow a step-by-step procedure. First, they examine each account in light of the situation that existed at the very end of the accounting period to determine whether the ending balances are appropriate. Second, when they find accounts that have inappropriate balances, they must determine the amount by which they need to increase or decrease those accounts. Finally, they make an adjusting entry in the general journal to change the ending account balances to the appropriate amount.

worksheet A tool used by the accountant to accumulate the necessary information used to prepare the financial statements.

As part of the adjusting process, accountants frequently use a **worksheet** to help them prepare financial statements. We will examine the details of the worksheet later in this chapter.

Once the accounting staff has made all the necessary adjusting entries, the account balances are ready to prepare the adjusted trial balance.

Discussion Question

6–3. List and discuss two situations that would result in the need to adjust accounting records even though all the company's accounting had been done properly.

STEP 6. PREPARING AN ADJUSTED TRIAL BALANCE

adjusted trial balance A trial balance that is prepared after all of the adjusting entries have been made.

The **adjusted trial balance** is a trial balance that is prepared after all of the adjusting entries have been made. It is like any other trial balance except that it reflects account balances that are up to the minute and as accurate as reasonably possible. The adjusted trial balance provides the accounting staff with the account balances they need to prepare the company's financial statements.

STEP 7. PREPARING FINANCIAL STATEMENTS

Once the company accountant is satisfied that the account balances are correct as of the balance sheet date, he or she prepares the financial statements. The accountant uses the amounts from the adjusted trial balance to prepare the income statement, the statement of owners' equity, and the balance sheet.

Discussion Questions

6–4. Imagine that you own a large retail stereo and electronics business. With respect to your need for information, how often do you think your company should prepare financial statements?

6–5. Assume your stereo and electronics business has borrowed a substantial sum from ***Bank of America.*** How often do you think the bank will want your business to provide them with financial statements?

STEP 8. PREPARING AND POSTING CLOSING ENTRIES

The closing process involves closing out one year of business and getting ready for the next. To understand the closing process, we must first understand a little bit about how accounts are used to provide information. Revenue and expense accounts are what we might call "accumulator accounts." This is because they accumulate, or keep a running total of the revenues and expenses a company has had during the year. Similarly, distributions to owners accounts, such as dividends, keep a running total of the amounts distributed to owners throughout the year. Once a fiscal (business) year comes to a close, it is time to prepare the company's books so that new running totals can be maintained for the next year. What this means is that revenues, expenses, and dividends should begin the new year with a blank slate—that is, zero balances. To accomplish this, accountants make a series of **closing entries** to reset revenues, expenses, and dividends to zero. The entries ultimately move the balances in revenue, expense, and dividend accounts into retained earnings.

Accounts that are closed during the closing process—generally, revenues, expenses, and dividends—are called **temporary** (or **nominal**) **accounts.** The closing entries zero out temporary account balances much like a trip-switch zeros out the mileage on an automobile trip odometer. We do not close all general ledger accounts, however. Unlike income statement accounts (temporary accounts) that keep running totals of business activity, balance sheet accounts represent what a company has (its assets), what it owes (its liabilities), and the owners' interest in the company (its equity) as of a moment in time. Balance sheet accounts present a picture of "what is." Balance sheet accounts are called **permanent** (or **real**) **accounts** because they are not closed during the closing process. Permanent accounts include asset, liability, and equity accounts, except for distributions to owners such as the dividend account.

The closing process consists of four steps and uses a temporary account called *income summary.* As you can see by the following list of closing steps for a corporation, the income summary account is created and then closed during the closing process.

1. Close the revenue accounts to income summary.
2. Close the expense accounts to income summary.
3. Close income summary to retained earnings.
4. Close the dividends account to retained earnings.

Although it might not seem so, the closing process is really quite interesting. In prior chapters, we said that net income increases owners' equity and distributions to owners' decreases it. If you examine the four steps of the closing process, you will see just how owners' equity, through retained earnings, is increased by net income (revenues less expenses) and decreased by distributions to owners (dividends.) An understanding of this concept will be critically important as you are learning how and why debits and credits affect revenues, expenses, and dividends.

Discussion Question

6–6. We have said that income increases owners' equity in a business. Why are the owners entitled to the income instead of the employees who worked to earn the income in the first place?

STEP 9. PREPARING THE POST-CLOSING TRIAL BALANCE

After we prepare the closing entries and post them to the general ledger, only the permanent accounts (the balance sheet accounts) will have balances remaining. Revenues, expenses, and any owner withdrawal or dividend accounts should have zero balances. As part of a final check of the closing process, we prepare a **post-closing trial balance** after posting closing entries to confirm that the closing entries have zeroed the temporary accounts. In a computerized system, this step is crucial to verify the integrity of the closing process and to ensure that the accounting equation remains in balance.

Marginal glossary definitions:

closing entries A series of entries to reset revenues, expenses, and dividends to zero in preparation for a new accounting year.

temporary (nominal) accounts The general ledger accounts that are closed to a zero balance at the end of the fiscal year as the net income or net loss is transferred to the appropriate equity account. Temporary accounts include revenues, expenses, gains, losses, owner withdrawal, and dividend accounts.

permanent (real) accounts The general ledger accounts that are never closed. The permanent accounts include assets, liabilities, and equity accounts except for owner withdrawals.

post-closing trial balance A trial balance prepared after all closing entries have been posted, which proves that the only accounts remaining in the general ledger are the permanent accounts and that the accounting equation remains in balance.

Before we look at the specifics of how the accounting cycle works, let's see how accountants use debits and credits to increase and decrease account balances.

Part II: Application of Accounting Procedures

Now that you are familiar with the accounting cycle's nine steps, we are ready to explore the details of how accountants transform transaction data into useful accounting information.

Learning Objectives

After completing your work on Part II of this chapter, you should be able to do the following:

1. Understand the effects of debits and credits and use them to make accounting entries.
2. Make accounting entries using T-accounts and the general journal.
3. Post journal entries to the general ledger.
4. Prepare a trial balance.
5. Prepare adjusting journal entries and reconcile a bank account.
6. Prepare a worksheet and an adjusted trial balance.
7. Prepare financial statements from a worksheet or an adjusted trial balance.
8. Prepare closing journal entries and a post-closing trial balance.

◆ DEBITS AND CREDITS

Accountants do not use pluses (+) and minuses (−) to increase and decrease dollar amounts in accounting records; instead they use a system of *debits* and *credits*. This is because the debit and credit system enables accountants to keep the accounting system in balance more readily than would the use of pluses and minuses. At any given point in the accounting process, whether we examine a single accounting entry or the balances in an entire accounting system, the total dollar amount of the debits should equal the total dollar amount of the credits.

Making debit and credit entries is not really difficult, but to be successful, it requires you to bring three important areas of understanding together. These areas are:

1. You must understand the accounting elements and accounts. As we mentioned earlier, the accounting elements basically comprise a system for classifying economic events and transactions. The accounting elements are further broken down into subclassifications called accounts or general ledger accounts.
2. You must understand how to analyze economic events and transactions to determine their impact, if any, on the accounting elements and specific general ledger accounts.
3. You must understand how debits and credits increase and decrease account balances.

Knowing any one or two of the areas is not enough; you must understand all three. By now, you should have a firm grasp of the accounting elements we covered in the first five chapters of this book. If not, review them before proceeding further. You are probably less familiar with how accountants analyze transactions, so we provide several step-by-step examples in the remainder of this chapter. If you are like most people who take a beginning accounting course, you probably don't know much about debits and credits at all, so our coverage of this topic will be extensive.

◆ THE IMPACT OF DEBITS AND CREDITS ON ASSETS, LIABILITIES, AND EQUITY

Accounting and accounting entries are based on the accounting equation we first presented in Chapter 1 (Assets = Liabilities + Equity). As we know from mathematics, a change in one side of the equation requires a change in the other side to keep the equation in balance. This concept is the basis of the double-entry bookkeeping.

The double-entry system we use today is based on the writings of Luca Pacioli of Venice, Italy. In his book, *Summa de Arithmetica, Geometria, Proportioni et Proportionalita* (Everything About Arithmetic, Geometry and Proportion), published in 1494, Pacioli described the double-entry system of bookkeeping being used by merchants in Venice at that time. The ledger he described was very similar to the ones we use in modern accounting today. It included notations for the date and a description of the event, with debits on the left side (*deve dare*) and credits on the right (*deve avere*). Even today, debits are always on the left and credits are always on the right.

When we apply this debits on the left, credits on the right logic to the accounting equation, assets (the accounting element on the left side of the equation) are on the debit (left) side of the equation, while liabilities and equity (the elements on the right side of the equation) are on the credit (right) side of the equation. When an accounting system is in balance, the debits equal the credits; left equals right.

$$\text{Assets} = \text{Liabilities} + \text{Equity}$$
$$\text{Left Side of the Equation} = \text{Right Side of the Equation}$$
$$\text{Debit Side} = \text{Credit Side}$$

Because of their position in the accounting equation, assets normally have debit balances and liabilities and equity accounts normally have credit balances. The debit or credit balance an account typically has is called the account's **normal balance.**

normal balance The balance of the account derived from the type of entry (debit or credit) that increases the account.

$$\text{Assets} = \text{Liabilities} + \text{Equity}$$
Normal Balances: $\text{Debit Balance} = \text{Credit Balance*} + \text{Credit Balance*}$

An account's normal balance dictates the type of entry that increases the account; debits increase debit balance accounts and credits increase credit balance accounts. Accounts that are increased by debits are decreased by credits and accounts that are increased by credits are decreased by debits. Exhibit 6–4 shows a summary of normal account balances and the effects of debits and credits on assets, liabilities, and equity.

EXHIBIT 6–4 Effects of Debits and Credits on Assets, Liabilities, and Equity			
	Assets	*Liabilities*	*Equity*
Normal Balance	Debit	Credit	Credit
Increased by:	Debits	Credits	Credits
Decreased by:	Credits	Debits	Debits

Understanding how debits and credits affect account balances is essential. Through logic or memorization, you must comprehend how debits and credits work to increase and decrease account balances. With this knowledge and a familiarity with the accounting elements and accounts, and an ability to analyze transactions, you can make debit and credit entries in asset, liability, and equity accounts. But first, you will need to know an acceptable format for your debit/credit entries. The format we will use initially is the T-account.

THE T-ACCOUNT

The T-account gets its name because it is nothing more than a big "T" drawn under an account name with space for debits on the left and credits on the right. T-accounts for cash and supplies are presented below:

Cash

Debit	Credit
side	side

Supplies

Debit	Credit
side	side

---
*The two credit balances must equal the debit balance.

To debit a T-account, all we have to do is to place the dollar amount of the debit on the left side of the T-account account. To credit a T-account, we place the dollar amount on the right side. Dollar signs ($) are not necessary for T-account entries. For example, assume **Holiday Isle Resorts** buys $300 dollars worth of supplies for cash and they wish to make a T-account entry for this transaction. The company is receiving supplies in exchange for cash so we should increase the supplies account and decrease the cash account. Both supplies and cash are asset accounts, and, as we already know, assets are increased by debits and decreased by credits, so the T-account entry would appear as follows:

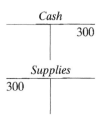

As we have already mentioned, whenever you make an accounting entry, in whatever format, debits will always be on the left while credits will always be on the right. In addition, the total dollar amount of the debits should always equal the total dollar amount of the credits.

When we said debit cash for $300 to increase it, the entry may have seemed entirely backwards to you. The reason debits and credits seem to work backwards to a lot of us is that the account records we generally see are not our own, but rather those of banks or credit card companies. So, the debits and credits you have seen in the past on your bank statement are from the *bank's* perspective, *not yours*. What you probably do not realize is that when you look at your bank statement, you are not really looking at a *cash* account at all, but rather the bank's *liability* account to you. The bank has a liability to you because the bank has your money and, at some point, must pay it back. To increase a liability, the bank credits the liability account. So the reason debits and credits may seem backwards to you is that, probably for the first time, you are viewing the situation from the perspective of making entries in your own accounting records (or those of the company for which you are doing the accounting) rather than from the perspective of a bank or credit card company.

THE IMPACT OF DEBITS AND CREDITS ON REVENUES, EXPENSES, AND DIVIDENDS

By now you should be familiar with how debits and credits affect assets, liabilities, and equity. But what about making debit and credit entries to revenue and expense accounts? To understand how debits and credits affect revenues and expenses, we need to bear in mind that revenues and expenses are really part of equity. In a corporate setting, revenues and expenses are a part of retained earnings. The more revenue a company has, the more its retained earnings will increase. The more expenses a company has, the more retained earnings will decrease. So, revenues increase retained earnings while expenses decrease it. We should also mention that dividends also decrease retained earnings.

Remember, equity normally carries a credit balance, and because it is part of equity, so does retained earnings. What this means is that credits increase retained earnings while debits decrease it. Revenues are the source of credits that increase retained earnings and expenses and dividends are the sources of debits that decrease retained earnings. So, revenues normally have credit balances while expenses and dividends normally have debit balances. Exhibit 6–5 shows the accounting equation and how the debits and credits from revenues, expenses, and dividends affect equity.

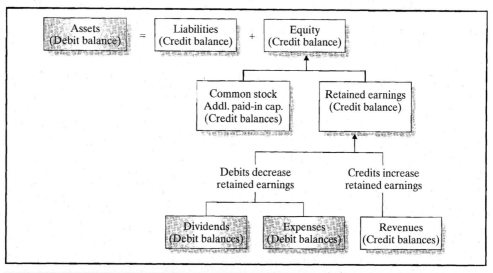

EXHIBIT 6–5   The Accounting Equation and the Effects of Debits and Credits to Revenues, Expenses, and Dividends on Equity

Exhibit 6–5 shows the logic of how debits and credits affect revenues, expenses, and dividends. To put this knowledge to use, we will make T-account entries to record the following three transactions for A. R. Oddo Leasing Corporation.

a. On July 31, 2004, Oddo Leasing collected $500 for July rent.
b. On July 31, the company paid $200 for July's property taxes.
c. On July 31, the company paid dividends of $120 to its owners.

```
                    Cash
        (a.) 500 |  200 (b.)
                 |  120 (c.)


                Rent Revenue
                 |  500 (a.)


                 Property
                Tax Expense
        (b.) 200 |


                 Dividends
        (c.) 120 |
```

Although a basic understanding of how debits and credits increase and decrease account balances is essential, don't be concerned if you have yet to fully understand how debits and credits work. You will have plenty of opportunities to enhance your understanding as we proceed through each step of the accounting cycle.

Exhibit 6–6 summarizes the effects of debits and credits on assets, liabilities, equity, revenues, expenses, and dividends.

EXHIBIT 6–6   Effects of Debits and Credits on Account Balances

	Assets	*Liabilities*	*Equity*	*Revenues*	*Expenses*	*Dividends*
Normal Balance	Debit	Credit	Credit	Credit	Debit	Debit
Increased by:	Debits	Credits	Credits	Credits	Debits	Debits
Decreased by:	Credits	Debits	Debits	Debits	Credits	Credits

Although T-accounts worked well to introduce debits and credits, in accounting, their use is generally limited to informal illustrations of accounting entries and procedures; they are not a formal part of an accounting system. Instead of using T-accounts, businesses initially record transactions in a journal. As we indicated earlier in this chapter, there are several types of journals. For simplicity, in this chapter, we will use only the general journal, because the general journal can be used to record virtually any accounting entry. Before you begin to make accounting entries, you must first understand the correct format for entries in the general journal. Exhibit 6–7 illustrates a general journal and shows the entry to record the 2004 transactions for A. R. Oddo Leasing Corporation that we previously showed in T-account form.

EXHIBIT 6–7 Sample General Journal Entry

Date 2004	Description	Post. Ref.	Debit	Credit
Jul 31	Cash		500	
	Rent revenue			500
	To record rent collected for July.			
31	Property tax expense		200	
	Cash			200
	To record July property taxes.			
31	Dividends		120	
	Cash			120
	To record cash dividends paid to owners.			

General Journal — Page xx

The date column of the general journal provides information about the effective date of the entry. It is not necessarily the date that the accounting staff made the entry; rather it is the date the accounting staff wants the entry to take effect. As a practical matter, accounting entries are often made after an economic event has occurred. When dating a journal entry, the year is placed at the top of the date column, followed by an abbreviation for the month, and finally the day. Once the month has been indicated on the journal, it need not be entered again until it changes.

The description column of the general journal provides space for the account names and for an optional description of the entry. Accounting custom dictates that the debits for an entry are made first, followed by the credits. Then an optional description may be presented to provide additional detail about the transaction. Note that the title of the credited account has been indented. This indenting is one of the indications that the account was credited. Making the debit part of the general journal entry first and indenting the credited account title are two important accounting customs.

The posting reference column of the general journal is not used when the entry is originally recorded in the journal; rather it is used when the entry is posted to the general ledger. As part of the posting process, accountants record the account number that corresponds to the account to which the transaction was posted.

The general journal's debit column is used to record the dollar amount of the debit entries and the credit column is used to record the dollar amount of the credits. Note that it is not necessary to use dollar signs ($) when making entries in a journal.

◆ ANALYZING AND JOURNALIZING TRANSACTIONS

As part of the process of making the accounting entries, we must analyze each of the company's economic events and transactions. As we said earlier in this chapter, analyzing a transaction entails a common sense look at the situation to determine if a transaction has occurred and, if one has, the transaction's impact on the general ledger accounts. To help you analyze transactions and make general journal entries, we suggest the following four steps:

1. Determine if and when a transaction occurred, what accounts were affected, which account balances should increase, which should decrease, and by how much.
2. Determine which accounts should be debited and which should be credited.
3. Make the journal entry.
4. Review the entry to ensure it is in proper form and that the debits equal the credits.

We will follow these four steps as we examine a series of transactions for the Collins Container Corporation. As we proceed, try to develop the skills necessary to analyze transactions and make the entries on your own. Keep in mind that the entries we show are a small sample of the thousands that are possible. Accordingly, try to develop a technique for analyzing events and transactions and then making appropriate entries, rather than trying to memorize the entries we make for our example transactions. We will begin with the transactions listed in Exhibit 6–8. These initial transactions affect only assets, liabilities, and equity.

EXHIBIT 6–8 Transactions a. Through h. for the Collins Container Corporation

a. On January 1, 2004, Collins Container Corporation began by issuing 1,000 shares of its $1 par common stock in exchange for $10,000 in cash.

b. On January 1, the company borrowed cash of $20,000 on a 9%, one-year promissory note from *Bank of America.*

c. On January 1, the company purchased a one-year insurance policy for $2,400 cash.

d. On January 1, the company purchased a $15,000 delivery truck for cash.

e. On January 4, the company ordered $4,200 worth of shipping supplies. The shipping supplies are to be delivered in early February.

f. On January 7, the company purchased office supplies for $2,000 on account (on a charge account).

g. On January 8, the company purchased merchandise inventory costing $16,000 on account.

h. On January 12, the company paid $750 on account toward the office supplies purchased on January 7, 2004, in item f.

---

a. On January 1, 2004, Collins Container Corporation began by issuing 1,000 shares of its $1 par common stock in exchange for $10,000 in cash.

1. This transaction took place on January 1, 2004, and affects cash, common stock, and additional paid-in capital. The balances of each of the accounts should be increased: cash by $10,000, common stock by $1,000, and additional paid-in capital by $9,000.

2. Because cash is an asset account, it is on the left side of the accounting equation and is increased with a debit. Common stock and additional paid-in capital are both equity accounts and are on the right side of the accounting equation, so they are increased by credits.

3. The general journal entry:

2004
Jan 1   Cash   10,000
*   Common stock   1,000*
*   Additional paid-in capital   9,000*

4. A final check of the entry reveals that we dated the entry, we made the debit part of the entry first, we indented the credit account titles, we did not use dollar signs, and the dollar amount of the debits equals that of the credits.

b. On January 1, 2004, the company borrowed cash of $20,000 on a 9 percent, one-year promissory note from *Bank of America*.

1. This transaction took place on January 1, 2004, and affects cash and notes payable. The balances of both accounts should be increased by $20,000. (*Note*: Because Collins has just borrowed the money, no time has passed for interest to accrue, so we need not include interest in the entry we are making at this time.)

2. Because cash is an asset account, it is on the left side of the accounting equation and is increased with a debit. Notes payable, a liability account, is on the right side of the accounting equation, so it is increased by a credit.

3. The general journal entry:

Jan 1   Cash   20,000
*   Notes payable   20,000*

4. A final check of the entry reveals that the entry is in good form and the dollar amount of the debits equals that of the credits.

c. On January 1, 2004, the company purchased a one-year insurance policy for $2,400 cash.

1. This transaction took place on January 1, 2004. With this $2,400 payment, the company now owns an insurance policy that will benefit the company for the next 12 months. Therefore, the payment for this insurance has future value to the company and we should consider it an asset. Expenses paid in advance are called *prepaid expenses*, so in this case, prepaid insurance and cash are affected by the transaction. The balance of the prepaid insurance account should be increased by $2,400 and the balance of the cash account should be decreased by $2,400.

2. Because prepaid insurance is an asset account, it is on the left side of the accounting equation and is increased by a debit. Cash is also an asset account, and, because assets are on the left side of the accounting equation, they are decreased by credits. In this case, we want to decrease the account, so the cash account is credited.

3. The general journal entry:

Jan 1   Prepaid insurance   2,400
*   Cash   2,400*

4. A final check of the entry reveals that the dollar amount of the debits equals that of the credits.

Discussion Question

6–7. When accountants review an entry to make sure it balances, they check to see that debits equal credits. Why couldn't they do the same thing with pluses and minuses?

d. On January 1, 2004, the company purchased a $15,000 delivery truck for cash.

1. This transaction took place on January 1, 2004. Based on this transaction, Collins Container Corporation owns a new asset, a delivery truck. In addition, cash was used to pay for the truck, so cash should be decreased. The delivery truck account should be increased by the $15,000 cost of the truck and the cash account should be decreased by the $15,000 paid for the truck.

2. Because the delivery truck account is an asset account, it is on the left side of the accounting equation and is increased by a debit. Cash is also an asset account, and, because assets are on the left side of the accounting equation, they are decreased by credits. In this case, we want to decrease the account, so the cash account is credited.

3. The general journal entry:

Jan 1 Delivery truck   15,000
           Cash   15,000

4. A final check of the entry reveals that the entry is in good form and the dollar amount of the debits equals that of the credits.

e. On January 4, the company ordered $4,200 worth of shipping supplies. The shipping supplies are to be purchased for cash in early February.

1. Actually, a transaction has not yet occurred with respect to item e. Merely ordering material such as supplies does not impact an accounting element or account. The transaction will occur when Collins Container Corporation purchases the supplies in February. No accounting entry is necessary at this time. This item does not change the balance in any account. We have not purchased the supplies and do not own them yet, so we should *not* increase the shipping supplies account balance. In addition, we have not yet paid any cash for the supplies, so we should *not* decrease the cash account. Again, no entry should be made for this item at this time, so our analysis can end here.

f. On January 7, 2004, the company purchased office supplies for $2,000 on account (on a charge account).

1. This transaction took place on January 7, 2004. In this transaction, the company purchased office supplies that it can use in the future. The company has not paid for the office supplies however; rather, it purchased them "on account," so a liability (accounts payable) has been created. The balance of the office supplies account should be increased by the $2,000 cost of the supplies acquired. The accounts payable account should be increased by the $2,000 the company now owes on account.

2. Because office supplies is an asset account, it is on the left side of the accounting equation and is increased by a debit. Accounts payable is a liability account and on the right side of the accounting equation, so it is increased by a credit.

3. The general journal entry:

Jan 7 Office supplies   2,000
           Accounts payable   2,000

4. A final check of the entry reveals that the dollar amount of the debits equals that of the credits.

g. On January 8, the company purchased merchandise inventory costing $16,000 on account.

1. This transaction took place on January 8, 2004. In this transaction, the company purchased merchandise that it will sell to customers in the future. Merchandise inventory, an asset, should be increased, and, because the company has not yet paid for the merchandise, accounts payable should be increased for the purchase. The balance of the merchandise inventory account should be increased by the

$16,000 cost of the merchandise purchased. The accounts payable account should be increased by the $16,000 the company now owes on account for this purchase.

2. Because merchandise inventory is an asset account, it is on the left side of the accounting equation and is increased by a debit. Accounts payable is a liability account, so it is on the right side of the accounting equation and is increased by a credit.

3. The general journal entry:

Jan 8	Merchandise inventory	16,000	
	Accounts payable		16,000

4. A final check of the entry reveals that the dollar amount of the debits equals that of the credits.

h. On January 12, 2004, the company paid $750 on account toward the office supplies purchased on January 7, 2004, in item f.

1. This transaction took place on January 12, 2004. In this transaction, the company is paying part of its $2,000 accounts payable liability. The company is paying with cash, so cash should be reduced. Also, the amount the company owes will be reduced by the payment, so accounts payable should also be reduced. Both the cash account and accounts payable account should be reduced by the $750 paid. Note that the company is *not* acquiring more office supplies, it is simply paying the liability incurred for the office supplies it purchased previously. Accordingly, the office supplies account is not affected by this entry.

2. Accounts payable is a liability account, so it is on the right side of the accounting equation and is decreased by a debit. Because cash is an asset account, it is on the left side of the accounting equation and is decreased by a credit.

3. The general journal entry:

Jan 12	Accounts payable	750	
	Cash		750

4. A final check of the entry reveals that the dollar amount of the debits equals that of the credits.

Now we continue our Collins Container Corporation example with some additional items that impact not only assets, liabilities, and equities, but also revenues and expenses as well. See Exhibit 6–9.

EXHIBIT 6–9 Transactions i. Through p. for the Collins Container Corporation

i. On January 22, Collins Container Corporation received cash of $8,000 for merchandise it sold and delivered to customers that day. The merchandise originally cost Collins $5,000.

j. Collins Container Corporation billed customers $12,600 for merchandise delivered to customers on January 26. This merchandise originally cost Collins $7,400.

k. Collins Corporation provides delivery services to some neighboring businesses to help utilize its delivery truck. On January 26, Collins Corporation billed one of these businesses $300 and collected cash of $150 from another business for delivery services. Thus, the total for delivery services for neighboring businesses was $450.

l. On January 27, the company paid $90 for gasoline used in the company's delivery truck during the month of January.

m. On January 27, the company paid wages to employees of $1,500.

n. On January 28, the company received a $2,700 order from a customer for goods to be delivered in February.

o. On January 31, the company paid $500 for January's rent.

p. On January 31, the company paid a dividend to its shareholders of $300.

i. On January 22, Collins Container Corporation received cash of $8,000 for merchandise it sold and delivered to customers that day. The merchandise originally cost Collins $5,000.

1. This transaction took place on January 22, 2004. Generally speaking, sales transactions have two distinct parts we must deal with. First, the company has sold merchandise for cash, so we should increase both sales and cash. Second, the company has delivered merchandise to the customer from its inventory, so we should decrease merchandise inventory and increase cost of goods sold. The amount of the sale and the cash received is $8,000, so we should increase the sales account and the cash account by this amount. The company's cost of the inventory it sold is $5,000, so we should decrease the merchandise inventory account and increase the cost of goods sold account by this amount.

2. As you know, because cash is an asset account, we increase it with a debit. Sales is a revenue account and revenue increases equity. Equity accounts are increased with a credit, so we should credit the sales revenue account. Cost of goods sold is an expense account and expenses decrease equity. Therefore, we increase expense accounts such as cost of goods sold with a debit. Merchandise inventory is an asset account, so we decrease it with a credit. This item actually requires two separate entries, or an entry that includes multiple parts. Entries that include multiple parts are called **compound entries.**

compound entries

Entries recorded in the general journal that contain more than two accounts.

3. The two separate entries are:

Jan 22	Cash	8,000	
	Sales		8,000
22	Cost of goods sold	5,000	
	Merchandise inventory		5,000

Or, to accomplish the same changes to the account balances, we can make the following compound entry:

Jan 22	Cash	8,000	
	Cost of goods sold	5,000	
	Sales		8,000
	Merchandise inventory		5,000

4. A final check of both sets of entries reveals that the dollar amount of the debits equals that of the credits. You can make either two separate entries or a compound entry for an item such as this. The choice is yours.

j. Collins Container Corporation billed customers $12,600 for merchandise delivered to customers on January 26. This merchandise originally cost Collins $7,400.

1. This transaction took place on January 26, 2004. As we said before, sales transactions generally have two distinct parts. In this case, the company has sold merchandise on account, so we should increase sales and accounts receivable. Also, the company has delivered merchandise to the customer from its inventory, so we should decrease merchandise inventory and increase cost of goods sold. The amount of the sale and the amount that the customer owes Collins is $12,600, so we should increase the sales account and the accounts receivable account by this amount. The company's cost of the inventory it sold is $7,400, so we should decrease the merchandise inventory account and increase the cost of goods sold account by this amount.

2. Accounts receivable is an asset account, so we increase it with a debit. We increase sales, a revenue account, with a credit. Cost of goods sold is an expense account, so we increase it with a debit. Merchandise inventory is an asset account, so we decrease it with a credit.

3. Like **item *i,*** this item requires two separate entries or a compound entry. The entries are:

Jan 26	Accounts receivable	12,600	
	Sales		12,600
26	Cost of goods sold	7,400	
	Merchandise inventory		7,400

Or, to accomplish the same changes to the account balances, we can make the following compound entry:

Jan 26	Accounts receivable	12,600	
	Cost of goods sold	7,400	
	Sales		12,600
	Merchandise inventory		7,400

4. A final check of both sets of entries reveals that the dollar amount of the debits equals that of the credits. Just as was the case for **item h,** you can make either two separate entries or a compound entry for an item such as this.

Discussion Question ●

6–8. You may have noticed that when we make an entry to record a sale and its associated cost of goods sold, we do not subtract the cost from the sale amount to determine the income on the sale. When *would* we subtract cost of goods sold from sales to determine gross profit on sales?

k. **Collins Corporation provides delivery services to some neighboring businesses to help utilize its delivery truck. On January 26, Collins Corporation billed one of these businesses $300 and collected cash of $150 from another business for delivery services. Thus, the total for delivery services for neighboring businesses totaled $450.**

1. This transaction took place on January 26, 2004. In this transaction, Collins received some cash, so cash should be increased. The company has also billed customers, so accounts receivable should be increased. The company has earned revenue from providing delivery services, so delivery service revenue should be increased. The amount of cash received was $150, billings to customers on account were $300, and the total delivery service revenue earned was $450.

2. We increase the cash account and accounts receivable with debits, while the delivery service revenue account is increased with a credit.

3. The journal entry:

Jan 26	Cash	150	
	Accounts receivable	300	
	Delivery service revenue		450

Or, to accomplish the same changes to the account balances, we can make the following two entries:

Jan 26	Cash	150	
	Delivery service revenue		150
	Accounts receivable	300	
	Delivery service revenue		300

4. A final check of both sets of entries reveals that the dollar amount of the debits equals that of the credits. Again, you can make either a compound entry or two separate entries for an item such as this.

l. **On January 27, the company paid $90 for gasoline used in the company's delivery truck during the month of January.**

1. This transaction took place on January 27, 2004. The company paid cash for the fuel, so cash should be decreased. The company purchased and used the fuel, so gasoline expense should be increased. The cash account should be decreased by

the $90 paid for the gasoline. The gasoline expense account should be increased by the $90 cost of the gasoline purchased and used.

2. We increase the gasoline expense account with a debit and we decrease the cash account with a credit.

3. The general journal entry:

Jan 27	Gasoline expense	90	
	Cash		90

4. A final check of the entry reveals that the dollar amounts of the debits and credits are equal.

m. On January 27, the company paid wages to employees of $1,500.

1. This transaction took place on January 27, 2004. The company paid cash for wages, so cash should be decreased and wages expense should be increased. The cash account should be decreased by $1,500 and the wages expense account increased by the $1,500 paid for the wages.

2. We increase the wages expense account with a debit and decrease the cash account with a credit.

3. The general journal entry:

Jan 27	Wages expense	1,500	
	Cash		1,500

4. A final check of the entry reveals that the dollar amounts of the debits and credits are equal.

n. On January 28, the company received a $2,700 order from a customer for goods to be delivered in February.

1. This item does not affect any accounts or accounting elements. Although an entry will be required in February when the sale actually takes place, no entry should be made at this time.

o. January 31, the company paid $500 for January's rent.

1. This transaction took place on January 31, 2004. Collins paid cash for rent, so we should increase the rent expense account and decrease the cash account by the amount of the $500 rent payment.

2. We increase the rent expense account with a debit and decrease the cash account with a credit.

3. The general journal entry:

Jan 31	Rent expense	500	
	Cash		500

4. A final check of the entry reveals that the dollar amounts of the debits and credits are equal.

Discussion Question ●

6–9. If Collins Corporation paid $1,500 on January 31 for rent for February, March, and April, should it debit rent expense? If not, what type of account should it debit? Why?

p. On January 31, the company paid a dividend to its shareholders of $300.

1. This transaction took place on January 31, 2004. Collins is making a cash dividend distribution to its owners, so we should decrease cash and increase dividends. We should increase the dividends account and decrease the cash account by the $300 amount of the dividend.

contra-account   An account that carries a normal balance that decreases the accounting element in which it is classified.

2. Although the dividends account is an equity account, its normal balance actually works to decrease equity. An account that carries a normal balance that decreases the accounting element in which it is classified is called a **contra account.** Dividends, a contra equity account, decreases equity, so we increase the dividend account with a debit. We decrease the cash account, of course, with a credit.

3. The general journal entry:

Jan 31	Dividends	300	
	Cash		300

4. A final check of the entry reveals that the dollar amounts of the debits and credits are equal.

Exhibit 6–10 shows the general journal for Collins Container Corporation with all the journal entries we have made so far.

EXHIBIT 6–10   General Journal for Collins Container Corporation

	General Journal			Page 1
Date 2004	Description	Post. Ref.	Debit	Credit
Jan 1	Cash		10,000	
	Common stock			1,000
	Additional paid-in capital			9,000
	To record the sale of 1,000 shares of			
	$1 par common stock for $10,000 cash.			
1	Cash		20,000	
	Notes payable			20,000
	To record $20,000, 9%, one-year promissory			
	note to Bank of America.			
1	Prepaid insurance		2,400	
	Cash			2,400
	To record the purchase of a one-year			
	insurance policy effective January 1.			
1	Delivery truck		15,000	
	Cash			15,000
	To record purchase of a delivery truck for			
	cash.			
7	Office supplies		2,000	
	Accounts payable			2,000
	To record the purchase of office supplies on			
	account.			
8	Merchandise inventory		16,000	
	Accounts payable			16,000
	To record the purchase of merchandise on			
	account.			
12	Accounts payable		750	
	Cash			750
	To record $750 payment on account.			

General Journal				Page 2
Date 2004	Description	Post. Ref.	Debit	Credit
Jan 22	Cash		8,000	
	Sales			8,000
	Cost of goods sold		5,000	
	Merchandise inventory			5,000
	To record $8,000 sale for cash of goods that cost $5,000.			
26	Accounts receivable		12,600	
	Sales			12,600
	Cost of goods sold		7,400	
	Merchandise inventory			7,400
	To record $12,600 sale on account of goods that cost $7400.			
26	Cash		150	
	Accounts receivable		300	
	Delivery service revenue			450
	To record revenue for miscellaneous deliveries.			
27	Gasoline expense		90	
	Cash			90
	To record the purchase of gasoline for cash.			
27	Wages expense		1,500	
	Cash			1,500
	To record the payment of wages to employees.			
31	Rent expense		500	
	Cash			500
	To record the payment of January's rent.			
31	Dividends		300	
	Cash			300
	To record payment of dividends to common stockholders.			

EXHIBIT 6-10 *Continued*

Now that the transactions have been journalized, we can post them to the general ledger.

STEP 3. POSTING THE TRANSACTIONS TO THE GENERAL LEDGER

Posting transactions to the general ledger is a simple process of transcribing entries from company journals to the general ledger. Although it is tedious and time consuming, the posting process presents no serious challenge. Posting requires attention to detail, and the accounting staff generally follows procedures similar to the following:

1. Locate the account in the general ledger.
2. Record the transaction date on the account's general ledger page. When posting from the general journal, we use the date of the journal entry.

3. The description column of the general ledger is often left blank. However, you can enter a notation about the transaction in this column if you feel that such information will be valuable in the future.

4. The posting reference column is very important. The notation in this column is the key to tracing an entry in the general ledger back to the original entry in the journal. Identifying the journal and the page number of original entry in the general ledger's posting reference column does this. For example, if the entry was originally journalized on page 212 of the general journal, GJ 212 is entered in the posting reference column on the general ledger.

5. Next, you record the amount of the entry in the appropriate debit or credit column. It is not necessary to use dollar signs ($) when posting amounts to the general ledger.

6. The last step in the posting process is a bit unusual but critically important. It is unusual because, instead of making this final notation in the *general ledger*, you make the entry back in the *journal*. In this step, we record the general ledger account number in the journal's posting reference column. Like the ledger's posting reference notations, the journal's posting references are critical in tracing journal entries forward to the appropriate general ledger account.

EXHIBIT 6-11   Posting to the General Ledger

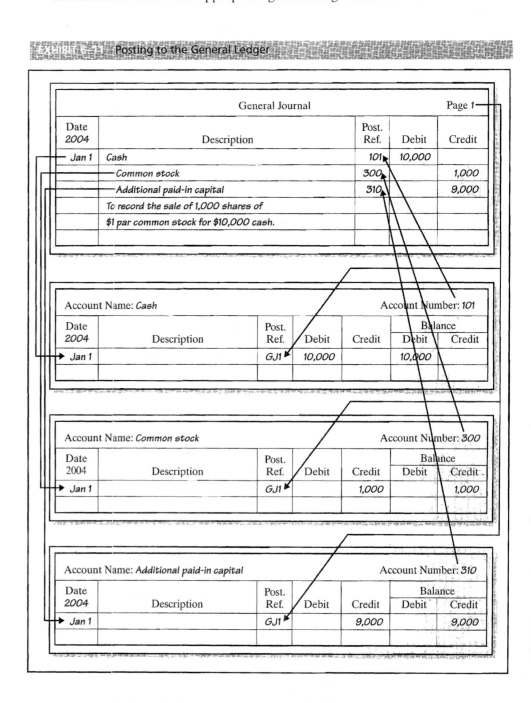

Exhibit 6–11 shows the posting of Collins Container Corporation's first journal entry. Then, Exhibit 6–12 presents the general ledger for the Collins Container Corporation once we have posted all the entries from the general journal. Once all the entries are posted, we can prepare a trial balance.

EXHIBIT 6–12   General Ledger for Collins Container Corporation

Account Name: *Cash*   Account Number: *101*

Date 2004	Description	Post. Ref.	Debit	Credit	Balance Debit	Balance Credit
Jan 1		GJ1	10,000			
1		GJ1	20,000			
1	Ck. #101	GJ1		2,400		
1	Ck. #102	GJ1		15,000		
12	Ck. #103	GJ1		750		
22		GJ2	8,000			
26		GJ2	150			
27	Ck. #104	GJ2		90		
27	Ck. #105	GJ2		1,500		
31	Ck. #106	GJ2		500		
31	Ck. #107	GJ2		300	17,610	

Account Name: *Accounts receivable*   Account Number: *110*

Date 2004	Description	Post. Ref.	Debit	Credit	Balance Debit	Balance Credit
Jan 26		GJ2	12,600			
26		GJ2	300		12,900	

Account Name: *Merchandise inventory*   Account Number: *120*

Date 2004	Description	Post. Ref.	Debit	Credit	Balance Debit	Balance Credit
Jan 8		GJ1	16,000			
22		GJ2		5,000		
26		GJ2		7,400	3,600	

Account Name: *Office supplies*   Account Number: *130*

Date 2004	Description	Post. Ref.	Debit	Credit	Balance Debit	Balance Credit
Jan 7		GJ1	2,000		2,000	

Account Name: *Prepaid insurance*   Account Number: *140*

Date 2004	Description	Post. Ref.	Debit	Credit	Balance Debit	Balance Credit
Jan 1		GJ1	2,400		2,400	

continued

Account Name: Delivery truck — Account Number: 150

Date 2004	Description	Post. Ref.	Debit	Credit	Balance Debit	Balance Credit
Jan 1		GJ1	15,000		15,000	

Account Name: Accounts payable — Account Number: 200

Date 2004	Description	Post. Ref.	Debit	Credit	Balance Debit	Balance Credit
Jan 7		GJ1		2,000		
8		GJ1		16,000		
12		GJ1	750			17,250

Account Name: Notes payable — Account Number: 250

Date 2004	Description	Post. Ref.	Debit	Credit	Balance Debit	Balance Credit
Jan 1		GJ1		20,000		20,000

Account Name: Common stock — Account Number: 300

Date 2004	Description	Post. Ref.	Debit	Credit	Balance Debit	Balance Credit
Jan 1		GJ1		1,000		1,000

Account Name: Additional paid-in capital — Account Number: 310

Date 2004	Description	Post. Ref.	Debit	Credit	Balance Debit	Balance Credit
Jan 1		GJ1		9,000		9,000

Account Name: Dividends — Account Number: 325

Date 2004	Description	Post. Ref.	Debit	Credit	Balance Debit	Balance Credit
Jan 31		GJ2	300		300	

EXHIBIT 6–12   Continued

Account Name: Sales					Account Number: 400	
Date 2004	Description	Post. Ref.	Debit	Credit	Balance Debit	Credit
Jan 22		GJ2		8,000		
26		GJ2		12,600		20,600

Account Name: Delivery service revenue					Account Number: 410	
Date 2004	Description	Post. Ref.	Debit	Credit	Balance Debit	Credit
Jan 26		GJ2		450		450

Account Name: Cost of goods sold					Account Number: 500	
Date 2004	Description	Post. Ref.	Debit	Credit	Balance Debit	Credit
Jan 22		GJ2	5,000			
26		GJ2	7,400		12,400	

Account Name: Wages expense					Account Number: 620	
Date 2004	Description	Post. Ref.	Debit	Credit	Balance Debit	Credit
Jan 27		GJ2	1,500		1,500	

Account Name: Rent expense					Account Number: 630	
Date 2004	Description	Post. Ref.	Debit	Credit	Balance Debit	Credit
Jan 27		GJ2	500		500	

Account Name: Gasoline expense					Account Number: 650	
Date 2004	Description	Post. Ref.	Debit	Credit	Balance Debit	Credit
Jan 27		GJ2	90		90	

EXHIBIT 6–12 *Continued*

STEP 4. PREPARING A TRIAL BALANCE

To prepare the trial balance, we simply list the general ledger accounts and their balances, include an appropriate heading, and provide totals for the debit and credit columns. You may have noticed that we are not yet using some accounts shown on Collins Container Corporation's chart of accounts. When we prepare a trial balance, we only list the accounts that we are currently using and that have balances. The trial balance for Collins Container Corporation appears in Exhibit 6–13. The fact that the debit and credit columns equal is an indication that our general ledger is in balance.

EXHIBIT 6–13   Trial Balance for the Collins Container Corporation

Collins Container Corporation
Trial Balance
January 31, 2004

Account	Debit	Credit
101 Cash	$17,610	
110 Accounts receivable	12,900	
120 Merchandise inventory	3,600	
130 Office supplies	2,000	
140 Prepaid insurance	2,400	
150 Delivery truck	15,000	
200 Accounts payable		$17,250
250 Notes payable		20,000
300 Common stock		1,000
310 Additional paid-in capital		9,000
325 Dividends	300	
400 Sales		20,600
410 Delivery service revenue		450
500 Cost of goods sold	12,400	
620 Wages expense	1,500	
630 Rent expense	500	
650 Gasoline expense	90	
Total	$68,300	$68,300

Discussion Questions

6–10. If the debits equal the credits on the trial balance, does this mean that everything in the general ledger is correct? Explain your answer.

6–11. If the debits do not equal the credits, what might have caused the imbalance?

STEP 5. ADJUSTING THE GENERAL LEDGER ACCOUNT BALANCES

We examine each account to see whether the balance is reasonable and to determine whether any accrual, deferral, or some other adjusting entry is needed. As we mentioned earlier in this chapter, the adjusting process basically consists of three steps:

1. **Examine each account and determine the appropriate ending account balances.** Examine each account in light of the situation as it exists on the last day of the accounting period to determine whether the ending account balances are appropriate. If an account's ending balance is not appropriate for the situation that exists at the end of the accounting period, determine the appropriate ending account balance.

2. **Determine the required increase or decrease.** Determine the amount by which the account should be increased or decreased so the account reflects the appropriate balance.

3. **Make an adjusting entry.** Make the adjusting journal entries to change the ending account balances to the appropriate amounts.

Accountants develop various techniques and procedures to ensure that they have made all of the adjusting entries needed. An accountant might begin by reviewing last year's adjusting entries, and then he or she might examine the trial balance and the general ledger. Accountants also collect additional information by talking to managers and employees throughout the company to determine the present state of business affairs and whether the general ledger account balances reflect these affairs.

For Collins Container Corporation, we will methodically examine each account listed on Collins Container Corporation's chart of accounts, beginning with cash. The idea is to use the chart of accounts to direct our attention to each business area so we can determine the adjusting entries required.

Cash The best way to determine whether the cash account's balance is appropriate is to reconcile it to the bank statement. Conceptually, the bank reconciliation is simple. We compare the amounts on the bank statement to those on our books to determine the differences that exist. For each of those differences, we need to indicate whether the bank's balance or our general ledger cash balance should be adjusted, and by how much.

Each month, banks send statements to each of their customers. These statements trace bank account balances from the beginning of the month to the end of the month and show each and every addition and deduction that affected each customer's account. Although there are some miscellaneous items, the additions consist primarily of deposits and the deductions consist primarily of checks the bank has paid from the accounts.

When you review your bank statement, the debits and credits may seem to be the exact opposite of what you have learned so far in this chapter. This may surprise you, but you are not looking at a cash account, but rather at the bank's liability account to you. That's right, the statement you receive from your bank reflects its liability to you, not a cash account. With this in mind, the debits and credits on the statement make perfect sense.

There are many acceptable formats that you could use to reconcile a bank account. As Exhibit 6–14 on page F–228 shows, we will use one that reflects the bank's cash balance and our own general ledger cash balance, followed by the changes required to adjust each of these balances to the correct cash amount.

Before we get started, we should make sure we have all the documents and information we need to do the reconciliation. To do the bank reconciliation, you need:

1. The prior month's bank reconciliation
2. The bank statement
3. The company's cash records. Generally, this would include the company's general ledger cash account and its journals if the ledger does not provide enough detail.

For our example, we will need to collect the appropriate documents for Collins Container Corporation. Although the bank statement and general ledger are available for the company, Collins is a new company and just opened its bank account in January, so we will not have a prior month's bank reconciliation.

Reconciling a bank statement uses the following process:

1. Record the ending general ledger cash account balance on the appropriate space on the bank reconciliation form.
2. Match and check off each item on the prior month's bank reconciliation to the bank statement and the company's records to determine whether the items have been resolved and the appropriate entries made.

Company Name
Bank Reconciliation
For the Month of _____ ____

Balance per bank statement $ _____ ____
Add:
  Deposits in transit:
  _____ ___ $ _____ ____
  _____   _____
  _____   _____   _____ ____
  Other reconciling items:
  _____ ___   _____   _____ ____
Deduct:
  Outstanding checks:
  _____ ___   _____
  _____ ___   _____
  _____ ___   _____
  _____ ___   _____   _____ ____
  Other reconciling items:
  _____   _____   _____ ____
Correct cash balance $ _____
Balance per bank statement $ _____ ___
Add:
  _____ ___ $ _____
  _____   _____
  _____   _____
  _____ ___   _____
Deduct:
  Bank service charge   _____
  Other reconciling items:
  _____   _____
  _____ ___   _____
  _____ ___   _____
Correct cash balance $ _____

EXHIBIT 6–14   Sample Bank Reconciliation Form

3. Match and check off each item on the bank statement to the company's cash records (the general ledger or, if necessary, the journals) to determine which items appear on the statement, but not on the company's books, or vice versa.

4. Examine the prior month's bank reconciliation, the bank statement, and the company's cash records (the general ledger cash account, or, if necessary, the journals) in search of any cash items that you could not check off in steps 2 and 3. This is a very important step because we are actively seeking items that are causing the difference between the bank's balance and our own. We will list these items, called **reconciling items,** in the appropriate places on our bank reconciliation form.

5. Any item on the prior month's bank reconciliation that you did not check off was probably not recorded by the bank or the company. Place such items on the current bank reconciliation in the same position they occupied on the prior month's reconciliation.

6. If the bank statement appropriately reflects an item but the company's cash account does not, you should add or subtract the item as appropriate on the company's part of the reconciliation.

7. If the company's cash account appropriately reflects an item but the bank statement does not, you should add or subtract the item on the bank's part of the reconciliation.

8. Once you have entered all the reconciling items on the bank reconciliation, you are ready to determine the correct cash balance. To do this, adjust the bank's bal-

reconciling items   Items that are causing the difference between a bank's cash balance and the balance shown on a company's records. These items are listed in the appropriate places on the company's bank reconciliation form.

ance and the general ledger cash balance shown on the reconciliation as appropriate by the reconciling items. When you are done, both parts of the reconciliation should arrive at the same amount as the correct cash balance.

If your bank reconciliation does not balance, you will have to recheck your work. You should look for the following types of problems:

a. *Not checking an item.* Look for items that you should have checked off but did not.
b. *Checking an item by mistake.* Look for items that you should not have checked off but you did.
c. *Forgetting to put an item on the bank reconciliation.* Look for items that you did not check off that you failed to place on the bank reconciliation.
d. *Putting an item in the wrong place on the bank reconciliation.* Look for items that you put in the wrong place on the bank reconciliation form. Remember, if the item is on the bank statement but not on our books, we need to include it in our books (to our side of the bank reconciliation), and if an item is on our books but not on the bank statement, we need to include it on the bank's side of the reconciliation.
e. *Mathematical errors.* Review the bank reconciliation to ensure you have added items that should have been added and subtracted the items that should have been subtracted, and that your math is correct. Also, look for transposed numbers—a distinct possibility if the unreconciled difference is divisible by 9.

Exhibit 6–15 on page F–230 shows Collins Container Corporation's bank statement and general ledger cash account for January with the appropriate items checked off.

Once the bank reconciliation is complete, the next step is to make the appropriate entries in the general journal to adjust the cash account to the correct amount. The bank reconciliation for Collins Container Corporation in Exhibit 6–16 on page F–231 indicates that we need to make two entries to our cash account: one to increase cash and increase interest revenue and the other to decrease cash and increase bank service charge expense. Therefore, we should make the following adjusting entries.

a.	Jan 31	Cash	28	
		Interest revenue		28
	31	Bank service charge	32	
		Cash		32

Often, the items that appear on the bank's part of the bank reconciliation are due to timing differences. Timing differences are those that resolve themselves in due course as the bank finally pays our checks and records our deposits. Sometimes, however, in addition to the adjustments we make in our books, we may also need to call the bank to tell them about mistakes they have made or adjustments they need to make.

Now that we have made the adjusting entries to the company's cash account, we will continue down the trial balance and review each of the other general accounts.

Accounts Receivable Try to verify the correctness of the accounts receivable balance by actively seeking any transactions where "sales" on account were recorded but the sale was not actually made and where sales were actually made but, for one reason or another, were not recorded. In addition, we should verify that all collections on account are properly recorded. In the case of Collins Container Corporation, the accounts receivable balance appears to include all the appropriate entries, and therefore, no adjusting entry seems to be needed.

Merchandise Inventory As we will explore in Chapter 8, companies generally compare the balance of the inventory account to a physical count of the inventory. Accountants then make adjusting entries as needed for the differences. In addition, accountants must ensure that the inventory account includes all of the inventory the company owns, and no more. In the case of Collins Container Corporation, the ending inventory account balance seems appropriate, so no adjusting entry is required.

Bank of America

555 Any Street   Anytown, TX

Page 1 of 1
Statement Period:
01-01-04 through 01-31-04

Collins Container Corporation
1234 Any Road
Anytown, TX

Account Number: 123 456789

Your Account Balance at a Glance

Beginning Balance on 01-01-04	$	0
Deposits and Other Additions +	+	38,028
Checks Posted	–	19,650
Other Subtractions	–	32
Ending Balance on 01-31-04	$	18,346

Account Additions and Subtractions

Date	Amount ($)	Resulting Balance	Transaction
01-02	✓20,000+	20,000	Deposit
01-02	✓10,000+	30,000	Deposit
01-03	✓15,000–	15,000	Check 102
01-06	✓2,400–	12,600	Check 101
01-15	✓750–	11,850	Check 103
01-23	✓8,000–	19,850	Deposit
01-29	✓1,500–	18,350	Check 105
01-31	32–	18,318	Service Charge
01-31	28+	18,346	Interest

Account Name: *Cash*   Account Number: *101*

Date 2004	Description	Post. Ref.	Debit	Credit	Balance Debit	Balance Credit
Jan 1		GJ1	✓10,000			
1		GJ1	✓20,000			
1	Ck. #101	GJ1		✓2,400		
1	Ck. #102	GJ1		✓15,000		
12	Ck. #103	GJ1		✓750		
22		GJ2	✓8,000			
26		GJ2	150			
27	Ck. #104	GJ2		90		
27	Ck. #105	GJ2		✓1,500		
31	Ck. #106	GJ2		500		
31	Ck. #107	GJ2		300	17,610	

EXHIBIT 6–15 Collins Container Corporation's Bank Statement and General Ledger Cash Account

Office Supplies   On January 31, employees at Collins Container Corporation counted the office supplies that remained in the storage cabinet. They found that office supplies costing $1,650 were unused and still on hand at January 31, 2004. If the company originally purchased $2,000 worth of supplies and $1,650 are left, they must have used $350 worth of supplies. We should make an adjusting entry for these office supplies used during the month. As the following calculations show, the adjusting entry should

```
                        Collins Container Corporation
                             Bank Reconciliation
                        For the Month of January, 2004

Balance per bank statement                                        $      18,346
Add:
  Deposits in transit:
  January 26                                      $        150

                                                                           150
  Other reconciling items:


Deduct:
  Outstanding checks:
  104                                                       90
  106                                                      500
  107                                                      300
                                                                           890
  Other reconciling items:


Correct cash balance                                              $      17,606

Balance per books (per general ledger cash account)              $      17,610
Add:
  January interest                                $         28

                                                                            28
Deduct:
  Bank service charge                                       32
  Other reconciling items:



                                                                            32

Correct cash balance                                             $      17,606
```

decrease office supplies to the amount on hand at January 31 and increase office supplies expense for the $350 worth of supplies used.

Office Supplies:		
Unadjusted Account Balance	$2,000	Debit
Adjusted Account Balance	1,650	Debit
Required Adjusting Entry	$ 350	Credit
Office Expense:		
Unadjusted Account Balance	$ 0	
Adjusted Account Balance	350	Debit
Required Adjusting Entry	$ 350	Debit

Adjusting entry to accrue wages:

b.   Jan 31   *Office supplies expense*   350
                  Office supplies   350

Prepaid Insurance   The company's $2,400 insurance policy covers a 12-month time period. Since January has passed, only 11 of those months remain. Therefore, the prepaid insurance account's balance should only include the 11 months' worth of insurance. As the following calculations show, the adjusting entry to record the expiration of insurance during January should decrease prepaid insurance and increase insurance expense by $200.

Prepaid Insurance:
Unadjusted Account Balance (12 months)	$2,400	Debit
Adjusted Account Balance (11 months)	2,200	Debit
Required Adjusting Entry (1 month)	$ 200	Credit

Insurance Expense:
Unadjusted Account Balance	$ 0	
Adjusted Account Balance	200	Debit
Required Adjusting Entry	$ 200	Debit

Adjusting entry to accrue wages:

c.   Jan 31   Insurance expense   200
                    Prepaid insurance   200

Delivery Truck   The delivery truck account correctly reflects the fact that the company owns a delivery truck, so the account balance seems correct and no adjusting entry is necessary.

Accumulated Depreciation on Delivery Truck   Since the company used the truck to earn revenue for a month, we should make an adjusting entry to record one month's depreciation. As we learned in Chapter 5, one way we can compute the depreciation is to subtract the truck's residual value from its cost and divide the result by the estimated useful life of the truck. In this case, the truck cost $15,000, its estimated useful life is five years or 60 months, and its estimated residual value is $1,500. Therefore, the truck's depreciation expense equals $225 for January calculated as follows:

$$\text{Depreciation Expense} = \frac{\text{Asset's Cost} - \text{Estimated Residual Value}}{\text{Estimated Useful Life of the Asset}}$$

$$\frac{\$15,000 - \$1,500}{60 \text{ Months}} = \$225$$

As the following calculations show, the adjusting entry to record depreciation expense should increase both accumulated depreciation and depreciation expense. Keep in mind that accumulated depreciation is a *contra asset* account because, although it is part of the asset classification, it works to reduce the total asset balance. Unlike regular asset accounts that are increased with debits, contra asset accounts work to decrease total assets, so they are increased with credits. Depreciation expense, like any other expense, should be increased with a debit.

Accumulated Depreciation on Delivery Truck:
Unadjusted Account Balance	$ 0	
Adjusted Account Balance	225	Credit
Required Adjusting Entry	$225	Credit

Depreciation Expense:
Unadjusted Account Balance	$ 0	
Adjusted Account Balance	225	Debit
Required Adjusting Entry	$225	Debit

Adjusting entry for delivery truck depreciation:

d.   Jan 31   Depreciation expense   225
                    Accumulated depreciation on delivery truck   225

Accounts Payable   After reviewing its suppliers' accounts, Collins determines that this account includes everything it should, and no more, so its balance seems appropriate. No adjusting entry is needed.

Wages Payable   Collins Container Corporation hired its employees on Tuesday, January 21, 2004, and pays them $300 per day based on a five-day workweek. The company paid its employees on Tuesday, January 28, for their work up to Monday, January 27. The company did not pay its employees until February 4 for their work on January 28, 29, 30, and 31. Therefore, we should accrue wages of $1,200 for the four days at $300 per day. As the following calculations show, the adjusting entry to record the $1,200 wage accrual should increase both wages payable and wages expense.

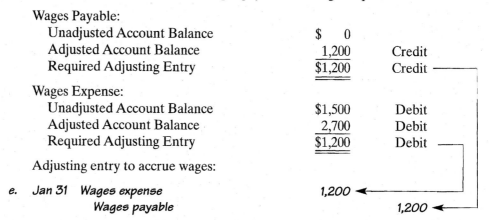

Wages Payable:
Unadjusted Account Balance — $ 0
Adjusted Account Balance — 1,200 — Credit
Required Adjusting Entry — $1,200 — Credit

Wages Expense:
Unadjusted Account Balance — $1,500 — Debit
Adjusted Account Balance — 2,700 — Debit
Required Adjusting Entry — $1,200 — Debit

Adjusting entry to accrue wages:

e. Jan 31 Wages expense — 1,200
    Wages payable — 1,200

Interest Payable   On January 1, 2004, Collins Container Corporation signed a one-year, 9 percent promissory note to **Bank of America** for $20,000. Because the company used the loan to fund its business operations during January, we should accrue interest for the month. We compute January's loan interest as follows:

$$\text{Interest} = \text{Principal } \$20,000 \times \text{Rate } 9\% \times \text{Time } 1/12 = \$150$$

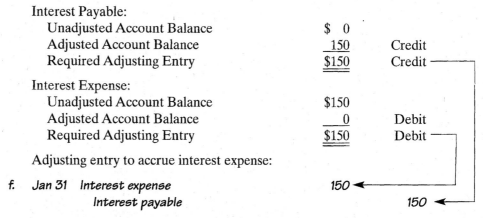

Interest Payable:
Unadjusted Account Balance — $ 0
Adjusted Account Balance — 150 — Credit
Required Adjusting Entry — $150 — Credit

Interest Expense:
Unadjusted Account Balance — $150
Adjusted Account Balance — 0 — Debit
Required Adjusting Entry — $150 — Debit

Adjusting entry to accrue interest expense:

f. Jan 31 Interest expense — 150
    Interest payable — 150

Accrued Expenses   Let's assume that on February 3, the company received an electric bill for $120 dated January 31, 2004. The bill is for electricity the company used during the month of January, so it should be included in electricity expense for January. When bills and invoices are recorded as part of the adjusting process, instead of including their liability in accounts payable, a liability account called **accrued expenses** is used. Make a special effort to remember that *accrued expenses* is a liability account, not an expense account, because this is a common point of confusion. As the following calculations show, the adjusting entry to record the accrual of the $120 electric bill should increase both the accrued expenses liability account and electricity expense.

accrued expenses
Expenses appropriately recognized under accrual accounting in one income statement period although the associated cash will be paid in a later income statement period.

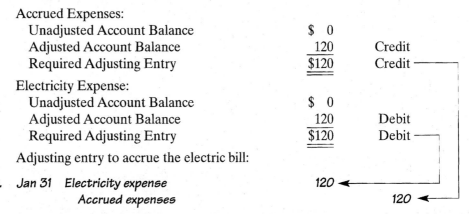

Accrued Expenses:
Unadjusted Account Balance — $ 0
Adjusted Account Balance — 120 — Credit
Required Adjusting Entry — $120 — Credit

Electricity Expense:
Unadjusted Account Balance — $ 0
Adjusted Account Balance — 120 — Debit
Required Adjusting Entry — $120 — Debit

Adjusting entry to accrue the electric bill:

g. Jan 31 Electricity expense — 120
    Accrued expenses — 120

Unearned Revenue   Unearned revenue is a liability account used to defer (put off) the recognition of revenue. We use it when customers pay in advance for products or

unearned revenue   A liability account used to record a company's liability to provide goods or services, which customers have paid for but have not yet received.

services yet to be delivered. In such cases, the seller has the cash but has not yet earned the revenue—the revenue is *unearned*. As was the case with accrued expenses, avoid making a common error by noting that **unearned revenue** is a liability account, not a revenue account. To determine if any revenue has been recorded but not earned, company accountants must seek out any situations in which customers have paid and revenue has been recorded, but the company has yet to perform. In the case of Collins Container Corporation, let's assume we have discovered that of the $450 of delivery service revenue, only $375 has been earned because $75 of the delivery service revenue recorded in January is actually for a delivery the company will make in February. As the following calculations show, the adjusting entry to defer the recognition of the unearned $75 delivery service revenue should increase unearned revenue and decrease delivery service revenue.

Unearned Revenue:
Unadjusted Account Balance	$ 0	
Adjusted Account Balance	75	Credit
Required Adjusting Entry	$ 75	Credit

Delivery Service Revenue:
Unadjusted Account Balance	$ 450	Credit
Adjusted Account Balance	375	Credit
Required Adjusting Entry	$ 75	Debit

Adjusting entry to accrue the electric bill:

h.   Jan 31   Delivery service revenue   75
                   Unearned revenue   75

Notes Payable   This account includes everything it should include, and no more, so its balance seems appropriate.

Common Stock   This account includes everything it should include, and no more, so its balance seems appropriate.

Additional Paid-in Capital   This account includes everything it should include, and no more, so its balance seems appropriate.

Retained Earnings   We will determine the appropriate balance for retained earnings when we do the statement of stockholders' equity for Collins Container Corporation. Generally, aside from closing entries, we seldom change or adjust the retained earnings account.

Dividends   We have already recorded all the dividends paid, so this account includes everything it should, and no more. No adjustment is needed.

Sales   This account includes everything it should include, and no more, so its balance seems appropriate.

Delivery Service Revenue   We made the adjusting entry to this account when we reviewed unearned revenue.

Interest Revenue   We made the adjusting entry to interest revenue when we reviewed cash.

Cost of Goods Sold   This account includes everything it should include, and no more, so its balance seems appropriate.

Wages Expense   We made the adjusting entry to wages expense when we reviewed wages payable.

Rent Expense   This account includes everything it should include, and no more, so its balance seems appropriate.

Electricity Expense   We made the adjusting entry to electricity expense when we reviewed accrued expenses.

Gasoline Expense This account includes everything it should include, and no more, so its balance seems appropriate.

Depreciation Expense We made the adjusting entry to depreciation expense when we reviewed accumulated depreciation.

Bank Service Charge Expense We made the adjusting entry to bank service charge expense when we reviewed cash.

Interest Expense We made the adjusting entry to interest expense when we reviewed interest payable.

Next, we will enter the adjusting entries on the worksheet. As we mentioned earlier, the worksheet is an optional step in the accounting cycle. It is an informal procedure that accountants often perform before they formally journalize and post each of the adjusting entries. Exhibit 6–17 on page F–236 shows the worksheet for Collins Container Corporation including all of January's adjusting entries.

To prepare the worksheet:

1. We begin with an appropriate heading.
2. Then we list all the accounts included on the company's chart of accounts. Alternatively, we could copy the trial balance onto the worksheet, but then we would have to leave space to add accounts as they are needed.
3. Next, we enter the account balances from the trial balance and total them to assure that they are in balance.
4. We then enter the adjusting entries in the appropriate columns next to the accounts we are adjusting. We then total the adjusting entries columns to make sure our adjusting entries balance.
5. Once we enter all the adjusting entries on the worksheet, we add across each line to determine the amounts for the adjusted trial balance columns. We then total the adjusted trial balance columns to assure that our worksheet still balances.
6. Once we determine that the adjusted account balances, we place the adjusted balance for each account in the income statement and balance sheet columns as appropriate. Of course, income statement accounts go in the income statement columns and balance sheet accounts go in the balance sheet columns.
7. In the final steps of preparing the worksheet, we total the income statement and balance sheet columns but, at this point, they do *not* balance. For these columns to balance, we must enter the net income figure as shown on the worksheet and then calculate our final totals.

Do not make the mistake of believing that the trial balance totals or any other worksheet totals provide significant information aside from an indication that debits and credits equal. They do not. Except for assuring us that our debits equal our credits and that our worksheet is in balance, none of the worksheet totals really mean much.

In summary, the work sheet begins with the unadjusted trial balance and includes columns for the adjusting entries. Then the adjusting entries are incorporated into the account balances to arrive at the adjusted trial balance. Finally, the adjusted trial balances are moved over to the appropriate income statement or balance sheet columns and each column on the worksheet is totaled to ensure that debits equal credits.

STEP 6. JOURNALIZING AND POSTING THE ADJUSTING ENTRIES AND PREPARING THE ADJUSTED TRIAL BALANCE

Whether or not we use a worksheet, we must formally journalize all of the adjusting entries and post them to the general ledger. Then we prepare a trial balance called the adjusted trial balance. The adjusted trial balance is prepared after all the adjusting entries are journalized and posted to the general ledger. Exhibit 6–18 on page 237 shows the adjusted trial balance for Collins Container Corporation.

EXHIBIT 6-17 Worksheet for Collins Container Corporation

Collins Container Corporation
Worksheet
For the Month Ended January 31, 2004

Account	Trial Balance Debit	Trial Balance Credit	Adjusting Entries Debit	Adjusting Entries Credit	Adjusted Trial Balance Debit	Adjusted Trial Balance Credit	Income Statement Debit	Income Statement Credit	Balance Sheet Debit	Balance Sheet Credit
101 Cash	17,610			32	17,606				17,606	
110 Accounts receivable	12,900				12,900				12,900	
120 Merchandise inventory	3,600				3,600				3,600	
130 Office supplies	2,000			350	1,650				1,650	
140 Prepaid insurance	2,400			200	2,200				2,200	
150 Delivery truck	15,000				15,000				15,000	
155 Accumulated depreciation				225		225				225
200 Accounts payable		17,250				17,250				17,250
210 Wages payable				1,200		1,200				1,200
220 Interest payable				150		150				150
240 Accrued expenses				120		120				120
245 Unearned revenue				75		75				75
250 Notes payable		20,000				20,000				20,000
300 Common stock		1,000				1,000				1,000
310 Additional paid-in capital		9,000				9,000				9,000
320 Retained earnings										
325 Dividends	300				300				300	
400 Sales		20,600				20,600		20,600		
410 Delivery service revenue		450	75			375		375		
420 Interest revenue				28		28		28		
500 Cost of goods sold	12,400				12,400		12,400			
620 Wages expense	1,500		1,200		2,700		2,700			
630 Rent expense	500				500		500			
640 Electricity expense			120		120		120			
645 Office supplies expense			350		350		350			
650 Gasoline expense	90				90		90			
655 Insurance expense			200		200		200			
660 Depreciation expense			225		225		225			
670 Bank service charge expense			32		32		32			
680 Interest expense			150		150		150			
Total	68,300	68,300	2,380	2,380	70,023	70,023	16,767	21,003	53,256	49,020
Net income							4,236			4,236
Total							21,003	21,003	53,256	53,256

Collins Container Corporation
Adjusted Trial Balance
January 31, 2004

Account	Debit	Credit
101 Cash	$17,606	
110 Accounts receivable	12,900	
120 Merchandise inventory	3,600	
130 Office supplies	1,650	
140 Prepaid insurance	2,200	
150 Delivery truck	15,000	
155 Accumulated depreciation on delivery truck		$ 225
200 Accounts payable		17,250
210 Wages payable		1,200
220 Interest payable		150
240 Accrued expenses		120
245 Unearned revenue		75
250 Notes payable		20,000
300 Common stock		1,000
310 Additional paid-in capital		9,000
320 Retained earnings		
325 Dividends	300	
400 Sales		20,600
410 Delivery service revenue		375
420 Interest revenue		28
500 Cost of goods sold	12,400	
620 Wages expense	2,700	
630 Rent expense	500	
640 Electricity expense	120	
645 Office supplies expense	350	
650 Gasoline expense	90	
655 Insurance expense	200	
660 Depreciation expense	225	
670 Bank service charge expense	32	
680 Interest expense	150	
Total	$70,023	$70,023

EXHIBIT 6–18   Adjusted Trial Balance for Collins Container Corporation

STEP 7. PREPARING FINANCIAL STATEMENTS

The trial balance, or the worksheet if we have prepared one, includes all the information we need to prepare formal financial statements. Exhibit 6–19 on page F–238 shows the income statement, the statement of owners' equity, and the balance sheet for Collins Container Corporation using information from the adjusted trial balance as of January 31, 2004.

STEP 8. PREPARING AND POSTING CLOSING ENTRIES

As we mentioned earlier, companies close their books at the end of each business year to prepare them for the next business year. The four steps of the closing process for a corporation are:

1. Close all revenue and gain accounts to income summary.
2. Close all expense and loss accounts to income summary.

Collins Container Corporation
Income Statement
For the Month Ended January 31, 2004

Sales		$20,600
Less: Cost of goods sold		12,400
Gross margin		8,200
Operating expenses:		
Wages expense	$2,700	
Rent expense	500	
Electricity expense	120	
Office supplies expense	350	
Gasoline expense	90	
Insurance expense	200	
Depreciation expense	225	
Total operating expense		(4,185)
Operating income		4,015
Other revenues:		
Delivery service revenue	375	
Internet revenue	28	403
Other expenses:		
Bank service charge expense	32	
Internet expense	150	(182)
Net income		$ 4,236

Collins Container Corporation
Statement of Stockholders' Equity
For the Month Ended January 31, 2004

	Common Stock	Additional Paid-in Capital	Retained Earnings	Total Stockholders' Equity
Balance, January 1, 2004	$ 0	$ 0	$ 0	$ 0
Stock issued	1,000	9,000		10,000
Net income			4,236	4,236
Dividends (distributions to owners)			(300)	(300)
Balance, January 31, 2004	$1,000	$9,000	$3,936	$13,936

Collins Container Corporation
Balance Sheet
January 31, 2004

Assets:			Liabilities:		
Cash		$17,606	Accounts payable		$17,250
Accounts receivable		12,900	Wages payable		1,200
Merchandise inventory		3,600	Interest payable		150
Office supplies		1,650	Accrued expenses		120
Prepaid insurance		2,200	Unearned revenue		75
Delivery truck	15,000		Notes payable		20,000
Less accumulated depreciation	(225)		Total liabilities:		$38,795
Delivery truck, net		14,775	Stockholders' equity:		
			Common stock	1,000	
			Additional paid-in capital	9,000	
			Total contributed capital	10,000	
			Retained earnings	3,936	
			Total stockholders' equity		13,936
Total assets		$52,731	Total liabilities and stockholders' equity		$52,731

EXHIBIT 6–19   Financial Statements for Collins Container Corporation

3. Close the income summary account to retained earnings.
4. Close the dividends account to the retained earnings.

Although it is unrealistic for a business to end its business year one month after the company was established, for demonstration purposes, we will assume that Collins Container Corporation ends its business year on January 31. The adjusted trial balance in Exhibit 6–18 on page F–237 provides us with all the information we need to make the closing entries. The closing entries for Collins Container Corporation are as follows:

Step 1. Close all revenue and gain accounts to income summary.

Jan 31	Sales	20,600	
	Delivery service revenue	375	
	Interest revenue	28	
	Income summary		21,003

Step 2. Close all expense and loss accounts to income summary.

Jan 31	Income summary	16,767	
	Cost of goods sold		12,400
	Wages expense		2,700
	Rent expense		500
	Electricity expense		120
	Office supplies expense		350
	Gasoline expense		90
	Insurance expense		200
	Depreciation expense		225
	Bank service charge expense		32
	Interest expense		150

Step 3. Close the income summary account to retained earnings.

Jan 31	Income summary	4,236	
	Retained earnings		4,236

Step 4. Close the dividends account to the retained earnings.

Jan 31	Retained earnings	300	
	Dividends		300

The closing process is quite interesting in that we finally see how income actually becomes part of equity as the balances of revenues and expenses are transferred into retained earnings. Once we have made the closing entries, it is a good idea to prepare a post-closing trial balance to ensure that all temporary accounts are closed and all permanent accounts still remain.

STEP 9. PREPARING THE POST-CLOSING TRIAL BALANCE

We have reached the final step in the process. We prepare a post-closing trial balance to verify that each temporary account is closed, that all the permanent accounts remain, and that the general ledger remains in balance. The account balances on the post-closing trial balance become the opening balances for the new fiscal year. Exhibit 6–20 on page F–240 shows the January 31, 2004, post-closing trial balance for Collins Container Corporation.

Discussion Question

6–12. In addition to closing temporary accounts, why don't we also close permanent accounts? Wouldn't it be better to begin the new year with a blank slate for all accounts? Discuss your answers.

Collins Container Corporation
Post-Closing Trial Balance
January 31, 2004

Account	Debit	Credit
101 Cash	$17,606	
110 Accounts receivable	12,900	
120 Merchandise inventory	3,600	
130 Office supplies	1,650	
140 Prepaid insurance	2,200	
150 Delivery truck	15,000	
155 Accumulated depreciation on delivery truck		$ 225
200 Accounts payable		17,250
210 Wages payable		1,200
220 Interest payable		150
240 Accrued expenses		120
245 Unearned revenue		75
250 Notes payable		20,000
300 Common stock		1,000
310 Additional paid-in capital		9,000
320 Retained earnings		3,936
Total	$52,956	$52,956

EXHIBIT 6–20 Post-Closing Trial Balance for Collins Container Corporation

In this chapter, we have examined how accountants and their staff analyze, classify, and record transactions. In addition, we have reviewed the entire accounting cycle from its beginnings, through the preparation of financial statements, to closing entries.

Summary ●

Every business has hundreds if not thousands of transactions and economic events each year. To record these transactions and events and to convert these raw data into useful information, company accountants utilize an accounting system—a mechanism used to subclassify the accounting elements (assets, liabilities, etc.) that are affected by these various transactions. These subclassifications are called accounts or general ledger accounts.

Each account in the general ledger is assigned a title. These account titles are not dictated by generally accepted accounting principles or by any other accounting rules. Accounts are not only given descriptive names (cash, sales, rent expense, etc.), they are usually assigned account numbers as well. Companies generally develop a numbering system that groups similar types of accounts together. A reference document that lists all of the company's accounts and their account numbers is called a chart of accounts.

We journalize an economic event or transaction when it affects one or more accounting elements or accounts. Journalizing transactions means recording accounting transactions in a journal. A journal is a chronological record of the economic events and transactions that affect the accounting elements (the accounts) of a company. Special journals help to streamline the accounting process and greatly enhance accounting efficiency. If a company has no special journals, all transactions are recorded in the general journal. Periodically, the transactions recorded in a company's journals are transferred (posted) to the general ledger.

Accountants use a system of debits and credits to record transactions and events in journals and post to the general ledger. The accounting system records transactions as either debits or credits. Debit means left side and credit means right side, referring to the sides of the accounting equation. Debits must always equal credits in each transaction, each journal, and the general ledger to keep the equation in balance. Debits increase assets, expenses, and dividends and decrease liabilities, equity, and revenue. Credits increase liabilities, equity, and revenues and decrease assets and expenses.

Companies have some transactions and economic events that occur daily, some monthly, and some annually. As one year ends and the next begins, the process begins anew. The recording and reporting of these various transactions is called the accounting cycle. The steps in the accounting cycle are as follows:

Step 1: Analyze economic events and transactions
Step 2: Journalize transactions
Step 3: Post transactions to the general ledger
Step 4: Prepare a trial balance
Step 5: Prepare, journalize, and post adjusting entries
Step 6: Prepare an adjusted trial balance
Step 7: Prepare financial statements
Step 8: Prepare, journalize, and post closing entries
Step 9: Prepare the post-closing trial balance

These steps, when followed consistently, allow a company's accounting system to keep track of all the transactions and economic events the company experiences, and to produce accounting reports economic decision makers can use to make informed decisions.

Key Terms

- accounts, F–201
- accrued expenses, F–233
- adjusted trial balance, F–206
- adjusting entries, F–206
- book of original entry, F–203
- chart of accounts, F–201
- closing entries, F–207
- compound entries, F–217
- computerized accounting system, F–203

- contra account, F–220
- general journal, F–204
- general ledger, F–201
- general ledger accounts, F–201
- journal, F–203
- manual accounting system, F–203
- normal balance, F–209
- permanent (real) accounts, F–207
- post-closing trial balance, F–207

- posting, F–204
- reconciling items, F–228
- special journal, F–204
- temporary (nominal) accounts, F–207
- trial balance, F–205
- unearned revenue, F–234
- worksheet, F–206

Review the Facts—Part I

A. What is a general ledger account?
B. What information does a chart of accounts provide?
C. List the nine steps in the accounting cycle.
D. Describe the differences between a journal and a ledger.
E. Explain the purposes of special journals.
F. List the important elements of a general journal entry.
G. What is posting?
H. What information is shown on a trial balance?
I. Why do accountants make adjusting entries?
J. What is the difference between an unadjusted trial balance and an adjusted trial balance?
K. What is the difference between temporary and permanent accounts?
L. What is the purpose of the closing entries?
M. Describe the contents of the post-closing trial balance and explain its purpose.

Review the Facts—Part II ●

N. Distinguish between debits and credits and explain how they relate to the accounting equation.

O. Explain how a T-account is used.

P. What are the four steps for making general journal entries?

Q. What is the purpose of the general ledger?

R. How are posting references helpful?

S. With respect to bank reconciliations, what are deposits in transit? What are outstanding checks?

T. What type of account is accrued expenses? What is it used for?

U. Describe the information contained on the worksheet.

V. What are the four steps of the closing process?

Apply What You Have Learned—Part I ● ● ● ● ● ● ● ● ● ● ● ● ● ● ● ● ● ●

LO PART I, 1: ACCOUNT CLASSIFICATION

6–13. **Required:** Indicate the classification of each of the accounts as follows. Each letter may be used more than once.

a. Asset		d. Revenue	
b. Liability		e. Expense	
c. Equity			

1. _____ Prepaid taxes
2. _____ Notes payable
3. _____ Advertising expense
4. _____ Retained earnings
5. _____ Bonds payable
6. _____ Depreciation expense
7. _____ Rent revenue
8. _____ Land
9. _____ Automotive equipment
10. _____ Additional paid-in capital
11. _____ Sales
12. _____ Truck expense
13. _____ Accounts payable
14. _____ Gasoline expense
15. _____ Common stock

LO PART I, 1: ACCOUNT CLASSIFICATION

6–14. **Required:** Indicate the classification of each of the accounts as follows. Each letter may be used more than once.

a. Asset		d. Revenue	
b. Liability		e. Expense	
c. Equity			

1. _____ Accounts receivable
2. _____ Sales
3. _____ Notes payable
4. _____ Prepaid rent
5. _____ Supplies inventory
6. _____ Delivery service revenue
7. _____ Insurance expense
8. _____ Income tax expense
9. _____ Wages payable
10. _____ Additional paid-in capital

LO PART I, 2: THE ACCOUNTING CYCLE

6–15. Identify and list in order of occurrence the steps of the accounting cycle.

LO PART I, 1, 3, 4, 5, & 6: TERMINOLOGY

6–16. Define the following terms:

    a. Journal
    b. Ledger
    c. Posting
    d. Trial balance
    e. Adjusting entries
    f. Closing entries

LO PART I, 1, 2, 3, & 4: TERMINOLOGY

6–17. Below is a list of items relating to the concepts discussed in this chapter, followed by definitions of those items in scrambled order:

    a. Accounting cycle   e. Journalizing
    b. General journal   f. Account
    c. General ledger   g. Chart of accounts
    d. Trial balance   h. Posting

    1. _____ A subclassification of the broad accounting elements such as asset, liabilities, and equity
    2. _____ The series of steps repeated each accounting period to enable a business entity to record, classify, and summarize financial information
    3. _____ A book of original entry
    4. _____ A device used to sort accounting data into similar groupings
    5. _____ The process of recording into the general ledger from a journal
    6. _____ The process of recording transactions into the book of original entry
    7. _____ A listing to prove the equality of debits and credits
    8. _____ The complete list of the account titles used by an entity

Required: Match the letter next to each item on the list with the appropriate definition. Use each letter only once.

LO PART I, 6: PERMANENT OR TEMPORARY ACCOUNTS

6–18. Examine the following accounts:

    1. _____ Cash
    2. _____ Accounts payable
    3. _____ Additional paid-in capital
    4. _____ Sales revenue
    5. _____ Prepaid insurance
    6. _____ Merchandise inventory
    7. _____ Dividends
    8. _____ Rent expense
    9. _____ Income tax expense
    10. _____ Income taxes payable
    11. _____ Common stock

Required: In the space provided, indicate whether the type of account is permanent (P) or temporary (T).

LO PART I, 6: PERMANENT OR TEMPORARY ACCOUNTS

6–19. Examine the following accounts:

    1. _____ Accounts receivable
    2. _____ Notes payable
    3. _____ Dividends
    4. _____ Sales
    5. _____ Service revenue
    6. _____ Prepaid rent
    7. _____ Supplies inventory
    8. _____ Insurance expense
    9. _____ Income tax expense

10. _____ Wages payable
11. _____ Retained earnings

Required: In the space provided, indicate whether the type of account is permanent (P) or temporary (T).

Apply What You Have Learned—Part II ✺ ✺ ✺ ✺ ✺ ✺ ✺ ✺ ✺ ✺ ✺ ✺ ✺ ✺ ✺ ✺ ✺ ✺

LO PART I, 1 AND LO PART II, 1 & 5: ACCOUNT CLASSIFICATION

6–20. **Required:** Indicate the classification of each of the accounts as follows. Each letter may be used more than once.

a. Asset
b. Contra asset
c. Liability
d. Equity

e. Contra equity
f. Revenue
g. Expense

1. _____ Cash
2. _____ Accounts payable
3. _____ Accumulated depreciation
4. _____ Additional paid-in capital
5. _____ Revenues
6. _____ Prepaid insurance
7. _____ Unearned revenue
8. _____ Dividends
9. _____ Merchandise inventory
10. _____ Rent expense
11. _____ Income tax expense
12. _____ Income taxes payable
13. _____ Preferred stock

LO PART II, 1: NORMAL ACCOUNT BALANCES

6–21. Examine the following accounts:

1. _____ Accounts receivable
2. _____ Notes payable
3. _____ Dividends
4. _____ Sales
5. _____ Prepaid rent
6. _____ Supplies inventory
7. _____ Insurance expense
8. _____ Income tax expense
9. _____ Wages payable
10. _____ Retained earnings

Required: In the space provided, indicate whether the normal balance of each account is a debit (DR) or credit (CR).

LO PART II, 1: NORMAL ACCOUNT BALANCES

6–22. Examine the following accounts:

1. _____ Cash
2. _____ Accounts payable
3. _____ Additional paid-in capital
4. _____ Revenues
5. _____ Prepaid insurance
6. _____ Merchandise inventory
7. _____ Rent expense
8. _____ Income tax expense
9. _____ Income taxes payable
10. _____ Common stock

Required: In the space provided, indicate whether the normal balance of each account is a debit (DR) or credit (CR).

LO PART II, 1: NORMAL ACCOUNT BALANCES

6–23. Examine the following accounts:

1. _____ Prepaid taxes
2. _____ Advertising expense
3. _____ Retained earnings
4. _____ Depreciation expense
5. _____ Rent revenue
6. _____ Automotive equipment
7. _____ Allowance for doubtful accounts
8. _____ Truck expense
9. _____ Gasoline expense
10. _____ Common stock

Required: In the space provided, indicate whether the normal balance of each account is a debit (DR) or credit (CR).

LO PART II, 2: SIMPLE T-ACCOUNT ENTRIES—BALANCE SHEET ACCOUNTS ONLY

6–24. **Required:** Prepare T-account entries for the following transactions:

Jan 1 Borrowed $10,000 from the bank for two years at 8 percent.
   1 Purchased merchandise inventory for $2,800 on account.
   2 Purchased equipment for $2,000 cash.
   3 Purchased supplies for $1,000 cash.
  10 Paid for the merchandise purchased on January 1.

LO PART II, 2: SIMPLE GENERAL JOURNAL ENTRIES—BALANCE SHEET ACCOUNTS ONLY

6–25. **Required:** Prepare general journal entries for the following transactions:

Feb 1 Sold 1,000 shares of the company's no-par common stock for $5,000 cash.
   5 Purchased a delivery truck for $18,000 by signing a promissory note for the entire $18,000.
   6 Purchased supplies for $200 on account.
   9 Paid $2,400 cash for a one-year insurance policy.
  16 Paid for the supplies purchased on February 6.

LO PART II, 2: SIMPLE GENERAL JOURNAL ENTRIES—BALANCE SHEET ACCOUNTS ONLY

6–26. **Required:** Prepare general journal entries for the following transactions:

Mar 1 Sold 1,000 shares of the company's no-par preferred stock for $9,000 cash.
   1 Borrowed $10,000, signing a promissory note.
   7 Purchased production equipment for $11,000 cash.
   8 Purchased inventory for $1,400 on account.
   9 Purchased office furniture for $3,000 cash.
  18 Paid for the inventory supplies purchased on March 8.

LO PART II, 2: SERVICE COMPANY SIMPLE T-ACCOUNT ENTRIES—BALANCE SHEET AND INCOME STATEMENT ACCOUNTS

6–27. **Required:** Prepare T-account entries for the following transactions:

Apr 1 Borrowed $8,000, signing a promissory note.
   7 Purchased lawn equipment for $2,000 cash.
   8 Billed a customer $300 for lawn services performed.
   9 Received $150 from cash customers for lawn services performed.
   9 Paid wages to helpers of $120.

LO PART II, 2: SERVICE COMPANY SIMPLE GENERAL JOURNAL ENTRIES—BALANCE SHEET AND INCOME STATEMENT ACCOUNTS

6–28. **Required:** Prepare general journal entries for the following transactions:

May 1 Sold 500 shares of $1 par common stock for $7,000 cash.
   2 Purchased computer equipment for $3,500 on account.
  18 Collected $600 cash for word processing services performed.
  29 Billed a customer $400 for word processing services performed.
  30 Paid $90 for electricity used in May.

LO PART II, 2: SERVICE COMPANY SIMPLE GENERAL JOURNAL ENTRIES—BALANCE SHEET AND INCOME STATEMENT ACCOUNTS

6–29. **Required:** Prepare general journal entries for the following transactions:

Jun 1 Sold 1,000 shares of $2 par common stock for $8,000 cash.
   2 Purchased equipment for $3,500 on account.
   2 Purchased garage supplies for $300 cash.
  15 Billed Smith for $1,900 for repair services performed.
  27 Received $1,200 cash from Jones for repair services performed.
  30 Paid $120 for electricity used in June.

LO PART II, 2: MERCHANDISING COMPANY SIMPLE T-ACCOUNT ENTRIES—BALANCE SHEET AND INCOME STATEMENT ACCOUNTS

6–30. **Required:** Prepare T-account entries for the following transactions:

Jul 1 Borrowed $12,000 on a promissory note.
   2 Purchased merchandise inventory for $8,500 on account.
   2 Purchased store supplies for $800 cash.
  15 Sold merchandise that cost $2,000 for $4,500 cash.
  27 Sold merchandise that cost $1,500 on account for $3,250.
  30 Paid wages of $300.

LO PART II, 2: MERCHANDISING COMPANY SIMPLE GENERAL JOURNAL ENTRIES—BALANCE SHEET AND INCOME STATEMENT ACCOUNTS

6–31. **Required:** Prepare general journal entries for the following transactions:

Aug 1 Sold 2,000 shares of no-par common stock for cash of $11,000.
   3 Purchased store equipment for $2,800 cash.
   3 Purchased merchandise inventory on account for $9,000.
  10 Sold merchandise that cost $3,000 for cash of $5,000.
  30 Sold merchandise that cost $2,000 on account for $4,000.
  30 Paid sales salaries of $300.

LO PART II, 2: MERCHANDISING COMPANY SIMPLE GENERAL JOURNAL ENTRIES—BALANCE SHEET AND INCOME STATEMENT ACCOUNTS

6–32. **Required:** Prepare general journal entries for the following transactions:

Sept 1 Sold 200 shares of $100 par preferred stock for cash of $20,300.
   2 Paid $3,600 for a one-year insurance policy.
   3 Purchased merchandise inventory on account for $18,000.
  15 Sold merchandise that cost $9,000 for cash of $15,000.
  29 Sold merchandise that cost $5,000 on account for $8,000.
  30 Paid sales salaries of $1,500.
  30 Paid $450 for electricity used in September.

LO PART II, 2: TRANSACTION ANALYSIS AND JOURNAL ENTRIES

6–33. On May 1, Bill Simon Computer Repair was begun when the company sold 1,000 shares of its no-par common stock for $7,000 cash. Also on May 1, the company paid two months' rent in advance totaling $400. On May 3, the company purchased computer repair supplies for $700 cash and three computers at a total cost of $4,500 on account. On May 3, the company hired a student helper, agreeing to pay the helper $1,000 per month. On May 12, the company billed a customer $700 for repair services rendered. The company paid the helper $500 on May 15. On May 25, the company paid $200 for a newspaper advertisement, which appeared in the paper a week earlier to announce the opening of the business. On May 31, the company paid another $500 to the helper. On May 31, the company received cash of $2,800 for repair services rendered to another customer.

Required: Prepare journal entries to record these transactions.

LO PART II, 2: TRANSACTION ANALYSIS AND JOURNAL ENTRIES

6–34. On July 1, Mead Travel Agency, Inc., was established when it sold 3,000 shares of no-par common stock for $10,000 cash. On July 2, the company paid $500 for one month's rent. On July 5, the company purchased office supplies for $700 on account and three desks at a total cost of $1,500 cash. On July 6, the company hired a travel consultant, agreeing to pay her $20 per hour. The consultant worked 100 hours in July, which the company will pay on August 1. The company paid $100 on July 29 for a newspaper advertisement that had appeared in the paper the week before to announce the opening of its business. On July 22, the company received $800 from East Coast Cruise Lines for commission revenue in connection with bookings Mead Travel made in July. On July 31, the company borrowed $12,000 from the **Bank of America** for two years at 7 percent.

Required: Prepare journal entries to record these transactions.

LO PART II, 2: TRANSACTION ANALYSIS AND JOURNAL ENTRIES

6–35. On December 1, 2004, Wayne Cox Enterprises, Inc., was established when the company sold 500 shares of no-par common stock for cash of $5,000. Also on December 1, the company paid office rent for December 2004 and January and February 2005 totaling $900. On December 2, the company purchased office furniture for cash of $1,500 and bought $250 worth of office supplies on account. The company also purchased computer equipment by signing a three-year, 6 percent promissory note for $1,500.

Required: Prepare journal entries to record these transactions.

LO PART II, 2: T-ACCOUNT AND JOURNAL ENTRIES

6–36. The transactions for September 2004 for Frank Collins Two Mile High Flight School are as follows:

Sept 1 Sold 25,000 shares of its $1 par common stock for $125,000 cash.
 1 Purchased an airplane for cash of $80,000.
 2 Paid $260 for a newspaper advertisement.
 2 Paid $3,000 for six months rent on an airplane hangar.
 5 Collected $900 for lessons given to students.
 5 Borrowed $10,000 from the bank for two years at 8 percent.
 6 Purchased office supplies for $250 cash.
 8 Collected $1,100 for lessons given to students.
 12 Paid a dividend of $850.
 20 Ordered $320 of repair parts for the airplane.
 23 Received the parts ordered on the 20th, paying cash.
 29 Paid cash of $400 for the fuel the airplane used in September.
 29 Paid September's electric bill for $150.

Required:

    a. Prepare T-account entries for the above transactions.
    b. Prepare general journal entries for the above transactions.

LO PART II, 3 & 4: CONTINUATION OF 6–36—CHART OF ACCOUNTS, POSTING TRANSACTIONS, TRIAL BALANCE

6–37. Refer to problem 6–36 for Frank Collins Two Mile High Flight School.

Required:

    a. Prepare a chart of accounts for the company based on the accounts you used for the journal entries.
    b. Post the transactions in the general ledger.
    c. Prepare a trial balance after completion of the posting process.

LO PART II, 2: RECORDING TRANSACTIONS—COMMON AND PREFERRED STOCK

6–38. Transactions for XXX Pest Control for October 2005 are as follows:

Oct 1 XXX Pest Control was formed when the company sold 3,500 shares of its $1 par stock for cash of $35,000.

1 The company sold 100 shares of its $100 par preferred stock for $10,500 cash.

1 Purchased a truck for $18,000 cash.

1 Borrowed $8,000 from the bank using the truck as collateral. Interest of 9 percent will be paid monthly on the first day of each month.

2 Purchased spraying equipment for the truck costing $3,500 cash including $400 of chemicals ($3,100 for the equipment and $400 for the chemicals).

2 Paid $600 for a newspaper advertisement to run each week in October.

2 Paid rent on an office for six months in advance totaling $6,000.

5 Collected $75 upon completion of spraying a new residence.

5 Billed a customer $150 upon completion of spraying the lawn.

6 Purchased office supplies for $200 cash.

8 Collected $100 for a termite inspection.

9 Collected the $150 from the customer on the 5th.

12 Paid a $500 dividend.

20 Ordered $1,000 of chemicals.

23 Received the chemicals ordered on the 20th with payment due in 10 days.

28 Collected $2,300 for completed termite inspections done for a loan company and billed an apartment complex $1,200 upon completion of spraying 40 units.

29 Paid the power company $135 for electricity used in October.

Required: Prepare general journal entries for the above transactions.

LO PART II, 3 & 4: CONTINUATION OF 6–38—CHART OF ACCOUNTS, POSTING TRANSACTIONS, TRIAL BALANCE

6–39. Refer to problem 6–38 for XXX Pest Control.

Required:

a. Prepare a chart of accounts for the company based on the accounts you used for the journal entries.

b. Post the transactions in the general ledger.

c. Prepare a trial balance after completion of the posting process.

LO PART II, 2: RECORDING TRANSACTIONS

6–40. The transactions for December 2004 for Brad Sanders Auto Repair Shop are as follows:

Dec 1 Sold 5,000 shares of $5 par common stock for $45,000 cash.

1 Purchased a wrecker for $30,000 cash.

1 Borrowed $25,000 on a one-year, 8 percent note from the bank. Interest is payable monthly on the first day of the month.

2 Purchased shop equipment for cash of $12,500.

2 Paid $360 for a newspaper advertisement to announce the opening of his business.

2 Paid rent on garage and office for six months in advance totaling $8,100.

5 Signed a contract to perform maintenance service on all auto equipment for a car rental agency.

5 Billed a customer $250 upon completion of auto repairs.

6 Purchased office supplies for $250 cash.

8 Billed the rental agency $2,500 upon completion of work performed.

10 Collected the $250 from the customer billed on the 5th.

12 Paid a cash dividend of $500.

15 Paid the December's telephone bill of $300.

21 Paid the local parts distributor $600 for parts already used on repair jobs (parts expense).

21 Ordered $1,300 of parts for parts inventory.

25 Received the parts ordered on the 21st and paid cash on delivery.

29 Paid $320 to the power company for electricity used in December.

31 Billed the rental agency $3,600 upon completion of repair services. Used $680 worth of the parts inventory for these repairs.

Required: Prepare general journal entries for the preceding transactions.

LO PART II, 3 & 4: CONTINUATION OF 6–40—CHART OF ACCOUNTS, POSTING TRANSACTIONS, TRIAL BALANCE

6–41. Refer to problem 6–40.

Required:

    a. Prepare a chart of accounts for the company based on the accounts you used for the journal entries.

    b. Post the transactions in the general ledger.

    c. Prepare a trial balance after completion of the posting process.

LO PART II, 5: SIMPLE ACCRUAL ADJUSTING ENTRIES

6–42. The Carlos Garcia Company had the following accrual information available at the end of the year 2004:

    a. Wages earned but unrecorded and unpaid as of December 31, 2004, were $2,500.

    b. Unpaid and unrecorded interest to date on a bank loan was $1,000.

    c. On January 12, 2005, the company received a $280 electric bill for December's electricity. The amount is unrecorded and unpaid.

    d. A customer owed one year's interest on a note to Garcia for $400 as of December 31. No entry has been made to record this transaction.

    e. As of December 31, 2004, Garcia has completed $2,300 of repair service in connection with a service contract. The amount will not be billed until January when the rest of the work is completely done.

Required: Prepare the appropriate general journal entries with explanations to record the above adjustments as of December 31, 2004.

LO PART II, 5: ADJUSTING ENTRIES

6–43. The Ray Placid Corporation had the following information available for the year ended December 31, 2004:

    a. The accountant completed the 2004 depreciation schedule, which showed the total depreciation expense of $10,520 for the year. The depreciation expense account has a balance of $8,500.

    b. Commissions for December of $22,000 will be paid to Placid's sales staff on January 5. The commissions payable account has a zero balance.

    c. The company loaned $20,000 to a customer on July 1 for one year at 8 percent interest. The customer will pay the principal and interest on the loan on June 30, 2005. No interest in connection with this loan has been recorded.

    d. On July 1, Placid paid an entire year's rent of $14,000 for a warehouse. In July, the bookkeeper recorded this payment as rent expense.

Required: Prepare the appropriate general journal entries with explanations to record the above adjustments as of December 31, 2004.

LO PART II, 5: ADJUSTING ENTRIES

6–44. The Butler Company has the following information available for the year ended December 31, 2004:

    a. Wages earned by employees but not paid at year end is $4,000.

    b. A one-year insurance policy was paid for on October 1 for $2,520. The insurance expense account's current balance is $2,520.

    c. Service revenue earned but not collected at year end is $14,000. Accounts receivable has a zero balance.

    d. Real estate taxes unrecorded and unpaid at year end are $3,900.

    e. Interest owed to the bank but not recorded or paid at year end is $2,200.

Required: Prepare the appropriate general journal entries with explanations to record the above adjustments as of December 31, 2004.

LO PART II, 5: DEFERRAL ADJUSTING ENTRIES

6–45. The Cohen Company's trial balance at June 30, 2004, has the following balances before adjustments:

Unearned rental revenue	$7,200
Prepaid rent expense	3,600
Prepaid insurance	4,800
Supplies inventory	1,200

a. On May 1, the company paid the rent for one year in the amount of $3,600.
b. On April 1, the company collected rental revenue in advance for the following 24 months in the amount of $7,200.
c. On June 1, the company paid for its one-year business insurance policy in the amount of $4,800.
d. At June 30, 2004, the physical count of the supplies inventory indicated that $295 of supplies were on hand.

Required: Prepare the appropriate adjusting entries with explanations to record the above information as of June 30, 2004.

LO PART II, 5: DEFERRAL ADJUSTING ENTRIES

6–46. As of June 30, 2004, the Jones Company has the following account balances before adjustments:

Unearned rental revenue	$4,800
Prepaid rent	3,600
Insurance expense	2,400
Prepaid insurance	0
Supplies inventory	700

a. On January 1, the company paid the rent expense of $3,600 for one year's rent in advance.
b. On March 1, the company collected 24 months' rent in advance totaling $4,800.
c. On May 1, the company paid $2,400 for a one-year catastrophe insurance policy. This was the only policy in force.
d. On June 30, the physical count of the supplies inventory on hand was $400.

Required: The company's year end is June 30. Prepare the appropriate adjusting entries as of June 30, 2004, with explanations to record the above adjustments.

LO PART II, 5: COMPLEX DEFERRAL ADJUSTING ENTRIES

6–47. In the first few days of January 2004, *Hearty Cooking* magazine sold 1,000 annual subscriptions to its monthly magazine for $16 each. It also sold 500 two-year subscriptions for $25 each and 250 three-year subscriptions for $32 each.

Required:

a. Prepare the appropriate adjusting entries with explanations to record the adjustments necessary at December 31, 2004, and at December 31, 2005. Assume the subscriptions were all sold at the beginning of January 2004 and were originally recorded as income in the subscriptions revenue account.
b. Prepare the appropriate adjusting entries with explanations to record the adjustments necessary at December 31, 2004, and at December 31, 2005. Assume the subscriptions were all sold at the beginning of January 2004 and were originally recorded as a liability in the unearned subscriptions revenue account.

LO PART II, 5: SIMPLE DEPRECIATION ADJUSTING ENTRIES

6–48. On January 1, 2004, the Stevens Company purchased a copy machine for $2,000. The firm believed the machine would have an estimated useful life of six years and a residual value of $200. The firm also purchased a delivery van costing $28,000 with an estimated useful life of four years and a residual value of $4,000. The company uses straight-line depreciation for all of its assets.

Required: Prepare the appropriate entries with explanations to record the depreciation expense for the first year for the copy machine and delivery van.

LO PART II, 5: SIMPLE DEPRECIATION ADJUSTING ENTRIES

6–49. On January 1, 2004, the Bishop Company purchased equipment for $3,000. The firm believed the equipment would have an estimated useful life of four years and a residual value of $200. The firm also purchased a tractor costing $56,000 with an estimated useful life of six years and a residual value of $2,000. The company uses straight-line depreciation for all of its assets.

Required: Prepare the appropriate adjusting entries with explanations to record the depreciation adjustment for December 31, 2004, for the equipment and the tractor.

LO PART II, 5: SIMPLE DEPRECIATION ADJUSTING ENTRIES

6–50. At the start of the year 2004, the Mitchell Corporation purchased a piece of equipment for $36,000. The firm believed the machine would have an estimated useful life of five years and a residual value of $6,000. The firm also purchased a building costing $200,000 with an estimated useful life of 40 years and no residual value. The company uses straight-line depreciation for all of its assets.

Required: Prepare the appropriate adjusting entries with explanations to record the depreciation adjustment at the end of the first year for the equipment and the building.

LO PART II, 4 & 5: ADJUSTING ENTRIES USING TRIAL BALANCE AND SUPPLEMENTAL INFORMATION

6–51. The following is a partial trial balance for the Weiss Company as of December 31, 2004:

The Weiss Company
Partial Trial Balance
December 31, 2004

	Debit	Credit
Prepaid insurance	$18,000	
Prepaid rent expense	12,000	
Interest receivable	0	
Wages payable		$10,000
Unearned service revenue		36,000
Interest revenue		0

Additional information includes the following:

a. As of December 31, 2004, seven months remain on the 12-month insurance policy that originally cost $18,000.
b. Weiss has a note receivable with $2,500 of interest due and payable on January 1, 2005.
c. The books show that two thirds of the fees paid in advance by a customer on June 30 have now been earned. Only one customer has paid Weiss Company in advance during 2004.
d. The company prepaid its rent of $12,000 for nine months on July 1.
e. The wages payable on December 31, 2004, were $7,000. The amount in the wages payable account is from December 31, 2003.

Required: Record the adjusting entries required based on the above information as of December 31, 2004.

LO PART II, 5: ADJUSTING ENTRIES USING TRIAL BALANCE AND SUPPLEMENTAL INFORMATION

6–52. The following is a partial trial balance for the Brown Company as of December 31, 2005:

The Brown Company
Partial Trial Balance
December 31, 2005

	Debit	Credit
Prepaid insurance	$ 7,200	
Prepaid rent expense	10,000	
Interest payable		$ 0
Subscription revenue		72,000
Wages expense	25,000	
Interest expense	0	

Additional information includes the following:

    a. The company paid a $7,200 premium on a one-year business insurance policy on July 1, 2005.

    b. Brown borrowed $200,000 on January 2, 2005, and must pay 12 percent interest on January 2, 2006, for the entire year of 2005.

    c. Of the $72,000 of subscription revenue, $60,000 was earned as of December 31, 2005, and the balance will be earned in 2006.

    d. The company prepaid 10 months' rent in advance on November 1, 2005, to take advantage of a special discount that reduced the rent to $1,000 per month.

    e. Wages for work done by employees on December 31, 2005, of $3,000 will be paid to the employees on January 6, 2006.

Required: Record the adjusting entries required based on the above information as of December 31, 2005.

LO PART II, 5: ADJUSTING ENTRIES USING TRIAL BALANCE AND SUPPLEMENTAL INFORMATION

6–53. The following is a partial trial balance for the Mendoza Company as of December 31, 2004:

The Mendoza Company
Partial Trial Balance
December 31, 2004

	Debit	Credit
Office supply inventory	$ 1,400	
Wages payable		$0
Office supply expense	36,000	
Wage expense	45,500	

Additional information includes the following:

    a. Office supplies on hand at year end were $1,230.

    b. The total payroll cost for the year 2004 was $50,000. At December 31, 2004, the company owed employees $4,500 for wages earned in 2004.

Required: Record the adjusting entries required at December 31, 2004, based on the above information.

LO PART II, 5: SIMPLE BANK RECONCILIATION

6–54. The Clarke Company showed a balance for cash on their books of $2,517 on November 30, 2004. The company received the bank statement dated November 30, 2004, that showed a balance of $2,750. The differences between the company's book balance of cash and the bank statement balance are:

- A deposit of $500 that was made on November 30 was not included in the bank statement.
- Outstanding checks on November 30 were $1,280.
- Regular bank service charges imposed by the bank were $35.
- Bank service charge for credit card collections was $512.

Required:

    a. Prepare the bank reconciliation for the Clarke Company for November 30, 2004.

    b. Prepare any necessary adjusting journal entries at November 30, 2004.

LO PART II, 5: SIMPLE BANK RECONCILIATION

6–55. The Clifford Company received the bank statement for October 2004. The following information is available as of October 31, 2004:

Cash balance per general ledger	$7,500
Cash balance per bank statement	8,023
Interest earned shown on the bank statement but unrecorded by Clifford	18
Outstanding checks total	2,365

Deposits in transit	1,800
Bank charges	60

Required:

    a. Prepare the bank reconciliation for the Clifford Company for October 31, 2004.

    b. Prepare any necessary adjusting journal entries at October 31, 2004.

LO PART II, 5: SIMPLE BANK RECONCILIATION

6–56. The Patten Company showed a cash balance of $1,838 on its books as of December 31, 2004, but the December 31, 2004, bank statement showed a balance of $2,116. The differences between the company's book balance for cash and the bank statement's balance include:

    1. A deposit of $300 that was made on December 31 was not included in the bank statement.

    2. Outstanding checks on December 31 were $1,280.

    3. Bank service charges imposed by the bank were $28.

    4. The bank included a debit memo for bank charges for credit card handling fees totaling $690.

    5. The bank statement reflected interest revenue of $16.

Required:

    a. Prepare the bank reconciliation for the Patten Company for December 31, 2004.

    b. Prepare any adjusting journal entries at December 31, 2004.

LO PART II, 5: BANK RECONCILIATION

6–57. The following bank statement and cash journal are for the Whitaker Company's first month of business during 2004:

Any Bank

555 Any Street   Narberth, PA

Whitaker Company
1234 Any Road
Anytown, PA

Page 1 of 1
Statement Period:
11-01-04 through 11-30-04

Account Number: 123 456789

Your Account Balance at a Glance

Beginning Balance on 11-01-04	$	0
Deposits and Other Additions +	+	10,773
Checks Posted	–	1,603
Other Subtractions	–	45
Ending Balance on 11-30-04	$	9,125

Account Additions and Subtractions

Date	Amount ($)	Resulting Balance	Transaction
11-02	1,500+	1,500	Deposit
11-02	128–	1,372	Check 1001
11-03	1,254+	2,626	Deposit
11-06	425–	2,201	Check 1002
11-15	550–	1,651	Check 1004
11-23	8,000+	9,651	Deposit
11-29	500–	9,151	Check 1005
11-30	45–	9,106	Service Charge
11-30	19+	9,125	Interest

Account Name: *Cash*					Account Number: *111*	
Date 2004	Description	Post. Ref.	Debit	Credit	Balance Debit	Balance Credit
Nov 1	Deposit	GJ1	1,500			
1	Deposit	GJ1	1,254			
1	Ck. #1001	GJ1		128		
1	Ck. #1002	GJ1		425		
12	Ck. #1003	GJ1		785		
22	Deposit	GJ2	8,000			
26	Deposit	GJ2	150			
27	Ck. #1004	GJ2		550		
27	Ck. #1005	GJ2		500		
30	Ck. #1006	GJ2		95		
30	Ck. #1007	GJ2		130	8,291	

Required:

a. Prepare the bank reconciliation for the Whitaker Company for November 30, 2004.
b. Prepare any necessary adjusting journal entries at November 30, 2004.

LO PART II, 5: BANK RECONCILIATION

6–58. The following bank statement and cash journal are for the Levine Company's first month of business:

University Bank

555 Dixie Highway   Coral Gables, FL

Page 1 of 1
Statement Period:
11-01-04 through 11-30-04

Levine Company
317 Jenkins Drive
Coral Gables, FL

Account Number: 123 456789

Your Account Balance at a Glance

Beginning Balance on 11-01-04	$	0
Deposits and Other Additions +	+	6,362
Checks Posted	–	5,441
Other Subtractions	–	36
Ending Balance on 11-30-04	$	885

Account Additions and Subtractions

Date	Amount ($)	Resulting Balance	Transaction
11-02	2,750+	2,750	Deposit
11-02	3,000+	5,750	Deposit
11-03	2,250–	3,500	Check 2001
11-06	1,125–	2,375	Check 2002
11-15	55–	2,320	Check 2004
11-22	1,965–	355	Check 2003
11-23	600+	955	Deposit
11-29	46–	909	Check 2006
11-30	12+	921	Interest
11-30	36–	885	Service Charge

Account Name: Cash					Account Number: 111	
Date 2004	Description	Post. Ref.	Debit	Credit	Balance Debit	Credit
Nov 1	Deposit	GJ1	2,750			
1	Deposit	GJ1	3,000			
1	Ck. #2001	GJ1		2,250		
1	Ck. #2002	GJ1		1,125		
12	Ck. #2003	GJ1		1,965		
22	Deposit	GJ2	600			
27	Deposit	GJ2	1,150			
27	Ck. #2004	GJ2		55		
28	Ck. #2005	GJ2		79		
30	Ck. #2006	GJ2		46		
30	Ck. #2007	GJ2		122		
30	Ck. #2008	GJ2		139		
30	Deposit	GJ2	750		2,469	

Required:

a. Prepare the bank reconciliation for the Levine Company for November 30, 2004.
b. Prepare any necessary adjusting journal entries at November 30, 2004.

LO PART II, 5: ADJUSTING ENTRIES USING TRIAL BALANCE AND SUPPLEMENTAL INFORMATION, FINANCIAL STATEMENT IMPACT

6–59. The Thompson Company has the following account balances for the year ended December 31, 2004 (all have normal balances):

Prepaid insurance	$ 6,000
Insurance expense	0
Rental revenue	44,800
Unearned revenue	0
Wages expense	7,660
Wages payable	0
Interest revenue	2,325
Interest receivable	0

The company also has the following information available at the end of the year:

1. $4,000 of the prepaid insurance has now expired.
2. Of the $44,800 of rental revenue, $2,200 has not yet been earned.
3. The company must accrue an additional $1,500 of wages expense.
4. The company has earned an additional $500 of interest revenue.

Required:

a. Prepare the adjusting journal entries necessary based on the above information.
b. Use T-accounts to compute the account balances of the income statement and balance sheet accounts.

LO PART II, 5: ADJUSTING ENTRIES USING TRIAL BALANCE AND SUPPLEMENTAL INFORMATION, FINANCIAL STATEMENT IMPACT

6–60. The Carol Levine Company has the following account balances for the year ended December 31, 2004 (all have normal balances):

Insurance expense	$4,000
Prepaid insurance	0
Unearned rental revenue	3,800
Rental revenue	135,200

Wages payable	0
Wages expense	53,800
Property tax expense	4,398
Property tax payable	0
Depreciation expense	0
Accumulated depreciation	17,486

The company also has the following information available at the end of the year:

1. $1,000 of the insurance policy has not yet expired.
2. $1,600 of the unearned rental revenue has now been earned.
3. As of the end of the year, the company owes employees $1,200 of wages.
4. The company owes an additional $4,900 in real estate taxes.
5. Depreciation expense for the year totals $8,743.

Required:

a. Prepare any necessary adjusting journal entries based on the above information at December 31, 2004.
b. Use T-accounts to compute the account balances of the income statement and balance sheet accounts at December 31, 2004.

LO PART II, 5: ADJUSTING ENTRIES USING TRIAL BALANCE AND SUPPLEMENTAL INFORMATION, FINANCIAL STATEMENT IMPACT

6–61. The Alvarez Company has the following account balances for the year ended December 31, 2004 (all have normal balances):

Insurance expense	$ 5,400
Prepaid insurance	0
Unearned service revenue	3,525
Service revenue	235,750
Wages payable	0
Wage expense	64,820
Advertising expense	9,500
Prepaid advertising	0
Depreciation expense	0
Accumulated depreciation	24,000

The company also has the following information available at the end of the year:

1. $3,200 of the company's insurance has not yet expired.
2. $1,200 of the unearned service revenue was earned in the last month of the year.
3. The company must accrue an additional $1,800 of wages expense.
4. The company paid $6,000 for advertisements that will run for the next six months beginning next month. The $6,000 is included in the advertising expense account balance.
5. Depreciation expense for the year is a total of $8,000.

Required:

a. Prepare any necessary adjusting journal entries based on the above information at December 31, 2004.
b. Use T-accounts to compute the account balances of the income statement and balance sheet accounts.

LO PART II, 5: ADJUSTING ENTRIES USING TRIAL BALANCE AND SUPPLEMENTAL INFORMATION, FINANCIAL STATEMENT IMPACT

6–62. The Holmes Company has the following account balances for the year ended December 31, 2005 (all have normal balances):

Supplies expense	$2,000
Supplies	730
Unearned subscription revenue	3,758
Prepaid rent expense	4,950
Depreciation expense	0
Accumulated depreciation	24,652

The company also has the following information available at the end of the year:

1. Only $500 of the supplies are still on hand.
2. $1,785 of the unearned subscription revenue has now been earned.
3. With respect to prepaid rent, there are two months' rent remaining at $850 per month.
4. Depreciation expense for the year totals $12,326.

Required:

a. Prepare any necessary adjusting journal entries based on the above information at December 31, 2005.
b. Use T-accounts to compute the account balances of the income statement and balance sheet accounts.

LO PART II, 8: CLOSING ENTRIES

6–63. **Required:** Prepare closing entries based on the following information available for the year ended December 31, 2004:

	Debit	Credit
Cash	$20,180	
Supplies	4,340	
Prepaid expenses	1,685	
Notes payable		$ 2,400
Common stock		1,200
Additional paid-in capital—common		3,404
Retained earnings		7,680
Dividends	20,000	
Sales		129,850
Salaries expense	68,458	
Rent expense	18,082	
Rent revenue		2,000
Interest expense	280	
Income tax expense	13,509	

LO PART II, 8: CLOSING ENTRIES

6–64. **Required:** Prepare closing entries based on the following information available for the year ended June 30, 2005:

	Debit	Credit
Cash	$3,500	
Inventory	12,000	
Equipment	9,000	
Notes payable		$ 2,000
Common stock		500
Additional paid-in capital—common		3,500
Retained earnings		12,000
Dividends	1,000	
Sales		100,000
Cost of goods sold	60,000	
Wages expense	15,000	
Rent expense	9,000	
Electricity expense	4,000	
Telephone expense	2,000	
Income tax	2,500	

LO PART II, 8: CLOSING ENTRIES

6–65. **Required:** Prepare closing entries based on the following information available for the year ended December 31, 2005:

	Debit	Credit
Cash	$ 1,980	
Inventory	8,540	
Equipment	13,850	
Notes payable		$ 7,000

Common stock		1,350
Additional paid-in capital—common		2,820
Retained earnings		10,840
Dividends	250	
Sales		34,620
Cost of goods sold	22,860	
Wages expense	6,500	
Rent expense	1,180	
Interest expense	600	
Income tax expense	870	

LO PART II, 8: CLOSING ENTRIES

6–66. **Required:** Prepare closing entries based on the following information available for the year ended December 31, 2004 (all have normal balances):

Cash	$ 5,800
Accounts receivable	12,300
Inventory	26,800
Supplies	575
Land	40,650
Building	88,450
Accumulated depreciation—building	20,000
Equipment	4,950
Accumulated depreciation—equipment	1,100
Computer system	1,850
Accumulated depreciation—computer system	300
Delivery truck	29,960
Accumulated depreciation—delivery truck	3,000
Accounts payable	6,860
Notes payable	5,000
Common stock	1,000
Additional paid-in capital—common	95,520
Retained earnings	64,580
Dividends	2,900
Sales	260,500
Cost of goods sold	182,530
Wages expense	33,000
Depreciation expense	15,000
Electricity expense	3,500
Telephone expense	1,500
Rent revenue	2,100
Interest expense	4,570
Income tax	5,625

LO PART II, 8: CLOSING ENTRIES

6–67. **Required:** Prepare closing entries based on the following information available for the year ended June 30, 2005 (all have normal balances):

Cash	$ 2,680
Inventory	8,880
Equipment	12,640
Accumulated depreciation—equipment	3,000
Computer system	4,850
Accumulated depreciation—computer system	1,100
Delivery truck	18,600
Accumulated depreciation—delivery truck	6,000
Accounts payable	5,480
Notes payable	4,500
Common stock	2,000
Additional paid-in capital—common	10,312
Retained earnings	12,850
Dividends	500
Sales	56,250

Cost of goods sold	24,630
Salaries expense	18,400
Depreciation expense	4,400
Rent expense	2,400
Electricity expense	1,260
Telephone expense	625
Interest expense	900
Income tax expense	727

LO PART II, 8: CLOSING ENTRIES

6–68. **Required:** Prepare closing entries based on the following information available for the year ended December 31, 2004 (all have normal balances):

Cash	$ 1,920,650
Accounts receivable	263,520
Inventory	2,462,250
Supplies	1,200
Land	750,520
Building	1,685,520
Accumulated depreciation—building	300,000
Equipment	385,220
Accumulated depreciation—equipment	120,000
Accounts payable	1,985,640
Notes payable	736,580
Bonds payable	500,000
Preferred stock	200,000
Common stock	998,590
Retained earnings	2,460,350
Dividends	25,000
Sales	12,856,850
Cost of goods sold	9,458,560
Salaries expense	2,771,518
Depreciation expense	190,000
Rent expense	105,642
Electricity expense	24,995
Telephone expense	36,795
Rent revenue	36,000
Interest expense	13,340
Income tax expense	99,280

Mini Practice Sets ●

LO PART II, 1, 2, 3, 4, 5, & 7: JOURNALIZE AND POST TRANSACTIONS, AND TRIAL BALANCE AND FINANCIAL STATEMENT PREPARATION

6–69. The Best Home Improvement Center began operations on November 1, 2004. Transactions for the month of November are as follows:

Nov 1 Best Home Improvement Center sold 1,500 shares of $1 par Best common stock for cash of $45,000.

    1 Borrowed $5,000 from ***First National Bank,*** signing a 9 percent, 90-day note with interest payable on the first day of each month.

    1 Purchased a forklift to move merchandise for $5,000 cash.

    5 Best signed a lease on a store and paid six months' rent in advance beginning November 1, $9,450.

    6 Purchased $500 of office supplies from Helen's Office Supply on account.

    8 Purchased merchandise for $25,000 from Associated Supply on account.

   11 Paid $175 for a radio ad to run in November to announce the store's opening.

   14 Sold merchandise for cash of $4,000 that cost $2,400.

   15 Sold merchandise that cost $1,750 for $2,500 on a 30-day account to J. Park.

   17 Sold merchandise that cost $1,950 for $3,000 on a 30-day account to H. Clark.

   19 Purchased $10,000 merchandise from the Sun Company on account.

   20 Sold merchandise that cost $13,200 for $20,000 cash.

   21 Paid Helen's Office Supply for purchase on November 6th.

23 Paid Associated Supply for the purchase on the 8th.
24 Collected payment in full from H. Clark.
25 Paid Sun Company for the purchase on the 19th.
25 Received payment in full from J. Park.
28 Paid $800 to the power company for electricity used in the month of November.
29 Paid all the wages for the month of $4,000.
30 Paid a cash dividend of $1,000.

Required:

a. Journalize the transactions for the month of November in the general journal.
b. Open the general ledger accounts and post the November transactions to the appropriate accounts in the general ledger.
c. Prepare an unadjusted trial balance at November 30, 2004.
d. Prepare adjusting general journal entries and post them to the ledger accounts. The following additional information is available:

1. Best depreciated the forklift for the month of November, using straight-line depreciation with a $200 residual value and an eight-year (96-month) estimated life.
2. Best accrued the interest on the bank loan for November. The interest will be paid on December 1.
3. On December 8, Best received the phone bill for November phone service for $190.

e. Prepare an income statement, a statement of stockholders' equity, and a balance sheet for the month of November.

LO PART II, 1, 2, 3, 4, 5, 6, & 7: JOURNALIZE AND POST TRANSACTIONS, AND TRIAL BALANCE, WORKSHEET, AND FINANCIAL STATEMENT PREPARATION

6–70. Robertson Distributing, Inc., began operations on December 1, 2004. Transactions for the month of December are as follows:

Dec 1 Robertson Distributing, Inc., sold 7,500 shares of its $2 par value common stock for $75,000 cash.
1 Borrowed $10,000 from **First National Bank,** signing a 10 percent, 180-day note.
1 Robertson signed a lease on a warehouse and paid $6,000 for six months' rent in advance.
1 Purchased a truck to deliver merchandise for $14,000 cash.
5 Purchased $1,500 of office supplies from Market Office Supply on account.
7 Purchased merchandise for $15,000 from Acme Supply on account.
11 Paid the *Time Express* newspaper $350 for an ad to announce the grand opening of the distribution center. The ad ran in December.
13 Sold merchandise that cost $6,300 for $8,200 cash.
14 Sold merchandise that cost $3,725 for $5,000 to M. Real on account.
16 Sold merchandise that cost $3,050 for $4,000 to E. Johnson on account.
17 Purchased merchandise for $20,000 from the Davis Company on account.
19 Sold merchandise that cost $7,950 for $10,000 cash.
21 Paid Market Office Supply for the purchase on the 5th.
22 Paid Acme Supply for the purchase on the 7th.
24 Collected payment in full from M. Real.
26 Paid Davis Company for the purchase on the 17th.
27 Received payment in full from E. Johnson.
30 Paid the power company $1,800 for electricity used in December.
31 Paid wages for the month of $7,000.
31 Paid a cash dividend of $1,800.

Required:

a. Journalize the transactions for the month of December in the general journal.
b. Open the necessary accounts in the general ledger and post the December transactions to the appropriate accounts in the general ledger.
c. Prepare an unadjusted trial balance at December 31, 2004.

d. Prepare a worksheet and adjusting general journal entries and post them to the ledger accounts. In addition to information from the entries you made previously, the following additional information is available:

1. Robertson depreciated the truck for the entire month of December, using straight-line depreciation with a $1,400 residual value and a 5-year (60-month) estimated life.
2. Robertson accrued the interest on the bank loan for the month of December.
3. As of December 31, Robertson owes wages of $1,900 for the month of December.

e. Prepare an income statement and a statement of stockholders' equity for the month ended December 31, 2004, and prepare a balance sheet as of December 31, 2004.

LO PART II, 1, 2, 3, 4, 5, & 7: PROPRIETORSHIP JOURNAL ENTRIES, POSTING, TRIAL BALANCE, ADJUSTING ENTRIES, AND FINANCIAL STATEMENTS

6–71. John Fox began his retail clothing business, Fineries, on November 1, 2004, as a sole proprietorship. The post-closing trial balance at November 30, 2004, appeared as follows:

Fineries
Post-Closing Trial Balance
November 30, 2004

	Debits	Credits
Cash	$38,500	
Prepaid rent	200	
Merchandise inventory	24,000	
Equipment	6,000	
Accumulated depreciation		$ 1,000
Common stock (no par)		67,700
Totals	$68,700	$68,700

The following transactions occurred in the month of December, 2004:

Dec 1 Fineries sold an additional 5,000 shares of stock for $100,000 cash.
1 Bought equipment on account from the Acme Company for $13,600.
1 Paid six months' rent in advance, $12,000.
5 Purchased $28,000 of merchandise on account from Rose Company.
7 Paid for a 12-month contents policy for fire damage at a cost of $1,440.
8 Purchased merchandise for resale for $25,000 cash.
10 Sold merchandise costing $6,300 to M. Powers on account for $12,600.
12 Paid the balance due to Rose Company.
15 Cash sales for the first half of the month totaled $27,500 for merchandise costing $13,750.
16 Sold merchandise costing $5,000 to Alan Foster on account for $10,000.
16 Paid wages for the first half of the month totaling $5,500.
18 Purchased merchandise on account from King Company for $9,500.
20 Purchased office supplies totaling $250 cash.
22 Received a check from M. Powers for her invoice.
25 Received a check from Alan Foster for payment of invoice.
28 Sold merchandise costing $4,300 to Paul Munter for $8,600 on account.
28 Paid cash of $300 for electricity used in December.
28 Received but did not pay a $100 telephone bill for December's phone service.
28 Paid King Company for the invoice of December 18.
31 Recorded cash sales for the second half of December totaling $44,900 for merchandise costing $22,450.
31 Paid wages for the second half of December, $4,500.
31 Received a bill for delivery expense for December, $250.

Required:

a. Journalize the transactions for the month of December in the general journal.
b. Open the necessary accounts in the general ledger and post the December transactions to the appropriate accounts.
c. Prepare an unadjusted trial balance at December 31, 2004.

d. Prepare adjusting general journal entries and post them to the ledger accounts. In addition to the entries you have previously made, the following information is also available:

1. The company owes wages of $900 for work done in the last three days of the month.
2. Depreciation expense to be recorded for the month of December is $250.

e. Prepare an adjusted trial balance for the company.
f. Prepare a balance sheet as of December 31, 2004, and an income statement and a statement of owners' equity for the month ended December 31, 2004.

LO PART II, 1, 2 ,3, 4, 5, 7, & 8: JOURNAL ENTRIES, POSTING, TRIAL BALANCE, ADJUSTING ENTRIES, FINANCIAL STATEMENTS INCLUDING STATEMENT OF CASH FLOWS, CLOSING ENTRIES

6–72. Michael Sharpe started a retail hardware store, Sharpe's Home Haven, Inc., on December 1, 2005. The following transactions occurred in the month of December:

Dec 1   Sharpe's Home Haven, Inc., sold Michael 100,000 shares of its common stock for cash of $200,000. The stock has a par value of $1 per share, and there were 200,000 shares authorized.
1   Bought store equipment on account from the Ace Company for $22,000.
1   Paid three months' rent in advance, $9,000.
5   Purchased merchandise on account from Taylor Company for $50,000.
7   Paid $1,200 for a 12-month insurance policy.
8   Purchased merchandise for resale for $30,000 cash.
10   Sold merchandise costing $12,000 to Hill on account, $24,000.
12   Paid the balance due to Taylor Company.
15   Cash sales for the first half of the month totaled $30,000 for merchandise costing $15,000.
16   Sold merchandise costing $2,500 to Scott Dunn Company on account, $5,000.
16   Paid wages for the first half of the month totaling $7,000.
18   Purchased merchandise on account from M. Lynne Company for $18,000.
20   Purchased office supplies for cash of $400.
22   Received a check from Hill for payment of the December 10 invoice.
25   Received a check from Scott Dunn for payment of invoice.
28   Sold merchandise that cost $6,300 for $12,600 to David Brown Supply on account.
28   Paid cash of $600 for electricity used in December.
28   Received but did not pay the telephone bill for $200 for the month of December. It is due on January 12.
28   Paid M. Lynne Company for the invoice of December 18.
31   Recorded cash sales for the second half of December totaling $35,200 for merchandise that cost $17,600.
31   Paid wages for the second half of December, $7,500.
31   Received a bill for delivery expense for December for $400 due January 10.
31   Paid a $.10 per share cash dividend.

Required:

a. Journalize the transactions for the month of December in the general journal.
b. Open the necessary accounts in the general ledger and post the December transactions to the appropriate accounts.
c. Prepare an unadjusted trial balance at December 31, 2005.
d. Prepare adjusting general journal entries and post them to the ledger accounts. In addition to the entries you have previously made, the following information is also available:

1. As of December 31, Sharpe owes wages of $900 for the last two days of December.
2. Equipment is depreciated using the straight-line method over five years with $2,200 residual value.

e. Prepare an adjusted trial balance for the company.
f. Using the information from the adjusted trial balance, prepare an income statement and a statement of retained earnings for the month of December 2005 and a balance sheet as of December 31, 2005.

g. Using information from the cash entries on the general journal, prepare a statement of cash flows for the company.

h. Prepare and post the closing entries as of December 31, 2005, to close the year.

i. Prepare a post-closing trial balance at December 31, 2005.

LO PART II, 1, 2 ,3, 4, 5, 7, & 8: JOURNAL ENTRIES, POSTING, TRIAL BALANCE, ADJUSTING ENTRIES, FINANCIAL STATEMENTS INCLUDING STATEMENT OF CASH FLOWS, CLOSING ENTRIES

6–73. James and William Blues began a management consulting business on October 1, 2005, called Blues Brothers Consulting, Inc. The following transactions occurred in the month of October 2005:

Oct 1 Blues Brothers Consulting, Inc., sold 1,000 shares of its $1 par common stock for $10,000 cash.

　　 1 Purchased office equipment for $5,000, paying $1,000 cash and signing a 10 percent, one-year promissory note for the balance. The equipment has an expected life of five years with a $500 residual value.

　　 1 Paid three months' rent in advance totaling $3,000.

　　 5 Purchased office supplies on account from Spring Company for $700.

　　 6 Paid $600 for a one-year insurance policy.

　　 10 Performed consulting services and billed Sam Hall Company $14,000 on account.

　　 11 Provided consulting services for Betty Collins Corporation receiving cash of $4,000.

　　 15 Paid for the office supplies purchased from Spring Company on the 5th.

　　 15 Provided consulting services to Lynne Munter Interior Design, Inc., receiving cash of $2,000.

　　 15 Billed Gary Sumter Enterprises $5,000 for consulting fees earned.

　　 16 Paid secretary wages for the first half of the month totaling $1,000.

　　 19 Purchased computer supplies on account from Dale Company, $400.

　　 20 Purchased office supplies for cash totaling $400.

　　 20 Received payment from Sam Hall for payment of his October 10 invoice.

　　 25 Received a check from Gary Sumter Enterprises for payment of invoice.

　　 28 Provided services on account to Dan Lee for $1,600.

　　 28 Paid $300 for electricity used during October.

　　 28 Received telephone bill for $250 for telephone service for the month of October.

　　 28 Paid Dale Company for the invoice of October 19.

　　 31 Paid wages for the second half of October, $1,500.

　　 31 Received a bill from *Kinko's* for October's copy services for $100.

　　 31 Paid cash dividends of $2,700.

Required:

a. Journalize the transactions for the month of October in the general journal.

b. Open the necessary accounts in the general ledger and post the October transactions to the appropriate accounts.

c. Prepare an unadjusted trial balance at October 31, 2005.

d. Prepare adjusting general journal entries and post them to the ledger accounts. In addition to the entries you have previously made, the following information is also available:

　 1. Office supplies of $100 were on hand at October 31.

　 2. There were no computer supplies left at year end.

e. Prepare an adjusted trial balance.

f. Using the information from the adjusted trial balance, prepare an income statement and statement of stockholders' equity for the month of October 2005 and a balance sheet as of October 31, 2005.

g. Using information from the cash entries on the general journal, prepare a statement of cash flows for the company.

h. Assume that Blues Brothers Consulting, Inc., selected October 31 as the year end. Prepare and post the closing entries to close the year.

i. Prepare a post-closing trial balance at October 31, 2005.

ANNUAL REPORT PROJECT

6–74. Section 6—Finding Peer Companies and Peer Company Comparisons

By now you have learned a lot about the company you selected for your annual report project. For this assignment, you will select another company in the same industry, a peer company. Peer companies are companies that are similar to one another, usually in the same industry and of similar size, which analysts use for financial comparisons.

Required:

a. Select a peer company. Sometimes peer companies are obvious. For example, if you were analyzing a large airline like *American,* it is fairly obvious that you would select another large airline like *United.* If you are having trouble selecting a peer company, one way you can find one is to use the Securities and Exchange Commission's (SEC's) Electronic Data Gathering, Analysis, and Retrieval (EDGAR) system. In case you need it, we have listed the step-by-step instructions to help you find a peer company using the SEC's EDGAR system.

Step-by-step instructions to find peer companies using the SEC's Web site:

1. Go to the SEC's home page at *www.sec.gov.*
2. Click on *Search for Company Filings* (listed under *"Filings and Forms (EDGAR)"*).
3. Click on *Search Companies and Filings.*
4. Enter your company's name (the name of the company you selected for your project) in the appropriate place and click *Find Companies.*
5. The company's Standard Industrial Classification (SIC) code and a description of the company's industry will appear just under the company's name in the upper left area of the page. For example, for *Pier 1 Imports, Inc.,* the following information appears on the Web page just under the SEC's logo and seal:

```
PIER 1 IMPORTS INC
SIC: 5700 - Retail - Home Furniture, Furnishings & Equipment Stores
```

6. Click on your company's SIC code. In *Pier 1*'s case, you would click on 5700.
7. A list of companies classified under that SIC code will appear.
8. Click on several of the companies and examine their Form 10-K to find a company that is a good fit. Try to find a company of similar size (based on sales revenues or total assets) in a business that appears to closely match that of the company you selected for your annual report project.

b. Once you have selected a peer company, locate its latest Form 10-K in the EDGAR system. You will need to print out the peer company's Form 10-K to obtain the information necessary to calculate financial ratios for this and later sections of this annual report project.

c. Prepare a report that compares the following ratios for your company with those of the peer company you selected. Keep in mind that you have already calculated each of the ratios for your company in earlier sections of this project.

- Debt ratio for two years
- Debt-to-equity ratio for two years
- Gross profit margin ratios for three years
- Net profit margin ratios for three years
- Rate of return on assets ratio for the latest year
- Rate of return on common equity ratio for the latest year
- Dividend payout ratio for three years
- Earnings per share for three years
- Price-to-earnings ratio for the latest year

d. Comment in your report on the information that the comparison of each one of the ratios provides. How does your company compare to its peer? And where applicable, comment on how your company has performed over time relative to the peer company you selected.

e. Your report should conclude with comments regarding what you think of your company and how you think your company compares to its peer in light of the work you did in connection with this assignment.

CHAPTER 7

Long-Lived Depreciable Assets— A Closer Look

Let's say you are about to invest in one of two moving and storage companies. Both companies appear interesting, but you would like to review some of the companies' financial information before you make a decision. At your request, the companies, Straight-Line Movers and Accelerated Movers, provide you with 2002 financial statements, the data from which appear in Exhibit 7–1 on page F–266.

After reviewing the two companies' financial statements, you conclude that Straight-Line Movers definitely appears to be the stronger of the two. Not only does Straight-Line have greater net income, but its assets and its equity are greater as well. The investment decision seems easy. But is it really that simple? Is Straight-Line Movers really a more solid company than Accelerated? Upon closer examination, you notice that depreciation expense plays a major role in the differences between the two companies. You need to have a good understanding of depreciation before you can tell for sure which company is stronger. This chapter will provide you with a basic understanding of the most popular depreciation methods and will help you understand depreciation's influence on the amounts that appear on financial statements.

In virtually every context except accounting, the word depreciation is associated with the declining value of assets over time. One might say that his or her car depreciates by $2,000 a year, meaning that the car's value declines each year by $2,000. In accounting, however, the word depreciation has an entirely different meaning. As you recall from Chapter 5, in an accounting context, **depreciation** is defined as a systematic and rational allocation of the cost of a long-lived asset. You must know about the accounting implications of depreciation because it is a component of the financial reports of *Target, Eastman Kodak, Sprint,* and every other company in the United States.

depreciation The systematic and rational conversion of a long-lived asset's cost from asset to expense in the income statement periods benefited.

In this chapter, we will extend our coverage of depreciation by considering several issues that further complicate the depreciation process. In Chapter 5, we mentioned that management must estimate an asset's useful life and its residual value in order to calculate annual depreciation expense. In this chapter, we will explore how these estimates affect depreciation expense, net income, and the book value of assets. In addition, we will explore the two most popular methods of depreciation, which are the straight-line method and the double-declining-balance method. Finally, we will look at the gains and losses that occur when a company sells a depreciable asset and how management's estimates and their choice of depreciation method greatly impact the gains or losses the company will recognize.

Learning Objectives

After completing your work on this chapter, you should be able to do the following:

1. Explain the process of depreciating long-lived assets.
2. Determine depreciation expense using the straight-line and the double-declining-balance depreciation methods.
3. Describe how the use of different depreciation methods affects the income statement and the balance sheet.

	Income Statements For the Year Ended December 31, 2002	
	Straight-Line Movers	Accelerated Movers
Sales	$ 769,000	$ 769,000
LESS: Cost of goods sold	295,500	295,500
Gross margin	$ 473,500	$ 473,500
Wages expense	$ 67,500	$ 67,500
Utilities expense	31,000	31,000
Depreciation expense	34,000	114,000
Total operating expenses	(132,500)	(212,500)
Operating income	$ 341,000	$ 261,000
Other revenues and expenses:		
Interest expense	(120,000)	(120,000)
Net income	$ 221,000	$ 141,000

	Balance Sheets December 31, 2002	
	Straight-Line Movers	Accelerated Movers
Assets:		
Cash	$226,000	$ 226,000
Accounts receivable	198,000	198,000
Inventory	223,000	223,000
Trucks	$228,000	$228,000
Accumulated depreciation	(34,000)	(114,000)
Trucks, net	194,000	114,000
Total assets	$841,000	$ 761,000
Liabilities:		
Accounts payable	$ 22,000	$ 22,000
Notes payable	61,000	61,000
Total liabilities	$ 83,000	$ 83,000
Owners' equity:		
Common stock	$200,000	$ 200,000
Additional paid-in capital	194,000	194,000
Contributed capital	$394,000	$ 394,000
Retained earnings	364,000	284,000
Total shareholders' equity	758,000	678,000
Total liabilities and owners' equity	$841,000	$ 761,000

EXHIBIT 7–1   2002 Financial Statements of Straight-Line Movers and Accelerated Movers

4. Compare and contrast gains and losses with revenues and expenses.
5. Calculate gains and losses on the disposal of depreciable assets.
6. Describe the true meaning of gains and losses on the disposal of depreciable assets.
7. Prepare journal entries associated with long-lived depreciable assets. (Appendix)

◆ DEPRECIATION

As we've said, *depreciation* is a systematic and rational allocation of the cost of a long-lived asset to the accounting periods benefited. Companies initially record the cost of long-lived property, plant, and equipment as assets. This is appropriate because, like all assets, the property, plant, and equipment have future value. Firms can use these long-lived assets for years to come, usually to help earn revenue. As a company benefits from the use of property, plant, and equipment, accountants use depreciation as a means of transferring their cost from assets to expense. In this way, a company recognizes expense in the period benefited by the use of the asset. As a result, depreciation helps match the expense of using long-lived assets with the revenues the assets helped to produce. What this means is that when **Southwest Airlines** depreciates one of its airplanes, it is trying to match the cost of the aircraft to the revenue that aircraft helped to produce.

When a company determines that it will use an item for more than one income statement period, the company should not recognize the item's entire cost as an expense immediately. Instead, the company should record the item as an asset. Then, in each year of the asset's *useful life*, the company should recognize a portion of the item's cost as an expense. Just how much the company should recognize as expense in a given year depends on several factors, including the company's estimates for the asset's useful life, its residual value (what the company estimates it will be able to sell the asset for at the end of its useful life), and the company's choice of depreciation method.

THE EFFECT OF ESTIMATES

depreciable base   The total amount of depreciation expense that is allowed to be claimed for an asset during its useful life. The depreciable base is the cost of the asset less its residual value.

A company's estimates of the length of the asset's useful life and the amount of its residual value directly affect the amount of depreciation expense the company will recognize each year. For example, assume a division of **3Com** purchases a new copy machine for $20,000. If management estimates that the copier has a residual value of $4,000, the asset has a depreciable base of $16,000. An asset's **depreciable base** is the asset's cost less its estimated residual value (also commonly referred to as *salvage value* or *scrap value*). The depreciation expense a company recognizes will differ if it estimates a $3,000 residual value rather than $4,000. By the same token, the amount of depreciation expense a company recognizes each year will differ if the company estimates a useful life of four years rather than five. Exhibit 7–2 shows examples of how residual value and useful life estimates can impact depreciation expense.

EXHIBIT 7–2   Effects of Estimates on Depreciation

Options	Depreciable Base	Annual Expense
Residual value: $4,000, useful life: 4 years	$16,000	$4,000
Residual value: $4,000, useful life: 5 years	$16,000	$3,200
Residual value: $3,000, useful life: 4 years	$17,000	$4,250
Residual value: $3,000, useful life: 5 years	$17,000	$3,400

Discussion Questions

7–1. What factors do you think a company should consider when it determines the estimated useful life of a long-lived asset? How do you think a company determines the asset's estimated residual value?

7–2. Assume that you are the manager of the **3Com** division that has just purchased the $20,000 copy machine. How would the depreciation estimates you make affect how your division's performance appears on the company's financial reports? Would you have any control over this?

7–3. Consider a long-lived asset that costs $30,000. How would net income be affected by using an estimated useful life of four years and an estimated residual value of $5,000 rather than a five-year estimated useful life and a residual value of $5,000? Explain.

As you review financial information, be aware that the estimates companies use for calculating depreciation vary. For example, **UAL Corporation (United Air Lines)** typically depreciates its aircraft over four to 30 years while **Delta** depreciates its flight equipment over 15 to 25 years.

THE EFFECTS OF DIFFERENT DEPRECIATION METHODS

Within generally accepted accounting principles (GAAP), there is some latitude permitted so companies can select accounting procedures that are best suited to fit their needs. Companies may use any of several acceptable methods of depreciation. However, GAAP require companies to provide information about their depreciation estimates and the depreciation methods they choose to use. This information is not generally on the face of the financial statements; it is usually found in the financial statement notes. For example, you won't find the words "depreciation expense" on **General Mills**' income statement, but on page 6, note B, of its 2001 annual report, the company reports it depreciates buildings over 40 to 50 years and equipment over three to 15 years, primarily using the straight-line method. The note goes on to say that depreciation charges for 2001 were $194 million. Although **General Mills** does not specifically show the depreciation expense of $194 million on its income statement, the company includes the amount as part of cost of goods sold, selling, general and administrative expense, and perhaps as other expense classifications as well.

Most companies have more than one depreciable asset, and they are free to choose one method of depreciation for one asset and a totally different method for another. Although many companies use the same depreciation method for all their depreciable assets, some do choose to use more than one depreciation method.

As users of the financial accounting information, it is important that you understand the impact of depreciation method choice on financial statements. To illustrate these effects, we will explore in detail the two most commonly used depreciation methods. The first method we will examine is **straight-line depreciation,** which records an equal amount of depreciation expense in each year of an asset's life. Not only is this the simplest method of depreciation, it is also the one most widely used by companies in the United States. Of the 600 companies surveyed by the authors of *Accounting Trends and Techniques* in 2001, 96 percent used the straight-line method to calculate depreciation expense reported in their financial statements for the year 2000 for at least some of their assets.

The second depreciation method we will study records a larger amount of depreciation expense in the early years of an asset's life and less in the later years. There are several depreciation methods that work this way, and collectively, they are known as **accelerated depreciation methods.** During 2000, about 14 percent of the companies surveyed by the authors of *Accounting Trends and Techniques* used some type of accelerated depreciation for some of their assets. Remember, some companies use more than one type of method. For example, **Chevron Corporation** generally uses an accelerated method to depreciate its plant and equipment in the United States and the straight-line method to depreciate international plant and equipment.

How do companies choose between using straight-line depreciation and an accelerated depreciation method? Recall that a basic premise of accrual accounting is that we should match expenses to the revenues they help produce. Theoretically, then, companies should use straight-line depreciation for assets that produce the same amount of revenue in each period of their useful lives. Conversely, companies should use accelerated depreciation methods for assets that produce more revenue in the early years and a lesser amount as time goes by. However, companies are more likely to choose one depreciation method over another based on the anticipated effect on the financial statements during the asset's useful life. Exhibit 7–3 contrasts straight-line depreciation expense to the amount recorded if an accelerated method is used.

As we explore different depreciation methods, you will see the significant impact a company's choice of depreciation method can have on the accounting information offered to economic decision makers. To illustrate this impact on financial statements, we will contrast straight-line depreciation with the most popular accelerated depreciation method—the double-declining-balance method. We will explore the application of these methods so you can learn the mechanics of how to use them and, more importantly, to demonstrate their impact on reported net income.

straight-line depreciation A method of calculating periodic depreciation. The depreciable base of an asset is divided by its estimated useful life. The result is the amount of depreciation expense to be recognized in each year of the item's useful life: (Cost − Residual Value)/N = Annual Depreciation Expense.

accelerated depreciation methods Those methods that record more depreciation expense in the early years of an asset's life and less in the later years.

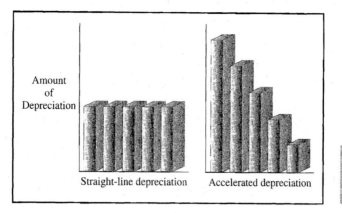

EXHIBIT 7–3 Straight-Line versus Accelerated Depreciation

STRAIGHT-LINE DEPRECIATION

In Chapter 5, we introduced the concept of depreciation with an example of the straight-line method. To review how straight-line depreciation is calculated, assume Barlow Paving Corporation purchased an asphalt paving machine on January 2, 2002, for a total cost of $300,000.

In accounting, when we calculate the cost of a depreciable asset, we include all the costs to bring an asset to a usable state. This includes the invoice price, applicable sales tax, installation costs, cost of insurance while in transit, shipping costs, and cost of training personnel to use the machine. It does not include repairs and maintenance or insurance once the asset becomes productive.

Barlow's management estimates the useful life of this machine to be five years, at the end of which the machine will be sold for an estimated $25,000. For simplicity, we will assume that this machine is the only long-lived asset Barlow owns.

Using the straight-line method, Barlow's yearly depreciation expense is $55,000. To calculate this amount, we determine the depreciable base of $275,000 ($300,000 cost less the $25,000 estimated residual value) and then divide that base by the five-year estimated useful life ($275,000/5 years = $55,000 per year).

What this means is that for each of the five years, $55,000 is removed from the asset total on the balance sheet and is shown as depreciation expense on the income statement. While accountants could accomplish the transfer by decreasing the asset amount itself, they don't. Instead, they use a separate account called *accumulated depreciation* to record the reduction. This way, a company can determine the asset's original cost at any time by simply examining the asset account, in this case, the machine account. Additionally, the company can determine the asset's depreciation to date by examining the accumulated depreciation account, in this case, the accumulated depreciation—machine account. So, the total depreciation expense recognized since the asset was put in service is called **accumulated depreciation.** In other words, accumulated depreciation keeps a running total of all the depreciation that has ever been taken on an asset. When we examine the financial statements for Barlow Paving Corporation, we will see depreciation expense on the income statements of $55,000 for each year and a yearly increase in the balance of accumulated depreciation for the same amount. To illustrate this point, we present Barlow Paving Corporation's income statements and balance sheets for the years 2002 through 2006 using straight-line depreciation in Exhibit 7–4 on page F–270. For ease of interpretation, we have kept the financial statement items not affected by depreciation constant.

Regardless of what else happened in Barlow's operations for the years 2002 through 2006, the depreciation expense remained the same amount each year. Constant depreciation expense is one of the main characteristics of straight-line depreciation. Also note that there is a direct relationship between the yearly depreciation expense on the income statement and the machine's book value on the balance sheets. You will recall from Chapter 5 that **book value** is the cost of a long-lived asset less all the depreciation expense recognized since the asset was placed in service. Therefore,

Cost − Accumulated Depreciation = Book Value

accumulated depreciation The total amount of cost that has been systematically converted to expense since a long-lived asset was first purchased.

book value The original cost of a long-lived asset less its accumulated depreciation. This item is often shown on the balance sheet.

	Income Statements				
	2002	2003	2004	2005	2006
Sales	$755,000	$755,000	$755,000	$755,000	$755,000
Cost of goods sold	422,000	422,000	422,000	422,000	422,000
Gross margin	$333,000	$333,000	$333,000	$333,000	$333,000
Operating expenses other than depreciation	(236,000)	(236,000)	(236,000)	(236,000)	(236,000)
Depreciation expense	(55,000)	(55,000)	(55,000)	(55,000)	(55,000)
Net income	$ 42,000	$ 42,000	$ 42,000	$ 42,000	$ 42,000

	Balance Sheets				
	2002	2003	2004	2005	2006
Assets:					
Cash	$ 50,000	$ 96,000	$157,000	$213,000	$289,000
Accounts receivable	206,000	257,000	293,000	334,000	355,000
Inventory	77,000	77,000	77,000	77,000	77,000
Machine	300,000	300,000	300,000	300,000	300,000
LESS: Accumulated depreciation	(55,000)	(110,000)	(165,000)	(220,000)	(275,000)
Total assets	$578,000	$620,000	$662,000	$704,000	$746,000
Liabilities and stockholders' equity:					
Accounts payable	$206,000	$206,000	$206,000	$206,000	$206,000
Notes payable	170,000	170,000	170,000	170,000	170,000
Common stock	100,000	100,000	100,000	100,000	100,000
Additional paid-in capital	10,000	10,000	10,000	10,000	10,000
Retained earnings	92,000	134,000	176,000	218,000	260,000
Total liabilities and stockholders' equity	$578,000	$620,000	$662,000	$704,000	$746,000

EXHIBIT 7–4   Barlow Paving Corporation's Financial Statements Using Straight-Line Depreciation

Each year, as the company recognizes $55,000 in depreciation expense, the balance of accumulated depreciation increases by that amount. The net effect is a reduction in the asset's book value by that same $55,000. This example illustrates that straight-line depreciation causes the book value of assets to decrease by the same amount each year. Barlow recorded a total of $275,000 in depreciation expense. The book value at the end of 2006 is $25,000 ($300,000 cost − $275,000 accumulated depreciation). An asset's depreciable base is equal to the total amount of depreciation expense allowed throughout the asset's life. Once all of the allowable depreciation expense has been recognized for an assets entire useful life, the asset is **fully depreciated.** So you see, it is no coincidence that the book value of a fully depreciated asset is equal to the asset's estimated residual value.

fully depreciated When all of the allowable depreciation expense has been recognized for an asset's entire useful life.

Discussion Question ●●●●●●●●●●●●●●●●●●●●●●●●●●●●●●●●●●●

7–4. Refer to Exhibit 7–2, which illustrates *3Com*'s four estimate options for its new copy machine. For each option, determine what the book value would be after three years of straight-line depreciation.

Obviously, a different estimated useful life or a different estimated residual value would cause the amount of yearly depreciation expense to be different. So, too, would the selection of a different method of calculating yearly depreciation expense. To demonstrate the effect of selecting one depreciation method over another, we will now explore the most widely used accelerated depreciation method.

DOUBLE-DECLINING-BALANCE DEPRECIATION

double-declining-balance method An accelerated depreciation method in which depreciation expense is twice the straight-line percentage multiplied by the book value of the asset.

The **double-declining-balance method** got its name because it calculates depreciation expense at twice the straight-line depreciation rate. Note that we said twice the straight-line *rate*, not twice the straight-line *amount*. The difference is subtle, but very important. If you don't pick up on that difference (which we'll demonstrate shortly), you will fall into the trap of thinking that double-declining-balance depreciation records twice as much depreciation expense each year as the amount recorded using straight-line depreciation.

Rather than using the depreciable base to calculate yearly depreciation expense as the straight-line method does, double-declining-balance calculates depreciation expense for a given year by applying a percentage depreciation rate to the current book value of the asset. As a result, the double-declining-balance method ignores the estimated residual value in the depreciation calculation—though, as we will see, companies using this method must be careful not to depreciate an asset beyond its residual value.

There are three steps to calculating depreciation using the double-declining-balance method:

1. Determine the straight-line rate of depreciation as a percentage. (100% / N, where N = number of years in the asset's useful life.)
2. Double the straight-line percentage.
3. Apply that percentage to the current book value of the asset. Book value declines with the deduction of each year's depreciation so that even though the percentage applied is constant, the amount of depreciation expense decreases each year.

As an example, let's use the double-declining-balance method to determine the depreciation expense for Barlow's paving machine.

1. 100% / 5 = 20% (per year)
2. 20% × 2 = 40% (per year)
3. $300,000 × 40% = $120,000 (for the first year)

For 2002, Barlow Paving Corporation would record $120,000 depreciation expense using the double-declining-balance method.

Note that in the first year of the asset's useful life, before any depreciation has been recorded, the book value of the asset we use in Step 3 equals the cost of the asset. In later years, however, the book value of the asset equals the asset's cost minus its accumulated depreciation.

Exhibit 7–5 shows how yearly depreciation expense would be calculated on Barlow's $300,000 machine using double-declining-balance depreciation, a $25,000 residual value, and a five-year estimated useful life.

EXHIBIT 7–5   Book Value and Double-Declining-Balance Depreciation Calculations

	Book Value Calculation			Depreciation Calculation		
Year	Cost	Accumulated Depreciation	Book Value	Book Value	Rate	Depreciation Expense
2002	$300,000 − $ 0 =		$300,000	$300,000 ×	40% =	$120,000
2003	$300,000 − $120,000 =		$180,000	$180,000 ×	40% =	$ 72,000
2004	$300,000 − $192,000 =		$108,000	$108,000 ×	40% =	$ 43,200
2005	$300,000 − $235,200 =		$ 64,800	$ 64,800 ×	40% =	$ 25,920
2006	$300,000 − $261,120 =		$ 38,880			$ 13,880
2007	$300,000 − $275,000 =		$ 25,000			$ 0
				Total depreciation expense		$275,000

As you examine the calculations in the exhibit, note several points. First, the book value of the machine declines each year by the amount of depreciation expense of the prior year. For example, the book value at the beginning of 2002 is the full $300,000 cost of the machine. At the beginning of 2003, the book value drops to $180,000 (the $300,000 cost − $120,000 depreciation for 2002). The book value of the machine continues to drop until, at the beginning of 2006, it is $38,880.

The second thing to note in Exhibit 7–5 is that depreciation expense for 2006 ($13,880) is not 40 percent of the book value at the beginning of the year. The amount of depreciation expense in 2006 is limited to $13,880 because companies are not allowed to depreciate assets beyond the point at which the book value of the asset is equal to its estimated residual value. In other words, the book value of an asset may never be lower than its residual value. As Exhibit 7–5 shows, total depreciation over the five-year life of the asset is $275,000, and it is not by chance that this amount is the asset's depreciable base. Even when double-declining-balance depreciation is used, total depreciation expense over the life of the asset cannot exceed the asset's depreciable base (cost − residual value). As the book value declines toward the residual value of the asset and the accumulated depreciation rises toward the maximum depreciation allowed, we must be careful not to exceed the limits. When the double-declining-balance depreciation method is used, the last year's depreciation expense is not equal to the asset's book value times the double-declining-balance rate; rather, it is the amount required to reduce the book value of the asset to its estimated residual value. This is the maximum depreciation expense allowed in that period. At that point, the asset is fully depreciated.

The third point to note about the double-declining-balance calculations is that during an asset's useful life, yearly depreciation expense starts out high but quickly decreases. This decrease is characteristic of all accelerated depreciation methods and has a profound effect on the financial statements of companies using accelerated depreciation. Exhibit 7–6 illustrates this with Barlow Paving Corporation's income statements and balance sheets for 2002 through 2006, this time using the double-declining-balance depreciation method. As with our straight-line depreciation presentation, we have kept the items not affected by the company's choice of depreciation method constant from year to year.

Discussion Questions ●

7-5. Based on Barlow Paving Corporation's financial statements in Exhibit 7–6, and assuming no dividends were declared during 2002, what was the balance in retained earnings at the beginning of 2002?

7-6. Prepare the 2002 statement of retained earnings assuming Barlow Paving Corporation had not recorded *any* depreciation on its paving machine.

UNDERSTANDING THE IMPACT OF DEPRECIATION METHOD CHOICE

When you compare Barlow Paving Corporation's financial statements using straight-line depreciation (Exhibit 7–4) with Barlow's financial statements for the same period using double-declining-balance depreciation (Exhibit 7–6), notice several differences and several similarities:

- There is a significant difference in Barlow's depreciation expense in each of the five years.
- There is a significant difference in Barlow's net income in each of the five years.
- *Total* depreciation expense and *total* net income over the entire five-year period are exactly the same regardless of which depreciation method Barlow uses. The differences occur in the individual years but balance out by the time the asset is fully depreciated.
- There is a significant difference in the amounts of accumulated depreciation on the balance sheets for each of the years from 2002 through 2005. The 2006 balance

Income Statements

	2002	2003	2004	2005	2006
Sales	$755,000	$755,000	$755,000	$755,000	$755,000
Cost of goods sold	422,000	422,000	422,000	422,000	422,000
Gross margin	$333,000	$333,000	$333,000	$333,000	$333,000
Operating expenses other than depreciation	(236,000)	(236,000)	(236,000)	(236,000)	(236,000)
Depreciation expense	(120,000)	(72,000)	(43,200)	(25,920)	(13,880)
Net income	$(23,000)	$ 25,000	$ 53,800	$ 71,080	$ 83,120

Balance Sheets

	2002	2003	2004	2005	2006
Assets:					
Cash	$ 50,000	$ 96,000	$157,000	$213,000	$289,000
Accounts receivable	206,000	257,000	293,000	334,000	355,000
Inventory	77,000	77,000	77,000	77,000	77,000
Machine	300,000	300,000	300,000	300,000	300,000
LESS: Accumulated depreciation	(120,000)	(192,000)	(235,200)	(261,120)	(275,000)
Total assets	$513,000	$538,000	$591,800	$662,880	$746,000
Liabilities and stockholders' equity:					
Accounts payable	$206,000	$206,000	$206,000	$206,000	$206,000
Notes payable	170,000	170,000	170,000	170,000	170,000
Common stock	100,000	100,000	100,000	100,000	100,000
Additional paid-in capital	10,000	10,000	10,000	10,000	10,000
Retained earnings	27,000	52,000	105,800	176,880	260,000
Total liabilities and stockholders' equity	$513,000	$538,000	$591,800	$662,880	$746,000

EXHIBIT 7–6 Barlow Paving Corporation's Financial Statements Using Double-Declining-Balance Depreciation

sheet, however, shows exactly the same amount of accumulated depreciation in both presentations. In fact, the 2006 balance sheets in the two presentations are identical.

We are not saying that one method of depreciation is better than the other. But our presentation does point out that, if we look at a company's financial statements from one year to the next, the company's choice of one depreciation method over another will affect its reported net income and certain amounts that appear on its balance sheets.

Discussion Questions

7–7. Examine Exhibits 7–4 and 7–6 and explain why the 2006 balance sheets on the exhibits are identical even though they reflect different depreciation methods. Also explain why all five income statements and the first four years' balance sheets are different.

7–8. Examine Exhibits 7–4 and 7–6. How does the amount of cash Barlow shows using straight-line depreciation each year compare to what the company shows when we assume it uses double-declining-balance depreciation? Explain your findings.

We have now seen how Barlow's machine would be depreciated using either the straight-line method or the double-declining-balance method. Exhibit 7–7 summarizes the results by presenting a comparison of the depreciation expense, net income, and book value of the machine using the two different methods.

EXHIBIT 7–7 Straight-Line vs. Double-Declining-Balance Depreciation—A Comparison of Depreciation Expense, Net Income, and Book Value

	Straight-Line			Double-Declining-Balance		
Year	Depreciation Expense	Net Income	Book Value of Machine	Depreciation Expense	Net Income	Book Value of Machine
2002	$ 55,000	$ 42,000	$245,000	$120,000	($ 23,000)	$180,000
2003	$ 55,000	$ 42,000	$190,000	$ 72,000	$ 25,000	$108,000
2004	$ 55,000	$ 42,000	$135,000	$ 43,200	$ 53,800	$ 64,800
2005	$ 55,000	$ 42,000	$ 80,000	$ 25,920	$ 71,080	$ 38,880
2006	$ 55,000	$ 42,000	$ 25,000	$ 13,880	$ 83,120	$ 25,000
Total	$275,000	$210,000		$275,000	$210,000	

We used double-declining-balance depreciation to demonstrate the impact of accelerated depreciation on financial statements. Other accelerated methods include the 150 percent-declining-balance method and the sum-of-the-year's-digits method. **Boeing,** for example, uses the 150 percent-declining-balance method for buildings and land improvements and the sum-of-the-year's-digits method for machinery and equipment. Although we will not delve into the calculations for these methods, if you see them in financial reports, you should know that although they are not as aggressive as the double-declining-balance method, they are accelerated depreciation methods all the same.

Discussion Question ●

7–9. Assume that Exhibit 7–7 depicts information from two different companies, one using straight-line and the other double-declining-balance. If you were making an investment decision based solely on information available up to 2002, which company would *appear* to be the most attractive investment? Explain why this appearance could be deceptive.

◆ DISPOSAL OF DEPRECIABLE ASSETS

In a perfect world, a company would use a depreciable asset for exactly the time it had originally estimated, and then it would sell the asset for an amount equal to the asset's original estimated residual value. In reality, this almost never happens. The actual useful life of an asset may differ greatly from its estimated useful life. In fact, a company may dispose of (sell or scrap) an asset at any time, even long before the asset reaches the end of its estimated useful life. No laws prohibit a company from selling an asset before the end of its depreciable life, nor must a company stop using or dispose of an asset when it is fully depreciated. For example, the fact that **UPS** estimates the useful life of its delivery vans to be five years does not mean that the company cannot use the vans for a longer period of time. From a business perspective, **UPS** should continue to use a delivery van as long as the van is economically serviceable regardless of the van's estimated useful life.

historical cost principal
The accounting principal that requires balance sheet amounts generally to be shown at acquisition price rather than fair value.

According to the conceptual framework's **historical cost principal,** amounts are generally shown on the balance sheet at acquisition price, not at fair value. Therefore it is unlikely that an asset will be sold for the amount shown on the balance sheet. Additionally, there is no guarantee that a company will receive an amount equal to the asset's estimated residual value when it finally sells the asset. When companies sell their used equipment, machinery, trucks, and other depreciable assets, they may sell them for more or less than their estimated residual value. Companies try to sell these assets for as much as they reasonably can, but they do not limit their selling price by the estimated residual value, nor do they insist on receiving an amount equal to the asset's residual value when the asset is just not worth that much. They sell the assets for what they can get. Generally, estimated useful lives and estimated residual values used for depreciation calculation are not significant considerations in decisions regarding whether or not a company should dispose of an asset or the amount for which depreciable assets should be sold.

Disposing of depreciable assets is usually not associated with a company's ongoing major or central activity. Rather, this type of transaction is most often incidental or peripheral to the day-to-day operation of the business. For this reason, we do not normally classify any increase in equity from the disposal of depreciable assets as revenue, or any decrease in equity associated with this type of transaction as expense. Instead, accountants classify net inflows from the disposal of depreciable assets as gains and net outflows from the disposal of depreciable assets as losses.

GAINS AND LOSSES

Gains and losses are two of the accounting elements discussed by the Financial Accounting Standards Board (FASB) in its *Conceptual Framework of Accounting* (see Exhibit 7–8 on page F–276). As we discuss these two elements, we will provide the actual FASB definitions in italics, followed by a brief explanation of each.

gains Net inflows resulting from peripheral activities of a company. An example is the sale of an asset for more than its book value.

- **Gains**—*Increases in equity from peripheral or incidental transactions of an entity and from all other transactions and other events and circumstances affecting the entity except those that result from revenues or investments by owners* (Statement of Financial Accounting Concepts No. 6, paragraph 82). As you may recall from our discussion of revenue recognition in Chapter 5, gains are very similar to revenues because both are inflows of assets. The source of the inflows is what distinguishes these two elements from one another. Revenues are generated by the company's major business activities while gains result from peripheral or incidental business activities. As we will soon learn, another distinction between revenues and gains is that revenues generally represent only inflows of assets, but gains often represent the netting of inflows and outflows associated with a particular transaction or type of transaction.

losses Net outflows resulting from peripheral activities of a company. An example is the sale of an asset for less than its book value.

- **Losses**—*Decreases in equity from peripheral or incidental transactions of an entity and from all other transactions and other events and circumstances affecting the entity except those that result from expenses or distributions to owners* (Statement of Financial Accounting Concepts No. 6, paragraph 83). Recall from our discussion of expense recognition in Chapter 5 that losses are very similar to expenses because both are outflows of assets. As was the case with gains and revenues, losses and expenses differ by source. Expenses are the results of the company's major business activity, whereas losses generally result from other activities. Unlike gains, which are always associated with peripheral or incidental transactions, losses are sometimes associated with a company's major business activity. Losses of this type generally reflect the decline in value of operating assets, such as inventory. Another distinction between expenses and losses is that expenses generally represent only outflows of assets, but losses often represent the netting of the inflows and outflows associated with a particular transaction or type of transaction.

Keep in mind that an income statement provides information about the past performance of a company. This type of information can help decision makers better predict a company's future performance. Because all gains and many losses are incidental to a company's central operations, they may be less significant to decision makers than the revenues and expenses from the company's central operations. To allow decision makers to evaluate the inflows from a company's major or central operations (revenues) separately from the inflows from incidental activities (gains), the two are reported separately on the income statement. For example, *AMC Entertainment, Inc.*, reported a $664,000 gain on the disposal of assets in 2002 separately from theater admissions and concession revenue. The same treatment applies to expenses and

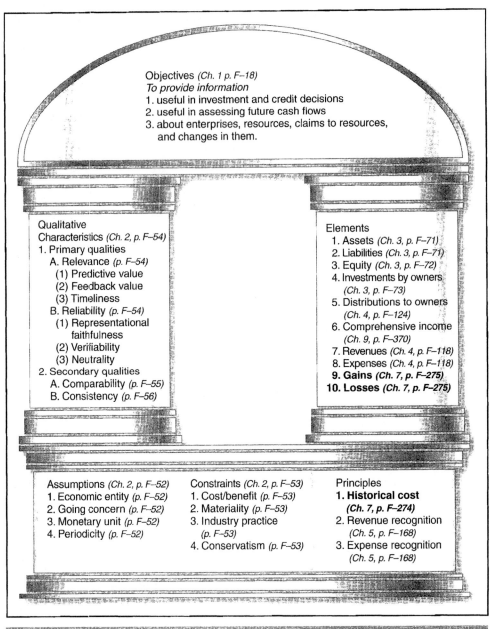

losses. The income statement reports the outflows from major or central business operations (expenses) separately from outflows from incidental activities (losses).

Although the income statement reports revenues separate from gains, and expenses separate from losses, gains affect net income in exactly the same way that revenues do, and the effect of losses is exactly the same as that of expenses. With the addition of gains and losses, we can expand the income statement equation introduced in Chapter 4 as follows:

$$\text{Revenues} + \text{Gains} - \text{Expenses} - \text{Losses} = \text{Net Income}$$

CALCULATING GAINS AND LOSSES

Calculating gains and losses that result from the disposal of depreciable assets is straightforward. When a company sells a depreciable asset, the difference between the amount the company receives (most often cash) and the book value of the asset sold is the amount of gain or loss on the sale. Let's return once again to the Barlow Paving Corporation and its $300,000 paving machine. Assume Barlow depreciated this machine using the straight-line method over a five-year estimated useful life, with an estimated residual value of $25,000 (Exhibit 7–4). Assume further that it is now January 2, 2007, and Barlow is selling the machine. As of the end of 2006, the machine has a $25,000 book value ($300,000 cost − $275,000 accumulated depreciation). For how much should Barlow sell the machine? If your answer is $25,000, you should reconsider—$25,000 is the book value of the machine, not its market value. Barlow will sell the machine for as much as it can get. The book value is based on an estimate made way back in 2002. In truth, potential buyers will neither know nor care about the book value as reflected in Barlow's records. A buyer will pay what she or he thinks the item is worth. This amount will depend on a number of factors, such as the condition of the machine, the state of technology, and the selling prices of comparable used machines. It's highly unlikely that Barlow will receive exactly $25,000, but we do not have enough information to determine whether Barlow will receive more or less.

Gain on Disposal

Assume Barlow is able to sell the machine for a cash price of $32,000. Because Barlow has received more than the book value of the machine, there is a gain, which we calculated as $7,000 ($32,000 cash received − $25,000 book value). Barlow will report the $7,000 as a gain on its income statement for the year 2007. Exhibit 7–9 shows Barlow's income statements and balance sheets for 2006 and 2007 reflecting a $7,000 gain on the disposal of its machine.

EXHIBIT 7–9 Barlow Paving Corporation's Financial Statements Reflecting a Gain on the Sale of Machine

Barlow Paving Corporation
Income Statements

	2006	2007
Sales	$755,000	$941,000
Cost of goods sold	422,000	525,000
Gross margin	$333,000	$416,000
Operating expenses other than depreciation	(236,000)	(319,000)
Depreciation expense	(55,000)	0
Operating income	$ 42,000	$ 97,000
Gain on sale of machine	0	7,000
Net income	$ 42,000	$104,000

Balance Sheets

	2006	2007
Assets:		
Cash	$289,000	$225,000
Accounts receivable	355,000	313,000
Inventory	77,000	172,000
Machine	300,000	0
LESS: Accumulated depreciation	(275,000)	0
Total assets	$746,000	$710,000
Liabilities and stockholders' equity:		
Accounts payable	$206,000	$216,000
Notes payable	170,000	20,000
Common stock	100,000	100,000
Additional paid-in capital	10,000	10,000
Retained earnings	260,000	364,000
Total liabilities and stockholders' equity	$746,000	$710,000

As you examine the financial statements in Exhibit 7–9, there are several things to note:

- Barlow's 2007 income statement shows the $7,000 gain in a different place than it shows the revenues from its ongoing major operations.
- The $7,000 gain has exactly the same effect on net income as revenues from Barlow's ongoing major operations.
- Because Barlow no longer owns the machine, it has removed both the cost of the machine ($300,000) and the machine's accumulated depreciation ($275,000) from its balance sheet as of the end of 2007.

Discussion Question

7–10. Note that Barlow Paving Corporation's income statements are presented in a multiple-step format in Exhibit 7–9. What specific items on the income statements are unique to this format and would not appear on a single-step statement?

Loss on Disposal

Now assume Barlow is able to sell the machine for a cash price of only $19,000. Because the company received less than the book value of the machine, there is a loss, which we calculate as $6,000 ($19,000 cash received − $25,000 book value). Barlow will report the $6,000 as a loss on its income statement for the year 2007. Exhibit 7–10 shows Barlow's income statements and balance sheets for 2006 and 2007 reflecting the $6,000 loss on the disposal of its machine.

EXHIBIT 7–10 Barlow Paving Corporation's Financial Statements Reflecting a Loss on the Sale of Machine

Barlow Paving Corporation
Income Statements

	2006	2007
Sales	$755,000	$941,000
Cost of goods sold	422,000	525,000
Gross margin	$333,000	$416,000
Operating expenses other than depreciation	(236,000)	(319,000)
Depreciation expense	(55,000)	0
Operating income	$ 42,000	$ 97,000
Loss on sale of machine	0	(6,000)
Net income	$ 42,000	$ 91,000

Balance Sheets

	2006	2007
Assets:		
Cash	$289,000	$212,000
Accounts receivable	355,000	313,000
Inventory	77,000	172,000
Machine	300,000	0
LESS: Accumulated depreciation	(275,000)	0
Total assets	$746,000	$697,000
Liabilities and stockholders' equity:		
Accounts payable	$206,000	$216,000
Notes payable	170,000	20,000
Common stock	100,000	100,000
Additional paid-in capital	10,000	10,000
Retained earnings	260,000	351,000
Total liabilities and stockholders' equity	$746,000	$697,000

As you examine the financial statements in Exhibit 7–10, there are several things to note:

- Barlow's 2007 income statement shows the $6,000 loss in a different place than it shows the expenses required for its ongoing major operations.
- The $6,000 loss has exactly the same effect on net income as expenses required for Barlow's ongoing major operations.
- Because Barlow no longer owns the machine, it has removed both the cost of the machine ($300,000) and the accumulated depreciation ($275,000) from its balance sheet as of the end of 2007.

In our examples of both a gain and a loss, we have assumed that Barlow was able to sell its machine for some amount of cash. However, there are times when an asset has no market value, so the company must simply scrap it. If this were the case with Barlow's machine, it would result in a loss of $25,000 ($0 cash received − $25,000 book value).

Discussion Question ●

7–11. Refer to Barlow Paving Corporation's income statements and balance sheets in Exhibit 7–10. What items on the financial statements for the year 2007 would be different (and by how much) if Barlow had scrapped the machine?

Disposal with No Gain or Loss

Now let's assume Barlow is able to sell the machine for a cash price of $25,000. Because the company received exactly the book value of the machine, there is neither a gain nor a loss ($25,000 cash received −$25,000 book value = $0 gain or loss). As Exhibit 7–11 shows, under these circumstances, the sale of the machine will not directly affect the income statement for the year 2007, but it will affect the balance sheet.

EXHIBIT 7–11 Barlow Paving Corporation's Financial Statements Reflecting the Sale of Its Machine for Book Value

Barlow Paving Corporation
Income Statements

	2006	2007
Sales	$755,000	$941,000
Cost of goods sold	422,000	525,000
Gross margin	$333,000	$416,000
Operating expenses other than depreciation	(236,000)	(319,000)
Depreciation expense	(55,000)	0
Operating income	$ 42,000	$ 97,000
Gain (loss) on sale of machine	0	0
Net income	$ 42,000	$ 97,000

Balance Sheets

	2006	2007
Assets:		
Cash	$289,000	$218,000
Accounts receivable	355,000	313,000
Inventory	77,000	172,000
Machine	300,000	0
LESS: Accumulated depreciation	(275,000)	0
Total assets	$746,000	$703,000
Liabilities and stockholders' equity:		
Accounts payable	$206,000	$216,000
Notes payable	170,000	20,000
Common stock	100,000	100,000
Additional paid-in capital	10,000	10,000
Retained earnings	260,000	357,000
Total liabilities and stockholders' equity	$746,000	$703,000

As you examine the financial statements in Exhibit 7–11, there are two things to note:

- There is no gain or loss from the disposal of the machine on the income statement for the year 2007.
- Because Barlow no longer owns the machine, it has removed both the cost of the machine ($300,000) and the accumulated depreciation ($275,000) from its balance sheet as of the end of 2007.

Thus far, we have examined how to calculate gains and losses, as well as how these elements affect a company's financial statements. Next, we will explore how to interpret gains and losses from the sale of depreciable assets in light of the effects of depreciation estimates and the selection of one depreciation method over another.

◆ UNDERSTANDING THE TRUE MEANING OF GAINS AND LOSSES

To demonstrate the true meaning of gains and losses, let's assume there are two companies—Straight-Line Movers and Accelerated Movers—whose business activities are identical in almost every respect. The companies have the exact same sales for the year, and all their operating expenses (except depreciation) are the same.

Each company purchased a fleet of trucks for $228,000 on January 2, 2002. In addition, both companies estimated a useful life of four years and a residual value of $92,000 for the trucks. Because Straight-Line Movers uses—you guessed it—straight-line depreciation and Accelerated Movers uses the double-declining-balance (accelerated) method, we would expect to see differences in their financial statements. The 2002 income statement and balance sheet for each company appear in Exhibit 7–12.

Discussion Questions

Refer to Exhibit 7–12 to answer the following questions:

7–12. The income statements show the amount of depreciation expense for each company. Provide computations that show how each company determined its depreciation expense.

7–13. Between companies, four items on the income statements differ and six items on the balance sheets differ. Identify each item and explain the cause of the difference.

The impact of the choice of depreciation method becomes even more evident over time. Exhibit 7–13 on page F–282 shows the income statements and balance sheets of Straight-Line Movers and Accelerated Movers at the end of 2003. Again, we have held constant the items that are not affected by using different depreciation methods.

Discussion Question

7–14. Provide computations and an explanation to show how Accelerated Movers determined the depreciation expense of $22,000 shown in Exhibit 7–13.

As we have seen, the use of different depreciation methods causes a profound effect on depreciation expense and other financial statement amounts. An even more striking impact occurs when we examine the effect of the use of different depreciation methods on the gains and losses companies recognize when they sell depreciable assets. For example, suppose that Straight-Line Movers and Accelerated Movers both decide to sell their trucks on December 31, 2003. The assets the companies are selling are identical in age, condition, and market value. Each company receives $150,000 cash in exchange for its trucks, the market value of the trucks on the day of the sale. Even though the companies are selling their trucks, they still have to record depreciation for 2003 because they used the trucks all year. Therefore, the companies would still show depreciation expense on their financial statements for 2003, just as we showed in the previous exhibits.

Income Statements
For the Year Ended December 31, 2002

	Straight-Line Movers	Accelerated Movers
Sales	$769,000	$769,000
LESS: Cost of goods sold	295,500	295,500
Gross margin	$473,500	$473,500
Wages expense	$ 67,500	$ 67,500
Utilities expense	31,000	31,000
Depreciation expense	34,000	114,000
Total operating expenses	(132,500)	(212,500)
Operating income	$341,000	$261,000
Other revenues and expenses:		
Interest expense	(120,000)	(120,000)
Net income	$221,000	$141,000

Balance Sheets
December 31, 2002

	Straight-Line Movers	Accelerated Movers
Assets:		
Cash	$226,000	$226,000
Accounts receivable	198,000	198,000
Inventory	223,000	223,000
Trucks	$228,000	$228,000
Accumulated depreciation	(34,000)	(114,000)
Trucks, net	194,000	114,000
Total assets	$841,000	$761,000
Liabilities:		
Accounts payable	$ 22,000	$ 22,000
Notes payable	61,000	61,000
Total liabilities	$ 83,000	$ 83,000
Owners' equity:		
Common stock	$200,000	$200,000
Additional paid-in capital	194,000	194,000
Contributed capital	$394,000	$394,000
Retained earnings	364,000	284,000
Total shareholders' equity	758,000	678,000
Total liabilities and owners' equity	$841,000	$761,000

EXHIBIT 7–12   2002 Financial Statements of Straight-Line Movers and Accelerated Movers

Discussion Question

7–15. Were the companies wise to sell the assets? Did they get "a good deal"? Did one company make a better deal than the other? What information might you want before deciding whether each company made a smart move?

Even though Straight-Line Movers and Accelerated Movers' business activity is identical, the financial statement presentation of the results of the sale of their trucks would be quite different, as Exhibit 7–14 on page F–283 shows.

The most obvious financial statement impact of the different depreciation methods is the resulting gain or loss on the sale of the trucks. Note that Straight-Line Movers recorded a $10,000 loss, but the exact same activity resulted in a $58,000 gain for Accelerated Movers. The moral of the story is that smart financial statement users are not overly impressed by gains or overly alarmed by losses associated with the dis-

Income Statements For the Year Ended December 31, 2003	Straight-Line Movers	Accelerated Movers
Sales	$769,000	$769,000
LESS: Cost of goods sold	295,500	295,500
Gross margin	$473,500	$473,500
Wages expense	$ 67,500	$ 67,500
Utilities expense	31,000	31,000
Depreciation expense	34,000	22,000
Total operating expenses	(132,500)	(120,500)
Operating income	$341,000	$353,000
Other revenues and expenses:		
Interest expense	(120,000)	(120,000)
Net income	$221,000	$233,000

Balance Sheets December 31, 2003	Straight-Line Movers	Accelerated Movers
Assets:		
Cash	$ 426,000	$426,000
Accounts receivable	253,000	253,000
Inventory	223,000	223,000
Trucks	$ 228,000	$228,000
Accumulated depreciation	(68,000)	(136,000)
Trucks, net	160,000	92,000
Total assets	$1,062,000	$994,000
Liabilities:		
Accounts payable	$ 22,000	$ 22,000
Notes payable	61,000	61,000
Total liabilities	$ 83,000	$ 83,000
Owners' equity:		
Common stock	$ 200,000	$200,000
Additional paid-in capital	194,000	194,000
Contributed capital	$ 394,000	$394,000
Retained earnings	585,000	517,000
Total shareholders' equity	979,000	911,000
Total liabilities and owners' equity	$1,062,000	$994,000

EXHIBIT 7–13 2003 Financial Statements of Straight-Line Movers and Accelerated Movers

posal of depreciable assets. Such gains and losses are merely a result of the difference between the book value and the market value of assets sold. We cannot always assume that a gain from the sale of depreciable assets reflects something that was "good" for business. Likewise, we cannot assume that a loss means that management made a bad move. In our example, there is not enough information available to determine whether the sale of the trucks for $150,000 was a wise business decision or a poor one. Clearly, though, the sale was no wiser for one company than for the other.

Also note that the retained earnings balances for Straight-Line Movers and Accelerated Movers in Exhibit 7–14 are exactly the same—$575,000. As you know, the depreciation process transfers the cost of property, plant, and equipment from assets on the balance sheet to expense on the income statement. By claiming a larger amount of depreciation in the early years of an asset's life—as happens when a company uses accelerated depreciation—a company's net income will be less in those early years. In this way, the company also lowers the asset's book value, which then may be much

Income Statements
For the Year Ended December 31, 2003

	Straight-Line Movers	Accelerated Movers
Sales	$769,000	$769,000
LESS: Cost of goods sold	295,500	295,500
Gross margin	$473,500	$473,500
Wages expense	$ 67,500	$ 67,500
Utilities expense	31,000	31,000
Depreciation expense	34,000	22,000
Total operating expenses	(132,500)	(120,500)
Operating income	$341,000	$353,000
Other revenues and expenses:		
Gain on sale of truck		58,000
Loss on sale of truck	(10,000)	
Interest expense	(120,000)	(120,000)
Net income	$211,000	$291,000

Balance Sheets
December 31, 2003

	Straight-Line Movers	Accelerated Movers
Assets:		
Cash	$ 576,000	$ 576,000
Accounts receivable	253,000	253,000
Inventory	223,000	223,000
Trucks	0	0
Accumulated depreciation	0	0
Trucks, net	0	0
Total assets	$1,052,000	$1,052,000
Liabilities:		
Accounts payable	$ 22,000	$ 22,000
Notes payable	61,000	61,000
Total liabilities	$ 83,000	$ 83,000
Owners' equity:		
Common stock	$ 200,000	$ 200,000
Additional paid-in capital	194,000	194,000
Contributed capital	$ 394,000	$ 394,000
Retained earnings	575,000	575,000
Total shareholders' equity	969,000	969,000
Total liabilities and owners' equity	$1,052,000	$1,052,000

EXHIBIT 7–14   Impact of the Sale of Trucks at the End of 2003 on the Financial Statements of Straight-Line Movers and Accelerated Movers

lower than the asset's market value. In our example, the book value of Accelerated Movers' trucks was so low that the company registered quite a large gain on their sale. Conversely, if a company claims a smaller amount of depreciation in the early years—as happens when using the straight-line method—the asset's book value will be higher. In our example, the book value of Straight-Line Movers' trucks was so high at the time of sale that the company incurred a loss.

Exhibit 7–15 on page F–284 illustrates the effect of the method of depreciation on net income in our example. Note that there are differences between the amounts shown for the two companies in individual years, but over the entire period of owner-ship, the differences balance out, so the company's choice of depreciation method ulti-mately has no effect on net income.

	Straight-Line	Accelerated
2002 Depreciation expense	$(34,000)	$(114,000)
2003 Depreciation expense	(34,000)	(22,000)
2003 Gain or (loss) resulting from sale of asset	(10,000)	58,000
Total Impact of Asset Ownership	**$(78,000)**	**$ (78,000)**

EXHIBIT 7–15 Long-Term Impact of Depreciation Method on Net Income

Exhibit 7–15 illustrates why it isn't wise for decision makers to focus too much on the impact of gains and losses from the sale of assets without considering the bigger picture. Clearly, gains and losses that result from the sale of assets are only part of the overall financial impact of asset ownership.

◆ OTHER DEPRECIATION METHODS

Thus far, we have examined the two most popular depreciation methods. Although straight-line and double-declining-balance depreciation are the most widely used, there are other methods of depreciation that are worth looking at. These methods include the units-of-production depreciation method and the Modified Accelerated Cost Recovery System (MACRS), the depreciation method that income tax regulations permit.

UNITS-OF-PRODUCTION DEPRECIATION METHOD

units-of-production depreciation method
A straight-line depreciation method that uses production activity as the basis of allocating depreciation expense. Instead of using an amount of depreciation per year, an amount of depreciation per unit produced is used.

Instead of using the estimated useful life in years as the basis for their straight-line depreciation calculations, some companies use the estimated number of units of production. The **units-of-production depreciation method,** or *units-of-activity method* as it is sometimes called, is a straight-line depreciation method that uses production activity as the basis of allocating depreciation expense. Instead of calculating an amount of depreciation per year, when a company uses the units-of-production method, it calculates an amount of depreciation per unit produced. Here, we are using the word *production* to mean whatever the asset normally produces. For example, we would probably define the "production" of a delivery truck as the number of miles traveled and the production of a milling machine as the number of units of product manufactured. *Freeport-McMoran Copper & Gold, Inc.,* uses units-of-production depreciation for its copper mining equipment based on the estimated copper the machines will recover.

To demonstrate the calculations for the units-of-production depreciation method, assume that on January 2, 2003, Rodriguez Trucking purchased a long-haul delivery truck for $125,000. Rodriguez Trucking estimates that it will use the truck for 400,000 miles. At the end of the truck's useful life, Rodriguez estimates that it can sell the truck for $25,000. Using the units-of-production depreciation method, Rodriguez's depreciation expense is $.25 per mile. To calculate this amount, we determine the depreciable base of $100,000 ($125,000 cost less the $25,000 estimated residual value) and then divide that base by the estimated number of miles ($100,000/400,000 miles = $0.25 per mile). If Rodriguez Trucking drives the truck 94,000 miles in 2003, the depreciation expense would be $23,500 (94,000 × $.25). We would calculate depreciation in subsequent years in the same fashion as Exhibit 7–16 shows.

Exhibit 7–16 shows that we used 58,000 miles to calculate the depreciation expense for 2007. However, this does not necessarily mean Rodriguez drove the truck only 58,000 miles that year. Although the company may have used the truck for many more than the 58,000 miles we used to calculate the depreciation expense for 2007, once the company has recorded depreciation on a total of 400,000 miles, the truck is fully depreciated and it should not be depreciated further.

Year	Actual Miles Driven		Depreciation per Mile		Depreciation Expense
2003	94,000	×	$.25	=	$ 23,500
2004	88,000	×	.25	=	22,000
2005	84,000	×	.25	=	21,000
2006	76,000	×	.25	=	19,000
2007	58,000	×	.25	=	14,500
Total	400,000				$100,000

EXHIBIT 7–16   Units-of-Production Depreciation Method

DEPRECIATION AND FEDERAL INCOME TAXES

Federal income tax regulations permit companies to deduct depreciation expense as part of their taxable income calculation. However, the ***Internal Revenue Service (IRS)*** requires that businesses use either of two prescribed depreciation methods for income tax purposes. The first is an accelerated depreciation method originally called the Accelerated Cost Recovery System (ACRS) when it was adopted by the federal government in 1981. ACRS was modified somewhat in 1986 and became known as the **Modified Accelerated Cost Recovery System (MACRS).** The other depreciation method allowed under IRS regulations is a form of the straight-line method.

Modified Accelerated Cost Recovery System (MACRS) Depreciation method taxpayers use to calculate depreciation expense for tax purposes.

Under MACRS, companies must use ***IRS***-mandated service lives regardless of how long the company feels its assets will last. Additionally, the residual value assigned to assets is zero under MACRS. Bear in mind that the purpose of tax regulations, and MACRS for that matter, is to provide a conduit for collecting taxes. MACRS is a departure from generally accepted accounting principles (GAAP) because it does not allow companies to estimate appropriate useful lives or residual values for their assets, and it is not designed to enhance the information provided to economic decision makers. Accordingly, the use of MACRS is not generally used for financial accounting purposes.

◆ DEPRECIATION'S IMPACT ON CASH

Depreciation expense has an important characteristic that distinguishes it from most other expenses. Depreciation does *not* require the outflow of cash. That is, depreciation is a *noncash* expense. Think about it. Expenses like wages expense, electricity expense, and rent expense all require the outflow of cash. But no company has to pay cash to anyone for depreciation expense. Depreciation is an allocation process that transfers the cost of an asset from assets to expense. No cash changes hands in that allocation process.

The fact that depreciation expense does not require an outflow of cash has tremendous implications to economic decision makers. They must think of depreciation expense differently than they do other expenses as they attempt to predict a company's future cash flows. In fact, banks and other lending institutions typically eliminate depreciation expense from the income statement and treat it as though it is not an expense at all. This is accomplished by *adding back* depreciation expense to net income. Exhibit 7–17 on page F–286 shows 2006 and 2007 income statements for Barlow Paving Corporation with depreciation added back for 2006. You will recall that in the Barlow examples we held everything constant from one year to the next except the items affected by depreciation. There was no depreciation in 2007, so once the depreciation is added back for 2006, the adjusted income for 2006 equals the new income for 2007.

In this chapter, we demonstrated that depreciation and the disposal of depreciable assets can have a significant impact on a company's net income and other financial

Barlow Paving Corporation Income Statements		
	2006	2007
Sales	$755,000	$941,000
Cost of goods sold	422,000	525,000
Gross margin	$333,000	$416,000
Operating expenses other than depreciation	(236,000)	(319,000)
Depreciation expense	(55,000)	0
Operating income	$ 42,000	$ 97,000
Gain (loss) on sale of machine	0	0
Net income	$ 42,000	$ 97,000
Add back depreciation expense	55,000	0
Adjusted net income	$ 97,000	$ 97,000

EXHIBIT 7-17   Barlow Paving Corporation's Net Income—Depreciation Expense Added Back

information. Economic decision makers must understand depreciation if they are to use financial statements for predicting a company's future or assessing its past performance.

Depreciation is but one of the complex areas that affect accrual basis financial statements. We will continue our discussion of these complications in Chapter 8, where we consider issues associated with sale of merchandise inventory.

Summary

Depreciation is the process of allocating the cost of long-lived assets to the periods in which the assets help to earn revenues. When a company purchases property, plant, and equipment, it records it as an asset and shows it on its balance sheet. As time passes, the cost is transferred from an asset on the balance sheet to an expense on the income statement. Recording depreciation expense accomplishes this transfer. The amount of an asset's accumulated depreciation represents the total of all of the asset's depreciation expense recognized thus far. Accumulated depreciation is reported on the balance sheet as a reduction of the asset cost.

GAAP rules allow several depreciation methods. The straight-line method allocates cost evenly over the life of the asset being depreciated. Accelerated depreciation methods, such as the double-declining-balance method, recognize a greater amount of depreciation expense in the early years of an asset's life and a smaller amount in later years.

The choice of depreciation methods affects companies' financial statements. In total, over the useful life of an asset, straight-line and double-declining-balance depreciation methods record the same amount of depreciation expense. However, in any particular period, different depreciation methods usually result in different amounts of depreciation expense, and this causes a difference in reported net income. Because the amount of depreciation expense affects accumulated depreciation, the balance sheets of companies using different depreciation methods will also be different during most of the life of the assets.

From time to time, companies sell some of their depreciable assets, and these transactions often result in gains or losses. Gains and losses affect net income in a manner similar to that of revenues and expenses, but they are shown as separate items on the income statement. Gains and losses result from activities peripheral to the major activity of the company; revenues and expenses are direct results of the company's primary business activity.

An asset's book value is its cost less the amount of its accumulated depreciation. If an asset is sold for more than its book value, the transaction results in a gain. Conversely, selling an asset for less than its book value results in a loss.

If the disposal of an asset results in a gain or loss, that outcome is reported on the income statement. If, however, an asset is sold for exactly its book value, the transaction results in no gain or loss. In any case, when a company disposes of an asset, both the asset and its corresponding accumulated depreciation account are removed from the balance sheet.

If the sale of an asset results in a gain, it cannot be assumed that this was a "wise move" or that management received a good price for the asset. A gain simply indicates that the asset was sold for more than its book value. Conversely, disposing of an asset at a loss is not necessarily an indication of poor management. Losses result when less than the book value is received for the asset. Depreciation method choice and estimates of the useful life and residual value of the asset affect book values of assets. Selling price is determined by what the buyer is willing to pay for the asset. Gains and losses are merely an indication of the relationship between book value and selling price. They should not be interpreted as anything more than that.

Recording Long-Lived Assets and Depreciation

After completing your work on this chapter appendix, you should be able to prepare the journal entries associated with long-lived depreciable assets.

DEPRECIABLE ASSET ENTRIES

The recording process for depreciable assets involves three basic types of transactions:

Transaction 1 — The purchase or other acquisitions of long-lived depreciable assets.
Transaction 2 — The depreciation of long-lived assets.
Transaction 3 — The sale or other disposals of depreciable assets.

To record these transactions, accountants generally use the following general ledger accounts:

1. *Long-lived asset accounts.* In our example, the account we will use is "Machine."
2. *An accumulated depreciation account for each asset account.* In our example, we will use "Accumulated depreciation — machine."
3. *Depreciation expense*
4. *Gain on disposal of assets*
5. *Loss on disposal of assets*

Recall that debits increase assets, expenses, and losses, and credits increase liabilities, equity, revenues, and gains. Also recall that debits and credits must equal for each journal entry. We will now examine the journal entries that the Barlow Paving Corporation would make to record the transactions for its asphalt paving machine. The first set of transactions illustrates Barlow's purchase of the machine, its use of straight-line depreciation, and its sale of the machine for $32,000. Where it is appropriate and nonrepetitive, we will analyze each transaction using the four steps we introduced in Chapter 6.

1. Determine if and when a transaction occurred, what accounts were affected, which account balances should increase, which should decrease, and by how much.
2. Determine which accounts should be debited and which should be credited.
3. Make the journal entry.
4. Review the entry to ensure it is in proper form and that the debits equal the credits.

DEPRECIABLE ASSET ENTRIES—ASSUMING STRAIGHT-LINE DEPRECIATION

Transaction 1: On January 2, 2002, Barlow Paving Corporation purchased an asphalt paving machine for cash of $300,000.

1. This transaction took place on January 2, 2002. The transaction affects the machine account and cash. The balance of the machine account should be increased by $300,000 and the balance in cash should be decreased by the same amount.
2. Because the machine account is an asset account, it is on the left side of the accounting equation and increased with a debit. Cash is also an asset account and should be decreased with a credit.
3. The general journal entry:

2002			
Jan 2	Machine	300,000	
	Cash		300,000

4. A final check of the entry reveals that we dated it correctly, made the debit part of the entry first, indented the credit account title, and the dollar amount of the debits equals that of the credits. The entry is fine.

Transaction 2: On December 31, 2002, Barlow Paving Corporation records straight-line depreciation for its paving machine in the amount of $55,000.

1. This "transaction" took place a little at a time, each day of the year. Companies can record depreciation on a routine basis, say monthly, or they can wait until the end of the year and use the balance sheet date for depreciation entries, even though they are recording depreciation for an entire accounting period. In this case, we will assume

Barlow records its depreciation at the end of the year, so we will use December 31, 2002. Depreciation transfers the cost of an asset from assets to expense. Although we could accomplish the transfer by decreasing the asset account itself, in accounting, we use a separate account called accumulated depreciation to record the reduction. In this case, the account would be accumulated depreciation—machine. This way, we can determine the asset's original cost at any time by simply examining the asset account, in this case, the machine account. Additionally, we can determine the asset's depreciation to date by examining the accumulated depreciation account. So, the transaction affects depreciation expense and the contra-asset account, accumulated depreciation—machine. We should increase the depreciation expense account by $55,000. What about accumulated depreciation? To determine the machine's book value, we subtract its accumulated depreciation from the machine account. Therefore, to reduce the machines book value, accumulated depreciation—machine should be increased by $55,000.

2. To increase depreciation expense, we debit it, and to increase accumulated depreciation—machine, a contra-asset account, we credit it.
3. The general journal entry:

        2002
        Dec 31 Depreciation expense   55,000
                Accumulated depreciation—machine   55,000

4. A final check of the entry reveals that the entry is fine.

We are not going to prepare entries for each year's depreciation because, except for the date, the depreciation entries for 2003, 2004, 2005, and 2006 would be identical to the one we made for December 31, 2002.

Recording a Gain on Disposal of Assets

Before we record the disposal of an asset, we must record depreciation up to the moment the asset is taken out of service. Because Barlow's paving machine was fully depreciated at the time of its sale, no additional depreciation entry is needed.

The entry we make to record the disposal of the paving machine removes the asset and the accumulated depreciation associated with the asset from Barlow's books. Removing the asset and its accumulated depreciation from Barlow's books is reasonable because, once the machine is sold, Barlow no longer owns it. The entry also records the gain or loss on the sale of the asset.

Transaction 3: Barlow sold its paving machine on January 2, 2007, for cash of $32,000 resulting in a $7,000 gain.

1. This transaction took place on January 2, 2007. Since Barlow is selling the paving machine, we should remove it and its accumulated depreciation from Barlow's books. We should also record the cash Barlow receives and the resulting gain or loss on the disposal. Accordingly, we should decrease the machine account and accumulated depreciation—machine and increase cash. In this particular disposal transaction, we should increase gain on disposal of assets because the proceeds from the sale of the asset exceed its book value. We should increase cash by the $32,000 Barlow received. We should decrease the machine account and accumulated depreciation—machine by $300,000 and $275,000, respectively, to reduce their balance to zero. We should increase gain on disposal of assets by the amount that the proceeds from the sale exceed the book value of the asset, in this case, $7,000.
2. We increase cash with a debit, decrease accumulated depreciation—machine with a debit, decrease machine with a credit, and increase gain on disposal of assets with a credit.
3. The general journal entry:

        2007
        Jan 2   Cash   32,000
                Accumulated depreciation—machine   275,000
                    Machine   300,000
                    Gain on disposal of assets   7,000

4. A final check of the entry reveals that the entry is fine.

Exhibit 7A–1 on page F–290 shows T-account entries for the Barlow machine assuming the company used straight-line depreciation. Keep in mind that for this presentation, we show all of the depreciation entries in the depreciation expense account even though the company would actually close the depreciation expense account to zero at the end of each year as part of the closing process.

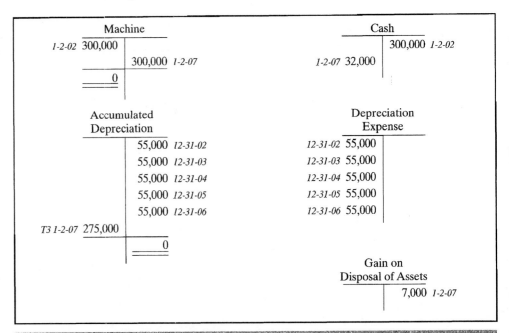

EXHIBIT 7A–1 T-Account Entries for Barlow's Paving Machine Assuming Straight-Line Depreciation

Recording a Loss on Disposal of Assets

To demonstrate recording a loss on disposal of assets, let's assume that instead of receiving $32,000 for its paving machine, Barlow only received $19,000 (transaction 3). This change would not affect the acquisition entry or the depreciation entries, but, as we show below, the entry to record the disposal of the paving machine is different under this assumption.

Transaction 3: Assume Barlow sold its paving machine on January 2, 2007, for cash of $19,000 resulting in a $6,000 loss.

1. This transaction took place on January 2, 2007. As before, since we are selling the paving machine, we should remove it and its accumulated depreciation. We should also record the cash received and the resulting gain or loss on the disposal. In this particular disposal transaction, *loss* on disposal of assets should be increased because the proceeds from the sale of the asset are less than its book value. We should increase cash by the $19,000 Barlow received. We should decrease the machine account and accumulated depreciation—machine by $300,000 and $275,000, respectively, to reduce their balance to zero. We should increase loss on disposal of assets by the amount that the book value of the asset sold exceeds the proceeds from the sale, in this case, $6,000.
2. We increase cash with a debit, decrease accumulated depreciation—machine with a debit, and increase loss on disposal of assets with a debit. We decrease machine with a credit.
3. The general journal entry:

```
2007
Jan 2   Cash                                      19,000
        Accumulated depreciation—machine         275,000
        Loss on disposal of assets                 6,000
             Machine                                        300,000
```

4. The entry seems fine.

Next we will record the disposal of Barlow's paving machine assuming the company sold it for $25,000.

Sale of an Asset for Book Value

When the selling price of an asset is exactly equal to the asset's book value, there is no gain or loss. The following entry shows a journal entry to record the sale of Barlow's paving machine for an amount exactly equal to its book value. This is an unlikely event indeed.

Transaction 3: Assume Barlow sold its paving machine on January 2, 2007, for cash of $25,000, an amount equal to the machine's book value.

1. This transaction took place on January 2, 2007. The increases and decreases for this version of Transaction 3 are the same as they were for the first two versions except that there is no gain or loss to record. We should increase cash by the $25,000 Barlow received. Again, we should decrease the machine account and accumulated depreciation—machine by $300,000 and $275,000, respectively. There is no gain or loss to record on this version of the transaction because we assume that Barlow sold the asset for an amount equal to its book value.
2. We increase cash with a debit, decrease accumulated depreciation—machine with a debit, and decrease machine with a credit.
3. The general journal entry:

2007			
Jan 2	Cash	25,000	
	Accumulated depreciation—machine	275,000	
	Machine		300,000

4. The entry seems fine.

Depreciable Asset Entries—Assuming Double-Declining-Balance Depreciation

The entries associated with depreciable assets are basically the same regardless of the depreciation method the company uses. So, whether a company uses the double-declining-balance depreciation method or straight-line, its depreciable asset entries will be pretty much the same except for the dollar amounts. The entries follow the same format and use the same accounts. The only differences are associated with the amount of annual depreciation expense. Because the double-declining-balance entries are so similar to straight-line entries, to avoid repetition, we will not present them.

Appendix Summary

When recording transactions for long-lived assets, the accounts companies use include a long-lived asset account, accumulated depreciation, depreciation expense, and a gain or loss account for disposal of assets. Companies record the original purchase of an asset as a debit to the asset account. Recording annual depreciation results in a debit to depreciation expense and a credit to accumulated depreciation, a contra-asset account. When a company sells an asset, it must record depreciation up to the moment the asset is taken out of service, then the company debits the asset received (usually cash), debits accumulated depreciation, credits the asset sold, and credits a gain on the sale or debits a loss on the sale to balance the journal entry.

Key Terms

- accelerated depreciation methods, F–268
- accumulated depreciation, F–269
- book value, F–269
- depreciable base, F–267
- depreciation, F–265
- double-declining-balance method, F–271
- fully depreciated, F–270
- gains, F–275
- historical cost principle, F–274
- losses, F–275
- Modified Accelerated Cost Recovery System (MACRS), F–285
- straight-line depreciation, F–268
- units-of-production depreciation method, F–284

Review the Facts

A. Provide three examples of long-lived depreciable assets.
B. In an accounting context, how is depreciation defined?
C. What two estimates made by management will affect the amount of depreciation recorded each period?
D. What is the depreciable base of an asset?
E. Explain what is meant by an accelerated depreciation method.
F. Theoretically, in what situation is an accelerated depreciation method the appropriate choice?
G. Explain how the amount of depreciation expense is calculated using straight-line depreciation.

H. What is meant by an asset's book value?

I. What does the amount of accumulated depreciation represent?

J. Describe the process of determining depreciation expense using the double-declining-balance method.

K. Compared to straight-line depreciation, what is the effect of an accelerated depreciation method on the balance sheet? On the income statement?

L. Regardless of what depreciation method is used, at what point is an asset considered "fully depreciated"?

M. On what financial statement do gains and losses appear?

N. What is the difference between a revenue and a gain? A loss and an expense?

O. How is a gain or loss calculated for the sale of an asset?

P. Describe the units-of-production method of depreciation.

Q. How do MACRS depreciation and depreciation under GAAP differ?

Apply What You Have Learned ●

LO 1, 2, 3, & 4: TERMINOLOGY

7–16. Presented below is a list of items relating to the concepts discussed in this chapter, followed by definitions of those items in scrambled order:

a. Accelerated depreciation   f. Straight-line depreciation
b. Book value   g. Gains
c. Gain on sale of asset   h. Loss on sale of asset
d. Losses   i. Depreciable base
e. Estimated useful life   j. Production method

1. _____ A factor determining how much of an asset's cost will be allocated to the periods supposedly benefited.

2. _____ A depreciation method that uses activity instead of time as the basis of allocation.

3. _____ More of the cost of a long-lived asset is converted to expense in the early years of its life than in later years.

4. _____ The cost of a long-lived asset less the estimated residual value.

5. _____ Results when a depreciable asset is sold for more than its book value.

6. _____ An equal amount of a long-lived asset's cost is converted to expense in each year of its useful life.

7. _____ Net inflows resulting from peripheral activities.

8. _____ The cost of a long-lived depreciable asset less its accumulated depreciation.

9. _____ Results when a depreciable asset is sold for less than its book value.

10. _____ Net outflows resulting from peripheral activities.

Required: Match the letter next to each item on the list with the appropriate definition. Use each letter only once.

LO 1: DEPRECIATION PROCESS

7–17. Evaluate the following statement and write a brief response: "The depreciation process is an accounting process designed to value fixed assets on the balance sheet."

LO 2: COMPUTE DEPRECIATION EXPENSE—STRAIGHT-LINE METHOD

7–18. **Required:** Compute annual straight-line depreciation expense for the following situation:

Equipment cost	$74,840
Estimated residual value	$12,000
Estimated useful life	5 Years

LO 2: COMPUTE DEPRECIATION EXPENSE—STRAIGHT-LINE METHOD

7–19. **Required:** Compute annual straight-line depreciation expense for the following situation:

Machinery cost	$643,778
Estimated residual value	$50,000
Estimated useful life	7 Years

LO 2: COMPUTE DEPRECIATION EXPENSE—STRAIGHT-LINE METHOD

7–20. **Required:** Compute annual straight-line depreciation expense for the following situation:

Production equipment cost	$207,888
Estimated residual value	$20,000
Estimated useful life	8 Years

LO 2: COMPUTE DEPRECIATION EXPENSE—STRAIGHT-LINE METHOD

7–21. Jerry Proctor and Company purchased a lathe for use in its manufacturing operation. The machine cost $150,000, has a five-year estimated useful life, and will be depreciated using the straight-line method. The only thing remaining to be determined before yearly depreciation expense can be calculated is the lathe's estimated residual value.

The alternatives are

1. $10,000 estimated residual value
2. $20,000 estimated residual value
3. $30,000 estimated residual value

Required:

a. Calculate the yearly depreciation expense for the new lathe under each of the alternatives given.
b. Which of the three alternatives will result in the highest net income?
c. How long will the new lathe be useful as an asset to Proctor and Company? What factors could change this time period?

LO 2: COMPUTE DEPRECIATION EXPENSE—STRAIGHT-LINE METHOD

7–22. Betty Hart Company, Inc., has just purchased a computer for use in its manufacturing operation. The machine cost $75,000, has a four-year estimated useful life, and will be depreciated using the straight-line method. The only thing remaining to be determined before yearly depreciation expense can be calculated is the estimated residual value.

The alternatives are

1. $7,500 estimated residual value
2. $12,500 estimated residual value
3. $17,500 estimated residual value

Required:

a. Calculate the yearly depreciation expense for the new computer under each of the alternatives given.
b. Which of the three alternatives will result in the highest net income? Which of the three alternatives will result in the lowest net income?
c. How long will the new computer be useful as an asset to Hart? What factors could change this time period?

LO 2: COMPUTE DEPRECIATION EXPENSE—STRAIGHT-LINE METHOD

7–23. Carl Young Publishing Company purchased a new printing press for a total installed cost of $700,000. The printing press will be depreciated using the straight-line method. Michael Hoff, the corporate controller, is trying to decide on an estimated useful life and an estimated residual value for the asset.

The alternatives are

1. A six-year estimated useful life with a $40,000 estimated residual value
2. A five-year estimated useful life with a $100,000 estimated residual value
3. A four-year estimated useful life with a $140,000 estimated residual value

Required:

a. Calculate the yearly depreciation expense for the new printing press under each of the alternatives given.
b. Which of the three alternatives will result in the lowest yearly net income? Which of the three alternatives will result in the highest yearly net income?
c. What should be the deciding factor in selecting among the three alternatives?

LO 2: COMPUTE DEPRECIATION EXPENSE—STRAIGHT-LINE METHOD

7–24. The Pizzeria Restaurant Company purchased a new walk-in freezer for a total installed cost of $250,000. The walk-in freezer will be depreciated using the straight-line method. Richard Porter, the corporate controller, is trying to determine an estimated useful life and residual value for the asset.

His alternatives are

1. A five-year estimated useful life with a $10,000 estimated residual value
2. A four-year estimated useful life with a $25,000 estimated residual value
3. A three-year estimated useful life with a $50,000 estimated residual value

Required:

a. Calculate the yearly depreciation expense for the new freezer under each of the alternatives given.
b. Which of the three alternatives will result in the lowest yearly net income? Which of the three alternatives will result in the highest yearly net income?
c. What should be the deciding factor in selecting among the three alternatives?

LO 2: COMPUTE DEPRECIATION EXPENSE—DOUBLE-DECLINING-BALANCE METHOD

7–25. **Required:** Based on the following information, prepare a table that shows the depreciation expense for each year using the double-declining-balance method:

Computer equipment cost	$36,000
Estimated residual value	$6000
Estimated useful life	5 Years

LO 2: COMPUTE DEPRECIATION EXPENSE—DOUBLE-DECLINING-BALANCE METHOD

7–26. **Required:** Based on the following information, prepare a table that shows the depreciation expense for each year using the double-declining-balance method:

Machinery cost	$76,000
Estimated residual value	$5,000
Estimated useful life	4 Years

LO 2: COMPUTE DEPRECIATION EXPENSE—DOUBLE-DECLINING-BALANCE METHOD

7–27. **Required:** Based on the following information, prepare a table that shows the depreciation expense for each year using the double-declining-balance method:

Production machinery cost	$16,000
Estimated residual value	$2,000
Estimated useful life	5 Years

LO 2: COMPUTE DEPRECIATION EXPENSE—STRAIGHT-LINE AND DOUBLE-DECLINING-BALANCE METHODS

7–28. The following information is available:

Machinery cost	$203,475
Estimated residual value	$25,000
Estimated useful life	5 Years

Required:

a. Compute annual straight-line depreciation expense.
b. Prepare a table that shows the depreciation expense for each year using the double-declining-balance method.

LO 2: COMPUTE DEPRECIATION EXPENSE—STRAIGHT-LINE AND DOUBLE-DECLINING-BALANCE METHODS

7–29. The following information is available for Oxy's of Pinecrest, Inc.:

Equipment cost	$5,932
Estimated residual value	$900
Estimated useful life	4 Years

Required:

a. Compute annual straight-line depreciation expense.
b. Prepare a table that shows the depreciation expense for each year using the double-declining-balance method.

LO 2: COMPUTE DEPRECIATION EXPENSE—STRAIGHT-LINE AND DOUBLE-DECLINING-BALANCE METHODS

7–30. The following information is available:

Truck cost	$46,390
Estimated residual value	$7,000
Estimated useful life	5 Years

Required:

a. Compute annual straight-line depreciation expense.
b. Prepare a table that shows the depreciation expense for each year using the double-declining-balance method.

LO 2: COMPUTE DEPRECIATION EXPENSE AND BOOK VALUE— DOUBLE-DECLINING-BALANCE METHOD

7–31. Cramer Company purchased a high-tech assembler on January 2, 2004, for a total cost of $600,000. The assembler has an estimated useful life to the company of five years. Cramer thinks it can sell the used assembler for $60,000 after five years. The company chose to depreciate the new assembler using the double-declining-balance method.

Required:

a. Prepare a schedule showing the amount of depreciation expense for each of the five years of the estimated useful life.
b. What will be the book value of the assembler at the end of the five-year estimated useful life?
c. What does book value represent?

LO 2: COMPUTE DEPRECIATION EXPENSE AND BOOK VALUE— DOUBLE-DECLINING-BALANCE METHOD

7–32. Winch Company purchased an earthmoving machine on January 2, 2003, for a total cost of $900,000. The earthmover has an estimated useful life to the company of four years. Winch believes it can sell the used earthmover for $80,000 after four years. The company selected the double-declining-balance method of depreciation.

Required:

a. Prepare a schedule showing the amount of depreciation expense for each of the four years of the estimated useful life.
b. What will be the book value of the earthmover at the end of the four-year estimated useful life?
c. What does book value represent?

LO 2: COMPUTE DEPRECIATION EXPENSE—STRAIGHT-LINE AND DOUBLE-DECLINING-BALANCE METHODS

7–33. Danielle Company purchased a sophisticated stamping machine on January 2, 2004, for $480,000. The estimated useful life of the stamping machine is six years. Danielle estimates the machine's residual value is $54,000.

Required:

    a. Calculate the yearly depreciation expense for the stamping machine assuming the company uses the straight-line depreciation method.

    b. Prepare a schedule showing the amount of depreciation expense for each of the six years of the estimated useful life assuming the company uses the double-declining-balance depreciation method.

LO 2: COMPUTE DEPRECIATION EXPENSE—STRAIGHT-LINE AND DOUBLE-DECLINING-BALANCE METHODS

7–34. Hal Clark, Inc., purchased a pasteurizing machine on January 2, 2004, for $375,000. The estimated useful life of the machine is four years with a residual value of $45,000.

Required:

    a. Calculate the yearly depreciation expense for the machine assuming the company uses the straight-line depreciation method.

    b. Prepare a schedule showing the amount of depreciation expense for each of the four years of the estimated useful life assuming the company uses the double-declining-balance depreciation method.

LO 1, 2, & 3: COMPUTE DEPRECIATION EXPENSE—STRAIGHT-LINE AND DOUBLE-DECLINING-BALANCE METHODS

7–35. David Brown, Inc., purchased a fleet of delivery trucks on January 2, 2004, for $700,000. The estimated useful life of the fleet is four years, after which Brown estimates it can sell the entire fleet for $50,000.

Required:

    a. Calculate the yearly depreciation expense for the fleet of vehicles assuming the company uses the straight-line depreciation method.

    b. Prepare a schedule showing the amount of depreciation expense for each of the four years of the estimated useful life assuming the company uses the double-declining-balance depreciation method.

    c. Address the following questions:

        1. Double-declining-balance calculates depreciation at twice the straight-line rate. Why is the amount of depreciation expense in 2004 under double-declining-balance not exactly twice the amount under straight-line for 2004?

        2. Over the four-year estimated useful life of the vehicles, how much depreciation expense will be charged against income using the straight-line method? How much will be charged against income using the double-declining-balance method?

        3. Discuss the impact on the net income of each method of depreciation in the first two years of the life of the asset.

LO 1, 2, & 3: COMPUTE DEPRECIATION EXPENSE—STRAIGHT-LINE AND DOUBLE-DECLINING-BALANCE METHODS

7–36. Mandy and Jessie, Inc., purchased equipment on January 2, 2004, for $600,000. The corporation estimates the useful life of the equipment is three years, after which it can sell the equipment for $51,000.

Required:

    a. Calculate the yearly depreciation expense for the equipment assuming the company uses the straight-line depreciation method.

    b. Prepare a schedule showing the amount of depreciation expense for each of the three years of the estimated useful life assuming the company uses the double-declining-balance depreciation method.

    c. Address the following questions:

        1. Double-declining-balance calculates depreciation at twice the straight-line rate. Why is the amount of depreciation expense in 2004 under double-declining-balance not exactly twice the amount under straight-line for 2004?

2. Over the three-year estimated useful life of the equipment, how much depreciation expense will be charged against income using the straight-line method? How much will be charged against income using the double-declining-balance method?
3. Discuss the impact on the net income of each method of depreciation in the first two years of partial year life of the asset.

LO 2 & 5: COMPUTE PARTIAL YEAR DEPRECIATION EXPENSE AND GAIN OR LOSS—STRAIGHT-LINE METHOD

7–37.   Roberts Company purchased a machine in January 2003 for $200,000. When originally purchased, the machine had an estimated useful life of five years and an estimated residual value of $30,000. The company uses straight-line depreciation. It is now June 30, 2006, and the company has decided to dispose of the machine.

Required:

   a. Calculate the book value of the machine as of June 30, 2006.
   b. Calculate the gain or loss on the sale of the machine assuming Roberts sells it for $102,000.
   c. Calculate the gain or loss on the sale of the machine assuming Roberts sells it for $25,000.

LO 2 & 5: COMPUTE PARTIAL YEAR DEPRECIATION EXPENSE AND GAIN OR LOSS—STRAIGHT-LINE METHOD

7–38.   Cohen Company purchased a machine in January 2004 and paid $150,000 for it. When originally purchased, the machine had an estimated useful life of four years and an estimated residual value of $10,000. The company uses straight-line depreciation. It is now September 30, 2006, and the company has decided to dispose of the machine.

Required:

   a. Calculate the book value of the machine as of September 30, 2006.
   b. Calculate the gain or loss on the sale of the machine assuming Cohen sells it for $172,000.
   c. Calculate the gain or loss on the sale of the machine assuming Cohen sells it for $25,000.

LO 2 & 5: COMPUTE DEPRECIATION EXPENSE AND GAIN OR LOSS—STRAIGHT-LINE METHOD

7–39.   Colton Company purchased a machine in January 2003 for $450,000. When originally purchased, the machine had an estimated useful life of 10 years and an estimated residual value of $60,000. The company uses straight-line depreciation. It is now January 2, 2009, and the company has decided to dispose of the machine.

Required:

   a. Calculate the book value of the machine as of December 31, 2008.
   b. Calculate the gain or loss on the sale of the machine assuming Colton sells it for $130,000.
   c. Calculate the gain or loss on the sale of the machine assuming Colton sells it for $30,000.

LO 1, 2, 3, 4, 5, & 6: IMPACT OF DEPRECIATION METHOD ON GAINS AND LOSSES

7–40.   Pam and Cam are twins. Each of them has her own company. Three years ago, on the same day, they each purchased copiers for use by their companies. The machines were identical in every way and cost exactly the same amount ($28,000). The machines had the same estimated useful life (five years) and the same estimated residual value ($3,000). The only difference was the depreciation method chosen. Nails by Pam chose to depreciate its copier using the straight-line method, while Cam's Sportswear chose an accelerated depreciation method.

   Due to technological developments in copy machines, at the end of two years, Pam decided to sell her old machine and buy a new one. Cam decided to do the same thing. In fact, they each received exactly the same amount when they sold their machines ($16,500). Later, while they were having lunch together, Cam mentioned that when she sold her copier, she had a gain of $6,420 on the sale. Pam kept quiet but was confused because she knew she had sold her copier for exactly the same amount as Cam, yet the sale of her copier had resulted in a loss of $1,500.

Required: Explain how Pam could have had a loss of $1,500 on the sale of her copier, while Cam had a sizable gain.

LO 2, 3, 5, & 6: IMPACT OF DEPRECIATION METHOD ON GAINS AND LOSSES

7–41. Leroy Bowden and Bill Hudik each ran their own automotive repair shop. On January 2, 2004, each of them bought a new hydraulic vehicle lift costing $10,000. Each of the lifts was expected to have an eight-year life and a $2,000 residual value. Bowden Auto Repair used straight-line depreciation, and Hudik Automotive Service used the double-declining-balance method. At the end of three years, each of them sold their lifts for $5,500.

Required:

  a. Compute the depreciation for both Bowden and Hudik through the third year.
  b. Compute the gain or loss that each would recognize on the sale of their machine.
  c. If the gain or loss is different for each of them, explain why.

LO 2, 3, 5, & 6: IMPACT OF DEPRECIATION METHOD ON GAINS AND LOSSES

7–42. Penny and Linda each ran their own cooking school. Each bought a new piece of equipment costing $20,000 on January 2, 2004. The equipment was expected to have a five-year useful life and a $2,000 residual value. Cooking with Penny used straight-line depreciation and Linda's Kitchen used double-declining-balance depreciation. At the end of three years, each of them sold their equipment for $11,000.

Required:

  a. Compute the depreciation for both Penny and Linda through the third year.
  b. Compute the gain or loss that each would recognize on the sale of the equipment.
  c. If the gain or loss is different for each of them, explain why.

LO 2, 3, 5, & 6: IMPACT OF DEPRECIATION METHOD ON GAINS AND LOSSES

7–43. Jerry and Pete each ran their own construction business. Each bought a new piece of equipment costing $40,000 on January 2, 2004. The equipment was expected to have a five-year useful life and $4,000 residual value. Jerry's Home Repairs used straight-line depreciation and Pete's Custom Kitchens used double-declining-balance depreciation. At the end of three years, each of them sold their machines for $22,000.

Required:

  a. Compute the depreciation for both Jerry and Pete through the third year.
  b. Compute the gain or loss that each would recognize on the sale of the machine.
  c. If the gain or loss is different for each of them, explain why.

LO 4: MEANING OF GAINS AND LOSSES

7–44. Explain in your own words what a gain or loss on the sale of long-lived depreciable assets means and how the gain or loss relates to depreciation expense.

LO 2: COMPUTE DEPRECIATION EXPENSE—UNITS-OF-PRODUCTION METHOD

7–45. Strickland, Inc., purchased a delivery truck on January 2, 2003, for $70,000. Strickland estimates the useful life of the vehicle is 200,000 miles and the residual value at $10,000. The truck is driven 40,000 miles in 2003; 45,000 miles in 2004; 60,000 miles in 2005; and 65,000 miles in 2006.

Required: Calculate the yearly depreciation expense for the vehicle assuming the company uses the units-of-production depreciation method.

LO 2: COMPUTE DEPRECIATION EXPENSE—UNITS-OF-PRODUCTION METHOD

7–46. McLeod, Inc., purchased a printing press on January 2, 2003, for $95,000. McLeod estimates the useful life of the press is 2,000,000 pages or five years, after which he can sell the press for $5,000. The press produces 500,000 pages in 2003; 400,000 pages in 2004; 430,000 pages in 2005; 600,000 pages in 2006; and 350,000 pages in 2007.

Required: Calculate the yearly depreciation expense for the press assuming the company uses the units-of-production depreciation method.

LO 2: COMPUTE DEPRECIATION EXPENSE—UNITS-OF-PRODUCTION METHOD

7–47. Patten, Inc., purchased a lathe on January 2, 2003, for $200,000. Patten estimates its useful life as 10,000 hours or four years and its residual value at $4,000. He uses the lathe for 2,000 hours in 2003; 2,800 hours in 2004; 3,200 hours in 2005; and 2,600 hours in 2006.

Required: Calculate the yearly depreciation expense for the machine assuming the company uses the units-of-production depreciation method.

LO 2 & 7: APPENDIX—RECORDING ASSETS AND STRAIGHT-LINE DEPRECIATION

7–48. On January 2, 2004, Cunningham Corporation purchased a new piece of equipment for $60,000 cash. Cunningham uses straight-line depreciation and estimates the useful life of the equipment at five years with a residual value of $10,000.

Required:

    a. Prepare the journal entry to record the purchase of the asset.

    b. Prepare the journal entries to record the depreciation for the first year of life of the asset.

LO 2 & 7: APPENDIX—RECORDING ASSETS AND STRAIGHT-LINE DEPRECIATION

7–49. On January 2, 2004, Holzmann, Inc., purchased a new piece of equipment for $560,000. The company paid $125,000 in cash and signed a promissory note to finance the balance. Holzmann uses straight-line depreciation and estimates the useful life of the equipment at six years with a residual value of $50,000.

Required:

    a. Prepare the journal entry to record the purchase of the asset.

    b. Prepare the journal entry to record the depreciation for the first year of life of the asset.

LO 2 & 7: APPENDIX—RECORDING ASSETS AND STRAIGHT-LINE DEPRECIATION

7–50. On January 2, 2004, Miceli Corporation purchased a new piece of equipment for $75,000 cash. Miceli uses straight-line depreciation and estimates the useful life of the equipment at seven years with a residual value of $5,000.

Required:

    a. Prepare the journal entry to record the purchase of the asset.

    b. Prepare the journal entry to record the depreciation for the first year of life of the asset.

LO 2 & 7: APPENDIX—RECORDING ASSETS AND STRAIGHT-LINE DEPRECIATION

7–51. On January 2, 2004, Chris Scott Corporation purchased a new piece of equipment for $85,000. The company paid $8,000 in cash and signed a promissory note for the balance. Scott uses straight-line depreciation and estimates the useful life of the equipment at seven years with a residual value of $11,500.

Required:

    a. Prepare the journal entry to record the purchase of the asset.

    b. Prepare the journal entry to record the depreciation for the first year of the life of the asset.

LO 2, 5, & 7: APPENDIX—COMPUTE GAIN OR LOSS, STRAIGHT-LINE DEPRECIATION, RECORD SALE OF ASSET

7–52. On January 2, 2005, Esposito, Inc., purchased a new piece of equipment for $650,000. The company paid $130,000 in cash and borrowed the remainder from the bank. Esposito uses straight-line depreciation and estimates the useful life of the equipment at six years with a residual value of $75,000.

Required:

    a. Compute the gain or loss if the company uses straight-line depreciation and sells the equipment for $86,000 at the end of the fourth year.

    b. Prepare the journal entry to record the sale of the equipment.

LO 2, 5, & 7: APPENDIX—COMPUTE DOUBLE-DECLINING-BALANCE DEPRECIATION, COMPUTE GAIN OR LOSS, RECORD SALE OF ASSET

7–53. On January 2, 2004, Allen Corporation purchased a new piece of equipment for $75,000. The company paid $5,000 in cash and borrowed the remainder from the bank. Allen estimates the useful life of the equipment at seven years with a residual value of $12,000.

Required:

    a. Compute the gain or loss if the company uses double-declining-balance depreciation and sells the equipment for $8,000 at the end of the fourth year.

    b. Prepare the journal entry to record the sale of the equipment.

LO 2, 5, & 7: APPENDIX—COMPUTE AND RECORD STRAIGHT-LINE DEPRECIATION, COMPUTE GAIN OR LOSS, RECORD SALE OF ASSET

7–54. J. T. Company purchased a stamping machine on January 2, 2004, for $480,000. The estimated useful life of the stamping machine is five years. The machine has an estimated residual value of $40,000.

Required:

    a. Calculate the yearly depreciation expense for the stamping machine assuming the company uses the straight-line depreciation method.

    b. Record the journal entries for the depreciation that would be required each year.

    c. Prepare the required journal entries to record the sale of the machine at the end of two years for $350,000.

LO 2, 5, 6, & 7: APPENDIX—COMPUTE AND RECORD DOUBLE-DECLINING-BALANCE DEPRECIATION, COMPUTE GAIN OR LOSS, RECORD SALE OF ASSET

7–55. Cooke Company purchased a pasteurizing machine on January 2, 2004, for $375,000. The estimated useful life of the machine is five years. The machine has an estimated residual value of $40,000.

Required:

    a. Calculate the yearly depreciation expense for the machine assuming the company uses the double-declining-balance depreciation method and prepare the journal entries to record depreciation each year.

    b. Assuming the machine is sold at the end of December 2006 for $50,000, prepare the required entry to record the sale.

    c. Assuming the machine is sold at the end of April 2006 for $50,000, prepare the required entry to record the sale.

    d. Is it better to sell the machine in April or December? Explain your answer.

LO 2, 5, 6, & 7: APPENDIX—COMPUTE AND RECORD STRAIGHT-LINE DEPRECIATION, COMPUTE GAIN OR LOSS, RECORD SALE OF ASSET

7–56. Suzanne, Inc., purchased a delivery truck on January 2, 2004, for $70,000. The estimated useful life of the vehicle is four years, after which Suzanne thinks it will be able to sell it for $5,000.

Required:

    a. Calculate the yearly depreciation expense for the vehicle assuming the company uses the straight-line depreciation method and prepare the journal entries to record the depreciation.

    b. Assume the truck is sold at the end of December of the fourth year for $7,000. Prepare the journal entry to record the transaction.

    c. Assume the truck is sold on March 31, 2007, for $3,000. Prepare the journal entry to record the transaction.

    d. Is it better to sell the truck at the end of December of the fourth year or on March 31, 2007? Explain your answer.

LO 2, 3, 5, & 7: APPENDIX—COMPUTE AND RECORD STRAIGHT-LINE AND DOUBLE-DECLINING-BALANCE DEPRECIATION, COMPUTE GAIN OR LOSS, RECORD SALE OF ASSET

7–57. Jerry and Pete each run their own construction business. Each bought a new piece of equipment costing $40,000 on January 2, 2004. The equipment is expected to have a five-year useful life and a $4,000 residual value. Jerry's Home Repairs uses straight-line depreciation and Pete's Custom Kitchens uses double-declining-balance depreciation. On June 30, 2007, each of them sold their machines for $22,000.

Required:

    a. Compute the depreciation for both Jerry and Pete through the date of sale.

    b. Compute the gain or loss that each would recognize on the sale of the equipment.

    c. Prepare the journal entries necessary to record the purchase, annual depreciation, and sale of Jerry's and Pete's equipment.

Financial Reporting Exercises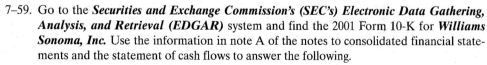

7–58. Go to *Pier 1*'s annual report on page F–503. Look in the notes to consolidated financial statements section under the subheading Properties, Maintenance, and Repairs to answer the following.

Required:

    a. For which of the items listed does ***Pier 1 Imports, Inc.,*** use depreciation?

    b. How long are the average useful lives for the items listed?

    c. For which of the items listed does ***Pier 1 Imports, Inc.,*** not use depreciation? Why?

    d. What type of depreciation calculations do they use?

    e. What were their total depreciation costs in 2000–2002?

    f. What do they do when they sell/dispose of an asset that has been partially or fully depreciated?

7–59. Go to the ***Securities and Exchange Commission's (SEC's) Electronic Data Gathering, Analysis, and Retrieval (EDGAR)*** system and find the 2001 Form 10-K for ***Williams Sonoma, Inc.*** Use the information in note A of the notes to consolidated financial statements and the statement of cash flows to answer the following.

Required:

    a. What type of depreciation method does ***Williams Sonoma, Inc.,*** employ?

    b. What are the useful lives assigned to the different types of assets by ***Williams Sonoma, Inc.?***

    c. What was its total depreciation cost in 2000–2002?

7–60. Go to the SEC's EDGAR system and find the 2001 Form 10-K for ***Bed Bath & Beyond, Inc.*** Use the information in the notes to consolidated financial statements to answer the following.

Required:

    a. Determine the type of depreciation methods used for different types of long-lived assets.

    b. What are the useful lives assigned to the different types of assets by ***Bed Bath & Beyond, Inc.?***

    c. What was its total depreciation cost in 2000–2002?

7–61. Continuation of problems 7–58, 7–59, and 7–60.

Required:

    a. Prepare a list that compares the depreciation methods and amounts of depreciation of ***Pier 1 Imports, Inc., Williams Sonoma, Inc.,*** and ***Bed Bath & Beyond, Inc.***

    b. What are the similarities or significant differences that you see? What do you think they mean?

ANNUAL REPORT PROJECT

7–62. Section 7—Long-Lived Assets

This section of the annual report project focuses on your company's property, plant, and equipment and its depreciation.

Required: Prepare a report that includes the following information:

    a. A schedule that presents and compares the property, plant, and equipment of your company and the peer company you selected for the assignment for Section 6. For example, include a presentation of each company's property, plant, and equipment for the two years listed in the financial reports. Also, present the total of accumulated depreciation associated with property, plant, and equipment for each company for each year. You can find information about property, plant, and equipment and depreciation in the balance sheet and the notes to the financial statements.

    b. Identify the method or methods of depreciation used by the two companies. In addition, comment on the significance of any similarities or differences between the depreciation methods used by the two companies.

    c. Comment on the estimates used by the two companies for depreciation calculations. For example, what are the estimates used by each company? Comment on the significance of any similarities or differences between the estimates used by the two companies.

    d. A schedule that presents and compares the intangible assets of your company and the peer company you selected. Comment on the intangible assets of each company. For example, which is most significant? Has either company recognized any sizable losses due to the impaired value of intangible assets? If so, read the notes to the financial statements and fully explain the circumstances relating to the loss. For example, did the loss relate to a new accounting pronouncement? Does the company comment on whether it is likely that such a loss will occur again in the future?

    e. Your report should conclude with comments regarding what you think of your company and how you think your company compares to its peer in light of the work you did in connection with this assignment.

CHAPTER 8

Accounting for Inventory

Palmer Nursery has been in business for over 20 years. It sells the same products— plants, shrubs, trees, and garden supplies—year in and year out. But the owners feel that because the company's business practices might be out of step with the times, their sales may be suffering. They hire you, a business consultant, to suggest ways they can improve performance.

One of the first things you do is review Palmer's financial statements. You notice that the dollar amount of inventory shown on their balance sheet seems quite low. Surely, you reason, such a low dollar value can't represent much in the way of salable product. You are alarmed by this, so you check other companies in the industry and confirm that there must be a problem. These other companies (which are of comparable size to Palmer) all show much higher dollar amounts of inventory on their balance sheets. You wonder if Palmer's low inventory might be resulting in lost sales. When you make your first site visit, you are surprised to see that Palmer has plenty of saleable merchandise on hand. In fact, they may have *too much*! There are trees, shrubs, shovels, and hoses everywhere. How, you ask yourself, can there be so much physical inventory on hand when the balance sheet shows such a low inventory dollar amount? So you approach the company's bookkeeper and ask her to explain it. She looks at you and says one word: LIFO.

You decide—wisely—that you had better go back to your office and learn more about accounting for inventory before you say much more to the folks at Palmer.

In Chapter 7, we explored the impact that the latitude generally accepted accounting principles (GAAP) permit in accounting for long-lived depreciable assets has on financial statements. Similarly, GAAP permit a considerable degree of latitude in accounting cost of products companies sell, and this latitude also can have a significant effect on financial statements.

Accrual accounting generally requires companies to recognize revenue when it is earned and when it is realized or realizable. Therefore, accrual accounting requires companies to match expenses—in this case, the cost of the product sold—with the revenues the expenses helped generate. GAAP permit companies to select from a variety of acceptable accounting methods to match sales revenue with the cost of the goods sold. In this chapter, we will look at three of them. Like depreciation, this is an example of how the financial statements of companies may vary under accrual accounting. In fact, the way companies account for the flow of merchandise inventory costs can have a direct and significant impact on their reported net income and on the dollar amounts they show for inventory on their balance sheets.

Learning Objectives

After completing your work on this chapter, you should be able to do the following:

1. Describe goods available for sale and name its components.
2. Explain the relationship between ending inventory and cost of goods sold.

3. Differentiate between the physical flow of merchandise and the cost flow of merchandise.

4. Explain the differences between periodic and perpetual inventory systems.

5. List three different inventory cost flow assumptions and contrast how they affect net income.

6. Calculate cost of goods sold and the cost of ending inventory using FIFO, LIFO, and average cost inventory cost flow assumptions.

7. Calculate and interpret the inventory turnover ratio.

8. Describe the impact of payment terms and freight terms. (Appendix A)

9. Prepare journal entries associated with the purchase and sale of merchandise inventory. (Appendix B)

◆ TRACKING INVENTORY COSTS

merchandise inventory
The physical units (goods) a company buys to resell as part of its business operation. Also called inventory.

inventory The stockpile of tangible product that a company has on hand to sell.

In Chapter 1, we introduced the three major types of businesses—manufacturing firms, merchandising firms, and service firms. Recall that manufacturers make the products they sell, merchandisers buy the products they sell, and service companies sell services rather than tangible products. The stockpile of tangible products that a merchandiser has on hand to sell is called **merchandise inventory,** or simply **inventory.** For example, ***Wal-Mart Corporation***'s inventory includes toys, lawnmowers, clothing, and thousands of other products. ***Bassett Furniture Company***'s inventory includes beds, dressers, tables, desks, and chairs. ***General Motors*** owns desks and chairs also, but these items are not inventory because they are things ***General Motors*** uses, not things it sells. Inventory is the stock of items a company holds for resale. The inventory of ***General Motors*** includes cars, trucks, vans, and a variety of automotive parts and accessories.

The terms *merchandise inventory* and *inventory* are often used to describe the *cost* of the items as well as the items themselves. Therefore, when you see the term *merchandise inventory*, you will have to determine whether it is describing the actual physical units of inventory or the cost of that inventory.

We should mention that a company's inventory cost generally includes the cost of the product itself, plus any additional costs for freight to bring the product in, plus any other costs associated with getting the product ready to sell. For example, if Carolina's Shoe Store pays $10,000 for shoes, $200 for freight to have the shoes delivered to the store, and another $300 to put the shoes into custom shoe boxes to get them ready to sell, the company's total cost for the inventory is $10,500. Only costs that are directly related to obtaining the product or getting the product ready to sell should be treated as part of inventory cost. Accordingly, the cost of inventory generally should not include operating expenses such as store rent, sales salaries, and electricity expense.

beginning inventory
The amount of merchandise inventory (units or dollars) on hand at the beginning of the income statement period.

purchases The amount of merchandise inventory bought during the income statement period.

goods available for sale
The total amount of merchandise inventory a company has available to sell in a given income statement period.

Beginning inventory is the amount of salable merchandise a company has on hand at the first moment of a particular accounting period. **Purchases** is the amount of salable merchandise a company buys during that particular period. Again, both of these terms may refer to the cost of products or to the products themselves. **Goods available for sale** is the amount of merchandise a company starts with (beginning inventory) plus the amount it buys (purchases) during the accounting period. Goods available for sale represents the total amount of merchandise inventory a company could sell in a given income statement period. Once again, the term *goods available for sale* describes both the physical amount of merchandise inventory and the cost of that inventory. Whether we are referring to the physical amount of inventory or its cost, the following relationship among beginning inventory, purchases, and goods available for sale holds true:

Beginning Inventory + Purchases = Goods Available for Sale

Companies report the inventory they have on hand as an asset because it has probable future benefit (it should generate future sales revenues). **Cost of goods sold**

cost of goods sold The cost of the product sold as the primary business activity of a company.

cost of sales Another name for cost of goods sold.

(sometimes called **cost of sales**) is the cost of all of the merchandise (products) a company has transferred (sold) to its customers during a particular income statement period. When a company sells some of its inventory, we should transfer the cost of the merchandise sold from inventory, an asset on the balance sheet, to cost of goods sold, an expense on the income statement. We can determine cost of goods sold by subtracting the amount of inventory on hand at the end of the period, called ending inventory, from goods available for sale. In other words, the total amount that we could have sold (goods available for sale) minus the amount we still had at the end of the period (ending inventory) equals the amount we must have sold (cost of goods sold):

$$\text{Goods Available for Sale} - \text{Ending Inventory} = \text{Cost of Goods Sold}$$

Conversely, if we know a company's goods available for sale and its cost of goods sold, we can determine a company's ending merchandise inventory:

$$\text{Goods Available for Sale} - \text{Cost of Goods Sold} = \text{Ending Inventory}$$

Again, these relationships are true whether we are considering the amount of physical units of inventory or the cost of the inventory. Exhibit 8–1 shows an example of these relationships in terms of both units and dollar amounts.

EXHIBIT 8–1   Relationships Among Goods Available for Sale, Ending Inventory, and Cost of Goods Sold in Both Units and Dollars

	Units	Cost
Beginning Inventory	20	$200
+ Purchases	70	700
= Goods Available for Sale	90	900
− Less: Ending Inventory	(15)	(150)
= Cost of Goods Sold	75	$750

OR

	Units	Cost
Beginning Inventory	20	$200
+ Purchases	70	700
= Goods Available for Sale	90	900
− Less: Cost of Goods Sold	(75)	(750)
= Ending Inventory	15	$150

In the first calculation, we subtract ending inventory to arrive at units sold and cost of goods sold. In the second calculation, we subtract units sold and cost of goods sold to determine ending inventory. It is important to learn from these two calculations that *the total of ending inventory and cost of goods sold always equals goods available for sale.*

To illustrate, consider the ***Virgin Record Store.*** All the CDs and tapes in the store on January 1 (beginning inventory) plus any new CDs and tapes the store buys during January (purchases) equals the total of all the CDs and tapes the store has available to sell (goods available for sale). By the end of January, the products that constituted goods available for sale are either gone or still in the store. If items are gone, we presume the store sold them and consider them part of cost of goods sold. (*Note:* Some of the items could have been broken or stolen, but generally companies consider this cost as part of cost of goods sold.) The CDs and tapes that are still in the store at the end of January are the store's ending inventory. What this means is that *all goods available for sale become either cost of goods sold or ending inventory.*

Exhibit 8–2 on page F–306 shows the movement of inventory through a merchandising operation. Notice that beginning inventory and purchases comprise goods avail-

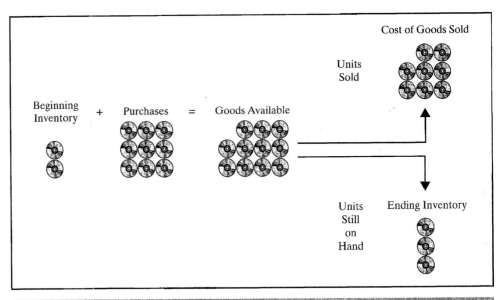

able for sale. By the end of the period, goods available for sale becomes either cost of goods sold or ending inventory.

Discussion Question •

8–1. Assume that you decide to throw a party and begin to plan for it by checking out what's in the house. You find you have some hot dogs, rolls, and pretzels. That's a good start, but you go to the store to buy soda, chips, dip, peanuts, and ice cream. The party is a great hit. Your guests devour all the food and drinks, except for the ice cream—it was never touched! In terms of the party items we have mentioned, what was your:

  a. beginning inventory?
  b. purchases?
  c. goods available?
  d. ending inventory?
  e. "cost" of the party?

Now, let's look closer at the process of tracking a company's inventory and its cost as items are bought and sold.

◆ PHYSICAL FLOW OF INVENTORY (REALITY)

Assume that Computer Exchange, Inc., purchased a computer on January 17, 2003, for $800 and placed it in its warehouse. Also assume the company sold the computer to a customer on February 6, 2003, for $1,500.

Because Computer Exchange purchased the computer for the purpose of reselling it, the company should consider the computer merchandise inventory. Had the company bought the computer for its own use, the company would have considered it a long-lived depreciable asset instead of inventory. Exhibit 8–3 illustrates the physical

EXHIBIT 8–3   Physical Movement of a Computer Purchased by Computer Exchange

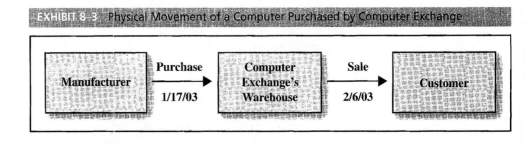

movement of the computer from the time Computer Exchange purchased it until the company sold it and delivered it to the customer.

For many companies, it is important to "rotate their stock"—to sell old merchandise before they sell newer merchandise. This is particularly true of companies selling perishable products such as produce and dairy products. We could describe this physical flow as first-in, first out (FIFO).

Discussion Question

8–2. For what other products would it be important for the first units of merchandise purchased to be the first ones sold? Explain.

For some products, it is unimportant or impractical to sell the first units purchased first. For example, it is both unimportant and impractical for a nursery to sell its oldest sand before it sells sand purchased later. When a truckload of sand arrives, the driver dumps the new sand right on top of the remnants of the old sand pile. It would be silly to dig down into the pile and attempt to sell the oldest sand first. In such cases, goods may be sold in random order, or perhaps the merchandise is sold from the top of the pile so that the last units in are the first units taken out of inventory and sold. We could describe this physical flow as last-in, first out (LIFO).

Sometimes it is impossible to tell which units were sold first because the product becomes so intermixed. This is the case with liquid or gas products such as gasoline and propane. For example, it would be impossible for Chevron to tell which gasoline it was selling first from one of its huge storage tanks, and impossible for Chevron's retailers to tell which gasoline it is selling first from its underground tanks. When the retailer receives the load of gasoline, the new product simply blends together with the old. The gasoline she or he sells will consist of a blend of the old and new. We could describe this physical flow as an average of old product and new product.

Discussion Questions

8–3. Once again, assume you are Palmer Nursery's consultant. With respect to the physical units themselves, would you advise Palmer to use LIFO for its potting soil? Do you think LIFO is acceptable for all of the nursery's products or should it use FIFO or average for some of them? Explain your answers.

8–4. If you owned a retail camera shop, what possible reasons would you have for insisting that your employees sell the first Nikon cameras received before the ones that arrived at the store later?

You might suppose that accounting rules require that the flow of inventory costs through a company's accounting records reflect the reality of how the physical units flow through the company's warehouse. For example, if a company sells bread, it will sell older loaves before newer ones to ensure product freshness. It seems logical to expect that the company would be required to recognize the cost of the older product as expense before it recognizes the cost of the newer product. However, accounting rules *do not* require that the cost flow for inventory mirror the physical flow of inventory. There are several acceptable cost flow methods allowed by GAAP, and we will discuss four of them a little later in this chapter. For now, we will introduce you to the inventory cost flow in a very general way.

◆ INVENTORY COST FLOW (MEASUREMENT OF REALITY)

Let's return to our Computer Exchange example. Under accrual accounting, Computer Exchange must attempt to match expenses to the same income statement period as the revenues they help generate. For this reason, the company would not recognize the cost of the $800 computer as an expense when it was purchased. Instead, the company would consider the computer and its $800 cost as an asset.

As of January 31, 2003, the company had not sold the computer—it was in the company's warehouse. Therefore, the company should show the computer's cost on the balance sheet prepared at the end of January as merchandise inventory. The company would not report anything related to the computer on its January income statement. The calculations below show the cost of goods sold and ending inventory for Computer Exchange, Inc., assuming the company purchased the computer but has not sold it yet.

	Units	Cost
Beginning Inventory, January 1	0	$ 0
+ Purchases	1	800
= Goods Available for Sale	1	800
− Cost of Goods Sold	0	0
= Ending Inventory, January 31	1	$800

Exhibit 8–4 shows Computer Exchange's income statement for the month of January 2003 and its balance sheet at January 31, 2003, assuming the company had no business transactions during January except those related to the computer and warehouse rent.

Discussion Question ●

8–5. Can you tell how long Computer Exchange, Inc., has been in business by looking at the income statement and balance sheet in Exhibit 8–4? Explain.

EXHIBIT 8–4 Computer Exchange's Financial Statements—Before Sale of Computer

Computer Exchange, Inc.
Income Statement
For the Month Ended January 31, 2003

Sales	$ 0
LESS: Cost of goods sold	0
Gross margin	$ 0
Operating expenses:	
Warehouse rent	$ (200)
Net income (loss)	$ (200)

Computer Exchange, Inc.
Statement of Retained Earnings
For the Month Ended January 31, 2003

Beginning retained earnings	$ 0
Net income (loss)	(200)
	$ (200)
Less dividends	$ 0
Ending retained earnings	$ (200)

Computer Exchange, Inc.
Balance Sheet
January 31, 2003

Assets:	
Cash	$22,000
Merchandise inventory	800
Total assets	$22,800
Liabilities and stockholders' equity:	
Common stock	$15,000
Additional paid-in capital	8,000
Retained earnings	(200)
Total liabilities and stockholders' equity	$22,800

Recall that Computer Exchange sold the computer for $1,500 on February 6, 2003, and delivered it to the customer on that day. The calculations below show the cost of goods sold and ending inventory for Computer Exchange at the end of February.

	Units	Cost
Beginning Inventory, January 1	0	$ 0
+ Purchases	1	800
= Goods Available for Sale	1	800
− Cost of Goods Sold	1	800
= Ending Inventory, February 28	0	$ 0

Exhibit 8–5 shows Computer Exchange's income statement for the month of February 2003 and its balance sheets at January 31, 2003, and February 28, 2003, assuming the company had no business transactions during February except those related to the computer and the warehouse rent.

We have included the presale (January 31) balance sheet as well as the postsale (February 28) balance sheet in Exhibit 8–5 to demonstrate how the $800 cost of the computer flowed through the financial statements. Computer Exchange reported the $800 as an asset (merchandise inventory) on the January 31 balance sheet. Because the company sold the computer during February and has no other merchandise to sell, there is no merchandise inventory on the February 28 balance sheet. Instead, Computer Exchange shows the computer's $800 cost as an expense and reports it on

EXHIBIT 8–5 Computer Exchange's Financial Statements Showing Effects of Sale of Computer

Computer Exchange, Inc.
Income Statement
For the Month Ended February 28, 2003

Sales	$ 1,500
LESS: Cost of goods sold	800
Gross margin	$ 700
Operating expenses:	
Warehouse rent	$ (200)
Net income (loss)	$ 500

Computer Exchange, Inc.
Statement of Retained Earnings
For the Month Ended January 31, 2003

Beginning retained earnings	$ (200)
Net income (loss)	500
	$ 300
Less dividends	$ 0
Ending retained earnings	$ 300

Computer Exchange, Inc.
Balance Sheets
January 31, 2003, and February 28, 2003

Assets:	January 31	February 28
Cash	$22,000	$21,800
Accounts receivable	-0-	1,500
Merchandise inventory	800	0
Total assets	$22,800	$23,300
Liabilities and stockholders' equity:		
Common stock	$15,000	$15,000
Additional paid-in capital	8,000	8,000
Retained earnings	(200)	300
Total liabilities and stockholders' equity	$22,800	$23,300

the February income statement as cost of goods sold. As you can see, cost of goods sold affects the gross margin, and thus the net income as well. The February 28 balance sheet reflects the $500 net income as an increase in both the total assets and total liabilities and stockholders' equity. The company's total assets increased by $500 because, while the company sacrificed $1,000 of assets during February ($800 cost of goods sold and $200 rent on the warehouse), those sacrifices generated a $1,500 asset (accounts receivable). As the arrow in Exhibit 8–5 shows, stockholders' equity increases by $500 as a result of combining the net income figure for February with the previous retained earnings balance (which in this case was negative) to arrive at the updated retained earnings balance of $300.

Discussion Question

8–6. Can you tell by looking at the income statement and balance sheets in Exhibit 8–5 whether the customer who purchased the computer from Computer Exchange has paid for it by the end of February 2003? Explain.

Exhibit 8–3 on page F–306 illustrates the physical movement of the computer from the time Computer Exchange purchased it to the time it was sold to the customer. Exhibit 8–6 shows both the physical flow of the computer and the flow of the cost associated with the computer.

Computer Exchange purchased a computer and put it in the company's warehouse. This is reality. Then, Computer Exchange sold the computer, took it out of the warehouse, and delivered it to its customer. This, too, is reality. The company initially reported the computer's $800 cost on its balance sheet as an asset. When it sold the computer, the company transferred the $800 cost to an expense, cost of goods sold, on the income statement. This is the measurement of reality. As Exhibit 8–6 shows, in this simple example involving only one unit of inventory, the physical flow of the merchandise inventory and the flow of the cost associated with the merchandise inventory coincide. As we will see later in this chapter, however, when a company has many units of inventory, the physical flow of merchandise (reality) and the cost flow of that merchandise (measurement of reality) do not necessarily coincide. This situation is another source of variation among companies' accounting information. To some degree, a company's financial information is influenced by its choice of one inventory costing method over another.

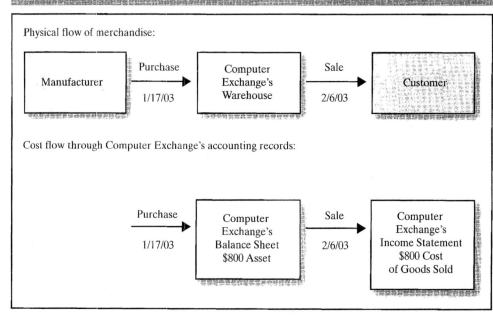

EXHIBIT 8–6 The Physical Movement of the Computer from the Time Computer Exchange Purchased It to the Time It Was Sold to the Customer

INVENTORY SYSTEMS

In our previous example, Computer Exchange, Inc., transferred the $800 cost of the computer from an asset to an expense when the item was sold on February 6, 2003. Over time, two major inventory systems have been developed to account for this transfer. As we will see, each has advantages and disadvantages in comparison to the other.

PERIODIC INVENTORY SYSTEM

periodic inventory system An inventory system in which all inventory and cost of goods sold calculations are done at the end of the income statement period.

Under a **periodic inventory system,** companies do their inventory and cost of goods sold calculations at the end of the income statement period. When a company uses a periodic inventory system, it does not update the detailed inventory records during the period. Further, the accounting records of a company using this system do not provide up-to-date information about which products have been sold during the period and which remain in inventory. Under this system, only at the end of the accounting period, when a company prepares its financial statements, does it calculate the cost of its ending inventory and its cost of the goods sold. It is only then that the company adjusts its accounting records to reflect the cost of ending inventory to show on its balance sheet and the cost of goods sold to show on its income statement.

The strength of the periodic inventory system is that it involves relatively little record keeping. Its greatest weakness is that it does not provide the company with any day-to-day information about the status of its inventory or its cost of goods sold.

Prior to the computer age, virtually all companies used the periodic inventory system because keeping detailed inventory records manually was too time consuming. Now, however, the availability of powerful and affordable computer technology makes the task of keeping daily inventory records an efficient process. For this reason, most companies now use the perpetual inventory system. Because of its overwhelming popularity, all our remaining examples are based on the perpetual inventory system.

PERPETUAL INVENTORY SYSTEM

perpetual inventory system An inventory system in which both the physical count of inventory units and the cost classification (asset or expense) are updated when a transaction involves inventory.

Under a **perpetual inventory system,** companies update their inventory records continually to keep track of both the physical count of inventory units and the cost of those units. The inventory records are updated whenever there is a transaction involving inventory. What this means is that when a company uses the perpetual system, it updates its accounting records to provide up-to-date information about which products it has sold and which products still remain in inventory. To illustrate, let's return to our example of Computer Exchange. Under a perpetual system, Computer Exchange would have an inventory report similar to the one shown in Exhibit 8–7.

EXHIBIT 8-7 Inventory Control Report Under Perpetual Inventory System Merchandise

		Purchases			Cost of Goods Sold			Inventory Balance		
Date	Explanation	Units	Unit Cost	Total Cost	Units	Unit Cost	Total Cost	Units	Unit Cost	Total Cost
1/17	Purchase	1	$800	$800				1	$800	$800
2/06	Sale				1	$800	$800	0		$0

Since the report keeps a running balance of merchandise inventory (the far right side of the report), the company can tell the number of physical units it has on hand at any time. The report also shows the dollar amount that the company has transferred from assets (merchandise inventory) on the balance sheet to expense (cost of goods sold) on the income statement.

Computer Exchange uses a computerized accounting system to generate its inventory reports automatically. Purchases and sales of inventory are registered either by keyboard entries or by a bar-code scanning device. Retailers use scanners to read bar codes—formally known as universal product codes, or UPCs—printed on their inventory. Companies program their computers to assign a given cost to each inventory item and to perform the necessary functions to update their inventory records. Chances are, when you purchased this book, the clerk at the bookstore's checkout counter scanned the UPC on the book's back cover. In addition to ringing up the sale of the book, the bookstore's computer probably also updated the bookstore's inventory records. The bookstore's computer made entries to update the number of physical units on hand and to transfer the book's cost from merchandise inventory to cost of goods sold. By utilizing this technology, the bookstore's computer can provide employees with valuable information about the number of books sold and the number of books remaining on the shelf. If everything in the system works correctly, the bookstore's management can tell how many books are on the shelf without having to physically count them.

Discussion Question

8–7. Assume the inventory report at the bookstore for this textbook shows 25 books remaining on the shelf. Just to make sure, the bookstore manager goes over to the shelf, counts the remaining books, and finds there are only 22. What might explain the discrepancy?

◆ THE NECESSITY OF A PHYSICAL INVENTORY COUNT

book inventory The amount of ending inventory (units and dollars) resulting from transactions recorded by a perpetual inventory system.

The inventory amounts in units and dollars that a company's perpetual inventory system shows is called **book inventory.** Book inventory may or may not coincide with the merchandise inventory actually on hand at the end of the period. Errors in recording inventory transactions and theft of inventory are two potential causes of differences between book inventory and actual inventory. Others are damaged and discarded inventory and, in the case of perishable inventory, spoilage. Because discrepancies between book inventory and the actual physical inventory on hand are bound to occur, companies must physically count their inventory. Accounting rules dictate that every company governed by GAAP must take a physical count of its inventory at least annually.

Results of a physical inventory count take precedence over the book inventory the inventory system generates. Companies must adjust their book inventory to match the actual physical inventory on hand. To accomplish such an adjustment, the book inventory is adjusted and offset by a corresponding adjustment of cost of goods sold. To illustrate, Exhibit 8–8 shows the calculation of cost of goods sold and ending inventory generated by a perpetual inventory system.

EXHIBIT 8–8 Record of Ending Inventory Based on Book Inventory

	Units	Cost
Beginning Inventory, January 1	20	$200
+ Purchases	70	700
= Goods Available for Sale	90	900
− Cost of Goods Sold	75	750
= Ending Inventory, February 28	15	$150

The figures in this exhibit came from the company's records. The ending inventory of 15 units and $150 is the company's book inventory. However, a physical count reveals that there are only 13 units on hand. In this case, the company must adjust its records to reflect reality. The amount the balance sheet shows as ending inventory must be the amount the company actually had on hand. Since we know that cost of goods available for sale ($900 in this example) will end up as either cost of goods sold or ending inventory, a change in the ending inventory amount will cause a change in the amount of cost of goods sold. After the necessary adjustments, the company's records would look like Exhibit 8–9.

	Units	Cost
Beginning Inventory, January 1	20	$200
+ Purchases	70	700
= Goods Available for Sale	90	900
− Cost of Goods Sold	77	770
= Ending Inventory, February 28	13	$130

EXHIBIT 8–9 Adjusted Record of Ending Inventory After Physical Count

The cost of goods sold the company reports as an expense on its income statement for the period would be $770. The merchandise inventory the company reports as an asset on its balance sheet would be $130, which reflects the reality of the number of units actually on hand at the end of the period. With this adjustment, the company's financial statement will more accurately reflect reality.

Some accountants argue that because the book inventory under a perpetual inventory system is adjusted to the physical count periodically, all companies really end up using a form of the periodic inventory method.

Discussion Question

8–8. If careless employees break inventory items and discard them, or dishonest employees steal inventory items, how is a company's income statement affected?

◆ INVENTORY COST FLOW METHODS

Now that we have introduced you to the two inventory systems and have discussed the flow of inventory costs through a company's accounting records in a general way, we will now present four different inventory costing methods companies use, depending on their circumstances. The first of these methods is the specific identification method.

SPECIFIC IDENTIFICATION COST FLOW METHOD

specific identification method The method of inventory cost flow that identifies each item sold by a company.

Under the **specific identification method,** company accountants move the actual cost of individual units of inventory through the company's accounting records to exactly match the physical flow of units through the company's inventory. In other words, when a company uses the specific inventory method, its cost of goods sold is the actual cost of specific units of inventory the company sold, and the cost the company assigns to its ending inventory is the actual cost of specific units still on hand. Generally, this method is used only by companies that sell expensive, unique items such as airplanes, antiques, and boats. As an example, assume that Dobbs Motor Company sells antique automobiles and appropriately uses the specific identification method. Exhibit 8–10 shows the details of the automobiles in inventory at the beginning of March, those Dobbs purchased in March, and those Dobbs sold during the month.

EXHIBIT 8–10 Dobbs Motor Company's Detailed Inventory Information

Date Purchased	Description	Cost	Date Sold	Selling Price
Beginning Inventory				
10-15-2002	1926 Bentley	$35,000	03-05-2003	$45,000
12-20-2002	1960 Mercedes	15,000		
01-25-2003	1955 Thunderbird	25,000	03-09-2003	38,000
02-10-2003	1929 Model A Ford	24,000	03-18-2003	36,000
Purchases				
03-10-2003	1955 Cadillac	20,000		
03-25-2003	1964 Corvette	31,000		
Cost of Goods Available		$150,000		

When a company uses the specific identification inventory method, it keeps track of the cost of the actual units of inventory it sold. Let's assume that Dobbs sold the Bentley, the Thunderbird, and the Model A Ford during March. Exhibit 8–11 shows a summary of the sales and the cost of the automobiles sold.

EXHIBIT 8–11 Specific Identification Sales and Cost of Goods Sold

	Date Sold	Selling Price	Cost
1926 Bentley	03-05-2003	$ 45,000	$35,000
1955 Thunderbird	03-09-2003	38,000	25,000
1929 Model A Ford	03-18-2003	36,000	24,000
Total		**$119,000**	**$84,000**

The dollar amount assigned to the ending inventory under specific identification consists of the cost of the actual units of inventory still on hand at the end of the accounting period. In Dobbs's case, the ending inventory consists of the Mercedes, the Cadillac, and the Corvette. Exhibit 8–12 shows the cost that Dobbs would assign to its ending inventory.

EXHIBIT 8–12 Specific Identification Ending Inventory

Date Purchased	Description	Cost	Date Sold	Selling Price
12-20-2002	1960 Mercedes	$15,000		
3-10-2003	1955 Cadillac	20,000		
3-25-2003	1964 Corvette	31,000		
Ending Inventory Cost		$66,000		

Exhibit 8-13 presents a summary of the inventory cost flow for Dobbs Motor Company under the specific identification inventory method.

EXHIBIT 8–13 Dobbs Motor Company's Inventory Amounts Using Specific Identification

Beginning Inventory	$ 99,000
+ Purchases	51,000
= Goods Available for Sale	150,000
− Cost of Goods Sold	84,000
= Ending Inventory	$ 66,000

The specific identification method is both logical and intuitive. It is logical because it adheres to a rational set of procedures, and it is intuitive because the flow of costs through the accounting records is exactly the same as the physical flow of inventory. In many instances, however, it is impractical, unnecessary, or even impossible for the cost flow to exactly correspond to the physical flow of units through the inventory. GAAP do not require the flow of costs through a company's accounting records to reflect the reality of how the physical units flow through the company's inventory, as was the case with the antique car example we just used. Rather, these accounting rules allow companies to cost their products based on some *assumption* of how units of product physically flow through the company.

COST FLOW ASSUMPTIONS

Over time, the accounting profession has developed several cost flow assumptions to account for the movement of product cost through a company's accounting system. The three we will discuss in this chapter are the first-in, first-out (FIFO) method, the last-in, first-out (LIFO) method, and the average cost method. These cost flow assumptions are logical because they adhere to rational procedures. They are not, however, as intuitive as the specific identification method, because the flow of costs is not in any way related to how the physical inventory moves through a company. For example, **Holsum Bakery** makes certain it sells its oldest bread first. If it sold its freshest bread first, the older bread would go stale, leaving **Holsum** with merchandise it couldn't sell. For product costing purposes, however, **Holsum** can use any cost flow assumption it wishes without regard to how its inventory physically flows through the bakery. That is, accounting rules do not require the flow of inventory costs through accounting records to mirror the flow of physical units. Accounting rules permit companies to use any cost flow assumption—FIFO, LIFO, or average cost—regardless of the physical flow of inventory through their warehouses. This is yet another example of how reality and the measurement of reality may differ, and this difference can result in a difference between reality and the measurement of reality in accrual accounting. As financial statement users, you need to understand how companies track their inventory costs and how they arrive at the amounts they present on their financial statements. We will now explore three acceptable cost flow assumptions and the impact they have on inventory, cost of goods sold, and net income.

Generally, product costs change over time. For some products, prices rise regularly; wholesalers often warn the retailers to whom they sell goods of price increases months in advance. Products based on technology often fall in price as more and more companies offer the products and competition drives prices down. Prices may rise or fall over time, or they may fluctuate in unexpected patterns, but rarely will they remain constant for long periods.

When prices are changing, the cost flow assumption a company chooses will have a dramatic impact on its cost of goods sold and ending inventory. To illustrate, we will examine the effect of three cost flow assumptions on a product sold by Montoya Emergency Equipment Corporation. As the company's name implies, Montoya sells various kinds of emergency equipment to hospitals, ambulance services, and governments at the local and state level. The product we will focus on is the model EG241 emergency generator, which provides electric power whenever regular electricity service is unavailable. Montoya purchases these generators directly from the manufacturer and then sells them to its customers. For purposes of this example, we will assume that Montoya's cost for the generators is increasing, but due to competition, Montoya is unable to increase its retail selling price.

Montoya began March 2003 with only one model EG241 generator in stock. The company's cost for this generator was $800. During March, the company purchased five more generators. As Exhibit 8–14 shows, Montoya's cost for the generators is increasing even though the five generators purchased in March are identical to the one the company had on hand at the beginning of the month.

EXHIBIT 8–14 Montoya's March Beginning Inventory and March Purchases

Date		Quantity	Cost per Unit
March 1	Beginning Inventory	1	$ 800
March 3	Purchase	2	1,000
March 17	Purchase	1	1,200
March 26	Purchase	1	1,300
March 29	Purchase	1	1,400

Montoya Emergency Equipment sold one generator on March 22 and another on March 30 for $1,500 each. Remember, though, that because of competition, Montoya is unable to raise its $1,500 selling price per generator. Exhibit 8–15 on page F–316 shows Montoya's beginning inventory, its purchases, and the two sales.

Considering what you know about when Montoya purchased the generators and the dates of the two sales, which one do you think Montoya Emergency Equipment Corporation sold on March 22 and which do you think it sold on March 30? Different

Date		Quantity	Cost per Unit
March 1	Beginning Inventory	1	$ 800
March 3	Purchase	2	1,000
March 17	Purchase	1	1,200
March 22	Sale	(1)	
March 26	Purchase	1	1,300
March 29	Purchase	1	1,400
March 30	Sale	(1)	
March 31	Ending Inventory	4	

EXHIBIT 8-15   Montoya's March Beginning Inventory, March Purchases, and March Sales

answers are possible, but the generators the company actually sold were probably the ones most conveniently located in the warehouse (i.e., those closest to the door). In this case, the generators are identical, so it doesn't really matter which ones are sold first. About the only thing you can determine for sure is that the generator Montoya sold on March 22 was either the $800 one, one of the $1,000 ones, or the $1,200 one; and that the one Montoya sold on March 30 was one of the five still in the warehouse on that day.

Discussion Question ● ○ ● ○ ● ○ ● ● ○ ● ○ ● ● ○ ● ○ ● ○ ● ○ ● ○ ● ● ○ ● ○ ● ○ ● ● ○ ● ○ ●

8–9. Why must the generator sold on March 22 have been one costing $800, $1,000, or $1,200?

Because Montoya's cost of the generators varied, it is impossible for us to determine the cost of the actual physical goods sold if we don't know exactly which generators the company sold. What we need is a method to calculate cost of goods sold that will work regardless of which specific products were sold.

In the sections that follow, we discuss three acceptable inventory cost flow assumptions. Before we do so, however, we must make three important points:

1. None of the three methods we discuss attempts to reflect the physical movement of the actual units of merchandise inventory.
2. Our discussions of the three methods are not intended to be exhaustive. Our aim is to give you a basic understanding of these methods so that you will understand how a particular inventory cost flow assumption can significantly affect a company's financial statements.
3. Our illustrations of cost flow methods assume that a perpetual inventory system is in place. Accordingly, we will keep a running inventory balance and we will calculate cost of goods sold each time a generator is sold.

The number of generators Montoya Emergency Equipment Corporation purchased, the date they were purchased, and their cost to Montoya are all facts. Likewise, the quantity of generators Montoya sold and when it sold them are also facts. The cost flow assumption Montoya uses cannot change these facts. What we *can* change is our *assumption* of which particular generator Montoya sold for product costing purposes. The cost flow assumptions we make will affect the amount Montoya records as cost of goods sold and also the amount Montoya shows as the cost of its ending inventory.

As we mentioned earlier in this chapter, cost of goods available for sale is the total cost of the inventory on hand at the beginning of the period plus the cost of inventory purchased during the period. Exhibit 8–16 shows the calculation of Montoya Emergency Equipment Corporation's cost of goods available for sale for March 2003.

The various cost flow assumptions we will apply to this situation will separate the $6,700 into two portions: (1) the cost that we will assign to the two generators Montoya sold (cost of goods sold), and (2) the cost we will assign to the four generators Montoya still has on hand at the end of March (ending inventory). Each cost flow assumption will take a different approach to determining which items we assume were sold on March 22 and March 30 and, thus, to determining the cost of goods sold for the month.

Date		Quantity	Cost per Unit	Total Cost
March 1	Beginning Inventory	1	$ 800	$ 800
March 3	Purchase	2	1,000	2,000
March 17	Purchase	1	1,200	1,200
March 26	Purchase	1	1,300	1,300
March 29	Purchase	1	1,400	1,400
	Total Goods Available for Sale			$6,700

EXHIBIT 8–16 Montoya Emergency Equipment Corporation's Cost of Goods Available for Sale

Because we will use the perpetual inventory system, we will determine the cost of goods sold at the time of each sale. The portion of the cost of goods available for sale not included in cost of goods sold, then, must be the cost of ending inventory.

FIRST-IN, FIRST-OUT (FIFO) METHOD

first-in, first-out (FIFO)
The inventory flow concept based on the assumption that the first units of inventory purchased are the first ones sold.

The **first-in, first-out (FIFO)** inventory cost flow method is so named because it *assumes* that the first units placed in inventory are the first units sold. Let's apply the FIFO inventory method to our example.

The first sale took place on March 22. One generator was sold, but which one? What inventory items were available on the sale date? Exhibit 8–17 answers that question. Then, applying FIFO logic, we assume that the generator sold on March 22 must have been the oldest one, the one from beginning inventory. That is, the first generator in was the first one out. Therefore, cost of goods sold for the March 22 sale was $800.

EXHIBIT 8–17 Inventory Items Available for Sale on March 22

Date		Quantity	Cost per Unit	Total Cost
March 1	Beginning Inventory	1	$ 800	$ 800
March 3	Purchase	2	1,000	2,000
March 17	Purchase	1	1,200	1,200

The next sale took place on March 30. What inventory items were on hand at the time of the sale? Exhibit 8–18 answers that question. Under FIFO, which of the generators should we assume was sold on March 30? At this point in time, the first generator into inventory was one of those Montoya purchased on March 3, so we assume one of those was sold. Therefore, cost of goods sold for the March 30 sale is $1,000.

EXHIBIT 8–18 Inventory Items Available for Sale on March 30 Under FIFO Assumption

Date		Quantity	Cost per Unit	Total Cost
March 3	Purchase	2	$1,000	$2,000
March 17	Purchase	1	1,200	1,200
March 26	Purchase	1	1,300	1,300
March 29	Purchase	1	1,400	1,400

We can now calculate the cost of goods sold that Montoya Emergency Equipment Corporation should report on its March income statement. Since cost of goods sold for the month is the total of the cost of goods sold for each sale, Montoya should report cost of goods sold of $1,800 ($800 + $1,000). Exhibit 8–19 on page F–318 summarizes Montoya's inventory cost flow under the FIFO inventory method.

At the time of each sale, cost of goods sold is determined using the assumption that the first items into inventory are the first ones to be sold. As Exhibit 8–19 shows, we assume that the generator from beginning inventory was the one Montoya sold on March 22 and one of the generators Montoya purchased on March 3 was sold on March 30. Montoya's ending inventory consists of the cost of the four unsold generators: one of the generators it purchased on March 3 and the ones it purchased on

Goods Available

Date		Quantity	Cost per Unit	Total Cost
March 1	Beginning Inventory	1	$ 800	$ 800
March 3	Purchase	2	1,000	2,000
March 17	Purchase	1	1,200	1,200
March 26	Purchase	1	1,300	1,300
March 29	Purchase	1	1,400	1,400
	Total Cost of Goods Available for Sale			$6,700

Cost of Goods Sold

Date	Quantity	Cost per Unit	Total Cost
March 22 Sale	1	$ 800	$ 800
March 30 Sale	1	$1,000	1,000
Total Cost of Goods Sold	2		$1,800

Ending Inventory

Date		Quantity	Cost per Unit	Total Cost
March 3	Purchase	1	$1,000	$1,000
March 17	Purchase	1	1,200	1,200
March 26	Purchase	1	1,300	1,300
March 29	Purchase	1	1,400	1,400
March 31	Ending Inventory	4		$4,900

EXHIBIT 8–19   Cost of Goods Sold and Ending Inventory Cost Under FIFO

March 17, 26, and 29. By totaling the costs of these four generators, we determine that the cost of Montoya's ending inventory for March is $4,900.

Discussion Question

8-10. If Montoya Emergency Equipment Corporation sells two more generators before purchasing any more, which two would we assume the company sold under FIFO?

Even if we didn't identify and cost the items we assumed were remaining in ending inventory as we did in Exhibit 8–19, we could determine the ending inventory cost. Since we know the cost of goods available for sale is $6,700 and the cost of goods sold is $1,800, we can determine the cost of the company's ending inventory for March 2003 by subtracting cost of goods sold from the cost of goods available:

Cost of Goods Available − Cost of Goods Sold = Ending Inventory
$6,700 − $1,800 = $4,900

Note that we separated cost of goods available for sale ($6,700) into cost of goods sold ($1,800) and cost of ending inventory ($4,900). Cost of goods sold is shown as an expense on the income statement, and ending inventory is shown as an asset on the balance sheet.

Exhibit 8–20 shows Montoya's financial statements assuming it used the FIFO inventory method and had no business transactions during March except those related to the generators and its rent payment.

We included both the February 28 and the March 31 balance sheets in Exhibit 8–20 to demonstrate how the cost of inventory flows through the financial statements. Montoya had only $800 in merchandise inventory on February 28, as its balance sheet reflects. This was the beginning inventory for March. During March, the company purchased five generators for a total of $5,900. Some of the $6,700 cost of goods available for sale becomes part of the merchandise inventory on the March

Montoya Emergency Equipment Corporation
Income Statement
For the Month Ended March 31, 2003

Sales	$ 3,000
LESS: Cost of goods sold	1,800
Gross margin	$1,200
Operating expenses:	
Warehouse rent	$ (200)
Net income (loss)	$ 1,000

Montoya Emergency Equipment Corporation
Balance Sheets
February 28, 2003, and March 31, 2003

Assets:	February 28	March 31
Cash	$21,000	$22,300
Accounts receivable	1,500	3,000
Merchandise inventory	800	4,900
Total assets	$23,300	$30,200
Liabilities and stockholders' equity:		
Accounts payable	$ 0	$ 5,900
Common stock	15,000	15,000
Additional paid-in capital	8,000	8,000
Retained earnings	300	1,300
Total liabilities and stockholders' equity	$23,300	$30,200

EXHIBIT 8–20   Montoya Emergency Equipment Corporation's Financial Statements—FIFO Inventory Method

balance sheet ($4,900) while the rest becomes cost of goods sold on the March income statement ($1,800). The $4,900 merchandise inventory on the March 31 balance sheet represents the unsold generators, while the $1,800 cost of goods sold represents the two generators Montoya sold in March. The cost of goods sold affects the gross margin and thus the net income as well. We combine the $1,000 net income with the previous retained earnings balance of $300 to arrive at the March 31 retained earnings balance of $1,300.

Discussion Question

8–11. Can you tell by looking at Montoya's financial statements in Exhibit 8–20 whether, as of March 31, the company had paid for the five generators purchased during March 2003? Explain.

As you can see, even though it may not be intuitive, FIFO is logical because it adheres to a rational set of procedures. Next, we will explore the LIFO method, which is no less logical than FIFO but results in different amounts for cost of goods sold and ending inventory.

LAST-IN, FIRST-OUT (LIFO) METHOD

last-in, first-out (LIFO)
The inventory flow concept based on the assumption that the last units of inventory purchased are the first ones sold.

The **last-in, first-out (LIFO)** method is so named because it *assumes* that the last units placed in inventory are the first units sold. In other words, regardless of the physical flow of merchandise through the warehouse, under LIFO, the cost of the goods most recently purchased is the first cost recognized as cost of goods sold. Exhibit 8–21 shows Montoya Emergency Equipment Corporation's goods available for sale when the company makes its first sale of the month on March 22.

Date		Quantity	Cost per Unit	Total Cost
March 1	Beginning Inventory	1	$ 800	$ 800
March 3	Purchase	2	1,000	2,000
March 17	Purchase	1	1,200	1,200

EXHIBIT 8–21 Inventory Items Available for Sale on March 22

Applying LIFO logic, we assume that the generator sold on March 22 was the one Montoya purchased on March 17. That is, the last one in was the first one out. Therefore, cost of goods sold for the March 22 sale was $1,200.

The next sale took place on March 30. Exhibit 8–22 shows what inventory items were on hand at the time of the sale.

EXHIBIT 8–22 Inventory Items Available for Sale on March 30 Under LIFO Assumption

Date		Quantity	Cost per Unit	Total Cost
March 1	Purchase	1	$ 800	$ 800
March 3	Purchase	2	1,000	2,000
March 26	Purchase	1	1,300	1,300
March 29	Purchase	1	1,400	1,400

Under LIFO, we assume that the generator sold on March 30 was the last one into inventory—that is, the generator Montoya purchased on March 29. Therefore, cost of goods sold for the March 30 sale is $1,400.

We can now calculate the cost of goods sold that Montoya Emergency Equipment Corporation should report on its March income statement: $2,600 ($1,200 + $1,400). Montoya's ending inventory cost consists of the cost of the four unsold generators. Exhibit 8–23 summarizes Montoya's inventory cost flow under the LIFO inventory method.

EXHIBIT 8–23 Cost of Goods Sold and Ending Inventory Cost Under LIFO

Goods Available

Date		Quantity	Cost per Unit	Total Cost
March 1	Beginning Inventory	1	$ 800	$ 800
March 3	Purchase	2	1,000	2,000
March 17	Purchase	1	1,200	1,200
March 26	Purchase	1	1,300	1,300
March 29	Purchase	1	1,400	1,400
	Total Cost of Goods Available for Sale			$6,700

Cost of Goods Sold

Date	Quantity	Cost per Unit	Total Cost
March 22 Sale	1	$1,200	$1,200
March 30 Sale	1	1,400	1,400
Total Cost of Goods Sold	2		$2,600

Ending Inventory

Date		Quantity	Cost per Unit	Total Cost
March 1	Beginning Inventory	1	$ 800	$ 800
March 3	Purchase	2	1,000	2,000
March 26	Purchase	1	1,300	1,300
March 31	Ending Inventory	4		$4,100

As Exhibit 8–23 indicates, we assume that the generator purchased on March 17 was sold on March 22 and the generator purchased on March 29 was sold on March 30. The generators remaining in ending inventory are the one from beginning inventory, the two Montoya purchased on March 3, and the one it purchased on March 26. By adding up the costs of these four generators, we determine that the cost of Montoya's ending inventory is $4,100.

Discussion Question

8–12. If Montoya sells two more generators before purchasing any more, under LIFO, which two would we assume the company sold next?

Even if we didn't identify and cost the items we assumed were remaining in ending inventory as we did in Exhibit 8–23, we could determine Montoya's ending inventory cost. Since we know the cost of goods available for sale is $6,700 and the cost of goods sold is $2,600, we can determine the cost of the company's ending inventory for March 2003 by subtracting cost of goods sold from the cost of goods available:

$$\text{Cost of Goods Available} - \text{Cost of Goods Sold} = \text{Ending Inventory}$$
$$\$6,700 \quad - \quad \$2,600 \quad = \quad \$4,100$$

Exhibit 8–24 shows Montoya's financial statements assuming the company used the LIFO inventory method and had no business transactions during March except those related to the generators and its rent payment.

EXHIBIT 8–24 Montoya Emergency Equipment Corporation's Financial Statements—LIFO Inventory Method

Montoya Emergency Equipment Corporation
Income Statement
For the Month Ended March 31, 2003

Sales	$ 3,000
LESS: Cost of goods sold	2,600
Gross margin	$ 400
Operating expenses:	
Warehouse rent	(200)
Net income (loss)	$ 200

Montoya Emergency Equipment Corporation
Balance Sheets
February 28, 2003, and March 31, 2003

Assets:	February 28	March 31
Cash	$21,000	$22,300
Accounts receivable	1,500	3,000
Merchandise inventory	800	4,100
Total assets	$23,300	$29,400
Liabilities and stockholders' equity:		
Accounts payable	$ 0	$ 5,900
Common stock	15,000	15,000
Additional paid-in capital	8,000	8,000
Retained earnings	300	500
Total liabilities and stockholders' equity	$23,300	$29,400

As with the FIFO presentation, we included both the February 28 and March 31 balance sheets in Exhibit 8–24 to demonstrate how the cost of inventory items flows through the financial statements. The $800 in merchandise inventory Montoya had on February 28 becomes the company's beginning inventory for March. During March, Montoya purchased $5,900 of generators. Some of the $6,700 cost of goods available for sale becomes part of the merchandise inventory on the March balance sheet ($4,100), while the rest becomes cost of goods sold on the March income statement

($2,600). The $4,100 merchandise inventory on the March 31 balance sheet represents the unsold generators, while the $2,600 cost of goods sold represents the two generators Montoya sold in March. We combine the $200 net income with the previous retained earnings balance of $300 to arrive at the March 31 retained earnings balance of $500. Now let's compare the financial statements prepared for Montoya Emergency Equipment Corporation using FIFO (Exhibit 8–20) with those prepared using LIFO (Exhibit 8–24). Remember, the two sets of financial statements are based on exactly the same facts. Yet, applying the FIFO inventory method, the company reports net income of $1,000, whereas under the LIFO inventory method, the company reports net income of $200. Moreover, using FIFO, we see results in total assets on the March 31 balance sheet of $30,200, while using LIFO results in total assets on the March 31 balance sheet of $29,400. This demonstrates that when prices are increasing, using FIFO results in both higher reported net income and a higher reported inventory amount. When prices are decreasing, however, LIFO would result in higher reported net income and a higher reported inventory amount. Keep in mind that companies may use either LIFO or FIFO, regardless of their inventory's physical flow.

Discussion Questions

8–13. The FIFO financial statements in Exhibit 8–20 show Montoya Emergency Equipment Corporation to be more profitable than do the LIFO financial statements in Exhibit 8–24. Is the company really more profitable if it uses the FIFO method rather than the LIFO method? Explain.

8–14. How would you explain the differences between these two sets of financial statements to someone who did not know the facts behind them?

8–15. In a time of rising prices, which inventory method would you choose for your company if you were trying to impress a banker with your company's success?

The third cost flow assumption we will discuss is the average cost method. It is as logical as both FIFO and LIFO, and many people also think it is more intuitive.

AVERAGE COST METHOD

average cost method
The inventory cost flow method that assigns an average cost to the units of inventory on hand at the time of each sale.

The **average cost method** is so named because it uses an average cost per unit to determine the cost of goods sold and the cost of goods in ending inventory. Under this method, the average cost per unit for a product changes each time more of that product is purchased and added to inventory. As a practical matter, companies generally calculate a new average cost per unit at the time of each sale or when they otherwise need to know the cost per unit. As Exhibit 8–25 shows, we calculate the average cost per unit by dividing the cost of goods available for sale by the total number of units available for sale.

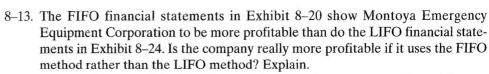

EXHIBIT 8–25   Average Cost per Unit Calculation for Montoya's March 22 Sale

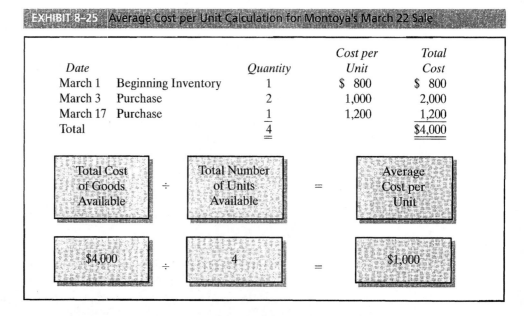

Date		Quantity	Cost per Unit	Total Cost
March 1	Beginning Inventory	1	$ 800	$ 800
March 3	Purchase	2	1,000	2,000
March 17	Purchase	1	1,200	1,200
Total		4		$4,000

Total Cost of Goods Available	÷	Total Number of Units Available	=	Average Cost per Unit
$4,000	÷	4	=	$1,000

Montoya sold one generator on March 22, and we assigned each of the four generators on hand at that time an average cost of $1,000. Therefore, cost of goods sold for the generator sold on March 22 was $1,000. After the March 22 sale, there are three generators in inventory at an average cost of $1,000 each.

The next sale of a generator took place on March 30. But before that, Montoya purchased two more generators—one on March 26 and one on March 29. We must consider these purchases when we calculate the new average cost per unit for the March 30 sale. So, on March 30, in total, there were five generators in inventory at a total cost of $5,700 resulting in an average cost per unit of $1,140. So, the cost of goods sold for the generator sold on March 30 is $1,140.

Exhibit 8–26 shows the calculation for the new average cost per unit at the time of the March 30 sale. We can now calculate the cost of goods sold that should be reported on Montoya's March income statement. Cost of goods sold for the month is the total of the cost of goods sold for each sale. Therefore, cost of goods sold is:

$$\$1,000 + \$1,140 = \$2,140$$

We can also now calculate the cost of ending inventory. After the March 30 sale, the four generators that were left constitute ending inventory. Therefore, the cost of the company's ending inventory for March is:

$$4 \text{ Units} \times \$1,140 = \$4,560$$

There is an alternative to this ending inventory calculation. As we indicated for both the FIFO and LIFO methods, by knowing the amount of cost of goods available for sale ($6,700) and the cost of goods sold ($2,140), we can determine the cost of the company's ending inventory for March 2003:

$$\text{Cost of Goods Available} - \text{Cost of Goods Sold} = \text{Ending Inventory}$$
$$\$6,700 \qquad - \qquad \$2,140 \qquad = \qquad \$4,560$$

EXHIBIT 8–26 Average Cost per Unit Calculation for Montoya's March 30 Sale

Date		Quantity	Cost per Unit	Total Cost
March 22	Inventory	3	$1,000	$3,000
March 26	Purchase	1	1,300	1,300
March 29	Purchase	1	1,400	1,400
Total		5		$5,700

Total Cost of Goods Available	÷	Total Number of Untits Available	=	Available Cost per Unit
$5,700	÷	5	=	$1,140

Discussion Question

8–16. If Montoya Emergency Equipment Corporation sells two more generators before purchasing any more, which two would we assume the company sold under the average cost method?

Exhibit 8–27 shows Montoya's financial statement assuming it used the average cost method and had no business transactions during March except those related to the generators and its rent payment.

As with the FIFO and LIFO presentations, we have included both the February 28 and the March 31 balance sheets in Exhibit 8–27 to demonstrate how the cost of inventory items flows through the financial statements. The $800 in merchandise inventory

Montoya Emergency Equipment Corporation
Income Statement
For the Month Ended March 31, 2003

Sales	$ 3,000
LESS: Cost of goods sold	2,140
Gross margin	$ 860
Operating expenses:	
Warehouse rent	$ (200)
Net income (loss)	$ 660

Montoya Emergency Equipment Corporation
Balance Sheets
February 28, 2003, and March 31, 2003

Assets:	February 28	March 31
Cash	$21,000	$22,300
Accounts receivable	1,500	3,000
Merchandise inventory	800	4,560
Total assets	$23,300	$29,860
Liabilities and stockholders' equity:		
Accounts payable	$ 0	$ 5,900
Common stock	15,000	15,000
Additional paid-in capital	8,000	8,000
Retained earnings	300	960
Total liabilities and stockholders' equity	$23,300	$29,860

EXHIBIT 8–27   Montoya Emergency Equipment Corporation's Financial Statements—Average Cost Method

Montoya had on February 28 becomes the beginning inventory for March. During March, the company purchased $5,900 of generators. Some of the $6,700 cost of goods available for sale becomes part of the merchandise inventory on the March balance sheet ($4,560), while the rest becomes cost of goods sold on the March income statement ($2,140). The $4,560 of merchandise inventory on Montoya's March 31 balance sheet represents the unsold generators, while the $2,140 cost of goods sold represents the two generators Montoya sold in March. We combine the $660 net income with the previous retained earnings balance of $300 to arrive at the March 31 retained earnings balance of $960.

Discussion Question

8–17. Using Montoya Emergency Equipment Corporation's financial statements in Exhibit 8–27, explain the increase in cash from $21,000 to $22,300.

We have explored four popular inventory approaches and have seen how they result in different cost of goods sold and ending inventory amounts. Now we will further explore how the inventory cost flow method a company selects affects its financial statements.

◆ THE EFFECTS OF INVENTORY COST FLOW METHOD CHOICE

The financial statements we prepared for Montoya Emergency Equipment Corporation using the average cost method (Exhibit 8–27) are based on exactly the same set of facts as the ones we prepared using FIFO (Exhibit 8–20) and LIFO (Exhibit 8–24). That is, the reality is the same. What differs is the measurement of that reality. Exhibit 8–28 summarizes the differences that result from using the three different cost flow assumptions.

	FIFO	LIFO	Average Cost
Goods Available for Sale	$6,700	$6,700	$6,700
Income Statement:			
Cost of Goods Sold	$1,800	$2,600	$2,140
Net Income	$1,000	$200	$660
Balance Sheet:			
Ending Inventory	$4,900	$4,100	$4,560
Retained Earnings	$1,300	$ 500	$ 960

EXHIBIT 8–28   Effect of Inventory Cost Flow Assumptions

It appears that Montoya Emergency Equipment Corporation is most profitable if it employs the FIFO method and least profitable if it uses the LIFO method. The average cost method results in profits somewhere between FIFO and LIFO. In reality, a company is no "better off" when it selects one cost flow method over another. Let's take a closer look at the two opposite ends of the inventory spectrum, FIFO and LIFO.

EFFECTS OF FIFO

As you have seen, FIFO matches the oldest product cost with current sales revenue. What this means is that, when inventory prices are changing, it is probable that sales revenue will be matched with costs that are different (older) than the current replacement costs of the products sold. This is because FIFO assumes that the earliest goods were sold first and that the most current costs are associated with goods left in ending merchandise inventory. Financial statement users should be aware of this when they are trying to determine the future earnings potential of a company that uses FIFO.

FIFO provides good information to decision makers trying to determine the present condition of a company because it values inventory with costs that are the most recent and up to date. When a company uses FIFO, it assigns the most current product cost to ending inventory. Therefore, the ending inventory cost shown on a company's balance sheet would closely approximate the current value of the inventory.

EFFECTS OF LIFO

As you have seen, LIFO matches the most recent product cost with sales revenue. LIFO probably provides the best information available for financial decision makers trying to determine the future earnings potential of a company. However, over time, LIFO may distort the dollar amount companies assign to inventory on their balance sheets because the costs used to value LIFO ending inventories may be so old they are severely outdated. For example, if a company has had a product in inventory continually for 20 years, at least part of the cost assigned to that product will be cost from 20 years ago. If prices are increasing, the dollar amount the balance sheet shows for inventory will be unrealistically low. This is what happened at Palmer Nursery, the example we used in the opening vignette for this chapter. Remember that you were concerned when you looked at the company's balance sheet because the dollar amount of inventory was so low. And yet, when you made your site visit, you found a huge amount of physical inventory. To demonstrate how this happened at Palmer (and could happen in any company), we will look at just one item from Palmer's operation, an aloe vera plant.

Let's say that Palmer purchased 1,000 aloe vera plants at the beginning of 1983 for $1.00 each. Since 1983, the company has purchased and sold countless aloe vera plants but always keeps a minimum of 1,000 plants in inventory. So, at the end of 2003, Palmer has 1,000 aloe vera plants on hand. Now, you know that these are not the same 1,000 plants Palmer purchased in 1983. Those were sold long ago, as were the ones Palmer bought in 1984, 1985, and so on. Remember, that is physical flow and we're talking here about cost flow. Now let's assume that the cost of nursery plants has increased by about 3 percent each year. Exhibit 8–29 shows how Palmer's cost per aloe vera plant has increased since 1983.

Year	Cost at Beginning of Year	Percent Increase	Cost at End of Year
1983	$1.00	103%	$1.03
1984	1.03	103%	1.06
1985	1.06	103%	1.09
1986	1.09	103%	1.13
1987	1.13	103%	1.16
1988	1.16	103%	1.19
1989	1.19	103%	1.23
1990	1.23	103%	1.27
1991	1.27	103%	1.30
1992	1.30	103%	1.34
1993	1.34	103%	1.38
1994	1.38	103%	1.43
1995	1.43	103%	1.47
1996	1.47	103%	1.51
1997	1.51	103%	1.56
1998	1.56	103%	1.60
1999	1.60	103%	1.65
2000	1.65	103%	1.70
2001	1.70	103%	1.75
2002	1.75	103%	1.81
2003	1.81	103%	1.86

EXHIBIT 8-29   Cost Increase of Aloe Vera Plants Since 1983

Even though Palmer's 2003 replacement cost for the 1,000 aloe vera plants is $1,860 (1,000 × $1.86), under LIFO, Palmer would value the plants on hand at the end of 2003 at $1,000 (1,000 × $1.00) for its December 31, 2003, inventory. This is because Palmer uses the cost of the most recently purchased products for its cost of goods sold (last-in, first-out), and it uses the cost of the inventory it purchased earliest to value its ending inventory. A plant that costs Palmer $1.86 today cost the company only $1.00 in 1983. Because the physical inventory of plants has never fallen below 1,000 units, the 1,000 aloe vera plants on hand at the end of 2003 each carry a 1983 cost ($1.00). If this were the case for all of the products in Palmer's inventory, the total dollar amount of inventory reported on the company's balance sheet would be dramatically lower than the replacement cost of the inventory. This is why LIFO does not provide the best information for decision makers trying to determine the present condition of a company because LIFO values inventory with costs that can be years out of date.

When the authors of *Accounting Trends and Techniques* surveyed 600 companies to determine which inventory cost flow method they used for the year 2000, this was the response:

FIFO	386
LIFO	283
Average Cost	180
Other	38
Total	887

The total of 887 far exceeds the number of companies surveyed because many companies have more than one type of inventory and use more than one method. Montoya, for example, might use the average cost method on its generators, but FIFO on the emergency food supplies it sells.

As was the case with accounting for depreciation of long-lived assets, accounting for the cost of merchandise inventory affects the net income a company reports for a given period. The amount of inventory a company reports is also affected. Remember that the total cost of goods available for sale will be shown as either cost of goods sold (expense on the income statement) or as the cost of ending inventory (asset on the balance sheet). If more of that total cost is shown as expense on the income statement (as would be the case with LIFO in a time of rising prices), then less of that total cost will be shown as the asset inventory on the balance sheet. Informed users of financial statements must have an understanding of the effect of the various inventory cost flow methods if they hope to use accounting information to its fullest potential.

◆ STATEMENT OF CASH FLOWS

As we mentioned in previous chapters, the operating activities section of the statement of cash flows includes cash flows for the revenues and expenses that are associated with a company's ongoing business operations. With respect to the sale of merchandise inventory, operating activities include cash received from customers for sales and cash payments to suppliers for merchandise. In the case of Montoya Emergency Equipment Corporation, cash flow from operating activities for March 2003 does not equal the company's income from operations because of two important factors. First, Montoya's March sales were credit sales rather than cash sales. Second, Montoya purchased the generators in March on account instead of paying cash for them. Rather than confusing you at this point by presenting the statement of cash flows with these complicating factors, we will cover the handling of such complications (and others) in Chapter 10, when we take a closer look at the statement of cash flows.

◆ USING FINANCIAL INFORMATION

Next, we will present a measure that economic decision makers use to evaluate inventory levels—the inventory turnover ratio. As an example, we will use the financial statements for Palmer Nursery we show in Exhibit 8–30.

EXHIBIT 8–30 Palmer Nursery, Inc.'s Financial Statements—LIFO Inventory Method

Palmer Nursery, Inc.
Income Statement
For the Year Ended December 31, 2003

Sales	$1,850,000
LESS: Cost of goods sold	1,125,000
Gross margin	$ 725,000
Operating expenses	(577,000)
Net income (loss)	$ 148,000

Palmer Nursery, Inc.
Balance Sheets
As of December 31, 2003 and 2002

	2003	2002
Assets:		
Cash	$175,000	$116,000
Merchandise inventory	100,000	106,000
Other assets	415,000	315,000
Total assets	$690,000	$537,000
Liabilities:		
Accounts payable	$ 75,000	$ 70,000
Stockholders' equity:		
Common stock	$ 25,000	$ 25,000
Additional paid-in capital	10,000	10,000
Retained earnings	580,000	432,000
Total stockholders' equity	$615,000	$467,000
Total liabilities and stockholders' equity	$690,000	$537,000

INVENTORY TURNOVER RATIO

inventory turnover ratio
A liquidity ratio that indicates how long a company holds its inventory.

The **inventory turnover ratio** expresses the theoretical number of times the complete inventory was sold during the year. For example, if cost of goods sold is $400,000 and average inventory is $100,000, the inventory turned over or was sold four times ($400,000/$100,000). The formula for this ratio is:

$$\text{Inventory turnover ratio} = \frac{\text{Cost of goods sold}}{\text{Average inventory}}$$

The cost of goods sold figure in the numerator comes from the income statement. The denominator is normally based on the inventory shown on the balance sheet. However, if we are analyzing a company that uses the LIFO inventory method (as Palmer does), it is a common practice to use the company's FIFO inventory value when computing the inventory turnover ratio. By doing so, the inventory turnover calculation is based on the most current costs for both cost of goods sold and inventories. We use an average amount for this ratio for the same reason we used an average amount in earlier ratios. Since the cost of goods sold in the numerator occurred throughout 2003, we should use the amount of inventory throughout the year. We will assume that Palmer has disclosed in its notes to the financial statements that the FIFO value of its 2002 and 2003 inventories were $191,860 and $186,000, respectively, so we determine the average inventory of $188,930 ($191,860 + $186,000 = $377,860/2 = $188,930). We calculate Palmer's inventory turnover ratio for 2003 as:

$$\frac{\$1,125,000}{\$188,930} = 5.95 \text{ times}$$

The inventory turnover ratio for Palmer indicates that its inventory turns over 5.95 times per year. That is, in theory, the company sells its entire inventory the equivalent of nearly six times each year. Inventory turnover varies greatly from industry to industry and company to company, but generally, the higher the inventory turnover without sacrificing customer satisfaction, the better.

You might note that because Palmer's LIFO inventory value is so low, the company's inventory turnover would have been 10.92 times per year had we used its LIFO inventory values. Now, if you think back to the opening vignette of this chapter, you can see how Palmer's inventory value as shown on the balance sheet might have appeared to be too low when in fact the company had plenty of product (maybe even too much).

Palmer's inventory turnover of 5.95 times per year becomes easier to comprehend if we extend the calculation to determine average length of time product is held in inventory before it is sold. To calculate the **average inventory holding period,** we divide the inventory turnover ratio into 365 (the number of days in a year). Palmer's average inventory holding period is:

average inventory holding period The average length of time product is held in inventory.

$$\text{Average inventory holding period in days} = \frac{365}{\text{Inventory turnover ratio}}$$

$$\frac{365}{5.95} = 61.34 \text{ days}$$

This calculation indicates that Palmer's inventory turns over every 61.34 days. That is, in theory, the company sells the equivalent of its entire inventory every 61.34 days. In general, the fewer days sales in inventory, the better, as long as the company has enough inventory to maintain the desired level of customer satisfaction.

Now that you have an understanding of some of the issues and situations that impact financial statements, in Chapter 9, we will explore the balance sheet and income statement in more detail.

Summary ●

The term *merchandise inventory* (or *inventory*) refers to the physical units of goods that a company plans to sell. Inventory on hand at the beginning of a given income statement period (beginning inventory) and the inventory bought during the period (purchases) constitute the total amount of goods the company could sell (goods available for sale). Goods available for sale will either be on hand at the end of the period or be assumed sold.

Under accrual accounting, when inventory is purchased, its cost is considered an asset to the company and is listed as such on the balance sheet. As inventory is sold, its cost is converted from an asset to an expense, which is listed on the income statement as cost of goods sold. It follows, then, that the total cost of goods available for sale will end up either as ending inventory (an asset on the balance sheet) or as cost of goods sold (an expense on the income statement).

Two types of systems have been developed to track the cost of inventory. The periodic system counts inventory and traces costs only at the end of each income statement period, while the perpetual system updates inventory counts and costs each time a sale or purchase is made. Perpetual inventory systems usually make use of computer technology and scanners that read UPCs. Even though inventory records are updated often when a perpetual system is in place, physical inventory counts are still necessary. Determining the actual amount of inventory on hand may uncover theft, damage, or spoilage of inventory.

The physical flow of inventory can be quite different from the flow of inventory costs. Several methods have been developed to trace inventory costs as they move from the balance sheet to the income statement. Of the four methods we presented in this chapter, only under the specific identification method is the physical flow and the cost flow the same. The other three methods are cost flow assumptions that prescribe which inventory items are assumed to be the ones sold. The first-in, first-out (FIFO) method assumes that the first units of inventory purchased are the first ones sold. Conversely, the last-in, first-out (LIFO) method assumes that the last units of inventory purchased are the first sold. The average cost method assigns an average cost to the units of inventory on hand at the time of each sale. Companies may choose to use any of these cost flow methods. If the price they pay for inventory items varies during the period, the choice will impact several amounts reported on the company's financial statements.

Inventory Purchasing Issues

This appendix covers two important issues that companies must contend with when they purchase merchandise inventory—payment terms and freight terms.

PAYMENT TERMS AND CASH DISCOUNTS

Suppliers frequently encourage their customer to pay invoices more quickly by offering a relatively small discount, say 2 percent, in exchange for the customer's prompt payment. Sellers spell out such discounts in their *payment terms*. Payment terms are also called *terms of sale, sales terms*, or simply *terms*. Sellers devise payment terms that best suit their needs and appeal to their customers. Sometimes payment terms are spelled out and easy to understand. For example, the terms might say: *A 2% discount is allowed if paid within 10 days, net invoice amount is due if paid within 30 days.* Or the same terms may be presented in a popular, yet more cryptic, fashion as follows: *2/10, N/30*. In either case, the terms specify that a 2 percent discount is allowed if paid within 10 days from the invoice date; otherwise, full payment is due 30 days after the invoice date. Terms of *1/10, EOM, net 60 days EOM* means that a 1 percent discount is allowed if paid within 10 days after the end of the month (EOM) of the sale; otherwise, full payment is due 60 days from the end of the month of the sale.

To demonstrate, let's return to the Montoya Emergency Equipment Corporation example we used in the chapter to present the cost flow assumptions. Recall that Montoya purchased two generators on March 3 for $1,000 each. If that purchase had terms of 2/10, net 30, Montoya must pay the invoice by March 13 to receive a 2 percent discount. Otherwise, Montoya could wait until April 3 but would have to pay the full invoice amount.

To take advantage of the prompt payment discount, more commonly called the *cash discount*, Montoya would pay 98 percent of $2,000, or $1,960 ($2,000 × .98), by March 13. In this case, the discount amounts to $40 (2% × $2,000). Cash discounts are considered part of inventory acquisition cost and therefore reduce the cost of inventory purchases.

Although cash discounts seem relatively small—commonly 1, 2, or 3 percent for example—on an annualized basis, the amounts are substantial. Let's consider cash terms of 2 percent 10 days, net 30 days. In this situation, the seller is offering a 2 percent discount if the buyer will pay within 10 days. If the buyer does not take advantage of the discount, the buyer must pay the invoice in 30 days, or 20 days after the prompt payment date has passed. Therefore, the 2 percent is offered in return for paying the invoice 20 days earlier. This means that the buyer gets 2 percent for a short 20-day investment. There are 18.25 20-day periods in a year (365/20) and if the buyer could get 2 percent for each of these periods, the buyer would earn a 36.5 percent (18.25 × 2%) return on an annualized basis.

FREIGHT TERMS

Freight terms define the point at which title passes from the seller to the buyer. FOB (free on board) shipping point indicates that the title passes when the merchandise leaves the seller's shipping dock. FOB destination indicates that the title passes when the merchandise arrives at the purchaser's unloading dock.

Freight cost may be paid by either the buyer or seller. If the shipment is made *freight collect*, the buyer must pay the freight costs. On the other hand, if the shipment is made *freight prepaid*, the seller pays the freight costs. Freight costs that the buyer pays are considered part of inventory acquisition cost and therefore increase the cost of inventory purchases.

In some cases, the point at which title transfers to the buyer is used as an indication of which party is responsible for the shipping cost. In such a case, if the terms are FOB shipping point, title passes at the sellers shipping dock and the buyer bears the freight expense. If the terms are FOB destination, the seller owns the goods until delivery and bears the freight expense. Keep in mind that this is not always the case, however. For example, when **Eastman Kodak Company** ships merchandise from its warehouse in Rochester to **Pitman Photo Supply** in Miami, **Kodak** ships it FOB shipping point, freight prepaid. In this case, title passes to **Pitman** as soon as the trucking company picks up the merchandise, but **Kodak** pays the freight bill.

If Montoya Emergency Equipment Corporation bought two generators from Taylor Equipment, Inc., on March 3 with terms of FOB shipping point, freight collect, Montoya will pay the shipping costs directly to the freight company (sometimes called the *common carrier* or simply the *carrier*). This is freight paid to ship merchandise *in* to Montoya—in this case, Montoya is the buyer—and therefore the company should increase its cost of the generators accordingly.

We should not confuse freight paid to ship merchandise *in* with freight paid to ship merchandise *out* to customers. Freight paid to ship merchandise out to customers—when Montoya is selling merchandise—would be considered part of selling expense.

✦✦✦ Appendix B

Recording Inventory Transactions

The accounting procedures in Part II of Chapter 6 and those in this chapter (including Appendix A) have prepared you to understand the following entries regarding the purchase and sale of merchandise inventory. After completing your work on this appendix, you should be able to prepare the journal entries associated with purchase and sale of merchandise inventory.

The recording process for merchandise inventory involves seven basic types of transactions:

Transaction 1: Purchasing inventory
Transaction 2: Paying freight charges on purchases
Transaction 3: Paying the vendor for merchandise
Transaction 4: Returning merchandise
Transaction 5: Selling merchandise to customers
Transaction 6: Receiving cash from customer
Transaction 7: Adjusting inventory records to the physical count

To record these transactions, accountants use the following general ledger accounts:

- Asset accounts:

  Inventory or *Merchandise inventory*

- Expense accounts:

  Cost of goods sold
  Purchase discounts (a contra-account to *Cost of goods sold*)
  Freight-out (a selling expense)

- Revenue accounts:

  Sales or *Sales revenue*
  Sales returns and allowances
  Sales discounts

Recall that debits increase assets, expenses, and losses, and credits increase liabilities, equity, revenues, and gains. You should also recall that debits and credits must equal for each journal entry. We will now examine the journal entries that the Montoya Emergency Equipment Corporation would make to record the transactions for its purchase and sale of merchandise inventory. The entries in this appendix demonstrate the perpetual inventory system, which is far and away the system most commonly used today. Where it is appropriate and nonrepetitive, we will analyze each transaction using the four steps we introduced in Chapter 6.

1. Determine if and when a transaction occurred, which accounts were affected, which account balances should increase and which should decrease, and by how much.
2. Determine which accounts should be debited and which should be credited.
3. Make the journal entry.
4. Review the entry to ensure it is in proper form and that the debits equal the credits.

Transaction 1: On March 3, Montoya Emergency Equipment Corporation purchased two generators on account for $2,000, 2/10, net 30, FOB destination, freight collect.

1. This transaction took place on March 3, 2003. The transaction affects merchandise inventory and accounts payable. We should increase the balances of both merchandise inventory and accounts payable by $2,000.
2. We increase merchandise inventory, an asset account, with a debit, and we increase accounts payable, a liability account, with a credit.
3. The general journal entry:

```
2003
Mar 3   Merchandise inventory                    2,000
             Accounts payable                              2,000
```

4. A final check of the entry reveals that we dated it correctly, we made the debit part of the entry first, and the entry is in balance. The entry is fine.

Transaction 2: On March 4, Montoya paid the freight bill of $125 from UPS to deliver the generators purchased on March 3 to Montoya's warehouse.

1. This transaction took place on March 4, 2003. Because the freight is for shipping the generators to Montoya's warehouse, it is treated as part of the cost of the merchandise. Therefore, we should increase merchandise inventory. Also, Montoya paid UPS, so it should decrease cash. We should increase the balance of merchandise inventory and decrease cash by $125.
2. We increase merchandise inventory with a debit and decrease cash with a credit.
3. The general journal entry:

```
2003
Mar 4   Merchandise inventory                     125
             Cash                                          125
```

4. A final check of the entry reveals that it is fine.

Transaction 3: First Assumption: Assume that on March 12, 2003, Montoya paid for the generators it purchased on March 3. Note that Montoya paid the invoice within the discount period.

1. This transaction took place on March 12, 2003. Montoya took the 2 percent cash discount of $40 ($2,000 × .02) and paid only the remaining 98 percent of the invoice, which amounts to $1,960 ($2,000 × .98). The transaction affects accounts payable, cash, and, because the discount is considered a reduction in the inventory's acquisition cost, merchandise inventory. Instead of affecting the merchandise inventory account, some companies use an account called *purchase discounts*. We should decrease the balance of accounts payable by the amount of the liability satisfied by the payment. In this case, even though Montoya is paying less than the full invoice amount, the payment satisfies the entire liability. Therefore, we should decrease accounts payable by $2,000, decrease cash by the $1,960 paid, and decrease merchandise inventory by the $40 cash discount.
2. We decrease accounts payable with a debit, and we decrease both cash and inventory with credits.
3. The general journal entry:

```
2003
Mar 12   Accounts payable                          2,000
              Cash                                          1,960
              Merchandise inventory (or purchase discounts)     40
```

4. A final check of the entry reveals that it is fine.

Transaction 3: Second Assumption: Now assume that Montoya didn't pay for the generators it purchased on March 3 until April 2, 2003. Note that under this assumption, Montoya did not pay for the generators in time to earn the cash discount.

1. Under this assumption, this transaction took place on April 2, 2003. Because Montoya did not pay for the generators within the discount period, it paid the full invoice amount and took no discount. Therefore, the transaction affects accounts payable and cash. We should decrease the balances of both accounts payable and cash by the $2,000 Montoya paid.
2. We decrease accounts payable with a debit, and we decrease cash with a credit.
3 The general journal entry:

```
2003
Apr 2   Accounts payable                          2,000
             Cash                                          2,000
```

4. A final check of the entry reveals that it is fine.

Transaction 4: Now let's assume that instead of paying for the generators, Montoya returned them to the manufacturer on March 8, 2003.

1. This transaction took place on March 8, 2003. When a company uses a perpetual inventory system, the entry to record a return of merchandise is simply a reversal of the entry made to record the purchase. Therefore, the entry affects accounts payable and merchandise inventory. We should decrease the balances of both accounts payable and merchandise inventory by the $2,000 cost of the merchandise Montoya returned.

2. We decrease accounts payable with a debit, and we decrease merchandise inventory with a credit.

3. The general journal entry:

2003			
Mar 8	Accounts payable	2,000	
	Merchandise inventory		2,000

4. A final check of the entry reveals that it is fine.

Transaction 5: On March 17, Montoya sold a generator to Earheart Industries for $1,500 on account with terms of 2/10, net/30.

1. This transaction took place on March 17, 2003. Montoya sold the generator to Earheart on account, so the transaction affects sales and accounts receivable. Also, under the perpetual method, we must make an entry to move the cost of the sold generator from merchandise inventory to cost of goods sold. We should increase both sales and accounts receivable by the $1,500 selling price. In addition, assuming Montoya Emergency Equipment Corporation uses FIFO, we should increase cost of goods sold and decrease merchandise inventory by the generator's $800 cost.

2. We increase accounts receivable with a debit and increase sales with a credit. Also, we increase cost of goods sold, an expense, with a debit, and we decrease merchandise inventory with a credit.

3. The general journal entry:

2003			
Mar 17	Accounts receivable	1,500	
	Sales		1,500
17	Cost of goods sold	800	
	Merchandise inventory		800

4. A final check of the entry reveals that it is fine.

Transaction 6: First Assumption: Assume that on March 26 Earheart Industries paid Montoya for the generator it purchased on March 17, 2003. Note that under this assumption, Earheart paid Montoya for the generator within the discount period.

1. This transaction took place on March 26, 2003. The customer deducted the 2 percent cash discount of $30 ($1,500 3 .02) from its payment, so Montoya will receive a payment of $1,470, which is 98 percent of the sale amount ($1,500 3 .98). This transaction affects cash and accounts receivable, and, when a customer takes a discount for prompt payment, the sales discounts account is used. We should increase cash by the $1,470 received and increase sales discounts by the $30 discount. We should decrease the balance of accounts receivable by the amount of the receivable satisfied by the customer's payment. In this case, even though the customer paid less than the full invoice amount, the payment satisfies the entire liability. Therefore, we should decrease accounts receivable by $1,500.

2. We increase cash with a debit, and we also increase sales discounts, a contra-revenue account, with a debit. We decrease accounts receivable with a credit.

3. The general journal entry:

2003			
Mar 26	Cash	1,470	
	Sales discounts	30	
	Accounts receivable		1,500

4. A final check of the entry reveals that it is fine.

Transaction 6: Second Assumption: Now we will assume that Earheart Industries did not pay for the generator it purchased from Montoya until April 16, 2003. Note that under this assumption, Earheart paid Montoya too late to take the prompt payment discount.

1. This transaction took place on April 16, 2003. The customer paid too late to take advantage of the cash discount, so it paid Montoya the full $1,500. Therefore, this transaction affects only cash and accounts receivable. We should increase cash and decrease accounts receivable by the $1,500 Montoya received.
2. We increase cash with a debit, and we decrease accounts receivable with a credit.
3. The general journal entry:

```
2003
Apr 16   Cash                              1,500
              Accounts receivable                    1,500
```

4. A final check of the entry reveals that it is fine.

Transaction 7: Assume that on December 31, 2003, Montoya's accounting records reflected a perpetual inventory balance of nine generators at $1,400 each. Assume further that the company took a physical count of its inventory and discovered only eight generators in stock. Montoya Emergency Equipment Corporation must adjust its perpetual inventory records to reflect the reality of having only eight generators in inventory.

1. It would be difficult, if not impossible, to determine when the missing generator disappeared. The discrepancy was detected when the physical inventory was taken on December 31. Therefore, we use December 31, 2003, as the date for the entry to adjust the perpetual inventory records to match the physical count. Generally, we adjust cost of goods sold and merchandise inventory as necessary to bring the accounting records in balance with the physical inventory count. In this case, since there is an inventory shortage, we decrease merchandise inventory and increase cost of goods sold by $1,400.
2. We increase cost of goods sold with a debit, and we decrease merchandise inventory with a credit.
3. The general journal entry:

```
2003
Dec 31   Cost of goods sold                1,400
              Merchandise inventory                  1,400
```

4. A final check of the entry reveals that it is fine.

In Transaction 7, we assumed that the perpetual inventory records reflected a lower amount of inventory than Montoya actually had in stock. If, on the other hand, Montoya's December 31 physical inventory count had revealed that the actual inventory was *more* than the amount the perpetual inventory reflected, the adjustment would have been a debit to merchandise inventory, and cost of goods sold would have been credited.

Key Terms •

- average cost method, F–322
- average inventory holding period, F–328
- beginning inventory, F–304
- book inventory, F–312
- cost of goods sold, F–305

- cost of sales, F–305
- first-in, first-out (FIFO), F–317
- goods available for sale, F–304
- inventory, F–304
- inventory turnover ratio, F–328
- last-in, first-out (LIFO), F–319

- merchandise inventory, F–304
- periodic inventory system, F–311
- perpetual inventory system, F–311
- purchases, F–304
- specific identification method, F–313

Review the Facts

A. Define the terms *inventory* and *merchandise inventory*.

B. What two amounts are added to determine goods available for sale?

C. Goods available for sale is allocated to two places in financial statements. Name them.

D. Under accrual accounting, the cost of inventory still on hand at the end of the period is shown on which financial statement?

E. Under accrual accounting, the cost of inventory no longer on hand at the end of the period is shown on which financial statement?

F. Explain the difference between the physical flow of merchandise and the cost flow of merchandise.

G. What are the two types of inventory systems? Explain the differences between them.

H. List three causes of differences between book inventory and the results of a physical inventory count.

I. Why are FIFO, LIFO, and average cost referred to as "assumptions"?

J. Describe in your own words the differences among the FIFO, LIFO, and average cost methods.

K. Name the financial ratio used to evaluate inventory. What does it tell you?

L. Describe what is meant by sales terms of 2/10, n/30. (Appendix A)

M. What is the difference between FOB shipping point and FOB destination? (Appendix A)

N. Describe the entry that would be necessary if a company's perpetual inventory records indicated a greater amount of inventory than what physically exists. (Appendix B)

Apply What You Have Learned

LO 1: TERMINOLOGY

8–18. Below is a list of items relating to the concepts presented in this chapter, followed by definitions of those items in scrambled order:

a. Periodic inventory system
b. Perpetual inventory system
c. Goods available for sale
d. Cost of goods sold

e. Merchandise inventory
f. First-in, first-out method
g. Last-in, first-out method
h. Average cost method

1. _____ The total amount of merchandise inventory a company can sell during a particular income statement period.

2. _____ All inventory and cost of goods sold calculations are done at the end of the period.

3. _____ Cost of goods sold is determined based on the assumption that the first units acquired are the first ones sold.

4. _____ Updates both the physical count of inventory units and the cost classification of those units when a transaction involves inventory.

5. _____ The physical units of product a company buys and then resells as part of its business operation.

6. _____ Cost of goods sold is based on the assumption that the last units acquired are the first ones sold.

7. _____ Cost of goods sold is determined based on the total cost of inventory units divided by the number of units.

8. _____ The cost of merchandise inventory that has been converted from an asset on the balance sheet to an expense on the income statement.

Required: Match the letter next to each item on the list with the appropriate definition. Each letter will be used only once.

LO 1: ELEMENTS OF GOODS AVAILABLE FOR SALE

8–19. Identify the various components of goods available for sale and define each component.

LO 1: ELEMENTS OF COST OF GOODS SOLD

8–20. Ned Flanders Company began the month of March 2004 with 304 units of product on hand at a total cost of $9,120. During the month, the company purchased an additional 818 units at $30 per unit. Sales for March were 732 units at a total cost of $21,960.

Required: From the information provided, complete the following schedule:

	Units	Cost
+ Beginning Inventory	_____	$_____
+ Purchases	_____	_____
= Goods Available for Sale	_____	_____
− Cost of Goods Sold	_____	_____
= Ending Inventory	_____	$_____

LO 7: CALCULATE INVENTORY TURNOVER RATIOS

8–21. This problem is a continuation of problem 8–20.

Required:

    a. Compute the inventory turnover ratio for the company.
    b. Compute the average inventory holding period for the company.

LO 1: ELEMENTS OF COST OF GOODS SOLD

8–22. Andrew D. Company began the month of June 2004 with 150 units of product on hand at a total cost of $3,000. During the month, the company purchased an additional 460 units at $20 per unit. Sales for June were 510 units at a total cost of $10,200.

Required: From the information provided, complete the following schedule:

	Units	Cost
+ Beginning Inventory	_____	$_____
+ Purchases	_____	_____
= Goods Available for Sale	_____	_____
− Ending Inventory	_____	_____
= Cost of Goods Sold	_____	$_____

LO 7: CALCULATE INVENTORY TURNOVER RATIOS

8–23. This problem is a continuation of problem 8–22.

Required:

    a. Compute the inventory turnover ratio for the company.
    b. Compute the average inventory holding period for the company.

LO 1: ELEMENTS OF COST OF GOODS SOLD

8–24. Bill Carter Company began the month of April 2005 with 452 units of product on hand at a cost of $54 per unit. During the month, the company purchased an additional 1,500 units at a total cost of $81,000. At the end of April, 616 units were still on hand at a cost of $33,264.

Required: From the information provided, complete the following schedule:

	Units	Cost
+ Beginning Inventory	_____	$_____
+ Purchases	_____	_____
= Goods Available for Sale	_____	_____
− Ending Inventory	_____	_____
= Cost of Goods Sold	_____	$_____

LO 1: ELEMENTS OF COST OF GOODS SOLD

8–25. Jones and Mosley Company began the month of July 2004 with 412 units of product on hand at a cost of $34 per unit. During the month, the company purchased an additional 1,300 units at a total cost of $44,200. At the end of July, 712 units were still on hand at a cost of $24,208.

Required: From the information provided, complete the following schedule:

	Units	Cost
+ Beginning Inventory	_____	$_____
+ Purchases	_____	_____
= Goods Available for Sale	_____	_____
− Ending Inventory	_____	_____
= Cost of Goods Sold	_____	$_____

LO 1: ELEMENTS OF COST OF GOODS SOLD

8–26. Nancy Keegan and Company began the month of February 2004 with 650 units of product on hand at a total cost of $11,050. During the month, the company purchased an additional 1,884 units at $17 per unit. Sales for February were 1,734 units at $64 per unit. The total cost of the units sold was $29,478, and operating expenses totaled $18,900.

Required:

a. From the information provided, complete the following schedule:

	Units	Cost
+ Beginning Inventory	_____	$_____
+ Purchases	_____	_____
= Goods Available for Sale	_____	_____
− Ending Inventory	_____	_____
= Cost of Goods Sold	_____	$_____

b. Prepare Nancy Keegan and Company's income statement for the month ended February 28, 2004.

LO 1: ELEMENTS OF COST OF GOODS SOLD

8–27. Bill Matheis and Company began the month of October 2005 with 470 units of product on hand at a total cost of $15,980. During the month, the company purchased an additional 1,244 units at $34 per unit. Sales for October were 1,280 units at $60 per unit. The total cost of the units sold was $43,520, and operating expenses totaled $11,300.

Required:

a. From the information provided, complete the following schedule:

	Units	Cost
+ Beginning Inventory	_____	$_____
+ Purchases	_____	_____
= Goods Available for Sale	_____	_____
− Ending Inventory	_____	_____
= Cost of Goods Sold	_____	$_____

b. Prepare Bill Matheis and Company's income statement for the month ended October 31, 2005.

LO 3 & 4: COST FLOW VERSUS PHYSICAL FLOW OF GOODS

8–28. Mary Reed TV Sales and Service began the month of March with two identical TV sets in inventory. During the month, six additional TV sets (identical to the two in beginning inventory) were purchased as follows:

2 on March 9
1 on March 13
3 on March 24

The company sold two of the TV sets on March 12, another one on March 17, and two more on March 28.

Required:

    a. Assume the company uses a perpetual inventory system and the first-in, first-out cost flow method, from a cost flow perspective:

        1. Which two TV sets were sold on March 12?
        2. Which one was sold on March 17?
        3. Which two TV sets were sold on March 28?
        4. The cost of which three TV sets will be included in Reed's inventory at the end of March?

    b. If the company uses a perpetual inventory system and the last-in, first-out cost flow method, the cost of which three TV sets will be included in Reed's inventory at the end of March?

LO 3 & 4: COST FLOW VERSUS PHYSICAL FLOW OF GOODS

8–29. Pfeiffer's Piano Sales & Service began the month of February with two identical pianos in inventory. During the month, six additional pianos (identical to the two in beginning inventory) were purchased as follows:

2 on February 10
1 on February 20
3 on February 26

The company sold two of the pianos on February 12, another one on February 17, and two more on February 28.

Required:

    a. Assume the company uses a perpetual inventory system and the first-in, first-out cost flow method, from a cost flow perspective:

        1. Which two pianos were sold on February 12?
        2. Which one was sold on February 17?
        3. Which two pianos were sold on February 28?
        4. The cost of which three pianos will be included in Pfeiffer's inventory at the end of February?

    b. If the company uses a perpetual inventory system and the last-in, first-out cost flow method, the cost of which three pianos will be included in Pfeiffer's inventory at the end of February?

LO 4: INVENTORY COST

8–30. The Tomlin Company purchased 500 drill presses from the Falcon Machinery Company. Each drill press cost $350. The presses are to be sold for $700 each. Tomlin paid $1,850 for freight to have them shipped in from Falcon and $260 for freight insurance while the presses were in transit. Tomlin Company hired two more salespeople for a cost of $4,000 per month.

Required: Calculate the cost of the inventory of drill presses to be recorded in the books and records.

LO 4: INVENTORY COST

8–31. The Baker Company acquired 4,000 hand saws from the Snaggletooth Saw Company. Each saw cost $10. The saws are to be sold for $25 each. Baker paid $750 for freight and $250 for insurance while the saws were in transit. Baker Company ran a special newspaper ad costing $800 to advertise the saws.

Required: Calculate the cost of the inventory of saws to be recorded in the books and records.

LO 4: INVENTORY COST

8–32. The Winter Company acquired 10,000 cases of wine from the Sonoma Wine Company. Each case of wine cost $130 and contains 12 bottles. The wine will sell for $20 per bottle.

Sonoma paid $1,200 for freight and $550 for freight insurance while the wine was in transit. Winter Company ran a special newspaper ad costing $1,800 to advertise the wine.

Required: Calculate the cost of the inventory of wine to be recorded in the books and records.

LO 4: INVENTORY COST

8–33. The Zeus Grocery Store began operations on July 1. The following transactions took place in the month of July.

   a. Cash purchases of merchandise during July were $500,000.
   b. Purchases of merchandise on account during July were $400,000.
   c. The cost of freight to bring the product in to Zeus was $25,000.
   d. Zeus returned $22,000 of merchandise purchased in part b to the supplier.
   e. The grocery store manager's salary is $3,000 for the month.

Required: Determine the amount that Zeus Grocery should use to calculate the cost of its merchandise inventory.

LO 4: INVENTORY COST

8–34. Chang's Gift Shop began operations on September 1. The following transactions took place in the month of September.

   a. Cash purchases of merchandise during September were $175,000.
   b. Purchases of merchandise on account during September were $225,000.
   c. The cost of freight to bring the merchandise in to Chang's was $5,000.
   d. Electricity cost totaled $800 for the month.
   e. Store rent was $2,400 for the month.
   f. Chang's returned $13,000 of merchandise purchased in part b to the supplier.
   g. The store manager's salary is $3,000 for the month.
   h. Advertising for the month of September totaled $4,000.

Required: Calculate the amount that Chang's should include in the valuation of its merchandise inventory.

LO 6: VERY SIMPLE FIFO, LIFO, AND AVERAGE INVENTORY CALCULATIONS— ONE SALE

8–35. The following information pertains to the inventory records of Gene's Pool Supply:

Date	Purchases (Units)	Cost per Unit	Total Cost
June 1	2,400	$100	$240,000
June 20	3,600	120	432,000
June 27	1,500	130	195,000
Total Goods Available for Sale	7,500		$867,000

The company's only sale occurred on June 30 when it sold 5,925 units. Inventory at the end of June was 1,575 units.

Required: Compute the cost of the inventory at June 30 and the cost of goods sold for the month of June under each of the following cost flow assumptions:

   a. FIFO
   b. LIFO
   c. Average cost method

LO 7: CALCULATE INVENTORY TURNOVER RATIOS

8–36. This problem is a continuation of problem 8–35.

Required:

    a. Compute the inventory turnover ratios for the company under FIFO, LIFO, and the average inventory cost methods.

    b. Compute the average inventory holding period for the company under FIFO, LIFO, and the average inventory cost methods.

    c. How does management's choice of inventory cost flow assumption impact the results of the inventory ratio calculations?

LO 6: VERY SIMPLE FIFO, LIFO, AND AVERAGE INVENTORY CALCULATIONS— ONE SALE

8–37. The following information pertains to one of the products sold by Casey's Computer Supply:

Date	Purchases (Units)	Cost per Unit	Total Cost
November 1	110	$28	$ 3,080
November 12	310	22	6,820
November 25	80	15	1,200
Total Goods Available for Sale	500		$11,100

The company's only sale occurred on November 30 when it sold 385 units. Inventory at the end of November was 115 units.

Required: Compute the cost of the inventory at November 30 and the cost of goods sold for the month of November under each of the following cost flow assumptions:

    a. FIFO

    b. LIFO

    c. Average cost method

LO 6: VERY SIMPLE FIFO, LIFO, AND AVERAGE INVENTORY CALCULATIONS— ONE SALE

8–38. The following information pertains to one of the products sold by William's Wholesale Supply:

Date	Purchases (Units)	Cost per Unit	Total Cost
December 1	800	$3.20	$2,560.00
December 17	750	3.55	2,662.50
December 29	950	3.95	3,752.50
Total Goods Available for Sale	2,500		$8,975.00

The company's only sale occurred on December 31 when it sold 1,580 units. Inventory at the end of December was 920 units.

Required: Compute the cost of the inventory at December 31 and the cost of goods sold for the month of December under each of the following cost flow assumptions:

    a. FIFO

    b. LIFO

    c. Average cost method

LO 6: SIMPLE FIFO, LIFO, AND AVERAGE INVENTORY CALCULATIONS— ONE SALE

8–39. Penny's Precious Metals Company purchases silver to sell by the ounce. During the month of August, its first month of operations, Penny's purchased the following silver:

Date	Purchases	Cost per Unit	Total Cost
August 1	50 ounces	$35.00	$1,750
August 8	25 ounces	39.00	975
August 19	30 ounces	42.00	1,260
August 22	15 ounces	43.00	645
August 29	20 ounces	45.00	900
Total Goods Available for Sale	140 ounces		$5,530

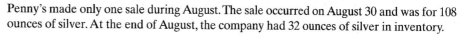

Penny's made only one sale during August. The sale occurred on August 30 and was for 108 ounces of silver. At the end of August, the company had 32 ounces of silver in inventory.

Required: Assuming the company uses a perpetual system, compute the cost of the inventory at August 31 and the cost of goods sold for the month of August under each of the following cost flow assumptions:

a. FIFO
b. LIFO
c. Average cost method

LO 7: CALCULATE INVENTORY TURNOVER RATIOS

8–40. This problem is a continuation of problem 8–39.

Required:

a. Compute the inventory turnover ratios for the company under the FIFO inventory cost flow assumption.
b. Compute the average inventory holding period for the company under the FIFO inventory cost flow assumption.
c. What do the results of these ratios tell you about the company?

LO 6: SIMPLE FIFO, LIFO, AND AVERAGE INVENTORY CALCULATIONS— ONE SALE

8–41. The Repo Rock Company purchases rock by the ton to sell to construction companies. During the month of June, its first month of operations, Repo purchased the following:

Date	Purchases (Tons)	Cost per Ton	Total Cost
June 1	700	$100	$ 70,000
June 6	250	120	30,000
June 17	300	125	37,500
June 24	150	130	19,500
June 29	200	145	29,000
Total Goods Available for Sale	1,600		$186,000

Repo Rock's only sale was on June 30. On June 30, the company sold 1,370 tons of rock. Inventory at the end of June was 230 tons.

Required: Assuming the company uses a perpetual system, compute the cost of the inventory at June 30 and the cost of goods sold for the month of June under each of the following cost flow assumptions:

a. FIFO
b. LIFO
c. Average cost method

LO 7: CALCULATE INVENTORY TURNOVER RATIOS

8–42. This problem is a continuation of problem 8–41.

Required:

a. Compute the inventory turnover ratios for the company under the FIFO inventory cost flow assumption.
b. Compute the average inventory holding period for the company under the FIFO inventory cost flow assumption.
c. What do the results of these ratios tell you about the company?

LO 2, 5, & 6: FIFO AND LIFO INVENTORY CALCULATIONS—MULTIPLE SALES

8–43. Majestic Commercial Supply reported the following information for the year 2004 for one of its products:

Date		Units	Unit Cost	Total Cost
Jan 2	Beginning Inventory	1,000	$10	$10,000
Jan 15	Purchased	1,500	11	16,500
Jan 20	Sold 1,400 Units			
Mar 23	Purchased	1,200	12	14,400
Apr 2	Sold 1,300 Units			
Jun 10	Purchased	1,000	13	13,000
Aug 18	Purchased	1,100	15	16,500
Sep 12	Sold 2,100 Units			
Dec 1	Purchased	1,400	16	22,400
Dec 20	Sold 600 Units			
Total Goods Available for Sale		7,200		$92,800

At the end of the year, a physical count is taken and there are 1,800 units left on December 31, 2004.

Required: Use the perpetual inventory system and determine the ending inventory and the cost of goods sold at December 31, 2004, using:

a. FIFO cost flow method
b. LIFO cost flow method

LO 2, 5, & 6: FIFO AND LIFO INVENTORY CALCULATIONS—MULTIPLE SALES

8–44. The Speace Electrical Supply Company reported the following information for the year 2005 for X-rite Switches:

Date		Units	Unit Cost	Total Cost
Jan 2	Beginning Inventory	500	$10	$ 5,000
Jan 23	Purchased	800	11	8,800
Mar 14	Purchased	600	12	7,200
Mar 18	Sold 1,000 Units			
Jul 5	Purchased	500	13	6,500
Aug 10	Purchased	1,100	14	15,400
Sep 2	Sold 1,300 Units			
Dec 15	Purchased	1,200	15	18,000
Dec 19	Sold 1,800 Units			
Total Goods Available for Sale		4,700		$60,900

A physical count taken on December 31, 2005, revealed that 600 units remained in inventory.

Required: Determine the ending inventory and the cost of goods sold at December 31, 2005, using:

a. FIFO cost flow method
b. LIFO cost flow method

LO 7: CALCULATE INVENTORY TURNOVER RATIOS

8–45. This problem is a continuation of problem 8–44.

Required:

a. Compute the inventory turnover ratios for the company under the FIFO inventory cost flow assumption.
b. Compute the average inventory holding period for the company under the FIFO inventory cost flow assumption.
c. What do the results of these ratios tell you about the company?

LO 2, 5, & 6: FIFO AND LIFO INVENTORY CALCULATIONS—MULTIPLE SALES

8–46. The Kundrat Widget Company reported the following information for the month of January, regarding widgets:

Date		Units	Unit Cost	Total Cost
Jan 1	Beginning Inventory	500	$71	$ 35,500
Jan 3	Purchased	800	73	58,400
Jan 6	Sold 1,020 Units			
Jan 10	Purchased	700	75	52,500
Jan 14	Sold 540 Units			
Jan 22	Purchased	600	80	48,000
Jan 25	Purchased	1,100	85	93,500
Jan 27	Sold 1,190 Units			
Jan 29	Purchased	1,200	87	104,400
Jan 30	Sold 1,315 Units			
Total Goods Available for Sale		4,900		$392,300

At the end of January, a physical count was taken revealing that there were 835 widgets left in inventory.

Required: Determine the January ending inventory and the cost of goods sold using:

    a. FIFO cost flow method
    b. LIFO cost flow method

LO 2, 5, & 6: FIFO, LIFO, AND AVERAGE COST INVENTORY CALCULATIONS— MULTIPLE SALES

8–47. The Spring Sales Company reported the following information for the year 2005, regarding their No. 123 spring:

Date		Units	Cost per Spring	Total Cost
Jan 2	Beginning Inventory	5,000	$15	$ 75,000
Purchases:				
Jan 23		8,000	14	112,000
Mar 14		7,000	13	91,000
Jul 5		6,000	11	66,000
Aug 10		11,000	9	99,000
Dec 15		12,000	8	96,000
Total Goods Available for Sale		49,000		$539,000

Sales of No. 123 springs occurred as follows:

Jan 28	Sold	6,000 springs
Feb 15	Sold	3,000 springs
Jul 6	Sold	15,000 springs
Aug 12	Sold	10,000 springs
Dec 24	Sold	6,600 springs

At the end of the year, a physical count is taken and there are 8,400 springs left on December 31, 2005.

Required: Use the perpetual inventory system and determine the December 31, 2005, ending inventory and the cost of goods sold using:

    a. FIFO cost flow method
    b. LIFO cost flow method
    c. Average cost method

LO 2, 5, & 6: FIFO, LIFO, AND AVERAGE COST INVENTORY CALCULATIONS— MULTIPLE SALES

8–48. During the month of August, the first month of its operations, Maupin Mercantile Company had the following transactions:

Date		Units Purchased	Cost per Unit	Total Cost
August 1	Purchased	50	$35	$1,750
August 3	Sold 40 Units			
August 8	Purchased	25	40	1,000
August 11	Sold 20 Units			
August 19	Purchased	30	42	1,260
August 20	Sold 18 Units			
August 22	Purchased	10	43	430
August 29	Sold 30 Units			
August 30	Purchased	20	45	900
Total Goods Available for Sale		135		$5,340

Maupin's has 27 units left in inventory at the end of August.

Required: Assuming the company uses a perpetual system, compute the cost of the inventory at August 31 and the cost of goods sold for the month of August under each of the following cost flow assumptions:

a. FIFO cost flow method
b. LIFO cost flow method
c. Average cost method

LO 2, 5, & 6: FIFO, LIFO, AVERAGE COST INVENTORY CALCULATIONS—MULTIPLE SALES

8–49. During the month of June, its first month of operations, Walker Company had the following inventory transactions:

		Purchases (Units)	Cost per Unit	Total Cost
June 1	Purchased	700	$100	$ 70,000
June 3	Sold 400 units			
June 6	Purchased	250	105	26,250
June 17	Purchased	300	115	34,500
June 20	Sold 400 units			
June 24	Purchased	150	118	17,700
June 26	Sold 570 units			
June 30	Purchased	200	125	25,000
Total Goods Available for Sale		1,600		$173,450

Walker had 230 units left in inventory at the end of June. Assume a perpetual system of inventory.

Required: Compute the cost of the inventory at June 30 and the cost of goods sold for the month of June under each of the following cost flow assumptions:

a. FIFO cost flow assumption
b. LIFO cost flow assumption
c. Average cost method

LO 5 & 6: CALCULATION AND COMPARISON OF COST FLOW ASSUMPTIONS—INCREASING PRICES

8–50. Cox Company buys and then resells a product that is subject to rather severe cost increases. Following is information concerning Cox's inventory activity during the month of July 2005:

July 1: 431 units on hand, $3,017
July 2: Sold 220 units
July 9: Purchased 500 units @ $8.00 per unit
July 12: Purchased 200 units @ $8.50 per unit
July 16: Sold 300 units
July 21: Purchased 150 units @ $9.00 per unit

July 24: Purchased 50 units @ $9.75 per unit
July 29: Sold 500 units

Required:

a. Assuming Cox employs a perpetual inventory system, calculate cost of goods sold for the month of July 2005 and ending inventory at July 31, 2005, using the following:

1. FIFO cost flow assumption
2. LIFO cost flow assumption
3. Average cost method (round all unit cost calculations to the nearest penny)

b. Which of the three methods resulted in the highest cost of goods sold for July?
c. Which one would result in the highest net income for the company?
d. Which one would provide the highest ending inventory value for Cox's balance sheet?
e. In times of rising prices, which inventory cost flow assumption should Cox select if the company's intention is to favorably impress its banker?

LO 5 & 6: CALCULATION AND COMPARISON OF COST FLOW ASSUMPTIONS— DECREASING PRICES

8–51. The following information is available concerning Elsea Computer Component Company's inventory activity for the month of October 2005:

October 1:   216 units on hand @ $14 per unit
October 5:   Sold 80 units
October 7:   Purchased 150 units @ $13 per unit
October 11: Purchased 100 units @ $12 per unit
October 15: Sold 200 units
October 21: Purchased 300 units @ $10 per unit
October 25: Purchased 50 units @ $8 per unit
October 29: Sold 350 units

Required:

a. Assuming Elsea employs a perpetual inventory system, calculate cost of goods sold (units and cost) for the month of October using the following:

1. FIFO cost flow assumption
2. LIFO cost flow assumption
3. Average cost method (round all unit cost calculations to the nearest penny)

b. Which of the three methods resulted in the highest cost of goods sold for October?
c. Which one will provide the highest net income?
d. Which one will provide the highest ending inventory value for Elsea's balance sheet?
e. If the price of the products Elsea sells generally decreases over time, which inventory cost flow assumption should the company select if its intention is to favorably impress its banker?

LO 5 & 6: CALCULATION AND COMPARISON OF COST FLOW ASSUMPTIONS— INCREASING PRICES

8–52. Zingle's buys and then resells a single product as its primary business activity. Following is information concerning the Zingle's inventory activity for the product during August 2004:

August 1:   210 units on hand @ $5.10 per unit
August 5:   Sold 80 units
August 7:   Purchased 160 units @ $5.25 per unit
August 11: Purchased 110 units @ $5.30 per unit
August 15: Sold 200 units
August 21: Purchased 55 units @ $5.70 per unit
August 25: Purchased 290 units @ $5.80 per unit
August 29: Sold 350 units

Required:

    a. Assuming Zingle's employs a perpetual inventory system, calculate cost of goods sold (units and cost) for the month of August using the following:

        1. FIFO cost flow assumption
        2. LIFO cost flow assumption
        3. Average cost method (round all unit cost calculations to the nearest penny)

    b. Which of the three methods resulted in the highest inventory amount for Zingle's August 31 balance sheet?

    c. How would the differences among the three methods affect Zingle's income statement and balance sheet for the month?

LO 5 & 6: CALCULATION AND COMPARISON OF COST FLOW ASSUMPTIONS— DECREASING PRICES

8–53. David Harris Company buys and then resells a single product as its primary business activity. Following is information concerning the David Harris Company's inventory activity for the product during August 2005:

    August 1:   200 units on hand @ $18 per unit
    August 5:   Sold 80 units
    August 7:   Purchased 170 units @ $17 per unit
    August 11: Purchased 90 units @ $15 per unit
    August 15: Sold 200 units
    August 21: Purchased 275 units @ $14 per unit
    August 25: Purchased 90 units @ $12 per unit
    August 29: Sold 350 units

Required:

    a. Assuming Harris employs a perpetual inventory system, calculate cost of goods sold (units and cost) for the month of August using the following:

        1. FIFO cost flow assumption
        2. LIFO cost flow assumption
        3. Average cost method (round all unit cost calculations to the nearest penny)

    b. Which of the three methods resulted in the highest inventory amount for Harris's August 31 balance sheet?

    c. How would the differences among the three methods affect Harris's income statement and balance sheet for the month?

LO 5 & 6: CALCULATION AND COMPARISON OF COST FLOW ASSUMPTIONS— STABLE PRICES

8–54. Dennis Lee Company buys and then resells a single product as its primary business activity. Following is information concerning Lee's inventory activity for the product during the month of July 2004:

    July 1:   220 units on hand @ $4 per unit
    July 5:   Sold 80 units
    July 7:   Purchased 140 units @ $4 per unit
    July 11: Purchased 85 units @ $4 per unit
    July 15: Sold 200 units
    July 21: Purchased 320 units @ $4 per unit
    July 25: Purchased 40 units @ $4 per unit
    July 29: Sold 350 units

Required:

    a. Assuming Lee employs a perpetual inventory system, calculate cost of goods sold (units and cost) for the month of July using the following:

        1. First-in, first-out method
        2. Last-in, first-out method
        3. Average cost method (round all unit cost calculations to the nearest penny)

  b. Which of the three methods resulted in the highest cost of goods sold for July?
  c. Describe the differences among income statements and balance sheets prepared under the three cost flow assumptions.

LO 2 & 3: IMPACT OF DIFFERENCES BETWEEN PERPETUAL INVENTORY RECORDS AND PHYSICAL INVENTORY

8–55. The Corning Company's perpetual inventory records indicate that the ending inventory should be $160,000. In fact, when Corning Company's staff completed their annual physical inventory, they discovered that the inventory on hand was actually $156,000.

Required:

  a. With respect to the company's accounting records, what action should the Corning Company's accounting staff take regarding the difference between their perpetual inventory records and the inventory that is actually on hand?
  b. If no action is taken, how would this situation adversely impact the usefulness of the company's financial statements?

LO 2 & 3: IMPACT OF DIFFERENCES BETWEEN PERPETUAL INVENTORY RECORDS AND PHYSICAL INVENTORY

8–56. The Ace Company's perpetual inventory system reflected the following amounts for the year ended December 31, 2004:

Ending Inventory	$1,750,000
Cost of Goods Sold	$15,380,000

The staff completed a physical inventory and found that the inventory was actually $1,680,000.

Required:

  a. Name at least two possible reasons for the difference between the company's perpetual inventory records and the actual physical inventory on hand.
  b. With respect to security issues, name at least two actions the company could take to prevent such a thing from happening in the future.
  c. With regard to the company's accounting records, what action should the company take before it publishes its financial statements regarding the difference?
  d. If the company had already published its financial statements for 2004 when it discovered the difference, how would the situation adversely impact the usefulness of the financial statements? Be specific. Indicate which financial statement amounts would be in error and how much the error would be.

LO: COMPREHENSIVE

8–57. Benny Blades Company and Emeril Behar Company both began their operations on January 2, 2005. Both companies experienced exactly the same reality during 2005: They purchased exactly the same number of units of merchandise inventory during the year at exactly the same cost, and they sold exactly the same number of inventory units at exactly the same selling price during the year. They also purchased exactly the same type and amount of property, plant, and equipment and paid exactly the same amount for those purchases. At the end of 2005, the two companies prepared income statements for the year. Blades reported net income of $92,000 and Behar reported net income of $55,000.

Required: List and discuss all items you can think of that might have caused the reported net income for the two companies to be different. (*Note:* Do not restrict yourself only to items covered in Chapter 8.)

LO: COMPREHENSIVE

8–58. Pete Rush Merchandising Company uses a perpetual inventory system. Both the number of inventory units and the inventory costs are updated whenever an inventory transaction occurs. The company's perpetual inventory accounting records provide the following information for October 2005:

	Units	Cost
+ Beginning Inventory	200	$ 600
+ Purchases	1,700	5,100
= Goods Available for Sale	1,900	5,700
− Ending Inventory	400	1,200
= Cost of Goods Sold	1,500	$4,500

On October 31, 2005, Rush conducted a physical count of its inventory and discovered there were only 375 units of inventory actually on hand.

Required:

a. Show Rush's schedule of cost of goods sold and ending inventory as it should be, to reflect the results of the physical inventory count on October 31.
b. Explain what the company should do regarding its accounting records in light of the physical count.
c. If Rush takes no action regarding its accounting records and the inventory difference, what financial statement amounts will be in error on its October 31 financial reports?
d. What are some possible causes of the difference between the inventory amounts in Rush's accounting records and the inventory amounts from the physical count?

LO 8: APPENDIX A—FREIGHT TERMS AND CASH DISCOUNTS

8–59. The Young Company made the following purchases from the Greene Company in August of the current year:

Aug 2   Purchased $5,000 of merchandise, terms 1/10, n/30, FOB shipping point. The goods were received on August 8.
Aug 5   Purchased $2,000 of merchandise, terms 2/10, n/45, FOB shipping point. The goods were received on August 15.
Aug 10 Purchased $4,000 of merchandise, terms 3/10, n/15, FOB destination. The goods were received on August 18.

Required: For each of the listed purchases, answer the following questions:

a. By what dates should the company pay each invoice in order to take advantage of the discount?
b. When is the payment of each invoice due if the company does not intend to take advantage of the discount?
c. What is the amount of the total cash discounts allowed?
d. Assuming the freight charges are $250 on each purchase and the seller pays freight on FOB destination orders and the buyer pays the freight on FOB shipping point orders and the company takes advantage of all the discounts, what is the total amount of inventory costs for the month of August?

LO 8: APPENDIX A—FREIGHT TERMS AND CASH DISCOUNTS

8–60. The Gruber Company made the following purchases from the Cope Company in May of the current year:

May 2   Purchased $3,000 of merchandise, terms 2/10, n/30, FOB destination. The goods were received on May 10.
May 10 Purchased $2,800 of merchandise, terms 2/10, n/60, FOB shipping point. The goods were received on May 19.
May 20 Purchased $6,000 of merchandise, terms 3/10, n/20, FOB destination. The goods were received on May 23.

Required: For each of the listed purchases, answer the following questions:

a. When is the payment for each invoice due assuming the company would like to take advantage of the discount?
b. When is the payment of each invoice due assuming the company does not intend to take advantage of the discount?
c. What is the total amount of the cash discounts allowed?
d. Assuming the freight charges are $400 on each purchase and the seller pays freight on FOB destination orders and the buyer pays the freight on FOB shipping point orders and the company takes advantage of all the discounts, what is the total amount of inventory costs for the month?

LO 8: APPENDIX A—FREIGHT TERMS AND CASH DISCOUNTS

8–61. The Payne Company made the following purchases from the Metz Company in July of the current year:

July 3   Purchased $7,000 of merchandise, terms 2/10, n/15, FOB shipping point. The goods were received on July 9.

July 7   Purchased $1,700 of merchandise, terms 1/10, n/60, FOB shipping point. The goods were received on July 17.

July 20   Purchased $9,000 of merchandise, terms 4/10, n/30, FOB destination. The goods were received on July 23.

Required: For each of the listed purchases, answer the following questions:

a. When is the payment for each invoice due assuming the company would like to take advantage of the discount?

b. When is the payment of each invoice due assuming the company does not intend to take advantage of the discount?

c. What is the total amount of the cash discounts allowed?

d. Assuming the freight charges are $100 on each purchase and the seller pays freight on FOB destination orders and the buyer pays the freight on FOB shipping point orders and the company takes advantage of all the discounts, what is the total amount of inventory costs for the month?

LO 8: APPENDIX B—SIMPLE JOURNAL ENTRIES—PURCHASES AND SALES OF INVENTORY

8–62. The Edwards Company had the following transactions during June:

June 1   Purchased 1,000 radios for cash of $20 each for a total of $20,000.

June 3   Purchased 2,500 clocks on account for $10 each for a total of $25,000.

June 5   Sold 250 of the radios that cost $20 each for cash of $8,000.

June 7   Sold, on account, 500 of the clocks that cost $10 each for a total of $7,000.

June 13   Paid for the clocks purchased on June 3.

June 19   Payment received for the June 7 sale.

Required: Prepare the general journal entries to record the June transactions using the perpetual inventory system.

LO 8: APPENDIX B—SIMPLE JOURNAL ENTRIES—PURCHASES AND SALES OF INVENTORY

8–63. The Scofield Wholesale Company had the following transactions during July:

July 7   Purchased 500 cookware sets on account for $56 each for a total of $28,000.

July 9   Purchased 750 cutting boards for cash of $8 each for a total of $6,000.

July 15   Sold 50 of the cookware sets that cost $56 each for cash of $4,150.

July 16   Sold, on account, 150 of the cutting boards that cost $8 each for a total of $1,800.

July 17   Paid for the cookware sets purchased on July 7.

July 27   Payment received for the July 16 sale.

Required: Prepare the general journal entries to record the July transactions using the perpetual inventory system.

LO 8: APPENDIX B—SIMPLE JOURNAL ENTRIES—PURCHASES AND SALES OF INVENTORY

8–64. Manny's Wholesale Sales had the following transactions during May:

May 4   Purchased, on account, inventory for $12,900.

May 5   Inventory purchased for cash of $3,800.

May 14   Sold, on account, merchandise that cost $880 for a total selling price of $1,390.

May 17   Merchandise sold that cost $750 for cash of $1,220.

May 24   Paid for the inventory purchased on May 4.

May 25   Payment received for the May 14 sale.

Required: Prepare the general journal entries to record the May transactions using the perpetual inventory system.

LO 8: APPENDIX B—JOURNAL ENTRIES—PURCHASES, PURCHASE RETURNS, FREIGHT, AND SALES

8–65. The Pierno Trading Company had the following transactions during May:

May 5   Purchased, on account, inventory for $11,900.
May 5   Paid cash in the amount of $120 for freight on inventory purchased.
May 6   Inventory purchased for cash of $1,800.
May 7   Returned and received credit for $900 of the inventory purchased on May 5.
May 11   Sold, on account, merchandise that cost $125 for a total selling price of $275.
May 16   Merchandise sold that cost $250 for cash of $430.
May 25   Paid for the inventory purchased on May 5.
May 27   Payment received for the May 11 sale.

Required: Prepare the general journal entries to record the May transactions using the perpetual inventory system.

LO 8: APPENDIX B—JOURNAL ENTRIES—PURCHASES, PURCHASE RETURNS, FREIGHT, AND SALES

8–66. Tatum Sales, Inc., had the following transactions during July:

July 2   Inventory purchased for cash of $880.
July 3   Sold, on account, merchandise that cost $220 for a total selling price of $330.
July 12   Inventory purchased on account for $950.
July 12   Paid cash of $40 for freight on inventory purchased.
July 16   Sold merchandise that cost $300 for cash of $450.
July 17   Returned and received credit for $130 of the inventory purchased on July 12.
July 25   Paid for the inventory purchased on July 12.
July 27   Payment received for the July 3 sale.

Required: Prepare the general journal entries to record the July transactions using the perpetual inventory system.

LO 8: APPENDIX B—JOURNAL ENTRIES—PURCHASES, PURCHASE RETURNS, FREIGHT, AND SALES

8–67. Florence Company had the following transactions during June:

June 5   Inventory purchased on account for $800.
June 5   Paid cash of $56 for freight on inventory purchased.
June 6   Inventory purchased for cash of $250.
June 7   Returned and received credit for $130 of the inventory purchased on June 5.
June 11   Sold, on account, merchandise that cost $260 for a total selling price of $520.
June 16   Sold merchandise that cost $420 for cash of $840.
June 25   Paid for the inventory purchased on June 5.
June 27   Payment received for the June 11 sale.

Required: Prepare the general journal entries to record the June transactions using the perpetual inventory system.

LO 8 & 9: APPENDIX B—RECORDING PURCHASE AND PURCHASE DISCOUNTS

8–68. Rodgers Company made the following purchases during August:

Aug 2   Purchased $1,000 of merchandise, terms 1% 10, net 30.
Aug 5   Purchased $3,000 of merchandise, terms 2% 10, net 45.
Aug 10   Purchased $7,000 of merchandise, terms 3% 10, net 50.

Required:

a. Prepare journal entries to record each of the purchase transactions.
b. Prepare the journal entries to record the payment of each of the transactions assuming the discount was taken.
c. Prepare the journal entries to record the payment of each of the transactions assuming the discount was not taken.

LO 8 & 9: APPENDIX B—RECORDING PURCHASE AND PURCHASE DISCOUNTS

8–69. Butterfield Wholesale Company made the following purchases during January:

Jan 1 Purchased $22,000 of merchandise, terms 2/10, n/30.
Jan 3 Purchased $33,500 of merchandise, terms 2/10, n/45.
Jan 5 Purchased $127,000 of merchandise, terms 3/10, n/60.

Required:

a. Prepare journal entries to record each of the purchase transactions.
b. Prepare the journal entries to record the payment of each of the transactions assuming the discount was taken.
c. Prepare the journal entries to record the payment of each of the transactions assuming the discount was not taken.

LO 8 & 9: APPENDIX B—RECORDING PURCHASE AND PURCHASE DISCOUNTS

8–70. Daisy Trading Company made the following purchases from the Alonso Company in November:

Nov 1 Purchased $22,000 of merchandise, terms 2/10, n/30.
Nov 3 Purchased $33,500 of merchandise, terms 1/10, n/45.
Nov 5 Purchased $127,000 of merchandise, terms 2/15, n/60.

Required:

a. Prepare journal entries to record each of the purchase transactions.
b. Prepare the journal entries to record the payment of each of the transactions assuming the discount was taken.
c. Prepare the journal entries to record the payment of each of the transactions assuming the discount was not taken.

LO 9: APPENDIX B—JOURNAL ENTRIES—PURCHASES, PURCHASE DISCOUNTS, FREIGHT, SALES, AND SALES DISCOUNTS

8–71. The Steve's Retailing Company had the following transactions:

May 1 Purchased inventory on account for $5,250, terms 2% 10, net 30.
May 1 Paid cash of $225 for freight on inventory purchased.
May 3 Purchased inventory on account for $8,300, terms 2% 20, net 45.
May 12 Sold merchandise that cost $1,600 for $2,200, terms 2% 10, net 30.
May 13 Paid for the inventory purchased on May 3. (Steve's took the discount.)
May 16 Sold merchandise that cost $1,900 for $3,800, terms 2% 10, net 30.
May 17 Returned and received credit for $250 of the inventory purchased on May 1.
May 22 Payment received for the May 12 sale. (Customer took the discount.)
May 22 Paid for inventory purchased on May 3. (Steve's took the discount.)
June 1 Paid for the balance of the inventory purchased on May 1. (Steve's did not take the discount.)
June 27 Received payment for the May 16 sale. (Customer did not take the discount.)

Required: Prepare the general journal entries to record the May and June transactions using the perpetual inventory system.

LO 9: APPENDIX B—JOURNAL ENTRIES—PURCHASES, PURCHASE DISCOUNTS, FREIGHT, SALES, AND SALES DISCOUNTS

8–72. Real Company had the following transactions:

June 5 Purchased inventory on account for $1,800, terms 2% 10, net 30.
June 6 Purchased inventory on account for $3,500, terms 2% 10, net 30.
June 6 Paid cash of $158 for freight on inventory purchased.
June 7 Returned and received credit for $800 of the inventory purchased on June 5.
June 11 Sold merchandise that cost $125 for $250, terms 2% 10, net 30.
June 16 Sold merchandise that cost $425 for $850, terms 2% 10, net 30.
June 14 Paid for the balance of the inventory purchased on June 5. (Real took the discount.)
June 21 Payment received for the June 11 sale. (Customer took the discount.)
July 6 Paid for the inventory purchased on June 6. (Real did not take the discount.)
July 29 Received payment for the June 16 sale. (Customer did not take the discount.)

Required: Prepare the general journal entries to record the June and July transactions using the perpetual inventory system.

LO 9: APPENDIX B—JOURNAL ENTRIES—PURCHASES, PURCHASE DISCOUNTS, FREIGHT, SALES, AND SALES DISCOUNTS

8–73. The Moon Merchandising Company had the following transactions:

- May 5 Purchased inventory on account for $2,500, terms 2% 10, net 30.
- May 6 Purchased inventory on account for $4,500, terms 2% 10, net 30.
- May 6 Cash paid in the amount of $200 for freight on inventory purchased.
- May 7 Returned and received credit for $250 of the inventory purchased on May 5.
- May 11 Sold merchandise that cost $600 for $1,200, terms 2% 10, net 30.
- May 16 Sold merchandise that cost $900 for $1,800, terms 2% 10, net 30.
- May 14 Paid for the balance of the inventory purchased on May 5. (Moon took the discount.)
- May 21 Payment received for the May 11 sale. (Customer took the discount.)
- June 6 Paid for the inventory purchased on May 6. (Moon did not take the discount.)
- June 29 Received payment for the May 16 sale. (Customer did not take the discount.)

Required: Prepare the general journal entries to record the May and June transactions using the perpetual inventory system.

LO 9: APPENDIX—ADJUSTING ENTRY FOR THE DIFFERENCE BETWEEN PERPETUAL INVENTORY RECORDS AND PHYSICAL INVENTORY COUNT

8–74. Dowers Company manufactures seats for the aircraft industry. At the end of the year, the company's perpetual inventory records showed the following balances:

Cost of Goods Sold	$996,000
Ending Inventory	$287,000

A physical count of the company's inventory revealed that the actual inventory in the warehouse at December 31, 2004, was $298,000.

Required: Prepare an appropriate adjusting journal entry in light of the discrepancy between the perpetual inventory records and the physical inventory on hand.

LO 9: APPENDIX—ADJUSTING ENTRY FOR THE DIFFERENCE BETWEEN PERPETUAL INVENTORY RECORDS AND PHYSICAL INVENTORY COUNT

8–75. Charles Company's perpetual inventory records indicate that the ending inventory should be $1,688,000. In fact, when Charles' staff completed their annual physical inventory, they discovered that the inventory on hand was actually $1,682,000.

Required:

a. Prepare the adjusting entry for the difference between the perpetual inventory records and the inventory that is actually on hand.
b. If no action is taken, how would this situation adversely impact the usefulness of the company's financial statements?

LO 9: APPENDIX—ADJUSTING ENTRY FOR THE DIFFERENCE BETWEEN PERPETUAL INVENTORY RECORDS AND PHYSICAL INVENTORY COUNT

8–76. The Alana Bradley Company's perpetual inventory system reflected the following amounts for the year ended December 31, 2004:

Ending Inventory	$1,680,000
Cost of Goods Sold	$15,900,000

The staff completed a physical inventory and found that the inventory was actually $1,676,000.

Required:

a. Name at least two possible reasons for the difference between the company's perpetual inventory records and the actual physical inventory on hand.

b. With respect to security issues, name at least two actions the company could take to prevent such a thing from happening in the future.

c. Prepare a journal entry to address the difference between the perpetual inventory and the actual physical inventory on hand.

d. If the company fails to make the entry you propose in part c, how would the situation adversely impact the usefulness of the financial statements? Be specific. Indicate which financial statement amounts would be in error and how much the error would be.

Financial Reporting Exercises

8–77. Go to the Securities and Exchange Commission's (SEC's) Electronic Data Gathering, Analysis, and Retrieval (EDGAR) system and find the Inventories section under the Summary of Significant Accounting Policies in the 2001 Form 10-K for *Wal-Mart Stores, Inc.* Use that information to answer the following.

Required:

a. What kind of cost flow assumptions does *Wal-Mart Stores, Inc.,* use?

b. For each cost flow assumption used, list for what purpose it is used and why you think it is better for that specific purpose.

c. What potential problems do *Wal-Mart Stores, Inc.,* list that may affect future inventory? Come up with a situation that would lead to each of the problems listed for one product that they sell.

8–78. Go to the SEC's EDGAR system and find the financial statements and inventories section in the 2001 Form 10-K for *Home Depot, Inc.* Use that information to answer the following.

Required:

a. What cost flow assumption does *Home Depot, Inc.,* use?

b. What was their cost of goods sold for 2001?

c. What was their inventory at the end of 2001?

d. Using b and c, what was their goods available for sale for 2001?

8–79. Go to the SEC's EDGAR system and find the financial statements and inventories section in the 2001 Form 10-K for *General Electric Co.* Use that information to answer the following.

Required:

a. What cost flow assumption does the GE segment of the company mostly use? The GECS segment?

b. Using the inventory amounts listed for 2001 and 2000 on the financial statements, what is the inventory turnover for *General Electric Co.* assuming the LIFO adjustments have already been made?

c. Compute the inventory turnover ratio for the company.

d. Compute the average inventory holding period for the company.

e. Do the company's inventory ratios seem favorable? Why or why not?

ANNUAL REPORT PROJECT

8–80. Section 8—Inventory and Cost of Goods Sold

This section of the annual report project focuses on one of the most important costs for any merchandiser or manufacturer—the cost of inventory.

Required: Prepare a report that includes the following information:

a. A schedule that lists the various inventories for your firm and for those of the peer company you selected. List the inventory descriptions and dollar amounts for each year presented in the balance sheets.

b. Comment on the significance of the inventory. For example, relative to the other assets listed on the balance sheets, are inventories significant? How does your company's inventory compare to the peer company you are using? Over time, are the inventories increasing or decreasing? Are the products in your company's inventories perishable? If so, are they perishable because they are prone to spoilage like food, or because they are prone to technological obsolescence like computer processing chips?

c. Identify the inventory cost flow assumption or assumptions used by your company and those used by its peer. List the cost of goods sold and the gross profit for the two companies. Does the inventory cost flow assumption seem to have created any difference between your company and its peer company? Explain your reasoning. If one or both of the companies uses the LIFO inventory cost flow assumption, locate the financial statement note that relates to inventories and use the information it contains to prepare a schedule listing the LIFO inventory values, the inventory amounts had the inventories been valued under FIFO, and the difference between the LIFO and FIFO inventory values.

d. Calculate the inventory turnover ratio for your company and its peer for the current year. Comment on the information the ratio calculations provide.

e. Discuss which company seems to be using its investment in inventory more efficiently? Explain your reasoning.

f. Your report should conclude with comments regarding what you think of your company and how you think your company compares to its peer in light of the work you did in connection with this assignment.

CHAPTER 9

The Balance Sheet and Income Statement— A Closer Look

Your brother-in-law just sent you the annual report of a company that he believes will be the next *Microsoft.* He wants you to get in on the ground floor. You've looked at annual reports before, but none seemed this complex. The balance sheet includes a lot of "intangible" assets, but what are they? The income statement has numerous items after operating income. Should you really care about those figures? To top it off, the earnings per share has six different amounts! How can that be when you know earnings per share is the company's net income divided by the number of shares of common stock? Which one of them should you use to evaluate the stock's market price? The highest is only $0.45 a share, and your brother-in-law wants you to pay $12 per share for this stock. That is almost 27 times the annual income per share, if you are looking at the right one. Without an understanding of these financial statement complications, it is difficult to tell whether the investment your brother-in-law suggests is the right one for you.

Balance sheets and income statements are generally more complex than the ones we have explored so far, but they are organized in a manner that serves to clarify rather than complicate the information they provide to economic decision makers. An understanding of the organization of these two financial statements is crucial. In this chapter, we will explore the details and organization of the balance sheet and income statement.

Learning Objectives

After completing your work on this chapter, you should be able to do the following:

1. Describe how the balance sheet and income statement were developed as financial statements.

2. Explain the organization and purpose of the classified balance sheet.

3. Explain why recurring and nonrecurring items are presented separately on the income statement.

4. Interpret the net of tax disclosure of discontinued operations, extraordinary items, and accounting changes.

5. Calculate earnings per share and describe how it is presented on the income statement.

6. Describe the additional information provided by comparative financial statements.

7. Calculate several financial ratios based on income statement and balance sheet information.

Human beings have kept track of their business affairs by accounting for economic events and transactions ever since they began living in organized societies. They recorded them first on stone or clay tablets, then on papyrus, then on paper, and now via computer technology.

Accounting records were originally kept to help business owners run their companies; accounting was not generally intended to provide information to outsiders. Amounts owed to suppliers, for example, were recorded primarily so a company could keep track of what had and had not been paid. As time went on, however, more and more companies turned to outsiders for financing and other needs. These outsiders were unwilling to become involved with a company blindly. They wanted to evaluate company financial information before they would put their funds at risk, so record keeping was expanded for the specific purpose of providing financial information to outsiders. Eventually, financial statements were developed to communicate this information. In *A History of Accounting Thought*, Michael Chatfield describes this transition as follows:

> *More than most accounting tools, financial statements are the result of cumulative historical influences. Before the Industrial Revolution they were usually prepared as arithmetic checks of ledger balances. Afterward the roles were reversed and it was account books which were reorganized to facilitate statement preparation. As statements became communication devices rather than simple bookkeeping summaries, the journal and ledger evolved from narratives to tabulations of figures from which balances could easily be taken.*[1]

Accounting has been with us since about 5000 B.C., but financial statements as we know them are a relatively recent phenomenon. The balance sheet's function as a financial statement only emerged during the Renaissance, around A.D. 1600. For the next several hundred years, the balance sheet was the primary output of the accounting process. Accountants developed the income statement in the late 1800s, but did not consider the information nearly as important as the balance sheet figures. In his landmark work, *Accounting Evolution to 1900*, A. C. Littleton makes the following observation:

> *. . . it seems that the primary motive for separate financial statements was to obtain information regarding capital; this was the center of the interest of partners, shareholders, lenders, and the basis of the calculation of early property taxes. Thus balance-sheet data were stressed and refined in various ways, while expense and income data were incidental—in fact, the latter in the seventeenth century were presented merely as a "proof of estate"—to demonstrate by another route the correctness of the balance sheet.*[2]

At the beginning of the 20th century, most U.S companies were financed by banks, so at this time, banks (i.e., creditors) were the primary users of financial statements. These creditors looked at balance sheets to help them evaluate a company's ability to repay its debts. During the first two decades of the 1900s, U.S. companies began to rely less on debt financing and more on equity financing. Companies began to borrow less from banks and issue more capital stock. When selling stock became an important source of external financing, stockholders became major users of financial statements. Stockholders were interested in the earnings of companies and the potential for earnings distributions (dividends), and the value of the company's stock. Stockholders focused on net income and considered the income statement more important than the balance sheet. Over time, creditors also realized that earning power was crucial to debt

---

[1]Michael Chatfield, *A History of Accounting Thought* (Huntington, NY: R. E. Kriger Publishing Co., 1974), 164.

[2]A. C. Littleton, *Accounting Evolution to 1900* (New York: Russell & Russell, 1966), 153.

repayment, so they also began to rely more on the income statement than on the balance sheet.

By the 1930s, it became apparent that neither the balance sheet nor the income statement is more important than the other; they are best used together. Each provides valuable information for economic decision makers. By learning more about the detailed structure of the balance sheet and income statement, you can make the best use of the information they provide.

In introducing the balance sheet in Chapter 3, we used this simple equation:

$$\text{Assets} = \text{Liabilities} + \text{Owners' equity}$$

The equation does not distinguish one asset from another or one liability from another. A balance sheet prepared for Eliason and Company, a chain of specialty furniture stores, at December 31, 2004, using the basic format would look like Exhibit 9–1.

EXHIBIT 9–1   Eliason and Company Balance Sheet

Eliason and Company
Balance Sheet
December 31, 2004

Total assets	$1,566,800
Liabilities	$ 901,000
Stockholders' equity	665,800
Total liabilities and stockholders' equity	$1,566,800

Remember that economic decision makers are attempting to predict the amount and timing of future cash flows. The balance sheet in Exhibit 9–1 provides economic decision makers little useful information about the financial position of Eliason and Company at December 31, 2004. Even if the $1,566,800 of assets is all cash, we see no indication of how soon the $901,000 of liabilities must be paid or how much of the $665,800 of stockholders' equity represents contributed capital and how much represents retained earnings. In response to users' needs for additional information, accountants developed a more detailed balance sheet, called the classified balance sheet.

THE CLASSIFIED BALANCE SHEET

classified balance sheet
A balance sheet that provides a breakdown of the composition of the items the balance sheet includes.

A **classified balance sheet** provides a breakdown of the composition of the items included. Rather than just presenting the totals of assets, liabilities, and owners' equity, this type of balance sheet provides much more detail about the nature of the assets, liabilities, and equities that make up the totals. Exhibit 9–2 on page F–358 shows a classified balance sheet prepared from the same accounting data as that used for the balance sheet in Exhibit 9–1. Notice that the assets still total $1,566,800; total liabilities are still $901,000; and stockholders' equity is still $665,800. The difference between the two balance sheet presentations is the amount of detail the balance sheets disclose.

We will refer to Eliason and Company's classified balance sheet presented in Exhibit 9–2 on page F–358 as we describe how the classified balance sheet is organized.

Discussion Question

9–1. Which of the two balance sheet presentations for Eliason and Company do you think would be more useful in predicting the future and timing of the company's cash flow? Provide three specific examples to support your position.

ASSETS

current assets Assets that are cash, will become cash, or will be consumed within the longer of one year or the current operating cycle.

Under GAAP, assets shown on the balance sheet at their historical cost and are grouped as either current assets or long-term assets. **Current assets** are defined as assets that either are cash already or are expected to become cash within one year or

Eliason and Company
Balance Sheet
December 31, 2004

ASSETS:

Current assets:

Cash			$ 100
Accounts receivable			251,000
Inventory			298,900
Prepaid expenses			50,000
Total current assets			$ 600,000
Long-term investments			34,000

Property, plant, and equipment:

Land		$125,000	
Plant and equipment	$1,075,000		
Less: Accumulated depreciation	(283,200)		
Plant and equipment, net		791,800	
Total property, plant, and equipment			916,800
Intangible asset—copyright			16,000
Total assets			$1,566,800

LIABILITIES:

Current liabilities:

Accounts payable		$ 501,000
Short-term notes payable		50,000
Total current liabilities		$ 551,000

Long-term liabilities:

Bonds payable		350,000
Total liabilities		$ 901,000

STOCKHOLDERS' EQUITY:

Contributed capital:

Common stock, $1 par value, 100,000 authorized, 10,000 shares issued and outstanding	$ 10,000	
Additional paid-in capital	390,000	
Total contributed capital	$400,000	
Retained earnings	265,800	
Total stockholders' equity		665,800
Total liabilities and stockholders' equity		$1,566,800

EXHIBIT 9–2 Classified Balance Sheet

one operating cycle, whichever is longer. An operating cycle is the length of time it takes for an entity to complete one revenue-producing cycle. For a manufacturer, a revenue cycle is the length of time from receiving raw materials to producing and selling the final product to collecting cash from its customers. For a merchandiser, the operating cycle is the time it takes from receiving merchandise to collecting the cash from its customers. Most businesses have several operating cycles within a year. Some businesses, such as wineries, timber operations, or long-term construction companies, have operating cycles that last five years or even longer. As you can see from Exhibit 9–2, cash, accounts receivable, inventory, and prepaid expenses are examples of current assets. Prepaid expenses that will be used within one year are included because, even though they will not become cash, they will benefit the company without requiring additional cash outflows. Although our example company does not have any, short-term investments would also be included in current assets. Short-term investments may be listed as trading securities, marketable securities, or short investments. It is also permissible for companies to show cash along with marketable securities that will be converted into cash within 90 days as a single balance sheet amount labeled *cash and cash equivalents*.

long-term assets   Assets that are expected to benefit the company for longer than one year.

Long-term assets are defined as those assets that are expected to benefit the organization for more than one year, or that are not anticipated to become cash within one year. Although our example company does not use all of the classifications, there are several. The following long-term asset classifications are the ones most commonly used by businesses today.

long-term investments
Sometimes called *investments*. Investments in securities such as stocks, bonds, and long-term notes receivable; investments in fixed assets that are not currently being used in operations; special funds established to set aside financial resources.

property, plant, and equipment   Physical long-lived assets used by the business including land, buildings, equipment, machinery, vehicles, and furniture.

intangible assets   Things that have future value but lack physical presence such as patents, copyrights, trademarks, and purchased goodwill.

- **Long-term investments,** sometimes simply called *investments* include:
  - Investments in securities such as stocks, bonds, and long-term notes receivable
  - Investments in fixed assets such as land, buildings, and equipment that are not currently being used in operations
  - Special funds established to set aside financial resources (money) to pay for pension obligations, plant expansion, or to repay debt
- **Property, plant, and equipment** includes physical long-lived assets used by the business. Examples include land, buildings, equipment, machinery, vehicles, and furniture. As we learned in Chapter 7, except for land, accountants depreciate these durable assets to expense their cost in the periods they helped produce revenue.
- **Intangible assets** include the company's cost of things that have future value but lack physical presence. Examples include patents, copyrights, trademarks, and purchased goodwill. We say *purchased* goodwill because goodwill can only be recorded in company accounting records when a business is purchased and the purchase price exceeds the fair value of the individual assets acquired. For example, assume that Gourmet Outlets, Inc., purchases Smith Produce, a very successful gourmet grocery store for $300,000. The fair value of Smith's assets is only $100,000, but Gourmet Outlets is willing to pay the $300,000 because Smith's business is so successful. In this situation, the $200,000 ($300,000 − $100,000) Gourmet Outlets pays in excess of the fair value of Smith's assets is goodwill.

Like property, plant, and equipment, accountants systematically expense the cost of intangible assets in the accounting periods benefited by the use of the asset. As you know, for property, plant, and equipment, this systematic cost allocation is called depreciation. The systematic allocation of the cost of an intangible from assets to expense is called amortization. Not all intangible assets are amortized, however. According to the Financial Accounting Standards Board's (FASB's) Statement of Financial Accounting Standards (SFAS) Number 142 issued in June 2001, while intangible assets that have limited (finite) useful lives, such as patents, are amortized, intangible assets that have an indefinite useful life, such as goodwill, are not amortized.

SFAS 142 also requires companies to review their intangible assets for impairment at least annually. In other words, every company must evaluate its intangible assets to assure that the amount the company reflects on its balance sheet does not exceed the value of the intangible assets. The impact of impairment tests can be significant. For example, in the first quarter of 2002, **AOL Time Warner** posted one of the largest losses in history because it was forced to record a write-down of goodwill amounting to approximately $54 billion.

other assets   Long-term assets that do not fit into any other asset classification.

- **Other assets** are any long-term assets that do not fit into any other asset classification. Examples include property held for sale and long-term rent receivable.

Assets are listed on a classified balance sheet in order of decreasing liquidity. Liquidity means nearness to cash. Notice that we always list cash first on the balance sheet because by definition it is the most liquid asset. Generally, the farther down an item is found in the asset section of a classified balance sheet, the less likelihood there is that that item will be converted to cash in the near future. Because of the classified balance sheet's organization, users can tell in a glance just which assets (and their dollar amounts) the company thinks will be turned into cash within the next year (current assets) and which ones are not expected to be converted into cash (long-term assets).

In the case of Eliason and Company, current assets total $600,000 and property, plant, and equipment total $916,800. We would expect the $600,000 to be converted into cash before the $916,800.

Discussion Questions ●

9–2. Are there any items listed as current assets on Eliason's December 31, 2004, classified balance sheet (Exhibit 9–2) that you think will never be converted into cash? If there are, why do you think they are classified as current assets?

9–3. Property, plant, and equipment is not a current asset. Does this mean Eliason cannot sell one of its buildings in 2005? Explain your reasoning.

LIABILITIES

Generally, the balance sheet lists liabilities in order of how quickly they must be paid. Those liabilities that must be settled (paid or otherwise satisfied) first are listed first. Settlement often requires the payment of cash but may require other performance such as providing goods or services.

current liabilities
Liabilities that require settlement (payment) within one year or the current operating cycle, whichever is longer.

Current liabilities are those that require settlement within one year or the current operating cycle, whichever is longer. The operating cycle for the overwhelming majority of companies is less than one year, so the one-year criterion is the one most often used. Eliason and Company classifies the $501,000 it owes to suppliers (accounts payable) as a current liability because the suppliers expect Eliason to pay them within one year. Commercial suppliers usually require payment within 10 to 90 days, and the trend is to require payment sooner rather than later.

long-term liabilities
Liabilities that will not require settlement within one year or the current operating cycle.

Long-term liabilities are those that do not require settlement within one year or the current operating cycle. Eliason's bonds payable are not due within a year, so the company classifies the liability as long-term. If part of the bond liability was due within one year, the company would classify that part as current. In other words, current liabilities includes the current portion of any long-term debt.

Because of the way the balance sheet is organized, users can tell at a glance which liabilities are expected to be retired within the next year (current liabilities) and which ones are not (long-term liabilities). This enables them to assess future cash flows. Eliason's current liabilities total $551,000 and long-term liabilities total $350,000, so it must pay the $551,000 fairly soon, but the $350,000 is not due for at least a year. Exhibit 9–3 illustrates the current and long-term classifications of assets and liabilities.

EXHIBIT 9–3   Examples of Current and Long-Term Assets and Liabilities

Assets		Liabilities	
Current	**Long-Term**	**Current**	**Long-Term**
Cash	Long-term investments	Accounts payable	Notes payable
Marketable securities	Property, plant, and	Notes payable	Mortgages payable
Accounts receivable	equipment	Accrued expenses	Bonds payable
Inventory	Intangible assets	Unearned revenue	Others
Prepaid expenses	Other long-term assets	Payable for:	
		Wages	
		Taxes	
		Interest	
		Others	
		Current portion of long-term debt	

Discussion Questions

9–4. Provide two examples of current liabilities and two examples of long-term liabilities not shown on the Eliason and Company balance sheet in Exhibit 9–2.

9–5. Eliason shows $600,000 of current assets and $551,000 of current liabilities. Who might be interested in these amounts, and why?

OWNERS' EQUITY

contributed capital
Total amount invested in a corporation by its shareholders. Also called paid-in capital.

The stockholders' equity section of a classified balance sheet is also separated into two categories: contributed capital and retained earnings. **Contributed capital** (sometimes called *paid-in capital*) is the amount paid into the company by its owners in exchange for their ownership interest. In other words, contributed capital is the amount a company's stockholders paid for the stock they purchased. The contributed or paid-in capital section of equity generally begins with preferred stock. This is because preferred stockholders have first priority when it comes to dividends or distributions upon liquidation. Common stock is listed next, followed by the remaining contributed capital amounts. If the company has reacquired any of its capital stock (treasury stock), it is shown in the equity section of the balance sheet as a reduction in equity. In the case of Eliason and Company, we first list the $10,000 classified as common stock. The $10,000 is the amount associated with the stock's par value. The amount the company received in excess of a stock's par value ($390,000) is classified as additional paid-in capital. After listing all of the contributed capital items, we list retained earnings next.

retained earnings
Constitutes the earnings reinvested by the corporation and not distributed to owners in the form of dividends.

As we mentioned in Chapter 4, **retained earnings** constitutes the earnings reinvested by the corporation and not distributed to owners in the form of dividends. At December 31, 2004, Eliason and Company had a retained earnings balance of $265,800.

Discussion Questions

9–6. Explain the exact meaning of the $265,800 of retained earnings on Eliason and Company's balance sheet.

9–7. On average, how much did Eliason and Company receive for each share of stock sold?

9–8. Does Eliason's balance sheet provide an indication of the current market value of the company's stock? Explain your reasoning.

◆ ORGANIZATION OF THE INCOME STATEMENT

When we introduced the income statement in Chapter 4, we used the following simple equation:

$$\text{Revenues} - \text{Expenses} = \text{Net income}$$

An income statement prepared for Eliason and Company for the year ended December 31, 2004, using this simple format would look like the one in Exhibit 9–4.

EXHIBIT 9–4   Income Statement Prepared for Eliason and Company for the Year Ended December 31, 2004—Simple Format

Eliason and Company
Income Statement
For the Year Ended December 31, 2004

Revenue	$752,500
Less: Expenses	840,400
Net loss	$ (87,900)

Net income or net loss, of course, is the "bottom line" and discloses whether or not a company has been profitable for a given period. This is important, and we would never suggest otherwise. However, for Eliason and Company, there is more to the story than that told by the $87,900 loss.

The accounting profession follows established guidelines so income statements provide a fairly complete and relevant picture of what happens to businesses during an income statement period. Income statements that conform to these guidelines provide important information about the characteristics of the revenues and expenses they present. Exhibit 9–5 shows an income statement for Eliason and Company that conforms to the current income statement guidelines (except that the required earnings per share presentation is omitted).

EXHIBIT 9–5 Expanded Format Income Statement

Eliason and Company
Income Statement
For the Year Ended December 31, 2004

Sales revenue		$ 752,500
Less: Cost of goods sold		352,800
Gross profit on sales		$ 399,700
Less: Operating expenses:		
Selling	$60,250	
General and administrative	96,250	
Total operating expenses		(156,500)
Operating income		$ 243,200
Less other expenses:		
Interest expense		(30,650)
Income before taxes and extraordinary item		$ 212,550
Less: Income taxes		(64,660)
Income before extraordinary item		$ 147,890
Extraordinary loss (less: income taxes of $87,420)		(235,790)
Net loss		$ (87,900)

nonrecurring item
Results of activities that are not expected to occur again and, therefore, should not be used to predict future performance.

Although this income statement bears little resemblance to the one presented earlier in our discussion, revenues still total $752,500; total deductions from revenues still total $840,400; and the net loss is still $87,900. By now, this format should look familiar to you. In fact, only the last few lines are new.

Discussion Questions ●

9–9. Is Exhibit 9–5 a single-step or multiple-step income statement? How can you tell?

9–10. If you were considering some kind of economic involvement with Eliason and Company, which number on the expanded income statement would you consider most reliable in predicting the company's future profitability? Explain.

RECURRING AND NONRECURRING ITEMS

Besides presenting more detail concerning Eliason and Company's regular revenues and expenses for 2004, the income statement in Exhibit 9–5 shows an extraordinary loss of $235,790, which is separated from the company's regular, recurring revenues and expenses. An extraordinary gain or loss is one of the items the accounting profession has determined should be shown separately as a nonrecurring item on the income statement.

A **nonrecurring item** is any item (either positive or negative) that should not be considered a normal part of continuing operations because it is not expected to recur. Let's explore the logic of separating nonrecurring from recurring items on the income statement.

Suppose something—good or bad—happened to a company during the income statement period that was not expected to recur. The company must report it because it happened. In Eliason's case, the extraordinary loss reported on the 2004 income statement was caused by a flood that wiped out one of the company's retail outlets. This store was located in Phoenix, Arizona, where floods are *extremely* rare, so Eliason carried no flood insurance. If you were attempting to predict the company's ability to generate future profits and cash flows, and the company lumped this one-time "something" in with all its other revenues and expenses, you might be misled. Therefore, if nonrecurring items *do not* represent the ongoing results of a company's operations, it makes sense to report them separately from what *does* represent the company's ongoing business.

If the extraordinary (flood) loss is truly a nonrecurring item for Eliason, then the net loss of $87,900 for 2004 is not a good predictor of future profitability and cash flow. In fact, the best predictive number on Eliason's income statement is probably the $147,890 listed as income before extraordinary item.

Extraordinary items are but one type of nonrecurring item. Actually, there are three general types of nonrecurring items, listed in their order of presentation on the income statement:

1. Discontinued operations
2. Extraordinary items
3. Cumulative effect of changes in accounting principles

In the sections that follow, we will more fully explain the presentation and interpretation of these nonrecurring items and how they appear on a company's income statement. Throughout our discussion, we will use the income statement of Toy Box, Inc., a retailer specializing in top-of-the-line children's toys, as an example. The company's 2005 income statement is presented in Exhibit 9–6.

EXHIBIT 9–6   Income Statement for Toy Box, Inc., for the Year Ended December 31, 2005

Toy Box, Inc.
Income Statement
For the Year Ended December 31, 2005

Sales		$858,600
Less: Cost of goods sold		456,800
Gross profit on sales		$401,800
Less: Operating expenses:		
Selling expense	$94,450	
General and administrative expense	116,050	
Total operating expenses		(210,500)
Operating income		$191,300
Less: Interest expense		(30,650)
Income from continuing operations before taxes		$160,650
Less: Income taxes		(64,260)
Income from continuing operations		$ 96,390
Discontinued operations:		
Income from discontinued operations		
($118,800, less: income taxes of $47,520)	$71,280	
Loss on disposal of discontinued operation		
($90,000, less: income taxes of $36,000)	(54,000)	17,280
Income before extraordinary item and cumulative		
effect of a change in accounting principle		$113,670
Extraordinary gain ($220,000, less: income taxes of $88,000)		132,000
Income before cumulative effect of a change in accounting principle		245,670
Cumulative effect of a change in accounting principle		
($62,000, less: income taxes of $24,800)		(37,200)
Net income		$208,470

Income statements broadly separate the activities they report into those that are expected to recur and those that are not. The first half of Toy Box's income statement, up to income from continuing operations, reflects results of activities that will probably continue in the future.

The income tax of $64,260 is the tax on income from ongoing activities of the company. In practice, determining the amount of income tax associated with reported income is quite complex. First, company accountants must determine the revenue that is taxable according to the income tax regulations of the **Internal Revenue Service (IRS)**. Next, the accountants must determine the costs the **IRS** allows to be deducted from taxable revenue to determine taxable income. Then, the accountants subtract the deductible costs from taxable revenue to determine taxable income. Finally, the amount of tax is calculated. The specifics for calculating the amount of income tax a company should pay or the amount it should report as income tax expense is beyond the scope of this course. But to get an approximation of income tax expense that is good enough for academic purposes, you can multiply income by an assumed income tax rate as we show below:

$$\text{Income} \times \text{Tax rate} = \text{Income tax expense}$$

We will use the above equation to calculate income tax whenever we need to determine a tax amount for something on Toy Box's income statement. The rough calculation to determine income tax expense for income from continuing operations is shown below:

Income from continuing operations before tax	× Tax rate =	Income tax on income from operations
$160,650	× 40% =	$64,260

The $96,390 identified as *income from continuing operations* represents the net results of Toy Box's ongoing operations. We are probably safe to assume that this figure has a predictive value for future earnings. Information on the income statement below this point relates to nonrecurring items. The income from continuing operations is the dividing line between the recurring and nonrecurring activities. If a company does not have discontinued operations but does have extraordinary items, the company would use a title such as *income before extraordinary items*. If a company had no discontinued items and no extraordinary items but did have an accounting change to disclose, the company would use a title such as *income before cumulative effect of changes in accounting principle*. Regardless of the title, nonrecurring items always come after the income tax expense.

Proper classification of items as recurring or nonrecurring is critical to the usefulness of the accounting information. A company might be tempted to treat an item as nonrecurring because it reduces net income or to include an item with recurring revenues when it increases net income. To prevent companies from confusing the users of financial statements this way, the accounting profession restricts the items that may be considered nonrecurring. We will consider the criteria for each of these items after we discuss the income tax effects of these nonrecurring items.

INCOME TAX DISCLOSURE

We mentioned earlier that Toy Box's tax expense associated with the ongoing, recurring operation of the business income is $64,260. But how should the company disclose the income tax effect of the nonrecurring items shown on the income statement? The nonrecurring events cannot escape income tax consequences, and those consequences must be disclosed. Lumping together the income tax associated with nonrecurring items with that of income tax expense for continuing operations would distort the information. For example, the total of all income tax on Toy Box's income statement is $138,980 ($64,260 + $47,520 − $36,000 + $88,000 − $24,800). If Toy Box mistakenly presented the entire $138,980 as though all of it were associated with income from continuing operations, this part of the income statement would appear as follows:

Income from continuing operations before taxes		$160,650
Less:		
Income taxes on continuing operations	$64,260	
Income taxes on income from discontinued operations	47,520	
Income tax reduction from loss on disposal of discontinued operations	(36,000)	
Income taxes on extraordinary gain	88,000	
Income tax reduction from change in accounting principle	(24,800)	138,980
Income from continuing operations		$ 21,670

This presentation makes it appear that Toy Box is paying out about 86.5 percent ($138,980/$160,650) of its income from continuing operations for income taxes. That leaves a disproportionately small $21,670 for income from continuing operations after tax. The trouble with the preceding presentation is that it distorts the picture of continuing operations by including tax that is associated with nonrecurring items. To eliminate the distortion and confusion, the accounting profession decided that the only tax expense shown on the income statement as a separate line item will be the amount associated with continuing operations. Therefore, the three major types of nonrecurring items included on the income statement are shown "less income tax" or "net of tax."

net of tax The amount remaining for an item after income tax has been deducted.

Net of tax means the income tax has already been deducted from the amount shown for an item. For example, assume a company has an extraordinary gain of $100,000 and the income tax on the gain is $30,000. The extraordinary gain, net of tax would be $70,000 ($100,000 − $30,000). Next, we will calculate the income tax associated with the nonrecurring items for Toy Box, Inc.

Current accounting rules require that the tax effect of each of these nonrecurring items be disclosed either on the face of the income statement or in the related notes to the financial statements. Although it is not always the case, Toy Box's income statement shows the full amount of each nonrecurring item and its associated income tax. If the income statement does not show the full amount of a nonrecurring item, a financial statement user can calculate the amount by adding the item's net-of-tax amount to its associated income tax.

As we have already mentioned, we will calculate tax expense by simply multiplying the income by the effective tax rate. Before you can calculate the income tax for the nonrecurring items, you need to know each of their full amounts. As we show below, we can use the same basic calculation to determine the income tax expense for gains and the income tax savings associated with losses.

Income from operation of discontinued operations	$118,800 × 40% = $47,520
Disposal of discontinued operation	$ 90,000 × 40% = $36,000
Extraordinary gain	$220,000 × 40% = $88,000
Cumulative effect of accounting principle change	$ 62,000 × 40% = $24,800

When a business experiences a gain, the total income of the business increases and the *IRS* will require more taxes. The gain increases the amount of taxes owed, which in turn reduces the amount of the gain (see Exhibit 9–7 on page F–366). When a business experiences a loss, the total income of the business decreases and the *IRS* will require less taxes. The loss decreases the amount of taxes owed, which in turn reduces the amount of the loss. Therefore, we subtract income tax from the original amount of the nonrecurring item to get its net-of-tax amount.

Now look again at the income statement for Toy Box, Inc., in Exhibit 9–6. Notice that the statement includes examples of the three major types of nonrecurring items, and the statement presents each of them in the same general way: Each is shown below the *income from continuing operations*, and each is shown "net of tax." We now explore the criteria for, and specific presentation of, each type of nonrecurring item.

discontinued operations The disposal of a business segment. One of the nonrecurring items shown net of tax on the income statement.

DISCONTINUED OPERATIONS

When a company eliminates a *major segment* of its business, that segment is called **discontinued operations.** When a company formally decides to dispose of a major seg-

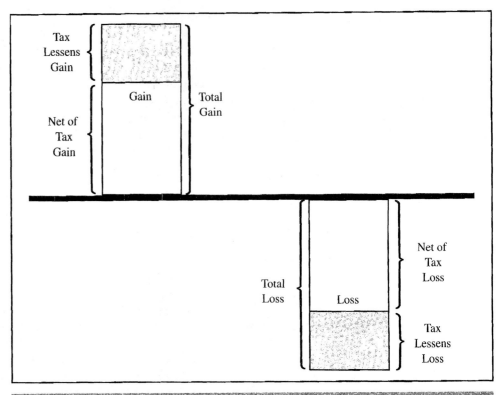

EXHIBIT 9–7 Effect of Tax on Gains and Losses

ment of its business, the income or loss on the operations of the segment that is to be eliminated and any gain or loss from the actual disposal of that business segment are reported as nonrecurring items on the income statement. A **business segment** may be a portion of an entity representing either a separate major line of business or a class of customer.

business segment A portion of an entity representing either a separate major line of business or a class of customer.

> *The part of the business being eliminated is considered a business segment provided that its assets, results of operations, and activities can be clearly distinguished, physically and operationally and for financial reporting purposes, from the other assets, results of operations, and activities of the entity.*[3]

The following examples of situations meeting the criteria for disposal of a business segment will help you understand the application of these criteria.

1. *A sale by a diversified company of a major division, which represents the company's only activities in the electronics industry.*
2. *A sale by a meat packing company of a 25% interest in a professional football team.*
3. *A sale by a communications company of all its radio stations, which represent 30% of gross revenues. The company's remaining activities are three television stations and a publishing company.*
4. *A food distributor disposes of one of its two divisions. One division sells food wholesale primarily to supermarket chains and the other division sells food through its chain of fast food restaurants, some of which are franchised and some of which are company-owned.*[4]

Once a company determines that the disposal of a business segment should be considered a discontinued operation, generally accepted accounting principles (GAAP) require certain disclosures on the income statement. To illustrate, Toy Box, Inc., buys and resells toys. Many years ago, for reasons no one in the company's management even remembers, Toy Box purchased a company that manufactured hats. Although the hat manufacturing portion of the business has always been profitable,

---

[3]APB Opinion No. 30, paragraph 13.

[4]AICPA Accounting Interpretations, AIN-APB30, #1.

current management does not believe that the hat business fits into the corporation's strategic plans and sells it during 2005. Toy Box includes two items on its 2005 income statement to reflect the hat division's operation and disposal.

1. Toy Box reports income from discontinued operations of $71,280. In 2005, prior to being sold, the hat operation had revenues of $220,100 and expenses of $101,300. So its pretax income for the time Toy Box owned it during the year was $118,800 ($220,100 revenues − $101,300 expenses). Income taxes on the results of discontinued operations totaled $45,720, so the amount shown for income from discontinued operations on the income statement is $71,280 ($118,800 − $45,720).

2. Toy Box also reports a $54,000 loss on the disposal of discontinued operations. When the company sold the hat operation, it incurred a $90,000 pretax loss on the sale. Because this loss was deductible on the company's income tax return, it resulted in a reduction of $36,000 in income taxes for the year. The after-tax loss (the real loss to Toy Box) was $54,000 ($90,000 − $36,000).

After Toy Box reports the two components of the results of discontinued operations, it nets the two amounts. In other words, the company combines the $71,280 income from discontinued operations and the $54,000 loss on disposal of the discontinued operation, which results in a net gain of $17,280 under discontinued operations.

Discontinued operations occur more often than you might think. Of the 600 companies surveyed by the authors of *Accounting Trends and Techniques* in 2001, 60 companies reported discontinued operations in their 2000 income statements, including such companies as **American Home Products Corporation, Eaton Corporation,** and **International Multifoods Corporation.** It would be a mistake to think any time a company disposes of a major business segment, it is because that segment is unprofitable. **American Home Products,** for example, sold its crop protection and pest control products business in 2000 and reported after-tax profits from this discontinued operation of over $103 million in 2000. Sometimes, as was the case with Toy Box when it discontinued its hat manufacturing operation, the segment being disposed of just doesn't fit into the company's strategic plans.

EXTRAORDINARY ITEMS

extraordinary item
A gain or loss that is both unusual in nature and infrequent in occurrence. One of the nonrecurring items shown net of tax on the income statement.

In accounting, the word extraordinary has a very special meaning. Accounting rules define an **extraordinary item** as an event that is both *unusual* in nature and *infrequent* in occurrence. It can't be just one or the other, it must be both. When applying the criterion of "unusual in nature," accountants must consider the operating environment of the business entity.

> *The environment of an entity includes such factors as the characteristics of the industry or industries in which it is operating, the geographical location of its operations, and the nature and extent of government regulation. Thus, an event or transaction may be unusual in nature for one entity but not for another because of differences in their respective environments.*[5]

So, a gain or loss that would be considered unusual for one company might be considered an ordinary event for another company.

Accountants must also consider the operating environment of the entity when applying the criterion of "infrequent in occurrence." To be considered infrequent, an event must be neither a recurrence of reasonably recent past events, nor should it be expected to recur in the foreseeable future. Earlier in this chapter, for example, we looked at Eliason and Company's income statement for 2004. Included in the statement was an extraordinary loss resulting from a flood in Phoenix, Arizona. Well, floods are both unusual and infrequent in Phoenix, so this loss can probably be considered extraordinary. However, if the store destroyed by a flood had been located in the flood plains of Iowa, where floods are quite common, the loss would not qualify as extraordinary.

---

[5]APB Opinion No. 30, paragraph 21.

According to *Accounting Trends and Techniques*, of the 600 companies surveyed in 2001, 55 companies reported extraordinary items in their 2000 income statements, including such companies as **Ingram Micro Inc., United Stationers,** and **ExxonMobil Corporation.**

What if an item is either unusual in nature *or* infrequent in occurrence, but not both? If the item is significant, the company should list it as a separate item, usually under other gains or other losses as appropriate. And, like the rest of the items included in other gains and other losses, the unusual *or* infrequent item should not be shown net of tax.

Although they are not necessarily unusual and infrequent, prior to May 2002, accounting rules required that any gain or loss that results from extinguishment of debt must be reported as extraordinary. Because companies do have gains and losses from extinguishment of debt from time to time, and because it is unlikely that any event would be both unusual in nature and infrequent in occurrence, in the past, the most popular extraordinary items companies reported were those associated with debt extinguishments. However, in April 2002, the FASB issued Statement No. 145, eliminating the requirement to treat all gains and losses related to extinguishments of debt as extraordinary. As a result, for financial statements issued on or after May 15, 2002, gains and losses from extinguishment of debt should be classified as extraordinary items only if they meet the criteria for treatment as an extraordinary item. That is, they must be unusual and infrequent. According to *Accounting Trends and Techniques*, of the 55 companies that reported extraordinary items in 2000, 48 were reporting extraordinary items associated with debt extinguishments. Although gains and losses related to extinguishments of debt have historically been the most common extraordinary items, you will seldom see them listed as extraordinary on income statements published after May 2002.

Extinguishment of debt means nothing more than paying off debt. Sometimes when a company pays off debt, especially if it pays it earlier than the due date, the company will pay either more or less than the actual loan amount. For example, assume that Smith, Inc., has a $1 million liability for some 12 percent corporate bonds that it would like to pay off. It would like to extinguish (pay off) these bonds even though they are not yet due because interest rates have fallen and the company can now borrow funds at an interest rate of 9 percent. But, will the bondholders readily agree to accept early payment of the debt when they are earning such a high rate of interest relative to current rates? Probably not. Smith will have to entice the bondholders by offering to pay them more than the face value of the bonds. Let's assume that the bondholders will accept no less than $1,115,000 as payment. If Smith pays the $1,115,000 to retire the debt, the difference between the $1 million liability on Smith's books and the amount Smith pays is a loss on extinguishment of debt.

Aside from gains and losses from the extinguishment of debt, which happened from time to time prior to May 2002, companies seldom report extraordinary items. Given the catastrophic events of September 11, 2001, you might expect that the number of companies reporting extraordinary items for 2001 would greatly increase from 2000. This, however, was not the case, at least as a result of the terrorist attacks of 9/11. In a landmark (and somewhat baffling) decision, the FASB, through its Emerging Issues Task Force (EITF), ruled that no losses as a result of 9/11 could be classified as extraordinary.

As you use financial statement information, a basic appreciation of how these criteria are applied will enhance your ability to interpret the impact of extraordinary items. The following events or transactions meet the criteria of both unusual and infrequent and should therefore be presented as extraordinary items on the income statement.

1. A hailstorm destroys a large portion of a tobacco manufacturer's crops in an area where hailstorms are rare.
2. A steel fabricating company sells the only land it owns. The company acquired the land 10 years ago for future expansion but shortly thereafter abandoned all plans for expansion and held the land for appreciation in value instead.

3. A company sells a block of common stock of a publicly traded company. The block of shares, which represents less than 10 percent of the publicly held company, is the only security investment the company has ever made.

4. An earthquake in Texas destroys one of the oil refineries owned by a large multinational oil company. (*Note*: Earthquakes generally do not occur in Texas.)

Discussion Question ●

9–11. The following examples do not qualify as extraordinary items. For each one, explain specifically what criterion/criteria have not been met.

    a. A citrus grower's Florida crop is damaged by frost ...

    b. A company that operates a chain of warehouses sells excess land around one of its warehouses. Normally, when the company buys land for a new warehouse, it buys more land than it needs for the warehouse expecting that the land will appreciate in value ...

    c. A large diversified company sells from its portfolio a block of shares, which it has acquired for investment purposes. This is the first sale from its portfolio of securities ...

    d. A textile manufacturer with only one plant moves to another location. It has not relocated a plant in 20 years and has no plans to do so in the foreseeable future ...[6]

The income statement for Toy Box, Inc. (Exhibit 9–6) reports an extraordinary gain of $132,000 ($220,000 less income taxes of $88,000). This gain resulted from the city government's purchase of Toy Box's land adjacent to the municipal airport. The government expropriated the land to complete an airport expansion, and Toy Box had no choice but to sell the property. Forced sales to government agencies will not create a taxable gain if the citizen or business entity replaces the property with property that costs as much as the proceeds of the sales. Because Toy Box decided not to replace the land, the transaction was taxable. This transaction is both unusual in nature and infrequent in occurrence for Toy Box. Therefore, the company appropriately reported it as an extraordinary item.

CHANGES IN ACCOUNTING PRINCIPLES

As we mentioned in Chapter 1, one of the secondary qualitative characteristics of useful accounting information is consistency. This means that companies should be consistent in their accounting and refrain from shifting from one accounting method to another. However, from time to time, business entities find it necessary to make changes. In fact, the FASB views changes in accounting principles or standards as part of accounting's natural progression. In its *Conceptual Framework*, the FASB stated:

> *Consistent use of accounting principles from one accounting period to another, if pushed too far, can inhibit accounting progress. No change to a preferred accounting method can be made without sacrificing consistency, yet there is no way that accounting can develop without change. Fortunately, it is possible to make the transition from a less preferred to a more preferred method of accounting and still retain the capacity to compare the periods before and after the change if the effects of the change of method are disclosed.*[7]

Disclosure of the effects of these changes results in the third major type of nonrecurring item that is shown on the income statement net of tax—cumulative effect of a change in accounting principle. This nonrecurring item can result from either of two

---

[6]AICPA Accounting Interpretations, AIN-APB30, #1.

[7]Statement of Accounting Concepts #2, paragraph 122.

scenarios. Bear in mind, however, that in both cases the company must be changing from one acceptable accounting treatment to another acceptable treatment.

The first scenario involves the adoption of a new accounting standard. When a company applies a new accounting method required by a new FASB standard, net income is often affected. Unless the FASB indicates otherwise, the change in net income is reported in the year the company implements the new accounting rule.

The second scenario springs from the fact that in many cases, companies can choose one of several acceptable methods of accounting, and from time to time, companies choose to change from one acceptable accounting method to another. For instance, in Chapter 7, we discussed two different methods for calculating periodic depreciation expense—straight-line and double-declining-balance. In Chapter 8, we presented four different methods of accounting for the cost of inventory—specific identification, FIFO, LIFO, and average cost. Changing from one accounting method to another can have a significant impact on reported net income. Therefore, companies should include the results of these changes on their income statements. We should also say that the decision to change accounting methods should be made after careful consideration. Investors, creditors, the Securities and Exchange Commission (SEC), and the IRS take a dim view of companies that change accounting methods without a good reason.

The required presentation for a cumulative effect of a change in accounting principle is the same whether the change was caused by a new accounting *rule* or was a discretionary *choice*. Often, a newly adopted accounting method impacts not only current income but past income as well. That is, if a company had used the newly adopted accounting procedures in prior years, the income in those past years would have been different. Except in a very few situations, accounting rules do not require or even permit companies to retroactively adjust the income reported in prior periods. Instead, the cumulative effect of the accounting change is presented on the current year's income statement. The **cumulative effect of an accounting change** is the total of the difference between the prior income a company actually reported and the income the company *would have* reported if the company had used the newly adopted accounting principle all along.

cumulative effect of an accounting change
Result of adopting a new accounting standard or changing from one acceptable method of accounting to another. One of the nonrecurring items shown net of tax on the income statement.

To illustrate, we return once again to Toy Box, Inc. Toy Box began operation in 1971, and from the beginning, it used the first-in, first-out (FIFO) method to account for its inventory transactions. Then, in 2005, Toy Box decided to change from FIFO to the average cost method. The effect of this change was a significant reduction in the company's cumulative net income. This arises because if we go back to 1971 and calculate the income as if the average cost method were used from 1971 to 2005, cost of goods sold would have been higher for the 30-year period, and therefore, net income would have been lower over that same time span.

Accounting rules require that the effect of Toy Box's change be reported in 2005. But to report the entire amount as an effect on cost of goods sold in 2005 would be misleading to those who use Toy Box's 2005 income statement to try to predict future results. Instead, the company rightly shows the cumulative effect of its change from FIFO to average cost as a nonrecurring item on its 2005 income statement (Exhibit 9–6).

Of the 600 companies surveyed by the authors of *Accounting Trends and Techniques* in 2001, 43 companies reported cumulative effect of accounting changes on their 2000 income statements, including such companies as ***Dillard's, Inc., Greif Bros. Corporation,*** and ***Intergraph Corporation.***

◆ COMPREHENSIVE INCOME

So far, when we have mentioned the word *income*, we have been talking about income that appears on the income statement. But you may be surprised to learn that accounting rules do not permit all "gains" and "losses" to appear on the income statement. So, the FASB created comprehensive income as a means to fully inform financial statement users of the change in equity from all nonowner transactions. Comprehensive income is one of the 10 accounting elements we began introducing in Chapter 3 (see Exhibit 9–8). As we have with the other nine elements, we will give the actual FASB definition in italics, followed by a less technical explanation.

comprehensive income
The change in equity during a period from nonowner sources.

Comprehensive income is *the change in equity of a business enterprise during a period from transactions and other events and circumstances from non-owner sources. It includes all changes in equity during a period except those resulting from investments by owners and distributions to owners* (Statement of Financial Accounting Concepts No. 6, paragraph 70). Comprehensive income includes all changes in equity during the accounting period *except* for investments by owners and distributions to owners. Comprehensive income not only includes net income from the income statement, but may also include some "gains" and "losses," called *other comprehensive income*, that the income statement doesn't show. There are three types of gains and losses that companies must report as direct adjustments to shareholders' equity, thus bypassing the income statement altogether. Although an understanding of these items is beyond the scope of this text, it may help you to know they are associated with accounting for foreign currency, certain pension liabilities, and unrealized holding gains and losses on certain securities (called available-for-sale securities).

EXHIBIT 9–8 Conceptual Framework with Comprehensive Income Highlighted

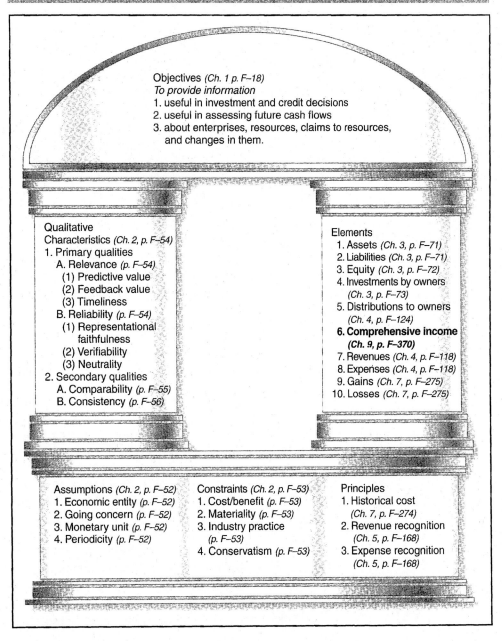

The FASB allows companies to choose from any one of the following three methods of disclosing comprehensive income:

1. A separate statement of comprehensive income
2. A combined statement of income and comprehensive income
3. Comprehensive income included in the statement of changes in stockholders' equity

Of the 600 companies surveyed by the authors of *Accounting Trends and Techniques* in 2001, 519 reported other comprehensive income for 2000. Of those companies, 65 prepared a separate statement, such as **Chevron Corporation** and **Enesco Group, Inc.** Thirty-two companies, including **Chesapeake Corporation** and **Metro-Goldwyn-Mayer,** combined comprehensive income with the income statement; and 422, like **Armstrong World Industries, Inc.,** and **PE Corporation,** included comprehensive income in the statement of stockholders' equity.

It appears that many firms will continue to select the third option because that has been the practice in recent years. An in-depth understanding of this issue is beyond the scope of this text, but we include the information because most of the annual reports you may examine will include comprehensive income in one of these places in the financial statements.

◆ EARNINGS PER SHARE

earnings per share (EPS)
The amount of a company's total earnings attributable to each share of common stock.

Many investors and other financial statement users rely on one statistic more than any other to measure a company's performance—earnings per share. GAAP require companies to disclose earnings per share on the face of their income statements. **Earnings per share (EPS)** is the amount of a company's earnings attributable to each share of common stock. Note, earnings per share is calculated for *common* stock only. Companies do not calculate earnings per share on preferred stock.

BASIC EARNINGS PER SHARE

basic earnings per share
Earnings per share based on the average number of common shares outstanding.

Basic earnings per share is earnings per common share based on the average number of common shares outstanding during the year. Companies use the following formula to calculate basic earnings per share:

$$\frac{\text{Net income} - \text{Preferred dividends}}{\substack{\text{Weighted average number of} \\ \text{common shares outstanding}}} = \text{Basic earnings per share}$$

Both the numerator and denominator in this calculation require a bit of explanation. In the numerator, dividends paid to preferred shareholders are subtracted from net income, because when a company computes earnings per share, it should only include income that it could possibly use to someday pay dividends to common shareholders. That is, it should only use the earnings available to common shareholders. Because the preferred dividends are paid to preferred shareholders and not available to common shareholders, they are deducted from income in the earnings per share calculation. The resulting amount is divided by the average number of common shares outstanding during the year.

There are a couple of reasons why the average number of shares of common stock is used as the denominator in the basic earnings per share calculation, rather than the number of shares outstanding at the end of the year. The first can be attributed to the desire every company has to show as high an earnings per share amount as possible. If you look back at the calculation, you will note that the way to make earnings per share higher is to either increase the numerator or decrease the denominator. Note also that the shares of stock used in the calculation are shares outstanding. That means shares actually owned by shareholders. If the number of shares outstanding at the end of the year were used in the calculation, a company could go out on the open market and repurchase shares of its own stock (called treasury stock), thereby reducing the number of shares outstanding and making earnings per share greater. Requiring companies to use the average number of shares outstanding for the year lessens a company's ability to manipulate earnings per share.

The second reason for using the average number of shares outstanding is that the net income included in the numerator was earned throughout the year (some in January, some in February, etc.), therefore, it makes sense to use the number of shares outstanding throughout the year. There are a number of ways to calculate the weighted average shares outstanding for the year. Maybe the simplest conceptually is to take the number of shares outstanding on January 1, add the number of shares outstanding on January 2, add those outstanding on January 3, and so on, all the way to December 31. Then divide the total by 365 (the number of days in the year), and the result will be the weighted average number of shares outstanding for the entire year.

We will use Toy Box, Inc., as our example for the earnings per share calculations we present. As you can see, to calculate Toy Box's basic earnings per share, we need three important pieces of information: net income, preferred dividends, and the weighted average number of common shares outstanding. As the income statement in Exhibit 9–6 shows, Toy Box's net income for 2006 was $208,470. Toy Box's partial balance sheet in Exhibit 9–9 shows that for 2005, the company had $500,000 worth of 4 percent preferred stock outstanding all year. In 2005, Toy Box paid preferred dividends of $20,000 ($500,000 × 4 percent).

Next, we determine the weighted average number of common shares outstanding during the year. Assume that during 2005, Toy Box had 85,000 common shares outstanding for three months of the year and 90,000 shares outstanding for the remaining nine months of the year. The weighted average number of common shares outstanding for Toy Box would be 88,750 shares calculated as follows:

Dates	Number of Shares Outstanding		Period of Time	Weighted Amount
January 1 to March 31	85,000	×	3/12	21,250
April 1 to December 31	90,000	×	9/12	67,500
	Weighted average shares			88,750

Now that we know Toy Box's net income, its preferred dividends, and its weighted average common shares outstanding, we can calculate the company's basic earnings per share as follows:

$$\text{Basic earnings per share} = \frac{\text{Net income} - \text{Preferred dividends}}{\text{Weighted average number of common shares outstanding}} = \frac{\$208,4702 - \$20,000}{88,750} = \$2.12 \text{ (Rounded)}$$

For some companies, basic earnings per share adequately informs financial statement users, but there are companies that have securities outstanding that can potentially reduce (dilute) earnings per share.

EXHIBIT 9–9 Stockholders' Equity Section of Toy Box, Inc.'s Balance Sheet

Toy Box, Inc.
Stockholders' Equity Section
December 31, 2005 and 2004

	2005	2004
Contributed capital:		
4% Preferred stock, $100 par value, 5,000 shares authorized, issued, and outstanding	$ 500,000	$ 500,000
Common stock, $10 par value, 100,000 shares authorized, 90,000 for 2005 and 85,000 for 2004 issued and outstanding	900,000	850,000
Additional paid-in capital	450,000	390,000
Total contributed capital	$1,850,000	$1,740,000
Retained earnings	794,050	675,580
Total stockholders' equity	$2,644,050	$2,415,580

DILUTED EARNINGS PER SHARE

Some companies sell securities or enter into contracts that may require the company to issue additional common stock. These securities have the potential to reduce (dilute) earnings per share because, if converted or exercised, they can increase the number of common shares outstanding. Potentially more common shares means potentially lower earnings per share. Securities that have the potential to reduce earnings per share are called **dilutive securities.**

dilutive securities
Securities that have the potential to reduce earnings per share.

diluted earnings per share A calculation of earnings per share that takes into account all potentially dilutive securities.

If a company has dilutive securities, GAAP require the company to report both basic earnings per share and diluted earnings per share. **Diluted earnings per share** is an *as if* calculation, meaning that it is calculated as if the dilutive securities had been converted into shares of common stock. There are two types of potentially dilutive securities:

- Convertible securities are debt and equity securities (generally corporate bonds and preferred stocks) that can be exchanged for specified amounts of common stock. When security holders trade these securities for common shares, we say the securities were *converted*.
- Securities such as stock options and stock warrants permit their holder to purchase shares of common stock from the company at a specified price, within a specified time period. When security holders acquire common shares under the terms of these securities, we say the securities were *exercised*.

The actual calculations for diluted earnings per share can be quite involved, and are beyond the scope of this text. The basic idea, however, is that diluted earnings per share should reflect the earnings per common share as though the dilutive securities had been converted or exercised at the beginning of the year even though in fact, they were not.

When a company calculates diluted earnings per share, it recalculates earnings per share under the *assumption* that dilutive securities were converted or exercised at the very beginning of the accounting period (or on the dilutive security's issue date if it was issued during the current accounting period). Keep in mind that the securities were not really converted or exercised and they are still outstanding on the balance sheet date. So what we do when we calculate diluted earnings per share is to calculate the earnings per share that would have resulted *if* the securities had been converted or exercised. To do this, we adjust preferred dividends and the weighted average number of common shares outstanding as necessary to reflect the situation that *would have existed* had the securities been converted.

As an example, assume that each of the 5,000 shares of Toy Box's 4 percent preferred stock is convertible to six shares of Toy Box common stock, a total of 30,000 shares. To calculate diluted earnings per share, we assume that the preferred stock was converted at the very first day of the year. If it had been converted, the preferred stock dividend would not have been paid. Additionally, the preferred stock would have been converted to 30,000 (5,000 preferred shares × 6) common shares, so the weighted average common shares outstanding would have increased by this amount. Accordingly, we calculate diluted earnings per share for Toy Box, Inc., as follows:

$$\text{Diluted earnings per share} = \frac{\text{Net income} - \text{Adjusted preferred dividends}}{\text{Adjusted weighted average number of common shares outstanding}} = \frac{\$208,470 - 0}{88,750 + (5,000 \times 6)} = \$1.76 \text{ (Rounded)}$$

To better understand the earnings per share calculation, look first to the numerator of the equation. If we assume the preferred stock was converted at the beginning of the year, there would have been no requirement to pay preferred dividends for the year. The denominator changes because, if we assume the preferred stock was converted, there would have been an additional 30,000 shares of common stock outstanding all year. The result lowers (dilutes) the earnings per share by $0.36 per share.

INCOME STATEMENT PRESENTATION

GAAP require that basic and diluted earnings per share be prominently displayed on the income statement for many of the items on the income statement that appear below income tax expense. If a company has nonrecurring items, where applicable, it should prominently present basic and diluted earnings per share amounts for income from continuing operations, income before extraordinary items, income before cumulative effect of changes in accounting principle, and net income on the face of its income statement. The remaining earnings per share amounts are required but can be presented either on the face of the income statement or in the accompanying notes. Exhibit 9–10 shows Toy Box, Inc.'s 2005 income statement with all earnings per share information included.

The income statement provides users with a great deal of information, but having only one year's information may prove inadequate for many of the economic decisions we have to make. For this reason, companies are required to present financial statements for more than one accounting period.

EXHIBIT 9–10 Income Statement for Toy Box, Inc., for the Year Ended December 31, 2005

Toy Box, Inc.
Income Statement
For the Year Ended December 31, 2005

Sales		$858,600
Less: Cost of goods sold		456,800
Gross profit on sales		$401,800
Less: Operating expenses:		
Selling expense	$ 94,450	
General and administrative expense	116,050	
Total operating expenses		(210,500)
Operating income		$191,300
Less: Interest expense		(30,650)
Income from continuing operations before taxes		$160,650
Less: Income taxes		(64,260)
Income from continuing operations		$ 96,390
Discontinued operations:		
Income from discontinued operations ($118,800, less: income taxes of $47,520)	$ 71,280	
Loss on disposal of discontinued operation ($90,000, less: income taxes of $36,000)	(54,000)	17,280
Income before extraordinary item and cumulative effect of a change in accounting principle		$113,670
Extraordinary gain ($220,000, less: income taxes of $88,000)		132,000
Income before cumulative effect of a change in accounting principle		245,670
Cumulative effect of a change in accounting principle ($62,000, less: income taxes of $24,800)		(37,200)
Net income		$208,470

Earnings per Common Share	*Basic*	*Diluted*
Income from continuing operations	$ 0.86	$ 0.81
Income from discontinued operation, net of income tax	0.80	0.60
Loss on disposal of discontinued operation, net of income tax	(0.61)	(0.45)
Gain from discontinued operation, net of income tax	$ 0.19	$ 0.15
Income before extraordinary item and cumulative effect of a change in accounting principle	$ 1.05	$ 0.96
Extraordinary gain, net of income tax	1.49	1.11
Income before cumulative effect of a change in accounting principle	$ 2.54	$ 2.07
Cumulative effect of a change in accounting principle, net of tax	(0.42)	(0.31)
Net income	$ 2.12	$ 1.76

◆ COMPARATIVE FINANCIAL STATEMENTS

comparative financial statements Financial statements showing results from two or more consecutive periods.

Comparative financial statements show results for two or more consecutive periods—usually years or quarters. As we will see in Chapter 11, financial statement users use information from comparative financial statements to apply analytical techniques that will help them develop a sense of the company's performance over time.

Companies registered with the SEC are required to present at least two years' balance sheets and three years' income statements and statements of cash flows plus selected financial information for at least five preceding years. The Committee on Accounting Procedure described the importance of comparative financial statements this way:

> *Such presentation emphasizes the fact that statements for a series of periods are far more significant than those for a single period and that the accounts for one period are but an installment of what is essentially a continuous history.*[8]

To illustrate the comparative financial statements, we provide the financial statements for Norton Tire Company, Inc., in Exhibit 9–11 (earnings per share omitted).

Discussion Questions

9–12. Using the comparative income statements and balance sheets of Norton Tire Company, Inc., presented in Exhibit 9–11, prepare the company's 2003 statement of retained earnings.

9–13. What specific information did this statement of retained earnings provide that was not apparent from Norton's income statements or balance sheets?

Comparative financial statements enhance the user's ability to analyze a company's past performance and present condition. And, as we will see in the next chapter, information from comparative financial statements is needed to prepare the statement of cash flows.

◆ USING FINANCIAL INFORMATION

Next, we will present several measures that economic decision makers use to evaluate items presented on the classified balance sheet and expanded income statement. As an example, we will use the financial statements for Norton Tire Company, Inc., in Exhibit 9–11.

ASSET TURNOVER RATIO

asset turnover ratio A financial ratio that shows the amount of sales produced for a given level of assets used.

The **asset turnover ratio** shows the amount of sales produced for a given level of assets used. It is good when a company can produce high sales with a low investment in assets. Therefore, companies should try to get the most out of every dollar invested in assets. The asset turnover ratio is important because it indicates how efficiently the company uses its total assets to generate sales. The formula for this ratio is:

$$\text{Asset turnover ratio} = \frac{\text{Net sales}}{\text{Average total assets}}$$

The net sales figure in the numerator of this ratio comes from the income statement. The amounts we use to calculate the denominator come from the balance sheet. We use an average amount for the same reason we did in earlier ratios. Since the sales in the numerator occurred throughout 2003, we want to know the amount of assets

---

[8]Accounting Research Bulletin No. 43, Chapter 2, paragraph 1.

employed throughout the year. We determine this by calculating the average of the total assets. This is done by adding the beginning balance of total assets to the ending balance of total assets and then dividing that number by two ($9,032 + $10,725 = $19,757/2 = $9,878.5). We calculate Norton's asset turnover ratio for 2003 as:

$$\frac{\$14,745}{\$9,878.5} = 1.49 \text{ times}$$

Our calculation indicates that Norton Tire Company, Inc., produced $1.49 in sales during 2003 for every dollar it had invested in assets. The higher the multiple, the more efficiently the company is using its assets to produce sales.

EXHIBIT 9-11   Comparative Financial Statements for Norton Tire Company, Inc.

Norton Tire Company, Inc.
Income Statements
For the Years Ended December 31, 2003, 2002, and 2001
(in thousands)

	2003	2002	2001
Sales	$14,745	$12,908	$10,888
Less: cost of goods sold	10,213	8,761	7,661
Gross profit on sales	$ 4,532	$ 4,147	$ 3,227
Selling, general, and administrative expenses	(3,627)	(2,997)	(2,087)
Operating income	$ 905	$ 1,150	$ 1,140
Interest expense	(145)	(138)	(107)
Income before taxes	$ 760	$ 1,012	$ 1,033
Income taxes	(266)	(354)	(362)
Net income	$ 494	$ 658	$ 671

Norton Tire Company, Inc.
Balance Sheets
December 31, 2003, and December 31, 2002
(in thousands)

	2003	2002
ASSETS:		
Current assets:		
Cash	$ 2,240	$ 1,936
Accounts receivable	2,340	2,490
Merchandise inventory	776	693
Prepaid expenses	200	160
Total current assets	$ 5,556	$ 5,279
Property, plant, and equipment:		
Buildings, net	$ 4,046	$ 2,889
Equipment, net	1,123	864
Total plant and equipment	$ 5,169	$ 3,753
Total assets	$10,725	$ 9,032
LIABILITIES:		
Current liabilities:		
Accounts payable	$ 1,616	$ 1,080
Notes payable	2,720	2,920
Total current liabilities	$ 4,336	$ 4,000
Long-term liabilities	2,000	1,600
Total liabilities	$ 6,336	$ 5,600
STOCKHOLDERS' EQUITY:		
Common stock, no-par value	$ 3,000	$ 2,400
Retained earnings	1,389	1,032
Total stockholders' equity	$ 4,389	$ 3,432
Total liabilities and stockholders' equity	$10,725	$ 9,032

RECEIVABLES TURNOVER RATIO

receivables turnover ratio An efficiency ratio that measures how quickly a company collects its accounts receivable.

The **receivables turnover ratio** measures how efficiently a company manages its accounts receivable. Accounts receivable is the amount a company is owed by its customers, and it is often a significant current asset. Companies need to convert accounts receivable to cash as quickly as possible because, for many companies, they represent interest-free loans to customers. The receivables turnover ratio indicates how quickly a company collects its receivables. The formula for this ratio is:

$$\text{Receivables turnover ratio} = \frac{\text{Net sales}}{\text{Average accounts receivable}}$$

The net sales figure in the numerator comes from Norton's 2003 income statement and the denominator is based on the accounts receivable shown on the balance sheet. We use an average amount for the denominator in this calculation for the same reason we did in earlier ratios. Since the sales used in the numerator occurred throughout 2003, we want to know the amount of accounts receivable throughout the year. We determine this by calculating the average of the accounts receivable shown on the 2002 and 2003 balance sheets. Our average accounts receivable calculation is ($2,490 + $2,340 = $4,830/2 = $2,415). We calculate Norton's receivables turnover ratio for 2003 as:

$$\frac{\$14,745}{\$2,415} = 6.11 \text{ times}$$

Our calculation indicates that Norton turns its receivables over an average of 6.11 times per year. A higher number would suggest that the company collects cash from its credit customers more quickly and is apparently managing its receivables better. On the other hand, a lower receivables turnover means the company manages its receivables less efficiently.

The information that Norton turns over its accounts receivable 6.11 times per year becomes easier to interpret if we extend it to determine the average collection period for its accounts receivable. We can do that by dividing the receivables turnover into 365 (the number of days in a year) to determine the average time it takes the company to collect its receivables or the **average accounts receivable collection period in days**:

average accounts receivable collection period in days The average time it takes a company to collect its receivables.

$$\frac{\text{Average accounts receivable}}{\text{collection period in days}} = \frac{365}{\text{Receivables turnover ratio}}$$

$$\frac{365}{6.11} = 59.74 \text{ days}$$

Our calculation shows that it takes Norton an average of 59.74 days from the sale date to collect cash from its customers.

CURRENT RATIO

current ratio A liquidity ratio that measures a company's ability to meet short-term obligations by comparing current assets to current liabilities.

The **current ratio** was probably the most widely used measure of a company's liquidity for much of the 20th century. Its purpose is to gauge a company's current assets relative to its current liabilities, thereby attempting to offer a measure of the company's ability to meet its short-term financial obligations (its current liabilities) with cash generated from current assets. The formula for this ratio is:

$$\text{Current ratio} = \frac{\text{Current assets}}{\text{Current liabilities}}$$

This ratio indicates the amount of current assets a company has for each dollar of current liabilities, and both the numerator and the denominator come directly from the balance sheet. We calculate Norton's current ratio for 2003 as:

$$\frac{\$5,556}{\$4,336} = 1.28 \text{ to } 1, \text{ or simply, } 1.28$$

A current ratio of 1.28 tells us that Norton had $1.28 of current assets for every $1.00 of current liabilities at the end of 2003.

The current ratio is a well-respected indicator of liquidity, but the problem with this measure is that a company does not pay its bills with accounts receivable, inventory, and other noncash items included in current assets. It must pay its bills with cash. For this reason, many financial analysts have begun questioning the importance of the current ratio.

QUICK RATIO

quick ratio A liquidity ratio that is similar to the current ratio, but a more stringent test of liquidity, because only current assets considered to be highly liquid (quickly converted to cash) are included in the calculation.

acid-test ratio Another name for the quick ratio.

The **quick ratio** (sometimes called the **acid-test ratio**) is similar to the current ratio. It is a more stringent test of liquidity, however, because it considers only current assets that are highly liquid (quickly convertible into cash) in the numerator. The calculations for this ratio vary because there is some debate as to what assets to include. This stems from the fact that the definition of "highly liquid" is quite subjective. The formula that we are using is one of the more conservative and it is quite popular among financial analysts. The formula for this ratio is:

$$\text{Quick ratio} = \frac{\text{Cash + Short-term investments + Current receivables}}{\text{Current liabilities}}$$

In the numerator of our equation, cash is obviously liquid. We also assume accounts receivable will be quickly converted to cash. However, if an analyst knows that any current receivable will not be quickly converted, it should not include that receivable in the calculation of this ratio. Since Norton shows no short-term investments on its balance sheet, cash and accounts receivable constitute the numerator for the company's quick ratio calculation. As was the case with the current ratio, the denominator of the quick ratio is total current liabilities. We calculate Norton's quick ratio for 2003 as:

$$\frac{\$2,240 + \$2,340}{\$4,336} = 1.06 \text{ to } 1$$

This ratio calculation tells us that Norton had $1.06 of quick assets for each $1.00 of current liabilities at the end of 2003. Note that Norton's quick ratio is lower than its current ratio. That is usually the case because we have removed assets that are not highly liquid from the numerator, while the denominator remains unchanged.

TIMES INTEREST EARNED RATIO

times interest earned ratio A financial ratio that indicates a company's ability to earn (cover) its periodic interest payments.

coverage ratio Same as the times interest earned ratio.

EBIT Earnings before interest and taxes.

The **times interest earned ratio** (often called the **coverage ratio**) indicates a company's ability to earn (cover) its periodic interest payments. It compares the amount of income available for interest payments to the interest requirements. Creditors use this ratio to assess the risk associated with lending money to a business. The formula for this ratio is:

$$\text{Times interest earned ratio} = \frac{\text{Earnings before interest and income taxes}}{\text{Interest expense}}$$

Earnings before interest and taxes, which is often called **EBIT,** is what Norton calls operating income. We calculate Norton's times interest earned ratio for 2003 as:

$$\frac{\$905}{\$145} = 6.23 \text{ times}$$

This ratio calculation tells us Norton's income available to pay interest expense was $6.23 for every $1.00 of interest expense. In other words, the income Norton had available to pay interest expense was 6.23 times the amount of interest the company reported on its income statement.

Many financial analysts believe a times interest earned ratio of at least four provides an appropriate degree of safety for creditors. This means a company's EBIT should be at least four times as great as its interest expense.

Summary ◦◦

The two primary financial statements we have explored thus far—the balance sheet and the income statement—provide important information for economic decision makers. The balance sheet provides a picture of a company's financial position on a given day. This statement outlines what the company owns (assets), what it owes (liabilities), and the residual amount that can be claimed by the owner(s) (equity). The income statement provides a report of the result of business activity during a specific period. Its disclosures of revenues, expenses, gains, and losses for the period are used to measure a company's past performance.

Both the balance sheet and income statement are useful tools. By learning more about the construction and organization of these statements, users of balance sheet and income statement information are able to use the information contained in the statements more effectively.

The classified balance sheet separates assets into four major categories: current, long-term, investments, and intangibles. Liabilities on a classified balance sheet are separated into current and long-term. These classifications provide additional information to users of the information.

Income statements often include items that are not part of the company's normal operations and are not expected to recur. Inflows or outflows of this type must be separated from results of activities that are expected to recur as part of the company's normal, ongoing operations. Reporting recurring items and nonrecurring items separately offers financial statement users additional useful information. Three major types of nonrecurring items (discontinued operations, extraordinary items, and changes in accounting principles) are presented below income from continuing operations and are shown net of tax. An item that is unusual or infrequent, but not both, is shown within the section of the income statement related to continuing operations but is identified as a special item.

Comprehensive income represents the change in equity from nonowner sources. GAAP now require that comprehensive income be prominently displayed in the financial statements. GAAP also require that basic and diluted earnings per share be disclosed on the income statement for each item of income from income from continuing operations through net income. Even with the additional detail offered by a classified balance sheet or an expanded format income statement, economic decision makers are not getting the "big picture" if they consider financial statement information from only one period. Comparative financial statements, providing information for two or more consecutive periods, offer a clearer view of a company's performance and financial position than a financial statement from a single period.

Key Terms ◦◦

- acid-test ratio, F–379
- asset turnover ratio, F–376
- average accounts receivable collection period in days, F–378
- basic earnings per share, F–372
- business segment, F–366
- classified balance sheet, F–357
- comparative financial statements, F–376
- comprehensive income, F–371
- contributed capital, F–361
- coverage ratio, F–379

- cumulative effect of an accounting change, F–370
- current assets, F–357
- current liabilities, F–360
- current ratio, F–378
- diluted earnings per share, F–374
- dilutive securities, F–374
- discontinued operations, F–365
- earnings per share (EPS), F–372
- EBIT, F–379
- extraordinary item, F–367
- intangible assets, F–359

- long-term assets, F–359
- long-term investments, F–359
- long-term liabilities, F–360
- net of tax, F–365
- nonrecurring item, F–362
- other assets, F–359
- property, plant, and equipment, F–359
- quick ratio, F–379
- receivables turnover ratio, F–378
- retained earnings, F–361
- times interest earned ratio, F–379

Review the Facts

A. What was the original purpose of accounting records?

B. What caused the shift in attention from the balance sheet to the income statement?

C. Explain why a decision maker may prefer a classified balance sheet to one using the simplest possible format.

D. What is the difference between current and long-term assets? Offer two examples of each.

E. In what order are assets presented on a classified balance sheet?

F. Describe investments and intangible assets and provide two examples of each.

G. Describe the difference between current and long-term liabilities and provide two examples of each.

H. Explain the difference between recurring and nonrecurring items on an income statement. Why are these items reported separately from one another?

 I. Identify the three major types of nonrecurring items that are shown net of tax on the income statement.

J. Explain the effect of taxes on gains and on losses.

K. With respect to discontinued operations, what is a business segment?

L. What criteria must be met for an item to be considered extraordinary?

M. What does the cumulative effect of a change in accounting principle represent?

N. What is comprehensive income? How does it differ from net income?

O. What is the difference between basic and diluted earnings per share?

P. Describe comparative financial statements and explain their benefits to economic decision makers.

Q. What is the focus of the asset turnover ratio and the receivables turnover ratio?

R. What can the current and quick ratios reveal about a company?

S. What does the times interest earned ratio indicate?

Apply What You Have Learned

LO 2: BALANCE SHEET TERMINOLOGY

9–14. Below are items related to the organization of the classified balance sheet, followed by the definitions of those items in scrambled order:

a. Liquidity	f. Long-term liabilities
b. Current assets	g. Stockholders' equity
c. Long-term assets	h. Total liabilities and stockholders' equity
d. Current liabilities	i. Plant and equipment, net
e. Intangible asset	j. Investments

1. _____ Obligations not requiring payment within the next year

2. _____ Items controlled by a company that are not expected to become cash within the next year

3. _____ Describes an item's nearness to cash

4. _____ The owners' residual interest in a corporation

5. _____ Long-lived tangible assets less all the depreciation expense ever recognized on those assets

6. _____ Obligations that must be retired within the next year

7. _____ Equal to total assets

8. _____ Items controlled by a company that are expected to become cash within the next year

9. _____ An investment in a contractual arrangement such as a patent

10. _____ A long-term commitment to ownership of other entities

Required: Match the letter next to each item with the appropriate definition. Use each letter only once.

LO 2: BALANCE SHEET ACCOUNTS

9–15. **Required:**

a. What are investments on a balance sheet and how are they classified?

b. Provide three examples of investments and discuss how they would be classified on the balance sheet.

LO 2: BALANCE SHEET ACCOUNTS

9–16. **Required:**

  a. Define intangible assets in your own words.
  b. Provide three examples of intangible assets and discuss how they would be classified on the balance sheet.
  c. What is the term applied to the process of matching the cost of an intangible with the periods of time benefited or with the revenues they help to create?

LO 2: BALANCE SHEET ACCOUNTS

9–17. Below are the major sections of the classified balance sheet, followed by a list of items normally shown on the balance sheet:

  a. Current assets   e. Long-term liabilities
  b. Long-term assets   f. Contributed capital
  c. Current liabilities   g. Retained earnings
  d. Intangible asset   h. Investments

  1. _____ Accounts payable
  2. _____ Common stock
  3. _____ Franchise
  4. _____ Accounts receivable
  5. _____ Notes payable due within one year
  6. _____ Prepaid expenses
  7. _____ Preferred stock
  8. _____ Notes payable due in two years
  9. _____ Amounts earned by the company but not yet distributed to the owners of the business
  10. _____ Amounts received in excess of par value on the sale of stock
  11. _____ Bonds held by the company to earn interest revenue
  12. _____ Land
  13. _____ Stock of a subsidiary
  14. _____ Wages payable
  15. _____ Vehicles
  16. _____ Copyright
  17. _____ Cash
  18. _____ Buildings
  19. _____ Bonds payable
  20. _____ Trademark

Required: Indicate where each item on the list should be shown on the classified balance sheet by placing the letter of the appropriate balance sheet section in the space provided. The letters may be used more than once.

LO 2: SIMPLE CLASSIFIED BALANCE SHEET PREPARATION

9–18. The following items relate to the Carol Strong Company at December 31, 2004:

Cash	$ 124,200
Accounts receivable	315,200
Inventory	864,800
Prepaid expenses	56,000
Land	620,000
Building	1,450,000
Accumulated depreciation—building	685,000
Accounts payable	546,500
Current notes payable	75,000
Long-term bonds payable	350,000
Common stock, $1 par	55,000
Additional paid-in capital—common	866,400
Retained earnings	852,300

Required:

    a. How many shares of Strong Company's common stock are outstanding at December 31, 2004? Explain how you determined your answer.

    b. How much cash did Strong Company receive from the sale of its common stock? Explain how you determined your answer.

    c. Prepare a classified balance sheet for Strong Company at December 31, 2004.

LO 7: CURRENT AND QUICK RATIO CALCULATIONS

9–19. This problem is a continuation of problem 9–18.

Required:

    a. Using information from the balance sheet you prepared for problem 9–18, calculate the following ratios for the company:

        1. The current ratio
        2. The quick ratio

    b. Based on ratios you calculated, what is your impression of the company's liquidity? Explain your answer.

LO 2: CLASSIFIED BALANCE SHEET PREPARATION

9–20. The following items relate to the Dana Corporation at December 31, 2004:

Land	$210,000
Cash	14,600
Accounts receivable	92,300
Accounts payable	74,000
Common stock (75,000 shares outstanding)	300,000
Bonds payable	100,000
Additional paid-in capital—common stock	10,000
Inventory	118,000
Prepaid expenses	11,200
Taxes payable	17,000
Short-term notes payable	50,000
Building	400,000
Accumulated depreciation—building	142,000
Retained earnings	117,300
Wages payable	35,800

Required:

    a. What is the par value of Dana Corporation's common stock? Explain how you determined your answer.

    b. How much cash did Dana Corporation receive from the sale of its common stock? Explain how you determined your answer.

    c. Prepare a classified balance sheet for Dana Corporation at December 31, 2004.

LO 7: CURRENT AND QUICK RATIO CALCULATIONS

9–21. This problem is a continuation of problem 9–20.

Required:

    a. Using information from the balance sheet you prepared for problem 9–20, calculate the following ratios for the company:

        1. The current ratio
        2. The quick ratio

    b. Based on ratios you calculated, what is your impression of the company's liquidity? Explain your answer.

LO 2: CLASSIFIED BALANCE SHEET PREPARATION

9–22. The following items relate to Murphy and Company at December 31, 2005:

Accounts payable	$172,000
Common stock ($2 par value)	400,000
Bonds payable	307,700
Prepaid expenses	9,800
Taxes payable	47,000
Short-term notes payable	70,000
Building	875,000
Accumulated depreciation—building	271,000
Additional paid-in capital—common stock	240,000
Land	490,000
Cash	124,200
Accounts receivable	212,000
Inventory	338,000
Retained earnings	463,700
Wages payable	77,600

Required:

a. How many shares of Murphy and Company's common stock are outstanding at December 31, 2005? Explain how you determined your answer.
b. How much cash did Murphy and Company receive from the sale of its common stock? Explain how you determined your answer.
c. Prepare a classified balance sheet for Murphy and Company at December 31, 2005.

LO 7: CURRENT AND QUICK RATIO CALCULATIONS

9–23. This problem is a continuation of problem 9–22.

Required:

a. Using information from the balance sheet you prepared for problem 9–22, calculate the following ratios for the company:

1. The current ratio
2. The quick ratio

b. Based on ratios you calculated, what is your impression of the company's liquidity? Explain your answer.

LO 2: BALANCE SHEET CLASSIFICATIONS

9–24. Many of the assets on a classified balance sheet are identified as current assets. Liabilities on the classified balance sheet are also identified as either current or long-term.

Required:

a. What criterion is used to determine whether an asset or liability is classified as current or long-term?
b. Explain in your own words why the following parties would be interested in the separation of current and long-term assets and liabilities on a company's balance sheet:

1. Short-term creditors (other businesses from whom the company buys inventory, supplies, etc.)
2. Long-term creditors (banks and others from whom the company borrows money on a long-term basis)
3. The company's stockholders
4. The company's management

LO 2: CLASSIFIED BALANCE SHEET

9–25. Stockholders' equity on the classified balance sheet of a corporation is divided into two major categories: contributed capital and retained earnings.

Required:

    a. Explain in your own words what each of the two major categories under stockholders' equity represents.

    b. Explain in your own words why the following parties would be interested in the relative amounts of contributed capital and retained earnings in the stockholders' equity section of a company's balance sheet:

        1. Short-term creditors (other businesses from whom the company buys inventory, supplies, etc.)

        2. Long-term creditors (banks and others from whom the company borrows money on a long-term basis)

        3. The company's stockholders

        4. The company's management

LO 3: INCOME STATEMENT TERMINOLOGY

9–26. Below are several sections of the multiple-step income statement, followed by several independent situations or transactions:

a. Sales	e. Discontinued operation
b. Cost of goods sold	f. Extraordinary item
c. Operating expenses	g. Change in accounting principle
d. Income from continuing operations	h. Not shown on income statement

    1. _____ A manufacturing company sells a warehouse with a book value of $20,000 for $20,000.

    2. _____ A company changed from the FIFO method to the average cost method of accounting for inventory cost flows.

    3. _____ A company sells units of inventory in the normal course of its business operation.

    4. _____ A company located in San Francisco, California, experiences a loss from earthquake damage. This loss is determined to be a "special" item.

    5. _____ A company disposes of a major segment of its business.

    6. _____ A company pays wages, rent, utilities, and so forth.

    7. _____ A company located in Columbia, South Carolina, experiences a loss from earthquake damage. This loss is determined to be both unusual in nature and infrequent in occurrence.

    8. _____ A company adopts a newly required accounting standard for accounting for postretirement benefits other than pensions. As a result, net income for the year is adversely affected.

Required: Indicate where the result of each situation or transaction should be shown on the multiple-step income statement by placing the letter of the appropriate income statement section in the space provided. The letters may be used more than once. *Note*: The results of some situations or transactions may not be shown on the income statement. If so, place the letter h in the space provided.

LO 3: INCOME STATEMENT TERMINOLOGY

9–27. Below are items related to the multiple-step income statement as discussed in this chapter, followed by the definitions of those items in scrambled order:

a. Gross profit on sales	e. Extraordinary item
b. Operating expenses	f. Change in accounting principle
c. Income from continuing operations	g. Recurring item
d. Discontinued operation	h. Nonrecurring item

    1. _____ A material gain or loss that is both unusual in nature and infrequent in occurrence

    2. _____ Generally, the difference between normal ongoing revenues and normal ongoing expenses

    3. _____ The difference between sales and cost of goods sold

    4. _____ Any item that should not be considered a normal part of continuing operations because it is not expected to happen again

    5. _____ Sacrifices incurred in the normal day-to-day running of a business

6. _____ Any item considered a normal part of continuing operations because it is expected to happen on an ongoing basis
7. _____ A change from a less preferred to a more preferred method of accounting
8. _____ The disposal of a business segment

Required: Match the letter next to each item with the appropriate definition. Use each letter only once.

LO 3: INCOME TAX DISCLOSURE

9–28. **Required:**

a. What is the purpose of reporting discontinued items, extraordinary gains and losses, and the cumulative effect of changes in accounting principle net of income taxes?
b. Discuss the meaning of the phrase "net of tax" and how this is reported on the income statement.

LO 3: DISCONTINUED OPERATIONS

9–29. On March 1, 2005, the board of directors of Photoception approved the disposal of a segment of its business. For the period of January 1 through February 28, 2005, the segment had revenues of $200,000 and expenses of $350,000. The company sold the assets of the segment at a loss of $100,000.

Required: Describe how the corporation should report the previous information on the financial statements. Be as specific as possible.

LO 3: DISCONTINUED OPERATIONS

9–30. On July 1, 2004, the board of directors of Donahue Company approved the sale of a segment of its business. For the period of January 1 through June 30, 2004, the segment had revenues of $1,100,000 and expenses of $1,500,000. The company sold the assets of the segment at a gain of $200,000.

Required: Describe how the corporation should report the previous information on the financial statements. Be as specific as possible.

LO 3: DISCONTINUED OPERATIONS

9–31. On October 1, 2005, the board of directors of Lopez Company approved the disposal of a segment of its business. For the period of January 1 through September 30, 2005, the segment had revenues of $1,500,000 and expenses of $2,500,000. The company sold the assets of the segment at a gain of $300,000.

Required: Describe how the corporation should report the previous information on the financial statements. Be as specific as possible.

LO 4: MULTIPLE-STEP INCOME STATEMENT

9–32. The following items relate to Kim Hahn, Inc., for the year ended December 31, 2004:

- Net sales for the year totaled $665,000.
- Cost of goods sold for the year totaled $271,000.
- Regular operating expenses for the year were $145,000.
- Interest expense for the year was $27,000.
- On February 18, 2004, one of Hahn's warehouses burned to the ground. The company's loss (after the insurance settlement) was $106,000 before any tax effect. This loss was determined to be both unusual in nature and infrequent in occurrence.
- During 2004, Hahn changed the way it depreciated its property, plant, and equipment from an accelerated method to the straight-line method. The cumulative effect of this change was a $93,000 increase in net income before any tax effect.
- Hahn's income tax rate is 40 percent on all items.

Required: Prepare Hahn's income statement for the year ended December 31, 2004, using the expanded multiple-step format presented in this chapter.

LO 7: ASSET TURNOVER, RECEIVABLES TURNOVER, AND TIMES INTEREST EARNED RATIO CALCULATIONS

9–33. This problem is a continuation of problem 9–32.

In addition to the information from the financial statements you prepared for 9–32, the following information is available:

- The average total assets for the company are $950,000.
- Average accounts receivable for the company are $140,000.

Required:

    a. Calculate the following ratios for the company:

        1. The asset turnover ratio
        2. The receivables turnover ratio
        3. The average accounts receivable collection period in days
        4. The times interest earned ratio

    b. Based on the ratios, what is your impression of the company? Explain your answer.

LO 4: MULTIPLE-STEP INCOME STATEMENT

9–34. The following items relate to Linda Jones and Company for the year ended December 31, 2005:

- Net sales for the year totaled $575,000.
- Cost of goods sold for the year totaled $372,500.
- Regular operating expenses for the year were $121,500.
- Interest expense for the year was $16,000.
- On September 5, 2005, Jones sold the only land it owned at a pretax gain of $50,000. The land was acquired in 1996 for future expansion, but shortly thereafter, the company abandoned all plans for expansion and held the land for appreciation.
- During 2005, Jones changed the way it accounted for inventory from the FIFO method to the average cost method. The cumulative effect of this change was an $80,000 decrease in net income before any tax effect.
- Jones's income tax rate is 30 percent on all items.

Required: Prepare Jones's income statement for the year ended December 31, 2005, using the expanded multiple-step format presented in this chapter.

LO 7: ASSET TURNOVER, RECEIVABLES TURNOVER, AND TIMES INTEREST EARNED RATIO CALCULATIONS

9–35. This problem is a continuation of problem 9–34.

In addition to the information from the financial statements you prepared for 9–34, the following information is available:

- The average total assets for the company are $360,000.
- Average accounts receivable for the company are $55,000.

Required:

    a. Calculate the following ratios for the company:

        1. The asset turnover ratio
        2. The receivables turnover ratio
        3. The average accounts receivable collection period in days
        4. The times interest earned ratio

    b. Based on the ratios, what is your impression of the company? Explain your answer.

LO 4: MULTIPLE-STEP INCOME STATEMENT

9–36. The following items relate to Mark Ripley Company for the year ended December 31, 2004:

- Net sales for the year totaled $1,075,000.
- Cost of goods sold for the year totaled $667,000.

- Operating expenses for the year were $102,500.
- Interest expense for the year was $43,000.
- On June 30, 2004, Ripley sold a major segment of its business at a loss of $95,000 before any tax effects. This segment of the company represented a major line of business that was totally separate from the rest of Ripley's operation.
- Prior to being sold, the business segment had sales during 2004 of $150,000, cost of goods sold of $90,000, and operating expenses of $45,000. These amounts are not included in the previous information provided.
- Ripley's income tax rate is 40 percent on all items.

Required: Prepare Ripley's income statement for the year ended December 31, 2004, using the expanded multiple-step format presented in this chapter.

LO 7: ASSET TURNOVER, RECEIVABLES TURNOVER, AND TIMES INTEREST EARNED RATIO CALCULATIONS

9–37. This problem is a continuation of problem 9–36.

In addition to the information from the financial statements you prepared for 9–36, the following information is available:

- The average total assets for the company are $390,000.
- Average accounts receivable for the company are $165,000.

Required:

a. Calculate the following ratios for the company:

1. The asset turnover ratio
2. The receivables turnover ratio
3. The average accounts receivable collection period in days
4. The times interest earned ratio

b. Based on the ratios, what is your impression of the company? Explain your answer.

LO 4: MULTIPLE-STEP INCOME STATEMENT

9–38. The following items relate to Andre Holmes, Inc., for the year ended December 31, 2005:

- Net sales for the year totaled $465,000.
- Cost of goods sold for the year totaled $239,000.
- Operating expenses for the year were $113,200.
- Interest expense for the year was $11,000.
- On July 16, 2005, Holmes sold a major segment of its business at a gain of $50,000 before any tax effects. This segment of the company represented a major line of business that was totally separate from the rest of Holmes's operation.
- Prior to being sold, the business segment had sales during 2005 of $60,000, cost of goods sold of $40,000, and operating expenses of $35,000. These amounts are not included in the previous information provided.
- Holmes's income tax rate is 30 percent on all items.

Required: Prepare Holmes's income statement for the year ended December 31, 2005, using the expanded multiple-step format presented in this chapter.

LO 7: ASSET TURNOVER, RECEIVABLES TURNOVER, AND TIMES INTEREST EARNED RATIO CALCULATIONS

9–39. This problem is a continuation of problem 9–38.

In addition to the information from the financial statements you prepared for 9–38, the following information is available:

- The average total assets for the company are $738,000.
- Average accounts receivable for the company are $47,000.

Required:

    a. Calculate the following ratios for the company:

        1. The asset turnover ratio
        2. The receivables turnover ratio
        3. The average accounts receivable collection period in days
        4. The times interest earned ratio

    b. Based on the ratios, what is your impression of the company? Explain your answer.

LO 4: DISCUSSION OF INCOME STATEMENT

9–40. The multiple-step income statement as presented in this chapter separates recurring items from nonrecurring items. Further, three major types of nonrecurring items are shown on the income statement net of tax.

Required:

    a. Explain in your own words the rationale behind showing recurring and nonrecurring items separately on the multiple-step income statement.
    b. Explain in your own words what the phrase "net of tax" means and why three major types of nonrecurring items are shown in this manner on the income statement.

LO 5: SIMPLE CALCULATION OF BASIC EARNINGS PER SHARE—SIMPLE CAPITAL STRUCTURE

9–41. The Tatum Company reported net income for the year ended December 31, 2005, of $337,600. At the end of the year 2005, the Tatum Company had the following shares of capital stock outstanding:

- Preferred stock, 5 percent, $200 par value, nonconvertible, 10,000 issued and outstanding.
- Common stock, $2 par value, 40,000 shares issued and outstanding.

Required: Assume the preferred dividends were paid and calculate basic earnings per share for 2005.

LO 5: BASIC EARNINGS PER SHARE—SIMPLE CAPITAL STRUCTURE

9–42. The Kreutzer Company reported net income for the year ended December 31, 2005, of $554,800. During the year 2005, the Kreutzer Company had the following shares of capital stock outstanding:

- Preferred stock, 6 percent, $100 par value, nonconvertible, 20,000 issued and outstanding.
- Common stock, $1 par value, 40,000 shares issued and outstanding on January 1, 2005.
- An additional 5,000 shares of common stock were issued on April 1, 2005.

Required: Assume the preferred dividends were paid and calculate basic earnings per share for 2005.

LO 5: BASIC EARNINGS PER SHARE—SIMPLE CAPITAL STRUCTURE

9–43. The Witt Company reported income after taxes for the year ended December 31, 2005, of $775,200. During the year 2005, the Witt Company had the following shares of capital stock outstanding:

- Preferred stock, 5 percent, $100 par value, nonconvertible, 20,000 issued and outstanding.
- Common stock, $3 par value, 80,000 shares issued and outstanding on January 1, 2005.
- An additional 10,000 shares of common stock were issued on July 1, 2005.

Required: Assume the preferred dividends were paid and calculate basic earnings per share for 2005.

LO 1, 2, & 5: INCOME STATEMENT, STATEMENT OF RETAINED EARNINGS, BALANCE SHEET WITH NO NONRECURRING ITEMS (SELECTED CHECK FIGURE PROVIDED)

9–44. The following information is taken from accounting records of Kevin's Toy Store as of the year ended December 31, 2004:

Income tax rate	34%
Net sales	$1,268,000
Cost of goods sold	975,000
Operating expenses	225,000
Rent revenue	6,000
Interest expense	5,000
Check figure—income tax	23,460
Beginning retained earnings balance	114,460
Dividends	10,000
Cash	126,000
Accounts receivable	185,000
Inventory	225,000
Other current assets	38,000
Property, plant, and equipment	875,000
Accumulated depreciation—property, plant, and equipment	350,000
Accounts payable	260,000
Current notes payable	30,000
Long-term notes payable	34,000
Common stock, $2 par, 50,000 shares authorized, 12,500 shares issued and outstanding	25,000
Additional paid-in capital—common	600,000
Check figure—ending retained earnings balance	150,000

Required:

a. Prepare an income statement for the company using a multiple-step format.
b. Calculate basic earnings per share and include it at the bottom of the income statement. Assume that the number of common shares outstanding remained constant all year.
c. Prepare a statement of retained earnings for the company.
d. Prepare a classified balance sheet for the company as of the end of the accounting period.

LO 7: FINANCIAL RATIO CALCULATIONS

9–45. This problem is a continuation of problem 9–44.

In addition to the information from the financial statements you prepared for 9–44, the following information is available:

• The company's assets totaled $1,027,000 at December 31, 2003.
• The company's accounts receivable totaled $165,000 at December 31, 2003.

Required:

a. Calculate the following ratios for the company:

1. The asset turnover ratio
2. The receivables turnover ratio
3. The average accounts receivable collection period in days
4. The current ratio
5. The quick ratio
6. The times interest earned ratio

b. Based on the ratios, what is your impression of the company? Explain your answer.

LO 1, 2, & 5: INCOME STATEMENT, STATEMENT OF RETAINED EARNINGS, BALANCE SHEET WITH NO NONRECURRING ITEMS (SELECTED CHECK FIGURE PROVIDED)

9–46. The following information is taken from accounting records of Kyle's Lawns, Inc., as of the fiscal year ended November 30, 2005:

Income tax rate	30%
Net sales	$3,000,000
Cost of goods sold	2,000,000
Operating expenses	380,000
Interest revenue	2,000
Interest expense	22,000
Income tax	180,000
Beginning retained earnings balance	122,000
Dividends	42,000
Cash	125,000
Accounts receivable	175,000
Merchandise inventory	245,000
Other current assets	25,000
Property, plant, and equipment	965,000
Accumulated depreciation—property, plant, and equipment	335,000
Accounts payable	285,000
Current notes payable	10,000
Wages payable	5,000
Long-term notes payable	50,000
Common stock, $1 par, 150,000 shares authorized, 95,000 shares issued and outstanding	95,000
Additional paid-in capital—common	255,000
Check figure—ending retained earnings balance	500,000

Required:

    a. Prepare an income statement for the company using a multiple-step format.

    b. Calculate basic earnings per share and include it at the bottom of the income statement. Assume that the number of common shares outstanding remained constant all year.

    c. Prepare a statement of retained earnings for the company.

    d. Prepare a classified balance sheet for the company as of the end of the accounting period.

LO 7: FINANCIAL RATIO CALCULATIONS

9–47. This problem is a continuation of problem 9–46.

In addition to the information from the financial statements you prepared for 9–46, the following information is available:

- The company's assets totaled $1,100,000 at November 30, 2004.
- The company's accounts receivable totaled $191,000 at November 30, 2004.

Required:

    a. Calculate the following ratios for the company:

        1. The asset turnover ratio
        2. The receivables turnover ratio
        3. The average accounts receivable collection period in days
        4. The current ratio
        5. The quick ratio
        6. The times interest earned ratio

    b. Based on the ratios, what is your impression of the company? Explain your answer.

LO 1, 2, & 5: INCOME STATEMENT, STATEMENT OF RETAINED EARNINGS, BALANCE SHEET WITH NO NONRECURRING ITEMS (SELECTED CHECK FIGURE PROVIDED)

9–48. The following information is taken from accounting records of Fashions by Christie as of the year ended December 31, 2004:

Income tax rate	30%
Net sales	$350,000
Cost of goods sold	150,000
Operating expenses	135,000
Interest revenue	1,000

Interest expense	16,000
Income tax	15,000
Beginning retained earnings balance	57,000
Dividends	17,000
Cash	62,000
Inventory	78,000
Property, plant, and equipment	186,000
Accumulated depreciation—property, plant, and equipment	26,000
Accounts payable	90,000
Current notes payable	10,000
Long-term notes payable	25,000
Common stock, $5 par, 10,000 shares authorized,	
1,000 shares issued and outstanding	5,000
Additional paid-in capital—common	95,000
Check figure—ending retained earnings balance	75,000

Required:

a. Prepare an income statement for the company using a multiple-step format.
b. Calculate basic earnings per share and include it at the bottom of the income statement. Assume that the number of common shares outstanding remained constant all year.
c. Prepare a statement of retained earnings for the company.
d. Prepare a classified balance sheet for the company as of the end of the accounting period.

LO 1, 2, 3, 4, & 5: INCOME STATEMENT, STATEMENT OF RETAINED EARNINGS, BALANCE SHEET WITH EXTRAORDINARY ITEM (SELECTED CHECK FIGURES PROVIDED)

9–49. The following information is taken from accounting records of Art by Nicole as of the year ended December 31, 2004:

Income tax rate	32%
Sales	$427,650
Cost of goods sold	255,340
Operating expenses	119,850
Rent revenue	1,240
Interest expense	3,000
Casualty loss (Both unusual and infrequent)	19,000
Beginning retained earnings balance	215,000
Dividends	2,000
Cash	18,000
Accounts receivable	63,500
Inventory	98,450
Other current assets	26,800
Property, plant, and equipment	230,000
Accumulated depreciation—property, plant, and equipment	40,000
Accounts payable	38,600
Current notes payable	25,000
Long-term bonds payable	50,000
Common stock, $1 par, 50,000 shares authorized,	
3,500 shares issued and outstanding	3,500
Additional paid-in capital—common	45,094
Check figure—ending retained earnings balance	234,556
Check figure—income tax amount for nonrecurring item	6,080
Check figure—income tax on income before extraordinary item	16,224

Required:

a. Prepare an income statement for the company using a multiple-step format.
b. Calculate basic earnings per share and include it at the bottom of the income statement. Assume that the number of common shares outstanding remained constant all year.
c. Prepare a statement of retained earnings for the company.
d. Prepare a classified balance sheet for the company as of the end of the accounting period.

LO 7: FINANCIAL RATIO CALCULATIONS

9–50. This problem is a continuation of problem 9–49.

In addition to the information from the financial statements you prepared for 9–49, the following information is available:

- The company's assets totaled $374,250 at December 31, 2003.
- The company's accounts receivable totaled $69,250 at December 31, 2003.

Required:

a. Calculate the following ratios for the company:

1. The asset turnover ratio
2. The receivables turnover ratio
3. The average accounts receivable collection period in days
4. The current ratio
5. The quick ratio
6. The times interest earned ratio

b. Based on the ratios, what is your impression of the company? Explain your answer.

LO 1, 2, 3, 4, & 5: INCOME STATEMENT, STATEMENT OF RETAINED EARNINGS, BALANCE SHEET WITH EXTRAORDINARY ITEM (SELECTED CHECK FIGURES PROVIDED)

9–51. The following information is taken from accounting records of Adrienne's Cosmetics as of the year ended December 31, 2004:

Income tax rate	36%
Net sales	$1,525,000
Cost of goods sold	925,000
Operating expenses	386,000
Interest revenue	3,000
Interest expense	15,000
Extraordinary casualty loss—flood damage	36,000
Beginning retained earnings balance	160,000
Dividends	20,000
Cash	126,500
Accounts receivable	186,500
Inventory	225,500
Other current assets	38,000
Property, plant, and equipment	875,000
Accumulated depreciation—property, plant, and equipment	350,000
Accounts payable	260,000
Current notes payable	30,000
Long-term notes payable	37,000
Common stock, $5 par, 100,000 shares authorized, 10,000 shares issued and outstanding	50,000
Additional paid-in capital—common	478,260
Check figure—ending retained earnings balance	246,240
Check figure—income tax amount for nonrecurring item	12,960
Check figure—income tax on income before extraordinary item	72,720

Required:

a. Prepare an income statement for the company using a multiple-step format.
b. Calculate basic earnings per share and include it at the bottom of the income statement. Assume that the number of common shares outstanding remained constant all year.
c. Prepare a statement of retained earnings for the company.
d. Prepare a classified balance sheet for the company as of the end of the accounting period.

LO 1, 2, 3, 4, & 5: INCOME STATEMENT, STATEMENT OF RETAINED EARNINGS, BALANCE SHEET WITH ACCOUNTING CHANGE (SELECTED CHECK FIGURES PROVIDED)

9–52. The following information is taken from accounting records of Jerry's Tile Depot as of the year ended December 31, 2004:

Income tax rate	34%
Sales	$2,300,000
Cost of goods sold	1,450,000
Operating expenses	787,000
Rent revenue	19,000
Interest expense	5,000
Gain from cumulative effect of accounting change	33,000
Beginning retained earnings balance	160,000
Dividends	15,000
Cash	126,500
Accounts receivable	186,500
Inventory	225,500
Other current assets	38,000
Property, plant, and equipment	875,000
Accumulated depreciation – property, plant, and equipment	350,000
Accounts payable	260,000
Current notes payable	25,000
Wages payable	5,000
Long-term notes payable	37,000
Common stock, $1 par, 100,000 shares authorized, 50,000 shares issued and outstanding	50,000
Additional paid-in capital – common	506,900
Check figure – ending retained earnings balance	217,600
Check figure – income tax amount for nonrecurring item	–$11,220
Check figure – income tax on income before cumulative effect of account change	26,180

Required:

a. Prepare an income statement for the company using a multiple-step format.
b. Calculate basic earnings per share and include it at the bottom of the income statement. Assume that the number of common shares outstanding remained constant all year.
c. Prepare a statement of retained earnings for the company.
d. Prepare a classified balance sheet for the company as of the end of the accounting period.

LO 1, 2, 3, 4, & 5: INCOME STATEMENT, STATEMENT OF RETAINED EARNINGS, BALANCE SHEET WITH DISCONTINUED OPERATION (SELECTED CHECK FIGURES PROVIDED)

9–53. The following information is taken from accounting records of Danielle's Shoes as of the year ended December 31, 2004:

Income tax rate	30%
Sales	$960,000
Cost of goods sold	575,600
Operating expenses	276,000
Interest expense	1,500
Discontinued operation	
Loss on operation of discontinued operation	8,500
Loss on disposal of discontinued operation	29,500
Beginning retained earnings balance	98,650
Dividends	4,823
Cash	68,500
Accounts receivable	140,000
Inventory	175,500
Other current assets	2,000
Equipment	185,000

Accumulated depreciation—equipment	32,000
Accounts payable	80,500
Current notes payable	2,000
Long-term notes payable	15,000
Preferred stock, $50 par, 5,000 shares authorized,	
2,400 shares issued and outstanding	120,000
Additional paid-in capital—preferred	3,000
Common stock, $1 par, 100,000 shares authorized,	
27,000 shares issued and outstanding	27,000
Additional paid-in capital—common	149,443
Check figure—ending retained earnings balance	142,057
Check figure—income tax amount for nonrecurring items	11,400
Check figure—income tax on income from continuing operations	32,070

Required:

a. Prepare an income statement for the company using a multiple-step format.
b. Calculate basic earnings per share and include it at the bottom of the income statement. Assume that the number of common shares outstanding remained constant all year.
c. Prepare a statement of retained earnings for the company.
d. Prepare a classified balance sheet for the company as of the end of the accounting period.

LO 1, 2, 3, 4, & 5: COMPLEX DETAILED INCOME STATEMENT, STATEMENT OF RETAINED EARNINGS, BALANCE SHEET WITH DISCONTINUED OPERATION, EXTRAORDINARY ITEM, AND ACCOUNTING CHANGE (SELECTED CHECK FIGURES PROVIDED)

9–54. The following information is taken from accounting records of Mark's Custom Decks and Ponds as of the fiscal year ended November 30, 2005:

Income tax rate	32%
Sales	$2,650,500
Cost of goods sold	1,825,000
Wages and salaries	420,000
Rent	108,000
Electricity	10,200
Telephone	4,200
Interest revenue	1,600
Interest expense	36,000
Discontinued operation	
Loss on operation of discontinued operation	1,000
Loss on disposal of discontinued operation	14,000
Extraordinary loss	22,000
Cumulative effect of accounting change—gain	5,000
Beginning retained earnings balance	43,116
Dividends	20,000
Cash	34,500
Accounts receivable	152,500
Inventory	231,232
Supplies	2,500
Land	100,000
Building	155,000
Accumulated depreciation—building	75,000
Equipment	20,300
Accumulated depreciation—equipment	10,000
Intangible assets—copyrights	15,000
Accounts payable	155,300
Current notes payable	5,000
Current bonds payable	31,000
Long-term bonds payable	150,000
Preferred stock, $100 par, 500 shares authorized,	
issued, and outstanding	50,000
Additional paid-in capital—preferred	5,000

Common stock, $1 par, 10,000 shares authorized,	
2,500 shares issued and outstanding	2,500
Additional paid-in capital—common	56,760
Check figure—ending retained earnings balance	170,472
Check figure—income tax on continuing operations	79,584

Required:

a. Prepare an income statement for the company using a multiple-step format.
b. Calculate basic earnings per share and include it at the bottom of the income statement. Assume that the number of common shares outstanding remained constant all year.
c. Prepare a statement of retained earnings for the company.
d. Prepare a classified balance sheet for the company as of the end of the accounting period.

LO 1, 2, 3, 4, & 5: COMPLEX VERY DETAILED INCOME STATEMENT, STATEMENT OF RETAINED EARNINGS, BALANCE SHEET WITH DISCONTINUED OPERATION, EXTRAORDINARY ITEM, AND ACCOUNTING CHANGE (SELECTED CHECK FIGURES PROVIDED)

9–55. The following information is taken from accounting records of Louie's Lumber as of the fiscal year ended June 30, 2005:

Income tax rate	30%
Net sales	$950,000
Cost of goods sold	596,500
Wages and salaries	123,000
Rent	36,000
Electricity	4,200
Telephone	1,800
Advertising	6,000
Interest revenue	1,000
Rent revenue	12,000
Interest expense	16,000
Casualty loss (infrequent but not unusual)	9,500
Discontinued operation	
Loss on operation of discontinued operation	8,000
Gain on disposal of discontinued operation	3,000
Extraordinary loss—storm damage	7,500
Cumulative effect of accounting change—gain	6,300
Beginning retained earnings balance	195,640
Dividends	17,000
Cash	68,520
Accounts receivable	104,640
Inventory	174,020
Supplies	2,500
Prepaid expenses	1,800
Long-term investments	34,000
Land	96,350
Building	128,750
Accumulated depreciation—building	29,000
Equipment	85,000
Accumulated depreciation—equipment	30,000
Intangible asset—copyright	2,400
Accounts payable	77,500
Current notes payable	5,000
Long-term notes payable	15,000
Long-term bonds payable	50,000
Preferred stock, $100 par, 5,000 shares authorized,	
500 shares issued and outstanding	50,000
Additional paid-in capital—preferred	2,000
Common stock, $2 par, 20,000 shares authorized,	
8,000 shares issued and outstanding	16,000
Additional paid-in capital—common	130,180

Check figure—ending retained earnings balance	293,300
Check figure—income tax amount for nonrecurring items	1,860
Check figure—income tax on income from continuing operations	51,000

Required:

a. Prepare an income statement for the company using a multiple-step format.
b. Calculate basic earnings per share and include it at the bottom of the income statement. Assume that the number of common shares outstanding remained constant all year.
c. Prepare a statement of retained earnings for the company.
d. Prepare a classified balance sheet for the company as of the end of the accounting period.

LO 7: FINANCIAL RATIO CALCULATIONS

9–56. This problem is a continuation of problem 9–55.

In addition to the information from the financial statements you prepared for 9–55, the following information is available:

- The company's assets totaled $620,000 at June 30, 2004.
- The company's accounts receivable totaled $92,000 at June 30, 2004.

Required:

a. Calculate the following ratios for the company:

1. The asset turnover ratio
2. The receivables turnover ratio
3. The average accounts receivable collection period in days
4. The current ratio
5. The quick ratio
6. The times interest earned ratio

b. Based on the ratios, what is your impression of the company? Explain your answer.

LO 7: FINANCIAL RATIO CALCULATIONS

9–57. The following information is available for Carter, Inc.:

Carter, Inc.
Income Statement
For the Year Ended December 31, 2004

Sales	$250,000
Cost of goods sold	130,000
Gross profit	120,000
Operating expenses	87,000
Operating income	33,000
Interest expense	3,000
Income before income tax	30,000
Income tax	6,000
Net income	$ 24,000

Statement of Retained Earnings
For the Year Ended December 31, 2004

Beginning retained earnings balance	$ 38,000
Net income	24,000
Dividends	(2,000)
Ending retained earnings	$ 60,000

Balance Sheet
December 31, 2004

ASSETS:
Current assets:

Cash	$ 14,000

Accounts receivable	48,000
Inventory	39,000
Supplies	1,000
Prepaid expenses	2,000
Total current assets	104,000
Property, plant, and equipment:	79,000
Accumulated depreciation—property, plant, and equipment	(13,000)
Property, plant, and equipment, net	66,000
Total assets	$ 170,000
LIABILITIES:	
Current liabilities:	
Accounts payable	$ 18,000
Current notes payable	27,000
Total current liabilities	45,000
Long-term liabilities:	
Notes payable	11,000
Total liabilities	56,000
EQUITY:	
Contributed capital:	
Common stock, $2 par, 100,000 shares authorized, 2,500 shares issued and outstanding	5,000
Additional paid-in capital—common	49,000
Total contributed capital	54,000
Retained earnings	60,000
Total equity	114,000
Total liabilities and equity	$ 170,000

Required: Assume the following:

- The company's assets totaled $160,000 at December 31, 2003.
- The company's accounts receivable totaled $44,000 at December 31, 2003.

a. Calculate the following ratios for the company:

1. The asset turnover ratio
2. The receivables turnover ratio
3. The average accounts receivable collection period in days
4. The current ratio
5. The quick ratio
6. The times interest earned ratio

b. Do any of the ratios reveal anything that you find troubling about the company?

LO 7: FINANCIAL RATIO CALCULATIONS

9–58. The president of Stacyjohn Industries, Inc., is expanding and would like to obtain additional external financing. The following information is available:

Stacyjohn Industries, Inc.
Income Statement
For the Year Ended December 31, 2004

Net sales	$12,188,720
Cost of goods sold	8,850,400
Gross profit	3,338,320
Operating expenses	(2,158,080)
Operating income	1,180,240
Interest expense	($32,690)
Income before income tax	1,147,550
Income tax	(413,118)
Net Income	$ 734,432

Statement of Retained Earnings
For the Year Ended December 31, 2004

Beginning retained earnings balance	$1,864,900
Net income	734,432
Dividends	0
Ending retained earnings	$2,599,332

Balance Sheet
December 31, 2004

ASSETS:

Current assets:

Cash	$ 236,580
Accounts receivable	1,235,500
Merchandise inventory	1,580,000
Prepaid expenses	56,000
Total current assets	3,108,080

Property, plant, and equipment:

Land	1,684,000
Building	1,968,000
Accumulated depreciation—building	(685,000)
Building, net	1,283,000
Total property, plant, and equipment	2,967,000
Total assets	$6,075,080

LIABILITIES:

Current liabilities:

Accounts payable	$ 546,500
Current portion of notes	50,000
Total current liabilities	596,500
Long-term liabilities—bonds payable	350,000
Total liabilities	946,500

EQUITY:

Contributed capital:

Common stock, $1 par, 200,000 shares authorized,	
85,000 shares issued and outstanding	85,000
Additional paid-in capital—common	2,444,248
Total contributed capital	2,529,248
Retained earnings	2,599,332
Total equity	5,128,580
Total liabilities and equity	$6,075,080

Required: Assume the following:

- The company's assets totaled $5,680,000 at December 31, 2003.
- The company's accounts receivable totaled $1,150,250 at December 31, 2003.

a. Calculate the following ratios for the company:

1. The asset turnover ratio
2. The receivables turnover ratio
3. The average accounts receivable collection period in days
4. The current ratio
5. The quick ratio
6. The times interest earned ratio

b. Based on the ratios you calculated, do you feel the company will have difficulty securing additional external financing? Explain your answer.

LO 7: FINANCIAL RATIO CALCULATIONS

9–59. The following information is available for the Fox Company, Inc.:

Fox Company, Inc.
Income Statement
For the Year Ended December 31, 2005

Sales	$6,500,000
Cost of goods sold	4,850,000
Gross profit	1,650,000
Operating expenses	(780,000)
Operating income	870,000
Other expenses—interest expense	(125,000)
Income before income tax	745,000
Income tax	(268,200)
Net income	$ 476,800

Statement of Retained Earnings
For the Year Ended December 31, 2005

Beginning retained earnings balance	$ 950,000
Net income	476,800
Dividends	(47,680)
Ending retained earnings	$1,379,120

Balance Sheet
December 31, 2005

ASSETS:	
Current assets:	
Cash	$ 126,000
Accounts receivable	750,000
Inventory	598,000
Supplies	12,000
Prepaid expenses	36,000
Total current assets	1,522,000
Property, plant, and equipment:	
Land	865,000
Building	2,350,000
Accumulated depreciation—building	(360,000)
Building, net of accumulated depreciation	1,990,000
Total property, plant, and equipment	2,855,000
Total Assets	$4,377,000
LIABILITIES:	
Current liabilities:	
Accounts payable	$ 550,000
Current notes payable	65,000
Total current liabilities	615,000
Long-term liabilities:	
Long-term notes payable	150,000
Long-term bonds payable	1,350,000
Total long-term liabilities	1,500,000
Total liabilities	2,115,000
EQUITY:	
Paid-in capital:	
Common stock, $5 par, 200,000 shares authorized,	
38,000 shares issued and outstanding	190,000
Additional paid-in capital—common	692,880
Total paid-in capital	882,880
Retained earnings	1,379,120
Total equity	2,262,000
Total liabilities and equity	$4,377,000

Required: Assume the following:

• The company's assets totaled $4,290,000 at December 31, 2004.
• The company's accounts receivable totaled $720,000 at December 31, 2004.

a. Calculate the following ratios for the company:

   1. The asset turnover ratio
   2. The receivables turnover ratio
   3. The average accounts receivable collection period in days
   4. The current ratio
   5. The quick ratio
   6. The times interest earned ratio

b. Based on the ratios, what is your impression of the company? Explain your answer.

Financial Reporting Exercises

9–60. Using the **SEC's Electronic Data Gathering, Analysis, and Retrieval (EDGAR)** system, obtain a copy of the **Office Depot, Inc.,** income statement and balance sheet from the company's Form 10-K from 2001.

Required:

a. Calculate the following ratios for the company for 2001:

   1. The asset turnover ratio
   2. The receivables turnover ratio
   3. The average accounts receivable collection period in days
   4. The current ratio
   5. The quick ratio
   6. The times interest earned ratio

b. What is the impression you get about the company from these ratios?
c. Look at the ratios calculated for **Office Depot, Inc.,** in problem 4–73. Did these ratios give you the same impression as those did? Why or why not and what do you think this means?

9–61. Using the **SEC's EDGAR** system, obtain a copy of the **OfficeMax, Inc.,** income statement and balance sheet from the company's Form 10-K from 2001.

Required:

a. Calculate the following ratios for the company for 2001:

   1. The asset turnover ratio
   2. The receivables turnover ratio
   3. The average accounts receivable collection period in days
   4. The current ratio
   5. The quick ratio
   6. The times interest earned ratio

b. What is the impression you get about the company from these ratios?
c. Look at the ratios calculated for **OfficeMax, Inc.,** in problem 4–74. Did these ratios give you the same impression as those did? Why or why not and what do you think this means?
d. Compare your impression of **OfficeMax, Inc.,** to that of **Office Depot, Inc.** Now that you have more information, which company would you be more likely to invest in and why? Is this the same as the company you chose in Chapter 4 and why or why not?

9–62. Using the **SEC's EDGAR** system, obtain a copy of the **Staples, Inc.,** income statement and balance sheet from the company's Form 10-K from 2001.

Required:

a. Calculate the following ratios for the company for 2001:

   1. The asset turnover ratio
   2. The receivables turnover ratio
   3. The average accounts receivable collection period in days
   4. The current ratio
   5. The quick ratio
   6. The times interest earned ratio using interest and other expense net for interest expense

b. What is the impression you get about the company from these ratios?

c. Look at the ratios calculated for *Staples, Inc.*, in problem 4–75. Did these ratios give you the same impression as those did? Why or why not and what do you think this means?

d. Compare the impressions of the *Office Depot, Inc., OfficeMax, Inc.,* and *Staples, Inc.* For each of the six ratios, choose which company you believe is most favorable and explain your answer. Now that you have more information, which company would you be most likely to invest in and why? Is this the same as the company you chose in Chapter 4 and why or why not? What does this tell you about using the ratios presented together?

ANNUAL REPORT PROJECT

9–63. Section 9—Financial Statements—A Closer Look

In this assignment, you will prepare a report that further explores information contained in your company's balance sheet and income statement.

Required: Prepare a report that includes the following information:

a. List your company's major asset classifications.

b. Describe how your company's asset classifications compare to those of its peer.

c. Discuss which of your company's assets is most significant? Discuss which is least significant? Does your company's asset holding seem excessive to you? Discuss why it would be risky for your company to hold more assets than it really needs.

d. List your company's major liability classifications.

e. Describe how your company's liabilities compare to those of its peer.

f. Discuss which of your company's liabilities is most significant? Discuss which is least significant? Does your company's liabilities seem excessive to you?

g. Does your company or the peer company you are using include any nonrecurring items on its income statements? In other words, do the income statements include any discontinued operations, extraordinary items, or cumulative effect of accounting changes? If so, provide information about each of them. Are there items or events mentioned by either your company or its peer's financial reports or that you happen to know about that you feel should give rise to a nonrecurring item, but did not? An example of such a situation would be when a company's annual report mentions major losses due to the massive freight delays in connection with the Longshoreman labor strike that occurred in 2002, and yet does not list the loss as extraordinary.

h. A schedule that includes the following ratios for your company with those of the peer company you selected:

   - Basic earnings per share for three years (use the amounts from the income statements)
   - Diluted earnings per share for three years (use the amounts from the income statements)
   - Asset turnover ratio for the current year
   - Receivables turnover ratio for the current year
   - Current ratio for two years
   - Quick ratio for two years
   - Times interest earned for three years

i. Comment in your report on the information that each one of the ratios provides. How does your company compare to its peer? And where applicable, comment on how your company has performed over time relative to the peer company you selected.

j. Your report should conclude with comments regarding what you think of your company and how you think your company compares to its peer in light of the work you did in connection with this assignment.

CHAPTER 10

The Statement of Cash Flows— A Closer Look

Net income is an opinion; cash is a fact.

—Anonymous

Your best friend Sally recently told about what she says is a "can't miss" investment opportunity. The company she described to you manufactures digital cameras and is extremely successful. It has had compounded sales growth of 25 percent per year since it began five years ago. More importantly, Sally says, profits have increased by 15 percent per year over that same period. "Buy some stock!" she urges. "The future prospects for the company are virtually unlimited. The cameras the company produces sell themselves!"

Even after poring over the income statements and balance sheets your friend provided, you are still not sure what to do. Everything *seems* to make sense. The sales and profits are certainly there, and you know Sally is really smart (she was, after all, an accounting major). Then it hits you—you can ask your Aunt Matilda's advice. She's a bit of a crotchety old goat, and she still pinches your cheek when she sees you, but you know she has made a lot of money in the stock market.

When you arrive at your auntie's mansion, the butler leads you to the den, where you find Aunt Matilda sitting in her easy chair watching a soap opera. Before you can even speak, she pinches your cheek. "What can I do for you, my darling niece?" Aunt Matilda asks. You explain the investment opportunity Sally has recommended. Throughout your lengthy discourse, your aunt sits quietly, her chin in her hand. You tell her all you know about the company—about the sales growth and the profits. "Should I buy some stock, Aunt Matilda?" you ask. With a wry smile on her face, your aunt leans forward, looks you straight in the eye, and says, "Profit schmofit, show me the cash." When you ask what she means by that, she laughs and says, "That you must figure out for yourself, my dear." Then she pinches your cheek and says she must get back to her soap opera.

In the first nine chapters of this text, we focused primarily on three major financial statements: the income statement, the statement of owners' equity, and the balance sheet. Each of these three financial statements developed over time in response to the needs of economic decision makers. Generally, the financial information presented in the financial statements we explored is produced using accrual accounting to measure results of business activity. Recall that we discussed a number of items that affect financial statements that are prepared using accrual accounting, including:

- The difficulties in determining when revenue should be recognized
- The difficulties in matching expenses to the same income statement period as the revenues they helped generate
- The estimates of useful life and residual value required for depreciation of property, plant, and equipment
- Choices of inventory cost flow method (e.g., first-in, first-out [FIFO], last-in, first-out [LIFO]) and depreciation method (e.g., straight-line, double-declining-balance).

These are just a few of the items that make periodic financial measurement under accrual accounting challenging. Although accrual accounting has advantages and it is the acceptable measurement basis under generally accepted accounting principles (GAAP), it is not perfect. Perhaps accrual accounting's most serious weakness is that it takes the financial statement user's eye off cash. To address this problem and bring the user's focus back to cash, a fourth financial statement was developed: the statement of cash flows. When information from the statement of cash flows is combined with the information contained in the other three financial statements, decision makers have a more complete picture of a company's financial health.

You should already be somewhat familiar with the statement of cash flows because we discussed parts of it as appropriate in earlier chapters. In this chapter, we will review some of the concepts introduced previously, introduce new topics relating to the statement of cash flows, and demonstrate how to prepare and use the statement.

Learning Objectives

After completing your work on this chapter, you should be able to do the following:

1. Explain the purpose of the statement of cash flows.
2. Describe the three types of activities that can either generate or use cash in any business.
3. Prepare a statement of cash flows using the indirect method for the operating activities section.
4. Evaluate and use the information the statement of cash flows provides.
5. Prepare a statement of cash flows using the direct method for the operating activities section. (Appendix)

◆ INTRODUCTION TO THE STATEMENT OF CASH FLOWS

In its present format, the statement of cash flows has existed since 1988. However, it existed in other forms for decades before that. These earlier forms were known by such names as the *Where-Got and Where-Gone Statement*, the *Funds Statement*, the *Statement of Sources and Application of Funds*, and the *Statement of Changes in Financial Position*.

All of these earlier versions had the same objectives as today's statement of cash flows. That is, their main purpose was to provide information about a company's cash receipts and cash payments during a specific period, because the balance sheet, income statement, and statement of owners' equity prepared using accrual accounting were not giving economic decision makers all the information they needed.

Discussion Question ⁎ ⁎ ⁎ ⁑ ⁑ ⁎ ⁑ ⁑ ⁑ ◉ ◉ ◉ ◉ ◉ ◉ ◉ ◉ ◉ ◉ ◉ ◉ ◉ ◉ ◉ ◉ ⁑ ⁑ ⁑

10–1. How do revenue recognition and expense recognition criteria under accrual accounting take the focus off cash?

Unlike the current statement of cash flows, which focuses exclusively on changes in cash, most of the earlier versions of this financial statement included other items as well. A good example of this is the Statement of Changes in Financial Position, which is the form of the statement that immediately preceded the currently used statement of cash flows. When the *Statement of Changes in Financial Position* was adopted as GAAP in 1971, companies had the choice of using either the cash format or the working capital format. The vast majority of companies chose to prepare the statement using the working capital format. This format was based on the assumption that **working capital,** which is defined as current assets less current liabilities, is a good predictor of future cash flows. Some argued that by examining items other than cash, the working capital format presented a broader picture of the changes a company experienced.

working capital The difference between current assets and current liabilities.

By the early 1980s, however, many financial analysts became increasingly concerned about cash flows because some companies with strong working capital positions had weak cash flow. The financial markets, too, became more concerned about companies' cash flows and, therefore, grew steadily more dissatisfied with the working capital format of the *Statement of Changes in Financial Position.* After years of mounting pressure on companies to provide more detailed information about the sources and uses of their cash, the new statement of cash flows was introduced in 1988.

In addition to providing information about a company's cash receipts and cash payments during a specific period, the statement of cash flows helps investors, creditors, and other external parties to:

1. Assess a company's ability to generate positive future net cash flows.
2. Assess a company's need for external financing and its ability to pay its debts and pay dividends.
3. Reconcile the differences between net income and the change in cash.

BASIC ORGANIZATION OF THE STATEMENT OF CASH FLOWS

How does the statement go about fulfilling its purpose? The statement of cash flows begins by disclosing what caused changes in the balance of cash from the beginning of the period to the end. Then the statement reflects the cash balance at the beginning of the period and incorporates the change in cash to arrive at the cash balance at the end of the period. As an example of the statement, Exhibit 10–1 on page F–406 shows the statement of cash flows for **The Rowe Companies,** a major furniture and home furnishings company.

As you recall from our discussions in prior chapters and as you can see in Exhibit 10–1, the statement of cash flows is grouping cash flows by three major business activities: operating activities, investing activities, and financing activities. Therefore, one of the most important tasks when preparing a statement of cash flows is to identify the cash flows associated with each of these activities. We have done a significant amount of work on this process in earlier chapters and we will now review each of the activities in turn.

Discussion Question

10–2. Imagine that you are the owner of a bookstore. What would constitute your bookstore's:

    a. operating activities?
    b. investing activities?
    c. financing activities?

Explain your reasons for the classifications you made.

OPERATING ACTIVITIES

operating activities
Activities centered on the day-to-day business transactions of the company.

Operating activities are those centered on the actual day-to-day business transactions of the company. A variety of transactions either generates or uses cash. Cash is received (inflows) from the sale of goods or services. For example, *McDonald's* receives cash when its customers buy hamburgers. *Bank of America* receives cash for interest it earns on loans it has made to individuals and companies, or when it receives dividends on investments it owns. Cash is paid by *Boeing* (outflows) to *Honeywell* and other suppliers for inventory, to employees for wages, to the government for taxes, to lenders for interest on loans, and to other parties for the expenses of running the company. For example, cash flow from operating activities for **The Rowe Companies** includes cash received from customers, cash paid to suppliers and employees, income taxes paid, interest paid, interest received, and other receipts.

When you think about it, all of the items listed in the previous paragraph appear on their company's income statements. Remember that the actual name of the income statement is the *Statement of Results of Operations.* So the operating activities section of the statement of cash flows is related to items presented on the income statement.

The Rowe Companies
Statement of Cash Flows
Year Ended December 31, 2000
(in thousands)
Increase (Decrease) in Cash

Cash flows from operating activities:

Cash received from customers	$379,400
Cash paid to suppliers and employees	(354,570)
Income taxes paid, net of refunds	(6,183)
Interest paid	(5,693)
Interest received	288
Other receipts—net	1,156
Net cash and cash equivalents provided by (used in) operating activities	14,398

Cash flows from investing activities:

Proceeds from sale of property and equipment	21
Capital expenditures	(9,155)
Payments to acquire businesses (Note 2)	(5,160)
Net cash used in investing activities	(14,294)

Cash flows from financing activities:

Net borrowings (payments) under line of credit	(164)
Proceeds from issuance of long-term debt	13,020
Payments to reduce long-term debt	(11,922)
Proceeds from issuance of common stock	51
Dividends paid	(1,849)
Purchase of treasury stock	(951)
Net cash provided by (used in) financing activities	(1,815)
Net increase (decrease) in cash and cash equivalents	(1,711)
Cash at beginning of year	5,104
Cash at end of year	$ 3,393

EXHIBIT 10-1   Statement of Cash Flows for *The Rowe Companies*

Discussion Questions •

10–3. Imagine once again that you own a bookstore. If you sold one of your customers several books on account and she had 30 days after she received the books to pay for them, how would this credit sale be reported by your company under the cash basis of accounting? How about under the accrual basis?

10–4. For your bookstore's statement of cash flows, how would you determine the net cash flow from operations on an accrual basis?

Under GAAP, there are two acceptable methods of preparing the operating activities section of the statement of cash flows: the direct method and the indirect method. Both arrive at exactly the same amount of cash flow from operations. The difference lies in how the information is presented.

DIRECT METHOD VERSUS INDIRECT METHOD

direct method The format of a statement of cash flows that provides detail about the individual sources and uses of cash associated with operating activities.

The **direct method** involves a series of calculations to determine the amount of cash inflow and cash outflow from each individual facet of operating activities. For example, under the direct method, accountants determine the cash collections from customers, cash received for interest earned on bank accounts or from making loans, cash received for rents, and so forth. Accountants also determine the cash paid for inventory, for wages, for electricity, for taxes, for interest, and for other expense items. The operating activities section of the statement of cash flows under the direct method consists of a summarized list of these individual cash inflows and outflows. The examples we presented in earlier chapters of this book and the statement of cash flows for **The Rowe Companies** in Exhibit 10–1 use the direct method of presenting cash flows from operating activities.

indirect method   The more widely used format of the statement of cash flows. This approach reconciles accrual net income to the cash provided by or used by operating activities.

The **indirect method** is more closely tied to accrual accounting than is the direct method. Unlike the direct method, it does not attempt to provide any detail about the individual inflows and outflows of cash associated with the company's operating activities. When a company uses the indirect method, the statement of cash flows begins with the accrual net income for the period. Remember, though, that if the company uses the accrual basis of accounting, the net income figure must be adjusted for any revenues that did not provide cash during the income statement period. Similarly, net income must be adjusted for any expenses that did not use cash during the period. Therefore, if you are attempting to determine **Microsoft**'s cash flows from operating activities using the indirect method, for example, the place to start is the company's net income as shown on the income statement. Then a series of adjustments are made to convert the accrual net income amount to cash flow from operating activities. In other words, adjustments are made for all items included in the calculation of net income that did not either generate or use cash. If this concept is not totally clear to you at this point, don't fret; we will show you how it works a little later in the chapter.

Now that you have an idea of the difference between the direct method and the indirect method, we should tell you that if a company uses the direct method, it must also include a reconciliation of net income to operating cash flows as a supplementary schedule to the statement of cash flows. Think about it. This reconciliation is the same thing as the indirect method. The Financial Accounting Standards Board (FASB) required this supplementary information because the reconciliation links (articulates) the statement of cash flows to the income statement. However, if a company uses the indirect method (which is the same as the reconciliation), it does not have to include the direct method, *but* it does have to include a supplementary schedule indicating the amount of cash paid for interest and taxes.

The direct method presents an easy-to-understand list of each cash inflow and outflow from operating activities. Many users (including students) find the direct method more logical and intuitive and therefore easier to read and understand than the indirect method. This is why all of our presentations of the operating activities section of the statement of cash flows in previous chapters used the direct method. In actual practice, however, very few companies use the direct method. *Accounting Trends and Techniques* reports that of the 600 companies it surveyed in 2001, only seven (slightly more than 1 percent of companies) used the direct method in preparing the statement of cash flows for 2000 (Exhibit 10–2 on page F–408).

As you have seen in prior chapters, the operating activities section of a statement of cash flows using the direct method is not overly challenging to prepare as long as you have a detailed list containing each of the operating cash flows. Since the vast majority of firms use the indirect method, however, this is the method we will concentrate on in this chapter. We have included an appendix to the chapter presenting calculation specifics for preparing the operating activities section of the statement using the direct method.

INVESTING ACTIVITIES

investing activities   Activities associated with buying and selling the investments used to support the operation of the business.

Investing activities are those associated with buying and selling the investments used to support the operation of the business. For many companies, the vast majority of this investment is in the assets required to operate the company. As with operating activities, investing activities include both outflows and inflows of cash. As examples of cash outflow, **Campbell Soup Company** uses cash to invest in the machinery it needs to can its soup, and **American Express** uses cash when it builds a transactions processing center. As we have discussed in previous chapters, the long-lived assets used in a company's operations are usually reported on the balance sheet in a category called *property, plant, and equipment* and include the buildings, vehicles, furniture, machinery, and other items a business uses to run its operations. The cash paid when a company buys this type of asset is an outflow from investing activities.

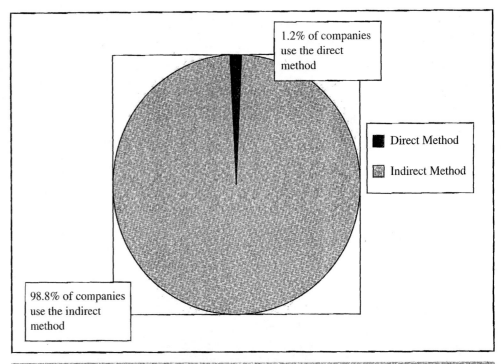

1.2% of companies use the direct method

Direct Method

Indirect Method

98.8% of companies use the indirect method

EXHIBIT 10–2 Direct Method versus Indirect Method of Preparing the Statement of Cash Flows

As we discussed in Chapter 7, companies sell long-lived assets from time to time when they are no longer needed. For example, *Campbell Soup* might sell a soup canning machine that it is no longer using, and *American Express* might sell one of its processing centers because it needs a bigger facility. The cash received when a company sells this type of asset is an inflow from investing activities.

While the cash received from selling property, plant, and equipment is a legitimate source of cash, a company cannot sell off assets it needs to run its operations because before long the cash generated through operating activities would be adversely affected. *American Airlines,* for example, could generate cash by selling all its airplanes, but if it did so, it would no longer be able to transport passengers and would go out of business. Instead of selling its property, plant, and equipment to generate cash, a growing and healthy company will likely use cash to acquire additional assets it can use in its operations. Therefore, the net cash flow from investing activities may very well be negative (net outflow) for companies that are experiencing healthy growth. For example, the statement of cash flows in Exhibit 10–1 for *The Rowe Companies* shows that the company received $21,000 from selling property and equipment while it spent $9,155,000 for capital expenditures (property and equipment) and $5,160,000 to acquire a business during the same year. Other companies, such as *Boeing, Procter & Gamble,* and *Target,* all very different kinds of companies, show significant investing activities related to their acquisition and disposal of property, plant, and equipment.

Besides investing in property, plant, and equipment, investments in stocks, bonds, and other financial investments are included as part of investing activities. For example, *Navistar International*'s cash flow associated with the purchase and sale of marketable securities would be included in the investing activities section of its statement of cash flows. A company receives cash (inflow) from investing activities when it sells equity or debt investments (stocks or bonds of other companies) it owns.

Logically, companies might classify the interest they earn on loans to others and the dividends they receive from investments in the stock of other companies as inflows in the investing activities section. However, because interest earned and dividends received are reported on the income statement of the period, *the cash a company receives from interest and dividends is almost always reported in the operating activities section.*

Think about the examples of investing activities we just mentioned. Notice that they involve items that are reported in the long-term asset section of the balance sheet. Therefore, if you are attempting to determine the cash flows from investing activities, you should analyze the long-term section of the company's balance sheets, paying particular attention to the changes in account balances from the beginning of the period to the end. Once again, do not be concerned if this is not totally clear to you at this point. We will demonstrate the process a little later in the chapter.

FINANCING ACTIVITIES

financing activities
Business activities, such as the issuance of debt or equity and the payment of dividends, that focus on the external financing of the company.

Recall from our discussion in Chapter 3 that the financing options available to any business are broadly classified as either internal or external. *Internal financing* comes from a company's profitable operation, that is, from income. The statement of cash flows reports the cash flows from internal financing in the operating activities section discussed earlier. Therefore, the **financing activities** section of the statement deals only with external financing. A company's *external financing* comes from either selling shares of the company's stock (common or preferred) or borrowing (from banks or by selling corporate bonds). *Verizon Communications* or *International Paper,* for example, can obtain cash (inflow) from selling shares of their stock or from borrowing.

Companies also report the cash outflows to repay loans and retire bonds, to pay dividends to shareholders, and to reacquire shares of common or preferred stock from their stockholders in the financing activities section of the statement of cash flows. Logically, you might think that companies classify the interest they pay as outflows in the financing activities section. However, because interest expense is reported on the income statement, the *cash payments (outflows) for interest are almost always reported in the operating activities section of the statement of cash flows.* Unlike interest expense, dividends paid to shareholders are not reported on the income statement. So dividends paid *are* included in financing activities.

Think about the examples of financing activities mentioned in the previous two paragraphs. Notice that they involve items that are reported in the long-term liabilities and owners' equity sections of the balance sheet. Therefore, when you are attempting to determine the cash flow from financing activities, analyze the long-term liabilities and equity sections of the balance sheets and pay particular attention to the changes in the accounts' balances that took place during the year. Once again, do not be concerned if this is not totally clear to you at this point. We will demonstrate the process a little later in the chapter.

Exhibit 10–3 on page F–410 lists examples of the cash flows associated with the three types of business activities reported in the statement of cash flows. Refer to this exhibit often as we discuss how to prepare and use the statement.

In practice, the inflows and outflows a particular company shows on its statement of cash flows may be more or less extensive than the list we have included in Exhibit 10–3. However, regardless of a company's complexity, we can classify every cash inflow and outflow as an operating activity, an investing activity, or a financing activity in the statement of cash flows.

◆ GATHERING INFORMATION TO PREPARE THE STATEMENT OF CASH FLOWS

In order to prepare a company's statement of cash flows for a particular income statement period, we need information from three important sources:

1. That period's income statement.
2. A set of comparative balance sheets (a balance from the current period and one from the previous period).
3. Additional information about transactions that is not explained by the income statement or comparative balance sheets mentioned above. For example, we would need information about the purchase and sale of investments and property, plant, and equipment that is too detailed to find on financial statements.

Operating Activities

Cash Inflows
From customers as a result of the sale of goods or services or rent received
From interest earned on loans to others
From dividends received from investment in the stock of other companies

Cash Outflows
To suppliers for the purchase of inventory
To employees for salaries and wages
To governments for taxes
To creditors for interest on loans
To others for operating expenses

Investing Activities

Cash Inflows
From the sale of property, plant, and equipment
From the sale of investments in debt or equity securities of other companies
From collecting on loans made to other companies

Cash Outflows
To purchase property, plant, and equipment
To purchase debt and equity investments in other companies
Making loans to other companies

Financing Activities

Cash Inflows
From selling shares of the company's own common or preferred stock
From bank loans or the sale of corporate bonds

Cash Outflows
To pay dividends to stockholders
To reacquire shares of the company's own stock from stockholders
To repay loans or redeem corporate bonds

EXHIBIT 10-3 Summary of the Three Business Activities Reported on the Statement of Cash Flows

For our example, we will gather information for Tsujimoto's Oriental Rug Factory, a rug manufacturer. We begin with Tsujimoto's income statement. Remember, in our discussion in this chapter, we will use the indirect method of preparing the operating activities section, which uses net income as its starting point. Exhibit 10–4 shows Tsujimoto's income statement for the year ended December 31, 2004.

EXHIBIT 10-4 Tsujimoto's Oriental Rug Factory's Income Statement for 2004

Tsujimoto's Oriental Rug Factory
Income Statement
For the Year Ended December 31, 2004
(in thousands)

Sales		$15,158
Cost of goods sold		11,151
Gross margin		4,007
Operating expenses:		
Depreciation expense	$ 231	
Selling and administration	3,047	
Total operating expenses		(3,278)
Operating income		729
Gain on sale of long-term investments		31
Less: Interest expense		(160)
Income before income taxes		600
Income tax expense		(180)
Net income		$ 420

In addition to the income statement, we also need information from the balance sheet. Exhibit 10–5 shows Tsujimoto's comparative balance sheets for 2004 and 2003. Keep in mind that the asset, liability, and stockholders' equity balances at the end of one period become the beginning balances in the next period. Thus, Exhibit 10–5 provides beginning and ending balances for Tsujimoto's balance sheet amounts for 2004—necessary information for preparing the company's statement of cash flows for that year.

EXHIBIT 10–5 Tsujimoto's Oriental Rug Factory's Comparative Balance Sheets for 2004 and 2003

Tsujimoto's Oriental Rug Factory
Balance Sheet
December 31, 2004, and December 31, 2003
(in thousands)

	2004	2003
ASSETS:		
Current assets:		
Cash	$ 981	$ 419
Accounts receivable	1,925	2,112
Merchandise inventory	1,022	858
Prepaid expenses	192	132
Total current assets	4,120	3,521
Long-term investments	21	73
Plant and equipment:		
Equipment	1,155	1,045
LESS: Accumulated depreciation	(851)	(620)
Equipment, net	304	425
Total assets	$4,445	$4,019
LIABILITIES:		
Current liabilities:		
Accounts payable	$ 820	$ 710
Accrued expenses	17	28
Income tax payable	25	10
Total current liabilities	862	748
Long-term liabilities:		
Notes payable	425	700
Bonds payable	1,100	900
Total long-term liabilities	1,525	1,600
Total liabilities	2,387	2,348
STOCKHOLDERS' EQUITY:		
Common stock, no-par value	1,332	1,228
Retained earnings	726	443
Total stockholders' equity	2,058	1,671
Total liabilities and stockholders' equity	$4,445	$4,019

Discussion Questions

Refer to Exhibit 10–5 to answer the following questions:

10–5. What was Tsujimoto's Oriental Rug Factory's balance in accounts receivable on January 1, 2004? Did accounts receivable increase or decrease during 2004?

10–6. What was Tsujimoto's balance in retained earnings on January 1, 2004?

10–7. What do you think caused retained earnings to increase during 2004?

Before we tackle the preparation of the statement of cash flows, there are a couple of things you should understand about Tsujimoto's income statement and balance sheet. First, look at the cash balances on the two balance sheets in Exhibit 10–5, and you will see that cash increased from the start of 2004 to the end of 2004 by $562 ($981 − $419). Note that Tsujimoto's Oriental Rug Factory's financial statements are presented "in thousands." This means that the $562 increase in cash is really $562,000. But what caused the increase? It was not the company's net income, because if you look at Tsujimoto's income statement in Exhibit 10–4, you will see that net income for the year ended December 31, 2004, was $420,000. Tsujimoto's Oriental Rug Factory uses accrual accounting, so it is no surprise that the company's net income for the year does not equal the change in cash. So, we ask again: What caused the $562,000 increase in cash in 2004? Well, the statement of cash flows we are about to prepare will answer this question. If properly prepared and analyzed, the statement of cash flows will tell us the amount by which cash changed, and what caused the change. Plus, it will reconcile the company's net income figure to the change in cash.

In addition to Tsujimoto's income statement and its balance sheet, we need some information that cannot be found on financial statements. For Tsujimoto's, three bits of additional information will be helpful as we create the company's statement of cash flows:

- During 2004, Tsujimoto's sold some of its long-term investments for $83,000 but did not purchase any.
- During 2004, Tsujimoto's purchased equipment for cash of $110,000.
- During 2004, Tsujimoto's paid $137,000 cash dividends to its stockholders.

We now have all the information necessary to prepare Tsujimoto's Oriental Rug Factory's statement of cash flows for 2004. The detailed presentation that follows is not intended to make you an expert preparer, but rather to help you become a wiser user of this financial tool. Knowing how the amounts on a statement of cash flows were determined will help you to assess their usefulness and impact on your decision making process.

◆ PREPARING THE STATEMENT OF CASH FLOWS

To give you an idea of what we will be doing as we prepare the statement of cash flows, we will begin by showing you the basic format of Tsujimoto's statement of cash flows (Exhibit 10–6).

EXHIBIT 10–6   Basic Format of the Statement of Cash Flows for Tsujimoto's Oriental Rug Factory

Tsujimoto's Oriental Rug Factory
Statement of Cash Flows
For the Year Ended December 31, 2004
(in thousands)

Cash Flows from Operating Activities:	
Net income	$420
Adjustments to reconcile net income to net cash provided by operating activities	
Net cash provided (used) by operating activities	?
Cash Flows from Investing Activities:	——
Net cash provided (used) by investing activities	?
Cash Flows from Financing Activities:	——
Net cash provided (used) by financing activities	?
Net increase (decrease) in cash during 2004	**$562**
Beginning cash balance, January 1, 2004	419
Ending cash balance, December 31, 2004	$981

There are two things to note about the statement's format. First, it is divided into the three broad types of activities that generate or use cash (operating, investing, and financing). Second, we have already put four amounts into the statement. Net income came directly from Tsujimoto's income statement in Exhibit 10–4. The beginning and ending cash balances came directly from Tsujimoto's balance sheets in Exhibit 10–5. We determined the change in cash by subtracting the beginning cash balance from the ending cash balance. Remember, the purpose of the statement of cash flows is not to disclose what the change in cash was, but to show what caused the change and also to reconcile the change in cash to the net income.

DETERMINING CASH FLOW FROM OPERATING ACTIVITIES

As we said earlier, we are going to use the indirect method of determining cash flow from operations because the vast majority of the statements of cash flows you will see are prepared using this method. The direct method is presented in an appendix to this chapter using the same Tsujimoto's Oriental Rug Factory example. Remember, the net cash flow from operating activities is the same using either the indirect method or the direct method. It's only the approach that is different.

When we determine cash flows from operating activities using the indirect method, we begin with net income because most items involved in net income either already affected cash (inflow or outflow) or will eventually affect cash (inflow or outflow). Because of the way accrual accounting recognizes revenues and expenses, however, net income for a particular income statement period does not equate to the change in cash for that same period. Remember from our discussion of revenue recognition in Chapter 5 that a company using accrual accounting may receive the cash associated with revenue before the revenue is recognized, at the time the revenue is recognized, or after the revenue is recognized. The same is true for expenses. A company using accrual accounting may pay the cash associated with expense before the expense is recognized, at the time the expense is recognized, or after the expense is recognized. For this reason, in determining net cash flow from operating activities for this period, we must adjust the net income figure for any revenues that did not generate cash during this period and any expenses that did not use cash during this period. This is a crucial concept, so before you proceed, read it again if you don't fully understand it.

Discussion Question ⊕ ⊕ ⊛ ⊛ ⊕ ⊕ ⊕ ⊕ ⊕ ⊛ ⊕ ⊕ ⊛ ⊕ ⊕ ⊕ ⊕ ⊕ ⊕ ⊕ ⊕ ⊕ ⊕ ⊕ ⊕ ⊕ ⊕ ⊕ ⊕ ⊕

10–8. Why are retained earnings not equal to cash?

To determine cash flow from operating activities using the indirect method, we make three basic adjustments to net income:

1. Add back depreciation expense and amortization expense if any exist.
2. Add back losses and subtract gains associated with the sale of investments or property, plant, and equipment.
3. Adjust for the changes in current assets and current liabilities that are associated with operating activities.

The information we need to make these adjustments is found in the income statement and the current assets and current liabilities sections of the balance sheet.

1. *Depreciation.* The first adjustment we will make to Tsujimoto's net income is for depreciation expense, because as we mentioned in Chapter 7, depreciation is a noncash expense. When we say *noncash*, we don't mean to imply that there never is cash paid for this expense, because there was (or will be); it just wasn't paid during this income statement period. To fully grasp this concept, you must remember just what depreciation is. It is an accrual accounting process of converting the cost of long-lived items (buildings and equipment in Tsujimoto's case) from asset to expense. It is completely unrelated to when the buildings and equipment were paid for (cash outflow). Therefore, to determine the cash flow

from Tsujimoto's operating activities, one of the things we must do is add the depreciation expense for the period to net income. We do this because depreciation is an expense that did not use cash in 2004, but which was included in the expenses subtracted from revenue to arrive at net income for 2004. If you look at Tsujimoto's income statement in Exhibit 10–4, you will see that the company had depreciation expense for 2004 of $231,000. The adjustment for depreciation expense for Tsujimoto's statement of cash flows is shown in Exhibit 10–7.

EXHIBIT 10–7   Statement of Cash Flows Adjustment for Depreciation Expense

Tsujimoto's Oriental Rug Factory
Partial Statement of Cash Flows
For the Year Ended December 31, 2004
(in thousands)

Cash Flows from Operating Activities:

Net income		$449
Adjustments to reconcile net income to net cash provided by operating activities:		
Depreciation expense	$231	
Net cash provided (used) by operating activities		?

2. *Gains and losses from disposal of long-lived assets.* Companies normally have a gain or a loss when they sell investments or property, plant, and equipment. This is because companies almost never sell an asset for an amount that exactly equals the asset's book value. Recall from Chapter 7 that if a company sells an asset for more than its book value, there is a gain. If the company sells the asset for less than its book value, there is a loss. The amount of the gain or loss is the *difference* between the amount of cash received for the sale and the book value of the asset sold. It is *not* the amount of cash received. For example, if a company were to sell an asset that had a book value of $1 million for cash of $990,000, the company would have a whopping $990,000 cash inflow, but its income statement would actually reflect a $10,000 loss. This example makes it easy to see that the gain or loss on the sale of assets does not equal cash flow from the sale. These gains and losses are included in the calculation of net income because gains are treated similarly to revenues, and losses are treated similarly to expenses. Because the gains and losses are not equal to cash flow and because the cash flow for such transactions should be in investing activities anyway, we adjust net income to remove the effect of gains and losses associated with the sale of investments and property, plant, and equipment. Since a gain shown on the accrual income statement served to increase net income, we must subtract the gain from net income. Since a loss shown on the accrual income statement served to decrease net income, we must add the loss to net income. The cash a company receives from selling a long-lived asset is reported in the investing activities section of the statement of cash flows, so if we don't adjust for the gain or loss in the operating activities section, we will effectively show the amount twice on the statement of cash flows. Tsujimoto had a gain of $31,000 for the sale of long-term investments. The adjustment for the gain for Tsujimoto's statement of cash flows is as shown in Exhibit 10–8.

3. *Changes in current assets and current liabilities.* Since most current assets and current liabilities are associated with the day-to-day operation of the company, they are related to the revenues and expenses that make up the income statement. The current asset and current liability sections from Tsujimoto's comparative balance sheets are shown in Exhibit 10–9. We have added a column that calculates the change in the balance of each item.

We will not consider the change in cash as an adjustment to net income because cash is the object of the entire statement of cash flows. In addition, if current liabilities included general borrowing such as notes payable or bonds payable, changes in such

Tsujimoto's Oriental Rug Factory
Partial Statement of Cash Flows
For the Year Ended December 31, 2004
(in thousands)

Cash Flows from Operating Activities:		
Net income		$449
Adjustments to reconcile net income		
to net cash provided by operating activities:		
Depreciation expense	$231	
Gain on sale of long-term investments	(31)	
Net cash provided (used) by operating activities		?

EXHIBIT 10–8   Adjustment for Gain on Sale of Investments for Tsujimoto's Oriental Rug Factory's Statement of Cash Flows

items would be treated as financing activities and not as adjustments to net income to calculate cash flows from operating activities. In our example, Tsujimoto's does not include any general borrowing in current liabilities.

A change in any of the other items listed in Exhibit 10–9 will require an adjustment to net income in determining the net cash provided by operating activities. The adjustments, however, will be exactly opposite of what you probably think they should be.

- Adjustments for current assets—An increase in a current asset item (except cash) is considered a use of cash, and a decrease in a current asset item (except cash) is considered a source of cash.
- Adjustments for current liabilities—An increase in a current liability item is considered a source of cash, and a decrease in a current liability item is considered a use of cash.

This adjustment process makes sense if you really ponder it. Consider accounts receivable, for example. Where do they come from? They come from selling to customers on a credit basis (i.e., customers pay some time after they purchase whatever they purchase). Now answer this question: What does a company *not have* when it sells on credit that it *would have had* if it had sold for cash instead? The answer, of course, is cash! We consider credit sales as revenue under accrual accounting and, therefore, use them in the calculation of net income. But remember, we are trying to determine the amount of cash

EXHIBIT 10–9   Current Assets and Current Liabilities Sections of Balance Sheets for Tsujimoto's Oriental Rug Factory for 2004 and 2003

Tsujimoto's Oriental Rug Factory
Partial Balance Sheets
December 31, 2004, and December 31, 2003
(in thousands)

ASSETS:	2004	2003	Increase/Decrease
Current assets:			
Cash	$ 981	$ 419	$562
Accounts receivable	1,925	2,112	(187)
Merchandise inventory	1,022	858	164
Prepaid expenses	192	132	60
Total current assets	$4,120	$3,521	
LIABILITIES:			
Current liabilities:			
Accounts payable	$ 820	$ 710	$110
Accrued expenses	17	28	(11)
Income tax payable	25	10	15
Total current liabilities	$ 862	$ 748	

generated by operating activities. Any increase in accounts receivable must be deducted from net income because such an increase represents the credit sales that have not been collected as of the end of the year. Accounts receivable decrease when customers pay the cash they owe, so a decrease in accounts receivable is a source of cash.

Now think about accounts payable. Where do they come from? They are created when a company buys merchandise inventory on a credit basis (it pays some time after the purchase). Now answer this question: What does a company *have* when it buys on credit that it *would not have* if it paid cash? The answer, again, is cash! Therefore, we consider an increase in accounts payable a source of cash. Accounts payable decrease as the company pays the cash it owes, so a decrease in accounts payable is a use of cash.

Now let's go through the specifics of the adjustments to net income caused by the changes in Tsujimoto's current assets and current liabilities:

a. *Accounts receivable*—According to Exhibit 10–9, accounts receivable decreased by $187,000 during 2004. Accounts receivable decrease when customers' payments during the income statement period are greater than the sales during that period. This means that the cash Tsujimoto's collected from its customers during 2004 was $187,000 *more* than the $15,158,000 revenue the accrual income statement used to calculate net income. Therefore, we must add $187,000 to net income.

b. *Merchandise inventory*—According to Exhibit 10–9, merchandise inventory increased by $164,000 during 2004. Inventory increases when a company buys more inventory than it sells. This means that during 2004, Tsujimoto's purchased $164,000 *more* inventory than the $11,151,000 cost of goods the accrual income statement used to calculate net income. It is possible, of course, that at least part of this $164,000 increase has not yet been paid for. If so, it will be reflected in accounts payable, which we will analyze a little later. For now, we will consider the increase in inventory as a use of cash. Therefore, we must deduct $164,000 from net income.

c. *Prepaid expenses*—According to Exhibit 10–9, prepaid expenses increased by $60,000 during 2004. Prepaid expenses, as you recall, are items that are not recognized as expense until some time after they are paid for. They are classified as assets at the time of purchase and then recognized as expense in a later income statement period as they are used up. Tsujimoto's classifies this expense as *selling and administration*. Undoubtedly, some of the prepaid expenses shown on Tsujimoto's 2003 balance sheet were recognized as selling and administration expense in 2004, which would cause the balance in prepaid expenses to decrease. The balance in prepaid expenses, however, increased by $60,000 from the end of 2003 to the end of 2004. Prepaid expenses increase during an income statement period when a company purchases more of them during that period than it recognizes as expense. This means that during 2004, Tsujimoto's purchased and paid cash for $60,000 *more* prepaid expense than it recognized as expense, so we must deduct $60,000 from net income.

d. *Accounts payable*—According to Exhibit 10–9, accounts payable increased by $110,000 during 2004. Accounts payable increase when a company's payments to suppliers during the income statement period are less than the purchases during that period. This means that the cash Tsujimoto's paid to its suppliers during 2004 was $110,000 *less* than the amount of its purchases. Therefore, we must add $110,000 to net income. This adjustment, coupled with the one we made for merchandise inventory, adjusts cost of goods sold on the income statement to the amount of cash Tsujimoto's actually paid to suppliers during 2004.

e. *Accrued expenses*—According to Exhibit 10–9, accrued expenses decreased by $11,000 during 2004. Accrued expenses is a liability amount that accountants use to reflect liabilities for expenses that they record at the last minute as they prepare company financial statements. For practical purposes, accrued expenses are the same as accounts payable. (Please refer to Chapter 6 to see a more detailed discussion of accrued expenses.) When accrued expenses increase, it means that the company's cash payments for expenses are less than the expense amount shown on the income statement. On the other hand, when accrued expenses decrease as they did for the Tsujimoto's Oriental Rug Factory, it means that the company's cash payments for expenses are more than the expense amount shown on the income statement. This means that the cash Tsujimoto's paid for operating expenses in 2004 was $11,000 *more* than the amount shown on its income statement. Therefore, we must subtract $11,000 from net income. Tsujimoto's actually paid this money to suppliers during 2004.

f. *Income taxes payable*—According to Exhibit 10–9, income taxes payable increased by $15,000 during 2004. Income taxes payable increase when a company's payments for income tax are less than the tax expense shown on the income statement for that period. Therefore, we must add $15,000 to net income.

Exhibit 10–10 shows the completed operating activities section of Tsujimoto's statement of cash flows after we include the adjustments for the changes in the current assets and current liabilities.

EXHIBIT 10–10   Partial Statement of Cash Flows for Tsujimoto's Oriental Rug Factory: Operating Activities Section

Tsujimoto's Oriental Rug Factory
Partial Statement of Cash Flows
For the Year Ended December 31, 2004
(in thousands)

Cash Flows from Operating Activities:

Net income		$420
Adjustments to reconcile net income to net cash provided by operating activities:		
Depreciation expense	$231	
Gain on sale of long-term investments	(31)	
Decrease in accounts receivable	187	
Increase in merchandise inventory	(164)	
Increase in prepaid expense	(60)	
Increase in accounts payable	110	
Decrease in accrued expenses	(11)	
Increase in income taxes payable	15	277
Net cash provided by operating activities		$697

We have now determined that Tsujimoto's Oriental Rug Factory generated a positive cash flow of $697,000 through its operating activities during 2004. Since cash increased during 2004 by only $562,000, there must have been cash outflow in one or both of the other types of activities (investing and financing). We will look at investing activities next.

DETERMINING CASH FLOW FROM INVESTING ACTIVITIES

Determining cash flow from investing activities requires an analysis of the noncurrent asset section of the balance sheet. Tsujimoto's Oriental Rug Factory has two classifications of assets that are noncurrent: long-term investments and property, plant, and equipment. Exhibit 10–11 on page F–418 shows that section of Tsujimoto's comparative balance sheets with a column added that calculates the change in each item from the end of 2003 to the end of 2004. If there were any investments in the current assets section of Tsujimoto's balance sheet, we would also list them here as they would be part of investing activities rather than operating activities.

We already know from the additional information provided about the company's activities earlier in the chapter that Tsujimoto's sold long-term investments for $83,000 and purchased equipment for $110,000 during 2004. But even if these details are not

Tsujimoto's Oriental Rug Factory
Partial Balance Sheets
December 31, 2004, and December 31, 2003
(in thousands)

	2004	2003	Increase/Decrease
Long-term investments	21	73	$ (52)
Plant and equipment:			
Equipment	1,155	1,045	110
LESS: Accumulated depreciation	(851)	(620)	231
Equipment, net	304	425	
Total noncurrent assets	$4,445	$4,019	

EXHIBIT 10–11 Noncurrent Asset Section of Balance Sheets for Tsujimoto's Oriental Rug Factory for 2004 and 2003

disclosed, it is sometimes possible to determine these amounts by noting the change in the account balances. An increase in a noncurrent asset balance would most likely be the result of a purchase of assets. For example, the balance shown on Tsujimoto's balance sheet for equipment increased by $110,000 as a result of the company's equipment purchase. On the other hand, a decrease in a noncurrent asset balance would likely be the result of a sale. To determine the resulting cash inflow when there is a sale of an investment activities item, we must combine the amount of the decrease in the item's balance with the gain or loss on the sale of that item. For example, Tsujimoto's long-term investments decreased by $52,000. This $52,000 decrease combined with the $31,000 gain equals the $83,000 cash inflow Tsujimoto's received when it sold the investments. However, determining the cash flows for investing activities by examining the changes in a balance sheet amount works only if the change is the result of a single transaction such as either a purchase or a sale. It would not work if the change in the balance were composed of multiple transactions such as a sale and a purchase together. In such a case, you would be forced to use additional information, which is not included in the financial statements themselves.

Aside from the long-term investments and equipment, there are no other items listed as noncurrent assets on Tsujimoto's balance sheets, so we know that the sale of the long-term investment securities and the purchase of equipment are the only items that will be in the investing activities section of the statement of cash flows. After including the investing activities section, Tsujimoto's Oriental Rug Factory's statement of cash flows is shaping up as shown in Exhibit 10–12.

If we combine the cash provided by operating activities and the cash used by investing activities, we arrive at a net cash inflow for 2004 of $670,000 (697,000 inflow − 27,000 outflow). This means there must have been cash outflow from financing activities, because we know that overall cash increased by $562,000 during 2004.

DETERMINING CASH FLOW FROM FINANCING ACTIVITIES

Determining cash flow from financing activities generally requires an analysis of the long-term liabilities and stockholders' equity sections of the balance sheet. Exhibit 10–13 shows those sections from Tsujimoto's Oriental Rug Factory's comparative balance sheets with a column added that calculates the change in each item from the end of 2003 to the end of 2004. If there was any general borrowing in the current liabilities section of Tsujimoto's balance sheet, we would have also listed it here as it would be part of financing activities.

Tsujimoto's cash flow from financing activities is made up of several elements. By examining the company's comparative balance sheets, we determine that notes payable decreased substantially. This is due to the company making principal payments on its promissory notes totaling $275,000. These payments are a cash outflow from financing activities. The increase in bonds payable is due to the company selling an

---

Tsujimoto's Oriental Rug Factory
Partial Statement of Cash Flows
For the Year Ended December 31, 2004
(in thousands)

Cash Flows from Operating Activities:

Net income		$420
Adjustments to reconcile net income to net cash provided by operating activities:		
Depreciation expense	$231	
Gain on sale of long-term investments	(31)	
Decrease in accounts receivable	187	
Increase in merchandise inventory	(164)	
Increase in prepaid expense	(60)	
Increase in accounts payable	110	
Decrease in accrued expenses	(11)	
Increase in income taxes payable	15	277
Net cash provided by operating activities		697
Cash Flows from Investing Activities:		
Sale of long-term investments	83	
Purchase of equipment	(110)	
Net cash used by investing activities		(27)

EXHIBIT 10–12 Partial Statement of Cash Flows for Tsujimoto's Oriental Rug Factory: Operating Activities and Investing Activities Sections

additional $200,000 in bonds. The sale of bonds results in a cash inflow from financing activities. Likewise, the $104,000 increase in common stock stems from the company selling additional shares of stock, a cash inflow from financing activities. All of these amounts can be determined simply by looking at the changes in those three items in Exhibit 10–13. In addition, there was a cash outflow from cash dividends paid during 2004 totaling $137,000. We know this amount because it was included in the additional information provided earlier in the chapter. But if we didn't already know the amount of dividends, we could determine it from information in Tsujimoto's income statement and balance sheets (Exhibits 10–4 and 10–5).

We know the balance in retained earnings at the end of 2003 is $443,000. We also know that the balance in retained earnings at the end of 2004 is $726,000. As discussed in earlier chapters, we know that the balance of retained earnings is increased by net income and decreased by dividends. We know from Tsujimoto's income statement that

EXHIBIT 10–13 Long-Term Liabilities and Stockholders' Equity Sections of Tsujimoto's Oriental Rug Factory's Balance Sheets for 2004 and 2003

Tsujimoto's Oriental Rug Factory
Partial Balance Sheets
December 31, 2004, and December 31, 2003
(in thousands)

	2004	2003	Increase/Decrease
Long-term liabilities:			
Notes payable	$ 425	$ 700	$(275)
Bonds payable	1,100	900	200
Total long-term liabilities	$1,525	$1,600	
Stockholders' equity:			
Common stock, no-par value	$1,332	$1,228	$ 104
Retained earnings	726	443	283
Total stockholders' equity	$2,058	$1,671	

the net income was $420,000, so the only amount we are missing is dividends. Therefore:

Retained earnings at 12/31/03	$443,000
PLUS: 2004 net income	420,000
LESS: Dividends paid during 2004	(?)
Equals retained earnings at 12/31/04	$726,000

The unknown amount of dividends must be $137,000. This calculation is based on the relationships we already know from the statement of retained earnings:

Beginning retained earnings + Net income − Dividends = Ending retained earnings

The net cash flow from financing activities, then, is $108,000. It is composed of the $275,000 outflow for the loan payments, the $200,000 inflow from the sale of bonds, the $104,000 inflow from the sale of Tsujimoto's common stock, and the outflow of $137,000 for the payment of dividends. If we have considered everything we were supposed to, the cash provided by operating activities combined with the cash used by investing activities and the cash used by financing activities should equal the change in cash from the end of 2003 to the end of 2004. Exhibit 10–14 shows the completed statement.

Tsujimoto's Oriental Rug Factory's statement of cash flows was a fairly simple one to prepare because there were relatively few things to consider. But whether simple or complex, all statements of cash flows assume the basic format we used for Tsujimoto's Oriental Rug Factory.

EXHIBIT 10–14 Tsujimoto's Oriental Rug Factory's Complete Statement of Cash Flows for 2004

Tsujimoto's Oriental Rug Factory
Statement of Cash Flows
For the Year Ended December 31, 2004
(in thousands)

Cash Flows from Operating Activities:		
Net income		$420
Adjustments to reconcile net income to		
net cash provided by operating activities:		
Depreciation expense	$231	
Gain on sale of long-term investments	(31)	
Decrease in accounts receivable	187	
Increase in merchandise inventory	(164)	
Increase in prepaid expense	(60)	
Increase in accounts payable	110	
Decrease in accrued expenses	(11)	
Increase in income taxes payable	15	277
Net cash provided by operating activities		697
Cash Flows from Investing Activities:		
Sale of long-term investments	83	
Purchase of equipment	(110)	
Net cash used by investing activities		(27)
Cash Flows from Financing Activities:		
Payments on long-term notes payable	(275)	
Proceeds from sale of bonds	200	
Proceeds from sale of common stock	104	
Payment of cash dividends	(137)	
Net cash used by financing activities		(108)
Net increase in cash during 2004		562
Cash balance at January 1, 2004		419
Cash balance at December 31, 2004		$981

SUPPLEMENTAL SCHEDULE

To complete the statement of cash flows disclosures for users, companies are required to include a supplemental schedule that outlines any significant noncash investing and financing activities during the period. Examples of such transactions include purchasing an asset by signing a promissory note instead of paying cash, using an asset other than cash to retire a loan, or trading one asset for another. In such transactions, no cash changes hands, but the transaction may have future cash consequences. If a company pays off a bond issue with common stock, that removes the future cash outflow required to repay the bond, because common stock has no maturity date or amount. On the other hand, dividend requirements will be increased in the future.

HOW TO USE THE STATEMENT OF CASH FLOWS

One of the two main purposes of the statement of cash flows is to disclose a company's sources of cash during a specific time period and what it used the cash for (the other being to reconcile accrual net income to the change in cash). One of the most important things the statement shows is a company's investment during the period and how that investment was financed. We are talking here mostly about a company's investment in long-lived assets that will be used to produce future revenues and, eventually, cash. The things the company invested in during the period are presented in the middle section of the statement (investing activities). How that investment was financed is presented in the top section of the statement (operating activities) and the bottom section of the statement (financing activities). To demonstrate this concept, we have extracted the cash flow totals for the three types of activities from Tsujimoto's Oriental Rug Factory's statement of cash flows from Exhibit 10–14:

Net cash provided by operating activities	$ 697,000
Net cash used by investing activities	$ (27,000)
Net cash provided by financing activities	$ (108,000)

Tsujimoto's Oriental Rug Factory has a net cash investment of $27,000 during 2004. This total is a bit misleading, because the company's actual investment in new equipment was $110,000. The total is reduced by the sale of long-term investments for $83,000. The company invested cash in the equipment to enhance the way it conducts its business by upgrading manufacturing facilities, entering into new markets, or developing new products. The point is there had to be a reason for Tsujimoto's to make this investment. We can't assess whether this investment was good or bad because we don't have enough information, but we can determine where the cash came from to finance it.

Aside from selling off investments, there are only two sources of cash available to any company, and Tsujimoto is no exception. A company either generates cash internally (from profitable operations) or it obtains it from external sources (borrowing or selling stock). In our example, virtually all of Tsujimoto's needed cash was generated internally through operating activities. In fact, the company's operations generated enough cash to pay down loans and to pay dividends, thus resulting in a net cash outflow for financing activities. With that in mind, focus on this important concept: *In the long run, all investment (disclosed in the middle section of the statement of cash flows) must be financed through operations (disclosed in the top section of the statement).* If a company wants or needs to invest, but does not generate enough cash from operations to pay for it, the only alternative is to go outside the company for the financing, by either borrowing or by selling shares of stock (disclosed in the bottom section of the statement). On the other hand, if a company does not generate enough cash from operations to pay for its investment, but either can't or doesn't want to go outside the company for financing, the only alternative is to cut back on the investment. However, this may not be a smart business decision. Remember why companies make these investments. The purpose of the investment is to generate cash from operations. If a company decides to cut back on its investment because it is not generating sufficient cash from operations to pay for it (and won't or can't finance the investment externally), the company may reduce its cash flow even further. We said earlier that Tsujimoto's invested $27,000 in 2004 to enhance the way the company conducts its business by upgrading manufacturing facilities, entering into new markets, or developing new products. If it hadn't made the investment, perhaps it couldn't upgrade its manufacturing facilities, enter new markets, or develop any new products. What might be the result of this decision? Well, the result may very well be declining cash flows from operations in subsequent years. This can cause an even more dramatic cutback in investment, which will likely lead to a further decline in cash generated by operations. Finally, the company may go bankrupt. Exhibit 10–15 illustrates this downward spiral using information extracted from the statements of cash flow for the years 1998 through 2003 for the Weiser Company, a videotape manufacturing firm.

EXHIBIT 10–15   The Downward Spiral of the Weiser Company

	2003	2002	2001	2000	1999	1998
Net cash provided by operating activities	$150	300	700	800	1,200	1,000
Net cash used by investing activities	(125)	(450)	(450)	(900)	(900)	(900)
Net cash provided by financing activities	(25)	60	(275)	150	(250)	(300)

Discussion Question

10–9. From what you see in Exhibit 10–15, what do you think Weiser Company's cash flow prospects are for 2004?

There are a couple of things we should note about the presentation in Exhibit 10–15. First, the *amount* of cash Weiser Company invests is not nearly as important as the *quality* of what it invests in. There is no information in the exhibit about the quality of any of this company's investments. The rapid decline in net cash provided by operating activities could be a result of the company investing in the wrong things in 1998 and 1999 (or even earlier years). If Weiser's investment in 1998 and 1999 was to upgrade its tape manufacturing equipment, the company may be in real trouble. Perhaps the investment in those years should have been in digital video disc (DVD) manufacturing equipment, because the DVD market is rapidly replacing the video tape market.

The second thing we should note about the presentation in Exhibit 10–15 is that the investing activities in a given year likely did not generate the cash from operating activities in that year. In other words, the $900 Weiser invested in 1998 probably did not generate the $1,000 cash from operating activities in 1998. The cash provided by operating activities in 1998 likely was a result of investments the company made in earlier years. What this means, of course, is that the rapid decline in Weiser's cash flows from operating activities in 2002 and 2003 may be due to the company's cutback in its investing activities in 2001 and 2002.

As you can see, the statement of cash flows provides valuable information to financial statement users. In and of itself, however, it cannot answer all an economic decision maker's questions about a company's past performance, present condition, or future prospects. As is the case with the other three financial statements we have discussed in this text, the statement of cash flows is best utilized in conjunction with the other statements and other pertinent information about the company.

◆ **USING FINANCIAL INFORMATION**

At the beginning of the chapter, we posed the hypothetical situation in which you were trying to decide whether to buy stock in the company your friend Sally has recommended. When you asked your Aunt Matilda's advice, her response was, "Profit, schmofit. Show me the cash." The statement of cash flows we have presented in this chapter provides you with solid information about a company's ability to generate positive cash flow. Additionally, analysts have developed certain ratios in recent years that focus on cash. In the remainder of this chapter, we will present two of them: the operating cash flow to current debt ratio and the operating cash flow coverage ratio. We will use the information from Tsujimoto's Oriental Rug Factory's financial statements to calculate these ratios for 2004.

Operating Cash Flow to Current Debt Ratio

operating cash flow to current debt ratio   A financial ratio that measures the sufficiency of cash flows from operating activities to meet current obligations.

The **operating cash flow to current debt ratio** measures the sufficiency of cash flows from operating activities to meet current obligations. In other words, it measures the company's ability to generate enough cash from operating activities to meet its current obligations. Whereas the current and quick ratios measure a firm's liquidity based on the financial resources the company has on hand (its assets), the operating cash flow to current debt ratio measures a company's ability to maintain liquidity by generating sufficient cash inflows from its operations. The formula for this ratio is:

$$\text{Operating cash flow to current debt ratio} = \frac{\text{Cash provided by operating activities}}{\text{Average current liabilities}}$$

The numerator for this ratio is cash provided by operating activities from the statement of cash flows. For Tsujimoto's, that amount is $697,000 as shown in Exhibit 10–14. The denominator is based on current liabilities from the balance sheet. We use an average for current liabilities for the same reason we used average amounts for ratios presented in earlier chapters. Since the cash provided by operating activities in the numerator occurred throughout 2004, we should use an approximation of the current liabilities outstanding throughout the year. We determine this by calculating the average of the current liabilities shown on the 2003 and 2004 balance sheets shown in Exhibit 10–5 ($748,000 + $862,000 = $1,610,000/2 = $805,000). We calculate Tsujimoto's operating cash flow to current debt ratio for 2004 as:

$$\frac{\$697,000}{\$805,000} = 0.87 \text{ to } 1$$

This ratio calculation tells us that Tsujimoto's operating activities generated $0.87 of cash in 2004 for each $1.00 of its average current liabilities. Generally speaking, generating a high amount of cash inflow from operating activities relative to current liabilities is a positive indication. Averages vary from company to company and industry to industry, but many analysts get a bit nervous if this ratio falls below $0.90 cash flow from operating activities to every $1.00 of average current liabilities.

Operating Cash Flow Coverage Ratio

operating cash flow coverage ratio   A financial ratio that indicates a company's capacity to repay its liabilities from the net cash generated by its operating activities.

The **operating cash flow coverage ratio** indicates a company's capacity to repay its liabilities from the net cash generated by its operating activities. The formula for this ratio is:

$$\text{Operating cash flow coverage ratio} = \frac{\text{Cash provided by operating activities}}{\text{Average total liabilities}}$$

As you can see, the numerator for this ratio is the same as for the operating cash flow to current liabilities ratio—cash provided by operating activities shown on the statement of cash flows. For Tsujimoto's, that amount is $697,000 as shown in Exhibit 10–14. The denominator is based on the total liabilities shown on the balance sheet. We use an average amount for the same reason we have in earlier ratios. Since the cash provided by operating activities in the numerator occurred throughout 2004, we want to know the total liabilities throughout the year. We determine this by calculating the average of the total liabilities shown on the 2003 and 2004 balance sheets as shown in

Exhibit 10–5 ($2,348,000 + $2,387,000 = $4,735,000/2 = $2,367,500). We calculate Tsujimoto's operating cash flow coverage ratio for 2004 as:

$$\frac{\$697,000}{\$2,367,500} = 0.29 \text{ to } 1$$

This ratio tells us that Tsujimoto's generated $0.29 of cash through its operation in 2004 for every $1.00 of its average total liabilities for 2004. The higher this ratio is, the more likely a company is to be able to service its debt without going outside the company for financing (by either borrowing additional funds or selling additional shares of its stock). Averages vary from company to company and industry to industry, but many analysts get a bit nervous if this ratio falls below $0.40 cash flow from operating activities to every $1.00 of average current liabilities.

Based on these two ratios, Tsujimoto's Oriental Rug Factory's cash position relative to its liabilities does not appear to be exceptionally good. In order to assess this, however, we must compare its ratios (and other financial information) to its industry, peer companies within that industry, and how these ratios have changed over time. This analysis is the subject of the next chapter.

Summary ◦

One of the disadvantages of accrual basis accounting is that it takes the financial statement reader's eye off cash. Over the past several decades, economic decision makers' interest in the cash flows of companies has risen. The accounting profession developed the statement of cash flows to give financial statement users information about the cash flows of companies during a particular period. This financial statement provides information about cash flows used by or provided by three major types of business activities: operating, investing, and financing. Information necessary for the development of a statement of cash flows can be found on a company's comparative balance sheets and the income statement of the period.

Cash flows provided or used by operating activities can be presented using either of two acceptable approaches—the indirect method or the direct method. The indirect method begins with net income. Adjustments to this figure are made for any revenue items not producing cash this period and expense items not using cash this period. The direct method provides detail about the individual sources and uses of cash associated with operating activities. Because the indirect method is the more widely used format, we presented this method in the chapter. A presentation of the direct method is found in an appendix to the chapter.

Results of investing activities can be found in the long-term asset section of the balance sheet. Typical transactions that are classified as investing activities are the purchase and sale of property, plant, and equipment.

The financing activities section of the statement of cash flows shows what types of external financing the company used to provide funds. Information showing the results of financing activities can be found in the long-term liability section and the owners' equity section of the balance sheet.

The statement of cash flows furnishes valuable information about the cash inflows and outflows of a business during a particular period. It provides an explanation of the changes in cash from the beginning to the end of a period. Therefore, the statement of cash flows can be considered a financial statement analysis tool as well as a financial statement.

Determining Cash Flows from Operating Activities— Direct Method

When the FASB introduced the statement of cash flows as one of the required financial statements in 1988, it recommended that companies use the direct method and include a supplemental schedule reconciling net income to the change in cash from operating activities. Recall that this reconciliation is the indirect method we presented in this chapter.

Many people (the authors of this text included) think it is unfortunate that the vast majority of companies use the indirect method. While the indirect method is every bit as logical as the direct method, it does not provide information regarding individual operating activity cash flows.

The direct method involves a series of calculations to determine the individual cash inflows from customers, interest earned on loans, dividends received from stock investments in other companies, and the like, and individual cash outflow for payments to suppliers, employees, creditors, and others. Remember, both the direct and the indirect methods deal only with the operating activities section of the statement of cash flows. The investing activities section and the financing activities section are the same, regardless of whether the direct or the indirect method is used for the operating activities section.

To determine net cash flow from operating activities using the direct method, we will, in effect, convert the accrual basis income statement into a cash basis income statement in order to get the focus back onto cash. To accomplish this, we examine the income statement along with the current assets and current liabilities on the comparative balance sheets. We will use Tsujimoto's Oriental Rug Factory as our example, so we have duplicated its 2004 income statement and the current assets and current liabilities sections of its balance sheets at the end of 2003 and 2004 as Exhibit 10A–1 on page F–426.

Exhibit 10A–2 on page F–427 shows the basic format of the cash flows from operating activities section of the statement of cash flows using the direct method.

As you can see from Exhibit 10A–2, we must determine five amounts to complete the operating activities section of Tsujimoto's statement of cash flows.

1. *Cash received from customers.* Credit sales increase accounts receivable, and cash received from customers that previously bought on account decreases accounts receivable. To determine the cash Tsujimoto's received from its customers during 2004, we combine the beginning balance in accounts receivable with sales to arrive at the total amount the company could have collected. Next, we subtract the amount they *did not* collect, namely the ending balance of accounts receivable to determine the total cash collected from customers.

Beginning accounts receivable balance (from the 2003 balance sheet)	$ 2,112
+ Sales during 2004 (from the 2004 income statement)	15,158
= Amount Tsujimoto's could have collected from customers in 2004	$17,270
− Ending accounts receivable balance (from the 2004 balance sheet)	(1,925)
= Total cash received from customers during 2004	$15,345

2. *Cash paid for merchandise inventory.* As it happens, rather than paying cash for the merchandise it sells, a company may sell the merchandise it has on hand. And, if it does buy merchandise, instead of paying for it, the company may buy some or all of the merchandise on account. Therefore, to determine the cash paid for merchandise during a period, we must examine cost of goods sold, merchandise inventory, and accounts payable together. Determining the cash Tsujimoto's paid its suppliers during 2004 is a two-step calculation. First, we must determine the cost of the merchandise the company purchased during the year. To do this, we take the company's cost of goods sold, reduce it by the amount of the beginning inventory, and then we add the ending balance in merchandise inventory. Second, we must determine the amount the company actually paid for the merchandise it purchased. To do this, we must consider the amount of merchandise purchased calculated in step one, in light of the beginning and ending balances in accounts payable. This two-step calculation is as follows:

Tsujimoto's Oriental Rug Factory
Income Statement
For the Year Ended December 31, 2004
(in thousands)

Sales		$15,158
Cost of goods sold		11,151
Gross margin		$ 4,007
Operating expenses:		
Depreciation expense	231	
Selling and administration	3,047	
Total operating expenses		(3,278)
Operating income		$ 729
Gain on sale of long-term investments		31
Less: Interest expense		(160)
Income before income taxes		$ 600
Income tax expense		(180)
Net income		$ 420

Tsujimoto's Oriental Rug Factory
Partial Balance Sheets
December 31, 2003, and December 31, 2003
(in thousands)

ASSETS:	2004	2003	Increase/Decrease
Current assets:			
Cash	$ 981	$ 419	$ 562
Accounts receivable	1,925	2,112	(187)
Merchandise inventory	1,022	858	164
Prepaid expenses	192	132	60
Total current assets	$4,120	$3,521	
LIABILITIES:			
Current liabilities:			
Accounts payable	$ 820	$ 710	$ 110
Accrued expenses	17	28	(11)
Income tax payable	25	10	15
Total current liabilities	$ 862	$ 748	

EXHIBIT 10A–1 Tsujimoto's Oriental Rug Factory's Income Statement for 2004 and Partial Balance Sheets for 2003 and 2004

Step One—Determine the amount of merchandise inventory purchased in 2004:

Cost of goods sold (from the 2004 income statement)	$11,151
– Beginning merchandise inventory balance (from the 2003 balance sheet)	(858)
= Amount of cost of goods sold purchased in 2004	10,293
+ Ending merchandise inventory balance (from the 2004 balance sheet)	1,022
= Merchandise inventory purchased in 2004	$11,315

Step Two—Determine the amount of merchandise inventory paid for in 2004:

Beginning accounts payable balance (from the 2003 balance sheet)	$ 710
+ Merchandise inventory purchased in 2004 (calculated in step one)	11,315
= Amount Tsujimoto's could have paid to suppliers in 2004	$12,025
– Ending accounts payable balance (from the 2004 balance sheet)	(820)
= Total cash paid for merchandise inventory in 2004	$11,205

3. *Cash paid for operating expenses.* Some of the operating expenses in Tsujimoto's 2004 income statement were not paid in 2004. Some were paid before 2004 and some might be paid after 2004. A company classifies operating expenses it pays for in advance (such as insurance or rent) as assets (prepaid expenses) on the balance sheet until they are subsequently recognized as expenses on the income statement. Conversely, when a company

Tsujimoto's Oriental Rug Factory
Partial Statement of Cash Flows
For the Year Ended December 31, 2004
(in thousands)

Cash Flows from Operating Activities:

Cash received from customers	$?	
Cash paid for:		
Merchandise inventory	?	
Operating expenses	?	
Interest	?	
Income taxes	?	
Net cash provided (used) by operating activities		$?

EXHIBIT 10A–2 Basic Format of Cash Flow from Operating Activities Section of the Statement of Cash Flows Using the Direct Method

recognizes operating expenses on its income statement (such as supplies, utilities, and wages) but has not paid for them by the end of the period, it classifies the amount owed for those expenses as a liability (accrued expenses) on the balance sheet. Accrued expenses is a liability very similar to accounts payable. To determine the cash Tsujimoto's paid for operating expenses in 2004, then, we must consider not only the operating expenses from the income statement, but prepaid expenses and accrued expenses from the balance sheets, as well.

One last thing we should mention before we demonstrate the calculation of cash paid for operating expenses is depreciation. Recall from our discussion in Chapter 7 that depreciation is a noncash expense. When we say *noncash*, we don't mean to imply that cash was never paid for this expense, because it was; it just wasn't paid during this income statement period. In fact, depreciation is associated with a very special prepaid expense, called property, plant, and equipment. The cash flow associated with property, plant, and equipment is reported in the investing activities section of the statement of cash flows so we exclude any treatment here. The calculation of Tsujimoto's Oriental Rug Factory's cash paid for operating expenses is as follows:

Operating expenses other than depreciation (from the 2004 income statement)	$3,047
− Beginning prepaid expenses balance (from the 2003 balance sheet)	(132)
+ Ending prepaid expenses balance (from the 2004 balance sheet)	192
+ Beginning accrued expenses balance (from the 2003 balance sheet)	28
− Ending accrued expenses balance (from the 2004 balance sheet)	(17)
= Total cash paid for operating expenses in 2004	$3,118

4. *Cash paid for interest.* To determine the amount of cash Tsujimoto's Oriental Rug Factory paid for interest in 2004, we must examine the beginning balance of accrued interest (from the 2003 balance sheet), interest expense (from the 2004 income statement), and the ending balance of accrued interest (from the 2004 balance sheet). Since there is no balance for accrued interest on either the 2003 or 2004 balance sheet, we can conclude that the cash Tsujimoto's paid for interest in 2004 is exactly the $160,000 shown as interest expense on the 2004 income statement. If there had been a balance in either the beginning or ending balance of accrued interest, we would need to do a calculation similar to the one we did for cash collected from customers.

5. *Cash paid for income taxes.* To calculate the amount of cash Tsujimoto's paid for income taxes in 2004, we must examine the beginning balance of taxes payable (from the 2003 balance sheet), income tax expense (from the 2004 income statement), and the ending balance of income taxes payable (from the 2004 balance sheet). The calculation of Tsujimoto's Oriental Rug Factory's cash paid for income taxes follows:

Income tax expenses (from the 2004 income statement)	$180
+ Beginning taxes payable (from the 2003 balance sheet)	10
− Ending taxes payable (from the 2004 balance sheet)	(25)
= Cash paid for income taxes	$165

Tsujimoto's Oriental Rug Factory
Statement of Cash Flows
For the Year Ended December 31, 2004
(in thousands)

Cash Flows from Operating Activities:

Cash received from customers	$15,345	
Cash paid for:		
Merchandise inventory	(11,205)	
Operating expenses	(3,118)	
Interest	(160)	
Income taxes	(165)	
Net cash provided (used) by operating activities		$697
Cash Flows from Investing Activities:		
Sale of long-term investments	83	
Purchase of equipment	(110)	
Net cash used by investing activities		(27)
Cash Flows from Financing Activities:		
Payments on long-term notes payable	(275)	
Proceeds from sale of bonds	200	
Proceeds from sale of common stock	104	
Payment of cash dividends	(137)	
Net cash used by financing activities		(108)
Net increase in cash during 2004		562
Cash balance at January 1, 2004		419
Cash balance at December 31, 2004		$981

EXHIBIT 10A–3 Statement of Cash Flows for Tsujimoto's Oriental Rug Factory: Operating Activities Section—Direct Method

With these five calculations, we can now complete the operating activities section of Tsujimoto's Oriental Rug Factory's statement of cash flows as shown in Exhibit 10A–3.

So you can more easily compare the operating activities section using the direct method with the operating activities section using the indirect method, Exhibit 10A–4 duplicates the indirect method statement of cash flows we presented earlier in the chapter.

As you can see by examining the two exhibits, the statements are exactly the same except for the operating activities sections. And even the operating activities sections are similar in that the net cash flows from operating activities is the same regardless of whether the indirect method or direct method was used. Remember, however, that the FASB requires that the reconciliation of net income to cash flow from operating activities (essentially, a presentation of the indirect method) also be presented when the direct method is employed.

Tsujimoto's Oriental Rug Factory
Statement of Cash Flows
For the Year Ended December 31, 2004
(in thousands)

Cash Flows from Operating Activities:

Net income		$420
Adjustments to reconcile net income to		
net cash provided by operating activities:		
Depreciation expense	$231	
Gain on sale of long-term investments	(31)	
Decrease in accounts receivable	187	
Increase in merchandise inventory	(164)	
Increase in prepaid expense	(60)	
Increase in accounts payable	110	
Decrease in accrued expenses	(11)	
Increase in income taxes payable	15	277
Net cash provided by operating activities		697
Cash Flows from Investing Activities:		
Sale of long-term investments	83	
Purchase of equipment	(110)	
Net cash used by investing activities		(27)
Cash Flows from Financing Activities:		
Payments on long-term notes payable	(275)	
Proceeds from sale of bonds	200	
Proceeds from sale of common stock	104	
Payment of cash dividends	(137)	
Net cash used by financing activities		(108)
Net increase in cash during 2004		562
Cash balance at January 1, 2004		419
Cash balance at December 31, 2004		$981

EXHIBIT 10A–4   Statement of Cash Flows for Tsujimoto's Oriental Rug Factory: Operating Activities Section—Indirect Method

Key Terms

- direct method, F–406
- financing activities, F–409
- indirect method, F–407
- investing activities, F–407
- operating activities, F–405
- operating cash flow coverage ratio, F–423
- operating cash flow to current debt ratio, F–423
- working capital, F–404

Review the Facts

A. When did the present format of the statement of cash flows come into existence?
B. What is the main purpose of the statement of cash flows?
C. Name the two methods of presenting the operating activities section of statement of cash flows. Which method is more commonly used by publicly traded companies?
D. What are the three activity classifications presented on the statement of cash flows?
E. Which category includes the cash inflows for interest received?
F. Which category includes the cash outflows for interest paid?
G. Which category includes the cash inflows for dividends received?
H. Which category includes the cash outflows for dividends paid?
I. Provide three examples of cash flows for each of the three activities shown on the statement of cash flows.

J. What is the starting point for calculating cash flows from operating activities under the indirect method?

K. When gathering information to prepare the operating activities section, where on the financial statements would you likely find most of the information you need?

L. Where would you find information to prepare the investing activities section?

M. Where would you find information to prepare the financing activities section?

N. Which section of the statement of cash flows shows cash outflows to acquire the property, plant, and equipment the company will use in its business operations?

O. According to the chapter, what ratios help financial statement users evaluate a company's operating cash flows? What do the ratios measure?

Apply What You Have Learned ●●●●●●●●●●●●●●●●●●●●●●●●●●●

LO 1 & 2: STATEMENT OF CASH FLOWS TERMINOLOGY

10–10. Below is a list of items relating to the concepts discussed in this chapter, followed by definitions of those items in scrambled order:

a. Operating activities
b. Indirect method
c. Depreciation expense
d. Comparative financial statements
e. Financing activities
f. Working capital
g. Direct method
h. Investing activities

1. _____ Provides a reconciliation of accrual net income to the cash provided by or used by operating activities
2. _____ Accounting reports providing information from two or more consecutive periods at once
3. _____ Activities centered around the actual day-to-day business transactions of a company
4. _____ Current assets less current liabilities
5. _____ Business activities related to long-term assets
6. _____ Provides detail as to the individual sources and uses of cash associated with operating activities
7. _____ An item that reduces reported net income, but does not require the use of cash
8. _____ Activities such as the issuance of debt or equity and the payment of dividends

Required: Match the letter next to each item on the list with the appropriate definition. Use each letter only once.

LO 2: IDENTIFICATION OF ACTIVITIES

10–11. Listed below are the three broad types of activities that can either generate or use cash in any business, followed by descriptions of various items:

a. Operating activities
b. Investing activities
c. Financing activities

1. _____ Payment of dividends
2. _____ Adjustment for depreciation
3. _____ Purchase of merchandise inventory
4. _____ Purchase of vehicles
5. _____ Repayment of loan principal
6. _____ Payment of loan interest
7. _____ Issuing capital stock
8. _____ Payment of wages to employees
9. _____ Payment of taxes
10. _____ Cash received from sale of property and equipment
11. _____ Cash paid for loans made to other companies
12. _____ Interest received on loans to other companies
13. _____ Adjustments for changes in most current asset and current liability items
14. _____ Cash from selling investments in other companies

Required: Classify each of the items listed above by placing the letter of the appropriate activity category in the space provided.

LO 2: IDENTIFICATION OF ACTIVITIES

10–12. Listed below are the three broad types of activities that can either generate or use cash in any business, followed by descriptions of various items:

   a. Operating activities
   b. Investing activities
   c. Financing activities

   1. _____ Adjustment to income for depreciation or amortization expense
   2. _____ Cash received for sale of merchandise inventory
   3. _____ Cash paid for merchandise inventory
   4. _____ Principal part of loan payments
   5. _____ Interest part of loan payments
   6. _____ Cash paid when a company buys common stock in another company
   7. _____ Cash paid when a company buys back its own common stock
   8. _____ Payment of rent on office space
   9. _____ Cash received for dividends
   10. _____ Cash paid for dividends
   11. _____ Cash paid for wages
   12. _____ Cash paid for income taxes
   13. _____ Cash paid for insurance on factory equipment
   14. _____ Cash paid to buy factory equipment
   15. _____ Cash received for the sale of factory equipment
   16. _____ Cash received from sale of treasury stock
   17. _____ Cash received when a company sells bonds of other companies, which were held for investment
   18. _____ Cash received when a company sells its own company bonds
   19. _____ Cash from the collection of accounts receivable

Required: Classify each of the items listed above by placing the letter of the appropriate activity category in the space provided.

LO 2: IDENTIFICATION OF SOURCES AND USES—INDIRECT METHOD

10–13. Following are the changes in some of George R. Violette Company's assets, liabilities, and equities from December 31, 2004, to December 31, 2005:

   1. _____ Accounts payable decreased.
   2. _____ Property and equipment increased.
   3. _____ Accounts receivable increased.
   4. _____ Long-term notes payable decreased.
   5. _____ Prepaid expenses decreased.
   6. _____ Notes payable increased.
   7. _____ Taxes payable decreased.
   8. _____ Common stock increased.
   9. _____ Wages payable increased.
   10. _____ Accrued expenses decreased.
   11. _____ Merchandise inventory decreased.

Violette is in the process of preparing the operating activities section of its statement of cash flows using the indirect method. Some of the items above will be included and others will not.

Required: Designate each of the items listed above as follows:

   S Place the letter S in the space next to each item that should be considered a source of cash in the operating activities section.
   U Place the letter U in the space next to each item that should be considered a use of cash in the operating activities section.
   N Place the letter N next to any item not included in the indirect method operating activities section.

LO 3: SIMPLE OPERATING ACTIVITIES SECTION PREPARATION

10–14. The Doran Company gathered the following information from its accounting records:

Collections from customers	$450,000
Payments to suppliers	150,000
Payments for income taxes	75,000
Interest received on investments	5,000
Payments to employees for wages	64,000
Payments for interest	85,000
Depreciation expense	50,000

Required: Prepare the operating activities section of the statement of cash flows for the Doran Company. (Use a format similar to the one in Exhibit 10–1.)

LO 3: SIMPLE OPERATING ACTIVITIES SECTION PREPARATION

10–15. The McDaniel Company gathered the following information from its accounting records:

Collections of accounts receivable	$350,000
Cash sales	85,000
Payments for merchandise	260,000
Payments for income taxes	45,000
Payments of electricity	40,000
Interest received on investments	15,000
Wage payments to employees	55,000
Interest payments	68,000
Depreciation expense	25,000

Required: Prepare the operating activities section of the statement of cash flows for the McDaniel Company. (Use a format similar to the one in Exhibit 10–1.)

LO 3: SIMPLE OPERATING ACTIVITIES SECTION PREPARATION

10–16. The PJ Boardman Company gathered the following information from its accounting records:

Payment for treasury stock	$200,000
Payments for dividends	100,000
Collections of accounts receivable	870,000
Cash sales	385,000
Payments to suppliers on account	738,000
Cash purchases of merchandise inventory	250,000
Payments for income taxes	245,000
Interest received on investments	95,000
Payments to employees for salaries	460,000
Payments for interest	35,000
Depreciation expense	125,000

Required: Prepare the operating activities section of the statement of cash flows for the PJ Boardman Company. (Use a format similar to the one in Exhibit 10–1.)

LO 3: SIMPLE INVESTING ACTIVITIES SECTION PREPARATION

10–17. In preparing its statement of cash flows for the year ended December 31, 2003, Debbie Hoffman Company gathered the following data:

Gain on sale of machinery	$ 18,000
Proceeds from sale of machinery	60,000
Purchase of new machinery	420,000
Purchase of Fred, Inc., bonds (face value $100,000)	80,000
Dividends declared and paid	40,000
Proceeds from the sale of common stock	50,000

Required: Prepare the investing activities section of the statement of cash flows for Debbie Hoffman Company. (Use a format similar to the one in Exhibit 10–1.)

LO 3: SIMPLE INVESTING ACTIVITIES SECTION PREPARATION

10–18. In preparing its statement of cash flows for the year ended December 31, 2004, Imelda Company gathered the following data:

Purchased new production equipment for cash	$128,000
Loss on sale of machinery	24,000
Proceeds from sale of old machinery	40,000
Purchase of *Eastman Kodak* bonds (face value $8,000)	9,000
Sold half of the Aka, Inc., bonds	5,000
Imelda Company dividends paid	96,000
Sold Imelda Company bonds	80,000

Required: Prepare the investing activities section of the statement of cash flows for Imelda Company. (Use a format similar to the one in Exhibit 10–1.)

LO 3: SIMPLE INVESTING ACTIVITIES SECTION

10–19. In preparing its statement of cash flows for the year ended December 31, 2004, Juliany Company gathered the following data:

Purchased *IBM* stock	$ 45,000
Purchased back some Juliany common stock	6,000
Received cash dividends from *IBM*	3,000
Paid Juliany cash dividends	28,000
Loss on sale of equipment	4,000
Proceeds from sale of equipment	20,000
Purchase of equipment	980,000

Required: Prepare the investing activities section of the statement of cash flows for Juliany Company. (Use a format similar to the one in Exhibit 10–1.)

LO 3: SIMPLE FINANCING ACTIVITIES SECTION PREPARATION

10–20. In preparing its statement of cash flows for the year ended December 31, 2004, Pat Van Liu Company gathered the following data:

Gain on sale of equipment	$ 4,000
Proceeds from sale of equipment	30,000
Cash paid to purchase equipment	280,000
Purchased *Dow Chemical* stock	32,000
Received cash dividends from *Dow Chemical*	2,000
Sold some of the *Dow Chemical* stock	15,000
Paid Pat Van Liu cash dividends	28,000
Sold Pat Van Liu common stock	60,000
Borrowed cash from *Bank Atlantic*	120,000

Required: Prepare the financing activities section of the statement of cash flows for Pat Van Liu Company. (Use a format similar to the one in Exhibit 10–1.)

LO 3: SIMPLE FINANCING ACTIVITIES SECTION PREPARATION

10–21. In preparing its statement of cash flows for the year ended December 31, 2004, Lori Beloff Company gathered the following data:

Loss on sale of equipment	$ 54,000
Proceeds from sale of equipment	230,000
Cash paid for *Eastman Kodak* stock	23,000
Proceeds from sale of Lori Beloff preferred stock	200,000
Paid Lori Beloff dividends	80,000
Proceeds from sale of Lori Beloff common stock	160,000
Proceeds from sale of part of the *Kodak* stock	9,000

Borrowed cash from **Ocean Bank**	300,000
Payment of interest on **Ocean Bank** loan	20,000
Repayment of principal on **Ocean Bank** loan	120,000

Required: Prepare the financing activities section of the statement of cash flows for Lori Beloff Company. (Use a format similar to the one in Exhibit 10–1.)

LO 3: SIMPLE FINANCING ACTIVITIES SECTION PREPARATION

10–22. In preparing its statement of cash flows for the year ended December 31, 2005, Marc Oliver Company gathered the following data:

Proceeds from sale of equipment	$115,000
Proceeds from sale of Oliver preferred stock	100,000
Paid Oliver dividends	75,000
Proceeds from sale of Oliver common stock	500,000
Proceeds from bank loan	200,000
Payment of interest on bank loan	14,000
Repayment of bank loan principal	100,000

Required: Prepare the financing activities section of the statement of cash flows for Marc Oliver Company. (Use a format similar to the one in Exhibit 10–1.)

LO 3: SIMPLE STATEMENT OF CASH FLOWS PREPARATION

10–23. The following information is from the records of the Greenfield Company for the year ended December 31, 2004:

Loaned $2,000 to Adams Company
Sold Greenfield Company stock for cash of $10,000
Purchased equipment for cash of $20,000
Cash sales to customers were $95,000
Sold equipment for cash of $4,000
Paid cash to employees for wages, $9,500
Paid cash for merchandise, $29,000
Paid a $2,000 cash dividend
Borrowed $6,000 from Friendly National Bank
Purchased **Ford Motor Company** stock, $5,000
Received a cash dividend from **Ford** of $200
Paid cash for other expenses, $8,000
Made a loan payment to Friendly Bank of $2,200, which included $200 interest
Cash balance at December 31, 2003, is $15,000

Required: Prepare a statement of cash flows for Greenfield Company for the year ended December 31, 2004. (Use a format similar to the one in Exhibit 10–1.)

LO 3: SIMPLE STATEMENT OF CASH FLOWS PREPARATION

10–24. The following information is from the records of the Jane Avery Company for the year ended December 31, 2005:

Purchased equipment for cash of $8,000
Cash sales to customers were $75,000
Sold Jane Avery Company stock for cash of $6,000
Loaned $1,000 to Denson Company
Sold equipment for cash of $1,000
Paid cash to employees for wages, $4,500
Borrowed $5,000 from Peoples National Bank
Paid cash for merchandise, $32,000
Paid a $500 cash dividend
Made a loan payment to Peoples Bank of $1,500, which included $100 interest
Purchased **DuPont Company** stock, $2,000
Received a cash dividend from **DuPont,** $100
Paid cash for other expenses, $3,000
Cash balance at December 31, 2004, is $7,500

Required: Prepare a statement of cash flows for Jane Avery Company for the year ended December 31, 2005. (Use a format similar to the one in Exhibit 10–1.)

LO 3: SIMPLE STATEMENT OF CASH FLOWS PREPARATION

10–25. The following information is from the records of the Beth Toland Company for the year ended December 31, 2005:

Paid cash to employees for wages, $7,000
Purchased equipment for cash of $3,000
Cash sales to customers were $80,000
Sold Beth Toland Company stock for cash of $9,000
Loaned $2,000 to Furman Company
Paid cash for merchandise, $24,000
Sold equipment for cash of $2,000
Borrowed $8,000 from Central National Bank
Paid a $100 cash dividend
Made a loan payment to Central Bank of $3,000, which included $500 interest
Purchased Lucent stock, $1,000
Received a cash dividend from Lucent, $50
Paid cash for other expenses, $2,000
Cash balance at December 31, 2004, is $4,500

Required: Prepare a statement of cash flows for Beth Toland Company for the year ended December 31, 2005. (Use a format similar to the one in Exhibit 10–1.)

LO 3: OPERATING ACTIVITIES SECTION PREPARATION—INDIRECT METHOD

10–26. Below are partial comparative balance sheets for Zhang Chinese Trading Company as of December 31, 2004, and 2003:

Zhang Chinese Trading Company
Partial Balance Sheets
December 31, 2004, and December 31, 2003
Current Assets and Current Liabilities Only
(in thousands)

	2004	2003	Increase (Decrease)
Current assets:			
Cash	$ 110	$ 150	$(40)
Accounts receivable	750	670	80
Merchandise inventory	620	680	(60)
Total current assets	$1,480	$1,500	$(20)
Current liabilities:	—	—	
Accounts payable	$ 550	$ 460	$ 90
Wages payable	28	38	(10)
Total current liabilities	$ 578	$ 498	$ 80

Additional Information: Net income for 2004 was $120,000. Included in the operating expenses for the year was depreciation expense of $30,000.

Required: Prepare the operating activities section of Zhang Chinese Trading Company's statement of cash flows for 2004 using the indirect method.

LO 3: OPERATING ACTIVITIES SECTION PREPARATION— INDIRECT METHOD

10–27. Following are partial comparative balance sheets for Sheridan Company as of December 31, 2005, and 2004:

Sheridan Company
Partial Balance Sheets
December 31, 2005, and December 31, 2004
Current Assets and Current Liabilities Only
(in thousands)

	2005	2004	Increase (Decrease)
Current assets:			
Cash	$3,400	$2,920	$480
Accounts receivable	1,825	2,212	(387)
Merchandise inventory	1,170	966	204
Prepaid expenses	240	270	(30)
Total current assets	$6,635	$6,368	$267
Current liabilities:	—	—	
Accounts payable	$2,321	$1,740	$581
Interest payable	0	200	(200)
Total current liabilities	$2,321	$1,940	$381

Additional Information: Net income for 2005 was $406,000. Included in the operating expenses for the year was depreciation expense of $175,000.

Required: Prepare the operating activities section of Sheridan Company's statement of cash flows for 2005 using the indirect method.

LO 3: OPERATING ACTIVITIES SECTION PREPARATION—INDIRECT METHOD

10–28. Below are partial comparative balance sheets for Vincent Scelta Company as of December 31, 2004, and 2003:

Vincent Scelta Company
Partial Balance Sheets
December 31, 2004, and December 31, 2003
Current Assets and Current Liabilities Only
(in thousands)

	2004	2003	Increase (Decrease)
Current assets:			
Cash	$2,110	$2,650	$(540)
Accounts receivable	1,254	977	277
Merchandise inventory	730	856	(126)
Prepaid expenses	127	114	13
Total current assets	$4,221	$4,597	$(376)
Current liabilities:	—	—	
Accounts payable	$1,054	$1,330	$(276)
Wages payable	125	75	50
Total current liabilities	$1,179	$1,405	$(226)

Additional Information: Net income for 2004 was $185,000. Included in the operating expenses for the year was depreciation expense of $102,000.

Required: Prepare the operating activities section of Scelta Company's statement of cash flows for 2004 using the indirect method.

LO 3: OPERATING ACTIVITIES SECTION PREPARATION—INDIRECT METHOD

10–29. Steven Hunter Corporation's worksheet for the preparation of its 2005 statement of cash flows included the following:

	January 1	December 31
Accounts receivable	$78,000	$71,000
Prepaid insurance	48,000	36,000
Inventory	56,000	75,000
Accounts payable	64,000	57,000

Steven Hunter Corporation reported net income of $450,000 for the year, and depreciation expense was $39,000.

Required: Prepare the operating activities section of Hunter Corporation's statement of cash flows for 2005 using the indirect method.

LO 3: INDIRECT METHOD PREPARATION OF THE STATEMENT OF CASH FLOWS

10–30. Use the balance sheets, income statement, and the additional information provided below to complete this problem.

Jim Boyd Company
Balance Sheets
As of December 31, 2005, and December 31, 2004
(in thousands)

	2005	2004
ASSETS:		
Current assets:		
Cash	$ 1,618	$1,220
Accounts receivable	1,925	2,112
Merchandise inventory	1,070	966
Prepaid expenses	188	149
Total current assets	$ 4,801	$4,447
Plant and equipment:		
Buildings	$4,818	$3,292
LESS: Accumulated depreciation	(361)	(300)
Buildings, net	$ 4,457	$2,992
Equipment	$1,434	$1,145
LESS: Accumulated depreciation	(141)	(100)
Equipment, net	$ 1,293	$1,045
Total plant and equipment	$ 5,750	$4,037
Total assets	$10,551	$8,484
LIABILITIES:		
Current liabilities:		
Accounts payable	$ 1,818	$ 1,686
Wages payable	900	1,100
Total current liabilities	$ 2,718	$ 2,786
Long-term liabilities	2,500	2,000
Total liabilities	$ 5,218	$4,786
STOCKHOLDERS' EQUITY:		
Common stock, no-par value	$ 3,390	$ 2,041
Retained earnings	1,943	1,657
Total stockholders' equity	$ 5,333	$3,698
Total liabilities and stockholders' equity	$10,551	$8,484

Jim Boyd Company
Income Statement
For the Year Ended December 31, 2005
(in thousands)

Net sales		$11,228
LESS: Cost of goods sold		7,751
Gross profit on sales		$ 3,477
Operating expenses:		
Depreciation—buildings and equipment	$ 102	
Other selling and administrative	2,667	
Total operating expenses		(2,769)
Operating income		$ 708
Interest expense		(168)
Income before taxes		$ 540
Income taxes		(114)
Net income		$ 426

Additional Information: There were no sales of plant and equipment during the year, and the company paid dividends to stockholders during the year of $140,000.

Required:

    a. Prepare Boyd Company's statement of cash flows for the year ended December 31, 2005, using the indirect method for operating activities.

    b. In which of the three categories of activities did Boyd use the majority of its cash during 2005?

    c. What does your answer to the previous question tell you about Boyd Company?

    d. From which of the three types of activities did Boyd obtain the majority of its cash during 2005?

    e. Is the activity you identified in the previous requirement an appropriate source of cash in the long run? Explain your reasoning.

LO 5: APPENDIX—DIRECT METHOD PREPARATION OF THE STATEMENT OF CASH FLOWS

10–31. Use the Boyd financial statements in 10–30 to complete the following requirements.

Required:

    a. Prepare Boyd Company's statement of cash flows for the year ended December 31, 2005, using the direct method for operating activities.

    b. In which of the three categories of activities did Boyd use the majority of its cash during 2005?

    c. What does your answer to the previous question tell you about Boyd Company?

    d. From which of the three types of activities did Boyd obtain the majority of its cash during 2005?

    e. Is the activity you identified in the previous requirement an appropriate source of cash in the long run? Explain your reasoning.

LO 4: FINANCIAL RATIO CALCULATIONS

10–32. This problem is a continuation of either problem 10–30 or 10–31. Use the financial statements in 10–30 and the statement of cash flows you prepared for problem 10–30 or 10–31 to complete the following requirements.

Required:

    a. Calculate operating cash flow to current debt ratio.

    b. Calculate the operating cash flow coverage ratio.

    c. What do these ratios tell you about the company? Explain your answer.

LO 4: INDIRECT METHOD PREPARATION OF THE STATEMENT OF CASH FLOWS

10–33. Use the balance sheets, income statement, and the additional information presented below to complete this problem.

Thomas Greco Company
Balance Sheets
As of December 31, 2005, and December 31, 2004
(in thousands)

	2005	**2004**
ASSETS:		
Current assets:		
Cash	$ 529	$ 660
Accounts receivable	1,006	1,011
Merchandise inventory	396	452
Prepaid expenses	38	62
Total current assets	$ 1,969	$ 2,185

Property, plant, and equipment:

Buildings	$2,000		$1,681	
LESS: Accumulated depreciation	(176)		(146)	
Buildings, net		$1,824		$1,535
Equipment	$ 809		$ 609	
LESS: Accumulated depreciation	(76)		(61)	
Equipment, net		733		548
Total plant and equipment		$2,557		$2,083
Total assets		$4,526		$4,268

LIABILITIES:

Current liabilities:

Accounts payable	$726	$ 809
Total current liabilities	$ 726	$ 809
Long-term liabilities		
Notes payable	2,250	1,800
Total long-term liabilities	2,250	1,800
Total liabilities	$2,976	$2,609

STOCKHOLDERS' EQUITY:

Common stock, no-par value	$1,300	$1,000
Retained earnings	250	659
Total stockholders' equity	$1,550	$1,659
Total liabilities and stockholders' equity	$4,526	$4,268

Thomas Greco Company
Income Statement
For the Year Ended December 31, 2005
(in thousands)

Sales		$6,391
LESS: Cost of goods sold		4,474
Gross profit on sales		$1,917
LESS: Operating expenses:		
Depreciation—buildings and equipment	$ 45	
Other selling and administrative	2,066	
Total operating expenses		(2,111)
Operating income		$ (194)
LESS: Interest expense		(145)
Income before taxes		$ (339)
Income taxes		0
Net loss		$ (339)

Additional Information: There were no sales of plant and equipment during the year, and the company paid dividends to stockholders during the year of $70,000.

Required:

a. Prepare Greco Company's statement of cash flows for the year ended December 31, 2005, using the indirect method for operating activities.

b. In which of the three broad activities did Greco use the majority of its cash during 2005?

c. What does your answer to the previous question tell you about Greco Company?

d. In which of the three broad activities did Greco obtain the majority of its cash during 2005?

e. Is the activity you identified in the previous requirement an appropriate source of cash in the long run? Explain your reasoning.

LO 5: APPENDIX—DIRECT METHOD PREPARATION OF THE STATEMENT OF CASH FLOWS

10–34. Use the Greco financial statements in 10–33 to complete the following requirements.

Required:

a. Prepare Greco Company's statement of cash flows for the year ended December 31, 2005, using the direct method for operating activities.

b. In which of the three broad activities did Greco use the majority of its cash during 2005?

c. What does your answer to the previous question tell you about Greco Company?

d. In which of the three broad activities did Greco obtain the majority of its cash during 2005?

e. Is the activity you identified in the previous requirement an appropriate source of cash in the long run? Explain your reasoning.

LO 3: INDIRECT METHOD PREPARATION OF THE STATEMENT OF CASH FLOWS

10–35. Use the balance sheets, income statement, and the additional information provided below to complete this problem.

Walton Imports
Balance Sheets
As of December 31, 2004, and December 31, 2003

	2004	2003
ASSETS:		
Current assets:		
Cash	$ 14,000	$ 26,400
Accounts receivable	48,000	38,000
Inventory	39,000	42,000
Prepaid expenses	10,000	15,000
Total current assets	$111,000	$121,400
Long-term investment	0	60,000
Property, plant, and equipment	$109,000	$53,000
LESS: Accumulated depreciation	(13,000)	(6,000)
Property, plant, and equipment, net	$ 96,000	$ 47,000
Total assets	$207,000	$228,400
LIABILITIES:		
Current liabilities:		
Accounts payable	$ 18,000	$ 49,000
Accrued expenses	11,650	10,650
Income taxes payable	3,750	5,750
Total current liabilities	$ 33,400	$ 65,400
Long-term liabilities:		
Notes payable	7,000	0
Bonds payable	30,000	110,000
Total long-term liabilities	37,000	110,000
Total liabilities	$ 70,400	$175,400
STOCKHOLDERS' EQUITY:		
Preferred stock, no par	10,000	8,000
Common stock, $1 par	$ 4,500	$ 3,500
Additional paid-in capital—common	17,500	13,500
Retained earnings	104,600	28,000
Total stockholders' equity	$136,600	$ 53,000
Total liabilities and stockholders' equity	$207,000	$228,400

Walton Imports
Income Statement
For the Year Ended December 31, 2004

Net sales		$585,000
Cost of goods sold		328,000
Gross profit on sales		$257,000
Operating expenses:		
Depreciation—buildings and equipment	$ 7,000	
Other selling and administrative	109,000	
Total operating expenses		(116,000)

Operating income	$141,000
Interest expense	(3,000)
Loss on sale of long-term investments	(20,000)
Income before taxes	$118,000
Income taxes	(35,400)
Net income	$ 82,600

Additional Information: Walton sold the long-term investments for cash of $40,000. There were no sales of property, plant, and equipment during the year. Walton paid cash dividends to stockholders during the year of $6,000.

Required:

    a. Prepare a statement of cash flows for Walton Imports for the year ended December 31, 2004, using the indirect method for operating activities.

    b. In which of the three categories of activities did Walton use the majority of its cash during 2004?

    c. What does your answer to the previous question tell you about Walton Imports?

    d. From which of the three types of activities did Walton obtain the majority of its cash during 2004?

    e. Is the activity you identified in the previous requirement an appropriate source of cash in the long run? Explain your reasoning.

LO 5: APPENDIX—DIRECT METHOD PREPARATION OF THE STATEMENT OF CASH FLOWS

10–36. Use the Walton Imports financial statements in 10–35 to complete the following requirements.

Required:

    a. Prepare a statement of cash flows for Walton Imports for the year ended December 31, 2004, using the direct method for operating activities.

    b. In which of the three categories of activities did Walton use the majority of its cash during 2004?

    c. What does your answer to the previous question tell you about Walton Imports?

    d. From which of the three types of activities did Walton obtain the majority of its cash during 2004?

    e. Is the activity you identified in the previous requirement an appropriate source of cash in the long run? Explain your reasoning.

LO 4: FINANCIAL RATIO CALCULATIONS

10–37. This problem is a continuation of either problem 10–35 or 10–36. Use the Walton Imports financial statements in 10–35 and the statement of cash flows you prepared for problem 10–35 or 10–36 to complete the following requirements.

Required:

    a. Calculate operating cash flow to current debt ratio.

    b. Calculate the operating cash flow coverage ratio.

    c. What do these ratios tell you about the company? Explain your answer.

LO 4: STATEMENT OF CASH FLOWS CONCEPTS

10–38. Below is Steve Frim Company's statement of cash flows for the year ended December 31, 2005:

Steve Frim Company
Statement of Cash Flows
For the Year Ended December 31, 2005
(in thousands)

Cash Flows from Operating Activities:

Net income		$ 389
Adjustments to reconcile net income		
to net cash provided by operating activities:		
Depreciation expense	$ 131	
Increase in accounts receivable	(287)	

Increase in merchandise inventory	(104)	
Increase in prepaid expense	(70)	
Decrease in accounts payable	(4)	(334)
Net cash provided by operating activities		$ 55

Cash Flows from Investing Activities:
Purchase of building	$(1,255)	
Purchase of equipment	(304)	
Net cash used by investing activities		(1,559)

Cash Flows from Financing Activities:
Proceeds from long-term loan	$ 800	
Proceeds from sale of common stock	300	
Payment of cash dividends	(100)	
Net cash provided by financing activities		1,000
Net decrease in cash during 2005		$ (504)
Cash balance, January 1, 2005		1,200
Cash balance, December 31, 2005		$ 696

Required: Respond to the following questions:

a. For which of the three broad types of activities did Frim use the majority of its cash during 2005?
b. What does your answer to the previous question tell you about Frim Company?
c. From which of the three broad types of activities did Frim obtain the majority of its cash during 2005?
d. Is the activity you identified in the previous requirement an appropriate source of cash in the long run? Explain your reasoning.

LO 4: FINANCIAL RATIO CALCULATIONS

10–39. Refer to problem 10–38. Use the statement of cash flows in problem 10–38 to complete the following requirements.

Required: Assume that average current liabilities total $338,000 and average total liabilities total $1,180,000.

a. Calculate operating cash flow to current debt ratio.
b. Calculate the operating cash flow coverage ratio.
c. What do these ratios tell you about the company? Explain your answer.

LO 4: STATEMENT OF CASH FLOWS CONCEPTS

10–40. Below is Flaherty Company's statement of cash flows for the year ended December 31, 2005:

Flaherty Company
Statement of Cash Flows
For the Year Ended December 31, 2005
(in thousands)

Cash Flows from Operating Activities:
Net income		$ 1,608
Adjustments to reconcile net income to net cash provided by operating activities:		
Depreciation expense	$ 218	
Increase in accounts receivable	(341)	
Decrease in merchandise inventory	81	
Increase in prepaid expense	(100)	
Increase in accounts payable	154	12
Net cash provided by operating activities		$ 1,620

Cash Flows from Investing Activities:
Purchase of building	$(1,000)	
Purchase of equipment	(200)	
Net cash used by investing activities		(1,200)

Cash Flows from Financing Activities:

Repayment of long-term loan	$ (350)	
Proceeds from sale of common stock	350	
Payment of cash dividends	(100)	
Net cash used by financing activities		(100)
Net increase in cash during 2005		$ 320
Cash balance, January 1, 2005		430
Cash balance, December 31, 2005		$ 750

Required: Respond to the following questions:

a. For which of the three types of activities did Flaherty use the majority of its cash during 2005?

b. What does your answer to the previous question tell you about Flaherty Company?

c. From which of the three types of activities did Flaherty obtain the majority of its cash during 2005?

d. Is the activity you identified in the previous requirement an appropriate source of cash in the long run? Explain your reasoning.

LO 4: FINANCIAL RATIO CALCULATIONS

10–41. Refer to problem 10–40. Use the statement of cash flows in problem 10–40 to complete the following requirements.

Required: Assume that average current liabilities total $680,000 and average total liabilities total $1,790,000.

a. Calculate operating cash flow to current debt ratio.

b. Calculate the operating cash flow coverage ratio.

c. What do these ratios tell you about the company? Explain your answer.

LO 4: ANALYSIS OF CASH FLOW INFORMATION

10–42. Below are the totals from the main three sections of Kay Carnes and Company's most recent statement of cash flows:

Net cash provided by operating activities	$ 1,812,000
Net cash used by investing activities	$(1,280,000)
Net cash used by financing activities	$ (153,000)

Required:

a. What do these totals tell you about Carnes and Company?

b. What additional information would you want to see before you analyze Carnes and Company's ability to generate positive cash flow in the future?

c. Did Carnes and Company have a net income or loss for the period? What additional information would you want before trying to predict the company's net income for the next period?

LO 4: ANALYSIS OF CASH FLOW INFORMATION

10–43. Below are the totals from the main three sections of Mary D. Maury and Company's most recent statement of cash flows:

Net cash used by operating activities	$ (835,000)
Net cash used by investing activities	$(1,280,000)
Net cash provided by financing activities	$ 2,153,000

Required:

a. What do these totals tell you about Maury and Company?

b. What additional information would you want to see before you analyze Maury and Company's ability to generate positive cash flow in the future?

c. Did Maury and Company have a net income or loss for the period? What additional information would you want before trying to predict the company's net income for the next period?

LO 4: ANALYSIS OF CASH FLOW INFORMATION

10–44. Below are the totals from the main three sections of Paul Smolenski and Company's most recent statement of cash flows:

Net cash used by operating activities	$(1,409,000)
Net cash provided by investing activities	$ 1,980,000
Net cash used by financing activities	$ (303,000)

Required:

    a. What do these totals tell you about Smolenski and Company?

    b. What additional information would you want to see before you analyze Smolenski and Company's ability to generate positive cash flow in the future?

LO 4: DISCUSSION

10–45. One of the main purposes of the statement of cash flows is to disclose a company's sources of cash during a specific time period and what it used the cash for. From this standpoint, the statement of cash flows is considered a tool of accounting. Such tools are developed to solve problems.

Required:

    a. Explain in your own words how the income statement and balance sheet using accrual accounting take the focus off cash.

    b. Describe how the statement of cash flows serves as a tool to bring the focus of economic decision makers back to cash.

LO 4: DISCUSSION—DIRECT METHOD VERSUS INDIRECT METHOD

10–46. Compare the two methods for preparing the statement of cash flows, the direct method and the indirect method. Which sections are different and which sections are the same?

LO 3: COMPLEX EQUIPMENT SALE AND PURCHASE CALCULATIONS

10–47. The Calvert Company is preparing a statement of cash flows for the year ended December 31, 2004. Selected beginning and ending account balances are as follows:

	Beginning	Ending
Machinery	$450,000	$475,500
Accumulated depreciation—machinery	(95,000)	(129,000)
Loss on sale of machinery		(2,000)

During the year, the company received $44,500 for a machine that cost $49,500 and purchased other items of equipment.

Required:

    a. Compute the depreciation on machinery for the year.

    b. Compute the amount of machinery purchases for the year.

LO 3: COMPLEX EQUIPMENT SALE AND PURCHASE CALCULATIONS

10–48. Charles Lewis Company is preparing a statement of cash flows for the year ended December 31, 2005. Selected beginning and ending account balances are as follows:

	Beginning	Ending
Machinery	$250,000	$280,000
Accumulated depreciation—machinery	(65,000)	(89,000)
Gain on sale of machinery		2,000

During the year, the company received $50,000 for a machine that cost $65,000 and purchased some other items of equipment.

Required:

    a. Compute the depreciation on machinery for the year.

    b. Compute the amount of machinery purchases for the year.

LO 3: COMPLEX EQUIPMENT SALE AND PURCHASE CALCULATIONS

10–49. The Morrissey Company is preparing a statement of cash flows for the year ended December 31, 2004. Selected beginning and ending account balances are as follows:

	Beginning	Ending
Computers	$300,000	$390,000
Accumulated depreciation—computers	165,000	215,000
Gain on sale of computers		12,000

During the year, the company received $20,000 for a computer that cost $40,000 and purchased other items of equipment.

Required:

   a. Compute the depreciation on computers for the year.
   b. Compute the amount of computer purchases for the year.

Financial Reporting Exercises

10–50. Using the ***Securities and Exchange Commission***'s (***SEC***'s) Electronic Data Gathering, Analysis, and Retrieval (EDGAR) system, obtain a copy of the ***Guess, Inc.,*** income statement and balance sheet for 2001 and 2000 from the company's Form 10-K from 2001.

Required:

   a. Does this company use the direct or indirect method for their operating cash flows?
   b. List the total cash flows for the operating, investing, and financing activities sections for 2001 and state whether you think the number is favorable or not.
   c. Calculate the operating cash flow to current debt ratio for 2001.
   d. Calculate the operating cash flow coverage ratio for 2001.
   e. Based on this information, what impression do you get about this company as an investment possibility?

10–51. Using the SEC's EDGAR system, obtain a copy of the ***Liz Claiborne, Inc.,*** income statement and balance sheet for 2001 and 2000 from the company's Form 10-K from 2001.

Required:

   a. Does this company use the direct or indirect method for their operating cash flows?
   b. List the total cash flows for the operating, investing, and financing activities sections for 2001 and state whether you think the number is favorable or not.
   c. Calculate the operating cash flow to current debt ratio for 2001.
   d. Calculate the operating cash flow coverage ratio for 2001.
   e. Based on the information about these two companies (***Guess, Inc.,*** and ***Liz Claiborne, Inc.***), circle for each ratio which number you think is more favorable. Which company would you be more likely to invest in?

10–52. Visit the PHLIP Web site for this book at *www.prenhall.com/werner* to locate the ***Walt Disney Company*** link. Find ***Disney***'s statement of cash flows to answer the following questions.

Required:

   a. List the total cash flows for operating, investing, and financing activities for each of the years shown in the report's statement of cash flows.
   b. Does the company use the direct or indirect method of preparing the statement of cash flows?
   c. Have the operating cash flows been positive?
   d. List the transactions that affect the cash flow for investing activities.
   e. List the transactions that affect the cash flow for financing activities.
   f. Write a brief report that summarizes your feelings regarding information provided by ***Disney***'s statements of cash flows.

10–53. Visit the PHLIP Web site for this book at *www.prenhall.com/werner* to find the ***Coca-Cola Company*** link. Find ***Coke***'s statement of cash flows to answer the following questions.

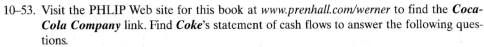

Required:

a. List the total cash flows for operating, investing, and financing activities for each of the years shown in the report's statement of cash flows.
b. Does the company use the direct or indirect method of preparing the statement of cash flows?
c. Have the operating cash flows been positive?
d. List the transactions that affect the cash flow for investing activities.
e. List the transactions that affect the cash flow for financing activities.
f. Write a brief report that summarizes your feelings regarding information provided by *Coca-Cola*'s statements of cash flows.

ANNUAL REPORT PROJECT

10–54. Section 10—The Statement of Cash Flows

In this assignment, you will prepare a report based on your company's statement of cash flows.

Required: Prepare a report that includes the following information:

a. A schedule that presents the cash flows from operating, investing, and financing activities for your company and that of its peer for the past three years.
b. Examine the operating cash flows. Have the operating cash flows been positive? Have the operating cash flows increased or decreased in the years presented? Are the operating cash flows sufficient to pay principal and interest on debt and meet other cash requirements? What method is used to prepare the operating activities section of the statement of cash flows, direct or indirect?
c. Examine investing cash flows. For each line presented in the investing section, discuss how it impacts the other financial statements and other parts of the annual report. Include the page number where you found the information. The management discussion and analysis may be a very good place to find this information.
d. Examine the financing cash flows. For each line presented in this section, discuss how it impacts other financial statements. The balance sheet and statement of stockholders' equity may be an excellent place to look.
e. Also comment on significant changes that have occurred over time regarding each company's sources and uses of cash. For example, have cash flows from operating activities been increasing or decreasing? Have cash flows from investing activities been increasing or decreasing? Have cash flows from financing activities been increasing or decreasing? Provide an explanation of the significance of the changes or the lack of change.
f. A schedule that presents the following ratios for your company with those of the peer company you selected:

   • Operating cash flows to current debt ratio for the current year
   • Operating cash flow coverage ratio for the current year

g. Comment in your report on the information that the comparison of each one of the ratios provides. How does your company compare to its peer?
h. Your report should conclude with a summary of what you think of your company's sources and uses of cash and your thoughts regarding how your company's statement of cash flows information compares to that of its peer.

CHAPTER 11

Financial Statement Analysis—A Closer Look

During lunch one day, your classmate Marcus tells you all about a company that has net income of $250,000. It's a small company owned by a mutual acquaintance, and you are both quite impressed with the profits the company has generated. You begin to dream about how wonderful it would be to own a company with that amount of income. It's a lot of money, and you think of all the nice things you could do with it.

A company that has a net income of $250,000 must be successful, stable, and profitable, right? Well, not necessarily. Even though income of $250,000 could be a sign of exceptional business performance, it could just as easily be the result of a dismal year of underachievement. For example, if the company had sales of $3 million and assets totaling $2 million, income of a quarter of a million dollars might be fine, but what if sales were a whopping $200 million or the investment in assets was a huge $100 million? In that case, an income of $250,000 would be unacceptably low. What's more, it's possible that the company's debt is so high and it generates so little cash that the owner will never get a dime of the company's profits.

In order to properly evaluate a company, we must not be tempted to use just one or two financial statement amounts to form our opinion. In fact, even if we examine every amount on an entire set of financial statements, it is unlikely that this alone will enable us to make a well-informed judgment regarding the company's potential for future success. Financial statements alone simply do not provide enough information to enable us to do this. We must consider other important factors such as general business conditions, the outlook for the company's industry, and the economic and political conditions that impact the business.

As we mentioned in previous chapters, the ***Securities and Exchange Commission (SEC)*** requires publicly traded companies to publish an annual report. It also requires companies to file other reports, such as an annual Form 10-K. These reports contain general information about the company and its business, at least five years of key financial information, income statements and statements of cash flows for three years, and balance sheets for two years. While these resources provide a wealth of information, gathering and reading it is just the first step in using the information to make a sound economic decision. For one thing, we need to look beyond the numbers. In other words, we can't just look at the financial statements—we must analyze them.

Financial statement analysis means looking beyond the face of the financial statements to gain additional insight into a company. In this chapter, we will focus primarily on ratio analysis—the most comprehensive form of financial statement analysis. Most of the material in this chapter will already be familiar to you. This is because in earlier chapters we introduced the computations of all the ratios we present in this chapter. In this chapter, we will show you something more important—how to use their results in proper combination with other information to make economic decisions.

Learning Objectives

After completing your work on this chapter, you should be able to do the following:

1. Identify the three major categories of users of financial statement analysis and describe the objectives of each.

2. Gather information to evaluate the political climate and general economic conditions and describe the ways each of them can affect business.

3. Locate sources of information about specific industries.

4. Describe the two industry classification systems and explain what a NAICS code or an SIC code indicates.

5. Describe the purpose of ratio analysis and the four aspects of business it helps users evaluate.

6. Calculate and use financial ratios designed to measure a company's profitability, efficiency, liquidity, and solvency, and evaluate a company's ratios compared to those of peer companies and industry averages.

7. Describe the limitations of financial statement analysis.

◆ FINANCIAL STATEMENT ANALYSIS—WHO DOES IT AND WHY

Why would someone take the time to analyze a company's financial statements? Well, usually because they are making an economic decision, and understanding the company's current position and what has happened to a company in the past can make that decision easier. The decision maker could be a potential creditor trying to decide whether to lend money to a company, a potential investor trying to decide whether to buy stock in the company, or a manager trying to select the best course of action for the company. Other decision makers include current and prospective employees, internal and external auditors, customers, suppliers, and government agencies. By providing additional insight, financial statement analysis helps decision makers reduce the risk of making poor choices. This is because financial statement analysis often uncovers financial strengths and weaknesses that would otherwise go unnoticed. Because there is an array of decision makers that might analyze financial statements, and because the objectives of each vary, their perspectives on the results of the analysis will differ.

In this chapter, we will focus on just three types of decision makers:

1. Creditors (short-term and long-term)
2. Equity investors (present and potential)
3. Company managers

Let's examine objectives of each of these economic decision makers.

OBJECTIVES OF CREDITORS

Some creditors make loans to companies for a relatively short period of time while others lend on a long-term basis. There are two major types of short-term creditors. One type, called *trade creditors*, provides goods and services to a business on credit and expects payment within whatever time period is customary in the industry (in most industries somewhere between 10 and 90 days). Normally, trade creditors don't charge interest, so the credit they extend to companies amounts to interest-free financing. Trade creditors analyze financial statements to determine whether they should grant or continue to grant credit to a particular customer. Their goal is to determine the likelihood that the customer will pay them promptly in the future.

Banks and other lending institutions also extend short-term credit to businesses. That is, they make short-term loans to companies, often in the form of credit lines that support the day-to-day operations of businesses. Unlike trade creditors, banks do charge interest. The objectives of both trade creditors and lending institutions, however, are quite similar. Both want to be assured that they will receive prompt payment for the credit they extend.

Long-term creditors have a very different perspective than short-term creditors. These creditors—generally banks and corporate bondholders—lend money to companies for relatively long time periods. Therefore, their principal objective in analyzing a company's financial statements is to acquire information to help them determine whether the company is likely to be financially healthy over the long haul. These creditors are trying to assure themselves that, in addition to making interest payments, their borrowers will be able to pay back loans when they finally come due.

OBJECTIVES OF EQUITY INVESTORS

In this context, equity investors are those who have purchased or might purchase an ownership interest in a company, meaning those that have already invested (current equity investors) and those that might invest in the future (potential equity investors). Equity investors expect a reasonable return *on* their investment and, ultimately, the return *of* their investment. As we mentioned in Chapter 3, the return for a corporate equity investor has two components:

1. Dividends—the distribution of corporate earnings to stockholders
2. Stock appreciation—the increase in the market value of stock between the time it is purchased and the time it is sold

Therefore, when analyzing financial statements, the principal objective of present and potential equity investors is to determine whether it is likely that the combination of dividends and stock appreciation will provide an adequate return. The return depends on the company's ability to generate income and cash in the future. This is because dividends can only be paid if a company has sufficient retained earnings and cash, both of which depend on a company's ability to generate earnings in the future. Further, many experts consider a company's ability to generate earnings to be the single most important factor affecting the value of its stock over time.

Both creditors and equity investors are external decision makers. However, financial statement analysis is also a useful tool for internal decision makers—namely, a company's management.

OBJECTIVES OF MANAGEMENT

management accounting The branch of accounting developed to meet the informational needs of internal decision makers.

financial accounting The branch of accounting developed to meet the informational needs of external decision makers.

Corporate managers are responsible for operating the company for the benefit of its owners. To make decisions on behalf of the company that maximize the use of company assets and to earn profits, managers rely on two types of information. Primarily, they use **management accounting** information—the information available only to insiders. Management accounting information also helps managers evaluate their company's performance. Corporate managers also use **financial accounting** information—the accounting information available to outsiders.

You may study management accounting as part of your later coursework, but for now, we will limit our discussion in this chapter to financial accounting information.

A corporate manager's performance is evaluated in large part by the financial success of his or her company as reflected in the company's financial statements. Therefore, these managers have a personal stake in seeing the company appear as successful as possible in the financial statements.

It is a legitimate objective to present the company in its best light, since a company's relationship with creditors, stockholders, and other outsiders is vital. However, a corporate manager's own self-interest combined with his or her justifiable desire to analyze the company's financial statements in a way that favorably impresses external parties can lead to managing the financial statements rather than managing the business. *Enron, WorldCom,* and *Global Crossing* quickly come to mind as examples of companies in which corporate managers ceased to manage the business and, instead, managed the numbers.

Some corporate executives have yielded to the pressure to show a strong financial picture by falsifying amounts that appear on their company's financial statements. This devastating practice not only compromises the managers' own personal integrity, but also the integrity of all accounting information. These unscrupulous managers have allowed greed and their desire for power, prestige, and wealth to damage part of the very fabric on which our economic markets are based—reliable financial information. If economic decision makers cannot rely on the information companies provide, they lose faith in the information and they also lose faith in the companies themselves.

Unfortunately, this loss of faith is not limited to the companies that have been implicated in such falsifications. It extends to other companies as suspicions grow and the integrity of all financial reporting comes into question. This is because decision makers who need to use the information are unable to tell the difference between information that includes falsifications and information that doesn't. The result is that everyone loses faith in all financial information as more and more cases of "aggressive accounting" and outright falsification of financial information surface.

Discussion Questions ●

11–1. What do you think the phrase "managing the financial statements rather than managing the business" means?

11–2. Assume you have invested $10,000 in Company A and $10,000 in Company B. Both are solid companies according to their financial statements. In fact, their financial statements look quite similar to one another. Then, Company A goes bankrupt, shocking the financial community. The value of your investment in Company A plummets to a fraction of what it once was. It turns out that the company's financial statements had been doctored in some way to conceal huge financial weaknesses. In light of what happened to your investment in Company A, how do you feel about your investment in Company B?

Now that we have discussed the basic objectives of three primary financial information users, we will explore how to gather the background information you will need for financial statement analysis.

◆ GATHERING BACKGROUND INFORMATION—AN IMPORTANT FIRST STEP

In the appendix to Chapter 1, we discussed how you could find background information on virtually any publicly traded company. If you want to do a thorough analysis of a company's financial statements, use the sources in that chapter's appendix to gather enough information to put the company's financial statement information in proper context. Businesses do not operate in a vacuum, so it is important to also gather background information about a company's external environment. In its *Conceptual Framework of Accounting*, the Financial Accounting Standards Board (FASB) warns that external factors can seriously affect a company's performance:

> *Those who use financial information for business and economic decisions need to combine information provided by financial reporting with pertinent information from other sources, for example, information about general economic conditions or expectations, political events and political climate, or industry outlook.*[1]

When we are analyzing data from financial statements, we should also consider the three factors mentioned by the FASB: general economic conditions, political events and the political climate, and the industry outlook.

GENERAL ECONOMIC CONDITIONS AND EXPECTATIONS

The general economic environment in which a company operates affects its business activity and therefore its financial results. For a company producing goods bought by the general public, bright economic conditions generally enhance sales. For a company manufacturing and selling equipment to other companies, an economy that encourages business growth is an important positive factor. So we must first consider general economic conditions and expectations when evaluating the performance and overall financial position of a business.

---

[1] Statement of Financial Accounting Concepts No. 1, paragraph 22.

The health of the American economy and information about anticipated changes in economic conditions receives widespread daily news coverage. Popular business periodicals such as *BusinessWeek*, the *Wall Street Journal*, and *Fortune* inform their readers about current economic conditions. Business analysts, economists, and politicians often voice their views on television and radio. Additionally, statistical data on measures of economic health (e.g., gross domestic product, consumer price index) are available in such books as *The Economic Indicators Handbook*. The U.S. Department of Commerce, in a monthly publication called *Survey of Current Business*, provides data from dozens of general economic and business cycle indicators. Remember, though, all of these "expert" predictions of the future of the United States and world economies are, in fact, nothing more than educated guesses. Use this information carefully!

Although general economic conditions certainly affect a company's performance, we should not totally excuse poor company performance because the economy is in a downturn. Neither should a company's exceptional performance be dismissed as simply the product of a healthy economy. *Kmart* declared bankruptcy at the same time business was booming at *Target* and *Wal-Mart*. *Lowe's Home Improvement* has been expanding rapidly over the past decade, while *Home Base* went out of business. And no one believes that *Enron*'s collapse was due totally to what was happening in the economy. Economic conditions provide *one context* within which we evaluate the results of business activity. We must also consider other external factors.

POLITICAL EVENTS AND POLITICAL CLIMATE

Politics is the second external factor mentioned by the FASB. The terms *political events* and *political climate* are closely related, yet they are different. A political event is an action that has already taken place, whereas a political climate is a situation that can lead to an action.

Each political party takes credit when the general economy improves and blames the others when it declines. That's the nature of politics. The truth is that both improvement and decline in the general economy result from many interrelated and complex factors. Indeed, the factors affecting the general economy are so complicated and intertwined that no political party can control it enough to take credit or blame. Still, there is no question that what goes on in politics, both domestic and foreign, has a significant influence on the general economy as well as on the world of business. The actions taken by Congress and the president on such matters as the amount of government regulation, income taxes, health care, and welfare reform have an enormous impact on the general economy. And we know that changes in the general economy will affect the level of business activity.

In the last decade of the 20th century, the collapse of the Soviet Union, the reunification of Germany, and other world political events that marked the end of the Cold War had strong repercussions in the U.S. economy. These foreign political events changed the entire defense industry, which created a ripple effect on many other industries and the communities that depend on them. Reduced purchases by the Pentagon of items used for national defense, for example, forced such companies as *Motorola, Lockheed,* and *Rockwell International* to make major adjustments in their businesses.

Certainly no one would question the impact the terrorist attack on the World Trade Center on September 11, 2001, had on the United States economy, and indeed, on that of the rest of the world. When President Bush announced the war on terrorism shortly after the attack, the implication for companies in the defense industry was enormous.

In the United States, the political climate is generally reflected in public opinion. For the past three decades, the public has scrutinized companies' positions on social and environmental issues. The concept of being "politically correct" arose from such public scrutiny. As we discussed in Chapter 1, a wise firm pays close attention to its social responsibility and frequently describes its corporate citizenship in its annual report. A growing number of investors have resolved to invest their money only in companies that have a genuine commitment to responsible behavior. This trend has generated a broader sense of social responsibility in American corporations.

Where, then, can you find accurate, objective information about a company's corporate citizenship? Your library most likely has publications intended to give you this information, but the evaluations you read will reflect the writer's views of corporate social responsibility, which may not coincide with your own. We suggest that instead of naively accepting such appraisals, you carefully consider the perspective of each author.

INDUSTRY OUTLOOK

The third factor to consider when using financial information is the industry in which a company operates, because industry affiliation may define the company's prospects for future growth. As Roy Taub, vice president of Standard and Poor's, once pointed out:

> *The industry is the environment in which the company operates and it defines both the opportunities the company may seize and the challenges it must face.*[2]

Industry opportunities and challenges are key considerations in evaluating a company's outlook. For example, a company in an industry that is facing an overall decline in demand may be powerless to take any action to ensure its own future growth. As we mentioned earlier, cuts in the federal defense budget resulted in reduced demand for such items as military aircraft and tanks, affecting the entire industry producing these goods. Certainly, this type of industry-wide trend touches all companies within the industry.

Government action is not the only force that produces industry-wide effects. Technological change often spurs spectacular growth within an industry. The field of telecommunications, for instance, has undergone a revolution in the past two decades. Just a few years ago, the fax machine was an expensive luxury—a form of communication reserved for "big business." Today, most personal computers come from the factory with internal fax capabilities.

Often, a technological change that opens the doors of opportunity in one industry closes them in another. For example, the development of personal computers has virtually wiped out opportunities for expansion among companies producing typewriters. But remember that each threat produces opportunity. Adaptable companies change their product mix to seize upon new opportunities and discontinue product lines that no longer have markets. So when considering a company's outlook for the future, it is important to learn what likely lies ahead for the entire industry.

Discussion Question

11–3. Changes in society, family structures, and the way people behave and interact have always had dramatic impact on business. Cite two examples of such changes in your lifetime, identify industries they have affected, and describe how they did so.

Not only does a company's industry affiliation affect its opportunities, but it may also define the challenges ahead. For example, a few decades ago, companies did not have to consider the environmental impact of their actions. After the Environmental Protection Agency (EPA) was established, however, many companies were forced to spend significant amounts of money to comply with EPA regulations. These regulations cost some industries more than others. For example, when the EPA banned the use of DDT as a pesticide, companies that manufactured this product either had to convert their factories to produce other products or they went out of business. The impact of this ban was also felt in agriculture, as farmers who had depended on DDT as their primary pesticide were forced to switch to less effective, sometimes more expensive, products.

The flip side of government regulation is deregulation. When the government suddenly discontinues its regulation and frees the market, this has an impact on all companies operating within the deregulated industry. For example, when the federal government deregulated the commercial airline industry in the early 1980s, all airlines were affected. Prior to deregulation, the federal government set standard airfares. All airlines flying passengers from one specific destination to another were required to charge the

[2]*S&P*, 1983, p. 2.

same fare. Companies competed on amenities (in-flight movies, food, drink, and the like), not on price. The government also required airlines to operate unprofitable flights for the convenience of customers in underpopulated areas. Fares of profitable flights were set high enough to offset the companies' losses from these unprofitable flights.

With deregulation came competition. Forced to make every flight profitable, airlines canceled many routes and began scrambling to attract customers. The result was a price war that forced several legendary carriers such as ***Pan American Airlines*** and ***Eastern Airlines*** out of business. Deregulation was seen by newer "upstart" companies such as ***Southwest Airlines*** and ***America West Airlines*** as an opportunity. Unregulated competition became an environment of survival of the fittest, and many companies—both new and old—did not survive.

Discussion Questions

11-4. Identify two industries and describe their similarities and their differences.
11-5. If two companies offered you upper-level management positions—one from each of the industries you identified in your response to question 11-4—which would you take? Why?
11-6. If you had $2,000 to invest and your only option was to invest it all in one of two companies—one from each of the industries you identified in your response to question 11-4—which would you choose? Explain your reasoning.

Where do you look for information about a particular industry? Several sources are available. *Standard and Poor's Industry Surveys* is composed of numerous sections with various types of information. One section offers recent articles about each industry written by professional business analysts or drawn from business publications. Another good source is the *U.S. Industry & Trade Outlook*, which offers background information and projections for the 10 fastest-growing and 10 slowest-growing industries, 40 service industries, and over 150 manufacturing industries. This book includes references to sources that contain more detailed information about each industry. *Mergent's Industry Review* provides comparative statistics on specific industries. These are three good examples available in your library.

Heeding the warning of the FASB, economic decision makers should gather background information regarding general economic conditions and expectations, political climate and events, and industry outlook. Anyone analyzing financial statements must consider the impact of each of these factors on a company's past performance and its future prospects, for they provide the context within which financial data should be evaluated.

Now we turn to actually analyzing financial statement information.

◆ ANALYZING FINANCIAL STATEMENTS—*PIER 1 IMPORTS*

In the sections that follow, we will analyze the financial statements of ***Pier 1 Imports, Inc.*** As you may know, ***Pier 1 Imports*** is an international specialty retailer of decorative home furnishings, furniture, and gifts. The company was established in 1962 and now has over 900 stores and more than 17,500 employees. A copy of ***Pier 1***'s 2002 annual report (on page F–503) is included as an appendix to this text. Since the computation of each ratio will be illustrated using the ***Pier 1*** financial statements presented in the company's 2002 annual report, take a look at it before you try to follow the ratio calculations and the way we analyze them. Be certain you understand how we determine which items from the balance sheet, income statement, and statement of cash flows we use for each ratio.

We will calculate 17 financial ratios using ***Pier 1 Imports***' 2002 financial statements as an example. As you recall, we included ratio calculations near the end of several earlier chapters. Because of this, you should have no difficulty understanding the calculations we present. In fact, the calculations are exactly the same as those in earlier chapters. Exhibit 11–1 on page F–454 presents a list of the 17 ratios we will use as we analyze ***Pier 1***'s financial statements.

EXHIBIT 11-1   Summary of Key Ratios

Ratio	Calculation	Purpose of Ratio	Reference
Profitability Ratios			
1. Gross profit margin ratio	$\dfrac{\text{Gross profit}}{\text{Net sales}}$	Measures the percentage gross profit generated by each sales dollar	Chapter 4, page F–134
2. Net profit margin ratio	$\dfrac{\text{Net income}}{\text{Net sales}}$	Measures the percentage profit generated by each sales dollar	Chapter 4, page F–134
3. Rate of return on assets ratio	$\dfrac{\text{Net income} + \text{Interest expense}}{\text{Average total assets}}$	Measures the rate of return earned on investment in assets	Chapter 4, page F–135
4. Rate of return on common equity ratio	$\dfrac{\text{Net income} - \text{Preferred dividend}}{\text{Average common stockholders' equity}}$	Measures the rate of return earned on investment in equity	Chapter 4, page F–135
5. Dividend payout ratio	$\dfrac{\text{Cash dividends}}{\text{Net income}}$	Indicates the proportion of net income paid out in dividends	Chapter 4, page F–136
6. Earnings per share	$\dfrac{\text{Net income} - \text{Preferred dividend}}{\text{Average common shares outstanding}}$	Measures the earning per common share of stock	Chapter 4, page F–136, and Chapter 9, page F–372
7. Price-to-earnings ratio	$\dfrac{\text{Average market price per share of stock}}{\text{Earnings per share}}$	A measure of the market price per common share compared to the earnings per share	Chapter 4, page F–137
Efficiency Ratios			
8. Asset turnover ratio	$\dfrac{\text{Net sales}}{\text{Average total assets}}$	Indicates a firm's ability to generate revenues from a given level of assets	Chapter 9, page F–376
9. Receivables turnover ratio	$\dfrac{\text{Net sales}}{\text{Average accounts receivable}}$	An indication of the quality of a company's accounts receivable; indicates how quickly a company collects its accounts receivable	Chapter 9, page F–378
10. Inventory turnover ratio	$\dfrac{\text{Cost of goods sold}}{\text{Average inventory}}$	An indication of the quality of a company's inventory; indicates how long a company holds inventory	Chapter 8, page F–328
Liquidity Ratios			
11. Current ratio	$\dfrac{\text{Current assets}}{\text{Current liabilities}}$	Indicates a company's ability to meet short-term obligation	Chapter 9, page F–378
12. Quick ratio	$\dfrac{\text{Cash} + \text{Short-term investments} + \text{Current receivables}}{\text{Current liabilities}}$	Measures short-term liquidity more stringently than the current ratio does	Chapter 9, page F–379
13. Operating cash flow to current debt ratio	$\dfrac{\text{Cash provided by operating activities}}{\text{Average current liabilities}}$	A measure of the sufficiency of cash provided by operating activities relative to current liabilities	Chapter 10, page F–423

Solvency Ratios			
14. Debt ratio	$\dfrac{\text{Total liabilities}}{\text{Total assets}}$	Measures the proportion of assets financed by debt	Chapter 3, page F–92
15. Debt-to-equity ratio	$\dfrac{\text{Total liabilities}}{\text{Total equity}}$	Compares the amount of debt financing to the amount of equity financing	Chapter 3, page F–93
16. Times interest earned ratio	$\dfrac{\text{Earnings before interest and income taxes}}{\text{Interest expense}}$	Indicates a company's ability to make its periodic interest payments	Chapter 9, page F–379
17. Operating cash flow coverage ratio	$\dfrac{\text{Cash provided by operating activities}}{\text{Average total liabilities}}$	A measure of the sufficiency of cash provided by operating activities relative to total liabilities	Chapter 10, page F–423

EXHIBIT 11–1 *Continued*

A particular ratio for just one company for a single year doesn't tell you very much. Let's think of it this way. Suppose your friend Mark tells you that he walked from one end of Duval Street to the other in 20 minutes. Would you be impressed? You might be if you knew something about Duval Street. What if he told you that the first time he walked the length of Duval Street it took him over an hour, or what if you knew that it took three of your other friends 45 minutes to walk it? Once you had this additional information for comparison, you would probably be impressed that Mark was able to improve his time so much and that he could walk the distance so much faster than his peers. For information to really take on life, we need a basis for judgment.

Once we calculate these 17 ratios for *Pier 1 Imports,* how will we use them to evaluate the business? Financial ratios are bits of data that only become valuable information when they are used in comparison to prior years' ratios, to peer companies, or to industry averages. This kind of interpretation is what we would call the "art of ratio analysis."

After we show how to calculate each ratio, we will present a chart that depicts that ratio for as many years as we have data. Since we are using only the information included in *Pier 1*'s annual report published in 2002, we have enough data to calculate many ratios for five years. For other ratios, we will be forced to present fewer years due to the lack of data.

In addition to presenting *Pier 1*'s ratios, we will compare the results with the ratios of two peer companies. **Peer companies** are companies that are similar to one another, usually in the same industry and of similar size, which analysts use for financial comparisons.

It would be best if the peer companies we use are in the same industry as *Pier 1.* Therefore, before we discuss the selection of peer companies, you need to understand something about the systems that are used to classify companies into industry groupings.

peer companies
Companies that are similar to one another, usually in the industry and of similar size.

INDUSTRY CLASSIFICATIONS

Industry classifications are a key component of selecting peer companies. In the United States, there are two widely used industry classification systems: the *North American Industry Classification System (NAICS),* and the *Standard Industrial Classification (SIC)* system.

NAICS (pronounced Nakes) is rapidly becoming the most widely accepted industry classification system in the United States. NAICS was developed by representatives of the governments of the United States, Canada, and Mexico (hence the name North American Industry Classification System) in 1997 to replace the Standard Industrial

Classification (SIC) system. The SIC system was established by the United States Office of Management and Budget in 1987.

NAICS uses six-digit codes to specify the industry in which a company operates. In developing NAICS, the United States, Canada, and Mexico agreed that the first five digits of the code would be universal and useful for comparing industry information among the three countries. They further agreed that the sixth digit would allow each country to further subdivide the industries specified in the five-digit categories. In the United States, all NAICS codes have six digits, and if there is no subdivision of a particular industry, the sixth digit is a zero.

You might think that as soon as NAICS was put in place the SIC system (which uses four-digit codes) would quickly go by the wayside. Such has not been the case. Many financial institutions, publications, and government agencies continue to use the four-digit SIC system. For example, federal agencies such as the Occupational Safety and Health Administration (OSHA) and the SEC still use the SIC system. Further, even though NAICS has been in existence since 1997, many business publications either have not yet switched to NAICS or have done so only recently. For example, the *Almanac of Business and Industrial Financial Ratios*, a leading annual business publication, did not switch from the SIC system to NAICS until its 2002 edition.

Any business can be classified by industry using the NAICS or SIC system. If you would like to find the industry classification for a publicly traded company, all you have to do is visit the SEC's Web site at *www.sec.gov.* This Web site can provide the SIC code for a particular company, and in addition, it can provide a list of companies within the same SIC classification. For example, **Pier 1 Imports**' SIC code on the SEC's Electronic Data Gathering, Analysis, and Retrieval (EDGAR) system is 5700.

But what if the company we are analyzing is not registered with the SEC? You can visit the NAICS Web site. As long as you have some knowledge regarding the company's line of business, you can determine an appropriate industry classification code for any company. To find **Pier 1**'s classification code, let's begin with the assumption that we know **Pier 1** is a retailer and that it sells household furnishings, furniture, and gifts. Type in the address, *www.census.gov/epcd/www/naicstab.htm,* or type "NAICS" into almost any Internet browser. For **Pier 1,** the closest NAICS code description is *Retail Trade, Furniture and Home Furnishings Stores,* which corresponds to NAICS code 442000. If you know a company's SIC code and wish to find the corresponding NAICS code, visit the NAICS Web site and click on *Correspondence between NAICS and SIC.* Then, follow the prompts until you find the corresponding NAICS code.

By now, you probably know more about industry classification systems than you ever wanted to know, but if you still want to learn more about the background and development of NAICS, or want more information about the differences between NAICS and the SIC, visit the U.S. Census Web site at *www.census.gov/epcd/www/naicsdev.htm.*

FINDING PEER COMPANIES

Once we know a company's NAICS code or SIC, how can we find peer companies to use as comparisons in our financial analysis? There are several ways, and we are going to show you how to find peer companies using the SEC's Web site. It's really quite simple. First, visit the SEC's Web site at *www.sec.gov,* and use the EDGAR system to look up the company you are analyzing. Then all you have to do is to click on the company's SIC code, 5700 for **Pier 1,** and a list of all the companies in that industry classification will appear. You can use that list to find peer companies for financial comparisons.

We looked at the 10-Ks (which include annual financial statements) for several companies listed by the SEC for SIC 5700. We were trying to find companies that were about the same size as **Pier 1** and that had a fairly similar business style. After eliminating many of the companies because they were too small or their line of business didn't seem close enough, we chose **Bed Bath & Beyond** and **Williams-Sonoma** as the peer companies we would use as comparisons to evaluate **Pier 1 Imports.** These two companies are classified along with **Pier 1** under SIC 5700. Although they do not sell the exact same products as **Pier 1 Imports,** they are of similar size. Like **Pier 1,** their products cover a limited spectrum (as opposed to a department store that sells just about every kind of product), and like **Pier 1,** they compete with independent businesses and selected departments of major department stores. In addition, all three companies have assets and sales in the billions of dollars.

INDUSTRY AVERAGES

We can also compare the company we are analyzing to the ratios for its entire industry. The *Almanac of Business and Industrial Financial Ratios* (hereafter referred to simply as "the Almanac") is a book published annually that lists selected key ratios for over 190 industries and is the publication we will use for industry comparisons in this chapter. Other widely used sources of industry averages include the **Risk Management Association**'s (**RMA**'s) *Annual Statement Studies* and **Dunn & Bradstreet**'s *Industry Norms and Key Business Ratios.*

Regardless of the source, your first step in making an industry comparison is to determine the company's NAICS code or SIC. Although the Almanac began using NAICS in its 2002 edition, it includes an appendix that cross-references the SIC system to NAICS.

Data in the Almanac are compiled from approximately 4.8 million corporate federal income tax returns. Gathering data from the **IRS** rather than other publicly available sources of financial information has two distinct advantages: (1) Information about all active corporations is included (other sources include only large or publicly held corporations); and (2) because of substantial penalties for misreporting, corporate data submitted to the **IRS** are generally more reliable than that from other sources.

Information provided in the Almanac for each industry is reported in two tables. Table I provides an analysis of all companies in the particular industry, regardless of whether they had any net income or a net loss. Table II provides the same information items as Table I, but it considers only companies that showed a net income. Exhibit 11–2 on page F–458 shows a portion of Table II for industry classification 442000, the NAICS code for **Pier 1 Imports,** from the 2002 edition of the Almanac.

Note that Table II in Exhibit 11–2 arranges the ratios in 13 columns. The first column ("Total") provides industry averages for all companies in the industry. The other columns provide averages for companies based on their total assets. When we compare **Pier 1**'s ratios to industry averages, we will use the first column (the total column) and the last column (for companies with assets in excess of $250 million). This is because we would like to see how **Pier 1** compares with the entire industry and to companies of somewhat similar size.

Now that we have selected our peer companies and we know something about industry averages, we are ready to present the calculations and interpretations of the financial ratios we will use to evaluate **Pier 1 Imports, Inc.**

◆ CALCULATING FINANCIAL RATIOS AND INTERPRETING THEIR RESULTS

Ratio analysis, as we explained earlier, is a method of analyzing the relationship between two items from a company's financial statements. We said important relationships may exist between two items on the same financial statement or between two items from different financial statements. All the ratios we calculate here are based on information from the balance sheets, income statements, and statements of cash flows for **Pier 1 Imports, Inc., Bed Bath & Beyond,** and **Williams-Sonoma** published in 2002.

Understand that the absolute numbers resulting from the calculations are of little value in themselves. It's like the friend telling you that he walked the length of Duval Street in 20 minutes. So what! It is the *analysis* and *interpretation* of the numbers—the art of ratio analysis—that provides the usefulness. For the ratios to be truly useful to economic decision makers, an analyst must compare those ratios to other information, such as the company's ratios in past years, the ratios of peer companies, or industry averages. So, in addition to calculating the ratios for just a single year, we will present a

Table II
Corporations with Net Income
Furniture and Home Furnishings Stores
Money Amounts and Size of Assets in Thousands of Dollars

Item Description for Accounting Period 7/98 Through 6/99		Total	Zero Assets	Under 100	100 to 250	251 to 500	501 to 1,000	1,001 to 5,000	5,001 to 10,000	10,001 to 25,000	25,001 to 50,000	50,001 to 100,000	100,001 to 250,000	250,001 and over
Number of Enterprises	1	23738	132	6982	6338	3840	3523	2509	250	107	25	0	0	11
Revenues ($ in Thousands)														
Net Sales	2	56154823	434489	2525522	4771410	5055847	6555770	13112347	5018841	4406253	2563686	0	0	7861403
Interest	3	191413	691	60	23	2630	22699	48531	12025	7076	1731	0	0	60554
Rents	4	20227	0	0	0	0	431	2826	0	3316	2	0	0	7076
Royalties	5	21163	0	0	0	0	0	0	16395	4	0	0	0	2856
Other Portfolio Income	6	136135	1203	40	398	3111	10442	2661	5127	27783	303	0	0	68422
Other Receipts	7	519773	1183	2998	3390	16228	27008	110639	52879	83083	47852	0	0	99952
Total Receipts	8	57043534	437566	2528620	4776221	5077816	6616350	13277004	5105267	4527515	2613574	0	0	8100263
Average Total Receipts	9	2403	3315	362	753	1322	1878	5292	2041	42313	104543	•	•	736388
Operating Costs/Operating Income (%)														
Cost of Operations	10	62.6	63.3	62.0	64.7	61.5	63.6	63.0	67.0	66.6	69.2	•	•	55.0
Salaries and Wages	11	10.9	8.3	5.4	5.6	9.7	10.5	11.8	11.8	12.0	11.9	•	•	13.3
Taxes Paid	12	2.2	1.9	2.8	2.5	2.5	2.4	2.0	1.6	1.7	1.4	•	•	2.6
Interest Paid	13	0.8	0.5	0.2	0.5	0.4	0.8	0.7	0.4	0.6	0.9	•	•	1.5
Depreciation	14	1.0	0.3	0.9	0.9	0.6	0.9	0.8	0.7	1.0	0.8	•	•	2.3
Amortization and Depletion	15	0.1	0.1	0.0	0.1	0.0	0.0	0.0	0.0	0.0	0.0	•	•	0.4
Pensions and Other Deferred Comp.	16	0.2	•	0.1	0.0	0.2	0.5	0.2	0.3	0.3	0.1	•	•	0.2
Employee Benefits	17	0.6	0.1	0.4	0.3	0.5	0.6	0.5	0.0	0.5	0.0	•	•	1.1
Advertising	18	3.5	4.2	2.3	2.4	2.9	3.2	3.4	3.8	3.6	2.6	•	•	4.1
Other Expenses	19	12.4	10.4	15.0	15.2	14.2	10.9	11.2	10.4	10.1	10.4	•	•	14.6

EXHIBIT 11-2 Continued

20 Officers' Compensation	0.9	•	1.0	2.0	2.1	3.7	4.7	4.6	3.5	6.0	1.8	3.0
21 Operating Margin	4.1	•	1.1	1.7	1.3	2.7	2.1	3.0	4.3	4.9	9.1	2.7
22 Operating Margin Before Officers' Comp.	5.0	•	2.1	3.6	3.4	6.3	6.8	7.6	7.8	10.9	10.9	5.7

Selected Average Balance Sheet ($ in Thousands)

23 Net Receivables	53893	•	10154	3795	1871	446	136	59	35	7	0	175
24 Inventories	174356	•	12879	5197	2413	880	292	183	76	9	0	352
25 Net Property, Plant, and Equipment	148291	•	6020	2907	301	316	112	41	20	14	0	105
26 Total Assets	542318	•	35076	15125	6702	2063	724	357	165	48	0	944
27 Notes and Loans Payable	105536	•	10587	3065	1131	495	160	75	48	18	0	210
28 All Other Liabilities	181895	•	14278	5746	2331	668	196	115	59	16	0	311
29 Net Worth	255087	•	10212	6314	3240	900	368	168	59	15	0	423

Selected Financial Ratios (Times to 1)

30 Current Ratio	1.4	•	1.5	1.6	1.8	1.9	2.6	2.6	1.8	1.9	•	1.8
31 Quick Ratio	0.5	•	0.7	0.8	1.0	0.8	1.1	1.0	0.7	1.3	•	0.8
32 Net Sales to Working Capital	8.9	•	12.9	9.6	8.1	6.6	5.4	7.1	13.3	23.4	•	8.0
33 Coverage Ratio	5.6	•	4.5	8.4	8.4	6.5	4.9	10.2	9.3	21.4	21.4	6.7
34 Total Asset Turnover	1.3	•	2.9	2.7	3.0	2.5	2.6	3.7	4.6	7.5	•	2.5
35 Inventory Turnover	2.3	•	5.5	5.3	5.6	3.7	4.1	4.4	6.4	23.8	•	4.2
36 Receivables Turnover	•	•	•	•	•	•	•	•	•	•	•	•
37 Total Liabilities to Net Worth	1.1	•	2.4	1.4	1.1	1.3	1.0	1.1	1.8	2.2	•	1.2
38 Current Assets to Working Capital	3.6	•	3.2	2.6	2.2	2.1	1.6	1.6	2.3	2.2	•	2.2
39 Current Liabilities to Working Capital	2.6	•	2.2	1.6	1.2	1.1	0.6	0.6	1.3	1.2	•	1.2

EXHIBIT 11–2 *Continued*

Item Description for Accounting Period 7/98 Through 6/99		Total	Zero Assets	Under 100	100 to 250	251 to 500	501 to 1,000	1,001 to 5,000	5,001 to 10,000	10,001 to 25,000	25,001 to 50,000	50,001 to 100,000	100,001 to 250,000	250,001 and over
Working Capital to Net Sales	40	0.1	•	0.0	0.1	0.1	0.2	0.2	0.1	0.1	0.1	•	•	0.1
Inventory to Working Capital	41	1.2	•	0.6	1.3	1.0	0.8	1.1	1.0	1.2	1.6	•	•	2.2
Total Receipts to Cash Flow	42	8.4	6.4	6.6	7.8	8.1	9.6	9.5	10.2	9.2	9.6	•	•	6.6
Cost of Goods to Cash Flow	43	5.2	4.0	4.1	5.1	5.0	6.1	6.0	6.9	6.2	6.7	•	•	3.6
Cash Flow to Total Debt	44	0.5	•	1.6	0.9	0.9	0.5	0.5	0.6	0.5	0.4	•	•	0.4
Selected Financial Factors (in Percentages)														
Debt Ratio	45	55.2	•	69.1	64.5	53.0	49.2	56.4	51.7	58.3	70.9	•	•	53.0
Return on Total Assets	46	12.7	•	39.6	22.3	14.1	9.7	11.8	10.2	13.6	11.5	•	•	11.4
Return on Equity Before Income Taxes	47	24.1	•	122.0	56.1	27.0	15.3	22.9	18.7	28.8	30.7	•	•	19.9
Return on Equity After Income Taxes	48	20.8	•	120.6	55.4	26.1	13.8	20.8	15.5	26.9	27.9	•	•	13.4
Profit Margin (Before Income Tax)	49	4.3	9.8	5.0	4.4	3.4	3.0	3.9	3.0	4.4	3.1	•	•	7.1
Profit Margin (After Income Tax)	50	3.7	8.3	5.0	4.3	3.3	2.7	3.6	2.5	4.1	2.8	•	•	4.8

series of charts depicting *Pier 1*'s ratios for several years along with the ratios of the two peer companies we selected. Then we will briefly discuss the implications of the information presented in the chart. Seeing the charted ratios for three peer companies, for several years when possible, will bring meaning to the ratios and help you readily comprehend their implications.

Using the resources available over the internet, we could calculate ratios for each company going back 10 years or even more. However, for this introduction to financial statement analysis, we will limit our presentation to ratios that can be calculated using data from the annual reports published in 2002. In annual reports, the SEC requires companies to present selected financial information for five years, income statements and statements of cash flows for three years, and balance sheets for only two years. What this means is that we will be able to present five years of information for some ratios, three or four years for others, and only one year for still others. As we will see, if a ratio requires an average balance sheet amount, such as average inventory, with only two years of balance sheets available, we can calculate the average for only one year. You can track each of the ratios we present for *Pier 1 Imports* back to the annual report included with this text.

Let's address two more items before we begin computing the ratios:

- First, there is a lack of consistency among analysts in the way they calculate various ratios. Even when two analysts use the same name for a particular ratio, the calculations they use for the ratios may be different from one another. This inconsistency often makes it difficult to compare ratios calculated by different analysts or financial publications.

  One popular difference in the way ratios are calculated has to do with using average amounts for certain balance sheet items. In practice, many analysts use year-end amounts instead of averages when they calculate their ratios. For example, the analyst will use the year-end amount for total assets instead of average total assets. This way, the ratio calculations are simpler and the results are generally adequate. When completing the exercises in this text, use averages unless instructed otherwise.

- Second, virtually all ratios were developed by financial analysts, not accountants. What this means is that some of the ratio language (from analysts) does not match exactly with financial statement language (from accountants). For example, financial analysts may use the word *profit* in the ratios, whereas accountants may use the words *net income* in the financial statements. The two terms are synonymous but can cause confusion. As we proceed through the ratios, we will make certain to reconcile the descriptive terms used in the ratios with what they represent in the financial statement information.

Decision makers calculate a variety of ratios to gain meaningful insight into a company's past performance and current financial position. Don't get the idea that the 17 ratios we present represent a complete list of the financial ratios analysts use. In fact, there are so many useful and revealing financial ratios that it was difficult to limit our presentation to just 17 of them.

To fully assess a company's well-being, it is critically important that the analyst evaluate four important characteristics of the business: profitability, efficiency, liquidity, and solvency. The 17 ratios we present will provide you with a solid overview of *Pier 1*'s performance in each of those areas.

MEASURING PROFITABILITY

profitability The ease with which a company generates income.

Profitability is the ease with which a company generates income. If a company generates a high level of income very easily, it is said to have high profitability. All companies must maintain at least a minimum level of profitability to meet their obligations, such as servicing long-term debt and paying dividends to stockholders. Profitability ratios measure a firm's past performance. This past performance is generally helpful in predicting a company's future profitability level. Present stockholders, potential stockholders, and long-term creditors, therefore, use these ratios to evaluate investments.

Company managers use profitability ratios to monitor and evaluate their company's performance. A growing concern, however, is that some managers may be trying too desperately to improve their company's apparent performance and, thus, their profitability ratios. There are two potential reasons for this. First, managers may want to make the company's financial results look more appealing to external decision makers. Second, at least a portion of their own compensation may be directly tied to these profitability ratios, for often managers receive bonuses based on the level of profitability achieved by the company.

Stockholders and creditors also want the company to be profitable, but profitability ratios are based on short-term results (usually one year), and the only way to boost them is to attain the highest possible profit for any given year. That doesn't sound so bad, does it? Well, profits are not bad, but remember this:

> ### *A Preoccupation with Short-Term Profits is Detrimental to the Long-Term Value of a Business!*

Stockholders and creditors, then, generally take a longer-term view of the company's health than can be measured by profitability alone.

As you look at the profitability ratios in this section, focus both on what they should reveal about a company and on how they might encourage shortsighted behavior by management. It is quite common for managers to slant business decisions toward that which makes the ratios "look better" to the decision makers who are using their company's financial statements. In 2001, for example, *WorldCom* made itself appear more profitable by not including $3.8 billion of expenses in its income statement.

Discussion Question ●●●●●●●●●●●●●●●●●●●●●●●●●●●●●●●●●●

11–7. Give an example of a management decision that would be made differently depending on whether the manager is concerned with short-term profits versus the long-term well-being of the company. Explain the impact of the two different perspectives on the outcome of the decision.

Gross Profit Margin Ratio

gross profit margin ratio
A profitability ratio that expresses a company's gross profit (often called gross margin on the financial statements) as a percentage of sales revenue.

net sales
Total sales less any discounts or reductions due to returns or sales allowances.

Introduced in Chapter 4, the **gross profit margin ratio** expresses a company's gross profit (often called gross margin on the financial statements) as a percentage of net sales. **Net sales** is total sales less any discounts or reductions due to returns or sales allowances. The formula for this ratio is:

$$\text{Gross profit margin ratio} = \frac{\text{Gross profit}}{\text{Net sales}}$$

Both the numerator and denominator for this ratio come from the income statement information in *Pier 1*'s annual report. Recall that we calculate gross margin (gross profit) by subtracting cost of goods sold (cost of sales) from net sales. Unfortunately, *Pier 1* does not include gross margin as a subtotal on its income statement on page 34 of the annual report. In fact, the company has lumped cost of sales with the other operating expenses, including the cost of buying merchandise and store occupancy. The notes to *Pier 1*'s financial statements fail to provide enough information for us to distinguish the company's cost of sales from its other costs. Even the gross profit figure of $649.8 million that *Pier 1* presents in its Financial Summary on page 21 is calculated using cost of sales *including* the buying and store occupancy costs ($1,548,556 − $898,795 = $649,761 rounded to $649.8 million). Returning to the income statement on page 34, we have no choice but to calculate gross profit by subtracting cost of sales *including* the buying and store occupancy costs from net sales ($1,548,556 − $898,795 = $649,761). Using this amount and the net sales figure from the income statement, we calculate *Pier 1*'s gross profit margin ratio for 2002 as:

$$\frac{\$649,761}{\$1,548,556} = .4196 \text{ or } 41.96\%$$

This ratio calculation tells us that after covering the cost of product sold during 2002, *Pier 1* had 41.96 percent of each sales dollar remaining to cover all the company's operating expenses, interest cost, and income taxes. You can also look at it this way: For every one dollar of sales, the company had about 42 cents remaining after it paid for the merchandise it sold. The 42 cents is what *Pier 1* has left to pay all its other costs. Gross profit margin ratios vary from industry to industry, but, clearly, the higher the gross profit margin percentage, the better.

As we mentioned earlier in this chapter, where possible, we will compare *Pier 1*'s ratios to industry averages taken from the 2002 edition of the Almanac. Unfortunately, we can't compare *Pier 1*'s gross profit margin to industry averages because the Almanac does not include this ratio in the industry statistics it publishes. Frankly, this is not uncommon because different publications present different ratios. If we really wanted to see how *Pier 1*'s gross profit margin ratio compares to its industry average, we would need to refer to one of the other publications.

So the question remains, how does *Pier 1*'s gross profit margin ratio measure up when compared to other large specialty retailers? And what has happened to *Pier 1*'s gross profit margin over time? Has it been increasing, staying the same, or is it declining? To answer these important questions, we calculated the gross profit margins for *Pier 1, Bed Bath & Beyond,* and *Williams-Sonoma* for each of the five years ending with their financial statements published in 2002. We then created a bar chart graph to illustrate our findings. Exhibit 11–3 shows the chart we created for the gross profit margin ratio for the three companies.

EXHIBIT 11-3 Gross Profit Margin Ratio for 1998 Through 2002

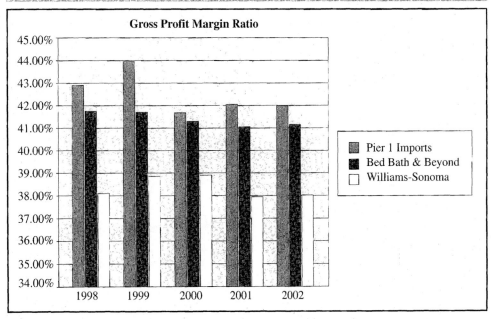

As the chart in Exhibit 11–3 shows, all three companies have consistently high gross profit margin ratios. All of them seem to be performing well by this measure; however, *Pier 1*'s gross profit margin ratio is consistently higher than those of *Bed Bath & Beyond* and *Williams-Sonoma.* The chart in Exhibit 11–3 also shows that *Pier 1*'s gross profit percentage has been fairly constant—between about 42 and 44 percent.

Net Profit Margin Ratio

net profit margin ratio
A profitability ratio that expresses a company's net profit (almost always called either net income or net earnings on the financial statements) as a percentage of sales revenue. It indicates the amount of net income generated by a dollar of sales.

Introduced in Chapter 4, the **net profit margin ratio** expresses a company's net profit (almost always called either net income or net earnings on the financial statements) as a percentage of sales revenue. It indicates the amount of net income generated by a dollar of sales. The formula for this ratio is:

$$\text{Net profit margin ratio} = \frac{\text{Net profit}}{\text{Net sales}}$$

Both the numerator and denominator for this ratio come from the income statement on page 34 of *Pier 1*'s annual report. We calculate *Pier 1*'s net profit margin ratio for 2002 as:

$$\frac{\$100,209}{\$1,548,556} = .0647 \text{ or } 6.47\%$$

This ratio tells us that during 2002, *Pier 1* had 6.47 percent of each sales dollar remaining as profit after covering the cost of products sold, all operating expenses, interest cost, and income taxes. In other words, it reveals the percentage of each sales dollar remaining after *all* the costs of running the business for the year. So for every one dollar of sales, *Pier 1* had about 6.5 cents (of each sales dollar) remaining after it paid its costs for the year. Net profit margin ratios vary from industry to industry, but clearly, the higher the net profit margin percentage, the better. As Dennis E. Logue suggests in the *Handbook of Modern Finance*:

> *The profit margin percentage measures a firm's ability to (1) obtain higher prices for its products relative to competitors and (2) control the level of operating costs, or expenses, relative to revenues generated. By holding down costs, a firm increases the profits from a given amount of revenue and thereby improves its profit margin percentage.*[3]

Compared to the industry averages for furniture and home furnishings stores published in the Almanac for 2002, *Pier 1*'s net profit margin ratio is quite strong. The industry's average net profit margin ratio (called the "profit margin after tax" in the Almanac) for all companies in Table II is 3.7 percent, and the industry average for companies with assets in excess of $250 million is 4.8 percent. Clearly *Pier 1*'s 6.47 percent net profit margin ratio is substantially higher than the industry averages.

We will next see how *Pier 1*'s net profit margin ratio compares to our peer companies and how it has changed over time. To do this, we calculated the net profit margins for *Pier 1, Bed Bath & Beyond,* and *Williams-Sonoma* for each of the five years ending with information from their financial statements published in 2002. Then we created a bar chart to summarize the information, shown in Exhibit 11–4.

As you can see by the chart in Exhibit 11–4, *Pier 1*'s net profit margin ratio is consistently between about 6 and 7 percent. It is clearly higher than *Williams-Sonoma*'s net profit margin, but in the last three years, *Bed Bath & Beyond*'s ratio has edged out *Pier 1*'s. All in all, the graph shows that *Pier 1* has a strong and consistent net profit compared to its peer companies.

EXHIBIT 11–4 Net Profit Margin Ratio for 1998 Through 2002

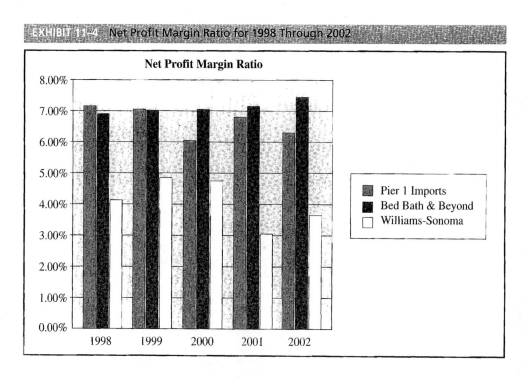

---

[3]Dennis E. Logue, *Handbook of Modern Finance*.

rate of return on assets ratio   A profitability ratio that shows the amount of profit (net income) produced for a given level of assets.

Rate of Return on Assets Ratio

Introduced in Chapter 4, the **rate of return on assets ratio** shows the amount of profit (net income) produced for a given level of assets. This is an important ratio because it indicates how effectively the company uses its total assets to generate net income. The formula for this ratio is:

$$\text{Rate of return on assets ratio} = \frac{\text{Net income}}{\text{Average total assets}}$$

The net income amount we use in the numerator of this ratio comes directly from the income statement. The amount we use as the denominator requires a bit of explanation. Since the net income in the numerator was earned throughout 2002 (some in January, some in February, etc.), we want to know the amount of assets employed throughout the year. We determine this by calculating the average of the total assets shown on the 2001 and 2002 balance sheets on page 35 of the annual report ($735,710 + $862,672 = $1,598,382/2 = $799,191). We calculate *Pier 1*'s rate of return on assets for 2002 as:

$$\frac{\$100,209}{\$799,191} = .1254 \text{ or } 12.54\%$$

This ratio calculation tells us that during 2002, *Pier 1* had a 12.54 percent return on its investment in assets. This is an important measure because, after all, the reason companies invest in assets is to produce revenue and ultimately profit (net income).

Compared to the industry averages for furniture and home furnishings stores published in the Almanac for 2002, *Pier 1*'s rate of return on assets ratio is stronger than the industry average for companies with assets over $250 million, but slightly less than the average of all companies in Table II. The industry average for the rate of return on assets ratio for all companies in Table II is 12.7 percent and the industry average for companies with assets in excess of $250 million is 11.4 percent. *Pier 1*'s 12.54 percent return on assets ratio is on par with the industry averages.

Next we will examine how *Pier 1*'s rate of return on assets ratio compares to the peer companies. The chart in Exhibit 11–5 shows how *Pier 1, Bed Bath & Beyond,* and *Williams-Sonoma*'s rate of return on assets has faired from 1999 to 2002.

Although *Pier 1*'s rate of return on assets has been somewhat lower than that of *Bed Bath & Beyond,* it has been quite stable, if not increasing. In contrast, even though their rates of return on assets are still strong, the other two company's rates have been declining somewhat.

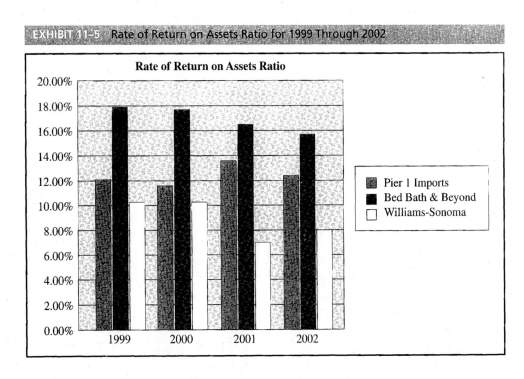

EXHIBIT 11–5   Rate of Return on Assets Ratio for 1999 Through 2002

Rate of Return on Common Equity Ratio

Introduced in Chapter 4, the **rate of return on common equity ratio** shows the amount of profit (net income) in relation to the amount of investment by the company's owners. The purpose of this ratio is similar to that of the rate of return on assets ratio except that it focuses on the assets provided by the owners, rather than total assets. The formula for this ratio is:

$$\text{Rate of return on common equity ratio} = \frac{\text{Net income} - \text{Preferred dividends}}{\text{Average common stockholders' equity}}$$

The net income used in the numerator of this ratio comes from the income statement, but it must be adjusted for any preferred stock dividend requirement, because that amount is not available to common stockholders. Since *Pier 1* has no preferred stock (we determine this by looking at the shareholder' equity section of the balance sheet), there are no preferred stock dividends to deduct in our calculation. We use an average amount for the denominator in this calculation for the same reason we did in the rate of return on assets ratio. Since the net income in the numerator was earned throughout 2002, we want to know the amount of common equity throughout the year. We determine this by calculating the average of the common stockholders' equity shown on the 2001 and 2002 balance sheets ($581,879 + $585,656 = $1,167,535 /2 = $583,767.5). We calculate *Pier 1*'s rate of return on common equity ratio for 2002 as:

$$\frac{\$100,209}{\$583,767.5} = .1717 \text{ or } 17.17\%$$

This ratio tells us that during 2002, *Pier 1* had a 17.17 percent return on the owners holdings in the company. Do not confuse this with what the owners themselves earned on their investment. The owners' return is a combination of the dividends they receive and appreciation of the stock's price in the marketplace. The company's rate of return on common equity does, however, greatly influence the market price of the company's stock and, therefore, the stockholders' return on their investment.

Compared to the industry averages for furniture and home furnishings stores published in the Almanac for 2002, *Pier 1*'s 17.17 percent rate of return on common equity ratio is substantially higher than the 13.4 percent industry average for companies with assets over $250 million, but somewhat less than the 20.8 percent industry average of all companies in Table II.

Now let's look at the rate of return on common equity ratio for *Pier 1 Imports, Bed Bath & Beyond,* and *Williams-Sonoma.* Exhibit 11–6 shows the rates of return on equity for our peer companies for 1999 to 2002.

Pier 1 Imports' rate of return on common equity ratio is consistently between about 17 percent and 20 percent. Although it is below that of *Bed Bath & Beyond,* it has surpassed that of *Williams-Sonoma* and is holding steady.

Dividend Payout Ratio

Introduced in Chapter 4, the **dividend payout ratio** shows what portion of a company's net income for a given year was paid to its owners as cash dividends during that year. The formula for this ratio is:

$$\text{Dividend payout ratio} = \frac{\text{Cash dividends}}{\text{Net income}}$$

We could determine the amount of cash dividends to use in the numerator by examining the stockholders' equity section of the balance sheet and calculating the amount. A better way, however, is to simply look for the amount of cash dividends paid in the financing section of the statement of cash flows on page 36 of the annual report. The denominator is simply net income from the income statement. We calculate *Pier 1*'s dividend payout ratio for 2002 as:

$$\frac{\$15,134}{\$100,209} = .1510 \text{ or } 15.10\%$$

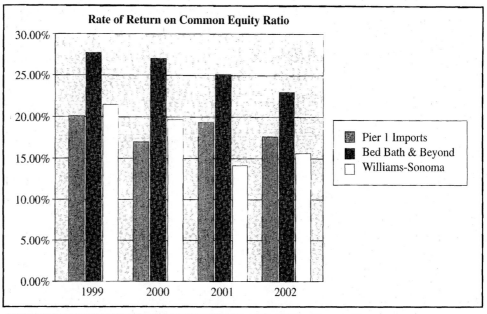

EXHIBIT 11-6 Rate of Return on Common Equity Ratio for 1999 Through 2002

This ratio tells us that during 2002, ***Pier 1*** paid out 15.10 percent of its net income to its stockholders as dividends. On the surface, it might seem that a high dividend payout ratio is better than a low one, and for some investors this is true (those who count on dividends as a significant portion of their yearly income). Many investors and analysts, however, believe a low dividend payout ratio is superior to a high one. The reason is actually pretty simple. Remember that a company can do only two things with the profits it earns. It can either distribute them to the stockholders as dividends or it can reinvest them in the business in the form of property, plant, and equipment or new products and processes. A high dividend payout ratio may indicate that a company is not investing sufficiently for the future.

The Almanac does not publish industry averages for the dividend payout ratio, but we will compare ***Pier 1***'s dividend payout to our peer companies. Exhibit 11–7 shows ***Pier 1, Bed Bath & Beyond,*** and ***Williams-Sonoma***'s dividend payout ratio for 2000 through 2002.

EXHIBIT 11-7 Dividend Payout Ratio for 2000 Through 2002

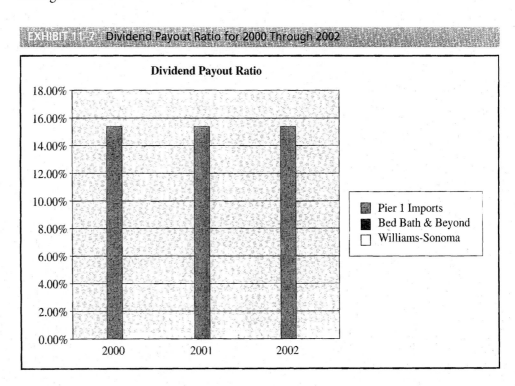

It is likely that the comparison of *Pier 1*'s dividend payout ratio with those of *Bed Bath & Beyond* and *Williams-Sonoma* yields results that may look quite strange to you. This is because *Pier 1* pays a dividend of about 15 percent of net income and neither *Bed Bath & Beyond* nor *Williams-Sonoma* pays a dividend at all. Now, we must caution you that paying no dividend is not a sign of financial weakness. Both *Bed Bath & Beyond* and *Williams-Sonoma* are reinvesting earnings instead of distributing them. You may ask which is better, a company that pays dividends or one that doesn't. Well, there is no one correct answer to that question because some investors desire a greater distribution of profits than others. Those who want a greater distribution view a high dividend payout ratio as good. Other investors prefer to see a company reinvest a higher percentage of its profits so the company can continue to grow. These folks view a low dividend payout ratio as good.

Earnings per Share

earnings per share ratio
The amount of a company's total earnings attributable to each share of common stock.

Introduced in Chapter 4 and discussed further in Chapter 9, the **earnings per share ratio** expresses a company's net income as a per common share amount. The formula for this ratio is:

$$\text{Earnings per share} = \frac{\text{Net income} - \text{Preferred dividend}}{\text{Average common shares}}$$

We demonstrated very simple earnings per share (EPS) calculations in Chapter 4 and more complicated basic and diluted earnings per share calculations in Chapter 9. When you are evaluating a company whose stock is publicly traded, however, you will *never* have to calculate earnings per share, because the SEC requires that the company calculate it for you and include it in the annual report. *Pier 1*'s basic and diluted earnings per share for 2002 were:

Basic earnings per share = $1.06
Diluted earnings per share = $1.04

Clearly, all interested parties desire a company's earnings per share to be as high as possible. The Almanac does not publish industry averages for earnings per share, but we will compare *Pier 1*'s earnings per share to that of *Bed Bath & Beyond* and *Williams-Sonoma.* When we look at the annual reports for *Pier 1 Imports, Bed Bath & Beyond,* and *Williams-Sonoma,* we find that all three companies disclose diluted earnings per share information for the past five years (see Exhibit 11–8).

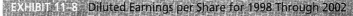

EXHIBIT 11–8 Diluted Earnings per Share for 1998 Through 2002

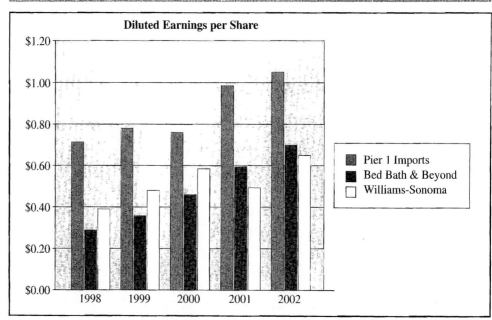

The chart in Exhibit 11–8 shows that *Pier 1*'s earnings per share is clearly the highest, but the earnings per share for each of our three companies has generally increased over time.

Price-to-Earnings Ratio

price-to-earnings ratio
A profitability ratio that is often called simply the PE ratio that expresses the relationship between a company's earnings per share and the market value of the company's stock.

Introduced in Chapter 9, the **price-to-earnings ratio** (often referred to as simply the PE ratio) expresses the relationship between a company's earnings per share and the market value of the company's stock. Financial analysts use this measure to decide whether a company's stock is *under*valued or *over*valued. The formula for this ratio is:

$$\text{Price-to-earnings ratio} = \frac{\text{Average market price per share of stock}}{\text{Earnings per share}}$$

The numerator for this ratio is not found in any of a company's financial statements. We can, however, calculate it from the market price and dividend information found on page 51 of the annual report. Analysts can use the current market price per share or they can use an average price to calculate the PE ratio. We will use an average price per share from amounts for the fourth quarter only. We calculate the average the same way we did in previous ratios, except this time we will use the high and low market prices, rather than the beginning and ending market prices ($20.24 high + $14.50 low = $34.74/2 = $17.37). The denominator is earnings per share from the income statement. We calculate *Pier 1*'s PE ratio for 2002 as:

$$\frac{\$17.37}{\$1.06} = 16.39 \text{ times}$$

This ratio calculation tells us that *Pier 1*'s stock was selling for 16.39 times its earnings per share in 2002 (at least during the fourth quarter). The Almanac does not include industry averages for earnings per share, but Exhibit 11–9 shows the price-to-earnings ratios for *Pier 1 Imports, Bed Bath & Beyond,* and *Williams-Sonoma* for 2001 and 2002.

This is a difficult ratio to interpret because it means different things to different analysts. A high PE ratio may indicate that the stock is overvalued (and may be an unwise investment), whereas a low PE ratio may indicate that is undervalued (and may be a wise investment). Since the market value of a stock is not directly related to earn-

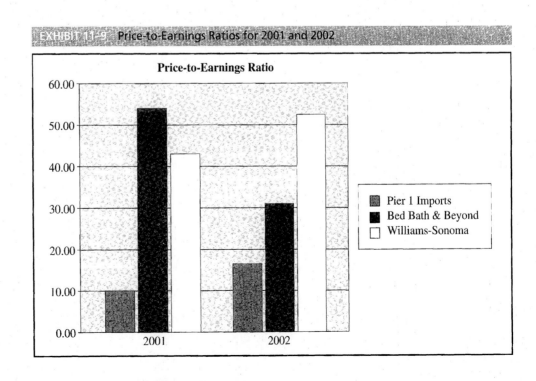

EXHIBIT 11–9   Price-to-Earnings Ratios for 2001 and 2002

ings per share, smart analysts evaluate this ratio in conjunction with many other factors. In any case, *Pier 1*'s PE ratio is clearly much lower than those of *Bed Bath & Beyond* and *Williams-Sonoma.*

MEASURING EFFICIENCY

efficiency ratios Financial ratios that measure the investment in assets relative to business activity.

Companies use resources (assets) to conduct business. The more business a company can generate with a given amount of assets, the better. For example, when a company can generate a tremendous amount of revenue with a relatively small amount of assets, the company must be using those assets efficiently. **Efficiency ratios** measure the investment in assets relative to business activity. For example, assume that Custom Ride Inc., plans to sell 5,200 hydraulic cylinders during the next year. If we assume that each cylinder costs $100, Custom Ride would have to invest $520,000 (5,200 × $100) in inventory if the company purchases all 5,200 cylinders on January 1. Although the company would have the cylinders in stock and ready to sell throughout the year, this plan would result in a very inefficient use of company assets. Instead of buying all of the cylinders at the very beginning of the year, Custom Ride could buy just a two-week supply at a time. On average, the company sells about 100 cylinders per week (5,200/52 weeks), so buying a two-week supply (200 cylinders) rather than a one-year supply would reduce the company's investment in inventory from $520,000 to $20,000 (200 × $100). The idea here is that the company will buy 200 cylinders, sell the 200 cylinders, then buy 200 more cylinders, and sell those 200 cylinders. In other words, their inventory of cylinders would *turn over* every two weeks, or 26 times per year. The higher the asset turnover, the more efficiently the company is using its investment in assets. This is because high asset turnover signifies that the company is doing more business with a smaller investment in assets. We will examine the efficiency ratios for total assets, accounts receivable, and inventory.

Asset Turnover Ratio

asset turnover ratio An efficiency ratio that shows the amount of sales produced for a given level of assets used.

Introduced in Chapter 9, the **asset turnover ratio** shows the amount of sales produced for a given level of assets used. It is good when a company can produce high sales with a low investment in assets. Therefore, companies should try to get the most out of every dollar invested in assets. In considering *Pier 1,* we are talking about getting the most sales. The asset turnover ratio is important because it indicates how efficiently the company uses its total assets to generate sales. The formula for this ratio is:

$$\text{Asset turnover ratio} = \frac{\text{Net sales}}{\text{Average total assets}}$$

The net sales figure in the numerator of this ratio comes from the income statement. The amounts we use to calculate the denominator come from the balance sheet. We use an average amount for the same reason we did in earlier ratios. Since the sales in the numerator occurred throughout 2002, we want to know the amount of total assets employed throughout the year. We determine this by calculating the average of the total assets shown on the 2001 and 2002 balance sheets ($735,710 + $862,672 = $1,598,382/2 = $799,191). We calculate *Pier 1*'s asset turnover ratio for 2002 as:

$$\frac{\$1,548,556}{\$799,191} = 1.94 \text{ times}$$

Our calculation indicates that *Pier 1* produced 1.94 times as many dollars in sales during 2002 as it had invested in assets. The higher the multiple, the more efficiently the company is using its assets to produce sales.

Compared to the industry averages for furniture and home furnishings stores published in the Almanac for 2002, *Pier 1*'s asset turnover ratio of 1.94 times is higher than the industry average of 1.3 times for companies with assets over $250 million, but less than the industry average of 2.5 times for all companies in Table II. *Pier 1* is doing better than companies with assets in excess of $250 million, but not as well as the industry as a whole.

Now let's look at the asset turnover ratio for ***Pier 1 Imports, Bed Bath & Beyond,*** and ***Williams-Sonoma.*** The chart in Exhibit 11–10 depicts the asset turnover ratios for the three peer companies for 1999 through 2002.

EXHIBIT 11–10   Asset Turnover Ratios for 1999 Through 2002

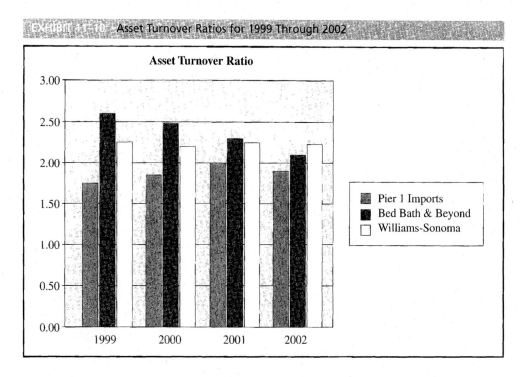

Over the past four years, ***Pier 1***'s asset turnover ratio has improved steadily. Currently, the asset turnover ratio of all three companies is around two, which indicates that ***Pier 1*** compares favorably with the peer companies we are using.

Receivables Turnover Ratio

receivables turnover ratio   An efficiency ratio that measures how quickly a company collects its accounts receivable.

Introduced in Chapter 9, the **receivables turnover ratio** measures how efficiently a company manages its accounts receivable. Accounts receivable is the amount a company is owed by its customers, and it is often a significant current asset. Companies need to convert accounts receivable to cash as quickly as possible because, for many companies, they represent interest-free loans to customers. The receivables turnover ratio indicates how quickly a company collects its receivables. The formula for this ratio is:

$$\text{Receivables turnover ratio} = \frac{\text{Net sales}}{\text{Average accounts receivable}}$$

The net sales figure in the numerator comes from the income statement, and the denominator is based on the accounts receivable shown on the balance sheet. We use an average amount for the denominator in this calculation for the same reason we did in earlier ratios. Since the sales used in the numerator occurred throughout 2002, we want to know the amount of accounts receivable throughout the year. We determine this by calculating the average of the accounts receivable shown on the 2001 and 2002 balance sheets. ***Pier 1*** shows two classifications of its accounts receivable on the balance sheets (beneficial interest in securitized receivables and other accounts receivable). If we look in the notes to the financial statements on page 39 of the annual report, we find three paragraphs explaining what the securitized receivables represent. After reading each of the three paragraphs several times to try and figure out what they are talking about, we are satisfied that these receivables should be included in our calculation. Our average accounts receivable calculation, then, is ($75,403 + $8,370 + $44,620 + $6,205 = $134,598/2 = $67,299). We calculate ***Pier 1***'s receivables turnover ratio for 2002 as:

$$\frac{\$1,548,556}{\$67,299} = 23.01 \text{ times}$$

Our calculation indicates that *Pier 1* turns its receivables over an average of 23.01 times per year. A higher number would suggest that the company collects cash from its credit customers more quickly and is apparently managing its receivables better. On the other hand, a lower receivables turnover means the company manages its receivables less efficiently.

Although the Almanac publishes industry averages for receivables turnover, it does not calculate the ratio for furniture and home furnishings stores. This is probably because the credit sales these businesses make are generally through credit card companies. Therefore, companies in this industry generally collect their receivables almost immediately. This would explain why *Pier 1*'s receivables turnover is so high.

The information that *Pier 1* turns over its accounts receivable 23.01 times per year becomes easier to interpret if we extend it to determine the average collection period for its accounts receivable. We can do that by dividing the receivables turnover into 365 (the number of days in a year) to determine the average time it takes the company to collect its receivables:

$$\text{Average accounts receivable collection period in days} = \frac{365}{\text{Receivables turnover ratio}}$$

$$\frac{365}{23.01} = 15.86 \text{ days}$$

Our calculation shows that it takes *Pier 1* an average of 15.86 days from the sale date to collect cash from its customers. In addition to our calculations for *Pier 1*, we also calculated the average accounts receivable collection period in days for *Williams-Sonoma* for 2002. *Bed Bath & Beyond* shows no accounts receivable on their balance sheet, so the company either has no current receivables or they are insignificant and included in other current assets. Exhibit 11–11 shows a chart for the average accounts receivable collection period in days for *Pier 1* and *Williams-Sonoma* for 2002.

EXHIBIT 11–11 Average Accounts Receivable Collection Period in Days for 2002

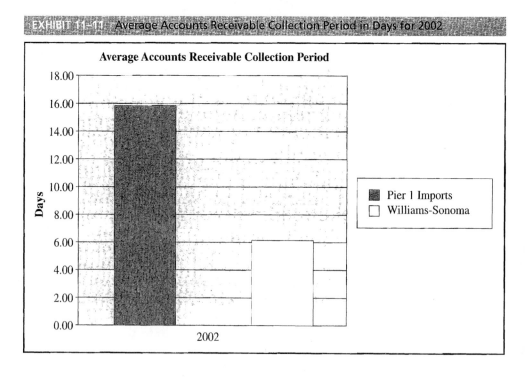

This ratio tells us that the average collection period for receivables is quite short for both *Pier 1 Imports* and *Williams-Sonoma*. The reason for this is that most of the credit sales for the two companies are done through credit card companies such as *American Express, MasterCard,* and *VISA*. We can tell from the chart in Exhibit 11–11 that both of the companies are collecting their receivables very quickly, so it appears that neither is having difficulties with collections.

Inventory Turnover Ratio

inventory turnover ratio
An efficiency ratio that indicates how long a company holds its inventory.

Introduced in Chapter 8, the **inventory turnover ratio** measures how efficiently a company uses its investment in inventory. Inventory is often a sizable current asset, and every dollar tied up in inventory is a dollar that can't be used for some other purpose. A company should strive to keep its investment in inventory as low as possible by, for example, purchasing a one-month supply instead of a year's worth of inventory at a time. This way, the company would have to make inventory purchases more often, but the investment in inventory would be substantially less. The inventory turnover ratio indicates the number of times total merchandise inventory is purchased and sold during a period. If a company keeps a one-year supply of inventory on hand, the inventory would turn over once a year. On the other hand, if a company keeps only a one-month supply on hand, the inventory would turn over 12 times per year. The formula for this ratio is:

$$\text{Inventory turnover ratio} = \frac{\text{Cost of goods sold}}{\text{Average inventory}}$$

The cost of goods sold (cost of sales) figure in the numerator comes from the income statement. Remember that *Pier 1* has lumped cost of sales with its buying and store occupancy costs. However, since that is the best amount we have for cost of goods sold—the only amount really—we will use it as this ratio's numerator. The denominator is based on the inventory shown on the balance sheet. We use an average amount for this ratio for the same reason we used an average amount in earlier ratios. Since the cost of sales in the numerator occurred throughout 2002, we should use the amount of inventory throughout the year. We determine this by calculating the average of the inventory shown on the 2001 and 2002 balance sheets ($310,704 + $275,433 = $586,137/2 = $293,068.5). We calculate *Pier 1*'s inventory turnover ratio for 2002 as:

$$\frac{\$898,795}{\$293,068.5} = 3.07 \text{ times}$$

This ratio calculation tells us that *Pier 1* turns its inventory an average of 3.07 times per year. A higher ratio suggests the company requires a lower investment in inventory and is, therefore, using its inventory more efficiently. On the other hand, a lower inventory turnover means the company is using its inventory less efficiently.

Compared to the industry averages for furniture and home furnishings stores published in the Almanac for 2002, *Pier 1*'s inventory turnover ratio of 3.07 times is higher than the industry average of 2.3 times for companies with assets over $250 million, but less than the industry average of 4.2 times for all companies in Table II. *Pier 1* is doing better than companies with assets in excess of $250 million, but not as well as the industry as a whole.

Pier 1's inventory turnover of 3.07 times per year becomes easier to comprehend if we extend the calculation to determine average length of time a product is held in inventory before it is sold. To calculate the average inventory holding period, we divide the inventory turnover ratio into 365 (the number of days in a year). *Pier 1*'s average inventory holding period is:

$$\text{Average inventory holding period in days} = \frac{365}{\text{Inventory turnover ratio}}$$

$$\frac{365}{3.07} = 118.89 \text{ days}$$

This ratio tells us that, on average, 118.89 days pass between the time *Pier 1* purchases inventory and the time it sells that inventory. Exhibit 11–12 on page F–474 shows the average inventory holding period in days for *Pier 1 Imports, Bed Bath & Beyond,* and *Williams-Sonoma* for 2002.

Exhibit 11–12 shows that *Pier 1*'s average inventory holding period is in line with the two peer companies we are using. All three companies have substantial inventories relative to their sales, but *Pier 1*'s average inventory holding period falls between that of *Williams-Sonoma* (about 70 days) and *Bed Bath & Beyond* (just over 140 days).

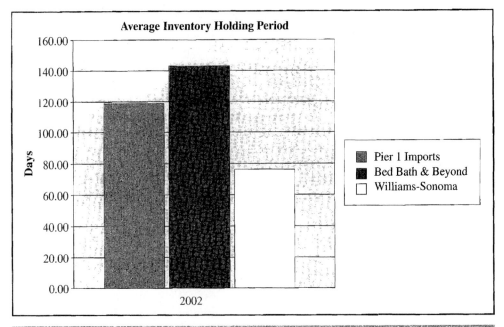

Average Inventory Holding Period

- Pier 1 Imports
- Bed Bath & Beyond
- Williams-Sonoma

2002

EXHIBIT 11–12   Average Inventory Holding Period in Days for 2002

MEASURING LIQUIDITY

liquidity   An item's nearness to cash.

Cash is the lifeblood that flows through every business. **Liquidity** refers to a company's ability to generate the cash needed to meet its short-term obligations. If a company is very liquid, it means that the company has or can generate enough cash to meet its short-term requirements for cash—it can easily pay its bills on time. If a company is not liquid, it means that the company has difficulty generating enough cash to pay its bills. The bills we are talking about here are those due in the near term, primarily the company's current liabilities. Clearly, all economic decision makers must consider a firm's liquidity, because if a company can't meet its current obligations, it may not be around long enough to prove whether or not it will be profitable in the long run. Short-term creditors and a company's management, however, tend to be those who pay most careful attention to liquidity.

Current Ratio

current ratio   A liquidity ratio that measures a company's ability to meet short-term obligations by comparing current assets to current liabilities.

Introduced in Chapter 9, the **current ratio** was probably the most widely used measure of a company's liquidity for much of the 20th century. Its purpose is to gauge a company's current assets relative to its current liabilities, thereby attempting to offer a measure of the company's ability to meet its short-term financial obligations (its current liabilities) with cash generated from current assets. The formula for this ratio is:

$$\text{Current ratio} = \frac{\text{Current assets}}{\text{Current liabilities}}$$

This ratio indicates the amount of current assets a company has for each dollar of current liabilities, and both the numerator and the denominator come directly from the balance sheet. We calculate *Pier 1*'s current ratio for 2002 as:

$$\frac{\$605,153}{\$208,396} = 2.90 \text{ to } 1, \text{ or simply, } 2.9$$

A current ratio of 2.9 tells us that *Pier 1* had $2.90 of current assets for every $1.00 of current liabilities at the end of 2002.

Compared to the industry averages for furniture and home furnishings stores published in the Almanac for 2002, *Pier 1*'s current ratio of 2.9 to 1 is higher than both the industry average of 1.4 to 1 for companies with assets over $250 million and the industry average of 1.8 to 1 for all companies in Table II. Analysts that are focusing on *Pier 1*'s ability to pay its short-term obligations would be pleased that *Pier 1*'s current ratio is outpacing the industry by so much. On the other hand, analysts focusing on effi-

cient use of assets might argue that a current ratio that is too high is a sign of inefficiency and that the company has too much invested in current assets.

Exhibit 11–13 shows a chart of the current ratios for *Pier 1, Bed Bath & Beyond,*
and *Williams-Sonoma* for 2001 and 2002.

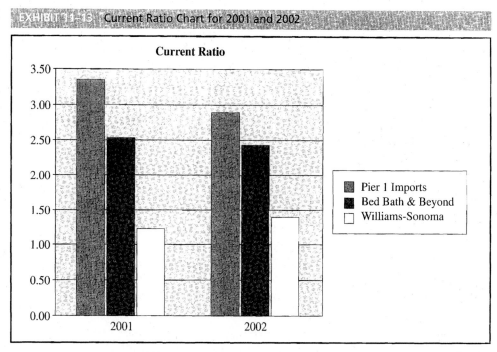

EXHIBIT 11–13   Current Ratio Chart for 2001 and 2002

It is clear from the chart in Exhibit 11–13 that *Pier 1* has a higher current ratio and,
therefore, more current assets relative to their liabilities than the other two companies.
This is an indication that *Pier 1* is probably in a stronger position when it comes to
their ability to pay current debt. The question then becomes, does the company have
too much invested in current assets. Analysts use the efficiency ratios we calculated in
the previous section to evaluate how efficiently a company uses its assets. If a company
has too much invested in current assets, the current ratio looks better, but the company's efficiency ratios suffer.

The current ratio is a well-respected indicator of liquidity, but the problem with
this measure is that a company does not pay its bills with accounts receivable, inventory, and other noncash items included in current assets. It must pay its bills with cash.
Recall our discussion in Chapter 10 of the renewed focus on cash flow in the 1980s.
Part of that renewed focus was that many financial analysts began questioning the
importance of the current ratio.

Discussion Question

11–8. If *Pier 1* was to borrow money to pay its current liabilities, it would have to pay
interest on the borrowed funds. What effect (if any) would the additional interest expense have on the following ratios:

a. Gross profit margin?
b. Net profit margin?
c. Rate of return on assets?
d. Rate of return on common equity?
e. Asset turnover?

Quick Ratio

Introduced in Chapter 9, the **quick ratio** (sometimes called the **acid-test ratio**) is similar to the current ratio. It is a more stringent test of liquidity, however, because it considers only current assets that are highly liquid (quickly convertible into cash) in the
numerator. The calculations for this ratio vary because there is some debate as to what
assets to include. This stems from the fact that the definition of "highly liquid" is quite

quick ratio A liquidity
ratio that is similar to the current ratio, but a more stringent
test of liquidity, because only
current assets considered to be
highly liquid (quickly converted to cash) are included in
the calculation.

acid-test ratio Another
name for the quick ratio.

subjective. The formula that we are using is one of the more conservative, and it is quite popular among financial analysts. The formula for this ratio is:

$$\text{Quick ratio} = \frac{\text{Cash + Short-term investments + Current receivables}}{\text{Current liabilities}}$$

In the numerator of our equation, cash is obviously liquid. We also assume accounts receivable will be quickly converted to cash. However, if an analyst knows that any account receivable will not be quickly converted, it should not include that receivable in the calculation of this ratio. For our calculation, ***Pier 1*** has two classifications of accounts receivable, both of which are included. Marketable securities (temporary investments) held in a company's trading portfolio are usually highly liquid and often represent excess cash that the company plans to use in the near future. As was the case with the current ratio, the denominator of the quick ratio is total current liabilities. We calculate ***Pier 1***'s quick ratio for 2002 as:

$$\frac{\$235,609 + \$44,620 + \$6,205}{\$208,396} = 1.37 \text{ to } 1$$

This ratio calculation tells us that ***Pier 1*** had $1.37 of quick assets for each $1.00 of current liabilities at the end of 2002. Note that ***Pier 1***'s quick ratio is lower than its current ratio. That is usually the case because we have removed assets that are not highly liquid from the numerator, while the denominator remains unchanged.

Compared to the industry averages for furniture and home furnishings stores published in the 2002 edition of the Almanac, ***Pier 1***'s quick ratio of 1.37 to 1 is higher than both the industry average of 0.5 to 1 for companies with assets over $250 million and the industry average of 0.8 to 1 for all companies in Table II. ***Pier 1***'s high quick ratio relative to the industry is a positive indication regarding the company's ability to pay its short-term obligations. But again, some analysts would argue that a quick ratio that is too high is a sign of inefficiency and that the company has too much invested in current assets.

Exhibit 11–14 shows a chart for the quick ratios for ***Pier 1, Bed Bath & Beyond,*** and ***Williams-Sonoma*** for 2001 and 2002.

EXHIBIT 11–14   Quick Ratio Chart for 2001 and 2002

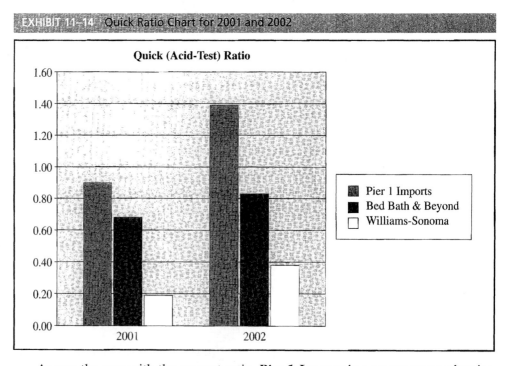

As was the case with the current ratio, ***Pier 1 Imports*** has a very strong showing for the quick ratio. The fact that ***Pier 1***'s quick ratio is higher than those of ***Bed Bath & Beyond*** and ***Williams-Sonoma*** is an indication that ***Pier 1*** is in a better position to pay its short-term liabilities using quick assets.

Discussion Questions

11–9. Besides the three assets—cash, accounts receivable, and notes receivable—considered in our version of the quick ratio, what other quick assets might a company have?

11–10. How would holding an excessive amount of inventory affect the following ratios:

    a. Gross profit margin?

    b. Net profit margin?

    c. Rate of return on assets?

    d. Rate of return on common equity?

    e. Asset turnover?

    f. Current ratio?

    g. Quick ratio?

Operating Cash Flow to Current Debt Ratio

operating cash flow to current debt ratio A financial ratio that measures the sufficiency of cash flows from operating activities to meet current obligations.

Introduced in Chapter 10, the **operating cash flow to current debt ratio** measures the sufficiency of cash flows from operating activities to meet current obligations. In other words, it measures the company's ability to generate enough cash from operating activities to meet its current obligations. Whereas the current and quick ratios measure liquidity based on the financial resources the company has on hand (its assets), the operating cash flow to current debt ratio measures a company's ability to maintain liquidity by generating sufficient cash inflows from its operations. The formula for this ratio is:

$$\text{Operating cash flow to current debt ratio} = \frac{\text{Cash provided by operating activities}}{\text{Average current liabilities}}$$

As you can see, the numerator is cash provided by operating activities from the statement of cash flows and the denominator is based on current liabilities from the balance sheet. We use an average for current liabilities for the same reason we used average amounts for earlier ratios. Since the cash provided by operating activities in the numerator occurred throughout 2002, we should use an approximation of the current liabilities outstanding throughout the year. We determine this by calculating the average of the current liabilities shown on the 2001 and 2002 balance sheets ($144,110 + $208,396 = $352,506/2 = $176,253). We calculate **Pier 1**'s operating cash flow to current debt ratio for 2002 as:

$$\frac{\$244,324}{\$176,253} = 1.39 \text{ to } 1$$

This ratio calculation tells us that **Pier 1**'s operating activities generated $1.39 of cash in 2002 for each $1.00 of its average current liabilities. Generally speaking, generating a high amount of cash inflow from operating activities relative to current liabilities is a positive indication. But, how does **Pier 1**'s operating cash flow to current debt ratio of 1.39 stack up compared to other companies? Unfortunately, the Almanac does not publish industry averages for this ratio, so we will have to rely solely on our peer company comparison. Exhibit 11–15 on page F–478 shows a chart for the operating cash flow to current debt for **Pier 1 Imports, Bed Bath & Beyond,** and **Williams-Sonoma.**

As Exhibit 11–15 shows, **Pier 1**'s operating cash flows to current debt is consistently above that of the peer companies we are using. This means that **Pier 1**'s cash inflow from operating activities relative to current liabilities is higher than those of **Bed Bath & Beyond** and **Williams-Sonoma.**

MEASURING SOLVENCY

solvency A company's ability to meet the obligations created by its long-term debt obligations.

Solvency refers to a company's ability to meet its long-term financial obligations. Debt obligations include both paying back the amount borrowed and paying interest on the debt. Over time, analysts have developed a set of solvency ratios, some focusing on the

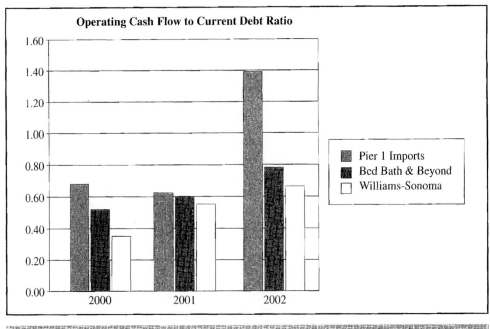

EXHIBIT 11-15 Operating Cash Flow to Current Debt Chart for 2000 Through 2002

overall level of debt a company carries, while others measure a company's ability to make interest payments. Solvency ratios are of most importance to economic decision makers interested in the long-term outlook for the company. These decision makers include stockholders, long-term creditors, and, of course, company management.

Debt Ratio

debt ratio A solvency ratio that indicates what proportion of a company's assets is financed by debt.

Introduced in Chapter 3, the **debt ratio** measures the proportion of a company's assets financed by debt. All of a company's assets are financed by either creditors (debt) or by the owners (equity). This can be demonstrated by looking once again at the accounting (business) equation:

$$\text{Assets} = \text{Liabilities} + \text{Owners' equity}$$
$$100 \text{ percent} = \text{Some percent} + \text{Some percent}$$

Or:

$$\text{Assets} = \text{Liabilities} + \text{Owners' equity}$$
$$100\% = \text{Some }\% + \text{Some }\%$$

The debt ratio calculates the percentage of a company's assets that are financed by debt. Like other ratios, the exact formula for the debt ratio varies somewhat depending on the analyst. Some analysts exclude interest-free financing from liabilities, for example. In our example, we will include all liabilities so the formula is:

$$\text{Debt ratio} = \frac{\text{Total liabilities}}{\text{Total assets}}$$

As you know, both assets and liabilities are found on the balance sheet; however, in *Pier 1*'s case, the balance sheet does not show a total liabilities amount. We can calculate it two ways: One way is to add up all the liabilities (current liabilities of $208,396 + long-term debt of $25,356 + other noncurrent liabilities of $43,264 = $277,016). A second, simpler way to calculate total liabilities is to subtract the shareholders' equity amount from total liabilities and shareholders' equity (total liabilities and shareholders' equity of $862,672 − shareholders' equity of $585,656 = $277,016). As you can see, either approach yields the same amount for total liabilities. We calculate *Pier 1*'s debt ratio for 2002 as:

$$\frac{\$277,016}{\$862,672} = 0.3211 \text{ or } 32.11\%$$

This ratio calculation tells us that as of the end of 2002, 32.11 percent of **Pier 1**'s assets are financed by debt. By extension then, 67.89 percent of the company's assets are financed by equity.

Compared to the industry averages for furniture and home furnishings stores published in the Almanac for 2002, **Pier 1**'s debt ratio of 32.11 percent is lower than both the industry average of 53.0 percent for companies with assets over $250 million and the industry average of 55.2 percent for all companies in Table II. Analysts that are focusing on **Pier 1**'s ability to meet its obligations would be pleased that **Pier 1**'s debt ratio is so low relative to the industry.

Now let's see how **Pier 1**'s debt ratio compares to our two peer companies. Exhibit 11–16 shows how **Pier 1**'s debt ratio compares to those of **Bed Bath & Beyond** and **Williams-Sonoma.**

EXHIBIT 11–16   Debt Ratio Chart for 1998 Through 2002

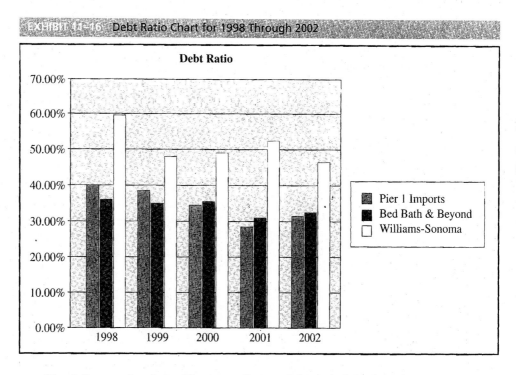

Pier 1 Imports has less of its assets financed through debt than the two peer companies we are using. It is also interesting to note the **Pier 1**'s debt ratio has generally decreased over the past five years. There is no hard-and-fast rule concerning what amount of a company's assets should be financed through debt. Creditors tend to feel better when a company's debt ratio is on the low, more conservative side. Equity investors may feel the same way, but in some situations, the equity investors would like more debt. Remember, the company pays a certain amount, a certain interest rate for its debt financing. For example, if a company borrows funds at 8 percent, say, it pays the 8 percent and no more. If the company uses the funds it has borrowed and earns a return of say, 20 percent, 12 percent of the return (20% − 8%) is available to equity investors. This situation, called *financial leverage,* is a very interesting phenomenon because the equity investors are earning a return on funds they did not even invest. That is, by virtue of owning stock in the company, the shareholders are able to earn a return on not only their equity investment, but also on the investment made by creditors. Of course, if the company earns a return that is less than the fixed interest rate it must pay on borrowed funds, any shortfall comes from the return that would otherwise be available to equity investors. Most analysts would agree that less debt is more conservative and in many cases the best approach. Although all of the companies in Exhibit 11–16 are all within a reasonably close range, **Pier 1 Imports** is in the most conservative debt position of the three. A company's debt ratio must be evaluated in light of peer companies in the industry, the maturity of the company (new businesses tend to have more debt relative to equity), and management's philosophy concerning the appropriate balance between debt financing and equity financing.

debt-to-equity ratio A solvency ratio that expresses the proportional relationship between liabilities and equity.

Debt-to-Equity Ratio

Introduced in Chapter 3, the **debt-to-equity ratio** expresses the proportional relationship between liabilities and equity. Many financial publications call this ratio the *total liabilities to net worth ratio*. You must remember this, because many of these publications do not include a ratio called the debt-to-equity ratio. They have the ratio, but call it something else. The formula for this ratio is:

$$\text{Dept-to-equity ratio} = \frac{\text{Total liabilities}}{\text{Total equity}}$$

Both the items necessary to calculate the debt-to-equity ratio come from the balance sheet. As you can see, the numerator, total liabilities, is the same as it is for the debt ratio, and for the denominator, we use total shareholders' equity. We calculate *Pier 1*'s debt-to-equity ratio for 2002 as:

$$\frac{\$277,016}{\$585,656} = .4730 \text{ to } 1$$

This ratio tells us that at the end of 2002, *Pier 1* had $0.47 of debt for every $1.00 of equity. This ratio reveals essentially the same information as the debt ratio but presents it slightly different. The lower the debt-to-equity ratio, the lower total debt is relative to total equity.

Compared to the industry averages for furniture and home furnishings stores published in the Almanac for 2002, *Pier 1*'s debt-to-equity ratio (called the *total liabilities to net worth ratio* in the Almanac) of .4730 to 1 is lower than both the industry average of 1.1 to 1 for companies with assets over $250 million and the industry average of 1.2 to 1 for all companies in Table II. Analysts that are focusing on *Pier 1*'s ability to meet its obligations would be pleased that *Pier 1*'s debt-to-equity is so low relative to the industry.

Now let's see how *Pier 1*'s debt-to-equity ratio compares to our two peer companies. Exhibit 11–17 shows a chart for *Pier 1, Bed Bath & Beyond,* and *Williams-Sonoma*'s debt-to-equity ratios for 1998 through 2002.

EXHIBIT 11–17 Debt-to-Equity Ratio for 1998 Through 2002

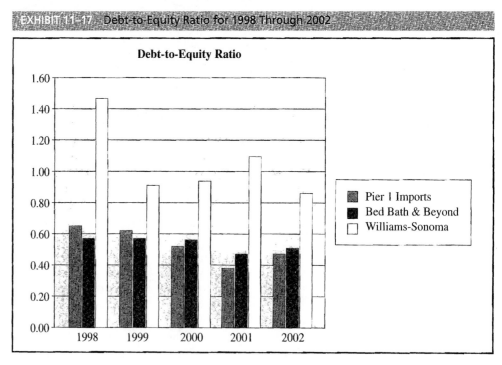

As we would expect after looking at the debt ratio for the three companies, we see that *Pier 1*'s debt is lower in proportion to equity than that of *Bed Bath & Beyond* or *Williams-Sonoma.* And, once again, there is no hard-and-fast rule concerning what a company's debt should be relative to its equity. A company's debt-to-equity ratio must be evaluated in light of peer companies in the industry, the maturity of the company (new businesses tend to have more debt relative to equity), and management's philosophy concerning the appropriate balance between debt financing and equity financing.

Times Interest Earned Ratio

Introduced in Chapter 9, the times interest earned ratio (often called the **coverage ratio**) indicates a company's ability to earn (cover) its periodic interest payments. It compares the amount of income available for interest payments to the interest requirements. Creditors use this ratio to assess the risk associated with lending money to a business. The formula for this ratio is:

$$\text{Times interest earned ratio} = \frac{\text{Earnings before interest and income taxes}}{\text{Interest expense}}$$

Earnings before interest and taxes, which is often called *EBIT*, can be calculated by taking net income and adding back income taxes and interest. In the case of *Pier 1,* EBIT is $161,297 (net income of $100,209 + income taxes of $58,788 and interest expense of $2,300). We calculate *Pier 1*'s times interest earned ratio for 2002 as:

$$\frac{\$161,297}{\$2,300} = 70.13 \text{ times}$$

This ratio calculation tells us *Pier 1*'s income available to pay interest expense was a whopping $70.13 for every $1.00 of interest expense. In other words, the income *Pier 1* had available to pay interest expense was 70.13 times the amount of interest the company reported on its income statement.

Compared to the industry averages for furniture and home furnishings stores published in the Almanac for 2002, *Pier 1*'s times interest earned ratio (called the *coverage ratio* in the Almanac) of 70.13 times is much higher than both the industry average of 5.6 times for companies with assets over $250 million and the industry average of 6.7 times for all companies in Table II. This is because *Pier 1*'s debt is almost entirely comprised of interest-free financing through short-term creditors. Analysts that are focusing on *Pier 1*'s ability to pay interest would have no concern whatsoever that *Pier 1* could meet this obligation.

Now let's see how *Pier 1*'s times interest earned ratio compares to our two peer companies. Exhibit 11–18 shows a chart depicting the times interest earned for *Pier 1 Imports, Bed Bath & Beyond,* and *Williams-Sonoma* for 2000 through 2002.

EXHIBIT 11–18 Times Interest Earned for 2000 Through 2002

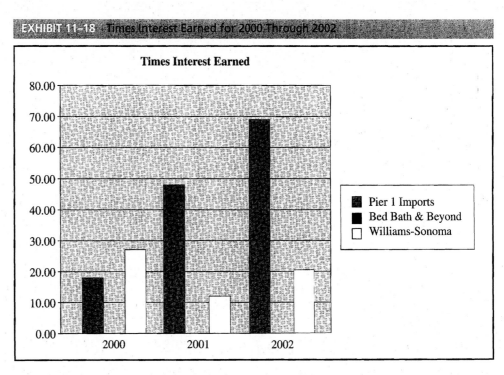

Many financial analysts believe a times interest earned ratio of at least four provides an appropriate degree of safety for creditors. This means a company's EBIT should be at least four times as great as its interest expense. The chart in Exhibit 11–18 reveals that both *Pier 1* and *Williams-Sonoma* far exceed that level. *Bed Bath &*

Beyond does not even appear on the chart because the company has virtually no interest expense.

Operating Cash Flow Coverage Ratio

operating cash flow coverage ratio A financial ratio that indicates a company's capacity to repay its liabilities from the net cash generated by its operating activities.

Introduced in Chapter 10, the **operating cash flow coverage ratio** indicates a company's capacity to repay its liabilities from the net cash generated by its operating activities. The formula for this ratio is:

$$\text{Operating cash flow coverage ratio} = \frac{\text{Cash provided by operating activities}}{\text{Average total liabilities}}$$

As you can see, the numerator is cash provided by operating activities shown on the statement of cash flows. The denominator is based on the total liabilities shown on the balance sheet. We use an average amount for the same reason we did in earlier ratios. Since the cash provided by operating activities in the numerator occurred throughout 2002, we want to know the total liabilities throughout the year. We determine this by calculating the average of the total liabilities shown on the 2001 and 2002 balance sheets ($203,831 + $277,016 = $480,847/2 = $240,423.5). We calculate *Pier 1*'s operating cash flow coverage ratio for 2002 as:

$$\frac{\$244,324}{\$240,423.5} = 1.02 \text{ to } 1$$

This ratio tells us that *Pier 1* generated $1.02 of cash through its operation in 2002 for every $1.00 of its average total liabilities for 2002. The higher this ratio is, the more likely a company is to be able to service its debt without going outside the company for financing (by either borrowing additional funds or selling additional shares of its stock).

Although the Almanac publishes some industry averages for cash flow ratios, it defines cash flows as *the difference between cash receipts and cash disbursements*. Unlike the ratio we are using, the Almanac does not focus specifically on cash flow from operating activities. Therefore, we will have to rely on our peer companies as comparisons to evaluate *Pier 1*'s operating cash flow coverage ratio. A chart depicting the operating cash flow coverage ratio for *Pier 1 Imports, Bed Bath & Beyond,* and *Williams-Sonoma* appears in Exhibit 11–19.

EXHIBIT 11–19 Operating Cash Flow Coverage Ratio for 2000 Through 2002

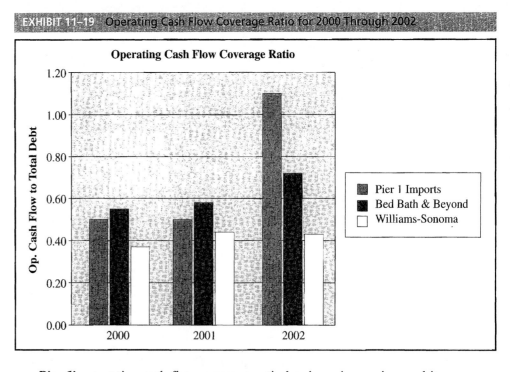

Pier 1's operating cash flow coverage ratio has been improving, and it compares favorably to the ratios of the peer companies we have been examining. As Exhibit 11–19 shows, *Pier 1*'s operating cash flow coverage ratio is currently above that of the peer

companies we are using. This means that *Pier 1*'s cash inflow from operating activities relative to total debt is higher than those of *Bed Bath & Beyond* and *Williams-Sonoma.*

Discussion Questions

11–11. Assume you had to decide to invest in one of two companies with no information other than values of four of their financial ratios. Which four would you want to know? Explain the reasons for your choices.

11–12. Carol Company and Cindy Corporation are in the same line of business. However, Carol uses straight-line depreciation, whereas Cindy uses an accelerated depreciation method. If this is the only difference in the business activity of the two companies, how should their financial ratios compare at the end of their first year of operations? Explain the effect of the difference in depreciation methods on each of the 17 ratios described in this chapter.

Analysts use ratio analysis to evaluate the company's current levels of profitability, efficiency, liquidity, and solvency. Ratios can send up red flags that warn management, creditors, and investors of trouble ahead. An unprofitable company becomes illiquid because it cannot generate profits and cash, which eventually leads to insolvency. Insolvency leads to bankruptcy. When red flags appear, management can initiate corrective action to prevent future troubles. Next, we will summarize our findings concerning *Pier 1*'s profitability, efficiency, liquidity, and solvency.

SUMMARIZING *PIER 1*'S RATIO ANALYSIS

In the following section, we summarize the results of our ratio analysis and try to rate *Pier 1*'s performance relative to the furniture and home furnishings stores industry and the two peer companies we used as comparisons. Where appropriate, to make the summaries a little easier to follow, we will use the following performance descriptions:

Very strong
Strong
Fairly strong
Average
Fairly weak
Weak
Very weak

We are only using these descriptions to help you understand the explanations that follow. They are not official financial analysis rankings of any kind.

Profitability

Gross profit margin ratio—Very strong. *Pier 1*'s gross profit margin ratio is consistently higher than those of *Bed Bath & Beyond* and *Williams-Sonoma*. *Pier 1*'s gross profit percentage has been fairly constant between about 42 and 44 percent. Note that the Almanac does not publish industry averages for this ratio.

Net profit margin ratio—Strong. Clearly, *Pier 1*'s 6.47 percent net profit margin ratio is substantially higher than the industry averages of 3.7 percent for all companies and 4.8 percent for companies with assets in excess of $250 million. *Pier 1*'s net profit margin ratio is consistently between about 6 and 7 percent. This is higher than *Williams-Sonoma*'s net profit margin but, in the last three years, *Bed Bath & Beyond*'s ratio has edged out *Pier 1*'s.

Rate of return on assets ratio—Strong. *Pier 1*'s 12.54 percent rate of return on assets ratio is on par with the industry averages of 12.7 percent for all companies and 11.4 percent for companies with assets in excess of $250 million. *Pier 1*'s rate of return on assets is clearly higher than that of *Williams-Sonoma* but somewhat lower than that of *Bed Bath & Beyond*. *Pier 1*'s return on assets ratio has been quite stable, if not increasing. This contrasts to those of the two peer company's rates, which have been declining somewhat.

Rate of return on common equity ratio—Strong. **Pier 1**'s 17.17 percent rate of return on common equity ratio is less than the industry average of 20.8 percent for all companies, but much stronger than the 13.4 percent for companies with assets in excess of $250 million. **Pier 1**'s rate of return on common equity is consistently between about 17 and 20 percent. Although it is below that of **Bed Bath & Beyond,** it has surpassed that of **Williams-Sonoma,** and it is holding steady.

Dividend payout ratio—Strong. **Pier 1** consistently pays a dividend of about 15 percent of net income, while neither **Bed Bath & Beyond** nor **Williams-Sonoma** pays a dividend at all. Note that the Almanac does not publish industry averages for this ratio.

Earnings per share—Very strong. **Pier 1**'s earnings per share is clearly the highest of the three peer companies, and the earnings per share for each of our three companies has generally increased over time. Note that the Almanac does not publish industry averages for earnings per share.

Price-to-earnings ratio—Rating not possible because it is too subjective. **Pier 1**'s PE ratio is clearly lower than those of **Bed Bath & Beyond** and **Williams-Sonoma.** Although it is not always the case, a high PE ratio *may* indicate that the stock is overvalued, whereas a low PE ratio may indicate that it is undervalued. Note that the Almanac does not publish industry averages for this ratio.

Efficiency

Asset turnover ratio—Fairly strong. Compared to the industry averages, **Pier 1**'s asset turnover ratio of 1.94 times is higher than the industry average of 1.3 times for companies with assets over $250 million, but less than the industry average of 2.5 times for all companies. **Pier 1** is doing better than companies with assets in excess of $250 million, but not as well as the industry as a whole. Over the past five years, **Pier 1**'s asset turnover ratio has improved steadily. Currently, the asset turnover ratio of all three companies is around two, which indicates that **Pier 1** compares favorably with the peer companies we are using.

Receivables turnover ratio—Very strong. This ratio tells us that the average collection period for receivables is quite short for both **Pier 1 Imports** and **Williams-Sonoma.** Both of the companies are collecting their receivables so quickly that it appears that neither is having difficulties with collections. Note that there were no receivables listed in **Bed Bath & Beyond**'s annual report. Due to the lack of data for this industry, the Almanac does not publish industry averages for this ratio for furniture and home furnishings stores.

Inventory turnover ratio—Fairly strong. Compared to the industry averages published in the 2002 edition of the Almanac, **Pier 1**'s inventory turnover ratio of 3.07 times is higher than the industry average of 2.3 times for companies with assets over $250 million, but less than the industry average of 4.2 times for all companies in Table II. This is an indication that **Pier 1** is doing better than the industry average for companies with assets in excess of $250 million, but not as well as the industry as a whole. With respect to the peer company comparison, all three companies have substantial inventories relative to their sales, and **Pier 1**'s average inventory holding period of 118.89 days falls between that of **Williams-Sonoma** (about 70 days) and **Bed Bath & Beyond** (just over 140 days).

Liquidity

Current ratio—Very strong. Compared to the industry, **Pier 1**'s current ratio of 2.9 to 1 is higher than both the industry average of 1.4 to 1 for companies with assets over $250 million and the industry average of 1.8 to 1 for all companies in Table II. In the peer company comparison, it is also clear that **Pier 1 Imports** has a higher current ratio than the other two companies. This is an indication that **Pier 1** is probably in a stronger position when it comes to its ability to pay current debt. However, if a company has too much invested in current assets, the current ratio looks better, but the company's efficiency ratios suffer.

Quick ratio—Very strong. Compared to the industry averages, **Pier 1**'s quick ratio of 1.37 to 1 is higher than both the industry average of 0.5 to 1 for companies with assets over $250 million and the industry average of 0.8 to 1 for all companies in Table II. **Pier 1**'s high quick ratio relative to the industry is a positive indication regarding the company's ability to pay its short-term obligations. With respect to the peer company comparison, **Pier 1 Imports** has a very strong showing for the quick ratio. The fact that **Pier 1**'s quick ratio is higher than those of **Bed Bath & Beyond** and **Williams-Sonoma** is an indication that **Pier 1** is in a better position to pay its short-term liabilities using quick assets. Some analysts would argue, however, that a quick ratio that is too high is a sign of inefficiency and that the company has too much invested in current assets.

Operating cash flows to current debt ratio—Very strong. The Almanac does not publish industry averages for this ratio, so we will have to rely solely on our peer company comparison. **Pier 1**'s operating cash flows to current debt ratio is consistently above those of **Bed Bath & Beyond** and **Williams-Sonoma,** indicating that **Pier 1**'s cash inflow from operating activities relative to current liabilities is higher than that of the two peer companies.

Solvency

Debt ratio—Very strong. Compared to the industry averages, **Pier 1**'s debt ratio of 32.11 percent is lower than both the industry average of 53.0 percent for companies with assets over $250 million and the industry average of 55.2 percent for all companies in Table II. With respect to our peer company comparison, **Pier 1** has less of its assets financed through debt than **Bed Bath & Beyond** and **Williams-Sonoma.** Also, **Pier 1**'s debt ratio has generally decreased over the past five years. Although there is no hard-and-fast rule concerning what amount of a company's assets should be financed through debt, analysts that are focusing on **Pier 1**'s ability to meet its obligations would be pleased that **Pier 1**'s debt ratio is so low relative to the industry and its peer companies.

Debt-to-equity ratio—Very strong. Compared to the industry averages, **Pier 1**'s debt-to-equity ratio (called the *total liabilities to net worth ratio* in the Almanac) of .4730 to 1 is lower than both the industry average of 1.1 to 1 for companies with assets over $250 million and the industry average of 1.2 to 1 for all companies in Table II. With respect to our peer company comparison, **Pier 1**'s debt is lower in proportion to equity than that of **Bed Bath & Beyond** or **Williams-Sonoma.** Once again, there is no hard-and-fast rule concerning what a company's debt should be relative to its equity; however, analysts that are focusing on **Pier 1**'s ability to meet its obligations would be pleased that **Pier 1**'s debt-to-equity ratio is so low relative to the industry and its peer companies.

Times interest earned ratio—Very strong. Compared to the industry averages, **Pier 1**'s times interest earned ratio (called the *coverage ratio* in the Almanac) of 70.13 times is much higher than both the industry average of 5.6 times for companies with assets over $250 million and the industry average of 6.7 times for all companies in Table II. With respect to our peer comparisons, **Bed Bath & Beyond** has virtually no interest expense, but **Pier 1**'s times interest earned ratio compared favorably with that of **Williams-Sonoma.** Additionally, **Pier 1**'s times interest earned ratio has increased substantially over the past three years. All of this indicates that **Pier 1** is in a very strong position when it comes to its ability to meet its obligation to pay interest.

Operating cash flow coverage ratio—Very strong. The Almanac does not publish industry averages for this ratio, so we will have to rely solely on our peer company comparison. **Pier 1**'s operating cash flow coverage ratio has been improving, and it compares favorably to the ratios of the peer companies we have been examining. At 1.02 to 1, **Pier 1**'s operating cash flow coverage ratio is currently above that of the peer companies we are using. This means that **Pier 1**'s cash inflow from operating activities relative to total debt is higher than those of **Bed Bath & Beyond** and **Williams-Sonoma.**

CONSIDERING THE INDUSTRY ENVIRONMENT—A CRUCIAL STEP IN FINANCIAL ANALYSIS

Any change in political or economic forecasts will have a ripple effect and impact most industries. *Pier 1 Imports Inc.*, is a specialty retailer operating three store chains under the names *Pier 1 Imports, The Pier,* and *Cargo,* selling furniture, decorative home furnishings, dining and kitchen goods, and bath and bedding accessories. When researching the industry outlook, we find the outlook for SIC 5700 in Chapter 42 of the *U.S. Industry & Trade Outlook 2000* (a Standard & Poor's publication). This chapter includes the outlook for retail trade covering SIC codes 5200 through 5999. It predicts moderate growth for retailers through the year 2004 with a 4.5 percent average growth rate. This growth rate is due to a slight slowdown in spending on new homes and related durable and nondurable home furnishings. Standard & Poor's suggests that a successful retailer will have to increase its market share by offering fair prices, creating value for its customers, being convenient for busy shoppers, and emphasizing customer service.

Standard & Poor's produces another publication, *Industry Surveys*, which is more specific to individual industry groups. It contains weekly and monthly updates in a loose leaf publication format. In the July 2002 issue ("Monthly Investment Review," p. 64), S&P discusses that the retail specialty stores industry has outperformed the total stock market with a stock price increase of 7.6 percent contrasted with the 9.3 percent decrease in the S&P 1500 stocks. The companies' stocks, which are classified in this industry, have risen 7.6 percent, while their home furnishing sales during the same time period have increased only 1 percent. Since consumers are spending more time at home, *Industry Surveys* predicts neutral to slightly favorable short-term results for home furnishing retailers and forecasts that internet sales will become increasingly important for future growth. It suggests that firms with value, a strong brand name, aggressive brand support, and internet sales market will prosper in the long run.

Industry Surveys focuses on one area in each publication, such as the January 31, 2002, issue that focused on specialty retailing. Specialty stores increased slightly in the market share of home furnishings. More consumers are precision shoppers who go after what they want and are less likely to make impulse purchases.

Now that we have analyzed *Pier 1*'s financial information and we have reviewed the outlook for the company's industry, we can draw some conclusions.

FINANCIAL ANALYSIS CONCLUSIONS

The conclusions that an analyst draws depends largely on individual perceptions and the analysts objectives. Remember, the objectives of financial analysts differ. But, generally, we can draw the flowing conclusions from our analysis of *Pier 1 Imports, Inc.*

1. *Pier 1* is an industry leader with strong profitability and liquidity and a very strong solvency picture.
2. If *Pier 1* can maintain its leadership position and hold down its debt, it might be a survivor in the tough competitive industry in which it operates.
3. We expect the furniture and home furnishings stores industry to continue to be at least neutral or perhaps slightly positive.
4. If we choose to invest in a specialty retail company, *Pier 1* is one to consider.

◆ LIMITATIONS OF FINANCIAL STATEMENT ANALYSIS

Ratio analysis is an excellent tool for gathering additional information about a company, but it does have its limitations.

1. Attempting to predict the future using past results depends on the predictive value of the information we use. Changes in the general economy, in the economy of the particular industry being studied, and in the company's management present some of the uncertainties that can cause past results to be an unreliable predictor of the future.

2. The financial statements used to compute the ratios are based on historical cost. In a time of rapidly changing prices, comparison between years might be difficult.

3. Figures from the balance sheet (i.e., assets, liabilities) used to calculate the ratios are year-end numbers. Because most businesses have their fiscal year-end in the slowest part of the year, the balances in such accounts as receivables, payables, and inventory at year-end may not be representative of the rest of the year. Even when averages are used instead of year-end amounts, the problem is not eliminated, for averages are typically based on year-end numbers from two consecutive years.

4. Industry peculiarities create difficulty in comparing the ratios of a company in one industry with those of a company in another industry. Even comparison of companies within an industry may not be reasonable at times because different companies use different accounting methods (e.g., depreciation methods).

5. Lack of uniformity concerning what is to be included in the numerators and denominators of specific ratios makes comparison to published industry averages extremely difficult.

Perhaps the greatest single limitation of ratio analysis is that people tend to place too much reliance on the ratios. Financial ratios should not be viewed as a magical checklist in the evaluation process. Ratio analysis only enriches all the other information decision makers should consider when making credit, investment, and similar types of decisions.

Summary ❀

In response to the need to reduce uncertainty in the decision making process, analysts developed several techniques to assist economic decision makers as they evaluate financial statement information. Creditors (short-term and long-term), equity investors (present and potential), and company management comprise the three major categories of financial statement users. Because their objectives vary, their perspectives on the results of financial statement analysis will differ.

Three external factors—general economic conditions and expectations, political events and political climate, and industry outlook—affect business performance and should be considered when evaluating results of any type of financial statement analysis.

One important method of financial statement analysis is ratio analysis, a technique for analyzing the relationship between two items from a company's financial statements for a given period. We compute ratios by dividing the dollar amount of one item from the financial statements by the dollar amount of the other item from the statements.

Analysts have developed a great many ratios over time to help economic decision makers assess a company's financial health. Because not all ratios are relevant in a given decision situation, decision makers must take care to select appropriate ratios to analyze. Ratio values, in and of themselves, have very little meaning and become meaningful only when compared to other relevant information, such as industry averages or the company's ratio values from other years.

We broadly classify financial ratios as profitability ratios, efficiency ratios, liquidity ratios, and solvency ratios. Profitability ratios measure the ease with which companies generate income. Efficiency ratios measure the investment in assets relative to business activity. Liquidity ratios measure a company's ability to generate positive cash flow in the short run to pay off short-term liabilities. Solvency ratios measure a company's ability to meet the obligations created by its long-term debt.

Each of the profitability, efficiency, liquidity, and solvency ratios provides valuable information for both internal and external decision makers. Ratio analysis does have its limitations, however. Placing too much reliance on the financial statements and the ratios derived from them without putting the information in the proper political, economic, and industry perspective can lead to poor decisions. Ratio analysis is an important financial analysis tool, but as with the other tools we have discussed throughout this book, it must be used wisely and in the proper context.

Key Terms ◦

- acid-test ratio, F–475
- asset turnover ratio, F–470
- coverage ratio, F–481
- current ratio, F–474
- debt ratio, F–478
- debt-to-equity ratio, F–480
- dividend payout ratio, F–466
- earnings per share ratio, F–468
- efficiency ratios, F–470
- financial accounting, F–449

- gross profit margin ratio, F–462
- inventory turnover ratio, F–473
- liquidity, F–474
- management accounting, F–449
- net profit margin ratio, F–463
- net sales, F–462
- operating cash flow coverage ratio, F–482
- operating cash flow to current debt ratio, F–477

- peer companies, F–455
- price-to-earnings ratio, F–469
- profitability, F–461
- quick ratio, F–475
- rate of return on assets ratio, F–465
- rate of return on common equity ratio, F–466
- receivables turnover ratio, F–471
- solvency, F–477
- times interest earned ratio, F–481

Review the Facts ◦

A. What is the purpose of financial statement analysis?
B. List the three financial statement user groups discussed in the chapter and describe what each group hopes to learn from financial statement analysis.
C. Describe the three types of external factors the Financial Accounting Standards Board (FASB) warns users of financial information to consider, and explain how each factor can impact a company's performance.
D. Briefly describe the purpose and meaning of NAICS.
E. How does NAICS relate to the SIC code system?
F. Describe how you could find publicly traded peer companies to use for financial comparisons.
G. Name three sources of financial industry averages.
H. Define profitability.
 I. List the seven profitability ratios discussed in the chapter. Describe the calculation and the purpose of each.
J. Describe the calculation and the purpose of each of the three efficiency ratios mentioned in the chapter.
K. Define liquidity.
L. List the three liquidity ratios discussed in the chapter. For each one, describe the calculation used and the purpose of the ratio.
M. What is the difference between the current ratio and the quick ratio? What is the purpose in examining both?
N. Define solvency.
O. List the four solvency ratios discussed in the chapter. For each one, describe the calculation used and the purpose of the ratio.
P. How are the debt ratio and debt-to-equity ratio related?
Q. What information can be learned from a company's times interest earned ratio?
R. Describe five limitations of ratio analysis discussed in the chapter.

Apply What You Have Learned ◦

LO 1: IDENTIFY FINANCIAL STATEMENT ANALYSIS USERS

11–13. Identify the three major categories of financial statement analysis users and describe the basic objectives of each group.

LO 2: GATHERING BACKGROUND INFORMATION

11–14. Discuss how one goes about gathering background information on a company.

LO 1 & 4: MATCHING

11–15. Listed below are items relating to the concepts presented in this chapter, followed by definitions of those items in scrambled order:

a. Financial statement analysis
b. Ratio analysis
c. Short-term creditors
d. Long-term creditors
e. Stockholders
f. Management
g. Profitability

h. Profitability ratios
i. Liquidity
j. Liquidity ratios
k. Solvency
l. Solvency ratios
m. Standard Industrial Classification
n. NAICS

1. _____ Designed to measure a firm's ability to generate sufficient cash to meet its short-term obligations.
2. _____ A method for analyzing the relationship between two items from a company's financial statements for a given period.
3. _____ Designed to measure the ease with which a company generates income.
4. _____ Focus on interest payments and the overall debt load a company carries.
5. _____ The old system to indicate a company's industry.
6. _____ The new system to indicate a company's industry.
7. _____ Looking beyond the face of the financial statements to gather additional information.
8. _____ Those who own an equity interest in a corporation.
9. _____ The ease with which an item, such as an asset, can be converted into cash.
10. _____ Trade creditors and lending institutions such as banks.
11. _____ A company's ability to meet the obligations created by its long-term debt.
12. _____ Bondholders and lending institutions such as banks.
13. _____ The ease with which companies generate income.
14. _____ Responsible for a company's day-to-day operations.

Required: Match the letter next to each item on the list with the appropriate definition. Each letter will be used only once.

LO 5: MATCHING

11–16. Listed below are all the ratios discussed in this chapter, followed by explanations of what the ratios are designed to measure in scrambled order:

a. Gross profit margin ratio
b. Net profit margin ratio
c. Rate of return on assets ratio
d. Rate of return on common equity
e. Dividend payout ratio
f. Earnings per share
g. Price-to-earnings ratio
h. Asset turnover ratio
i. Receivables turnover ratio

j. Inventory turnover ratio
k. Current ratio
l. Quick ratio
m. Operating cash flow to current debt ratio
n. Debt ratio
o. Debt-to-equity ratio
p. Times interest earned
q. Operating cash flow coverage ratio

1. _____ Most common ratio used to measure a company's ability to meet short-term obligations.
2. _____ Measures a company's ability to make periodic interest payments.
3. _____ Measures the return earned on investment in assets.
4. _____ A more stringent test of short-term liquidity than the current ratio.
5. _____ Measures the amount of after-tax net income generated by a dollar of sales.
6. _____ Indicates the proportion of assets financed by debt.
7. _____ Measures a company's ability to generate revenues from a given level of assets.
8. _____ Compares the amount of debt financing with the amount of equity financing.
9. _____ Indicates how long a company holds its inventory.
10. _____ Measures how quickly a company collects amounts owed to it by its customers.
11. _____ Measures operating cash flow relative to current debt.
12. _____ Measures operating cash flow relative to total debt.
13. _____ Expresses the relationship between per share earnings and stock price.

Required: Match the letter next to each item on the list with the appropriate explanation. Use a letter only once. Not all letters will be used.

LO 5: MATCHING

11–17. Listed below are all the ratios discussed in this chapter:

1. _____ Debt ratio
2. _____ Rate of return on common equity ratio
3. _____ Quick ratio
4. _____ Dividend payout ratio
5. _____ Operating cash flow coverage ratio
6. _____ Price-to-earnings ratio
7. _____ Gross profit margin ratio
8. _____ Asset turnover ratio
9. _____ Times interest earned ratio
10. _____ Inventory turnover ratio
11. _____ Net profit margin ratio
12. _____ Current ratio
13. _____ Rate of return on assets ratio
14. _____ Operating cash flow to current debt ratio
15. _____ Earnings per share
16. _____ Debt-to-equity ratio
17. _____ Receivables turnover ratio

Required: Identify each of the 17 ratios as a profitability ratio (P), efficiency ratio (E), a liquidity ratio (L), or a solvency ratio (S) by assigning it the appropriate letter.

LO 6: FINANCIAL RATIO CALCULATIONS

11–18. Below are partial comparative balance sheets of P.J. Boardman Company at December 31, 2005, and 2004:

P.J. Boardman Company
Partial Balance Sheets
December 31, 2005, and December 31, 2004
Current Assets and Current Liabilities Only
(in thousands)

	2005	*2004*
Current assets:		
Cash	$3,400	$2,920
Accounts receivable	1,825	2,212
Merchandise inventory	1,170	966
Supplies	240	270
Total current assets	$6,635	$6,368
Current liabilities:		
Accounts payable	$2,321	$1,740
Notes payable	3,100	3,300
Total current liabilities	$5,421	$5,040

Required:

a. Calculate Boardman's current ratios for 2005 and 2004.
b. Calculate Boardman's quick ratios for 2005 and 2004.
c. Which financial statement users are most interested in these two sets of ratios? Explain why the ratios are considered important to these users.
d. Assume that the average company in Boardman's industry has a current ratio of 2:1 and a quick ratio of 1.25:1. If you were evaluating Boardman's liquidity, what could you learn from comparing Boardman's ratios to the industry averages?

LO 6: CURRENT AND QUICK RATIO CALCULATIONS

11–19. Following are partial comparative balance sheets of Stephen Deitmer Company at December 31, 2005, and 2004:

Stephen Deitmer Company
Partial Balance Sheets
December 31, 2005, and December 31, 2004
Current Assets and Current Liabilities Only
(in thousands)

	2005	2004
Current assets:		
Cash	$2,110	$2,650
Accounts receivable	1,254	977
Merchandise inventory	730	856
Prepaid insurance	127	114
Total current assets	$4,221	$4,597
Current liabilities:		
Accounts payable	$1,054	$1,330
Notes payable	2,100	1,750
Total current liabilities	$3,154	$3,080

Required:

a. Calculate Deitmer's current ratios for 2005 and 2004.
b. Calculate Deitmer's quick ratios for 2005 and 2004.
c. Which financial statement users are most interested in these two sets of ratios? Explain why the ratios are considered important to these users.
d. Assume that the average company in Deitmer's industry has a current ratio of 2.5:1 and a quick ratio of 1:1. If you were evaluating Deitmer's liquidity, what could you learn by comparing Deitmer's ratios to those of the industry averages?
e. What, if anything, could you determine by comparing Deitmer's current ratio and quick ratio for 2004 with the same ratios for 2005? Explain your reasoning.

LO 6: LIQUIDITY EVALUATION

11–20. A five-year comparative analysis of the Amy Whitaker Company's current ratio and quick ratio is as follows:

	2000	2001	2002	2003	2004
Current ratio	1.24	1.95	2.55	3.68	4.13
Quick ratio	1.20	1.06	0.96	0.77	0.51

Required:

a. What does this analysis tell you about the overall liquidity of the Amy Whitaker Company over the five-year period?
b. What does this analysis tell you about what has happened to the composition of Whitaker's current assets over the five-year period?

LO 6: LIQUIDITY EVALUATION

11–21. A five-year comparative analysis of the Margaret Elsea Company's current ratio and quick ratio is as follows:

	2000	2001	2002	2003	2004
Current ratio	4.24	3.95	2.95	2.68	1.93
Quick ratio	0.51	0.86	1.03	1.33	1.68

Required:

a. What does this analysis tell you about the overall liquidity of the Margaret Elsea Company over the five-year period?
b. What does this analysis tell you about what has happened to the composition of Elsea's current assets over the five-year period?

LO 6: PROFITABILITY EVALUATION

11–22.   A five-year comparative analysis of the Annie Todd Company's gross profit margin ratio and net profit margin ratio is as follows:

	2000	*2001*	*2002*	*2003*	*2004*
Gross profit margin ratio	13.83	13.65	13.34	12.75	12.53
Net profit margin ratio	2.22	2.95	3.41	3.77	4.12

Required:

a. What does this analysis indicate about the company's performance over the five-year period?

b. Which of the following groups would be interested in this analysis? Include in your answer a brief discussion of how you think each of them would interpret this analysis.

1. Trade creditors
2. Long-term creditors
3. Stockholders
4. Company managers

LO 6: PROFITABILITY EVALUATION

11–23.   A five-year comparative analysis of Juan Rodriguez Company's gross profit margin ratio and net profit margin ratio is as follows:

	2000	*2001*	*2002*	*2003*	*2004*
Gross profit margin ratio	11.28	9.16	8.48	7.01	5.78
Net profit margin ratio	9.33	8.59	6.14	5.72	3.89

Required:

a. What does this analysis indicate about Rodriguez's performance over the five-year period?

b. Which of the following groups would be interested in this analysis? Include in your answer a brief discussion of how you think each of them would interpret this analysis.

1. Trade creditors
2. Long-term creditors
3. Stockholders
4. Company managers

LO 6: SOLVENCY EVALUATION

11–24.   A five-year comparative analysis of the Kasey Sheehan Company's debt-to-equity ratio and debt ratio is as follows:

	2000	*2001*	*2002*	*2003*	*2004*
Debt-to-equity ratio	2.75	2.50	2.25	1.50	1.00
Debt ratio	73.33	71.43	69.23	60.00	50.00

Required:

a. What does this analysis indicate about Kasey Sheehan Company's capital structure over the five-year period?

b. Which of the following groups would be interested in this analysis? Include in your answer a brief discussion of how you think each of them would interpret this analysis.

1. Trade creditors
2. Long-term creditors
3. Stockholders
4. Company managers

LO 6: SOLVENCY EVALUATION

11–25. A five-year comparative analysis of the Jane Avery Company's debt-to-equity and debt ratio is as follows:

	2000	*2001*	*2002*	*2003*	*2004*
Debt-to-equity ratio	1.50	1.15	2.65	2.25	1.90
Debt ratio	60.00	53.49	72.60	69.23	65.52

Required:

a. What does this analysis indicate about Avery's capital structure over the five-year period?

b. Which of the following groups would be interested in this analysis? Include in your answer a brief discussion of how you think each of them would interpret this analysis.

1. Trade creditors
2. Long-term creditors
3. Stockholders
4. Company managers

LO 6: FINANCIAL RATIO CALCULATIONS

11–26. Below are the comparative balance sheets for Oscar Holzmann Company at December 31, 2005, and 2004. Also included is Oscar Holzmann's income statement for the year ended December 31, 2005:

Oscar Holzmann Company
Balance Sheets
December 31, 2005, and December 31, 2004
(in thousands)

	2005	*2004*
ASSETS:		
Current assets:		
Cash	$ 1,618	$1,220
Accounts receivable	1,925	2,112
Merchandise inventory	1,070	966
Prepaid expenses	188	149
Total current assets	$ 4,801	$4,447
Property, plant, and equipment:		
Buildings, net	$ 4,457	$2,992
Equipment, net	1,293	1,045
Total property, plant, and equipment	$5,750	$4,037
Total assets	$10,551	$8,484
LIABILITIES:		
Current liabilities:		
Accounts payable	$ 1,818	$1,686
Notes payable	900	1,100
Total current liabilities	$ 2,718	$2,786
Long-term liabilities	2,500	2,000
Total liabilities	$ 5,218	$4,786
STOCKHOLDERS' EQUITY:		
Common stock, no-par value	$ 3,390	$2,041
Retained earnings	1,943	1,657
Total stockholders' equity	$5,333	$3,698
Total liabilities and stockholders' equity	$10,551	$8,484

Oscar Holzmann Company
Income Statement
For the Year Ended December 31, 2005
(in thousands)

Sales revenue	$11,228
LESS: Cost of goods sold	7,751
Gross profit on sales	$ 3,477

LESS: Operating expenses:		
Depreciation—buildings and equipment	$ 102	
Other selling and administrative	2,667	
Total operating expenses		2,769
Income from operations		$ 708
LESS: Interest expense		168
Income before taxes		$ 540
Income taxes		114
Net income		$ 426

Additional Information:

Dividends paid during 2005 totaled $140,000.
Cash flows from operating activities for 2005 totaled $504,000.
Average number of common shares outstanding for 2005 was 3,550,000 shares.
Average market price per common share for 2005 was $1.02.

Required: Compute the following ratios for 2005:

1. Gross profit margin ratio
2. Net profit margin ratio
3. Rate of return on assets ratio
4. Rate of return on common equity ratio
5. Dividend payout ratio
6. Earnings per share
7. Price-to-earnings ratio
8. Asset turnover ratio
9. Receivables turnover ratio
10. Inventory turnover ratio
11. Current ratio
12. Quick ratio
13. Operating cash flow to current debt ratio
14. Debt ratio
15. Debt-to-equity ratio
16. Times interest earned ratio
17. Operating cash flow coverage ratio

LO 6: FINANCIAL RATIO CALCULATIONS

11–27. Below are the comparative balance sheets for the Tom Robinson Company at December 31, 2005, and 2004, and the income statements for the years ended December 31, 2005, and 2004.

Tom Robinson Company
Balance Sheets
December 31, 2005, and December 31, 2004
(in thousands)

	2005	2004
ASSETS:		
Current assets:		
Cash	$1,292	$ 980
Accounts receivable	1,068	1,112
Merchandise inventory	970	906
Supplies	40	59
Prepaid expenses	48	50
Total current assets	$3,418	$3,107
Property, plant, and equipment:		
Buildings, net	$3,457	$2,442
Equipment, net	993	945
Total property, plant, and equipment	$4,450	$3,387
Total assets	$7,868	$6,494

LIABILITIES:

Current liabilities:

Accounts payable	$ 998	$ 786
Notes payable	600	500
Total current liabilities	$1,598	$1,286
Long-term liabilities	837	467
Total liabilities	$2,435	$1,753

STOCKHOLDERS' EQUITY:

Common stock, no-par value	$2,490	$2,000
Retained earnings	2,943	2,741
Total stockholders' equity	$5,433	$4,741
Total liabilities and stockholders' equity	$7,868	$6,494

Tom Robinson Company
Income Statements
For the Years Ended
December 31, 2005, and 2004
(in thousands)

	2005	2004
Net sales	$9,228	$8,765
LESS: Cost of goods sold	6,751	6,097
Gross profit on sales	$2,477	$2,668
LESS: Operating expenses:		
Depreciation—buildings and equipment	$ 80	$ 56
Other selling and administrative	1,667	1,442
Total operating expenses	$1,747	$1,498
Operating income	$ 730	$1,170
LESS: Interest expense	98	89
Income before taxes	$ 632	$1,081
Income taxes	190	357
Net income	$ 442	$ 724

Additional Information:

Dividends paid during 2005 totaled $240,000.

Average number of common shares outstanding for 2005 was 2,600,000 shares.

Cash flows from operating activities for 2005 totaled $835,000.

Average market price per common share for 2005 was $1.55.

Required:

a. Calculate the following ratios for 2005:

   1. Gross profit margin ratio
   2. Net profit margin ratio
   3. Rate of return on assets ratio
   4. Rate of return on common equity ratio
   5. Dividend payout ratio
   6. Earnings per share
   7. Price-to-earnings ratio
   8. Asset turnover ratio
   9. Receivables turnover ratio
   10. Inventory turnover ratio
   11. Current ratio
   12. Quick ratio
   13. Operating cash flow to current debt ratio
   14. Debt ratio
   15. Debt-to-equity ratio
   16. Times interest earned ratio
   17. Operating cash flow coverage ratio

b. Using the ratios you calculated in the previous requirement, complete the following comparison of Tom Robinson's ratios to those of its entire industry and companies of comparable asset size for 2005. Note that industry averages are not available for all the ratios you calculated previously. Accordingly, some of the ratios will not appear in your comparison.

	Total Industry	Assets Between $5 Million and $10 Million	Tom Robinson Company
Gross profit margin ratio			
Net profit margin ratio	4.99	4.61	
Rate of return on assets ratio	9.30	10.40	
Rate of return on common equity ratio	6.12	5.85	
Asset turnover ratio	1.76	1.42	
Receivables turnover ratio	7.83	6.54	
Inventory turnover ratio	5.73	5.47	
Current ratio	1.46	1.95	
Quick ratio	0.93	1.11	
Debt ratio	65.99	65.87	
Debt-to-equity ratio	1.94	1.93	
Times interest earned ratio	5.63	5.16	

c. Analyze the industry comparison you completed in the previous requirement as follows:

1. Identify any ratios you think do not warrant further analysis. Be sure to explain why any particular ratio is not going to be analyzed further.
2. For those ratios you felt deserved further analysis, assess whether Tom Robinson's ratios are better or worse relative to both the entire industry and companies of comparable asset size.

LO 6: RATIO ANALYSIS

11–28. Below is a comparison of certain ratios for the Paul Munter Company for the years 2000 through 2004:

	2000	2001	2002	2003	2004
Gross profit margin ratio	32.25%	31.04%	30.42%	29.22%	28.67%
Net profit margin ratio	8.66%	7.90%	7.14%	6.52%	2.28%
Rate of return on assets ratio	9.28%	8.44%	8.20%	7.68%	6.21%
Rate of return on common equity	8.31%	8.06%	7.22%	6.38%	4.77%
Asset turnover ratio	1.46	1.40	1.17	1.08	0.99
Receivables turnover ratio	8.93	7.41	6.52	5.87	5.34
Inventory turnover ratio	8.88	8.24	8.11	6.46	4.45
Current ratio	1.77	1.91	2.93	2.41	3.12
Quick ratio	1.40	1.26	1.08	0.94	0.79
Debt ratio	48.97%	54.95%	66.33%	68.85%	71.75%
Debt-to-equity ratio	0.96	1.22	1.97	2.21	2.54
Times interest earned ratio	6.90	6.91	5.76	5.24	3.49

Required: Analyze the five-year company comparison as follows:

a. Identify any ratios you think do not warrant further analysis. Be sure to explain why any particular ratio is not going to be analyzed further.
b. For each ratio you felt deserved further analysis, assess whether it has improved or worsened over the five-year period.
c. Based on your analysis of the five-year company comparison, comment briefly on the trend of Paul Munter Company's performance over the five-year period.

Problems 11–29 through 11–33 are based on the following comparative financial statements of Debbie Hoffman and Company:

Debbie Hoffman and Company
Balance Sheets
As of December 31, 2004, 2003, and 2002
(in thousands)

	2004	2003	2002
ASSETS:			
Current assets:			
Cash	$ 2,240	$1,936	$1,836
Accounts receivable	2,340	2,490	2,530

Merchandise inventory	776	693	520
Prepaid expenses	200	160	145
Total current assets	$ 5,556	$5,279	$5,031
Property, plant, and equipment	10,410	8,810	8,480
Accumulated depreciation	(5,241)	(5,057)	(4,810)
Property, plant, and equipment, net	$5,169	$3,753	$3,670
Total assets	$10,725	$9,032	$8,701
LIABILITIES:			
Current liabilities—accounts payable	$ 4,336	$4,000	$3,843
Long-term liabilities—notes payable	2,000	1,600	1,900
Total liabilities	$6,336	$5,600	$5,743
STOCKHOLDERS' EQUITY:			
Common stock, no-par value	$ 3,000	$2,400	$2,400
Retained earnings	1,389	1,032	558
Total stockholders' equity	$ 4,389	$3,432	$2,958
Total liabilities and stockholders' equity	$10,725	$9,032	$8,701

Debbie Hoffman and Company
Income Statements
For the Years Ended December 31, 2004, 2003, and 2002
(in thousands)

	2004	*2003*	*2002*
Net sales revenue	$14,745	$12,908	$11,800
LESS: Cost of goods sold	10,213	8,761	7,810
Gross profit on sales	$ 4,532	$ 4,147	$ 3,990
LESS: Operating expenses:			
Selling expense	$ 1,022	$ 546	$ 523
General and administrative	2,721	2,451	2,390
Total operating expenses	3,743	2,997	2,913
Operating income	789	$ 1,150	$ 1,077
Interest expense	172	137	127
Income before income taxes	$ 617	$ 1,013	$ 950
Income taxes	123	355	323
Net income	$ 494	$ 658	$ 627

Additional Information:

	2004	*2003*	*2002*
Dividends paid	$ 137,000	$184,000	$ 176,000
Cash flow from operating activities	$1,041,000	$914,000	$1,200,000
Average market price per common share	$1.41	$1.83	$1.62
Average number of common shares outstanding	2,470,000	2,350,000	2,160,000

LO 6: FINANCIAL RATIO CALCULATIONS

11–29. Using the Hoffman and Company financial statements, calculate the following ratios for 2004 and 2003:

1. Gross profit margin ratio
2. Net profit margin ratio
3. Rate of return on assets ratio
4. Rate of return on common equity ratio
5. Dividend payout ratio
6. Earnings per share
7. Price-to-earnings ratio
8. Asset turnover ratio
9. Receivables turnover ratio
10. Inventory turnover ratio

11. Current ratio
12. Quick ratio
13. Operating cash flow to current debt ratio
14. Debt ratio
15. Debt-to-equity ratio
16. Times interest earned ratio
17. Operating cash flow coverage ratio

LO 6: COMPARING RATIOS TO INDUSTRY AVERAGES

11–30. Below is a partially completed comparison of Hoffman's ratios to those of its entire industry and companies of comparable asset size for 2004:

	Total Industry	Assets Between $10 Million and $25 Million	Hoffman
Gross profit margin ratio			
Net profit margin ratio	4.49	2.61	
Rate of return on assets ratio	9.30	10.40	
Rate of return on common equity ratio	16.12	15.85	
Dividend payout ratio			
Earnings per share			
Price-to-earnings ratio			
Asset turnover ratio	1.76	1.42	
Receivables turnover ratio	7.83	6.54	
Inventory turnover ratio	5.78	5.77	
Current ratio	2.24	1.95	
Quick ratio	1.33	1.31	
Operating cash flow to current debt ratio			
Debt ratio	69.51	65.99	
Debt-to-equity ratio	2.28	1.94	
Times interest earned ratio	5.43	3.16	
Operating cash flow coverage ratio			

Required:

a. Complete the industry comparison by calculating each of Hoffman and Company's ratios for 2004 and recording them in the space provided. (*Note:* If you have completed problem 11–29, you have already done the calculations. Just use the ratios you have already calculated.)

b. Analyze the industry comparison you completed in the previous requirement as follows:

1. Identify any ratios you think do not warrant further analysis. Be sure to explain why any particular ratio is not going to be analyzed further.
2. For those ratios you felt deserved further analysis, assess whether Hoffman's ratios are better or worse relative to both the entire industry and companies of comparable asset size.
3. Based on your analysis of the industry comparison, comment briefly on how you think Hoffman and Company compares to other companies in its industry.

LO 6: FINANCIAL RATIO ANALYSIS

11–31. Below is a partially completed comparison of Hoffman's ratios for the years 2000 through 2004:

	2000	2001	2002	2003	2004
Gross profit margin ratio	34.16%	34.11%	33.81%		
Net profit margin ratio	5.35%	5.33%	5.31%		
Rate of return on assets ratio	5.22%	6.11%	8.67%		
Rate of return on common equity ratio	23.18%	22.62%	21.20%		
Dividend payout ratio	27.98%	28.02%	28.08%		
Earnings per share	$.32	$.30	$.29		

Price-to-earnings ratio	9.43	8.72	5.58
Asset turnover ratio	1.11	1.86	1.36
Receivables turnover ratio	4.80	4.99	4.66
Inventory turnover ratio	10.88	11.37	15.02
Current ratio	2.07	2.62	1.31
Quick ratio	1.00	1.09	1.14
Operating cash flow to current debt ratio	.45	.39	.31
Debt ratio	54.95%	62.26%	66.00%
Debt-to-equity ratio	1.22	1.65	1.94
Times interest earned ratio	6.31	5.44	8.48
Operating cash flow coverage ratio	.30	.26	.21

Required:

a. Complete the five-year company comparison by calculating each of Hoffman's ratios for 2003 and 2004 and recording them in the space provided. (*Note:* If you have completed problem 11–29, you have already done the calculations. Just use the ratios you have already calculated.)

b. Analyze the five-year company comparison you completed in the previous requirement as follows:

1. Identify any ratios you think do not warrant further analysis. Be sure to explain why any particular ratio is not going to be analyzed further.
2. For each ratio you felt deserved further analysis, assess whether it has improved or gotten worse over the five-year period.
3. Based on your analysis of the five-year company comparison, comment briefly on the trend of Hoffman and Company's performance over the five-year period.

COMPREHENSIVE

11–32. The financial statements for Debbie Hoffman and Company do not include a statement of cash flows. To assess the company's overall performance in 2004, however, you should also look at its statement of cash flows.

Required:

a. Using the 2003 and 2004 comparative balance sheets and the income statement for 2004, prepare Hoffman's 2004 statement of cash flows.
b. Which of the three broad activities (operating, investing, and financing) provided Hoffman with the majority of its cash during 2004?
c. Briefly discuss whether the activity you identified in the previous requirement is an appropriate source of cash in the long run.
d. In which of the three broad activities (operating, investing, and financing) did Hoffman use most of its cash during 2004?
e. Briefly discuss what your answer to the previous requirement reveals about Hoffman.

COMPREHENSIVE

11–33. The financial statements for Debbie Hoffman and Company did not include a statement of stockholders' equity. To assess the company's overall performance in 2004, however, you should also look at the company's statement of stockholders' equity.

Required:

a. Using the 2003 and 2004 comparative balance sheets and the income statement for 2004, prepare Hoffman's 2004 statement of stockholders' equity.
b. Briefly discuss how the statement of stockholders' equity demonstrates articulation among Hoffman's financial statements.

LO 7: LIMITATIONS OF RATIO ANALYSIS

11–34. The chapter discussed several limitations of ratio analysis, namely:

1. Using past results to predict future performance
2. Using historical cost as a basis for ratios

3. Using year-end balances as either the numerator or denominator for many ratios
4. Industry peculiarities
5. Lack of uniformity in defining the numerators and denominators used in calculating ratios
6. Giving too much credence to ratio analysis

Required: Explain why each of the six items listed limit the usefulness of ratio analysis.

Financial Reporting Exercises ⬤

LO 6: FINANCIAL RATIO CALCULATIONS AND EVALUATION

11–35. Using the **SEC's EDGAR** system, obtain a copy of the **Nautica, Inc.,** income statement, balance sheet, and statement of cash flows from the company's Form 10-K for 2001.

Required:

a. Using **Nautica**'s financial statements, calculate the 17 ratios presented in the chapter for the latest year presented.
b. Based on the ratios, write a summary of your impression of the company's profitability, efficiency, liquidity, and solvency.

LO 6: FINANCIAL RATIO CALCULATIONS AND EVALUATION

11–36. Using the **SEC's EDGAR** system, obtain a copy of the **Tommy Hilfiger, Inc.,** income statement, balance sheet, and statement of cash flows from the company's Form 10-K for 2001.

Required:

a. Using **Hilfiger**'s financial statements, calculate the 17 ratios presented in the chapter for the latest year presented.
b. Based on the ratios, write a summary of your impression of the company's profitability, efficiency, liquidity, and solvency?

LO 6: PEER COMPANY COMPARISON

11–37. Requires completion of problems 11–35 and 11–36.

Required:

a. For each of the two companies (**Nautica, Inc.,** and **Tommy Hilfiger, Inc.**), circle the ratio you think is more favorable.
b. Write a brief report that compares the two company's profitability, efficiency, liquidity, and solvency.
c. In which company would you rather invest? Explain.

LO 6: FINANCIAL RATIO CALCULATIONS AND EVALUATION (PART B REQUIRES A LIBRARY SOURCE FOR INDUSTRY AVERAGES.)

11–38. Visit the PHLIP Web site for this book at *www.prenhall.com/werner* to find the link for two companies in the same industry. Select an industry in which you are interested.

Required:

a. Calculate the 17 basic ratios presented in the chapter for the most current year for each of the companies.
b. Based on the ratios that you have computed, and the information presented in the chapter, how do these companies compare with each other and the industry averages on the basis of the ratios that you have computed. Industry averages may be obtained from the sources identified in the text, which are usually found in the reference section of the library.

LO 6: FINANCIAL RATIO CALCULATIONS AND EVALUATION

11–39. Visit the PHLIP Web site for this book at *www.prenhall.com/werner* and locate the links for **Ford Motor Company** and for **General Motors Corporation.**

Required:

a. Using the corporations' financial statements, calculate the following ratios for the latest year presented. (Assume minority interest is part of stockholders' equity.) Compute the following ratios:

1. Gross profit margin ratio
2. Net profit margin ratio
3. Rate of return on assets ratio
4. Rate of return on common equity ratio
5. Dividend payout ratio
6. Earnings per share
7. Price-to-earnings ratio
8. Asset turnover ratio
9. Receivables turnover ratio
10. Inventory turnover ratio
11. Current ratio
12. Quick ratio
13. Operating cash flow to current debt ratio
14. Debt ratio
15. Debt-to-equity ratio
16. Times interest earned ratio
17. Operating cash flow coverage ratio

b. Write a report comparing the two companies' profitability, efficiency, liquidity, and solvency. In your report's summary, indicate which company you feel is the stronger investment. Explain the reasons for your choice, or, the difficulty you had making a choice.

LO 6: FINANCIAL RATIO CALCULATIONS AND EVALUATION

11–40. Visit the PHLIP Web site for this book at *www.prenhall.com/werner* and locate the link for ***Ford Motor Company.***

Required:

a. Using the financial statements and the financial summary of ***Ford Motor Company,*** prepare a five-year ratio analysis. For several ratios, there will not be enough information provided for all five years. In such cases, write a brief explanation and place it at the end of your response to this requirement. (Assume any minority interest is part of stockholders' equity.)

b. Based on the ratios you prepared for the previous requirement:

1. Identify any ratios you think are improving.
2. Identify any ratios you think are getting worse.
3. Comment briefly on the trend of ***Ford***'s performance over the five-year period.

ANNUAL REPORT PROJECT

11–41. Section 11 – Summary, Conclusions, and Recommendations

In the first 10 sections of this annual report project, you gathered and reported on a variety of information. In addition, you calculated 17 ratios, compared those ratios to a peer company, and commented on each ratio and its comparison. Now it's time to bring all this information together for a final report on the company you selected.

Required:

a. Prepare a schedule that lists all of the ratios you calculated for your company and its peer. Your report should be arranged in the following order, which is the same arrangement as they appear in Chapter 11 and in Exhibit 11–1:

Profitability ratios:

- Gross profit margin ratio
- Net profit margin ratio
- Rate of return on assets ratio

- Rate of return on common equity ratio
- Dividend payout ratio
- Earnings per share
- Price-to-earnings ratio

Efficiency ratios:

- Asset turnover ratio
- Receivables turnover ratio
- Inventory turnover ratio

Liquidity ratios:

- Current ratio
- Quick ratio
- Operating cash flow to current debt ratio

Solvency ratios:

- Debt ratio
- Debt-to-equity ratio
- Times interest earned ratio
- Operating cash flow coverage ratio

b. Review Sections 1 through 10 of your annual report project. Based on the schedule of ratios you prepared and your review of your annual report project, prepare a report that summarizes what you have learned about your company. Your report should include a section with your overall conclusion. Be sure to mention your company's strengths, weaknesses, opportunities, and threats. What is your opinion regarding whether your company is a good investment candidate? Based on what you have learned about the company, do you think the company would be a good prospect for employment?

Pier 1 imports®

annual report 2002

Financial Highlights
For the three years ended March 2, 2002

Pier 1 Imports, as one of North America's largest specialty retailers of unique decorative home furnishings, gifts and related items, achieved record sales of over $1.5 billion and record net income of over $100 million in fiscal 2002. Pier 1 directly imports from over 40 countries around the world, displaying merchandise in a visually appealing setting in stores throughout the United States, Canada, Puerto Rico, the United Kingdom and Mexico.

	2002	2001	2000
	($ in millions except per share amounts)		
For the year:			
Net sales	$ 1,548.6	$1,411.5	$1,231.1
Gross profit	649.8	594.5	512.5
Operating expenses	490.9	442.9	389.4
Operating income	158.8	151.5	123.2
Nonoperating (income) and expenses, net	(0.2)	1.3	4.6
Income before income taxes	159.0	150.2	118.6
Net income	$ 100.2	$ 94.7	$ 74.7
Basic earnings per share	$ 1.06	$ .98	$ .78
Diluted earnings per share	$ 1.04	$ .97	$ .75
Weighted average diluted shares outstanding (millions)	96.2	98.0	103.3
Increase in same-store sales (1)	4.5%	7.8%	2.7%
At year-end:			
Number of stores worldwide (2)	974	899	834
North American retail square feet (millions)(3)	6.9	6.2	5.9

(1) Stores included in the same-store sales calculation are those stores opened prior to the beginning of the preceding fiscal year and that are still open, including qualifying relocated stores. For further explanation regarding the calculation of same-store sales, see Critical Accounting Policies in Management's Discussion and Analysis of Financial Condition and Results of Operations. Same-store sales amounts reflect a 52-week comparison for all periods presented. All other fiscal 2001 data includes 53 weeks of operations. For an explanation regarding the fluctuation in same-store sales increases from year to year, refer to Management's Discussion and Analysis of Financial Condition and Results of Operations for those years.

(2) Worldwide store count at fiscal 2001 year-end includes the acquisition of Cargo Furniture, Inc. on February 21, 2001. Results of operations for fiscal 2001 were not affected by this acquisition. By fiscal 2002 year-end, all Japan locations had been closed. Results of operations for all years presented include Japan's operations.

(3) North American retail square footage includes Pier 1 Imports' locations throughout the United States and Canada, along with Cargo stores.

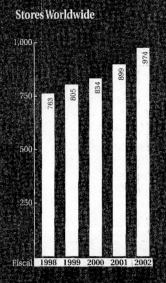

Stores Worldwide

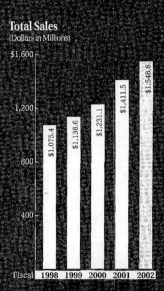

Total Sales
(Dollars in Millions)

Making ourselves at home.

The things that make up a home are simple. Whether they're family,

friends or a favorite chair, they fill empty spaces with warmth and love.

When someone brings home an armoire or rug from one of our stores,

we understand just how big a compliment that is. Invitations home

aren't given to casual acquaintances. They're reserved for those you're

most comfortable with. It's a statement from our customers that they're

at home with us and we're at home with them.

Pier 1 imports®

Fiscal year 2002 was a unique and exceptional year for Pier 1 Imports. The first half of the year was difficult, affected by soft economic conditions. Then the events of September 11th changed our nation forever. During that second half of the year, the influences of "cocooning" took hold in America. Individuals chose to retreat to the security and comfort of their homes. As a company, we moved ahead with even more compassion toward our associates, friends, family and customers. Pier 1 Imports has been a known and trusted brand for 40 years. I believe that we understand the importance of providing customers with value, quality and style that is found in a friendly and relaxing shopping experience.

We are proud that fiscal year 2002, notwithstanding the difficult first half, was a record year for the Company. Net income was over $100 million for the first time in Pier 1's history. Sales were $1.55 billion, an increase of 9.7% over last year's $1.4 billion. All-important same-store sales grew by 4.5%. Diluted earnings per share for the year was $1.04 compared to $.97 a year ago. The increases in traffic, transactions and average ticket for the year were supported by positive customer response to new merchandise assortments during the year and a very successful advertising campaign.

We continue to strengthen the Company's balance sheet, as evidenced by cash of $235.6 million at the end of fiscal 2002. Net income plus depreciation was $143 million, and working capital was a source of funds so that cash generated from operations was $244 million. We repurchased four million shares of the Company's stock during the year, and the Board of Directors recently authorized up to a total of $150 million of additional share repurchases. In keeping with our conservative financial strategy, we will continue to be prudent in our infrastructure investments and in funding the future growth of the Company.

The acceleration of new store growth continued in fiscal 2002, with 104 new Pier 1 stores opening and 20 closing or relocating to stronger trading areas. This year, fiscal 2003, we plan to open 115 to 120 Pier 1 stores and will close 30. Our research has identified more than 500 additional potential sites for Pier 1 stores throughout North America, which we plan to develop over the next eight to ten years. This represents a 65% increase in our current base of store locations at the end of fiscal 2002.

We ended fiscal 2002 with 910 Pier 1 stores in North America, 16 in Mexico, 7 in Puerto Rico, 23 stores in the United Kingdom operating as "The Pier" and 18 Cargo stores, for a total of 974 stores worldwide. In addition, we are prepared to begin the Cargo store rollout. During fiscal 2003, we plan to open eight to twelve new Cargo stores and have aggressive growth plans for over 300 Cargo stores in North America during the next ten years.

Pier 1 continued its successful national marketing campaign this year with television and print advertising. We increased the use of direct marketing by growing our proprietary database to over 7.5 million customers. Special incen-

Sales of our Komen Candle benefit breast cancer research.

tives targeted to our most valued customers were used to increase shopping frequency and average ticket. The Pier 1 preferred card continued to be widely accepted among our most loyal shoppers. Sales from the preferred card represent 30% of Pier 1 and Cargo's store sales, and the average amount spent on the card is more than three times that of a typical Pier 1 or Cargo customer. We continue to see growth from our e-commerce business. Pier1.com has become a valuable source for our customers in gaining product information, receiving promotional and sale event notifications, and for finding store locations throughout North America. Additionally, our e-marketing efforts are beginning to generate very positive results with the acquisition of more than 250,000 e-mail subscribers. As a whole, these integrated marketing initiatives have raised brand awareness for our unique selling proposition, resulting in a significant increase in customer traffic in Pier 1 stores.

Our support for UNICEF helps impoverished children and families.

Our charitable efforts extend internationally from the countries where we source merchandise, to national causes and local initiatives in our hometown that our associates and customers believe in and support. This year our philanthropic work took on a whole new meaning, as our Pier 1 associates, as well as our customers, reached out with added enthusiasm. Sales of 2001 UNICEF greeting cards generated almost $2 million, all of which was donated to help families, and especially children, that needed food, medicine and supplies in Third-World countries. Pier 1 also was a national box distributor for "Trick-or-Treat" for UNICEF, which raised an estimated $3.5 million for emergency relief for the children of Afghanistan. In November 2001, we donated an additional $100,000 to UNICEF to help save the lives of Afghan women and children.

Nationally, we also sell a specially designed candle in October, Breast Cancer Awareness Month, to help fund the Susan G. Komen Breast Cancer Foundation. In 2001, our contribution from the sale of these candles to the Komen foundation was over $144,000, which strengthens our belief that our customers share in our passion to help those in need. This is in addition to sponsoring thousands of Pier 1 associates to participate in Race for the Cure® events across the U.S. and Canada. In our headquarters city of Fort Worth, Texas, we continued to donate time and gifts to the United Way, Daggett Elementary (our Adopt-A-School) and other various organizations that support the community.

Since accepting my position as Chairman and CEO in 1998, I have worked very hard to enhance Pier 1's culture of unquestionable integrity and responsibility, expressed in both written codes and living example. Our retail business is simple and straightforward, and so are our financials. Many public companies, including ours, have reviewed current board and company policies. Your Board of Directors will continue to oversee the corporate governance and ethical principles of the Company in order to serve the interests of our shareholders and associates.

Tomorrow's successful retailers must be customer-centered with a focus on increasing *value*. Value means not only price, but quality, selection and an engaging shopping experience. This defines the Pier 1 Imports brand

and is the promise we will keep in satisfying our loyal and passionate customers. As we reflect on our 40 successful years in the retail business, I am pleased with our accomplishments ... but I believe the best is yet to come as we implement plans to grow in totally new ways and directions. To our customers, suppliers, associates, Board of Directors and shareholders who make it all possible: Thank you for your support.

Marvin J. Girouard
Chairman and Chief Executive Officer

Coming home to Pier 1 Imports. To an ever-broadening spectrum of consumers – including baby boomers and Gen-X and -Yers – there's no place like home.

A decade ago, business author/trend consultant Faith Popcorn dubbed this trend *cocooning*, defined as "the need to protect oneself from the unpredictable realities of the outside world." In this scenario, consumer spending focuses on safety, security … and comfort.

If there was ever any question about Popcorn's theory, all doubt seems to have been erased in the last year, as the "trend" has become a full-blown cultural phenomenon. Goods and services that responded to this lifestyle shift have experienced a strong market – a conclusion borne out by the fact that during the slumping economy in 2001, Pier 1 Imports and other retailers that addressed these needs performed quite well.

Pier 1's answers to the trend? An ever-changing mix of products that stimulates the senses, making homes not just warm and inviting, but also a reflection of individual style. A value proposition that promises a decorating resource that fits any budget. And refocused store location metrics that prove while we're already established and well-entrenched, there's still plenty of room for growth.

Our marketing campaign also meshes with this stay-at-home trend, conveying our brand position of casual comfort, style and fun. We have achieved success through marketing our preferred card, a national TV campaign, print advertising and database marketing, plus national programs for interior designers and bridal and gift registries. E-commerce initiatives are also growing, with online sales and e-mail marketing to a database that already includes 250,000 subscribers.

The proof of our efforts? Our customers have rewarded us by making Pier 1 Imports a part of their homes – resulting in record sales of $1.55 billion during fiscal 2002.

The marketplace has undergone a paradigm shift most evident in the past several months – a shift accelerated by recent eco events, terrorism and other uncertainties. People seem to be looking deeper inside to find what they really value. For this shift places us not just at the right place at the right time … but the right place for the future as well.

It was an uncomfortably hot Saturday in July when Darrell learned of Lisa's new love.

Well-built, good-looking. She said it would last. Darrell was generous in his response, even understanding. After all, the cabinet was perfect – like everything she'd fallen for from Pier 1.

A world of value. The success of the Pier 1 Imports brand is built upon offering unique and exclusive merchandise at a value. The brand is known for being casual, eclectic and culturally inspired.

Just as unique as our products are the people behind them. Stocking America's best-known chain of imported home fashions is no simple task – but it is a labor of love. Our merchandising team consists of some of the most-traveled people on the planet. Our buyers spend many a week far from home. Expertise and a sense of style are required to develop and select merchandise that will delight our customers' demanding tastes. Some items are created with designers abroad, others with our experienced in-house product development team.

Equally vital to our success is our exceptional network of 600+ suppliers in 40 countries worldwide. After all, not just any artisan can craft the captivating beauty of our wicker collections, or create the memorable fragrances of our popular candles. In many cases, our relationships with these suppliers have been built over the past 40 years. The longevity of these relationships helps us deliver consistent quality, value and results.

Of course, styles and trends are a moving target. Our merchandise assortment remains in a state of perpetual motion, with seasonal transitions that keep our product offerings fresh. As much as 65% of Pier 1's merchandise changes each year.

A typical Pier 1 store inventory forms multiple tiers. Broad-appeal items at entry-level price points break the ice with younger customers and those on a budget. A mid-level assortment of furniture and accessories includes our best-known products and is at the core of the Pier 1 brand. And to test new ideas and satisfy the cravings of trendier tastes, we devote a portion of our assortment to the more fashion-forward. Cash-and-carry convenience is a key strategy – the merchandise must be on hand in the store to close the sale when the customer is ready to buy.

Stroll through a Pier 1 store and you'll see a world of craftsmanship on display. Our wicker isn't produced by machine but by the age-old art of weaving by hand. Many of our dinnerware patterns are original pieces painted by artisans. Delivering of-a-kind products of this caliber could mean pricing most customers out of the picture. But our product development merchandising teams consider all aspects of design, manufacturing and country of origin for every item we sell. The result uncommon craftsmanship and quality at a surprisingly affordable value.

A lot has changed since Stan and Linda's kids left home.

Family vacations and Saturday soccer games have been replaced by a strange quiet in the house. And the odd group of chipped plates and bowls that screamed "tater tot casserole" has been replaced with a set of understated, beautiful dinnerware that whispers, "Maybe this empty nest isn't so bad, after all."

Growth in store. Merchandising a store might seem easy when you have such an exquisite array of countries and cultures on display. The product is key, of course, but our team of visual merchandisers continuously refines our store presentations with meticulous care to create a pleasing environment that sparks ideas and results in add-on sales.

Pier 1 Imports operates almost 1,000 stores, including the 18-store Cargo chain, in 48 states, Canada, Mexico, Puerto Rico and the United Kingdom. The store network is supported by six distribution centers that provide efficient access to the greatest concentrations of stores and major ports of entry. Enhanced warehouse management systems enable smarter inventory control that makes us more responsive to our customers and, ultimately, more profitable.

New store growth continues to sustain our momentum. Research has pointed to a compelling prospect: Thanks to residential development, as well as economic and demographic factors, markets once thought to be saturated plus undiscovered new markets are capable of supporting additional stores – adding sales volume and creating economies of scale for our distribution and marketing.

The implication is significant, with current projections calling for us to reach 1,500 Pier 1 stores by the end of the decade. Moving toward that goal, we added 84 net new stores in fiscal 2002 and project 85 to 90 more in fiscal 2003. Beyond 2003, we hope to average 70 to 80 net new Pier 1 stores and 15 to 20 new Cargo stores per year through 2010.

An average Pier 1 store is 8,000 to 12,000 square feet and produces approximately $1.6 million in annual sales. We are testing a new large-store format for product introductions and for offering merchandise designed for larger homes. We now have five of these new stores, which, at 12,000 to 17,000 square feet, are significantly larger than a typical Pier 1. Located in highly targeted areas, these stores are producing beyond expected results. An average Cargo store is 4,500 square feet and produces annual sales volume of approximately $1 million.

Over the last five years, Pier 1 Imports has enjoyed a compound annual growth rate in sales and diluted ear per share of almost 10%. Continued growth potential is promising, as younger consumers earn more buying p and our store base grows.

Brad saw the vase, and it said "Holly."

It spoke to everything he loves about his wife. Which is why Brad felt compelled to take it home, and Holly felt compelled to ask what got into Brad. We think it might have been the unique craftsmanship.

14

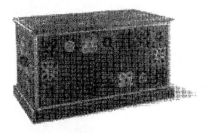

Traditional strengths, uncommon potential. Pier 1 got its start 40 years ago with one small store in San Mateo, California. During the '60s, it became a haven for the "flower children" of the baby-boom generation. We've moved way beyond beads and incense, but some products, like our famous Papasan chair, still help define us, thanks to their timeless appeal. It is promising for us to know that we've been embraced by baby-boomer children, and now their children, too.

Research tells us that these baby boomers have settled down and now appreciate the fundamental pleasures of family and home life. Gen-Xers are establishing homes at an earlier age. And college students are taking dorm décor to a new level – in fact, we've seen a marked increase in sales to these younger customers.

It's quite simple: We sell home furnishings. Success is predicated on our ability to source products that people want at prices that will make Pier 1 profitable. Our steady growth may not have seemed exciting during the days of skyrocketing tech stocks. In retrospect, we're pleased that our beliefs about the business and our strategies have been confirmed.

Putting customers first enables us to return value to our shareholders and employees, and to practice good corporate citizenship. We never lose sight of what got us where we are and where we want to go. Outstanding customer service, convenient locations and ever-changing merchandise at a value are our commitments to our customers.

Pier 1's corporate-giving activities are meant to touch the sensibilities of the customers we serve. Internationally, our su[for UNICEF, now 19 years strong, has raised over $16 million for children's charities. Nationally, sales of our Komen C[have raised over $250,000 for breast cancer research since 2000, and nearly 17,000 Pier 1 employees have partici[in Race for the Cure® events since 1991. And since 1985, in our headquarters city of Fort Worth, Texas, Pier 1 a[employees have donated over $3.7 million to the United Way of Metropolitan Tarrant County.

It was the one dorm room everyone gravitated to at the end of the day.

Sure, Cindy Parker was popular, and her roommate was tolerable. But for most of the girls in Livingston Hall, it was the classic comfort of their rattan furniture that had the most appeal.

Key Financial Statistics

For the five years ended March 2, 2002

Total Sales
(Dollars in Millions)

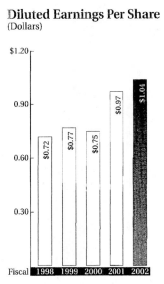

Fiscal	1998	1999	2000	2001	2002
	$1,075.4	$1,138.6	$1,231.1	$1,411.5	$1,548.6

Net Income
(Dollars in Millions)

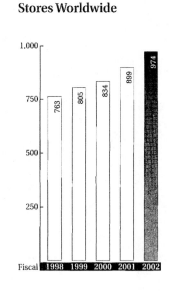

Fiscal	1998	1999	2000	2001	2002
	$78.0	$80.4	$74.7	$94.7	$100.2

Preferred Credit Card Sales
(Dollars in Millions)

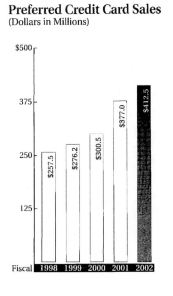

Fiscal	1998	1999	2000	2001	2002
	$257.5	$276.2	$300.5	$377.0	$412.5

Diluted Earnings Per Share
(Dollars)

Fiscal	1998	1999	2000	2001	2002
	$0.72	$0.77	$0.75	$0.97	$1.04

Stores Worldwide

Fiscal	1998	1999	2000	2001	2002
	763	805	834	899	974

Shareholders' Equity Per Share
(Dollars)

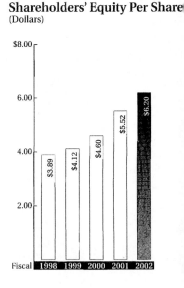

Fiscal	1998	1999	2000	2001	2002
	$3.89	$4.12	$4.60	$5.52	$6.20

Merchandise Sales Mix
For fiscal year 2002

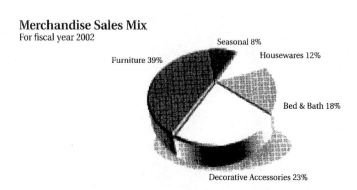

Furniture 39%
Seasonal 8%
Housewares 12%
Bed & Bath 18%
Decorative Accessories 23%

20

Pier 1 Imports, Inc.

FINANCIAL SUMMARY
($ in millions except per share amounts)

	4-Year Compound Annual Growth Rate	Year Ended				
		2002	2001(1)	2000	1999	1998
SUMMARY OF OPERATIONS:						
Net sales	9.5%	$ 1,548.6	1,411.5	1,231.1	1,138.6	1,075.4
Gross profit.................................	8.9%	$ 649.8	594.5	512.5	500.4	461.5
Selling, general and administrative expenses........	9.1%	$ 448.1	399.8	349.4	334.6	315.8
Depreciation and amortization...................	15.7%	$ 42.8	43.2	40.0	31.1	23.9
Operating income............................	6.9%	$ 158.8	151.5	123.2	134.7	121.7
Nonoperating (income) and expenses, net (2)........		$ (0.2)	1.3	4.6	5.0	(2.3)
Income before income taxes	6.4%	$ 159.0	150.2	118.6	129.6	124.0
Net income...................................	6.5%	$ 100.2	94.7	74.7	80.4	78.0
PER SHARE AMOUNTS (ADJUSTED FOR STOCK SPLITS AND DIVIDENDS):						
Basic earnings	8.3%	$ 1.06	.98	.78	.82	.77
Diluted earnings	9.6%	$ 1.04	.97	.75	.77	.72
Cash dividends declared.......................	15.5%	$ .16	.15	.12	.12	.09
Shareholders' equity...........................	12.4%	$ 6.20	5.52	4.60	4.12	3.89
OTHER FINANCIAL DATA:						
Working capital (3)	9.0%	$ 396.8	333.0	239.3	252.1	280.8
Current ratio (3)...............................	(3.2%)	2.9	3.3	2.4	2.9	3.3
Total assets..................................	7.2%	$ 862.7	735.7	670.7	654.0	653.4
Long-term debt (3)	(31.4%)	$ 25.4	25.0	25.0	96.0	114.9
Shareholders' equity...........................	10.5%	$ 585.7	531.9	440.7	403.9	392.7
Weighted average diluted shares outstanding (millions)........................		96.2	98.0	103.3	108.9	112.9
Effective tax rate		37.0%	37.0	37.0	38.0	37.1
Return on average shareholders' equity............		17.9%	19.5	17.7	20.2	21.8
Return on average total assets...................		12.5%	13.5	11.3	12.3	12.8
Pre-tax return on sales		10.3%	10.6	9.6	11.4	11.5

(1) Fiscal 2001 consisted of a 53-week year. All other fiscal years presented reflect 52-week years.
(2) Nonoperating (income) and expenses, net, were comprised of interest expense and interest and investment income in each fiscal year presented, and in addition, included net recoveries associated with trading activities in fiscal 1998.
(3) The reduction in fiscal 2000 working capital, current ratio and long-term debt was the result of the Company's call of its outstanding 5¾% convertible subordinated notes. The notes were primarily converted into shares of the Company's common stock in March 2000. Excluding the reclassification of the 5¾% notes from long-term to short-term, working capital would have been $278.5 million with a current ratio of 3.0 to 1 at fiscal 2000 year-end.

Pier 1 Imports, Inc.
MANAGEMENT'S DISCUSSION AND ANALYSIS OF FINANCIAL CONDITION AND RESULTS OF OPERATIONS

Pier 1 Imports, Inc. and its consolidated subsidiaries (the "Company") is one of North America's largest specialty retailers of unique decorative home furnishings, gifts and related items, with over 950 stores in 48 states, Canada, Puerto Rico, the United Kingdom and Mexico as of fiscal 2002 year-end. The Company directly imports merchandise from over 40 countries around the world and designs offerings that are proprietary to Pier 1 Imports. During fiscal 2002, the Company reported record sales of $1,548.6 million and record net income of $100.2 million, or $1.04 per diluted share. In February 2001, the Company acquired certain assets and assumed certain liabilities of Cargo Furniture, Inc. and formed New Cargo Furniture, Inc. ("Cargo"). Cargo, an 18-store retailer and wholesaler of casual lifestyle furniture, gifts and home décor, had no impact on the Company's fiscal 2001 operations due to the timing of the acquisition, but is reflected in the Company's fiscal 2002 and 2001 year-end balance sheets and fiscal 2002 results of operations.

FISCAL YEARS ENDED MARCH 2, 2002 AND MARCH 3, 2001

During the 52-week period of fiscal 2002, net sales increased $137.1 million, or 9.7%, to $1,548.6 million. Net sales for the 53-week period of fiscal 2001 were $1,411.5 million. Same-store sales for fiscal 2002 improved 4.5% over the prior year, excluding the 53rd week of sales in fiscal 2001. Despite a slow start in sales growth during the first half of the fiscal

year, the Company began to see improvements in customer traffic, average ticket and customer conversion in the third quarter. These sales trends began after the events of September 11th when consumers shifted their spending away from travel and entertainment and began making purchases for their homes. In addition to this change in consumer behavior, the Company believes that its value-oriented merchandising efforts and the success of its marketing campaign contributed to the sales increases experienced during fiscal 2002.

The Company's accelerated new store growth plans in North America also contributed to sales growth during fiscal 2002. The Company opened 104 and closed 20 North American Pier 1 stores during the fiscal year. The North American Pier 1 store count totaled 910 at the end of fiscal 2002 compared to 826 a year ago. Including Cargo and all other worldwide locations, the Company's store count totaled 974 at the end of fiscal year 2002 compared to 899 at the end of fiscal year 2001. Prior to the close of fiscal year 2002, the franchise agreement with Akatsuki Printing Co., Ltd. and Skylark Co., Ltd. expired without any additional costs or further obligations to the Company. As a result, the Company no longer has stores in Japan.

A summary reconciliation of the Company's stores open at the beginning of fiscal 2002, 2001 and 2000 to the number open at the end of each period follows:

	Pier 1 North American	International (1)	Cargo (2)	Total
Open at February 27, 1999	752	54	–	806
Openings (3)	63	5	–	68
Closings (3)	(30)	(10)	–	(40)
Open at February 26, 2000	785	49	–	834
Openings (3)	65	3	–	68
Closings (3)	(24)	–	–	(24)
Acquisition (February 2001)	–	–	21	21
Open at March 3, 2001	826	52	21	899
Openings (3)	104	3	3	110
Closings (3)	(20)	(9)	(6)	(35)
Open at March 2, 2002	910	46	18	974

(1) International stores were located in Puerto Rico, the United Kingdom, Mexico and Japan for fiscal 2000 and 2001. All Japan locations were closed by fiscal 2002 year-end.
(2) The Company's results of operations for fiscal 2001 were not affected by the acquisition of Cargo.
(3) Openings and closings include stores which were relocated.

Pier 1 Imports, Inc.

MANAGEMENT'S DISCUSSION AND ANALYSIS OF FINANCIAL CONDITION AND RESULTS OF OPERATIONS
(continued)

Sales on the Company's proprietary credit card for fiscal 2002 were $412.5 million compared to $377.0 million last year and accounted for 28.9% of U.S. store sales for both fiscal periods. Proprietary credit card customers spent an average of $153 per transaction, which was comparable to last year. The Company continues to encourage sales on its proprietary credit card by opening new accounts, including accounts on Cargo's new proprietary credit card, and developing customer loyalty through marketing promotions specifically targeted to cardholders, including deferred payment options on larger purchases. Although the proprietary credit card generates income, it primarily serves as a marketing and communication tool for the Company's most loyal customers.

Gross profit, after related buying and store occupancy costs, expressed as a percentage of sales, was 42.0% for fiscal 2002 compared to 42.1% a year ago. Merchandise margins for fiscal year 2002 remained unchanged at 54.2% of sales when compared to last fiscal year. Although the first half of fiscal 2002 was more promotional as a result of soft economic conditions, the second half of fiscal 2002 yielded sales with a more favorable blend of regular-priced merchandise and promotional items and merchandise margins rebounded accordingly. Store occupancy costs were 12.3% of sales in fiscal 2002 versus 12.1% of sales last fiscal year. This increase was primarily attributable to the effect of leveraging occupancy costs over an additional week of sales in fiscal year 2001 versus fiscal year 2002. This increase was also the result of additional store rental expense due to the sale and subsequent leaseback of six store properties previously owned by the Company. These sale-leaseback transactions also resulted, although to a lesser extent, in a reduction of depreciation expense, which is not classified as a component of store occupancy costs.

As a percentage of sales, selling, general and administrative expenses, including marketing, increased 60 basis points to 28.9% of sales for fiscal year 2002 from 28.3% of sales a year ago. Expenses that normally increase proportionately with sales and number of stores, such as store payroll, equipment rental, supplies and marketing expenses, were well controlled and declined 50 basis points to 19.7% of sales. Store payroll decreased 20 basis points as a percentage of sales, which was largely the result of a decrease in store

bonuses that are awarded based on sales gains over the prior year. Marketing as a percentage of sales decreased 10 basis points, to 4.5% of sales, due to lower television advertising rates negotiated by the Company. All other selling, general and administrative expenses increased 110 basis points to 9.3% of sales for the fiscal year. These increases were largely the result of increases in non-store payroll, medical, workers' compensation, and general insurance expenses, and the impact of Cargo's expenditures this year with no corresponding expense last year. The increases in non-store payroll resulted primarily from an enhancement to the field management structure in the first quarter of fiscal 2002 to provide for future growth.

Depreciation and amortization expense for fiscal 2002 was $42.8 million, or 2.8% of sales, compared to $43.2 million, or 3.1% of sales, last fiscal year. The decrease was primarily the result of store point of sale equipment, which became fully depreciated in March 2001, along with the sale of eight store properties previously owned, six of which were subsequently leased back by the Company.

Operating income improved to $158.8 million, or 10.3% of sales, in fiscal 2002 from $151.5 million, or 10.7% of sales, in fiscal 2001.

Interest income increased $0.6 million, or 10 basis points as a percentage of sales, to $2.5 million due to considerably higher average cash and investment balances during the current fiscal year compared to last fiscal year, partially offset by a decrease in interest rates. Interest expense was $2.3 million in fiscal year 2002 compared to $3.1 million in fiscal year 2001, a 10 basis point reduction. The decline in interest expense was due to lower average interest rates on a relatively fixed long-term debt balance along with no borrowings under the Company's revolving credit facility during fiscal 2002 compared to several months of outstanding balances on the revolver during fiscal 2001.

The Company's effective tax rate remained constant at 37% of income before income taxes for both fiscal 2002 and 2001.

Fiscal 2002 net income totaled $100.2 million, representing 6.5% of sales, or $1.04 per share on a diluted basis. In fiscal 2001, net income was 6.7% of sales and totaled $94.7 million, or $.97 per share on a diluted basis.

Pier 1 Imports, Inc.

MANAGEMENT'S DISCUSSION AND ANALYSIS OF FINANCIAL CONDITION AND RESULTS OF OPERATIONS
(continued)

FISCAL YEARS ENDED MARCH 3, 2001
AND FEBRUARY 26, 2000

During fiscal 2001, the Company recorded net sales of
$1,411.5 million, an increase of $180.4 million, or 14.7%,
over net sales of $1,231.1 million for the prior fiscal year.
Fiscal 2001 consisted of a 53-week year, while fiscal 2000
and 1999 were 52-week years. Same-store sales for fiscal
2001 improved 7.8%, excluding the 53rd week of sales.
The Company believes that its new advertising campaign,
proprietary credit card and other promotions, and continued
focus on a value pricing initiative, which began in fiscal
2000, resulted in higher customer traffic, average purchases
per customer and conversion ratios during fiscal 2001.

The Company's continued efforts to expand by opening new
stores also contributed to sales growth during fiscal 2001.
The Company opened 65 new stores and closed 24 stores
in North America during fiscal 2001, bringing the Pier 1
North American store count up to 826 at year-end. With
the addition of Cargo, the store count worldwide, including
North America, Puerto Rico, the United Kingdom, Mexico
and Japan, totaled 899 at the end of fiscal 2001 compared
to 834 at the end of fiscal 2000. A summary reconciliation
of the Company's stores open at the beginning of fiscal
2001, 2000 and 1999 to the number open at the end of each
period follows:

	Pier 1 North American	International (1)	Cargo (2)	Total
Open at February 28, 1998	719	45	–	764
Openings (3)	63	11	–	74
Closings (3)	(30)	(2)	–	(32)
Open at February 27, 1999	752	54	–	806
Openings (3)	63	5	–	68
Closings (3)	(30)	(10)	–	(40)
Open at February 26, 2000	785	49	–	834
Openings (3)	65	3	–	68
Closings (3)	(24)	–	–	(24)
Acquisition (February 2001)	–	–	21	21
Open at March 3, 2001	826	52	21	899

(1) International stores were located in Puerto Rico, the United Kingdom, Mexico and Japan.
(2) The Company's results of operations for fiscal 2001 were not affected by the acquisition of Cargo.
(3) Openings and closings include stores which were relocated.

Pier 1 Imports, Inc.

MANAGEMENT'S DISCUSSION AND ANALYSIS OF FINANCIAL CONDITION AND RESULTS OF OPERATIONS
(continued)

Increased use of the Company's proprietary credit card added to the Company's sales growth during fiscal 2001. Sales on the proprietary credit card were $377.0 million and accounted for 28.9% of U.S. store sales during fiscal 2001, an increase of $76.5 million over proprietary credit card sales in the prior year of $300.5 million, which represented 26.3% of U.S. store sales during that year. Proprietary credit card customers spent an average of $152 per transaction in fiscal 2001 compared to $142 per transaction in fiscal 2000. The Company attributed the growth in sales on the card to continued efforts to open new accounts, deferred payment options offered to cardholders during furniture promotions, and enhanced customer loyalty through targeted promotions.

Gross profit, after related buying and store occupancy costs, expressed as a percentage of sales, increased 50 basis points in fiscal 2001 to 42.1% from 41.6% in fiscal 2000. Merchandise margins, as a percentage of sales, declined from 54.6% in fiscal 2000 to 54.2% in fiscal 2001, a decrease of 40 basis points. The decrease was a result of management's concerted decision to continue to give value back to customers by offering unique merchandise at affordable prices. In addition, the effect of a full year of price reductions taken as a result of the value pricing initiative started in May 1999 which continued throughout fiscal 2000 created downward pressure on fiscal 2001 merchandise margins. This decline was also due in part to higher freight rates during the first half of fiscal 2001 as compared to the same period in fiscal 2000. The decreases in merchandise margins were more than offset by the leveraging of relatively fixed rental costs over a higher sales base, which included an additional week of sales in fiscal 2001. Store occupancy costs improved 90 basis points as a percentage of sales from 13.0% in fiscal 2000 to 12.1% in fiscal 2001.

As a percentage of sales, selling, general and administrative expenses, including marketing, improved 10 basis points to 28.3% in fiscal 2001 from 28.4% in fiscal 2000. In total dollars, selling, general and administrative expenses for fiscal 2001

increased $50.4 million over the prior fiscal year. Expenses that normally increase proportionately with sales and number of stores, such as marketing, store payroll, supplies and equipment rental, increased by $34.3 million, but as a percentage of sales declined nearly 20 basis points to 20.2% this fiscal year. Marketing as a percentage of sales decreased 20 basis points as a result of reduced spending on newspaper and magazine advertisements, along with leveraging marketing expenditures over a higher sales base. As a percentage of sales, the decrease in marketing expenses was offset by a 10 basis point increase in store payroll when comparing the two fiscal years. This increase was largely attributable to store bonuses awarded based on sales gains. All other selling, general and administrative expenses increased by $16.0 million, and increased 10 basis points as a percentage of sales. This increase was primarily due to an increase in information technology and other non-store salaries, partially offset by effective management of other administrative expenses and a reduction in net credit card costs.

Depreciation and amortization increased by $3.2 million to $43.2 million in fiscal 2001 primarily because of the Company's increased capital expenditures throughout fiscal 2001 and 2000, especially expenditures on technology-related assets which tend to have relatively short useful lives.

In fiscal 2001, operating income for the year improved to $151.5 million or 10.7% of sales, from $123.2 million or 10.0% of sales in fiscal 2000, an increase of 23.0% or $28.3 million.

Interest income decreased slightly to $1.9 million in fiscal 2001 from $2.3 million in fiscal 2000 due to lower average cash balances during the current fiscal year. Interest expense was $3.1 million in fiscal 2001 compared to $6.9 million in fiscal 2000, a decline of $3.8 million. The decrease in interest expense was primarily due to the repurchase of $28.6 million of the Company's 5¾% convertible subordinated notes during fiscal 2000 and the retirement of the remaining $39.2 million of these notes during the first quarter of fiscal 2001. *See Note 5 of the Notes to Consolidated Financial Statements.*

Pier 1 Imports, Inc.

MANAGEMENT'S DISCUSSION AND ANALYSIS OF FINANCIAL CONDITION AND RESULTS OF OPERATIONS
(continued)

The Company's effective tax rate remained constant at 37% of income before income taxes for both fiscal 2001 and 2000.

Net income in fiscal 2001 was $94.7 million, or $.97 per share on a diluted basis, an increase of $20.0 million, or 26.7%, as compared to fiscal 2000's net income of $74.7 million, or $.75 per share on a diluted basis. Net income, as a percentage of sales, improved from 6.1% in fiscal 2000 to 6.7% in fiscal 2001.

LIQUIDITY AND CAPITAL RESOURCES

The Company ended fiscal year 2002 with $235.6 million of cash compared to $46.8 million a year ago. Total cash generated from operations was $244.3 million compared to $107.5 million last year. Net income, adjusted for non-cash and non-operating related items, was $147.0 million and served as the Company's primary source of operating cash for the fiscal year. The Company's reduction in inventory levels provided cash of $34.8 million compared to a use of cash in the prior fiscal year of $39.1 million. The Company's ability to better manage inventory levels resulted in higher inventory turns and lower overall inventories this year compared to last year, with only a slight decline in average inventory per store. After a successful January clearance event, inventory levels were well positioned at the end of fiscal 2002, enabling a smooth transition into the spring selling season. Increases in accounts payable and accrued liabilities provided cash of $66.0 million. These increases were primarily the result of an increase in merchandise-related accounts payable, increased sales of the Company's gift cards and increases in federal and state income taxes payable resulting from a change in the timing of tax payments.

During fiscal 2002, the Company spent a net of $10.5 million on investing activities. Capital expenditures were $57.9 million, a majority of which was used for new and existing store development and investments in the Company's information systems. The Company opened a record 104 new Pier 1 stores in North America, as well as three international stores, and relocated three existing Cargo stores, which together

accounted for $27.9 million of the total amount expended for capital purchases. The Company remodeled five stores in fiscal 2002 at a cost of $5.1 million. Continuing with its commitment to invest in current store locations, the Company spent an additional $4.5 million to improve floor plans and upgrade fixtures on existing stores. The Company also spent $16.7 million on computer software and other system enhancements, including a new financial system, warehouse management system and customer relations management system. Proceeds from disposition of properties totaled $16.7 million, which included $12.6 million in proceeds from the sale-leaseback of six Company-owned properties throughout fiscal 2002. *See Note 9 of the Notes to Consolidated Financial Statements for additional discussion of the sale-leaseback transactions.*

As of March 2, 2002, the Company's beneficial interest in securitized receivables decreased $30.8 million from the balance at fiscal 2001 year-end. During the third quarter of fiscal 2002, the Company completed a new credit card securitization transaction through the Pier 1 Imports Credit Card Master Trust (the "Master Trust"). The Master Trust is not consolidated by the Company as it is a qualifying special-purpose entity under Statement of Financial Accounting Standards ("SFAS") No. 140, "Accounting for Transfers and Servicing of Financial Assets and Extinguishments of Liabilities." The Master Trust issued $100 million in trust certificates to a third party, which bear interest at a floating rate equal to the rate on commercial paper issued by the third party. As of the end of fiscal year 2002, this rate was 1.81%. In conjunction with this transaction, the Master Trust retired $50 million in previously issued certificates, which bore interest at a fixed rate of 6.74% and were scheduled to mature in May 2002. After the retirement of these certificates, the new transaction provided the Company with net proceeds of approximately $49 million. The sale of the additional $50 million of retained interest contributed to this decrease in beneficial interest in securitized receivables, but was partially offset by increases subsequent to the sale of the retained interest due to

Pier 1 Imports, Inc.

MANAGEMENT'S DISCUSSION AND ANALYSIS OF FINANCIAL CONDITION AND RESULTS OF OPERATIONS
(continued)

increased sales on the Company's proprietary credit card. The Company has continued to experience payment rates comparable to last fiscal year on its proprietary credit card receivables. *See Note 2 of the Notes to Consolidated Financial Statements.*

During fiscal 2002, the Company paid $44.1 million to repurchase 4,020,500 common shares under the Board of Directors-approved stock buyback program at an average price of $10.98, including fees. Subsequent to the end of fiscal 2002, the Company announced that its Board of Directors authorized share repurchases of up to $150 million of the Company's common stock. This authorization replaced the previously authorized 2.8 million shares that were remaining for repurchase at the end of fiscal 2002. These repurchases will be made in open market or private transactions over the next two to three years depending on prevailing market conditions, the Company's available cash, loan covenant restrictions and consideration of its corporate credit ratings. During the year, the Company continued to pay dividends and $15.1 million of cash was expended for dividend payments during fiscal 2002. Also, subsequent to the end of the fiscal year, the Company declared an increased quarterly cash dividend of $.05 per share payable on May 22, 2002 to shareholders of record on May 8, 2002. The Company expects to continue to pay cash dividends in fiscal 2003, but to retain most of its future earnings for expansion of the Company's business. Other financing activities, primarily the exercise of stock options, provided cash of $14.2 million during fiscal 2002.

At fiscal 2002 year-end, the Company's sources of working capital were cash flow from operations, sales of proprietary credit card receivables and bank lines of credit. The bank facilities include a $125 million credit facility, which expires in November 2003, all of which was available at fiscal 2002 year-end. The Company had no borrowings on this facility during fiscal 2002. Additionally, the Company has a $120 million short-term line of credit, which is primarily used to issue merchandise letters of credit. At fiscal 2002 year-end, approximately $64.6 million had been utilized, leaving $55.4 million available. The Company also has $28.7 million in credit lines used to issue other special-

purpose letters of credit, all of which were fully utilized at fiscal 2002 year-end. Of the $28.7 million in special-purpose letters of credit, $25.6 million related to the Company's industrial revenue bonds. *See Note 5 of the Notes to Consolidated Financial Statements.* Most of the Company's loan agreements require the Company to maintain certain financial ratios and limit certain investments and distributions to shareholders, including cash dividends and repurchases of common stock. The Company's current ratio was 2.9 to 1 at fiscal 2002 year-end compared to 3.3 to 1 at fiscal 2001 year-end.

A summary of the Company's other commercial commitments as of March 2, 2002 is listed below (in thousands):

	Total Amounts Committed	Amount of Commitment Expiration per Period	
		Less Than 1 Year	1 to 3 Years
Merchandise letters of credit	$ 64,640	$ 64,640	$ –
Standby letters of credit	28,740	3,175	25,565
Total other commercial commitments	$ 93,380	$ 67,815	$ 25,565

A summary of the Company's contractual cash commitments as of March 2, 2002 is listed below (in thousands):

Fiscal Year	Long-term Debt	Operating Leases
2003	$ 356	$ 162,315
2004	356	158,525
2005	–	145,608
2006	–	132,855
2007	–	118,102
Thereafter	25,000	426,946
Total contractual cash commitments	$ 25,712	$ 1,144,351

The present value of total existing minimum operating lease commitments discounted at 10% was $751.9 million at fiscal 2002 year-end. The Company plans to continue to fund these commitments from operating cash flow.

Pier 1 Imports, Inc.

MANAGEMENT'S DISCUSSION AND ANALYSIS OF FINANCIAL CONDITION AND RESULTS OF OPERATIONS
(continued)

The Company's securitization transaction accounts for a significant source of its funding, with a face amount of outstanding debt securities (the Class A Certificates) assumed by third parties of $100 million. The Company does not provide recourse to third-party investors that purchase the debt securities issued by the Master Trust. However, should the performance of the underlying credit card receivables held by the Master Trust deteriorate to a level that the Company's retained subordinated interests were insufficient to collateralize the Class A Certificates, the Master Trust would be contractually required to begin repayment of the Class A Certificates, thereby limiting the amount of receivables that could be sold to the Master Trust and limiting the securitization as a source of funding. However, this repayment would only be required to the extent that the Master Trust was out of compliance with its required performance measures. The performance measures that could trigger this repayment, such as payment rate, returns and fraud, portfolio yield and minimum transferor's interest, would have to decline significantly to result in such an early amortization event. In addition, if the Company was required to consolidate the Master Trust due to a change in accounting rules, the Company's operations for fiscal 2002 would not have been materially different than its reported results and both its assets and liabilities would have increased by approximately $100 million as of March 2, 2002.

The Company plans to open approximately 115 to 120 new Pier 1 stores during fiscal year 2003 and plans to close approximately 30 stores as their leases expire or otherwise end. A majority of the store closings are planned relocations within the same markets. In addition, the Company will begin its expansion plans for Cargo and will open eight to ten locations during fiscal 2003. New store buildings and land will be financed primarily through operating leases. Total capital expenditures for fiscal 2003 are expected to

be approximately $85 million. Of this amount, the Company expects to spend approximately $43 million on store development, $15 million on the replacement of its Savannah distribution facility, net of estimated proceeds from the disposal of the current facility, $15 million on information systems and $12 million on the land and other costs related to construction of the Company's new headquarters.

In summary, the Company's primary uses of cash in fiscal 2002 were to fund operating expenses, provide for new and existing store development and repurchase common stock of the Company. Historically, the Company has financed its operations primarily from internally generated funds and borrowings under the Company's credit facilities. The Company believes that the funds provided from operations, available lines of credit and sales of its proprietary credit card receivables will be sufficient to finance working capital and capital expenditure requirements throughout fiscal year 2003.

CRITICAL ACCOUNTING POLICIES

The preparation of the Company's consolidated financial statements in accordance with accounting principles generally accepted in the United States requires the use of estimates that affect the reported value of assets, liabilities, revenues and expenses. These estimates are based on historical experience and various other factors that are believed to be reasonable under the circumstances, the results of which form the basis for the Company's conclusions. The Company continually evaluates the information used to make these estimates as the business and the economic environment changes. Actual results may differ from these estimates under different assumptions or conditions. The use of estimates is pervasive throughout the consolidated financial statements, but the accounting policies and estimates considered most critical are as follows:

Pier 1 Imports, Inc.

MANAGEMENT'S DISCUSSION AND ANALYSIS OF FINANCIAL CONDITION AND RESULTS OF OPERATIONS
(continued)

Beneficial interest in securitized receivables - In February 1997, the Company sold all of its proprietary credit card receivables to a special-purpose wholly-owned subsidiary, Pier 1 Funding, Inc., predecessor to Pier 1 Funding, LLC ("Funding"), which transferred the receivables to the Pier 1 Imports Credit Card Master Trust (the "Master Trust"). The Master Trust is not consolidated by the Company as it meets the requirements of a qualifying special-purpose entity under SFAS No. 140. The Master Trust issues beneficial interests that represent undivided interests in the assets of the Master Trust consisting of the transferred receivables and all cash flows from collections of such receivables. The beneficial interests include certain interests retained by Funding, which are represented by Class B Certificates, and the residual interest in the Master Trust (the excess of the principal amount of receivables held in the Master Trust over the portion represented by the certificates sold to investors and the Class B Certificates). Gain or loss on the sale of receivables depends in part on the previous carrying amount of the financial assets involved in the transfer, allocated between the assets sold and the retained interests based on their relative fair value at the date of transfer. The beneficial interest in the Master Trust is accounted for as an available-for-sale security. The Company estimates the fair value of its beneficial interest in the Master Trust, both upon initial securitization and thereafter, based on the present value of future expected cash flows estimated using management's best estimates of key assumptions including credit losses and timeliness of payments. Although not anticipated by the Company, a significant deterioration in the financial condition of the Company's credit card holders, interest rates, or other economic conditions could result in other than temporary losses on the beneficial interest in future periods.

Inventories - The Company's inventory is comprised of finished merchandise and is stated at the lower of average cost or market; cost is determined on a weighted average method. Calculations of the carrying value of inventory are made on an item-by-item basis. The Company reviews its inventory levels in order to identify slow-moving merchandise and uses merchandise markdowns to clear such merchandise. Reserves are established to reduce the value of such slow-moving merchandise. The Company records inventory shrink expense based upon known inventory losses plus unknown losses estimated by reviewing historical experience of the results of its physical inventories. Although inventory shrink rates have not fluctuated significantly in recent years, should actual inventory shrink rates differ from the Company's estimates, revisions to the inventory shrink expense may be required. Most inventory purchases and commitments are made in U.S. dollars.

Income taxes - The Company records income tax expense using the liability method for taxes. The Company is subject to income tax in many jurisdictions, including the United States, various states and localities, and foreign countries. The process of determining tax expense by jurisdiction involves the calculation of actual current tax expense, together with the assessment of deferred tax expense resulting from differing treatment of items for tax and financial accounting purposes. Deferred tax assets and liabilities are recorded in the Company's consolidated balance sheets.

In accordance with Accounting Principles Board ("APB") Opinion No. 23, deferred federal income taxes, net of applicable foreign tax credits, are not provided on the undistributed earnings of foreign subsidiaries to the extent the Company intends to permanently reinvest such earnings abroad. The Company intends these earnings to be indefinitely reinvested in international operations. If future events require that certain assets associated with these earnings be repatriated to the United States, an additional tax provision will be required. Determination of the amount of additional taxes that would be payable if such earnings were not considered indefinitely reinvested is not practical due to the complexities in tax laws and the assumptions that would have to be made.

Pier 1 Imports, Inc.

MANAGEMENT'S DISCUSSION AND ANALYSIS OF FINANCIAL CONDITION AND RESULTS OF OPERATIONS
(continued)

Revenue recognition - The Company recognizes revenue upon customer receipt or delivery for retail sales, including sales under deferred payment promotions on its proprietary credit card. Credit card receivable deferrals are for approximately 90 days and have historically resulted in no significant increases in bad debt losses arising from such receivables. Revenue from gift cards, gift certificates and merchandise credits is deferred until redemption. The Company records an allowance for estimated merchandise returns based on historical experience and other known factors. Should actual returns differ from the Company's estimates and current provision for merchandise returns, revisions to the estimated merchandise returns may be required.

Same-store sales - Stores included in the same-store sales calculation are those stores opened prior to the beginning of the preceding fiscal year and that are still open. Also included are stores that are relocated during the year within a specified distance serving the same market, where there is not a significant change in store size and where there is not a significant overlap between the opening of one store and the closing of the existing store. Stores that are expanded or renovated are excluded from the same-store sales calculation during the period they are closed for such remodeling. When these stores re-open for business, they are included in the same-store sales calculation in the first full month after the re-opening if there is no significant change in store size. If there is a significant change in store size, the store continues to be excluded from the calculation until it meets the Company's established definition of a same-store. Sales over the internet are included, but clearance stores are omitted from the same-store sales calculation. Also, Cargo was not included in the operations of the Company for fiscal 2001 and was not included in the same-store sales calculation for fiscal 2002.

MARKET RISK DISCLOSURES

Market risks relating to the Company's operations result primarily from changes in foreign exchange rates and interest rates. The Company has only limited involvement with derivative financial instruments, does not use them for trading purposes and is not a party to any leveraged derivatives.

The Company periodically enters into forward foreign currency exchange contracts to hedge some of its foreign currency exposure. The Company uses such contracts to hedge exposures to changes in foreign currency exchange rates, primarily the EMU euro and British pounds, associated with purchases denominated in foreign currencies. The Company also uses contracts to hedge its exposure associated with repatriation of funds from its Canadian operations. Changes in the fair value of the derivatives are included in the Company's consolidated statements of operations. Forward contracts, which hedge merchandise purchases, generally have maturities not exceeding six months, and contracts which hedge the repatriation of Canadian funds have maturities not exceeding eighteen months. At March 2, 2002, the notional amount of the Company's forward foreign currency exchange contracts and contracts to hedge its exposure associated with repatriation of Canadian funds totaled approximately $3.9 and $12.2 million, respectively.

The Company manages its exposure to changes in interest rates by optimizing the use of variable and fixed rate debt. The Company had $25.0 million of variable rate borrowings at March 2, 2002. A hypothetical 10% adverse change in interest rates would have a negligible impact on the Company's earnings and cash flows.

Collectively, the Company's exposure to these market risk factors was not significant and did not materially change from March 3, 2001.

Pier 1 Imports, Inc.

MANAGEMENT'S DISCUSSION AND ANALYSIS OF FINANCIAL CONDITION AND RESULTS OF OPERATIONS
(continued)

IMPACT OF INFLATION AND CHANGING PRICES

Inflation has not had a significant impact on the operations of the Company during the preceding three years.

IMPACT OF NEW ACCOUNTING STANDARDS

In the first quarter of fiscal 2002, the Company adopted SFAS No. 133, "Accounting for Derivative Instruments and Hedging Activities," which was amended by SFAS No. 137 and SFAS No. 138. This statement establishes accounting and reporting guidelines for derivatives and requires the Company to record all derivatives as assets or liabilities on the balance sheet at fair value. The Company's use of derivatives is primarily limited to forward foreign currency exchange contracts, which the Company uses to mitigate exposures to changes in foreign currency exchange rates. The Company also uses contracts which hedge the repatriation of Canadian funds. Upon adoption of SFAS No. 133, the Company did not designate such derivatives as hedging instruments; thus, the changes in the fair value of the derivatives have been included in the consolidated statements of operations. Prior to adoption, the Company deferred all gains and losses on its derivative contracts and recognized such gains and losses as an adjustment to the transaction price. The adoption of SFAS No. 133 has not had a material impact on the Company's consolidated balance sheets or its statements of operations, shareholders' equity and cash flows.

The Company adopted SFAS No. 140, "Accounting for Transfers and Servicing of Financial Assets and Extinguishments of Liabilities," in the first quarter of fiscal 2002. This statement established new conditions for a securitization to be accounted for as a sale of receivables, changed the requirements for an entity to be a qualifying special-purpose entity, and modified the conditions for determining whether a transferor has relinquished control over transferred assets. SFAS No. 140 also requires additional disclosures related to securitized financial assets and retained interests in securitized financial assets.

See Note 2 of the Notes to Consolidated Financial Statements. Prior to adoption, the Company made the necessary amendments to its securitization agreements and continues to receive sale treatment for its securitized proprietary credit card receivables. The implementation of SFAS No. 140 did not have a material impact on the Company's consolidated balance sheets or its statements of operations, shareholders' equity and cash flows.

In June 2001, the Financial Accounting Standards Board ("FASB") issued SFAS No. 141, "Business Combinations," which supersedes APB Opinion No. 16, "Business Combinations," and SFAS No. 38, "Accounting for Preacquisition Contingencies of Purchased Enterprises." Statement No. 141 eliminates the pooling-of-interests method of accounting for business combinations and requires all such transactions to be accounted for under the purchase method. This statement also addresses the initial recognition and measurement of goodwill and other intangible assets acquired in a business combination and is effective for all business combinations initiated after June 30, 2001. The adoption of SFAS No. 141 did not have a material impact on the Company's consolidated balance sheets or its statements of operations, shareholders' equity and cash flows.

In June 2001, the FASB also issued SFAS No. 142, "Goodwill and Other Intangible Assets," which supersedes APB Opinion No. 17, "Intangible Assets." This statement addresses the initial recognition and measurement of intangible assets acquired outside of a business combination and the accounting for goodwill and other intangible assets subsequent to their acquisition. SFAS No. 142 also provides that intangible assets with finite useful lives be amortized and that goodwill and intangible assets with indefinite lives will not be amortized, but will rather be tested on an annual basis for impairment. The Company is required to adopt SFAS No. 142 for its fiscal year beginning March 3, 2002. The Company has analyzed the implementation requirements

Pier 1 Imports, Inc.
MANAGEMENT'S DISCUSSION AND ANALYSIS OF FINANCIAL CONDITION AND RESULTS OF OPERATIONS
(continued)

and does not anticipate that the adoption of SFAS No. 142 will have a material impact on the Company's consolidated balance sheets or its statements of operations, shareholders' equity and cash flows.

In October 2001, the FASB issued SFAS No. 144, "Accounting for the Impairment or Disposal of Long-Lived Assets," which replaces SFAS No. 121, "Accounting for the Impairment of Long-Lived Assets and for Long-Lived Assets to Be Disposed Of." Statement No. 144 retains the fundamental provisions of SFAS No. 121 with additional guidance on estimating cash flows when performing a recoverability test, requires that a long-lived asset to be disposed of, other than by sale, be classified as "held and used" until it is disposed of, and establishes more restrictive criteria to classify an asset as "held for sale." SFAS No. 144 also supersedes APB Opinion No. 30, "Reporting the Results of Operations – Reporting the Effects of Disposal of a Segment of a Business, and Extraordinary, Unusual and Infrequently Occurring Events and Transactions" regarding the disposal of a segment of a business and would extend the reporting of a discontinued operation to a "component of an entity" and requires the operating losses thereon to be recognized in the period in which they occur. The Company is required to adopt SFAS No. 144 for its fiscal year beginning March 3, 2002. The Company has analyzed the implementation requirements and does not anticipate that the adoption of SFAS No. 144 will have a material impact on the Company's consolidated balance sheets or its statements of operations, shareholders' equity and cash flows.

FORWARD-LOOKING STATEMENTS

Certain matters discussed in this annual report, other than historical information, may constitute "forward-looking statements" that are subject to certain risks and uncertainties that could cause actual results to differ materially from those described in the forward-looking statements. The Company may also make forward-looking statements in other reports filed with the Securities and Exchange Commission and in material delivered to the Company's shareholders. Forward-looking statements provide current expectations of future events based on certain assumptions. These statements encompass information that does not directly relate to any historical or current fact and often may be identified with words such as "anticipates," "believes," "expects," "estimates," "intends," "plans," "projects" and other similar expressions. Management's expectations and assumptions regarding planned store openings, financing of Company obligations from operations and other future results are subject to risks, uncertainties and other factors that could cause actual results to differ materially from the anticipated results or other expectations expressed in the forward-looking statements. Risks and uncertainties that may affect Company operations and performance include, among others, the effects of terrorist attacks or other acts of war, weather conditions that may affect sales, the general strength of the economy and levels of consumer spending, the availability of new sites for expansion along with sufficient labor to facilitate growth, the strength of new home construction and sales of existing homes, the ability of the Company to import merchandise from foreign countries without significantly restrictive tariffs, duties or quotas and the ability of the Company to ship items from foreign countries at reasonable rates in timely fashion. The foregoing risks and uncertainties are in addition to others discussed elsewhere in this annual report. The Company assumes no obligation to update or otherwise revise its forward-looking statements even if experience or future changes make it clear that any projected results expressed or implied will not be realized.

Pier 1 Imports, Inc.

REPORT OF INDEPENDENT AUDITORS

To the Board of Directors of Pier 1 Imports, Inc.

We have audited the accompanying consolidated balance sheets of Pier 1 Imports, Inc. as of March 2, 2002 and March 3, 2001, and the related consolidated statements of operations, shareholders' equity and cash flows for each of the three years in the period ended March 2, 2002. These financial statements are the responsibility of the Company's management. Our responsibility is to express an opinion on these financial statements based on our audits.

We conducted our audits in accordance with auditing standards generally accepted in the United States. Those standards require that we plan and perform the audit to obtain reasonable assurance about whether the financial statements are free of material misstatement. An audit includes examining, on a test basis, evidence supporting the amounts and disclosures in the financial statements. An audit also includes assessing the accounting principles used and significant estimates made by management, as well as evaluating the overall financial statement presentation. We believe that our audits provide a reasonable basis for our opinion.

In our opinion, the financial statements referred to above present fairly, in all material respects, the consolidated financial position of Pier 1 Imports, Inc. at March 2, 2002 and March 3, 2001, and the consolidated results of its operations and its cash flows for each of the three years in the period ended March 2, 2002, in conformity with accounting principles generally accepted in the United States.

Ernst + Young LLP

Fort Worth, Texas
April 8, 2002

REPORT OF MANAGEMENT

To our shareholders:

Management is responsible for the preparation and the integrity of the accompanying consolidated financial statements and related notes, which have been prepared in accordance with accounting principles generally accepted in the United States and include amounts based upon our estimates and judgments, as required. The consolidated financial statements have been audited by Ernst & Young LLP, independent certified public accountants. The accompanying independent auditors' report expresses an independent professional opinion on the fairness of presentation of management's financial statements.

The Company maintains a system of internal controls over financial reporting. We believe this system provides reasonable assurance that transactions are executed in accordance with management authorization and that such transactions are properly recorded and reported in the financial statements, that assets are properly safeguarded and accounted for, and that records are maintained so as to permit preparation of financial statements in accordance with accounting principles generally accepted in the United States. The Company also has instituted policies and guidelines, which require employees to maintain a high level of ethical standards.

In addition, the Board of Directors exercises its oversight role with respect to the Company's internal control systems primarily through its Audit Committee. The Audit Committee consists solely of outside directors and meets periodically with management, the Company's internal auditors and the Company's independent auditors to review internal accounting controls, audit results, financial reporting, and accounting principles and practices. The Company's independent and internal auditors have full and free access to the Audit Committee with and without management's presence. Although no cost-effective internal control system will preclude all errors and irregularities, we believe our controls as of and for the year ended March 2, 2002 provide reasonable assurance that the consolidated financial statements are reliable.

Marvin J. Girouard	Charles H. Turner
Chairman of the Board	Executive Vice President,
and Chief Executive Officer	Chief Financial Officer
	and Treasurer

Pier 1 Imports, Inc.

CONSOLIDATED STATEMENTS OF OPERATIONS
(in thousands except per share amounts)

	Year Ended		
	2002	**2001**	**2000**
Net sales	$ 1,548,556	$ 1,411,498	$ 1,231,095
Operating costs and expenses:			
Cost of sales (including buying and store occupancy costs)	898,795	817,043	718,547
Selling, general and administrative expenses	448,127	399,755	349,394
Depreciation and amortization	42,821	43,184	39,973
	1,389,743	1,259,982	1,107,914
Operating income	158,813	151,516	123,181
Nonoperating (income) and expenses:			
Interest and investment income	(2,484)	(1,854)	(2,349)
Interest expense	2,300	3,130	6,918
	(184)	1,276	4,569
Income before income taxes	158,997	150,240	118,612
Provision for income taxes	58,788	55,590	43,887
Net income	$ 100,209	$ 94,650	$ 74,725
Earnings per share:			
Basic	$ 1.06	$ .98	$ .78
Diluted	$ 1.04	$ .97	$ .75
Dividends declared per share	$ .16	$ .15	$ .12
Average shares outstanding during period:			
Basic	94,414	96,306	95,766
Diluted	96,185	97,952	103,297

The accompanying notes are an integral part of these financial statements.

Pier 1 Imports, Inc.

CONSOLIDATED BALANCE SHEETS
(in thousands except share amounts)

	2002	2001
ASSETS		
Current assets:		
Cash, including temporary investments of $213,488 and $31,142, respectively	$ 235,609	$ 46,841
Beneficial interest in securitized receivables	44,620	75,403
Other accounts receivable, net of allowance for doubtful accounts		
of $275 and $295, respectively	6,205	8,370
Inventories	275,433	310,704
Prepaid expenses and other current assets	43,286	35,748
Total current assets	605,153	477,066
Properties, net	209,954	212,066
Other noncurrent assets	47,565	46,578
	$ 862,672	$ 735,710
LIABILITIES AND SHAREHOLDERS' EQUITY		
Current liabilities:		
Current portion of long-term debt	$ 356	$ –
Accounts payable and accrued liabilities	208,040	144,110
Total current liabilities	208,396	144,110
Long-term debt	25,356	25,000
Other noncurrent liabilities	43,264	34,721
Shareholders' equity:		
Common stock, $1.00 par, 500,000,000 shares authorized, 100,779,000 issued	100,779	100,779
Paid-in capital	140,190	139,424
Retained earnings	429,910	344,809
Cumulative other comprehensive income	(4,702)	(3,115)
Less – 7,362,000 and 4,619,000 common shares in treasury, at cost, respectively	(80,521)	(49,933)
Less – unearned compensation	–	(85)
	585,656	531,879
Commitments and contingencies	–	–
	$ 862,672	$ 735,710

The accompanying notes are an integral part of these financial statements.

Pier 1 Imports, Inc.

CONSOLIDATED STATEMENTS OF CASH FLOWS
(in thousands except share amounts)

	Year Ended		
	2002	2001	2000
CASH FLOW FROM OPERATING ACTIVITIES:			
Net income	$ 100,209	$ 94,650	$ 74,725
Adjustments to reconcile to net cash provided by operating activities:			
Depreciation and amortization	42,821	43,184	39,973
Loss on disposal of fixed assets	4,205	6,514	5,828
Deferred compensation	3,697	2,072	1,543
Deferred taxes	(2,238)	735	1,724
Other	(1,707)	(184)	1,938
Change in cash from:			
Inventories	34,804	(39,127)	(10,133)
Other accounts receivable and other current assets	(2,983)	(5,847)	586
Accounts payable and accrued expenses	66,048	6,280	8,962
Other noncurrent assets	(32)	(378)	(2,382)
Other noncurrent liabilities	(500)	(390)	(911)
Net cash provided by operating activities	244,324	107,509	121,853
CASH FLOW FROM INVESTING ACTIVITIES:			
Capital expenditures	(57,925)	(42,745)	(48,219)
Proceeds from disposition of properties	16,682	353	19,425
Net cost from disposition of Sunbelt Nursery Group, Inc. properties	–	–	(439)
Acquisitions, net of cash acquired	–	(3,917)	–
Beneficial interest in securitized receivables	30,783	(21,583)	(12,820)
Net cash used in investing activities	(10,460)	(67,892)	(42,053)
CASH FLOW FROM FINANCING ACTIVITIES:			
Cash dividends	(15,134)	(14,494)	(11,504)
Purchases of treasury stock	(44,137)	(34,270)	(31,806)
Proceeds from stock options exercised, stock purchase plan and other, net	13,463	5,627	4,148
Borrowings under long-term debt	712	82,500	4,035
Repayments of long-term debt	–	(82,515)	(36,242)
Net cash used in financing activities	(45,096)	(43,152)	(71,369)
Change in cash and cash equivalents	188,768	(3,535)	8,431
Cash and cash equivalents at beginning of year	46,841	50,376	41,945
Cash and cash equivalents at end of year	$ 235,609	$ 46,841	$ 50,376
Supplemental cash flow information:			
Interest paid	$ 2,493	$ 3,171	$ 7,137
Income taxes paid	$ 35,951	$ 58,302	$ 40,883

During fiscal 2001, the Company issued 4,764,450 shares of its common stock upon the conversion of $39,164,000 principal amount of

5¾% convertible subordinated notes.

The accompanying notes are an integral part of these financial statements.

Pier 1 Imports, Inc.

CONSOLIDATED STATEMENTS OF SHAREHOLDERS' EQUITY
(in thousands except per share amounts)

	Common Stock Shares	Common Stock Amount	Paid-in Capital	Retained Earnings	Cumulative Other Comprehensive Income	Treasury Stock	Unearned Compensation	Total Shareholders' Equity
Balance February 27, 1999	97,672	$ 100,779	$ 159,631	$ 201,457	$ (1,850)	$ (54,654)	$ (1,469)	$ 403,894
Comprehensive income:								
Net income	–	–	–	74,725	–	–	–	74,725
Other comprehensive income, net of tax:								
Currency translation adjustments	–	–	–	–	314	–	–	314
Comprehensive income								75,039
Purchases of treasury stock	(4,393)	–	–	–	–	(31,806)	–	(31,806)
Restricted stock forfeits and amortization	(83)	–	709	–	–	(1,392)	1,168	485
Exercise of stock options, stock purchase								
plan and other	625	–	(4,629)	–	–	9,184	–	4,555
Cash dividends ($.12 per share)	–	–	–	(11,504)	–	–	–	(11,504)
Balance February 26, 2000	93,821	100,779	155,711	264,678	(1,536)	(78,668)	(301)	440,663
Comprehensive income:								
Net income	–	–	–	94,650	–	–	–	94,650
Other comprehensive income, net of tax:								
Currency translation adjustments	–	–	–	–	(1,579)	–	–	(1,579)
Comprehensive income								93,071
Purchases of treasury stock	(3,269)	–	–	–	–	(34,270)	–	(34,270)
Restricted stock amortization	–	–	–	–	–	–	216	216
Exercise of stock options, stock purchase								
plan and other	825	–	(1,774)	(25)	–	9,119	–	7,320
Cash dividends ($.15 per share)	–	–	–	(14,494)	–	–	–	(14,494)
Conversion of 5¾% convertible debt	4,764	–	(14,513)	–	–	53,886	–	39,373
Balance March 3, 2001	96,141	100,779	139,424	344,809	(3,115)	(49,933)	(85)	531,879
Comprehensive income:								
Net income	–	–	–	100,209	–	–	–	100,209
Other comprehensive income, net of tax:								
Currency translation adjustments	–	–	–	–	(1,587)	–	–	(1,587)
Comprehensive income								98,622
Purchases of treasury stock	(4,021)	–	–	–	–	(44,137)	–	(44,137)
Restricted stock amortization	–	–	–	–	–	–	85	85
Exercise of stock options, stock purchase								
plan and other	1,269	–	766	26	–	13,549	–	14,341
Cash dividends ($.16 per share)	–	–	–	(15,134)	–	–	–	(15,134)
Balance March 2, 2002	93,389	$ 100,779	$ 140,190	$ 429,910	$ (4,702)	$ (80,521)	$ –	$ 585,656

The accompanying notes are an integral part of these financial statements.

Pier 1 Imports, Inc.
NOTES TO CONSOLIDATED FINANCIAL STATEMENTS

NOTE 1 - SUMMARY OF SIGNIFICANT ACCOUNTING POLICIES

Organization - Pier 1 Imports, Inc. is one of North America's largest specialty retailers of imported decorative home furnishings, gifts and related items, with retail stores located in the United States, Canada, Puerto Rico, the United Kingdom and Mexico. Concentrations of risk with respect to sourcing the Company's inventory purchases are limited due to the large number of vendors or suppliers and their geographic dispersion around the world. The Company sells merchandise imported from over 40 different countries, with 35% of its sales derived from merchandise produced in China, 11% derived from merchandise produced in India and 29% derived from merchandise produced in Indonesia, Thailand, Brazil, Italy, the Philippines and Mexico. The remaining 25% of sales was from merchandise produced in various Asian, European, Central American, South American and African countries or was obtained from U.S. manufacturers.

Basis of consolidation - The consolidated financial statements of Pier 1 Imports, Inc. and its consolidated subsidiaries (the "Company") include the accounts of all subsidiary companies except Pier 1 Funding, LLC, which is a non-consolidated, bankruptcy remote, securitization subsidiary. *See Note 2 of the Notes to Consolidated Financial Statements.* Material intercompany transactions and balances have been eliminated.

Acquisitions - The Company completed its acquisition of certain assets and assumption of certain liabilities of Cargo Furniture, Inc. and formed New Cargo Furniture, Inc. ("Cargo") for $3,931,000, including cash acquired, on February 21, 2001. These assets and liabilities were included in the Company's consolidated balance sheet as of March 3, 2001; however, this acquisition had no effect on the Company's fiscal 2001 operations. Cargo is a retailer and wholesaler of casual lifestyle furniture, gifts and home décor with a focus on children's furniture. This acquisition was accounted for under the purchase method of accounting, and ultimately resulted in goodwill of $4,386,000, which has been amortized using the straight-line method over 20 years through fiscal 2002, at which time amortization ceases due to the adoption of Statement of Financial Accounting Standards ("SFAS") No. 142. The pro forma effect on the Company's results of operations, as if the acquisition had been completed at the beginning of fiscal 2001, was not significant. Cargo's operations for fiscal 2002 are fully consolidated with the Company's results.

Use of estimates - Preparation of the financial statements in conformity with accounting principles generally accepted in the United States requires management to make estimates and assumptions that affect the amounts reported in the financial statements and accompanying notes. Actual results could differ from those estimates.

Reclassifications - Certain reclassifications have been made in the prior years' consolidated financial statements to conform to the fiscal 2002 presentation.

Fiscal periods - The Company utilizes 5-4-4 (week) quarterly accounting periods with the fiscal year ending on the Saturday nearest the last day of February. Fiscal 2002 and 2000 consisted of 52-week years and fiscal 2001 was a 53-week year. Fiscal 2002 ended March 2, 2002, fiscal 2001 ended March 3, 2001 and fiscal 2000 ended February 26, 2000.

Cash and cash equivalents - The Company considers all highly liquid investments with an original maturity date of three months or less to be cash equivalents. The effect of foreign currency exchange rate fluctuations on cash is not material.

Translation of foreign currencies - Assets and liabilities of foreign operations are translated into U.S. dollars at fiscal year-end exchange rates. Income and expense items are translated at average exchange rates prevailing during the year. Translation adjustments arising from differences in exchange rates from period to period are included as a separate component of shareholders' equity and are included in comprehensive income.

Financial instruments - The fair value of financial instruments is determined by reference to various market data and other valuation techniques as appropriate. There were no significant assets or liabilities with a fair value different from the recorded value as of March 2, 2002 and March 3, 2001.

Risk management instruments: The Company may utilize various financial instruments to manage interest rate and market risk associated with its on- and off-balance sheet commitments.

The Company hedges certain commitments denominated in foreign currencies through the purchase of forward contracts. The forward contracts are purchased only to cover specific commitments to buy merchandise for resale. The Company also uses contracts to hedge its exposure associated with the repatriation of funds from its Canadian

Pier 1 Imports, Inc.

NOTES TO CONSOLIDATED FINANCIAL STATEMENTS
(continued)

operations. At March 2, 2002, the notional amount of the Company's forward foreign currency exchange contracts and contracts to hedge its exposure associated with repatriation of Canadian funds totaled approximately $3.9 million and $12.2 million, respectively. For financial accounting purposes, the Company has not designated such contracts as hedges. Thus, changes in the fair value of both of these forward contracts are included in the Company's consolidated statements of operations.

The Company enters into forward foreign currency exchange contracts with major financial institutions and continually monitors its positions with, and the credit quality of, these counterparties to such financial instruments. The Company does not expect non-performance by any of the counterparties, and any losses incurred in the event of non-performance would not be material.

Beneficial interest in securitized receivables - In February 1997, the Company sold all of its proprietary credit card receivables to a special-purpose wholly-owned subsidiary, Pier 1 Funding, Inc., predecessor to Pier 1 Funding, LLC ("Funding"), which transferred the receivables to the Pier 1 Imports Credit Card Master Trust (the "Master Trust"). The Master Trust is not consolidated by the Company as it meets the requirements of a qualifying special-purpose entity under SFAS No. 140. The Master Trust issues beneficial interests that represent undivided interests in the assets of the Master Trust consisting of the transferred receivables and all cash flows from collections of such receivables. The beneficial interests include certain interests retained by Funding, which are represented by Class B Certificates, and the residual interest in the Master Trust (the excess of the principal amount of receivables held in the Master Trust over the portion represented by the certificates sold to investors and the Class B Certificates).

Gain or loss on the sale of receivables depends in part on the previous carrying amount of the financial assets involved in the transfer, allocated between the assets sold and the retained interests based on their relative fair value at the date of transfer. A servicing asset or liability was not recognized in the Company's credit card securitizations (and thus was not considered in the gain or loss computation) since the Company received adequate compensation relative to current market servicing prices to service the receivables sold. Initial transaction costs for credit card securitizations were deferred and are being amortized over the expected life of the securitization.

The beneficial interest in the Master Trust is accounted for as an available-for-sale security. The Company estimates fair value of its beneficial interest in the Master Trust, both upon initial securitization and thereafter, based on the present value of future expected cash flows estimated using management's best estimates of key assumptions including credit losses and timeliness of payments. As of March 2, 2002, the Company's assumptions included credit losses of 5% of the outstanding balance and expected payment within a six-month period using a discount rate of 15% to calculate the present value of the future cash flows. A sensitivity analysis was performed assuming a hypothetical 20% adverse change in both interest rates and credit losses, which had an immaterial impact on the fair value of the Company's beneficial interest.

Inventories - Inventories are comprised of finished merchandise and are stated at the lower of average cost or market; cost is determined on a weighted average method.

Properties, maintenance and repairs - Buildings, equipment, furniture and fixtures, and leasehold interests and improvements are carried at cost less accumulated depreciation. Depreciation is computed using the straight-line method over estimated remaining useful lives of the assets, generally thirty years for buildings and three to seven years for equipment, furniture and fixtures. Amortization of improvements to leased properties is based upon the shorter of the remaining primary lease term or the estimated useful lives of such assets. Depreciation costs were $41,047,000, $41,882,000 and $38,672,000 in fiscal 2002, 2001 and 2000, respectively.

Expenditures for maintenance, repairs and renewals, which do not materially prolong the original useful lives of the assets, are charged to expense as incurred. In the case of disposals, assets and the related depreciation are removed from the accounts and the net amount, less proceeds from disposal, is credited or charged to income.

Revenue recognition - Revenue is recognized upon customer receipt or delivery for retail sales, including sales under deferred payment promotions on the Company's proprietary credit card. An allowance has been established to provide for estimated merchandise returns. Revenue from gift cards, gift certificates and merchandise credits is deferred until redemption.

39

Pier 1 Imports, Inc.

NOTES TO CONSOLIDATED FINANCIAL STATEMENTS
(continued)

Advertising costs - Advertising costs are expensed the first time the advertising takes place. Advertising costs were $64,414,000, $59,721,000 and $54,970,000 in fiscal 2002, 2001 and 2000, respectively. Prepaid advertising at the end of fiscal years 2002 and 2001 was $2,303,000 and $2,086,000, respectively, consisting primarily of production costs for advertisements not yet run.

Income taxes - The Company records income tax expense using the liability method for taxes. Under this method, deferred tax assets and liabilities are recognized based on differences between financial statement and tax bases of assets and liabilities using presently enacted tax rates. Deferred federal income taxes, net of applicable foreign tax credits, are not provided on the undistributed earnings of foreign subsidiaries to the extent the Company intends to permanently reinvest such earnings abroad.

Stock-based compensation - The Company grants stock options and restricted stock for a fixed number of shares to employees with stock option exercise prices equal to the fair market value of the shares on the date of grant. The Company accounts for stock option grants and restricted stock grants in accordance with Accounting Principles Board ("APB") Opinion No. 25, "Accounting for Stock Issued to Employees," and, accordingly, recognizes no compensation expense for the stock option grants.

Earnings per share - Basic earnings per share amounts were determined by dividing net income by the weighted average number of common shares outstanding for the period. Diluted earnings per share amounts were similarly computed, but included the effect, when dilutive, of the Company's weighted average number of stock options outstanding and the average number of common shares that would be issuable upon conversion of the Company's convertible securities. To determine diluted earnings per share, interest and amortization of debt issue costs related to the subordinated notes, net of any applicable taxes, have been added back to net income to reflect assumed conversions.

The following earnings per share calculations reflect the effect of the Company's conversion of its 5¾% convertible subordinated notes, which were primarily converted, without interest, on or before March 23, 2000. Earnings per share amounts are calculated as follows (in thousands except per share amounts):

	2002	2001	2000
Net income	$100,209	$ 94,650	$ 74,725
Plus interest and debt issue costs, net of tax, on the assumed conversion of the 5¾% subordinated notes	–	–	2,237
Diluted net income	$100,209	$ 94,650	$ 76,962
Average shares outstanding:			
Basic.....................	94,414	96,306	95,766
Plus assumed exercise of stock options	1,771	1,325	644
Plus assumed conversion of the 5¾% subordinated notes ...	–	321	6,887
Diluted	96,185	97,952	103,297
Earnings per share:			
Basic.....................	$ 1.06	$ .98	$ .78
Diluted	$ 1.04	$ .97	$ .75

Stock options for which the exercise price was greater than the average market price of common shares were not included in the computation of diluted earnings per share as the effect would be antidilutive. At the end of fiscal years 2002, 2001 and 2000, there were 433,800, 1,078,200 and 1,157,025, respectively, stock options outstanding with exercise prices greater than the average market price of the Company's common shares.

Impact of recently issued accounting standards - In the first quarter of fiscal 2002, the Company adopted SFAS No. 133, "Accounting for Derivative Instruments and Hedging Activities," which was amended by SFAS No. 137 and SFAS No. 138. This statement establishes accounting and reporting guidelines for derivatives and requires the Company to record all derivatives as assets or liabilities on the balance sheet at fair value. The Company's use of derivatives is primarily limited to forward foreign currency exchange contracts, which the Company uses to mitigate exposures to changes in foreign currency exchange rates. The Company also uses contracts which hedge the repatriation of Canadian funds. Upon adoption of SFAS No. 133, the Company did not designate such derivatives as hedging instruments; thus, the changes in the fair value of the derivatives have been included in the consolidated statements of operations. Prior

Pier 1 Imports, Inc.
NOTES TO CONSOLIDATED FINANCIAL STATEMENTS
(continued)

to adoption, the Company deferred all gains and losses on its derivative contracts and recognized such gains and losses as an adjustment to the transaction price. The adoption of SFAS No. 133 has not had a material impact on the Company's consolidated balance sheets or its statements of operations, shareholders' equity and cash flows.

The Company adopted SFAS No. 140, "Accounting for Transfers and Servicing of Financial Assets and Extinguishments of Liabilities," in the first quarter of fiscal 2002. This statement established new conditions for a securitization to be accounted for as a sale of receivables, changed the requirements for an entity to be a qualifying special-purpose entity, and modified the conditions for determining whether a transferor has relinquished control over transferred assets. SFAS No. 140 also requires additional disclosures related to securitized financial assets and retained interests in securitized financial assets. *See Note 2 of the Notes to Consolidated Financial Statements.* Prior to adoption, the Company made the necessary amendments to its securitization agreements and continues to receive sale treatment for its securitized proprietary credit card receivables. The implementation of SFAS No. 140 did not have a material impact on the Company's consolidated balance sheets or its statements of operations, shareholders' equity and cash flows.

In June 2001, the Financial Accounting Standards Board ("FASB") issued SFAS No. 141, "Business Combinations," which supersedes Accounting Principles Board ("APB") Opinion No. 16, "Business Combinations," and SFAS No. 38, "Accounting for Preacquisition Contingencies of Purchased Enterprises." Statement No. 141 eliminates the pooling-of-interests method of accounting for business combinations and requires all such transactions to be accounted for under the purchase method. This statement also addresses the initial recognition and measurement of goodwill and other intangible assets acquired in a business combination and is effective for all business combinations initiated after June 30, 2001. The adoption of SFAS No. 141 did not have a material impact on the Company's consolidated balance sheets or its statements of operations, shareholders' equity and cash flows.

In June 2001, the FASB also issued SFAS No. 142, "Goodwill and Other Intangible Assets," which supersedes APB Opinion No. 17, "Intangible Assets." This statement addresses the initial recognition and measurement of intangible

assets acquired outside of a business combination and the accounting for goodwill and other intangible assets subsequent to their acquisition. SFAS No. 142 also provides that intangible assets with finite useful lives be amortized and that goodwill and intangible assets with indefinite lives will not be amortized, but will rather be tested on an annual basis for impairment. The Company is required to adopt SFAS No. 142 for its fiscal year beginning March 3, 2002. The Company has analyzed the implementation requirements and does not anticipate that the adoption of SFAS No. 142 will have a material impact on the Company's consolidated balance sheets or its statements of operations, shareholders' equity and cash flows.

In October 2001, the FASB issued SFAS No. 144, "Accounting for the Impairment or Disposal of Long-Lived Assets," which replaces SFAS No. 121, "Accounting for the Impairment of Long-Lived Assets and for Long-Lived Assets to Be Disposed Of." Statement No. 144 retains the fundamental provisions of SFAS No. 121 with additional guidance on estimating cash flows when performing a recoverability test, requires that a long-lived asset to be disposed of, other than by sale, be classified as "held and used" until it is disposed of and establishes more restrictive criteria to classify an asset as "held for sale." SFAS No. 144 also supersedes APB Opinion No. 30, "Reporting the Results of Operations – Reporting the Effects of Disposal of a Segment of a Business, and Extraordinary, Unusual and Infrequently Occurring Events and Transactions," regarding the disposal of a segment of a business and would extend the reporting of a discontinued operation to a "component of an entity" and requires the operating losses thereon to be recognized in the period in which they occur. The Company is required to adopt SFAS No. 144 for its fiscal year beginning March 3, 2002. The Company has analyzed the implementation requirements and does not anticipate that the adoption of SFAS No. 144 will have a material impact on the Company's consolidated balance sheets or its statements of operations, shareholders' equity and cash flows.

NOTE 2 - PROPRIETARY CREDIT CARD INFORMATION
The proprietary credit card receivables, securitized as discussed below, arise primarily under open-end revolving credit accounts issued by the Company's subsidiary, Pier 1 National Bank, to finance purchases of merchandise and services offered by the Company. These accounts have various billing and payment structures, including varying

Pier 1 Imports, Inc.

NOTES TO CONSOLIDATED FINANCIAL STATEMENTS
(continued)

minimum payment levels. The Company has an agreement with a third party to provide certain credit card processing and related credit services, while the Company maintains control over credit policy decisions and customer service standards.

As of fiscal 2002 year-end, the Company had approximately 5,178,000 proprietary cardholders and approximately 1,205,000 customer credit accounts considered active (accounts with a purchase within the previous 12 months). The Company's proprietary credit card sales accounted for 28.9% of total U.S. store sales in fiscal 2002. Net proprietary credit card income is included in selling, general and administrative expenses on the Company's statements of operations. The Company has sold virtually all of its proprietary credit card receivables. The following information presents a summary of the Company's proprietary credit card results for each of the last three fiscal years on a managed basis (in thousands):

	2002	2001	2000
Income:			
Finance charge income, net of debt service costs.........	$ 24,124	$ 21,759	$ 16,780
Insurance and other income	231	253	287
	24,355	22,012	17,067
Costs:			
Processing fees.........	14,197	13,608	10,763
Bad debts..............	6,977	5,285	4,664
	21,174	18,893	15,427
Net proprietary credit card income..........	$ 3,181	$ 3,119	$ 1,640
Proprietary credit card sales...................	$412,469	$377,045	$300,462
Costs as a percent of proprietary credit card sales..............	5.13%	5.01%	5.13%
Gross proprietary credit card receivables at year-end...............	$140,713	$122,876	$100,095
Proprietary credit card sales as a percent of total U.S. store sales	28.9%	28.9%	26.3%

In February 1997, the Company securitized its entire portfolio of proprietary credit card receivables (the "Receivables"). The Company sold all existing Receivables to a special-purpose wholly-owned subsidiary, Pier 1 Funding, Inc., predecessor to Pier 1 Funding, LLC ("Funding"), which transferred the Receivables to the Pier 1 Imports Credit Card Master Trust (the "Master Trust"). The Master Trust issues beneficial interests that represent undivided interests in the assets of the Master Trust consisting of the Receivables and all cash flows from collections of the Receivables. On a daily basis, the Company sells to Funding and Funding transfers to the Master Trust all newly generated Receivables, except those failing certain eligibility criteria, and receives as the purchase price payments of cash (funded from previously undistributed principal collections from the Receivables in the Master Trust) and retains residual interests in the Master Trust. Cash flows received from the Master Trust for each of the last three fiscal years are as follows (in thousands):

	2002	2001	2000
Proceeds from collections reinvested in revolving securitizations	$ 366,228	$ 347,404	$ 303,340
Proceeds from new securitizations	$ 49,226	$ –	$ –
Servicing fees received	$ 2,381	$ 2,189	$ 1,820
Cash flows received on retained interests.....	$ 172,473	$ 199,619	$ 147,314

Gains or losses resulting from the sales of the Company's proprietary credit card receivables were not material in any of the periods presented. The Company's exposure to deterioration in the performance of the receivables is limited to its retained beneficial interest in the Master Trust. As such, the Company has no corporate obligation to reimburse Funding, the Master Trust or purchasers of any certificates issued by the Master Trust for credit losses from the Receivables.

Funding was capitalized by the Company as a special-purpose wholly-owned subsidiary that is subject to certain covenants and restrictions, including a restriction from engaging in any business or activity unrelated to acquiring and selling interests in receivables. The Master Trust is not consolidated with the Company.

Pier 1 Imports, Inc.
NOTES TO CONSOLIDATED FINANCIAL STATEMENTS
(continued)

In the initial sale of the Receivables, the Company sold all of its Receivables and received cash and beneficial interests in the Master Trust. The Master Trust sold to third parties $50.0 million of Series 1997-1 Class A Certificates, which bore interest at 6.74% and were scheduled to mature in May 2002. Funding retained $14.1 million of Series 1997-1 Class B Certificates, which were subordinated to the Class A Certificates. Funding also retained the residual interest in the Master Trust.

In September 2001, the Master Trust negotiated the purchase of all of the Series 1997-1 Class A Certificates from their holders. Subsequently the Master Trust retired both the Series 1997-1 Class A and Class B Certificates in connection with the issuance of $100 million in 2001-1 Class A Certificates to a third party. The 2001-1 Class A Certificates bear interest at a floating rate equal to the rate on commercial paper issued by the third party. As of March 2, 2002, this rate was 1.81%. Funding continued to retain the residual interest in the Master Trust and $9.3 million in 2001-1 Class B Certificates, which are subordinated to the 2001-1 Class A Certificates. As a result of this securitization transaction, the Company effectively sold a portion of its beneficial interest for net proceeds of $49.2 million. As of March 2, 2002 and March 3, 2001, the Company had $44.6 million and $75.4 million, respectively, in beneficial interests (comprised primarily of principal and interest related to the underlying Receivables) in the Master Trust.

Under generally accepted accounting principles, if the structure of the securitization meets certain requirements, these transactions are accounted for as sales of receivables. As the Company's securitizations met such requirements as discussed above, they were accounted for as sales. Gains or losses from sales of these receivables were not material during fiscal 2002, 2001 and 2000. The Company expects no material impact on net income in future years as a result of the sales of receivables, although the precise amounts will be dependent on a number of factors such as interest rates and levels of securitization.

NOTE 3 - PROPERTIES

Properties are summarized as follows at March 2, 2002 and March 3, 2001 (in thousands):

	2002	2001
Land	$ 16,458	$ 22,353
Buildings	51,747	59,716
Equipment, furniture and fixtures	238,454	207,956
Leasehold interests and improvements	183,676	171,021
	490,335	461,046
Less accumulated depreciation and amortization	280,381	248,980
Properties, net	$209,954	$212,066

NOTE 4 - ACCOUNTS PAYABLE AND ACCRUED LIABILITIES/OTHER NONCURRENT LIABILITIES

The following is a summary of accounts payable and accrued liabilities and other noncurrent liabilities at March 2, 2002 and March 3, 2001 (in thousands):

	2002	2001
Trade accounts payable	$ 78,961	$ 52,637
Accrued payroll and other employee-related liabilities	36,999	33,685
Accrued taxes, other than income	16,815	15,576
Gift cards, gift certificates and merchandise credits outstanding	29,288	18,989
Accrued income taxes payable	29,738	7,786
Other	16,239	15,437
Accounts payable and accrued liabilities	$208,040	$144,110
Accrued average rent	$ 19,230	$ 17,590
Other	24,034	17,131
Other noncurrent liabilities	$ 43,264	$ 34,721

NOTE 5 - LONG-TERM DEBT AND AVAILABLE CREDIT

Long-term debt is summarized as follows at March 2, 2002 and March 3, 2001 (in thousands):

	2002	2001
Industrial revenue bonds	$ 25,000	$ 25,000
Other	712	–
	25,712	25,000
Less – portion due within one year	356	–
Long-term debt	$ 25,356	$ 25,000

Pier 1 Imports, Inc.

NOTES TO CONSOLIDATED FINANCIAL STATEMENTS
(continued)

In fiscal 1987, the Company entered into industrial revenue development bond loan agreements aggregating $25 million. Proceeds were used to construct three warehouse distribution facilities. The loan agreements and related tax-exempt bonds mature in the year 2026. The Company's interest rates on the loans are based on the bond interest rates, which are market driven, reset weekly and are similar to other tax-exempt municipal debt issues. The Company's weighted average interest rates were 3.8% and 5.7% for fiscal 2002 and 2001, respectively.

In September 1996, the Company issued $86.3 million principal amount of 5¾% convertible subordinated notes due October 1, 2003. The notes were convertible at any time prior to maturity, unless previously redeemed or repurchased, into shares of common stock of the Company at a conversion price of $8.22 per share, adjusted for stock splits. The Company had the option to redeem the notes, in whole or in part, on or after October 2, 1999, at a redemption price (expressed as a percentage of principal amount) of 103% of par value which was scheduled to decline annually to 100% of par value at the maturity date. Interest on the notes was payable semiannually on April 1 and October 1 of each year. In February 2000, the Company announced its intention to call the remaining $39.2 million outstanding principal amount of these notes for redemption on March 23, 2000. The notes were convertible into common stock of the Company at any time prior to the close of business on March 22, 2000, at a conversion price of $8.22 per share. During March 2000, the Company converted $39,164,000 of the notes into 4,764,450 shares of the Company's common stock and redeemed $15,000 of the notes for cash at a redemption price of 103% of par value. The conversion and redemption of these notes during fiscal 2001 reduced the Company's debt by $39.2 million and increased its capitalization by $39.4 million. Accordingly, these notes are not detailed in the above schedule as the notes were fully redeemed at fiscal 2001 year-end.

In November 2001, the Company executed a note payable in the original principal amount of £500,000. The note bears interest at 4.0% per annum and has a maturity date of April 2003. Interest is payable in semiannual installments and principle is payable in two installments, June 2002 and April 2003. At March 2, 2002, this note was valued at $712,000.

Long-term debt matures as follows (in thousands):

Fiscal Year	Long-term Debt
2003	$ 356
2004	356
2005	–
2006	–
2007	–
Thereafter	25,000
Total long-term debt	$ 25,712

The Company has a $125 million unsecured credit facility available, which expires in November 2003. The interest rate on borrowings against this facility is determined based upon a spread from LIBOR that varies depending upon either the Company's senior debt rating or leverage ratio. All of the $125 million revolving credit facility was available at fiscal 2002 year-end. The Company had no borrowings under this facility during fiscal 2002. The weighted average interest rate on borrowings outstanding for fiscal 2001 was 7.2%.

The Company has a $120 million short-term line of credit, which is primarily used to issue merchandise letters of credit. At fiscal 2002 year-end, approximately $64.6 million had been utilized for letters of credit, leaving $55.4 million available. The Company also has $28.7 million in credit lines used to issue other special-purpose letters of credit, all of which were fully utilized at fiscal 2002 year-end. Of the $28.7 million in special-purpose letters of credit, $25.6 milllion related to the Company's industrial revenue bonds.

Most of the Company's loan agreements require that the Company maintain certain financial ratios and limit specific payments and equity distributions including cash dividends, loans to shareholders and repurchases of common stock. The Company is in compliance with all debt covenants.

NOTE 6 - EMPLOYEE BENEFIT PLANS

The Company offers a qualified, defined contribution employee retirement plan to all its full- and part-time personnel who are at least 18 years old and have been employed for a minimum of six months. Employees contributing 1% to 5% of their compensation receive a matching Company contribution of up to 3%. Company contributions to the plan were $1,734,000, $1,790,000 and $1,753,000 in fiscal 2002, 2001 and 2000, respectively.

Pier 1 Imports, Inc.

NOTES TO CONSOLIDATED FINANCIAL STATEMENTS
(continued)

In addition, a non-qualified retirement savings plan is available for the purpose of providing deferred compensation for certain employees whose benefits under the qualified plan are limited under Section 401(k) of the Internal Revenue Code. The Company's expense for this non-qualified plan was not significant for fiscal 2002, 2001 and 2000.

The Company maintains supplemental retirement plans (the "Plans") for certain of its executive officers. The Plans provide that upon death, disability or reaching retirement age, a participant will receive benefits based on highest compensation and years of service. The Company recorded expenses related to the Plans of $2,488,000, $1,850,000 and $1,409,000 in fiscal 2002, 2001 and 2000, respectively.

Measurement of plan assets and obligations for the Plans are calculated as of each fiscal year-end. The discount rates used to determine the actuarial present value of projected benefit obligations under such plans were 7.25% and 7.50% as of March 2, 2002 and March 3, 2001, respectively. The assumed weighted average rate increase in future compensation levels under such plans was 5.0% as of both March 2, 2002 and March 3, 2001. The following provides a reconciliation of benefit obligations and funded status of the Plans as of March 2, 2002 and March 3, 2001 (in thousands):

	2002	2001
Change in projected benefit obligation:		
Projected benefit obligation, beginning of year	$ 12,962	$ 8,944
Service cost	569	434
Interest cost	1,055	779
Actuarial loss	1,278	–
Plan amendments	–	2,805
Projected benefit obligation, end of year	$ 15,864	$ 12,962
Reconciliation of funded status:		
Funded status	$ (15,864)	$ (12,962)
Unrecognized net loss	1,338	60
Unrecognized net transitional obligation	–	2
Unrecognized prior service cost	7,086	7,948
Accrued pension cost	(7,440)	(4,952)
Additional minimum liability	(3,980)	(5,663)
Accrued benefit liability	$ (11,420)	$ (10,615)
Amounts recognized in the balance sheets:		
Accrued benefit liability	$ (11,420)	$ (10,615)
Intangible asset	3,980	5,663
Net amount recognized	$ (7,440)	$ (4,952)

Net periodic benefit cost included the following actuarially determined components during fiscal 2002, 2001 and 2000 (in thousands):

	2002	2001	2000
Service cost	$ 569	$ 434	$ 459
Interest cost	1,055	779	543
Amortization of unrecognized prior service cost	862	635	374
Amortization of net obligation at transition	2	2	2
Recognized net actuarial loss	–	–	31
	$ 2,488	$ 1,850	$ 1,409

NOTE 7 - MATTERS CONCERNING SHAREHOLDERS' EQUITY

Stock purchase plan - Substantially all employees and directors are eligible to participate in the Pier 1 Imports, Inc. Stock Purchase Plan under which the Company's common stock is purchased on behalf of employees at market prices through regular payroll deductions. Each employee participant may contribute up to 10% of the eligible portions of compensation and directors may contribute part or all of their directors' fees. The Company contributes from 10% to 100% of the participants' contributions, depending upon length of participation and date of entry into the plan. Company contributions to the plan were $985,000, $921,000 and $954,000 in fiscal years 2002, 2001 and 2000, respectively.

Restricted stock grant plans - In fiscal 1998, the Company issued 238,500 shares of its common stock to key officers pursuant to a Management Restricted Stock Plan, which provides for the issuance of up to 415,600 shares. The fiscal 1998 restricted stock grant vested over a four-year period of continued employment. The fair value at the date of grant of these restricted stock shares was expensed over the afore-mentioned vesting period. The fair value at the date of grant of the restricted shares granted in fiscal 1998 was $3,000,000. Shares not vested were returned to the plan if employment was terminated for any reason. To date, 107,184 shares have been returned to the plan.

In fiscal 1991, the Company issued 726,804 shares of its common stock to key officers pursuant to a Restricted Stock

Pier 1 Imports, Inc.
NOTES TO CONSOLIDATED FINANCIAL STATEMENTS
(continued)

Grant Plan, which provided for the issuance of up to 1,037,214 shares. These shares vested, and the fair value at the date of grant was expensed, over a ten-year period of continued employment. Unvested shares are returned to the plan upon employment termination. As of March 2, 2002, 407,742 shares have been returned to the plan. In fiscal 2000, the Restricted Stock Grant Plan was terminated by the Board of Directors and is no longer available for issuance of common stock to key officers. The final vesting period was March 2000.

Total compensation expense for both of the restricted stock grant plans was $85,000, $216,000 and $485,000 for fiscal 2002, 2001 and 2000, respectively.

Stock option plans - In June 1999, the Company adopted the Pier 1 Imports, Inc. 1999 Stock Plan (the "Plan"). The Plan will ultimately replace the Company's two previous stock option plans, which were the 1989 Employee Stock Option Plan (the "Employee Plan") and the 1989 Non-Employee Director Stock Option Plan (the "Director Plan").

The Plan provides for the granting of options to directors and employees with an exercise price not less than the fair market value of the common stock on the date of the grant. Options may be either Incentive Stock Options authorized under Section 422 of the Internal Revenue Code or non-qualified options, which do not qualify as Incentive Stock Options. Current director compensation provides for non-qualified options covering 6,000 shares to be granted once each year to each non-employee director. Additionally, the Plan authorizes a Director Deferred Stock Program. As the program is currently implemented by the Board of Directors, each director must defer a minimum of 50% and may defer up to 100% of the director's cash fees into a deferred stock account. The amount deferred receives a 50% matching contribution from the Company. The Plan provides that a maximum of 7,000,000 shares of common

stock may be issued under the Plan, of which not more than 250,000 may be issued in exchange for deferred stock units. Options issued to non-director employees vest equally over a period of four years while directors' options are fully vested at the date of issuance. Additionally, employee options will fully vest upon retirement or, under certain conditions, a change in control of the Company. As of March 2, 2002 and March 3, 2001, respectively, there were 1,026,978 and 3,520,887 shares available for grant under the Plan, of which 171,673 and 200,381 may be used for deferred stock issuance. Additionally, outstanding options covering 894,200 and 429,600 shares were exercisable and 78,327 and 49,619 shares were issuable in exchange for deferred stock units at fiscal years ended 2002 and 2001, respectively. The Plan will expire in June 2009, and the Board of Directors may at any time suspend or terminate the Plan or amend the Plan, subject to certain limitations.

Under the Employee Plan, options may be granted to qualify as Incentive Stock Options under Section 422 of the Internal Revenue Code or as non-qualified options. Most options issued under the Employee Plan vest over a period of four to five years. As of March 2, 2002 and March 3, 2001, outstanding options covering 2,303,198 and 2,318,042 shares were exercisable and 932,684 and 878,059 shares were available for grant, respectively. The Employee Plan expires in June 2004. The Director Plan expired in fiscal 2000. As of March 2, 2002 and March 3, 2001, outstanding options covering 48,264 and 61,764 shares, respectively, were exercisable under the Director Plan. Due to the expiration of the Director Plan during fiscal 2000, no shares are available for future grants. Both plans were subject to adjustments for stock dividends and certain other changes to the Company's capitalization.

A summary of stock option translations related to the stock option plans during the three fiscal years ended March 2, 2002 is as follows:

46

Pier 1 Imports, Inc.
NOTES TO CONSOLIDATED FINANCIAL STATEMENTS
(continued)

	Shares	Weighted Average Exercise Price	Weighted Average Fair Value at Date of Grant	Exercisable Shares Number of Shares	Weighted Average Exercise Price
Outstanding at February 27, 1999	4,597,830	$ 9.20		1,810,819	$ 6.66
Options granted	2,379,500	6.20	$3.18		
Options exercised	(134,936)	4.63			
Options cancelled or expired	(793,187)	10.63			
Outstanding at February 26, 2000	6,049,207	7.94		2,214,717	7.28
Options granted	1,589,000	10.49	5.31		
Options exercised	(569,326)	5.38			
Options cancelled or expired	(351,900)	8.47			
Outstanding at March 3, 2001	6,716,981	8.73		2,809,406	8.07
Options granted	2,711,500	8.32	4.59		
Options exercised	(937,619)	7.06			
Options cancelled or expired	(314,125)	9.90			
Outstanding at March 2, 2002	8,176,737	8.74		3,245,662	8.81

For shares outstanding at March 2, 2002:

Ranges of Exercise Prices	Total Shares	Weighted Average Exercise Price	Weighted Average Remaining Contractual Life	Shares Currently Exercisable	Weighted Average Exercise Price – Exercisable Shares
$2.85 - $ 8.19	2,732,912	$ 5.96	5.82	1,794,112	$ 5.89
$8.26 - $ 8.50	3,026,475	8.29	9.15	289,600	8.49
$9.08 - $18.50	2,417,350	12.45	7.51	1,161,950	13.39

The Company accounts for its stock options using the intrinsic value-based method of accounting prescribed by APB Opinion No. 25, but is required to disclose the pro forma effect on net income and earnings per share as if the options were accounted for using a fair value-based method of accounting. The fair values for options issued in fiscal 2002, 2001 and 2000 have been estimated as of the date of grant using the Black-Scholes or a similar option pricing model with the following weighted average assumptions for 2002,

2001 and 2000, respectively: risk-free interest rates of 3.75%, 5.68% and 5.79%, expected stock price volatility of 60.25%, 55.86% and 51.50%, expected dividend yields of 0.8%, 1.0% and 1.0% and weighted average expected lives of six years from date of grant to date of exercise for all options. For purposes of computing pro forma net income and earnings per share, the fair value of the stock options is amortized on a straight-line basis as compensation expense over the vesting periods of the options. The pro forma effects on net

Pier 1 Imports, Inc.

NOTES TO CONSOLIDATED FINANCIAL STATEMENTS
(continued)

income and earnings per share are as follows (in thousands except per share amounts):

	2002	2001	2000
Pro forma net income	$ 95,863	$ 91,573	$ 72,317
Pro forma basic earnings per share	$ 1.02	$ .95	$ .76
Pro forma diluted earnings per share	$ 1.00	$ .93	$ .72

Option valuation models are used in estimating the fair value of traded options that have no vesting restrictions and are fully transferable. In addition, option valuation models require the input of highly subjective assumptions, including the expected stock price volatility and the average life of options. Because the Company's stock options have characteristics significantly different from those of traded options, and because changes in the subjective input assumptions can materially affect the fair value estimate, in management's opinion, the existing models do not necessarily provide a reliable single measure of the fair value of its stock options. In addition, the pro forma net income and earnings per share amounts shown above for fiscal 2002, 2001 and 2000 do not include the effect of any grants made prior to fiscal 1996.

Share purchase rights plan - On December 9, 1994, the Board of Directors adopted a Share Purchase Rights Plan and declared a dividend of one common stock purchase right (a "Right") payable on each outstanding share of the Company's common stock on December 21, 1994, and authorized the issuance of Rights for subsequently issued shares of common stock. The Rights, which will expire on December 21, 2004, are initially not exercisable, and until becoming exercisable will trade only with the associated common stock. After the Rights become exercisable, each Right entitles the holder to purchase at a specified exercise price one share of common stock. The Rights will become exercisable after the earlier to occur of (i) ten days following a public announcement that a person or group of affiliated

or associated persons have acquired beneficial ownership of 15% or more of the outstanding common stock or (ii) ten business days (or such later date as determined by the Board of Directors) following the commencement of, or announcement of an intention to make, a tender or exchange offer the consummation of which would result in beneficial ownership by a person or group of 15% or more of the outstanding common stock. If the Company were acquired in a merger or other business combination transaction or 50% or more of its consolidated assets or earning power were sold, proper provision would be made so that each Right would entitle its holder to purchase, upon the exercise of the Right at the then current exercise price (currently the exercise price is $14.81), that number of shares of common stock of the acquiring company having a market value of twice the exercise price of the Right. If any person or group were to acquire beneficial ownership of 15% or more of the Company's outstanding common stock, each Right would entitle its holder (other than such acquiring person whose Rights would become void) to purchase, upon the exercise of the Right at the then current exercise price, that number of shares of the Company's common stock having a market value on the date of such 15% acquisition of twice the exercise price of the Right. The Board of Directors may at its option, at any time after such 15% acquisition but prior to the acquisition of more than 50% of the Company's outstanding common stock, exchange all or part of the then outstanding and exercisable Rights (other than those held by such acquiring person whose Rights would become void) for common stock at an exchange rate per Right of one-half the number of shares of common stock receivable upon exercise of a Right. The Board of Directors may, at any time prior to such 15% acquisition, redeem all the Rights at a redemption price of $.01 per Right.

Shares reserved for future issuances - As of March 2, 2002, the Company had approximately 114,416,000 shares reserved for future issuances under the stock plans and the share purchase rights plan.

Pier 1 Imports, Inc.

NOTES TO CONSOLIDATED FINANCIAL STATEMENTS
(continued)

NOTE 8 - INCOME TAXES

The provision for income taxes for each of the last three fiscal years consists of (in thousands):

	2002	2001	2000
Federal:			
Current................	$ 56,207	$ 50,455	$ 39,463
Deferred..............	(2,110)	583	355
State:			
Current................	3,909	3,368	1,890
Deferred..............	(128)	152	1,370
Foreign:			
Current................	910	1,032	809
	$ 58,788	$ 55,590	$ 43,887

Deferred tax assets and liabilities at March 2, 2002 and March 3, 2001 are comprised of the following (in thousands):

	2002	2001
Deferred tax assets:		
Inventory	$ 2,166	$ 1,727
Deferred compensation..............	9,129	7,292
Accrued average rent	8,476	7,784
Losses on a foreign subsidiary	3,948	3,301
Self insurance reserves...............	2,408	910
Fixed assets, net	–	795
Other	2,470	2,326
	28,597	24,135
Valuation allowance....................	(3,948)	(3,301)
Total deferred tax assets..............	24,649	20,834
Deferred tax liabilities:		
Fixed assets, net	(1,577)	–
Total deferred tax liabilities...........	(1,577)	–
Net deferred tax assets.................	$ 23,072	$ 20,834

The Company has settled and closed all Internal Revenue Service ("IRS") examinations of the Company's tax returns for all years through fiscal 1999. An IRS audit of fiscal years 2000 and 2001 is expected to begin in the first quarter of fiscal year 2003. For financial reporting purposes, a valuation allowance exists at March 2, 2002 to offset the deferred tax asset relating to the losses of a foreign subsidiary.

Undistributed earnings of the Company's non-U.S. subsidiaries amounted to approximately $22.6 million at March 2, 2002. These earnings are considered to be indefinitely reinvested and, accordingly, no additional U.S. income taxes or non-U.S. withholding taxes have been provided. Determination of the amount of additional taxes that would be payable if such earnings were not considered indefinitely reinvested is not practical.

The difference between income taxes at the statutory federal income tax rate of 35% in fiscal 2002, 2001 and 2000, and income tax reported in the consolidated statements of operations is as follows (in thousands):

	2002	2001	2000
Tax at statutory federal			
income tax rate	$ 55,649	$ 52,584	$ 41,514
State income taxes,			
net of federal benefit	3,387	3,200	2,526
Work opportunity tax			
credit, foreign tax			
credit and R&E credit....	(202)	(207)	(283)
Net foreign income taxed			
at lower rates...........	(101)	(1,048)	(960)
Other, net	55	1,061	1,090
	$ 58,788	$ 55,590	$ 43,887

NOTE 9 - COMMITMENTS AND CONTINGENCIES

Leases - The Company leases certain property consisting principally of retail stores, warehouses and material handling and office equipment under leases expiring through the year 2021. Most retail store locations are leased for initial terms of 10 to 15 years with varying renewal options and rent escalation clauses. Certain leases provide for additional rental payments based on a percentage of sales in excess of a specified base. The Company's lease obligations are considered operating leases, and all payments are reflected in the accompanying consolidated statements of operations.

During fiscal 2002, the Company sold certain store properties for $12.6 million. These stores were leased back from unaffiliated third parties for periods of approximately ten years. The resulting leases are being accounted for as operating leases. The Company deferred gains of $5.1 million

Pier 1 Imports, Inc.

NOTES TO CONSOLIDATED FINANCIAL STATEMENTS
(continued)

in fiscal 2002 on these sale-leaseback transactions; the gains are being amortized over the initial lives of the leases. Future minimum lease commitments of these operating leases are included in the summary below of the Company's operating leases. The Company had no sale-leaseback transactions in fiscal 2001.

At March 2, 2002, the Company had the following minimum lease commitments in the years indicated (in thousands):

Fiscal Year	Operating Leases
2003	$ 162,315
2004	158,525
2005	145,608
2006	132,855
2007	118,102
Thereafter	426,946
Total lease commitments	$ 1,144,351
Present value of total operating lease commitments at 10%	$ 751,919

Rental expense incurred was $159,461,000, $144,035,000 and $131,835,000, including contingent rentals of $921,000, $979,000 and $794,000, based upon a percentage of sales, and net of sublease incomes totaling $1,191,000, $2,650,000 and $2,141,000 in fiscal 2002, 2001 and 2000, respectively.

Legal matters - There are various claims, lawsuits, investigations and pending actions against the Company and its subsidiaries incident to the operations of its business. Liability, if any, associated with these matters is not determinable at March 2, 2002; however, the Company considers them to be ordinary and routine in nature. The Company maintains liability insurance against most of these claims. While certain of the lawsuits involve substantial amounts, it is the opinion of management, after consultation with counsel, that the ultimate resolution of such litigation will not have a material adverse effect on the Company's financial position, results of operations or liquidity.

NOTE 10 - SELECTED QUARTERLY FINANCIAL DATA (UNAUDITED)

Summarized quarterly financial data for the years ended March 2, 2002 and March 3, 2001 are set forth below (in thousands except per share amounts):

Fiscal 2002	Three Months Ended			
	6/2/01	9/1/01	12/1/01	3/2/02
Net sales	$ 325,387	357,248	387,360	478,561
Gross profit	$ 134,914	137,539	165,408	211,900
Net income	$ 12,345	13,802	25,046	49,016
Basic earnings per share	$ .13	.15	.27	.53
Diluted earnings per share	$ .13	.14	.26	.51

Fiscal 2001	Three Months Ended			
	5/27/00	8/26/00	11/25/00	3/3/01
Net sales	$ 299,528	337,991	343,493	430,486
Gross profit	$ 126,646	135,616	147,160	185,033
Net income	$ 16,877	17,715	23,569	36,489
Basic earnings per share	$ .17	.18	.25	.38
Diluted earnings per share	$ .17	.18	.24	.38

Pier 1 Imports, Inc.
SHAREHOLDER INFORMATION

EXECUTIVE OFFICES

Suite 600

301 Commerce Street

Fort Worth, Texas 76102

(817) 252-8000

www.pier1.com

COMMON STOCK

Approximately 40,000 shareholders of record

Traded on the New York Stock Exchange

Symbol: PIR

INVESTOR RELATIONS AND FORM 10-K REPORT

A copy of the Pier 1 Imports, Inc. Form 10-K report filed with
the Securities and Exchange Commission is available by
writing the Investor Relations Department at:

Pier 1 Imports, Inc.

P.O. Box 961020

Fort Worth, Texas 76161-0020

or by calling (817) 252-7835

Toll Free (888) 80-PIER1

(888) 807-4371

Investor inquiries also may be directed to that department.

INDEPENDENT AUDITORS

Ernst & Young LLP

Fort Worth, Texas

TRANSFER AGENT

Mellon Investor Services

85 Challenger Road

Ridgefield Park, New Jersey 07660

Shareholder Line Toll Free (888) 884-8086

ANNUAL MEETING

The annual meeting of shareholders will be held at
10 a.m. Central Daylight Time, Thursday, June 27, 2002,
in the Brazos Room at the Renaissance Worthington Hotel,
Fort Worth, Texas.

MARKET PRICE AND DIVIDEND INFORMATION

The Company's common stock is traded on the New York Stock Exchange. The following tables show the high and low closing sale
prices on such Exchange, as reported in the consolidated transaction reporting system, and the dividends paid per share, for each
quarter of fiscal 2002 and 2001.

Fiscal 2002	Market Price		Cash Dividends Per Share (1)	Fiscal 2001	Market Price		Cash Dividends Per Share (1)
	High	Low			High	Low	
First quarter	$ 14.5500	$ 11.1000	$ .04	First quarter	$ 11.8750	$ 7.8750	$ .03
Second quarter	12.6500	10.3000	.04	Second quarter	12.7500	8.5000	.04
Third quarter	14.7000	8.1300	.04	Third quarter	14.0000	10.4375	.04
Fourth quarter	20.2400	14.5000	.04	Fourth quarter	13.8750	8.1875	.04

(1) *For restrictions on the payments of dividends, see Management's Discussion and Analysis of Financial Condition and Results of Operations – Liquidity and
Capital Resources.*

Pier 1 Imports, Inc.
DIRECTORS AND OFFICERS

BOARD OF DIRECTORS	EXECUTIVE OFFICERS
Marvin J. Girouard Chairman and Chief Executive Officer	**Marvin J. Girouard** Chairman and Chief Executive Officer
John H. Burgoyne Principal Burgoyne and Associates	**Charles H. Turner** Executive Vice President, Chief Financial Officer and Treasurer
James D. Carreker Owner JDC Holdings	**Robert A. Arlauskas** Executive Vice President, Stores
Dr. Michael R. Ferrari Chancellor Texas Christian University	**Jay R. Jacobs** Executive Vice President, Merchandising
James M. Hoak, Jr. Chairman Hoak Capital Corporation	**J. Rodney Lawrence** Executive Vice President, Legal Affairs and Corporate Secretary
Karen W. Katz President and Chief Executive Officer Neiman Marcus Direct	**Phil E. Schneider** Executive Vice President, Marketing
Tom M. Thomas Senior Partner Kolodey, Thomas & Blackwood, LLP	**David A. Walker** Executive Vice President, Logistics and Allocations
	E. Mitchell Weatherly Executive Vice President, Human Resources

Pier1 imports℠

Suite 600
301 Commerce Street
Fort Worth, Texas 76102
www.pier1.com

Glossary of Accounting Terms in Introduction to Financial Accounting

accelerated depreciation methods Those methods that record more depreciation expense in the early years of an asset's life and less in the later years.

accounting A service activity that has the function of providing quantitative information, primarily financial in nature, about economic entities that is intended to be useful in making economic decisions.

accounting information Raw data concerning transactions that have been transformed into financial numbers that can be used by economic decision makers.

accounts Subclassifications used to classify and record economic events and transactions. For example, some accounts that may be found under assets are accounts receivable, office supplies, and property, plant, and equipment. Under expenses, we may find wages, rent, and advertising.

accrual basis accounting A method of accounting in which revenues are recognized when they are earned, regardless of when the associated cash is collected. The expenses incurred in generating the revenue are recognized when the benefit is derived rather than when the associated cash is paid.

accruals Adjustments made to record items that should be included on the income statement but have not yet been recorded.

accrue As used in accounting, to come into being as a legally enforceable claim.

accrued expenses Expenses appropriately recognized under accrual accounting in one income statement period although the associated cash will be paid in a later income statement period.

accrued revenues Revenues appropriately recognized under accrual accounting in one income statement period although the associated cash will be received in a later income statement period.

accumulated depreciation The total amount of cost that has been systematically converted to expense since a long-lived asset was first purchased.

acid-test ratio Another name for the quick ratio.

additional paid-in capital The amount in excess of the stock's par value received by the corporation when par value stock is issued.

adjusted trial balance A trial balance that is prepared after all of the adjusting entries have been made.

adjusting entries The entries to modify account balances so that all revenue earned and all expenses incurred are recorded and all asset, liability, and equity accounts are properly stated as of the balance sheet date.

adjustments Changes made in recorded amounts of revenues and expenses in order to follow the guidelines of accrual accounting.

annual report A corporate document that provides interested parties with a variety of information including financial statements and a host of general information about the company and its management.

articulation The links among the financial statements.

asset turnover ratio A financial ratio that shows the amount of sales produced for a given level of assets used.

assets An accounting element that is one of the three components of a balance sheet. Assets are probable future economic benefits controlled by an entity as a result of previous transactions or events—that is, what a company has.

authorized shares The maximum number of shares of stock a corporation has been given permission to issue under its corporate charter.

average accounts receivable collection period in days The average time it takes a company to collect its receivables.

average cost method The inventory cost flow method that assigns an average cost to the units of inventory on hand at the time of each sale.

average inventory holding period The average length of time product is held in inventory.

balance sheet The financial tool that focuses on the present condition of a business.

basic earnings per share Earnings per share based on the average number of common shares outstanding.

beginning inventory The amount of merchandise inventory (units or dollars) on hand at the beginning of the income statement period.

bond An interest-bearing debt instrument that allows corporations to borrow large amounts of funds for long periods of time and creates a liability for the borrower.

book inventory The amount of ending inventory (units and dollars) resulting from transactions recorded by a perpetual inventory system.

book of original entry The same thing as a journal.

book value The original cost of a long-lived asset less its accumulated depreciation. This item is often shown on the balance sheet.

business Depending on the context, the area of commerce or trade, an individual company, or the process of producing and distributing goods and services.

business segment A portion of an entity representing either a separate major line of business or a class of customer.

capital A factor of production that includes the buildings, machinery, and tools used to produce goods and services. Also, sometimes used to refer to the money used to buy those items.

capitalism An example of a market economy. A *market economy* is one that relies on competition to determine the most efficient way to allocate the economy's resources.

cash basis accounting A basis of accounting in which cash is the major criterion used in measuring revenue and expense for a given income statement period. Revenue is recognized when the associated cash is received, and expense is recognized when the associated cash is paid.

chart of accounts A list of all the accounts used by a business entity. The list usually contains the name of the account and the account number.

classified balance sheet A balance sheet that provides a breakdown of the composition of the items the balance sheet includes.

closing entries A series of entries to reset revenues, expenses, and dividends to zero in preparation for a new accounting year.

collateral   Something of value that will be forfeited if a borrower fails to make payments as agreed.

commercial borrowing   The process that businesses go through to obtain financing.

common stock   A share of ownership in a corporation. Each share represents one vote in the election of the board of directors and other pertinent corporate matters.

communism   An example of a planned economy. A *planned economy* is one with a strong centralized government that controls all or most of the natural resources, labor, and capital used to produce goods and services.

comparability   A quality needed to meaningfully assess the relative performance on *two different entities*. The requirement that every company provide accounting information in conformity with a fairly uniform structure enables decision makers to compare one company to another.

comparative financial statements   Financial statements showing results from two or more consecutive periods.

compound entries   Entries recorded in the general journal that contain more than two accounts.

comprehensive income   The change in equity during a period from nonowner sources.

computerized accounting system   An accounting system in which the accountants and bookkeepers make entries in a computer system where the journals and ledgers consist of listings of transactions on computer printouts or in files in the computer's memory.

Conceptual Framework of Accounting   A framework created by the FASB to establish the objectives of financial reporting and the qualitative characteristics of useful accounting information, and to define the accounting elements, assumptions, principles, and constraints.

conservatism   Provides a guideline in difficult valuation or measurement situations. Accountants should guard against accounting treatments that unjustly overstate financial position or earnings.

consistency   A quality that is needed to meaningfully assess the performance of a *single entity* over time. Consistent application of accounting rules enables us to track a single company's performance over time.

consumer borrowing   Loans obtained by individuals to buy homes, cars, or other personal property.

contra-account   An account that carries a normal balance that decreases the accounting element in which it is classified.

contract rate   *See* nominal interest rate.

contributed capital   Total amount invested in a corporation by its shareholders. Also called paid-in capital.

corporation   A business that is a separate legal entity from its stockholders (owners).

cost of goods sold   The cost of the product sold as the primary business activity of a company.

cost of products sold   *See* cost of goods sold.

cost of sales   *See* cost of goods sold.

cost/benefit   Deals with the trade-off between the rewards of selecting a given alternative and the sacrifices required to obtain those rewards.

coupon rate   *See* nominal interest rate.

coverage ratio   Same as the times interest earned ratio.

cumulative effect of an accounting change   Result of adopting a new accounting standard or changing from one acceptable method of accounting to another. One of the nonrecurring items shown net of tax on the income statement.

current assets   Assets that are cash, will become cash, or will be consumed within the longer of one year or the current operating cycle.

current liabilities   Liabilities that require settlement (payment) within one year or the current operating cycle, whichever is longer.

current ratio   A liquidity ratio that measures a company's ability to meet short-term obligations by comparing current assets to current liabilities.

data   The raw results of transactions. Facts and figures that are not organized enough to be useful to decision makers.

date of declaration   The date upon which a corporation announces plans to distribute a dividend. At this point, the corporation becomes legally obligated to make the distribution: A liability is created.

date of payment   The date a corporate dividend is actually paid. The payment date is generally announced on the date of declaration.

date of record   Owners of the shares of stock on this day are the ones who will receive the dividend announced on the date of declaration.

debenture bond   An unsecured bond payable.

debt financing   Acquiring funds for business operations by borrowing. Debt financing is one type of external financing.

debt ratio   A solvency ratio that indicates what proportion of a company's assets is financed by debt.

debt-to-equity ratio   A financial ratio that expresses the proportional relationship between liabilities and equity.

deferrals   Situations in which cash is either received or paid, but the income statement effect is delayed until some later period. Deferred revenues are recorded as liabilities, and deferred expenses are recorded as assets.

deferred expenses   Expenses created when cash is paid before any benefit is received. Because the benefit to be derived is in the future, the item is recorded as an asset. Later, when the benefit is received from the item, it will be recognized as an expense.

deferred revenues   Revenues created when cash is received before the revenue is earned. Because the cash received has not yet been earned, an obligation is created and a liability is recorded. Later, when the cash is deemed to have been earned, it will be recognized as a revenue.

depreciable base   The total amount of depreciation expense that is allowed to be claimed for an asset during its useful life. The depreciable base is the cost of the asset less its residual value.

depreciation   The systematic and rational conversion of a long-lived asset's cost from asset to expense in the income statement periods benefited.

diluted earnings per share   A calculation of earnings per share that takes into account all potentially dilutive securities.

dilutive securities   Securities that have the potential to reduce earnings per share.

direct method   The format of a statement of cash flows that provides detail about the individual sources and uses of cash associated with operating activities.

discontinued operations   The disposal of a business segment. One of the nonrecurring items shown net of tax on the income statement.

discount   If a bond's selling price is below its par value, the bond is being sold at a discount.

distributions to owners   Decreases in equity resulting from transferring assets to the owners of an enterprise.

dividend payout ratio   A financial ratio that shows what portion of a company's net income for a given year was paid to its owners as cash dividends during that year.

dividends   A distribution of earnings from a corporation to its owners. Dividends are most commonly distributed in the form of cash.

double-declining-balance method An accelerated depreciation method in which depreciation expense is twice the straight-line percentage multiplied by the book value of the asset.

drawings Distributions to the owners of proprietorships and partnerships. Also called withdrawals.

earned equity The total amount a company has earned since its beginning, less any amounts distributed to the owner(s). In a corporation, this amount is called retained earnings.

earnings per share A calculation indicating how much of a company's total earnings is attributable to each share of common stock.

earnings per share (EPS) The amount of a company's total earnings attributable to each share of common stock.

EBIT Earnings before interest and taxes.

economic entity The assumption that economic activities can be identified with a particular enterprise.

effective interest rate The rate of interest actually earned by a lender. This amount will be different from the nominal interest rate if a bond is bought at a discount or premium, or a note is discounted. Also called yield rate or market interest rate.

efficiency ratios Financial ratios that measure the investment in assets relative to business activity.

Electronic Data Gathering, Analysis, and Retrieval (EDGAR) A system operated by the SEC to facilitate the collection and, more importantly, the dissemination of corporate information to all interested parties. Access to EDGAR is available over the Internet at *www.sec.gov.*

entrepreneurship The factor of production that brings the other three factors—natural resources, labor, and capital—together to form a business.

equity An accounting element that is one of the three components of a balance sheet. Equity is the residual interest in the assets of an entity that remains after deducting liabilities. Also called net assets.

equity financing Acquiring funds for business operations by giving up ownership interest in the company. For a corporation, this means issuing capital stock. Equity financing is one type of external financing.

expense An accounting element representing the outflow of assets resulting from an entity's ongoing major or central operations. These are the sacrifices required to attain the rewards (revenues) of doing business.

exports Goods produced in a country but sold outside that country.

external decision makers Economic decision makers outside a company who make decisions about the company. The accounting information they use to make those decisions is limited to what the company provides them.

external financing Acquiring funds from outside the company. Equity and debt financing are the two major types of external financing.

extraordinary item A gain or loss that is both unusual in nature and infrequent in occurrence. One of the nonrecurring items shown net of tax on the income statement.

factors of production The four major items needed to support economic activity: natural resources, labor, capital, and entrepreneurship.

feedback value A primary characteristic of relevance. To be useful, accounting must provide decision makers with information that allows them to assess the progress of an investment.

financial accounting The branch of accounting developed to meet the informational needs of external decision makers.

Financial Accounting Standards Board (FASB) The organization that is principally responsible for establishing accounting guidelines and rules in the United States at the present time.

financial statement analysis The process of looking beyond the face of the financial statements to gather more information.

financing activities Business activities, such as the issuance of debt or equity and the payment of dividends, that focus on the external financing of the company.

first-in, first-out (FIFO) The inventory flow concept based on the assumption that the first units of inventory purchased are the first ones sold.

Form 10-K Less glamorous than the annual report, this corporate document includes additional financial and nonfinancial details that are invaluable to external decision makers.

fully depreciated When all of the allowable depreciation expense has been recognized for an asset's entire useful life.

gains Net inflows resulting from peripheral activities of a company. An example is the sale of an asset for more than its book value.

general journal A book of original entry in which is recorded all transactions not otherwise recorded in special journals.

general ledger A book of final entry that contains a page for each account listed in the chart of accounts.

general ledger accounts The same thing as accounts.

generally accepted accounting principles (GAAP) Guidelines for presentation of financial accounting information designed to serve external decision makers' need for consistent and comparable information.

going concern The assumption that unless there is persuasive evidence otherwise, a particular business enterprise will stay in business indefinitely.

goods available for sale The total amount of merchandise inventory a company has available to sell in a given income statement period.

gross margin An item shown on a multiple-step income statement, calculated as: Sales − Cost of goods sold.

gross profit *See* gross margin.

gross profit margin ratio A financial ratio that expresses a company's gross profit (often called gross margin on the financial statements) as a percentage of sales revenue.

historical cost principal The accounting principle that requires balance sheet amounts generally to be shown at acquisition price rather than fair value.

hybrid companies Those companies involved in more than one type of activity (manufacturing, merchandising, service).

imports Foreign products brought into a country.

income from operations *See* operating income.

income statement A financial statement providing information about an entity's past performance. Its purpose is to measure the results of the entity's operations for some specific time period.

income tax A tax based on the amount of income a company has earned.

indenture The legal agreement made between a bond issuer and a bondholder that states repayment terms and other details.

indirect method The more widely used format of the statement of cash flows. This approach provides accrual net income to the cash provided by or used by operating activities.

industry practice The notion that the peculiar nature of some industries actually causes adherence to GAAP to have misleading results, and therefore, these industries have developed accounting treatments for certain items that depart from GAAP.

information   Facts and figures that are sorted, arranged, and summarized and otherwise put into a form that is useful to decision makers.

intangible assets   Things that have future value but lack physical presence such as patents, copyrights, trademarks, and purchased goodwill.

internal decision makers   Economic decision makers within a company who make decisions for the company. They have access to much or all of the accounting information generated within the company.

internal financing   Providing funds for the operation of a company through the earnings process of that company.

inventory   The stockpile of tangible product that a company has on hand to sell.

inventory turnover ratio   A liquidity ratio that indicates how long a company holds its inventory.

investing activities   Business activities related to long-term assets. Examples are the purchase and sale of property, plant, and equipment.

investments by owners   That part of owners' equity generated by the receipt of cash (or other assets) from the owners.

issued shares   Stock that has been distributed to the owners of the corporation in exchange for cash or other assets.

journal   A book of original entry used to record the economic events and transactions that affect the accounts of a company.

labor   The mental and physical efforts of all workers performing tasks required to produce and sell goods and services. This factor of production is also called the human resource factor.

last-in, first-out (LIFO)   The inventory flow concept based on the assumption that the last units of inventory purchased are the first ones sold.

liabilities   An accounting element that is one of the three components of a balance sheet. Liabilities are probable future sacrifices of assets arising from present obligations of an entity as a result of past transactions or events—that is, what a company owes.

liquidity   An item's nearness to cash.

long-term assets   Assets that are expected to benefit the company for longer than one year.

long-term investments   Sometimes called *investments.* Investments in securities such as stocks, bonds, and long-term notes receivable; investments in fixed assets that are not currently being used in operations; special funds established to set aside financial resources.

long-term liabilities   Liabilities that will not require settlement within one year or the current operating cycle.

losses   Net outflows resulting from peripheral activities of a company. An example is the sale of an asset for less than its book value.

management accounting   The branch of accounting developed to meet the informational needs of internal decision makers.

manual accounting system   An accounting system in which the accountants and bookkeepers write all of the entries by hand in pen and ink.

manufacturing   The business activity that converts purchased raw materials into some tangible, physical product.

market interest rate   *See* effective interest rate.

market price (of bonds)   The amount that investors are actually willing to pay for a bond. A bond's selling price.

matching   Accounting principle that relates the expenses to the revenues of a particular income statement period. Once it is determined in which period a revenue should be recognized, the expenses that helped to generate the revenue are matched to that same period.

materiality   Something that will influence the judgment of a reasonable person.

merchandise inventory   The physical units (goods) a company buys to resell as part of its business operation. Also called inventory.

merchandising   The business activity involving the selling of finished goods produced by other businesses.

Modified Accelerated Cost Recovery System (MACRS)   Depreciation method taxpayers use to calculate depreciation expense for tax purposes.

monetary unit   The assumption that all economic transactions and events can be measured by some monetary unit. In the United States, for example, the dollar is used.

mortgage   A document that states the agreement between a lender and a borrower who has secured the loan by offering something of value as collateral.

multiple-step income statement   An income statement format that highlights gross margin and operating income.

natural resources   Land and the materials that come from the land, such as timber, mineral deposits, oil deposits, and water. One of the factors of production.

net assets   *See* equity.

net cash flow   The difference between cash inflows and cash outflows; it can be either positive or negative.

net earnings   *See* net income.

net income   The amount of profit that remains after all costs have been considered. The net reward of doing business for a specific time period.

net loss   The difference between revenues and expenses of a period in which expenses are greater than revenues.

net of tax   The amount remaining for an item after income tax has been deducted.

net profit   *See* net income.

net profit margin ratio   A financial ratio that expresses a company's net profit (almost always called either net income or net earnings on the financial statements) as a percentage of sales revenue. It indicates the amount of net income generated by a dollar of sales.

net sales   Total sales less any discounts or reductions due to returns or sales allowances..

net worth   *See* equity.

neutrality   A primary characteristic of reliability. To be useful, accounting information must be free of bias.

nominal interest rate   The interest rate set by the issuers of bonds, stated as a percentage of the par value of the bonds. Also called the contract rate.

nonrecurring item   Results of activities that are not expected to occur again and, therefore, should not be used to predict future performance.

normal balance   The balance of the account derived from the type of entry (debit or credit) that increases the account.

operating activities   Activities that result in cash inflows and outflows generated from the normal course of business.

operating cash flow coverage ratio   A financial ratio that indicates a company's capacity to repay its liabilities from the net cash generated by its operating activities.

operating cash flow to current debt ratio   A financial ratio that measures the sufficiency of cash flows from operating activities to meet current obligations.

operating income   Income produced by the major business activity of the company. An item shown on the multiple-step income statement.

opportunity cost   The benefit or benefits forgone by not selecting a particular alternative. Once an alternative is selected in a decision situation, the benefits of all rejected alternatives become part of the opportunity cost of the alternative selected.

other assets Long-term assets that do not fit into any other asset classification.

outstanding shares Shares of stock actually held by shareholders. The number may be different than that for issued shares because a corporation may reacquire its own stock (treasury stock).

paid-in capital Total amount invested in a corporation by its shareholders.

paid-in capital in excess of par Same thing as additional paid-in capital.

par value (bonds) The amount that must be paid back upon maturity of a bond. Also called face value or maturity value.

par value (stock) An arbitrary amount assigned to each share of stock by the incorporators at the time of incorporation.

partnership A business form similar to a proprietorship, but having two or more owners.

peer companies Companies that are similar to one another, usually in the same industry and of similar size.

periodic inventory system An inventory system in which all inventory and cost of goods sold calculations are done at the end of the income statement period.

periodicity The assumption that the economic activities of an entity can be traced to some specific time period and results of those activities can be reported for any arbitrary time period chosen.

permanent (real) accounts The general ledger accounts that are never closed. The permanent accounts include assets, liabilities, and equity accounts except for owner withdrawals.

perpetual inventory system An inventory system in which both the physical count of inventory units and the cost classification (asset or expense) are updated when a transaction involves inventory.

post-closing trial balance A trial balance prepared after all closing entries have been posted, which proves that the only accounts remaining in the general ledger are the permanent accounts and that the accounting equation remains in balance.

posting The process of transcribing information from journals to the ledger.

predictive value A primary characteristic of relevance. To be useful, accounting must provide information to decision makers that can be used to predict the future and timing of cash flows.

preferred stock A share of ownership in a corporation that has preference over common stock as to dividends and as to assets upon liquidation of the corporation. Usually nonvoting stock.

premium If a bond's selling price is above its par value, the bond is being sold at a premium.

price-to-earnings ratio A financial ratio that is often called simply the PE ratio that expresses the relationship between a company's earnings per share and the market value of the company's stock.

principal In the case of notes and mortgages, the amount of funds actually borrowed.

profit The excess of benefit over sacrifice. A less formal name for net income or net profit.

profitability The ease with which a company generates income.

promissory note A written promise to repay a loan.

property, plant, and equipment Physical long-lived assets used by the business including land, buildings, equipment, machinery, vehicles, and furniture.

proprietorship Same thing as a sole proprietorship.

purchases The amount of merchandise inventory bought during the income statement period.

quick ratio A liquidity ratio that is similar to the current ratio, but a more stringent test of liquidity, because only current assets considered to be highly liquid (quickly converted to cash) are included in the calculation.

quotas A limit on the quantities of particular items that can be imported.

rate of return on assets ratio A financial ratio that shows the amount of profit (net income) produced for a given level of assets.

rate of return on common equity ratio A financial ratio that shows the amount of profit (net income) in relation to the amount of investment by the company's owners.

ratio analysis A technique for analyzing the relationship between two items from a company's financial statements for a given period.

receivables turnover ratio An efficiency ratio that measures how quickly a company collects its accounts receivable.

recognition The process of recording an event in your records and reporting it on your financial statements.

reconciling items Items that are causing the difference between a bank's cash balance and the balance shown on a company's records. These items are listed in the appropriate places on the company's bank reconciliation form.

relevance Pertinent to the decision at hand. The capability of making a difference in a decision by helping users to form predictions or to adjust their expectations.

reliability A characteristic of information whereby decision makers can depend on information actually depicting the reality of a given situation.

representational faithfulness A primary characteristic of reliability. To be useful, accounting information must reasonably report what actually happened.

retained earnings Constitutes the earnings reinvested by the corporation and not distributed to owners in the form of dividends.

revenue An accounting element representing the inflows of assets as a result of an entity's ongoing major or central operations. These are the rewards of doing business.

risk/reward trade-off The relationship between uncertainty and reward. It indicates that the higher the risk, the higher the reward required to induce the risk taking.

sales revenue The revenue generated from the sale of a tangible product as a major business activity.

Securities and Exchange Commission (SEC) The government agency empowered to regulate the buying and selling of stocks and bonds and to establish accounting rules, standards, and procedures, and the form and content of published financial reporting.

selling price (of bonds) *See* market price (of bonds).

separate entity assumption The assumption that economic activity can be identified with a particular economic entity and that the results of activities for each entity will be recorded separately.

service company A business that performs a service as its major business activity.

single-step income statement A format of the income statement that gathers all revenues into "total revenues" and all expenses into "total expenses." Net income is calculated as a subtraction of total expenses from total revenues.

sole proprietorship An unincorporated business that is owned by one person. Also called a proprietorship.

solvency A company's ability to meet the obligations created by its long-term debt obligations.

special journal A book of original entry designed to record a specific type of transaction.

specific identification method The method of inventory cost flow that identifies each item sold by a company.

stakeholder Anyone who is affected by the way a company conducts its business.

stated rate *See* nominal interest rate.

statement of capital   A statement of owner's equity for a proprietorship.

statement of cash flows   A financial statement that provides information about the causes of a change in the company's cash balance from the beginning to the end of a specific period.

statement of owners' equity   The financial statement that reports activity in the capital accounts of proprietorships and partnerships and in the stockholders' equity accounts of corporations. The statement of owners' equity serves as a bridge between the income statement and the balance sheet.

statement of partners' capital   A statement of owners' equity for a partnership.

statement of results of operations   *See* income statement.

statement of retained earnings   A corporate financial statement that shows the changes in retained earnings during a particular period.

statement of stockholders' equity   The financial statement that shows the changes in owners' equity for a corporation for a given time period.

straight-line depreciation   A method of calculating periodic depreciation. The depreciable base of an asset is divided by its estimated useful life. The result is the amount of depreciation expense to be recognized in each year of the item's useful life:

(Cost − Residual Value)/N = Annual Depreciation Expense.

tariffs   Taxes that raise the price of imported products to about the same as similar domestic products.

temporary (nominal) accounts   The general ledger accounts that are closed to a zero balance at the end of the fiscal year as the net income or net loss is transferred to the appropriate equity account. Temporary accounts include revenues, expenses, gains, losses, owner withdrawal, and dividend accounts.

timeliness   A primary characteristic of relevance. To be useful, accounting information must be provided in time to influence a particular decision.

times interest earned ratio   A financial ratio that indicates a company's ability to earn (cover) its periodic interest payments.

title   Legal ownership of something.

treasury stock   Corporate stock that has been issued and then reacquired by the corporation.

trial balance   The listing of the general ledger account balances, which proves that the general ledger and therefore the accounting equation is in balance.

unearned revenue   A liability account used to record a company's liability to provide goods or services, which customers have paid for but have not yet received.

units-of-production depreciation method   A straight-line depreciation method that uses production activity as the basis of allocating depreciation expense. Instead of using an amount of depreciation per year, an amount of depreciation per unit produced is used.

verifiability   A primary characteristic of reliability. Information is considered verifiable if several individuals, working independently, would arrive at similar conclusions using the same data.

withdrawals   *See* drawings.

working capital   The difference between current assets and current liabilities.

worksheet   A tool used by the accountant to accumulate the necessary information used to prepare the financial statements.

yield rate   *See* effective interest rate.

Company Index: Financial Accounting

Real company names are in bold type.

A

Accelerated Movers, F-265, 266, 280–283
Ace Company, F-347
Ace Corporation, F-111
A&C Enterprises, F-103
Adrienne's Cosmetics, F-393
Alana Bradley Company, F-352–353
Alberto Pons, F-191
Alex's Baseball Card Shop, F-141–142
Allen Corporation, F-300
Al's Boating Supplies, F-142
Alto Corporation, F-110–111
Alvarez Company, F-256
Alvin Smith Company, F-144–145
Amanda's Cooking Supplies, F-100
AMC Entertainment, F-275
American Airlines, F-264, 408
American Express, F-37, 407, 408
American Home Products, F-367
America West Airlines, F-453
Amy Whitaker Company, F-491
Andersen, F-20
Andre Holmes, Inc., F-388–389
Andrew D. Company, F-336
Annie Todd Company, F-492
AOL Time Warner, F-359
A.R. Oddo Leasing Corporation, F-211, 212
Armstrong World Industries, F-372
Art by Nicole, F-392–393
Arthur Johnson Enterprises, F-103
AT&T, F-1
Avonia's Clothes, F-192

B

Baker Company, F-338
Banana Republic, F-11
Bank of America, F-11, 41, 117, 405
Barlow Paving Corporation, F-269–273,
    277–280, 288–291
Barnes & Nobles, F-114–115
Bassett Furniture Company, F-304
Bea's Pet Shop, F-144
Bed Bath & Beyond, F-301, 302, 456–485
Belski & Miglio, F-192
Ben Jones Company, F-145
Bennett Corporation, F-108–109
Benny Blades Company, F-347
Best Buy, F-74–75, 78, 89–91, 121
Best Home Improvement Center,
    F-259–260
Beth Toland Company, F-435
Betty Hart Company, F-293
Big Company, F-109
Bill Carter Company, F-336
Bill Matheis and Company, F-337
Bill Simon Computer Repair, F-246–247
Bishop Company, F-251
Bishop Corporation, F-148
Blockbuster, F-115–116
Blues Brothers Consulting, F-263
Bob Franks and Company, F-189–190
Boeing, F-10, 405, 408
Boston Brothers, F-83
Brad Sanders Auto Repair Shop, F-248

Brandess-Kalt-Aetna Corporation, F-11
Brown Company, F-251–252
BusinessWeek, F-26, 451
Butler Company, F-249
Butterfield Wholesale Company, F-351

C

Calvert Company, F-444
Campbell Soup Company, F-407, 408
Cam's Sportswear, F-297–298
Cargo, F-486
Carlos Garcia Company, F-249
Carl Smythe Company, F-145
Carlson Company, F-345–346
Carl Young Publishing Company, F-293
Carnival Cruise Lines, F-197
Carole's Delivery Service, F-194
Carol Levine Company, F-255–256
Carol Strong Company, F-382–383
Carter, Inc., F-397–398
Casey's Computer Supply, F-340
Chang's Gift Shop, F-339
Charles Company, F-352
Charles Lewis Company, F-444
Chesapeake Corporation, F-372
Chevron, F-268, 372
Chevy, F-65
Chris Scott Corporation, F-299–300
Citibank, F-82
Clarke Company, F-252
Clifford Company, F-252–253
Coca-Cola, F-72, 81, 445, 446
Cohen Company, F-250, 297
Coke, F-445
Collins Container Corporation, F-201, 202,
    213–240
Colton Company, F-297
Computer Center of America, F-31
Computer Exchange, Inc., F-306–311
Cooke Company, F-300
Cooking with Penny, F-298
Corning Company, F-347
Cox Company, F-344–345
Cramer Company, F-295
Cronin Corporation, F-162–163
Cunningham Corporation, F-299
Cupcake's Specialty Bakery, F-154

D

Daisy Trading Company, F-351
Dale's Computer Center, F-111
Dana Corporation, F-383
Danielle Company, F-295–296
Danielle's Shoes, F-394–395
Davenport Corporation, F-192
David Brown, Inc., F-296
David Harris Company, F-346
David Luza Corporation, F-105
David Watts and Company, F-62
Debbie Hoffman and Company, F-432–433,
    496–499
Delta, F-268
Dennis Lee Company, F-346–347
Dillard's, Inc., F-370

Dillon Corporation, F-62
Dobbs Motor Company, F-313–314
Doran Company, F-432
Dow Chemical, F-81
Dowers Company, F-352
Dunn & Bradstreet, F-457
DuPont, F-9

E

Eastern Airlines, F-453
Eastman Kodak, F-265, 330
Eaton Corporation, F-367
Edwards Company, F-349
Einstein Corporation, F-148
Eliason and Company, F-357–363
Elizabeth Arden, F-116
Elsea Computer Component Company, F-345
Elsea Corporation, F-110
Emerson Radio Corporation, F-115
Enesco Group, F-372
Enron, F-16, 20, 449, 451
Ericsson, F-1
Esposito, Inc., F-300
ExxonMobil, F-368

F

Fashions by Christie, F-391–392
Fineries, F-261–262
First Union, F-41
Fisher, Inc., F-193
Flaherty Company, F-442–443
Flemming Real Estate Company, F-193
Florence Company, F-350
Ford Motor Company, F-11, 500, 501
Fowks Company, F-194
Fox Company, F-156, 399–401
Foxmore Company, F-111
Frank Collins Two Mile High Flight School,
    F-247
Fred Berfel Enterprises, F-103
Freeport-McMoran Copper & Gold, F-284
Friedman Corporation, F-196–197

G

Gap, F-9, 11, 24
Gaylord Corporation, F-98
General Electric, F-353
General Mills, F-48
General Motors, F-11, 304, 500
Gene's Pool Supply, F-339–340
George R. Violette Company, F-431
Gerner Enterprises, F-112
Gina's Nail Salon, F-142–143
Glenna Corporation, F-196
Global Crossing, F-16, 449
Goodyear, F-10, 81
Gourmet Outlets, F-359
Grand Oil Company, F-109
Green Corporation, F-196
Greenfield Company, F-434
Greif Brothers, F-370
Gruber Company, F-348
Guess, F-445

Subject Index: Financial Accounting

Introduction
to Management
Accounting

A User Perspective

1

Management Accounting: Its Environment and Future

Times have changed! In the last three decades of the 20th century, the United States experienced serious erosion in its position as the world's business leader. Industry after industry in the United States suffered from the effects of significant foreign competition. At the time, experts offered many reasons to explain what was happening; among them were low labor costs in foreign countries, excessively high labor costs at home, too much government regulation of U.S. industries, and too little government regulation of U.S. industries.

Because the "reasons" were simplistic, the "solutions" were simplistic. U.S. industries lobbied Congress for tariffs on imported products (essentially a form of tax) to offset the low labor costs in foreign countries. The issue of excessively high labor rates was used by U.S. companies in negotiating labor costs with their employees, either to hold the line on wage increases, or in some instances to actually negotiate lower wage rates. Throughout the 1970s and 1980s, the U.S. government alternatively deregulated and then re-regulated some American industries to try and increase U.S. companies' competitiveness globally.

Eventually, as these simplistic approaches did not solve the competition crisis, managers in the United States began to see that the problem arose from differences between American businesses' organizational structure and worker productivity and those of their foreign competitors. Consider the following comparison of U.S. auto manufacturers and the Japanese auto manufacturer Toyota in the mid-1980s.[1]

Ford Produced an average of two engines a day per employee. Daily production required 777 square feet of plant space. **Chrysler** Had about 500 in-plant job classifications. **A Typical U.S. Auto Plant** A change from metal-stamping one model to another required six hours.	**Toyota** Produced an average of nine engines a day per employee. Daily production required 454 square feet of plant space. **Toyota** Had seven in-plant job classifications. **Toyota** The same change required three to five minutes.

Because of more efficient production techniques, a small Toyota car cost $1,700 less to produce than a comparable U.S. car. This cost difference made it difficult for U.S. automakers to effectively compete against Toyota and the other car companies employing more efficient manufacturing methods.

---

[1]John Lee, *Managerial Accounting Changes for the 1990s* (Addison-Wesley, 1987, p. 14.)

The automobile industry was by no means alone. By the mid-1980s, U.S. companies in many different industries had realized the need to change business operations to remain competitive. Beginning in the last half of the 1980s and continuing throughout the 1990s, many of those businesses began to take significant steps to increase their competitiveness. Our focus will be not on the specific changes that managers made but rather on the way these changes have affected their accounting needs and how accounting information has responded.

Learning Objectives

After completing your work on this chapter, you should be able to do the following:

1. Describe management accounting and contrast it with financial accounting.
2. Explain major historical developments that have affected management accounting.
3. Discuss what may have led to the stagnation in the development of management accounting.
4. Describe how changes in management accounting affect today's businesses.
5. Explain how businesspeople use management accounting information and skills.

◆ WHAT IS MANAGEMENT ACCOUNTING?

management accounting
The branch of accounting designed to provide information to internal economic decision makers (managers).

Management accounting is the branch of accounting designed to provide information to a firm's internal economic decision makers, or managers. It is also sometimes called managerial accounting or cost accounting. Because these three terms are often used interchangeably in accounting literature, confusion can result. Management accounting is

> ... the process of identification, measurement, accumulation, analysis, preparation, interpretation, and communication of financial information used by management to plan, evaluate, and control ... an organization ...

STATEMENT ON MANAGEMENT ACCOUNTING (NO. LA. IMA, 1981)

managerial accounting
Another name for management accounting.

Management accounting and **managerial accounting** mean exactly the same thing. We will use the term *management accounting* throughout our discussions of the subject. However, in references to other writings, you may see the term *managerial accounting*.

cost accounting A narrow application of management accounting dealing specifically with procedures designed to determine how much a particular item (usually a unit of manufactured product) costs.

The third term, **cost accounting,** is really a narrow application of management accounting. Cost accounting deals specifically with procedures designed to determine how much a particular item (usually a unit of manufactured product) costs.

◆ CONTRASTING FINANCIAL AND MANAGEMENT ACCOUNTING

financial accounting The branch of accounting designed to provide information to external decision makers such as stockholders and creditors.

Financial accounting provides useful information, generally economic in nature, to external decision makers—people outside the company. Management accounting, in contrast, provides information to internal decision makers. Exhibit 1–1 lists only some of the many external and internal users of a company's accounting information.

Discussion Questions

1-1. For each of the external parties listed in Exhibit 1–1, suggest one economic decision they might make regarding a company.
1-2. Name two external parties in addition to those listed in Exhibit 1–1, and provide an example of an economic decision each might make regarding a company.
1-3. For each of the internal parties listed in Exhibit 1–1, describe one economic decision they might make regarding their company.
1-4. Name two internal parties in addition to those listed in Exhibit 1–1, and give an example of an economic decision each might make regarding the company.

External	Internal
• Stockholders (present and potential)	• Marketing managers
• Bankers and other lending institutions	• Salespersons
• Bondholders (present and potential)	• Production managers
• Suppliers	• Production supervisors
• Customers	• Strategic planners
• Competitors	• Company president
	• Company engineers

EXHIBIT 1-1 External and Internal Decision Makers

Discussion Questions 1–1 through 1–4 highlight the different nature of the decisions made by external and internal parties. If you review your answers to these questions, you will discover that the decisions external parties make focus on the company as a whole, whereas the decisions internal parties make usually center on some part of the company. Because people use financial accounting information and management accounting information differently, the nature of the two differs.

Traditionally, financial accounting has focused primarily on a company's overall profitability, solvency, and liquidity. Management accounting, on the other hand, focuses on the efficiency, productivity, and product or service quality of a company's various operating functions. Logically, increasing efficiency, productivity, and product or service quality should ultimately lead to increased profitability, solvency, and liquidity. The emphasis of management accounting, however, is on the means to those ends, not the ends themselves.

ACCOUNTING RULES

Financial accounting information must be prepared in accordance with rules known as generally accepted accounting principles (GAAP). These rules are necessary to provide assurance to external parties that the information they receive from a company has been prepared in conformance with a consistently applied set of standards. No such rules apply to management accounting. Because management accounting information is prepared for use by those working within the company, its users can question the content, meaning, level of detail, and validity of the accounting information they receive. They can also determine the format of the information. In sum, internal decision makers can generally make certain the information they receive is exactly what they want. External decision makers must accept the financial accounting information they receive, like it or not.

LEVEL OF DETAIL

In contrast to the general-purpose nature of financial accounting information, firms prepare management accounting information to address specific company issues. Therefore, it is often much more detailed than financial accounting information. For example, it may be fine for a potential investor to know that *IBM*'s sales were $81.2 billion in 2002, but this information would be nearly useless to the national sales manager for *IBM*'s ThinkPad™, the company's line of notebook computers, who needs to know that product's sales numbers for 2002.

Discussion Question ●

1–5. In addition to sales information, what other accounting information would you want if you were the national sales manager for *IBM*'s ThinkPad™?

In addition to preparing general purpose financial statements for the public, a company's accountants also prepare management accounting information for the managers or employees who need it. For a given internal decision, a user may need specific information from a division, product line, product, or department. The company's accountants should be able to customize information to fit the needs of the user.

For example, ***Honeywell International, Inc.*** has a production facility on 59th Avenue and Bell Road in Phoenix, Arizona. This facility requires various types of maintenance, including mowing the lawn and weeding the flower beds outside the buildings. This maintenance costs money. The amount spent for grounds maintenance at this Phoenix facility is totally irrelevant to external parties. The maintenance supervisor at that facility, however, would find that amount quite relevant. ***Honeywell***'s accountants should be able to customize a report providing the supervisor with pertinent cost information.

TIMELINESS

Timeliness is important to both financial and management accounting information users. Regardless of whether the user is external or internal, accounting information is useful only if it is available in time to help the decision maker.

Because it has become customary, users of financial accounting information expect that financial results will be available quarterly. However, managers making frequent decisions need information much more often. They need information monthly, weekly, or even daily, so they can make informed decisions. Because of the fast pace of business decision making, sometimes it is better to forfeit precision in favor of speed. Management accountants must strike a balance between information accuracy and timeliness to provide managers with information that is accurate enough to make good decisions, and yet timely enough to make a difference.

FUTURE ORIENTATION

Although financial accounting information should have predictive value, it primarily presents historical results. In contrast, management accounting has a forward-looking orientation. Management accounting focuses on estimating future revenues, costs, and other measures to forecast future activities and their results. Firms use these forecasts to plan their courses of action toward company goals.

As you can see, because of the fundamental differences between the information needs of external and internal parties, financial and management accounting differ. Exhibit 1–2 summarizes the differences we have discussed.

EXHIBIT 1–2   Contrast of Financial and Management Accounting

	Financial Accounting	Management Accounting
• Principal users	External parties	Internal parities
• Rules and regulations	Governed by GAAP	No rules
• Level of detail	Deals with the company as a whole	Deals with various parts of the company
• Timeliness	Quarterly and annually	As users need
• Orientation	The past	The future

◆ WHERE ACCOUNTING FITS IN A COMPANY

Exhibit 1–3 presents a typical corporate organizational structure. Note where financial and management accounting fit within a company. When you think of accounting, the corporate officers that probably come to mind are the treasurer and the controller. Generally, the **treasurer** is responsible for managing cash and credit and in charge of obtaining external financing and making investments for the company. The **controller**

treasurer The corporate officer who is responsible for cash and credit management and in charge of obtaining external financing and making investments for the company.

controller A company's chief accountant, who is responsible for the preparation of accounting reports for both external and internal decision makers.

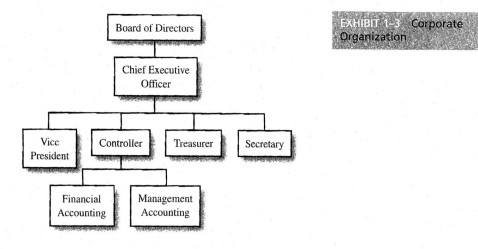

EXHIBIT 1-3 Corporate Organization

is a company's chief accountant. This person is responsible for preparing accounting reports for both external and internal decision makers.

In a large company, such as **Sara Lee** or **Rockwell,** the treasurer and controller are both likely to have large staffs reporting to them. In small firms, one person may perform all the controller's functions, while another performs all the treasurer's functions.

Discussion Question

1–6. What possible problems may arise when the same accountants prepare reports for both external parties and internal parties?

THE ORIGIN AND EVOLUTION OF MANAGEMENT ACCOUNTING

Accounting and accounting records have existed since the dawn of civilization. Indeed, formal accounting systems have been in use for thousands of years. The need for accounting information for management decision making purposes, however, did not exist until the early 19th century. Before that time almost all businesses were proprietorships or small partnerships. Businesses had no permanent employees to speak of and no management as we know it today. Management usually consisted of the proprietor or partners and immediate family members. Because businesses had no management, they had no need for management accounting information. Virtually all transactions were between the company and parties outside the company. Transactions with external parties such as suppliers, contract labor, and customers were easy to measure and evaluate: A company was successful if it collected more cash from its customers than it paid to suppliers and contract laborers.

In the 100 years between 1825 and 1925, however, four significant changes took place in business operation and organization: the emergence of permanent employees, the Industrial Revolution, the rise of scientific management, and diversification. These changes altered the nature of management accounting.

EMERGENCE OF PERMANENT EMPLOYEES

For the most part, businesses had few employees before the 1880s. Businesses purchased labor with a piece-rate contract and hired independent contractors to complete most of their production functions. A chair manufacturer, for example, purchased wood at a certain price per board foot. Then the company contracted someone to turn the wood into legs, arms, seats, and backs at some specified rate per item. When the pieces were produced and paid for, the company contracted someone else to assemble the chairs, and paid that person some specified amount per chair assembled.

Determining the cost of a chair produced was very simple—the sum of the wood is cost, the amount paid per component piece (arm, leg, and so on), and the cost of assembling it. The company was not terribly interested in how long it took any of these contractors to complete their tasks, so long as they met the needs of the company.

Gradually, however, companies began hiring permanent employees to fill the role of the independent contractors. Why the switch to permanent employees happened and whether it was positive or negative has been hotly debated by scholars for over 100 years. From the company's standpoint, moving from a contract system to a wage system gave the firm greater control of the production process and, in fact, created what we now know as the factory. From the laborer's standpoint, the change was likely an exchange of freedom for security.

Discussion Questions

1-7. In what ways do you think hiring permanent employees gives a company greater control of the production process?
1-8. What kinds of freedom do you think permanent employees exchange for security?

When we see the word *factory*, we tend to think of the huge factories of today. Actually, early factories were still small businesses. Management accounting did not develop because of the size or complexity of the organization. Rather, it developed because the accounting systems then in existence did not provide businesspeople with enough information to determine the cost of a manufactured product. Nor did these systems provide information about a company's efficiency, productivity, and product or service quality.

Discussion Question

1-9. Why do you think the emergence of the factory (even a small one) made it more difficult to determine the cost of a manufactured product?

THE INDUSTRIAL REVOLUTION

Industrial Revolution A term used to describe the transition in the United States from an agricultural-based economy to a manufacturing-based economy.

The **Industrial Revolution** was the 19th-century transition of the United States from an agricultural-based economy to a manufacturing-based economy. From 1825 to 1925, businesses greatly increased their investment in property, plant, and equipment and began to rely more on machines instead of human labor to produce products. As companies grew in size and complexity, owners found it impossible to be in all places at all times. They were forced to create hierarchical levels of management for their organizations. These managers sought needed information to control costs and production processes. Over time, businesses developed methods to measure the conversion of raw materials into units of finished product. These methods were the foundation for present-day management accounting. Their focus was on the effectiveness and efficiency of various internal processes, rather than on the overall profitability of the company.

SCIENTIFIC MANAGEMENT

scientific management A management philosophy based on the notion that factories were run by machines—some mechanical and some human. Scientific management experts believed they could improve production efficiency by establishing standards of performance for workers.

The scientific management movement began near the end of the 19th century and had a tremendous influence on business management and management accounting. **Scientific management** was a philosophy based on the notion that factories were run by machines—some mechanical and some human. You may think it insensitive to treat employees as nothing more than machines plugged into the production process. Nonetheless, scientific management took this view. Experts in this area believed they could improve production efficiency by establishing standards of performance for workers. In a tool-manufacturing company, for instance, experts conducted time-and-motion studies to set a standard for the time workers should take to convert a given amount of resources into a finished product, such as a hammer.

These standards of performance were quickly adapted to accounting for the purpose of determining how much it should cost to manufacture a product. The experts, often engineers, determined how much material, labor, and other resources a business needed to manufacture a single unit of product. This information served as a yardstick to measure whether resources were used efficiently or squandered during the production process. Such standards were the beginning of what is referred to as standard costing, one of the most important developments in management accounting. We will discuss standard costing in greater detail in Chapter 10.

Discussion Questions

Assume a company manufactures tables. Scientific management studies show that each tabletop requires four square feet of wood, and it takes a worker 45 minutes to convert the wood into a tabletop.

1–10. If the wood costs the company $2 per square foot and the company's workers are paid $10 per hour, how much does each tabletop cost to produce?

1–11. What other costs should be considered in the calculation of the cost to produce the tabletop? Explain.

DIVERSIFICATION

During the first two decades of the 20th century, companies began to diversify. Before this time, virtually all companies undertook only one activity. For example, railroad companies were strictly in the railroad business, and steel companies were strictly in the steel business. The primary investment decision for these single-activity companies was whether to expand. The emergence of diversified, multiactivity companies changed the nature of decision making.

Discussion Question

1–12. Why do you think companies began to diversify in the early years of the 20th century?

Owners of diversified companies could not directly manage all the various business operations. Instead, they relied on others to manage operations that they could not personally oversee; and they obtained additional management accounting information from the various parts of the business so they could plan, control, and evaluate performance. Company accountants tailored reports to meet the needs of managers at each level of the organization. Lower-level managers, such as production supervisors, received reports that focused on production efficiencies. Higher-level managers received reports that focused on product profits.

DEVELOPMENT STOPS (OR AT LEAST DRAMATICALLY SLOWS)

Institute of Management Accountants (IMA) The leading professional organization devoted to management accounting. The IMA provides similar professional support to management accountants as the AICPA provides to financial accountants.

In 1919, the formation of the **Institute of Management Accountants (IMA)**—formerly the National Association of Accountants—signified that management accounting was a recognized branch of the accounting profession separate and distinct from financial accounting. Among other purposes, the IMA provided the same sort of professional support and status for management accountants as the *American Institute of Certified Public Accountants (AICPA)* did for financial accountants.

In approximately 1925, however, something curious occurred—development of new management accounting techniques virtually ceased. Essentially all management accounting tools in use as late as 1985 were already in place by 1925. Certainly, the business environment changed between 1925 and 1985. Why then were so few management accounting techniques developed to respond to those changing needs? This question has been the subject of much analysis and debate over the past decade by both accountants and business leaders.

Possibly, the slowdown was caused by the dominance of financial accounting in the 20th century. The growth of publicly held corporations, the stock market crash of 1929, and the Great Depression that followed led to the creation of the Securities and Exchange Commission (SEC) and the establishment of GAAP. The new rules and regulations governed financial reporting to external parties and required that corporations file audited financial statements with the SEC prepared in accordance with GAAP. The rules and regulations led to the design of accounting systems that could provide financial information and reports to outsiders. These financial accounting systems, however, ignored (or at least underrepresented) information managers could use to make decisions about the internal processes of their companies.

Companies could have maintained two systems—one that generated and gathered information to meet external reporting requirements, and another that generated the information managers needed to manage and control the operation of the company. Or a common system could collect data and then customize the information to conform to the informational needs of both internal and external users. The cost of creating and maintaining a dual-purpose system, however, would have been prohibitive before computers, which is when GAAP and the SEC came into being.

Consider also the legal environment existing in the 1930s after the creation of the SEC. If a company failed to have an accounting system designed to produce financial accounting information for external parties in accordance with GAAP, there would be serious legal consequences. If a company's accounting system did not produce management accounting information, however, there were no legal consequences. Given this situation, it is not surprising that at that time financial accounting requirements drove the creation and use of accounting information.

Throughout the 20th century, most management accountants had a financial accounting background. It stands to reason, then, that these accountants tended to approach management accounting from a financial accounting perspective.

Discussion Question ◦◦◦◦◦◦◦◦◦◦◦◦◦◦◦◦◦◦◦◦◦◦◦◦◦◦◦◦◦◦◦◦◦◦◦

1–13. What possible problems do you think arise when a company's single accounting system is designed to produce financial accounting information?

Another possible reason for the slowdown in the development of management accounting techniques is that companies often focus on short-term financial accounting measures (usually profits) in the performance evaluation of managers. Managers are bright people. It doesn't take them long to learn how to manipulate the financial results of operations to maximize a short-run performance measure. Think about it. It seems reasonable to expect managers to focus on short-term financial accounting measures if their compensation and career advancement rely on these items.

Bonus programs that motivate key managers to perform better seem reasonable, except that most bonuses are heavily weighted in favor of short-term, not long-term, performance. As Charles W. Mulford and Eugene E. Comisky noted in their book *The Financial Numbers Game: Detecting Creative Accounting Practices*:

> Incentive compensation plans for corporate officers and key employees are typically stock option and/or stock appreciation rights plans. With such plans, employees receive stock or the right to obtain stock, or cash, tied to the company's share price. When properly structured, such plans successfully link the officers' and employees' interest with those of other shareholders'. Occasionally companies use a measure of earnings—for example pretax income—in calculating a cash or stock bonus. When such bonus schemes are tied to reported earnings, officers and employees have an incentive to employ creative accounting practices in an effort to maximize the bonuses received.[2]

These incentives encourage managers to focus on improving financial statement measures rather than on improving productivity, efficiency, and quality measures. Preoccupation with financial accounting income has diminished their interest in demanding new management accounting techniques.

The problem of the short-term view is compounded by the mobility of management. Managers used to stay in their jobs longer than they do today. It was not uncommon in the early 1900s for a manager to occupy the same position for 10 or even 20

[2]Charles W. Mulford and Eugene E. Comisky, *The Financial Numbers Game*: Detecting Creative Accounting Practices (New York: John Wiley & Sons, 2002, p. 6).

years. For such managers, taking actions that would result in an impressive short-term performance at the expense of the long run made no sense. Today, however, many managers believe they will stay in a particular position for only a few years, so their objective is often to maximize short-term measures and not worry about what will happen in 5 or 10 years.

A lack of competitive pressure may also be a reason new management accounting techniques were not developed. Until the 1970s, the lack of competition from outside the country allowed U.S. companies to flourish, despite management's short-term perspective. Because many industries lacked serious competition, many decisions—even those made without adequate management accounting information—led to favorable financial results. If satisfactory decisions could be made without more sophisticated accounting information, why would management even recognize that improvements were needed? Even business executives who were convinced of the weaknesses in their management accounting systems did not believe changes were worth making because they felt they were no worse off than their competition.

By the early 1980s, however, competition from foreign companies with more sophisticated management accounting systems forced U.S. companies to pay more attention to the relevance of the accounting information they were using to make short-term and long-term business decisions.

◆ CHALLENGES AND TRENDS IN MANAGEMENT ACCOUNTING

The first step in solving a problem is to recognize that a problem exists. By the mid-1980s, U.S. companies had certainly recognized that they had a problem—the management accounting techniques they were using were not providing the information needed to make solid business decisions. Since that time they have made great strides toward solving that problem.

First, businesses began using production and management techniques that were initiated in other countries, most notably Japan and what used to be West Germany. Second, companies became more innovative. Automobile manufacturers in the United States are much more efficient in their production processes than they were a decade ago. In the area of inventory control alone, American auto manufacturers have drastically reduced the level of inventories on hand, thereby reducing their annual inventory holding cost by hundreds of millions of dollars. This reduced cost translates into cars that are cheaper to manufacture.

As businesses examined and reorganized their operations to become more competitive, they also examined the way they use accounting information to make decisions. Managers and accountants are making or considering many changes in management accounting as a result. Some of these recent developments, such as just-in-time inventory (JIT), activity-based costing (ABC), and the balanced scorecard, are topics covered in later chapters of this text. One of the more dynamic developments in the past 15 years is a management concept known as value based management.

VALUE BASED MANAGEMENT

value based management (VBM) A mechanism by which managers can make strategic and tactical decisions that serve to maximize the long-term value of an organization.

Value based management (VBM) is a mechanism by which managers can make strategic and tactical decisions that serve to maximize the long-term value of the organization. It is an approach to management that aligns a company's operational decision making with that of the investment community by focusing the enterprise's efforts on identifying, securing, and managing value-creating opportunities, while eliminating business, projects, or activities that tend to destroy value.

Essentially, the VBM philosophy is that real value is created in any organization by focusing on creating value for three parties—shareholders, customers, and employees, as shown in Exhibit 1–4.

As you can see in the exhibit, the enterprise receives capital (money) from its shareholders. The company uses this capital to operate the business. As the company creates value for its employees through compensation and self-fulfillment, these employees develop products and processes that create value for the customers. If the

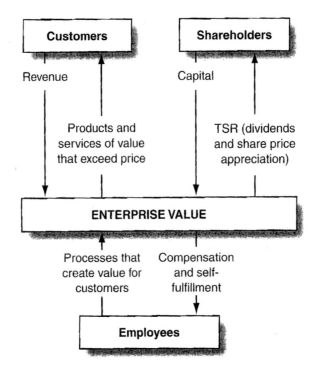

EXHIBIT 1–4 Creating the Value Enterprise

company provides products and services for its customers where the quality exceeds the price, the customers reward the company by providing revenue. As the company prospers, value is created for the shareholders. This increased shareholder value is called *total shareholder return (TSR)* and is a combination of dividends and appreciation of the company's stock price in the stock market.

This value creation cycle is like a three-legged stool. If any of the legs on a three-legged stool is missing or weak, the stool collapses. Well, the VBM philosophy holds that if a company does not create value for all three of the interested parties, that company cannot have any real long-term value. Creating real value for shareholders is a function of creating real value for customers and employees.

Creating Value for Customers
Companies have long understood that to be successful, they must produce products and services for their customers wherein the quality exceeds the price. Virtually every company mission statement contains a phrase such as "total customer satisfaction" or "quality is our top priority." Until fairly recently, however, companies have not really attempted to measure the value they are creating (or not creating) for their customers. Historically, companies have relied on customer satisfaction surveys, the number of customer complaints, and the amount of sales returns to learn what customers are thinking. Only in the last few years have companies begun to try and find out what their customers really desire and how well they are meeting those needs. Total Quality Management (TQM) and measures of the cost of poor quality are two examples of the increased focus on creating value for customers.

Creating Value for Employees
First, it is important to understand that we are talking about the value of the company to the employees and not the value of the employees to the company. This is perhaps the least well understood facet of VBM. In order to create real value for customers and shareholders, a company must create real value for its employees. Relatively few employees stay with one company throughout their entire careers anymore. When asked why this is so, most managers respond that that is just the way things are, that we live in a mobile society, and people have many more options than they did 100 years ago. VBM's response to this assertion is that the mobile society facilitates such chang-

ing of jobs, but does not cause it. The reason employees leave one company for another is that their needs are not being fulfilled. That is, there is insufficient value being created for them where they are.

In recent years, companies have begun to focus on creating value for their employees because they have realized how costly it is to hire and train new employees. Certainly, competitive compensation and benefits are important elements of creating value for employees, but increasingly the focus is on other areas, such as a safe, rewarding work environment and a comfortable, attractive workplace. Flexible work schedules, on-site day care centers, and enhanced cafeterias are all examples of benefits companies are now offering to attract and keep the best employees.

Value Based Management and Accounting

Value based management is a subject that could easily take a full semester to cover adequately. Our purpose here is only to introduce the topic as an example of the events taking place in the world of business today. Why are we discussing VBM and accounting? Much of the VBM philosophy concerns items that have traditionally not been considered accounting topics. Accounting information has been used in measuring the creation of shareholder value—financial statements, financial analysis, and the like. Management accountants have also been involved in certain aspects of value creation for customers—product cost reports, for example. Other items, such as the cost of poor quality and determining what customers want and are willing to pay for, have not been considered accounting topics at all. Value creation for employees has been largely ignored by accountants. If you ask any competent management accountant, for example, if she or he can calculate the cost savings of a layoff, the answer will be yes. If, on the other hand, you asked that same accountant if she or he can calculate the *cost* of a layoff, the answer will almost certainly be no. And yet, there are costs associated with a layoff. These costs include decreased morale and disruption of processes. So there are two reasons we talk about VBM in this text. First, some of you will eventually become accountants. We think it is important for you to learn early on about the changing landscape of your discipline. The second reason we are introducing the VBM topic is that many of you will not become accountants. But since you are taking this course, it's likely you intend to major in some area of business, so it is important for you to begin thinking about this subject and the ways you can use the accounting function to help you in your chosen career.

With all this talk about new and exciting management techniques, you may get the impression that any technique in use prior to the Great Awakening of the 1980s has no relevance in today's business environment. This would be a serious blunder. Much of traditional management accounting is as relevant today as it has ever been. Therefore, in addition to our discussion of the newer techniques, we will also explore many of the traditional management accounting topics in this text.

◆ CONSUMERS OF MANAGEMENT ACCOUNTING INFORMATION

To make effective decisions, business managers must understand the firm's management accounting system, know whether the information is reliable, and recognize that no system will provide perfect information. Decision making by its very nature is forward looking, and the future always contains an element of uncertainty. Managers should look for ways to reduce the level of that uncertainty.

Every decision results in an outcome. Sometimes, even sound decisions result in bad outcomes. For example, say that you are about to get in the checkout line at the grocery store. You evaluate the lines leading to open cash registers and, after counting the number of people in line and eyeballing the amount of groceries each customer is about to buy, you select what appears to be the shortest line—an express, "cash-only" line. Your decision is sound, based on the information available. Just as the person ahead of you is about to pay, checkout disaster strikes. The customer has only a credit card—no cash. The register has no credit card scanner, so the cashier cannot easily make an exception. You must now wait for the manager to arrive and resolve the problem (a process that seems to take as long as college registration) before the cashier can help you. Quickly, you look to see whether you can jump to another line, but it is too late: The other lines are now too long, and you must wait it out. Did you make a poor decision? No, you made the best decision you could with the available information. Your good decision simply led to a poor outcome.

Regardless of your career, at some point you will probably use accounting information to make a decision. If you are studying marketing, you may start as an assistant who helps prepare and implement marketing programs. As you advance in the firm, you may manage a staff of people who handle marketing programs, so you will need the accounting tools to make well-informed decisions. When you are responsible for the well-being of a company, department, division, or management team, you will face decisions that depend on your using management accounting information. The following chapters will teach you to be a careful consumer of accounting information.

Summary

Management accounting is the process of identifying, measuring, and communicating financial information used by managers to plan, evaluate, and control their organization.

Financial accounting, which is intended for use by external parties, is subject to generally accepted accounting principles (GAAP). No such rules apply to management accounting, which is intended for use by internal parties. The general-purpose financial statements produced by financial accounting focus on past results. Reports produced by management accounting are much more detailed and focus on the future of the organization.

Although accounting and accounting records have existed since the dawn of civilization, the need for accounting information for use by management did not exist prior to the early 19th century. The emergence of permanent employees, the Industrial Revolution, scientific management, and the diversification by businesses all contributed to significant development of management accounting techniques between 1825 and 1925.

Around the year 1925, there was a dramatic slowdown in the development of new management accounting techniques. Some of the contributing factors often cited for this slowdown are the dominance of financial accounting, a focus by many companies on short-term financial results, and the lack of competitive pressure on U.S. businesses. However, great strides have been made in the past 15 years toward developing improved management accounting techniques.

American companies face significant competitive challenges in the 21st century, and the role of management accounting information in helping these companies will be critical. Therefore, managers and accountants are developing new, more modern management accounting techniques. Some recent developments include just-in-time inventory (JIT), activity-based costing (ABC), and the balanced scorecard. Value based management (VBM) is another important management concept developed in response to competition. It is a mechanism by which mangers can make strategic and tactical decisions that serve to maximize the long-term value of the organization.

To make effective decisions, business managers must understand the firm's management accounting system. Decision making by its very nature is forward looking, and the future always contains an element of uncertainty. Management accounting provides useful information that helps managers to reduce the amount of that uncertainty.

Key Terms

- controller, M–7
- cost accounting, M–4
- financial accounting, M–4
- Industrial Revolution, M–8
- Institute of Management Accountants (IMA) M–9
- management accounting, M–4
- managerial accounting, M–4
- scientific management, M–8
- treasurer, M–7
- value based management (VBM), M–11

Review the Facts

A. What are the differences among management accounting, managerial accounting, and cost accounting?

B. What is the purpose of management accounting?

C. What are the primary differences between financial accounting and management accounting?

D. Financial accounting information must be prepared in conformity with GAAP. Why are there no such rules for management accounting?

E. List four significant changes in business that led to the development of management accounting.

F. What is the IMA and what is its purpose?

G. Describe three factors that possibly led to the stagnation of management accounting development.

H. Explain the difference between a good decision and a good outcome.

I. Why is an understanding of management accounting an important ingredient of success in your career?

Apply What You Have Learned ●

LO 1: CONTRAST MANAGEMENT ACCOUNTING AND FINANCIAL ACCOUNTING

1–14. Following are certain characteristics of either financial accounting information or management accounting information.

    1. _____ Must conform to GAAP.

    2. _____ Tends to be quite detailed.

    3. _____ Generally limited to presenting historical information.

    4. _____ Need not conform to a formal set of rules and standards.

    5. _____ Information prepared primarily for external users.

    6. _____ Tends to include only a limited amount of detail.

    7. _____ Information prepared on a quarterly or yearly basis.

    8. _____ Information prepared on a monthly, weekly, or daily basis.

    9. _____ Information often includes future projections.

    10. _____ Information prepared for use by internal parties.

Required: Designate each of the characteristics as pertaining to (a) financial accounting information or (b) management accounting information.

LO 1: DESCRIBE MANAGEMENT ACCOUNTING

1–15. Is management accounting important for not-for-profit organizations as well as for-profit organizations? Explain.

LO 1: DESCRIBE MANAGEMENT ACCOUNTING

1–16. If you were the manager of a ***Blockbuster Entertainment*** Store, what accounting information would you desire to help you do your job better?

LO 3: STAGNATION IN DEVELOPMENT OF MANAGEMENT ACCOUNTING

1–17. Explain why managers tend to focus on improving short-term financial results.

LO 4: CHANGES IN MANAGEMENT ACCOUNTING

1–18. Explain why there has been a renewed emphasis on the development of management accounting in the United States in the last decade.

LO 1: CONTRAST MANAGEMENT ACCOUNTING AND FINANCIAL ACCOUNTING

1–19. Following are examples of users of financial accounting information and users of management accounting information.

    1. _____ Sales supervisor

    2. _____ Salespersons

3. _____ Wall Street analyst
4. _____ Suppliers
5. _____ Current shareholders
6. _____ Potential shareholders
7. _____ Personnel manager
8. _____ Maintenance supervisor
9. _____ Maintenance worker
10. _____ Loan officer at a company's bank

Required: Designate each of the users of accounting information as either (a) external party or (b) internal party.

CHAPTER

2

Classifying Costs

Suppose for a moment that you work for a large toy store chain that offers mail-order service. Your boss has asked you to organize the catalog of all the toys the company sells. You need to categorize the toys so users of your catalog will be able to find information easily. After thinking about your task for a while, you make a list of toy classifications—design, price, gender of user, and age of user. It looks like this:

Classification	Type of Toys
Age of User	Toys for infants Toys for toddlers ages 1 to 3 Toys for children ages 3 to 5 Toys for children ages 5 to 9 Toys for children ages 10 and older
Gender of User	Toys designed for girls Toys designed for boys Toys for all children
Price	Toys that cost less than $10 Toys that cost $10 to $50 Toys that cost $51 to $99 Toys that cost more than $100
Design	Electronic toys Bikes and scooters Games Learning toys

Your boss wants you to pick only one or two categories by which to organize the catalog. You scan your list to see which classifications will be most useful, but you realize that the catalog must include all of them to be as useful as possible, because purchasers may need different information for different decisions. For instance, let's say someone is choosing toys to donate to the annual toy drive for needy children. They may want to focus on price so they can donate several toys, and may want to use the gender classification to find toys for all children because they would not know in advance whether the child receiving the toy is a girl or a boy.

Another shopper may be looking for a birthday present intended for a 2-year-old relative, so he would need to use the age classification to find an appropriate toy. And because he has a budget, this shopper will also want to use the price category to help decide on the gift. As these examples show, even in making just one decision, more than one classification may provide useful information.

Like our hypothetical toy buyers, managers must have information to make effective planning and controlling decisions. Cost information is one of the key components of financial decision making, but what exactly is a cost? In accounting, a cost is how much we have to give up to get something. Put more formally, a **cost** is the dollar amount of resources forfeited to receive some goods or services. Note that cost is different from price. Price is what we charge; cost is what we pay.

Business managers classify costs in many different ways because, just like the vast array of toys, there are many types of costs. Each classification can provide managers with useful information. In this chapter, we explore several different cost classifications that managers use to make decisions.

cost The resources forfeited to receive some goods or services.

Learning Objectives

After completing your work on this chapter, you should be able to do the following:

1. Classify costs by cost objects, and distinguish between direct and indirect costs.
2. Distinguish between product costs and period costs, and contrast their accounting treatment.
3. Explain the differences between product cost for a merchandiser and for a manufacturer.
4. Describe the components of the costs included in each of the three types of inventory in a manufacturing operation.
5. Calculate cost of goods manufactured and cost of goods sold.
6. Describe the components of the cost of services provided by a service firm.
7. Prepare basic journal entries for a manufacturer. (Appendix)

◆ MAJOR COST CLASSIFICATIONS

Businesses incur various costs as they operate, and there are many useful ways to classify these costs. As managers make each internal business decision, they must determine what cost classifications will help them most. We will first identify important cost terms and investigate several cost classifications.

ASSIGNING COSTS TO COST OBJECTS

cost object Any activity or item for which a separate cost measurement is desired.

One of the most useful classifications of cost is by cost object. A **cost object** is any activity or item for which we desire a separate cost measurement. Think of any noun associated with business and you have a potential cost object. Exhibit 2–1 lists some cost objects commonly used by companies.

We identify a cost object to determine the cost of that particular object. Such classification can provide useful information. For example, *Prestone* may need information about the cost of the antifreeze and other products it manufactures. In this case, the individual products are the cost objects. All costs associated with a particular product are grouped to determine the full cost of that product. Managers may also want to determine the cost associated with a group of products, such as a fleet of delivery trucks.

EXHIBIT 2–1 Common Cost Object Designations

Cost Object	Examples
• Activity	• Repairing equipment, testing manufactured products for quality
• Product	• Paper towels, personal computers, automobiles (These can be either purchased or manufactured products.)
• Service	• Performing surgery, accounting work, legal work
• Project	• Constructing a bridge, designing a house
• Geographic region	• A state, a city, a county
• Department	• Marketing department, accounting department

When we assign costs to cost objects, we classify costs as direct or indirect. A cost that is easily traced to individual cost objects is a **direct cost.** Many times, however, a cost may benefit more than one cost object, so tracing that cost to individual cost objects becomes difficult or even impossible. A cost that supports more than one cost object is an **indirect cost.** An indirect cost may also be called a **common cost,** because it is common to more than one cost object.

direct cost A cost that can be easily traced to an individual cost object.

indirect cost A cost that supports more than one cost object.

common cost Another name for indirect cost.

To illustrate the difference between direct and indirect costs, consider 12 *Target* stores in New York. Each store has a manager who is responsible for the day-to-day operation of that store. *Target* also has a general manager who is responsible for the operation of all the stores in the state. If we define each of the 12 stores as cost objects, the salary of each store manager is a direct cost to his or her store. The salary of the *general manager*, however, is not incurred to support any one of the 12 stores—rather, it supports all 12 stores. Therefore, the general manager's salary is an indirect cost to each cost object (the individual stores).

Discussion Questions

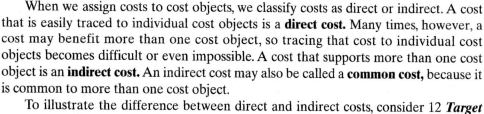

Assume that instead of defining each individual *Target* store as a cost object, we define the entire *Target* operation in New York as a cost object.

2–1. In this case, would the salaries of the 12 store managers be considered direct or indirect costs? Explain your reasoning.

2–2. Would the salary of the general manager be considered a direct or an indirect cost? Explain your reasoning.

2–3. Why do you think managers at various levels in a company would find it useful to classify costs as direct or indirect?

PRODUCT COST

product cost The cost of the various products a company sells.

When you see inventory on store shelves, you know the store did not get the inventory for free. Rather, each unit of product had some cost. The cost of the various products a company sells is called **product cost.** More specifically, product costs are the costs associated with making the products available and ready to sell. For a bookstore, such as *B. Dalton Booksellers* or *Waldenbooks,* product cost is the cost of the books it purchases for resale, the freight to get the books to the store (also known as freight-in), and other costs involved in getting the books ready to sell.

inventoriable costs Another name for product cost.

Product costs are also known as **inventoriable costs** because they become part of a company's inventory until the goods associated with those costs are sold. Because a product held for sale is considered an asset, its cost is shown on the balance sheet (inventory) until the product is actually sold. When the goods are sold, the product cost is converted from an asset on the balance sheet to an expense (cost of goods sold) on the income statement.

For example, when *Payless Shoe Source* buys shoes to sell, the cost of the shoes is a product cost and is added to inventory on the balance sheet. The cost remains in inventory on the balance sheet until the shoes are sold. When the shoes are sold, the reality of the reduced inventory caused by the sale is reflected in the company's accounting records by reducing inventory on the balance sheet and increasing cost of goods sold on the income statement.

PERIOD COST

period costs All costs incurred by a company that are not considered product cost. Includes selling and administrative cost.

Period costs are all the costs a company incurs that are not considered product costs. They include selling and administrative expenses, but not any costs associated with acquiring product or getting it ready to sell. For *Payless Shoe Source* this would include costs of employees in accounting, finance, marketing, advertising, and executives.

Selling Cost

selling cost The cost of locating customers, attracting customers, convincing customers to buy, and the cost of necessary paperwork to document and record sales.

Selling cost includes the cost of locating customers, attracting them, convincing them to buy, and the cost of necessary paperwork to document and record sales. Examples of selling cost include salaries paid to members of the sales force, sales commissions, and advertising.

Two selling costs are less obvious: the cost of delivering product to customers (also known as freight-out) and the cost of storing merchandise inventory. The reason delivery cost is considered a selling cost is that companies probably would not provide delivery unless it helped sell more product. If customers would buy with or without free delivery, the seller would likely not offer it.

Do not confuse freight-out (period cost) with freight-in (product cost). The key to keeping the two straight is to think about when they are incurred. Freight-in is a cost incurred before the product is ready to sell and is therefore a product cost. Freight-out is incurred after the product is ready for sale and is therefore classified as a period cost. For a company like *Dell Computers,* freight-in is the cost to get the raw materials to assemble the computers and freight-out is the cost from a free shipping promotion for customers to get the finished computer.

The cost of storing inventory that is ready to sell is also classified as a selling cost, because merchandise in stock enhances its sales potential. Businesses cannot easily sell what they do not have. For example, if you go to your local music shop to buy a compact disc and the salesperson tells you, "We don't keep that CD in stock, but we'll be glad to order it for you," you may decide to go to another store that carries a better-stocked inventory of CDs rather than wait. Because providing delivery and having merchandise inventory on hand enhance sales, both of these items are considered selling costs.

Administrative Cost

administrative cost All costs incurred by a company that are not product costs or selling costs. The cost of areas that provide support to the product and selling areas such as the cost of accounting, finance, employee relations, and executive functions.

Administrative cost includes all costs that are not product or selling costs. These costs are typically associated with support functions—areas that offer support to the product and selling areas, such as accounting, finance, human resources, and executive functions.

Generally, period costs are shown as operating expenses (selling and administrative expenses) on the income statement. Most period costs—administrators' salaries, for example—are presented as expenses when the expenditure is made. When long-lived assets that will be used for selling or administrative functions are purchased, a slightly different treatment is necessary. At the time they are purchased, the cost of long-lived assets is shown on the balance sheet. As time passes, the depreciation expense associated with these assets becomes part of selling and administrative expense.

Discussion Questions ●

Assume that you are using a felt-tip highlighter to mark this book as you read it. Assume further that you purchased the marker at the college bookstore.

2–4. What costs associated with the marker do you think the bookstore would consider to be product costs? Explain your reasoning for each cost you included.

2–5. What costs associated with operating the bookstore do you think would be considered period costs (selling and administrative)? Explain your reasoning for each cost you included.

COMPARING PRODUCT AND PERIOD COSTS

The distinction between product cost and period cost is based on whether the cost in question benefits the process of getting products ready for sale (product cost), or the selling and administrative functions (period cost). Let's look at some examples to make sure you understand the distinction. The cost of a factory security guard is a product cost because it benefits the manufacturing facility. Conversely, the cost of a security guard in the sales office is a selling expense, which is a period cost. The classification depends on the area of the company that benefits from the cost.

What about the salary of the vice president of manufacturing? Even though vice president of manufacturing may sound like an administrative position, the cost benefits the manufacturing function, so it is a product cost. Further, all costs associated with that position, including, for example, the depreciation on the vice president's desk, the cost of his or her support personnel, and travel costs, are classified as product costs. Likewise, the salary of the vice president of marketing and the costs of that position are period costs, as they benefit the sales area of the company.

Next, we examine how manufacturing, merchandising, and service firms identify their product costs.

◆ PRODUCT COST IDENTIFICATION FOR MERCHANDISING FIRMS

Merchandising firms, whether wholesale or retail, purchase products ready to sell, add a markup, and resell the goods. They generate profits by selling merchandise for a price that is higher than its cost. Wholesalers generally buy products from manufacturers (or other wholesalers) and then sell them to retailers. Retailers buy from manufacturers or wholesalers and sell their products to the final consumers. In this section we explore how a merchandising company identifies product costs and how those product costs flow through the balance sheet and income statement.

For a merchandising firm, product cost includes the cost of the merchandise itself, freight costs to obtain the merchandise, and any other costs incurred to get the product ready to sell. Because merchandisers buy goods for resale, often the cost of getting products ready to sell is minor or nonexistent. Product cost does not include any cost incurred after the product is in place and ready to sell.

Product cost is often the most significant of all costs for a merchandiser. It is not uncommon for merchandising companies to have cost of goods sold as high as 80 percent of the selling price of the product sold, meaning that they have a gross profit as low as 20 percent. Besides increasing sales, managers are always interested in reducing expenses, which is impossible without an understanding of what items are included in product cost. Efforts to reduce total cost of goods sold may focus on any component of that expense, that is, any component of product cost.

THE FLOW OF PRODUCT COST—MERCHANDISING COMPANY

If you were responsible for the profitability of a product or group of products, not only would you want to know total product cost, but you would also want to know and understand the various components of each product's cost. With this understanding, you could analyze reports detailing these products' cost components and work to isolate costs that could be reduced or eliminated. The diagram in Exhibit 2–2 illustrates the flow of costs in a merchandising operation.

Exhibit 2–2 indicates that as goods are purchased, their cost is classified as merchandise inventory. In fact, all product costs are originally shown like those in Exhibit 2–2, as an asset on the balance sheet. Typically, a merchandising firm has only one inventory classification, which is usually referred to as *merchandise inventory* or, sim-

EXHIBIT 2–2 Flow of Product Costs— Merchandising Company

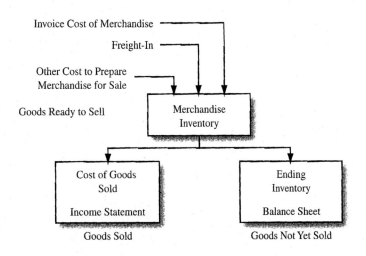

ply, *inventory*. As the units of product are sold, their cost is converted to an expense and shown on the income statement as the cost of goods sold.

COST OF GOODS SOLD

Exhibit 2–3 is a cost of goods sold schedule for Jason's Supply Company. As the exhibit shows, Jason adds purchases to the inventory on hand at the beginning of the period to arrive at the goods available for sale. Generally, one of two things can happen to the goods available for sale: They are either sold (cost of goods sold) or remain on hand at the end of the period (ending inventory). Thus, when ending inventory is subtracted from the goods available for sale, Jason can determine the cost associated with the products that have been sold—that is, the company can determine the cost of goods sold.

EXHIBIT 2–3   Cost of Goods Sold Schedule

Jason's Supply Company
Cost of Goods Sold Schedule
For the Year Ending December 31, 2004

	Beginning Inventory at January 1, 2004	$ 23,000
+	Purchases during 2004	300,000
=	Goods Available for Sale in 2004	$323,000
−	Ending Inventory at December 31, 2004	(30,000)
=	Cost of Goods Sold for 2004	$293,000

The January 1, 2004, beginning inventory amount shown in Exhibit 2–3 is actually the ending inventory from Jason's balance sheet at December 31, 2003, and the ending inventory amount shown is from Jason's balance sheet at December 31, 2004. The cost of goods sold amount is included as an expense item on the company's income statement for the year ending December 31, 2004.

Discussion Question ●

2-6. Accounting for the flow of product cost for a merchandiser seems to be a lot of bother. If all merchandise inventory will eventually be sold anyway, why not just record it as an expense (cost of goods sold) on the income statement when it is purchased?

Any company that sells tangible, physical product must sell its product for more than the product cost or it will eventually go bankrupt. This may seem very obvious, and in fact, good business managers are well aware of this necessity. Understanding the need is one thing; making sure it happens is another. Competitive pressures in most industries cause companies to sell their products for less than they would like to. Managers of these businesses must have a solid understanding of the relationship between the selling price of their products and the cost of those products, or they may actually sell a product for less than it costs.

It's like two guys—Harry and George—who bought watermelons for $1 each and were selling them for $0.90 each. Business was certainly brisk because they were underselling all their competition. Still, they were not making a profit. Finally, George turned to his friend and said, "Harry, we need to get a bigger truck." What George and Harry didn't understand is that they could never sell enough watermelons at $0.90 each to be profitable because they were selling each melon for less than it cost. Without a thorough understanding of the relationship between the cost of a product and the selling price of that product, managers cannot hope to make prudent business decisions.

Virtually all the products that consumers purchase have undergone some manufacturing process. In this section we explore how a manufacturing company identifies product costs and how those product costs flow through the balance sheet and income statement. As in merchandising firms, product cost for a manufacturer includes all costs associated with acquiring the product and getting it ready to sell. For manufacturers, however, getting the product ready to sell is usually an extensive process requiring the use of factory facilities such as production machinery and factory workers.

For a manufacturer, units of product are normally considered cost objects, and their cost encompasses three distinct elements. We will introduce them briefly here and then discuss each of them in more detail a bit later. As we present each of the elements, think back to our discussion earlier in the chapter about cost objects and direct versus indirect costs.

direct materials cost The cost of all raw materials that can be traced directly to a unit of manufactured product.

1. **Direct materials cost.** Direct materials cost is the cost of all raw materials that can be traced directly to a single unit of manufactured product. For **Ford Motor Company**'s Mustang this would include the metal, tires, engine, belts, seats, etc. Direct materials cost, however, is not the cost of all materials used in the manufacture of the product. In most manufacturing operations some materials costs are incurred for multiple cost objects. These costs are indirect materials cost, which we consider a part of manufacturing overhead.

direct labor cost The cost of all production labor that can be traced directly to a unit of manufactured product.

2. **Direct labor cost.** Direct labor cost is the cost of all production labor that can be traced directly to a unit of manufactured product. Direct labor is also sometimes called *touch labor* because it is the cost of the workers who actually touch the product being manufactured. For **Ford**'s Mustang, this would include the assembly line workers. Direct labor cost is not the cost of all labor incurred in the manufacture of product. In most manufacturing operations, some labor costs are incurred for multiple cost objects. That type of cost is indirect labor cost, which we consider a part of manufacturing overhead, discussed next.

manufacturing overhead cost All costs associated with the operation of the manufacturing facility besides direct materials cost and direct labor cost. It is composed entirely of indirect manufacturing cost incurred to support multiple cost objects.

3. **Manufacturing overhead cost.** Manufacturing overhead is all the costs associated with the operation of the manufacturing facility other than direct materials cost and direct labor cost. It is composed entirely of indirect manufacturing cost—that is, manufacturing cost incurred to support multiple cost objects. Among others, manufacturing overhead includes indirect materials and indirect labor as discussed in items 1 and 2. For **Ford**'s Mustang, this would include a portion of the factory's security, telephone, electricity, paper towels, factory, etc.

INVENTORY CLASSIFICATIONS

As with merchandising firms, product costs for a manufacturer are inventoriable costs. However, manufacturing companies have not just one, but three types of inventory: raw materials, work in process, and finished goods. Note that these three types of inventory are not the same as the three elements of manufactured product we just introduced. Rather, these inventory classifications specify where manufactured product is at any given time in the production process.

As we discuss the three inventory classifications used by manufacturers, consider the following thoughts. First, our discussion in this chapter is intended to serve only as a broad introduction to the flow of product cost through a manufacturing company. The next two chapters deal with specific methods used to accumulate product cost for a manufacturer. Second, there is a difference between reality and the measurement of reality. Reality is the physical units of product moving through the production process, separate from our attempt to measure that reality.

Raw Materials Inventory
Raw materials inventory, sometimes called **material stores,** consists of materials that have been purchased but have not yet entered the production process. Raw

raw materials inventory
Materials that have been purchased but have not yet entered the production process.

material stores Another name for raw materials inventory.

materials inventory includes all the materials that will eventually be accounted for as either direct or indirect materials. For example, ***Steelcase, Inc.,*** manufactures metal desks, filing cabinets, and other metal office furniture. Raw materials inventory consists of the sheet metal, screws, paint, and glue ***Steelcase*** has on hand with which to make metal office furniture. It would not include any of the material in the office furniture the company has begun to manufacture but has not yet finished, nor would it include the material in the office furniture that has been completed and ready for sale. Until raw materials actually enter the production process, the cost associated with those materials is classified as raw materials inventory, an asset on the balance sheet.

Work-in-Process Inventory

work-in-process inventory Products that have entered the production process but have not yet been completed.

Work-in-process inventory consists of products that have entered the production process but have not yet been completed—those units currently on the production line or in the production process. In our ***Steelcase*** example, work-in-process inventory consists of the desks, filing cabinets, and other metal office furniture that have been started but are not yet finished. The reality is partially completed desks, filing cabinets, and other metal office furniture. The measurement of reality counts the costs associated with these partially completed units of product and classifies them as work-in-process inventory on the balance sheet. These costs include the cost of the materials associated with these units, the labor cost incurred so far in the production process, and some amount of manufacturing overhead applied to each of the partially completed units of product.

Work-in-process inventory does not include the cost of raw materials that have not yet entered the production process, nor does it include the cost associated with products that have been completed and ready for sale.

Finished Goods Inventory

finished goods inventory
Products that have been completed and are ready to sell.

Finished goods inventory, as you might imagine, consists of products that have been completed and are ready to sell. With respect to ***Steelcase,*** finished goods inventory consists of the pieces of metal office furniture completed but not yet sold. Remember, these are real units of finished product: They are reality. They have completed the production process and are sitting in a warehouse somewhere waiting to be sold. The measurement of that reality is a classification of inventory on the balance sheet called finished goods inventory, an asset. Included in that amount are all the materials, labor, and manufacturing overhead costs accumulated for those units completed, but not yet sold.

Discussion Question

2–7. Why do you think managers of a manufacturing firm would find it beneficial to separate the amount and cost of inventory items into raw materials, work-in-process, and finished goods?

If managers in manufacturing businesses are to make prudent production decisions, they must have relevant information. The decisions they must make include how much and what type of materials they need to purchase, how many production workers are needed, what skill level these workers must possess, and whether production capacity is sufficient to produce the product required. The information managers need to help them make these and many other production decisions includes the amount and cost of raw materials on hand, the composition of the labor force, the capacity and cost of production facilities, and the amount and cost of both work-in-process and finished goods inventory.

Although much of the relevant information managers need to make these decisions is provided by nonaccountants such as marketing and sales personnel, accountants provide vital information concerning the cost of raw materials, work-in-process, and finished goods. All three classifications of inventory have one or more of the product cost elements introduced earlier: direct material, direct labor, and manufacturing overhead. We will now discuss each of those elements in more detail.

DIRECT MATERIAL

direct material The raw material that becomes a part of the final product and can be easily traced to the units produced.

Direct material is the raw material that becomes part of the final product and can be easily traced to the individual units produced. Obviously, direct materials cost is the cost of these raw materials. Examples of direct materials used in the manufacture of automobiles are sheet metal, plastic, and window glass. In the manufacture of computers, direct materials include circuit boards, cathode ray tubes, and other items. At **Steelcase,** direct materials include the sheet metal used to manufacture the desks, filing cabinets, and other metal office furniture.

Often, the final product of one company is purchased by another to be used as part of its raw material in the manufacturing process. For example, direct materials used in the manufacture of **Cessna** aircraft include aluminum, wheels, tires, cables, and engines. The tires that **Cessna** uses as raw materials in the manufacture of its aircraft are the finished product of one of the company's suppliers, **Goodyear Tire and Rubber Company.**

Discussion Questions

2–8. In addition to the tires supplied by **Goodyear,** what other finished products do you think **Cessna** uses in its production of small aircraft? What companies might produce these products?

2–9. Name three additional pairs of manufacturing companies that have a supplier–buyer relationship—that is, the finished product of one company becomes the raw material of another company.

When materials are purchased for use in the manufacture of products, their cost at first is added to raw materials inventory. Once the material has entered the production process (reality), its cost is removed from raw materials inventory and added to work-in-process inventory (measurement of reality). Thus, in our **Steelcase** example, as sheet metal is purchased, its cost is added to raw materials. Once the metal has been used to make a desk or other piece of office furniture, its cost is removed from raw materials inventory and becomes part of work-in-process inventory. When the goods are completed, their cost is moved from work-in-process inventory to finished goods inventory.

DIRECT LABOR

direct labor hours The time spent by production workers as they transform raw materials into units of finished products.

Direct labor hours are defined as the time spent by production workers as they transform raw materials into units of finished products. Direct labor costs are the salaries and wages paid to these workers, which can be easily traced to the products they produce.

Think about some article of clothing, say a pair of pants, you are wearing right now. Certainly there is material in the pants. But how did the pants become pants? Well, you may not know all the steps, but you do know that somewhere, someone sat at a sewing machine and stitched the cut material into a pair of pants. The money paid to that person, whether in Taiwan, Korea, or New Jersey, is considered direct labor, because her or his efforts (and therefore cost) can easily be traced to that single cost object (the pair of pants).

The accounting treatment of direct labor cost may surprise you. Direct labor needed to get products ready to sell is a product cost that enhances the value of direct material. Because product costs are inventoriable costs, direct labor cost is added to the value of work-in-process inventory, along with the cost of direct material. Why? Because the work of production-line personnel increases the value of material as it is fabricated, assembled, painted, or processed. As a result, the cost of production-line labor should increase the value of inventory, shown as an asset on the balance sheet and ultimately as cost of goods sold on the income statement. In our **Steelcase** example, then, wages paid to workers who actually make the desks, filing cabinets, and other metal office furniture is considered direct labor and added to work-in-process inventory.

Thus far, we have explored two elements of product costs for a manufacturing firm: direct material and direct labor. Next, we consider the third and last element of manufacturers' product costs—manufacturing overhead.

MANUFACTURING OVERHEAD

manufacturing overhead
All activities involved in the manufacture of products besides direct materials or direct labor.

factory overhead Another name for manufacturing overhead cost.

factory burden Another name for manufacturing overhead cost.

overhead In a manufacturing company, another name for manufacturing overhead cost; in a service type business, the indirect service cost.

indirect manufacturing cost Another name for manufacturing overhead cost.

indirect materials Materials consumed in support of multiple cost objects.

indirect labor The labor incurred in support of multiple cost objects.

Manufacturing overhead is defined as all activities involved in the manufacture of products besides direct materials or direct labor. Manufacturing overhead cost, then, is the cost of these indirect manufacturing activities. It is also referred to as **factory overhead, factory burden,** or simply **overhead.** In recent years, manufacturing companies have begun to call the cost of manufacturing overhead **indirect manufacturing cost,** which is certainly more descriptive than any of its other names. Old habits die hard, however, so we will call it manufacturing overhead because this term has been and remains universally understood in business.

To be considered part of manufacturing overhead, a cost must be associated with the manufacturing facility, not some other aspect of the company such as selling or administrative functions. Manufacturing overhead includes three groups of costs—indirect materials, indirect labor, and other indirect manufacturing costs.

Indirect Material

Indirect materials are those consumed in a manufacturing facility in support of multiple cost objects. There are two types of indirect material costs in manufacturing. The first is the cost of raw materials so insignificant that the added benefit of physically tracing these materials to individual products is not worth the effort. Examples include glue, rivets, solder, small nails, and caulking. In fact, businesses could physically trace all material cost to their products. In the case of indirect materials, however, the effort required to trace the cost outweighs the benefit of the additional information. The second type of indirect material is factory supplies. These are materials used in the manufacturing facility but not incorporated into the product. Examples include paper towels, janitorial supplies, and lubricants for production machinery. The cost of all indirect materials, whether or not the materials actually become part of manufactured product, is added to the cost of the product as part of manufacturing overhead.

Indirect Labor

Indirect labor is labor incurred in a manufacturing facility in support of multiple cost objects. As was the case with indirect material costs, there are two types of indirect labor in manufacturing. The first is the cost associated with factory workers who are neither on the production line nor directly involved in the manufacturing process. Examples include the cost of materials handlers, production supervisors, plant security personnel, plant janitorial personnel, factory secretarial and clerical personnel, and the vice president of manufacturing. Although the effort of these workers is important to the production process, their labor costs are not easily traceable to products. They are therefore classified as indirect labor.

The second type of indirect labor is the cost of wages paid to direct labor employees when they are doing something other than working on the product they produce. These activities might include setting up equipment for production runs or sweeping up at the end of a shift. The idea is that direct labor should include only the cost of direct labor personnel when they are actually working on the product. The cost of all indirect labor is added to the cost of the product as part of manufacturing overhead.

Some manufacturers in the United States now consider *all* labor as indirect labor. In some types of operations, the direct labor element of a manufactured product is as low as 4 percent of the total manufacturing cost. If managers believe labor cost is insignificant, they may choose not to separate it into direct and indirect labor cost and may instead classify all labor costs as indirect.

Other Overhead Costs

In addition to indirect material and indirect labor, manufacturing overhead includes other costs associated with the production facility. Examples include depreciation on the factory building, rent paid for production equipment, factory insurance, property taxes for the factory, and telephone service for the factory. All the costs in this category are associated with the operation of the production facility.

We have seen that manufacturing overhead is the sum of all indirect material, indirect labor, and other overhead costs. Manufacturing overhead costs are necessary costs to produce products and enhance the value of the goods being manufactured. Accordingly, as products are being manufactured, manufacturing overhead costs are added to work-in-process inventory.

Discussion Question

2–10. The textbook you are reading was published (manufactured) by *Prentice Hall, Inc.* What costs of manufacturing this book do you think *Prentice Hall* would include as

   a. direct materials?
   b. direct labor?
   c. manufacturing overhead?

THE FLOW OF PRODUCT COST—MANUFACTURING COMPANY

In a manufacturing environment, just as in merchandising operations, managers must understand the flow of product costs to successfully control and plan for them. Product cost information is also an essential element of the information needed when making pricing and sales decisions. How could a business price a product if none of its managers knew how much the product cost to produce? Having the information is not enough, though. Managers must also understand the components of product cost and the way these costs will affect the company's assets as reported on the balance sheet and the profits as on the income statement. Exhibit 2–4 shows the flow of product costs through a manufacturing operation.

EXHIBIT 2–4 The Flow of Product Costs—Manufacturing Company

```
Raw Materials
Purchases
   |
Raw Materials ──── Direct Materials Cost ────┐
Inventory           Direct Labor Costs ────┐  |
   |                                        |  |
   |     MANUFACTURING OVERHEAD COST        |  |
   |     • Indirect Materials               |  |
   |     • Indirect Labor                   |  |
   |     • Factory Rent                     |  |
   |     • Depreciation                     |  |
   |     • Factory Taxes                    |  |
   |     • Factory Insurance                |  |
   |     • Other Factory Costs              |  |
   |                                        |  |
   |                        Work-in-Process ┘  |
   |                        Inventory          |
   |                             |             |
   |                        Finished Goods     |
   |                        Inventory          |
   |                             |             |
Ending    Ending    Ending      Cost
Raw Mat.  Work-in-  Finished     of
Inventory Process   Goods       Goods
          Inventory Inventory    Sold
   |         |         |          |
   Balance Sheet              Income Statement
```

Exhibit 2–4 looks more complicated than it really is. In fact, this exhibit summarizes our entire discussion of product cost identification for a manufacturer. Let's take some time to walk through the diagram.

As raw materials are purchased, they become part of raw materials inventory (a).

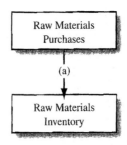

When materials actually enter the production process, we classify their cost as either direct materials (b) or indirect materials (c), depending on the type of material. We classify the cost of any raw materials still on hand at the end of the production period as ending raw materials inventory on the balance sheet at the end of the period (d).

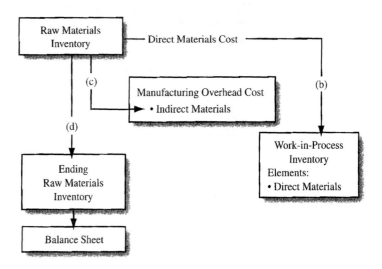

Note that we add the cost of direct materials to work-in-process inventory at this point, whereas the cost of indirect materials is classified as manufacturing overhead. We will return to manufacturing overhead in a moment.

We now have one of the three elements of product cost in work-in-process inventory (direct materials). The next element added is labor. Note that we add direct labor (e) directly to work-in-process inventory, whereas indirect labor (f) is classified as manufacturing overhead.

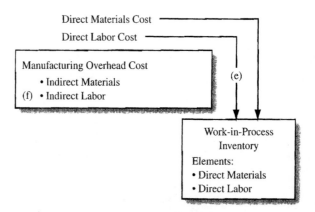

We now have two of the three elements of product cost in work-in-process inventory (direct materials and direct labor). The last element added is manufacturing overhead. In addition to indirect materials and indirect labor (which we classified as manufacturing overhead earlier), all other indirect manufacturing costs are classified as manufacturing overhead (g). The ones we have provided in Exhibit 2–4 are representative only. In reality, the list is almost endless.

Once we accumulate the manufacturing overhead items and amounts, we add the cost of manufacturing overhead to work-in-process (h).

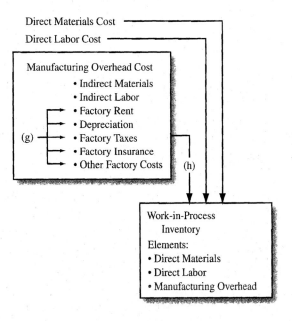

Work-in-process inventory, then, consists of the direct material, direct labor, and manufacturing overhead cost associated with goods that are currently in production. As units are completed, we transfer the cost associated with these units from work-in-process inventory to finished goods inventory (i). We classify the cost of product still in production at the end of the production period as ending work-in-process inventory on the balance sheet at the end of the period (j).

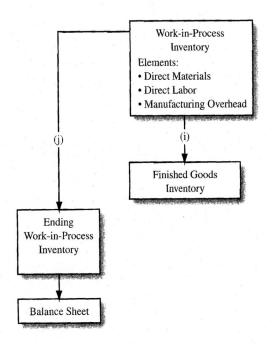

Once finished units of product (and their cost) have been transferred to finished goods inventory, usually only one of two things will happen to the actual units—either they will be sold by the end of the accounting period or they will not be sold. If they are sold, we transfer the cost associated with them to cost of goods sold (k). We classify the cost of the finished product still on hand at the end of the accounting period as ending finished goods inventory on the balance sheet at the end of the period (1).

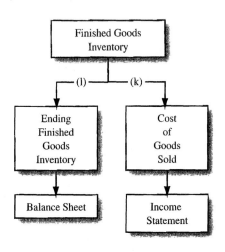

For most manufacturers, inventory is a sizeable asset requiring considerable financial resources. A walk through a manufacturing facility would make you aware of the significance of inventory, because you would see stacks of it sitting there. Raw materials, work-in-process, and finished goods are all important assets of a manufacturer. Proper measurement of these assets is crucial if managers are to make good decisions about inventory management. For this reason, businesspeople should understand the component costs of each type of inventory.

COST OF GOODS MANUFACTURED

We have seen that a manufacturer's product cost consists of direct material, direct labor, and manufacturing overhead. These three product classifications are summarized on the cost of goods manufactured schedule. You will find a typical presentation of this schedule for Lowell Manufacturing, Inc., in Exhibit 2–5.

Although this schedule looks quite involved, it consists of four relatively simple parts.

1. *Direct Materials Section.* This section is similar in format to the cost of goods sold section of the income statement. In both cases, we deal with costs stored in inventory to determine the cost of the inventory that has been used.

Lowell Manufacturing, Inc.
Cost of Goods Manufactured Schedule
Direct Materials Section
For the Year Ending December 31, 2004

Direct Materials:		
Beginning Direct Material Inventory	$ 13,000	
+ Purchases During 2004	400,000	
= Materials Available During 2004	$413,000	
− Ending Direct Material Inventory	(20,000)	
= Direct Materials Used During 2004		$393,000

2. *Direct Labor Section.* We see that the direct labor section of Lowell Manufacturing's cost of goods manufactured schedule consists of only one line, which is a common

---

Lowell Manufacturing, Inc.
Cost of Goods Manufactured Schedule
For the Year Ending December 31, 2004

Direct Materials:		
Beginning Direct Material Inventory	$ 1,3000	
+ Purchases During 2004	400,000	
= Materials Available During 2004	$413,000	
− Ending Direct Material Inventory	(20,000)	
= Direct Materials Used During 2004		$ 393,000
Direct Labor During 2004		220,000
Manufacturing Overhead Cost:		
Indirect Materials	$ 5,000	
Indirect Labor	20,000	
Factory Rent	144,000	
Depreciation of Equipment	250,000	
Repairs and Maintenance on Equipment	40,000	
Utilities	39,000	
Property Taxes	15,000	
Total Manufacturing Overhead Cost During 2004		513,000
Manufacturing Cost for Current Period		$1,126,000
+ Beginning Work-in-Process Inventory (1/1/04)		41,000
= Cost of Goods Available to Be Finished in 2004		$1,167,000
− Ending Work-in-Process Inventory (12/31/04)		(65,000)
= Cost of Goods Manufactured During 2004		$1,102,000

EXHIBIT 2-5   Cost of Goods Manufactured Schedule

way to present this information. Remember, direct labor represents the cost of employees directly involved in the production process.

Lowell Manufacturing, Inc.
Cost of Goods Manufactured Schedule
Direct Labor Section
For the Year Ending December 31, 2004

Direct Labor During 2004   220,000

3. *The Manufacturing Overhead Section.* This section lists manufacturing overhead costs by functional description. Depending on the level of detail desired, this section can be as short as one line, which depicts total manufacturing overhead. Lowell's cost of goods manufactured schedule provides several lines detailing the various components of manufacturing overhead.

Lowell Manufacturing, Inc.
Cost of Goods Manufactured Schedule
Manufacturing Overhead Section
For the Year Ending December 31, 2004

Manufacturing Overhead Cost:		
Indirect Materials	$ 5,000	
Indirect Labor	20,000	
Factory Rent	144,000	
Depreciation of Equipment	250,000	
Repairs and Maintenance on Equipment	40,000	
Utilities	39,000	
Property Taxes	15,000	
Total Manufacturing Overhead Cost During 2004		513,000

4. *Cost Summary and Work-in-Process Section.* The last section of the cost of goods manufactured schedule summarizes the current period's product cost and incorporates the beginning and ending work-in-process inventory balances. Note that as in a cost of goods sold schedule, beginning inventory is added and ending inventory is subtracted to arrive at inventory used.

Lowell Manufacturing, Inc.
Cost of Goods Manufactured Schedule
Cost Summary and Work-in-Process Section
For the Year Ending December 31, 2004

Manufacturing Cost for Current Period	$1,126,000
+ Beginning Work-in-Process Inventory (1/1/04)	41,000
= Cost of Goods Available to Be Finished in 2004	$1,167,000
− Ending Work-in-Process Inventory (12/31/04)	(65,000)
= Cost of Goods Manufactured During 2004	$1,102,000

Using the information from the cost of goods manufactured schedule, we can prepare a cost of goods sold schedule, such as the one for Lowell Manufacturing, Inc. shown in Exhibit 2–6.

EXHIBIT 2–6   Cost of Goods Sold Schedule

Lowell Manufacturing, Inc.
Cost of Goods Sold Schedule
For the Year Ending December 31, 2004

Beginning Finished Goods Inventory	$ 70,000
+ Cost of Goods Manufactured During 2004	1,102,000
= Goods Available for Sale in 2004	$1,172,000
− Finished Goods Inventory	(28,000)
= Cost of Goods Sold for 2004	$1,144,000

♦ PRODUCT COST IDENTIFICATION FOR SERVICE FIRMS

In contrast to both merchandisers and manufacturers, service-type businesses such as law firms, health care providers, airlines, and accounting firms do not sell tangible, physical products. Many service firms are huge. For example, **Hilton Hotels Corporation** is a diversified service company in the hospitality industry. The company reported revenues from hotel and casino services of over $3.8 billion for 2002.

Service companies offer their customers a product just as real as those sold by merchandisers and manufacturers, but service products lack physical substance. Determining the cost of its product is just as important for a service company as it is for merchandisers and manufacturers, but the procedures differ because service-type businesses have no inventory.

Costs can be accumulated for almost any facet of a service company's operation. To illustrate, let's consider the Marston Medical Clinic. The three doctors at the clinic (Dr. Helen Marston and two of her medical school classmates) perform routine physical exams, examinations in response to specific patient symptoms, immunizations, and minor surgery (they perform major surgery at a local hospital) with the assistance of five nurses. Any one of these services can be designated as a cost object, and cost can be accumulated for a particular service provided to an individual patient. Likewise, costs can be accumulated for a particular category of procedure, for a department or a particular area of the medical practice, or for each of the three doctors or the five nurses.

The three broad cost classifications included in the cost of services provided are materials, labor, and indirect service cost (sometimes called overhead). The cost classifications for a service firm are very similar to the classifications used in costing manufactured products, but there are some important differences.

MATERIALS

The materials used in performing services are normally incidental supplies, and the cost of these materials is relatively insignificant compared to the direct materials used in the production of manufactured products. In the case of Marston Medical Clinic, materials include items such as tongue depressors, needles, serum, and bandages.

Some service companies separate material that is significant enough to trace to individual cost objects from insignificant material that they simply treat as indirect overhead cost. In many cases, however, the materials used in performing a service are actually more like the indirect materials used by a manufacturer. Whereas a manufacturer such as **Steelcase** might consider glue and screws to be indirect materials, a legal firm would probably consider legal pads, computer disks, and pens as indirect materials, and all costs of materials are treated as indirect (overhead) cost.

LABOR

Generally, service businesses are labor intensive, meaning that the largest component of product cost for service organizations is often labor cost. It includes costs of those people who perform part or all of the service. In the case of Marston Medical Clinic, labor cost certainly includes the salaries of the three doctors and the five nurses. It does not, however, include the amount paid to the receptionist or bookkeeper. Even though their work is important, these employees do not perform the health care services provided by the clinic. The labor cost of the receptionist and bookkeeper, then, is a period cost.

OVERHEAD OR INDIRECT SERVICE COSTS

The overhead costs in a service business are similar to those for a manufacturer. They are costs that are associated specifically with performing the services provided but that cannot easily be traced to one specific cost object. In the case of the Marston Clinic, rent on the clinic building is an indirect cost of providing health care—the building is necessary to provide patient services. However, its cost is difficult to trace to one cost object, so it is considered an overhead cost.

Discussion Question

2-11. Airline companies such as **Delta Airlines,** often define the routes they fly as cost objects. Given that definition, consider a specific route from New York to Los Angeles and describe the costs you believe **Delta** would include as
   a. materials
   b. labor
   c. overhead

THE FLOW OF SERVICE COST—SERVICE COMPANY

Just as managers in manufacturing and merchandising operations must understand the flow of costs associated with products they sell, managers of service-type businesses must understand the flow of service costs if they are to control and plan for them. Also, service cost information is an essential element of the information needed when making pricing and sales decisions. Having the information is not enough, though. Managers must also understand how these costs will affect the company's assets reported on the balance sheet and profits on the income statement. The flow of costs through a typical service firm is shown in Exhibit 2-7.

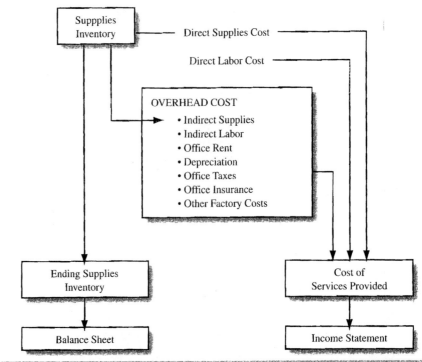

EXHIBIT 2-7 The Flow of Service Costs—Service Company

COST OF SERVICES

As Exhibit 2–7 indicates, cost of services has three parts: direct labor, overhead, and supplies. With this in mind, we can easily create a schedule computing the cost of service products. As an example, the schedule in Exhibit 2–8 computes the cost of medical services for Marston Medical Clinic.

EXHIBIT 2-8 Cost of Services Schedule

Marston Medical Clinic
Cost of Services Schedule
For the Year Ending December 31, 2004

Direct Labor Cost		$ 940,000
Overhead Cost:		
Indirect Supplies	$12,000	
Office Rent	24,000	
Depreciation	18,000	
Office Taxes	2,000	
Office Insurance	8,000	
Other Indirect Costs	6,000	
Total Overhead Cost		70,000
Direct Supplies Cost		$ 20,000
Cost of Services Provided		$1,030,000

Exhibit 2–8 shows that the cost of services for Marston Medical Clinic was $1,030,000 for the year ended December 31, 2004. The total cost included the three components of service product cost: direct labor, overhead, and direct supplies.

We have examined how service firms identify product costs and how those costs flow through the firm. We now turn briefly to hybrid firms, which produce both goods and services.

◆   HYBRID FIRMS

hybrid firms   Companies that generate revenue from both providing services and selling products.

Some companies, called **hybrid firms,** generate revenue from both providing services and selling products. For example, although the majority of *Blockbuster Entertainment*'s revenue comes from its movie rental service, the company also generates significant revenue from DVD and videotape product sales. In accounting for an operation that combines service and products, companies such as *Blockbuster* must incorporate techniques used by both service and merchandising firms. A single company, such as *General Motors,* might actually be a manufacturer (making cars and trucks), a merchandiser (selling floor mats and other accessories to *GM* dealers), and a service-type business (offering *GMAC Financing*).

◆   MERCHANDISING, MANUFACTURING, AND SERVICE—A COMPARISON

Now that we have explored how merchandising, manufacturing, and service businesses identify their product costs and how those costs flow through each type of operation, we can see how these businesses present product costs and period costs on their income statements. We begin with a merchandising operation, and then we look at a manufacturer and a service business.

Exhibit 2–9 illustrates how a merchandiser reports its product costs and period costs on an income statement. This exhibit shows the 2004 income statement for Jason's Supply Company and includes the cost of goods sold schedule we developed for Jason earlier in the chapter (presented as Exhibit 2–3 on page M–22).

EXHIBIT 2–9   Product Costs and Period Costs on the Income Statement—Merchandiser

Jason's Supply Company
Cost of Goods Sold Schedule
For the Year Ending December 31, 2004

	Beginning Inventory at January 1, 2004	$ 23,000
+	Purchases During 2004	300,000
=	Goods Available for Sale in 2004	$323,000
−	Ending Inventory at December 31, 2004	(30,000)
=	Cost of Goods Sold for 2004	$293,000

Jason's Supply Company
Income Statement
For the Year Ending December 31, 2004

Sales		$673,000
Cost of Goods Sold		293,000
Gross Profit		$380,000
Operating Expenses:		
Selling Expense	$120,000	
Administrative Expense	80,000	
Total Operating Expenses		(200,000)
Operating Income		$180,000

As Exhibit 2–9 indicates, the amount of product cost Jason recognized as expense (cost of goods sold) on its 2004 income statement ($293,000) is calculated in the cost of goods sold schedule. The period cost recognized is the total of the operating expenses ($200,000).

Exhibit 2–10 illustrates how a manufacturer reports its product costs and period costs on an income statement. This exhibit shows the 2004 income statement for Lowell Manufacturing, Inc., and includes the cost of goods manufactured schedule (presented as Exhibit 2–5 on page M–31) and cost of goods sold schedule (presented as Exhibit 2–6 on page M–32) we developed for Lowell earlier in the chapter.

EXHIBIT 2–10   Product Cost and Period Cost on the Income Statement—Manufacturer

Lowell Manufacturing, Inc.
Cost of Goods Manufactured Schedule
For the Year Ending December 31, 2004

Direct Materials:		
Beginning Direct Material Inventory	$ 13,000	
+ Purchases During 2004	400,000	
= Materials Available During 2004	$413,000	
− Ending Direct Material Inventory	(20,000)	
= Direct Materials Used During 2004		$ 393,000
Direct Labor During 2004		220,000
Manufacturing Overhead Cost:		
Indirect Materials	$ 5,000	
Indirect Labor	20,000	
Factory Rent	144,000	
Depreciation of Equipment	250,000	
Repairs and Maintenance on Equipment	40,000	
Utilities	39,000	
Property Taxes	15,000	
Total Manufacturing Overhead Cost During 2004		513,000
Manufacturing Cost for Current Period		$1,126,000
+ Beginning Work-in-Process Inventory (1/1/04)		41,000
= Cost of Goods Available to Be Finished in 2004		$1,167,000
− Ending Work-in-Process Inventory (12/31/04)		(65,000)
= Cost of Goods Manufactured During 2004		$1,102,000

Cost of Goods Sold Schedule
For the Year Ending December 31, 2004

Beginning Finished Goods Inventory		$ 70,000
+ Cost of Goods Manufactured During 2004		1,102,000
= Goods Available for Sale in 2004		$1,172,000
− Finished Goods Inventory		(28,000)
= Cost of Goods Sold for 2004		$1,144,000

Income Statement
For the Year Ending December 31, 2004

Sales		$1,884,000
Cost of Goods Sold		1,144,000
Gross Profit		$ 740,000
Operating Expenses:		
Selling Expense	$250,000	
Administrative Expense	180,000	
Total Operating Expenses		(430,000)
Operating Income		$ 310,000

As Exhibit 2–10 indicates, the amount of product cost Lowell recognized as expense (cost of goods sold) on its 2004 income statement ($1,144,000) is calculated in the cost of goods manufactured schedule and the cost of goods sold schedule. The period cost recognized is the total of the operating expenses ($430,000).

Exhibit 2–11 illustrates how a service-type company reports its cost of services and period costs on an income statement. This exhibit shows the 2004 income statement for Marston Medical Clinic and includes the cost of services schedule we developed for Marston earlier in the chapter (presented as Exhibit 2–8 on page M–34).

EXHIBIT 2–11 Cost of Services and Period Costs on the Income Statement—Service-Type Company

Marston Medical Clinic
Cost of Services Schedule
For the Year Ending December 31, 2004

Direct Labor Cost		$ 940,000
Overhead Cost:		
Indirect Supplies	$12,000	
Office Rent	24,000	
Depreciation	18,000	
Office Taxes	2,000	
Office Insurance	8,000	
Other Indirect Costs	6,000	
Total Overhead Cost		70,000
Direct Supplies Cost		$ 20,000
Cost of Services Provided		$1,030,000

Income Statement
For the Year Ending December 31, 2004

Service Revenue		$1,260,000
Cost of Services		1,030,000
Gross Margin on Services		$ 230,000
Operating Expenses:		
Selling Expense	$ 45,000	
Administrative Expense	130,000	
Total Operating Expenses		175,000
Operating Income		$ 55,000

As Exhibit 2–11 indicates, the amount of services cost Marston recognized as expense (cost of services) on its 2004 income statement ($1,030,000) is calculated in the cost of services schedule. The period cost recognized is the total of the operating expenses ($175,000).

Whether the costs are related to products purchased for sale, products manufactured for sale, or services provided, cost information is an important input in the decision making process. Remember that management accounting information helps internal decision makers plan and control the firm's future. In the chapters that follow, you will see how the cost classifications and cost flows you learned about in this chapter will help you understand and apply management accounting decision making techniques.

Summary ⦿

Businesses incur many different costs as they operate in the modern business world. These costs can be classified in a variety of ways and managers must determine what cost classifications will be most helpful if they are to make effective planning and control decisions.

Costs can be accumulated by cost object, which is any activity or item for which we desire a separate cost measurement. Some of the costs associated with a cost object can be traced directly to that cost object. These are called direct costs. Other costs incurred to support multiple cost objects are known as indirect costs.

The classification of costs as either product cost or period cost is very important because it determines how costs are reported on a company's financial statements. Product cost is the sum of all costs required to make the products available and ready to sell and is reported on the income statement as cost of goods sold. Period costs are all costs a company incurs that are not classified as product cost. Period costs are divided into selling and administrative costs and are reported on the income statement as expenses.

There are significant differences in the way product cost is determined for merchandising companies and for manufacturing companies. For a merchandiser, product cost includes the cost of the merchandise itself and freight costs to obtain the merchandise. For a manufacturer, product cost includes the direct materials, direct labor, and manufacturing overhead required to produce finished units of product.

Manufacturing companies have additional cost classification challenges because they have three distinct types of inventory: raw materials that have been purchased but have not yet entered the production process, work-in-process units that have begun the production process but are not yet complete, and units that have been completed and are ready for sale.

Cost of services performed for a service type business is similar in many ways to product cost for a manufacturer. It includes the cost of materials, labor, and overhead required to perform services.

Recording Manufacturing Costs

To fully understand the material in this appendix, it is best if you have a basic understanding of debit and credit accounting procedures including general journal entries and the use of T-accounts. If this is not the case, we suggest that you review Chapter 6 of our financial accounting text or the accounting procedures section of any introductory financial accounting text.

After completing your work on this chapter appendix, you should be able to prepare basic manufacturing journal entries.

The recording process for manufacturing involves six basic types of transactions:

Transaction 1: Purchasing raw material
Transaction 2: Using direct material in the manufacturing process
Transaction 3: Using direct labor in the manufacturing process
Transaction 4: Using manufacturing overhead in the manufacturing process
Transaction 5: Transferring the cost of completed units from work-in-process to finished goods
Transaction 6: Selling finished goods

To record these transactions, accountants generally use the following general ledger accounts:

1. Cash
2. Accounts receivable
3. Raw materials inventory
4. Work-in-process inventory
5. Finished goods inventory
6. Accounts payable
7. Sales
8. Cost of goods sold

Remember that debits increase assets, expenses, and losses and credits decrease those elements. Further recall that credits increase liabilities, equity, revenues, and gains and debits decrease those accounting elements. Lastly, also recall that debits and credits must equal for each journal entry.

We will now examine a series of journal entries that a manufacturer would make. When it is appropriate and nonrepetitive, we will analyze each transaction using the following four steps.

1. Determine if and when a transaction occurred, what accounts were affected, which account balances should increase, which should decrease, and by how much.
2. Determine which accounts we should debit and which we should credit.
3. Make the journal entry.
4. Review the entry to ensure it is in proper form and that the debits equal the credits.

Transaction 1: Purchased $90,000 of raw material on account on January 2, 2004.

1. This transaction took place on January 2, 2004. The transaction affects the raw materials inventory account and the accounts payable account. We should increase the balances of both accounts by $90,000.
2. Because raw materials inventory is an asset account we increase it with a debit. Accounts payable is a liability account so we increase it with a credit.
3. The general journal entry:

2004			
Jan 2	Raw Materials Inventory	90,000	
	Accounts Payable		90,000
	To record the purchase of raw material		

4. A final check of the entry reveals that we dated it correctly, made the debit part of the entry first, indented the credit account title, and the dollar amount of the debits equals that of the credits. The entry is fine.

Transaction 2: Transferred $70,000 of direct material to production on January 3, 2004.

1. This transaction took place on January 3, 2004. The transaction affects the work-in-process inventory and raw materials inventory accounts. We should increase the balance of the work-in-process inventory account by $70,000 and decrease the balance of the raw materials inventory account by the same amount.
2. Because work-in-process inventory is an asset account we increase it with a debit. Raw materials inventory is also an asset account so we decrease it with a credit.
3. The general journal entry:

```
2004
Jan 3   Work-in-Process Inventory          70,000
            Raw Material Inventory                      70,000
        To record the transfer of direct material to production
```

4. A final check of the entry reveals the entry is fine.

Transaction 3: On January 31, paid $80,000 for direct labor cost incurred during January 2004.

1. For this entry, we will use January 31, the date we paid the wages as the transaction date. Recall that direct labor cost becomes part of work-in-process inventory so the transaction affects the work-in-process inventory account and the cash account. We should increase the work-in-process inventory account by $80,000 and decrease the cash account by the same amount.
2. Because work-in-process materials inventory is an asset account we increase it with a debit. Cash is also an asset account so we decrease it with a credit.
3. The general journal entry:

```
2004
Jan 31  Work-in-Process Inventory          80,000
            Cash                                        80,000
        To record wages paid for direct labor in January
```

4. A final check of the entry reveals the entry is fine.

Transaction 4: Incurred various factory overhead costs totaling $110,000 during January 2004. Assume that $10,000 of the overhead costs were paid in cash and the balance of $100,000 was on account.

To keep the example simple, we will record the manufacturing overhead directly in work-in-process inventory. As you will see in the appendix of Chapter 3, manufacturing overhead is generally allocated to production which necessitates using more complicated accounting procedures.

1. So that our example remains straightforward, we will make a single journal entry on January 31 for all of the manufacturing overhead cost incurred during the period. In practice, a manufacturing company would make an entry each time an overhead cost is incurred. Recall that manufacturing overhead costs become part of work-in-process inventory so the transaction affects the work-in-process inventory account. They also affect the cash and accounts payable accounts. We should increase the balance in the work-in-process inventory account by $110,000. We should decrease the balance in the cash account for the $10,000 of manufacturing overhead costs paid for, and we should increase the balance of the accounts payable account by $100,000 for the manufacturing overhead on account.
2. Because work-in-process materials inventory is an asset account we increase it with a debit. Cash is also an asset account, so we decrease it with a credit. Accounts payable is a liability, so we increase it with a credit.
3. The general journal entry:

```
2004
Jan 31  Work-in-Process Inventory          110,000
            Cash                                        10,000
            Accounts Payable                            100,000
        To record manufacturing overhead for January
```

4. A final check of the entry reveals the entry is fine.

Transaction 5: On January 31, transferred goods costing $230,000 from work-in-process to finished goods.

1. On January 31, goods costing $230,000 to manufacture were completed and transferred to finished goods inventory so the transaction took place on January 31, 2004. The transaction affects the finished goods inventory and work-in-process inventory accounts. We should increase the balance of the finished goods inventory account by $230,000 and decrease the balance of the work-in-process inventory account by the same amount.
2. Because finished goods inventory is an asset account, we increase it with a debit. Work-in-process inventory is also an asset account, so we decrease it with a credit.
3. The general journal entry:

```
2004
Jan 31  Finished Goods Inventory              230,000
            Work-in-Process Inventory                      230,000
        To transfer completed goods from
        production to finished goods
```

4. A final check of the entry reveals the entry is fine.

Transaction 6: On January 31, the company sold finished goods that cost it $210,000 to manufacture for a selling price of $300,000. The goods were sold on account.

1. This transaction took place on January 31. Generally, transactions for the sale of goods have two distinct parts. First, the transaction affects the accounts receivable and sales accounts, and we should increase the balances of both these accounts by $300,000. Second, the transaction also affects the cost of goods sold and finished goods inventory accounts because the company has delivered merchandise to the customer from its inventory. We should increase the balance of the cost of goods sold account by $210,000 and decrease the balance of the finished goods inventory account by the same amount.
2. Accounts receivable is an asset account, so we increase it with a debit. Sales is a revenue account, so we increase it with a credit. Cost of goods sold is an expense account so we increase it with a debit. Finished goods inventory is an asset account so we decrease it with a credit.
3. This transaction requires two separate entries or a compound entry. The entries are:

```
2004
Jan 31  Accounts Receivable                  300,000
            Sales                                         300,000
        To record sales on account


     31  Cost of Goods Sold                   210,000
            Finished Goods Inventory                      210,000
        To record the cost of goods sold
```

Or, to accomplish the same changes to the account balances, we can make the following compound entry:

```
2004
Jan 31  Accounts Receivable                  300,000
        Cost of Goods Sold                   210,000
            Sales                                         300,000
            Finished Goods Inventory                      210,000
        To record sales on account and cost
        of goods sold
```

4. A final check of both sets of entries reveals that the dollar amount of the debits equals that of the credits. You can make either two separate entries or a compound entry for a transaction such as this.

The following selected T-accounts depict balances after recording all of the entries including the $300,000 sale and the $210,000 cost of goods sold.

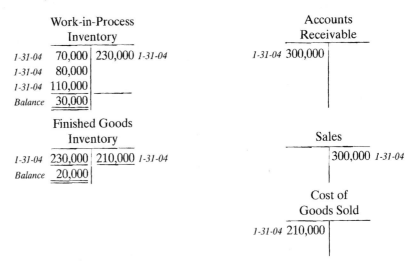

	Work-in-Process Inventory				Accounts Receivable	
1-31-04	70,000	230,000 *1-31-04*		*1-31-04*	300,000	
1-31-04	80,000					
1-31-04	110,000					
Balance	30,000					

	Finished Goods Inventory				Sales	
1-31-04	230,000	210,000 *1-31-04*			300,000 *1-31-04*	
Balance	20,000					

		Cost of Goods Sold	
1-31-04	210,000		

◆ **APPENDIX SUMMARY**

Recording basic manufacturing entries involves eight accounts: cash, accounts receivable, accounts payable, raw materials inventory, work-in-process inventory, finished goods inventory, cost of goods sold, and sales. The basic flow through the accounts is depicted in Exhibit 2–Al. We record the purchase of raw material with a debit to raw material inventory. We debit work-in-process inventory to record the transfer of direct material to production and the incurrence of direct labor and manufacturing overhead costs. When goods are completed, we credit work-in-process inventory and debit finished goods inventory for the amount of the cost of the goods manufactured. When the finished goods are sold, we make separate entries to reflect the sale and to reflect the decrease in finished goods inventory and the increase in cost of goods sold.

EXHIBIT 2–A1 Basic Flow of Costs Through Manufacturing Accounts

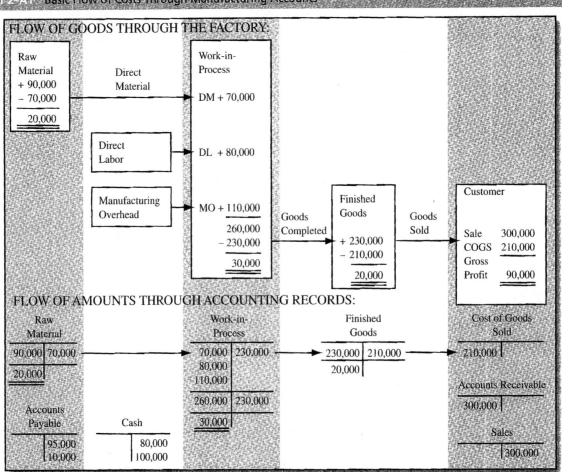

Key Terms

- administrative cost, M–20
- common cost, M–19
- cost, M–18
- cost object, M–18
- direct cost, M–19
- direct labor cost, M–23
- direct labor hours, M–25
- direct material, M–25
- direct materials cost, M–23

- factory burden, M–26
- factory overhead, M–26
- finished goods inventory, M–24
- hybrid firms, M–35
- indirect cost, M–19
- indirect labor, M–26
- indirect manufacturing cost, M–26
- indirect materials, M–26
- inventoriable costs, M–19

- manufacturing overhead, M–26
- manufacturing overhead cost, M–23
- material stores, M–24
- overhead, M–26
- period costs, M–19
- product cost, M–19
- raw materials inventory, M–24
- selling cost, M–19
- work-in-process inventory, M–24

Review the Facts

A. What is a cost object?

B. What is the difference between a direct cost and an indirect cost?

C. What is product cost?

D. What is period cost?

E. Why is the cost of delivering merchandise to customers included in selling expense?

F. Why is the cost of storing inventory that is ready to sell included in selling expense?

G. What classification includes costs that are neither product costs nor costs directly associated with selling activities?

H. Why are product costs called inventoriable costs?

I. Describe the difference between the accounting treatment for product costs and period costs.

J. Describe the flow of inventory costs for a merchandising operation as goods are bought and then sold.

K. What are the inventory classifications for a manufacturing-type firm?

L. What are the three main cost components included in product cost for a manufacturing-type firm?

M. What is the difference between direct material and indirect material?

N. What is the difference between direct labor and indirect labor?

O. In which product cost classification would you most likely find indirect material and indirect labor?

P. With respect to the cost of goods sold section of an income statement, what is the similarity between purchases for a merchandising-type company and cost of goods manufactured for a manufacturing-type company?

Q. What is included in the cost of services provided for a service-type firm?

Apply What You Have Learned

LO 1: DISTINGUISH BETWEEN DIRECT AND INDIRECT COSTS

2–12. Brittany operates a small chain of five children's shoe stores called Baby Feet. She employs a store manager and two sales clerks for each store. In addition, she rents office space which houses her office, the personnel department, and the bookkeeping department for the chain. Brittany has collected the following information regarding the stores and has asked you to determine which costs are direct and which are indirect costs.

Required: For each of the following items, indicate which would describe a direct cost (D) for the store at the corner of Elm Street and Main and which would describe an indirect cost (I) for an individual store.

1. _____ Rent for the office space
2. _____ Rent for the store
3. _____ Brittany's salary
4. _____ The store manager's salary
5. _____ The company personnel manager's salary
6. _____ Bookkeeper's salary
7. _____ Maintenance cost for the store
8. _____ Depreciation on sales equipment

9. _____ Depreciation on bookkeeping computer
10. _____ Sales clerks' salaries
11. _____ Cost of shoes
12. _____ Advertising cost for the chain

LO 1: DISTINGUISH BETWEEN DIRECT AND INDIRECT COSTS

2–13. Sue Lee is the president of Baby Care. The company operates a chain of four child care centers in southern Florida. In addition to the four Baby Care locations, the company rents office space which is used by the company's bookkeeper and Sue Lee.

Required:

    a. List four costs that would be considered direct costs of one of the four child care centers.

    b. List four costs that would be considered indirect costs of one of the four child care centers.

LO 1: DISTINGUISH BETWEEN DIRECT AND INDIRECT COSTS

2–14. Blue Water Travel operates a chain of travel agent offices in the eastern United States. Blue Water Travel's home office is in New York. There are six sales offices and a district office located in Florida.

Required: If the cost object is one of the sales offices in Florida, indicate which of the following would describe a direct cost (D) and which would describe an indirect cost (I).

1. _____ Rent for the Florida district office building
2. _____ Rent for the home office building in New York
3. _____ Rent for the sales office
4. _____ The company president's salary
5. _____ The salary of the vice president in charge of the Florida division
6. _____ The salary of a sales office manager
7. _____ The salary of a sales associate

LO 2: TYPES OF COST FOR A MANUFACTURER

2–15. Following are several representative costs incurred in a typical manufacturing company. For each of the costs, indicate in the space provided whether the cost is a direct material (DM), direct labor (DL), manufacturing overhead (MO), selling (S), or administrative (A) cost.

1. _____ Material incorporated into products
2. _____ Sales supplies
3. _____ Supplies used in the factory
4. _____ Wages of plant security guard
5. _____ Wages of security guard for the sales office
6. _____ Depreciation on a file cabinet used in the factory
7. _____ Depreciation on a file cabinet used in the general accounting office
8. _____ President's salary
9. _____ Salary of the president's secretary
10. _____ Manufacturing vice president's salary
11. _____ Salary of the manufacturing vice president's secretary
12. _____ Wages paid to production-line workers
13. _____ Factory rent
14. _____ Accounting office rent
15. _____ Depreciation on a copy machine used in the sales department
16. _____ Depreciation on a copy machine used to copy work orders in the factory
17. _____ Salary of plant supervisor

LO 2: TYPES OF COST FOR A MANUFACTURER

2–16. Following are several representative costs incurred in a typical manufacturing company. For each of the costs, indicate in the space provided whether the cost is a product cost (PR) or a period cost (PE).

1. _____ Material incorporated into products
2. _____ Sales supplies
3. _____ Supplies used in the factory
4. _____ Wages of plant security guard
5. _____ Wages of security guard for the sales office
6. _____ Depreciation on a file cabinet used in the factory
7. _____ Depreciation on a file cabinet used in the general accounting office
8. _____ President's salary
9. _____ Salary of the president's secretary
10. _____ Manufacturing vice president's salary
11. _____ Salary of the manufacturing vice president's secretary
12. _____ Wages paid to production-line workers
13. _____ Factory rent
14. _____ Accounting office rent
15. _____ Depreciation on a copy machine used in the sales department
16. _____ Depreciation on a copy machine used to copy work orders in the factory
17. _____ Salary of plant supervisor

LO 5: CALCULATE COSTS FOR A MANUFACTURER, NO INVENTORIES

2–17. The following data pertain to the Anderson Table Manufacturing Company for January 2003. The company made 1,000 tables during January, and there are no beginning or ending inventories.

Wood used in production	$25,000
Cleaning supplies used in the factory	300
Machine lubricants used in the factory	100
Factory rent	2,000
Rent on the sales office	3,000
Sales salaries	20,000
Production-line labor cost	50,000
Plant security guard cost	1,200
Plant supervision	2,500
Sales office supervision	3,000
Depreciation on production equipment	4,000
Depreciation on sales office equipment	1,000

Required:

a. What is the cost of direct material used in production during January 2003?
b. What is the cost of direct labor for January 2003?
c. What is the cost of manufacturing overhead for January 2003?
d. What is the total cost of tables manufactured in January 2003?
e. What is the cost of each table manufactured in January 2003?
f. Do you think the cost per table is valuable information for Carole Anderson, the company's owner? How might she use this information?

LO 5: CALCULATE ENDING INVENTORY

2–18. Steinmann Window Company makes aluminum window units. At the beginning of November, the company's direct material inventory included 900 square feet of window glass. During November, Steinmann purchased another 12,000 square feet of glass. Each completed window unit requires 9 square feet of glass. During November, 9,900 square feet of glass was transferred to the production line.

Required: How many square feet of glass remain in the ending direct material inventory?

LO 4: ANALYZING INVENTORY

2–19. Van Kirk Manufacturing Company has been in business for many years. Dottie Van Kirk, the company president, is concerned that the cost of raw material is skyrocketing. The production foreman assured Van Kirk that the use of direct material actually dropped in 2005.

Van Kirk has engaged your services to provide insight into what she thinks may be a sizable problem. Not only does it seem that the cost of direct material is increasing, but it also seems that her production foreman is being less than honest with her.

The following information is available:

Van Kirk Manufacturing Company
Direct Materials Schedule
For the Year Ending December 31, 2004

Beginning Direct Material Inventory	$ 25,000
Purchases During 2004	435,000
Materials Available During 2004	$460,000
Ending Direct Material Inventory	(30,000)
Direct Materials Used During 2004	$430,000

Van Kirk Manufacturing Company
Direct Materials Schedule
For the Year Ending December 31, 2005

Beginning Direct Material Inventory	$ 30,000
Purchases During 2005	501,000
Materials Available During 2005	$531,000
Ending Direct Material Inventory	(103,000)
Direct Materials Used During 2005	$428,000

Required: Examine the information presented and write a brief report to Dottie Van Kirk detailing your findings relative to her concerns.

LO 3: ANALYZE COSTS OF A MERCHANDISER

2–20. Ralph Brito opened Brito Auto Sales several years ago. Since then, the company has grown and sales have steadily increased. In the last year, however, income has declined despite successful efforts to increase sales. In addition, the company is forced to borrow more and more money from the bank to finance the operation.

The following information is available:

Brito Auto Sales
Income Statement
For the Year Ending December 31, 2005

Sales		$758,000
Cost of Goods Sold		
Beginning Inventory	$ 66,000	
+ Cost of Goods Purchased	639,000	
= Goods Available for Sale	$705,000	
− Ending Inventory	(85,000)	
= Cost of Goods Sold		620,000
Gross Profit		$138,000
Operating Expense:		
Selling Expense	$ 55,000	
Administrative Expense	60,000	(115,000)
Operating Income		$ 23,000

Brito Auto Sales
Income Statement
For the Year Ending December 31, 2006

Sales		$890,000
Cost of Goods Sold		
Beginning Inventory	$ 85,000	
+ Cost of Goods Purchased	799,000	
= Goods Available for Sale	$884,000	
− Ending Inventory	(123,000)	
= Cost of Goods Sold		761,000
Gross Profit		$129,000
Operating Expense:		
Selling Expense	$ 66,000	
Administrative Expense	60,000	(126,000)
Operating Income		$ 3,000

Required: Assume that you are hired by Mr. Brito as a consultant. Review the Brito income statement and write a report to Mr. Brito that addresses his concerns.

LO 4: CALCULATE ENDING DIRECT MATERIAL INVENTORY FOR A MANUFACTURER

2–21. Matheis Designs, Inc. manufactures swimming suits. At the beginning of October 2004, the company had $1,450 worth of cloth on hand which was included in its direct material inventory. During October, Matheis purchased cloth costing $12,360 and used material costing $12,750 in production.

Required: What is the cost of the ending direct material inventory of cloth for Matheis Designs, Inc.?

LO 4: CALCULATE DIRECT MATERIAL USED

2–22. The following information relates to the Penny Manufacturing Company.

Beginning direct material inventory	$ 540,000
Ending direct material inventory	$ 480,000
Direct material purchased on account	$4,680,000

Required:

    a. Compute the cost of direct material used in production.
    b. Appendix: Prepare the journal entry dated January 3, 2004, to record the purchase of the direct material.
    c. Appendix: Prepare a journal entry dated January 31, 2004, to record the use of direct material in production.

LO 4: CALCULATE DIRECT MATERIAL USED

2–23. The following information relates to the Montoya Manufacturing Company.

Beginning direct material inventory	$ 40,000
Ending direct material inventory	$ 48,000
Direct material purchased on account	$437,000

Required:

    a. Compute the cost of direct material used in production.
    b. Appendix: Prepare the journal entry dated June 3, 2004, to record the purchase of the direct material
    c. Appendix: Prepare a journal entry dated June 30, 2004, to record the use of direct material used in production.

LO 4: CALCULATE THE COST OF SUPPLIES USED

2–24. The following information relates to Pons Maintenance Service.

Maintenance supplies at January 1, 2004	$ 4,210
Maintenance supplies at December 31, 2004	$ 3,840
Maintenance supplies purchased during 2004	$27,530

Required: What was the cost of maintenance supplies consumed by Pons Maintenance Service during 2004?

LO 6: CALCULATE COST OF MATERIALS USED BY A SERVICE COMPANY

2–25. On January 1, 2003, Bowden Auto Repair had $3,560 worth of auto parts on hand. During the year, Bowden purchased auto parts costing $286,000. At the end of 2003, the company had parts on hand amounting to $4,260.

Required: What was the cost of the auto parts used by Bowden Auto Repair during 2003?

LO 3: CALCULATE THE COST OF GOODS SOLD FOR A MERCHANDISER

2–26. On January 1, 2004, the cost of merchandise on hand at Margaret's Fashions was $56,530. Purchases during the month amounted to $488,668 and the cost of merchandise on hand at the end of January was $52,849.

Required: Determine January's cost of goods sold for Margaret's Fashions.

LO 5: INVENTORY AND PRODUCTION COSTS FOR A MANUFACTURER

2–27. The following data pertain to the Hudik Manufacturing Company for the year ended December 31, 2004. The company made 115,000 light fixtures during 2004. There are no beginning or ending inventories.

Metal used in production	$750,000
Wire used in production	40,000
Factory supplies used	5,200
Depreciation on the factory	48,000
Depreciation on the sales office	3,000
Sales salaries	90,000
Assembly-line labor cost	960,000
Factory security guard cost	8,200
Factory supervision	62,500
General accounting cost	43,000
Depreciation on production equipment	454,850
Depreciation on sales office equipment	9,200

Required:

a. What is the cost of direct material used during 2004?
b. What is the cost of direct labor during 2004?
c. What is the cost of manufacturing overhead during 2004?
d. What is the total product cost for 2004 production?
e. What is the cost per light fixture for 2004?

LO 5: INVENTORY AND PRODUCTION COSTS INCLUDING COST OF GOODS MANUFACTURED AND COST OF GOODS SOLD

2–28. The following data pertain to the Elsea Manufacturing Company for the year ended December 31, 2004. The company made 60,000 SW20 switching units during 2004.

Beginning direct material inventory	$ 42,000
Ending direct material inventory	48,000
Beginning work-in-process inventory	84,000
Ending work-in-process inventory	93,000
Beginning finished goods inventory	124,000
Ending finished goods inventory	133,000
Direct material purchased	850,000
Indirect material used in production	4,000
Factory supplies used	6,200
Depreciation on the factory	60,000
Depreciation on the sales office	4,000
Depreciation on the administrative office	3,000
Sales salaries	120,000
Assembly-line labor cost	820,000
Factory security guard cost	12,000
Factory supervision	82,600
Depreciation on production equipment	560,000
Depreciation on sales office equipment	22,200

Required:

a. What is the cost of direct material used during 2004?
b. What is the cost of direct labor during 2004?
c. What is the cost of manufacturing overhead for 2004?
d. What is total manufacturing cost incurred during 2004?
e. What is the cost of goods manufactured for 2004?
f. What is the cost of goods sold for 2004?

LO 5: INVENTORY AND PRODUCTION COSTS INCLUDING COST OF GOODS MANUFACTURED AND COST OF GOODS SOLD

2–29. The following data pertain to the Miami Manufacturing Company for the year ended December 31, 2004.

Beginning finished goods inventory	$ 255,000
Ending finished goods inventory	270,000
Beginning direct material inventory	82,000
Ending direct material inventory	98,000
Beginning work-in-process inventory	164,000
Ending work-in-process inventory	184,000
Direct material purchased	1,740,000
Indirect material used in production	3,000
Factory supplies used	12,500
Depreciation on the factory	134,000
Depreciation on the sales office	14,000
Depreciation on the administrative office	9,000
Sales salaries	350,000
Assembly-line labor cost	2,120,000
Factory security guard cost	22,000
Factory supervision	183,500
Depreciation on production equipment	1,340,000
Depreciation on administrative office equipment	52,200

Required:

a. What is the cost of direct material used during 2004?
b. What is the cost of direct labor during 2004?
c. What is the cost of manufacturing overhead for 2004?
d. What is total manufacturing cost incurred during 2004?
e. What is the cost of goods manufactured for 2004?
f. What is the cost of goods sold for 2004?

LO 5: INVENTORY AND PRODUCTION COSTS INCLUDING COST OF GOODS MANUFACTURED AND COST OF GOODS SOLD

2–30. The following data pertain to the Seth Levine Manufacturing Company for the year ended December 31, 2004.

Beginning direct material inventory	$ 2,000
Ending direct material inventory	3,000
Beginning work-in-process inventory	4,000
Ending work-in-process inventory	5,000
Beginning finished goods inventory	9,500
Ending finished goods inventory	8,000
Direct material purchased	22,000
Factory supplies used	12,500
Depreciation on the factory	34,000
Assembly-line labor cost	120,000
Depreciation on production equipment	42,000
Other indirect factory costs	12,000

Required:

a. What is the cost of direct material used during 2004?
b. What is the cost of direct labor during 2004?
c. What is the cost of manufacturing overhead for 2004?
d. What is total manufacturing cost incurred during 2004?
e. What is the cost of goods manufactured for 2004?
f. What is the cost of goods sold for 2004?

LO 5: INVENTORY AND PRODUCTION COSTS INCLUDING COST OF GOODS MANUFACTURED AND COST OF GOODS SOLD

2–31. The following data pertain to the Sexton Manufacturing Company for the year ended December 31, 2005.

Beginning direct material inventory	$ 22,000
Ending direct material inventory	28,000
Beginning finished goods inventory	30,000
Ending finished goods inventory	28,000
Beginning work-in-process inventory	16,000
Ending work-in-process inventory	15,000
Direct material purchased	280,000
Production worker labor cost	290,000
Depreciation on production equipment	80,000
Factory rent	24,000
Other indirect factory costs	36,000

Required:

  a. What is the cost of direct material used during 2005?
  b. What is the cost of direct labor during 2005?
  c. What is the cost of manufacturing overhead for 2005?
  d. What is total manufacturing cost incurred during 2005?
  e. What is the cost of goods manufactured for 2005?
  f. What is the cost of goods sold for 2005?

LO 5: PREPARATION OF COST OF GOODS MANUFACTURED AND COST OF GOODS SOLD SCHEDULES

2–32. The following data pertain to the Adler Manufacturing Company for the year ended December 31, 2004.

Beginning direct material inventory	$ 12,000
Ending direct material inventory	13,000
Beginning work-in-process inventory	24,000
Ending work-in-process inventory	25,000
Beginning finished goods inventory	29,500
Ending finished goods inventory	28,000
Direct material purchased	122,000
Factory utilities	2,500
Rent on the factory	64,000
Assembly worker labor cost	86,000
Depreciation on production equipment	92,000
Other indirect factory costs	22,000

Required:

  a. Prepare a cost of goods manufactured schedule for 2004.
  b. Prepare a cost of goods sold schedule for 2004.

LO 5: PREPARATION OF COST OF GOODS MANUFACTURED AND COST OF GOODS SOLD SCHEDULES

2–33. The following data pertain to the Clifford Manufacturing Company for the year ended December 31, 2005.

Beginning direct material inventory	$ 2,300
Ending direct material inventory	3,400
Beginning work-in-process inventory	5,500
Ending work-in-process inventory	4,100
Beginning finished goods inventory	6,500
Ending finished goods inventory	5,100
Direct material purchased	12,300
Factory supplies used	500
Depreciation on the factory	22,000

Assembly-line labor cost	48,600
Depreciation on production equipment	12,000
Other indirect factory costs	4,700

Required:

   a. Prepare a cost of goods manufactured schedule for 2005.
   b. Prepare a cost of goods sold schedule for 2005.

LO 5: PREPARATION OF COST OF GOODS MANUFACTURED SCHEDULE, COST OF GOODS SOLD SCHEDULE, AND MULTIPLE-STEP INCOME STATEMENT

2–34. The following data pertain to the Lowell Manufacturing Company for the year ended December 31, 2005.

Sales	$1,267,000
Beginning direct material inventory	40,000
Ending direct material inventory	50,000
Beginning work-in-process inventory	70,000
Ending work-in-process inventory	60,000
Beginning finished goods inventory	90,000
Ending finished goods inventory	80,000
Direct material purchased	350,000
Indirect material used in production	24,000
Factory supplies used	6,000
Depreciation on the factory	90,000
Depreciation on the sales office	24,000
Depreciation on the administrative office	36,000
Sales salaries	110,000
Assembly-line labor cost	220,000
Factory security guard cost	22,000
Factory supervision	42,000
Depreciation on production equipment	160,000
Depreciation on general accounting office equipment	16,000

Required:

   a. Prepare a cost of goods manufactured schedule for 2005.
   b. Prepare a cost of goods sold schedule for 2005.
   c. Prepare a multiple-step income statement for 2005.

LO 5: PREPARATION OF COST OF GOODS MANUFACTURED SCHEDULE, COST OF GOODS SOLD SCHEDULE, AND MULTIPLE-STEP INCOME STATEMENT

2–35. The following data pertain to the Quintana Manufacturing Company for the year ended December 31, 2005.

Sales	$1,302,000
Beginning finished goods inventory	93,000
Ending finished goods inventory	86,000
Beginning direct material inventory	45,000
Ending direct material inventory	56,000
Beginning work-in-process inventory	72,000
Ending work-in-process inventory	77,000
Direct material purchased	370,000
Indirect material used in production	34,000
Depreciation on production equipment	145,000
Depreciation on administrative office equipment	19,000
Factory supplies used	8,000
Depreciation on the factory	96,000
Depreciation on the sales office	34,000
Depreciation on the administrative office	30,000
Sales salaries	122,000
Assembly-line labor cost	240,000
Factory security guard cost	32,000
Factory supervision	48,000

Required:

    a. Prepare a cost of goods manufactured schedule for 2005.
    b. Prepare a cost of goods sold schedule for 2005.
    c. Prepare a multiple-step income statement for 2005.

LO 5: PREPARATION OF COST OF GOODS MANUFACTURED SCHEDULE, COST OF GOODS SOLD SCHEDULE, AND MULTIPLE-STEP INCOME STATEMENT

2–36. The following data pertain to the Rodriguez Manufacturing Company for the year ended December 31, 2004.

Sales	$1,124,000
Beginning direct material inventory	55,000
Ending direct material inventory	56,000
Beginning finished goods inventory	83,000
Ending finished goods inventory	96,000
Beginning work-in-process inventory	62,000
Ending work-in-process inventory	67,000
Direct material purchased	290,000
Direct labor cost	220,000
Manufacturing overhead	286,000
Selling expense	122,000
Administrative expense	140,000

Required:

    a. Prepare a cost of goods manufactured schedule for 2004.
    b. Prepare a cost of goods sold schedule for 2004.
    c. Prepare a multiple-step income statement for 2004.

LO 5: PREPARATION OF COST OF GOODS MANUFACTURED SCHEDULE, COST OF GOODS SOLD SCHEDULE, AND MULTIPLE-STEP INCOME STATEMENT

2–37. The following data pertain to the Avener Manufacturing Company for the year ended December 31, 2004.

Sales	$333,000
Beginning direct material inventory	5,000
Ending direct material inventory	4,000
Beginning work-in-process inventory	6,000
Ending work-in-process inventory	7,000
Beginning finished goods inventory	8,000
Ending finished goods inventory	10,000
Direct material purchased	56,000
Direct labor cost	96,000
Manufacturing overhead	86,000
Selling expense	46,000
Administrative expense	34,000

Required:

    a. Prepare a cost of goods manufactured schedule for 2004.
    b. Prepare a cost of goods sold schedule for 2004.
    c. Prepare a multiple-step income statement for 2004.

LO 5: PREPARATION OF COST OF GOODS MANUFACTURED SCHEDULE COST OF GOODS SOLD SCHEDULE, AND JOURNAL ENTRIES

2–38. The following information is for Megan Hat Manufacturing Company.

Inventory information:

	January 1, 2005	December 31, 2005
Raw materials inventory	$ 9,000	$11,000
Work-in-process inventory	22,000	18,000
Finished goods inventory	42,000	38,000

Other information:

Direct materials purchases	$120,000
Direct labor cost	250,000
Manufacturing overhead	140,000

Required:

  a. What is the cost of direct material used in production?
  b. Prepare a cost of goods manufactured schedule.
  c. Prepare a cost of goods sold schedule.
  d. Appendix: Prepare journal entries to record the following:

   1. The purchase of direct material assuming it was purchased on account
   2. The use of direct material in production
   3. Direct labor cost
   4. Manufacturing overhead cost (Use "various accounts" for the credit side of the entry.)
   5. The cost of goods manufactured
   6. The sale of finished goods assuming the sale price was $600,000 and the sale was on account.

LO 5: PREPARATION OF COST OF GOODS MANUFACTURED SCHEDULE, COST OF GOODS SOLD SCHEDULE, AND JOURNAL ENTRIES

2–39. The following information is for Friedman Shelving Manufacturing Company.

Inventory information:

	January 1, 2005	December 31, 2005
Raw materials inventory	$22,000	$24,000
Work-in-process inventory	42,000	43,000
Finished goods inventory	82,000	78,000

Other information:

Direct materials purchases	$280,000
Direct labor cost	540,000
Manufacturing overhead	240,000

Required:

  a. What is the cost of direct material used in production?
  b. Prepare a cost of goods manufactured schedule.
  c. Prepare a cost of goods sold schedule.
  d. Appendix: Prepare journal entries to record the following:

   1. The purchase of direct material assuming it was purchased on account
   2. The use of direct material in production
   3. Direct labor cost
   4. Manufacturing overhead cost (Use "various accounts" for the credit side of the entry.)
   5. The cost of goods manufactured
   6. The sale of finished goods assuming the sale price was $1,400,000 on account

LO 5: PREPARATION OF COST OF GOODS MANUFACTURED SCHEDULE AND JOURNAL ENTRIES

2–40. The following information is for Tatum Manufacturing Company.

Inventory information:

	January 1, 2005	December 31, 2005
Raw materials inventory	$2,000	$4,000
Work-in-process inventory	4,000	3,000
Finished goods inventory	8,000	6,000

Other information:

Direct materials purchases	$ 8,000
Direct labor cost	12,000
Manufacturing overhead	9,000

Required:

    a. Prepare a cost of goods manufactured schedule.

    b. Appendix: Prepare journal entries to record the following:

        1. The purchase of direct material on account

        2. The use of direct material in production

        3. Direct labor cost

        4. Manufacturing overhead cost (Use "various accounts" for the credit side of the entry.)

        5. The cost of goods manufactured

        6. The sale of finished goods assuming the sale price was $40,000 and it was a cash sale

LO 5: PREPARATION OF COST OF GOODS MANUFACTURED SCHEDULE AND JOURNAL ENTRIES

2–41. The following information is for Munter Manufacturing Company.

Inventory information:

	January 1, 2005	December 31, 2005
Raw materials inventory	$6,000	$5,000
Work-in-process inventory	3,000	4,000
Finished goods inventory	7,000	9,000

Other information:

Direct materials purchases	$ 9,000
Direct labor cost	10,000
Manufacturing overhead	11,000

Required:

    a. Prepare a cost of goods manufactured schedule.

    b. Appendix: Prepare journal entries to record the following:

        1. The purchase of direct material on account

        2. The use of direct material in production

        3. Direct labor cost

        4. Manufacturing overhead cost (Use "various accounts" for the credit side of the entry.)

        5. The cost of goods manufactured

        6. The sale of finished goods assuming the sale price was $39,000 on account

LO 5: PREPARATION OF COST OF GOODS MANUFACTURED SCHEDULE AND MULTIPLE-STEP INCOME STATEMENT

2–42. The following information is for Collins Manufacturing Company.

Inventory information:

	January 1, 2005	December 31, 2005
Raw materials inventory	$16,000	$14,000
Work-in-process inventory	23,000	25,000
Finished goods inventory	33,000	36,000

Other information:

Sales	$760,000
Direct materials purchases	159,000
Direct labor cost	110,000
Manufacturing overhead	221,000
Selling expense	62,000
Administrative expense	47,000

Required:

    a. Prepare a cost of goods manufactured schedule.

    b. Prepare a multiple-step income statement in good form.

LO 5: PREPARATION OF COST OF GOODS MANUFACTURED SCHEDULE AND MULTIPLE-STEP INCOME STATEMENT

2–43. The following information is for Richard Manufacturing Company.

Inventory information:

	January 1, 2005	December 31, 2005
Raw materials inventory	$14,000	$16,000
Work-in-process inventory	25,000	28,000
Finished goods inventory	32,000	36,000

Other information:

Sales	$790,000
Direct materials purchases	162,000
Direct labor cost	140,000
Manufacturing overhead	234,000
Selling expense	72,000
Administrative expense	57,000

Required:

a. Prepare a cost of goods manufactured schedule.
b. Prepare a multiple-step income statement in good form.

LO 3: PREPARATION OF A MULTIPLE-STEP INCOME STATEMENT FOR A MANUFACTURER

2–44. Bonnie's Pet Cage Company has the following information for 2004:

Sales	$300,000
Cost of goods manufactured	200,000
Selling expense	30,000
Administrative expense	25,000
Beginning finished goods inventory	21,000
Ending finished goods inventory	28,000

Required: Prepare a multiple-step income statement for Bonnie's Pet Cage Company for 2004.

LO 3: PREPARATION OF A MULTIPLE-STEP INCOME STATEMENT FOR A MANUFACTURER

2–45. Albert's Manufacturing Company has the following information for 2004:

Beginning finished goods inventory	$ 41,000
Ending finished goods inventory	58,000
Sales	600,000
Cost of goods manufactured	400,000
Selling expense	90,000
Administrative expense	60,000

Required: Prepare a multiple-step income statement for Albert's Manufacturing Company for 2004.

LO 5: PREPARATION OF A MULTIPLE-STEP INCOME STATEMENT FOR A MERCHANDISER

2–46. Phillips Merchandising Company has the following information for 2004:

Sales	$400,000
Cost of merchandise purchased	300,000
Selling expense	30,000
Administrative expense	20,000
Beginning merchandise goods inventory	40,000
Ending merchandise goods inventory	50,000

Required: Prepare a multiple-step income statement for Phillips Merchandising Company for 2004.

LO 5: PREPARATION OF A MULTIPLE-STEP INCOME STATEMENT FOR A MERCHANDISER

2–47. Robinson Merchandising Company has the following information for 2005:

Beginning merchandise goods inventory	$ 60,000
Ending merchandise goods inventory	50,000
Sales	840,000
Cost of merchandise purchased	630,000
Selling expense	90,000
Administrative expense	40,000

Required: Prepare a multiple-step income statement for Robinson Merchandising Company for 2005.

LO 6: DETERMINE THE COST OF SERVICES PROVIDED AND PREPARATION OF A SINGLE-STEP INCOME STATEMENT FOR A SERVICE COMPANY

2–48. Butterfield's Bookkeeping Service began operations on January 1, 2005. The following information is taken from its accounting records as of December 31, 2005.

Bookkeeping service revenue	$80,000
Bookkeeping salaries	42,000
Bookkeeping office rent	12,000
Depreciation on bookkeeping equipment	2,000
Bookkeeping supplies used	700
Advertising	800

Required:

a. What is the cost of services provided?

b. Prepare a single-step income statement for Butterfield's Bookkeeping Service for 2005.

LO 6: DETERMINE THE COST OF SERVICES PROVIDED AND PREPARATION OF A SINGLE-STEP INCOME STATEMENT FOR A SERVICE COMPANY

2–49. Tony's Film Delivery Service began operations on January 1, 2005. The following information is taken from its accounting records as of December 31, 2005.

Delivery revenue	$40,000
Driver wages	22,000
Depreciation on truck	4,000
Fuel cost	2,700
Advertising	800
Bookkeeping cost	240

Required:

a. What is the cost of services provided?

b. Prepare a single-step income statement for Tony's Film Delivery Service.

LO 3: PREPARATION OF A MULTIPLE-STEP INCOME STATEMENT FOR A MERCHANDISER

2–50. Cam's Swimsuit Shop provided the following information for 2005.

Merchandise inventory, January 1, 2005	$16,000
Merchandise inventory, December 31, 2005	19,000
Sales	190,000
Advertising	1,200
Store rent	2,400
Purchases of merchandise	82,000
Sales salaries	22,000
Store utilities	3,600
Sales supplies used during 2005	1,000
Sales supplies on hand, December 31, 2005	500
Administrative office rent	800
Administrative salaries	18,000

Required: Prepare a multiple-step income statement for Cam's Swimsuit Shop for 2005.

LO 3: PREPARATION OF A MULTIPLE-STEP INCOME STATEMENT FOR A MERCHANDISER

2–51. Leroy's Auto Parts provided the following information for 2005.

Merchandise inventory, January 1, 2005	$ 19,000
Merchandise inventory, December 31, 2005	21,000
Sales	280,000
Advertising	2,200
Depreciation on the store	18,000
Purchases of merchandise	182,000
Sales salaries	21,000
Store utilities	1,200
Depreciation on administrative office building	4,000
Administrative salaries	15,000
Administrative office utilities	600

Required: Prepare a multiple-step income statement for Leroy's Auto Parts for 2005.

LO 6: PREPARATION OF A SINGLE-STEP INCOME STATEMENT FOR A SERVICE COMPANY

2–52. Dan's Security Service provided the following information for 2005.

Security revenue	$480,000
Advertising	12,000
Depreciation on the home office building	12,000
Security guard wages	362,000
Administrative salaries	21,000
Sales salaries	24,000
Utilities	1,200

Required: Prepare a single-step income statement for Dan's Security Service for 2005.

LO 3: PREPARATION OF A MULTIPLE-STEP INCOME STATEMENT FOR A MERCHANDISER

2–53. Margaret's Flower Shop provided the following information for 2005.

Merchandise inventory, January 1, 2005	$ 1,000
Merchandise inventory, December 31, 2005	1,200
Sales	42,400
Advertising	3,200
Store rent	1,200
Purchases of merchandise	18,000
Sales salaries	21,000
Utilities	1,300
Sales supplies used during 2005	9,000
Sales supplies on hand, December 31, 2005	300

Required: Prepare a multiple-step income statement for Margaret's Flower Shop for 2005.

LO 2, 3, & 4: UNDERSTANDING COST OF GOODS SOLD

2–54. The management of Diversified Incorporated is concerned that few of its employees understand cost of goods sold. The company president has decided that a series of presentations will be made focusing on cost of goods sold.

Assume that the company has formed two teams, Team A and Team B. You and several of your classmates have been assigned to Team B.

Team A is given the responsibility of preparing a presentation detailing the cost of goods sold pertaining to a subsidiary that operates a chain of hardware stores. Team B, your team, has been given the responsibility of preparing a presentation detailing the cost of goods sold of a subsidiary that manufactures electronic calculators.

In short order, Team A has completed its assignment and is ready to make its presentation. Your team, however, is still working. Company executives question why Team A is so far ahead of your team's progress.

Required: Working as a group, develop a response to the concerns relating to your team's slow progress. Explain why Team A could complete their assignment so quickly and why your team will have to work longer.

LO 6: UNDERSTANDING SERVICE COMPANY COSTS

2–55. Assume that you are the manager of an accounting practice. You are concerned about billing your clients so that the company covers all costs and makes a reasonable profit.

Required:

a. What information might you desire to help develop a method of billing clients?
b. How would you use the information to ensure that costs are covered and profits result?

LO 1, 2, & 4: UNDERSTANDING INVENTORY COST CLASSIFICATIONS

2–56. The inventory of a manufacturer is typically grouped into one of three classifications—raw material inventory, work-in-process inventory, and finished goods inventory.

Required: Discuss why it provides more useful information for a manufacturer to use three classifications of inventory rather than one.

LO 1, 2, & 4: UNDERSTANDING INVENTORY COSTS

2–57. Assume that you work for the Acme Wire Manufacturing Company. Some employees in the company are unsure of which costs should be included in inventories and which costs should not. There is also some confusion regarding the logic of including some items while excluding others.

You have been assigned to a group that is responsible for making a presentation on which of Acme's costs would properly be classified as inventory costs and which would not.

Required: Prepare a presentation describing the type of items that would be included in inventories and those that would not. Comment on the logic of including some cost items in inventory while excluding others.

LO 1, 2, & 3: GENERAL INVENTORY AND COST ANALYSIS

2–58. One year ago, Herb Smith quit his job at Adcox Medical where he earned $28,000 a year as a health care technician to start the Super CD Store. He invested almost his entire life's savings in the venture and is now concerned. He notes that when his money was in the bank, he earned about 4% interest. Now, when he compares his company profits to the amount invested in the store, the profits seem lower than what he could have earned if he had simply left the money in the bank. The following information is available for the company's first year of business:

Sales	$600,000
Cost of goods sold	450,000
Selling expense	90,000
Administrative expense	50,000
Inventory at year end	300,000
Other assets at year end	30,000
Total liabilities at year end	50,000

The administrative expense includes $30,000 received by Herb in the form of salary. Herb's friend Bill has suggested that a simple $5,000 computer might help with company record keeping and ordering inventory.

Herb has indicated that he does not mind the added work or ordering the merchandise without a computer. In fact, when it comes to ordering product, he seems quite proud of the job he is doing as he almost always has the CDs his customers want. Herb has engaged your services as a consultant to determine whether his feelings are correct about the low earnings of the company and to suggest some possibilities to improve the situation. Also, Herb would like some input regarding the computer.

Required: Prepare a report for Herb addressing each of his concerns.

LO 1, 2, & 3: GENERAL INVENTORY AND COST ANALYSIS

2–59. Alberto Manufacturing Company has been in business for many years. Toward the end of 2004, management began to notice that the company had to rely increasingly on borrowing to support the cash flow needs of the operation. Although sales increased in 2005, profits declined and the cash flow problem worsened. The company president is very concerned that the cash shortfall is caused by mismanagement of the daily operation of the factory. Managers argue that the company's operations are quite satisfactory. They cite that expenses have increased only slightly as sales have risen, and that production levels have been dictated by customer demand.

The president has hired your team of consultants to review the situation and comment on the possible problems that exist. The following information is available for 2004 and 2005.

Alberto Manufacturing Company
Schedule of Cost of Goods Manufactured
For the Year Ending December 31, 2004

Direct Materials:		
Beginning Direct Material Inventory	$ 15,000	
Purchases During 2004	420,000	
Materials Available During 2004	$435,000	
Ending Direct Material Inventory	(45,000)	
Direct Materials Used During 2004		$ 390,000
Direct Labor During 2004		225,000
Total Manufacturing Overhead Cost During 2004		415,000
Manufacturing Cost for Current Period		$1,030,000
Beginning Work-in-Process Inventory 1/1/04		40,000
Cost of Goods Available to Be Finished		$1,070,000
Ending Work-in-Process Inventory 12/31/04		(82,000)
Cost of Goods Manufactured During 2004		$ 988,000

Alberto Manufacturing Company
Income Statement
For the Year Ending December 31, 2004

Sales		$1,758,000
Cost of Goods Sold		
Beginning Finished Goods Inventory	$ 65,000	
+ Cost of Goods Manufactured	988,000	
= Goods Available for Sale in 2004	$1,053,000	
− Ending Finished Goods Inventory	(75,000)	
= Cost of Goods Sold for 2004		978,000
Gross Profit		$ 780,000
Operating Expense:		
Selling Expense	$ 355,000	
Administrative Expense	190,000	(545,000)
Operating Income		$ 235,000

Alberto Manufacturing Company
Schedule of Cost of Goods Manufactured
For the Year Ending December 31, 2005

Direct Materials:		
Beginning Direct Material Inventory	$ 45,000	
Purchases During 2005	457,000	
Materials Available During 2005	$502,000	
Ending Direct Material Inventory	(73,000)	
Direct Materials Used During 2005		$ 429,000
Direct Labor During 2005		263,000
Total Manufacturing Overhead Cost During 2005		450,000
Manufacturing Cost for Current Period		$1,142,000
Beginning Work-in-Process Inventory 1/1/05		82,000
Cost of Goods Available to Be Finished		$1,224,000
Ending Work-in-Process Inventory 12/31/05		(154,000)
Cost of Goods Manufactured During 2005		$1,070,000

Alberto Manufacturing Company
Income Statement
For the Year Ending December 31, 2005

Sales		$1,772,000
Cost of Goods Sold		
Beginning Finished Goods Inventory	$ 75,000	
+ Cost of Goods Manufactured During 2005	1,070,000	
= Goods Available for Sale in 2005	$1,143,000	
– Ending Finished Goods Inventory	(93,000)	
= Cost of Goods Sold for 2005		$1,052,000
Gross Profit		720,000
Operating Expense:		
Selling Expense	$ 365,000	
Administrative Expense	228,000	(593,000)
Operating Income		$ 127,000

Required: Your team should review the provided information and comment on problems
that exist. It may help to segment the statements into sections and assign group
members to a particular area. For example, a group member might be assigned
to review the purchase and use of direct material, another member might be
assigned the direct labor and manufacturing overhead areas, and so forth. Each
group member should comment on his or her assigned area as it pertains to
cash flow and income.

CHAPTER 3

Determining Costs of Products

Every year *Fortune* magazine compiles a list of the top 500 publicly traded companies in the United States. This prestigious list is called the *Fortune 500*. Of the top 25 *Fortune* 500 companies, most are manufacturing companies, demonstrating that manufacturing plays a pivotal role in our economy.

In recent years, however, manufacturing companies from outside the United States have begun to exert significant competitive pressure on U.S. manufacturers. The new global marketplace has forced U.S. manufacturers to take a hard look at both the way they operate and the way the results of their operations are measured and evaluated.

One area of vital importance to manufacturing companies is determining the cost of the products they manufacture. If you are the sales manager for *IBM*'s laptop computer division, for example, you must be sure that the selling price you establish is high enough to earn a profit. To ensure that the selling price of each computer exceeds its cost, you need accurate product cost information.

Besides the product pricing decision, there are several other uses of information about product cost. First, a company must determine the cost of products to compute cost of goods sold on its income statement for a particular period. Second, a company must have product cost information to determine the value of inventories shown on its balance sheet. Third, product cost information helps managers evaluate the efficiency and productivity of a company's manufacturing facility.

In Chapter 2, we stated that the three elements of product cost for a manufacturer are direct material, direct labor, and manufacturing overhead. We also presented an overview of the product costing process. In this chapter, we will delve more deeply into the methods that manufacturers use to determine the cost of the individual units of product they produce.

Learning Objectives

After completing your work on this chapter, you should be able to do the following:

1. Compare and contrast process costing with job order costing.
2. Describe how process costing and job order costing work.
3. Describe the documents used to help control the costs of manufacturing products.
4. Describe how overhead costs are allocated to products.
5. Determine the cost of products using job order costing.
6. Determine the cost of products using process costing.
7. Prepare basic manufacturing journal entries. (Appendix)

◆ ACCUMULATING PRODUCT COST—COST ACCOUNTING

The process of assigning manufacturing costs to manufactured products is called *cost accounting*. When we first introduced this term in Chapter 1, we said that it is often used interchangeably with the terms *management accounting* and *managerial accounting*, but that cost accounting is a narrow application of management accounting dealing with costing products. Cost accounting information can help managers plan and control their operations; make decisions about investments in property, plant, and equipment; establish selling prices; and determine the value of inventories on the balance sheet. Cost accounting information also affects reported net income on the income statement, because the cost of the products sold during the income statement period is reported as cost of goods sold.

◆ UNITS OF PRODUCT AS COST OBJECTS

Recall from Chapter 2 that a cost object is any activity or item for which a separate cost measurement is desired. For our purposes in this chapter, we will consider a unit of manufactured product as the cost object. As we said earlier, the cost of a unit of manufactured product includes the cost of the direct material, direct labor, and manufacturing overhead required to produce that unit of product. The amount of direct material included in each unit of production can actually be traced to finished products. Assigning the cost of direct material to production is relatively simple, then, as long as the company keeps track of the amount of material used to produce each unit of product. Similarly, if a company keeps track of the amount of direct labor used to produce each unit of product, it can readily assess the cost of direct labor used to produce each unit. Unlike direct material and direct labor, however, the amount of manufacturing overhead cost associated with particular units of production is quite abstract.

Manufacturing overhead cost includes all manufacturing cost except direct material and direct labor costs. Accordingly, it includes a wide assortment of factory-related items. Some examples are production design and setup, plant security, supervisory salaries, raw materials storage, building maintenance, and factory supplies.

◆ PRODUCT COSTING METHODS

Manufacturers generally use one of two methods for determining the cost of products—the job order cost method or the process cost method. Although both methods are used, they are not interchangeable. A company must select the method best suited to the type of products it makes and to the manufacturing process itself. The key consideration for choosing between process costing and job order costing is whether the goods produced consume similar enough amounts of factory resources (direct material, direct labor, and manufacturing overhead) that an average cost per unit would be an accurate reflection of the product's cost. This is process costing. An example of a product that would use process costing is *Colgate* White Strips. If the units consume very different amounts of factory resources, an average cost per unit is meaningless, and job order costing should be used. An example of a product that would use job order costing is a ship manufactured for *Carnival Cruise Lines.*

JOB ORDER COSTING BASICS

job order costing A costing method that accumulates cost by a single unit or batch of units.

Job order costing accumulates the cost of production for each job, each individual unit of production, each order, or each batch of product. This method is used to accumulate the cost of one-of-a-kind and custom-made goods such as custom furniture, custom cabinets, ships, airplanes, bridges, buildings, and advertising posters. For instance, when *Boeing* manufactured the five *Boeing* 777-200 passenger jets ordered by *Air China,* the airplane manufacturer used job order costing to determine how much each plane cost.

Under job order costing, managers keep close track of the material and labor associated with each job. The "job" may consist of a single unit or a batch of units. For example, a job for *Boeing* would consist of a single airplane. For *Perlmuter Printing,* however, a job may consist of a batch of 20,000 advertising posters. In either case, the cost of direct material, direct labor, and overhead are accumulated and totaled for each job. (See Exhibit 3–1)

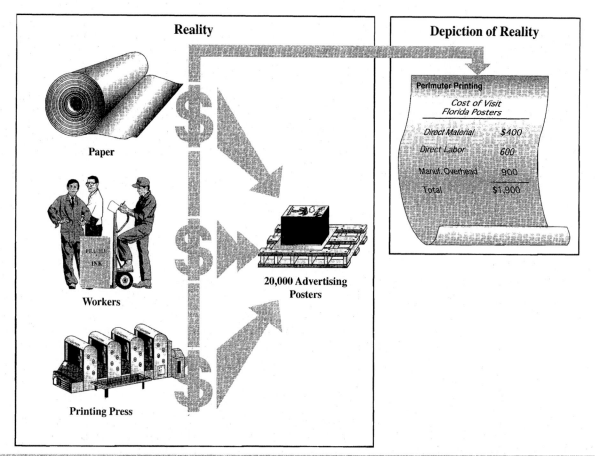

EXHIBIT 3–1   Cost of Advertising Posters

PROCESS COSTING BASICS

process costing   A method of allocating manufacturing cost to products to determine an average cost per unit.

Process costing is a method of allocating manufacturing cost to products to determine an average cost per unit. Companies use process costing when units of production are identical, or almost identical, and each unit of production receives the same manufacturing input as the next. Examples of such products are milk, soda, canned goods, breakfast cereal, household cleaners, motor oil, and gasoline. For example, *Eastman Kodak* uses process costing to determine the cost of the color film it produces.

Under process costing, total manufacturing cost is divided by the number of units produced to arrive at a per-unit cost. For example, if a toothbrush factory makes 2 million toothbrushes and the total production cost is $400,000, then the cost per toothbrush is $0.20, computed as follows:

$$\frac{\text{Total production cost}}{\text{Number of units produced}} = \text{Cost per unit}$$

$$\frac{\$400,000}{2,000,000 \text{ Units produced}} = 0.20 \text{ per unit}$$

The reason this simple method is adequate for a product such as toothbrushes is that each toothbrush is identical to, and consumes the same amount of resources as the next. Accordingly, an average cost per toothbrush provides an accurate unit cost.

Discussion Questions

3–1. Name four products (other than those mentioned in the text) for which process costing would be appropriate.

3–2. Name four products (other than those mentioned in the text) for which job order costing would be appropriate.

3–3. Are any products difficult to classify? List some and explain the difficulty.

The first product costing method we will explore in detail is job order costing. As we cover job order costing, we will also look at the documents manufacturers use to control factory resources and accumulate the cost of products.

◆ JOB ORDER COSTING

We have seen that in job order costing the job may be the production of a single unit or a batch of units. The key is that the units produced for one job are dissimilar from the units produced for another job, and that cost information is gathered for each individual production job.

Keeping track of product cost is not as challenging as it may seem. Particular documents help keep track of the direct material, direct labor, and manufacturing overhead associated with each production job. For example, a company that makes custom boats would keep a list of the direct materials used (amount and cost) and direct labor hours (amount and cost) used to make a boat. It would also keep track of the manufacturing overhead associated with each boat made. The firm would total the direct material, direct labor, and overhead costs to determine the boat's cost.

Managers use a system of documents to track the cost of units produced and to control the costs incurred in the factory. We will review these documents and explore job order costing procedures in the following sections, using *Manta Power Boats* for our example. *Manta Power Boats* is a top-quality, custom boat manufacturer located in Hollywood, Florida. In contrast to production-line boats—boats made in large quantities that are nearly identical—*Manta*'s boats are manufactured to each customer's specifications. Customers select the boat style, interior, engines, construction material, and paint scheme they want. No two boats are alike.

DOCUMENTATION RELATING TO JOB ORDER COSTING

job cost sheet A document that tracks the cost of products and organizes and summarizes the cost information for each job.

When a company uses job order costing, a document called a **job cost sheet** simplifies tracking the costs of products because it organizes and summarizes the cost information for each job. An example of a job cost sheet is shown in Exhibit 3–2.

EXHIBIT 3–2 Job Cost Sheet for *Manta Power Boats*

Manta Power Boats
Job Cost Sheet

Job #: _97384_ Date Promised: _7–11–04_

Customer: _Bill Hudik_ Date Started: _6–2–04_

Product Description: _28 Open Fisherman_

Direct Material			Direct Labor		Manufacturing Overhead			
Date	Req #	Amount	Date	Amount	Base	Rate	Amount	Total
		$		$			$	$
Total		$		$			$	$

Date Completed: _____

The job cost sheet in Exhibit 3–2 lists the manufacturing costs for Job Number 97384, a 28-foot Open Fisherman. An entry is made on the job cost sheet each time direct material, direct labor, and manufacturing overhead costs are incurred in connection with this job. *Manta*'s managers can refer to a job cost sheet any time they need information about the cost of producing a particular boat.

Job cost sheets not only help keep track of the costs of current production, but they also provide historical information that can help managers estimate the cost of future production. For example, if an order is received for a boat similar to one that *Manta* has made in the past, the company's owner, Tom Greco, can look at the first boat's job cost sheet to help estimate how much the next boat will cost.

Now let's look at how these costs are monitored and measured. We begin with an analysis of direct material.

Cost Information for Raw Material

Manufacturers such as *Manta* generally keep close track of raw material cost because it is such a large percentage of manufacturing cost. The raw materials *Manta* needs to build power boats include fiberglass cloth, polyester resin, wood, plastic, aluminum, engines, and much more. Because these materials are so costly, *Manta,* like other manufacturers, does not allow just any employee to buy raw material on behalf of the company. An unqualified employee might buy too much or too little, or they may buy the wrong raw material altogether. In most manufacturing companies, the employee in charge of monitoring the raw material inventory levels makes a request for material. This person may be in charge of the materials storeroom or perhaps is the production supervisor. At *Manta,* Carl Bevans is that person. Carl monitors the amount of material on hand, and when polyester resin is needed, Carl requests that more be purchased. This purchase request comes in the form of a purchase requisition.

purchase requisition A request form that lists the quantity and description of the materials needed.

A **purchase requisition** is a request form that lists the quantity and description of the materials needed. This form helps to control and monitor all material requested to ensure that the company secures the right amount and quality. Copies of the completed purchase requisition are forwarded to *Manta*'s purchasing department and to the accounts payable clerk in charge of paying the company's bills. Exhibit 3–3 shows the completed materials requisition for *Manta Power Boats.*

EXHIBIT 3-3 Purchase Requisition for *Manta Power Boats*

Manta Power Boats	
Purchase Requisition	

Number: 1001

Date: 6-4-04

Name: Carl Bevans

Department: Production Material Stores

Quantity	Description
110 Gal.	Polyester Resin

Signature: Carl Bevans

purchasing department
A specialized department that purchases all the goods required by a company.

purchase order A formal document used to order material from a vendor.

The **purchasing department** is a specialized department that purchases all the goods the company requires. In the purchasing department, trained individuals called purchasing agents or buyers contact several competing vendors (suppliers) to obtain the highest-quality material at the lowest price.

Once the purchasing agent has selected a vendor, the agent issues a **purchase order,** a formal document created to order material from a vendor. The purchase order specifies the quantity, type, and cost of the materials. Copies of the purchase order are distributed to the receiving department, the accounts payable department, and the vendor. A sample purchase order for *Manta Power Boats* is shown in Exhibit 3–4.

EXHIBIT 3–4 Purchase Order for *Manta Power Boats*

Manta Power Boats Purchase Order			

PO #: _06059702_

Vendor: _Pitman Sales Company_	Order Date: _6–5–04_
Address: _8650 S W 132 Street_	Delivery Date: _6–7–04_
Miami, FL 33156	
Phone: _305_ – _256_ – _9558_	

Purchase Requisition #: _1001_   Department: _Prod. Mat. Stores_

Quantity	Description	Unit Cost	Total Cost
110 Gal.	Polyester Resin	$6.00	$660.00

Purchasing Agent: _Bob Pass_

receiving report A document that indicates the quantity of each item received.

When *Manta*'s receiving department receives the material from the supplier, the receiving clerk compares the material received to the purchase order and completes a receiving report. The **receiving report** is a document that indicates the quantity of each item the company receives. It is used to note any differences between the goods ordered and the goods received. Lauren Elsea, *Manta*'s receiving clerk, completes a receiving report for each delivery received as shown in Exhibit 3–5.

Manta Power Boats
Receiving Report

Vendor: *Pitman Sales Company*

Number: 1234

Purchase Order #: *06059702*

Date Received: *6-7-04*

Quantity	Description
110 Gal.	Polyester Resin

Receiving Clerk: *Lauren Elsea*

EXHIBIT 3-5 Receiving Report for *Manta Power Boats*

A copy of the receiving report is sent to the accounts payable department. *Manta*'s accounts payable clerk now has three documents related to the purchase: (1) the purchase requisition, (2) the purchase order, and (3) the receiving report. When the accounts payable clerk receives the vendor's invoice for the materials, information on the invoice is matched to these three documents. If everything is correct, the clerk pays the invoice according to the payment terms.

Discussion Question ●●●●●●●●●●●●●●●●●●●●●●●●●●●●●●●●●

3-4. The accounts payable department verifies that the information on the vendor's invoice matches the purchase requisition, the purchase order, and the receiving report. In each of the following situations, what would the discrepancy indicate?

a. The receiving report conflicts with the vendor's invoice.
b. The purchase order conflicts with the receiving report.
c. The purchase requisition conflicts with the purchase order.

Once the materials have been checked in, they are stored in the materials stores warehouse until they are needed for production. Generally, such storage space is quite secure to protect the raw material from damage and theft.

When material is needed for production, *Manta*'s production manager, Kevin Dunn, completes a materials requisition. The **materials requisition** is a formal request to transfer material from the raw materials storage area to production. This document lists the type of material and the quantity needed. To begin work on the 28-foot Open Fisherman boat for Job Number 97384, Kevin needs polyester resin, so he prepares the materials requisition shown in Exhibit 3-6 to transfer this material into production.

Keep in mind that a *materials requisition* is different from a *purchase requisition*. The purchase requisition is a request to purchase material, whereas the materials requisition is a request by manufacturing personnel to transfer previously purchased material from the materials stores warehouse to production.

materials requisition A formal request for material to be transferred from the raw materials storage area to production.

Manta Power Boats
Materials Requisition

Req #: 98765

Job #: ___97384___

Date: ___6–16–04___

Quantity	Item #	Description	Unit Cost	Total Cost
55 Gal.	PR55X	Polyester Resin	$6.00	$330.00

Issued By: ___Carl Bevans___

Received By: ___Kevin Dunn___

EXHIBIT 3–6   Materials Requisition for *Manta Power Boats*

The materials requisition is a useful tool for accumulating the cost of products. Materials requisitions show how much material is being used, for what purpose, and at what cost. The information from the materials requisitions is transferred to the job cost sheets to show the quantity and cost of material used for each job. Exhibit 3–7 shows how the accounting department at *Manta Power Boats* transfers information from the materials requisition to the job cost sheet for Job Number 97384.

Materials requisitions are also valuable tools for controlling the movement of materials in the factory. Because the movement is documented, it is easier to monitor employees' use of material. This record helps prevent theft, waste, or other inappropriate use of material.

Cost Information for Direct Labor

Once raw material enters the production process, factory workers begin working with it, converting the material into finished product. Remember from Chapter 2 that the cost of the raw material incorporated into the product *and* the labor of production workers increase the value of the goods in work-in-process inventory. Therefore, in accounting records, work-in-process inventory is increased not only by the cost of direct material, but also by the cost of direct labor.

labor time ticket   A document used to track the amount of time each employee works on a particular production job or a particular task in the factory.

Manufacturers use **labor time tickets** to track the amount of time each employee works on a particular production job or a particular task in the factory. Exhibit 3–8 (on page 70) shows a sample labor time ticket for *Manta Power Boats.*

Labor time tickets include information regarding the amount of direct labor associated with each production job. As was the case with the materials requisitions, company accountants transfer cost information from the labor time tickets to the job cost sheet for each job. Exhibit 3–9 (on page 70) shows the transfer of information from the labor time tickets to the job cost sheet for Job Number 97384 at *Manta Power Boats.*

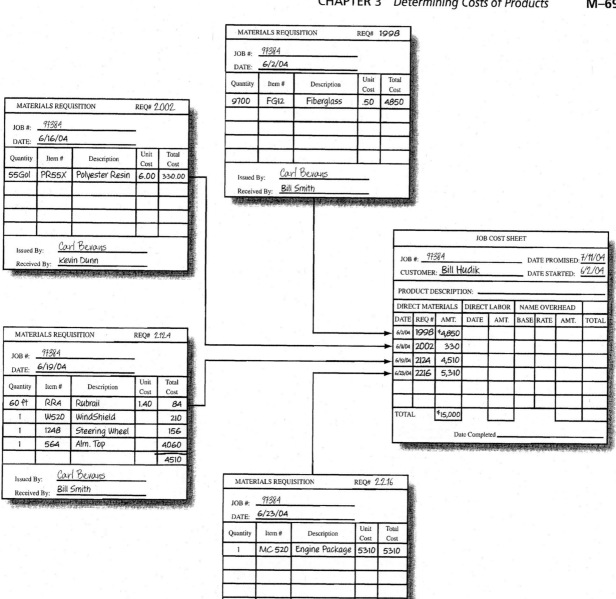

EXHIBIT 3–7 Transfer of Information from Materials Requisitions Form to a Job Cost Sheet

Many companies now use computer technology to make entries on labor time tickets. They issue identification cards to employees that are scanned by a card reader. The employees then enter codes to indicate the duties they are performing and the job or jobs to which these duties relate. Information from the electronic labor time tickets is stored in a computer file and transferred electronically to electronic job cost sheets.

The information from the materials requisitions and labor time tickets makes it easy to trace direct material cost and direct labor cost to individual jobs. Tracing manufacturing overhead is not quite as straightforward. What follows is a general treatment of the topic of manufacturing overhead allocation. The subject is presented in greater detail in the next chapter.

MANUFACTURING OVERHEAD

Manufacturing overhead generally benefits the factory as a whole and therefore all units produced. It is very difficult to accurately assign overhead costs to units produced because the benefit of these expenditures cannot be traced to individual jobs or units of production. Because it can't be traced to individual units, manufacturing overhead

EXHIBIT 3–8 Labor Time Ticket for *Manta Power Boats*

Manta Power Boats
Labor Time Ticket

Employee: *Edward Clark*

Employee Number: *127*   Week Ending: *6-8-04*

Job #	M	T	W	T	F	S	S	Total
97384	8	8	4		8			28
97383			4	8				12

Supervisor: *Seth Levine*   Receiving Clerk: *Edward Clark*

EXHIBIT 3–9 Transfer of Information from Labor Time Tickets to a Job Cost Sheet at *Manta Power Boats*

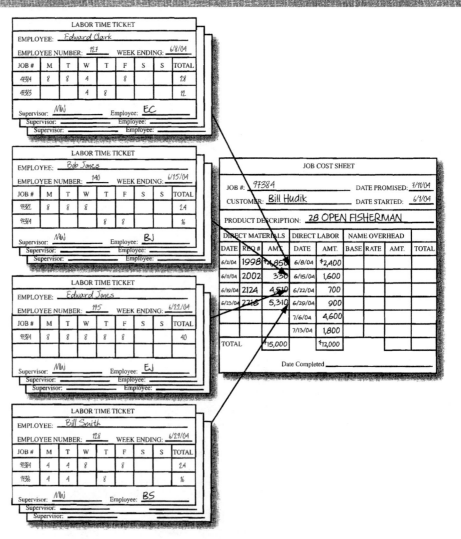

must be allocated to the units produced based on some reasonable basis of distribution. This allocation has traditionally been a two-stage process.

cost pool   An accumulation of the costs associated with a specific cost object.

The first stage is to gather manufacturing overhead into a cost pool. A **cost pool** is an accumulation of the costs associated with a specific cost object—in this instance, all manufacturing overhead costs. The second stage is to allocate the overhead to the units of product produced by way of an application rate. Determining this rate requires the selection of some allocation base. An **allocation base** is some item or activity used to proportionately distribute manufacturing overhead cost to the product being produced. Companies attempt to identify an allocation base that indicates the relative amounts of indirect factory resources consumed in the manufacture of individual units of product.

allocation base   An amount associated with cost objects that can be used to proportionately distribute manufacturing overhead costs to each cost object.

As seen in Exhibit 3–10, generally the cost to be allocated is divided by the total allocation base to determine the amount to allocate per occurrence of the allocation base.

EXHIBIT 3–10   General Formula to Allocate a Cost

$$\frac{\text{Cost to be allocated}}{\text{Total occurences of the allocation base}} = \text{Cost per occurrence of the allocation base}$$

Choosing an appropriate allocation base is critical if a company is to establish a reasonable application rate. One alternative is to use the number of units produced as the allocation base.

If we use the number of units produced as an allocation base, we divide the manufacturing overhead by the number of units to arrive at an amount of overhead per unit. This method of allocation provides an equal amount of overhead cost for each unit of production. When the products a company produces are different from one another, however, a uniform cost per unit is generally inadequate. If the manufacturing overhead for *Manta Power Boats,* for instance, is $75,000 and the company makes five boats, the overhead per boat would be $15,000 for each boat produced, as calculated in Exhibit 3–11 (on page 72).

However, this allocation of $15,000 per boat is not appropriate because the boats are so different from one another. It stands to reason that building a large boat would consume more factory resources and should receive a higher manufacturing overhead cost allocation than a small boat. It would be more accurate to allocate the overhead cost according to the resources consumed instead of allocating the exact same amount to each boat produced.

When we select an allocation base, we should strive to find one that will distribute manufacturing overhead cost fairly. The best allocation base would be one that *causes* the cost that is to be allocated; but, when a single cost pool is used for manufacturing overhead, it is impossible to find a single allocation base that causes all the cost in the pool. Instead, we attempt to find an allocation base that has the second-best attribute for cost allocation—an allocation base that is correlated to the incurrence of cost. Thus, we should try to find an allocation base that is correlated to the amount of overhead resources consumed by each unit produced. Direct labor hours, direct labor cost, and machine hours have traditionally been used as allocation bases.

Taking a closer look at our boat company example, we note that no two boats are identical and manufacturing a larger or more complicated boat would, in all likelihood, consume more manufacturing overhead than a smaller or less complicated boat. As a start, we should find an allocation base that would apportion more overhead to a boat that uses up more factory overhead resources and less to a boat that likely uses less. It seems reasonable that a correlation exists between the amount of direct labor cost and the amount of manufacturing overhead resources consumed to make each boat. Therefore, for our example, we will use *Manta Power Boats'* direct labor cost as the allocation base for manufacturing overhead.

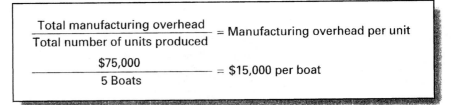

$$\frac{\text{Total manufacturing overhead}}{\text{Total number of units produced}} = \text{Manufacturing overhead per unit}$$

$$\frac{\$75,000}{5 \text{ Boats}} = \$15,000 \text{ per boat}$$

Manufacturing overhead cost

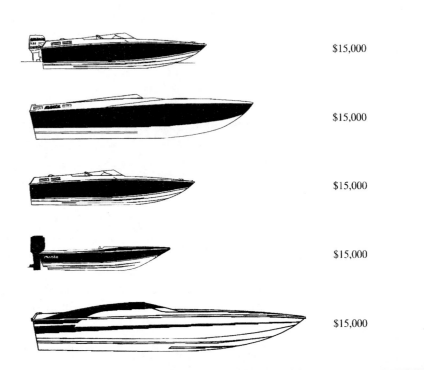

$15,000

$15,000

$15,000

$15,000

$15,000

EXHIBIT 3-11 Allocating Manufacturing Overhead Based on the Number of Units Produced

actual cost system
System in which product cost reflects actual direct material cost, actual direct labor cost, and actual overhead cost.

When we calculate product cost using actual amounts for direct material, direct labor and manufacturing overhead, the system is called an **actual cost system.** Manufacturing overhead is allocated to production based on actual overhead cost and the actual amount of the allocation base. For example, we use actual direct labor to allocate actual manufacturing overhead.

Unfortunately, when we do this, several problems emerge. First, managers must wait until the end of the production period to obtain actual cost information. Another problem is that the overhead allocation rate fluctuates as actual overhead and direct labor fluctuate. The overhead allocation rate will be different for each month if it is calculated using these fluctuating actual amounts. This results in identical products having different cost amounts unless they were made during the same production period.

normal cost system
System in which product cost reflects actual direct material cost, actual direct labor cost, and estimated overhead costs.

predetermined overhead application rate An overhead allocation rate calculated using estimated annual manufacturing overhead cost and the annual estimated amount for the allocation base.

To eliminate these problems, we use estimated annual amounts. In this approach, called a **normal cost system,** product cost reflects actual direct material cost, actual direct labor cost, and estimated manufacturing overhead costs. We use estimated annual manufacturing overhead cost and the estimated annual amount for the allocation base to calculate a **predetermined overhead application rate.**

Manta Power Boats allocates overhead using a normal cost system and has selected direct labor cost as its allocation base. Suppose that *Manta*'s estimated annual overhead is $1 million and estimated annual direct labor cost is $1,250,000. In this case, the predetermined overhead application rate is 80 percent ($1,000,000 ÷ $1,250,000) of direct labor cost. To determine the overhead cost for the 28-foot Open Fisherman boat for Job Number 97384, we must know the direct labor cost. According to the job cost sheet in Exhibit 3–9, the direct labor cost for this job was $12,000. Using the predetermined overhead application rate of 80 percent of direct labor cost, we calculate the manufacturing overhead associated with this job as follows: $12,000 \times 80\% = \$9,600$.

The total cost for Job Number 97384 is $15,000 for direct material, $12,000 for direct labor, and $9,600 for manufacturing overhead. These costs are summarized in the job cost sheet in Exhibit 3–12.

EXHIBIT 3–12   Completed Job Cost Sheet for Job 97384

Manta Power Boats
Job Cost Sheet

Job #: _97384_   Date Promised: _7–11–04_

Customer: _Bill Hudik_   Date Started: _6–2–04_

Product Description: _28 Open Fisherman_

Direct Material			Direct Labor		Manufacturing Overhead			
Date	Req #	Amount	Date	Amount	Base	Rate	Amount	Total
6–2–04	1998	$ 4,850	6–8–04	$ 2,400	DL$	80%	$ 1,920	$
6–16–04	2002	330	6–15–04	1,600	DL$	80%	1,280	
6–19–04	2124	4,510	6–22–04	700	DL$	80%	560	
6–23–04	2216	5,310	6–29–04	900	DL$	80%	720	
			7–6–04	4,600	DL$	80%	3,680	
			7–13–04	1,800	DL$	80%	1,440	
Total		$ 15,000		$ 12,000			$ 9,600	$ 36,600

Date Completed: _7–11–04_

A normal cost system generally is superior to an actual cost system because it smooths out the fluctuations in product cost due to monthly differences in manufacturing overhead cost and the allocation base. In addition, because the predetermined application rate is calculated at the very beginning of the year, there is no need to wait until actual overhead cost information is available to determine product cost.

OVER- OR UNDERAPPLIED OVERHEAD

As you might imagine, the actual amount of manufacturing overhead cost a company incurs will be different than the amount applied to production. In a given month, the actual amount of overhead may be more than the amount allocated, and in another month it may be less. The hope is that the differences will just about balance out during the year. If the amount allocated to production exceeds the actual overhead amount, overhead is **overapplied.** If the amount applied to production is less than the actual overhead amount, overhead is **underapplied.** The under- or overapplication of overhead is monitored during the year, but generally no accounting entries are made to dispense with the amount until the end of the year. In most cases, an accounting entry is made at year end to close the manufacturing overhead incurred, and manufacturing overhead is applied to cost of goods sold. Because the amount of under- or overapplied overhead is generally relatively small, and most product cost ends up in cost of goods sold by year end, closing the overhead accounts to cost of goods sold is adequate for most companies.

overapplied manufacturing overhead When more manufacturing overhead cost is applied to production than actual manufacturing overhead costs incurred.

underapplied manufacturing overhead When less manufacturing overhead cost is applied to production than actual manufacturing overhead costs incurred.

Recall that with process costing we allocate cost to products by dividing the total manufacturing cost of the period by the number of units produced to arrive at an average per-unit cost. The basic method is simple—just add up the direct materials, direct labor, and manufacturing overhead, and divide the total by the number of units produced.

For example, to determine the cost of each tube of toothpaste made in a toothpaste factory, we first determine the total manufacturing cost and then divide it by the number of units produced. Assume that the total manufacturing cost for toothpaste is $100,000 and the total number of units produced is 1 million. The cost per tube is $0.10 ($100,000 ÷ 1,000,000 = $0.10). Because each tube of toothpaste is identical to the next, the $0.10 per unit would be an accurate measure of the cost of each unit. This method works well only if all the units produced are the same, that is, if each unit of production is identical to the next, with the exception of minor variations such as color.

Process costing presents some challenges, however, because there are usually some units of product that are only partially completed at the end of the production period. These partially completed units remain in work-in-process inventory. To reflect reasonably accurate cost amounts, process costing calculations must accommodate situations in which some units are only partially completed.

Like job order costing, process costing is simply a method to help managers determine the cost of products. It provides several key items of information:

1. The number of equivalent units of production
2. The cost per equivalent unit of production
3. The cost of the units that remain in ending work-in-process inventory
4. The cost of the completed units

Understanding how process costing works is a necessary foundation to using product cost information wisely. Let's take a closer look at process costing and the complexities related to beginning and ending work-in-process inventories.

Ross Atkinson Company manufactures decorative pink flamingos. The process to make the decoration is simple. A worker coats the inside of a two-part mold with hot plastic, and then, when the plastic has cooled and hardened, another worker pulls the mold apart and removes the bird figure. The bird is finished by employees who trim off the excess plastic, paint the eyes and beaks, and add the legs.

EQUIVALENT UNITS

Atkinson must calculate the number of units produced before it can determine a cost per unit. For our example, assume that 10,000 flamingos were completed during the production period and another 1,000 were only partially completed at the end of the period. The 1,000 units still in production comprise the work-in-process inventory. Obviously, the 10,000 units completed should be included in the number of units produced, but what about the 1,000 units that were not yet finished? By definition, units in ending work-in-process inventory are incomplete. Thus, it would be inaccurate to assign the same cost per unit to these units as to the completed units. They did, however, require expenditures for direct material, direct labor, and manufacturing overhead to bring them to their present state of completion. So, some cost should be assigned to these units.

The 1,000 flamingos in work-in-process inventory are at various stages of completion. It would be impractical to determine the percentage of completeness for each individual unit of production, so Atkinson calculates an average. In this example, on average, the flamingos in work-in-process inventory are approximately 40 percent complete.

Because the flamingos are only 40 percent complete, Atkinson should not include the entire 1,000 units in the number of units produced. The company is interested in the portion of units complete, which we can calculate by multiplying the number of units in ending work-in-process inventory by their average completion percentage.

Because the 1,000 flamingos are on average 40 percent complete, they are the equivalent of 400 completed flamingos (1,000 × 40% = 400 equivalent units).

In process costing, **equivalent units** are the number of units that would have been completed if all production efforts resulted in only completed units. We can calculate the number of equivalent units by adding the number of completed units to the number of units in ending work-in-process inventory times their percentage complete. In the Atkinson example, the calculations for the number of equivalent units of production, 10,400 units, is as follows:

equivalent units The number of units that would have been completed if all production efforts resulted in only completed units.

	Number of Raw Units		Percent Complete		Equivalent Units
Units completed	10,000	×	100%	=	10,000
Ending work-in-process	1,000	×	40%	=	400
Total equivalent units					10,400

In actual practice, the percentage of completion for direct material is likely different from that of direct labor or manufacturing overhead. Product costs would be more accurate if we used separate completion percentages for direct material, direct labor, and overhead. Manufacturers do, in fact, calculate separate completion percentages to determine equivalent units of production. Such precise calculations greatly complicate process costing, so to keep our example simple and understandable, we will use a single percentage to represent the degree of completion for direct material, direct labor, and manufacturing overhead.

COST PER EQUIVALENT UNIT

Generally accepted accounting principles allow companies to use the first in–first out (FIFO), last in–first out (LIFO), or the average cost flow method for inventories. In process costing, the FIFO and average cost flow methods are popular. The method chosen can have a significant impact on the cost per equivalent unit calculation. For example, the FIFO cost flow method assumes that the cost of the first units added to inventory is the first cost removed from inventory. Thus, the cost of units must be tracked through the inventory records so the first cost in is the first cost out. As you might expect, this complicates process costing calculations. To keep our example simple, we will assume that Ross Atkinson Company uses the average inventory cost flow method to calculate its inventory amounts.

Now let's examine the cost associated with producing the 10,400 equivalent units in Atkinson's flamingo factory. Assume the production costs are $5,408, as summarized in Exhibit 3–13.

EXHIBIT 3-13 Summary of Production Cost

Cost of beginning work-in-process	$ 500
Current month's production cost	4,908
Total production cost	$5,408

To compute cost per unit when the average cost flow method is used in process costing, we divide the total production cost by the number of equivalent units as follows:

$$\frac{\text{Total production cost}}{\text{Equivalent units}} = \text{Cost per equivalent unit}$$

$$\frac{\$5,408}{10,400\ \text{Equivalent units}} = \$0.52 \text{ per equivalent unit}$$

In our example we see that Atkinson's cost per flamingo is $0.52. Now that we know the cost of each unit produced, we can determine the cost of the ending work-in-process inventory and the cost of the units completed. Barring theft or other losses, units of production are either completed and transferred to finished goods inventory, or they remain in ending work-in-process inventory. Therefore, it stands to reason that production costs are associated either with completed units or with units in ending work-in-process inventory.

COST OF ENDING WORK-IN-PROCESS INVENTORY

The cost of ending work-in-process inventory is shown as an asset on the balance sheet. To determine this cost, we multiply the number of equivalent units in ending work-in-process inventory by the cost per unit. For Atkinson, 400 equivalent units are in ending work-in-process inventory and the cost per unit is $0.52. Therefore, the cost of the ending work-in-process inventory is $208 as follows:

Number of Equivalent Units	×	Cost per Unit	=	Cost of Ending Work-in-Process Inventory
400	×	$0.52	=	$208

COST OF COMPLETED UNITS

To determine the cost of completed units, we multiply the number of completed units by the cost per unit. For Atkinson, the 10,000 completed units are multiplied by the $0.52 cost per unit. The cost of the completed units then is $5,200, calculated as follows:

Number of Units	×	Per-Unit Cost	=	Cost of Units Completed and Transferred to Finished Goods Inventory
10,000	×	$0.52	=	$5,200

The cost of completed units is important because initially it becomes part of finished goods inventory. Then, as products are sold, the cost of sold units becomes part of cost of goods sold on the income statement.

Assuming no units are spoiled, stolen, or otherwise lost, the cost of production is either transferred to finished goods inventory or remains as the cost of ending work-in-process inventory. If no units are lost or spoiled during production, the actual units are completed and physically transferred to finished goods or they remain in ending work-in-process inventory. In our Atkinson example, the total manufacturing cost was $5,408. As we see in Exhibit 3–14, part of the total manufacturing cost is transferred to finished goods inventory and the remainder reflects the cost of the units that remain in ending work-in-process inventory.

EXHIBIT 3-14   Flow of Manufacturing Cost

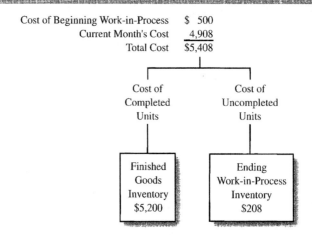

Once the units are completed, their cost remains in finished goods inventory until they are sold. Once they are sold, the cost of the units is transferred to cost of goods sold. Therefore, if Atkinson sells 8,500 of the completed units for $0.75 each, sales would total $6,375 (8,500 × $0.75) and cost of goods sold would be $4,420 (8,500 × $0.52). Therefore, the gross profit on the sale would be $1,955 ($6,375 – $4,420).

As we said at the beginning of this chapter, it is important for managers, such as the sales manager for ***IBM***'s laptop computer division, to know how much products cost. Otherwise, how could managers know which products are profitable and which are not? Whether it is being used to determine the company's cost of goods sold, the cost of inventories shown on the balance sheet, or to help set selling prices and determine the profitability of individual products, accurate product cost information is essential.

Summary ◦

As American manufacturing companies experience increasing competition—both domestic and foreign—accurate costing of the products they produce becomes ever more important. Information about the cost of manufactured product is useful in establishing a selling price for the products, determining cost of goods sold on the income statement, and valuing of inventories on the balance sheet.

The cost of a manufactured product is composed of the cost of direct materials, direct labor, and manufacturing overhead associated with the units of product produced. Although accounting for the cost of direct materials and direct labor is relatively straightforward, determining the amount of manufacturing overhead to include in a unit of manufactured product is more difficult because these costs must be allocated to the units produced.

The traditional method of allocating manufacturing overhead to product uses a two stage process. First, we accumulate overhead cost in a single cost pool. Second, we develop an overhead application rate based on some allocation base. Using that application rate, we then apply manufacturing overhead to production.

Job order costing is one of two main methods used to accumulate product costs and is most appropriate when units or batches of production are unique. Under this method, cost information is gathered for each production job. The second of the two main product costing methods is called process costing and is more appropriate when units of production are identical and each unit of production receives the same manufacturing input as the next.

Regardless of whether the job order costing method or the process costing method is used, the overall purpose of accumulating product costs is to provide managers with the information they need to make many of the decisions necessary to plan and control their operations.

Recording Manufacturing Costs

To fully understand the material in this appendix, it is best if you have a basic understanding of debit and credit accounting procedures including general journal entries and the use of T-accounts. If this is not the case, we suggest that you review Chapter 6 of our financial accounting text or the accounting procedures section of any introductory financial accounting text.

This appendix reviews some of the entries included in the appendix to Chapter 2. The main difference lies in the treatment of manufacturing overhead. In the appendix to Chapter 2, manufacturing overhead was recorded directly in work-in-process inventory. This appendix demonstrates the entries manufacturers use when actual manufacturing overhead costs are recorded in a *manufacturing overhead* account and then allocated to work in process using the allocation procedures described in this chapter.

After completing your work on this chapter appendix, you should be able to prepare basic manufacturing journal entries, including those to record manufacturing overhead allocation.

The recording process for manufacturing costs including overhead allocation involves eight basic types of transactions:

> Transaction 1—Purchasing raw material
> Transaction 2—Using direct material to manufacture goods
> Transaction 3—Using direct labor to manufacture goods
> Transaction 4—Incurring manufacturing overhead costs
> Transaction 5—Allocating manufacturing overhead cost to production
> Transaction 6—Transferring completed units or jobs from work in process to finished goods
> Transaction 7—Selling finished goods
> Transaction 8—Closing manufacturing overhead accounts

To record these transactions, we will use the following general ledger accounts:

1. Cash
2. Raw materials inventory
3. Work-in-process inventory
4. Manufacturing overhead incurred
5. Manufacturing overhead applied
6. Finished goods inventory
7. Accumulated depreciation
8. Accounts payable
9. Sales
10. Cost of goods sold

As we demonstrate the series of journal entries a manufacturer would make, we will analyze each transaction using the following four steps.

1. Determine if and when a transaction occurred, what accounts were affected, which account balances should increase, which should decrease, and by how much.
2. Determine which accounts we should debit and which we should credit.
3. Make the journal entry.
4. Review the entry to ensure it is in proper form and that the debits equal the credits.

The following transactions are based on information from the ***Manta Powerboats*** example presented in this chapter. For example, the first entry records the June 7 purchase of raw material. The remaining entries are based on other transactions that occurred in connection with ***Manta***'s 28 Open Fisherman, Job Number 97384.

Transaction 1: $660 of raw material was purchased on account on June 7, 2004. (See Exhibits 3–4 and 3–5.)

1. This transaction took place on June 7, 2004. The transaction affects the raw materials inventory account and the accounts payable account. We should increase the balances of both these accounts by $660.
2. Because raw materials inventory is an asset account we increase it with a debit. Accounts payable is a liability account so we increase it with a credit.

3. The general journal entry:

```
2004
Jun 7   Raw Materials Inventory              660
             Accounts Payable                            660
        To record the purchase of raw material.
```

4. A final check of the entry reveals that we dated it correctly, made the debit part of the entry first, indented the credit account title, and the dollar amount of the debits equals that of the credits. The entry is fine.

Transaction 2: Based on the information from Materials Requisition in Exhibit 3–6 (on page M–68), Direct material costing $330 was transferred to production on June 16, 2004.

1. This transaction took place on June 16, 2004. The transaction affects the work-in-process inventory and raw materials inventory accounts. We should increase the balance of the work-in-process inventory account by $330 and decrease the balance of the raw materials inventory account by the same amount.

2. Because work-in-process materials inventory is an asset account, we increase it with a debit. Raw materials inventory is also an asset account so we decrease it with a credit.

3. The general journal entry:

```
2004
Jun 16  Work-In-Process Inventory            330
             Raw Material Inventory                     330
        To record the transfer of direct
        material to production for Job 97384.
```

4. A final check of the entry reveals the entry is fine.

Transaction 3: Based on information from the Job Cost Sheet in Exhibit 3–12 (on page M–73), we determine that *Manta* paid $1,600 on June 15 for direct labor for Job Number 97384.

1. This transaction took place on June 15, 2004. Recall that direct labor cost becomes part of work-in process inventory so the transaction affects the work-in-process inventory account. It also affects the cash account. We should increase the balance of the work-in-process inventory account by $1,600 and decrease the balance of the cash account by the same amount.

2. Because work-in-process inventory is an asset account we increase it with a debit. Cash is also an asset account so we decrease it with a credit.

3. The general journal entry:

```
2004
Jun 15  Work-In-Process Inventory            1,600
             Cash                                        1,600
        To record wages paid for direct labor.
```

4. A final check of the entry reveals the entry is fine.

Transaction 4: Let's assume that *Manta*'s actual manufacturing overhead cost for June was $75,000 made up of the following items:

Factory rent paid on June 30	$33,000
Factory utilities paid on June 30	11,000
Indirect labor costs such as factory supervision paid on June 30	23,000
Depreciation on production equipment for June	8,000
Total actual manufacturing overhead cost	$75,000

1. We will assume that these transactions occurred on June 30, 2004. They affect the manufacturing overhead incurred account, the cash account, and the accumulated depreciation account. As you learned in Chapter 2 and in this chapter, manufacturing overhead eventually becomes part of the cost of goods in work-in-process inventory. But when a manufacturer *allocates* cost to production using an overhead application rate, the company initially records actual manufacturing overhead costs in an account called *manufacturing overhead cost incurred* or another similar title. In practice, a manufacturer would make separate entries for each of the manufacturing overhead costs incurred, so recording actual manufacturing overhead costs consists of a series of many entries. For each of *Manta*'s manufacturing overhead costs, we should increase the balance of the manufacturing overhead incurred account. We should decrease the balance of the cash account by $33,000, $11,000, and $23,000 for the paid items. We should increase the balance of the accumulated depreciation account by $8,000 for the depreciation on production equipment.

2. We increase the manufacturing overhead cost incurred account with debits. We decrease the cash account with credits and we increase the accumulated depreciation account with a credit.

3. The general journal entries:

```
2004
Jun  30 Manufacturing Overhead Cost Incurred          33,000
            Cash                                                33,000
         To record factory rent for June.

     30 Manufacturing Overhead Cost Incurred          11,000
            Cash                                                11,000
         To record factory utilities for June.

     30 Manufacturing Overhead Cost Incurred          23,000
            Cash                                                23,000
         To record indirect labor for June.

     30 Manufacturing Overhead Cost Incurred           8,000
            Accumulated Depreciation                             8,000
         To record depreciation on production
         equipment for June.
```

4. A final check of the entries reveals that they are fine.

Transaction 5: According to the Job Cost Sheet in Exhibit 3–12 (on page M–73), *Manta* allocated manufacturing overhead cost of $9,600 to Job 97384. To keep our example simple, we will allocate the entire amount in a single entry dated July 11, 2004.

1. The manufacturing overhead cost allocated to production becomes part of work-in-process inventory so this transaction affects the work-in-process inventory account. Because *Manta* uses a normal cost system, the transaction also affects an account called *manufacturing overhead applied*. When we allocate manufacturing overhead to production in a normal cost system, we use a different account than the one we used when we recorded the actual overhead costs. By using two separate accounts, managers can keep track of both the actual overhead costs incurred and the amount applied to production. We should increase the balances of both the work-in-process and the manufacturing overhead applied accounts by $9,600.

2. We increase the work-in-process inventory account with a debit and the manufacturing overhead applied account with a credit.

3. The general journal entry:

```
2004
Jul 11   Work-In-Process Inventory                     9,600
             Manufacturing Overhead Applied                     9,600
         To record the allocation of manufacturing
         overhead to production.
```

4. A final check of the entry reveals the entry is fine.

Transaction 6: On July 11, 2004, Job Number 97384 was completed and transferred from work-in-process inventory to finished goods. According to the job cost sheet in Exhibit 3–12, the total cost of the job was $36,600.

1. This transaction took place on July 11, 2004. The transaction affects the finished goods inventory account and the work-in-process inventory account. We should increase the balance of the finished goods inventory account by $36,600 and decrease the balance of the work-in-process inventory account by the same amount.

2. We increase the finished goods inventory account with a debit and decrease the work-in-process inventory account with a credit.

3. The general journal entry:

> 2004
>
> Jul 11   Finished Goods Inventory   36,600
>   Work-In-Process Inventory   36.600
>   To transfer Job 97384 from work-
>   in-process inventory to finished goods.

4. A final check of the entry reveals the entry is fine.

Transaction 7:   Assume that on July 12, 2004, *Manta* sold the 28 Open Fisherman boat for cash of $50,000. In other words, Job Number 97384 which cost $36,600 to manufacture was sold for $50,000.

1. This transaction took place on July 12. As we mentioned in Chapter 2, transactions for the sale of goods have two distinct parts. First, this transaction affects the cash and sales accounts, and we should increase the balances of both these accounts by $50,000. Second, the transaction also affects the cost of goods sold and finished goods inventory accounts because the company has delivered merchandise to the customer from its inventory. We should increase the balance of the cost of goods sold account by $36,600, and decrease the balance of the finished goods inventory account by the same amount.

2. We increase the cash account with a debit and the sales account with a credit. We increase the cost of goods sold account with a debit and decrease the finished goods inventory account with a credit.

3. This transaction requires two separate entries or a compound entry. The entries are:

> 2004
>
> Jul 12   Cash   50,000
>   Sales   50,000
>   To record the sale of Job 97384 for cash.
>
>   12   Cost of Goods Sold   36,600
>   Finished Goods Inventory   36,600
>   To record the cost of goods sold for
>   Job 97384.

Or, to accomplish the same changes to the account balances, we can make the following compound entry:

> 2004
>
> Jul 12   Cash   50,000
>   Cost of Goods Sold   36,600
>   Sales   50,000
>   Finished Goods Inventory   36,600
>   To record the cash sale of Job 97384
>   and cost of goods sold.

4. A final check of both sets of entries reveals that the dollar amount of the debits equals that of the credits. You can make either two separate entries or a compound entry for this type of transaction.

Transaction 8:   On December 31, *Manta* closed its underapplied overhead. Assume that the year-end balance in the manufacturing overhead incurred account is $1,091,000 debit and the balance in the manufacturing overhead applied accounts is a credit of $1,072,000. In this case, manufacturing overhead is underapplied by $19,000.

1. This transaction took place on December 31, 2004. Recall from our discussion of this topic in the chapter that the two overhead accounts are usually closed to cost of goods sold, so the closing process affects the manufacturing overhead incurred account, the manufacturing overhead applied account, and the cost of goods sold account. We should decrease the balance of the manufacturing overhead incurred account by $1,091,000 (making the balance zero) and decrease the balance of the manufacturing overhead applied account by $1,072,000 (making the balance zero). We should increase the bal-

ance of the cost of goods sold account by $19,000 (the amount of the under applied overhead).

2. The manufacturing overhead incurred account has a debit balance so we decrease it with a credit. The manufacturing overhead applied account has a credit balance so we decrease it with a debit. We increase the cost of goods sold account with a debit.

3. This transaction can be recorded in a single entry, or two separate entries. The entries are:

2004			
Dec 31	Manufacturing Overhead Applied	1,072,000	
	Cost of Goods Sold	19,000	
	Manufacturing Overhead Incurred		1,091,000
	To close manufactured overhead		
	incurred to cost of goods sold.		

Or, to accomplish the same thing, the following two entries can be made:

2004			
Dec 31	Cost of Goods Sold	1,091,000	
	Manufacturing Overhead Incurred		1,091,000
	To close manufactured overhead		
	incurred to cost of goods sold.		
31	Manufacturing Overhead Applied	1,072,000	
	Cost of Goods Sold		1,072,000
	To close manufactured overhead		
	applied to cost of goods sold.		

4. A final check reveals that the entries are fine.

◆ APPENDIX SUMMARY

Work-in-process inventory is debited to record the transfer of direct material to production and to record direct labor cost. Manufacturing overhead incurred is debited to record the actual amount of manufacturing overhead cost incurred. To apply manufacturing overhead to production, work-in-process is debited and manufacturing overhead applied is credited. If the amount applied to production exceeds the actual overhead amount, overhead is overapplied. If the amount applied to production is less than the actual overhead amount, overhead is underapplied. Manufacturers generally make an accounting entry at year end to close the manufacturing overhead incurred and manufacturing overhead applied accounts to cost of goods sold. When products are completed, finished goods is debited and work-in-process is credited for the cost of those products.

Key Terms ◦

- actual cost system, M–72
- allocation base, M–71
- cost pool, M–71
- equivalent units, M–75
- job cost sheet, M–64
- job order costing, M–62
- labor time ticket, M–68

- materials requisition, M–67
- normal cost system, M–72
- overapplied manufacturing overhead, M–73
- predetermined overhead application rate, M–72
- process costing, M–63

- purchase order, M–66
- purchase requisition, M–65
- purchasing department, M–66
- receiving report, M–66
- underapplied manufacturing overhead, M–73

Review the Facts ◦

A. What are the general characteristics of products for which process costing would be used?
B. What are the general characteristics of products for which job order costing would be used?
C. What is the purpose of a job cost sheet?
D. Which form is sent to a vendor to order materials and supplies?
E. What is the purpose of a receiving report?
F. What is the difference between a purchase requisition and a materials requisition?
G. What is the difference between an actual cost system and an normal cost system?
H. Which type of form is used to track the amount of labor associated with various jobs?
I. List the four key items of information provided by process costing.
J. Define the term *equivalent units* as used in process costing.

Apply What You Have Learned ◦

LO 1: COMPARE PROCESS COSTING WITH JOB ORDER COSTING

3–5. Following is a list of several products.

1. _____ Commercial jetliners
2. _____ Hair spray
3. _____ Oil tankers
4. _____ Breakfast cereal
5. _____ Office buildings
6. _____ Aspirin
7. _____ Dog food
8. _____ Advertising posters
9. _____ Custom kitchen cabinets
10. _____ Gasoline

Required: For each item, indicate whether job order costing (J) or process costing (P) would be the preferred costing method.

LO 4: CALCULATE AND DESCRIBE HOW OVERHEAD COSTS ARE ALLOCATED TO PRODUCTS

3–6. The Jessie Lynne Company manufactures playground equipment. For 2004, budgeted manufacturing overhead is $240,000. Budgeted direct labor is 30,000 hours at a cost of $384,000. Budgeted machine hours are 12,500.

Required:

a. When production begins on January 1, 2004, would it be a good idea for the managers to determine the cost of the manufacturing overhead associated with each swing set produced, or should managers wait for this information until actual overhead cost amounts are available at the end of the year? Explain your reasoning.
b. If we assume that managers need to know the manufacturing overhead cost associated with the playground equipment as soon as the equipment is manufactured, would actual overhead cost information be available when the first few swing sets are made in January? Explain your reasoning.

c. If we assume managers need to know the overhead cost associated with the playground equipment as soon as the equipment is made, and it is too early in the year to have actual overhead cost information, what overhead cost information must be used to allocate overhead cost to playground equipment produced by the company?

d. Determine the overhead application rates based on the following:

1. Direct labor hours
2. Direct labor cost
3. Machine hours

e. If you were asked to help select an allocation base for the Jessie Lynne Company, which of the three used in (d) would you recommend? Which would you not recommend? Why?

LO 4: CALCULATE TRADITIONAL OVERHEAD ALLOCATION

3–7. The Griswald Company allocates manufacturing overhead to production based on direct labor hours. The following information is available for Griswald:

Estimated manufacturing overhead	$403,200
Actual manufacturing overhead	$378,000
Estimated direct labor hours	21,000
Actual direct labor hours	20,000

Required:

a. Compute Griswald's overhead application rate.
b. Assuming that Griswald's overhead application rate is $19, calculate the amount of overhead that should be allocated to production.

LO 7: APPENDIX—PREPARE MANUFACTURING OVERHEAD JOURNAL ENTRIES

3–8. This problem is a continuation of problem 3–7 and requires journal entries based on the overhead calculations for the Griswald Company.

Required: Appendix: Prepare the following journal entries:

1. Record the actual manufacturing overhead. (Use "various accounts" for the credit side of the entry.)
2. Assuming that Griswald's overhead application rate is $19, record the overhead allocated to production.
3. Close the over- or underapplication of overhead.

LO 4: CALCULATE OVERHEAD ALLOCATION

3–9. The Anderson Company allocates manufacturing overhead to production based on machine hours. The following information is available for Anderson:

Estimated manufacturing overhead	$2,000,000
Actual manufacturing overhead	$2,100,000
Estimated machine hours	125,000
Actual machine hours	140,000

Required:

a. Compute Anderson's overhead allocation rate.
b. Assume that Anderson's overhead application rate is $18. Calculate the amount of overhead that should be allocated to production.

LO 7: APPENDIX—PREPARE MANUFACTURING OVERHEAD JOURNAL ENTRIES

3–10. This problem is a continuation of problem 3–9 and requires journal entries based on the overhead calculations for the Anderson Company.

Required: Appendix: Prepare the following journal entries:

1. Record the actual manufacturing overhead. (Use "various accounts" for the credit side of the entry.)
2. Assuming that Anderson's overhead application rate is $18, record the overhead allocated to production.
3. Close the over- or underapplication of overhead.

LO 4: CALCULATE TRADITIONAL OVERHEAD ALLOCATION

3–11. The Nunez Company allocates manufacturing overhead to production based on cost of direct labor. The following information is available for Nunez:

Estimated manufacturing overhead	$3,500,000
Actual manufacturing overhead	3,485,000
Estimated cost of direct labor	1,750,000
Actual cost of direct labor	1,700,000

Required:

    a. Compute the overhead allocation rate for the Nunez Company.

    b. Assume that the overhead allocation rate for Nunez is 190%. Calculate the amount of overhead that should be allocated to production.

LO 4 & 5: CALCULATE TRADITIONAL OVERHEAD ALLOCATION AND DETERMINE THE COST OF PRODUCTS USING JOB ORDER COSTING

3–12. Slater Industries makes custom optical glass equipment. The company began two jobs during January 2004. There was no beginning inventory. The following information is available:

	Job 7	Job 8
Direct material	$7,250	$3,640
Direct labor	$4,251	$5,125
Direct labor hours	212	234

Slater's estimated manufacturing overhead for 2004 is $110,400, and the company estimates that labor force will work 9,200 direct labor hours. Slater applies overhead to production based on direct labor hours.

Required:

    a. Calculate the cost of Job 7.

    b. Calculate the cost of Job 8.

LO 4 & 5: CALCULATE TRADITIONAL OVERHEAD ALLOCATION AND DETERMINE THE COST OF PRODUCTS USING JOB ORDER COSTING

3–13. Willig-Davis Cleaning Equipment began two jobs during March 2004. There was no beginning inventory. The following information is available:

	Job 10	Job 15
Direct material	$14,350	$23,530
Direct labor	$ 7,231	$15,125
Machine hours	124	236

The company estimated manufacturing overhead for 2004 is $307,200, and the company estimates that 4,800 machine hours will be used during the year. Willig-Davis applies overhead to production based on machine hours.

Required:

    a. Calculate the cost of Job 10.

    b. Calculate the cost of Job 15.

LO 4 & 5: CALCULATE OVERHEAD ALLOCATION AND DETERMINE THE COST OF PRODUCTS USING JOB ORDER COSTING—NO BEGINNING WORK-IN-PROCESS INVENTORY

3–14. Williams Company began operations in June 2004. During that month, two jobs were started. The following costs were incurred:

	Job 101	Job 202
Direct material	$3,000	$4,000
Direct labor	6,000	7,000

Factory overhead is applied at 60% of direct labor cost. During the month, Job 101 was completed but not sold. Job 202 is yet to be completed.

Required:

    a. Calculate the cost of the ending work-in-process inventory as of June 30, 2004.

    b. Calculate the cost of the finished goods inventory as of June 30, 2004.

LO 4 & 5: CALCULATE OVERHEAD ALLOCATION AND DETERMINE PRODUCT COSTS AND INVENTORY VALUES USING JOB ORDER COSTING—NO BEGINNING WORK-IN-PROCESS INVENTORY

3–15. Seth Levine Manufacturing began operations in August 2004. During that month, two jobs were started. The following costs were incurred:

	Job 1	Job 2
Direct material	$5,400	$8,900
Direct labor	6,500	9,000

Factory overhead is applied at 50% of direct labor cost. During the month, Job 1 was completed but not sold. Job 2 has not been completed.

Required:

    a. Calculate the cost of the ending work-in-process inventory as of August 31, 2004.

    b. Calculate the cost of the finished goods inventory as of August 31, 2004.

LO 4 & 5: CALCULATE OVERHEAD ALLOCATION AND DETERMINE PRODUCT COSTS AND INVENTORY VALUES USING JOB ORDER COSTING—NO BEGINNING WORK-IN-PROCESS INVENTORY

3–16. Stacy Sexton Manufacturing began operations in September 2004. During that month, two jobs were started. The following costs were incurred:

	Job A	Job B
Direct material	$2,500	$5,000
Direct labor	7,000	9,500

Factory overhead is applied at 120% of direct labor cost. During the month, Job A was completed but not sold. Job B has not been completed.

Required:

    a. Calculate the cost of the ending work-in-process inventory as of September 30, 2004.

    b. Calculate the cost of the finished goods inventory as of September 30, 2004.

LO 7: APPENDIX—PREPARE MANUFACTURING JOURNAL ENTRIES

3–17. This problem is a continuation of problem 3–16. Prepare journal entries based on the calculations in problem 3–16 for Stacy Sexton Manufacturing.

Required: Prepare the following journal entries:

    1. Record direct materials for each job.

    2. Record direct labor for each job.

    3. Record the allocation of manufacturing overhead for each job.

    4. Record the transfer to finished goods of Job A.

LO 4 & 5: CALCULATE OVERHEAD ALLOCATION AND DETERMINE PRODUCT COSTS AND INVENTORY VALUES USING JOB ORDER COSTING—NO BEGINNING WORK-IN-PROCESS INVENTORY

3–18. Mendelsohn Manufacturing began two jobs during the month of January 2004. There was no beginning inventory. The following costs were incurred:

	Job A	Job B
Direct material	$2,000	$3,000
Direct labor	4,000	5,000

Mendelsohn's estimated manufacturing overhead for 2004 is $117,000, and the estimated direct labor cost is $90,000. Mendelsohn applies overhead to production based on direct labor cost. During the month, Job A was completed but not sold. Job B has not been completed.

Required:

    a. Calculate the cost of the ending work-in-process inventory as of January 31, 2004.

    b. Calculate the cost of the finished goods inventory as of January 31, 2004.

LO 7: APPENDIX—PREPARE MANUFACTURING JOURNAL ENTRIES

3–19. This problem is a continuation of problem 3–18. Prepare journal entries based on the calculations in problem 3–18 for Mendelsohn Manufacturing.

Required: Appendix: Prepare the following journal entries:

    1. Record direct materials for each job.

    2. Record direct labor for each job.

    3. Record the allocation of manufacturing overhead for each job.

    4. Record the transfer to finished goods of Job A.

LO 4 & 5: DETERMINE PRODUCT COSTS AND INVENTORY VALUES USING JOB ORDER COSTING—INCLUDES BEGINNING WORK-IN-PROCESS INVENTORY

3–20. Speace Automotive Security converts regular automobiles to armored cars. Each car is custom made to conform to the needs of each individual customer. Modifications may be as minor as the addition of bullet-resistant windows or as extravagant as full armor. The following information is presented for March 2004.

Beginning work-in-process inventory:

Job 2727	Direct material	$24,000
	Direct labor	9,000
	Manufacturing overhead	5,400

Cost for current month:

	Direct Material	Direct Labor	Manufacturing Overhead
Job 2727	$ 8,000	$4,000	$2,400
Job 2728	11,000	6,000	3,600

Job 2727 was completed and sold in March, and Job 2728 was not complete as of March 31.

Required:

    a. What is the cost of the beginning work-in-process inventory for March 2004?

    b. What is the cost of the ending work-in-process inventory for March 2004?

    c. 1. What is the cost of Job 2727?

       2. How would Job 2727 appear on the March 2004 financial statements?

LO 4 & 5: CHALLENGING—CALCULATE OVERHEAD ALLOCATION AND DETERMINE PRODUCT COSTS AND INVENTORY VALUES USING JOB ORDER COSTING—INCLUDES BEGINNING WORK-IN-PROCESS INVENTORY

3–21. Crespin Brothers Equipment Company began two jobs during March 2004. At the beginning of March, Job 303 was the only job in work-in-process inventory. There was no finished goods inventory. The cost in beginning work-in-process inventory for Job 303 consisted of $5,450 in direct material cost, $8,825 in direct labor cost, and manufacturing overhead cost of $7,354. The following information is available for costs added during March:

	Job 303	Job 304	Job 305
Direct material	$4,350	$12,650	$11,300
Direct labor	$8,400	$ 8,125	$ 6,750
Direct labor hours	560	520	480

Job 303 was completed and sold during March. Job 304 was completed but has yet to be sold, and Job 305 remains in production.

    Crespin's estimated manufacturing overhead for 2004 is $225,000, and the company estimates that the labor force will work 18,000 hours during the year. Crespin applies overhead to production based on direct labor hours.

Required:

    a. Calculate the cost of the ending work-in-process inventory as of March 31, 2004.
    b. Calculate the cost of the finished goods inventory as of March 31, 2004.
    c. Calculate the cost of goods sold for March.

LO 4 & 5: CHALLENGING—CALCULATE OVERHEAD ALLOCATION AND DETERMINE PRODUCT COSTS AND INVENTORY VALUES USING JOB ORDER COSTING—INCLUDES BEGINNING WORK-IN-PROCESS INVENTORY

3–22. Greenberg and Son Manufacturing began two jobs during July 2004. At the beginning of July, Job 227 was the only job in work-in-process inventory. There was no finished goods inventory. The cost in beginning work-in-process inventory for Job 227 consisted of $1,500 in direct material cost, $2,000 in direct labor cost, and manufacturing overhead cost of $4,500. Total manufacturing overhead for the month was $16,054. The following information is available for costs added during July:

	Job 227	Job 228	Job 229
Direct material	$ 935	$2,850	$1,300
Direct labor	$1,840	$3,225	$1,975
Direct labor hours	184	310	204

Job 227 was completed and sold during July. Job 228 was completed but has yet to be sold, and Job 229 remains in production.

    Greenberg's estimated manufacturing overhead for 2004 is $180,000, and the company estimates that the labor force will work 8,000 hours during the year. Greenberg applies overhead to production based on direct labor hours.

Required:

    a. Calculate the cost of the ending work-in-process inventory as of July 31, 2004.
    b. Calculate the cost of the finished goods inventory as of July 31, 2004.
    c. Calculate the cost of goods sold for July.

LO 4 & 5: CHALLENGING—CALCULATE OVERHEAD ALLOCATION AND DETERMINE PRODUCT COSTS AND INVENTORY VALUES USING JOB ORDER COSTING—INCLUDES BEGINNING WORK-IN-PROCESS INVENTORY

3–23. Baillie Manufacturing began two jobs during May 2004. At the beginning of May, Job 411 was the only job in work-in-process inventory. There was no finished goods inventory. The cost in beginning work-in-process inventory for Job 411 consisted of $4,000 in direct material cost, $6,000 in direct labor cost, and manufacturing overhead cost of $8,000. Total manufacturing overhead for the month was $22,050. The following information is available for costs added during May:

	Job 411	Job 412	Job 413
Direct material	$2,000	$4,000	$6,000
Direct labor	$2,500	$6,500	$8,500
Direct labor hours	225	570	780

Job 411 was completed and sold during May. Job 412 was completed but has yet to be sold, and Job 413 remains in production.

    Baillie's estimated manufacturing overhead for 2004 is $277,875, and the company estimates that the labor force will work 19,500 hours during the year. Baillie applies overhead to production based on direct labor hours.

Required:

    a. Calculate the cost of the ending work-in-process inventory as of May 31, 2004.
    b. Calculate the cost of the finished goods inventory as of May 31, 2004.
    c. Calculate the cost of goods sold for May.

LO 4 & 5: CHALLENGING—CALCULATE OVERHEAD ALLOCATION AND DETERMINE PRODUCT COSTS AND INVENTORY VALUES USING JOB ORDER COSTING—INCLUDES BEGINNING WORK-IN-PROCESS INVENTORY

3–24. LHE Custom Truck Bodies makes aluminum truck bodies for medium and large trucks. The estimated manufacturing overhead for 2004 is $40,000, and the estimated direct labor cost is $60,000. Manufacturing overhead is applied to production based on direct labor cost.

The following information pertains to truck bodies manufactured during February 2004.

Beginning work-in-process inventory:

Job 101	Direct material	$1,000
	Direct labor	2,000
Job 102	Direct material	750
	Direct labor	1,200

Cost for current month:

Direct material	Job 101	$ 500
	Job 102	1,100
	Job 103	2,300
Direct labor	Job 101	$ 800
	Job 102	1,300
	Job 103	3,200

Job 101 was completed and sold in February and Job 102 was completed, but has not been sold. Job 103 remains in production.

Required:

a. What is the cost of LHE's beginning work-in-process inventory for February 2004?
b. What is the cost of LHE's ending work-in-process inventory for February 2004?
c. 1. What is the cost of Job 101?
   2. How would Job 101 appear on LHE's February 2004's financial statements?
d. 1. What is the cost of Job 102?
   2. How would Job 102 appear on LHE's February 2004's financial statements?

LO 6: DETERMINE THE COST OF PRODUCTS USING PROCESS COSTING—NO BEGINNING OR ENDING INVENTORY

3–25. Daysi's Specialty Food Company makes canned chili. The following cost information is available for March 2004:

Units produced	25,000 units
Direct material cost	$8,000
Direct labor cost	$3,000
Manufacturing overhead costs	$2,000

There were no beginning or ending inventories.

Required:

a. What is the total production cost for Daysi's Specialty Food Company?
b. What is the cost per unit?
c. If the chili sold for $0.82 per can, what is the gross profit for the company?

LO 6: DETERMINE THE NUMBER OF EQUIVALENT UNITS

3–26. The following information relates to the Collins Company for 2005:

	Units	Percent Complete
Units completed	138,000	
Work-in-process at December 31	17,000	50%

Required: Calculate the number of equivalent units of production.

LO 6: DETERMINE THE NUMBER OF EQUIVALENT UNITS

3–27. The following information relates to the Munter Company for June 2004:

	Units	Percent Complete
Units completed	1,850,000	
Work-in-process at June 30	65,000	30%

Required: Calculate the number of equivalent units of production.

LO 6: DETERMINE THE NUMBER OF EQUIVALENT UNITS

3–28. The following information relates to the Holder Company for July 2004:

	Units	Percent Complete
Units completed	72,000	
Work-in-process at July 31	3,000	20%

Required: Calculate the number of equivalent units of production.

LO 6: DETERMINE THE NUMBER OF EQUIVALENT UNITS

3–29. The following information relates to the Mayber Company for May 2004:

	Units	Percent Complete
Work-in-process at May 1	5,000	45%
Units started into production	77,000	
Units completed	70,000	
Work-in-process at May 31	12,000	35%

Required: Calculate the number of equivalent units of production.

LO 6: DETERMINE THE NUMBER OF EQUIVALENT UNITS

3–30. The following information relates to the Strayform Company for August 2004:

	Units	Percent Complete
Work-in-process at August 1	7,000	95%
Units started into production	87,000	
Units completed	87,500	
Work-in-process at August 31	6,500	25%

Required: Calculate the number of equivalent units of production.

LO 6: DETERMINE THE NUMBER OF EQUIVALENT UNITS

3–31. The following information relates to the Golden Company for February 2005:

	Units	Percent Complete
Work-in-process at February 1	22,500	80%
Units started into production	185,000	
Units completed	193,000	
Work-in-process at February 28	14,500	25%

Required: Calculate the number of equivalent units of production.

LO 6: DETERMINE THE COST OF PRODUCTS USING PROCESS COSTING—WITH BEGINNING INVENTORY

3–32. The following information relates to the Smithfield Company for July 2004:

	Units	Percent Complete
Units completed in July	231,000	
Work-in-process at July 31	8,500	40%
Cost information:		
Cost of the beginning work-in-process		$ 7,020
Current month's production cost		$166,436

Required:

    a. Calculate the number of equivalent units of production.
    b. Calculate the cost per equivalent unit of production.
    c. Calculate the cost of the ending work-in-process inventory.
    d. Calculate the cost of the completed units.

LO 6: DETERMINE THE COST OF PRODUCTS USING PROCESS COSTING—WITH BEGINNING INVENTORY

3–33. The following information relates to the Richard Renick Company for 2005:

	Units	Percent Complete
Units completed in 2005	390,000	
Work-in-process at December 31	72,000	20%
Cost information:		
Cost of the beginning work-in-process		$ 14,280
Current year's production cost		$248,580

Required:

    a. Calculate the number of equivalent units of production.
    b. Calculate the cost per equivalent unit of production.
    c. Calculate the cost of the ending work-in-process inventory.
    d. Calculate the cost of the completed units.

LO 6: DETERMINE THE COST OF PRODUCTS USING PROCESS COSTING—WITH BEGINNING INVENTORY

3–34. The following information relates to the Robert Lewis Manufacturing Company for 2004:

	Units	Percent Complete
Units completed in 2004	1,290,000	
Work-in-process at December 31	130,000	70%
Cost information:		
Cost of the beginning work-in-process		$ 40,200
Current year's production cost		$1,768,910

Required:

    a. Calculate the number of equivalent units of production.
    b. Calculate the cost per equivalent unit of production.
    c. Calculate the cost of the ending work-in-process inventory.
    d. Calculate the cost of the completed units.

LO 6: DETERMINE THE COST OF PRODUCTS USING PROCESS COSTING—WITH BEGINNING INVENTORY

3–35. The cost of the work-in-process inventory at January 1 for Ralph Robinson Manufacturing was $7,420. An additional 130,000 units were started into production during the year. The cost of material, labor, and overhead added during the year amounted to $280,680. The units completed and transferred to finished goods totaled 125,000. The ending work-in-process inventory consisted of 15,000 units which were 60% complete.

Required:

    a. Calculate the number of equivalent units of production.
    b. Calculate the cost per equivalent unit of production.
    c. Calculate the cost of the ending work-in-process inventory.
    d. Calculate the cost of the completed units.

LO 6: DETERMINE THE COST OF PRODUCTS USING PROCESS COSTING—WITH BEGINNING INVENTORY

3–36. The cost of the work-in-process inventory at January 1 for Jim Mays Manufacturing was $61,875. An additional 150,000 units were started into production during the year. The cost of material, labor, and overhead added during the year amounted to $1,872,855. The units completed and transferred to finished goods totaled 145,000. The ending work-in-process inventory consisted of 16,000 units, which were 65% complete.

Required:

    a. Calculate the number of equivalent units of production.
    b. Calculate the cost per equivalent unit of production.
    c. Calculate the cost of the ending work-in-process inventory.
    d. Calculate the cost of the completed units.

LO 6: DETERMINE THE COST OF PRODUCTS USING PROCESS COSTING—WITH BEGINNING INVENTORY

3–37. The cost of the work-in-process inventory at January 1 for Hanamura Manufacturing was $119,805. An additional 750,000 units were started into production during the year. The cost of material, labor, and overhead added during the year amounted to $2,627,820. The units completed and transferred to finished goods totaled 790,000. The ending work-in-process inventory consisted of 72,500 units, which were 25% complete.

Required:

    a. Calculate the number of equivalent units of production.
    b. Calculate the cost per equivalent unit of production.
    c. Calculate the cost of the ending work-in-process inventory.
    d. Calculate the cost of the completed units.
    e. Appendix: Prepare a journal entry to transfer the cost of completed goods from work-in-process.

LO 6: DETERMINE THE COST OF PRODUCTS USING PROCESS COSTING—WITH BEGINNING INVENTORY

3–38. The following information relates to the Zhang Manufacturing Company for 2004:

	Units	Cost
Work-in-process at January 1	18,500	$ 35,668
Units started into production	190,000	
Units completed in 2004	187,000	
Work-in-process at December 31	21,500	
Current production cost		$1,873,052

The beginning work-in-process inventory is 20% complete, and the ending work-in-process inventory is 55% complete.

Required:

    a. Calculate the number of equivalent units of production.
    b. Calculate the cost per equivalent unit of production.
    c. Calculate the cost of the ending work-in-process inventory.
    d. Calculate the cost of the completed units.
    e. Appendix: Prepare a journal entry to transfer the cost of completed goods from work-in-process.

LO 6: DETERMINE THE COST OF PRODUCTS USING PROCESS COSTING—WITH BEGINNING INVENTORY

3–39. The following information relates to the Mathias Manufacturing Company for 2004:

	Units	Cost
Work-in-process at January 1	77,000	$ 107,415
Units started into production	602,500	
Units completed in 2004	587,500	
Work-in-process at December 31	92,000	
Current production cost		$2,979,922

The beginning work-in-process inventory is 30% complete, and the ending work-in-process inventory is 80% complete.

Required:

  a. Calculate the number of equivalent units of production.
  b. Calculate the cost per equivalent unit of production.
  c. Calculate the cost of the ending work-in-process inventory.
  d. Calculate the cost of the completed units.
  e. Appendix: Prepare a journal entry to transfer the cost of completed goods from work-in-process.

LO 6: DETERMINE THE COST OF PRODUCTS USING PROCESS COSTING—WITH BEGINNING INVENTORY

3–40. The following information relates to the Heromi Manufacturing Company for 2004:

	Units	Cost
Work-in-process at January 1	13,000	$ 4,368
Units started into production	83,500	
Work-in-process at December 31	7,500	
Units completed in 2004	89,000	
Current production cost		$37,262

The beginning work-in-process inventory is 70% complete, and the ending work-in-process inventory is 20% complete.

Required:

  a. Calculate the number of equivalent units of production.
  b. Calculate the cost per equivalent unit of production.
  c. Calculate the cost of the ending work-in-process inventory.
  d. Calculate the cost of the completed units.
  e. Appendix: Prepare a journal entry to transfer the cost of completed goods from work-in-process.

LO 6: DETERMINE THE COST OF PRODUCTS USING PROCESS COSTING—WITH BEGINNING INVENTORY

3–41. Dunn Electronic Manufacturing Company makes low-cost calculators. The following information is available for January 2004:

	Units	Percent Complete	Cost
Beginning work-in-process inventory	700	40%	$224
Ending work-in-process inventory	900	60%	?
Units completed	12,000 calculators		

Manufacturing cost for January 2004 is $10,659.

Required:

  a. What is the number of equivalent units of production for January 2004?
  b. What is the cost per equivalent unit?
  c. What is the cost of the 900 calculators in the ending work-in-process?
  d. What is the cost of the calculators that were completed during January?

e. If 11,000 of the completed calculators were sold for $1.12 each, what is the gross profit for the Dunn Electronic Manufacturing Company?

f. 1. Do you think there is a benefit for Dunn's managers to know the cost of the calculators that are in ending work-in-process inventory? Explain.

2. Where would the cost of the ending inventory appear on the financial statements?

3. Do you think there is a benefit for Dunn's managers to know the cost of the calculators completed during January? Explain.

4. Where would the cost of the 11,000 sold calculators be found on the financial statements?

5. Where would the cost of the calculators that were completed, but not yet sold be found on the financial statements?

LO 6: DETERMINE THE COST OF PRODUCTS USING PROCESS COSTING—WITH BEGINNING INVENTORY

3–42. The following information is for Suzanne's Volleyball Manufacturing Company for February 2004:

	Units	Percent Complete	Cost
Beginning work-in-process inventory	2,400	80%	$2,304
Ending work-in-process inventory	3,200	50%	

64,000 volleyballs were completed in February. Manufacturing cost for February is $86,256.

Required:

a. What is the number of equivalent units of production for February?

b. What is the cost per equivalent unit for February?

c. What is the cost of the 3,200 volleyballs in the ending work-in-process inventory for February?

d. What is the cost of the volleyballs that were completed during February?

e. If 50,000 of the completed volleyballs were sold for $1.80 each, what is the gross profit for Suzanne's Volleyball Manufacturing Company?

LO 6: DETERMINE THE COST OF PRODUCTS USING PROCESS COSTING—WITH NO BEGINNING INVENTORY

3–43. Valentine's Manufacturing makes candy. During 2005, the company's first year of operations, the company completed 200,000 boxes of candy and incurred direct material cost of $160,800, direct labor cost of $40,200, and manufacturing overhead cost of $60,300. There were 2,000 boxes of candy that were 50% in the production process at the end of the year.

Required:

a. What is the number of equivalent units of production for 2005?

b. What is the cost per equivalent unit of production for 2005?

c. What is the cost of the 2005 ending work-in-process inventory?

d. What is the cost of the boxes of candy that were completed in 2005?

4

Cost Allocation and Activity-Based Costing

Jim Smith is a product manager for the Buck Slade Company, a manufacturer of cutting blades used in knives, scissors and industrial machinery. In recent years, profits at Slade have begun to decline and Jim is trying to improve the situation. Jim's plan is to determine which of the company's products are the most profitable, and then focus the company's sales efforts on these profitable products. He may also discontinue some of the less profitable products to preserve company resources for those that are more lucrative. But how can Jim determine which products to promote and which to discontinue? This is where the company's management accounting system comes into play. Jim calls upon the company's cost accounting department to provide revenue and cost information for the various products the company manufactures. Jim is hoping that he will be able to use the information to make the decisions that will curb the declining profit trend.

After reviewing the revenue and cost information, Jim notices that the reports generally indicate that complex, low volume products are much more profitable than the simple, high volume ones. Jim thinks this is because Slade charges a premium price for its complex products such as their complex cutters. Other manufacturers are not as competitive with these products, so customers seldom complain about the higher prices Slade charges. In fact, the company recently raised its selling price on complex cutters by 10 percent and, although some customers voiced their displeasure about the price hike, not one switched to another supplier. On the other hand, simple, high-volume products, such as Slade's simple trimming blades, are very price competitive. It seems that there are many other manufacturers making this type of product, and price competition is fierce. In fact, Slade must sell many of its simple, high-volume products at cost or even below cost just to be competitive in the marketplace. Exhibit 4–1 shows revenue and cost information for a typical complex, low-volume product and a simple, high-volume product.

EXHIBIT 4–1 Revenue and Cost Report for Representative Complex, Low-Volume, and Simple, High-Volume Products

	Complex Cutters		Simple Trimming Blades	
Sales		$19,500		$53,000
Cost:				
Direct material cost	$4,500		$10,000	
Direct labor cost	1,200		6,000	
Manufacturing overhead cost	8,000		40,000	
Total cost		(13,700)		(56,000)
Gross profit		$ 5,800		$ (3,000)

Slade uses job-order costing, which we demonstrated in Chapter 3, to cost its products. The company's cost accounting department traces direct material and direct labor costs directly to individual products while manufacturing overhead is allocated to various products based on direct labor hours.

Assuming that Exhibit 4–1 is representative of the profitability of the company's simple and complex products, what does the information suggest? Based on the information Jim received from his cost accounting department, what should Jim do to improve company profits? Well, the information clearly indicates that Jim should focus the company's efforts on shifting production and sales toward complex, low-volume products and that he should probably discontinue producing and selling simple, high-volume products. Management accounting information seems to make Jim's decisions easier because it is, in effect, telling Jim what to do. But is it telling him the right thing to do?

As we learned in Chapter 3, direct material and direct labor cost can be traced directly to individual products or batches of products. Manufacturing overhead, however, is another matter. Because manufacturing overhead is an indirect cost and benefits more than one product, it is difficult if not impossible to determine the true overhead cost associated with individual products produced. For example, it is easy for **Wilson Sporting Goods** to trace the direct material and direct labor costs to a batch of its basketballs, but it is nearly impossible for the company to trace overhead costs such as the cost of factory insurance, electricity, and production machine depreciation to individual batches of production.

The resources included in manufacturing overhead are an important component of manufacturing products. Even though their cost cannot easily be traced to individual units of production, manufacturing overhead resources are all necessary to produce products, and therefore, their cost should be included in the cost of products produced. The problem is, however, that the cost of manufacturing overhead resources and activities cannot be traced directly to the units of product produced. Their cost, therefore, must be allocated to production.

Consider the cost of factory lighting, for example. As units of product make their way through the production process, the factory lights are illuminated and lighting cost is incurred. Without light, it would be impossible for workers to manufacture the products, so it follows that a certain amount of the cost for lighting should be included in the cost of each unit of product manufactured. Unfortunately, when the power company sends the bill at the end of the month, there is no breakdown of the lighting cost for each unit of product. The bill shows only the total cost of electricity used, say $10,000. The manufacturer has to determine how to allocate some portion of the lighting cost to each unit produced. **Manufacturing overhead allocation** is a process of assigning or allotting an amount of manufacturing overhead cost to each unit of product produced using some reasonable basis of distribution.

manufacturing overhead allocation The process of assigning or allotting an amount of manufacturing overhead cost to each unit of product produced based on some reasonable basis of distribution.

Learning Objectives

After completing your work on this chapter, you should be able to do the following:

1. Describe how overhead costs are traditionally allocated to products.
2. Describe how overhead costs are allocated to products using activity-based costing.
3. Define the term *cost driver*.
4. Compare and contrast activity-based costing with traditional overhead allocation.
5. Describe how activity-based costing helps improve product cost accuracy.
6. Describe when activity-based costing will result in more accurate product costs.
7. Describe how activity-based costing helps companies to control costs.
8. Compare the complexity and cost of activity-based costing with traditional overhead allocation.

actual cost system
System in which product cost reflects actual direct material cost, actual direct labor cost, and actual overhead cost.

normal cost system
System in which product cost reflects actual direct material cost, actual direct labor cost, and estimated overhead costs.

predetermined overhead application rate An overhead allocation rate calculated using estimated annual manufacturing overhead cost and the annual estimated amount for the allocation base.

As we discussed in Chapter 3, when we allocate overhead using actual amounts for direct material, direct labor, and manufacturing overhead, the system is called an **actual cost system.** Unfortunately, using the actual amount of overhead and the actual amount of the allocation base to allocate manufacturing overhead has several problems. First, managers must wait until the end of the accounting period to receive actual cost information. Another problem with using actual amounts to allocate overhead is that the overhead allocation rate would fluctuate as actual overhead and the allocation base fluctuate. The overhead allocation rate will be different for each period if it is calculated using these fluctuating actual amounts. This will result in identical products having different cost amounts unless they were made during the same production period.

To eliminate these problems we use estimated annual amounts. In this approach, called a **normal cost system**, product cost reflects actual direct material cost, actual direct labor cost, and estimated overhead costs. Estimated annual manufacturing overhead cost and the annual estimated amount for the allocation base are used to calculate a **predetermined overhead application rate.**

◆ TRADITIONAL MANUFACTURING OVERHEAD ALLOCATION

cost pool An accumulation of the costs associated with a specific cost object.

Overhead allocation has traditionally been a two-stage process. The first stage is to gather overhead cost into a cost pool. A **cost pool** is an accumulation of the costs associated with a specific cost object. Traditionally, the cost of manufacturing overhead has been gathered into one large cost pool, including all manufacturing costs except for direct material and direct labor.

The second stage is to assign the manufacturing overhead cost gathered in the pool to units of product manufactured. Manufacturers attempt to allocate the amount of manufacturing overhead cost that corresponds to the overhead resources consumed to make the product. For example, if $1,000 of manufacturing overhead resources were consumed to manufacture a pool table, then, ideally, $1,000 should be allocated to that pool table and shown on the pool table's cost reports. (See Exhibit 4–2.)

EXHIBIT 4–2 Overhead Cost and Related Factory Resources Used

Manufacturing Overhead Resources Used To Make a Pool Table:		Manufacturing Overhead Cost Report For the Pool Table
• Factory Supplies		• Cost of Factory Supplies Used
• Factory Supervision		• Cost of Factory Supervision Used
• Factory Lighting		• Cost of Factory Lighting Used
• Production Equipment		• Cost of Production Equipment Used
• Materials Handling		• Cost of Materials Handling Used
• Setting up Production Equipment		• Cost of Setting up Production Equipment
• Product Quality Testing		• Cost of Product Quality Testing Done
		• Total $1,000

allocation base An amount associated with cost objects that is used to proportionately distribute manufacturing overhead costs to each cost object.

Because it is impractical if not impossible for managers to know the exact cost of the manufacturing overhead resources used to make each unit of product, an equitable basis for cost allocation must be determined.

An **allocation base** is an amount associated with cost objects that is used to proportionately distribute manufacturing overhead costs to each cost object. The traditional approach to allocating these costs to units produced is to identify some item, activity, or cost to serve as an indicator of the relative amounts of indirect factory resources used to make each unit of production. That is, to find some other item, activity, or cost that is correlated to the consumption of manufacturing overhead resources, and then use it as the allocation base. Direct labor hours, direct labor cost, and machine hours are common traditional manufacturing overhead allocation bases.

It seems logical that a larger unit of production would require the use of more factory resources than a smaller unit of production, which may mean more direct labor, direct materials, machine time, or some combination of these. The idea behind using an allocation base such as direct labor hours is that if a unit of product requires a large number of direct labor hours, it follows that its manufacture would probably use a large amount of overhead resources. So the relative amount of direct labor hours may be a good indication of the relative amount of manufacturing overhead resources used to make the product. If it took a lot of labor hours to make a particular product, it probably took a lot of overhead resources, too.

As an example, we will take a closer look at the Buck Slade Company and examine how the company's accounting department determined the manufacturing overhead costs presented in Exhibit 4–1. Slade uses direct labor hours as the allocation base for manufacturing overhead. Assume Slade estimates that its annual manufacturing overhead will be $1 million, and direct labor hours are expected to total 10,000 for the year. Slade can express the relationship between these two costs by dividing the $1 million manufacturing overhead by the 10,000 direct labor hours. Notice that we are dividing the cost we wish to allocate (the $1 million manufacturing overhead) by the allocation base (the 10,000 direct labor hours). The result is the company's overhead application rate. Slade will allocate overhead cost to the units of manufactured product at a rate of $100 per direct labor dollar as follows:

$$\frac{\text{Estimated annual manufacturing overhead cost}}{\text{Estimated annual allocation base}} = \text{Overhead application rate}$$

$$\frac{\$1,000,000}{10,000 \text{ Direct labor hours}} = \$100 \text{ per direct labor hour}$$

What this means is that for every direct labor hour it takes to manufacture a product, $100 of manufacturing overhead cost will be added to the product's cost. A product that requires little direct labor will receive a small allocation for manufacturing overhead. The total direct material cost, direct labor cost, and the total allocated manufacturing overhead cost are then added together to determine the cost of the manufactured product.

As an example, let's calculate the cost of the two Buck Slade products mentioned earlier in the chapter. Assume that it takes 80 direct labor hours to make the 15,000 complex cutters and 400 direct labor hours to make the 100,000 simple trimming blades. Based on the fact that the complex cutters required a total of 80 direct labor hours, the manufacturing overhead allocation would be $8,000, calculated as follows:

Direct labor hours	×	Overhead application rate	=	Total overhead allocation
80	×	$100	=	$8,000

The 100,000 simple trimming blades required 400 direct labor hours so the manufacturing overhead allocation for them would be $40,000, calculated as follows:

Direct labor hours	×	Overhead application rate	=	Total overhead allocation
400	×	$100	=	$40,000

Using the total sales, the direct material cost, and the direct labor cost included in Exhibit 4–1 along with the manufacturing overhead allocations we have calculated, we can calculate the gross profit for each of the two Slade products. (See Exhibit 4–3.)

	Complex Cutters		Simple Trimming Blades	
Sales		$19,500		$53,000
Cost:				
Direct material cost	$4,500		$10,000	
Direct labor cost	1,200		6,000	
Manufacturing overhead cost	8,000		40,000	
Total cost		(13,700)		(56,000)
Gross profit		$ 5,800		$(3,000)

EXHIBIT 4–3 Summary of Gross Profit Calculations for Buck Slade Products Using Traditional Manufacturing Overhead Allocation

Exhibit 4–3 presents the exact same information that we presented in the opening to this chapter. Only this time we know how the company calculated the manufacturing overhead cost for each of the products. Note that the complex cutter—a complex, low-volume product—earned a gross profit of $5,800, while the simple trimming blade—a simple, high-volume product—had a negative gross profit of $3,000.

The manufacturing overhead allocation technique we just examined uses a single manufacturing overhead cost pool and a single, plant-wide application rate. Virtually all manufacturers in the United States used this method until the mid-1980s, and many still do today.

During the mid-1980s, some companies realized that a plant-wide application rate has significant weaknesses. The difficulty is that manufacturing overhead costs are typically caused by (or related to) many different activities—the activity that drives one cost may be totally different from the activity that drives another cost. To use one activity (such as direct labor hours) as the allocation base for applying *all* manufacturing overhead cost will likely cause some products to be overcosted and others to be undercosted. For example, assume that a company uses direct labor hours to allocate all manufacturing overhead cost, and its factory has five machines, two of which use significant amounts of water for cooling. The overhead cost per direct labor hour will include an amount for cooling water. The amount will be allocated to products whether they are produced on a machine that requires cooling water or not. Therefore, products that are produced on machines that do not require cooling water will be overcosted. Also, because some of the cost of cooling water is allocated to products produced on the machines that do not require cooling water, products produced on machines that do require cooling water will be undercosted.

In an attempt to improve the accuracy of their overhead allocation, some companies now study their business activities and the costs these activities cause. The result is a costing method that provides more realistic and reasonable cost for units of manufactured product. This new method is called activity-based costing.

◆ ACTIVITY-BASED COSTING

activity-based costing (ABC) A technique to allocate indirect cost to cost objects based on activities that cause the cost to occur. It is more accurate than traditional cost allocation.

Activity-based costing (ABC) is a more accurate technique of allocating indirect cost to cost objects based on activities that cause the cost to occur.

Activity-based costing (ABC) improves on traditional overhead allocation in two ways. First, an analysis of activities, costs, and the causes of cost may result in the reclassification of certain costs from manufacturing overhead to direct material, direct labor, or some other direct cost classification. That is, some costs traditionally viewed as indirect can actually be traced directly to units of product and need not be allocated. This contributes to a more accurate unit cost because less cost remains to be allocated. Second, ABC allocates manufacturing overhead more accurately. ABC achieves a more accurate allocation by breaking total manufacturing overhead down into small cost pools and then allocating them based on activities that cause the costs to occur. Rather than allocating all manufacturing overhead to products using one plant-wide allocation base, ABC allocates various overhead costs using cost drivers. A **cost driver** is an activity used as an allocation base for a particular cost pool that actually *causes* the cost to occur. Therefore, unlike traditional overhead allocation that allocates cost using allocation bases that are believed to be correlated to the incurrence of cost, ABC allocates costs using activities that cause cost. This results in more accurate cost allocation.

◆ DETERMINING PRODUCT COST USING ABC

As an example of how companies determine product costs when they use ABC, let's revisit the Buck Slade Company. Recall that Buck Slade had total estimated annual manufacturing overhead cost of $1 million and 10,000 direct labor hours. To allocate manufacturing overhead costs using ABC we need some additional information. Once we gather the information we will proceed step by step to employ ABC. (See Exhibit 4–4.)

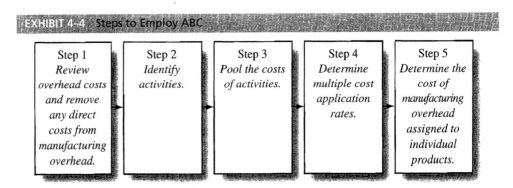

EXHIBIT 4–4 Steps to Employ ABC

| Step 1 *Review overhead costs and remove any direct costs from manufacturing overhead.* | Step 2 *Identify activities.* | Step 3 *Pool the costs of activities.* | Step 4 *Determine multiple cost application rates.* | Step 5 *Determine the cost of manufacturing overhead assigned to individual products.* |

STEP 1: *REVIEW OVERHEAD COSTS AND REMOVE ANY DIRECT COSTS FROM MANUFACTURING OVERHEAD*

Companies usually establish an activity-based cost system to assign cost to products more accurately. When manufacturing overhead includes costs that can actually be traced to individual products, removing these costs from overhead and treating them as direct product cost is a good first step in improving product cost accuracy. For example, when it is determined that indirect material and indirect labor costs included in overhead can actually be traced to individual products, these costs should be removed from manufacturing overhead and treated as direct material or direct labor. By the same token, if the benefit of a particular overhead cost other than indirect material or indirect labor can be traced to an individual product, that cost should be removed from overhead and treated as a direct cost of the product benefited. Let's say **Honeywell** uses a particular machine solely to manufacture a circuit board for one of its government contracts. The cost associated with the machine should not be included in manufacturing overhead, but rather should be treated as a direct cost of manufacturing the circuit boards. Further, if **Honeywell** uses a particular instrument solely to test these same circuit boards, the cost of the instrument should not be included in manufacturing overhead but should also be treated as a direct cost of manufacturing the circuit boards.

With respect to our Buck Slade example, assume that the company has analyzed its manufacturing overhead and has reclassified $220,000 of the $1 million in manufacturing overhead to direct cost because the company found that, using modern technology, it could readily trace those costs directly to units of product as they are produced.

STEP 2: *IDENTIFY ACTIVITIES*

Once any direct costs have been removed from overhead, the next step is to determine business activities. For example, depending on the company, manufacturing activities may include designing how products will be manufactured, setting up production machinery, moving raw material into production, manufacturing product, testing for product quality, and moving the goods in production from one manufacturing station to the next and then to finished goods. Manufacturing activities will vary from one company to the next. Exhibit 4–5 lists the estimated activities for the Buck Slade Company.

Number of parts	750,000
Number of production runs	25
Number of machine hours	2,000
Number of components tested	25,000
Number of direct labor hours	10,000

EXHIBIT 4-5 Estimated Annual Activities for the Buck Slade Company

STEP 3: *POOL THE COSTS OF ACTIVITIES*

In this step the cost of the resources consumed by each activity should be determined. Once determined, cost pools are formed for each activity.

Slade determines the cost of the resources consumed by each activity and groups the cost into a cost pool for each. Recall that Slade reclassified $220,000 from manufacturing overhead to direct cost. The remaining $780,000 manufacturing overhead cost consists of the items listed in Exhibit 4–6.

EXHIBIT 4-6 Remaining Overhead for Buck Slade Company

Costs associated with activities listed in Step 2:	
Materials purchasing and handling cost	$ 75,000
Production engineering and design	60,000
Production machine setup	40,000
Production machine depreciation	300,000
Production machine maintenance	50,000
Quality testing	100,000
Costs not associated with the activities listed in Step 2:	
Plant security	25,000
Plant supervision	70,000
Building maintenance	10,000
Factory supplies	20,000
Factory insurance	30,000
Total manufacturing overhead	$780,000

STEP 4: *DETERMINE MULTIPLE COST APPLICATION RATES*

Instead of using one plant-wide application rate and a single allocation base, ABC uses several application rates. Basically, this is done by dividing the amount of each cost pool determined in Step 3 by its corresponding activity from Step 2. When an activity is used to allocate overhead cost it is called a cost driver. As we have already mentioned, a cost driver is an activity that causes a cost that is used to allocate that cost.

Sometimes it is impossible or impractical to determine cost drivers for every overhead cost. This is because it may be difficult to determine the activity that causes a particular cost, or perhaps the activity that causes a cost is not really related to products or is not otherwise suitable to be used as a cost driver. For example, consider the cost of maintenance of the factory building. A fresh coat of paint on the cafeteria walls is not related to any product that the factory produces. For such situations, the company will probably continue using a traditional allocation base such as direct labor hours, direct labor cost or machine hours.

Costs should be paired with activities that cause the cost to occur. In other words, companies should pair costs with cost drivers. In the Buck Slade example, one of the logical pairs would be production machine set-up cost and the number of production runs. This is because production runs cause set-up cost to occur. Think about it. If the company had no production runs, there would be no need to set up production equipment and therefore, no set-up cost would occur. On the other hand, if the company has many production runs, the production machines must be set up for each run, so set-up cost would be substantial.

As we have already mentioned, sometimes it is impossible or impractical to find cost drivers for each and every overhead cost. For Slade, we will use direct labor hours to allocate these costs. Exhibit 4–7 shows our pairing of cost pools with their respective cost drivers.

EXHIBIT 4–7 Pairing of Cost Pools and Cost Drivers for The Buck Slade Company

Overhead Cost Pool	Cost Driver
Pool 1 Materials Purchasing and Handling Cost	Number of Parts
Pool 2 Production Engineering and Design Cost and Production Machine Set-up Cost	Number of Production Runs
Pool 3 Production Machine Depreciation and Production Machine Maintenance	Number of Machine Hours
Pool 4 Quality Testing	Number of components tested
Pool 5 Remaining Manufacturing Overhead Costs	Because it is impossible or impractical to determine cost drivers for these remaining costs, a traditional allocation base, direct labor hours, will be used.

As we have already mentioned, the basic calculation to allocate manufacturing overhead is to divide the total estimated overhead amount by the total estimated allocation base. This basic calculation is also used for ABC. Therefore, to calculate the application rate for an individual cost pool for Slade, we divide the estimated annual cost of the cost pool by the estimated number of occurrences of its cost driver.

$$\frac{\text{Estimated annual overhead cost}}{\text{Estimated annual occurances of the cost driver}} = \text{Overhead application rate}$$

Exhibit 4–8 shows the overhead application rate calculations for Slade.

Based on the calculations in Exhibit 4–8 we know that for every part added to a unit of product, $0.10 of manufacturing overhead cost is added to the product as well (Pool 1). Every time a production run is made, $4,000 is added to the cost of the products in that production run (Pool 2). For every machine hour devoted to the unit of product, $175 of manufacturing overhead is added; and for every component tested, $4 of manufacturing overhead is added (Pools 3 and 4). For every hour of direct labor, $15.50 of manufacturing overhead is added to the cost of the product (Pool 5).

STEP 5: *DETERMINE THE COST OF MANUFACTURING OVERHEAD ASSIGNED TO INDIVIDUAL PRODUCTS*

In this step we determine the manufacturing overhead for each product by multiplying the application rate determined in Step 4 by the number of occurrences of the cost

Manufacturing Overhead Pool	Cost Driver Allocation Base	Application Rate Based on Occurrence of the Cost Driver
POOL 1 Materials purchasing and handling cost	Number of parts	$75,000 \div 750,000 =$ $0.10 per part
POOL 2 Production engineering and design Production machine setup	Number of production runs	$100,000 \div 25 =$ $4,000 per prod. run
POOL 3 Production machine depreciation Production machine maintenance	Number of machine hours	$350,000 \div 2,000 =$ $175 per machine hour
POOL 4 Quality testing	Number of components tested	$100,000 \div 25,000 =$ $4 per comp. tested
POOL 5 Plant security Plant supervision Building maintenance Factory supplies Factory insurance	Number of direct labor hours	$155,000 \div 10,000 =$ $15.50 per direct labor hour

EXHIBIT 4-8   Overhead Application Rate Calculations for the Buck Slade Company

driver for each product. To allocate Slade's manufacturing overhead cost, we need to know more about the activities required to manufacture each of the example products. Exhibit 4–9 shows information for the two Buck Slade products mentioned earlier in this chapter.

	Complex Cutters	Simple Trimming Blades
Number of units produced	15,000	100,000
Number of parts per unit	3	1
Number of production runs	1	1
Number of machine hours	16	48
Number of components tested	1,000	100
Number of direct labor hours	80	400

EXHIBIT 4-9   Information for Buck Slade's Complex Cutters and Simple Trimming Blades

As Exhibit 4–9 shows, each complex cutter is made of three parts. In addition, it takes 16 machine hours and 80 direct labor hours to produce the 15,000 cutters. Also, during production a sample consisting of 1,000 cutters is tested for sharpness. To calculate the overhead cost allocation for the cutters, we will multiply each activity by the corresponding application rate. Exhibit 4–10 shows the manufacturing overhead cost allocated to the cutters under ABC.

Manufacturing Overhead Pool	Cost Allocation
POOL 1 Materials purchasing and handling cost	$15{,}000 \times 3 \times \$0.10 = \$4{,}500$
POOL 2 Production engineering and design Production machine setup	$1 \times \$4{,}000 = \$4{,}000$
POOL 3 Production machine depreciation Production machine maintenance	$16 \times \$175 = \$2{,}800$
POOL 4 Quality testing	$1{,}000 \times \$4 = \$4{,}000$
POOL 5 Plant security Plant supervision Building maintenance Factory supplies Factory insurance	$80 \times \$15.50 = \$1{,}240$
Total manufacturing overhead for 15,000 cutters Manufacturing overhead per cutter ($16,540 ÷ 15,000)	$\underline{\$16{,}540}$ $\$1.10$ (Rounded)

EXHIBIT 4–10 ABC Manufacturing Overhead Cost Allocation for Complex Cutters

Notice that the $16,540 of overhead allocated for the complex cutters under ABC is more than double the $8,000 allocated when a traditional allocation method is used. The cutters are not more expensive to make when ABC is used; rather, the amount of overhead allocated to the cutters under ABC more accurately represents the true cost of producing the cutters.

Now let's turn our attention to Slade's 100,000 simple trimming blades. As Exhibit 4–9 (on page M–103) shows, each blade is made of one part. In addition, it takes 48 machine hours and 400 direct labor hours to produce the 100,000 blades. Finally, a sample of 100 blades is tested for sharpness. Exhibit 4–11 shows the manufacturing overhead cost allocated to the blades under ABC.

Notice that the manufacturing overhead allocated to the simple trimming blades assuming traditional overhead allocation was used is $40,000 while the overhead allocated under ABC is only $29,000.

Discussion Questions

4–1. Why is the amount of overhead allocated to the simple trimming blades under ABC different from what it was under traditional overhead allocation?

4–2. Which overhead allocation do you think more accurately reflects the cost of the manufacturing overhead resources consumed to make the simple trimming blades? Why?

With the manufacturing overhead amounts we have determined, we can calculate the gross profit for each of the two Slade products under ABC. Exhibit 4–12 shows a comparison of the gross profit calculations for Buck Slade using traditional overhead allocation and ABC.

Manufacturing Overhead Pool	Cost Allocation
POOL 1 Materials purchasing and handling cost	$100{,}000 \times 1 \times \$0.10 = \$10{,}000$
POOL 2 Production engineering and design Production machine setup	$1 \times \$4{,}000 = \$4{,}000$
POOL 3 Production machine depreciation Production machine maintenance	$48 \times \$175 = \$8{,}400$
POOL 4 Quality testing	$100 \times \$4 = \$400$
POOL 5 Plant security Plant supervision Building maintenance Factory supplies Factory insurance	$400 \times \$15.50 = \$6{,}200$
Total manufacturing overhead for the 100,000 blades	$\underline{\underline{\$29{,}000}}$
Manufacturing overhead per blade ($\$29{,}000 \div 100{,}000$)	$\underline{\underline{\$\quad.29}}$

EXHIBIT 4-11   ABC Manufacturing Overhead Cost Allocation for Simple Trimming Blades

EXHIBIT 4-12   Summary of Gross Profit Calculations for Buck Slade Products Using Traditional Overhead Allocation and ABC

Costs Using Traditional Overhead Allocation:

	Complex Cutters		Simple Trimming Blades	
Sales		$19,500		$53,000
Cost:				
Direct material cost	$4,500		$10,000	
Direct labor cost	1,200		6,000	
Manufacturing overhead cost	8,000		40,000	
Total cost		(13,700)		(56,000)
Gross profit		$ 5,800		$ (3,000)

Costs Using ABC for Overhead Allocation:

	Complex Cutters		Simple Trimming Blades	
Sales		$19,500		$53,000
Cost:				
Direct material cost	$ 4,500		$10,000	
Direct labor cost	1,200		6,000	
Manufacturing overhead cost	16,540		29,000	
Total cost		(22,240)		(45,000)
Gross profit		$ (2,740)		$ 8,000

In Exhibit 4–12 the cost information for Slade using traditional overhead allocation shows that the complex cutters are quite profitable, while the simple trimming blades are not. But there is a catch. Although the information is prepared using accepted and popular management accounting techniques, it is terribly flawed. This is because when a single plant-wide overhead application rate is used, costs are allocated to products whether they consume a particular overhead resource or not. On the other hand, our ABC calculations show that in reality, the simple, high-volume products are more profitable than the complex, low-volume ones. This is because ABC results in more accurate product costs because it allocates cost to products based on factory resources used to make the product.

If Jim bases his decisions on the flawed costs achieved using traditional overhead allocation, Slade's profits will disappear and losses will skyrocket. The trouble with the cost information under traditional overhead allocation lies in the fact that allocating manufacturing overhead cost to production using a single allocation base does not do a good job of accurately assigning manufacturing overhead cost to the products that consume the factory's overhead resources.

When ABC is used, products are more realistically charged for the overhead resources they use. For example, if one product requires more inspections than another, as is the case with the complex cutters, because the allocation is based on the use of the resource (the number of inspections, for example), the product is charged more. Because products are allocated cost based on the overhead resources they use, product costs are more accurate.

◆ COMPARISON OF TRADITIONAL AND ABC OVERHEAD ALLOCATION

Let's compare a traditional overhead allocation method with the ABC overhead allocation method. (See Exhibit 4–13.)

EXHIBIT 4–13   Comparison of Traditional Overhead Allocation Method and ABC Overhead Allocation Method

	Traditional Overhead Allocation	ABC Overhead Allocation
Number of cost pools	One or few	Several
Number of allocation bases	One or few	Several
Relationship of allocation base with cost	Correlative	Causal
Product cost accuracy	Could be accurate enough for the company as a whole, but the cost of individual products may not be very accurate.	More accurate because costs are allocated to products based on the factory resources they use.
Cost control	Does not aid in cost reduction	Aids in cost reduction
Cost system complexity and cost	Simpler, less costly allocation system	More complex, more expensive cost allocation system

PRODUCT COST ACCURACY

Is traditional overhead allocation good enough? Well, for financial reporting and general purpose financial statements, it is accurate enough. This may be why using a single plant-wide allocation base is so popular. Unfortunately, however, the costs of products that result when a single allocation base is used are generally not accurate enough for many management decisions. For example, if Jim, Buck Slade's product manager, had shifted the company's focus based on information presented in Exhibit 4–1, it is likely that the company's profits would have disappeared.

When Does ABC Result in More Accurate Product Costs?

When a company manufactures products that differ or when manufacturing processes differ from one product to the next, that is, when diversity exists, ABC will probably result in more accurate product cost. On the other hand, when a company manufactures only one product or when products and processes to manufacture those products are nearly identical, activity-based costing will probably not result in more accurate product costs. For example, if each of the tires that *Goodyear Tire and Rubber Company* makes in one of its factories are identical to one another, ABC would not render more accurate product costs. On the other hand, since the models of tire *Goodyear* makes differ from one another with respect to the production machinery used, production processes, and production volumes, ABC would render more accurate product costs.

Diversity in manufacturing can take many forms. A company has diversity due to product complexity when it manufactures some simple products and some complex ones. Differences in complexity can be as subtle as manufacturing some products that require many component parts and manufacturing other products that require few. Alternatively, products could require varying amounts of engineering, materials handling, or quality testing. Diversity also exists when some products require the use of more costly factory resources than others. For example, some products must be produced on a machine that costs $1 million, while others can be made on a machine that costs only $100,000. Diversity may also be in the form of volume, as in a company that produces both low-volume and high-volume products.

When diversity exists, using activity-based costing will usually result in more accurate product costs. This is because each product is costed based on the activities required to make that product. For example, if diversity exists because some products require more quality inspections than others, activity-based costing will allocate cost based on the number of inspections required to make each product. Products requiring more inspections will receive a high inspection cost allocation, while products requiring fewer inspections will receive an allocation that is lower.

REDUCING COST BY USING ABC

ABC can actually help firms reduce costs in at least three ways. First, costs are more closely scrutinized when ABC is used. Second, the smaller ABC cost pools make it more difficult to hide questionable costs. And third, to reduce costs allocated to their products, managers will attempt to reduce the allocation base, which for ABC are cost causes. Reducing the activities that cause cost will lead to actual cost reduction. Let's look at each of these more closely.

Closer Cost Scrutiny

Under ABC, costs are more closely scrutinized, especially during the process of establishing an ABC system. As you recall, when an ABC system is established, managers attempt to determine which costs can be removed from overhead and treated as direct costs. In addition, managers work to separate manufacturing overhead into several smaller cost pools and to match these cost pools with cost drivers. With all this cost examination, managers are bound to find unnecessary costs. For example, a cost that has been the norm for years, such as the cost of maintaining and changing decorative plants in factory offices, may become a candidate for elimination when it fails to fit into a cost pool that is associated with an activity that benefits the company's products or services.

Smaller Cost Pool Makes It Difficult to Hide Cost

Costs that may be hidden in a single huge cost pool are more difficult to hide in smaller ABC cost pools. Under traditional overhead allocation, a single huge cost pool is often used for all overhead costs. Even sizable expenditures can be hidden in such a massive cost pool. For example, $20,000 in expenditures for traveling to trade shows may never be noticed in a $1 million cost pool, but may be detected if it is part of one of ten smaller, say $100,000 cost pools. The fact that costs are more likely to be detected in smaller ABC cost pools may cause managers to think twice before they allow questionable expenditures to occur.

Cost Control by Controlling the Allocation Base

If a company uses a predetermined overhead application rate, managers cannot really reduce the overhead cost associated with their products by reducing manufacturing overhead costs directly. For example, assume that a particular **Dow Chemical** plant uses direct labor hours to allocate manufacturing overhead. If a **Dow** production manager changes the way his products are made so that it takes less electricity, overhead cost to the company will be reduced, but the cost *allocated* to the manager's product will not change. This is because **Dow**'s predetermined overhead application rate would have been established before the year even began. The rate for the next year might be a little lower, but the current year's rate will remain unchanged by the reduced cost of electricity.

Because of the way overhead allocation works, managers who desire to reduce the overhead cost allocated to their products must reduce the incurrence of the allocation base. In our **Dow Chemical** example, the manager could reduce the overhead cost allocated to her products by reducing the number of direct labor hours.

Under traditional overhead allocation, reducing the incurrence of the allocation base will not reduce the amount the company actually pays for overhead cost, however. Unfortunately, in our **Dow Chemical** example, reducing direct labor hours may reduce labor cost, but it is unlikely that it will reduce the amount **Dow** spends for overhead. In fact, as the manager calls upon her factory engineers to find ways to reduce direct labor hours, the actual amount **Dow** pays for overhead may increase instead of decrease. Overhead cost will likely increase due to the added cost of the engineers (an overhead cost), and perhaps the added cost of updating or replacing equipment with new labor-saving devices. So, while the overhead cost allocated to the manager's product would decrease, overhead spending for the company as a whole may actually increase.

Under ABC, reducing the incurrence of the allocation base, the cost driver, *will* likely reduce the amount the company actually pays for overhead cost. Now let's assume that our **Dow Chemical** plant uses ABC to allocate its overhead cost and that the cost driver for inspection cost is the number of inspections. If the production manager would like to reduce the inspection cost allocated to his product, he would attempt to reduce the incurrence of the cost driver, the number of inspections. And, most importantly, since the cost driver (the number of inspections) causes the inspection cost, when the cost driver is reduced the amount the company pays for inspection cost is reduced. By reducing the cost driver, which is a cause of the cost, it actually saves the company money. But how can a manager reduce the number of inspections without hindering product quality? Let's assume that in the **Dow Chemical** example, the production manager determined that the blemishes to the product were caused by an uneven cooling process. Assume further that the manager corrected the problem so that blemishes would no longer occur and therefore the inspections from that time forward found no blemished product. Without the potential for product blemishes, inspections were no longer necessary. Reducing the cost driver (the number of inspections) actually reduced overhead cost to the company.

ADDED COMPLEXITY AND COST OF ABC

As you have seen with the Buck Slade example, an ABC system is much more complex than a traditional overhead allocation system. The added complexity begins with establishing the ABC system itself. Costs must be examined, direct costs must be removed from the overhead cost, and cost pools and cost drivers must be established. Then, once the cost pools and cost drivers are established, the company must design and establish systems to properly classify costs, to capture data regarding the occurrences of the various cost drivers, and to allocate the costs. This makes ABC considerably more complex than traditional overhead allocation.

The added complexity of an ABC system makes it considerably more costly than traditional overhead allocation. It is expensive to design and establish an ABC system, and the time and effort required to examine overhead cost and to establish cost pools and cost drivers can be substantial.

◆ ABC AND JOB ORDER COSTING—ANOTHER LOOK AT *MANTA POWER BOATS*

Let's further explore how activity based costing works by revisiting our *Manta Power Boats* example introduced in Chapter 3. *Manta*'s boats are made of fiberglass and plastic resin formed in molds. A series of molds is used to make the necessary components of each boat. Before a mold can be used, it must be cleaned and waxed to keep the fiberglass and polyester resin from sticking. The process of preparing molds to make a boat is part of *Manta*'s setup.

When a manufacturer uses activity-based costing, the cost of each manufacturing activity is accumulated in a dedicated cost pool. In the case of *Manta Power Boats,* overhead costs are examined and all costs associated with setup are separated out and grouped in a cost pool. Now set-up cost can be allocated to products separately from other overhead costs. Assume the annual set-up cost at *Manta* is $117,000.

Next a cost driver must be selected to allocate set-up cost. Assume that *Manta* has decided that the number of molds used is that cost driver. The number of molds required to make a single boat varies depending on each boat design. As Exhibit 4–14 shows, one boat requires the use of 12 molds, while another requires the use of only five molds.

The effort and cost of setup varies from boat to boat depending on the number of molds required. By using the number of molds as the cost driver, we can reflect the differing amounts of set-up effort in the costs of each boat produced. For example, the

EXHIBIT 4–14   Number of Molds Used for Each Basic Boat Design

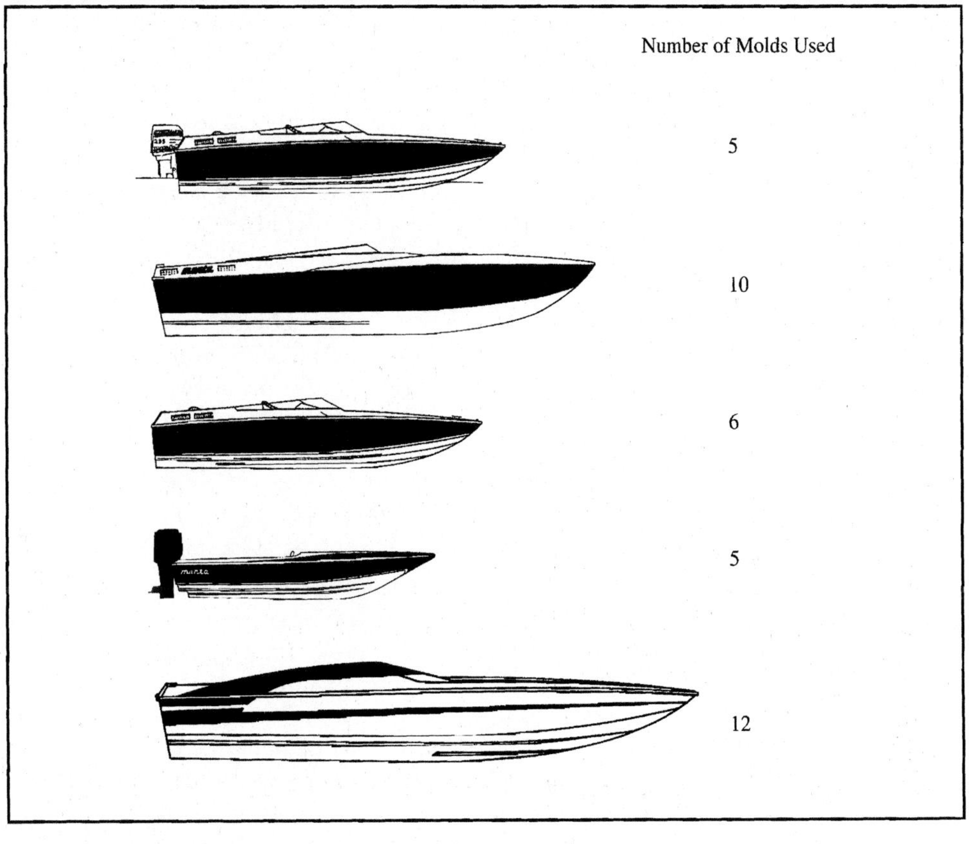

set-up cost for a boat that requires 12 molds will be twice as much as the set-up cost for a boat that requires six molds. The calculations for allocating an overhead cost pool using a cost driver are similar to the calculations using a traditional allocation base. The total estimated annual cost for the cost pool is divided by the estimated annual activity of the cost driver to arrive at an application rate per occurrence of the cost driver. The general formula is as follows:

$$\frac{\text{Estimated annual overhead cost}}{\substack{\text{Estimated annual occurrences of} \\ \text{the cost driver}}} = \substack{\text{Overhead application per occurrence} \\ \text{of the cost driver}}$$

Based on past experience, **Manta** estimates that it will need 360 mold preparations this year to produce 45 boats. Recall that **Manta**'s estimated total annual set-up cost is $117,000. With those two numbers, we can find **Manta**'s application rate for setup. **Manta** divides the estimated total set-up cost by the estimated number of mold preparations for the year to determine the application rate for set-up cost.

$$\frac{\text{Annual estimated set-up cost}}{\text{Annual estimated number of mold preparations}} = \text{Cost per mold preparation}$$

$$\frac{\$117,000}{360 \text{ Mold preparations}} = \$325 \text{ per mold preparation}$$

We find that with an estimated annual set-up cost of $117,000 and a total number of mold preparations of 360, the application rate is $325 per mold used.

Discussion Questions ●

4–3. If you owned a factory, would you prefer that employees spend time setting up production equipment or producing product? Explain.

4–4. If the production manager was able to use one less mold when making a boat, would the cost allocated to that boat be less? Is it likely that the company's actual set-up cost would also be less? Explain.

Using the activity-based costing application rate, we can now allocate set-up cost to each boat based on the number of molds required. For example, boat 1 requires the use of five molds, so its set-up cost would be $1,625 (5 × $325 = $1,625). The set-up cost allocated to boat 2 would be $3,250 based on the use of 10 molds (10 × $325 = $3,250). The more molds required to make a boat, the higher the allocation for set-up cost.

In a traditional cost system, a manager can reduce manufacturing overhead cost associated with a given product by reducing the allocation base used to allocate the cost. For example, if manufacturing overhead is allocated using machine hours, a manager could reduce the overhead allocated to his or her product by reducing the amount of machine time it takes to make the product. This process would reduce the manufacturing overhead cost allocated to the given product, but it would generally not affect the various overhead costs actually incurred by the company. As we mentioned earlier in this chapter, reducing machine hours has no significant effect on the amount the company spends for manufacturing overhead items such as property taxes, plant insurance, plant security, indirect material, indirect labor, and so forth. Even though accounting records would indicate a lower cost for that product's manufacturing overhead, the reduced machine hours would have little effect on the dollars the company spent for manufacturing overhead.

Let's say that **Manta Power Boats** uses activity-based costing and would like to reduce the set-up cost of a particular boat. The manager, then, would try to decrease the number of molds used. For instance, if the number of molds used to make boat 2 were reduced by one mold, the cost allocated to that boat would be reduced by $325. With this cost-reduction technique, the decrease in the allocation base (the cost driver) actually reduces the amount of cost incurred by the company. That is, reducing the number of molds used actually reduces the amount of work that must be done to make a boat. In general, this reduction in work contributes to true cost savings for the company.

Summary

Direct material and direct labor cost can be traced directly to individual products or batches of products. Because manufacturing overhead is an indirect cost and benefits more than one product, it is difficult, if not impossible to determine the true overhead cost associated with individual products produced.

The resources included in manufacturing overhead are an important component of manufacturing product. Even though their cost cannot easily be traced to individual units of production, manufacturing overhead resources are all necessary to produce products, and therefore, their cost should be included in the cost of products produced. The problem is, however, that the cost of manufacturing overhead resources and activities cannot be traced directly to the units of product produced. Their cost, therefore, must be allocated to production.

When allocating overhead using actual amounts for direct material, direct labor and manufacturing overhead, the system is called an actual cost system. Unfortunately, using the actual amount of overhead and the actual amount of the allocation base to allocate manufacturing overhead has several problems. Using a normal cost system, product cost reflects actual direct material cost, actual direct labor cost, and estimated overhead costs. Estimated annual manufacturing overhead cost and the estimated annual amount for the allocation base are used to calculate a predetermined overhead application rate.

Overhead allocation has traditionally been a two-stage process. The first stage is to gather overhead cost into a cost pool. The second stage is to assign the manufacturing overhead cost gathered in the pool to units of product manufactured. Manufacturers attempt to allocate the amount of manufacturing overhead cost that corresponds to the overhead resources consumed to make the product.

Because it is impractical if not impossible for managers to know the exact cost of the manufacturing overhead resources used to make each unit of product, an equitable basis for cost allocation must be determined. An allocation base is an amount associated with cost objects that is used to proportionately distribute costs to each cost object. Direct labor hours, direct labor cost, and machine hours are common traditional manufacturing overhead allocation bases.

Traditional overhead allocation uses a single manufacturing overhead cost pool and a single, plant-wide application rate. Virtually all manufacturers in the United States used this method until the mid-1980s, and many still do today.

During the mid-1980s, some companies realized that a plant-wide application rate has significant weaknesses. To use one activity (such as direct labor hours) as the allocation base for applying *all* manufacturing overhead cost will likely cause some products to be overcosted and others to be undercosted. In an attempt to improve the accuracy of their overhead allocation, many companies have begun to study their business activities and the costs these activities cause. This new method is activity-based costing. When ABC is used, products are more realistically charged for the overhead resources they use. Because products are allocated cost based on the overhead resources they use, product costs are more accurate.

Traditional overhead allocation may be accurate enough for financial reporting and general purpose financial statements but, unfortunately, the costs of products that result when a single allocation base is used are generally not accurate enough for many management decisions. When diversity exists, that is, when products differ or manufacturing processes differ from one product to the next, ABC will usually result in more accurate product cost because each product is costed based on the activities required to make that product.

Key Terms ●

- activity-based costing (ABC), M–99
- actual cost system, M–97
- allocation base, M–97
- cost driver, M–100

- cost pool, M–97
- manufacturing overhead allocation, M–96
- normal cost system, M–97

- predetermined overhead application rate, M–97

Review the Facts ●

A. Describe two problems associated with using actual amounts instead of estimated annual amounts for allocating manufacturing overhead.
B. What is a cost pool?
C. What is a manufacturing overhead allocation base?
D. List the allocation bases typically used in traditional manufacturing overhead allocation.
E. What is the significant weakness of a plant-wide allocation base?
F. What is activity-based costing?
G. In what two ways does activity-based costing improve upon the traditional approach to manufacturing overhead allocation?
H. Describe a cost driver.
I. What is the difference between a plant-wide cost pool and multiple cost pools?
J. Under what circumstances would ABC probably result in more accurate product costs?
K. List the three ways ABC can actually help firms reduce cost.
L. Which overhead allocation system, traditional or ABC, is more costly to establish and operate?

Apply What You Have Learned ●

LO 4: CALCULATE TRADITIONAL AND ABC OVERHEAD ALLOCATION

4–5. The president of Simple Products, Inc. is attending a management seminar and has just heard about activity-based costing. He wonders whether it would help his company.

Simple Products, Inc. uses common machinery to manufacture two simple products. Each year, there are two production runs for each product requiring similar set-up effort. Manufacturing overhead includes set-up cost of $50,400 per year. Total overhead for the company including the set-up cost is $198,000 annually and direct labor hours are expected to total 18,000 for the year.

The following information is available for products A and B.

	Product A	Product B
Units produced	1,000	8,000
Direct material cost per unit	$14	$14
Direct labor cost per unit	$24	$24
Machine hours per unit	1	1
Direct labor hours per unit	2	2

Required:

a. Calculate the cost per unit for each product using traditional overhead allocation.
b. Calculate the cost per unit for each product using activity-based costing.
c. Do you believe activity-based costing would benefit Simple Products, Inc.? Explain your answer.

LO 4: CALCULATE TRADITIONAL AND ABC OVERHEAD ALLOCATION

4–6. The president of Complex Products, Inc. is attending a management seminar and has just heard about activity-based costing. She wonders whether it would help her company.

Complex Products, Inc. uses common machinery to manufacture two complex products. Each year, there are two production runs for each product requiring similar set-up effort. Manufacturing overhead includes set-up cost totaling $52,000. To maintain a competitive edge, these products are updated periodically to conform to the latest technological advancements. These engineering changes are considered part of manufacturing overhead and cost $26,000 per year. Total overhead for the company including the cost of setup and engineering changes is $175,000 per year. Direct labor hours total 7,000 for the year.

The following information is available for products C and D:

	Product C	Product D
Units produced	1,000	1,000
Direct material cost per unit	$24	$24
Direct labor cost per unit	$36	$48
Machine hours per unit	6	8
Direct labor hours per unit	3	4
Engineering changes per year	6	2

Required:

    a. Calculate the cost per unit for each product using traditional overhead allocation.
    b. Calculate the cost per unit for each product using activity-based costing.
    c. Do you believe activity-based costing would benefit Complex Products, Inc.? Explain your answer.

LO 4: CALCULATE TRADITIONAL AND ABC OVERHEAD ALLOCATION

4–7. The following estimates are available for Violette Manufacturing for 2004.

Violette Manufacturing
Estimated Manufacturing Overhead
For the Year Ended December 31, 2004

Materials handling cost	$ 50,000
Product engineering	110,000
Production machine setup	200,000
Production machine depreciation	450,000
Quality testing	100,000
Other overhead cost	250,000
Total manufacturing overhead	$1,160,000

Estimated Overhead Activities
For the Year Ended December 31, 2004

Number of material movements	200,000
Number of product engineering hours	4,400
Number of machine setups	100
Number of machine hours	18,000
Number of tests performed	125,000
Number of direct labor hours	25,000

The following information is available for production runs of two products, the FPl11 and the FP222:

	FP111	FP222
Selling price per unit	$ 23	$ 26
Number of units produced	5,000	500
Total direct material cost	$60,000	$6,000
Total direct labor cost	$14,400	$1,440
Number of material movements	10,000	1,000
Number of product engineering hours	100	100
Number of machine setups	1	1
Number of machine hours	200	20
Number of tests performed	1,250	125
Number of direct labor hours	800	80

    Violette Manufacturing uses a traditional overhead allocation system. Manufacturing overhead is allocated based on direct labor hours.

    Violette Manufacturing's sales manager has submitted a proposal that would shift the marketing focus to low-volume products such as the FP222. The proposal is prompted by the higher markups that can be charged for these products without customer complaint.

The company president is concerned that the company's cost per unit may be sending the wrong message. He recently learned of activity-based costing and wonders if it might help. Assume that you are part of a group that has been assigned to review the situation.

Required:

a. Determine the per unit cost for FP111 and FP222 using direct labor hours as the allocation base for all manufacturing overhead cost.

b. Determine the per unit cost for FP111 and FP222 using activity-based costing to allocate manufacturing overhead cost. (*Note:* Allocate other overhead cost based on direct labor hours.)

c. Discuss the marketing manager's proposal in light of your findings. Discuss what would happen if the marketing manager's sales strategy was adopted.

LO 4: CALCULATE TRADITIONAL AND ABC OVERHEAD ALLOCATION

4–8. The following estimates are available for George Manufacturing for 2004:

George Manufacturing
Estimated Manufacturing Overhead
For the Year Ended December 31, 2004

Production machine setup	$ 75,000
Production machine depreciation	240,000
Quality testing	25,000
Other overhead cost	150,000
Total manufacturing overhead	$490,000

Estimated Overhead Activities
For the Year Ended December 31, 2004

Number of machine setups	100
Number of machine hours	3,200
Number of tests performed	5,000
Number of direct labor hours	16,000

The following information is available for production of two products, the AA1 and the BB2:

	AA1	BB2
Selling price per unit	$ 2.40	$3.25
Number of units produced	10,000	500
Total direct material cost	$ 5,000	$ 250
Total direct labor cost	$ 6,400	$ 320
Number of machine setups	1	1
Number of machine hours	100	5
Number of tests performed	100	50
Number of direct labor hours	400	20

George Manufacturing uses a traditional overhead allocation system. Manufacturing overhead is allocated based on direct labor hours. George Manufacturing's sales manager has submitted a proposal that would shift the marketing focus to low-volume products such as the BB2. The proposal is prompted by the higher markups and lack of competition, even at high selling prices.

The company president is concerned that the company's cost per unit may be sending the wrong message. He recently learned of activity based costing and wonders if it might help.

Assume that you are a member of a work team that has been assigned to review the situation.

Required:

a. Determine the per unit cost for AAI and BB2 using direct labor hours as the allocation base for all manufacturing overhead cost.

b. Determine the per unit cost for AAI and BB2 using activity-based costing to allocate manufacturing overhead cost. (*Note:* Allocate other overhead cost based on direct labor hours.)

c. Discuss the marketing manager's proposal in light of your findings. Discuss what would happen if the marketing manager's sales strategy was adopted.

LO 4 & 5: CALCULATE TRADITIONAL AND ABC OVERHEAD ALLOCATION AND DETERMINE THE COST OF PRODUCTS USING JOB ORDER COSTING

4–9. Salter Equipment Company began the following jobs during March 2004:

	Job 303	Job 304
Direct material	$2,000	$2,000
Direct labor	$3,120	$6,240
Direct labor hours	260	520
Machine hours machine A	5	30
Machine hours machine B	20	0
Machine setups	2	1
Engineering changes	22	9

Estimated overhead cost for 2004:

Depreciation machine A	$ 100,000
Depreciation machine B	500,000
Machine setup cost	50,000
Engineering cost	200,000
Other overhead cost	150,000
Total	$1,000,000

Estimated activities for 2004:

Machine hours machine A	1,000
Machine hours machine B	1,000
Number of setups	80
Number of engineering changes	800
Number of direct labor hours	20,000

Required:

    a. Calculate the cost of each job using direct labor hours as the allocation base for all overhead.

    b. Calculate the cost of each job using activity-based costing. Use direct labor hours as the allocation base for "other overhead cost."

LO 4 & 5: CALCULATE TRADITIONAL AND ABC OVERHEAD ALLOCATION AND DETERMINE THE COST OF PRODUCTS USING JOB ORDER COSTING

4–10. Jack Klett Equipment Company began the following jobs during August 2004:

	Job 500	Job 600
Direct material	$1,000	$1,000
Direct labor	$1,800	$3,000
Direct labor hours	120	200
Machine hours machine A	10	50
Machine hours machine B	50	0
Machine setups	2	1
Material movements	200	75

Estimated overhead cost for 2004:

Depreciation machine A	$ 50,000
Depreciation machine B	300,000
Machine setup cost	75,000
Material handling cost	100,000
Other overhead cost	80,000
Total	$605,000

Estimated activities for 2004:

Machine hours machine A	500
Machine hours machine B	500
Number of setups	75
Number of material movements	5,000
Number of direct labor hours	10,000

Required:

    a. Calculate the cost of each job using direct labor hours as the allocation base for all overhead.

    b. Calculate the cost of each job using activity-based costing. Use direct labor hours as the allocation base for "other overhead cost."

LO 4 & 5: CALCULATE TRADITIONAL AND ABC OVERHEAD ALLOCATION AND DETERMINE THE COST OF PRODUCTS USING JOB ORDER COSTING

4–11. Vazquez Manufacturing Company began the following jobs during July 2004:

	Job 901	Job 922
Direct material	$3,000	$3,000
Direct labor	$1,800	$3,000
Direct labor hours	250	100
Machine hours machine A	20	12
Machine hours machine B	0	8
Machine setups	1	2
Material movements	90	300

Estimated overhead cost for 2004:

Depreciation machine A	$ 150,000
Depreciation machine B	600,000
Machine setup cost	175,000
Material handling cost	150,000
Other overhead cost	180,000
Total	$1,255,000

Estimated activities for 2004:

Machine hours machine A	700
Machine hours machine B	700
Number of setups	100
Number of material movements	5,000
Number of direct labor hours	10,000

Required:

    a. Calculate the cost of each job using direct labor hours as the allocation base for all overhead.

    b. Calculate the cost of each job using activity-based costing. Use direct labor hours as the allocation base for "other overhead cost."

CHAPTER 5

Cost Behavior

Laura Jorgensen is the newly elected social chairperson of her mountain climbing club. Her first duty is to plan the club's big kickoff party for the upcoming year. Funds are limited, so she must plan well and estimate costs carefully. Laura's first step in estimating the total cost of the party is to identify the individual costs involved. As she begins the planning process, she identifies two major costs:

1. Entertainment — A live band is a must.
2. Food and drinks — Plenty for everyone is essential.

When Laura checks the records of last year's social chairperson, she discovers he spent $3,650 on these two items for last year's party ($525 for entertainment and $3,125 for food and drinks). Assuming the prices for entertainment and food and drinks have remained the same, the club should be able to have this year's party for $3,650. In fact, Laura has money to spare because the spending limit for this year's event is $5,500.

But wait. . . . The mountain climbing club has grown, so about 175 guests are expected to attend this year's party, compared to the 125 guests who attended last year. Laura must estimate the party's cost for 175 guests, not 125. How should she begin? To determine the total expected cost of the party, Laura needs to know which costs are affected by the number of guests attending and which costs are not. Let's examine Laura's two major costs for the party:

1. Entertainment: Will the band charge more if more guests attend? No.
2. Food and drinks: Will the caterer charge more if the number of guests increases? Yes.

How should Laura determine the cost of this year's party? She knows her cost for the item that is unaffected by the attendance level (the band), but what about the cost that *is* affected by a change in attendance level (food and drinks)? This chapter will demonstrate how to determine these amounts.

As managers plan for business success, they must know which costs will vary with changes in business activity and which will remain constant. In this context, we are using the term *business activity* in a very broad sense. "Business activity" can refer to almost anything happening in a business. In the mountain climbing club example, the activity is the number of guests attending the party. For a manufacturer, the activity could be the number of products produced; for a shipping department, it could be the number of packages shipped; and for a sales office, it could be the number of sales orders processed. Increases and decreases in any business activity will impact some costs and not others. That is, some costs will increase as business activity increases and others will not. To help them predict and control costs, managers must be able to determine how costs will behave as business activity changes. **Cost behavior** is the reaction of costs to changes in levels of business activity.

cost behavior The reaction of costs to changes in levels of activity.

Learning Objectives

After completing your work on this chapter, you should be able to do the following:

1. Describe the differences between fixed costs and variable costs.
2. Classify costs by cost behavior.
3. Explain the concept of relevant range and its effect on cost behavior information.
4. Describe the characteristics of a mixed cost and the four basic approaches to separating a mixed cost into its fixed and variable components.
5. Determine the fixed and variable components of a mixed cost using scatter graphs and the high–low method.
6. Use *Microsoft* Excel's Chart Wizard to prepare a behavior scatter graph.

◆ COMMON COST BEHAVIOR PATTERNS

Costs may react in various ways to changes in activity levels, creating many different cost behavior patterns. In this chapter we describe and compare the two most common patterns: fixed and variable.

FIXED COSTS

fixed costs Costs that remain constant in total regardless of the level of activity.

Fixed costs are costs that remain constant *in total* regardless of the level of activity. In our chapter-opening example, the entertainment cost is a fixed cost. As the number of guests increases, this cost does not change. The band will cost $525 for the night, regardless of how many guests attend the club's party.

Suppose Laura is interested in determining the fixed cost *per guest*. Would the fixed cost amount change per guest as the number of guests changes? Let's take a look.

	125 Guests	175 Guests
Total fixed cost	$525	$525
Cost per guest	$525 ÷ 125 = $4.20	$525 ÷ 175 = $3.00

As you can see, the fixed cost *per unit* (in this case, the entertainment cost per guest) changes as the activity level changes. A fixed cost, then, is a cost that remains constant in total, but changes per unit as the activity level changes. Fixed cost per unit decreases as activity increases.

Discussion Question

5-1. Consider the costs involved in operating a fast-food restaurant such as *McDonald's.* What are three examples of fixed costs?

VARIABLE COSTS

variable costs Costs that change in total proportionately with changes in the level of activity.

Variable costs are costs that change *in total* proportionately with changes in the level of activity. As activity increases, total variable cost also increases. In our party example, the variable cost is the catering cost of $25 per guest. We know this because the total cost for food and drinks last year was $3,125 for 125 guests, and $3,125 ÷ 125 = $25. For each additional guest added to the party, the total cost for food and drinks will increase by $25.

If 175 guests attend, the total catering cost is as follows:

$$175 \text{ Guests} \times \$25 = \$4{,}375$$

Variable cost *per unit* stays the same as activity changes. In our example, the catering cost per guest remains constant regardless of how many guests attend. A variable cost, then, is a cost that increases in total, but remains constant per unit as activity increases.

Discussion Question

5–2. Consider the costs involved in operating a fast-food restaurant such as ***McDonald's.*** What are three examples of variable costs and the activity or activities that cause them to change?

COMPARISON OF COST BEHAVIORS

Cost and activity can be plotted on a graph to yield a visual representation of cost behavior. When doing so, we plot the activity on the horizontal axis (the x axis) and the type of cost on the vertical axis (the y axis). You may recall from past math classes that x is the independent variable, and y is the dependent variable, which means that the item depicted on the x axis (activity) affects the item shown on the y axis (cost).

A graphic representation of a fixed cost is as follows:

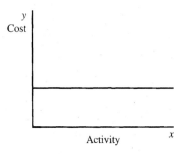

Examples of activities and fixed costs are shown in Exhibit 5–1. Notice that each example in Exhibit 5–1 suggests a cost that remains constant even if the level of the activity changes.

EXHIBIT 5–1   Examples of Fixed Costs

Activity	Fixed Cost
Production	Rent on the factory building
Production	Depreciation on production equipment
Sales	Salary of vice president of sales
Delivery	Vehicle insurance

From our party example, we can graph the cost of the band as an example of a fixed cost, as shown in Exhibit 5–2.

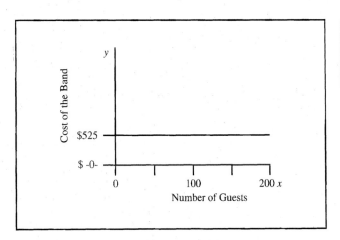

EXHIBIT 5–2   Graph of Fixed Cost Behavior Pattern of Entertainment at the Climbing Club Party

The horizontal line on the graph in Exhibit 5–2 shows that the fixed cost of entertainment stays constant no matter how the number of guests changes.

A graphic representation of variable cost is as follows:

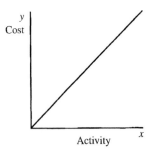

Examples of activities and variable costs are shown in Exhibit 5–3. Notice that for each example in Exhibit 5–3, a change in the level of the activity results in a change in the total cost.

EXHIBIT 5-3 Examples of Variable Costs

Activity	Variable Cost
Production	Direct material
Production	Direct labor
Sales	Sales commissions
Delivery	Gasoline

From our party example, we can graph the cost of catering as an example of a variable cost, as shown in Exhibit 5–4. The upward sloping line shows us that as the number of guests increases from 125 to 175, the catering cost increases proportionately.

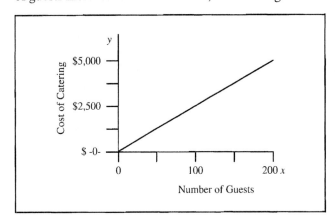

EXHIBIT 5–4 Graph of Variable Cost Behavior Pattern for Catering Cost at the Climbing Club Party

Discussion Question

5–3. Identify four additional costs of hosting the mountain climbing club party and describe the cost behavior of each if the number of guests changes.

In this section, we defined and compared the two most common types of cost behavior. Next, we see how to estimate the total cost of an activity.

DETERMINING TOTAL COST

Once managers classify costs according to cost behavior, they can determine the total cost of an activity. The formula for finding total cost is as follows:

$$\text{Total cost} = \text{Fixed cost} + \text{Variable cost}$$

Recall from our example that we have $525 of fixed cost for the band, and $4,375 of variable cost for the food and drinks (based on 175 guests). Using this information, Laura can calculate the total cost of the party as $4,900, as follows:

$$\$4,900 = \$525 + \$4,375$$

The total cost of the party is shown on the graph in Exhibit 5–5.

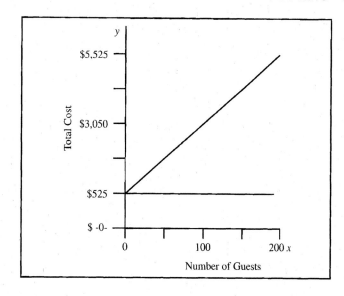

EXHIBIT 5–5   Graph of
Total Climbing Party Cost

The graph in Exhibit 5–5 shows both the horizontal line depicting the fixed cost of the band and the upward sloping line representing the variable cost of the food and drinks. Exhibit 5–5, then, is actually a combination of the graphs in Exhibits 5–2 and 5–4. These graphs are consistent with the statement that total cost equals fixed cost plus variable cost.

Since the budget for the event was $5,500, and Laura plans to spend only $4,900, she must have planned well, right? Not necessarily. Keep in mind that the numbers only tell part of the story. As a decision maker, Laura must not be lulled into thinking that she has made the most effective spending choices just because she failed to spend every budgeted dollar. Is it wise to spend nearly $5,000 on one event? Could some costs be reduced? To make sound decisions, managers must consider all issues—not just whether the budget has been met. In this chapter, we examine cost behaviors to equip you with a cost estimation tool. Remember, however, that when making decisions the numbers tell part, not all, of a story.

Discussion Question

5–4. The total cost of $4,900 covers the cost of 175 guests. Based on the cost behavior information available, what is the largest possible number of guests that could attend the party within the $5,500 budget?

◆ RELEVANT RANGE

Are there any situations when a cost behavior might change? Well, let's reexamine the cost of entertainment in the party example to answer this question. We assumed the cost of the band would remain fixed if the number of guests attending the party increased; however, if the number of guests increased well outside normal expectations to 500 or 1,000, the guests could not be entertained with a single band. At least two bands would be needed. Once the number of guests exceeds a certain range, the entertainment cost does not remain fixed at $525.

relevant range   The range of activity within which cost behavior assumptions are valid.

The range of activity within which cost behavior assumptions are valid is called the **relevant range.** In the party example, the relevant range might be up to 250 guests. If more than 250 guests attend, Laura will need more than one band. For a business, we usually consider the relevant range to be the normal range of activity for the company.

Activity that is outside the relevant range can affect costs in a business setting. For example, in Exhibit 5–1, we described rent for a factory building as a fixed cost relative to production. This fixed cost behavior holds true only within the relevant range. On the one hand, if production dropped to two units there would be no point in having a factory. Work could be contracted to an outside party. Conversely, if the factory building provided just enough space to produce 1,000 units per month, and production requirements increased to 1,500 units per month, a second factory would be needed. If the activity level were higher than the relevant range, factory rent would no longer be fixed at the original cost level.

Variable costs also have a relevant range. To illustrate, we return to the catering costs for the party example. The caterer charged the club $25 per guest for food and drinks for a party with 125 to 175 guests. Would the caterer offer the same service for $25 per guest if the event were a private evening with only six people attending? Probably not. The caterer's fee is based on a relatively large number of guests. Conversely, the caterer might be willing to provide food and drinks for less than $25 per guest if the crowd were significantly larger. For example, the caterer might offer a $25 per guest charge for groups of 50 to 200, and a $20 per guest charge for groups of more than 200. In such a case, the relevant range of the variable cost of $25 per guest would be from 50 to 200 guests.

In business settings, similar types of quantity discounts exist. For example, if **IBM** were to purchase just enough electrical wire to manufacture one computer, it would likely pay a higher price for the wire than if it were buying enough to make 1,000 computers. Buying enough electrical wire to make 1,000 computers allows **IBM** to get quantity discounts that would be unavailable otherwise. At the other extreme, if **IBM** were to make such a large number of computers that it outstripped its normal source for wire and had to resort to secondary, more expensive suppliers, the cost for electrical wire per computer could actually increase as production increased.

With these examples in mind, how can fixed cost be described as a cost that remains constant in total, and variable cost be described as cost that remains constant per unit regardless of activity? For most decision situations, the fixed and variable cost information provided to managers assumes activity will be within the relevant range, that is, the normal operating range for the company. The relevant range can be depicted graphically as shown in Exhibit 5–6.

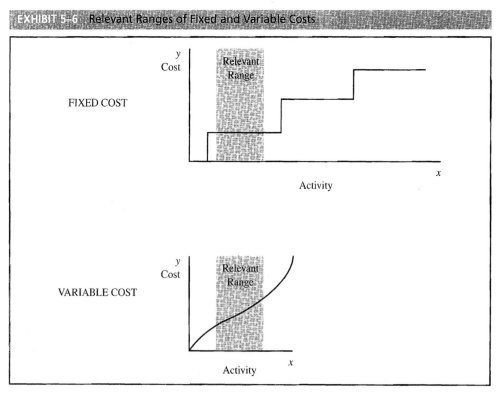

EXHIBIT 5–6   Relevant Ranges of Fixed and Variable Costs

As shown in Exhibit 5–6, the fixed cost remains constant in total and the variable cost is constant per unit within the relevant range.

Decision makers usually assume activity levels will be within a company's relevant range. Activity levels may exceed or fall below the relevant range, such as when growth in production activity is significant. However, unless some evidence suggests the contrary, you should assume in our text discussion and assignment material that the activity levels will be within the relevant range.

◆ MIXED COSTS ·

mixed cost An individual cost that has both a fixed cost and a variable cost component.

The costs we have discussed thus far have been either completely fixed or completely variable. Some costs, however, are actually a combination of fixed and variable cost, and are known as mixed costs. A **mixed cost** is a cost that has elements of both fixed and variable costs.

For decision making purposes, it is useful to identify the fixed and variable components of a mixed cost. For example, consider the cost of electricity consumed in a manufacturing facility. When production lines are completely shut down on weekends, production is zero. Even without any production, however, the facility still requires minimal electricity to operate water heaters, refrigerators, and security lighting. This minimum cost of keeping the factory ready for use is the fixed portion of electricity cost. When production begins and production machinery cranks up, much more electric power is used. This incremental cost, which is driven by the actual use of the manufacturing facility, is the variable portion of electricity cost. Exhibit 5–7 shows a graph of a mixed cost.

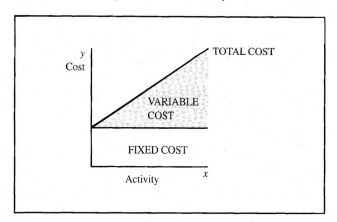

EXHIBIT 5–7 Graph of a Mixed Cost

Exhibit 5–7 shows that even when the activity level is at zero (the intercept of the *x* axis and the *y* axis), cost is incurred. This cost is the fixed element of the mixed cost. As activity increases, the cost rises from that initial point. This cost is the variable component of the mixed cost.

You may have observed that the graph in Exhibit 5–7 is quite similar to that in Exhibit 5–5 depicting the total cost of the climbing club party. This similarity occurs because total cost (which is composed of its fixed costs and its variable costs) could be described as one giant mixed cost.

Discussion Questions ●

5–5. Consider the costs involved in operating a fast-food restaurant such as *McDonald's.* What are three examples of activities that would have mixed costs?

Assume you are the sales manager for the Hinds Wholesale Supply Company, and you are trying to estimate the cost of operating the fleet of delivery vehicles for the coming year. The only information you have is that $110,000 was spent last year to operate the fleet.

5–6. Would it help you to know which delivery vehicle costs are fixed and which are variable? Why?

5–7. What other information would you need to gather before being able to estimate next year's costs?

5–8. Why would the sales manager at Hinds Wholesale Supply Company be concerned about the cost of delivery vehicles?

◆ IDENTIFYING THE FIXED AND VARIABLE ELEMENTS OF A MIXED COST

Even if we know that a cost is a combination of both fixed and variable costs, we have no information to tell us how much of the cost is unaffected by the level of activity (fixed) and how much of it will increase as activity increases (variable). Cost information is much more useful for cost control, planning, and decision making purposes if the manager can determine which part of a mixed cost is fixed and which is variable. In this section we will discuss four methods commonly used to identify the fixed and variable elements of a mixed cost: the engineering approach, scatter graphing, the high–low method, and regression analysis.

THE ENGINEERING APPROACH

engineering approach
A method used to separate a mixed cost into its fixed and variable components using experts who are familiar with the technical aspects of the activity and associated cost.

The **engineering approach** relies on engineers or other professionals who are familiar with the technical aspect of the activity and the associated cost to analyze the situation and determine which costs are fixed and which are variable. This approach may employ time-and-motion studies or other aspects of scientific management.

For example, experts in the field of aviation and aircraft operations could analyze the cost of operating a corporate aircraft to determine which portion of the operating cost increases as aircraft usage increases and which portion of the cost remains constant. Based on the experts' industry experience and evaluations, they would then separate the fixed and variable components of this mixed cost.

Analysts would be likely to use flying time as the activity level base because hours of use will affect costs. They would then classify the cost of insurance and of renting hangar space in which to store the plane as fixed costs. Why? The insurance and rental costs are unaffected by the number of hours the plane may be flown. The cost of the airplane's battery will likely be classified as a fixed cost because the deterioration of this item and the need for replacement are affected more by the passing of time and very little by the number of flight hours.

Aviation experts would probably classify fuel costs and certain expected maintenance and repair costs as variable costs, as both depend on usage. For example, experts may estimate that a plane's engines require an overhaul every 2,000 hours of flight time.

Discussion Questions ●

Again assume you are a sales manager for the Hinds Wholesale Supply Company trying to estimate the cost of operating the fleet of delivery vehicles for the coming year.

5–9. Would you engage the services of an automotive expert to help separate costs into fixed and variable? Why or why not?

5–10. List four costs you (or the automotive expert) would identify as part of the cost of operating the fleet of delivery trucks. Classify each by its cost behavior and the activity to which it relates.

5–11. If an expert determined that the fixed cost of operating each vehicle is $3,000 per year and the variable cost is $0.10 per mile, what would be the expected cost of operating the fleet? (Assume there are eight trucks, and they are each driven an average of 25,000 miles per year.)

The engineering approach to separating mixed cost relies on an expert's experience and judgment to classify costs as fixed or variable. It is often used when the company has no past experience concerning a cost's reaction to activity. In contrast, the other three methods we examine use historical data and mathematical computations to approximate the fixed and variable components of mixed cost.

SCATTER GRAPHING

scatter graph approach
A method used to separate a mixed cost into its fixed and variable components by plotting historical activity and cost data to determine how a cost relates to various levels of activity.

The **scatter graph approach** plots historical activity and cost data on a graph to see how a cost relates to various levels of activity. An analyst places a straight line through the visual center of the points plotted on the graph as shown in Exhibit 5–8. Then using some simple calculations, the analyst can approximate the fixed and variable elements of the cost being analyzed.

To demonstrate how scatter graphing works, imagine you are again the sales manager for the Hinds Wholesale Supply Company with the task of estimating the

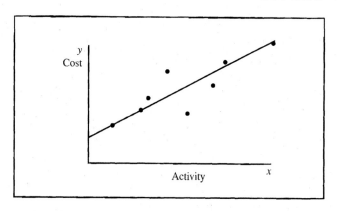

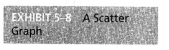
EXHIBIT 5-8 A Scatter Graph

expected delivery vehicle operating cost for 2005. One of the operating costs is vehicle maintenance, which you think is a mixed cost, so you need to determine how much of that cost is fixed and how much is variable. Your first step is to obtain relevant historical cost data. At your request, the accounting department provides you with the following maintenance cost information about the company's delivery vehicles for 2004:

Truck Number	Maintenance Cost
202	$2,000
204	1,600
205	2,200
301	2,400
422	2,600
460	2,200
520	2,000

You now ask yourself a couple of questions. First, is vehicle maintenance cost a fixed cost? Clearly it is not a fixed cost, because the cost is not the same for all trucks. Second, is this cost a variable cost? Well, if it is a variable cost, it varies based on some activity. After careful consideration, you determine that activity might be either (1) the number of miles driven or (2) the number of packages delivered. On request, the accounting department provides you with the following expanded data for 2004:

Truck Number	Miles Driven	Packages Delivered	Maintenance Cost
202	15,000	1,200	$2,000
204	11,000	1,000	1,600
205	24,000	1,500	2,200
301	30,000	1,500	2,400
422	31,000	500	2,600
460	26,000	1,000	2,200
520	20,000	2,000	2,000

Remember, if a cost is truly variable, it changes proportionately as activity changes. Let's consider miles driven first and see whether there is a proportional change in total vehicle maintenance cost as activity changes. Compare trucks 202 and 301. The miles driven for truck 301 are exactly twice as many as for truck 202. If vehicle maintenance cost is variable based on miles driven, then the cost for truck 301 should be twice the cost for truck 202, but it is not.

Now we look at packages delivered as the activity. Compare truck 204 with truck 422. Truck 204 delivered twice as many packages as truck 422. If vehicle maintenance cost is variable based on the number of packages delivered, the cost for truck 204 should be exactly twice the cost for truck 422. Again, it is not.

If a cost is neither fixed nor variable, then it is mixed, meaning it has both a fixed element and a variable element. This is the case with Hinds' delivery vehicle maintenance cost. Therefore, you must find a way to estimate the amount of fixed and variable costs associated with the maintenance cost if you are to reasonably predict the vehicle maintenance cost for 2005.

To use the scatter graph method to determine the fixed and variable elements of the vehicle maintenance cost, the first step is to plot the information for each observation (in this case, each delivery vehicle) on a graph. Remember, the vertical axis on a graph is the y axis (total cost), and the horizontal axis is the x axis (activity). Recall also that the independent variable, shown as the x axis, is not affected by a change in y. However, the dependent variable value, shown on the y axis, depends on the numerical value of the x variable. The assumption is that a change in x will lead to a change in y.

If a truck driver travels 1,000 miles, for example, Hinds must spend money on gasoline. In our case, driving is the independent (x) variable and the company's gasoline cost is the dependent (y) variable. Driving affects the company's gasoline cost; however, the reverse does not hold true. The mere purchase of gasoline, which increases the dependent (y) variable, will not cause a change in the number of miles driven.

For mixed cost calculations, the y variable is the cost affected by the activity and it is the cost you are trying to estimate. The x variable represents the activity you believe will affect the cost behavior. Do not fall into the trap of thinking that the dependent variable (y) will be measured in dollars and the independent variable (x) will not. It is possible to predict a cost such as sales commissions, expressed in dollars, based on an activity such as sales, also expressed in dollars.

For the Hinds Wholesale Supply Company example, the data has two possible activity–cost pairs. The first pair is the number of miles driven and vehicle maintenance cost. The second pair is the number of packages delivered and vehicle maintenance cost.

We begin by graphing maintenance cost and miles driven. When we plot the data on a graph, we plot each observation as a pair of values. The maintenance cost for a particular vehicle—the dependent variable—is plotted using the index on the y axis. The miles driven for the same vehicle—the independent variable—are plotted using the index on the x axis. The position on the graph occupied by the plotted pair of numbers is called a *coordinate*. As the graph in Exhibit 5–9 indicates, each observation is represented by a dot.

The next step is to place a straight line through the visual center of the plotted coordinates, which we have done in Exhibit 5–10.

In Exhibit 5–10 it is easy to place the straight line through the points on the graph because they seem to line up in a nearly straight line on their own. This straight line effect occurs when the relationship of the two variables is relatively constant, or linear. The graph in Exhibit 5–10 suggests a relatively constant relationship between the miles driven (x) and maintenance cost (y). The straight line represents the behavior of maintenance cost as it relates to the number of miles driven.

Now that we have a completed scatter graph for Hinds' vehicle maintenance cost, we can employ some simple calculations to approximate the fixed and variable portion of that cost. As you recall from earlier in the chapter:

$$\text{Total cost} = \text{Fixed cost} + \text{Variable cost}$$

For total mixed costs we can modify the equation slightly as follows:

$$\text{Total mixed cost} = \text{Fixed cost element} + \text{Variable cost element}$$

When using the scatter graph method, we identify the fixed element of the maintenance cost first. Note that in Exhibit 5–10 the straight line that indicates the relationship of miles driven and maintenance cost intercepts the y axis at $1,100. At this point, the x variable (miles) is zero, which suggests that when activity is zero, maintenance cost will still be $1,100. That $1,100 represents fixed cost. In the scatter graph method, we determine fixed cost simply by noting where the straight line intercepts the y axis. Thus, in our example we now know the following information:

$$\text{Total mixed cost} = \$1,100 + \text{Variable cost element}$$

Next, we find the variable cost per mile using simple mathematics. First we choose two points from anywhere along the *scatter graph line* to determine the effect of the x

DATA:	Truck Number	Miles Driven	Maintenance Cost
	202	15,000	$2,000
	204	11,000	1,600
	205	24,000	2,200
	301	30,000	2,400
	422	31,000	2,600
	460	26,000	2,200
	520	20,000	2,000

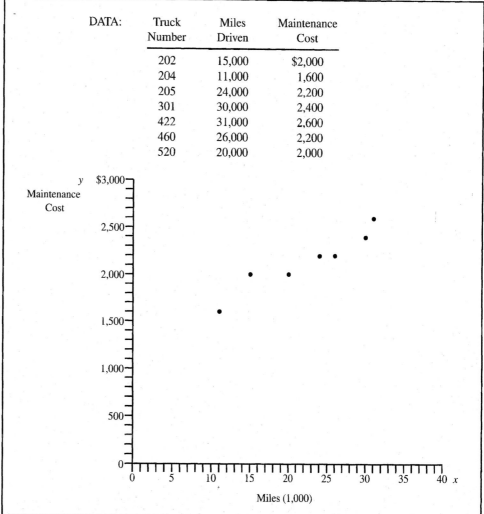

EXHIBIT 5–9   Scatter Graph for Hinds Company Vehicle Maintenance Cost and Miles Driven

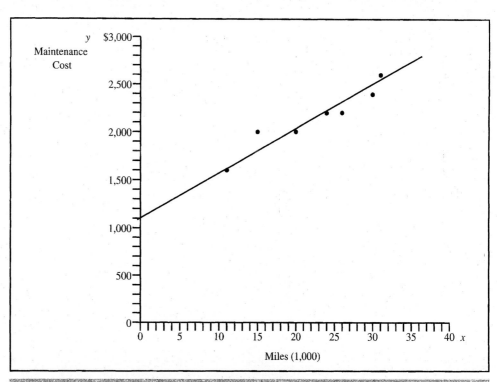

EXHIBIT 5–10   Scatter Graph for Vehicle Maintenance Cost and Miles Driven

variable on the *y* variable. *Note*: Because the points must be directly on the line, we can't use any of the points from our original data (unless one happens to be exactly centered on the scatter graph line). Any two positions on the line are fine, but it is better to select points that are somewhat separated. That way, the error caused by our visual estimation in reading the graph will be small relative to the numerical difference between the two points selected.

As one coordinate for our variable cost per unit calculations, we select the point at which activity is zero and cost is $1,100. We then choose as our second point the coordinate at which the activity level is 34,000 miles and cost is $2,700. As the graph in Exhibit 5–11 indicates, we determined that coordinate by choosing a position on the line and following the lines to the *x* axis and the *y* axis. The locations on these axes indicate the cost and activity level represented by that position on the line.

EXHIBIT 5-11 Scatter Graph with Activity Points Selected

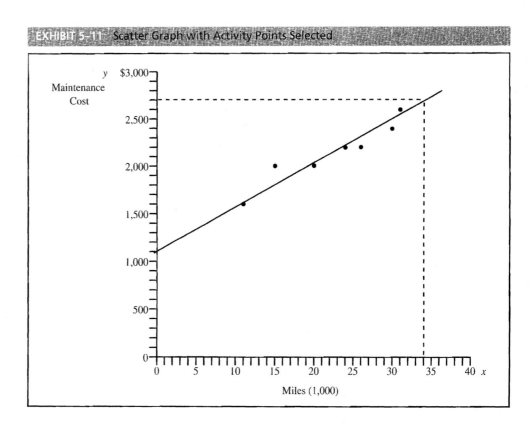

Miles (1,000)

The next step is to determine the mathematical difference between the two coordinates.

Miles	Cost
34,000	$ 2,700
(____0)	(1,100)
34,000	$ 1,600

We can see from our calculations that the maintenance cost at 34,000 miles is $1,600 higher than it is for zero miles. What do you think caused the $1,600 difference? We assume that the increase was caused exclusively by driving the 34,000 miles.

Now we can calculate the average amount of maintenance cost per mile caused by the additional activity. We do this by dividing the 34,000 mileage difference into the $1,600 increased maintenance cost:

$$\$1,600 \div 34,000 = \$0.047059, \text{ or about 4.7 cents per mile}$$

The calculations show that each additional mile of driving causes maintenance cost to rise by $0.047. If we combine this information with the fixed cost information determined earlier, we can create a cost formula for vehicle maintenance cost:

Vehicle maintenance cost = $1,100 + ($0.047 per mile driven)

We have now used scatter graphing to separate maintenance cost into its fixed and variable components. With this information, we can project maintenance cost at any level of activity. To do this, we add the fixed cost to the activity multiplied by the cost per unit of activity. For example, the estimated maintenance cost for a single delivery truck that will be driven 28,000 miles is $2,416, calculated as follows:

$$\$2,416 = \$1,100 + (\$0.047 \times 28,000)$$

Discussion Questions ●

5–12. Based on the information obtained from the scatter graph, what would be the maintenance cost of operating one delivery truck if we expected the truck to be driven 25,000 miles next year?

5–13. Based on the information obtained from the scatter graph, what would be the maintenance cost of operating a fleet of delivery trucks? (Assume there are eight trucks, and they are driven an average of 25,000 miles each.)

Now we turn to the information the accounting department provided about the number of packages delivered. Then we use the scatter graphing method to plot maintenance cost as the dependent (*y*) variable and packages delivered as the independent (*x*) variable. Exhibit 5–12 shows a scatter graph of the maintenance cost and packages delivered.

EXHIBIT 5–12   Scatter Graph for Vehicle Maintenance Cost and Packages Delivered

DATA:	Truck Number	Packages Delivered	Maintenance Cost
	202	1,200	$2,000
	204	1,000	1,600
	205	1,500	2,200
	301	1,500	2,400
	422	500	2,600
	460	1,000	2,200
	520	2,000	2,000

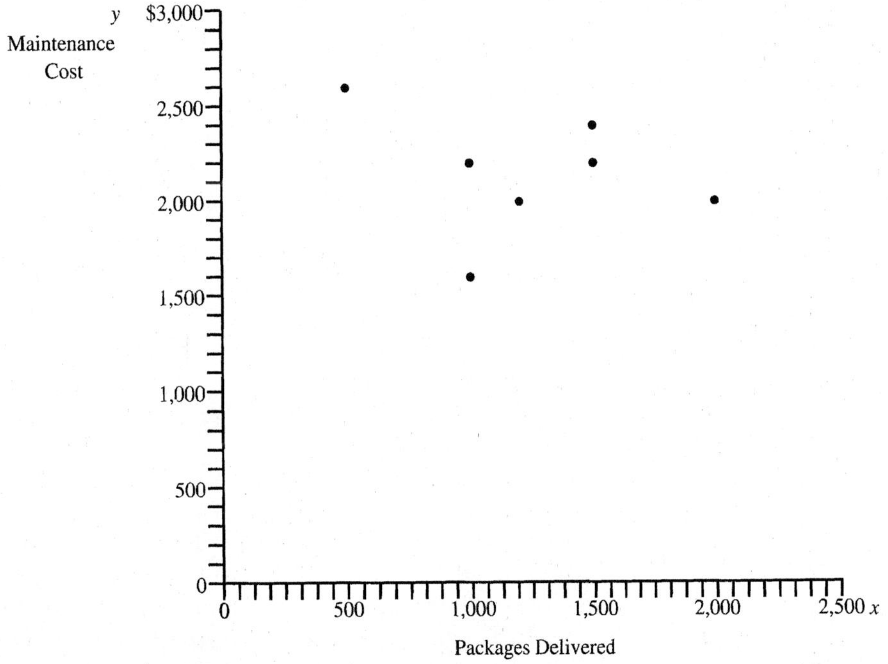

We draw a straight line through the points depicted by the observations, as in Exhibit 5–13.

Note in Exhibit 5–13 that placing a straight line through the points on this graph is considerably more challenging than in the previous scatter graphs. This is because a straight line could take any one of several paths through the points on the graph. Each of the lines seems to depict the relationship between maintenance cost and packages delivered, but none does a very good job. The reason for the difficulty is that the relationship between the variables is not linear. How do we use this method if the data do not have a clear linear relationship? Well, we don't. Before we determine fixed and variable cost using the scatter graph method, we must be sure the activity we have chosen has a relatively linear relationship with the cost in question. If we plot points on a graph and the coordinates resemble a random pattern with little linearity, the data do not indicate a constant relationship between the activity and the cost. In the case of a random pattern, any conclusions drawn from the data will be useless for predicting future cost, and may cause trouble if used. Once we see that random pattern, then, we should not use the packages delivered data to estimate the fixed and variable elements of vehicle maintenance cost.

EXHIBIT 5–13   Scatter Graph for Vehicle Maintenance Cost and Packages Delivered

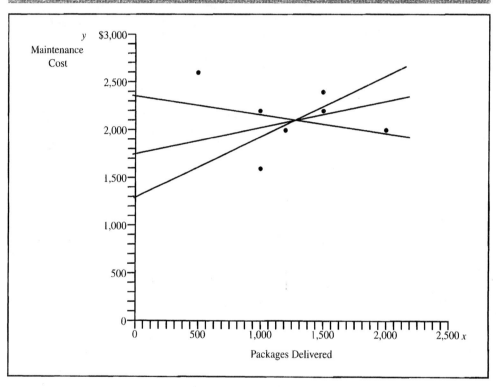

Even if a scatter graph appears to represent a linear relationship between an activity and a cost, we must be cautious to not imply relationships that do not exist. For instance, if we tried to determine cost behavior of vehicle maintenance cost by relating it to an activity such as the number of direct labor hours worked, we might possibly get mathematically reasonable results. However, common sense tells us that no relationship exists between direct labor hours and vehicle maintenance cost, so the results would be meaningless. A random guess would provide as good or better information. The activity and cost should have a clear, common sense relationship.

THE HIGH–LOW METHOD

high–low method   A method used to separate a mixed cost into its fixed and variable components using the mathematical differences between the highest and lowest levels of activity and cost.

Like the scatter graph approach, the **high–low method** uses historical data and mathematical computations to approximate the fixed and variable components of mixed cost. To illustrate the steps required by the high–low method, we review the following vehicle maintenance cost and activity data gathered for the Hinds Wholesale Supply Company:

Truck Number	Miles Driven	Maintenance Cost
202	1,200	$2,000
204	1,000	1,600
205	1,500	2,200
301	1,500	2,400
422	500	2,600
460	1,000	2,200
520	2,000	2,000

The high–low method focuses on the mathematical differences between the highest and lowest observations. Unless one or both of them is an outlier. That is, unless one of them is clearly too high or too low to be representative of the rest of the data. In such a case, we would select the next highest or lowest observation. If we examine the data list, we see that the highest observation is 31,000 miles with maintenance cost of $2,600. The lowest observation is 11,000 miles with maintenance cost of $1,600.

Remember, our purpose is to find the amount of the fixed and variable elements of a mixed cost. With the high–low method, we focus on determining the variable component of the cost first. The calculations to determine variable cost per unit are similar to those used in scatter graphing. By comparing the differences in activity and cost between the highest observation and the lowest observation, we can calculate a per unit cost that describes the relationship shown by these differences as follows:

	Miles	Cost
High	31,000	$ 2,600
Low	(11,000)	(1,600)
Difference	20,000	$1,000

Notice the mileage difference of 20,000 miles is accompanied by a cost difference of $1,000. So, to drive the extra 20,000 miles, the company spent $1,000 more in maintenance cost. We assume that the $1,000 increase in maintenance cost was caused exclusively by the increase in the number of miles from 11,000 to 31,000 miles. The cost per mile, then, is simply the $1,000 increased cost divided by the 20,000 additional miles as shown here:

$$\$1,000 \div 20,000 = \$0.05, \text{ or 5 cents per mile}$$

Before we calculate the fixed cost element, recall that total mixed cost is total fixed cost plus total variable cost (Total mixed cost = Fixed cost element + Variable cost element). The variable cost element can be calculated by multiplying the variable cost per unit by the activity. In this case we multiply the variable cost per mile by the number of miles. With what we have determined thus far, we can begin to construct a cost formula for vehicle maintenance cost as follows:

Total mixed cost = Fixed cost element + ($0.05 per mile driven)

For each of our observations (high and low), we know the total mixed cost and variable cost element. Therefore, we can easily determine the fixed cost element with simple calculations. Let's determine the fixed cost element associated with the high observation used in our example.

Total mixed cost = Fixed cost element + ($0.05 per mile driven)

$$\$2,600 = ? + (\$0.05 \times 31,000)$$
$$\$2,600 = ? + \quad \$1,550$$

To solve the equation, the fixed cost element must be $2,600 − $1,550, or $1,050, shown as follows:

Total mixed cost = Fixed cost element + ($0.05 per mile driven)

$$\$2,600 = \$1,050 + \$1,550$$

We now know both the variable cost per mile and the total fixed cost of operating one of the delivery vehicles. To check our math, we can do the same calculation for the low observation, as follows:

Total mixed cost = Fixed cost element + ($0.05 per mile driven)

$1,600 = ? + ($0.05 × 11,000)
$1,600 = ? + $550

For the low observation, to solve the equation, fixed cost must be $1,600 − $550, or $1,050, as we see next.

Total mixed cost = Fixed cost element + ($0.05 per mile driven)

$1,600 = $1,050 + $550

Note that you must use either the high or the low to determine the fixed cost. Using an observation other than the ones you used for the variable cost calculation will provide an erroneous fixed cost amount.

The high–low method yields a fixed cost for maintenance of $1,050, and a variable cost of 5 cents per mile. As with scatter graphing, to estimate the mixed cost at a particular level of activity we add the fixed cost to the activity multiplied by the cost per unit of activity. For example, the estimated maintenance cost for a single delivery truck that will be driven 28,000 miles is $2,450, calculated as follows:

$2,450 = $1,050 + ($0.05 × 28,000)

Discussion Questions ●

5–14. Using the high–low method and the data from our example, what would be the maintenance cost for operating one of the delivery trucks if we expected the truck to be driven 25,000 miles next year?

5–15. Using the high–low method and the information from our Hinds Company example, what would be the maintenance cost for operating the fleet of eight trucks, if each is to be driven 25,000 miles on average?

When we compare the scatter graph method with the high–low method, we find that the fixed and variable cost results are somewhat different. If you were going to present your cost estimates to the vice president of marketing, which method would you use? Which provides the more dependable information? The scatter graph method is based on visual estimation, whereas the high–low method is based on hard mathematics with no visual estimation. Does that make the high–low method better? No, because the high–low method considers only two observations. What if these two observations are not representative of the data in general? Then the cost behavior conclusions will be flawed and possibly misleading.

Another drawback to the high–low method is that users cannot assess whether the data items have a linear relationship, which is necessary to find meaningful results. Because the scatter graph method considers all observations and indicates whether the data items have a linear relationship, practitioners regard it as superior to the high–low method, despite the fact that it is more time consuming to use and it is based on visual estimation.

REGRESSION ANALYSIS

regression analysis A method used to separate a mixed cost into its fixed and variable components using complex mathematical formulas.

least-squares method
Another name for *regression analysis*.

Regression analysis, also called the **least-squares method** or **linear regression analysis,** is a mathematical approach to determining fixed and variable cost with statistical accuracy. The mathematical computations are complex and beyond the scope of this text. However, it is important to note that regression analysis is a more reliable estimation technique than either the scatter graph method or the high–low method. Regression analysis uses the information contained in all the observations in a data set. This thoroughness makes it superior to the high–low method. Because it considers all these points of observation mathematically, rather than visually, regression analysis is also superior to the scatter graph method. The basic mathematical equation for regression analysis follows:

linear regression analysis
Another name for *regression analysis.*

$$y = a + bx$$

Where:

y = The dependent variable, or the variable that changes in response to a change in x

a = The y intercept, or the amount for y when x is zero

b = The slope coefficient, or the amount by which y changes when x is increased by one

x = The independent variable

When applying regression analysis to find the fixed and variable elements of a mixed cost, the variables in the regression equation are defined as follows:

y = Total cost
a = Fixed cost
b = Unit variable cost
x = Activity level

Results of regression analysis would provide answers to the same questions that we posed for the scatter graph and the high–low methods. In fact, the results of regression analysis allow us to determine total cost, y, for any given level of activity, x. Reexamine the basic regression analysis formula and compare it with the total cost equation. When we rewrite the equation, we see that it translates directly to our earlier total cost equation, as follows:

$$y \quad = \quad a \quad + \quad bx$$
Total cost = Fixed cost + (Unit variable cost × Activity level)

Although regression analysis is difficult to compute manually, almost all business calculators, such as the ***Hewlett-Packard 12c***, are programmed to compute linear regression problems. By reading your calculator's instruction manual and practicing a little, you can easily determine fixed and variable cost components of a mixed cost using linear regression. In addition, most spreadsheet software packages provide easy-to-use regression functions. In the following section we will briefly demonstrate how you can use ***Microsoft*** Excel, a very popular spreadsheet program, to prepare cost behavior scatter graphs.

MICROSOFT EXCEL—PREPARING AN EXCEL SCATTER GRAPH

Basically, all we are going to do here is to use ***Microsoft*** Excel to prepare the charts that we prepared by hand when we covered the scatter graph approach. As we did with the manual scatter graph approach, we will use historical data and let Excel's Chart Wizard do the graphing and mathematical computations to approximate costs at various levels of activity.

Microsoft Excel's Chart Wizard uses a four-step sequence to prepare the graphs we need. Fortunately for most of us, the Chart Wizard is similar to most other ***Microsoft*** Wizards—it is so easy to use that even computer novices can easily prepare professional-looking charts with just a little practice.

To illustrate the use of Excel, we will again use the following vehicle maintenance cost and activity data gathered for the Hinds Wholesale Supply Company:

Truck Number	Miles Driven	Maintenance Cost
202	15,000	$2,000
204	11,000	1,600
205	24,000	2,200
301	30,000	2,400
422	31,000	2,600
460	26,000	2,200
520	20,000	2,000

To begin, you must open a new spreadsheet and enter the data in columns. You may also enter labels, such as column headings and the truck numbers, but these will not be used to prepare the Excel chart. For our example, we will enter column headings, truck numbers, and the number of miles driven in one column and the cost of operating the maintenance department in the adjacent column. To label the contents of each column, enter *Truck No.* in cell A1, in cell B1 enter *Miles*, and in cell C1 enter *Cost*. Then place the first truck's number in cell A2, the number of miles for the first truck in cell B2, and its cost in cell C2. Do the same thing for the second truck by placing its truck number in cell A3, the miles for the second truck in cell B3, and its cost in cell C3. Do this for all of the remaining trucks. It is critical that the amounts for the independent variable (the activity) be entered in the column just before the column for the amounts for the dependent variable (the mixed cost). This is why we used column B for the activity (the miles) and the next column, column C, for the mixed cost (the maintenance cost). When you are done, your spreadsheet should look like the one in Exhibit 5–14.

	A	B	C
1	Truck Number	Miles	Cost
2	202	15,000	$2,000
3	204	11,000	1,600
4	205	24,000	2,200
5	301	30,000	2,400
6	422	31,000	2,600
7	460	26,000	2,200
8	520	20,000	2,000

EXHIBIT 5–14 *Microsoft* Excel Spreadsheet with Data for Hinds Wholesale Supply Company

Next, highlight all the cells that include the activity and cost data. For our example, highlight only the cells that contain amounts for the number of miles and maintenance costs. Your highlighted spreadsheet should look like the one in Exhibit 5–15.

	A	B	C
1	Truck Number	Miles	Cost
2	202	15,000	$2,000
3	204	11,000	1,600
4	205	24,000	2,200
5	301	30,000	2,400
6	422	31,000	2,600
7	460	26,000	2,200
8	520	20,000	2,000

EXHIBIT 5–15 *Microsoft* Excel Spreadsheet with Highlighted Data for Hinds Wholesale Supply Company

Next select the **Insert** pull-down menu and click on **Chart,** which is about one third of the way down the list. The Chart Wizard box will appear. Note that the box is labeled **Chart Wizard—Step 1 of 4.** From the list of **Chart** types, click **XY (Scatter)** and the Wizard's default scatter graph. This will be the scatter graph without any lines connecting the plotted points. Once you have clicked **XY (Scatter),** click **Next.**

You are now at **Chart Wizard—Step 2 of 4.** This step is to set date ranges for rows and columns. For this step, simply click **Next.**

You are now at **Chart Wizard—Step 3 of 4.** In this step, you can customize the labels on your chart so it looks professional. To begin, for chart title, enter something like *Hinds Company Vehicle Maintenance Cost and Miles Driven.* For **Value (X) axis** enter *Miles Driven,* and for **Value (Y) axis** enter *Maintenance Cost.* On the **Legend** tab, click the **Show legend** box to remove the checkmark. Then click **Next.**

You are now at **Chart Wizard—Step 4 of 4.** Unless you would like the chart to appear on another sheet of your workbook, simply click **Finish.** Your chart should look like the one in Exhibit 5–16.

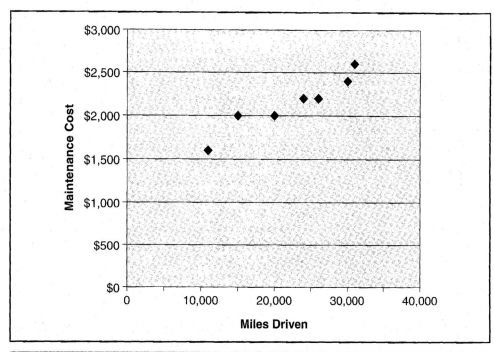

EXHIBIT 5-16   *Microsoft* Excel Scatter Graph for the Hinds Company

There is one more element to add to the chart. So that it can be used to predict costs, we now add a regression line, or what Excel calls a trend line. To do this, select the **Chart** pull-down menu and click on **Add Trendline.** The **Add Trendline** box will appear. Go with the default trend line (the straight one) and then click on the **Options** tab. It's a good idea to extend the trend line backward to the *y* axis and forward beyond its highest point. Otherwise, the trend line will end at the graph's lowest and highest plotted points. To extend the trend line backward to the *y* axis, in the box for **Forecast Backward,** enter the lowest *x* value from your data set. Using the Hinds example, enter 11,000, which is the *x* value for the truck with the fewest miles. In the box for **Forecast Forward,** we will enter 2,000 for this example, which represents the number of miles to extend the trend line forward. Once you have entered the values for **Forecast Backward** and **Forecast Forward,** click **OK.** At this point, your chart should look like the one in Exhibit 5–17.

EXHIBIT 5-17   *Microsoft* Excel Scatter Graph with Trend Line for the Hinds Company

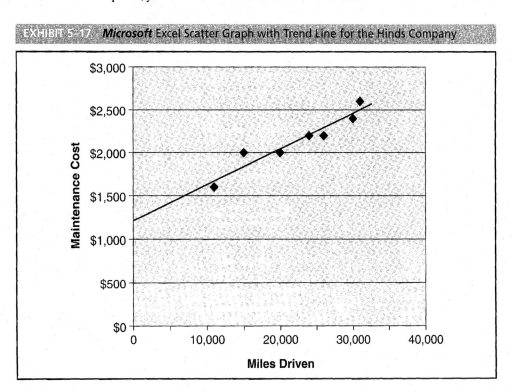

The Excel chart you have just prepared is very similar to the manually prepared ones we demonstrated earlier in this chapter. The most significant difference is that Excel uses regression analysis to precisely plot the chart's trend line, whereas we used visual estimation to plot it manually. Most people are more confident using an Excel chart because it is prepared with statistical accuracy and without any visual estimation.

Once you have prepared a chart similar to the one in Exhibit 5–17, you can predict costs for any level of activity shown on the chart. For example, we can readily see that the fixed cost of vehicle maintenance for Hinds is about $1,200. And for a truck driven 25,000, the maintenance cost should be about $2,250.

We have presented only the most basic use of Excel's Chart Wizard capabilities. You can customize the chart, making it easier to use, by adding additional tick marks and making other modifications. Consult Excel's help screens to learn more about customizing the charts you prepare.

No matter which of the methods a company uses to separate mixed costs into fixed and variable elements, the outcome of the mixed cost analysis is useful information for controlling costs, setting prices, and assessing profitability. Indeed, a variety of internal users of accounting information, from marketing managers to production managers, will want access to such cost behavior information.

Whether large or small, simple or complex, managers of all companies must understand cost behavior. Production managers at companies as diverse as *Caterpillar Tractor* and *Campbell Soup Company* need this information to plan and control their operations. Marketing managers at companies as different as *General Motors* and *Gerber Baby Foods* must know how costs react to activity if they are to do their jobs properly.

Once a determination has been made as to a cost's behavior, an appropriate notation can be made in the accounting records to designate it as fixed, variable, or mixed. Then, the accounting system can produce reports sorted by cost behavior. Internal reports providing cost behavior information are valuable in a variety of decision making settings. We will explore several of these settings in more detail in the next chapter.

Summary

If managers are to plan and control their operations effectively, they must understand cost behavior. Cost behavior is the reaction of costs to changes in levels of business activity.

Common cost behavior patterns are fixed cost, variable cost, and mixed cost. A fixed cost is a cost that remains constant in total regardless of the level of activity within the relevant range. A variable cost is a cost that changes in total proportionately with changes in the level of activity within the relevant range. The relevant range is the range of activity within which fixed and variable cost assumptions are valid. A mixed cost is a cost that has both a fixed cost element and a variable cost element.

Several alternative methods are used to separate mixed costs into their fixed and variable components. The most commonly used methods are the engineering approach, scatter graphing, the high–low method, and regression analysis.

The engineering approach to separating a mixed cost into its fixed and variable components uses experts who are familiar with the technical aspects of the activity and associated cost. Scatter graphing separates a mixed cost into its fixed and variable components by plotting historical activity and cost data to see how a cost relates to various levels of activity. The high–low method uses the mathematical differences between the highest and lowest levels of activity and cost. Regression analysis uses complex mathematical formulas, but the results are more mathematically precise than those of the scatter graph or high-low method. *Microsoft* Excel uses regression analysis and an easy-to-use Chart Wizard to prepare precise, high-quality scatter graphs for mixed costs.

Regardless of the method that managers choose to separate mixed costs into fixed and variable elements, the analysis provides useful information for a myriad of business decisions.

Key Terms

- cost behavior, M–117
- engineering approach, M–124
- fixed costs, M–118
- high–low method, M–130

- least-squares method, M–132
- linear regression analysis, M–133
- mixed cost, M–123
- regression analysis, M–132

- relevant range, M–121
- scatter graph approach, M–124
- variable costs, M–118

Review the Facts

A. What is cost behavior?
B. For fixed costs, what happens to total cost as activity increases?
C. For fixed costs, what happens to the cost per unit as activity increases?
D. For variable cost, what happens to total cost as activity increases?
E. For variable cost, what happens to the cost per unit as activity increases?
F. With respect to cost behavior, what is the relevant range?
G. Does the relevant range pertain to fixed costs, variable costs, or both fixed and variable costs?
H. What are the two elements of a mixed cost?
I. What are the four methods of separating a mixed cost into its two cost components?
J. Compare the high–low method to the scatter graph method. Which provides the more dependable information?
K. What is the major limitation of the high–low method?
L. What is another name for regression analysis?
M. If you desired the reliability of the regression analysis method but did not want to suffer through the difficulty of doing the mathematics manually, what would you do?

Apply What You Have Learned

LO 2: CLASSIFYING COST BY COST BEHAVIOR

5–16. Indicate whether the following costs are more likely to be fixed (F), variable (V), or mixed (M) with respect to the number of units manufactured.

1. _____ Direct material
2. _____ Direct labor
3. _____ Cost of the plant security guard
4. _____ Straight line depreciation on production equipment
5. _____ Maintenance on production equipment
6. _____ Maintenance on factory building
7. _____ Cost of cleaning supplies used in the factory
8. _____ Rent on the factory building
9. _____ Salary for the two factory supervisors
10. _____ Vice president of manufacturing's salary
11. _____ Cost of electricity used in the factory
12. _____ Cost of production machine lubricants

LO 2: CLASSIFYING COST BY COST BEHAVIOR

5–17. Assume that you are trying to analyze the costs associated with driving your car. Indicate whether the following costs are more likely to be fixed (F), variable (V), or mixed (M) with respect to the number of miles driven.

1. _____ Cost of the car
2. _____ Insurance cost
3. _____ Maintenance cost
4. _____ Cost of gasoline
5. _____ The cost of a college parking permit
6. _____ AAA membership

LO 2: CLASSIFYING COST BY COST BEHAVIOR

5–18. Assume that you are planning a large party. As you are trying to figure out how much the party will cost, you decide to separate the costs according to cost behavior. Indicate whether the following costs are more likely to be fixed (F), variable (V), or mixed (M) with respect to the number of guests attending the party.

1. _____ Rent for the party hall
2. _____ Cost of the band
3. _____ Cost of cold drinks
4. _____ Cost of food
5. _____ Cost of party decorations
6. _____ Cost of renting tables and chairs

LO 2: CLASSIFYING COST BY COST BEHAVIOR

5–19. Assume that you have been assigned to analyze the costs associated with operating the law firm of Moore & Moore and Company. The law firm just moved into a new, large office building that it purchased last year. Indicate whether the following costs are more likely to be fixed (F), variable (V), or mixed (M) with respect to the number of attorneys working for the firm.

1. _____ Cost of the new office building
2. _____ Basic telephone service
3. _____ Cost of attorney salaries
4. _____ Cost of the receptionist's wages

LO 2: CLASSIFYING COST BY COST BEHAVIOR

5–20. Assume that you have been assigned to analyze the costs of a retail merchandiser, Auto Parts City. Indicate whether the following costs are more likely fixed (F), variable (V), or mixed (M) with respect to the dollar amount of sales.

1. _____ Cost of store rent
2. _____ Basic telephone service
3. _____ Cost of salaries for the two salespeople
4. _____ Cost of advertising
5. _____ Cost of store displays
6. _____ Cost of electricity
7. _____ Cost of merchandise sold

LO 4: EVALUATING A MIXED COST SITUATION

5–21. Assume that you work for Wilma Manufacturing Company and have been asked to review the cost of delivery truck maintenance. The company president, Wilma Hudik, is dissatisfied with the accounting department's reluctance to calculate the fixed and variable cost of truck maintenance as it pertains to the number of units produced in the factory. The accounting department prepared the following scatter graph:

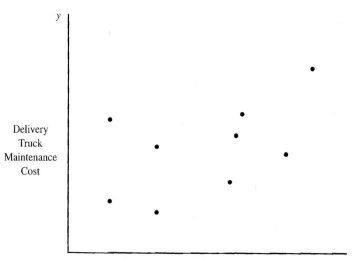

The accounting department personnel seem unable to use the graph to determine fixed and variable cost. The company president knows that regression analysis will provide mathematically accurate amounts for the fixed and variable truck maintenance cost, but no one in the accounting department seems to know how to do it.

Required: Prepare a short memo to the president that details the feasibility of using the scatter graph and regression analysis to determine the fixed and variable components of delivery truck maintenance relative to the amount of factory production. In addition, your memo should recommend an alternative approach that could be used to evaluate the cost and cost behavior of truck maintenance.

LO 5: USE OF A SCATTER GRAPH FOR SEPARATING MIXED COST

5–22. Consider the following scatter graphs:

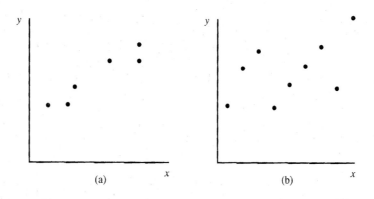

(a)   (b)

Required: Which of the scatter graphs (a or b) do you think would be more appropriate for determining the fixed and variable portions of a mixed cost? Explain your reasoning.

LO 5: SEPARATING MIXED COST USING THE HIGH–LOW METHOD

5–23. The following information pertains to Jacobs Incorporated:

2004 Information:	
Sales	$2,300,000
Selling expense	347,000

2005 Information:	
Sales	$2,860,000
Selling expense	369,400

Required: Using the high–low method, determine the following:

a. The variable cost element for selling expense
b. The fixed selling expense
c. The selling expense that can be expected if sales are $2,500,000

LO 5: SEPARATING MIXED COST USING THE HIGH–LOW METHOD

5–24. The following information pertains to the Robin Rappaport Company:

2004 Information:	
Units packaged	14,500
Packaging cost	$32,567

2005 Information:	
Units packaged	15,300
Packaging cost	$33,191

Required: Using the high–low method, determine the following:

a. The variable cost element for packaging cost
b. The fixed packaging cost
c. The packaging cost that can be expected if 15,000 units are packaged

LO 5: SEPARATING MIXED COST USING THE HIGH–LOW METHOD

5–25. The inspection department at the Rose Spiegel Company inspects every third unit produced. The following information is available for the inspection department:

2004 Information:
Number of inspections	41,950
Inspection cost	$77,273

2005 Information:
Number of inspections	48,600
Inspection cost	$83,790

Required: Using the high–low method, determine the following:

a. The variable cost element for inspection cost
b. The fixed inspection cost
c. The inspection cost that can be expected if 45,000 units are inspected

LO 5: SEPARATING MIXED COST USING THE HIGH–LOW METHOD

5–26. The plant manager has asked you to analyze the cost of electricity used in the manufacturing facility. Information for 2004 and 2005 follows:

	2004	2005
Machine hours	100,000	120,000
Cost of electricity	$188,000	$221,600

Required: Using the high–low method, determine the following:

a. The variable rate for electricity per machine hour.
b. The total fixed cost of electricity.
c. The estimated cost of electricity for next year if machine hours are expected to be 122,500.

LO 5: SEPARATING MIXED COST USING THE HIGH–LOW METHOD

5–27. The office manager has asked you to analyze the cost of service and supplies for the office copy machines. Information for 2004 and 2005 follows:

	2004	2005
Number of copies produced	52,550	77,800
Cost of service and supplies	$1,961.57	$2,592.82

Required: Using the high–low method, determine the following:

a. The variable cost per copy.
b. The total fixed cost for service and supplies for the copy machines.
c. The estimated cost of service and supplies for next year if 75,000 copies are made.

LO 5: SEPARATING MIXED COST USING THE HIGH–LOW METHOD

5–28. The production manager has asked you to analyze the cost of materials handling. Information for 2004 and 2005 follows:

	2004	2005
Number of parts handled	154,300	185,400
Materials handling cost	$9,244.77	$10,675.37

Required: Using the high–low method, determine the following:

a. The variable cost per part handled.
b. The total fixed cost for materials handling.
c. The estimated cost of materials handling if 160,000 parts are handled next year.

LO 5: SEPARATING MIXED COST USING THE HIGH–LOW METHOD

5–29. The sales manager has asked you to estimate the shipping cost that can be expected for 2006. Following is information for 2004 and 2005:

	2004	2005
Sales in units	15,000	18,000
Shipping cost	$30,000	$35,400

Required: Estimate 2006 shipping cost assuming sales of 16,500 units.

LO 5: SEPARATING MIXED COST USING THE HIGH–LOW METHOD

5–30. The transportation manager has asked you to estimate the operating cost that can be expected for the company jet for 2006. Following is information for 2004 and 2005:

	2004	2005
Flight time in hours	1,250	1,875
Aircraft operating cost	$1,563,750	$2,148,125

Required: Estimate the cost of operating the company jet for 2006 assuming that flight time will be 1,500 hours.

LO 5: SEPARATING MIXED COST USING THE HIGH–LOW METHOD

5–31. Tom Robinson is the owner of Robinson Fishing Guide Service. He is trying to estimate the cost of operating his fishing service next year. He expects to have 185 charters during 2006. The following information is available:

	2004	2005
Number of charters	150	190
Operating cost	$7,741	$8,601

Required: Determine the estimated operating cost for 2006.

LO 5: SEPARATING MIXED COST USING THE HIGH–LOW METHOD

5–32. The following information pertains to Picon Manufacturing for 2003 and 2004:

	Number of Purchase Orders Issued	Cost of Operating the Purchasing Department
Fourth quarter of 2003	2,500	$130,000
First quarter of 2004	1,000	80,000
Second quarter of 2004	1,500	110,000
Third quarter of 2004	2,000	115,000
Fourth quarter of 2004	3,000	140,000

Required: Using the high–low method, determine the following:
  a. The variable cost per purchase order.
  b. The fixed cost of operating the purchasing department for one quarter.
  c. The estimated cost of operating the purchasing department in 2005 assuming that 7,000 purchase orders will be issued. (*Hint*: Remember that the fixed cost for one year is four times the amount of fixed cost for one quarter.)

LO 5: SEPARATING MIXED COST USING THE SCATTER GRAPH METHOD

5–33. Refer to the information from problem 5–32.

Required: Using the scatter graph method, determine the following:
  a. The variable cost per purchase order.
  b. The fixed cost of operating the purchasing department for one quarter.
  c. The estimated cost of operating the purchasing department in 2005 assuming that 7,000 purchase orders will be issued. (*Hint*: Remember that the fixed cost for one year is four times the amount of fixed cost for one quarter.)

LO 6: SCATTER GRAPH USING *MICROSOFT* EXCEL'S CHART WIZARD

5–34. Refer to the information from problem 5–32.

Required:

a. Use *Microsoft* Excel to prepare a scatter graph for the data presented.
b. Estimate the fixed cost of operating the purchasing department for one quarter.
c. Estimate the cost of operating the purchasing department for a quarter assuming that 1,500 purchase orders are issued.

LO 5: SEPARATING MIXED COST USING THE HIGH–LOW METHOD

5–35. The following information pertains to Mendelsohn Bottled Spring Water:

	Number of Sales Invoices Processed	Cost of Operating the Invoicing Department
Fourth quarter of 2003	10,500	$49,310.65
First quarter of 2004	11,000	50,332.12
Second quarter of 2004	15,000	58,120.19
Third quarter of 2004	12,000	51,939.73
Fourth quarter of 2004	9,000	46,240.19

Required: Using the high–low method, determine the following:

a. The variable cost per invoice processed.
b. The fixed cost of operating the invoicing department for one quarter.
c. The estimated cost of operating the invoicing department in 2005 assuming that 45,000 invoices will be processed. (*Hint*: Remember that the fixed cost for one year is four times the amount of fixed cost for one quarter.)

LO 5: SEPARATING MIXED COST USING THE HIGH–LOW METHOD

5–36. The following information pertains to Jillian Munter & Associates:

	Number of Computers Repaired	Cost of Operating the Repair Department
Fourth quarter of 2003	125	$26,100.91
First quarter of 2004	130	26,529.16
Second quarter of 2004	110	25,400.65
Third quarter of 2004	105	25,212.91
Fourth quarter of 2004	115	25,799.88

Required: Using the high–low method, determine the following:

a. The variable cost per computer repair.
b. The fixed cost of operating the repair department for one quarter.
c. The estimated cost of operating the repair department in 2005 assuming that 450 invoices will be processed. (*Hint*: Remember that the fixed cost for one year is four times the amount of fixed cost for one quarter.)

LO 5: SEPARATING MIXED COST USING THE HIGH–LOW METHOD

5–37. The following information is taken from Sweepy Broom Manufacturing Company:

	Number of Brooms Produced	Total Production Cost
January	9,800	$17,100
February	7,000	15,000
March	8,000	16,000
April	7,500	15,500
May	10,100	17,200

June	9,000	17,000
July	10,500	19,000
August	11,600	20,000
September	10,600	18,200
October	8,500	16,800
November	12,100	20,500
December	11,000	18,000

Required: Using the high–low method, determine the following:

    a. The variable production cost per unit.
    b. The total fixed production cost.
    c. The expected production cost to produce 12,000 brooms.

LO 5: SEPARATING MIXED COST USING THE SCATTER GRAPH METHOD

5–38. Refer to the information in problem 5–37.

Required: Using the scatter graph method, determine the following:

    a. The variable production cost per unit.
    b. The total fixed production cost.
    c. The expected production cost to produce 12,000 brooms.

LO 6: SCATTER GRAPH USING *MICROSOFT* EXCEL'S CHART WIZARD

5–39. Refer to the information in problem 5–37.

Required:

    a. Use *Microsoft* Excel to prepare a scatter graph for the data presented.
    b. Estimate the total fixed production cost.
    c. Estimate the expected production cost to produce 12,000 brooms.

LO 5: SEPARATING MIXED COST USING THE HIGH–LOW METHOD

5–40. Ace Computer Training offers short computer courses. The number of course sessions offered depends on student demand. The following information pertains to 2005:

	Number of Sessions	Cost
First quarter	30	$ 75,000
Second quarter	35	78,000
Third quarter	15	42,000
Fourth quarter	20	48,000
Total	100	$243,000

Required: Using the high–low method, determine the following:

    a. The variable cost per session.
    b. The total fixed cost of operating the company.
    c. The expected cost for a quarter if 25 sessions are offered.

LO 5: SEPARATING MIXED COST USING THE SCATTER GRAPH METHOD

5–41. Refer to the information in problem 5–40.

Required: Using the scatter graph method, determine the following:

    a. The variable cost per session.
    b. The total fixed cost of operating the company.
    c. The expected cost for a quarter if 25 sessions are offered.

LO 6: SCATTER GRAPH USING *MICROSOFT* EXCEL'S CHART WIZARD

5–42. Refer to the information in problem 5–40.

Required:

   a. Use *Microsoft* Excel to prepare a scatter graph for the data presented.

   b. Estimate the total fixed cost of operating the company.

   c. Estimate the expected cost for a quarter if 25 sessions are offered.

LO 5: SEPARATING MIXED COST USING THE HIGH–LOW METHOD

5–43. The following information is taken from Miami Avionics Testing Service:

	Number of Tests Performed	Total Cost of Testing
January	61,000	$1,420,000
February	55,000	1,340,000
March	50,000	1,290,000
April	72,000	1,430,000
May	78,000	1,440,000
June	81,000	1,540,000
July	90,000	1,590,000
August	108,000	1,610,000
September	111,000	1,700,000
October	128,000	1,720,000
November	140,000	1,860,000
December	132,000	1,810,000

Required: Using the high–low method, determine the following:

   a. The variable cost per test.

   b. The total fixed cost of operating the testing facility.

   c. The expected cost for a month if 125,000 tests are performed.

LO 5: SEPARATING MIXED COST USING THE SCATTER GRAPH METHOD

5–44. Refer to the information in problem 5–43.

Required: Using the scatter graph method, determine the following:

   a. The variable cost per test.

   b. The total fixed cost of operating the testing facility.

   c. The expected cost for a month if 125,000 tests are performed.

LO 6: SCATTER GRAPH USING *MICROSOFT* EXCEL'S CHART WIZARD

5–45. Refer to the information in problem 5–43.

Required:

   a. Use *Microsoft* Excel to prepare a scatter graph for the data presented.

   b. Estimate the total fixed cost of operating the testing facility.

   c. Estimate the expected cost for a month if 125,000 tests are performed.

LO 5: SEPARATING MIXED COST USING THE HIGH–LOW METHOD

5–46. The following information is for the Valdez Supply Company:

	2005	2006
Sales	$1,000,000	$1,150,000
Costs:		
Cost of goods sold	$ 800,000	$ 920,000
Sales commissions	15,000	17,250
Store rent	3,000	3,000
Depreciation	20,000	20,000
Maintenance cost	3,800	4,100
Office salaries	34,000	35,500

Required: Assuming sales is the activity base, use the high–low method to determine the variable cost element and the fixed cost element of each of the costs just listed.

LO 5: SEPARATING MIXED COST USING THE HIGH–LOW METHOD

5–47. The following information is for the General Production Company:

	2005	2006
Units produced	257,000	326,000
Costs:		
Direct material	$ 611,660	$ 775,880
Direct labor	1,662,790	2,109,220
Manufacturing overhead	1,781,820	1,868,760

Required: Assuming units produced is the activity base, use the high–low method to determine the variable cost element and fixed cost element of each of the costs just listed.

LO 5: SEPARATING MIXED COST USING THE HIGH–LOW METHOD

5–48. The following information is for the Maupin Gift Shop:

	2005	2006
Sales	$100,000	$150,000
Costs:		
Cost of goods sold	$ 75,000	$112,500
Sales commissions	5,000	7,500
Store rent	1,000	1,000
Depreciation	500	500
Maintenance cost	200	250
Office salaries	5,000	6,000

Required:

a. Assuming sales is the activity base, use the high–low method to determine the variable cost element and the fixed cost element of each of the costs just listed.
b. Why is it useful to know the information requested in requirement a?

LO 4: COMPONENTS OF MIXED COST

5–49. Consider the following mathematical formula:

$$y = a + bx$$

Required: Match the variables to the correct descriptions. Some variables have two correct matches.

1. _____ y	a. Independent variable
2. _____ a	b. Variable cost per unit
3. _____ b	c. Dependent variable
4. _____ x	d. Total fixed cost
	e. Activity
	f. Total cost

LO 4: DESCRIBING THE METHODS OF SEPARATING MIXED COST

5–50. Mr. Robinson, the director of Medical Diagnostics Clinic, is preparing a presentation to the clinic's board of directors about the fee charged for thallium stress tests. Part of the presentation will include information about the variable cost element and fixed costs associated with the tests. The accounting department has provided the director with a report which details the monthly costs associated with the thallium stress tests and the number of tests performed each month. Mr. Robinson is contemplating whether to use the scatter graph method, the high–low method, or regression analysis to separate the cost into its variable cost element and fixed cost. The director has asked your help in choosing an appropriate method.

Required: Prepare a short report to Mr. Robinson providing insight into the strengths and weaknesses of the scatter graph method, the high–low method, and regression analysis.

LO 1, 2, 4, & 5: ANALYZING A SITUATION USING COST BEHAVIOR

5–51. Accents Furniture Company has been in business for two years. When the business began, Accents established a delivery department with a small fleet of trucks. The delivery department was designed to be able to handle the substantial future growth of the company. As expected, sales for the first two years of business were low and activity in the delivery department was minimal.

In an effort to control costs, Accents Furniture Company's store manager is considering a proposal from a delivery company to deliver the furniture sold by Accents for a flat fee of $30 per delivery.

The following information is available regarding the cost of operating Accents's delivery department during its first two years of business.

	2002	2003
Number of deliveries	600	700
Cost of operating the delivery department	$25,480	$26,480

Sales and the number of deliveries are expected to increase greatly in the coming years. For example, sales in 2004 will require an estimated 1,250 deliveries, while in 2005, it is expected that 1,775 deliveries will be required.

Due to the high growth rate, the store manager is concerned that the delivery cost will grow out of hand unless the proposal is accepted. He states that the cost per delivery was about $42.47 ($25,480/600) in 2004 and $37.83 ($26,480/700) in 2005. Even at the lower cost of $37.83, it seems the company can save about $7.83 ($30.00 − $37.83) per delivery. For 2005, the store manager believes the proposal can save the company about $13,898.25 (1,775 × $7.83).

Required: Assume that you have been assigned to a group which has been formed to analyze the delivery cost of Accents Furniture Company. Your group should prepare a report and presentation that indicates the advantage or disadvantage of accepting the proposed delivery contract. Your report and presentation should not only include calculations to support your recommended course of action, but should also address the non-monetary considerations of contracting with an outside source for delivery services.

LO 1, 2, 3, & 4: ADDRESSING A SITUATION USING COST BEHAVIOR CONCEPTS

5–52. Mr. Reed is considering starting his own business. He has worked for a large corporation all his life and desires a change of pace. He is most interested in retail merchandising, but does not know what products his new business should sell. Mr. Reed is unsure about how to proceed with this major change in his life and has hired a consulting firm to help. Assume that you have been assigned to the consulting group that will advise Mr. Reed.

Required: Your group is to prepare a report that recommends a particular product line for Mr. Reed's new retail merchandising business. In addition, your report should recommend ways for Mr. Reed to gather information about the various costs associated with the merchandising business you have recommended. Finally, your report should explain how costs are classified as variable, fixed, and mixed costs, and why such classification by cost behavior is important.

LO 1, 2, & 4: ANALYZING A SITUATION USING COST BEHAVIOR

5–53. The Bowl-O-Mat operates a small chain of bowling alleys in southern Florida. Bowl-O-Mat's president, Al Palmer, is considering adding a supervised playground facility to each of the bowling alley properties. The playgrounds would require that a small addition be built onto each of the bowling alley buildings. Each playground would include a swing, a slide, climbing bars, and some other small-scale playground equipment. Each child would be charged an admission fee to use the facility. It is expected that parents will stay at the bowling alleys longer while their children are occupied in the playground area.

Mr. Palmer is interested in obtaining cost information relative to the proposed playground project. He understands that the more hours each playground area is open for business, the higher the cost of operating the playground will be. Beyond that, he knows nothing of cost behavior patterns.

Required: Prepare a memorandum to Mr. Palmer that describes the following:

    a. The various variable, fixed, and mixed costs that are likely to be associated with the new playground facilities.

    b. The concept of fixed costs, variable costs, and mixed costs.

    c. Why an understanding of the methods available for estimating cost behavior patterns will help him to better plan and control his operations.

CHAPTER 6

Business Decisions Using Cost Behavior

Claudia June owns the Beachside T-Shirt Shop, one of many souvenir shops along Highway A1A in Daytona Beach, Florida. Beachside sold 3,000 T-shirts during 2003 (the company's first year of operation), and Claudia's accountant prepared the following multiple-step income statement for the year.

Beachside T-Shirt Shop
Income Statement
For the Year Ended December 31, 2003

Sales		$ 36,000
Cost of Goods Sold		21,600
Gross Profit		$ 14,400
Operating Expense:		
Selling Expense	$9,500	
Administrative Expense	7,900	(17,400)
Operating Loss		$ (3,000)

Claudia was satisfied with the results for 2003 because she didn't expect the store to be profitable in its first year. As she planned for 2004, Claudia figured she needed to increase sales by only 625 T-shirts to break even for the year. Her reasoning? Each T-shirt cost $7.20 and sold for $12, resulting in $4.80 gross profit per T-shirt ($12.00 − $7.20 = $4.80). If the shop sold 3,625 T-shirts, it would earn a gross profit of $17,400 (3,625 × $4.80), which would be exactly enough to cover the selling and administrative expenses of $17,400. If Claudia met her sales goal, the store would break even in its second year of operation. As luck would have it, Beachside T-Shirt Shop sold exactly 3,625 T-shirts during 2004. Each T-shirt sold for exactly $12 and cost the company exactly $7.20. Confident that the shop had broken even for the year, Claudia excitedly opened the envelope from her accountant and found the following multiple-step income statement for 2004.

Beachside T-Shirt Shop
Income Statement
For the Year Ended December 31, 2004

Sales		$ 43,500
Cost of Goods Sold		26,100
Gross Profit		$ 17,400
Operating Expense:		
Selling Expense	$10,438	
Administrative Expense	8,897	(19,335)
Operating Loss		$ (1,935)

Claudia was disappointed and discouraged when she saw an operating loss of $1,935 for the year. She rechecked the arithmetic and her assumptions about what it would take to break even for 2004 and could not understand why the store had an operating loss. Claudia wasn't aware of cost behavior. She failed to consider that some costs are affected by changes in activity level and others are not. In this chapter, we explore cost–volume–profit analysis and how businesspeople use this analytical technique to predict financial performance effectively.

Learning Objectives

After completing your work on this chapter, you should be able to do the following:

1. Describe the differences between a functional income statement and a contribution income statement.

2. Determine per unit amounts for sales, variable cost, and the contribution margin.

3. Determine the contribution margin ratio and explain its importance as a management tool.

4. Prepare and analyze a contribution income statement for a merchandising firm.

5. Describe cost–volume–profit (CVP) analysis and explain its importance as a management tool.

6. Use CVP analysis to determine the amount of sales required to break even or to earn a targeted profit.

7. Use CVP to perform sensitivity analysis.

◆ THE CONTRIBUTION INCOME STATEMENT

functional income statement An income statement that classifies cost by function (product cost and period cost).

As discussed in Chapter 5, classifying costs by cost behavior provides managers insight about forecasting cost at different levels of business activity. You can't find this valuable cost behavior information readily, however, in either the multiple-step or the single-step income statement. The traditional income statement, called a **functional income statement**, separates costs (expenses) as either product costs or period costs, and is used for financial reporting to external parties. For example, the income statement in the annual report for ***Barnes & Noble*** would have information about period and product costs. Management accountants have developed a special income statement format for internal use that categorizes costs by behavior (fixed cost and variable cost) rather than by function (product cost and period cost). It is called a **contribution income statement**. ***Barnes & Noble*** may use this kind of income statement as well, which would include information about fixed and variable costs. However it would be for internal use only. This new format is no more complicated than the income statements you studied in earlier chapters. The main difference between the two is that the contribution income statement lists variable costs first, followed by fixed costs. Note that generally accepted accounting principles (GAAP) do not permit businesses to use the contribution income statement for financial accounting—it is used only for internal decision making purposes.

contribution income statement An income statement that classifies cost by behavior (fixed cost and variable cost).

PURPOSE OF THE CONTRIBUTION INCOME STATEMENT

Let's return to the Beachside T-Shirt Shop example to see how a contribution income statement could have helped Claudia better predict the future profitability of her merchandising company. The two income statements presented for Beachside (2003 and 2004) were functional income statements. Beachside's 2003 functional income statement is reproduced as Exhibit 6–1.

We see that the cost information in Exhibit 6–1 is separated into product cost (cost of goods sold) and period cost (selling expenses and administrative expenses). Next we will examine how Claudia can convert her functional income statement into a contribution income statement.

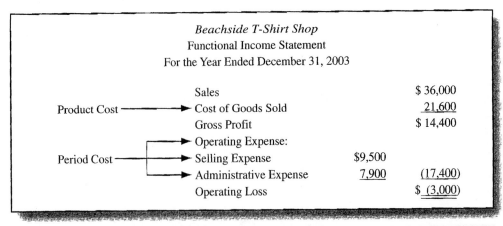

Beachside T-Shirt Shop
Functional Income Statement
For the Year Ended December 31, 2003

	Sales	$ 36,000
Product Cost ———→	Cost of Goods Sold	21,600
	Gross Profit	$ 14,400
	Operating Expense:	
Period Cost ———→	Selling Expense	$9,500
	Administrative Expense	7,900 (17,400)
	Operating Loss	$ (3,000)

EXHIBIT 6–1 Beachside's 2003 Functional Income Statement

First, Claudia needs additional information about the cost behavior of the expenses in Beachside's 2003 functional income statement. On request, Claudia's accountant provides the following information:

Cost of goods sold	All variable
Selling expense	40% variable, so 60% must be fixed
Administrative expense	$6,300 fixed, so $1,600 must be variable

Discussion Question ●

6–1. With the cost behavior information just presented, discuss how you could determine the change in profit if the company sells 5,000 shirts in 2005. (Remember to look at the 2004 income statement shown at the beginning of the chapter.)

Now that she has Beachside's cost behavior information, Claudia can prepare a contribution income statement for 2003. The contribution income statement lists sales first, with variable costs listed next. These costs are subtracted from sales to arrive at the contribution margin. **Contribution margin** is the amount remaining after all variable costs have been deducted from sales revenue. The contribution margin is an important piece of information for managers, because it tells them how much of their company's original sales dollars remain after deducting variable costs. This remaining portion of the sales dollars contributes to fixed costs and, once fixed costs have been covered, to profit. The contribution margin, then, is the amount available to contribute to covering fixed costs and ultimately toward profits.

contribution margin The amount remaining after all variable costs have been deducted from sales revenue.

Finally, fixed costs are listed and subtracted from the contribution margin to arrive at operating income, as shown in Exhibit 6–2.

Like a functional income statement, the contribution income statement can be detailed or condensed depending on the needs of the information users. We can also prepare it showing the per unit costs and percentage of sales calculations. A condensed version of Beachside's 2003 contribution income statement, including per unit and percentage of sales figures, is presented as Exhibit 6–3.

Throughout the rest of the chapter we will use a condensed version of the contribution income statement.

Discussion Question ●

6–2. How does the gross profit found on the functional income statement differ from the contribution margin found on the contribution income statement?

Looking at the per unit column in Exhibit 6–3, we note that the contribution margin per unit is $3. We calculate this by dividing the total contribution margin of $9,000 by the number of units sold—in this case 3,000 ($9,000 ÷ 3,000 = $3). The $3 per unit

Beachside T-Shirt Shop
Contribution Income Statement
For the Year Ended December 31, 2003

Sales		$ 36,000
Variable Cost:		
Cost of Goods Sold	$21,600	
Variable Selling Expense ($9,500 × 40%)	3,800	
Variable Administrative		
Expense ($7,900 − $6,300)	1,600	
Total Variable Cost		(27,000)
Contribution Margin (Sales Less Total Variable Cost)		$ 9,000
Fixed Cost:		
Fixed Selling Expense ($9,500 × 60%)	$ 5,700	
Fixed Administrative Expense	6,300	
Total Fixed Cost		(12,000)
Operating Loss		$ (3,000)

EXHIBIT 6–2   Beachside's Completed 2003 Contribution Income Statement

contribution margin means that for every T-shirt sold, the sale generates $3 to contribute toward fixed costs. Then, once fixed costs have been covered, $3 per T-shirt sold contributes to profit. The contribution margin contributes toward fixed cost first, then to profits.

Note in the percentage column of Exhibit 6–3 that the contribution margin is 25 percent of sales. When the contribution margin is expressed as a percentage of sales, it is called the **contribution margin ratio.**

contribution margin ratio
The contribution margin expressed as a percentage of sales.

We can calculate the contribution margin ratio by dividing the total contribution margin by total sales, or by dividing the per unit contribution margin by per unit selling price, as follows:

$$\frac{\text{Total contribution margin}}{\text{Total sales}} = \text{Contribution margin ratio}$$

or

$$\frac{\text{Per unit contribution margin}}{\text{Per unit selling price}} = \text{Contribution margin ratio}$$

EXHIBIT 6–3   Beachside's Condensed 2003 Contribution Income Statement

Beachside T-Shirt Shop
Contribution Income Statement
For the Year Ended December 31, 2003

	Total	Per Unit	Percent of Sales
Sales in Units	3,000	1	
Sales	$36,000	$12.00	100
Variable Cost	(27,000)	(9.00)	(75)
Contribution Margin	$ 9,000	$ 3.00	25
Fixed Cost	(12,000)		
Operating Loss	$ (3,000)		

In the case of Beachside T-shirt Shop, the calculations are as follows:

$$\frac{\$9,000}{\$36,000} = 25\%$$

or

$$\frac{\$3}{\$12} = 25\%$$

The contribution margin ratio is the same whether we compute it using total figures or per unit figures, because we base the contribution margin on sales minus only variable costs. Variable costs and contribution margin change in direct proportion to sales and this proportional relationship holds true whether we are using per unit amounts or amounts in total.

In our example, the 25 percent contribution margin ratio means that, of each sales dollar, 25 percent (or 25 cents) is available to contribute toward fixed cost and then toward profit.

Discussion Question

6–3. If Beachside's sales increase by $20,000 and the contribution margin ratio is 25 percent, by how much will profits increase?

PREDICTING PROFITS USING THE CONTRIBUTION INCOME STATEMENT

Let's assume that Beachside expects to sell 7,500 shirts in 2005. Claudia can quickly predict the expected profit at that sales level by preparing a contribution income statement, such as that in Exhibit 6–4. To do this, the sales figure equals the number of T-shirts multiplied by the selling price per unit (7,500 × $12 = $90,000). Variable cost is the number of T-shirts sold multiplied by the variable cost per unit (7,500 × $9 = $67,500). The fixed cost of $12,000 remains the same in total. With these three figures in place, simple arithmetic gave us the expected profit of $10,500 if 7,500 T-shirts are sold.

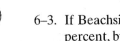

EXHIBIT 6–4   Beachside's Condensed 2005 Projected Contribution Income Statement

Beachside T-Shirt Shop
Projected Contribution Income Statement
For the Year Ended December 31, 2005

	Total	Per Unit	Percent of Sales
Sales in Units	7,500	1	
Sales	$ 90,000	$12.00	100
Variable Cost	(67,500)	(9.00)	(75)
Contribution Margin	$ 22,500	$ 3.00	25
Fixed Cost	(12,000)		
Operating Income	$ 10,500		

If we did not want to take the time to prepare an actual contribution income statement, we could calculate the company's operating income using the following basic equation.

Sales	− Variable costs	− Fixed costs	= Profit
(7,500 × $12) −	(7,500 × $9) −	$12,000	= Profit
$90,000 −	$67,500 −	$12,000	= $10,500

The sales figure in this calculation is the number of T-shirts multiplied by the selling price per unit (7,500 × $12 = $90,000). Variable cost is the number of T-shirts sold multiplied by the variable cost per unit (7,500 × $9 = $67,500). The fixed cost of

$12,000 remains the same in total. With these three figures in place, simple arithmetic gave us the expected profit of $10,500 if 7,500 T-shirts are sold.

The contribution income statement is a wonderful management tool because it allows managers to clearly see the amounts of fixed and variable costs incurred by the company. For example, using the contribution income statement, a manager at *DuPont* could assess the amount of costs that remain constant regardless of activity and the amount of costs that will change as business activity changes, allowing her to make more well-informed management decisions. Understanding which costs are variable and which are fixed is essential if managers are to reasonably predict future costs. More importantly, a solid understanding of the contribution income statement approach and the concept of the contribution margin and contribution margin ratio is the backbone of another important decision-making tool: cost–volume–profit analysis.

◆ COST–VOLUME–PROFIT ANALYSIS

cost–volume–profit (CVP) analysis The analysis of the relationship between cost and volume and the effect of these relationships on profit.

As its name implies, **cost–volume–profit (CVP) analysis** is the analysis of the relationships between cost and volume (the level of sales), and the effect of those relationships on profit. In this section, we examine how managers can use CVP concepts to predict sales levels at which a firm will break even or attain target profits. CVP analysis is a useful tool for managers, business owners, and potential business owners for determining the profit potential of a new company or the profit impact of changes in selling price, cost, or volume on current businesses.

Thousands of businesses are started every day. Unfortunately, most of them fail a short time later, and the people who start these businesses suffer significant financial and emotional hardship. Such hardships might be avoided if new business owners used CVP analysis to evaluate the potential profit of their business ventures. With CVP analysis, a potential business owner can discover impending disaster before starting the business, thereby preserving funds that could be used more productively elsewhere.

Throughout the remainder of this chapter we will use two basic CVP formulas. We will use these formulas to determine the sales required to earn a target profit amount. Both formulas work equally well, but one provides the dollar amount of sales while the other provides sales in units. Exhibit 6–5 shows the two CVP formulas we will use throughout the remainder of this chapter.

EXHIBIT 6–5 Cost-Volume-Profit Formulas

Formula	Calculation	Purpose
CVP Formula 1	$\dfrac{\text{Total fixed cost} + \text{target profit}}{\text{Contribution margin ratio}}$	To determine the required sales *in dollars* to achieve a target profit
CVP Formula 2	$\dfrac{\text{Total fixed cost} + \text{target profit}}{\text{Contribution margin per unit}}$	To determine the required sales *in units* to achieve a target profit

Notice that the first formula, the one that determines required sales in dollars, uses the *contribution margin ratio*, while the second formula, the one that determines sales in units, uses the *contribution margin per unit*.

Next, we will use these two formulas to determine sales required to break even.

breakeven Occurs when a company generates neither a profit nor a loss.

break-even point The sales required to achieve breakeven. This can be expressed either in sales dollars or in the number of units sold.

BREAKEVEN

Breakeven occurs when a company generates neither a profit nor a loss. The sales volume required to achieve break-even is called the **break-even point.** Because most businesses exist to earn a profit, why would managers be interested in calculating a break-even point? In at least two situations this kind of information is valuable. First, the break-even point tells managers how far sales can decline before the company will incur a loss. This information could provide the encouragement to continue in business, or may provide an early warning of impending business failure. Second, owners and managers may use break-even analysis when starting a business. For example, Claudia could have calculated Beachside's break-even point when she started the company. Even when Claudia tried to calculate the company's break-even point for its second year, she overlooked some important cost behavior considerations. Now, with our understanding of cost behavior and the contribution income statement, we can predict the correct sales level Beachside needs to break even for the year.

Let's look again at the 2003 contribution income statement for Beachside T-Shirt Shop, reproduced in Exhibit 6–6.

EXHIBIT 6–6 Beachside's Condensed 2003 Contribution Income Statement

Beachside T-Shirt Shop
Contribution Income Statement
For the Year Ended December 31, 2003

	Total	Per Unit	Percent of Sales
Sales in Units	3,000	1	
Sales	$36,000	$12.00	100
Variable Cost	(27,000)	(9.00)	(75)
Contribution Margin	$ 9,000	$ 3.00	25
Fixed Cost	(12,000)		
Operating Loss	$ (3,000)		

We can use either of the CVP formulas to calculate breakeven for Beachside. We will begin our presentation using CVP Formula 1. Remember that breakeven means that profit will be exactly zero. Therefore, we will use a target profit of zero in our break-even calculations for the Beachside T-Shirt Shop. To demonstrate the break-even calculation, we use the information provided by Beachside T-Shirt Shop's contribution income statement in Exhibit 6–6. Beachside's selling price per T-shirt is $12, its variable cost is $9 per shirt, the contribution margin ratio is 25 percent, and the company's fixed costs total $12,000 per year. With this information, we can use CVP Formula 1 to determine the sales in dollars that Beachside must have sell to break even by dividing the contribution margin ratio into the total fixed cost as follows:

CVP Formula 1—To Determine Required Sales in Dollars

$$\frac{\text{Total fixed cost} + \text{Target profit}}{\text{Contribution margin ratio}} = \text{Required sales in dollars}$$

$$\frac{\$12,000 + \$0}{25\%} = \$48,000$$

Using CVP Formula 1, we determined the sales must total $48,000 for Beachside to break even, but what if we wanted to know the number of units the company must sell? Once we know sales in dollars, and we know the selling price per unit, we can simply divide the total sales in dollars by the per unit selling price to determine the number of units the company must sell. Therefore, Beachside must sell 4,000 units ($48,000 ÷ $12) in order to break even.

For situations in which it is more convenient to use the per unit contribution margin rather than the contribution margin ratio, we can use CVP Formula 2. This might occur when the contribution margin ratio does not round to an even percentage and per unit amounts are available.

To illustrate how to find the break-even point in units using CVP Formula 2, we will once again use the information in Exhibit 6–6 for the Beachside T-Shirt Shop. Beachside's selling price per T-shirt is $12, its variable cost is $9 per shirt, the contribution margin is $3 per T-shirt, and the company's fixed costs total $12,000 per year. With this information, we can determine the number of T-shirts Beachside must sell to achieve a break-even point by dividing the contribution margin per unit into the total fixed cost, as follows:

CVP Formula 2—To Calculate Required Sales in Units

$$\frac{\text{Total fixed cost} + \text{Target profit}}{\text{Contribution margin per unit}} = \text{Required sales in units}$$

$$\frac{\$12,000 + \$0}{\$3.00} = 4,000 \text{ T-shirts}$$

As the calculation shows, Beachside must sell 4,000 T-shirts to break even. To determine sales in dollars, we simply multiply the number of units by the per unit selling price. For Beachside to break even, the company's sales in dollars must be $48,000 (4,000 units × $12).

Notice that we can determine sales in dollars and sales in units by using either one of the two CVP formulas. But how do we know that our calculations are correct? We can prepare a condensed contribution income statement to check our answers. We have already determined the sales figures for this contribution income statement (4,000 T-shirts, totaling sales of $48,000). Variable cost is the number of T-shirts sold multiplied by the variable cost per unit (4,000 × $9 = $36,000). The fixed cost of $12,000 remains the same in total. As the contribution income statement in Exhibit 6–7 shows, with these figures in place, profit will be zero if 4,000 T-shirts are sold.

EXHIBIT 6–7   Beachside's Condensed Contribution Income Statement at Breakeven

Beachside T-Shirt Shop
Projected Contribution Income Statement
For the Year Ended December 31, 2005

	Total	Per Unit	Percent of Sales
Sales in Units	4,000	1	
Sales (4,000 × $12)	$48,000	$12.00	100
Variable Cost (4,000 × $9)	(36,000)	(9.00)	(75)
Contribution Margin	$12,000	$ 3.00	25
Fixed Cost	(12,000)		
Operating Income	$ -0-		

We have examined the calculations for break-even point, but as we said earlier, companies are usually not in business to break even. Rather, they are usually interested in earning profits. In the next section, we will discuss how to use the CVP formulas to determine the sales needed to meet a specific profit objective. We will call this profit objective *target profit*. As with the break-even point, we can apply CVP analysis to determine the sales needed to meet target profits in either units or sales dollars.

DETERMINING SALES REQUIRED TO MEET A PROFIT OBJECTIVE

When we determined the break-even point, we calculated the sales required to generate a large enough contribution margin to cover fixed cost. In our present discussion, we are looking for the sales required not only to cover the fixed cost, but also to achieve a specific target profit. To use CVP Formula 1, we simply add the target profit to the total fixed cost and then divide the sum by the contribution margin ratio. This calculation will tell us the sales in dollars Beachside must achieve to cover all its fixed cost and to attain the target profit. If we assume that Claudia targets $27,000 as Beachside's profit for 2005, the calculation is as follows:

CVP Formula 1—To Determine Required Sales in Dollars

$$\frac{\text{Total fixed cost} + \text{Target profit}}{\text{Contribution margin ratio}} = \text{Required sales in dollars}$$

$$\frac{\$12,000 + \$27,000}{25\%} = \$156,000 \text{ in sales dollars}$$

Discussion Question ●

6–4. Prove that Claudia's sales must total $156,000 to earn a $27,000 profit.

Using CVP Formula 1, we determined the sales dollars required to earn a profit of $27,000. If we want to know the number of units the company must sell, we simply divide the total sales in dollars by the per unit selling price to determine the number of units the company must sell. In our example, Beachside must sell 13,000 units ($156,000 ÷ $12) in order to earn the $27,000 target profit.

Now let's use CVP Formula 2 to determine the number of T-shirts Beachside must sell to earn a target profit of $27,000. Using CVP Formula 2 to calculate the number of units the company must sell, we simply add the target profit to the total fixed cost and then divide the sum by the contribution margin per unit. This calculation will tell us how many units Beachside must sell to cover all the fixed cost and to attain the target profit. Beachside's calculation is as follows:

CVP Formula 2—To Calculate Required Sales in Units

$$\frac{\text{Total fixed cost} + \text{Target profit}}{\text{Contribution margin per unit}} = \text{Required sales in units}$$

$$\frac{\$12,000 + \$27,000}{\$3.00} = 13,000 \text{ T-shirts}$$

Our calculations confirm that with a fixed cost of $12,000 and a contribution margin per unit of $3, Beachside must sell 13,000 T-shirts to earn $27,000 profit. To determine sales in dollars, we simply multiply the number of units by the per unit selling price. For Beachside to earn a target profit of $27,000, the company's sales in dollars must be $156,000 (13,000 units × $12).

Once again, we see that we can determine sales in dollars and sales in units using either one of the two CVP formulas. To test the accuracy of our calculations, we can prepare a condensed contribution income statement. We already know that the sales figures for this contribution income statement are $156,000 or 13,000 units. Variable cost is the number of T-shirts sold multiplied by the variable cost per unit (13,000 × $9 = $117,000). The fixed cost of $12,000 remains unchanged. As the contribution income statements in Exhibit 6–8 shows, with these figures in place, profit will be $27,000 if 13,000 T-shirts are sold.

EXHIBIT 6-8 Beachside's Condensed Contribution Income Statement to Earn a $27,000 Profit

Beachside T-Shirt Shop
Projected Contribution Income Statement
For the Year Ended December 31, 2005

	Total	Per Unit	Percent of Sales
Sales in Units	13,000	1	
Sales (13,000 × $12)	$ 156,000	$12.00	100
Variable Cost (13,000 × $9)	(117,000)	(9.00)	(75)
Contribution Margin	$ 39,000	$ 3.00	25
Fixed Cost	(12,000)		
Operating Income	$ 27,000		

If we did not want to take the time to prepare an actual contribution income statement, we could calculate the same operating income using the following basic equation.

$$
\begin{array}{rcl}
\text{Sales} & - \text{Variable costs} - \text{Fixed costs} & = \text{Profit} \\
(13{,}000 \times \$12) & - (13{,}000 \times \$9) - \$12{,}000 & = \text{Profit} \\
\$156{,}000 & - \$117{,}000 - \$12{,}000 & = \$27{,}000
\end{array}
$$

COST–VOLUME–PROFIT GRAPH

In addition to the calculations we have been studying, CVP analysis can also be depicted graphically. Exhibit 6–9 shows a CVP graph for Beachside T-Shirt Shop.

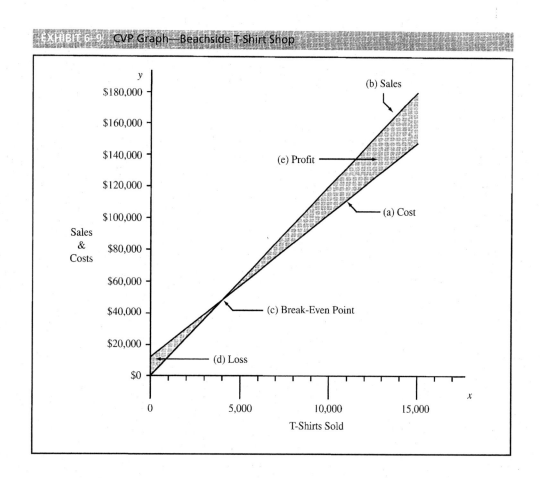

EXHIBIT 6–9 CVP Graph—Beachside T-Shirt Shop

The main difference between the CVP graph in Exhibit 6–9 and the cost behavior graphs in Chapter 5 is that the CVP graph shows sales in addition to variable and fixed costs. The cost line (a) on the graph is similar to those in Chapter 5. Note that this line intercepts the *y* axis at $12,000, the total fixed cost for Beachside T-Shirt Shop. Thus, Beachside incurs $12,000 fixed cost even if the company sells no T-shirts. The cost line slopes upward at $9 for each T-shirt sold (variable cost).

Now consider the sales line (b) on the graph. If Beachside sells no T-shirts, there would obviously be no sales dollars, which explains why the sales line intercepts the *y* axis at zero. The line slopes upward at $12 for every T-shirt sold. The point at which the cost line and the sales line cross (c) is Beachside's break-even point, which we know from our calculations in this chapter to be 4,000 T-shirts, or $48,000 in sales revenue. The loss area (d) on the graph and the profit area (e) represent a loss and profit, respectively, for Beachside. Thus, if Beachside sells fewer than 4,000 T-shirts, the company will experience a loss. If it sells more than 4,000 T-shirts, the company will earn a profit.

Discussion Question ●

6–5. Using the CVP graph in Exhibit 6–9, determine sales level (in units and dollars) where Beachside would earn a profit of

   a. $10,500
   b. $27,000

The CVP graph is a useful management tool. Although it should not take the place of the calculations we have demonstrated thus far in this chapter, it has a distinct advantage over the calculations in that it allows managers to view the entire cost–volume–profit picture. Claudia June can, for example, assess Beachside's profit potential at any level of business within the relevant range of activity.

Discussion Question ●

6–6. If Claudia is forced to lower her selling price to $11 per T-shirt, how much profit should she expect in 2005, assuming the company expects to sell 13,000 shirts and its cost structure stays the same?

To demonstrate the basics of CVP analysis, we have assumed that the selling price per unit, variable costs per unit, and total fixed cost all remained unchanged. Businesses, however, experience daily pressures that can cause each of these items to change. CVP analysis can adapt to any such change.

Now that we have covered the basics, we are ready to put CVP to perhaps its greatest use: sensitivity analysis.

SENSITIVITY ANALYSIS

sensitivity analysis A technique used to determine the effect on cost–volume–profit when changes are made in the selling price, cost structure (variable and/or fixed), and volume used in the CVP calculations. Also called *what if analysis*.

Sensitivity analysis is a technique used to determine the effect on CVP when changes are made in the selling price, cost structure (variable and/or fixed), and volume used in the calculations. Sensitivity analysis is also called *what if analysis*. Managers are often looking for answers to the following types of questions, in terms of the effect on projected profits: "What if we raised (or lowered) the selling price per unit?", "What if variable cost per unit increased (or decreased)?", and "What if fixed cost increased (or decreased)?" Sensitivity analysis can provide those answers. For example, **Radio Shack Corporation** may want to know what would happen to the profits of an individual store if the store's fixed cost increased by 3 percent.

To demonstrate sensitivity analysis, we return to Claudia June and the Beachside T-Shirt Shop example. Assume 2005 has ended. Exhibit 6-10 presents Beachside's contribution income statement for the year.

EXHIBIT 6–10	Beachside T-Shirt Shop's 2005 Contribution Income Statement

Beachside T-Shirt Shop
Contribution Income Statement
For the Year Ended December 31, 2005

	Total	Per Unit	Percent of Sales
Sales in Units	11,286	1	
Sales	$135,432	$12.00	100
Variable Cost	(101,574)	(9.00)	(75)
Contribution Margin	$ 33,858	$ 3.00	25
Fixed Cost	(12,000)		
Operating Income	$ 21,858		

Although it is less than she had hoped for, Claudia is satisfied with the $21,858 profit Beachside earned in 2005 and is aiming for a target profit of $27,000 in 2006 (the same target profit as 2005). However, a new T-shirt shop just opened three doors from

Beachside. Claudia feels she must lower her selling price to $11 due to competitive pressure and wants to know how many T-shirts her shop must now sell to attain the $27,000 target profit. Claudia can use CVP analysis to determine the required sales level to achieve a targeted profit even if she changes her selling price.

CHANGE IN SELLING PRICE

If the selling price changes but variable cost does not, sales required to attain a target profit can be determined using CVP Formula 1 and a recalculated contribution margin ratio based on the new selling price. In the case of Beachside T-Shirt Shop, the new per unit contribution margin is $2 (new selling price of $11 − variable cost of $9) and the new contribution margin ratio is 18.1818 percent (rounded), which we calculate by dividing the new $11 selling price into the new $2 contribution margin ($2 ÷ $11 = 18.1818%). We now apply this new information to CVP Formula 1. Remember that the target profit is still $27,000 and that fixed cost remains unchanged at $12,000.

CVP Formula 1—To Determine Required Sales in Dollars

$$\frac{\text{Total fixed cost} + \text{Target profit}}{\text{Contribution margin ratio}} = \text{Required sales in dollars}$$

$$\frac{\$12,000 + \$27,000}{18.1818\%} = \$214,500 \text{ sales dollars (rounded)}$$

By applying the revised contribution margin ratio to CVP Formula 1, we see that Beachside will need $214,500 in sales to achieve the target profit of $27,000. By dividing the $214,500 in sales by the new $11 per unit selling price we also determine that Beachside needs to sell 19,500 T-shirts to earn the $27,000 target profit.

Discussion Questions

6–7. Prove that Claudia's sales must equal $214,500 to earn a $27,000 profit if she reduces the selling price per T-shirt from $12 to $11.

6–8. Why must we calculate a new contribution margin ratio when the per unit selling price changes?

6–9. Under what other circumstances must we calculate a new contribution margin ratio?

We can also use CVP Formula 2 to calculate the number of units Beachside must sell to earn a target profit of $27,000. When the selling price changes but variable cost does not, the number of units required to attain a target profit is determined using CVP Formula 2 and a recalculated contribution margin based on the new selling price. In the case of Beachside T-Shirt Shop, the new contribution margin is $2 (new selling price of $11 − variable cost of $9). We now apply this contribution margin to the formula.

CVP Formula 2—Required Sales in Units

$$\frac{\text{Total fixed cost} + \text{Target profit}}{\text{Contribution margin per unit}} = \text{Required sales in units}$$

$$\frac{\$12,000 + \$27,000}{\$2.00} = 19,500 \text{ T-shirts}$$

Our calculations confirm that with the lower selling price and revised contribution margin per unit, Beachside must sell 19,500 T-shirts to attain the target profit of $27,000. By multiplying the 19,500 units by the new $11 selling price, we can also confirm that Beachside's sales need to total $214,500 to earn the $27,000 target profit.

If Claudia reduces her selling price to $11, then Beachside must sell 19,500 T-shirts in 2006 to earn the target profit of $27,000. Claudia believes it would be impossible to sell that many shirts, so she begins to consider alternative ways to earn the target profit of $27,000 in such a competitive environment.

Discussion Question •

6–10. If Claudia must lower her selling price to $11 per shirt to be competitive, and it would be impossible to sell 19,500 T-shirts, what are some of the alternatives she might consider to attain the $27,000 profit?

CHANGE IN VARIABLE COST AND FIXED COST

If Claudia does not want to change her selling price, there are alternatives–namely, changing variable cost or fixed cost. Because Claudia believes the selling price per T-shirt must be $11, either the variable cost per unit or the total fixed cost must be reduced. We start with an analysis of possible changes in variable cost.

First, let's analyze how Beachside determined its original variable cost. We determine per unit variable cost by dividing the total variable cost by the number of units sold. Recall from the earlier discussion and Exhibit 6–3 that Beachside sold 3,000 T-shirts during 2003, and its total variable cost was $27,000. Therefore, the variable cost per unit was $9 ($27,000 variable cost ÷ 3,000 units sold).

To analyze how a change in variable cost will affect the variable cost per unit of $9, we must look at the three components of per unit variable cost: the cost of each T-shirt, the variable selling expenses, and the variable administrative expenses. We need to know what portion of the $9 variable unit cost relates to each component. We can determine these portions by dividing the 3,000 units sold into each of the three cost components. We use 3,000 because that number of units caused these costs to be incurred. We find the cost of each variable cost component in the contribution income statement presented in Exhibit 6–3. The cost and per unit calculation for each component are presented in Exhibit 6–11.

EXHIBIT 6-11   Analysis of Beachside's Variable Cost Components

	Total Cost		Units Sold		Unit Cost
Cost of Goods Sold (T-shirts)	$21,600	÷	3,000	=	$7.20
Variable Selling Expenses	3,800	÷	3,000	=	1.27
Variable Administrative Expenses	1,600	÷	3,000	=	.53
Total Variable Cost	$27,000				$9.00 Per Unit

Claudia does not believe any change can be made in either the variable selling expenses or the variable administrative expenses. Any possible reduction in variable cost, then, must be in the cost of the T-shirts. Our calculations in Exhibit 6-11 show that the per unit cost of each T-shirt is $7.20.

Assume Claudia's shirt supplier has agreed to lower its price from $7.20 to $6 per T-shirt. This reduction of $1.20 ($7.20 − $6.00 = $1.20) will reduce Beachside's variable cost from $9 per shirt to $7.80 per shirt ($9.00 − $1.20 = $7.80). The new contribution margin is $3.20 ($11 selling price − $7.80 variable cost = $3.20), and the new contribution margin ratio is 29.091 percent ($3.20 contribution margin ÷ $11 selling price = 0.29091 or 29.091 percent rounded).

Now consider a change in Beachside's fixed cost. Recall that Beachside's total fixed cost is $12,000. Assume that Claudia has agreed to provide fellow businesswoman Susan Williams with space in her shop to sell bathing suits to Claudia's customers. Susan has agreed to pay Claudia $250 per month as rent for the space she will use. The $250 per month works out to be $3,000 per year ($250 per month × 12 months = $3,000). Thus, Beachside's total fixed cost decreases from $12,000 to $9,000.

Let's see what effect these changes would have on Claudia's company. To do this, again we will use CVP Formulas 1 and 2. We simply need to plug the new cost structures (variable and fixed) into the formulas as follows:

CVP Formula 1—Sales Dollars Required to Achieve Target Profits

$$\frac{\text{Total fixed cost} + \text{Target profit}}{\text{Contribution margin ratio}} = \text{Required sales in dollars}$$

$$\frac{\$9,000 + \$27,000}{29.091\%} = \$123,750 \text{ in sales (rounded)}$$

By using CVP Formula 1 (and Beachside's new variable and fixed cost structure), we found that if Beachside's sales total $123,750 in 2006, the company will earn a profit of $27,000. To calculate the unit sales required to attain Beachside's target profit of $27,000, we use the company's new contribution ratio and CVP Formula 2:

CVP Formula 2—Unit Sales Required to Achieve Target Profits

$$\frac{\text{Total fixed cost} + \text{Target profit}}{\text{Contribution margin per unit}} = \text{Required sales in units}$$

$$\frac{\$9,000 + \$27,000}{\$3.20} = 11,250 \text{ T-shirts}$$

With the changes in cost structure Claudia has negotiated, she will be able to earn $27,000 profit in 2006 even if her sales drop from 11,286 T-shirts (the 2005 sales level) to 11,250 T-shirts.

Discussion Questions

6–11. Prove that Claudia must have sales of $123,750 (11,250 T-shirts) to earn a $27,000 profit if she reduces the cost per T-shirt from $7.20 to $6 and reduces total fixed cost from $12,000 to $9,000.

6–12. If Claudia is more successful than anticipated in 2006 and sells 13,000 T-shirts by reducing her selling price to $11, and she also implements the variable and fixed cost changes described earlier, what will Beachside's profits be for 2006?

6–13. What complications do you foresee in using CVP analysis if, in addition to her existing line of shirts, Claudia begins selling a deluxe line of shirts that cost $11.50 each and sell for $17?

MULTIPLE PRODUCTS AND CVP

In reality, most companies sell more than one product. Companies that sell multiple products can estimate *total* variable cost and *total* sales, but their various per unit variable costs and selling prices are of little use when they employ CVP for the company as a whole. These companies can still use CVP analysis, but they must use CVP Formula 1 which uses the contribution ratio. CVP Formula 2 is useless in a multiproduct situation if the various products sold have different unit contribution margins as they do in most situations.

To demonstrate how managers use CVP analysis in a multiproduct situation or when per unit information is otherwise unavailable, let's consider the example of Margaret's Frame Factory. Margaret's Frame Factory makes and sells picture frames of various size and quality. Exhibit 6–12 presents Margaret's condensed contribution income statement for 2003.

There is a per unit variable cost and selling price for each of the frame models Margaret's manufactures, but they are not included in Exhibit 6–12. All we have are the totals. The $185,000 contribution margin comes from the sale of several different products, each with its own contribution margin. The 37 percent contribution margin ratio, then, is an average contribution margin ratio based on the sales mix of these different products. Even with this limited information, however, we can use CVP analysis to both calculate a break-even point and predict target profits.

Margaret's Frame Factory
Contribution Income Statement
For the Year Ended December 31, 2003

	Total	% of Sales
Sales	$500,000	100%
Variable Cost	(315,000)	(63%)
Contribution Margin	$185,000	37%
Fixed Cost	(143,000)	
Operating Income	$ 42,000	

EXHIBIT 6–12 Margaret's Condensed 2003 Contribution Income Statement

BREAK-EVEN POINT IN A MULTIPRODUCT SITUATION

To calculate the break-even point in a multiproduct situation, we use CVP Formula 1.

CVP Formula 1—Sales Dollars

$$\frac{\text{Total fixed cost} + \text{Target profit}}{\text{Contribution margin ratio}} = \text{Required sales in dollars}$$

$$\frac{\$143,000 + \$0}{37\%} = \$386,486 \text{ sales dollars (rounded)}$$

We know that Margaret's is well above the break-even point because the company earned a profit of $42,000 in 2003. The break-even calculation is still valuable to company management because it reveals how far sales could decline before the company would experience a loss. In this example, sales could decline by $113,514 ($500,000 2003 sales − $386,486 break-even point = $113,514 decline) before Margaret's would experience a loss.

DETERMINING REQUIRED SALES IN A MULTIPRODUCT SITUATION

Assume that Margaret's is interested in increasing profits to $80,000 in 2004. Based on the information contained in the 2003 contribution income statement presented in Exhibit 6–12, what would be the required sales to earn this target profit of $80,000? To find out, once again we use CVP Formula 1:

CVP Formula 1—Sales Dollars Required to Achieve Target Profits

$$\frac{\text{Total fixed cost} + \text{Target profit}}{\text{Contribution margin ratio}} = \text{Required sales in dollars}$$

Using the information from the contribution income statement of Margaret's Frame Factory, we know that total fixed cost is $143,000, the target profit is $80,000, and the contribution margin ratio is 37 percent. The calculation of the required sales dollars is as follows:

$$\frac{\$143,000 + \$80,000}{37\%} = \$602,703 \text{ sales dollars (rounded)}$$

Our calculations indicate that Margaret's Frame Factory will need $602,703 in sales to attain a target profit of $80,000.

Discussion Question ◦

6–14. Prove that Margaret's sales must total $602,703 to earn an $80,000 profit.

We have demonstrated how CVP analysis can provide useful information about how changes in selling price, variable cost, and fixed cost affect a company's break-even point. Managers can also use CVP analysis to see what sales (in either units or dollars) the company needs to attain target profits.

CVP analysis is highly adaptable. It works equally well when managers are trying to determine profit potential either of a small segment of a large business or of an entire company. Before a company expands an existing business market or makes the decision to enter new markets, management should invest some time in gathering revenue and cost data, separating the cost-by-cost behavior, developing a contribution income statement, and applying these simple CVP procedures.

◆ CVP ASSUMPTIONS

CVP analysis is a great "what if?" management tool because managers can use it to estimate a company's profit performance under a variety of different scenarios. It is, however, an estimation technique only, and the following assumptions are made when this type of analysis is used.

1. All costs can be classified as either fixed or variable. Implicit in this assumption is that a mixed cost can be separated into its fixed and variable components.
2. Fixed costs remain fixed throughout the range of activity.
3. Variable cost per unit remains the same throughout the range of activity.
4. Selling price per unit remains the same throughout the range of activity.
5. The average contribution margin ratio in a multiproduct company remains the same throughout the range of activity.

These assumptions rarely, if ever, match reality. Market pressures, inflation, and a myriad of other factors cause revenue and cost structures to change in ways that place limitations on CVP analysis. Notwithstanding these limitations, however, CVP helps managers make more realistic estimates of future profit potential. It is a technique available to managers of large and small companies worldwide as they attempt to better manage their businesses.

Summary

The functional income statement, which separates the costs shown into product cost and period cost, is limited in its usefulness to managers as they attempt to plan and control their operations. It does not take into account that some costs change as volume changes, and some do not. The contribution income statement is more useful to managers as a planning tool because it separates the costs presented into fixed costs and variable costs rather than into product costs and period costs.

An integral part of the contribution income statement is the contribution margin, which is the amount remaining after all variable costs have been deducted from sales revenue. When the contribution margin is presented as a percentage of sales, it is called the contribution margin ratio. Both the contribution margin and the contribution margin ratio are used in cost–volume–profit analysis.

Cost–volume–profit (CVP) analysis is the analysis of the relationships between cost and volume, and the effect of those relationships on profit. The first application of CVP analysis is the calculation of breakeven, which is the sales level resulting in neither a profit nor a loss. Breakeven can be calculated either in sales dollars or in the number of units of product that must be sold.

Cost–volume–profit analysis can also be used to calculate the sales level required to achieve a target profit. As was the case with breakeven, the sales level required to achieve a target profit can be calculated in both sales dollars and the number of units of product that must be sold.

Cost–volume–profit analysis can also be used to perform sensitivity analysis, which is a technique used to determine the effect on CVP when changes are made in the selling price, cost structure (variable and/or fixed), and volume used in the calculations.

Although CVP analysis is easier to perform in a single-product situation, it can also be used to calculate breakeven and sales required to achieve target profits in a multiple product situation.

Key Terms ●●●

- breakeven, M–153
- break-even point, M–153
- contribution income statement, M–149

- contribution margin, M–150
- contribution margin ratio, M–151
- cost–volume–profit (CVP) analysis, M–153

- functional income statement, M–149
- sensitivity analysis, M–158

Review the Facts ●●●

A. What is the difference between a contribution income statement and a functional income statement?

B. What is the contribution margin?

C. What does the contribution margin "contribute" toward?

D. How does total contribution margin differ from contribution margin per unit?

E. What is the contribution margin ratio, and how does it differ from the contribution margin?

F. What is cost–volume–profit (CVP) analysis?

G. What does the term *break-even point* mean?

H. In what ways does the calculation of the break-even point in units differ from the calculation of the break-even point in sales dollars?

I. How would you calculate the required sales in units to attain a target profit?

J. How would you calculate the required sales in dollars to attain a target profit?

K. What does the term *sensitivity analysis* mean in the context of CVP analysis?

L. What does the term *average contribution margin ratio* mean for a company that sells multiple products?

M. Which one of the two CVP formulas are used to calculate breakeven or sales required to attain target profits for a multiproduct company?

N. Why is one of the CVP formulas useless in a multiproduct situation when contribution margins for individual products are unknown?

Apply What You Have Learned ●●●●●●●●●●●●●●●●●●●●●●●●●●●●

LO 4: PREPARE A CONTRIBUTION INCOME STATEMENT

6–15. Fresh Baked Cookie Company sells cookies in a large shopping mall. The following multiple-step income statement was prepared for the year ending December 31, 2004.

Fresh Baked Cookie Company
Income Statement
For the Year Ended December 31, 2004

Sales		$36,000
Cost of Goods Sold		4,000
Gross Profit		$32,000
Operating Expense:		
Selling Expense	$18,000	
Administrative Expense	10,000	(28,000)
Operating Income		$ 4,000

Cost of goods sold is a variable cost. Selling expense is 20 percent variable and 80 percent fixed, and administrative expense is 5 percent variable and 95 percent fixed.

Required: Prepare a contribution income statement for the Fresh Baked Cookie Company.

LO 4: PREPARE A CONTRIBUTION INCOME STATEMENT

6–16. The following multiple-step income statement was prepared for Steinmann's Bait Shop for the year ending December 31, 2004.

Steinmann's Bait Shop
Income Statement
For the Year Ended December 31, 2004

Sales		$98,000
Cost of Goods Sold		22,000
Gross Profit		$76,000
Operating Expense:		
Selling Expense	$27,000	
Administrative Expense	36,000	(63,000)
Operating Income		$13,000

Cost of goods sold is a variable cost. Selling expense is 30 percent variable and 70 percent fixed, and administrative expense is 10 percent variable and 90 percent fixed.

Required: Prepare a contribution income statement for Steinmann's Bait Shop.

LO 4: PREPARE A CONTRIBUTION INCOME STATEMENT

6–17. Quality Fishing Gear Company sells high-quality fiberglass fishing rods to retailers. The following multiple-step income statement was prepared for the year ending December 31, 2004.

Quality Fishing Gear Company
Income Statement
For the Year Ended December 31, 2004

Sales		$540,000
Cost of Goods Sold		360,000
Gross Profit		$180,000
Operating Expense:		
Selling Expense	$88,000	
Administrative Expense	72,000	(160,000)
Operating Income		$ 20,000

Cost of goods sold is a variable cost. Selling expense is 65 percent variable and 35 percent fixed, and administrative expense is 25 percent variable and 75 percent fixed.

Required: Prepare a contribution income statement for Quality Fishing Gear Company.

LO 4: PREPARE A CONTRIBUTION INCOME STATEMENT

6–18. Ray Placid is considering opening the Placid Greeting Card Shop in a local mall. The store rent will be $550 per month, the cost of telephone service will be about $95 per month, and based on the size of the store, Ray believes that cost of electricity will average about $200 per month. Ray will be able to buy the greeting cards for $0.50 each and plans to sell them for $2 each. Salaries are expected to be $1,200 per month regardless of the number of cards sold. Ray estimates that other miscellaneous fixed costs will total $150 per month and miscellaneous variable cost will be $0.10 per card. Ray anticipates that he will be able to sell about 3,000 greeting cards per month. If Ray opens the store, his first month of business will be November 2004.

Required: Prepare a projected contribution approach income statement for November 2004.

LO 4: PREPARE A CONTRIBUTION INCOME STATEMENT

6–19. Joe's Pretzel Stand is located in the Orange Bowl stadium and sells pretzels during sporting events. The following information is available for 2004:

- Selling price per pretzel is $2.00.
- Cost of each pretzel is $0.25.
- Cost of renting the pretzel stand is $12,000 per year.
- Instead of an hourly wage, Joe pays college students $0.20 per pretzel sold to run the pretzel stand.

Required: Prepare a contribution income statement for 2004 assuming that 8,000 pretzels are sold.

LO 4: PREPARE A CONTRIBUTION INCOME STATEMENT

6–20. The following information is available for Blaire's Snow Cone Stand for 2004:

- Selling price per snow cone is $1.25.
- Cost of each snow cone is $0.30.
- Rent paid for the stand at a local flea market is $2,400 per year.
- Instead of an hourly wage, Blaire's pays high school students $0.40 per snow cone sold.

Required: Prepare a contribution income statement for 2004 assuming that 6,000 snow cones are sold.

LO 4: PREPARE A CONDENSED CONTRIBUTION INCOME STATEMENT

6–21. The following is the contribution income statement for The Bivans Company:

The Bivans Company
Contribution Income Statement
For the Year Ended December 31, 2005

Sales		$800,000
Variable Cost:		
Cost of Goods Sold	$420,000	
Variable Selling Expense	75,000	
Variable Administrative Expense	33,000	
Total Variable Cost		(528,000)
Contribution Margin		$272,000
Fixed Cost:		
Fixed Selling Expense	$128,000	
Fixed Administrative Expense	53,000	
Total Fixed Cost		(181,000)
Operating Income		$ 91,000

Required: Based on the contribution income statement for The Bivans Company, prepare a condensed contribution income statement.

LO 1: PREPARE A MULTIPLE-STEP INCOME STATEMENT

6–22. Refer to the information presented in problem 6–21.

Required: Prepare a multiple-step income statement for The Bivans Company.

LO 4: PREPARE A CONDENSED CONTRIBUTION INCOME STATEMENT

6–23. Following is the contribution income statement for The Lauren Company:

The Lauren Company
Contribution Income Statement
For the Year Ended December 31, 2005

Sales		$4,800,000
Variable Cost:		
Cost of Goods Sold	$2,320,000	
Variable Selling Expense	265,000	
Variable Administrative Expense	484,000	
Total Variable Cost		(3,069,000)
Contribution Margin		$1,731,000
Fixed Cost:		
Fixed Selling Expense	$ 648,000	
Fixed Administrative Expense	973,000	
Total Fixed Cost		(1,621,000)
Operating Income		$ 110,000

Required: Based on The Lauren Company's contribution income statement, prepare a condensed contribution income statement.

LO 1: PREPARE A MULTIPLE-STEP INCOME STATEMENT

6–24. Refer to the information presented in problem 6–23.

Required: Prepare a multiple-step income statement for The Lauren Company.

LO 4: PREPARE A CONDENSED CONTRIBUTION INCOME STATEMENT

6–25. The following is the contribution income statement for Karl's Athletic Shop:

Karl's Athletic Shop
Contribution Income Statement
For the Year Ended December 31, 2005

Sales		$422,000
Variable Cost:		
Cost of Goods Sold	$205,000	
Variable Selling Expense	55,000	
Variable Administrative Expense	22,000	
Total Variable Cost		(282,000)
Contribution Margin		$140,000
Fixed Cost:		
Fixed Selling Expense	$ 75,000	
Fixed Administrative Expense	34,000	
Total Fixed Cost		(109,000)
Operating Income		$ 31,000

Required: Based on this contribution income statement, prepare a condensed contribution income statement for Karl's Athletic Shop.

LO 1: PREPARE A MULTIPLE-STEP INCOME STATEMENT

6–26. Refer to the information presented in problem 6–25.

Required: Prepare a multiple-step income statement for Karl's Athletic Shop.

LO 4: PREPARE A CONTRIBUTION INCOME STATEMENT

6–27. Paradise Manufacturing makes weight-lifting equipment. During 2004, the following costs were incurred:

	Amount	Percentage Fixed	Percentage Variable
Direct material	$680,000	—	100
Direct labor	420,000	—	100
Variable manufacturing overhead	130,000	—	100
Fixed manufacturing overhead	900,000	100	—
Selling cost	300,000	20	80
Administrative cost	220,000	10	90

Sales for 2004 totaled $2,780,000 and there were no beginning or ending inventories.

Required: Prepare a contribution income statement for the year ended December 31, 2004.

LO 4: PREPARE A CONTRIBUTION INCOME STATEMENT

6–28. The following information is available for Nicole's Toy Manufacturing Company for 2004:

	Amount	Percent Fixed	Percent Variable
Direct material	$440,000	—	100
Direct labor	90,000	—	100
Variable manufacturing overhead	70,000	—	100
Fixed manufacturing overhead	800,000	100	—
Selling cost	950,000	45	55
Administrative cost	570,000	85	15

Sales for 2004 totaled $3,164,000 and there were no beginning or ending inventories.

Required: Prepare a contribution income statement for the year ended December 31, 2004.

LO 4: PREPARE A CONTRIBUTION INCOME STATEMENT

6–29. The following information is available for Rick's Watch Company for 2004:

	Amount	Percent Fixed	Percent Variable
Direct material	$534,000	—	100
Direct labor	129,000	—	100
Variable manufacturing overhead	397,000	—	100
Fixed manufacturing overhead	998,000	100	—
Selling cost	196,000	33	67
Administrative cost	243,000	78	22

Sales for 2004 totaled $2,745,000 and there were no beginning or ending inventories.

Required: Prepare a contribution income statement for the year ended December 31, 2004.

LO 4: PREPARE A CONTRIBUTION INCOME STATEMENT

6–30. Alumacraft Manufacturing makes aluminum serving carts for use in commercial jetliners. During 2005, the following costs were incurred:

	Amount	Percent Fixed	Percent Variable
Direct material	$2,600,000	100	—
Direct labor	1,820,000	100	—
Variable manufacturing overhead	540,000	—	100
Fixed manufacturing overhead	1,900,000	100	—
Selling cost	380,000	15	85
Administrative cost	230,000	5	95

Sales for 2005 totaled $7,900,000 and there were no beginning or ending inventories.

Required: Prepare a contribution income statement for the year ended December 31, 2005.

LO 6: DETERMINE BREAKEVEN AND SALES REQUIRED TO EARN TARGET PROFIT USING PER UNIT AMOUNTS

6–31. The following information is available for Medical Testing Corporation.

Amount charged for each test performed	$ 90
Annual fixed cost	200,000
Variable cost per test	25

Required:

a. Calculate how many tests Medical Testing Corporation must perform each year to break even.

b. Calculate how many tests Medical Testing Corporation must perform each year to earn a profit of $25,000.

LO 6: DETERMINE BREAKEVEN AND SALES REQUIRED TO EARN TARGET PROFIT USING PER UNIT AMOUNTS

6–32. The following information is available for Dottie's Donut Shop.

Amount charged per dozen doughnuts	$ 0.99
Annual fixed cost	385,000.00
Variable cost per dozen doughnuts	0.22

Required:

a. Calculate how many dozen doughnuts Dottie must sell each year to break even.

b. Calculate how many dozen doughnuts Dottie must sell each year to earn a profit of $35,000.

LO 6: DETERMINE BREAKEVEN AND SALES REQUIRED TO EARN TARGET PROFIT USING PER UNIT AMOUNTS

6–33. Jim is considering starting a small company to paint driveways. The following information is available:

Amount charged per square yard painted	$ 5
Annual fixed cost	3,000
Variable cost per square yard painted	2

Required:

    a. Calculate how many square yards of driveway Jim must paint each year to break even.

    b. Calculate how many square yards of driveway Jim must paint each year to earn a profit of $5,000.

LO 6: DETERMINE BREAKEVEN AND SALES REQUIRED TO EARN TARGET PROFIT USING PER UNIT AMOUNTS

6–34. Carbonnel Calendar Company is considering adding a new calendar design to their line. The following information is available:

Selling price	$ 3.97
Additional annual fixed cost	4,558.00
Variable cost per calendar	3.11

Required:

    a. Calculate how many calendars must be sold each year to break even.

    b. Calculate how many calendars must be sold each year to earn a profit of $2,580.

LO 3 & 6: USE RATIOS TO DETERMINE BREAKEVEN AND SALES REQUIRED TO EARN TARGET PROFIT

6–35. Melissa Valdez is planning to expand her clothing business by opening another store. In planning for the new store, Melissa believes that selling prices and costs of the various products sold will be similar to that of the existing store. In fact, she thinks that variable and fixed costs for the new store will be similar to that of the existing store, except that rent for the new store will be $300 per month more than the rent paid for the existing store. The following information is available for the existing store for the year ended December 31, 2004:

Sales	$200,000
Variable cost	130,000
Fixed cost	48,000

Required:

    a. Determine the sales required for the new store to break even.

    b. Determine the sales required for the new store to earn a profit of $20,000 per year. (*Hint*: Keep in mind that the $300 increase in rent is a monthly amount and the fixed cost of $48,000 is an annual amount.)

LO 3 & 6: USE RATIOS TO DETERMINE BREAKEVEN AND SALES REQUIRED TO EARN TARGET PROFIT

6–36. Emergency Medical, Inc. is considering opening a new emergency care facility. The fees charged and costs of the new facility will be similar to that of the existing facility. The only exception is that the annual fixed cost for the new facility is expected to be $75,000 more than that of the existing facility. The following information is available for Emergency Medical's existing facility for 2004:

Revenue	$1,250,000
Variable cost	600,000
Fixed cost	420,000

Required:

a. Determine the revenues required for the new emergency care facility to break even.
b. Determine the revenues required for the new emergency care facility to earn a profit of $120,000 per year.

LO 3 & 6: USE RATIOS TO DETERMINE BREAKEVEN AND SALES REQUIRED TO EARN TARGET PROFIT

6–37. Wendt Industries is considering opening a second school supply store. The annual fixed cost of the new store is expected to be $225,000 per year. The following information is available for Wendt's first school supply store for 2004:

Revenue	$3,650,000
Variable cost	1,387,000

Required:

a. Based on this information, what is the required revenue for the second store to break even?
b. Based on this information, what is the required revenue for the second store to earn a profit of $125,000?

LO 2, 4, & 6: USE PER UNIT AMOUNTS TO DETERMINE BREAKEVEN AND SALES REQUIRED TO EARN TARGET PROFIT AND PREPARE A CONTRIBUTION INCOME STATEMENT

6–38. Richard Davenport owns a clothing store and is considering renting a soda vending machine for his store. He can rent the soda machine for $125 per month. Richard would supply the soda for the machine which he can buy for $3 per twelve pack. Richard plans to charge $0.75 per can.

Required:

a. List the fixed costs for renting and stocking the soda machine.
b. List the variable costs for renting and stocking the soda machine.
c. Calculate the contribution margin per can of soda.
d. (1) Calculate how many cans of soda Richard must sell each month to break even.
   (2) Prepare a contribution income statement that proves the answer you just calculated.
e. (1) Calculate how many cans of soda Richard must sell each month to earn a profit of $50.
   (2) Prepare a contribution income statement that proves your answer to the previous requirement.

LO 2, 4, & 6: USE PER UNIT AMOUNTS TO DETERMINE BREAKEVEN AND SALES REQUIRED TO EARN TARGET PROFIT AND PREPARE A CONTRIBUTION INCOME STATEMENT

6–39. Erich Traebeecke owns the Kenpo Karate School in Miami. He is considering renting a candy vending machine for his school lobby. He can rent the candy machine for $90 per month. Erich would supply the candy bars for the machine. He can buy a box of eight candy bars for $1 per box. Erich plans to sell each candy bar for $0.35.

Required:

a. List the fixed costs of renting and stocking the candy machine.
b. List the variable costs of renting and stocking the candy machine.
c. Calculate the contribution margin per candy bar.
d. (1) Calculate how many candy bars must be sold each month to break even.
   (2) Prepare a contribution income statement that proves the answer you just calculated.
e. (1) Calculate how many candy bars must be sold each month to earn a profit of $180.
   (2) Prepare a contribution income statement that proves your answer to the previous requirement.

LO 2, 4, AND 6: USE PER UNIT AMOUNTS TO DETERMINE BREAKEVEN AND SALES REQUIRED TO EARN TARGET PROFIT AND PREPARE A CONTRIBUTION INCOME STATEMENT

6–40. Monica Llobet owns Monica's School of Dance. She is considering installing a cappuccino machine in the school's dance studio. Monica can rent the cappuccino machine for $48.88 per month. Coffee and supplies would cost about $.12 per cup of cappuccino. Monica plans to sell each cup of cappuccino for $2.

Required:

  a. List the fixed costs of renting and stocking the cappuccino machine.
  b. List the variable costs of renting and stocking the cappuccino machine.
  c. Calculate the contribution margin per cup of cappuccino.
  d. (1) Calculate how many cups of cappuccino must be sold each month to break even.
   (2) Prepare a contribution income statement that proves the answer you just calculated.
  e. (1) Calculate how many cups of cappuccino must be sold each month to earn a profit of $100. (Round your answer to the nearest unit.)
   (2) Prepare a contribution income statement that proves your answer to the previous requirement.

LO 2 & 6: USE PER UNIT AMOUNTS TO DETERMINE BREAKEVEN AND SALES REQUIRED TO EARN TARGET PROFIT

6–41. Alberto Pons is interested in selling pin-on buttons at school pep rallies. The button machine will cost $200, and the material to produce each button costs $0.15. In exchange for the right to sell the buttons, Alberto has agreed to donate $300 per year and $0.20 per button to the school's booster club. Alberto plans to sell the buttons for $1 each and to operate the service for four years. By then it will be time to graduate, and the button machine will be worn out.

Required:

  a. Assuming the button machine will be able to produce buttons for four years, calculate the cost per year for the button machine.
  b. Calculate the total fixed cost per year for Alberto's button business.
  c. Calculate the variable cost per button.
  d. Calculate the annual break-even point:
   1. In units.
   2. In dollars.
  e. Calculate how many buttons must be sold to earn an annual profit of $800.
  f. Calculate the sales in dollars required to earn an annual profit of $800.

LO 2 & 6: USE PER UNIT AMOUNTS TO DETERMINE BREAKEVEN AND SALES REQUIRED TO EARN TARGET PROFIT

6–42. Betty Lopez is interested in setting up a stand to sell Mylar helium balloons at a local roller rink. The stand would cost $250, and the material for each balloon would cost $0.75. In exchange for the right to sell the balloons, Betty has agreed to pay $500 per year and $0.50 per balloon to the roller rink's owner. Betty plans to sell the balloons for $3 each. Betty thinks the stand will last four years.

Required:

  a. Assuming the balloon stand has an estimated useful life of four years with no residual value, calculate the cost per year for the balloon stand.
  b. Calculate the total fixed cost per year for Betty's balloon business.
  c. Calculate the variable cost per balloon.
  d. Calculate the annual break-even point:
   1. In units.
   2. In dollars.
  e. Calculate how many balloons must be sold to earn an annual profit of $2,000.
  f. Calculate the sales in dollars required to earn an annual profit of $2,000.

LO 2 & 6: USE PER UNIT AMOUNTS TO DETERMINE BREAKEVEN AND SALES REQUIRED TO EARN TARGET PROFIT

6–43. Bill Smith is interested in selling ice cream bars at school events. The vendor stand will cost $800, and the ice cream bars cost $0.65. In exchange for the right to sell the ice cream bars, Bill has agreed to donate $600 per year and $0.25 per ice cream bar to the school's booster club. Bill plans to sell the ice cream bars for $1.50 each. Bill intends to sell the ice cream bars and run the stand for four years.

Required:

    a. Assuming the vendor stand can be used for four years with no residual value, calculate the cost per year for the vendor stand.

    b. Calculate the total fixed cost per year for Bill's ice cream business.

    c. Calculate the variable cost per ice cream bar.

    d. Calculate the annual break-even point:
        1. In units.
        2. In dollars.

    e. Calculate how many ice cream bars must be sold to earn an annual profit of $3,000.

    f. Calculate the sales in dollars required to earn an annual profit of $3,000.

    g. Calculate Bill's profit if sales were $8,000 for this year.

LO 3 & 6: DETERMINE THE CONTRIBUTION MARGIN RATIO AND DETERMINE BREAKEVEN AND SALES REQUIRED TO EARN TARGET PROFIT

6–44. Amanda is considering opening a gift shop. She has collected the following information:

Monthly rent	$2,800
Monthly sales salaries	1,200

In addition to the sales salaries, Amanda intends to pay sales commissions of 5 percent of sales to her sales staff. The cost of the merchandise sold is expected to be 40 percent of sales.

Required:

    a. Determine the following:
        1. Amanda's break-even point in monthly sales dollars.
        2. The monthly sales dollars required to earn a profit of $2,000 per month.
        3. Amanda's break-even point if she is able to reduce rent by $200.

    b. Assume in addition to the $200 reduction in rent, that Amanda has negotiated a 10 percent discount on all merchandise purchases. The new cost of merchandise will not change the selling price of product. Determine the following:
        1. The new contribution margin ratio.
        2. The new break-even point in monthly sales dollars.

LO 3 & 6: DETERMINE THE CONTRIBUTION MARGIN RATIO AND DETERMINE BREAKEVEN AND SALES REQUIRED TO EARN TARGET PROFIT

6–45. Noelle is considering opening a bookstore. She has collected the following information:

Monthly rent	$3,286
Monthly sales salaries	4,200

In addition to the sales salaries, Noelle intends to pay sales commissions of 10 percent of sales to her sales staff. The cost of the merchandise sold is expected to be 30 percent of sales.

Required:

    a. Determine the following:
        1. Noelle's break-even point in monthly sales dollars.
        2. The monthly sales dollars required to earn a profit of $1,500 per month.
        3. Noelle's break-even point if she is able to reduce rent by $300.

    b. Assume in addition to the $300 reduction in rent, that Noelle has negotiated a 5 percent discount on all merchandise purchases. The new cost of merchandise will not change the selling price of product. Determine the following:
        1. The new contribution margin ratio.
        2. The new break-even point in monthly sales dollars.

LO 2 & 6: USE PER UNIT AMOUNTS TO DETERMINE BREAKEVEN AND SALES REQUIRED TO EARN TARGET PROFIT

6–46. Clarice is considering buying a video rental business. If she finances the entire purchase price, the payments will be $2,900 per month. Store rent would be $2,000 per month and cost of sales clerks, replacement tapes, and other expenses would be $1,200 per month. Clarice plans to rent the tapes for $2 each.

Required:

    a. Calculate the variable cost (if any) per tape rental.
    b. Calculate the total fixed cost per month.
    c. Determine how many tapes Clarice must rent each month to break even.
    d. Determine how many tapes Clarice must rent each month to earn a profit of $1,000 per month.

LO 3 & 6: DETERMINE THE CONTRIBUTION MARGIN RATIO AND DETERMINE BREAKEVEN AND SALES REQUIRED TO EARN TARGET PROFIT

6–47. Margaret Pitman is considering opening a gift shop. She has collected the following information:

Monthly rent	$1,800
Monthly sales salaries	1,200

The cost of the merchandise sold is expected to be 55 percent of sales.

Required:

    a. What is the annual rent cost?
    b. What is the annual sales salaries cost?
    c. What is the contribution margin ratio?
    d. What is the break-even point in dollars?
    e. Determine the amount of sales needed to earn a profit of $12,000 for the year.

LO 3 & 6: DETERMINE THE CONTRIBUTION MARGIN RATIO AND DETERMINE BREAKEVEN AND SALES REQUIRED TO EARN TARGET PROFIT

6–48. Carol Jean is considering opening a frame shop. She has collected the following information:

Monthly rent	$ 600
Monthly sales salaries	1,100

The cost of the merchandise sold is expected to be 45 percent of sales.

Required:

    a. What is the annual rent cost?
    b. What is the annual sales salaries cost?
    c. What is the contribution margin ratio?
    d. What is the break-even point in dollars?
    e. Determine the amount of sales needed to earn a profit of $18,000 for the year.

LO 3 & 6: DETERMINE THE CONTRIBUTION MARGIN RATIO AND DETERMINE BREAKEVEN AND SALES REQUIRED TO EARN TARGET PROFIT

6–49. Birdie Musicus is considering opening Musicus Beauty Supply. She has collected the following information:

Monthly rent	$3,400
Monthly sales salaries	2,800

The cost of the merchandise sold is expected to be 68 percent of sales.

Required:

    a. What is the annual rent cost?
    b. What is the annual sales salaries cost?
    c. What is the contribution margin ratio?
    d. What is the break-even point in dollars?
    e. Determine the amount of sales needed to earn a profit of $36,000 for the year.

LO 3 & 6: DETERMINE THE CONTRIBUTION MARGIN RATIO AND DETERMINE BREAKEVEN AND SALES REQUIRED TO EARN TARGET PROFIT

6-50. Vivian Farias is considering opening Farias Music Store. She has collected the following information:

Monthly rent	$1,400
Monthly sales salaries	1,700

The cost of the merchandise sold is expected to be 52 percent of sales.

Required:

    a. What is the annual rent cost?
    b. What is the annual sales salaries cost?
    c. What is the contribution margin ratio?
    d. What is the break-even point in dollars?
    e. Determine the amount of sales needed to earn a profit of $36,000 for the year.

LO 2, 3, 4, & 5: ANALYZE A SITUATION USING CVP

6-51. Quality Instrument Company manufactures various industrial thermometers. Last year the company sold 600 model QI-22 thermometers for $129 each. Managers are concerned that the profits from the QI-22 were only $7,740 last year. Fixed costs for this product are $50,000 per year. In an effort to increase profits, the company raised the price of the QI-22 to $148. Based on annual sales of 600 units, managers are confident that profits from the QI-22 will be increased to $19,140 next year.

    The sales manager is concerned about the price increase. He believes the company should move more slowly in making the pricing decision and has suggested that a group be formed to explore the ramifications of such a pricing move.

Required: Assume that you have been assigned to the group who will evaluate the proposed price change. The group is to create a report discussing the various ramifications of the price increase including its effect on projected sales and profits. Your report should make recommendations that are supported by calculations similar to those found in this chapter.

LO 2, 3, 4, & 5: ANALYZE A SITUATION USING CVP

6-52. Reuben Escobar's Door Company manufactured and sold 1,000 model SD4896 doors for $88 each. Managers are concerned that the profits from the SD4896 doors were only $8,000 last year. In an effort to increase profits, the company raised the price of the SD4896 to $106. Based on annual sales of 1,000 units, managers are confident that profits from the SD4896 will increase to $26,000 next year. Fixed costs of $40,000 are allocated to the SD4896 based on the number of units produced.

    The sales manager is concerned about the price increase. He believes the company should move more slowly in making the pricing decision and has suggested that a group be formed to explore the ramifications of such a pricing move.

Required: Assume that you have been assigned to the group who will evaluate the proposed price change. The group is to create a report discussing the various ramifications of the price increase including its effect on projected sales and profits. Your report should make recommendations that are supported by calculations similar to those found in this chapter.

LO 2, 3, 4, & 5: ANALYZE A SITUATION USING CVP

6-53. Carol Werner is considering the purchase of a hot dog vending cart to sell hot dogs in a busy parking lot. The city of Panama City Beach requires that the cart be licensed at a cost of $500 per year.

Required:

    a. (1) How would Carol determine the cost to rent a small space in the parking lot to operate the hot dog cart?
        (2) How much do you think the monthly rent would be?

    (3) How much do you think the hourly wage would be for an employee to operate the stand?

    (4) How many hours per day do you think the stand should be open?

    (5) Based on your answers to 3 and 4, what would you estimate monthly wage cost to be for the hot dog stand?

    (6) How much do you think Carol should charge for each hot dog?

b. Answer the following questions using your answers to question 1.

    (1) What is the variable cost per hot dog?

    (2) What is the monthly fixed cost for operating the hot dog stand?

    (3) What is the contribution margin per hot dog?

    (4) What is the contribution ratio?

    (5) What is the variable cost percentage?

    (6) (a) How many hot dogs must Carol sell each month to break even?

       (b) Prepare a contribution income statement which proves your answer.

    (7) (a) How many hot dogs must Carol sell each month to earn a profit of $300?

       (b) Prepare a contribution income statement that proves your answer.

CHAPTER 7

Making Decisions Using Relevant Information

When managers make decisions, it is critical that they base them on *relevant* information, disregarding all *irrelevant* information. To be relevant, the information must be pertinent to the decision.

You may wonder why an entire chapter of this text is devoted to determining which costs and benefits are relevant. Isn't it understood that decision makers should disregard superfluous information and concentrate on the facts that relate to the decision at hand? Yes, but with so many considerations to muddy the water, determining what information is relevant is not always as easy as it might seem. For instance, consider an actual example about a couple who went to **Disney World** with their three-year-old daughter, Jessica. The family stayed at a **Disney** hotel to be close to the **Disney** attractions and to take advantage of the hotel's staff of baby-sitters. The baby-sitting service costs $14 per hour and requires a four-hour minimum. To get a sitter, you have to make arrangements well in advance and if you need to cancel, you must do it four hours in advance to avoid the $56 minimum fee. Jessica's parents planned to take her to the Magic Kingdom early in the day and then leave her with a sitter in the late afternoon while they visited EPCOT on their own.

Jessica and her parents went to **Disney**'s Magic Kingdom as they had planned and were having a wonderful time. As the day progressed, Jessica enjoyed the amusement park so much that her parents were having second thoughts about leaving her with the sitter. They had to make a decision: Should they take Jessica to EPCOT or leave her with the sitter as planned? What Jessica's parents really wanted to do was to take her to EPCOT. But, as they discussed the situation, the overwhelming focus of their decision became the troublesome $56 minimum charge for the sitter. Because it was too late to cancel the sitter and avoid the $56 cost, it seemed to follow that Jessica should stay with the sitter. But Jessica's parents were falling into a very common trap. They were allowing a cost that was actually irrelevant to sway their decision. Oddly enough, the element that had emerged as the central consideration, the $56, was in fact, irrelevant to their decision. This is because the $56 would have to be paid either way. That is, if Jessica's parents were to take her to the sitter, they would have to pay the $56 or if they were to take her to EPCOT, they would still have to pay the $56. Once Jessica's parents realized that the $56 cost was irrelevant to their decision, they dismissed the sitter and took Jessica to EPCOT with them.

In business, the issue of what is relevant often confuses even the most seasoned business executive. To make the best possible decisions, decision makers must learn to consider only relevant information.

Learning Objectives

After completing your work on this chapter, you should be able to do the following:

1. Identify the characteristics of a relevant cost and a relevant benefit.
2. Explain why sunk costs and costs that do not differ between alternatives are irrelevant costs.
3. Describe the qualitative factors that decision makers should consider when making a business decision.
4. Use accounting information to determine the relevant cost of various decisions.
5. Explain the effects of fixed costs and opportunity costs on outsourcing decisions.

◆ RELEVANT COSTS AND BENEFITS

relevant information
Information that is pertinent to a particular decision in that it has a bearing on which decision alternative is preferable.

relevant cost   A cost or outflow that is pertinent to a particular decision. A future cost that differs between alternatives.

relevant benefit   A benefit (a revenue or cash inflow) that is pertinent to a particular decision. A future benefit that differs between alternatives.

sunk costs   A past cost that cannot be changed by current or future actions.

Relevant information is information that is pertinent to a particular decision in that it has a bearing on which decision alternative is preferable. A **relevant cost** is a cost or cash outflow that is pertinent to a particular business decision. A **relevant benefit** is a benefit (revenue or cash inflow) that is pertinent to a particular business decision. Relevant costs and benefits possess two important characteristics: (1) The cost or benefit must be something that will happen in the future, and (2) the cost or benefit must differ between decision alternatives. A relevant cost is a future cost that differs between alternatives and a relevant benefit is a future benefit that differs between alternatives.

A relevant cost must be a future cost because current decisions have no effect on past expenditures. Expenditures that have already occurred are called **sunk costs,** and they cannot be changed by current or future actions. Because sunk costs are unaffected by current decisions, they are irrelevant and we should not consider them when evaluating current decision alternatives. For example, if your firm was deciding whether to replace an old printing press with a new, labor-saving model, the cost of the old press would be irrelevant. Why? The firm already bought the old press. The purchase of the new printing press would not lessen or change the amount paid for the old one. Whether the company purchases the new press or not, the cost of the old press is a sunk cost: Nothing you do now can change it. Sunk costs include both amounts paid in the past and past commitments to pay. That is, once there is a binding commitment to pay cash or otherwise transfer resources, the cost associated with that commitment is a sunk cost.

To be relevant, a future cost or benefit must differ between decision alternatives. If a future cost or benefit will be the same regardless of the alternative we choose, it is irrelevant. Again, consider the decision of whether to buy a new printing press or to keep the old one. If the new printing press will use the same quantity and type of ink as the old one, the cost of ink is irrelevant no matter how large the dollar figure. If the revenue earned will be the same whether or not you replace the printing press, that benefit is irrelevant.

Discussion Questions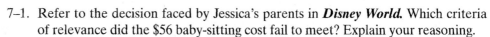

7–1. Refer to the decision faced by Jessica's parents in ***Disney World.*** Which criteria of relevance did the $56 baby-sitting cost fail to meet? Explain your reasoning.
7–2. Have you ever made a decision and later realized that you mistakenly let irrelevant factors affect your choice? Explain.

quantitative factors
Factors that can be measured by numbers.

qualitative factors
Factors that cannot be measured by numbers—they must be described in words.

Quantitative factors are those that can be represented by numbers. Almost all accounting information is quantitative, including relevant cost and benefit information. However, managers often consider additional factors that cannot be quantified. **Qualitative factors** are factors that cannot be measured numerically—they must be described in words. Examples include customer satisfaction, product quality, employee morale, and customer perceptions.

In addition to their financial impact, business decisions affect a multitude of nonfinancial areas. For example, closing an outdated factory may reduce production cost, but it may also adversely impact employee morale. The employees that remain after the plant closing may believe that the company's loyalty is to profits, not their well-being. Lower employee morale is likely to lead to less productivity and lower product quality. Qualitative factors should also be considered in smaller, routine decisions. For example, a furniture store manager considering a proposal to switch from company owned and operated delivery trucks to a delivery service should consider her lack of control if she uses the delivery service. Even though it may be less expensive to use a delivery service, the furniture store's manager may not want to lose the ability to select the most responsible truck drivers and to schedule deliveries exactly as she desires. When making decisions, managers should evaluate relevant quantitative and qualitative factors.

Discussion Questions

Assume you are planning a trip from Miami to Texas to visit some friends. You have a job, but your boss will let you take off as many days as you wish for the trip. Your car is unreliable, so you compare two alternatives—taking a bus or taking an airplane.

7–3. What are the relevant quantitative factors you should consider in making your decision?

7–4. What are the relevant qualitative factors you should consider in making your decision?

Decision makers must question the relevance of accounting information. As discussed in Chapter 1, managers do not always specify accounting information requirements. When they don't, accountants provide them with information based on accepted accounting techniques, and this information may or may not be relevant. Although management accounting information is generally relevant to internal decision makers, managers should be able to determine for themselves what information is relevant to their particular situation so they can make sound, well-informed decisions. As Exhibit 7–1 shows, whether an item is relevant or not hinges on the answers to two important questions: Is the item a future cost or benefit? Does the cost or benefit differ between decision alternatives?

EXHIBIT 7-1 Determining Relevant Cost and Benefit

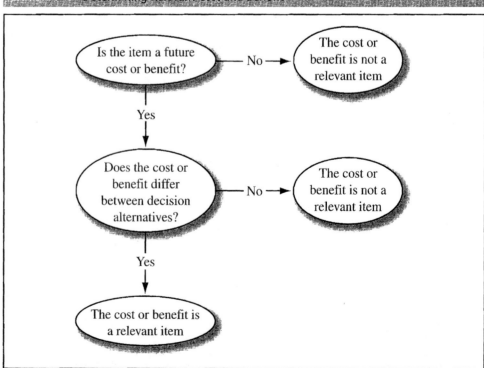

Throughout the remainder of this chapter, we will explore several common business situations to demonstrate how to determine relevant cost and benefit information and its importance to good decision making. For each example, we will gather all costs and benefits associated with the decision. Next, we will determine the relevant costs and benefits of each decision alternative. Finally, we will compare the relevant costs and benefits of the alternatives and determine the preferred alternative. The first example we will explore is an equipment replacement decision.

◆ EQUIPMENT REPLACEMENT

As an example of how to determine relevant information, we examine a proposed equipment replacement project. Our example highlights the treatment of depreciation, sunk costs, and future costs and benefits that do not differ between alternatives.

Bill Smith & Partners, a local law firm, purchased and installed a sophisticated computer system two weeks ago at a cost of $35,500. Bill's brother, John, stops by the law office to say hello. While there, he notices the new system. He remarks that it is too bad the system is not the latest and quickest because, if it were, the data input time could be cut in half. John suggests that Bill consider updating. Bill responds, "1 can't buy a new system. I just bought this one two weeks ago." John advises Bill to take a closer look before deciding.

GATHER ALL COSTS AND BENEFITS ASSOCIATED WITH THE DECISION

Bill turns to you for advice. He explains that the recently installed computer system cost $35,500 to purchase, has an estimated useful life of five years, with a residual value of $500. He notes that the firm plans to use straight-line depreciation, so it will recognize $7,000 depreciation per year. The cost of operating the recently installed system, which we will call the "old" system, includes two operators at $18,000 per year, and a maintenance contract at $1,000 per year. The maintenance agreement, however, can be canceled at any time. After calling around, Bill informs you that he can sell the old system now, but he will get only $10,000 for it (everyone wants the new model). The new model would cost $76,000 and also has an estimated useful life of five years with a $1,000 residual value. Using the straight-line method, annual depreciation would be $15,000. Because data entry is twice as fast, the new computer system would require only one operator at $18,000 per year. The maintenance contract on the new machine would cost $1,000 per year and would be cancelable at any time.

A summary of the cost and benefit of each system is shown in Exhibit 7–2. These items can be classified as start-up, operating, and shutdown.

EXHIBIT 7-2   Computer System Replacement Cost Summary

	Old System	Replacement System
Start-up:		
Cost of system	$ 35,500	$76,000
Operating:		
Annual depreciation	$ 7,000	$15,000
Total depreciation	35,000	75,000
Annual labor cost	36,000	18,000
Total labor cost	180,000	90,000
Annual maintenance cost	1,000	1,000
Total maintenance cost	5,000	5,000
Shutdown:		
Residual value of system	$ 500	$ 1,000
Current sale price of old system	10,000	

To help Bill make a wise decision about the new computer system, you must first look at each item and determine whether it is relevant. To make an informed decision, a manager must consider the total cost and benefit of each alternative, including all the costs and benefits over the life of the alternative. For our computer replacement decision, the annual costs associated with each system are multiplied by the number of years the system will be used to determine the total cost of the system over its lifetime.

DETERMINE THE RELEVANT COST AND BENEFIT OF EACH ALTERNATIVE

Next we determine the relevant cost and benefit of each decision alternative. As you consider each cost, try to determine whether it is relevant to the equipment replacement decision. Ask yourself the following two questions: (1) Is the cost a future cost? and (2) Does the cost or benefit differ between alternatives? We will examine the cost and benefit associated with the old computer system first.

Relevant Cost and Benefit of the Old Computer System

The $35,500 cost of the old system is not relevant because it is a sunk cost. Bill's decision to purchase or not to purchase the new computer system cannot change the past expenditure for the old one.

Although it may appear that depreciation is a future cost, it is nothing more than an allocation of an asset's original cost. The cost of an asset purchased in the past is a sunk cost, and depreciation simply allocates this sunk cost. Therefore, the depreciation for the old computer system is not relevant.

The total cost of $180,000 to pay for two operators is relevant, because it is a future cost and it differs between alternatives. The old system requires two operators, each costing $18,000 per year. Over the five-year expected life of the old system, that totals $180,000 (2 operators × $18,000 × 5 years).

The $5,000 total cost of the maintenance contract for the old system is irrelevant, because it does not differ between decision alternatives. The cost of the maintenance contract for the old system is the same as that for the new one. Therefore, although this is a future cost, it is irrelevant because it does not differ between alternatives.

The $500 residual value of the old system is relevant because it is a future benefit and it differs between alternatives. If Bill stays with the old computer system, he will be able to sell it at the end of its useful life for $500. If he buys the new one, however, he will sell the old one now for $10,000, and therefore he will be unable to sell it for its residual value in five years.

The $10,000 that Bill could get if he sells the old system now is a future benefit that differs between alternatives, and therefore it is relevant. If Bill buys the new computer system, he can sell the old one for $10,000, but if he does not buy the new system, he will need the old one so he would not sell it.

Relevant Costs and Benefits of the Replacement System

Next, we will analyze the start-up, operating, and shutdown of the replacement computer systems. In our example, the only start-up cost for the replacement system is the $76,000 to purchase and install it. This cost is relevant because it is a future cost and it differs between alternatives.

The $75,000 in total depreciation on the new computer system is an allocation of the replacement system's cost. Because we have already considered the cost of the new computer system, we avoid double counting by excluding its depreciation expense from our analysis of relevant costs.

The $90,000 ($18,000 × 5 years) total labor cost for the replacement system's one operator is relevant because it is a future cost that differs between alternatives. The labor cost for the old system is $180,000, whereas the labor cost for the replacement system is $90,000.

The total cost of the maintenance contract on the replacement system is $5,000. As it happens, the maintenance cost of the old system is also $5,000. In this situation, although maintenance cost is a future cost, it is irrelevant because it does not differ between alternatives.

The $1,000 residual value for the new computer system is relevant because it is a future benefit that differs between alternatives. If Bill replaces his current system with a new one, then he can sell the new system for $1,000 at the end of its useful life. If he does not buy the new one, he obviously can't sell it.

COMPARE THE RELEVANT INFORMATION AND SELECT AN ALTERNATIVE

Now that we have determined which costs and benefits are relevant for each alternative, we compare them to see which alternative is best for Bill's firm. For each of our relevant cost examples, we will use a simple format that includes a column for the relevant items for each decision alternative. Once we list all the relevant items in the appropriate column, we will calculate the difference between the relevant costs and benefits and select the best decision alternative. It is important to differentiate between inflows and outflows. In Exhibit 7–3 we use parentheses to identify outflows.

EXHIBIT 7-3 Relevant Cost and Benefit Comparison for an Equipment Replacement Decision

	Alternative One: Keep Old System	Alternative Two: Replace Old System
Start-up:		
Cost of new system		$ (76,000)
Operating:		
Labor cost:		
Old system (2 × $18,000 × 5)	$(180,000)	
New system (1 × $18,000 × 5)		(90,000)
Shutdown:		
Residual value of old system	500	
Sale price if old system sold now		10,000
Residual value of new system		1,000
Total relevant amounts	$(179,500)	$(155,000)
Difference in relevant costs and benefits		$24,500
		In favor of buying the new system

As this analysis shows, Bill would save $24,500 over the next five years by buying the new computer system. So he should buy the new system to save money, right? From a purely monetary point of view, he should. However, the replacement system is not cheap. Often, business decision makers determine the best alternative, only to learn the business does not have enough available cash to take advantage of a course of action that would save money in the long run. Considering only relevant costs and benefits in decision making will lead to better business decisions, but it will not necessarily enable a company to take advantage of what can be learned in the process.

Discussion Questions

7–5. Assuming all purchases and sales of computer systems are cash transactions, how much cash would Bill need to buy the new system?

7–6. Now that we know the relevant quantitative information associated with the computer replacement, what qualitative factors should Bill consider before he makes his final decision?

INTEREST—THE TIME VALUE OF MONEY

Equipment purchase decisions generally have long-term effects. Because of the long life of the equipment, the associated cash inflows and outflows will occur for many years. Therefore, decision makers should consider the interest-earning potential of the cash flows associated with equipment acquisitions. The interest-earning potential of cash is sometimes called the **time value of money.** In this chapter we are focusing on relevant costs and benefits and have ignored the time value of money. However, Chapter 8 covers special techniques developed to incorporate the effect of interest and the timing of cash flows.

time value of money
The interest-earning potential of cash.

◆ SPECIAL ORDERS

special order An order that is outside a company's normal scope of business activity.

Manufacturing businesses must often consider whether to accept a **special order**—an order that is outside its normal scope of business activity. As we will see, proper treatment of fixed cost is critical in making sound special order decisions.

Assume that your company, Alumafloat, makes small aluminum boats. Alumafloat has been in operation for almost 10 years and sells boats to marine supply stores in southern Florida. One day, a *Sears* representative approaches you with an interesting proposition. *Sears* is interested in purchasing 1,000 of your boats for $125 each. The largest order your company has received to date was for 100 boats, so obviously, this huge order requires special consideration.

GATHER ALL COSTS AND BENEFITS ASSOCIATED WITH THE DECISION

The $125 offer from *Sears* is considerably less than Alumafloat's normal selling price of $160 per boat. In fact, the boats cost $130 each to produce, so the company would lose $5 per boat if it accepts *Sears*'s $125 offer.

As you discuss the order with the representative from *Sears*, you tell her that you would be willing to sell the boats to *Sears* at a discounted price of $140 each because of the large quantity of boats they need. *Sears* refuses your offer. The store will pay only $125 per boat, and the representative expects you to accept or reject the order within five days.

You gather all the information necessary to make a wise decision. First, you meet with your company's cost accountant, who confirms that your cost per unit is $130. You also request a report detailing production cost so you can see how the cost per unit figure was calculated. Using expected total sales (excluding the special order from *Sears*) and production costs for the year, the cost accountant prepares the report shown in Exhibit 7–4.

EXHIBIT 7–4   Per Unit Cost and Sales Report for Alumafloat

Expected sales (5,500 units at $160 each)		$880,000
Less: Cost of goods sold (see detail below)		(715,000)
Expected gross margin		$165,000

Detailed calculation for cost of goods sold:

	Per Unit	Total
Number of units	1	5,500
Direct material	$ 50	$275,000
Direct labor	55	302,500
Variable manufacturing overhead	10	55,000
Fixed manufacturing overhead	15	82,500
Total cost of goods sold	$130	$715,000

We must determine the potential effect on Alumafloat's revenues and expenses of accepting the order. Which costs shown in Exhibit 7–4 would be affected by the decision to accept the special order from **Sears**? To determine which costs are relevant, we will again ask the following two questions: (1) Is the cost a future cost? and (2) Does the cost differ between alternatives?

DETERMINE THE RELEVANT COST AND BENEFIT OF EACH ALTERNATIVE

Next you must determine which costs and benefits are relevant. In this situation, the alternatives are to accept the order or reject it. Generally speaking, because no cost is associated with rejecting the order, our analysis focuses on the alternative to accept.

If you accept the order, sales will increase by $125,000 (1,000 boats × $125 per boat). The increase in sales due to the special order is a relevant benefit, because it is something that will happen in the future and it differs between alternatives.

All variable costs are relevant because they are future costs that differ between alternatives. If the special order is accepted, variable costs will be incurred to produce the 1,000 boats. In this example, variable cost includes direct material, direct labor, and variable manufacturing overhead.

Depending on the decision situation, fixed cost may or may not be relevant. Often, fixed manufacturing overhead costs are not relevant because total fixed cost for the company will be unaffected by the increase in production volume. This fact holds true unless specific fixed-cost increases occur due to the special order, or the order is so substantial that production would exceed the relevant range if the company accepts the order. As the report in Exhibit 7–4 indicates, the company expects total fixed costs to be $82,500. Assume in our example that the decision to accept or reject the special order from **Sears** would not affect total fixed cost. Therefore, in this case, fixed cost does not differ between alternatives and is irrelevant to the special order decision.

COMPARE THE RELEVANT COSTS AND BENEFITS AND SELECT AN ALTERNATIVE

Armed with information about relevant cost and benefit, you can make an informed decision about the **Sears** order. Exhibit 7–5 presents a schedule of relevant cost and benefit for this special order. The schedule excludes fixed costs because they are irrelevant.

EXHIBIT 7–5 Relevant Cost and Benefit for Special Order of 1,000 Boats

	Per Unit	Total
Sales from special order	$125	$125,000
Direct material	$(50)	$(50,000)
Direct labor	(55)	(55,000)
Variable manufacturing overhead	(10)	(10,000)
Total relevant manufacturing overhead	(115)	(115,000)
Total increase in profit	$ 10	$ 10,000

Alumafloat's profit will increase by $10,000 if you accept the special order.

The reasoning in the Alumafloat example may seem logical, but companies often reject special orders that would increase profits, because managers do not understand the concept of relevant cost as it pertains to fixed cost. To avoid making poor decisions, managers must carefully consider how a special order will affect fixed cost.

Accounting information must sometimes be tailored by the information user to provide information that is relevant to the decision at hand. Regarding a huge international sale an accountant for a **Fortune** 500 chemical company once remarked, "I can't believe that the product sales manager is selling below cost. He is disregarding fixed cost as he sets prices to move old stock." In fact, the manager may have made a good decision about the price of the product, depending on whether the fixed costs are relevant to the pricing decision. As a manager, you should know that routinely prepared accounting information cannot be relevant to every decision.

Discussion Questions

7–7. What would happen if you treated every order as a special order and routinely disregarded fixed cost considerations from your pricing decisions?

7–8. Assume that the production manager at Alumafloat reminds you that four years ago sales skyrocketed for a while. Demand was so great that production increased to the limit of the company's capacity. Alumafloat produced 6,950 boats in a 12-month period. What implications does this information have on your decision to accept the special order from **Sears**?

7–9. What qualitative factors should you consider regarding accepting an order to sell **Sears** the boats for less than the price you charge your regular customers? For example, what would your regular customers think if they found that **Sears** was selling the same style boat they buy from you?

◆ OUTSOURCING—THE MAKE OR BUY DECISION

Often, companies purchase subcomponents used to manufacture their products instead of making them in their in-house manufacturing facilities. Buying services, products, or components of products from outside vendors instead of producing them is called **outsourcing.** Decision makers considering whether to make or buy subcomponents must pay close attention to fixed costs. Also, because this make or buy decision does not directly affect revenues or cash inflow (relevant benefits), we focus solely on identifying relevant costs.

outsourcing Buying services, products, or components of products instead of producing them.

Assume you are a product manager at Microbake, a plant that manufactures various products including microwave ovens. A vendor has approached you about supplying the timer assemblies for your microwave ovens for $12 each. Currently, Microbake makes the timers in its own subassembly department. The subassembly department makes many of the small component parts for the various products manufactured at the plant. When you review the cost sheets for the timers, you discover that the company uses 80,000 timers each year and they cost $14 each to produce in-house.

GATHER ALL COSTS ASSOCIATED WITH THE DECISION

You call a meeting with Microbake's cost accounting department to discuss the situation and confirm that the $14 in-house manufacturing cost is correct. Even when pressed, the cost accountants are confident their cost figures are carefully prepared and accurate. In fact, they are surprised the company can buy the timers from the outside vendor for only $12 each. At your request, the cost accounting department prepares the cost breakdown for the timers shown in Exhibit 7–6.

EXHIBIT 7-6   Cost of Producing Oven Timers In-House

Number of timers produced each year		80,000
	Per Unit	**Total**
Direct material	$ 5	$ 400,000
Direct labor	4	320,000
Variable manufacturing overhead	1	80,000
Fixed manufacturing overhead	4	320,000
Total	$14	$1,120,000

DETERMINE THE RELEVANT COST OF EACH ALTERNATIVE

Once again we assess whether each cost is relevant by asking the following questions: (1) Is the cost a future cost? and (2) Does the cost differ between alternatives? The answers follow in Exhibit 7–7.

EXHIBIT 7-7 Selecting Relevant Costs of Producing Oven Timers

	Future?	Differs?	Relevant?
Direct material:	yes	yes	yes
Direct labor:	yes	yes	yes
Variable manufacturing overhead:	yes	yes	yes
Fixed manufacturing overhead:	yes	no	no

By definition, fixed manufacturing overhead remains constant in total regardless of the level of activity (in this case, "activity" is the number of units produced). The fixed cost presented by the cost accountants is an allocation of the total fixed overhead cost of the whole factory, or possibly of the subassembly department. If the company stops making the timers, the subassembly department will not go away and neither will its fixed cost, because the company needs the subassembly department to produce other components. Unless fixed cost changes based on management's decision to buy the timers, it is irrelevant.

COMPARE THE RELEVANT COSTS AND SELECT AN ALTERNATIVE

We compare the relevant costs of the make or buy decision in Exhibit 7–8.

EXHIBIT 7-8 Relevant Cost of Make or Buy Decision for Oven Timers

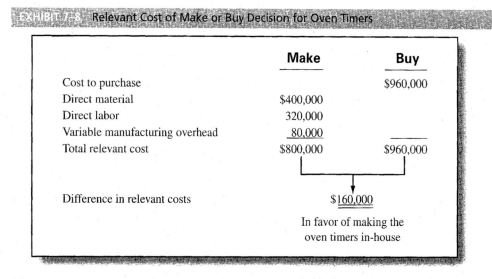

	Make	Buy
Cost to purchase		$960,000
Direct material	$400,000	
Direct labor	320,000	
Variable manufacturing overhead	80,000	
Total relevant cost	$800,000	$960,000
Difference in relevant costs		$160,000

In favor of making the
oven timers in-house

As Exhibit 7–8 indicates, once we have screened out the irrelevant fixed costs it becomes apparent that Microbake can save $160,000 per year by making the timers rather than buying them. Based on this relevant cost comparison, you decide to not purchase the timer assemblies from the outside vendor.

In a final effort to get the sale, the vendor contacts several people at Microbake informing them that you are squandering your company's money. The vendor points out to other Microbake managers that its price is $2 per unit less than your in-house production cost as determined by Microbake's highly trained cost accountants. Other managers are pressing to accept the outside vendor's proposal.

To settle the issue, you call a meeting of the managers and present your relevant cost findings. Several managers comment that your information disregards fixed manufacturing overhead. You explain that the fixed manufacturing overhead is irrelevant. The other managers argue that fixed manufacturing overhead is a very real part of business cost and that it should be included in your presentation. As it happens, this presents little problem. Including fixed manufacturing overhead, although irrelevant, may highlight how fixed costs are affected (or in this case, unaffected) by changes in production. You must demonstrate, however, that if the units are manufactured in-house, there will be fixed manufacturing overhead cost; and that if the units are purchased from the outside vendor, there will still be fixed manufacturing overhead cost. The relevant cost comparison can include the irrelevant fixed cost as shown in Exhibit 7–9.

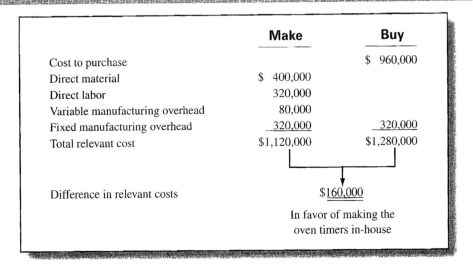

EXHIBIT 7–9 Relevant Cost of Make or Buy Decision for Oven Timers with Fixed Costs Shown

	Make	Buy
Cost to purchase		$ 960,000
Direct material	$ 400,000	
Direct labor	320,000	
Variable manufacturing overhead	80,000	
Fixed manufacturing overhead	320,000	320,000
Total relevant cost	$1,120,000	$1,280,000
Difference in relevant costs		$160,000

In favor of making the oven timers in-house

As Exhibit 7–9 shows, because fixed manufacturing overhead is the same for the two alternatives, the outcome of the comparison is the same as that in Exhibit 7–8. Microbake can save $160,000 by making the timers instead of buying them.

Discussion Question

7–10. What will happen to the cost of producing other Microbake products if your decision is overturned and the company outsources the timer assemblies?

SPECIAL RELEVANT COST CONSIDERATIONS FOR FIXED COSTS

In some situations, the alternative selected affects fixed costs. For example, suppose Microbake could eliminate an entire eight-hour production shift if it no longer made the timers. Eliminating that shift thus eliminates one line supervisor whose annual salary is $45,000 per year and reduces other fixed costs by $150,000. Therefore, fixed manufacturing overhead would decrease by $195,000 ($45,000 + $150,000). Exhibit 7–10 shows the relevant cost of the make or buy decision when the alternative to buy the timers enables the company to eliminate a production shift.

Exhibit 7–10 shows that the savings in fixed manufacturing overhead alters the cost comparison such that Microbake should opt to buy the timers. If the $195,000 reduction in fixed costs were realized, Microbake would save $35,000 by purchasing the timer assemblies from the vendor instead of making them.

Discussion Question

7–11. What qualitative factors should managers at Microbake consider with respect to their outsourcing decision?

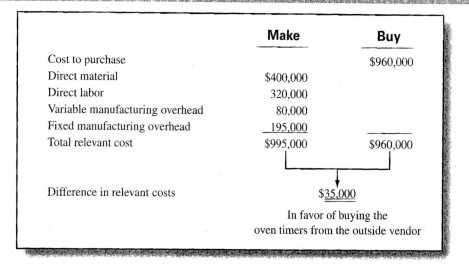

EXHIBIT 7–10 Relevant Cost of the Make or Buy Decision for Oven Timers with Relevant Fixed Costs

	Make	Buy
Cost to purchase		$960,000
Direct material	$400,000	
Direct labor	320,000	
Variable manufacturing overhead	80,000	
Fixed manufacturing overhead	195,000	
Total relevant cost	$995,000	$960,000
Difference in relevant costs		$35,000

In favor of buying the
oven timers from the outside vendor

CONSIDERING OPPORTUNITY COSTS

opportunity cost The benefit given up because one alternative is chosen over another.

An **opportunity cost** is the value of what a decision maker gives up because one alternative is chosen over another. For example, the opportunity cost of attending college rather than working full time is what you could have earned by working instead of going to college.

If Microbake buys the timer assemblies from an outside vendor, it may have an alternate use for the production capacity or assets used to make the timers—it may have an opportunity to enhance its earnings through an alternate use of the facilities. Assume that Microbake can use the production capacity freed up by purchasing the timers to make electronic alarm clocks. Assume further that the electronic alarm clocks would provide an annual contribution margin of $200,000 with no significant changes to fixed cost. If Microbake continues to make the timer assembles, it would lose the opportunity to earn the $200,000. The lost $200,000 contribution margin on the electronic alarm clocks is an opportunity cost.

Because opportunity cost is the cost of not doing something, it is not reflected in the accounting records of a business and is not reported in the company's external financial statements or internal management reports. This does not mean an opportunity cost is not real—remember, reality and the measurement of reality are not the same thing. Opportunity cost is an economic reality. Although it is not generally part of financial accounting measures, opportunity cost is a relevant consideration in business decisions.

Returning to the Microbake timer example, the relevant costs of making or buying the 80,000 timers, including the $200,000 lost opportunity, is presented in Exhibit 7–11.

Exhibit 7–11 suggests that if the $200,000 contribution margin from the production of alarm clocks could be realized, Microbake should buy the timer assemblies from the outside vendor. The production capacity no longer needed to produce the timers could then be used to produce the alarm clocks, resulting in a $40,000 difference in the relevant cost in favor of buying the timers.

Microbake's outsourcing problem is an example of a very real business dilemma. Managers cannot rely solely on the cost information from accountants. They themselves must have enough accounting knowledge to determine the relevant cost of each decision alternative.

Although we have explored relevant cost using only three examples, it is important to understand that relevant cost concepts apply to almost every business decision. Knowing how to determine which information is relevant is even helpful with personal decisions such as whether to attend summer school at a local university or enroll in a student exchange program and study abroad. Business situations and life in general provide an array of quantitative and qualitative considerations for every decision alter-

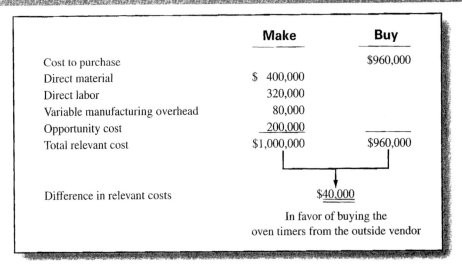

EXHIBIT 7-11 Relevant Cost of Make or Buy Decision for Oven Timers with Opportunity Cost

	Make	Buy
Cost to purchase		$960,000
Direct material	$ 400,000	
Direct labor	320,000	
Variable manufacturing overhead	80,000	
Opportunity cost	200,000	
Total relevant cost	$1,000,000	$960,000
Difference in relevant costs		$40,000

In favor of buying the
oven timers from the outside vendor

native. As a decision maker, you must be able to seek out the relevant considerations and disregard the irrelevant ones.

Summary

To make the best decision possible, a manager must attempt to consider only relevant information. What is relevant in one situation may not be relevant in another. A relevant cost or benefit is an item that makes a difference in a given decision situation. Relevant costs are always future costs, because past costs cannot be changed by any current or future actions. Further, a future cost or benefit must differ between alternatives to be considered relevant. Opportunity costs are often relevant and should be considered by managers making decisions. An opportunity cost is the value of benefits given up because one alternative is chosen over another.

In addition to the quantitative information managers must consider in making decisions, qualitative information such as customer satisfaction, product quality, and employee morale must also be considered. Oftentimes the qualitative considerations should outweigh purely quantitative considerations.

Key Terms

- opportunity cost, M–187
- outsourcing, M–184
- qualitative factors, M–177
- quantitative factors, M–177

- relevant benefit, M–177
- relevant cost, M–177
- relevant information, M–177
- special order, M–182

- sunk costs, M–177
- time value of money, M–182

Review the Facts

A. What is relevant information?
B. What is a relevant cost?
C. What is a relevant benefit?
D. What two important characteristics do all relevant costs possess?
E. What is a sunk cost?
F. Describe the difference between qualitative and quantitative factors.
G. When trying to determine whether a cost or benefit is relevant, what are the two questions the decision maker should ask?
H. Why is the depreciation for existing assets considered irrelevant for equipment replacement decisions?
I. What is the time value of money?
J. Why is the time value of money important for decisions involving the purchase of long-lived assets?
K. What would cause a fixed cost to be relevant for a special order decision?
L. What is outsourcing?
M. Define *opportunity cost.*
N. The concepts of selecting relevant information apply to what types of decisions?

Apply What You Have Learned

LO 1: DETERMINE WHICH ITEMS ARE RELEVANT

7–12. The production manager at Ace Manufacturing is contemplating whether he should upgrade some old production equipment. He is considering the following factors:

1. _____ The cost of the old equipment
2. _____ The cost of the new equipment
3. _____ Depreciation on the old equipment
4. _____ Depreciation on the new equipment
5. _____ Trade-in value of the old equipment
6. _____ Residual value of the old equipment
7. _____ Residual value of the new equipment

Required: For each item listed, indicate whether it is relevant (R) or irrelevant (I).

LO 3: QUANTITATIVE AND QUALITATIVE CONSIDERATIONS

7–13. Tom Robinson is thinking about buying a portable computer. He has a computer at home, but the portable computer would allow him to work during his frequent business trips. Tom is trying to convince his boss that the computer would save the company some money. Tom hopes that his company will pay at least part of the computer's purchase price and the monthly fee for an e-mail service.

Tom has asked a group of friends to help him think of all the advantages of buying the computer. Assume you are part of the group.

Group Requirements:

a. Prepare an informal schedule of the costs associated with the computer purchase.
b. List as many quantitative benefits as you can that the company will gain if Tom buys the portable computer.
c. List as many quantitative benefits as you can that Tom will gain if he buys the portable computer.
d. List as many qualitative benefits as you can that the company will gain if Tom buys the portable computer.

    e. List as many qualitative benefits as you can that Tom will gain if he buys the portable computer.

    f. How much of the computer's cost do you think Tom should pay? How much should Tom's employer pay?

LO 3 & 4: DETERMINE RELEVANT COST SCHEDULE AND QUALITATIVE FACTORS

7–14. Tina Alberts is thinking about trading her car for a new one. Her present car is only three years old, completely paid for, but out of warranty. The car's original cost was $22,000. Lately, the car has been somewhat undependable and the repair bills have been quite high. In the last three months, Tina paid over $1,200 for repairs. Tina intends to use her trade-in as the down payment and then finance the balance. She is looking at a new Nissan which she can get for about $23,000, less her trade.

    Tina has asked a group of close friends to help her think of all the relevant advantages and disadvantages of getting the new car. Assume you are part of this group.

Group Requirements:

    a. Prepare an informal schedule listing the relevant quantitative factors that Tina should consider. Do not limit your answer to the items found in the problem. Include all the factors you can think of. When possible, try to include estimated dollar amounts in your schedule.

    b. Prepare an informal schedule listing the relevant qualitative factors that Tina should consider.

    c. From a quantitative point of view, do you think Tina should buy the new car?

    d. Considering both quantitative and qualitative factors, do you think Tina should buy the new car?

LO 1: DETERMINE WHICH COSTS ARE RELEVANT

7–15. Jean Parks is a salesperson for Quality Food Products, Inc. She is considering a 250-mile trip to visit a potential customer, ByLots. Following are factors she is pondering.

    1. _____ The cost of traveling the 250 miles to ByLots
    2. _____ The time she will spend on the road
    3. _____ The time she will spend visiting with ByLots's executives
    4. _____ The amount of time already devoted to ByLots
    5. _____ The revenue potential from ByLots
    6. _____ The cost of her last visit to ByLots
    7. _____ The probability that her visit will result in new sales
    8. _____ The cost of lunch for herself if she visits ByLots
    9. _____ The cost of the lunch she would buy for ByLots' executives

Required: For each item listed, indicate whether it is relevant (R) or irrelevant (I).

LO 3: DETERMINE QUANTITATIVE AND QUALITATIVE FACTORS

7–16. This question is based on the same situation as 7–15. Jean Parks is a salesperson for Quality Food Products, Inc. She is considering a 250-mile trip to visit a potential customer, ByLots. Following are factors she is pondering.

    1. _____ The cost of traveling the 250 miles to ByLots
    2. _____ The time she will spend on the road
    3. _____ The time she will spend visiting with ByLots's executives
    4. _____ The amount of time already devoted to ByLots
    5. _____ The revenue potential from ByLots
    6. _____ The cost of her last visit to ByLots
    7. _____ The probability that her visit will result in new sales
    8. _____ The cost of lunch for herself if she visits ByLots
    9. _____ The cost of the lunch she would buy for ByLots's executives

Required: For each item listed, indicate whether it is quantitative (A) or qualitative (B).

LO 3: DETERMINE QUANTITATIVE AND QUALITATIVE FACTORS

7–17. Managers at Ace Manufacturing are considering upgrading some production equipment. They are considering the following factors:

1. _____ Maintenance cost
2. _____ Changes in product quality
3. _____ Residual value of the old equipment
4. _____ Cost of new equipment
5. _____ Difficulty of training employees to use new equipment
6. _____ Residual value of the new equipment
7. _____ The ill feelings due to the possible reduction in the labor force

Required: For each item listed, indicate whether it is quantitative (A) or qualitative (B).

LO 1, 2, 3, & 5: LIST COSTS, INDICATE RELEVANT COSTS, INDICATE QUALITATIVE FACTORS

7–18. Assume that you are deciding whether to live in a campus dormitory room or an off-campus apartment.

Required:

a. List all the costs that come to mind for each alternative as you think about this decision.
b. Review your list and indicate which costs are relevant and which are irrelevant to the decision.
c. What are some qualitative factors that you should consider when making this decision?

LO 1, 2, 3, & 5: LIST COSTS, INDICATE RELEVANT COSTS, INDICATE QUALITATIVE FACTORS

7–19. Assume that you are deciding what to do next summer. You are considering two alternatives: Go to summer school, or tour Europe.

Required:

a. List all the costs that come to mind for each alternative as you think about this decision.
b. Review your list and indicate which costs are relevant and which are irrelevant to your decision.
c. What are some qualitative factors that you should consider when making this decision?

LO 1, 2, 3, & 5: LIST COSTS, INDICATE RELEVANT COSTS, INDICATE QUALITATIVE FACTORS

7–20. George Binkley's car is seven years old. The car is no longer under warranty and requires frequent repairs. George is trying to decide whether to buy a new car. He has asked you what you think about his idea.

Required:

a. List all the costs that come to mind for each alternative as you think about his decision.
b. Review your list and indicate which costs are relevant and which are irrelevant to the decision.
c. What are some qualitative factors that he should consider when making this decision?

LO 4: DETERMINE RELEVANT COST FOR EQUIPMENT REPLACEMENT

7–21. The managers at Miami Manufacturing Company are considering replacing the industrial mixer used in the company's factory.

Information about the old mixer:

Cost	$28,000
Estimated useful life	10 years
Estimated residual value	$0
Current age	5 years
Estimated current fair value	$8,000
Annual operating cost	$15,000

Information about the new mixer:

Cost	$34,000
Estimated useful life	5 years
Estimated residual value	$0
Annual operating cost	$12,000

Required: Prepare a relevant cost schedule showing the benefit of keeping the old mixer or buying the new one.

LO 4: DETERMINE RELEVANT COST FOR EQUIPMENT REPLACEMENT

7–22. The managers at General Manufacturing Company are considering replacing the industrial lathe used in the company's factory.

Information about the old lathe:

Cost	$57,000
Estimated useful life	8 years
Estimated residual value	$0
Current age	2 years
Estimated current fair value	$32,000
Annual operating cost	$32,000

Information about the new lathe:

Cost	$61,000
Estimated useful life	6 years
Estimated residual value	$0
Annual operating cost	$24,000

Required: Prepare a relevant cost schedule showing the benefit of keeping the old lathe or buying the new one.

LO 4: DETERMINE RELEVANT COST FOR EQUIPMENT REPLACEMENT

7–23. John Paul Hudik, president of J. P. Hudik Boat Hauling, is considering replacing the company's industrial lift used to haul boats. The new lift would allow the company to lift larger boats out of the water.

Information about the old lift:

Cost	$94,000
Estimated useful life	12 years
Estimated residual value	$10,000
Current age	4 years
Estimated current fair value	$48,000
Annual contribution margin	$50,000

Information about the new lift:

Cost	$128,000
Estimated useful life	8 years
Estimated residual value	$25,000
Annual contribution margin	$65,000

Required: Prepare a relevant cost schedule showing the benefit of keeping the old lift or buying the new one.

LO 4: DETERMINE RELEVANT COST FOR EQUIPMENT REPLACEMENT

7–24. The managers at Wilma Manufacturing are considering replacing a printing press with a new, high-speed model.

Information about the old printing press:

Cost	$255,000
Estimated useful life	10 years
Estimated residual value	$25,000
Annual depreciation	$23,000
Current age	3 years
Accumulated depreciation to date	$69,000
Estimated current fair value	$150,000
Annual contribution margin	$110,000

Information about the new printing press:

Cost	$535,000
Estimated useful life	7 years
Estimated residual value	$45,000
Annual depreciation	$70,000
Annual contribution margin	$150,000

Required: Prepare a relevant cost schedule showing the benefit of keeping the old printing press or buying the new one.

LO 4: DETERMINE RELEVANT COST FOR NEW BUSINESS SEGMENT

7-25. Photo Express operates a small camera store in Ft. Lauderdale, Florida. The store has two departments, camera sales and photo finishing. Rent, utilities, and other operating expenses are allocated to the departments based on the square footage occupied by the department. Currently, the camera sales department occupies 3,000 square feet and the photo finishing department occupies 2,000 square feet.

Photo Express president, Billy Clifford, is thinking about buying a computer system to produce poster prints. The poster printing system would occupy 200 square feet of the store's floor space.

Budgeted monthly information for the store:

Store rent	$5,000
Salaries and wages	10,500
Utilities	750
Other operating expenses	3,000
Sales	125,000
Cost of goods sold	95,000

Information about the poster printing system:

Cost of the poster system	$25,700
Estimated useful life	5 years
Estimated residual value	$500
Floor space required	200 square feet
Monthly cost of electricity used by poster system	$50

Budgeted monthly amounts:

Poster sales revenue	$1,200
Poster supplies	200
Wages for poster operation	250
Store rent	200
Utilities	32
Other operating expenses	120

Clifford believes the company should not buy the poster system because it will show a loss every month. Because he is not sure, he has contacted a small consulting group to seek advice. Assume you are part of the consulting group.

Required:

a. Would the poster system show a loss every month as Clifford suggests? Prepare a schedule to substantiate your answer.

b. Would the company's overall monthly profits increase or decrease as a result of buying the poster system? Prepare a schedule to substantiate your answer.

c. Prepare a relevant cost schedule showing the advantage or disadvantage of buying the poster system.

LO 4: DETERMINE RELEVANT COST FOR NEW BUSINESS SEGMENT

7-26. The Largo Gift Hut operates a small souvenir shop in Key Largo, Florida. The shop has two departments, retail sales and mail order. Rent, utilities, and other operating expenses are allocated to the departments based on the square footage occupied by the department. Currently, the retail sales department occupies 5,000 square feet and the mail order department occupies 1,000 square feet.

Largo's president, Bobbye Kenyon, is thinking about buying a silkscreen machine to make souvenir T-shirts. The silkscreen machine would occupy 500 square feet of the souvenir shop's floor space.

Budgeted monthly information for the store:

Store rent	$5,100
Salaries and wages	8,500
Utilities	1,000
Other operating expenses	3,000
Sales	80,000
Cost of goods sold	57,000

Information about the silkscreen machine:

Cost of the silkscreen machine	$9,640
Estimated useful life	5 years
Estimated residual value	$400
Floor space required	500 square feet
Monthly cost of electricity used by silkscreen machine	$20

Budgeted monthly amounts:

T-shirt sales revenue	$1,700
Cost of T-shirts	450
Cost of T-shirt supplies	100
Wages for the T-shirt operation	250
Store rent	425
Utilities	85
Other operating expenses	250

Kenyon believes she should not buy the silkscreen machine because it will show a loss every month. Because she is not sure, she has contacted a small consulting group to seek advice. Assume you are part of the consulting group.

Required:

  a. Would the silkscreen machine show a loss every month as Kenyon suggests? Prepare a schedule to substantiate your answer.
  b. Would the company's overall monthly profits increase or decrease as a result of buying the silkscreen machine? Prepare a schedule to substantiate your answer.
  c. Prepare a relevant cost schedule showing the advantage or disadvantage of buying the silkscreen machine.

LO 4: DETERMINE RELEVANT COST FOR EQUIPMENT REPLACEMENT

7–27. Frank's Marine Service purchased a forklift five years ago for $16,000. When it was purchased the forklift had an estimated useful life of 10 years and a residual value of $4,000. The forklift can be sold now for $6,000. The operating cost for the forklift is $4,500 per year.

   Frank is thinking about buying a newer forklift for $17,000. The newer model would have an estimated useful life of five years and a residual value of $7,000. The operating cost for the newer forklift would be $3,000 per year.

Required:

  a. What are the relevant costs associated with the decision to replace the forklift?
  b. Prepare a relevant cost schedule showing the advantage or disadvantage of buying the forklift.

LO 4: DETERMINE RELEVANT COST FOR EQUIPMENT REPLACEMENT

7–28. Al Hart of Hart Engineering is considering whether to purchase a new copy machine. He purchased the old machine two years ago for $8,500. When purchased, the old machine had an estimated useful life of eight years and a residual value of $500. The operating cost of the old machine is $3,000 per year. The old machine can be sold today for $2,000. A new machine can be bought today for $10,000 and would have an estimated useful life of six years with a residual value of $1,000. The operating cost of the new copy machine is expected to be $1,500 per year.

Required:

  a. Prepare a schedule showing all the costs associated with the current copy machine.
  b. Prepare a schedule showing all the costs associated with the new copy machine.

    c. Prepare a schedule showing the relevant cost of the copy machine replacement decision and the favored alternative.

    d. Discuss the qualitative factors that Hart should consider.

    e. Would you buy the newer copy machine?

LO 4: DETERMINE RELEVANT COST FOR EQUIPMENT REPLACEMENT

7–29. Mike Thomlinson is considering whether to replace one of his delivery trucks. He purchased the current delivery truck four years ago for $24,000, and it came with a three-year, 75,000-mile warranty. When purchased, the current truck had an estimated useful life of five years and a residual value of $2,000. Thomlinson uses the straight-line method for depreciation. The new truck would be identical to the current truck, except it would be new and would have the new truck warranty. The operating cost for the current truck is $4,000 for fuel, $23,200 for the driver's salary, and maintenance cost is about $5,000 per year. If Thomlinson keeps the old truck, it will last another five years, but would require the $5,000 in maintenance each year. The current truck can be sold now for $4,000, or it can be sold in five years for $1,000. The new truck would cost $25,500, has an estimated useful life of five years, and can be sold at the end of the five years for $4,000. At the end of the warranty period, the new truck will require maintenance of $5,000 per year.

Required:

    a. Prepare a schedule showing all the costs associated with the current truck.

    b. Prepare a schedule showing all the costs associated with the new truck.

    c. Prepare a schedule showing the relevant cost of the truck replacement decision and the favored alternative.

    d. Discuss the qualitative factors that Thomlinson should consider.

    e. If the old truck had an estimated useful life of five years when it was purchased, and it has already been used for four years, discuss the ramifications of using the truck for another five years.

    f. Would you buy the new truck? Why or why not?

LO 4: DETERMINE RELEVANT COST FOR EQUIPMENT REPLACEMENT

7–30. Jack Owens is considering whether to replace a piece of production equipment with a new model. The new machine would cost $170,000, have an eight-year life, and have no residual value. The variable cost of operating the machine would be $180,000 per year. The present machine was purchased one year ago, and could be used for the next eight years. When it was purchased, the present machine had an estimated useful life of nine years and a residual value of zero. The present machine can be sold now for $28,000, but will have no residual value in eight years. The variable cost of operating the present machine is $200,000 per year.

Required:

    a. Prepare a schedule showing the costs associated with the present machine.

    b. Prepare a schedule showing the costs associated with the new machine.

    c. Prepare a schedule showing the relevant cost of the equipment replacement decision and the favored alternative.

    d. Discuss the qualitative factors that Owens should consider.

LO 3 & 4: DETERMINE THE RELEVANT COST OF BUYING A HOUSE AND LIST QUALITATIVE FACTORS

7–31. Lowell Elsea is in the process of buying a house. He is interested in two houses. One house is two miles from his work; the other is on the outskirts of town, 34 miles from work. Surprisingly, the two houses are nearly identical, except the closer house is much more expensive. The house that is two miles from Lowell's work is $127,000, whereas the other house is only $109,000. Maintenance, taxes, insurance, and other costs would be the same for both houses.

    Lowell goes to work about 250 days each year. Lowell has just traded his old car for a new one. Each time his car reaches 80,000 miles, Lowell trades it for a new model. Generally, he expects to pay about $20,000 when he trades for a new car. His cars usually get about 20 miles per gallon of regular, $1.25-per-gallon gasoline. Maintenance on his car runs about 5 cents per mile on average. Other than driving to and from work, Lowell drives about 15,000 miles each year.

Regardless of which house Lowell buys, he expects to be transferred to another area of the country in five years.

Lowell is about to buy the less expensive house when he asks your advice.

Required:

a. Which house should Lowell buy?

b. How much will Lowell save if he follows your advice? (Disregard the time value of money.)

c. What qualitative factors should Lowell consider?

LO 4: RELEVANT COST OF AN OUTSOURCING DECISION

7–32. Microline is considering buying computer cabinets from an outside vendor. Currently, Microline makes the cabinets in its own manufacturing facility. Microline can buy the cabinets for $15 each. The company uses 15,000 cabinets each year. Information about Microline's cost to manufacture the 15,000 cabinets follows:

	Per Unit	Total
Direct material	$ 4	$ 60,000
Direct labor	6	90,000
Variable overhead	7	105,000
Fixed overhead	5	75,000
Total	$22	$330,000

Fixed cost for Microline would not change if the company stopped making the cabinets.

Required: Prepare a relevant cost schedule that indicates whether Microline should buy the cabinets or continue to make them.

LO 4: RELEVANT COST OF AN OUTSOURCING DECISION

7–33. Gem Products is considering buying the casters it uses in the manufacture of office chairs from an outside vendor. Currently, Gem Products makes the casters in its own manufacturing facility. Gem Products can buy the casters for $1.15 each. The company uses 450,000 casters each year. Information about Gem Products' cost to manufacture the 450,000 casters follows:

	Per Unit	Total
Direct material	$ .50	$225,000
Direct labor	.10	45,000
Variable overhead	.40	180,000
Fixed overhead	.25	112,500
Total	$1.25	$562,500

Fixed cost for Gem Products would not change if the company stopped making the casters.

Required: Prepare a relevant cost schedule that indicates whether Gem Products should buy the casters or continue to make them.

LO 4: RELEVANT COST OF AN OUTSOURCING DECISION

7–34. RJ Manufacturing is considering buying the mounting brackets it uses to make its fire extinguishers from an outside supplier. Currently, RJ Manufacturing makes the brackets in its own manufacturing facility. RJ Manufacturing can buy the brackets for $0.75 each. The company uses 700,000 brackets each year. Information about RJ Manufacturing's cost to manufacture the 700,000 brackets follows:

	Per Unit	Total
Direct material	$.30	$210,000
Direct labor	.10	70,000
Variable overhead	.40	280,000
Fixed overhead	.15	98,000
Total	$.94	$658,000

Fixed cost for RJ Manufacturing would not change if the company stopped making the brackets.

Required: Prepare a relevant cost schedule that indicates whether RJ Manufacturing should buy the brackets or continue to make them.

LO 4: RELEVANT COST OF AN OUTSOURCING DECISION

7–35. Jumbo Chinese Restaurant operates a small laundry facility to launder the uniforms, tablecloths, and other linens used by its restaurant chain. Jumbo's laundry operation occupies space in an industrial area close to the company's home office and its largest restaurant. Jumbo is considering using a laundry service to perform the laundering needed by the company.

Jumbo's $180,000 administrative expense is allocated based on the number of employees. Jumbo employs 90 people. Information about the laundry facilities follows:

Direct cost information:	
Wages for two employees	$38,000
Cost of equipment	$7,500
Original estimated useful life of equipment	5 years
Estimated remaining useful life of equipment	1 year
Building rent per year	$3,000
Utilities	$2,000
Miscellaneous cost	$1,500
Indirect cost information:	
Administrative expense	$4,000

An outside laundry service has offered to provide Jumbo's laundering services for $50,000 per year. The fee is guaranteed for one year. If the offer is accepted, Jumbo will scrap the laundry equipment and close down its laundry operation completely.

Required: The president of Jumbo has asked you to prepare a report that details the qualitative and quantitative factors that should be considered in making the decision about whether to close the laundry operation. Your report should discuss the relevant qualitative and quantitative factors for each alternative and include a relevant cost schedule. Your report should conclude with a well-supported recommended course of action.

LO 4: RELEVANT COST OF AN OUTSOURCING DECISION

7–36. Fast Track Delivery Service operates a small auto repair facility to service its fleet of 35 delivery vehicles. Fast Track's repair facility occupies space in an industrial area close to the company's home office. Fast Track is considering using a local repair shop to service its vehicles. Fast Track's $120,000 administrative expense is allocated based on the number of employees. Fast Track employs 50 people. Information about the repair facility follows:

Direct cost information:	
Wages for three employees	$64,000
Cost of equipment used	$33,500
Original estimated useful life of equipment	12 years
Estimated remaining useful life of equipment	9 years
Building rent per year	$6,000
Utilities	$2,000
Cost of automobile parts	$30,000
Miscellaneous cost	$1,500
Indirect cost information:	
Administrative expense	$7,200

A dependable automotive service center has offered to provide maintenance contracts for each vehicle for $3,000 per vehicle. If Fast Track accepts the offer it would close the maintenance facility. The company estimates that it can sell the maintenance equipment for $10,000.

Required: The president of Fast Track has asked you to prepare a report that details the qualitative and quantitative factors that should be considered in making the decision about whether to close the maintenance facility. Your report should discuss the relevant qualitative and quantitative factors for each alternative and include a relevant cost schedule. Your report should conclude with a well-supported recommendation.

LO 3 & 4: RELEVANT BENEFIT AND COST AND QUALITATIVE FACTORS OF A SPECIAL ORDER DECISION

7–37. Abraham Manufacturing produces 22,000 rubber engine mounts each year for use in its electric cart manufacturing plant. Abraham's engine mounts have an excellent reputation for strength and durability. At a production level of 22,000, the cost per unit is as follows:

Direct material	$ .53
Direct labor	1.45
Variable overhead	.92
Fixed overhead	1.27
Total	$4.17

A competitor, Jenkins Cart Company, is interested in purchasing 14,000 rubber engine mounts from Abraham. Jenkins has offered to pay $4.17 each for the engine mounts. Abraham Manufacturing has the capacity and can easily manufacture the engine mounts for Jenkins.

Several managers at Abraham are concerned that there would be no financial benefit whatsoever for Abraham if the engine mounts are sold at cost.

Required:

a. Prepare a schedule that details the advantage or disadvantage of selling the 14,000 engine mounts to Jenkins.
b. Discuss the qualitative aspects of selling the parts to Jenkins.

LO 3 & 4: RELEVANT BENEFIT AND COST AND QUALITATIVE FACTORS OF A SPECIAL ORDER DECISION

7–38. Kelly Gas Grill Company produces 200,000 RV22 propane gas regulator and valve assemblies each year for use in its gas grill factory. Kelly's gas grills are known for quality and have a reputation of lasting a lifetime. At 200,000 units per year, the cost per unit is as follows:

Direct material	$ 3.02
Direct labor	2.44
Variable overhead	1.20
Fixed overhead	5.60
Total	$12.26

A competitor, Econo Grill, is interested in purchasing 80,000 RV22 assemblies from Kelly. Econo Grill has offered to pay $12.30 per unit. Kelly has the capacity and can easily manufacture the parts for Econo Grill.

Several managers at Kelly are concerned that there would be almost no financial benefit if the RV22 assemblies are sold for $12.30 each.

Required:

a. Prepare a schedule that details the advantage or disadvantage of selling the 80,000 RV22 assemblies to Econo Grill.
b. Discuss the qualitative aspects of selling the parts to Econo Grill.

LO 3 & 4: RELEVANT BENEFIT AND COST AND QUALITATIVE FACTORS OF A SPECIAL ORDER DECISION

7–39. Eiroa Marine Cable Company produces 400,000 feet of SS316 cable each year. At 400,000 feet per year, the cost per foot is as follows:

Direct material	$ .32
Direct labor	.14
Variable overhead	.08
Fixed overhead	.73
Total	$1.27

A competitor, Garcia Marine, is interested in purchasing 175,000 feet of SS316 cable from Eiroa. Garcia has offered to pay $0.92 per foot for the cable. Eiroa has the capacity and can easily manufacture the cable for Garcia Marine.

Frank Eiroa, president of Eiroa Marine Cable, thinks it would be detrimental for the company to sell the cable for only $0.92 per foot.

Required:

    a. Prepare a schedule that details the advantage or disadvantage of selling the 175,000 feet of cable to Garcia Marine.

    b. Discuss the qualitative aspects of selling the cable to Garcia.

LO 3 & 4: RELEVANT BENEFIT AND COST AND QUALITATIVE FACTORS OF A SPECIAL ORDER DECISION

7–40. Gator Corporation manufactures camping equipment. One of the Gator's most popular products is its T1012 tent which the company sells for $28 each. Gator sells about 9,000 T1012 tents each year through its mail-order business. Another camping equipment company, TreeClimb Corporation has approached Gator about purchasing 2,000 T1012 tents. The tents would be the same as the T1012 except they would bear the TreeClimb brand. TreeClimb is willing to pay $20 per tent. Although Gator has plenty of plant capacity to produce the additional 2,000 tents, the company's manufacturing cost is $23 per unit, or $3 more per tent than TreeClimb is willing to pay. The following per unit information pertains to Gator's cost to produce 9,000 T1012 tents:

Direct material	$ 9
Direct labor	4
Variable manufacturing overhead	2
Fixed manufacturing overhead	8
Total	$23

Required:

    a. By what amount would Gator's operating income increase or decrease if the company accepts the special order?

    b. Discuss the qualitative aspects of this special order decision.

LO 3 & 4: RELEVANT BENEFIT AND COST AND QUALITATIVE FACTORS OF A SPECIAL ORDER DECISION

7–41. Refer to problem 7–40. Assume that Gator Corporation would have to purchase an additional sewing machine to accept the special order from TreeClimb. The cost of the new sewing machine is $2,500.

Required:

    a. By what amount would Gator's operating income increase or decrease if the company accepts the special order under these circumstances?

    b. Discuss the qualitative aspects of this special order decision.

LO 4: RELEVANT BENEFIT AND COST OF A SPECIAL ORDER DECISION

7–42. Hi-Cast Corporation manufactures fishing rods. Part of Hi-Cast's sales success comes from a patented material, tuflex, used to make the fishing rods. Tuflex allows the fishing rods to be very flexible, yet nearly unbreakable. Hi-Cast sells about 150,000 fishing rods annually to wholesalers for $18 each. A major department store chain, Sale-Mart, is interested in purchasing 30,000 fishing rods that would bear the Sale-Mart's brand name. Sale-Mart is willing to pay only $9 per fishing rod, considerably less than Hi-Cast's normal selling price. Although Hi-Cast has plenty of plant capacity available to make the additional 30,000 fishing rods, the company's manufacturing cost is $11 per fishing rod, or $2 more per rod than Sale-Mart is willing to pay. Sale-Mart has indicated that the 30,000 fishing rods do not have to be as flexible and tough as the regular Hi-Cast rods. The following per unit information pertains to Hi-Cast's cost to produce 150,000 fishing rods:

Direct material:	
Tuflex	$ 4
Other material	1
Direct labor	3
Variable manufacturing overhead	1
Fixed manufacturing overhead	2
Total	$11

If fiberglass is used in place of tuflex, the direct material cost can be reduced by $2 per rod.

Required: By what amount would Hi-Cast's operating income increase or decrease if the company accepts the special order?

LO 3 & 4: RELEVANT COST AND QUALITATIVE FACTORS OF AN OUTSOURCING DECISION

7–43. John Tullis Equipment Company makes high-pressure pumps. Tullis makes 10,000 VI valve assembles per year for use in production. The manufacturing facilities used to make the VI valves are also used to produce a variety of other subassemblies and products. Accordingly, no special production equipment is needed to make the VI valves. The production cost for VI valve assembles is as follows:

Direct material	$ 55,000
Direct labor	140,000
Variable manufacturing overhead	70,000
Fixed manufacturing overhead	210,000
Total	$475,000

Sure Flow Valve Company has offered to supply the VI valve assemblies to Tullis for $32 each.

Required:
  a. Prepare a schedule that shows whether Tullis should buy the valves from Sure Flow or continue to make them.
  b. Discuss the qualitative factors that Tullis should consider in this make or buy decision.

LO 3 & 4: RELEVANT COST AND QUALITATIVE FACTORS OF AN OUTSOURCING DECISION

7–44. Refer to problem 7–43. Assume Tullis could use the manufacturing facilities which are no longer needed to make the VI valves to produce a new line of small pumps. The small pumps would provide a contribution margin of $60,000.

Required:
  a. Prepare a schedule that shows whether Tullis should buy the valves from Sure Flow or continue to make them.
  b. Discuss the qualitative factors that Tullis should consider in this make or buy decision.

LO 3 & 4: RELEVANT COST AND QUALITATIVE FACTORS OF AN OUTSOURCING DECISION

7–45. General Manufacturing Company makes residential aluminum windows. A company has offered to supply General with the window crank assembly it needs for $3.50 each. General uses 50,000 crank assemblies each year. The machinery used to make the window cranks is used to produce a variety of other subassemblies and products. The production cost for the window crank assemblies is as follows:

Direct material	$ 70,000
Direct labor	40,000
Variable manufacturing overhead	55,000
Fixed manufacturing overhead	35,000
Total	$200,000

Required:
  a. Prepare a schedule that shows the relevant cost and the preferred alternative of this make or buy decision.
  b. Discuss the qualitative factors that General should consider when deciding whether to buy the window cranks from the outside supplier.

LO 3 & 4: RELEVANT COST AND QUALITATIVE FACTORS OF AN OUTSOURCING DECISION

7–46. Hutchens Electric produces electric fans. Hutchens manufactures 19,000 small electric fan motors each year. Dalta Motor Company has offered to supply Hutchens with the small electric motors for $12.50 each. The facilities that Hutchens uses to make the small motors are used to make larger motors and other components. Hutchens's production cost for the small electric fan motors is as follows:

Direct material	$132,000
Direct labor	26,500
Variable manufacturing overhead	43,500
Fixed manufacturing overhead	77,500
Total	$279,500

Required:

a. Prepare a schedule that shows whether Hutchens Electric should buy the electric fan motors or continue to make them.
b. Discuss the qualitative factors that Hutchens should consider when making this make or buy decision.

LO 3 & 4: RELEVANT COST AND QUALITATIVE FACTORS OF AN OUTSOURCING DECISION

7–47. Refer to problem 7–46. Assume that Hutchens Electric can use the facilities freed up by purchasing the electric motors from Dalta Motor Company to produce a new model fan that would have a contribution margin of $95,000.

Required:

a. Prepare a relevant cost schedule that shows whether Hutchens Electric should buy the electric fan motors or continue to make them.
b. Discuss the qualitative factors that Hutchens should consider when making this make or buy decision.

LO 3 & 4: RELEVANT COST AND QUALITATIVE FACTORS OF AN OUTSOURCING DECISION

7–48. Nunez, Inc. requires 12,000 units of part X45 per year. At the current level of production, the cost per unit is as follows:

Direct material	$ 3
Direct labor	1
Variable overhead	2
Fixed overhead	4
Total	$10

JLW, Inc. has offered to sell Nunez 12,000 units of X45 for $8 each. If Nunez is no longer required to produce the X45s, a supervisor can be eliminated. The supervisor's salary of $24,000 is part of fixed overhead cost. Other fixed overhead costs would remain the same.

Required:

a. Prepare a schedule that details the advantage or disadvantage of buying the 12,000 units of X45 from JLW, Inc.
b. Discuss the qualitative aspects of purchasing the parts from JLW, Inc.

LO 3 & 4: RELEVANT COST AND QUALITATIVE FACTORS OF AN OUTSOURCING DECISION

7–49. Cox, Inc. requires 3,000 spindles per year. At the current level of production, the cost per unit is as follows:

Direct material	$ 38
Direct labor	12
Variable overhead	14
Fixed overhead	44
Total	$108

AMW, Inc. has offered to sell Cox the 3,000 spindles for $100 each. If Cox is no longer required to produce the spindles, a supervisor can be eliminated. The supervisor's salary of $36,000 is part of fixed overhead cost. Other fixed overhead costs would remain the same.

Required:

    a. Prepare a schedule that details the advantage or disadvantage of buying the 3,000 spindles from AMW, Inc.

    b. Discuss the qualitative aspects of purchasing the parts from AMW, Inc.

LO 3 & 4: RELEVANT COST AND QUALITATIVE FACTORS OF AN OUTSOURCING DECISION

7–50. Adcox, Inc. requires 4,000 switch assemblies per year. At the current level of production, the cost per unit is as follows:

Direct material	$ 3
Direct labor	3
Variable overhead	2
Fixed overhead	2
Total	$10

Camron, Inc. has offered to sell Adcox, Inc. the 4,000 switch assemblies for $9 each. If Adcox is no longer required to produce the switch assemblies, part of the building can be leased to another company for $10,000 per year. Other fixed overhead costs would remain the same.

Required:

    a. Prepare a schedule that details the advantage or disadvantage of buying the 4,000 switch assemblies from Camron, Inc.

    b. Discuss the qualitative aspects of purchasing the parts from Camron, Inc.

LO 1, 2, & 4: PREPARE A REPORT FOR EQUIPMENT REPLACEMENT DECISION

7–51. The Sakura Company operates a chain of Japanese restaurants. Restaurant managers are paid bonuses based on the financial profits of their restaurants.

    Last year, the manager of the South Miami Sakura Restaurant installed a new oven that cost $5,000. At the time, the oven had an estimated useful life of five years with no residual value. Annual repair and maintenance on the oven is $900, and the cost of electricity used by the oven is $3,400 per year. The old oven can be sold now for $1,500.

    A salesperson is trying to convince the store manager to replace the oven purchased last year with a new, energy-efficient model. The salesperson says the new oven will increase company profits. The new oven can be purchased for $6,000, and has an estimated useful life of four years with a residual value of $1,000. The annual repair and maintenance would be the same as the old oven, or $900 per year, but the annual cost of electricity used by the oven would drop to $1,800.

    The manager is not convinced by the salesperson. "If I buy this new oven, my financial income will drop and I'll never get my bonus. The loss in the first year will make me look like a fool!"

Required:

    a. Prepare a report showing the relevant cost of keeping the old oven versus buying the new one.

    b. Based on your report, what do you think of the restaurant manager's comments?

CHAPTER 8

The Capital Budget: Evaluating Capital Expenditures

Let's say you're considering two very different purchases: a compact disc and a new car. Certainly, each of these purchases will require different amounts of time and effort. For instance, you probably won't review your long-term goals and annual budget before you buy the CD, nor will you likely create a list of costs and benefits to determine which CD to buy. However, when thinking about buying a new car, you'll probably first spend considerable time deciding whether you really need one and whether you can afford one. Then, if you decide to go forward, you'll likely spend a significant amount of time determining what kind of car to buy.

The purchase of an expensive item such as a car warrants careful planning. For one thing, once you have bought something expensive it's usually costly to change your mind. In our example, you would have to sell or trade the new car, probably at a substantial loss. What is true in your personal financial decisions is also true in business. Unlike personal expenditures made for comfort or convenience, companies make business expenditures (large and small) to further the goals of the business. In fact, companies make most business expenditures to increase profits. For this reason, business expenditures are really investments, from which the company hopes to earn both a return *of* the investment and a return *on* the investment.

capital investments
Business expenditures to acquire expensive assets that will be used for more than one year.

Business expenditures for acquiring expensive assets that will be used for more than one year are called **capital investments.** Because of the cost and extended useful life of these assets, companies devote tremendous time and energy to evaluating potential capital investments. For example, according to information in its annual reports, **Motorola, Inc.**, invested approximately $11.5 billion in capital expenditures from 1992 to 1995. Even for a company as large as **Motorola**, $11.5 billion is an enormous amount of money. If **Motorola** made these investments in projects that did not perform as the company hoped they would, it could lead to disaster. Certainly, this magnitude of investment required serious analysis on the part of this company before it committed to the various projects those dollars represent.

capital projects Another name for capital investments.

capital budgeting The planning and decision process for making investments in capital projects.

Generally, capital investments—also known as **capital projects**—are investments in property, plant, and equipment. Examples include investments in computer equipment, production equipment, another factory, a new wing of a hospital, or a new campus dormitory. **Capital budgeting** is the planning and decision process for making investments in capital projects. Although we focus on business firms in our discussion, all types of organizations can use capital budgeting techniques—not-for-profit, for profit, and social organizations.

In this chapter, we explain how firms make capital budgeting decisions. Capital budgeting, however, is only part of a much more involved planning process, which we also discuss in this chapter.

Two of the evaluation techniques used to assess potential capital projects rely heavily on a knowledge of the time value of money. For this reason, we have included two appendices to the chapter that detail the time value of money. The first details calculation for the time value of money using financial tables and the second details similar calculations using a financial calculator.

Learning Objectives

After completing your work on this chapter, you should be able to do the following:

1. Describe the overall business planning process and where the capital budget fits in that process.
2. Explain in your own words the process of capital budgeting.
3. Discuss the four shared characteristics of all capital projects.
4. Describe the cost of capital and the concept of scarce resources.
5. Determine the information relevant to the capital budgeting decision.
6. Evaluate potential capital investments using four capital budgeting decision methods: net present value, internal rate of return, payback period, and accounting rate of return.
7. Determine present and future values using present value tables and future value tables. (Appendix A)
8. Determine present and future values using a financial calculator. (Appendix B)

◆ THE BUSINESS PLANNING PROCESS

Managers use accounting information for two main types of business decisions—planning and control. In this section, we give an overview of how organizations plan for the future. We discuss the why, the what, the how, and the who of business planning. Though management accounting information is used in all steps in the planning process, it is especially important to the what, the how, and the who decisions.

COMPANY GOALS: THE WHY

People form an organization to accomplish a purpose or several purposes—the organization's goals. These goals define *why* the organization exists; goals are the why of the business.

organizational goals
The core beliefs and values of the company. They outline why the organization exists and are a combination of financial and nonfinancial goals.

Organizational goals constitute the core beliefs and values of the company, so those goals should not be subject to short-term economic pressures. Examples of some organizational goals might be to earn money, to save lives, or to improve communication among employees. Most companies' goals are stated in general terms that are not easily quantified, which means that although progress toward fulfillment can be measured, it is not really possible to determine when the goals have been attained. For instance, a firm with the goal of earning money usually does not specify exactly how much money it must earn to meet its goal.

The goals of a business organization are usually a combination of nonfinancial and financial aspirations. Whether nonfinancial or financial, however, almost all goals have either a direct or indirect effect on the company's financial well-being. Does this sound strange? The next section explains why almost all goals can affect the financial health of a business.

NONFINANCIAL GOALS

Typically, nonfinancial goals do not mention money. Rather, they refer to activities that may or may not result in profits. A hospital's nonfinancial goals, for instance, might be to provide the best health care possible to its patients; to recruit and employ highly qualified workers; to provide a safe, pleasant environment for its employees and patients; and to create an atmosphere of caring for both the physical and the emotional concerns of its patients.

Discussion Questions

8–1. Consider the hospital's nonfinancial goals. What financial effect will occur if the hospital *does* work toward those goals?

8–2. What financial effect will result if the hospital *does not* work toward those goals?

8–3. Review the hospital's nonfinancial goals. How would you determine when those goals have been reached?

Note that the nonfinancial goals for the hospital are stated in very general language. More than specific results, these goals represent standards of conduct and performance toward which the hospital should always be striving. They are stated in such a way that it is very difficult, if not impossible, to determine when the goals have been attained.

FINANCIAL GOALS

For most business organizations, the primary financial goal is to earn a profit. What this really means, of course, is that the goal is to earn a return on investment for the business owner or owners. This goal may be worded as "achieving superior financial performance," "earning a reasonable return for the stockholders," "maximizing shareholder value," or similar language. As was the case with the nonfinancial goals, it is difficult to determine when these financial goals have been attained.

GOAL AWARENESS

mission statement A summary of the main goals of the organization.

Once goals have been set, the company should communicate them to every person in the organization. This communication maximizes the likelihood that a business will achieve its goals. Many companies use a **mission statement**—a summary of the main goals of the organization—to communicate the firm's goals to all employees. Exhibit 8–1 is a sample mission statement—from ***Johnson & Johnson.*** This mission statement is representative of those of many large companies.

The goals in the ***Johnson & Johnson*** mission statement address the concerns of all parties who have a stake in how the company conducts its business. For instance, ***Johnson & Johnson***'s stakeholders include health care providers, consumers, suppliers, employees, the community, and stockholders. ***Johnson & Johnson***'s mission statement communicates the firm's goals and presents the image of a responsible, ethical business.

Stating lofty goals in a mission statement is not a guarantee of reaching those goals. Businesses must act in a manner consistent with their goals to ensure progress. Consider the following two examples. In 1982, ***Johnson & Johnson*** demonstrated the company's commitment to its goals after two fatalities occurred in the Chicago area when someone placed cyanide into six bottles of Tylenol. Once aware of these events, ***Johnson & Johnson*** immediately responded by recalling all Tylenol nationwide. The company also instituted an advertising campaign advising consumers *not* to use Tylenol and provided full disclosure about the situation. In short, the company responded in a manner consistent with its goals.

Compare ***Johnson & Johnson***'s actions to ***Ford Motor Company***'s 1996 response to faulty ignition systems in some of its cars. These faulty ignition systems caught fire without warning and created a dangerous and potentially fatal situation. ***Ford***'s response was to wait for the federal government to tell the company which cars it had to recall. Legal? Certainly. A smart way to conduct business? Well, while it cost Ford less than a total recall of the affected vehicles, the company's reputation suffered, and many people agree that ***Ford*** did not conduct its business in a way consistent with its stated goal of total quality.

strategic plan A long-range plan that sets forth the actions a company will take to attain its organizational goals.

Once a business has set its goals, the firm must then create a **strategic plan**—a long-range plan that sets forth the actions the firm will take to attain its goals. In the following section, we explore briefly how firms develop strategic plans.

Our Credo

We believe our first responsibility is to the doctors, nurses and patients, to mothers and fathers and all others who use our products and services. In meeting their needs everything we do must be of high quality. We must constantly strive to reduce our costs in order to maintain reasonable prices. Customers' orders must be serviced promptly and accurately. Our suppliers and distributors must have an opportunity to make a fair profit.

We are responsible to our employees, the men and women who work with us throughout the world. Everyone must be considered as an individual. We must respect their dignity and recognize their merit. They must have a sense of security in their jobs. Compensation must be fair and adequate, and working conditions clean, orderly and safe. We must be mindful of ways to help our employees fulfill their family responsibilities. Employees must feel free to make suggestions and complaints. There must be equal opportunity for employment, development and advancement for those qualified. We must provide competent management, and their actions must be just and ethical.

We are responsible to the communities in which we live and work and to the world community as well. We must be good citizens—support good works and charities and bear our fair share of taxes. We must encourage civic improvements and better health and education. We must maintain in good order the property we are privileged to use, protecting the environment and natural resources.

Our final responsibility is to our stockholders. Business must make a sound profit. We must experiment with new ideas. Research must be carried on, innovative programs developed and mistakes paid for. New equipment must be purchased, new facilities provided and new products launched. Reserves must be created to provide for adverse times. When we operate according to these principles, the stockholders should realize a fair return.

Johnson & Johnson

EXHIBIT 8–1 *Johnson & Johnson* Mission Statement

THE STRATEGIC PLAN: THE WHAT

The steps outlined in the strategic plan, sometimes referred to as a long-range budget, are the *what* of doing business. The actions specified in the strategic plan describe what actions a business must take to implement its goals. To be effective, then, strategic plans should support—not conflict with—the company's goals.

Companies make long-range plans so they are well positioned to reach their goals as the future unfolds. For example, it can take ***Dow Chemical Company*** five years or longer to build a production facility, so ***Dow*** managers must anticipate product demand accurately in advance, in order to build a plant of the appropriate size in time to produce enough to meet consumer demand.

A company's strategic plan tends to have objectives that are quantifiable, as well as a time frame for attainment of the objectives. A company might specify, for instance, that it plans to replace its four least efficient production facilities over the next five years, reduce customer complaints by 20 percent over the next three years, or increase market share for its newest product by 25 percent within 10 years. As you can readily see, a firm can determine exactly when it has met all these objectives.

After an organization develops a strategic plan that specifies the actions it will take to reach its goals, the company then decides how to allocate its monetary resources to implement its strategies, and who will be responsible for the day-to-day activities of the business. This step in the planning process is the preparation of budgets.

THE CAPITAL BUDGET: THE HOW

capital budget The budget that outlines how a company intends to allocate its scarce resources over a five-year, 10-year, or even longer time period.

The capital budget is the *how* of the planning process. The **capital budget** is the budget that outlines how a firm intends to allocate its scarce resources over a 5-year, 10-year, or even longer time period.

The capital budget lays out plans for acquiring and replacing long-lived expensive assets such as land, buildings, machinery, and equipment. During the capital budgeting process, companies decide whether and what items they should purchase, how much they should spend, and how much profit the items can generate. Capital budgeting decisions, then, should further the strategic plan and goals of the business.

THE OPERATING BUDGET: THE WHO

operating budget The budget that plans a company's routine day-to-day business activities for one to five years.

Companies not only must budget for long-term activities, they also must plan and budget for day-to-day business activities. The budget that pertains to routine company operations for one to five years in the future is called the **operating budget.** The operating budget establishes who is responsible for the day-to-day operation of the organization, so we refer to it as the *who* of the planning process. The operating budget will be our focus in Chapter 9.

An important thing to understand about the planning process is the interrelationship among goals, strategic plan, capital budget, and operating budget. Exhibit 8–2 demonstrates that interrelationship.

EXHIBIT 8–2 Interrelationship Among the Planning Elements

The overall function of management accounting in this process is to provide a substantial portion of the information that company management needs not only to achieve the *what*, the *how*, and the *who*, but also to ensure that these functions are achieved within the context of the *why*.

THE CAPITAL BUDGET: WHAT IS IT?

capital assets Long-lived expensive items such as land, buildings, machinery, and equipment.

The capital budget plans for the acquisition and replacement of long-lived expensive items such as land, buildings, machinery, and equipment. These long-lived items are called **capital assets.** The capital budget focuses on the long-term operations of the company to determine how an organization intends to allocate its scarce resources over the next 5, 10, or even 20 years. Thus, we refer to this part of the planning process as the *how* of being in business and doing business.

During the capital budgeting process, companies decide whether they should purchase items, how much they should spend, and how much profit the items promise to generate. No decisions made in the capital budgeting process, however, should conflict with the company's strategic plan or organizational goals.

CAPITALIZING ASSETS

Capital budgeting deals with decisions regarding investments that will benefit the company for many years, so most companies do not use capital budgeting techniques for small purchases or for those that provide benefits for only the current year.

When a company makes an expenditure, the cost of the item purchased will be reflected either as an expense on the company's income statement for the year of purchase, or as an increase in the company's assets on its balance sheet. Theoretically, the distinction lies in whether the item purchased will provide economic value to the company beyond the year of purchase. If a purchased item is expected to provide economic benefits beyond the year in which it is purchased, it should be capitalized, which means that its cost has been recorded as an increase in long-term assets and will be depreciated (converted from asset to expense) over the item's estimated useful life. Conversely, if a purchased item is not expected to provide economic benefit to the company beyond the year of purchase, its cost should be reflected as an expense on the income statement for that year.

To illustrate, the cost of a delivery truck should be reflected as an increase in assets because the truck will likely be used for several years. In contrast, the cost of last month's lawn service does not provide any future value and therefore should be reflected as an expense immediately.

Judgment plays an important role in determining whether a purchased item should be capitalized or expensed. For example, how should a company record the cost of a $3 wastebasket with an estimated useful life of three years? Because the wastebasket will be used for several years, the item should theoretically be capitalized—its cost should be added to long-term assets and depreciated over the wastebasket's estimated useful life.

From a practical standpoint, it is senseless to expend the additional accounting effort to capitalize and then depreciate the wastebasket. Why? Because, whether the wastebasket is capitalized and depreciated over its estimated useful life or expensed immediately, the effect on a company's financial statements would be so minimal that no economic decision maker will be influenced by the alternative selected. Thus, the cost of the wastebasket is immaterial, so due to the modifying convention of materiality discussed in financial accounting, the wastebasket is expensed when purchased.

CAPITALIZATION AMOUNT

Generally, companies set a cost threshold that helps determine the appropriate accounting treatment for capitalizing long-lived items. For example, a company might say that any long-lived item costing less than $3,000 will be expensed when purchased, while those costing $3,000 or more will be capitalized. There are no hard-and-fast rules for setting the capitalization threshold, but most businesses choose an amount between $500 and $5,000 as their capitalization amount.

CHARACTERISTICS OF CAPITAL PROJECTS

Capital budgeting deals with planning for purchases of items that will be capitalized, meaning they will be classified as assets when purchased and then depreciated over their estimated useful lives. While the capitalization amount and the evaluation process for capital projects vary from company to company, all capital projects share certain characteristics. The four main shared characteristics include:

1. *Long life.* Capital projects are expected to benefit the company for at least two years, which is the whole idea behind capitalizing the cost of a purchased item. As discussed in the previous section, if a purchased item will benefit the company only in the year of purchase, the cost of the item is expensed immediately. If the item purchased is likely to benefit a company in years beyond the year of purchase, the cost of that item is capitalized. Usually, the kinds of purchases we are discussing in this chapter benefit the company longer than 2 years—perhaps 5, 10, or an even greater number of years.

2. *High cost.* Technically, the purchase of any long-lived item for which the cost exceeds a company's capitalization amount is considered a capital project. As stated earlier, this may be as low as $500 for some firms. As a practical matter, however, the capital budgeting techniques we consider in this chapter are used to evaluate high-cost projects. A good example is the cost of a new factory built by **Motorola** or **Intel.** Such a factory may cost $500 million or more. Another example is the decision by **Wal-Mart** or **Kmart** to open a new store in a particular location. Many millions of dollars are involved in opening a store for these companies.

3. *Quickly sunk costs.* Costs that cannot be recovered are called sunk costs. A capital project usually requires a firm to incur substantial cost in the early stages of the project. As new information about market size, technology, and so on becomes available, the company's management may decide the project should be abandoned. Unfortunately, the company may not be able to recoup much of the cost already incurred. For example, consider the case of a manufacturer that begins construction on a new factory with an estimated cost of $500 million. After spending $200 million on construction, the company decides the new factory is not needed because the product it planned to manufacture in the facility has become obsolete. The company cannot sell the partially completed factory and has no other use for it. The $200 million is a sunk cost because it cannot be recovered.

4. *High degree of risk.* Capital projects have a high degree of business risk because they involve the future, which always entails uncertainty. Because of the long lives, high costs, and sunk costs of capital projects, companies must try to estimate the returns from those projects in future years. These characteristics increase the likelihood of erroneous estimates. The uncertainty of the future coupled with the high initial investment make capital projects quite risky.

Discussion Question ·

Consider these questions: "Will I be paid?" "How much will I be paid?" and "When will I be paid?"

8–4. Why do you think these questions were extremely difficult for **Microsoft** to answer as the company considered the development of the *Windows XP* version of **Microsoft** Windows as a potential capital project?

◆ THE COST OF CAPITAL AND THE CONCEPT OF SCARCE RESOURCES

When you put money into a savings account, you expect to earn interest. This interest is the return on your investment. Like most people, you would like the return to be as high as possible. If you were going to deposit $5,000 in a savings account, you would probably shop for a secure bank, with a return as high as or higher than that of competing banks.

Businesses shop for capital projects the same way you would shop for a bank in which to deposit your $5,000. If it appears that a capital project will be profitable, how does a company determine whether it will be profitable enough to warrant investing its money? A proposed project should promise a return that is equal to or exceeds the firm's cost of capital.

cost of capital The cost of obtaining financing from all available financing sources.

cost of capital rate Another name for cost of capital.

required rate of return Another name for cost of capital.

hurdle rate Another name for cost of capital.

In evaluating potential capital projects, a company must determine a benchmark rate of return to help select which capital project or projects it will undertake. The benchmark return rate for selecting projects is usually the company's **cost of capital,** which is the cost of obtaining financing from all available financing sources. Cost of capital is also referred to as the **cost of capital rate,** the **required rate of return,** or the **hurdle rate.** For the sake of consistency, we use cost of capital throughout all our discussions in this chapter.

As you may recall from financial accounting, companies can obtain financing from two sources: borrowing from creditors (debt financing) and investments by owners (equity financing). When a company invests in a capital project, the money must come from one or both of these sources. Both creditors and owners require a return on the funding they provide to the company, and the company must seek investments that provide a return at least equal to the cost of obtaining funding from debt and equity sources. If a company borrows funds at an interest rate of 9 percent, then the expected return on a capital project must be at least 9 percent. Similarly, if a company's owners provide the financing and expect a return of 20 percent on their investment, then the expected return from a capital project should be at least 20 percent to be acceptable.

WEIGHTED AVERAGE COST OF CAPITAL

weighted average cost of capital The combined cost of debt financing and equity financing.

blended cost of capital Another name for the weighted average cost of capital.

cost of debt capital The interest a company pays on all forms of borrowing.

cost of equity capital The percentage return required to satisfy equity investors. An important consideration is what equity investors give up when they invest in one company rather than another.

The funding for a company's capital projects usually comes from a combination of debt and equity financing. The combined cost of debt and equity financing is called the **weighted average cost of capital.** The rate for the weighted average cost of capital represents the combined rate of the cost of both debt and equity financing. The weighted average cost of capital is sometimes called the **blended cost of capital.**

The **cost of debt capital** is the interest a company pays on all forms of borrowing. The interest rate, say 8 percent, is agreed upon when a company borrows from either the bank or the bond market. The amount of interest a company pays is easy to determine because it is reported on the company's income statement as interest expense.

The cost of a company's equity financing is more challenging to determine than the cost of its debt financing, because the **cost of equity capital** is what equity investors give up when they invest in one company rather than another. To illustrate, assume Elizabeth Todd has $5,000 to invest and she is considering the purchase of either Boardman Company stock or Hoffman Company stock. What does Elizabeth give up if she invests her $5,000 in Boardman? She relinquishes what she would have earned had she invested in Hoffman. That is, she lost the opportunity to earn whatever she would have earned had she purchased Hoffman's stock rather than Boardman's.

The amount an equity investor earns is a combination of dividends received and the appreciation in the market value of the stock the investor owns. In Elizabeth's case, the amount earned if she buys the Boardman Company stock is a combination of the dividends she receives from Boardman, plus any increase in the market value of the Boardman stock she owns.

Discussion Question

Assume Elizabeth buys the Boardman stock and consistently earns an 8 percent return on her investment (dividends plus appreciation of the Boardman stock).

8–5. If Elizabeth could earn a 17 percent return on an investment in Hoffman Company stock (or some other company), what would you advise her to do? Explain your reasoning.

It's all well and good for us to discuss this topic from the investor's point of view (in this case, Elizabeth Todd), but what has this to do with the cost of equity capital for Boardman Company? Well, if Boardman wants to keep Elizabeth as a stockholder, it must return to her an amount at least as great as she could earn by investing her money somewhere else. If Elizabeth can earn 17 percent from an investment in Hoffman, Boardman must give her that kind of return or she may sell her Boardman stock and invest in Hoffman (or some other company). Boardman, then, would use 17 percent as the cost of the equity capital it received from Elizabeth, because that is what she could earn elsewhere. In other words, that is what she gave up by investing in Boardman.

In a real-world situation, Boardman Company would not know about the alternatives being considered by Elizabeth Todd and her $5,000. Therefore, the company cannot determine the specific percentage return Elizabeth must earn to keep her happy. What Boardman must do is try to determine what percentage return equity investors can generally expect on their investments and use that percentage as the cost of equity capital.

Unlike debt financing costs (interest expense), the cost of equity financing is not reported in financial statements in its entirety. Firms do report profit distributions to stockholders in the form of dividends, but the larger part of the cost of equity capital is the appreciation in the market value of stockholders' ownership interest. This market value is not reported on financial statements.

To determine the full cost of equity capital, we must examine how stocks appreciate in value. We assume first that rational investors would desire a return on an investment in an individual company at least equal to the return they could receive from investing in other, similar publicly traded companies.

If all companies whose stocks are traded on recognized stock markets (NYSE, AMEX, NASDAQ, etc.) were separated based on the return they provide their stockholders, the breakdown would appear as shown in Exhibit 8–3.

HIGH-RETURN COMPANIES 25% of Firms
MEDIUM-RETURN COMPANIES 50% of Firms
LOW-RETURN COMPANIES 25% of Firms

EXHIBIT 8–3 High-, Medium-, and Low-Return Companies in the Stock Market

The high-return companies in Exhibit 8–3 represent one fourth of all the companies whose stock is publicly traded. The medium-return companies comprise one half of the companies, and the low-return companies represent one fourth of the total.

Discussion Question

8–6. If you owned stock in a publicly traded company, in which group of companies in Exhibit 8–3 would you want your company to be?

Most equity investors want to own stock in high-return companies because they naturally want their investment to earn the highest possible return. Many high-return companies in the stock market yield as high as 17 to 20 percent annually to their stockholders in the form of dividends and appreciation in stock value.

Discussion Questions

Assume you own stock in a publicly traded company and you consistently earn an 8 percent return on your investment (dividends plus appreciation of the company's stock).

8–7. If you are certain you could earn a 20 percent return on an investment in some other company's stock, what would you do? Explain your reasoning.

8–8. Because a publicly traded company receives money only when its stock is originally issued, why do you think it would care about the stock's market value in the stock market?

It is important to note here that the issue is not whether investors can, in fact, earn a 20 percent return by selling their stock in one company and investing in another. They only need to *think* they can earn the higher return.

If enough of a company's stockholders begin selling their stock, the market price of the stock will drop—the economic law of supply and demand at work. As the stock price drops, more stockholders may decide to sell their stock before the price drops even lower. This, of course, makes the stock price drop further.

Discussion Question ○

8–9. What would you think about a company whose stock was selling for $50 a share in January and $12 a share in December?

Stock analysts, customers, suppliers, and many other parties have a tendency to gauge a company's health by the market value of its stock. For this reason, companies have a vested interest in making sure the market value of their stock does not begin a downward spiral. Because the investors in the stock market think they can earn a 17 to 20 percent return by investing in the top performing companies, a company must return 17 to 20 percent annual return to its stockholders to be considered one of the high-performing companies. Publicly traded companies usually consider their cost of equity financing to be as high as 20 percent. This percentage is commonly used to compute the company's weighted average cost of capital.

To illustrate the calculation of the weighted average cost of capital, we consider the case of Adler Enterprises, which has $2 million in assets. A total of $1,200,000 (60 percent) of these assets was obtained using debt financing with an interest rate of 7.5 percent. The remaining $800,000 (40 percent) was financed through equity capital and the company uses a 20 percent cost of equity financing. We find the weighted average cost of capital for Adler Enterprises using the following calculation.

Method of Financing	Proportion of Financing Provided		Cost of Financing		Weighted Cost of Financing
Debt	60%	×	7.5%	=	4.5%
Equity	40%	×	20.0%	=	8.0%
			Weighted Average Cost of Capital		12.5%

We see that Adler's weighted cost of debt financing is the proportion of debt financing (60 percent) multiplied by the cost of that financing (7.5 percent). The company's weighted cost of equity financing is the proportion of equity financing (40 percent) times the cost of the equity financing (20 percent). Its weighted average cost of capital is the sum of the weighted cost of each type of financing—12.5 percent.

Firms use their weighted average cost of capital as a benchmark rate of return to evaluate capital projects. For example, suppose Adler Enterprises is considering a capital project that requires an investment of $200,000. If Adler decides to undertake this project, it must obtain $200,000 to fund it. Recall that Adler's weighted average cost of capital is 12.5 percent. Unless the expected rate of return on the project is 12.5 percent or higher, Adler's management will probably reject the project. Otherwise, it would cost more to fund the project than the project could earn.

Discussion Questions ○

8–10. When you consider that companies are generally in business to earn a profit, why might it be acceptable to select a capital project that promises a return that is just equal to the weighted average cost of capital?

8–11. Under what circumstances do you think a company might accept one capital project over another even though the project selected promises a lower return?

8–12. Do you think there would ever be a situation when a company should proceed with a capital project even though the project promises a return lower than the cost of capital? Explain your reasoning.

8–13. What do you think might cause a company to reject a proposed capital project even though it promises a return significantly higher than the cost of capital?

SCARCE RESOURCES

I'm so broke that if they was selling steamboats for a dime apiece, I could run up and down the bank saying "ain't that cheap."

—ROY CLARK

In our personal lives, what we buy is usually not limited by how much we want, but rather by how much money we have available to spend. Well, what is true for individuals is also true for businesses. The number and size of capital projects a company undertakes is not limited by a lack of viable alternative projects. What limits companies is that they simply do not have access to enough money to take advantage of all the opportunities available to them. This limitation on the amount available to spend is commonly called **scarce resources.** Even huge multinational companies must select only investments they consider most favorable from a virtually unlimited pool of possible investment opportunities, because firms do not have access to enough money to invest in every good project that comes along. Managers must carefully evaluate the alternative capital projects available to their companies so they can select the projects that promise the highest return (as long as the projects are consistent with the company's goals and strategies).

scarce resources   A term describing the limited amount of money a company has to invest in capital projects.

◆ EVALUATING POTENTIAL CAPITAL PROJECTS

Because capital projects are usually long lived, costly, and high risk, managers must carefully evaluate capital expenditure decisions, especially in light of their financial limitations. The evaluation process generally includes the following four steps:

1. Identifying possible capital projects
2. Determining the relevant cash flows for alternative projects
3. Selecting a method of evaluating the alternatives
4. Evaluating the alternatives and selecting the capital project or projects to be funded

Let's investigate each of these steps from the manager's point of view.

IDENTIFYING POSSIBLE CAPITAL PROJECTS

Businesses usually make capital expenditures to maximize profits by increasing revenue, reducing costs, or a combination of the two. A project that satisfies the company's desire to maximize profits will be identified as a potential capital expenditure.

Firms often generate revenue increases by investing in projects that increase capacity or draw more customers. For a hotel chain, an increase in available rooms might increase revenue. For a restaurant, revenue might be enhanced by investing in cooking equipment that prepares food more rapidly. For a hospital, the ability to provide additional services or increasing the number of beds might be the key to added revenue.

To reduce operating costs a manufacturer might upgrade production equipment so less direct labor or less electricity is required. An airline catering company could invest in more energy-efficient ovens to reduce food preparation cost. Reducing cost has exactly the same effect as increasing revenue. As Benjamin Franklin said, "A penny saved is a penny earned." If you think about it, this really makes sense. If a company saves $1 by reducing costs by $1, the cost reduction has the same impact on profits as increasing selling price to increase revenue by $1.

Although the majority of potential capital projects are intended to either increase revenue or reduce costs, in certain instances a company must make a capital expenditure that will result in neither. These projects are usually concerned with safety or environmental issues and may come as a result of governmental regulation requirements; or a company may simply determine that such an expenditure is necessary given its goal of worker safety or good corporate citizenship.

In any event, capital projects a company deems necessary but do not promise either to increase revenue or reduce costs are usually not evaluated using the same criteria as those projects that do promise increased profits. In this chapter, we restrict ourselves to the evaluation of potential capital projects that promise to either increase revenue or reduce costs.

As the need for increasing revenue or reducing costs presents itself, a company should explore all alternative courses of action. Brainstorming sessions and input from multiple sources both within and outside a firm can help generate ideas for alternative options.

DETERMINING RELEVANT CASH FLOWS FOR ALTERNATIVE PROJECTS

Throughout our discussion of capital budgeting, we have discussed capital projects that promise to increase a company's profits by either increasing revenue or reducing costs (expenses). Recall, however, that under accrual accounting, revenue is not the same as cash inflow, and expense is not the same as cash outflow in the short run.

net cash flow Cash inflow less cash outflow.

Because capital projects usually are long lived, most business managers believe it is appropriate to analyze an alternative using cash inflow and cash outflow over the life of the project. They do this by determining the **net cash flow** of a project—the project's expected cash inflows minus its cash outflows for a specific time period. For example, if a manager estimates that investing in a new production machine will yield $40,000 in cash inflows during the useful life of the machine but will require spending $30,000 for the same period, the net cash flow would be $10,000 ($40,000 − $30,000).

relevant net cash flows Future net cash flows that differ between or among the alternatives being considered.

Only relevant net cash flows should be considered in a capital budgeting decision. **Relevant net cash flows** are future cash flows that differ between or among alternatives. Thus, a relevant cash flow must be one that will occur in the future, not one that has already occurred, and it must be affected by the investment decision. Past cash flows, or cash flows that will not change as a result of the investment decision, are irrelevant and should not be considered in the decision process. This concept should seem familiar because it follows the same reasoning as our discussion of relevant costs, the subject of Chapter 7.

Once a company obtains and assesses the relevant cash flows for each alternative project, the next step is to choose a method to measure the value of each project.

SELECTING A METHOD OF EVALUATING THE ALTERNATIVES

Over time, accountants and managers have developed many capital budgeting decision methods to evaluate potential capital projects. In this chapter, we present four methods:

1. Net present value
2. Internal rate of return
3. Payback period
4. Accounting rate of return

Each of these methods offers a different way to measure a project's value, and sometimes the different methods render conflicting rankings. In such a case, managers should be aware of the strengths and weaknesses of each capital budgeting method. In the next major section, we discuss each of the four methods and the advantages and disadvantages of each.

SELECTING CAPITAL PROJECTS

To select a capital project, firms decide first whether to accept or reject a project using one or more capital budgeting methods to measure the project's value. If the project does not generate an acceptable rate of return, it will probably be rejected. Furthermore, a company should reject any proposed capital project that is inconsistent with the company's goals and strategic plan, even if the promised return on that project is higher than some other potential project.

Once a project has been accepted as viable, the project can then be ranked with other acceptable projects based on expected performance.

◆ CAPITAL BUDGETING DECISION METHODS

In this section, we present four capital budgeting methods: net present value, internal rate of return, payback period, and accounting rate of return. The first two methods, which are discounted cash flow methods, are used more frequently in business because they include the concept of the time value of money.

A dollar received or paid at some point in the future does not have the same value as a dollar received or paid today. The reason for the difference in value is that if cash

time value of money
The increase in the value of cash over time due to investment income.

is available now, it can be invested now and earn a return as time passes. This increase in the value of cash over time due to investment income is referred to as the **time value of money.** The concept of the time value of money is used to determine either the future value of money invested today or the present value of money to be received at some point in the future.

In the following discussion of net present value and internal rate of return, we assume you have a working knowledge of the time value of money, discussed in detail in Appendix A to this chapter. Refer to it now if you need to refresh your understanding. In addition, Appendix B to this chapter demonstrates how to do present value and future value calculations using a financial calculator. Throughout the remainder of this chapter, we will demonstrate present value calculations using both present value tables and a financial calculator. The amounts will differ somewhat due to rounding. Because not all students have access to a financial calculator, we will demonstrate both, but we will use only the amounts derived from using the tables.

Capital projects deal with cash flows that begin in the present and extend into the future, sometimes for many years. Therefore, the evaluation of these kinds of projects uses the concept of present value. Determining the present value of cash to be received or paid in future periods is called **discounting cash flows.**

discounting cash flows
Determining the present value of cash to be received in the future.

DISCOUNTED CASH FLOW METHODS

Business managers use two discounted cash flow methods to evaluate potential capital projects: net present value and internal rate of return.

Net Present Value

net present value (NPV)
The present value of all cash inflows associated with a proposed capital project minus the present value of all cash outflows associated with the proposed capital project.

The **net present value (NPV)** of a proposed capital project is the present value of cash inflows minus the present value of cash outflows associated with a capital project. Note that the NPV is different from the present value. The former is the difference between the present value of a capital project's cash inflow and the present value of its cash outflow. The latter is the amount a future payment or series of payments is in today's dollars evaluated at the appropriate discount rate. The NPV method is used to determine whether a proposed capital project's anticipated return is higher or lower than the weighted average cost of capital.

A company calculates the NPV of a capital project by discounting the net cash flows for all years of the project using the company's weighted average cost of capital as the discount rate. A positive net present value indicates that the expected return on a proposed project is higher than the company's cost of capital. A negative NPV indicates that the expected return on a proposed project is lower than the company's cost of capital. An NPV of zero shows that the expected return on a project is exactly equal to the company's cost of capital.

To illustrate the NPV calculations, assume Whitewater Adventure Company is considering a computer hardware upgrade that would require an investment of $100,000. Assume further that the enhanced speed of the computer is expected to save $31,000 annually in operator salaries. Remember, this reduction of cash outflow is a cash inflow in NPV analysis. The computer has an estimated useful life of five years with no residual value. The cash flows associated with the computer upgrade are shown in Exhibit 8-4.

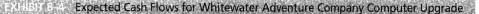
EXHIBIT 8-4 Expected Cash Flows for Whitewater Adventure Company Computer Upgrade

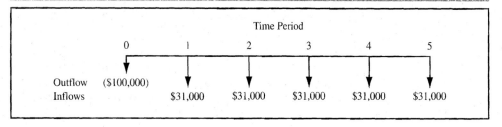

Notice in Exhibit 8–4 that the initial cash outlay of $100,000 occurs at "time 0." When working with present values, time 0 is considered today, or the present. Unless otherwise specified, we assume all other cash flows for this project will occur at the end of each period. We also ignore depreciation in our analysis because depreciation is a noncash expense under accrual accounting and the NPV method focuses on cash flow rather than accrual operating income.

Whitewater has a 14 percent weighted average cost of capital, so we use 14 percent as the discount rate to evaluate whether the company should accept the computer upgrade project; that is, we use a 14 percent discount rate to calculate the present value of the project's cash outflows and cash inflows. In this case, the project's $100,000 cash outflow occurs today (time 0), so that amount is already stated in present value terms.

Next, we must find the present value of the project's cash inflows, which occur at the end of each of the next five years. Because the stream of $31,000 positive cash flows constitutes an annuity, we use the *Present Value of an Annuity of $1 Table*, found in Exhibit A8–10 of Appendix A at the end of this chapter. In this case, we use the table to find the present value factor of a five-year annuity, with a discount rate of 14 percent. We have reproduced a portion of the table as Exhibit 8–5. As you can see from the highlighted portion in this exhibit, the factor for five years with a discount rate of 14 percent is 3.433.

EXHIBIT 8–5   Partial Present Value of an Annuity of $1 Table

Present Value of an Annuity of $1 Table

Period	8%	9%	10%	11%	12%	13%	14%	15%
1	0.926	0.917	0.909	0.901	0.893	0.885	0.877	0.870
2	1.783	1.759	1.736	1.713	1.690	1.668	1.647	1.626
3	2.577	2.531	2.487	2.444	2.402	2.361	2.322	2.283
4	3.312	3.240	3.170	3.102	3.037	2.974	2.914	2.855
5	3.993	3.890	3.791	3.696	3.605	3.517	3.433	3.352
6	4.623	4.486	4.355	4.231	4.111	3.998	3.889	3.784
7	5.206	5.033	4.868	4.712	4.564	4.423	4.288	4.160
8	5.747	5.535	5.335	5.146	4.968	4.799	4.639	4.487
9	6.247	5.995	5.759	5.537	5.328	5.132	4.946	4.772
10	6.710	6.418	6.145	5.889	5.650	5.426	5.216	5.019

We multiply $31,000, the amount of the annuity, by the 3.433 present value factor and find that the present value of the annuity is $106,423 ($31,000 × 3.433 = $106,423). See Exhibit 8–6 for instructions on how to use a financial calculator to determine this.

Finally, we find the NPV of the project by subtracting the present value of cash outflows from the present value of cash inflows. In our example, the NPV calculations are presented in Exhibit 8–7.

As Exhibit 8–7 shows, the positive NPV of $6,423 indicates that the project's expected return exceeds Whitewater's 14 percent weighted average cost of capital.

A word of caution here: A net present value of $6,423 does not mean that the project's return is only $6,423. Rather, it means that the project's return *exceeds* the company's 14 percent cost of capital by $6,423.

Discussion Questions

8–14. How would you explain the difference between present value and net present value?

8–15. Should a business accept or reject a project with an NPV of zero? Explain your reasoning.

EXHIBIT 8–6   How to Use a Financial Calculator

Using a Financial Calculator

To calculate the present value of the 31,000 payments using a financial calculator we would enter the information in our financial calculator and solve for a solution as follows:

Input: 5   14   ?   31,000   0

| n | i | PV | PMT | FV |

Answer: 106,426

Notice that the amount is $3 more than the amount we obtained when we used the present value table. This is because financial calculators typically round to 12 decimal places while our tables round to only three. What this means is that the answer we get from the calculator is more precise than the one from the tables. Although we will demonstrate each present value calculation using both tables and a financial calculator, because not all students have access to a financial calculator, throughout the remainder of the chapter we will use the amounts from the tables.

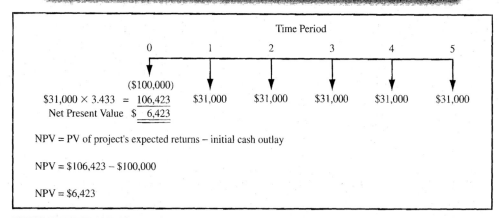

$31,000 × 3.433 = 106,423
Net Present Value $ 6,423

NPV = PV of project's expected returns − initial cash outlay

NPV = $106,423 − $100,000

NPV = $6,423

EXHIBIT 8–7   Net Present Value Calculations

NET PRESENT VALUE CALCULATIONS WITH UNEVEN CASH FLOWS

The Whitewater Adventure Company example was relatively easy to calculate because the project's expected cash flows were the same each year (an annuity). When the expected cash flows are uneven, we find the present value of each year's cash flow and then add those amounts. To demonstrate, assume that Whitewater's computer upgrade has expected annual returns of $31,000, but in year 3 the computer system will require $12,000 in maintenance fees (a cash outflow), and at the end of year 5, the system can be sold for $6,000 (a cash inflow). A timeline showing these additional cash flows is shown in Exhibit 8–8.

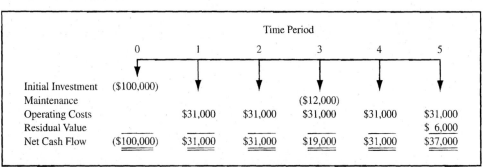

Each of the amounts for the five years shown in Exhibit 8–8 can be discounted to present value using the *Present Value of $1 Table*, found in Exhibit A8–5 of Appendix A, a portion of which is reproduced as Exhibit 8–9.

EXHIBIT 8–9 Present Value of $1 Table

Present Value of $1 Table

Period	8%	9%	10%	11%	12%	13%	14%	15%
1	0.926	0.917	0.909	0.901	0.893	0.885	0.877	0.870
2	0.857	0.842	0.826	0.812	0.797	0.783	0.769	0.756
3	0.794	0.772	0.751	0.731	0.712	0.693	0.675	0.658
4	0.735	0.708	0.683	0.659	0.636	0.613	0.592	0.572
5	0.681	0.650	0.621	0.593	0.567	0.543	0.519	0.497
6	0.630	0.596	0.564	0.535	0.507	0.480	0.456	0.432
7	0.583	0.547	0.513	0.482	0.452	0.425	0.400	0.376
8	0.540	0.502	0.467	0.434	0.404	0.376	0.351	0.327
9	0.500	0.460	0.424	0.391	0.361	0.333	0.308	0.284
10	0.463	0.422	0.386	0.352	0.322	0.295	0.270	0.247

The calculation of the present values, using the highlighted factors in the 14 percent discount rate column, is shown in Exhibit 8–10.

EXHIBIT 8–10 Net Present Value Calculations with Uneven Cash Flows

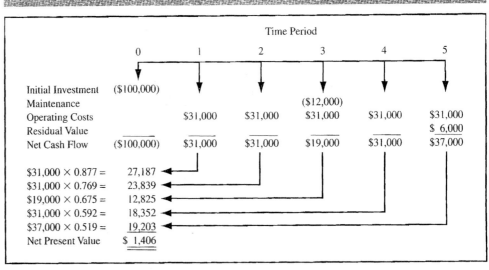

As Exhibit 8–10 demonstrates, the positive $1,406 NPV indicates that the computer upgrade exceeds Whitewater's 14 percent weighted average cost of capital. This positive NPV indicates that the project is acceptable for the company. See Exhibit 8–11 for instructions on calculating the present value using a financial calculator.

Although the net present value method indicates whether a proposed capital project is acceptable, it does have limitations as a ranking method to compare competing projects. A direct comparison of the NPVs of various projects may lead to poor decisions regarding project selection, because NPV is measured in dollars rather than percentages. For example, assume that management intends to select one of two projects, Project A and Project B. Calculations indicate that the NPV of Project A is $5,000, whereas the NPV of Project B is $6,000.

While choosing the project with the higher NPV seems wise, this is not always a good choice because NPV analysis does not consider the relative investments required by the projects. In our example, for instance, say the present value of Project A's cash inflows was $105,000 and the present value of its cash outflows was $100,000. Then suppose that the present value of Project B's cash inflows was $206,000 and the present value of its cash outflows was $200,000. We see that Project A requires an investment

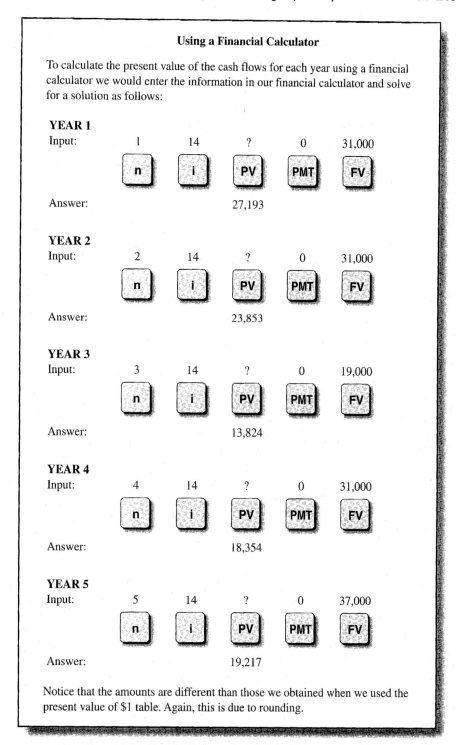

Using a Financial Calculator

To calculate the present value of the cash flows for each year using a financial calculator we would enter the information in our financial calculator and solve for a solution as follows:

YEAR 1

Input: 1 [n]   14 [i]   ? [PV]   0 [PMT]   31,000 [FV]

Answer: 27,193

YEAR 2

Input: 2 [n]   14 [i]   ? [PV]   0 [PMT]   31,000 [FV]

Answer: 23,853

YEAR 3

Input: 3 [n]   14 [i]   ? [PV]   0 [PMT]   19,000 [FV]

Answer: 13,824

YEAR 4

Input: 4 [n]   14 [i]   ? [PV]   0 [PMT]   31,000 [FV]

Answer: 18,354

YEAR 5

Input: 5 [n]   14 [i]   ? [PV]   0 [PMT]   37,000 [FV]

Answer: 19,217

Notice that the amounts are different than those we obtained when we used the present value of $1 table. Again, this is due to rounding.

EXHIBIT 8-11 Calculating the Present Value of the Cash Flows for Each Year

of $100,000, whereas Project B requires double that investment amount. In firms with scarce funds, the relatively small increase in the NPV from $5,000 to $6,000 may not justify selecting a project that requires double the amount of investment. How then can the NPV method be used when ranking various projects? We solve the problem of selecting among projects by using a profitability index.

Profitability Index

profitability index A method used to rank acceptable proposed capital projects.

The **profitability index** is an index of the values of alternative but acceptable capital budgeting projects, whose index values are calculated by dividing the present value of the project's cash inflows by the present value of its cash outflows. To illustrate, we return to our example of Projects A and B. We know that both projects have positive

NPVs and are acceptable projects. Suppose, however, we want to rank the projects in order of preference.

We find that the profitability index for Project A is 1.05 ($105,000 ÷ $100,000 = 1.05). The profitability index for Project B is 1.03 ($206,000 ÷ $200,000 = 1.03). We would rank Project A higher than Project B because Project A's index value is 1.05 compared to Project B's lower index value of 1.03. We see, then, how the profitability index is a tool that allows firms to rank competing projects.

Although the NPV method indicates whether a project's return is lower or higher than the required rate of return, it does not show the project's expected percentage return. Many managers find it helpful to know the expected rate of return of projects when making capital budgeting decisions. The internal rate of return method, discussed in the following section, is a capital budgeting method that provides this information.

Internal Rate of Return

internal rate of return (IRR)   The calculated expected percentage return promised by a proposed capital project.

real rate of return   Another name for internal rate of return.

time-adjusted rate of return   Another name for internal rate of return.

The **internal rate of return (IRR)** of a proposed capital project is the calculated expected percentage return promised by the project. Just like the NPV method, the IRR method considers all cash flows for a proposed project and adjusts for the time value of money. However, the IRR results are expressed as a percentage, not a dollar amount. This method, also known as the **real rate of return,** or the **time-adjusted rate of return,** determines the discount rate that makes the present value of a project's cash inflows and the present value of a project's outflows exactly the same.

To calculate a project's IRR, we use the same present value tables we use to calculate NPV, but we apply them differently. In this application, we use the tables to determine a discount rate (a percentage), rather than using a preselected discount rate to determine present value amounts (expressed in dollars).

As an example, assume that Project C requires an initial investment of $300,000 and will provide cash inflows of $56,232 per year for eight years. Because this project is an annuity, to determine the IRR we use the *Present Value of an Annuity of $1 Table* found in Exhibit A8–10 of Appendix A, a portion of which is reproduced as Exhibit 8–12.

EXHIBIT 8–12   Partial Present Value of an Annuity of $1 Table

Present Value of an Annuity of $1 Table

Period	7%	8%	9%	10%	11%	12%	13%	14%
1	0.935	0.926	0.917	0.909	0.901	0.893	0.885	0.877
2	1.808	1.783	1.759	1.736	1.713	1.690	1.668	1.647
3	2.624	2.577	2.531	2.487	2.444	2.402	2.361	2.322
4	3.387	3.312	3.240	3.170	3.102	3.037	2.974	2.914
5	4.100	3.993	3.890	3.791	3.696	3.605	3.517	3.433
6	4.767	4.623	4.486	4.355	4.231	4.111	3.998	3.889
7	5.389	5.206	5.033	4.868	4.712	4.564	4.423	4.288
8	5.971	5.747	5.535	5.335	5.146	4.968	4.799	4.639
9	6.515	6.247	5.995	5.759	5.537	5.328	5.132	4.946
10	7.024	6.710	6.418	6.145	5.889	5.650	5.426	5.216

First, we calculate the present value factor for the project as follows:

$$\frac{\text{Required initial investment}}{\text{Annual net cash inflow}} = \text{Present value factor}$$

$$\frac{\$300,000}{\$56,232} = 5.335 \text{ Present value factor}$$

Now that we know the present value factor, we can find Project C's IRR by moving down the time period column on the table in Exhibit 8–12 to eight periods, as that is the life of the project. Next, we follow across the row corresponding to eight periods until we find a factor that is close to the one we calculated (5.335). As we follow across the row for eight periods, we find a factor that is not just close but matches exactly. The factor of 5.335 is in the 10 percent column, which indicates that the IRR for Project C is 10 percent. Thus, the actual rate of return promised by Project C is 10 percent.

Once we determine the IRR, we compare it to the cost of capital to gauge the project's acceptability. An IRR that exceeds the firm's cost of capital indicates an acceptable project. For example, if the company's cost of capital is 9 percent, Project C's 10 percent IRR shows that the firm would find the project acceptable.

In the example for Project C, we contrived the dollar amounts so that the factor we calculated exactly equaled one of the factors in the present value table. In a real-life situation, the calculated factor will usually fall between two factors on the present value table. For example, assume that Project D would require an investment of $330,000 and would generate estimated annual returns of $64,900 for eight years. The present value factor for this project is 5.085, determined as follows:

$$\frac{\text{Required initial investment}}{\text{Annual net cash inflow}} = \text{Present value factor}$$

$$\frac{\$330,000}{\$64,900} = 5.085 \text{ Present value factor}$$

Returning to the table in Exhibit 8–12 and following across the year 8 row, we find that our calculated 5.085 factor is between the factors 5.146 (the 11 percent column) and 4.968 (the 12 percent column), but is closer to 5.146. Therefore, the project's return would fall between 11 and 12 percent, but would be closer to 11 percent. We estimate, then, that the IRR for Project D is slightly more than 11 percent.

For instructions on how to calculate the IRR using a financial calculator, see Exhibit 8–13.

EXHIBIT 8–13   Calculating the Internal Rate of Return

Using a Financial Calculator

To calculate the internal rate of return using a financial calculator, we simply enter all the data we have for the project, and solve for information we need. In other words, we enter the number of years (n = 8), the project's required initial investment (PV = –330,000), the project's annual net cash inflows (PMT = $64,900), the project's residual value, if any (FV = 0) and then solve for the project's rate or return, i. We would enter the information in our financial calculator and solve as follows:

Input:	8	?	–330,000	64,900	0
	n	i	PV	PMT	FV

Answer: 11.34%

When calculating the internal rate of return, a financial calculator not only makes the calculations easier to do, but the result is much more precise as well.

Comparing Projects Using the IRR Method

Managers can use the IRR method to rank projects. For example, the IRR of Project C (10 percent), can be compared to the approximate IRR of Project D (just over 11 percent). Assuming both projects were acceptable, Project D would be ranked higher than Project C because it promises a higher IRR.

Comparing the NPV and IRR Methods

Both the net present value method and the internal rate of return method are well-respected techniques used to determine the acceptability of a proposed capital project for two reasons. First, they are based on cash flows, not accounting income. Second, both methods consider the time value of money.

The NPV method is used to determine whether the promised return from a proposed capital project meets the minimum acceptable return requirements (cost of capital). A drawback of this method is that the calculated NPV is stated in dollars rather than percentages. Thus, comparison between projects of different size is difficult. The profitability index overcomes this difficulty.

The IRR method is used to calculate a proposed capital project's actual expected rate of return. Because this method is calculated using percentages rather than dollars, it can be used as a direct comparison of various proposed projects.

NONDISCOUNTED CASH FLOW METHODS

Decision makers generally consider the NPV and IRR methods the most reliable techniques available because they utilize the time value of money in their evaluation of potential capital projects. Other methods that ignore the time value of money exist, however, and many companies use them to some degree. We now discuss two of them—the payback period and the accounting rate of return method.

Payback Period

payback period
A capital budgeting technique that measures the length of time a capital project must generate positive cash flows that equal the original investment in the project.

As its name implies, the **payback period** is a capital budgeting technique that measures the length of time a capital project must generate positive net cash flows that equal, or "pay back," the original investment in the project. For instance, assume that a project's estimated initial outlay is $40,000. Assume further that the project is expected to generate a net cash inflow of $12,500 per year. When net cash inflows are equal from one year to the next, we determine the payback period by dividing the required initial investment by the annual cash inflows. In our example, we find that the payback period is 3.2 years. The calculations follow:

$$\frac{\text{Required initial investment}}{\text{Annual net cash inflow}} = \text{Payback period in years}$$

$$\frac{\$40,000}{\$12,500} = 3.2 \text{ Years}$$

If a project has uneven cash flows, we can determine the payback period by adding the cash inflows year by year until the total equals the required initial investment. For example, suppose a project requires an initial investment of $50,000 and is expected to generate the following net cash inflows:

2001	$12,000
2002	$15,000
2003	$18,000
2004	$15,000
2005	$12,000

We find the payback period by totaling the net cash inflows until we reach $50,000 as shown in Exhibit 8–14.

EXHIBIT 8–14 Payback Period with Uneven Cash Flows

Year	Cash Received in Prior Years		Cash Received in Current Year		Accumulated Cash Received
1	0	+	$12,000	=	$12,000
2	$12,000	+	$15,000	=	$27,000
3	$27,000	+	$18,000	=	$45,000
4	$45,000	+	$15,000	=	$60,000
5	$60,000	+	$12,000	=	$72,000

As Exhibit 8–14 shows, the initial investment will be "paid back" after the third year, but before the end of the fourth year. At the end of the third year, it is anticipated that $45,000, or all but $5,000 of the initial $50,000 investment will be recouped. The remaining $5,000 will be received during the fourth year as part of the $15,000 net cash inflows anticipated for that year. It will take about one third ($5,000 ÷ $15,000) of the fourth year to collect the final $5,000 to make up the $50,000 needed to payback the initial investment. Therefore, the payback period is 3⅓ years.

The payback period method highlights the liquidity of an investment, and companies use it as a screening device to reject projects with unreasonably low cash flow expectations. This method is simple to use, is easily understood, and offers some limited insight into a project's liquidity.

The payback period period method is not often used to make final capital investment decisions because it does not consider three crucial elements: (1) the expected returns of a project after the payback period, (2) how the returns will compare to the firm's cost of capital, or (3) the time value of money.

Because the payback period method ignores the firm's cost of capital, total cash flow, and time value of money concerns, managers do not normally accept or reject a project based solely on the payback period. If used at all, the payback period method is usually a screening device only to eliminate potential projects from further evaluation. Companies often establish a maximum payback period for potential projects. If a proposed capital project promises a payback of longer than the established maximum period, that project would be eliminated from further consideration. For example, assume a company has established a maximum payback period of three years. Using this standard, the project presented in Exhibit 8–14 would be rejected because its payback period is longer than three years.

Accounting Rate of Return

In our discussion so far, we have emphasized that the focus in capital budgeting decisions should be on cash flows. Over time, however, the net cash flow associated with a capital project should approximate operating income as determined using accrual accounting revenue and expense recognition. The **accounting rate of return** method uses accrual accounting operating income, rather than net cash flow, as the basis for evaluating alternative capital budgeting projects.

accounting rate of return
The rate of return for a capital project based on the anticipated increase in accounting operating income due to the project, relative to the amount of capital investment required.

The accounting rate of return is the rate of return for a capital project based on the anticipated increase in accounting operating income due to the project, relative to the amount of capital investment required.

This method focuses on a proposed project's required investment and how that project changes a company's operating income. As an example, let's reexamine the computer hardware upgrade project for the Whitewater Adventure Company discussed earlier in the chapter. As you recall, the computer hardware upgrade required an initial investment of $100,000. Additionally, the upgrade would reduce operating expenses by $31,000 per year for five years. The computer has an estimated useful life of five years with no residual value. Accounting operating income would be affected in two ways by the computer upgrade. First, the reduced operating expenses would increase operating income by $31,000 each year. Second, depreciation for the computer upgrade would decrease operating income by $20,000 each year ($100,000 ÷ 5 years). With this information, we can calculate the accounting rate of return as follows:

$$\frac{\text{Increase in operating income}}{\text{Required investment}} = \text{Accounting rate of return}$$

$$\frac{\$31,000 - \$20,000}{\$100,000} = 11\% \text{ Accounting rate of return}$$

The accounting rate of return is simple to calculate and provides some measure of a project's profitability; however, it has two major drawbacks. First, the accounting rate of return method focuses on accounting income rather than cash flow. In capital budgeting, most analysts generally believe that a focus on cash flow is preferred to a focus on accounting income. Second, like the payback method, the accounting rate of return does not consider the time value of money.

Many managers consider the accounting rate of return method to be superior to the payback period method because it offers at least a limited measure of a proposed capital project's rate of return. As with the payback period method, however, managers should not accept or reject a project based solely on the accounting rate of return. Both of these methods should be used only as screening devices or in conjunction with discounted cash flow methods of evaluating capital project alternatives.

♦ FACTORS LEADING TO POOR CAPITAL PROJECT SELECTION

The process of determining which capital projects to select is serious business for any company. If managers do not treat capital budgeting with the seriousness it deserves, they run the risk of making poor decisions as to the capital projects selected. At the very least, selecting the wrong capital projects is enormously costly. At worst, investing in the wrong projects can lead to financial ruin for any company, regardless of its size or past performance. Earlier in the chapter, we mentioned that **Motorola** reported investment in capital projects of about $11.5 billion from 1992 to 1995. We further stated that if **Motorola** made these investments in projects that did not perform as the company hoped they would, it could lead to disaster. Well, **Motorola**'s performance over the past four or five years can only be described as disappointing—so disappointing, in fact, that many experts are now questioning whether **Motorola,** so long the giant of the U.S. electronics industry, will survive in its present form. Most of those business analysts agree that one of the major contributing factors to **Motorola**'s problems was the poor capital project choices the company made from 1992 to 1995.

The two main factors leading to poor capital project selection are natural optimism on the part of managers and the tendency of some managers to turn the capital project evaluation process into a game.

NATURAL OPTIMISM

Human beings are essentially optimistic. As managers, they have a tendency to estimate both the cash inflows and outflows associated with a proposed project they are sponsoring with an overly optimistic outlook. This means they will likely overstate the estimated cash inflows and understate the estimated cash outflows. At the very minimum, this natural optimism limits the effectiveness of any of the evaluation techniques we have discussed in this chapter, because all of them use inflow and outflow estimates as the basis of evaluation.

There is nothing wrong with thinking positively. Optimism is, in fact, a desirable trait. Managers must understand, however, that such optimism can cloud their judgment as they assess potential capital projects. Good managers attempt to be as realistic as possible as they prepare proposals for the evaluation of potential capital projects.

CAPITAL BUDGETING GAMES

The managers who propose potential capital projects understand that there is usually not enough money available to fund all projects, even if they all promise a return greater than the cost of capital. A manager who proposes a capital project is, in fact, competing with other managers' projects for a limited number of capital investment dollars. For this reason, the capital project evaluation process is sometimes treated like some sort of game, with little consideration of the potentially disastrous consequences. Some managers manipulate the estimates of cash inflow and cash outflow to get "pet" projects approved, often at the expense of other, more deserving projects. Do not confuse this idea with the natural optimism we discussed a moment ago. The manipulation we are talking about here is an additional factor that can lead to selecting the wrong capital projects.

For example, consider the Electronics Division of Monolith Enterprises. This division has established a limit of $3 million for capital projects in 2005. Mary and Fred are the only two managers within the division who have potential capital projects to propose to division upper management. Both the potential projects will require an initial investment of $2 million, so only one of them is going to be approved.

Mary is in her office late one night putting the finishing touches on her proposal. She is reviewing the cash inflow and cash outflow estimates she has made for her project. As she goes over the estimates one last time, she is feeling a little guilty because she knows she has purposely overstated the inflows and understated the outflows to make her project look more favorable. She is convinced, however, that if she is totally realistic in her estimates, her project will stand no chance of being approved. Why? Because she knows Fred is in his office down the hall putting the finishing touches on his proposal, and she is sure he has manipulated the inflow and outflow estimates on his project to make it look better. To have any chance of approval, then, Mary must "play the game." The sad part of this situation is that Fred is down the hall in his office thinking exactly the same thing about Mary. He is certain she has manipulated her estimates, so he must also or his project has no chance of being approved. Now we introduce one more person to our scenario—Bill, the division controller. Bill is the person who will evaluate the proposed projects submitted by Mary and Fred and will decide which of the two projects will be funded. He knows from experience that both Mary and Fred have probably manipulated their estimates, so when he receives them, he compensates by arbitrarily revising their proposals or by using a higher cost of capital percentage in the NPV and IRR evaluations.

Does this seem to you to be an intelligent way to run a business? No, but this kind of game is played every day in many companies by bright and otherwise honest managers.

Discussion Question

Assume you have been hired as a consultant by Monolith Enterprises to help the company improve its capital project evaluation process.

8–16. What suggestions would you make to help Monolith eliminate the kind of "game" being played by Mary, Fred, and Bill?

How does a company make its capital project evaluation process more cooperative and less competitive? This question is difficult, if not impossible, to answer. What we do know, however, is that the global nature of business of the 21st century will not allow these kinds of budget games to continue. U.S. companies are competing with companies from all over the world, and the kind of behavior we have been discussing does not seem to exist in many of these businesses. If U.S. firms are to compete in this worldwide market, they must eliminate dysfunctional business practices. The stakes are simply too high for managers of these companies to continue this approach to capital budgeting.

In a very short time, you will occupy the position held by Mary, Fred, or Bill—not at Monolith, of course, because it is a fictitious company. The company that employs you, however, may approach capital budgeting the same way Monolith does. If so, you must do all you can to help the company find a better, more constructive capital budgeting process.

Summary

There are four elements in the overall planning process for any organization. These elements include establishing goals, formulating a strategic plan, preparing the capital budget, and preparing the operating budget.

The capital budgeting process has been described as the *how* of being in business and doing business, which means that the capital budget outlines how a company will allocate its scarce resources over the next 5, 10, or even 20 years.

All capital projects have at least four shared characteristics. Such projects are usually long-lived, carry with them high costs, have costs associated with the project that usually become sunk almost immediately, and usually involve a high degree of risk.

In the long run, the capital projects a company undertakes must cover at least the cost of the company's capital. The cost of capital is the cost of obtaining financing from both debt and equity sources. The combination of the cost of debt financing and equity financing is referred to as the weighted average cost of capital. If the capital project being considered does not at least return the cost of capital, it makes no sense, from a purely financial standpoint, to undertake it.

Over time, accountants and managers have developed several methods to evaluate potential capital projects. Among these are the net present value, the internal rate of return, the payback period, and the accounting rate of return. Each of these four methods has certain advantages and disadvantages relative to the other methods. Managers generally consider the NPV and IRR methods to be superior to the payback and accounting rate of return methods because they incorporate the time value of money in their approach to evaluating potential capital projects.

The Time Value of Money

THE TIME VALUE OF MONEY—THE CONCEPT OF INTEREST

Interest is an interesting thing—Those who understand it, get it.
Those who don't, pay it.

—ANONYMOUS

A dollar received or paid at some point in the future does not have the same value as a dollar received or paid today. If you were asked why this is so, you might think the change in value is due to inflation. Even if inflation did not exist, however, a dollar received or paid in the future would not have the same value as a dollar received or paid today. The reason for the difference in value is that if cash is available now, it can be invested now and earn a return as time passes. This increase in the value of cash over time, due to its earning potential, is referred to as the time value of money. We use the concept of the time value of money to determine either the future value of money invested today or the present value of money to be received at some point in the future.

Learning Objectives

After completing your work on this appendix, you should be able to do the following:

1. Explain the concept of simple interest and compound interest.
2. Determine the future value of a single amount invested today using a future value table.
3. Determine the present value of a single amount to be received at some point in the future using a present value table.
4. Describe the concept of an annuity.
5. Determine the future value of an annuity using a future value table.
6. Determine the present value of an annuity using a present value table.

Future Value

future value The value of a payment, or series of payments, at some future point in time calculated at some interest rate.

Future value is the value of a payment, or series of payments, at some future point in time calculated at some interest rate. For example, if you were to invest $2,000 at an annual interest rate of 10 percent, your investment would grow to $2,200 in one year. How? The amount of the increase is calculated by multiplying the principal—the original investment—by the interest rate. In our case the principal is $2,000, the interest rate is 10 percent, so the total return on your investment is $200. The $200 is added to the $2,000 investment for a total of $2,200. So far, so good. But suppose you left the investment untouched for three years. What would be its total value at the end of the three years? The answer depends on whether we calculate the interest as simple interest or compound interest.

simple interest Interest calculated on the original principal amount invested only.

Simple interest is interest calculated only on the original principal. A calculation of interest earned at 10 percent per year for three years on a $2,000 principal using simple interest is presented in Exhibit A8–1.

EXHIBIT A8–1 Simple Interest Calculation

	Year 1	Year 2	Year 3
Principal	$2,000	$2,000	$2,000
Times the interest rate	× 10%	× 10%	× 10%
Equals interest earned	$ 200	$ 200	$ 200

Note in Exhibit A8–1 that we calculate interest for each of the three years only on the original investment of $2,000. At the end of three years you would receive your $2,000 (return of your principal) and $600 interest (return on your investment).

compound interest
Interest calculated on the original principal amount invested plus all previously earned interest.

Compound interest is interest calculated on the investment principal *plus* all previously earned interest. Continuing with our example, a principal of $2,000 that earns a compounded rate of 10 percent interest per year for three years is shown in Exhibit A8–2.

EXHIBIT A8–2 Compound Interest Calculations

	Year 1	Year 2	Year 3
Principal	$2,000	$2,000	$2,000
Previously earned interest	+ 0	+ 200*	+ 420**
Total	2,000	2,200	2,420
Times the interest rate	× 10%	× 10%	× 10%
Equals interest earned	$ 200	$ 220	$ 242

*Interest earned in year 1 ($200) becomes part of the amount earning interest in year 2.
**Interest earned in year 1 ($200) and the interest earned in year 2 ($220) becomes part of the amount earning interest in year 3.

Note in Exhibit A8–2 that we calculate interest for each of the three years not only on the original investment of $2,000, but also on the interest earned in previous years. At the end of three years you would receive your $2,000 back (return of principal) and $662 interest (return on your investment). The difference of $62 between the interest earned using compound interest ($662) and the interest earned using simple interest ($600) is interest earned on your previously earned interest.

The power of compounding is tremendous. To demonstrate, let us extend our example of the $2,000 investment. Suppose Dick Gustufson invests $2,000 at 10 percent annual interest when he is 18 years old and leaves it untouched until he is 38 years old. Using the simple interest calculation, Dick's investment will earn interest of $4,000 ($2,000 × 10% × 20 years). If, however, the interest over that same 20 years is compounded, the total interest earned would be $11,454. The $7,454 difference in interest earned is due entirely to interest earning interest on previously earned interest.

Future Value of a Single Sum

We could calculate the amount of compound interest on Dick's investment by extending the three-year example presented in Exhibit A8–2 for another 17 years. This, however, would be cumbersome, time consuming, and tiresome. Fortunately, future value tables greatly simplify the calculation of compound interest.

Future value tables are previously calculated values of $1 at various rates of interest and time periods. The tables are used to determine either the future value of a single payment or the future value of an annuity—that is, a stream of equal payments made at equal intervals.

We use the *Future Value of $1 Table* (Exhibit A8–3) to determine the future value of a single amount deposited today. With this information, we can quickly determine the future value of Dick Gustufson's $2,000 investment at a 10 percent interest rate compounded annually.

As we see in Exhibit A8–3, by moving across the interest rate column headings to the 10 percent column, and then down the time period row to the 20 time periods row, we find a number on the table at the point where the row and column intersect, at a value of 6.727. This number is called a future value factor. Because we are using the *Future Value of $1 Table*, the 6.727 factor tells us that the value of a single dollar 20 years into the future is $6.727, or about $6.73. That is to say that if $1 is invested today at 10 percent, it will be worth $6.73 in 20 years.

But Dick invested $2,000, not $1. To determine the future value of $2,000, we multiply $2,000 by the factor of 6.727 to determine that $2,000 invested today at 10 percent will be worth $13,454 after 20 years ($2,000 × 6.727 = $13,454). If you subtract his initial investment of $2,000, the amount of interest he will earn is $11,454.

Future Value of an Annuity

We use the *Future Value of an Annuity of $1 Table*, presented as Exhibit A8–4, to determine the future value of a stream of cash flows when the stream of cash flows constitutes an annuity.

Future Value of $1 Table

Period	3%	4%	5%	6%	7%	8%	9%	10%	11%	12%	13%	14%	15%	16%	17%	18%
1	1.030	1.040	1.050	1.060	1.070	1.080	1.090	1.100	1.110	1.120	1.130	1.140	1.150	1.160	1.170	1.180
2	1.061	1.082	1.103	1.124	1.145	1.166	1.188	1.210	1.232	1.254	1.277	1.300	1.323	1.346	1.369	1.392
3	1.093	1.125	1.158	1.191	1.225	1.260	1.295	1.331	1.368	1.405	1.443	1.482	1.521	1.561	1.602	1.643
4	1.126	1.170	1.216	1.262	1.311	1.360	1.412	1.464	1.518	1.574	1.630	1.689	1.749	1.811	1.874	1.939
5	1.159	1.217	1.276	1.338	1.403	1.469	1.539	1.611	1.685	1.762	1.842	1.925	2.011	2.100	2.192	2.288
6	1.194	1.265	1.340	1.419	1.501	1.587	1.677	1.772	1.870	1.974	2.082	2.195	2.313	2.436	2.565	2.700
7	1.230	1.316	1.407	1.504	1.606	1.714	1.828	1.949	2.076	2.211	2.353	2.502	2.660	2.826	3.001	3.185
8	1.267	1.369	1.477	1.594	1.718	1.851	1.993	2.144	2.305	2.476	2.658	2.853	3.059	3.278	3.511	3.759
9	1.305	1.423	1.551	1.689	1.838	1.999	2.172	2.358	2.558	2.773	3.004	3.252	3.518	3.803	4.108	4.435
10	1.344	1.480	1.629	1.791	1.967	2.159	2.367	2.594	2.839	3.106	3.395	3.707	4.046	4.411	4.807	5.234
11	1.384	1.539	1.710	1.898	2.105	2.332	2.580	2.853	3.152	3.479	3.836	4.226	4.652	5.117	5.624	6.176
12	1.426	1.601	1.796	2.012	2.252	2.518	2.813	3.138	3.498	3.896	4.335	4.818	5.350	5.936	6.580	7.288
13	1.469	1.665	1.886	2.133	2.410	2.720	3.066	3.452	3.883	4.363	4.898	5.492	6.153	6.886	7.699	8.599
14	1.513	1.732	1.980	2.261	2.579	2.937	3.342	3.797	4.310	4.887	5.535	6.261	7.076	7.988	9.007	10.147
15	1.558	1.801	2.079	2.397	2.759	3.172	3.642	4.177	4.785	5.474	6.254	7.138	8.137	9.266	10.539	11.974
16	1.605	1.873	2.183	2.540	2.952	3.426	3.970	4.595	5.311	6.130	7.067	8.137	9.358	10.748	12.330	14.129
17	1.653	1.948	2.292	2.693	3.159	3.700	4.328	5.054	5.895	6.866	7.986	9.276	10.761	12.468	14.426	16.672
18	1.702	2.026	2.407	2.854	3.380	3.996	4.717	5.560	6.544	7.690	9.024	10.575	12.375	14.463	16.879	19.673
19	1.754	2.107	2.527	3.026	3.617	4.316	5.142	6.116	7.263	8.613	10.197	12.056	14.232	16.777	19.748	23.214
20	1.806	2.191	2.653	3.207	3.870	4.661	5.604	6.727	8.062	9.646	11.523	13.743	16.367	19.461	23.106	27.393
21	1.860	2.279	2.786	3.400	4.141	5.034	6.109	7.400	8.949	10.804	13.021	15.668	18.822	22.574	27.034	32.324
22	1.916	2.370	2.925	3.604	4.430	5.437	6.659	8.140	9.934	12.100	14.714	17.861	21.645	26.186	31.629	38.142
23	1.974	2.465	3.072	3.820	4.741	5.871	7.258	8.954	11.026	13.552	16.627	20.362	24.891	30.376	37.006	45.008
24	2.033	2.563	3.225	4.049	5.072	6.341	7.911	9.850	12.239	15.179	18.788	23.212	28.625	35.236	43.297	53.109
25	2.094	2.666	3.386	4.292	5.427	6.848	8.623	10.835	13.585	17.000	21.231	26.462	32.919	40.874	50.658	62.669

EXHIBIT A8-4 Future Value of an Annuity of $1 Table

Future Value of an Annuity of $1 Table

Period	3%	4%	5%	6%	7%	8%	9%	10%	11%	12%	13%	14%	15%	16%	17%	18%
1	1.000	1.000	1.000	1.000	1.000	1.000	1.000	1.000	1.000	1.000	1.000	1.000	1.000	1.000	1.000	1.000
2	2.030	2.040	2.050	2.060	2.070	2.080	2.090	2.100	2.110	2.120	2.130	2.140	2.150	2.160	2.170	2.180
3	3.091	3.122	3.153	3.184	3.215	3.246	3.278	3.310	3.342	3.374	3.407	3.440	3.473	3.506	3.539	3.572
4	4.184	4.246	4.310	4.375	4.440	4.506	4.573	4.641	4.710	4.779	4.850	4.921	4.993	5.066	5.141	5.215
5	5.309	5.416	5.526	5.637	5.751	5.867	5.985	6.105	6.228	6.353	6.480	6.610	6.742	6.877	7.014	7.154
6	6.468	6.633	6.802	6.975	7.153	7.336	7.523	7.716	7.913	8.115	8.323	8.536	8.754	8.977	9.207	9.442
7	7.662	7.898	8.142	8.394	8.654	8.923	9.200	9.487	9.783	10.089	10.405	10.730	11.067	11.414	11.772	12.142
8	8.892	9.214	9.549	9.897	10.260	10.637	11.028	11.436	11.859	12.300	12.757	13.233	13.727	14.240	14.773	15.327
9	10.159	10.583	11.027	11.491	11.978	12.488	13.021	13.579	14.164	14.776	15.416	16.085	16.786	17.519	18.285	19.086
10	11.464	12.006	12.578	13.181	13.816	14.487	15.193	15.937	16.722	17.549	18.420	19.337	20.304	21.321	22.393	23.521
11	12.808	13.486	14.207	14.972	15.784	16.645	17.560	18.531	19.561	20.655	21.814	23.045	24.349	25.733	27.200	28.755
12	14.192	15.026	15.917	16.870	17.888	18.977	20.141	21.384	22.713	24.133	25.650	27.271	29.002	30.850	32.824	34.931
13	15.618	16.627	17.713	18.882	20.141	21.495	22.953	24.523	26.212	28.029	29.985	32.089	34.352	36.786	39.404	42.219
14	17.086	18.292	19.599	21.015	22.550	24.215	26.019	27.975	30.095	32.393	34.883	37.581	40.505	43.672	47.103	50.818
15	18.599	20.024	21.579	23.276	25.129	27.152	29.361	31.772	34.405	37.280	40.417	43.842	47.580	51.660	56.110	60.965
16	20.157	21.825	23.657	25.673	27.888	30.324	33.003	35.950	39.190	42.753	46.672	50.980	55.717	60.925	66.649	72.939
17	21.762	23.698	25.840	28.213	30.840	33.750	36.974	40.545	44.501	48.884	53.739	59.118	65.075	71.673	78.979	87.068
18	23.414	25.645	28.132	30.906	33.999	37.450	41.301	45.599	50.396	55.750	61.725	68.394	75.836	84.141	93.406	103.740
19	25.117	27.671	30.539	33.760	37.379	41.446	46.018	51.159	56.939	63.440	70.749	78.969	88.212	98.603	110.285	123.414
20	26.870	29.778	33.066	36.786	40.995	45.762	51.160	57.275	64.203	72.052	80.947	91.025	102.444	115.380	130.033	146.628
21	28.676	31.969	35.719	39.993	44.865	50.423	56.765	64.002	72.265	81.699	92.470	104.768	118.810	134.841	153.139	174.021
22	30.537	34.248	38.505	43.392	49.006	55.457	62.873	71.403	81.214	92.503	105.491	120.436	137.632	157.415	180.172	206.345
23	32.453	36.618	41.430	46.996	53.436	60.893	69.532	79.543	91.148	104.603	120.205	138.297	159.276	183.601	211.801	244.487
24	34.426	39.083	44.502	50.816	58.177	66.765	76.790	88.497	102.174	118.155	136.831	158.659	184.168	213.978	248.808	289.494
25	36.459	41.646	47.727	54.865	63.249	73.106	84.701	98.347	114.413	133.334	155.620	181.871	212.793	249.214	292.105	342.603

annuity A stream of equal periodic cash flows.

An **annuity** is a stream of cash flows in which the dollar amount of each payment and the time interval between each payment are uniform.

To see how the table in Exhibit A8–4 is used, assume Susan King intends to deposit $2,000 in an account at the end of each year for four years at a compound interest rate of 12 percent per year. Using the *Future Value of an Annuity of $1 Table*, we determine that the factor for 4 years at 12 percent is 4.779. Accordingly, if Susan deposits $2,000 at the end of each year for four years at 12 percent, the account balance will be approximately $9,558 ($2,000 × 4.779).

Present Value (Discounting)

The basic premise of the present value of money is that it is more valuable to receive cash today (so it can be invested to receive interest) than to receive the cash later. The question is, just how valuable is it to receive cash sooner rather than later?

If we know the expected rate of return, we can actually calculate the value of receiving cash sooner rather than later. For example, if you are offered the option of receiving $1,000 today or $1,000 one year from now, how much more valuable is it to receive the $1,000 today? If the $1,000 received today can be invested in a savings account earning six percent interest, then it will grow by $60 during the year. At the end of one year, it will be worth $1,060 and you would be $60 richer than if you had opted to receive the $1,000 one year from now. The $60 growth in value over time exemplifies the time value of money. Clearly, if money is available and invested, it grows as time passes.

present value The amount future cash flows are worth today based on an appropriate interest rate.

If cash can be invested at six percent, $1,000 received today is equivalent to receiving $1,060 one year from now. The amount a future cash flow or stream of cash flows is worth today evaluated at the appropriate interest rate is the cash flow's **present value.** Determining the present value of an amount of cash to be received in the future is called *discounting*.

Present value tables greatly simplify the calculation of discounting to find the present value of a single amount or an annuity. Present value tables are previously calculated values of $1 at various interest rates and time periods. The tables are used to determine either the present value of a single amount or the present value of an annuity.

Present Value of a Single Sum

We use the *Present Value of $1 Table*, presented as Exhibit A8–5, to determine the present value of a single amount to be received at some point in the future.

To see how we use the *Present Value of $1 Table*, suppose you visit your rich Aunt Hattie and help her wash her dog. Your aunt is so touched by your kindness that she offers you a gift of $1,000. You are excited and hold out your hand for the money, but she informs you that she is not going to give you the money now. Rather, she intends to give you the money one year from now. Her only request is that you tell her how much to deposit in a six percent savings account today so that the account will equal $1,000 one year from now.

In this case, you know that the future value of the amount is $1,000 one year from now. The amount your Aunt Hattie wants to know is the present value, the amount that must be deposited today at six percent so that the account will be worth $1,000 in one year. To find out how much Aunt Hattie must deposit, we use the *Present Value of $1 Table* in Exhibit A8–5. We quickly scan the table to find the point of intersection between the six percent interest rate column and the number of time periods row, which is 1. The point of intersection, the present value factor, is 0.943. This factor indicates that the present value of one dollar discounted at six percent is $0.943, or about 94 cents. Thus, if $0.943 is invested today at six percent, it will be worth $1 one year from now.

But Aunt Hattie is going to give you $1,000, not $1. To determine the present value of $1,000, we simply multiply $1,000 by the factor of 0.943 to determine that $943 invested today at six percent will be worth $1,000 in one year, as shown by the timeline presentation in Exhibit A8–6.

Exhibit A8–6 shows that to have $1,000 a year from now, given an expected rate of interest of six percent per year, Aunt Hattie must deposit $943. So, the present value of $1,000 to be received one year from now at six percent is $943. The $943 will grow in value as it accumulates interest. This growth is the time value of money. You immediately inform Aunt Hattie that she must deposit $943 today at six percent to have the $1,000 gift ready for you one year from now.

Aunt Hattie is so happy with your quick response that she offers you an additional $1,000 gift. The second $1,000 gift, however, will be given two years from now, which means you will receive the first $1,000 gift at the end of year 1, and the second $1,000 gift at the end of year 2. You are thrilled, but again, Aunt Hattie requests that you tell her exactly how much she must deposit today at six percent to have the additional $1,000 in two years. We use the *Present Value of $1 Table* in Exhibit A8–5 to find that the present value factor for a time period of two and an

Present Value of $1 Table

Period	3%	4%	5%	6%	7%	8%	9%	10%	11%	12%	13%	14%	15%	16%	17%	18%
1	0.971	0.962	0.952	0.943	0.935	0.926	0.917	0.909	0.901	0.893	0.885	0.877	0.870	0.862	0.855	0.847
2	0.943	0.925	0.907	0.890	0.873	0.857	0.842	0.826	0.812	0.797	0.783	0.769	0.756	0.743	0.731	0.718
3	0.915	0.889	0.864	0.840	0.816	0.794	0.772	0.751	0.731	0.712	0.693	0.675	0.658	0.641	0.624	0.609
4	0.888	0.855	0.823	0.792	0.763	0.735	0.708	0.683	0.659	0.636	0.613	0.592	0.572	0.552	0.534	0.516
5	0.863	0.822	0.784	0.747	0.713	0.681	0.650	0.621	0.593	0.567	0.543	0.519	0.497	0.476	0.456	0.437
6	0.837	0.790	0.746	0.705	0.666	0.630	0.596	0.564	0.535	0.507	0.480	0.456	0.432	0.410	0.390	0.370
7	0.813	0.760	0.711	0.665	0.623	0.583	0.547	0.513	0.482	0.452	0.425	0.400	0.376	0.354	0.333	0.314
8	0.789	0.731	0.677	0.627	0.582	0.540	0.502	0.467	0.434	0.404	0.376	0.351	0.327	0.305	0.285	0.266
9	0.766	0.703	0.645	0.592	0.544	0.500	0.460	0.424	0.391	0.361	0.333	0.308	0.284	0.263	0.243	0.225
10	0.744	0.676	0.614	0.558	0.508	0.463	0.422	0.386	0.352	0.322	0.295	0.270	0.247	0.227	0.208	0.191
11	0.722	0.650	0.585	0.527	0.475	0.429	0.388	0.350	0.317	0.287	0.261	0.237	0.215	0.195	0.178	0.162
12	0.701	0.625	0.557	0.497	0.444	0.397	0.356	0.319	0.286	0.257	0.231	0.208	0.187	0.168	0.152	0.137
13	0.681	0.601	0.530	0.469	0.415	0.368	0.326	0.290	0.258	0.229	0.204	0.182	0.163	0.145	0.130	0.116
14	0.661	0.577	0.505	0.442	0.388	0.340	0.299	0.263	0.232	0.205	0.181	0.160	0.141	0.125	0.111	0.099
15	0.642	0.555	0.481	0.417	0.362	0.315	0.275	0.239	0.209	0.183	0.160	0.140	0.123	0.108	0.095	0.084
16	0.623	0.534	0.458	0.394	0.339	0.292	0.252	0.218	0.188	0.163	0.141	0.123	0.107	0.093	0.081	0.071
17	0.605	0.513	0.436	0.371	0.317	0.270	0.231	0.198	0.170	0.146	0.125	0.108	0.093	0.080	0.069	0.060
18	0.587	0.494	0.416	0.350	0.296	0.250	0.212	0.180	0.153	0.130	0.111	0.095	0.081	0.069	0.059	0.051
19	0.570	0.475	0.396	0.331	0.277	0.232	0.194	0.164	0.138	0.116	0.098	0.083	0.070	0.060	0.051	0.043
20	0.554	0.456	0.377	0.312	0.258	0.215	0.178	0.149	0.124	0.104	0.087	0.073	0.061	0.051	0.043	0.037
21	0.538	0.439	0.359	0.294	0.242	0.199	0.164	0.135	0.112	0.093	0.077	0.064	0.053	0.044	0.037	0.031
22	0.522	0.422	0.342	0.278	0.226	0.184	0.150	0.123	0.101	0.083	0.068	0.056	0.046	0.038	0.032	0.026
23	0.507	0.406	0.326	0.262	0.211	0.170	0.138	0.112	0.091	0.074	0.060	0.049	0.040	0.033	0.027	0.022
24	0.492	0.390	0.310	0.247	0.197	0.158	0.126	0.102	0.082	0.066	0.053	0.043	0.035	0.028	0.023	0.019
25	0.478	0.375	0.295	0.233	0.184	0.146	0.116	0.092	0.074	0.059	0.047	0.038	0.030	0.024	0.020	0.016

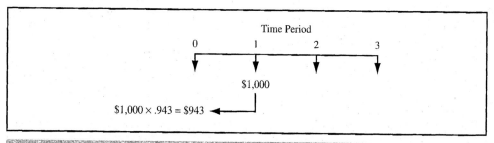

EXHIBIT A8–6   Timeline Presentation of Present Value of $1

interest rate of six percent is 0.890. Accordingly, the present value of $1,000 to be received two years from now is $890 ($1,000 × 0.890). You quickly inform your aunt that she must deposit a total of $1,833 ($943 + $890) today to pay both the $1,000 at the end of year 1 and the $1,000 at the end of year 2. The timeline and calculations are shown in Exhibit A8–7.

EXHIBIT A8–7   Timeline Presentation

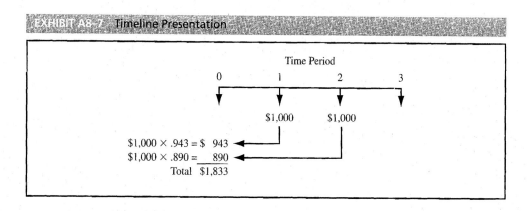

Now suppose your Aunt Hattie planned to give you a gift of $1,000 per year for the next three years. We could rely on the *Present Value of $1 Table* and add the totals for each year as shown in Exhibit A8–8.

EXHIBIT A8–8   Timeline Presentation

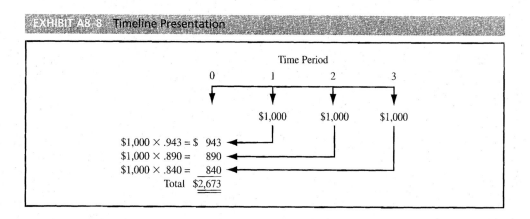

We can simplify the calculations, however, by multiplying the $1,000 by the sum of the three present value factors, which is 2.673. Accordingly, instead of multiplying $1,000 by 0.943, then $1,000 by 0.890, then $1,000 by 0.840, and summing the total, we simply multiply the $1,000 by the sum of the factors as shown in Exhibit A8–9.

Present Value of an Annuity

Because the stream of cash flows in our example is an annuity—three equal payments made at regular intervals of one year—we can use the *Present Value of an Annuity of $1 Table*, presented as Exhibit A8–10.

By examining the table in Exhibit A8–10, we find that the present value factor of an annuity for three periods at 6 percent is 2.673. Notice that the 2.673 equals the sum of the individual

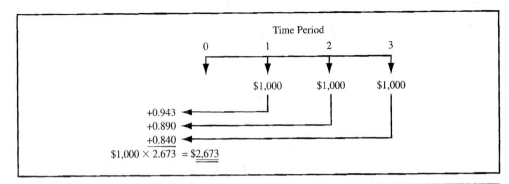

EXHIBIT A8–9 Timeline Presentation

present value of $1 factors for each of the three years in Exhibit A8–9. Next, we multiply the $1,000 by the 2.673 factor to find that the present value of Aunt Hattie's $1,000, three-year annuity paid yearly is $2,673.

As you use the future value and present value tables provided in this book, note that the number of interest rates and time periods is limited. Although these smaller tables are useful for learning the basics, in business practice future value and present value tables include a much larger number of interest rates and time periods. If needed, comprehensive tables are available at bookstores and office supply stores.

A working knowledge of present and future value concepts will be extremely important to you not only in your college coursework but also in your professional career. Whether the task is evaluating potential capital projects, as in this chapter, or any of its many other applications, you will find these concepts invaluable throughout your life.

Most computers can also be used to solve present value and future value problems. Many software packages now include modules that can handle simple and advanced calculations dealing with the time value of money.

As an alternative to using a computer or future and present value tables, we can compute future value and present value using nothing more than a handheld financial calculator. (It must be a financial or business calculator. Engineering and scientific calculators generally do not have present value and future value functions.) In the business world, most managers rely on calculators and computers to calculate future and present values. Appendix B of this chapter describes how to use a financial calculator for present value and future value computations.

Present Value of an Annuity of $1 Table

Period	3%	4%	5%	6%	7%	8%	9%	10%	11%	12%	13%	14%	15%	16%	17%	18%
1	0.971	0.962	0.952	0.943	0.935	0.926	0.917	0.909	0.901	0.893	0.885	0.877	0.870	0.862	0.855	0.847
2	1.913	1.886	1.859	1.833	1.808	1.783	1.759	1.736	1.713	1.690	1.668	1.647	1.626	1.605	1.585	1.566
3	2.829	2.775	2.723	2.673	2.624	2.577	2.531	2.487	2.444	2.402	2.361	2.322	2.283	2.246	2.210	2.174
4	3.717	3.630	3.546	3.465	3.387	3.312	3.240	3.170	3.102	3.037	2.974	2.914	2.855	2.798	2.743	2.690
5	4.580	4.452	4.329	4.212	4.100	3.993	3.890	3.791	3.696	3.605	3.517	3.433	3.352	3.274	3.199	3.127
6	5.417	5.242	5.076	4.917	4.767	4.623	4.486	4.355	4.231	4.111	3.998	3.889	3.784	3.685	3.589	3.498
7	6.230	6.002	5.786	5.582	5.389	5.206	5.033	4.868	4.712	4.564	4.423	4.288	4.160	4.039	3.922	3.812
8	7.020	6.733	6.463	6.210	5.971	5.747	5.535	5.335	5.146	4.968	4.799	4.639	4.487	4.344	4.207	4.078
9	7.786	7.435	7.108	6.802	6.515	6.247	5.995	5.759	5.537	5.328	5.132	4.946	4.772	4.607	4.451	4.303
10	8.530	8.111	7.722	7.360	7.024	6.710	6.418	6.145	5.889	5.650	5.426	5.216	5.019	4.833	4.659	4.494
11	9.253	8.760	8.306	7.887	7.499	7.139	6.805	6.495	6.207	5.938	5.687	5.453	5.234	5.029	4.836	4.656
12	9.954	9.385	8.863	8.384	7.943	7.536	7.161	6.814	6.492	6.194	5.918	5.660	5.421	5.197	4.988	4.793
13	10.635	9.986	9.394	8.853	8.358	7.904	7.487	7.103	6.750	6.424	6.122	5.842	5.583	5.342	5.118	4.910
14	11.296	10.563	9.899	9.295	8.745	8.244	7.786	7.367	6.982	6.628	6.302	6.002	5.724	5.468	5.229	5.008
15	11.938	11.118	10.380	9.712	9.108	8.559	8.061	7.606	7.191	6.811	6.462	6.142	5.847	5.575	5.324	5.092
16	12.561	11.652	10.838	10.106	9.447	8.851	8.313	7.824	7.379	6.974	6.604	6.265	5.954	5.668	5.405	5.162
17	13.166	12.166	11.274	10.477	9.763	9.122	8.544	8.022	7.549	7.120	6.729	6.373	6.047	5.749	5.475	5.222
18	13.754	12.659	11.690	10.828	10.059	9.372	8.756	8.201	7.702	7.250	6.840	6.467	6.128	5.818	5.534	5.273
19	14.324	13.134	12.085	11.158	10.336	9.604	8.950	8.365	7.839	7.366	6.938	6.550	6.198	5.877	5.584	5.316
20	14.877	13.590	12.462	11.470	10.594	9.818	9.129	8.514	7.963	7.469	7.025	6.623	6.259	5.929	5.628	5.353
21	15.415	14.029	12.821	11.764	10.836	10.017	9.292	8.649	8.075	7.562	7.102	6.687	6.312	5.973	5.665	5.384
22	15.937	14.451	13.163	12.042	11.061	10.201	9.442	8.772	8.176	7.645	7.170	6.743	6.359	6.011	5.696	5.410
23	16.444	14.857	13.489	12.303	11.272	10.371	9.580	8.883	8.266	7.718	7.230	6.792	6.399	6.044	5.723	5.432
24	16.936	15.247	13.799	12.550	11.469	10.529	9.707	8.985	8.348	7.784	7.283	6.835	6.434	6.073	5.746	5.451
25	17.413	15.622	14.094	12.783	11.654	10.675	9.823	9.077	8.422	7.843	7.330	6.873	6.464	6.097	5.766	5.467

Using a Financial Calculator

financial calculator A calculator that can provide an array of information regarding the time value of money including future and present values.

Once you have mastered Appendix A and know about the time value of money and how financial tables work, you are ready to learn about the modern-day equivalent of the tables—the financial calculator. A **financial calculator** can provide all the information that financial tables provide and more.

Learning Objectives

After completing your work on this appendix, you should be able to do the following:

1. Use a financial calculator for future value calculations.
2. Use a financial calculator for present value calculations
3. Use a financial calculator for auto loan calculations.
4. Use a financial calculator for home mortgage calculations.

Recall that in Appendix A we calculated several amounts as we demonstrated the future value and present value tables. In this appendix, we will use the same information to recalculate those same amounts, but this time we will use a financial calculator. In addition, we will demonstrate how to use the calculator for common situations such as auto financing and home mortgages. Once you understand how to use a financial calculator, calculating loan payments, present values, and future values will be quick and easy.

CALCULATOR DIFFERENCES

The way financial calculators works is quite simple. Generally, we know four of the variables and must use the calculator to solve for the one that's missing. Almost all financial calculators use the following five keys:

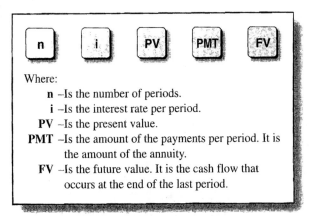

Where:
  n –Is the number of periods.
  i –Is the interest rate per period.
  PV –Is the present value.
  PMT –Is the amount of the payments per period. It is the amount of the annuity.
  FV –Is the future value. It is the cash flow that occurs at the end of the last period.

Although they all use the same financial keys (n, i, PV, PMT, and FV), not all financial calculators work exactly the same way. Consult your calculator's instruction manual to figure out just how your calculator works. Afterwards, it will be easy to do future value and present value calculations. Then, as you read this appendix, you can experiment with your calculator by entering each of our examples into it to make sure you get the same solution we do. Here are some of the calculator differences you may encounter:

Buttons vs. Display Many calculators have separate buttons on the face of the calculator for the financial function. On others, however, the financial function keys are shown on the display after the operator has accessed the calculator's present value menu.

Determining the Solution On many calculators you simply press the key corresponding to the amount you are trying to determine and the calculator provides the solution. But some calculators require that you press a *compute* key or *start* key and then the key corresponding to the amount you need to know.

Compounding Periods   Another difference among calculators has to do with the interest rate and compounding. In business, interest is most often compounded monthly. Accordingly, some calculators are programmed so that the calculator automatically converts the interest rate you enter to monthly compounding. With these calculators, when you enter the interest rate the calculator automatically converts it to a monthly rate by dividing the rate by 12. This is fine if you are truly doing a problem with monthly compounding of interest, but for academic problems, compounding is often assumed to occur yearly so you must either reprogram your calculator for yearly compounding or you can fool the calculator by multiplying the interest rate by 12 so that when the calculator divides it by 12 you end up with the correct rate.

Pluses and Minuses   Some calculators are programmed so the cash inflows and cash outflows offset each other. But for many calculators, the operator must indicate whether the cash flow is an inflow or an outflow or an error message may appear. If you notice that error messages appear, try entering all cash inflows as positive amounts and all cash outflows as negative amounts. This may solve the problem. For our examples, we will use positive and negative amounts to show inflows and outflows, respectively.

Timing of Cash Flows   All financial calculators are able to do future value and present value calculation assuming the cash flow takes place at the end of the period or at the beginning of the period. For this appendix, we will assume that cash flows take place at the end of each period. In the case of annuities, if the cash flow takes place at the end of each period it is sometimes called an *ordinary annuity*, and if the cash flow takes place at the beginning of each period it is often called an *annuity due*. For the calculations in this appendix, you should be sure your calculator is set to assume that cash flows take place at the end of the period. This is the default setting for most financial calculators.

In the following sections, we will recalculate each of the examples we presented in Appendix A. We will indicate the amounts we enter into our financial calculator followed by the solution.

FUTURE VALUE OF A SINGLE SUM

As we did in Appendix A, let's assume that Dick Gustufson invests $2,000 today at 10 percent interest compounded annually, and would like to know how much his investment will be worth in 20 years. Keep in mind that the when Dick invests, he has a $2,000 outflow because he is taking the cash and putting it into the investment. Therefore we will enter a negative amount in our calculator for this $2,000 outflow. We would enter the information in our financial calculator and solve as follows:

Input:	20	10	−2,000	0	?
	n	i	PV	PMT	FV
Answer:					13,455

In this case, we entered 20 for n, 10 for i, −2,000 for the PV, and 0 for PMT. We then press the FV key to determine that the future value of Dick's investment is $13,455. This amount is $1 more than the amount we obtained when we used the future value tables in Appendix A because the calculator rounds to 12 decimal places and our tables round to only three. What this means is that the answer we get from the calculator is more precise than the one from the tables.

What if Dick wanted to determine how much less he would earn if he could find only a 9 percent investment? The information is already in our calculator, but we need to change the interest rate from 10 percent to 9 percent. All we need to do is enter 9 for i and then press the FV key again to calculate the new future value. When an element of the calculation changes, we need to reenter only that element. If the other amounts stay the same, we need not reenter them.

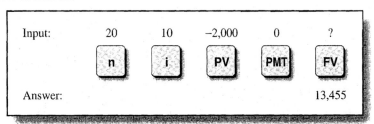

Already in Calculator	20	10	−2,000	0	13,455
New Input:		9			?
	n	i	PV	PMT	FV
Answer:					11,209

So if Dick can find only a 9 percent investment compounded annually, his $2,000 investment will be worth $11,209 at the end of 20 years.

FUTURE VALUE OF AN ANNUITY

As we did in Appendix A, let's say Susan King intends to deposit $2,000 in an account at the end of each year for four years at a compound interest rate of 12 percent per year. We would enter the information in our financial calculator and solve as follows:

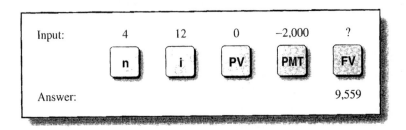

In this case, we entered 4 for n, 12 for i, 0 for the PV, and −2,000 for PMT. We then press the FV key to determine that the future value of Susan's investment is $9,559. As it happens, this is the same amount we obtained when we used the future value tables in Appendix A. Bear in mind, however, because financial calculators round to 12 decimal places and financial tables usually do not, differences between the results of the two methods are likely to occur. In all likelihood, the answers you get from a financial calculator will be more precise than those obtained from using financial tables.

PRESENT VALUE OF A SINGLE SUM

To demonstrate how to determine present value of a single sum, let's revisit the Aunt Hattie example in Appendix A. Remember that your aunt was touched by your kindness, so she offered to give you a gift of $1,000. Her only request is that you tell her how much to deposit in a six percent savings account today so that the account will equal $1,000 one year from now. We would enter the information in our financial calculator and solve as follows:

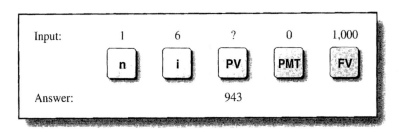

In this case, we entered 1 for n, 6 for i, 0 for PMT, and 1,000 for FV. We then press the PV key to determine that the present value, or the amount Aunt Hattie should deposit, is $943.

Now assume your Aunt Hattie is so happy with your quick response that she offers you an additional $1,000 gift. The second $1,000 gift, however, will be given two years from now, which means you will receive the first $1,000 gift at the end of year 1, and the second $1,000 gift at the end of year 2. As we enter the amounts in our calculator for the second $1,000 payment we should keep in mind that most of the amounts stay the same. Only the number of years changes. Accordingly, we would enter the information in our financial calculator and solve as follows:

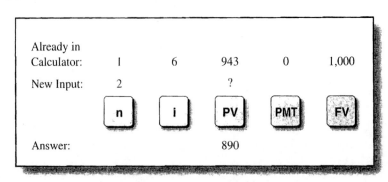

So your aunt must deposit a total of $1,833 ($943 + $890) today to pay both the $1,000 at the end of year 1, and the $1,000 at the end of year 2.

Now suppose your Aunt Hattie planned to give you a gift of $1,000 per year for the next three years. We would enter the information in our financial calculator and solve as follows:

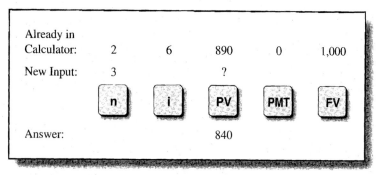

So your aunt must deposit a total of $2,673 ($943 + $890 + $840) today to pay $1,000 at the end of each of the next three years.

PRESENT VALUE OF AN ANNUITY

Because the stream of cash flows in our example is an annuity—three equal payments made at regular intervals of one year—we can find the present value of the stream of $1,000 payments using the PMT key instead of calculating the present value of each individual cash flow. We would enter the information in our financial calculator and solve as follows:

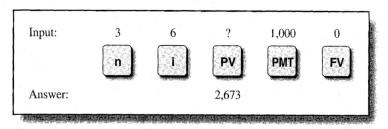

So again we determine that your aunt must deposit a total of $2,673 today to pay $1,000 at the end of each of the next three years.

COMMON USES OF A FINANCIAL CALCULATOR

Having a financial calculator and knowing the basics of how to use it provides you with a valuable business decision tool. The information a financial calculator offers can help you make adjustments in financing and investment situations so they best fit your needs and abilities. We have already discussed how to determine the future value and present value of investments. In the following sections, we will use a financial calculator to provide valuable information for auto loans and home mortgages.

Auto Loans

Let's say you're buying a new car. You have $6,000 as a down payment, and the total price of the car you have selected is $24,000. Accordingly, you intend to finance $18,000 ($24,000 − $6,000). The bank offers to make the loan at 7 percent. You have looked over your finances and feel you could pay $300 a month and would like the term of the auto loan to be four years, or 48 monthly payments. Unlike the academic problems we have been working so far, interest is compounded monthly for an auto loan, not annually. The bank's interest rate is an annual rate, not a monthly one. For some financial calculators, we must divide the 7 percent annual rate by 12 to determine the monthly rate of interest that we will enter for the i key. We would enter the information in our financial calculator and solve as follows:

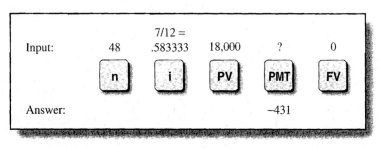

So we enter 48 for n, .583333 for i, 18,000 for PV and 0 for FV. Then we press the PMT key and the calculator determines that the payment will be $431. But wait. Although the loan term is 48 months, the monthly payment is more than our $300 limit. Let's assume that you decide that a longer-term loan would be easier to manage than a higher monthly payment. If you want to know how much the payments would be for a 60-month loan instead of a 48-month loan, just enter 60 for n and then press the PMT key again to calculate the new monthly payment amount. When only the length of the loan changes, the interest rate (i) and the amount of the loan (PV) stay the same, so we need not reenter them. Accordingly, we would enter the information in our financial calculator and solve as follows:

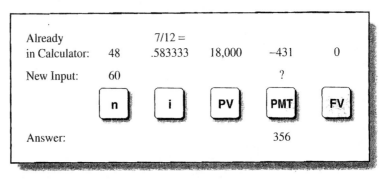

The monthly loan payment for a 60-month loan is $356. If the maximum we can pay per month is $300, how much can we borrow for 60 months? Well, to find out we enter an acceptable payment amount, the $300, and press PV to determine the amount we can borrow. All the other amounts in the calculator are fine and do not need to be changed. We would enter the information in our financial calculator and solve as follows:

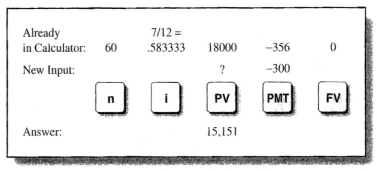

So for a 60-month loan at 7 percent interest with a monthly payment of $300, you can borrow $15,151. What this means is that, with your $6,000 down payment, you'd better look for a car that costs about $21,151 or less.

Home Mortgages

The calculations for a home mortgage are exactly the same as they are for an auto loan. The only difference is that the loan amounts and terms are usually much longer for home mortgages.

Assume that you are thinking about buying a home and have $10,000 available as the down payment. Assume further that you have found a house that you can buy for $150,000 and have been preapproved for a 6.5 percent, 30-year mortgage loan. Accordingly, you intend to finance $140,000 ($150,000 − $10,000). As was the case in the auto loan example, interest is compounded monthly for home mortgages. The bank's 6.5 percent interest rate is an annual rate, not a monthly one. For some financial calculators, we must divide the 6.5 percent annual rate by 12 to determine the monthly rate of interest that we will enter for the i key. We would enter the information in our financial calculator and solve as follows:

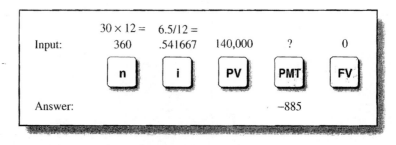

So we enter 360 for n, .541667 for i, 140,000 for PV, and 0 for FV. Then we press the PMT key and the calculator determines that the payment will be $885. Keep in mind that the $885 only pays the interest and principal on the loan. You will also have to pay homeowner's insurance and property taxes on the property, which could add significantly to the monthly payment. For our purposes, we will focus on the $885 principal and interest.

Assume that you feel the payment amount is affordable, but the term of the loan seems way too long. What if the term of the loan were cut in half? Instead of a 30-year loan, the term would be only 15 years. Will the payments nearly double if we have to pay the loan off in half the time? No, the monthly payment will increase substantially, but the new payment will be far less than double. We would enter the change in our financial calculator and solve as follows:

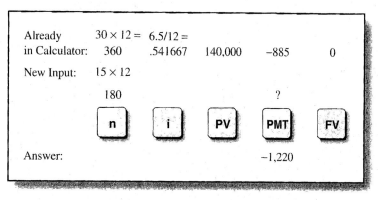

Assume that the $1,220 payment is acceptable and you inform the bank that you would like a 15-year loan. The interest rate for a 15-year loan will probably be less than that for a 30-year loan. Assume the bank reduces the rate to 6.25% due to the shorter loan term. We would enter the change in our financial calculator and solve as follows:

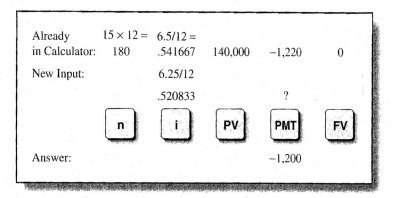

By reducing the interest rate from 6.5 percent to 6.25 percent, our monthly payment would go down by $20 per month.

Home Mortgages and Income Taxes   Although it is beyond the scope of this text, you should be aware that the interest paid on a home mortgage and home property taxes are deductible for federal income tax purposes. This basically means that within certain tax guidelines, taxpayers are permitted to reduce their taxable income by the amount of interest and taxes they pay on their home. On the $140,000, 15-year, 6.25 percent mortgage, the interest for the first year would be about $8,585. If we assume the property taxes are $1,200 annually then taxable income would be reduced by a total of 9,785 ($8,585 + $1,200). Assuming the taxpayer is in the 30 percent tax bracket, the tax savings for the first year is roughly $2,936, or, on average, about $245 per month. What this means to you is that when you are deciding whether to invest in a home instead of continuing to rent, don't overlook the tax savings associated with home ownership.

Whether you are evaluating potential capital projects or a home mortgage, a financial calculator can quickly and easily provide you with a wealth of valuable information. A financial calculator is truly worth every penny it costs, and learning how to use one is time very well spent.

Key Terms ●

- accounting rate of return, M–223
- annuity, M–231
- blended cost of capital, M–210
- capital assets, M–207
- capital budget, M–207
- capital budgeting, M–203
- capital investments, M–203
- capital projects, M–203
- compound interest, M–228
- cost of capital, M–209
- cost of capital rate, M–209
- cost of debt capital, M–210

- cost of equity capital, M–210
- discounting cash flows, M–215
- financial calculator, M–236
- future value, M–227
- hurdle rate, M–209
- internal rate of return (IRR), M–220
- mission statement, M–205
- net cash flow, M–214
- net present value (NPV), M–215
- operating budget, M–207
- organizational goals, M–204
- payback period, M–222

- present value, M–231
- profitability index, M–219
- real rate of return, M–220
- relevant net cash flows, M–214
- required rate of return, M–209
- scarce resources, M–213
- simple interest, M–227
- strategic plan, M–205
- time-adjusted rate of return, M–220
- time value of money, M–215
- weighted average cost of capital, M–210

Review the Facts ●

A. What constitutes a firm's goals?

B. What is a mission statement and how does it relate to a company's goals?

C. What is a strategic plan and how does it relate to a company's goals?

D. What is the purpose of a capital budget and how does it relate to the strategic plan and a company's goals?

E. What is the purpose of an operating budget and how does it relate to the capital budget, the strategic plan, and a company's goals?

F. What are capital investments?

G. What is the difference between a capital investment and a capital project?

H. What is the focus of the capital budget?

I. What does it mean when the cost of a purchased item is capitalized?

J. What does it mean when the cost of a purchased item is expensed?

K. What are the four shared characteristics of virtually all capital projects?

L. What are some other terms used to describe the cost of capital?

M. Describe what is meant by the net present value of an investment.

N. With respect to net present value calculations, what is the advantage of calculating the profitability index?

O. What is determined by the internal rate of return?

P. What is determined by the payback?

Q. What is the accounting rate of return?

R. What are two factors that can lead to poor capital project selection?

S. What is the basic difference between simple interest and compound interest? (Appendix)

T. What is an annuity? (Appendix)

Apply What You Have Learned ●

LO 1: MATCH ELEMENTS OF PLANNING TO CHARACTERISTICS

8–17. Following are the elements of the planning process as discussed in this chapter, with some characteristics pertaining to those elements.

a. Goals
b. Strategic plan
c. Capital budget
d. Operating budget

1. _____ Pertains to day-to-day activities
2. _____ Pertains to the allocation of scarce resources
3. _____ Consists of both financial and nonfinancial considerations
4. _____ Stated in terms that are not easily quantified
5. _____ Stated in terms that are easily quantified
6. _____ Constitutes the who of business planning
7. _____ Constitutes the why of business planning
8. _____ Constitutes the how of business planning
9. _____ Constitutes the what of business planning
10. _____ Relates to long-lived, expensive assets

Required: Match each element of the planning process with the appropriate characteristics. Each letter may be used more than once.

LO 4: DISCUSS AND CALCULATE THE COST OF CAPITAL

8–18. The Marcus Company is in the process of determining a return rate to use for its cost of capital. Upon review of the financial statements it was determined that the total interest bearing debt is $1,400,000 and total stockholders equity is $1,000,000. In addition, it was determined that the cost of debt financing is 8 percent, and the cost of equity financing is 18 percent.

Required:

    a. What proportion of the Marcus Company's total financing comes from debt?
    b. What proportion of the Marcus Company's total financing comes from equity?
    c. Calculate the Marcus Company's weighted average cost of capital rate.

LO 4: DISCUSS AND CALCULATE THE COST OF CAPITAL

8–19. The Byrne Company is in the process of determining a return rate to use for its cost of capital. Upon review of the financial statements it was determined that the total interest bearing debt is $4,800,000 and total stockholders' equity is $14,400,000. In addition, it was determined that the cost of debt financing is 7 percent, and the cost of equity financing is 22 percent.

Required:

    a. What proportion of The Byrne Company's total financing comes from debt?
    b. What proportion of The Byrne Company's total financing comes from equity?
    c. Calculate The Byrne Company's weighted average cost of capital rate.

LO 4: DISCUSS AND CALCULATE THE COST OF CAPITAL

8–20. The Cunningham Company is in the process of determining a return rate to use for its cost of capital.

    Upon review of the financial statements it was determined that the total interest bearing debt is $800,000 and total stockholders' equity is $1,700,000. In addition, it was determined that the cost of debt financing is 9 percent, and the cost of equity financing is 20 percent.

Required:

    a. What proportion of The Cunningham Company's total financing comes from debt?
    b. What proportion of The Cunningham Company's total financing comes from equity?
    c. Calculate The Cunningham Company's weighted average cost of capital rate.

LO 2: DETERMINE THE SEQUENCE OF EVALUATING CAPITAL EXPENDITURES

8–21. Following in random order are the four steps for evaluating a capital expenditure:

    a. _____ Identify alternative capital projects.
    b. _____ Select a method for evaluating the alternatives.
    c. _____ Evaluate the alternatives and select the project or projects to be funded.
    d. _____ Determine relevant cash inflow and cash outflow information.

Required: In the space provided, indicate a logical sequence of the steps for evaluating a capital expenditure.

LO 6 & 7: DETERMINE NET PRESENT VALUE, NO RESIDUAL VALUE

8–22. Florence Kundrat owns Discount Fashions. She is contemplating the purchase of a soda machine, which would be used to sell soft drinks to customers for $0.75 each. The following estimates are available:

Initial outlay	$3,500
Annual cash inflow	$1,000
Cost of capital	10%
Estimated life of the soda machine	5 years
Estimated residual value of the soda machine	$0

Required: Determine the net present value of the soda machine purchase.

LO 6 & 7: DETERMINE NET PRESENT VALUE, NO RESIDUAL VALUE

8–23. Brianna Garcia is contemplating the purchase of an ice cream vending machine, which would be used to sell ice cream to customers for $2 each. The following estimates are available:

Initial outlay	$4,000
Annual cash inflow	$1,200
Cost of capital	12%
Estimated life of the ice cream machine	5 years
Estimated residual value of the ice cream machine	$0

Required: Determine the net present value of the ice cream machine purchase.

LO 6 & 7: DETERMINE NET PRESENT VALUE, NO RESIDUAL VALUE

8–24. Javier Cruz is contemplating the purchase of a machine that will automate the production of baseball bats in his factory. The following estimates are available:

Initial outlay	$97,000
Annual reduction in manufacturing labor cost	$22,500
Cost of capital	14%
Estimated life of the baseball bat machine	8 years
Estimated residual value of the bat machine	$0

Required: Determine the net present value of the baseball bat machine purchase.

LO 6 & 7: DETERMINE NET PRESENT VALUE, NO RESIDUAL VALUE

8–25. Dahlia Garcia is contemplating the purchase of a machine that will automate the production of hosiery in her factory. The following estimates are available:

Initial outlay	$112,000
Annual reduction in manufacturing labor cost	$22,500
Cost of capital	12%
Estimated life of the hosiery machine	8 years
Estimated residual value of the hosiery machine	$0

Required: Determine the net present value of the hosiery machine purchase.

LO 6 & 7: DETERMINE NET PRESENT VALUE AND PROFITABILITY INDEX, VARIOUS RATES, NO RESIDUAL VALUE

8–26. Michael Diaz Sporting Goods is considering the purchase of a machine that is used to cut material to make baseball gloves. The cost of the machine is $265,000. The machine has an estimated useful life of eight years, with no residual value. Currently, the company leases a similar machine for $50,000 per year. If the new machine is purchased, the company's cost of labor would be reduced by $12,000 per year.

Required:

    a. Determine the net present value of the machine under each of the following assumptions:

        1. The cost of capital is 12 percent.
        2. The cost of capital is 14 percent.
        3. The cost of capital is 16 percent.

    b. Determine the profitability index under each of the following assumptions:

        1. The cost of capital is 12 percent.
        2. The cost of capital is 14 percent.
        3. The cost of capital is 16 percent.

LO 6 & 7: DETERMINE NET PRESENT VALUE AND PROFITABILITY INDEX, VARIOUS RATES, NO RESIDUAL VALUE

8–27. Carlos Urriola Manufacturing is considering the purchase of a computer-controlled manufacturing machine that is used in its factory. The cost of the machine $3,600,000. The machine has an estimated useful life of 10 years, with no residual value. If the new machine is purchased, the company's cost of labor would be reduced by $650,000 per year.

Required:

   a. Determine the net present value of the machine under each of the following assumptions:
1. The cost of capital is 10 percent.
2. The cost of capital is 12 percent.
3. The cost of capital is 14 percent.

   b. Determine the profitability index under each of the following assumptions:
1. The cost of capital is 10 percent.
2. The cost of capital is 12 percent.
3. The cost of capital is 14 percent.

LO 6 & 7: DETERMINE NET PRESENT VALUE, NO RESIDUAL VALUE

8–28. Frank Eiroa is considering the purchase of an engine lift for use in his marine repair business. He has determined that a used lift is available for $5,500. The engine lift has an estimated useful life of eight years and a residual value of zero. Currently, Frank rents engine lifts as needed. If the lift is purchased, annual rental payment of $1,400 would be saved. The cost of capital is 16 percent.

Required: Calculate the net present value of the engine lift purchase.

LO 6 & 7: DETERMINE NET PRESENT VALUE, NO RESIDUAL VALUE

8–29. Alfredo Lomando is considering the purchase of an industrial glass cutting machine for use in his business. He has determined that a used glass cutter is available for $25,800. The cutter has an estimated useful life of 10 years and a residual value of zero. Currently, Alfredo rents an industrial cutter for $4,400 annually. The cost of capital is 14 percent.

Required: Calculate the net present value of the industrial glass cutter.

LO 6 & 7: DETERMINE NET PRESENT VALUE, WITH RESIDUAL VALUE

8–30. The owner of Wynn Sports Cards is contemplating the purchase of a machine which will automate the production of baseball cards in her factory. The following estimates are available:

Initial outlay	$35,000
Annual reduction in manufacturing labor cost	$8,500
Cost of capital	14%
Estimated life of the card machine	5 years
Estimated residual value of the card machine	$2,000

Required: Determine the net present value of the baseball card machine purchase.

LO 6 & 7: DETERMINE NET PRESENT VALUE, WITH RESIDUAL VALUE

8–31. Kevin Petty owns Discount Parts, Inc. He is contemplating the purchase of a brake lathe that could be used to refurbish brake parts for customers. The following estimates are available:

Initial outlay	$6,500
Annual cash inflow	$1,500
Cost of capital	16%
Estimated life of the brake lathe	6 years
Estimated residual value of the brake lathe	$1,000

Required: Determine the net present value of the brake lathe purchase.

LO 6 & 7: DETERMINE NET PRESENT VALUE, WITH RESIDUAL VALUE

8–32. Paola Grillon owns Grillon Skin Care Products. She is contemplating the purchase of an industrial mixer that would be used to mix cosmetics in her factory. The following estimates are available:

Initial outlay	$78,500
Annual cash inflow	$19,500
Cost of capital	16%
Estimated life of the mixer	7 years
Estimated residual value of the mixer	$4,000

Required: Determine the net present value of the industrial mixer purchase.

LO 6 & 7: DETERMINE NET PRESENT VALUE, WITH RESIDUAL VALUE

8–33. Elianne Vinas owns Vinas Shoe Company. She is contemplating the purchase of a cutting machine that would be used to make shoes in her factory. The following estimates are available:

Initial outlay	$58,000
Annual cash inflow from reduced labor cost	$11,500
Cost of capital	12%
Estimated life of the cutter	8 years
Estimated residual value of the cutter	$2,000

Required: Determine the net present value of the cutting machine purchase.

LO 6 & 7: DETERMINE NET PRESENT VALUE AND PROFITABILITY INDEX, VARIOUS RATES, WITH RESIDUAL VALUE

8–34. George Gonzalez Construction Company is considering the purchase of a new road grader. The cost of the road grader is $68,000. The road grader has an estimated useful life of seven years and an estimated residual value of $5,000. Currently, the company rents road graders as needed. If the road grader is purchased, annual rental payments of $17,000 would be saved.

Required:

    a. Determine the net present value of the grader purchase under each of the following assumptions:

        1. The cost of capital is 12 percent.
        2. The cost of capital is 14 percent.
        3. The cost of capital is 16 percent.

    b. Determine the profitability index under each of the following assumptions:

        1. The cost of capital is 12 percent.
        2. The cost of capital is 14 percent.
        3. The cost of capital is 16 percent.

LO 6 & 7: DETERMINE NET PRESENT VALUE AND PROFITABILITY INDEX, VARIOUS RATES, WITH RESIDUAL VALUE

8–35. Wesley Parks Pencil Company is considering the purchase of a new machine to make pencils. The cost of the machine is $248,000. The pencil machine has an estimated useful life of 10 years and an estimated residual value of $25,000. Currently, the company leases a similar machine for $45,000 per year.

Required:

    a. Determine the net present value of the pencil machine purchase under each of the following assumptions:

        1. The cost of capital is 10 percent.
        2. The cost of capital is 12 percent.
        3. The cost of capital is 14 percent.

    b. Determine the profitability index under each of the following assumptions:

        1. The cost of capital is 10 percent.
        2. The cost of capital is 12 percent.
        3. The cost of capital is 14 percent.

LO 6 & 7: DETERMINE NET PRESENT VALUE AND PROFITABILITY INDEX, VARIOUS RATES, WITH RESIDUAL VALUE

8–36. Sylvia Heain's Catering Service is considering the purchase of new energy-efficient cooking equipment. The cost of the new equipment is $78,000. The equipment has an estimated useful life of eight years and an estimated residual value of $5,000. Currently, the company leases similar cooking equipment for $10,000 per year. If the new cooking equipment is purchased, the company's cost of electricity would be reduced by $8,000 per year.

Required:

  a. Determine the net present value of the cooking equipment under each of the following assumptions:

    1. The cost of capital is 12 percent.
    2. The cost of capital is 14 percent.
    3. The cost of capital is 16 percent.

  b. Determine the profitability index under each of the following assumptions:

    1. The cost of capital is 12 percent.
    2. The cost of capital is 14 percent.
    3. The cost of capital is 16 percent.

LO 6 & 7: DETERMINE INTERNAL RATE OF RETURN, VARIOUS RATES, NO RESIDUAL VALUE

8–37. Penny Williams is contemplating the purchase of a new computer system for her company, Williams Manufacturing. She has made the following estimates:

Initial outlay	$18,023.88
Annual cash savings	$5,000.00
Estimated life of the computer	5 years
Estimated residual value of the computer	$0

Required:

  a. Determine the internal rate of return for the computer purchase.
  b. Indicate whether the computer purchase should be accepted under each of the following assumptions.

    1. The cost of capital is 9 percent.
    2. The cost of capital is 11 percent.
    3. The cost of capital is 13 percent.
    4. The cost of capital is 15 percent.

LO 6 & 7: DETERMINE INTERNAL RATE OF RETURN, VARIOUS RATES, NO RESIDUAL VALUE

8–38. Valdez Moving and Storage is contemplating the purchase of a new delivery truck. The following estimates are available:

Initial outlay	$51,590
Annual cash flow from the new truck	$14,000.00
Estimated life of the truck	6 years
Estimated residual value of the truck	$−0

Required:

  a. Determine the internal rate of return for the truck purchase.
  b. Indicate whether the truck purchase should be accepted under each of the following assumptions.

    1. The cost of capital is 14 percent.
    2. The cost of capital is 16 percent.
    3. The cost of capital is 18 percent.

LO 6 & 7: DETERMINE INTERNAL RATE OF RETURN FOR THREE PROJECTS, SELECT PROJECT, NO RESIDUAL VALUE

8–39. Hank Maupin & Company is in the process of replacing its existing computer system. The following three proposals are being considered:

	System A	System B	System C
Initial outlay	$18,023.88	$22,744.72	$24,031.57
Annual cash savings	$5,000.00	$6,000.00	$7,000.00
Estimated useful life	5 years	5 years	5 years

The estimated residual value of all computer systems under consideration is zero.

Required:

    a. Determine the internal rate of return for each of the proposed computer systems.

    b. Which computer system would you recommend? Explain your reasoning.

LO 6 & 7: DETERMINE INTERNAL RATE OF RETURN FOR THREE PROJECTS, SELECT PROJECT, NO RESIDUAL VALUE

8–40. David Wilson Equipment Company is in the process of selecting some new manufacturing equipment. The following three proposals are being considered:

	Equipment A	Equipment B	Equipment C
Initial outlay	$14,902.92	$18,555.46	$26,674.63
Annual cash savings	$3,000.00	$4,000.00	$5,000.00
Estimated useful life	8 years	8 years	8 years

The estimated residual value of all equipment under consideration is zero.

Required:

    a. Determine the internal rate of return for each of the proposed pieces of equipment.

    b. Which piece of equipment would you recommend? Explain your reasoning.

LO 6 & 7: DETERMINE NET PRESENT VALUE, PROFITABILITY INDEX, AND INTERNAL RATE OF RETURN, VARIOUS RATES, NO RESIDUAL VALUE

8–41. Dunn Manufacturing Company is considering the purchase of a factory that makes valves. These valves would be used by Dunn to manufacture water pumps. The purchase would require an initial outlay of $1,564,800. The factory would have an estimated life of 10 years and no residual value. Currently, the company buys 500,000 valves per year at a cost of $1.50 each. If the factory were purchased, the valves could be manufactured for $0.90 each.

Required:

    a. Determine the net present value of the proposed project and whether it should be accepted under each of the following assumptions.

        1. The cost of capital is 12 percent.

        2. The cost of capital is 14 percent.

        3. The cost of capital is 16 percent.

    b. Determine the profitability index under each of the following assumptions.

        1. The cost of capital is 12 percent.

        2. The cost of capital is 14 percent.

        3. The cost of capital is 16 percent.

    c. Determine the internal rate of return of the proposed project and indicate whether it should be accepted under each of the following assumptions.

        1. The cost of capital is 12 percent.

        2. The cost of capital is 14 percent.

        3. The cost of capital is 16 percent.

LO 6: DETERMINE PAYBACK PERIOD, EVEN CASH FLOWS

✓ 8–42. Tom Robinson owns Discount Hardware. He is contemplating the purchase of a copy machine which would be used to make copies to sell to customers for five cents each. The following estimates are available:

Initial outlay	$4,500
Annual cash inflow	$1,800

Required: Determine the payback period for the copy machine purchase.

LO 6: DETERMINE PAYBACK PERIOD, EVEN CASH FLOWS

8–43. Rebecca Pons owns Pons Magic Makers Manufacturing. She is contemplating the purchase of a machine that would be used to manufacture various products that would be sold to magic shops. The following estimates are available:

Initial outlay	$23,539.20
Annual cash inflow	$7,356.00

Required: Determine the payback period for the machine purchase.

LO 6: DETERMINE PAYBACK PERIOD, EVEN CASH FLOWS

8–44. Claudia Vargas is contemplating the purchase of a machine that would be used in her business. The following estimates are available:

Initial outlay	$5,826.50
Annual cash inflow	$1,355.00

Required: Determine the payback period for the machine purchase.

LO 6: DETERMINE PAYBACK PERIOD, EVEN CASH FLOWS

8–45. Cesar Nieto is contemplating the purchase of a machine that would be used in his business. The following estimates are available:

Initial outlay	$323,400.00
Annual cash inflow	$33,000.00

Required: Determine the payback period for the machine purchase.

LO 6: DETERMINE PAYBACK PERIOD, UNEVEN CASH FLOWS

8–46. Junior Gonzales Racing Fuel is considering the purchase of a fuel truck that he would use to sell gasoline at motor sport racing events in Puerto Rico. He has determined that a used truck is available for $11,000. He believes that the cash inflows would grow each year as he is able to sign fuel supply contracts at more and more events. He has made the following cash inflow estimates:

First year	$3,000
Second year	$4,500
Third and subsequent years	$5,000

Required: Determine the payback period for the purchase of the fuel truck.

LO 6: DETERMINE PAYBACK PERIOD, UNEVEN CASH FLOWS

8–47. Veronica Torres is considering opening a ceramic studio. She has determined that it would require an investment of $14,000 to open the store. She believes that the cash inflows would grow each year as more and more people learn of the store. She has made the following cash inflow estimates:

First year	$2,000
Second year	$4,000
Third and subsequent years	$5,000

Required: Determine the payback period for the ceramic studio.

LO 6: DETERMINE PAYBACK PERIOD, UNEVEN CASH FLOWS

8–48. Karen Calloway is considering adding a new style of gym shorts to her product line. She has determined that it would require an investment of $22,000 to add the new style shorts. She believes that the cash inflows would grow each year as the new style becomes more popular. She has made the following cash inflow estimates:

First year	$4,000
Second year	$6,000
Third and subsequent years	$10,000

Required: Determine the payback period for the new style of gym shorts.

LO 6: DETERMINE ACCOUNTING RATE OF RETURN

8–49. BRV Construction Company is contemplating the purchase of scaffolding at the cost of $32,000. Currently, the company rents similar scaffolding for use at each of its construction sites. The scaffolding has an estimated useful life of five years and an estimated residual value of $2,000. By purchasing the scaffolding, BRV could save rental fees of $11,760 per year.

Required: Determine the accounting rate of return for BRV's investment in the scaffolding.

LO 6: DETERMINE ACCOUNTING RATE OF RETURN

8–50. Smith and Smith & Associates is contemplating the purchase of equipment that would cost $196,600. Currently, the company rents similar equipment for $45,076 per year. The proposed new equipment has an estimated useful life of eight years and an estimated residual value of $9,000.

Required: Determine the accounting rate of return for the Smith and Smith & Associates investment in the new equipment.

LO 6: DETERMINE ACCOUNTING RATE OF RETURN

8–51. Condore & Company is contemplating the purchase of a machine that would cost $142,790. The machine would provide an annual contribution margin of $47,262.55 each year. The proposed new machine has an estimated useful life of five years and an estimated residual value of $10,000.

Required: Determine the accounting rate of return for Condore & Company's investment in the new machine.

LO 5, 6, & 7: DETERMINE RELEVANT INFORMATION, NET PRESENT VALUE, SCREEN PROJECT, WITH RESIDUAL VALUE

8–52. Frank's Marine Service purchased a forklift five years ago for $16,000. When it was purchased, the forklift had an estimated useful life of 10 years and a residual value of $4,000. The forklift can be sold now for $6,000. The operating cost for the forklift is $4,500 per year.

Frank is thinking about buying a newer forklift for $17,000. The newer forklift would have an estimated useful life of five years and a residual value of $7,000. The operating cost for the newer forklift would be 3,000 per year.

The company's cost of capital is 10 percent.

Required:

a. Prepare a relevant cost schedule showing the benefits of buying the new forklift. (For this requirement, ignore the time value of money.)
b. How much must the company invest today to replace the old forklift?
c. If the company replaces the old forklift, what is the increase in the company's annual contribution margin?
d. If the company sells the old forklift now to make room for the new one, it will not receive the $4,000 residual value at the end of its useful life. Instead, the company will receive the $7,000 residual value from the new forklift. With this in mind, if the company buys the forklift, what is the change in the residual value the company is to receive at the end of the five-year life of the equipment?
e. Calculate the net present value of replacing the old forklift.
f. Do you think the company should replace the old forklift?

LO 5, 6, & 7: DETERMINE RELEVANT INFORMATION, NET PRESENT VALUE, SCREEN PROJECT, WITH RESIDUAL VALUE

8–53. Al Hart of Hart Engineering is considering the purchase of a new copy machine. He purchased the old machine two years ago for $8,500. When it was purchased the old machine had an estimated useful life of eight years and a residual value of $500. The operating cost of the old machine is $3,000 per year. The old machine can be sold today for $2,000. A new machine can be bought today for $10,000 and would have an estimated useful life of six years with a residual value of $1,000. The operating cost of the new copy machine is expected to be $1,500 per year. The company's cost of capital is 8 percent.

Required:

a. Prepare a relevant cost schedule showing the benefit of buying the new copy machine. (For this requirement, ignore the time value of money.)
b. How much must the company invest today to replace the old copy machine?
c. If the company replaces the old copy machine, what is the increase in the company's annual contribution margin?

d. If the company sells the old copy machine now to make room for the new one, it will not receive the $500 residual value at the end of its useful life. Instead, the company will receive the $1,000 residual value from the new copy machine. With this in mind, if the company buys the copy machine, what is the change in the residual value the company is to receive at the end of the six-year life of the equipment?

e. Calculate the net present value of replacing the old copy machine.

f. Do you think the company should replace the old copy machine?

LO 5, 6, & 7: DETERMINE RELEVANT INFORMATION, NET PRESENT VALUE, SCREEN PROJECT, NO RESIDUAL VALUE

8–54. The managers at AAA Manufacturing Company are considering replacing an industrial mixer used in the company's factory. The company's cost of capital is 10 percent.

Information about the old mixer:

Cost	$28,000
Estimated useful life	10 years
Estimated residual value	$0
Current age	5 years
Estimated current fair value	$8,000
Annual operating cost	$18,000

Information about the new mixer:

Cost	$34,000
Estimated useful life	5 years
Estimated residual value	$0
Annual operating cost	$12,000

Required:

a. Prepare a relevant cost schedule showing the benefit of buying the new mixer.

b. How much must the company invest today to replace the industrial mixer?

c. If the new mixer is purchased, how much would be saved in operating costs each year?

d. How much would the company receive at the end of the five-year useful life of the new mixer?

e. Calculate the net present value of replacing the old mixer.

f. Do you think the company should replace the old mixer?

LO 5, 6, & 7: DETERMINE RELEVANT INFORMATION, NET PRESENT VALUE, SCREEN PROJECT, NO RESIDUAL VALUE

8–55. The managers at General Manufacturing Company are considering replacing the industrial lathe used in the company's factory. The company's cost of capital is 12 percent.

Information about the old lathe:

Cost	$57,000
Estimated useful life	8 years
Estimated residual value	$0
Current age	2 years
Estimated current fair value	$32,000
Annual operating cost	$32,000

Information about the new lathe:

Cost	$61,000
Estimated useful life	6 years
Estimated residual value	$0
Annual operating cost	$24,000

Required:

a. Prepare a relevant cost schedule showing the benefit of buying the new lathe. (For this requirement, ignore the time value of money.)

b. How much must the company invest today to replace the old lathe?

c. If the company replaces the old lathe, how much will be saved in operating costs each year?

d. Calculate the net present value of replacing the old lathe.

e. Do you think the company should replace the old lathe?

LO 5, 6, & 7: DETERMINE RELEVANT INFORMATION, NET PRESENT VALUE, SCREEN PROJECT, WITH RESIDUAL VALUE

8–56. John Paul Hudik, president of Hudik Boat Hauling, is considering replacing the company's industrial lift used to haul boats. The new lift would allow the company to lift larger boats out of the water. The company's cost of capital is 14 percent.

Information about the old lift:

Cost	$94,000
Estimated useful life	12 years
Estimated residual value	$10,000
Current age	4 years
Estimated current fair value	$48,000
Annual contribution margin	$50,000

Information about the new lift:

Cost	$128,000
Estimated useful life	8 years
Estimated residual value	$25,000
Annual contribution margin	$65,000

Required:

a. Prepare a relevant cost schedule showing the benefit of buying the new lift. (For this requirement, ignore the time value of money.)
b. How much must the company invest today to replace the old lift?
c. If the company replaces the old lift, what is the increase in the company's annual contribution margin?
d. If the company sells the old lift now to make room for the new one, it will not receive the $10,000 residual value at the end of its useful life. Instead, the company will receive the $25,000 residual value from the new lift. With this in mind, if the company buys the new lift, what is the change in the residual value the company is to receive at the end of the eight-year life of the equipment?
e. Calculate the net present value of replacing the old lift.
f. Do you think the company should replace the old lift?

LO 5, 6, & 7: DETERMINE RELEVANT INFORMATION, NET PRESENT VALUE, SCREEN PROJECT, WITH RESIDUAL VALUE

8–57. The managers at Wilma Manufacturing are considering replacing a printing press with a new, high-speed model. The company's cost of capital is 12 percent.

Information about the old printing press:

Cost	$255,000
Estimated useful life	10 years
Estimated residual value	$25,000
Annual depreciation	$23,000
Current age	3 years
Accumulated depreciation to date	$184,000
Estimated current fair value	$150,000
Annual contribution margin	$110,000

Information about the new printing press:

Cost	$535,000
Estimated useful life	7 years
Estimated residual value	$45,000
Annual depreciation	$70,000
Annual contribution margin	$150,000

Required:

a. Prepare a relevant cost schedule showing the benefit of buying the new printing press. (For this requirement, ignore the time value of money.)
b. How much must the company invest today to replace the old printing press?
c. If the company replaces the old printing press, what is the increase in the company's annual contribution margin?

d. If the company sells the old printing press now to make room for the new one, it will not receive the $25,000 residual value at the end of its useful life. Instead, the company will receive the $45,000 residual value from the new printing press. With this in mind, if the company buys the printing press, what is the change in the residual value the company is to receive at the end of the seven-year life of the equipment?
e. Calculate the net present value of replacing the old printing press.
f. Do you think the company should replace the old printing press?

APPENDIX

LO 7: CALCULATE SIMPLE, COMPOUND INTEREST, FULL YEARS

8–58. Greg Gluck Marine borrowed $5,000 from National Bank on January 1, 2004.

Required:

a. Assuming 9 percent simple interest is charged, calculate interest for 2004, 2005, and 2006.
b. Assuming 9 percent compound interest is charged, calculate interest for 2004, 2005, and 2006.

LO 7: CALCULATE SIMPLE, COMPOUND INTEREST, FULL YEARS

8–59. Gary borrowed $8,000 from Orlando National Bank on January 1, 2004.

Required:

a. Assuming 8 percent simple interest is charged, calculate interest for 2004, 2005, and 2006.
b. Assuming 8 percent compound interest is charged, calculate interest for 2004, 2005, and 2006.

LO 7: CALCULATE SIMPLE, COMPOUND INTEREST, FULL YEARS

8–60. Cam borrowed $2,000 from Miami National Bank on January 1, 2004.

Required:

a. Assuming 6 percent simple interest is charged, calculate interest for 2004, 2005, and 2006.
b. Assuming 6 percent compound interest is charged, calculate interest for 2004, 2005, and 2006.

LO 7: CALCULATE FUTURE VALUE, SINGLE CASH FLOW, VARIOUS RATES AND MATURITIES

8–61. Susan Jones made the following investments on January 1, 2004:

1. $2,000 at 10 percent for 5 years
2. $12,000 at 4 percent for 8 years
3. $9,000 at 14 percent for 15 years

Assume the interest on each investment is compounded annually.

Required: Calculate the future value of each of the investments listed above at their maturity.

LO 7: CALCULATE FUTURE VALUE, SINGLE CASH FLOW, VARIOUS RATES AND MATURITIES

8–62. Ivan Zhang made the following investments on January 1, 2004:

1. $3,000 at 8 percent for 6 years
2. $4,000 at 6 percent for 8 years
3. $5,000 at 10 percent for 5 years

Assume the interest on each investment is compounded annually.

Required: Calculate the future value of each of the investments listed above at their maturity.

LO 7: CALCULATE FUTURE VALUE, SINGLE CASH FLOW, VARIOUS RATES AND MATURITIES

8–63. Orlando Gonzalez made the following investments on January 1, 2004:

1. $1,000 at 14 percent for 3 years
2. $2,000 at 10 percent for 5 years
3. $4,000 at 8 percent for 8 years

Assume the interest on each investment is compounded annually.

Required: Calculate the future value of each of the investments listed above at their maturity.

LO 7: CALCULATE FUTURE VALUE, YEARLY CASH FLOWS, VARIOUS RATES AND MATURITIES

8–64. Consider the following investments:

1. $2,000 at the end of each of the next five years at 10 percent interest compounded annually.
2. $12,000 at the end of each of the next eight years at 4 percent interest compounded annually.
3. $9,000 at the end of each of the next 15 years at 14 percent interest compounded annually.

Required: Calculate the future value of each of the investments listed above at their maturity.

LO 7: CALCULATE FUTURE VALUE, YEARLY CASH FLOWS, VARIOUS RATES AND MATURITIES

8–65. Consider the following investments.

1. $12,000 at the end of each of the next three years at 12 percent interest compounded annually.
2. $16,000 at the end of each of the next five years at 10 percent interest compounded annually.
3. $20,000 at the end of each of the next 10 years at 8 percent interest compounded annually.

Required: Calculate the future value of each of the investments listed above at their maturity.

LO 7: CALCULATE FUTURE VALUE, YEARLY CASH FLOWS, VARIOUS RATES AND MATURITIES

8–66. Consider the following investments.

1. $1,000 at the end of each of the next five years at 6 percent interest compounded annually.
2. $1,000 at the end of each of the next five years at 8 percent interest compounded annually.
3. $1,000 at the end of each of the next five years at 10 percent interest compounded annually.

Required: Calculate the future value of each of the investments listed above at their maturity.

LO 7: CALCULATE PRESENT VALUE, SINGLE CASH FLOW, SINGLE RATE

8–67. Jim Johnson is planning to buy a new car when he graduates from college in three years. He would like to invest a single amount now, in order to have the $24,000 he estimates the car will cost.

Required: Calculate the amount Jim must invest today, to have enough to buy the new car assuming his investment will earn 4 percent compounded annually for the three-year investment.

LO 7: CALCULATE PRESENT VALUE, SINGLE CASH FLOW, SINGLE RATE

8–68. Lowell Pitman needs to have $50,000 at the end of five years. Lowell would like to invest a single amount now, to have the $50,000 in five years.

Required: Calculate the amount Lowell must invest today to have the amount of money he needs assuming his investment will earn 8 percent compounded annually for the five-year investment.

LO 7: CALCULATE PRESENT VALUE, SINGLE CASH FLOW, SINGLE RATE

8–69. Lauren Elsea is planning to buy a house when she graduates from college. She would like to have $20,000 for the down payment. Lauren would like to invest a single amount now, to have the $20,000 at the end of three years.

Required: Calculate the amount Lauren must invest today, to have the amount of money she needs assuming her investment will earn 6 percent compounded annually for the three year investment.

LO 7: CALCULATE PRESENT VALUE, YEARLY CASH FLOWS, SINGLE RATE

8–70. Linda Chidister is planning to send her son, Edward, to college. While he is in college, Linda intends to give him $3,000 at the end of each year.

Required: How much must Linda invest today so she will have enough to give Edward $3,000 at the end of each of the next four years assuming the investment will earn 6 percent interest?

LO 7: CALCULATE PRESENT VALUE, YEARLY CASH FLOWS, SINGLE RATE

8–71. Alex Malpin is planning to spend the next three years doing research in China. An Asian studies research institute has agreed to pay Alex $20,000 at the end of each of the three years he is in China.

Required: How much must be invested today to have enough to pay Alex $20,000 at the end of each of the next three years assuming the investment will earn 10 percent interest.

LO 7: CALCULATE PRESENT VALUE, YEARLY CASH FLOWS, SINGLE RATE

8–72. Photo Factory is planning to purchase some photo processing equipment from Ace Equipment Company. The equipment will provide cash flow of $15,000 at the end of each of the next eight years.

Required: How much should Photo Factory pay for the equipment assuming it will provide $15,000 at the end of each of the next eight years and Ace has promised that it will earn a return of exactly 14 percent?

CHAPTER 9

The Operating Budget

operating budget A budget for a specific period, usually one to five years, that establishes who is responsible for the day-to-day operation of a business during that time.

master operating budget Another name for operating budget.

master budget Another name for operating budget.

Imagine that one morning midway through your accounting class, you and three of your classmates decide to go to Paris. The four of you stand up, excuse yourselves, and set out for the airport, where you discover that the next flight to France departs in four hours and that there are only three seats available. You buy three tickets, send one friend back to class, and head to the gate.

When you arrive in Paris, one of your friends asks, "Well, we're here. What now?" You respond, "I don't know, this was a spur-of-the-moment thing. We have the freedom to do whatever we want!" But suddenly your classmates are not feeling so spontaneous. In fact, they're riddled with concerns. "Where will we stay? Did you bring any money? Who has a French/English dictionary? Now that we're here, how long will we stay? What will we do? We didn't bring any clothes. How are we getting home?"

What's wrong with this adventure? Well, let's just say it could have used a bit more planning. Thoughtful planning increases the possibility of succeeding in almost anything we undertake.

Careful planning is, in fact, a key element of business success. Without planning, business activities founder and a company almost certainly loses direction. In Chapter 8 we described planning as the *why,* the *what,* the *how,* and the *who* of being in business. Recall that the *why* is the process of setting company goals. The *what* is the strategic plan to implement those goals in the long-term. These two planning elements were discussed in some detail in Chapter 8. The *how* is the process of capital budgeting to allocate scarce resources and was the major topic of Chapter 8.

The *who* is the final step—the operating budget. The **operating budget** is a budget for a specific time, usually one to five years, that establishes who is responsible for the day-to-day operation of the business during that time. This budget is also sometimes called the **master operating budget** or simply the **master budget.** For the sake of consistency, we will use the term *operating budget* throughout our discussions of this topic.

The operating budget will be an important part of your business life, regardless of your occupation or the type of company for which you choose to work. Whether the organization is for-profit or not-for-profit, and whether it is a service, merchandising, or manufacturing firm, budgeting has become increasingly important in charting the success of today's organizations. Gone are the days when companies could succeed on simple luck and optimism. Gone, too, are the days when a select group of top managers prepared operating budgets with little input from others in the organization. Many companies today involve all managers and employees in the budgeting process. *Fortune* 500 companies such as ***General Dynamics, Honeywell, General Motors,*** and others have recognized that better budgeting is achieved when they involve those who actually work in the area or function for which the budget is being prepared. As you read the pages that follow, we hope you remember that budgets will be an important ingredient in your personal business success, and that you will very likely be involved in the budgeting process much earlier in your career than you may expect.

This chapter is divided into two main parts. Part One is an overview of the operating budget, its purpose, and where it fits into the overall management process. Part Two is a detailed presentation of how the operating budget is actually prepared and how it should and should not be used by managers.

Learning Objectives

After completing your work on this chapter, you should be able to do the following:

1. Describe some of the benefits of the operating budget.
2. Describe the three budgeted financial statements contained in the operating budget and the other budgets that support the budgeted financial statements.
3. Compare and contrast various approaches to preparing and using the operating budget.
4. Describe the role of the sales forecast in the budgeting process.
5. Prepare various budgets included in the operating budget.
6. Describe the appropriate use of the operating budget in the overall management process.

Part I: An Overview of the Operating Budget

◆ THE OPERATING BUDGET: WHAT IS IT?

What exactly is an operating budget? We know it is the plan for a company's operating activities for some period of time, but what is in that plan? The operating budget includes a set of estimated financial statements.

Recall that the three main financial statements are the balance sheet, the income statement, and the statement of cash flows. Businesses prepare these statements at the end of a given time period to show the effects of past transactions and events. An operating budget contains those same three financial statements, except they are estimates—or forecasts—of future transactions and events. The forecasted financial statements in the operating budget are sometimes called pro forma financial statements. *Pro forma* is a Latin phrase meaning "provided in advance."

Because the operating budget is a set of estimated financial statements, much of what we will cover in this chapter will at least be familiar to you. The only difference between the financial statements businesses use to show the effects of past events and transactions and the ones you will explore in this chapter is that the budgeted financial statements are used to predict future events.

◆ BENEFITS OF BUDGETING

A well-prepared operating budget can create many benefits for the company. In this section, we will explore four of them. First, budgeting serves as a guide. Second, it helps organizations allocate resources. Third, it encourages communication and coordination. Fourth, it sets performance standards, or *benchmarks*.

SERVES AS A GUIDE

The operating budget should serve as a guide for a company to follow during the budgeted period. Recall the hypothetical trip to Paris we described in the chapter opener. Now lets assume that our travelers did have a plan after all. Suppose that while touring France, our travelers heard about a fantastic side trip (a terrific art show in Nice) not included in their original itinerary. Based on this new information, our travelers would probably adjust their original plan to allow for this side trip. And so it should be with a budget, because companies should adjust their budgets when desirable or necessary.

To illustrate, suppose the budget for Pam's Flower Shop forecasted sales revenue of $310,000 for the first three months of 2004. Business was better than expected and the flower shop had sales of $310,000 by the end of February. Should Pam close the flower shop until April 1 because she attained her budgeted sales figure for the quarter? Of course not. Or suppose Pam has the opportunity to purchase 20 dozen roses just before Valentine's Day at a bargain basement price. She can probably sell all of them for a whopping profit, but she didn't budget for this special purchase. What should she do? It may seem obvious that she should take advantage of this terrific opportunity, but a surprising number of businesses view the budget as "set in stone," so to speak, and meeting the budget becomes the primary business objective. An unwillingness to adjust a budget based on new information can be detrimental to a company because opportunities are missed and poor decisions made.

ASSISTS IN RESOURCE ALLOCATION

As discussed in Chapter 8, all organizations have scarce resources. No company can afford to do everything it desires, or even everything it needs to do within a given time period. A budget can help management decide where to allocate its limited resources.

The budgeting process may uncover potential bottlenecks and allow managers to address these issues in advance as the budget is being prepared, rather than as problems occur during the year. An example of a bottleneck in a manufacturing environment is presented for Montrose Manufacturing Company in Exhibit 9–1.

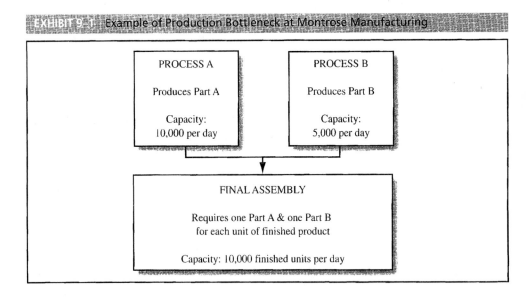

EXHIBIT 9–1 Example of Production Bottleneck at Montrose Manufacturing

As you can see from Exhibit 9–1, each unit of finished product Montrose manufactures requires one Part A and one Part B. The maximum number of finished units of product the company can produce per day is 5,000 even though the capacity of final assembly is 10,000 units per day. The limiting factor is Process B, which can produce only 5,000 parts per day. Montrose could increase the capacity of Process A from 10,000 parts per day to 100,000 parts per day and the company *still* could produce only 5,000 finished units per day because of the restriction caused by Process B. Process B is the bottleneck in this company's production process.

Assume Montrose Manufacturing Company moved some production machinery from Process A to Process B. This change reduces the capacity of Process A by 2,500 units per day, but increases the capacity of Process B by 2,500 units per day as reflected in Exhibit 9–2.

As you can see by looking at Exhibit 9–2, Montrose has increased its ability to produce finished units by 50 percent (from 5,000 units to 7,500 units) without adding any additional machinery to its operation, which is a significant factor if you recall our discussion of capital expenditures in Chapter 8.

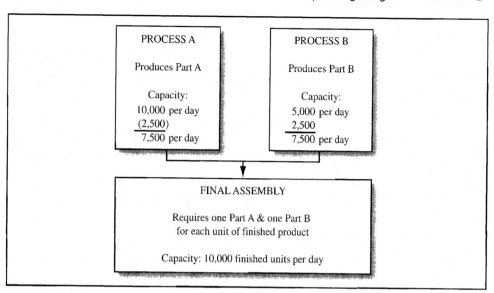

EXHIBIT 9-2   Elimination of Production Bottleneck at Montrose Manufacturing

The issue of resource allocation is also important for a merchandising business. For example, February may be so busy for Pam's Flower Shop that she will need extra workers. If Pam knows this in advance, she will have time to hire the needed workers at the least cost so she can offer quality service and sell more flowers. In contrast, if Pam does not plan for the February rush, she will find herself understaffed and unable to provide quality, timely service. She might lose customers before she could hire more workers, and sales could drop. Budgeting, then, helps Pam make good decisions about how to allocate her resources.

FOSTERS COMMUNICATION AND COORDINATION

As managers from different functional areas in an organization work together to prepare the budget, they gain a better understanding of the entire business. When managers from all areas learn of difficulties facing others and spot duplication of effort, the firm can then solve problems and coordinate efforts more effectively. Our previous example of Montrose Manufacturing Company and its production bottleneck points out the possibilities of increased communication and coordination through the budgeting process. In working to solve this production problem, the managers of Process A, Process B, and Final Assembly had the opportunity to view the production process from a broader perspective. Rather than concentrating only on their own part of the process, they were better able to understand the problems facing managers in other areas of the company's operations. They were forced to communicate with one another and to better coordinate their efforts.

Even for a small company like Pam's Flower Shop, success can depend on coordinating many activities. For example, Pam expects sales to increase in February because of Valentine's Day. She anticipates she will need more flowers to sell, and more labor to sell them. The number of extra workers, however, may depend on the amount of additional flowers ordered. When she prepares the budget, Pam speaks to the inventory manager and the personnel manager about the February rush to better coordinate their activities. Then the managers know in advance exactly what needs to be done.

ESTABLISHES PERFORMANCE STANDARDS

The operating budget also sets performance standards for an organization. As managers prepare budgets for their companies, they should establish performance goals that are lofty enough to be acceptable yet conservative enough to be attainable. If a company's actual sales, for example, are less than its budgeted sales for a particular period, the sales manager will review the deficit and ask why. Once she has learned why, she may be able to correct the problem causing the lagging sales, or she may find it necessary to adjust the budget for next time. Without a budget she might not notice the sales shortfall and therefore would not even know the problem exists.

Budgeted performance standards become benchmarks against which firms can compare actual results. Differences between the actual results and the budget can be explored and improvements made. The improvements may focus on performance, the budgeting process, or both.

Discussion Question

9–1. In what other ways do you think a company might benefit from preparing an operating budget?

◆ CONTENTS OF THE OPERATING BUDGET

Many of us have had to prepare a personal cash budget, in which we compare the amount of cash coming in to the amount of cash going out. Because of this personal experience with budgeting, many people think that business budgeting focuses only on budgeting for cash inflows and outflows. This view, however, is far too narrow. Remember, the operating budget is a set of estimated financial statements that includes the balance sheet, income statement, and statement of cash flows, regardless of whether the business preparing the budget is a manufacturer, a merchandiser, or a service company.

SALES BUDGET

sales forecast The prediction of sales in units or in dollars for the budget period.

sales budget Details the expected sales revenue from a company's primary operating activities during a certain time period.

The sales budget is the first budget prepared and is based on a sales forecast. A **sales forecast** is a prediction of sales in units or dollars for the budget period. We'll discuss the sales forecast in more detail later in this chapter. As the name implies, the **sales budget** details the expected sales revenue from a company's primary operating activities during a certain time period. Because manufacturers and merchandisers sell tangible, physical product, the sales budget is based on the number of units the firm expects to sell. The sales budget of a service business is based on the amount of services the firm expects to render.

Because sales revenue is an income statement item, companies use the information provided by the sales budget to construct the budgeted income statement.

PRODUCTION OR PURCHASES BUDGET

production budget Details the cost and number of units that must be produced by a manufacturer to meet the sales forecast and the desired ending inventory.

purchases budget Details the cost and number of units that must be purchased by a merchandiser to meet the sales forecast and the desired ending inventory.

For manufacturers, the budget that plans for the cost and number of units of product that must be manufactured to meet the sales forecast and the desired quantity of ending finished goods inventory is known as the **production budget.** For merchandisers this budget is called the **purchases budget,** because the two are functionally equivalent. Their names reflect the source of the items sold: Manufacturers produce the products they sell, and merchandisers purchase the products they sell.

The production budget and the purchases budget are simply pro forma versions of the cost of goods manufactured schedule and the cost of purchases schedule, as discussed in Chapter 2. A production budget is usually more complicated than a purchases budget because, as discussed in Chapter 2, costing manufactured product is more complicated than costing purchased product. A production budget includes schedules for materials, labor, and manufacturing overhead. An operating budget for a service business does not include a production budget or purchases budget because a service company does not sell tangible, physical product.

Only some of the product scheduled to be produced by a manufacturer or purchased by a merchandiser is intended to be sold during the period covered by the budget. The product not projected to be sold becomes *ending finished goods inventory* for a manufacturer and *ending merchandise inventory* for a merchandiser. In either case, this projected ending inventory is classified as an asset. Therefore, companies use some of the information provided by the production budget or purchases budget to construct the budgeted balance sheet.

The product that is projected to be sold during the period covered by the budget is classified as an expense item and will be shown on the budgeted income statement. As you recall, this expense item is called cost of goods sold. The cost of goods sold information needed to construct the budgeted income statement comes from the cost of goods sold budget.

COST OF GOODS SOLD OR COST OF SERVICES BUDGET

cost of goods sold budget   Calculates the total cost of all of the product a manufacturing or merchandising company estimates it will sell during the period covered by the budget.

A **cost of goods sold budget** calculates the total cost of all the product a company estimates it will sell during the period covered by the operating budget. This budget differs from the production (purchases) budget because of inventory requirements. Under accrual accounting, we do not recognize the cost of product as an expense (cost of goods sold) on the income statement until it is sold. Until then, we record it as an asset (inventory) and show it as such on the balance sheet. For a service type business, this budget is called the **cost of services budget.**

cost of services budget   Calculates the total cost of all the services a service-type business estimates it will provide during the period covered by the budget.

Whether we are talking about the cost of goods sold budget or the cost of services budget, they are similar to the schedules in Chapter 2 regarding the costing of products and services. The only difference is that the budgets discussed in this chapter pertain to the future.

Because cost of goods sold or cost of services is an income statement item, companies use the information provided by the cost of goods sold budget or cost of services budget to construct the budgeted income statement.

SELLING AND ADMINISTRATIVE EXPENSE BUDGET

selling and administrative expense budget   Calculates all costs other than the cost of product or services required to support a company's forecasted sales.

After a company makes its sales forecast and estimates its product (or service) cost, it can estimate all other costs needed to support that level of sales. A **selling and administrative expense budget** calculates all costs other than the cost of product or services required to support a company's forecasted sales. The kinds of items included in this budget are identical to those included in the income statements we have discussed throughout this text. They are what we described as period costs in Chapter 2 and include such items as advertising, administrative salaries, rent, and utilities.

BUDGETED INCOME STATEMENT

budgeted income statement   Shows the expected revenues, expenses, and income for the period covered by the operating budget.

A **budgeted income statement** shows the expected revenues, expenses, and income for the period covered by the operating budget. Companies prepare this budget using information from the sales budget, the cost of goods sold (or cost of services) budget, and the selling and administrative expense budget.

CASH BUDGET

cash budget   Shows whether the expected amount of cash generated by operating activities will be sufficient to pay anticipated expenses during the period covered by the operating budget.

A **cash budget** shows whether the expected amount of cash generated by operating activities will be sufficient to pay anticipated expenses during the period covered by the operating budget. It also reveals whether a company should expect a need for short-term external financing during the budget period. Be careful not to confuse the cash budget with the budgeted statement of cash flows, as discussed later in the chapter. The budgeted statement of cash flows is more comprehensive than a cash budget.

BUDGETED BALANCE SHEET

budgeted balance sheet   A presentation of estimated assets, liabilities, and owners' equity at the end of the budgeted period.

A **budgeted balance sheet** presents estimated assets, liabilities, and owners' equity at the end of the budgeted period. It is created the way a balance sheet based on actual historical results is prepared. At the start of the period being budgeted, a company has a balance sheet that presents its assets, liabilities, and owners' equity. The estimated results of operations (budgeted income statement) will change most (if not all) of the company's asset, liability, and equity items. The result is an estimated balance sheet at the end of the budget period.

Manufacturing and merchandising companies prepare the budgeted balance sheet using information from the actual balance sheet at the beginning of the period covered by the budget, the production (purchases) budget, and the budgeted income statement. Service-type companies have no production or purchases budget, so they prepare the budgeted balance sheet using information from the actual balance sheet at the beginning of the budget period and the budgeted income statement.

BUDGETED STATEMENT OF CASH FLOWS

budgeted statement of cash flows A statement of a company's expected sources and uses of cash during the period covered by the operating budget.

A **budgeted statement of cash flows** is a statement of a company's expected sources and uses of cash during the period covered by the operating budget. Manufacturers, merchandisers, and service companies create the budgeted statement of cash flows the same way they create the budgeted balance sheet. At the start of the period being budgeted, they report their cash balance. Based on the estimated results of operations (budgeted income statement) and other business activities that either generate or use cash, they estimate the cash balance at the end of the budget period. The purpose of the budgeted statement of cash flows is to explain what will cause that change in cash.

Discussion Question

9–2. In what ways do you think the cash budget described earlier differs from the budgeted statement of cash flows?

INTERRELATIONSHIP AMONG THE BUDGETS

The budgets we have discussed are closely interrelated. A change in any one of them will cause a ripple effect throughout all the others. Exhibit 9–3 shows the extent of this interrelationship.

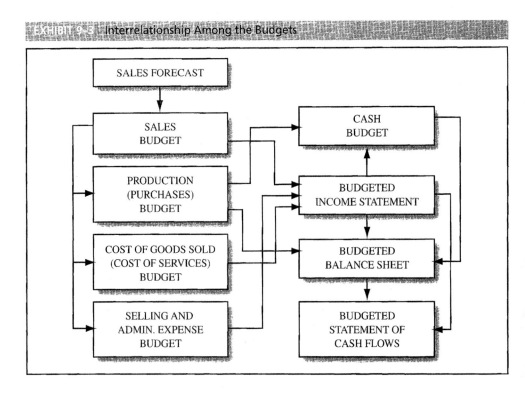

EXHIBIT 9–3 Interrelationship Among the Budgets

To demonstrate the interrelationship among the budgets, we return to Pam's Flower Shop for a moment. Because Pam's company is a merchandiser, the operating budget she prepares will include a sales budget, a purchases budget, a cost of goods sold budget, a selling and administrative expense budget, a cash budget, a budgeted income statement, a budgeted balance sheet, and a budgeted statement of cash flows.

Pam prepared the various budgets described for the first three months of 2004 based on the following sales forecast:

Pam's Flower Shop
Sales Forecast
For the Three Months Ended March 31, 2004

	January	February	March	Total
Sales	$90,000	$120,000	$100,000	$310,000

Discussion Question

9–3. From what you have learned so far about the operating budget, which of the budgets for Pam's Flower Shop will the amounts in this sales forecast affect? Explain how each is affected.

Now assume that a new flower shop opened just down the street from Pam's after she had prepared her operating budget. Pam believes that to be realistic in her planning, she needs to revise her sales forecast as follows:

Pam's Flower Shop
Revised Sales Forecast
For the Three Months Ended March 31, 2004

	January	February	March	Total
Sales	$75,000	$100,000	$90,000	$265,000

Discussion Question

9–4. Which of the budgets for Pam's Flower Shop will the changes in her sales forecast affect? Explain how each is affected.

Because sales revenue is changed in Pam's revised sales forecast, the sales budget will be different. Even without any information about purchases, you should intuitively recognize that lower sales probably means fewer flowers sold; therefore, Pam will need to purchase fewer flowers, meaning that the purchases budget must be revised. The same holds true for the cost of goods sold budget. The selling and administrative expense budget may need to be revised based on the new forecast, because lower sales probably means fewer salesclerks, at least. The cash budget will need to be revised because lower sales means less cash collected and lower purchases means less cash spent. The budgeted income statement must surely be revised, because we use the sales budget, the cost of goods sold budget, and the selling and administrative expense budget to construct the budgeted income statement. If those budgets must be revised, the budgeted income statement must also be revised. If the budgeted income statement is affected, the budgeted balance sheet must be revised because the results from the income statement are reflected in the balance sheet. If cash is affected in any way (and we already determined it would be), the budgeted statement of cash flows must be revised.

As you can see, a change in any of the budgets has a ripple effect throughout all the other budgets. Because the various budgets contained in the operating budget are so closely tied together, preparing the operating budget in most organizations is extremely time consuming and complicated. Depending on the size of the company, it may take several months to prepare the operating budget. For example, a manufacturer or merchandiser prepares a sales budget for each product the company sells. If the company sells 80 products, then 80 sales budgets must be prepared. If the company also has 80 sales territories, a whopping 6,400 sales budgets must be prepared (80 products × 80 sales territories). Companies must begin the budgeting process early enough to allow sufficient time for completion. If the budgeted period begins on January 1, 2004, for example, the budgeting process may begin in August or September 2003, or even earlier.

For some large, multinational companies, the process never ends. They work on the 2004 budget from January through December 2003. Then they turn right around in

January 2004 and begin work on the 2005 budget, and so on. It takes so long to complete the process that by they time they finish one year, it is time to start again for the next year.

◆ DIFFERENT APPROACHES TO BUDGETING

We now know what an operating budget is, but exactly how do businesse's prepare one? The answer depends on the needs of the business and the approach it takes to the budgeting process. Next we investigate seven budgeting approaches: perpetual, incremental, zero-based, top-down, bottom-up, imposed, and participative approaches.

PERPETUAL BUDGETING

perpetual budgeting
The budgeting approach of updating the budget every month.

continual budgeting
Another name for perpetual budgeting.

rolling budget   Another name for a perpetual budget.

Some companies continually update their operating budgets. As one month ends, another month's budget is added to the end of the budget. Therefore, at any given time, the budget projects 12 months into the future. This budgeting approach is called **perpetual budgeting,** sometimes called **continual budgeting** or a **rolling budget.** Companies that use perpetual budgeting always budget 12 months in advance.

One advantage of perpetual budgeting is that it spreads the workload for budget preparation evenly over the year, which allows employees to incorporate the work required to prepare the budget into their routine work schedule. Another advantage of a perpetual budget is that the budget always extends 12 months into the future. In contrast, when perpetual budgeting is *not* used, the new operating budget is typically prepared when only a couple of months are left on the old budget. One disadvantage of perpetual budgeting may be that the budget preparation process becomes so routine that employees lose the motivation and creativity required to prepare an innovative operating budget. An important aspect of solid budgeting is looking for better ways to do things. Think back to the example we used earlier for Montrose Manufacturing Company, which was able to restructure its production process because its managers were serious about looking for a better way. If preparing the budget becomes routine—just another bunch of forms to fill out—managers may stop this critical evaluation and become satisfied with the status quo. Another disadvantage is that many managers believe they do not have sufficient time to do all that is asked of them in their regular day-to-day responsibilities. Adding the responsibility of preparing a perpetual budget to a heavy workload can lead to sloppy budgeting.

INCREMENTAL BUDGETING

incremental budgeting
The process of using the prior year's budget or the company's actual results to build the new operating budget.

The process of using the prior year's budget or the company's actual results to build the new operating budget is called **incremental budgeting.** If, for example, a company's 2003 budget included $200,000 for maintenance and repairs on the machinery and equipment in its production facility, $200,000 becomes the starting point for this item in preparing the 2004 budget. The only question managers need to answer is whether the company needs to include *more* than $200,000 for repairs and maintenance in 2004. This budgeting approach is used by governmental entities, such as the federal government, and by many companies.

The trouble with the incremental budgeting approach is that if the prior year's budget includes unnecessary costs, or items that do not optimize performance, this waste may be simply rolled over into the next year's budget. The advantage to this approach is its simplicity. Some practitioners and many experts believe the disadvantages greatly outweigh the advantages.

Discussion Question ◦

9-5. In what ways, if any, do you think the federal government's use of incremental budgeting contributes to wasteful spending?

ZERO-BASED BUDGETING

zero-based budgeting
A process of budgeting in which managers start from scratch, or zero, when preparing a new budget.

An alternative to the incremental budgeting approach is zero-based budgeting. In **zero-based budgeting,** managers start from scratch, or zero, when preparing a new budget. Each item on the budget must be justified every year as though it were a new budget item. Zero-based budgeting is much more difficult and time consuming than incremental budgeting, but many organizations believe the results are worth that time and effort because managers are forced to reexamine the items included in the budget and justify their continuation.

TOP-DOWN VERSUS BOTTOM-UP BUDGETING

Budgeted information can flow either from the upper levels of management in a company down to managers and employees at lower levels, or vice versa. For fairly obvious reasons, the former approach is known as the top-down approach and the latter as the bottom-up approach. Each has distinct advantages and disadvantages.

Top-Down Budgeting

top-down budgeting A budget prepared by top managers in a company.

When top managers in the company prepare the budget, the process is called **top-down budgeting.** The top executives prepare the budget, and lower-level managers and employees work to meet that budget.

The top-down approach has several advantages. First, a company's upper management is usually most knowledgeable about the company's overall operation. It makes sense (on the surface, at least) that upper managers be responsible for the information contained in the operating budget because they are the most experienced and knowledgeable individuals in the company. Second, top management is keenly aware of company goals and strategic plans, so they will prepare the budget with these goals and plans in mind. Finally, the top-down budgeting approach involves fewer people, so it causes fewer disruptions, is more efficient, and is less time consuming than the bottom-up approach.

The top-down approach to budgeting has two major disadvantages. First, lower-level managers and employees are usually less accepting of budgets when they have no part in setting the standards. Second, top managers may be keenly aware of the big picture, but they do not have the working knowledge of daily activities needed to prepare the detailed budgets for all company activities.

Most large, publicly traded companies in the United States use some form of top-down budgeting. Why? If you recall our discussion of the cost of equity capital in Chapter 8, you know that a firm's top management fully understands the need to maximize returns for stockholders. Most of that return is in the form of stock appreciation (increase in the market price of the stock), rather than dividends. The greatest influence on the selling price of a company's stock price is company profits. So, to ensure maximum stock appreciation, a company must be as profitable as possible. The top management of these publicly traded companies generally have a better sense than lower-level managers and employees of how much profit the company must earn in a given year to maintain (or attain) a high return for stockholders. In top-down budgeting, the target profit figures become the starting point of the budgeting process.

imposed budget A budget in which upper management sets figures for operating activities that the rest of the company rarely, if ever, can negotiate.

Traditionally, most firms that used top-down budgeting also used an imposed budgeting process. An **imposed budget** is a budget in which upper management sets figures for operating activities that the rest of the company rarely, if ever, can negotiate. Top management expects all other managers to "do whatever it takes to make it happen." This type of budgeting process can do more harm than good, because it can lead to business practices that conflict with the company's stated goals. Today, however, not all top-down budgets are imposed budgets, as we will see shortly.

Bottom-Up Budgeting

bottom-up budgeting A budget initially prepared by lower-level managers and employees.

In **bottom-up budgeting,** lower-level managers and employees prepare the initial budget. For example, members of the sales force prepare the sales budget for their own sales territories. The sales manager then reviews these sales budgets, makes any necessary changes, and combines them to form the overall company sales budget. Likewise, employees in the production facility prepare budgets for production, including schedules for direct material, direct labor, and manufacturing overhead.

Bottom-up budgeting has three main advantages. First, the budget may be more realistic. Those who work in a functional area are usually better informed about what should be included in the budget than upper-level managers. If lower-level managers and employees take the budgeting process seriously, they are likely to create an operating budget based on accurate, realistic information. Second, lower-level managers and employees are more likely to work toward budgeted performance standards because they helped to set those standards. Third, as employees prepare the budget, they learn to think about the company's goals, how various activities can affect the future, and how they personally will participate. In short, they begin to think about the work they will need to do in the coming year.

Bottom-up budgeting has two disadvantages. First, employees at every level must take time from their day-to-day responsibilities to work on the budget as it is prepared, reviewed, revised, and approved—all of which adds up to substantial time and effort. Second, some employees may be tempted to prepare a budget that is so generous they can effortlessly outperform it. For example, sales representatives may budget sales of $300,000, when they can achieve sales of $350,000 with little effort. Thus, their actual sales performance looks great compared with budgeted sales. Manipulating the budget to make certain that the actual performance exceeds budgeted performance is one example of a budget game. A *budget game* is the game of using the budget to do things it was never intended to do, such as ensuring a strong performance appraisal.

participative budget A budget in which managers and employees at many levels of the company are involved in setting the performance standards and preparing the budget.

Bottom-up budgeting is always a participative budgeting process. A **participative budget** is one in which managers and employees at many levels of the company are involved in setting the performance standards and preparing the budget. Recent developments have expanded the use of participative budgeting to top-down budgeting, so it is beneficial to discuss imposed and participative budget philosophies a little further.

IMPOSED VERSUS PARTICIPATIVE BUDGETS

A bottom-up budget will always be a participative budget. Managers and employees at all levels of the company participate in preparing a bottom-up budget. A top-down budget, however, can be either imposed or participative.

In recent years, companies have discovered that by allowing more participation, they empower their employees. To empower employees means to give employees the authority to make decisions concerning their job responsibilities, including decisions about items in the operating budget.

A company committed to both top-down budgeting and empowered employees must combine the top-down and bottom-up approaches to budgeting. Rather than having all budget information flow from the top of the company downward to lower levels, upper management provides profit targets to managers at lower levels. These lower-level managers then prepare the operating budget for their functional areas, given the profit targets upper management provides.

Discussion Questions ◦

9–6. What possible positive results do you think can come from more empowerment:
   a. for the company? Explain your reasoning.
   b. for managers and employees? Explain your reasoning.

9–7. What possible negative results do you think can come from more empowerment:
   a. for the company? Explain your reasoning.
   b. for managers and employees? Explain your reasoning.

As an example of combining the top-down and bottom-up approaches to budgeting, we look at Preston Nydegger Company. Assume Nydegger is a publicly traded company that wants to be one of the top-performing companies (in terms of dividends and stock appreciation) in the stock market. Upper management has determined that the company must earn a profit of $1 million in the upcoming year to reach that goal. The company has three divisions (A, B, and C), and each must earn some part of the targeted $1 million profit. Division C is the smallest of the three, and corporate headquarters has assigned this division a target profit of $150,000 for the next year.

Now that Division C has received its target profit (this is the top-down part), the division manager, Joenne Moss, and her managers and employees set about to prepare the operating budget for the year (this is the participative part). When they have completed their budgeting process, the result in summary form is as follows:

Sales	$500,000
Expenses	(450,000)
Net Income	$150,000

Wait a minute! Something's wrong. The numbers just don't add up. Well, what we see is a conflict between the top-down target profit ($150,000) and what Joenne and her people at Division C think they can accomplish in the upcoming year ($500,000 in sales and $450,000 in expenses). What happens next will determine whether this budget is imposed or participative.

If the upper management of Nydegger Company refuses to negotiate and compromise with Division C, the budget becomes imposed. Remember, there is little room for negotiation between upper management and the rest of the company as to the amounts included in an imposed operating budget. If, however, upper management is willing to yield somewhat on its profit targets, the budget becomes participative.

It is unrealistic to think Nydegger will simply adjust its target from $150,000 to $50,000, which would certainly make the arithmetic in the budgeted income statement work. More than likely, Nydegger's upper management will meet with Joenne and her staff to negotiate a compromise target profit. Let's say they did just that, and the negotiations led to a revised target profit of $90,000 for the division. The revised summary budgeted income statement, then, would be as follows:

Sales	$500,000
Expenses	(450,000)
Net Income	$ 90,000

The math still doesn't work! Management at the division level must now either forecast more sales or find some way to reduce expected expenses (or some combination of the two) to project an additional $40,000 in profit for the year.

The key to making a top-down budget a participative budget is the ability and willingness on the part of upper management to negotiate and compromise.

Discussion Questions

9–8. If you were the chief executive officer of your company, would you prefer a top-down or bottom-up budgeting process? Why?

9–9. If you were in middle management, would you prefer a top-down or bottom-up budgeting process? Why?

9–10. If you were the company CEO, do you think it would be wise for you to spend time tending to the details of the various budgets, given all your other responsibilities?

The overall approach a company takes to preparing its operating budget may actually be a combination of several of the approaches we have discussed here. For example, one company may have a top-down, participative, zero-based budgeting approach. Another company may be committed to an incremental, participative, bottom-up, perpetual budgeting philosophy. The object is not to select a particular approach from a laundry list. Rather, managers must approach preparing the operating budget in a way that makes sense in the circumstances.

After analyzing all available data, the certified meteorologists at the U.S. Weather Service predicted sunny and warm weather for the next five days, with only a 10 percent chance of rain. It rained every day for the next five days.

What is true for predicting future weather conditions is also true for predicting a company's future sales performance. Although technological advances over the past 30 years have improved financial forecasting methods, predicting future sales still remains largely an educated guess. The prediction of sales for the period covered by the operating budget is called the sales forecast.

CORNERSTONE AND KEYSTONE OF BUDGETING

A solid, realistic sales forecast is perhaps the most critical feature of a solid, realistic operating budget. Why? Once the sales forecast has been developed, the business can prepare the sales budget, the production or purchases budget, the cost of goods sold or cost of services budget, the selling and administrative expense budget, the cash budget, and the three budgeted financial statements (income statement, balance sheet, and statement of cash flows).

The sales forecast is often called the cornerstone of budgeting. In the construction of a building, the first brick or stone laid is called the cornerstone. The remainder of the entire building is built off this cornerstone. If this brick is strong and placed properly the rest of the wall will be straight. In the construction of the operating budget, the sales forecast is the first step; all the budgets are built from the sales forecast. The sales forecast, then, is the cornerstone of the budgeting process, as depicted in Exhibit 9–4.

EXHIBIT 9–4 The Sales Forecast as the Cornerstone of Budgeting

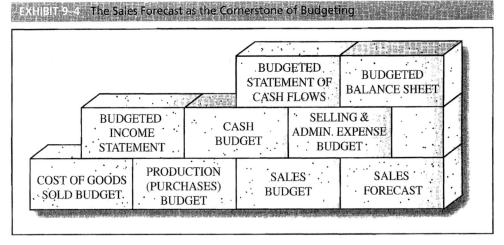

The sales forecast has also been called the keystone of budgeting. This description clearly reflects the importance of the forecast. In the building of a stone archway, the keystone is the stone placed at the exact center at the top of the arch. If this stone is strong and placed properly, the arch will last. In fact, some arches built without mortar in the Middle Ages are still standing. They are held together solely from the strength of the keystone. If the keystone is weak, however, or is improperly set, the arch will collapse; and so it is with budgeting. The quality of the entire operating budget depends on the quality and accuracy of the sales forecast as depicted in Exhibit 9–5.

As an archway made of stones depends on the keystone for its strength, the reliability of the operating budget depends on the strength of the sales forecast. If the sales forecast does not reasonably reflect the actual sales during the operating budget period, the budget will not reasonably estimate the actual results for the period. Thus, there will be differences between the actual income statement, balance sheet, and statement of cash flows and the budgeted income statement, balance sheet, and statement of cash flows.

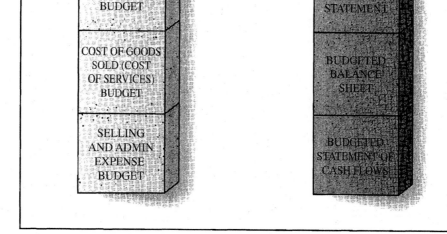

EXHIBIT 9-5   The Sales Forecast as the Keystone of Budgeting

FACTORS AFFECTING THE ACCURACY OF THE SALES FORECAST

Many factors influence the accuracy of the sales forecast. We have chosen four to discuss here: the economy, industry conditions, the competition, and technology.

General Economy

If the economy goes into a recession, consumer saving and spending patterns change. Sales forecasts are usually affected as a result. The problem is, most economists estimate that the economy can be entering or moving out of a recession for at least six to nine months before we realize it. Thus, when a firm creates its sales forecast for the next year's budget, it may be unaware of what the actual state of the economy will be throughout the period covered by the operating budget.

Industry Conditions

It is possible for the general economy to be healthy and a particular industry to be in a recession or for the economy to be unhealthy and the industry quite healthy.

Actions of Competitors

All companies take great pains to keep information about their plans from their competitors. Therefore, all companies make their sales forecasts without information that has a tremendous impact on the accuracy of the forecast. For example, imagine **Intel** is about to launch a revolutionary product that could absolutely blow its competitors away. **Motorola** does not know this, so it creates a sales forecast that is inaccurate because it is unaware of **Intel**'s planned actions.

Technological Developments

Technological developments can greatly influence the quality of the sales forecast. It is possible that the market for a particular product may not be as strong—or may not even exist—when the time the period being budgeted for arrives. When **Microsoft** introduced its *Windows 95* program, the need for products compatible with **Microsoft**'s old operating system sharply declined. Sales forecasts for software companies that did not expect the drop in demand for their products were rendered unreliable.

Discussion Question • ◦

9–11. What other factors can you think of that would influence the accuracy of a company's sales forecast?

We cannot overemphasize the importance of the sales forecast in the budgeting process, despite the difficulty of being completely accurate. It is worth the time and effort. Managers, however, must prepare and use the operating budget with a solid understanding of its limitations.

Part II: Preparing and Using the Operating Budget

◆ PREPARING A MASTER OPERATING BUDGET

Marcy's Surf Shop is a retail store that sells only one product (surfboards) and deals in only one product model. The company's fiscal year ends June 30. At Marcy's request, we will prepare the operating budget for the first quarter of the fiscal year ending June 30, 2005. Thus, we will be budgeting for the quarter ending September 30, 2004.

We start with Marcy's budgeted income statement and the budgets that provide information we use to construct that budgeted financial statement. We will then prepare the budgeted balance sheet along with all other budgets required to prepare the budgeted balance sheet. Finally, we will prepare the budgeted statement of cash flows.

Because we focus on a merchandising company rather than a manufacturer, we will work with a purchases budget rather than a production budget.

BUDGETED INCOME STATEMENT

To prepare the budgeted income statement, we need information about sales, cost of goods sold, and selling and administrative expenses for the period covered by the budget. Therefore, we must prepare a budget for each of those items before we can construct the budgeted income statement.

Sales Budget

The first information we need to build the budgeted income statement is found in the sales budget. Our first task, then, is to request that Marcy's marketing and sales personnel provide a sales forecast. They tell us that they will be happy to do so, but are not sure how. Should we suggest they take last year's sales numbers and increase them by, say, five percent? This would be incremental budgeting, and without a critical look at market factors that affect sales it is a poor approach to budgeting. If simply increasing last year's amounts by a constant percentage were adequate, a computer could easily be programmed to do the job.

Before Marcy's Surf Shop can forecast its sales realistically, sales management and the sales personnel must first consider the factors that influence market conditions. After much discussion, Marcy's staff decided to research the following items:

- Current customer spending patterns
- The ability to attract new customers through market promotions
- The introduction of any new products
- The discontinuation of any products
- The competition
- Price changes

- The general economy
- Technological changes

Marcy's sales team researches each of the items chosen for evaluation by the company and examines the results to make sales forecasting something more than just a guessing game. Once the sales team considers all its research, it develops a forecast of unit sales for each month in the quarter. The sales team forecasts sales for Marcy's Surf Shop of 30 units in July, 50 units in August, and 40 units in September, as shown in Exhibit 9–6.

EXHIBIT 9–6   Sales Forecast for Marcy's Surf Shop

Marcy's Surf Shop
Sales Forecast
For the Quarter Ended September 30, 2004

	July	August	September	Total
Forecasted Sales in Units	30	50	40	120

Based on this forecast, we can prepare Marcy's sales budget for the quarter, as shown in Exhibit 9–7.

EXHIBIT 9–7   Sales Budget for Marcy's Surf Shop

Marcy's Surf Shop
Sales Budget
For the Quarter Ended September 30, 2004

	July	August	September	Total
Forecasted Unit Sales	30	50	40	120
× Forecasted Sales Price	$ 200	$ 200	$ 200	$ 200
= Budgeted Sales Dollars	$6,000	$10,000	$8,000	$24,000

We simply used the sales forecast of unit sales and the projected selling price of $200 per surfboard to develop the sales budget.

A real sales budget for an actual company is somewhat more complicated than this one. This is primarily because, Marcy's sells only one product. Remember from our earlier discussion that if Marcy's sold 80 different products, the company would need to prepare 80 of these sales budgets. If Marcy's sold 80 different products in 80 different locations, the company would need to prepare 6,400 of these sales budgets (80 products × 80 locations).

Discussion Question

9–12. What factors should Marcy's management consider when setting the $200 budgeted selling price for its surfboards?

Cost of Goods Sold Budget

Once we know how many units Marcy's Surf Shop plans to sell, and the cost per unit, we can prepare a cost of goods sold budget. As its name implies, we use this budget to determine how much cost of goods sold should be based on forecasted sales. Preparing the cost of goods sold budget consists of multiplying forecasted unit sales by the cost per unit. The cost of goods sold budget for Marcy's Surf Shop is presented in Exhibit 9–8.

EXHIBIT 9–8 Cost of Goods Sold Budget for Marcy's Surf Shop

Marcy's Surf Shop
Cost of Goods Sold Budget
For the Quarter Ended September 30, 2004

	July	August	September	Total
Forecasted Unit Sales	30	50	40	120
× Forecasted Unit Cost	$ 120	$ 120	$ 120	$ 120
= Budgeted Cost of Goods Sold	$3,600	$6,000	$4,800	$14,400

Exhibit 9–8 shows that Marcy's forecasted cost of goods sold for the quarter is $14,400 ($3,600 + $6,000 + $4,800 = $14,400). The cost of goods sold budget provides the forecasted product cost information we use to prepare the budgeted income statement. This product cost information helps Marcy's management determine whether the company will be profitable based on its budget, or whether changes should be planned now to ensure profits in the budget period.

Discussion Questions

Compare the sales budget in Exhibit 9–7 with the cost of goods sold budget in Exhibit 9–8.

9–13. What are the similarities?

9–14. What are the differences?

Realistically, Marcy's will need to purchase more units of product than just the ones it expects to sell in July, August, and September. Thus, in addition to the budgets required to prepare the budgeted income statement, we will need to prepare a purchases budget. For our demonstration purposes, however, we will wait until after we have prepared the budgeted income statement to present the purchases budget. The only additional budget we need to prepare before we can prepare the budgeted income statement is the selling and administrative expense budget.

Selling and Administrative Expense Budget

The various expenses associated with the selling and administrative functions are estimated and used to prepare this budget. Selling and administrative expenses include salaries, advertising, rent, utilities, and so on. The selling and administrative expense budget for Marcy's Surf Shop is presented in Exhibit 9–9.

The types of items and the amounts included in the selling and administrative expense budget vary from company to company. As we said earlier, the items included in this budget are determined by what is required to support the level of sales in the sales budget.

Discussion Questions

9–15. If you were preparing a selling and administrative expense budget, what are some of the things you would consider as you mapped out strategies to increase sales?

9–16. Besides those included in Exhibit 9–9, what are some other administrative costs you think would normally be included in a selling and administrative expense budget?

Marcy's Surf Shop
Selling and Administrative Expense Budget
For the Quarter Ended September 30, 2004

	July	August	September	Total
Salaries and Wages	$1,600	$2,000	$1,800	$5,400
Rent	200	200	200	600
Depreciation	100	100	104	304
Others	800	1,000	900	2,700
Total	$2,700	$3,300	$3,004	$9,004

EXHIBIT 9-9   Selling and Administrative Expense Budget for Marcy's Surf Shop

9–17. What do you think might explain the increase in anticipated depreciation expense in September from $100 to $104?

BUILDING THE BUDGETED INCOME STATEMENT

To prepare the budgeted income statement, we use information from the sales, cost of goods sold, and selling and administrative expense budgets. The budgeted income statement depicts the amount of profit or loss a business can expect from its budgeted operating activities. First, we take the total forecasted sales revenue from the sales budget and subtract the forecasted cost of goods sold from the cost of goods sold budget. The result is a forecasted gross profit. We then subtract the total selling and administrative expense, which we get from the selling and administrative expense budget. The result is the company's budgeted net income for the period covered by the budget. The budgeted income statement for Marcy's Surf Shop is presented in Exhibit 9–10.

EXHIBIT 9-10   Budgeted Income Statement for Marcy's Surf Shop

Marcy's Surf Shop
Budgeted Income Statement
For the Quarter Ended September 30, 2004

		July	August	September	Total
	Sales	$6,000	$10,000	$8,000	$24,000
−	Cost of Goods Sold	3,600	6,000	4,800	14,400
=	Gross Profit	2,400	4,000	3,200	9,600
−	Selling and Admin. Expense	(2,700)	(3,300)	(3,004)	(9,004)
=	Net Income	$ (300)	$ 700	$ 196	$ 596

We see from Exhibit 9–10 that Marcy's Surf Shop is projecting a $300 net loss for July. In August Marcy's is projecting a net income of $700 and in September it is $196. The total net income for the quarter, then, is $596.

After Marcy's management team has looked at the budgeted income statement we have prepared, they may want to make some changes in their plans. For instance, management may find the $300 loss in July unacceptable. If so, they would review all the information used to build the budgeted income statement and either adjust their expectations or adjust the assumptions we used to prepare the budget.

Whatever the outcome of this evaluation, Marcy's Surf Shop has a better chance of planning for a successful future if management takes the budgeting process seriously. If budgets are used properly, managers will have an opportunity to see trouble spots in advance and make the required adjustments before it is too late.

BUDGETED BALANCE SHEET

Now that we have prepared the budgeted income statement, we have much of the information we need to prepare the budgeted balance sheet. First, however, we must prepare two more budgets: the purchases budget, as mentioned when we were preparing the budgeted income statement, and the cash budget.

PURCHASES BUDGET

The cost of goods sold budget we prepared accounts only for the units projected to be sold during the period covered by the budget. If Marcy's planned to begin and end the period covered by the budget with no inventory on hand and planned to purchase only the amount of inventory during the budgeted period sufficient to support the level of projected sales, there would be no need for a separate purchases budget. Rather, the company could just use the information from the cost of goods sold budget. This plan is unrealistic, however, because a company like Marcy's must begin and end each period with a certain amount of merchandise on hand. These inventory requirements create the need for the purchases budget. Marcy's purchases budget for the three months ended September 30, 2004, is presented as Exhibit 9–11.

EXHIBIT 9–11 Purchases Budget for Marcy's Surf Shop

Marcy's Surf Shop
Purchases Budget
For the Quarter Ended September 30, 2004

	July	August	September	Total	
Forecasted Unit Sales	30	50	40	120	(a)
+ Desired Ending Inventory*	20	16	24	24	(b)
= Total Units Needed	50	66	64	144	(c)
− Beginning Inventory	(8)	(20)	(16)	(8)	(d)
= Units to Be Purchased	42	46	48	136	(e)
× Cost per Unit	$ 120	$ 120	$ 120	$ 120	(f)
= Cost of Purchases	$5,040	$5,520	$5,760	$16,320	(g)

*40% of the next month's sales requirements

As you can see by looking at Exhibit 9–11, the purchases budget, even for a small company like Marcy's Surf Shop, can seem rather complicated. A line-by-line analysis, however, reveals that much of the information it contains is already known, and the new information is basically straightforward.

(a) *Forecasted Unit Sales.* These numbers should look familiar to you because you have seen them three times already. They come directly from the sales forecast presented in Exhibit 9–6 and we used them to construct the sales budget in Exhibit 9–7 and the cost of goods sold budget in Exhibit 9–8.

(b) *Desired Ending Inventory.* These numbers represent the number of units of product the company believes it needs on hand at the end of a given period to support sales in the early days of the next period. As the asterisk note in Exhibit 9–11 explains, Marcy's has decided it should have inventory of product on hand at the end of any given month equal to 40 percent of the next month's sales requirements.

At the end of July, for example, Marcy's desires an ending inventory of 20 units, which is 40 percent of August's sales of 50 units (50 × 40% = 20 units).

The amount of desired ending inventory is determined by at least two factors. First, the company must consider how long it usually takes to get product from the company's supplier. This information is obtained from the purchasing records and discussions with the purchasing department. Second, the company must estimate the number of units of product it will sell in the early days of each month. This information comes from historical sales records and discussions with sales personnel.

The desired ending inventory amounts for July, August, and September will be important to us when we construct the budgeted balance sheet, but we will defer our discussion of how they are used until we actually prepare that budget.

Discussion Question

9–18. Can you tell by looking at the purchases budget in Exhibit 9–11 how many surfboards Marcy's has forecasted it will sell in October? Explain your reasoning.

(c) *Total Units Needed.* This figure is the sum of (a) and (b).

(d) *Beginning Inventory.* Because the purpose of the purchases budget is to determine how many units of inventory Marcy's must purchase during each of the months included in the budget period, we must subtract any inventory forecasted to be on hand at the beginning of each month from the total units needed to determine how many units the company must purchase during the month.

The beginning inventory for any period is the ending inventory for the previous period. You will note in the purchases budget in Exhibit 9–11 that the beginning inventory for August (20 units) is the same as the desired ending inventory for July, and the beginning inventory for September (16 units) is the same as the desired ending inventory for August. You should also note that the beginning inventory in the total column (eight units) is the same as the beginning inventory for July, because the total column is for the entire quarter and the quarter begins in July.

Discussion Question

9–19. The purchases budget in Exhibit 9–11 indicates that Marcy's desires ending inventory equal to 40 percent of the next month's sales requirements. Because sales in July are expected to be 30 surfboards, the beginning inventory in July (which is the ending inventory for June) should be 12 units (30 × 40%). Why do you think the beginning inventory in July is only eight surfboards?

(e) *Units to Be Purchased.* This figure is simply (c) minus (d) and tells us the number of surfboards that Marcy's must purchase in each of the three months of the budget period and the total for the quarter.

(f) *Cost per Unit.* The cost per unit is what Marcy's must pay for each surfboard it purchases. Note that this cost is the same as the cost per unit used when we prepared the cost of goods sold budget presented in Exhibit 9–8.

(g) *Cost of Purchases.* This figure is simply (e) multiplied by (f) and tells us what the purchase of surfboards will cost Marcy's in each of the three months of the budget period and the total for the quarter.

CASH BUDGET

When a company uses accrual accounting, it recognizes revenue when it is earned rather than when the cash associated with that revenue is collected, and expenses when the benefit is received rather than when the cash associated with the expenses is paid. This means, of course, that while the budgeted income statement (including the sales budget, cost of goods sold budget, and the selling and administrative expense budget) provides information about Marcy's projected earnings activities for the budget period, it does not provide direct information about what is projected to happen during that period in terms of cash. Also, unless Marcy's pays cash for its purchase of surfboards, the purchases budget suffers from the same limitation.

Before we can prepare the budgeted balance sheet, we must determine the effect on cash of the budgets we have prepared so far. We do that by preparing a cash budget, which is composed of a cash receipts schedule and a cash payments schedule.

Cash Receipts Schedule

cash receipts schedule
Presents the amount of cash a company expects to collect during the budget period.

The **cash receipts schedule** presents the amount of cash a company expects to collect during the budget period from the sales of its product. Before we can prepare Marcy's cash receipts schedule, we must make certain estimates about the composition of the company's sales (cash or credit) and the pattern of collecting the accounts receivable created by the credit sales. We estimate that 25 percent of Marcy's sales are for cash and the remaining 75 percent are on account (credit sales). Of the sales on account, we estimate that 30 percent are collected in the month of the sale, 60 percent in the month following the sale, and 10 percent in the second month following the sale. Because of the lag between the time a credit sale is made and the time cash is collected, some of the cash for credit sales made in May and June will not have been collected by the end of June, which means that those amounts will be collected during the three months included in our budget period. Therefore, we need to know May credit sales were $4,500, and June credit sales were $6,000.

Using the credit sales figures from May and June, and our assumptions about when cash is collected, we can prepare Marcy's cash receipts schedule for the three months ended September 30, 2004, as shown in Exhibit 9–12.

Although the cash receipts schedule presented in Exhibit 9–12 seems quite complex, it is more straightforward than it first appears. It is broken into two major parts. The first presents the amount of cash collected from credit sales during the period covered by the schedule (a through c) and the second part presents the amount of cash collected from cash sales during the budget period (d).

Let's take a few minutes to examine this schedule and see where the numbers came from and what they mean.

a. *From Accounts Receivable at 6/30/04.* The accounts receivable balance at 6/30/04 is composed of receivables arising from sales in May and June. May's credit sales were $4,500. Based on our collection assumption, 30 percent of that amount was collected in May and 60 percent in June. If 90 percent had been collected by the end of June, the remaining $450 ($4,500 × 10%) had not and was included in the balance of accounts receivable at 6/30/04. Since July is the second month following the credit sales in May, the $450 balance is shown as a collection in July ($4,500 × 10%).

Credit sales in June totaled $6,000. Only $1,800 of that amount was collected in June ($6,000 × 30%). If 30 percent had been collected by the end of June, $4,200 ($6,000 × 70%) had not and was included in the balance of accounts receivable at 6/30/04. Since July is the month following the credit sales in June, $3,600 is shown as a collection in July ($6,000 × 60%); and because August is the second month following the credit sales in June, the remaining $600 balance is shown as a collection in August ($6,000 × 10%).

b. *From New Sales.* Recall from the sales budget in Exhibit 9–7 that budgeted sales for the three months covered by our budget example were $6,000 in July, $10,000 in August, and $8,000 in September. One of the assumptions we made as we began our discussion of the cash receipts schedule was that 75 percent of Marcy's sales were credit sales. Therefore, the amounts we are dealing with in this section of the schedule are $4,500 for July ($6,000 × 75%), $7,500 for August ($10,000 × 75%), and $6,000 for September ($8,000 × 75%).

The collection pattern for each of the three months is the same: 30 percent of credit sales are collected in the month of sale, 60 percent in the month following the sale, and 10 percent in the second month following the sale. So for

Marcy's Surf Shop
Cash Receipts Schedule
For the Quarter Ended September 30, 2004

	July	August	September	Total	
Credit Sales Collected:					
From Accounts Receivable					
at 6/30/04:					
May Credit Sales ($4,500)					
Collected in July (10%)	$ 450			$ 450	
June Credit Sales ($6,000)					
Collected in July (60%)	3,600			3,600	(a)
Collected in August (10%)		$ 600		600	
From New Credit Sales:					
July Credit Sales ($4,500)					
Collected in July (30%)	1,350			1,350	
Collected in August (60%)		2,700		2,700	
Collected in September (10%)			$ 450	450	
August Credit Sales ($7,500)					
Collected in August (30%)		2,250		2,250	(b)
Collected in September (60%)			4,500	4,500	
September Credit Sales ($6,000)					
Collected in September (30%)			1,800	1,800	
Budgeted Receipts from Credit Sales	$5,400	$5,550	$6,750	$17,700	(c)
Cash Sales:					
July Cash Sales	1,500			1,500	
August Cash Sales		2,500		2,500	(d)
September Cash Sales			2,000	2,000	
Budgeted Cash Receipts	$6,900	$8,050	$8,750	$23,700	(e)

EXHIBIT 9–12 Cash Receipts Schedule for Marcy's Surf Shop

July's credit sales, for example, the schedule shows $1,350 will be collected in July ($4,500 × 30%), $2,700 will be collected in August ($4,500 × 60%), and $450 ($4,500 × 10%) in September. The amounts projected to be collected for August and September credit sales are calculated exactly the same way.

c. *Budgeted Receipts from Credit Sales.* This figure is simply the sum of (a) and (b). It presents the total amount of cash Marcy's expects to collect during the period covered by the schedule from credit sales.

d. *Cash Sales.* This section is the least complicated of the schedule. For the three months included in the schedule it presents the portion of sales that will be cash sales. If 75 percent of the sales made in a given month are credit sales, then 25 percent will be cash sales. Therefore, in July the cash sales will be $1,500 ($6,000 × 25%) and that amount is shown as a cash receipt in July. The amount for August is $2,500 ($10,000 × 25%), and for September $2,000 ($8,000 × 25%).

e. *Budgeted Cash Receipts.* This figure is simply the sum of (c) and (d). As the description indicates, it presents the total amount of cash Marcy's plans to collect from the accounts receivable balance at 6/30/04, the credit sales it will have during the period covered by the schedule, and the cash sales made during the period.

cash payments schedule
Presents the amount of cash a company expects to pay out during the budget period.

Cash Payments Schedule

The **cash payments schedule** presents the amount of cash a company expects to pay out during the budget period. Before we can prepare Marcy's cash payments schedule, we must make certain assumptions about the company's pattern of cash payments. We assume that payment for the purchase of surfboards is made in the month following the purchase. Because of the lag time between the time a purchase is made and the time cash is paid, the purchases made in June will not have been paid by the end of June, which means that this amount will be paid in July, one of the months included in our budget period. Therefore, we need to know that purchases of merchandise in June totaled $5,200. All cash selling and administrative expenses are paid in the month incurred.

Using these assumptions about when cash is paid and the purchases figure from June, we can prepare Marcy's cash payments schedule for the three months ended September 30, 2004, as shown in Exhibit 9–13.

EXHIBIT 9–13   Cash Payments Schedule for Marcy's Surf Shop

Marcy's Surf Shop
Cash Payments Schedule
For the Quarter Ended September 30, 2004

	July	August	September	Total	
Purchases	$5,200	$5,040	$5,520	$15,760	(a)
Selling and Admin. Expense:					
Salaries and Wages	1,600	2,000	1,800	5,400	
Rent	200	200	200	600	(b)
Other Selling and Admin. Expense	800	1,000	900	2,700	
Purchase of Display Case		240			(c)
Budgeted Cash Payments	$7,800	$8,480	$8,420	$24,700	(d)

As you can see from Exhibit 9–13, the cash payments schedule is not nearly as complex as either the purchases budget or the cash receipts schedule. There are a couple of tricky parts, however, so let's examine the items included.

(a) *Purchases.* These are payments for the purchase of surfboards. Recall our assumption that payment for the purchase of merchandise is made in the month following purchase. The projected payment of $5,200 in July, then, is for purchases made in June, the payment of $5,040 in August will be for July purchases, and the $5,520 payment in September will be for August purchases.

Discussion Question

9–20. In our assumptions about cash payments, we said that June purchases of merchandise totaled $5,200 so it is easy to see where the July payment originated. Where do you suppose the payment amounts ($5,040 and $5,520) originated for August and September?

(b) *Selling and Administrative Expense.* These are payments for the support costs Marcy's anticipates for each month of the budget period. The amounts come directly from the selling and administrative expense budget in Exhibit 9–9.

Discussion Question

9–21. Look back at the selling and administrative expense budget in Exhibit 9–9. All the expense items included in that budget are included in the cash payments schedule except depreciation. Why do you think depreciation expense was included in the selling and administrative expense budget but excluded from the cash payments schedule?

(c) *Purchase of Display Case.* Evidently, Marcy's is planning to purchase a new display case for the showroom during the month of August. This purchase will be added to Marcy's property, plant, and equipment and will be important to us when we prepare the budgeted balance sheet and the budgeted statement of cash flows. Incidentally, the planned purchase of this display case is what caused depreciation expense in Exhibit 9–9 to increase by $4 in September.

(d) *Budgeted Cash Payments.* This figure is simply the sum of (a), (b), and (c). As the description indicates, it presents the total amount of cash Marcy's plans to pay out during the period covered by the schedule.

BUILDING THE CASH BUDGET

Now that we have prepared the cash receipts schedule and the cash payments schedule, we can prepare Marcy's cash budget for the quarter ended September 30, 2004. As was the case with the schedules, we must make some assumptions for the cash budget. First, we estimate that Marcy's Surf Shop will have a cash balance of $2,170 on June 30, 2004. Second, Marcy's desires to maintain a cash balance of at least $1,900 at all times. If cash falls below $1,900, the company will borrow from a local bank. Finally, we ignore the interest Marcy's would be required to pay on any borrowings from the bank.

Using the assumption about Marcy's desired minimum cash balance, and the information from the cash receipts schedule and the cash payments schedule, we can prepare the company's cash budget for the quarter ending September 30, 2004, as shown in Exhibit 9–14.

EXHIBIT 9–14   Cash Budget for Marcy's Surf Shop

Marcy's Surf Shop
Cash Budget
For the Quarter Ended September 30, 2004

		July	August	September	Total	
	Beginning Cash Balance	$2,170	$1,900	$ 1,900	$ 2,170	(a)
+	Cash Receipts	6,900	8,050	8,750	23,700	(b)
=	Cash Available	$9,070	$9,950	$10,650	$25,870	(c)
	Cash Payments	(7,800)	(8,480)	(8,420)	(24,700)	(d)
=	Balance before Borrowing	$1,270	$1,470	$ 2,230	$ 1,170	(e)
+/–	Borrowing/(Repayment)	$ 630	$ 430	$ (330)	$ 730	(f)
=	Ending Cash Balance	$1,900	$1,900	$ 1,900	$ 1,900	(g)

The cash budget itself is not as seemingly complicated as the purchases budget, the cash receipts schedule, or the cash payments schedule. There are, however, some potential pitfalls in your understanding of the way this budget is constructed, so we will take a few minutes and discuss the items included.

   a. *Beginning Cash Balance.* Like all balance sheet items, the beginning cash balance for any period is the ending cash balance for the previous period. As mentioned earlier, the ending cash balance for June will be $2,170. Therefore, July's beginning cash balance will be June's ending cash balance. The same pattern holds true for the other months presented. August's beginning balance is July's ending balance and September's beginning balance is August's ending balance. Note, however, that the beginning balance in the total column ($2,170) is the same as the beginning balance for July. Likewise, the ending balance in the total column ($1,900) is the same as the ending balance for September, because the total column represents the entire quarter. The beginning balance for the quarter is July's beginning balance and the ending balance for the quarter is September's ending balance.

b. *Cash Receipts.* The cash receipts amounts are taken directly from the budgeted cash receipts line of the cash receipts schedule shown in Exhibit 9–12.

c. *Cash Available.* This figure is simply the sum of (a) and (b). This amount represents the total cash Marcy's expects to be available before deducting any payments.

d. *Cash Payments.* The cash payments amounts are taken directly from the budgeted cash payments line of the cash payments schedule shown in Exhibit 9–13.

e. *Balance before Borrowing.* This amount is calculated by simply subtracting (d) from (c). It represents the anticipated ending cash balance before any adjustments for borrowing or loan payments.

f. *Borrowing/(Repayment).* Marcy's wants to maintain a cash balance of at least $1,900. If the balance before borrowing drops too low, Marcy's will borrow enough money from the bank to bring the balance up to the desired ending cash balance of $1,900. As you can see, July's balance before borrowing is expected to be only $1,270. Therefore, Marcy's can anticipate the need to borrow $630 to bring the balance up to $1,900. So, if the balance before borrowing is less than the desired ending cash balance, as it will be in July and again in August, the amount that must be borrowed to bring the cash balance to the desired amount can be easily calculated. If, on the other hand, the expected balance before borrowing is greater than $1,900, as is the case in September, any amount in excess of the desired ending cash balance will be used to repay the loan ($330 in this instance).

g. *Ending Cash Balance.* This figure is simply (e) plus the borrowing or less the repayment shown in (f). As we said earlier, this ending cash amount also becomes the next month's beginning cash balance.

Now we can use the information from the cash budget and other budgets to prepare the budgeted balance sheet.

BUILDING THE BUDGETED BALANCE SHEET

We assume that you already know the basics of how to construct a balance sheet, so for our presentation of the budgeted balance sheet, we focus on how to determine the various asset, liability, and equity items and dollar amounts for these items.

Although some of the amounts needed to prepare the budgeted balance sheet are taken directly from the budgets already prepared, many amounts are not specifically included in any of those budgets. For example, we have not prepared a budget or schedule that shows the ending balances for accounts receivable, inventory, property, plant, and equipment, accumulated depreciation, accounts payable, notes payable, common stock, additional paid-in capital, or retained earnings. For each of these items, we will present a brief discussion and a schedule to show how to calculate the amounts that should appear on the budgeted balance sheet. You will find as you examine each of these items that the budgeted ending balance is calculated by taking the beginning balance and adding or subtracting the changes that are expected to occur during the budget period. So, for each of these items, the beginning balance is our starting point. As discussed, the *beginning* balance of any balance sheet item is the prior month's *ending* balance. Therefore, all we need is the balance sheet for June 30 to determine the beginning balance for July. The balance sheet of June 30, 2004, for Marcy's Surf Shop is shown in Exhibit 9–15.

Using the June 30, 2004 balance sheet in Exhibit 9–15 and information from the other budgets we have prepared so far, we can prepare a budgeted balance sheet for each of the three months included in our budget period, as shown in Exhibit 9–16.

The balance sheets presented in Exhibit 9–16 are much like the other balance sheets you have seen throughout your studies. The essential difference is not the for-

Marcy's Surf Shop
Balance Sheet
As of June 30, 2004

Assets:	
Current Assets	
Cash	$ 2,170
Accounts Receivable	4,650
Inventory	960
Total Current Assets	$ 7,780
Property, Plant, and Equipment	
Equipment	6,000
Less Accumulated Depreciation	(1,200)
Equipment, Net	$ 4,800
Total Assets	$12,580
Liabilities:	
Current Liabilities	
Accounts Payable	$ 5,200
Total Liabilities	$ 5,200
Owner's Equity:	
Paid-in Capital	
Common Stock	$ 1,000
Additional Paid-in Capital	5,475
Total Paid-in Capital	$ 6,475
Retained Earnings	$ 905
Total Equity	$ 7,380
Total Liabilities and Equity	$12,580

EXHIBIT 9–15   Balance Sheet as of June 30, 2004, for Marcy's Surf Shop

mat, but rather, the time frame. These are projected balance sheets whereas the others have presented past results. There is no total column for this budget, because the balance sheet is a financial snapshot of a business taken at the end of a period. Therefore, in a very real sense, the snapshot taken at the end of September is the total column.

As we have done with the other budgets prepared in this chapter, we will now take a few minutes and explain how the items on the budgeted balance sheet were determined.

a. *Cash.* This amount is taken directly from the ending cash balance line of the cash budget shown in Exhibit 9–14. For example, the amount shown as the ending cash balance of $1,900 in the July column of the cash budget is shown as cash in the July column of the budgeted balance sheet.

b. *Accounts Receivable.* To determine the ending accounts receivable balance for each month shown in Exhibit 9–16, we simply take the beginning accounts receivable balance, add budgeted credit sales for that month, and subtract budgeted accounts receivable collections for that month.

	July	August	September
Beginning Balance	$4,650	$3,750	$ 5,700
+ Credit sales	4,500	7,500	6,000
− Collections	(5,400)	(5,550)	(6,750)
= Ending Balance	$3,750	$5,700	$4,950

Marcy's Surf Shop
Budgeted Balance Sheets
As of July 31, August 31, and September 30, 2004

	July	August	September	
Assets:				
Current Assets				
Cash	$ 1,900	$ 1,900	$ 1,900	(a)
Accounts Receivable, Net	3,750	5,700	4,950	(b)
Inventory	2,400	1,920	2,880	(c)
Total Current Assets	$ 8,050	$ 9,520	$ 9,730	
Property, Plant, and Equipment				
Equipment	$ 6,000	$ 6,240	$ 6,240	(d)
Less Accumulated Depreciation	(1,300)	(1,400)	(1,504)	(e)
Equipment, Net	$ 4,700	$ 4,840	$ 4,736	
Total Assets	$12,750	$14,360	$14,466	
Liabilities:				
Current Liabilities				
Accounts Payable	$ 5,040	$ 5,520	$ 5,760	(f)
Bank Loan Payable	630	1,060	730	(g)
Total Liabilities	$ 5,670	$ 6,580	$ 6,490	
Owner's Equity:				
Paid-in Capital				
Common Stock	$ 1,000	$ 1,000	$ 1,000	
Additional Paid-in Capital	5,475	5,475	5,475	(h)
Total Paid-in Capital	$ 6,475	$ 6,475	$ 6,475	
Retained Earnings	$ 605	$ 1,305	$ 1,501	(i)
Total Equity	$ 7,080	$ 7,780	$ 7,976	
Total Liabilities and Equity	$12,750	$14,360	$14,466	

EXHIBIT 9–16 Budgeted Balance Sheets for Marcy's Surf Shop

We can get the beginning accounts receivable balance of $4,650 for July from the June 30, 2004, balance sheet shown in Exhibit 9–15. The cash receipts budget provides the rest of the information we need. The cash receipts budget shows the projected credit sales, and the total expected to be collected from credit sales. For July, the cash receipts budget shows credit sales of $4,500 and a total of $5,400 collected from credit sales. After adding the credit sales of $4,500 to the beginning balance of $4,650, we subtract the collections of $5,400 to arrive at the ending accounts receivable balance of $3,750. This amount is shown on the budgeted balance sheet for July. The ending accounts receivable amounts for other months are calculated the same way.

c. *Inventory.* To determine the ending inventory balance for each month shown in Exhibit 9–16, we simply take the beginning inventory balance, add purchases made during the month, and subtract that month's cost of goods sold.

	July	August	September
Beginning Balance	$ 960	$2,400	$1,920
+ Purchases	5,040	5,520	5,760
− Cost of goods sold	(3,600)	(6,000)	(4,800)
= Ending Balance	$2,400	$1,920	$2,880

The beginning inventory balance for July of $960 is taken from the June 30, 2004, balance sheet shown in Exhibit 9–15. By looking at the purchases budget in Exhibit 9–11 and the cost of goods sold budget in Exhibit 9–8, we find that expected purchases for July are $5,040 and cost of goods sold are expected be

$3,600. After adding the purchases of $5,040 to the beginning balance of $960, we subtract the cost of goods sold of $3,600 to arrive at the ending inventory balance of $2,400. This amount is shown on the budgeted balance sheet for July. The ending inventory amounts for other months are calculated the same way.

d. *Equipment.* To determine the ending balance in the equipment, we adjust the beginning balance by adding the cost of equipment purchased and subtracting the cost of any equipment sold. In our example, the only change in equipment is the $240 for the showcase the company is planning to buy in August. We add $240 to the $6,000 beginning balance to arrive at the budgeted ending balance of $6,240.

e. *Accumulated Depreciation.* To determine the ending balance for accumulated depreciation, we adjust the beginning balance by adding the depreciation for the period and subtracting the accumulated depreciation associated with any assets that have been sold or scrapped. In our example, the company does not expect to sell or otherwise dispose of any equipment, so the only changes to accumulated depreciation are increases relating to the budgeted monthly depreciation. You might notice that the amount added to accumulated depreciation in September is slightly higher than that for July and August. This is so because of the added depreciation for the showcase the company expects to buy in August.

f. *Accounts Payable.* To determine the ending accounts payable balance for each month shown in Exhibit 9–16, we simply take the beginning accounts payable balance, add budgeted purchases for that month, and subtract budgeted payments for that month.

	July	August	September
Beginning Balance	$5,200	$5,040	$5,520
+ Purchases	5,040	5,520	5,760
− Payments	(5,200)	(5,040)	(5,520)
= Ending Balance	$5,040	$5,520	$5,760

The beginning accounts payable balance for July of $5,200 is taken from the June 30, 2004, balance sheet shown in Exhibit 9–15. By looking at the purchases budget in Exhibit 9–11 and the cash payments budget in Exhibit 9–13, we find that expected purchases for July are $5,040 and cash payments are expected to be $5,200. After adding the purchases of $5,040 to the beginning balance of $5,200, we subtract the cash payments of $5,200 to arrive at the ending accounts payable balance of $5,040. This amount is shown on the budgeted balance sheet for July. The ending accounts payable amounts for other months are calculated the same way.

g. *Bank Loan Payable.* To determine the ending notes payable balance for each month shown in Exhibit 9–16, we simply take the beginning notes payable balance, add the budgeted borrowing for that month, and subtract budgeted payments for that month.

	July	August	September
Beginning Balance	$ -0-	$ 630	$1,060
+ Borrowing	630	430	-0-
− Repayments	-0-	-0-	(330)
= Ending Balance	$630	$1,060	$ 730

The beginning notes payable balance for July would normally come from the June 30, 2004, balance sheet shown in Exhibit 9–15; however, in this example the beginning balance for notes payable on June 30, 2004, is zero, so notes payable does not appear. By looking at the cash budget in Exhibit 9–14, we find that borrowing of $630 is expected in July, borrowing of $430 is expected in August, and a repayment of $330 is expected in September.

h. *Common Stock and Additional Paid-in Capital.* In this example, no common stock or additional paid in capital transactions are expected during the budget period. Therefore, the beginning July balance for these items found on the June

30, 2004, balance sheet in Exhibit 9–15 remains unchanged during the budget period.

i. *Retained Earnings.* To determine the ending retained earnings balance, we add the income for the period or, if the company has a loss, subtract the loss and deduct dividends, if they exist, from the beginning retained earnings balance.

	July	August	September
Beginning Balance	$ 905	$ 605	$1,305
+ Income/Loss	(300)	700	196
− Dividends	-0-	-0-	-0-
= Ending Balance	$ 605	$1,305	$1,501

In our example, the $905 beginning balance of retained earnings is found on the June 30, 2004, balance sheet shown in Exhibit 9–15. To find the ending retained earnings that should appear on the budgeted balance sheet for July, we deduct the budgeted loss for that month of $300 from the beginning retained earnings balance of $905. That figure becomes the beginning balance in August. To determine the August ending balance of retained earnings we simply add August's budgeted net income. September's ending balance would be calculated the same way. There are no dividends in our example so the dividend amount is zero for each month presented.

BUDGETED STATEMENT OF CASH FLOWS

Now that we have prepared all the other budgets, we can prepare the budgeted statement of cash flows (SCF). This statement must be the final budget prepared because, as you recall from your earlier study of this financial statement, it is a form of financial statement analysis. An SCF prepared on historical results analyzes the income statement and the balance sheet to explain what caused cash to change from the beginning of a period to the end of the period. The budgeted SCF does exactly the same thing, except that it analyzes the budgeted income statement and the budgeted balance sheet to explain what will cause the projected change in cash from the start to the end of the budget period.

A budgeted SCF for Marcy's Surf Shop is presented as Exhibit 9–17.

We will not do a line-by-line analysis of the presentation in Exhibit 9–17 because we have explained all the items elsewhere in this chapter as we have constructed the other budgets. It is worthwhile, however, for us to discuss what this budget reveals in overall terms.

In the normal course of business, a company can obtain cash from only three sources: borrowing, owner contributions, and profitable operations. Ultimately, the only source of cash for any company, including Marcy's Surf Shop, is the profitable operation of the business. If a company does not generate enough cash from operations to run the business, it must seek outside financing (borrowing and owner contributions).

The budgeted statement of cash flows in Exhibit 9–17 reveals that for the three months covered by the budget, at least, Marcy's does not anticipate generating enough cash through operations to run the business and must, therefore, borrow the money. Three months is not a very long time, and all companies must obtain outside financing from time to time, but Marcy may not like what she sees when she looks at this budget. If she finds the prospects unacceptable, she may want to continue the budgeting process and make adjustments in how she plans to go about operating her business.

You will be delighted to know we are not going to do that for Marcy. We hope, however, that you have learned what a powerful tool the operating budget can be by going through the steps required to prepare one.

◆ USING (AND MISUSING) THE OPERATING BUDGET

We have seen that the operating budget can serve as a guide for the company to follow, assist a company in allocating its scarce resources, and foster communication and coor-

Marcy's Surf Shop
Budgeted Statement of Cash Flows
For the Quarter Ended September 30, 2004

	July	August	September	Total
Cash Flows From Operating Activities:				
Net Income	$ (300)	$ 700	$ 196	$ 596
Add: Depreciation	100	100	104	304
Changes in CA & CL:				
Accounts Receivable	900	(1,950)	750	(300)
Inventory	(1,440)	480	(960)	(1,920)
Accounts Payable	(160)	480		560
Net Cash Flow From Op Act	$ (900)	$ (190)	330	$ (760)
Cash Flow From Investing Activities:				
Cash Paid for Showcase	—	$ (240)	—	$ (240)
Net Cash Flow From Inv Act		$ (240)		$ (240)
Cash Flow From Financing Activities:				
Borrowing	$ 630	$ 430		$1,060
Loan Payments			$ (330)	(330)
Net Cash Flow From Fin Act	$ 630	$ 430	$ (330)	$ 730
Increase/(Decrease) in Cash	$ (270)	$ -0-	$ -0-	$ (270)
Budgeted Beginning Cash Balance	2,170	1,900	1,900	2,170
Budgeted Ending Cash Balance	$ 1,900	$1,900	$1,900	$1,900

EXHIBIT 9-17   Budgeted Statement of Cash Flows for Marcy's Surf Shop

dination among managers from different functional areas within the company. It can also establish performance standards, or benchmarks, against which the company can compare the actual results. This fourth application presents some serious challenges to managers, however. Misunderstanding how to set and use performance standards can lead to behavior that is actually detrimental to the organization.

Once upon a time, in the United States at least, someone figured out that the operating budget could be used as a means of controlling a company's activities. It's really a pretty simple concept. Once you establish the operating budget for the year, you keep one eye on the budget and one eye on the actual results. The idea is that if you prepare a solid budget and then perform to meet that budget, you will naturally keep control of your operation. Before long, this way of using the operating budget had become quite common among U.S. companies. As this practice became more popular, firms began evaluating the performance of their managers based on how they performed against the budget as well. This practice is known as the **performance to budget** evaluation. Salary increases, year-end bonuses, and promotions to senior management began to be dependent on a manager's ability to "meet or beat" the budget. By now, the operating budget had become the principal means used to control costs. It was felt that if managers performed well against the budget, they were doing a good job of controlling the operations they managed, which makes sense, right? Wrong! Unfortunately, that is not what happens when the budget is used as the primary control device in a company. What happens is that using the budget for this purpose actually encourages managers to make bad decisions and discourages them from making good decisions.

performance to budget
A process of evaluating managers and employees based on how they perform against the budget.

THE BUDGET PERFORMANCE REPORT

> *If I get bigger pants, does that mean I've lost weight?*
> —Paul Valenzuela

budget performance report   The evaluation instrument used to evaluate a manager's performance to budget.

As performance to budget became a popular way of measuring management performance, an instrument known as the **budget performance report** evolved to capture the information management thought was needed to perform the evaluation. A typical budget performance report has four columns as shown in Exhibit 9–18.

EXHIBIT 9–18   Budget Performance Report

(a) Description	(b) Budget	(c) Actual	(d) Variance
Salaries and Wages	$25,000	$23,000	$2,000 F
Office Rent	10,000	10,000	-0-
Office Supplies	1,000	1,200	200 U

variance   The difference between the amount budgeted and the actual amount.

As you can see, the report is not terribly complicated. The description column (a), lists the items for which the manager being evaluated is responsible. The budget column (b), lists the budgeted amount for each of those items. The actual column (c), lists the amount actually spent during the period covered by the budget. The difference between the amount budgeted and the actual amount is called a **variance.** The variances in our example appear in column (d). The letter F indicates a favorable variance and the letter U indicates an unfavorable variance.

Discussion Question ●

9–22. What do the words favorable and unfavorable mean to you?

The major problem with the budget performance report is not the report itself but rather the way it is used. As an example, say that Brian Sedgwick is the sales manager at Pepperwood Furniture Company. Among other things, Brian is responsible for gas and oil expenditures for the fleet of delivery trucks his company owns. These trucks are used to deliver products to customers. Say further that Brian is responsible for establishing the budget for this item, and he budgeted $50,000 for 2004. Now say that 2004 has ended and he spent $90,000 on gas and oil. Brian's budget performance report for this item would be as follows:

Description	Budget	Actual	Variance
Gas & Oil	$50,000	$90,000	$40,000 U

Now, what do you think might have caused this variance? Well, of the several possibilities, we will mention four.

1. Perhaps gas prices went through the roof. The budget was established based on what Brian *thought* gas and oil prices would be during the year.
2. Perhaps the budget Brian established was poorly done. Do not confuse this idea with the first possible explanation. In the first one, Brian did the best he could with the information he had—the information just turned out not to be reliable. This possibility comes from not taking the budgeting process seriously. Thus, for Brian, budgeting may mean filling out forms rather than being part of a real planning process.
3. Perhaps Brian was inefficient and wasted a lot of money. We would never want to forget this possibility. If he did waste money, he should be held accountable for his actions.

4. Perhaps business picked up significantly and the company had to make many more deliveries. This surely would have caused Brian to spend more money on gas and oil. Remember, the support costs in the budget are based on what is forecast to be sold.

Let's expand on the fourth possibility. Brian had an unfavorable variance caused by a good thing (greatly increased sales). This fact should help you understand that *unfavorable* in this context does not mean *bad*. It simply means *over budget*.

Brian Sedgwick's performance evaluation will depend on his company's attitude about what performance to budget means. Unfortunately, in all too many companies in the United States today, the evaluation begins with the variance column. If there are unfavorable variances, regardless of cause, Brian's performance evaluation will not be good. He may not get his bonus, he may not get that raise he was anticipating, and he may not be promoted.

Before we talk about how to overcome the problem we just described, let us look at another example using the same essential facts. Brian budgeted $50,000 for gas and oil expenditures for 2004, but only spent $30,000. His budget performance report would be as follows:

Description	Budget	Actual	Variance
Gas & Oil	$50,000	$30,000	$20,000 F

We will not discuss what might have caused this variance, but with the exception of the poor budgeting possibility (which is the same in either case), the reasons are just the opposite of what caused the $40,000 unfavorable variance in our first example. If you think about the fourth possibility, then, this favorable variance could have been caused by a decline in the company's business. In other words, Brian has a favorable variance caused by a bad thing. That should help you understand that *favorable* in this context does not mean *good*. It simply means *under budget*.

What about Brian's performance evaluation? Once again, it depends greatly on how his company management views the performance to budget. In all too many companies, he would be rewarded in two ways. First, he would receive congratulations from everyone involved in the evaluation on what a great job he did of controlling gas and oil costs for the year. Second, his gas and oil budget for next year will be cut by $20,000. The reasoning is that if that's all he needed for this year, that's all he will need for next year, as well. This is called "use it or lose it" and is a practice that flourishes in many companies in the United States today.

If this is how Brian's company views the evaluation process, it is in his best interest to make sure he does not have actual expenditures that are too far under budget. If Brian is smart, he will make certain that his performance report on gas and oil costs looks something like the following:

Description	Budget	Actual	Variance
Gas & Oil	$50,000	$50,000	-0-

This item will probably not be examined in any great detail during Brian's performance review, because the usual practice is to concentrate on the variance column. If no variance exists, it is assumed that the amount spent on the item was what should have been spent. This interpretation indicates efficient management, which is what Paul Valenzuela—a former executive of **Ford Motor Company**—meant in the quotation that opened this section. Buying bigger clothes makes it appear you have lost weight, when in fact you may not have lost any. The way this translates into the topic we are discussing is that if managers are able to secure a large budget for a particular item, they will appear to be efficient simply by spending less than, or exactly, the amount budgeted.

In many companies, then, the focus is on only items with large variances. Further, when these variances are investigated, the analysis usually focuses on the actual performance column of the performance report. If a large, unfavorable variance exists, managers are called on the carpet to explain why they spent more than the budget allowed. If a large, favorable variance exists, the item becomes a target for reducing costs next year, so the budget is cut.

What is bizarre about this method of using the budget performance report is that everybody knows budgets are established for the future. Everybody also knows that the future is to a great extent unknown to us. Yet, once the budget is established it becomes set in stone, so to speak, and any variance (favorable or unfavorable) between the budgeted cost and the actual cost is assumed to be because of the actual.

Are we suggesting that managers should be free to spend whatever amount they see fit on the cost items for which they are responsible? Absolutely not! This idea makes no sense, and it runs counter to everything we have said throughout this chapter, and indeed, throughout this book. Managers should be working every day to control costs and run their operations more efficiently. What we are saying is that this has very little to do with the operating budget. Cost control is an ongoing management process, of which the operating budget is only a part. Using the budget as the primary cost control device in a business is done in place of real control. Perhaps worse than that, using performance to budget as the evaluation instrument for managers encourages them to focus on the elimination of variances as their primary goal. As stated, because the budget is often considered to be set in stone, the only way to eliminate variances is to manipulate the actual performance to match the budget. This is what leads to silly budget games, such as the "use it or lose it" phenomenon we mentioned earlier.

If we lived in a perfect world where we could predict the future accurately, there would be no problem with the performance to budget evaluation technique. Unfortunately, we do not live in such a perfect world, and the future is largely unknown to us. When we prepare the operating budget we are attempting to predict the future. Differences are bound to exist between what we predict and what actually happens.

Earlier in the chapter we presented an exhibit that showed the interrelationship among all the budgets. We have reproduced that presentation as Exhibit 9–19.

As discussed during this interrelationship topic earlier in the chapter, a change in any one of the budgets has a ripple effect throughout all the other budgets. A little logic tells us that if there are variances in any one of the budgets there will also be a ripple effect throughout all the other budgets.

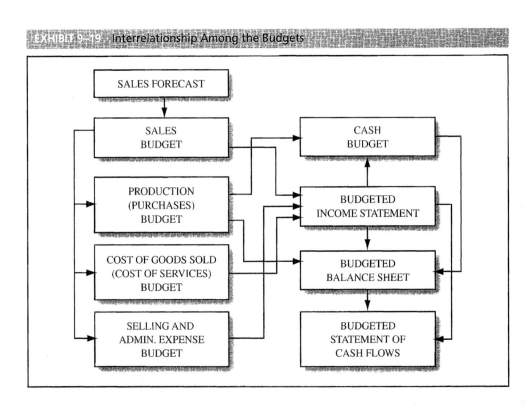

EXHIBIT 9–19 Interrelationship Among the Budgets

Perhaps a more important cause of variances than the interrelationship among the budgets is the role of the sales forecast in the budgeting process. Note in Exhibit 9–19 that all the budgets included in the operating budget are dependent upon the sales forecast, which explains why we described the sales forecast as both the cornerstone and the keystone of the operating budget in our earlier discussions.

The sales forecast is so critical in the budgeting process that we will end this section by sharing three truths with you about the sales forecast and the operating budget:

Truth 1: If the sales forecast is inaccurate, the operating budget will be inaccurate. Do not confuse *inaccurate* with *bad.* A bad sales forecast comes from lack of effort and attention. An inaccurate sales forecast comes about when the actual results are different from the operating budget because the future did not turn out the way company management predicted.

Truth 2: The sales forecast will be inaccurate. Recall the items we discussed earlier in the chapter that affect a company's ability to forecast sales. The state of the general economy, actions of competitors, technological developments, and many other factors make an accurate sales forecast literally impossible.

Truth 3: The operating budget will be inaccurate. Once again, do not confuse inaccurate with bad. Inaccurate simply means that the actual results are going to be different from what was budgeted, meaning, of course, that variances will always exist.

Some approaches to the budget performance report help overcome the variances caused by actual sales being different from budgeted sales. The most popular of these is the flexible budget performance report, which is covered in more advanced accounting courses. Note, however, that flexible budgeting does not eliminate the problem of using the budget in a way that was never intended, that is, as the primary control device in a business.

So, how do managers overcome the problems we have been discussing in this section? Well, they do it by using the budget as it was intended to be used—as a guide for the business. Managers must be prepared to respond to changing circumstances and updated information.

On June 6, 1944, the United States military and its allies invaded Europe in perhaps the largest and most complicated military action in the history of the world. Operation Overlord, as it was called, involved many thousands of troops, and the outcome of World War II was at stake. The allies, under the supreme command of General Dwight D. Eisenhower, spent well over a year preparing for D-Day. Every detail of the invasion was meticulously planned, and the various military units involved spent months practicing their roles. The plan called for split-second timing and total coordination among all units involved.

When the invasion was launched, however, almost nothing went according to plan. Landing craft carrying the soldiers missed their target beaches, some by as much as four miles. High winds caused paratroop units to land as far as ten miles behind enemy lines. Everything went wrong. And yet, the allies ultimately won a total and complete victory in the invasion of Normandy. When he was asked how this could be when nothing went according to plan, General Eisenhower (who later became president of the United States) responded with a statement that speaks volumes to the subject of planning and control. He said "Planning is everything—the plan is nothing." What he meant was that the planning and practice the military undertook to prepare for the invasion prepared them to respond and adjust to changing conditions.

As it was in the invasion of Europe, so must it be in business. Managers should not hesitate to adjust their budgets when desirable or necessary. Further, when the period covered by the operating budget is over, an analysis should be performed to compare the actual results to the budget. The focus of this analysis, however, should be on how to improve the budgeting process rather than on the inevitable variances that have occurred.

Summary ●

The operating budget is an integral part of the overall planning process for any company. Besides serving as a guide for the business throughout the period covered by the budget, the operating budget can assist management in the allocation of resources, foster communication and coordination among various segments of the company, and establish performance standards.

The operating budget is a set of estimated financial statements. These are the budgeted income statement, the budgeted balance sheet, and the budgeted statement of cash flows. Besides the budgeted financial statements, the operating budget includes several other budgets prepared to support the budgeted financial statements. These are the sales budget, the production (or purchases) budget, the cost of goods sold (or cost of services) budget, the selling and administrative expense budget, and the cash budget (including the cash receipts schedule and the cash payments schedule).

There are several different approaches to the preparation of the operating budget. Perpetual, incremental, zero-based, top-down, bottom-up, imposed, and participative approaches to budgeting are just some that have developed over time. Each approach has certain advantages and certain disadvantages relative to the other approaches.

All the budgets included in the operating budget are dependent on the sales forecast. Indeed, the accuracy of the entire budget is dependent on the accuracy of the forecast. Many factors, including the state of the general economy, the condition of the company's industry, the actions of competitors, and technological developments all influence a company's ability to forecast its sales reasonably.

The operating budget was never meant to be used as the principal cost control device in business. Using the budget for this purpose actually encourages managers to make decisions that are detrimental to the business. If used properly, however, as a guide and coordination instrument, the operating budget can be of tremendous benefit for any company.

Key Terms

- bottom-up budgeting, M–265
- budget performance report, M–286
- budgeted balance sheet, M–261
- budgeted income statement, M–261
- budgeted statement of cash flows, M–262
- cash budget, M–261
- cash payments schedule, M–278
- cash receipts schedule, M–276
- continual budgeting, M–264
- cost of goods sold budget, M–261
- cost of services budget, M–261
- imposed budget, M–265
- incremental budgeting, M–264
- master budget, M–256
- master operating budget, M–256
- operating budget, M–256
- participative budget, M–266
- performance to budget, M–285
- perpetual budgeting, M–264
- production budget, M–260
- purchases budget, M–260
- rolling budget, M–264
- sales budget, M–260
- sales forecast, M–260
- selling and administrative expense budget, M–261
- top-down budgeting, M–265
- variance, M–286
- zero-based budgeting, M–265

Review the Facts

A. What is the operating budget?
B. What is the master budget?
C. Which financial statements are part of the operating budget?
D. What is the difference between the financial statements included in the operating budget and other financial statements you have learned about in this course?
E. List the main benefits of budgeting.
F. What is the basic difference between the production budget and the purchases budget?
G. What are two advantages of perpetual budgeting?
H. What is a disadvantage of perpetual budgeting?
I. What is incremental budgeting?
J. What problem is associated with incremental budgeting?
K. What is zero-based budgeting?
L. Describe the differences between top-down and bottom-up budgeting.
M. Describe the differences between an imposed budget and a participative budget.
N. Why is the sales forecast often called the cornerstone of budgeting?

O. Why is the sales forecast often called the keystone of budgeting?

P. List three factors that should be considered when preparing the sales forecast.

Q. Why does the number of units budgeted to be purchased differ from the number of units budgeted to be sold?

R. When preparing the purchases budget, what two factors should be considered in determining the budgeted ending inventory?

S. What is presented on the cash receipts schedule?

T. For a particular budget period, why doesn't the budgeted cash collections from customers equal budgeted sales?

U. What is the basic difference between a budgeted balance sheet and an historical balance sheet?

V. In the normal course of business, what are the three sources from which a company can obtain cash?

W. What is a performance to budget evaluation?

Apply What You Have Learned

LO 3 & 4: DETERMINE ORDER OF OPERATING BUDGET PREPARATION

9–23. During the budgeting process, not all budgets are prepared at the same time. Following are several budgets included in the operating budget.

1. _____ Cash budget
2. _____ Budgeted financial statements
3. _____ Purchases budget
4. _____ Sales budget
5. _____ Administrative expense budget
6. _____ Selling expense budget

Required: Indicate a logical sequence for the preparation of the operating budget.

LO 3: INDICATE ADVANTAGES AND DISADVANTAGES OF TOP-DOWN, BOTTOM-UP APPROACHES

9–24. The master budget can be prepared using either the top-down or bottom-up approach. Following in random order are several advantages and disadvantages of each approach.

1. _____ Budgeting process forces managers at various levels to think about future activities.
2. _____ Top manager is more knowledgeable.
3. _____ Employees at various levels must take time from their schedules to work on the budget.
4. _____ Employees will be more eager to work toward goals they helped set.
5. _____ Employees feel more like part of the company team.
6. _____ Top manager is more aware of company goals.
7. _____ Employees may try to pad the budget.
8. _____ Employees are less accepting of budgeted goals if they had no part in setting them.
9. _____ Top manager lacks detailed knowledge required to prepare budgets.

Required: For each of these items, indicate whether it is associated with top-down (T) or bottom-up (B), and whether it is an advantage (A) or disadvantage (D).

LO 3: INDICATE BUDGETING APPROACHES

9–25. Following are approaches to budgeting, with a partial definition of those items in scrambled order.

a. Perpetual budgeting
b. Incremental budgeting
c. Zero-based budgeting
d. Top-down budgeting
e. Bottom-up budgeting

1. _____ Lower-level managers and employees initially prepare the budget.
2. _____ Each item on the budget must be justified each year.
3. _____ The budget is updated every month.

4. _____ Lower-level managers generally do not participate in budget preparation.
5. _____ Uses the prior year's budget to build the new budget.

Required: For each partial definition, identify the budgeting approach to which it refers.

LO 5: PREPARE A SALES BUDGET

9–26. For 2005, Tom Norris Computer Company expects to sell 6,000 games in the first quarter, 7,000 games in the second quarter, 9,000 games in the third quarter, and 12,000 games in the fourth quarter. Each game sells for $11.

Required: Prepare the 2005 sales budget for Tom Norris Computer Company.

LO 5: PREPARE A SALES BUDGET

9–27. For 2005, Paul Elsea's Barber Supply Company expects to sell 100 hair dryers in the first quarter, 90 hair dryers in the second quarter, 130 hair dryers in the third quarter, and 150 hair dryers in the fourth quarter. Each hair dryer sells for $67.

Required: Prepare the 2005 sales budget for hair dryers for Paul Elsea's Barber Supply Company.

LO 5: PREPARE A SALES BUDGET

9–28. For the first quarter of 2005, Taub Yo Yo Company expects to sell 20,000 units in January, 25,000 units in February, and 30,000 units in March. Each unit sells for $1.20.

Required: Prepare the sales budget for Taub Yo Yo Company for the first quarter of 2005.

LO 5: PREPARE A SALES BUDGET

9–29. The Golden Bird Cage Company intends to sell 11,500 bird cages during 2005. The budgeted selling price per cage is $88. The following sales forecast is available:

	Units
First quarter	2,500
Second quarter	2,100
Third quarter	3,800
Fourth quarter	3,100

Required: Prepare the 2005 sales budget for Golden Bird Cage Company.

LO 5: PREPARE A SALES BUDGET

9–30. Easy-Glide Strollers intends to sell 73,000 baby strollers in the first quarter of 2005. The budgeted selling price per stroller is $59. The following sales forecast is available:

	Units
January	22,500
February	22,500
March	28,000

Required: Prepare the sales budget for Easy-Glide Strollers for the first quarter of 2005.

LO 5: PREPARE A PURCHASES BUDGET

9–31. Florence Marie's Hat Shop plans to sell the following quantity of hats during the first four months of 2005.

	Units
January	200
February	250
March	300
April	320

Florence pays $6 for each hat and sells them for $15.

At the beginning of January, Florence plans to have 40 hats on hand, and to maintain an ending inventory equal to 20 percent of next month's sales.

Required: Prepare a purchases budget for the first quarter of 2005 for Florence Marie's Hat Shop. Remember, the first quarter is January, February, and March. April sales are provided only to help compute the ending inventory for March.

LO 5: PREPARE A SALES BUDGET AND COST OF GOODS SOLD BUDGET

9–32. Refer to the information in problem 9–31.

Required:

 a. Prepare a sales budget for the first quarter of 2005 for Florence Marie's Hat Shop.
 b. Prepare a cost of goods sold budget for the first quarter of 2005 for Florence Marie's Hat Shop.

LO 5: PREPARE A PURCHASES BUDGET

9–33. Cathy Norris Art Supplies plans to sell the following quantity of model AB222 airbrush during the first four months of 2005:

	Units
January	40
February	26
March	22
April	20

The company pays $44 for each airbrush and sells them for $65. At the beginning of January, Cathy Norris Art Supplies plans to have six airbrushes on hand, and intends to maintain an ending inventory equal to 15 percent of next month's sales.

Required: Prepare a purchases budget for the first quarter of 2005 for Cathy Norris Art Supplies. Remember, the first quarter is January, February, and March. April sales are provided only to help compute the ending inventory for March.

LO 5: PREPARE A SALES BUDGET AND COST OF GOODS SOLD BUDGET

9–34. Refer to the information in problem 9–33.

Required:

 a. Prepare a sales budget for the first quarter of 2005 for Cathy Norris Art Supplies.
 b. Prepare a cost of goods sold budget for the first quarter of 2005 for Cathy Norris Art Supplies.

LO 5: PREPARE A SALES BUDGET, COST OF GOODS SOLD BUDGET, AND PURCHASES BUDGET

9–35. Diaz Lumber plans to sell the following quantity of BC Grade 1/2-inch plywood during the first four months of 2005:

January	220 sheets
February	250 sheets
March	200 sheets
April	300 sheets

Diaz pays $7 for each sheet of plywood and sells them for $12. At the beginning of January, Diaz plans to have 66 sheets of plywood on hand, and intends to maintain an ending inventory equal to 30 percent of next month's sales.

Required:

 a. Prepare a sales budget for the first quarter of 2005 for Diaz Lumber.
 b. Prepare a cost of goods sold budget for the first quarter of 2005 for Diaz Lumber.
 c. Prepare a purchases budget for the first quarter of 2005 for Diaz Lumber.

LO 5: PREPARE A BUDGETED INCOME STATEMENT USING INFORMATION PROVIDED IN OTHER BUDGETS

9–36. Smith Manufacturing has prepared the following budgeted information for January 2005:

Smith Manufacturing
Sales Budget
For January 2005

Budgeted Sales in Units	3,300
× Budgeted Sales Price	$ 200
= Budgeted Sales Dollars	$660,000

Smith Manufacturing
Cost of Goods Sold Budget
For January 2005

Budgeted Sales in Units	3,300
× Budgeted Cost per Unit	$ 110
= Budgeted Cost of Goods Sold	$363,000

Smith Manufacturing
Selling and Administrative Expense Budget
For January 2005

Salaries and Wages	$101,500
Rent	64,000
Depreciation	53,200
Other	2,300
Budgeted S&A Expense	$221,000

Required: Prepare a budgeted income statement for January 2005 for Smith Manufacturing.

LO 5: PREPARE A BUDGETED INCOME STATEMENT USING INFORMATION PROVIDED IN OTHER BUDGETS

9–37. Gomez Sales Company has prepared the following budgeted information for March 2005:

Gomez Sales Company
Sales Budget
For March 2005

Budgeted Sales in Units	110,000
× Budgeted Sales Price	$ 4.95
= Budgeted Sales Dollars	$544,500

Gomez Sales Company
Cost of Goods Sold Budget
For March 2005

Budgeted Sales in Units	110,000
× Budgeted Cost per Unit	$ 3.35
= Budgeted Cost of Goods Sold	$368,500

Gomez Sales Company
Selling and Administrative Expense Budget
For March 2005

Sales Salaries	$ 51,500
Sales Commission	11,000
Other Salaries and Wages	35,000
Store Rent	24,000
Other Expenses	10,500
Budgeted S&A Expense	$132,000

Required: Prepare a budgeted income statement for March 2005 for Gomez Sales Company.

LO 5: PREPARE A BUDGETED INCOME STATEMENT USING INFORMATION PROVIDED IN OTHER BUDGETS

9–38. Copas Company has prepared the following budgeted information for December 2005:

Copas Company
Sales Budget
For December 2005

Budgeted Sales in Units	10,000
× Budgeted Sales Price	$ 12.00
= Budgeted Sales Dollars	$120,000

Copas Company
Cost of Goods Sold Budget
For December 2005

Budgeted Sales in Units	10,000
× Budgeted Cost per Unit	$ 800
= Budgeted Cost of Goods Sold	$ 80,000

Copas Company
Selling and Administrative Expense Budget
For December 2005

Sales Salaries	$ 18,500
Sales Commission	3,000
Store Rent	9,000
Other Expenses	1,500
Budgeted S&A Expense	$ 32,000

Required: Prepare a budgeted income statement for December 2005 for Copas Company.

LO 5: PREPARE A BUDGETED INCOME STATEMENT

9–39. For the first quarter of 2005, Philip's Sales Corporation has budgeted sales of $390,000 and budgeted cost of goods sold of $280,000. In addition, the budget for the first quarter of 2005 includes wages and salaries of $42,000, rent of $9,000, utilities of $2,000, maintenance of $1,000, and other expenses of $3,000.

Required: Prepare a budgeted income statement for the first quarter of 2005 for Philip's Sales Corporation.

LO 5: PREPARE A BUDGETED INCOME STATEMENT

9–40. For January 2005, Edwardo Manufacturing has budgeted sales of $1,200,000 and budgeted cost of goods sold of $980,000. In addition, the budget for January 2005 includes sales salaries of $98,000, administrative salaries of $54,000, rent of $24,000, utilities of $8,000, and other expenses of $9,000.

Required: Prepare a budgeted income statement for January 2005 for Edwardo Manufacturing.

LO 5: PREPARE A BUDGETED INCOME STATEMENT

9–41. For the year 2005, Martin Sales Corporation has budgeted sales of $3,500,000 and budgeted cost of goods sold of $2,800,000. In addition, the budget for 2005 includes sales salaries of $220,000, administrative salaries of $130,000, depreciation of $180,000, utilities of $38,000, and other expenses of $22,000.

Required: Prepare a budgeted income statement for 2005 for Martin Sales Corporation.

LO 5: PREPARE A BUDGETED INCOME STATEMENT FOR ONE QUARTER

9–42. The following budgets were prepared for Gary's Jean Store:

Gary's Jean Store
Sales Budget
For the Quarter Ended June 30, 2004

	Apr	May	Jun	Total
Budgeted Sales in Units	300	350	400	1,050
× Budgeted Sales Price	$ 27	$ 27	$ 27	$ 27
= Budgeted Sales Dollars	$8,100	$9,450	$10,800	$28,350

Gary's Jean Store
Cost of Goods Sold Budget
For the Quarter Ended June 30, 2004

	Apr	May	Jun	Total
Budgeted Sales in Units	300	350	400	1,050
× Budgeted Cost per Unit	$ 14	$ 14	$ 14	$ 14
= Budgeted Cost of Goods Sold	$4,200	$4,900	$5,600	$14,700

Gary's Jean Store
Selling and Administrative Expense Budget
For the Quarter Ended June 30, 2004

	Apr	May	Jun	Total
Salaries and Wages	$1,800	$2,200	$1,900	$5,900
Rent	500	500	500	1,500
Depreciation	100	100	100	300
Other	600	900	800	2,300
Budgeted Sales Dollars	$3,000	$3,700	$3,300	$10,000

Required: Prepare a budgeted income statement for the second quarter of 2004 for Gary's Jean Store.

LO 5: PREPARE A BUDGETED INCOME STATEMENT FOR ONE QUARTER

9–43. Franco's Cart Company manufactures small carts that are designed to be pulled behind a small tractor or riding lawn mower. The following budgets were prepared for Franco's Cart Company:

Franco's Cart Company
Sales Budget
For the Quarter Ended March 31, 2004

	Jan	Feb	Mar	Total
Budgeted Sales in Units	1,300	1,450	1,700	4,450
× Budgeted Sales Price	$ 186	$ 186	$ 186	$ 186
= Budgeted Sales Dollars	$241,800	$269,700	$316,200	$827,700

Franco's Cart Company
Cost of Goods Sold Budget
For the Quarter Ended March 31, 2004

	Jan	Feb	Mar	Total
Budgeted Sales in Units	1,300	1,450	1,700	4,450
× Budgeted Cost per Unit	$ 154	$ 154	$ 154	$ 154
= Budgeted Cost of Goods Sold	$200,200	$223,300	$261,800	$685,300

Franco's Cart Company
Selling and Administrative Expense Budget
For the Quarter Ended March 31, 2004

	Jan	Feb	Mar	Total
Salaries and Wages	$21,950	$22,200	$23,600	$67,750
Rent	4,000	4,500	4,500	13,000
Depreciation	3,200	3,200	3,200	9,600
Other	2,300	2,500	2,800	7,600
Budgeted S&A Expense	$31,450	$32,400	$34,100	$97,950

Required: Prepare a budgeted income statement for the first quarter of 2004 for Franco's Cart Company.

LO 5: PREPARE A BUDGETED INCOME STATEMENT FOR ONE QUARTER

9–44. The following budgets were prepared for Byrne Manufacturing:

Byrne Manufacturing
Sales Budget
For the Quarter Ended September 30, 2005

	Jul	Aug	Sep	Total
Budgeted Unit Sales	900	1,100	1,300	3,300
× Budgeted Sales Price	$ 225	$ 225	$ 225	$ 225
= Budgeted Sales Dollars	$202,500	$247,500	$292,500	$742,500

Byrne Manufacturing
Cost of Goods Sold Budget
For the Quarter Ended September 30, 2005

	Jul	Aug	Sep	Total
Budgeted Unit Sales	900	1,100	1,300	3,300
× Budgeted Cost per Unit	$ 204	$ 204	$ 204	$ 204
= Budgeted Cost of Goods Sold	$183,600	$224,400	$265,200	$673,200

Byrne Manufacturing
Selling and Administrative Expense Budget
For the Quarter Ended September 30, 2005

	Jul	Aug	Sep	Total
Salaries and Wages	$ 4,800	$ 5,200	$ 5,800	$15,800
Rent	2,400	2,400	2,400	7,200
Depreciation	1,150	1,150	1,150	3,450
Other	1,800	2,000	2,200	6,000
Budgeted S&A Expense	$10,150	$10,750	$11,550	$32,450

Required: Prepare a budgeted income statement for the third quarter of 2005 for Byrne Manufacturing.

LO 5: PREPARE A CASH RECEIPTS SCHEDULE FOR ONE QUARTER

9–45. The Deacon Company is preparing a cash receipts schedule for the first quarter of 2004. Sales for November and December 2003 are expected to be $180,000 and $200,000, respectively. Budgeted sales for the first quarter of 2004 are presented here.

The Deacon Company
Sales Budget
For the Quarter Ended March 31, 2004

	Jan	Feb	Mar	Total
Budgeted Sales	$220,000	$240,000	$260,000	$720,000

Twenty percent of sales are for cash, the remaining 80 percent are on account. Ten percent of the sales on account are collected in the month of the sale, 60 percent in the month following the sale, and the remaining 30 percent in the second month following the sale. There are no uncollectible accounts receivable.

Required: Prepare a cash receipts schedule for the first quarter of 2004.

LO 5: PREPARE A CASH RECEIPTS SCHEDULE FOR ONE QUARTER

9–46. The V&A Velez Company is preparing a cash receipts schedule for the first quarter of 2004. Sales for November and December 2003 are expected to be $300,000 and $310,000, respectively. Budgeted sales for the first quarter of 2004 are presented here.

The V&A Velez Company
Sales Budget
For the Quarter Ended March 31, 2004

	Jan	Feb	Mar	Total
Budgeted Sales	$220,000	$290,000	$340,000	$850,000

Ten percent of sales are for cash; the remaining 90 percent are on account. Twenty percent of the sales on account are collected in the month of the sale, 70 percent in the month following the sale, and the remaining 10 percent in the second month following the sale. There are no uncollectible accounts receivable.

Required: Prepare a cash receipts schedule for the first quarter of 2004.

LO 5: PREPARE A CASH RECEIPTS SCHEDULE FOR ONE QUARTER

9–47. The Arauz Company is preparing a cash receipts schedule for the first quarter of 2005. Sales for November and December 2004 are expected to be $30,000 and $50,000, respectively. Budgeted sales for the first quarter of 2005 are presented here.

The Arauz Company
Sales Budget
For the Quarter Ended March 31, 2005

	Jan	Feb	Mar	Total
Budgeted Sales	$20,000	$25,000	$40,000	$85,000

Fifteen percent of sales are for cash, the remaining 85 percent are on account. Twenty percent of the sales on account are collected in the month of the sale, 50 percent in the month following the sale, and the remaining 30 percent in the second month following the sale. There are no uncollectible accounts receivable.

Required: Prepare a cash receipts schedule for the first quarter of 2005.

LO 5: PREPARE A CASH RECEIPTS SCHEDULE FOR ONE QUARTER

9–48. The Phillips Company is preparing a cash receipts schedule for the first quarter of 2005. Sales for November and December 2004 are expected to be $33,000 and $55,000, respectively. Budgeted sales for the first quarter of 2005 are presented here.

The Phillips Company
Sales Budget
For the Quarter Ended March 31, 2005

	Jan	Feb	Mar	Total
Budgeted Sales	$20,000	$30,000	$45,000	$95,000

Fifteen percent of sales are for cash, the remaining 85 percent are on account. Twenty percent of the sales on account are collected in the month of the sale, 50 percent in the month following the sale, and the remaining 30 percent in the second month following the sale. There are no uncollectible accounts receivable.

Required: Prepare a cash receipts schedule for the first quarter of 2005.

LO 5: PREPARE A CASH RECEIPTS SCHEDULE FOR ONE QUARTER

9–49. The Aimin Company is preparing a cash receipts schedule for the first quarter of 2005. Sales for November and December 2004 are expected to be $40,000 and $80,000, respectively. Budgeted sales for the first quarter of 2005 are presented here.

The Aimin Company
Sales Budget
For the Quarter Ended March 31, 2005

	Jan	Feb	Mar	Total
Budgeted Sales	$30,000	$40,000	$50,000	$120,000

Ten percent of sales are for cash; the remaining 90 percent are on account. Fifteen percent of the sales on account are collected in the month of the sale, 60 percent in the month following the sale, and the remaining 25 percent in the second month following the sale. There are no uncollectible accounts receivable.

Required: Prepare a cash receipts schedule for the first quarter of 2005.

LO 5: PREPARE A CASH RECEIPTS SCHEDULE FOR ONE QUARTER

9–50. The Gabriel Diaz Company is preparing a cash receipts schedule for the first quarter of 2005. Sales on account for November and December 2004 are expected to be $500,000 and $750,000, respectively. Budgeted sales for the first quarter of 2005 are presented here.

The Gabriel Diaz Company
Sales Budget
For the Quarter Ended March 31, 2005

	Jan	Feb	Mar	Total
Budgeted Cash Sales	$ 40,000	$ 45,000	$ 55,000	$ 140,000
Budgeted Sales on Account	400,000	450,000	550,000	1,400,000
Total Sales	$440,000	$495,000	$605,000	$1,540,000

Expected collection pattern for sales on account:

15 percent in the month of sale
60 percent in the month following the sale
25 percent in the second month following the sale
 0 percent uncollectible

Required: Prepare a cash receipts schedule for the first quarter of 2005.

LO 5: PREPARE A CASH RECEIPTS SCHEDULE FOR ONE QUARTER

9–51. The Lila Steinman Company is preparing a cash receipts schedule for the first quarter of 2005. Sales on account for November and December 2004 are expected to be $200,000 and $400,000, respectively. Budgeted sales for the first quarter of 2005 are presented here.

The Lila Steinman Company
Sales Budget
For the Quarter Ended March 31, 2005

	Jan	Feb	Mar	Total
Budgeted Cash Sales	$ 20,000	$ 25,000	$ 27,000	$ 72,000
Budgeted Sales on Account	180,000	210,000	250,000	640,000
Total Sales	$200,000	$235,000	$277,000	$712,000

Expected collection pattern for sales on account:

10 percent in the month of sale
70 percent in the month following the sale
20 percent in the second month following the sale
 0 percent uncollectible

Required: Prepare a cash receipts schedule for the first quarter of 2005.

LO 5: PREPARE A CASH RECEIPTS SCHEDULE FOR ONE QUARTER

9–52. The Lowensohn Company is preparing a cash receipts schedule for the first quarter of 2005. Sales on account for November and December 2004 are expected to be $320,000 and $550,000, respectively. Budgeted sales for the first quarter of 2005 are presented here.

The Lowensohn Company
Sales Budget
For the Quarter Ended March 31, 2005

	Jan	Feb	Mar	Total
Budgeted Cash Sales	$120,000	$150,000	$125,000	$395,000
Budgeted Sales on Account	180,000	225,000	190,000	595,000
Total Sales	$300,000	$375,000	$315,000	$990,000

Expected collection pattern for sales on account:

30 percent in the month of sale
50 percent in the month following the sale
20 percent in the second month following the sale
 0 percent uncollectible

Required: Prepare a cash receipts schedule for the first quarter of 2005.

LO 5: PREPARE A CASH RECEIPTS SCHEDULE FOR ONE QUARTER

9–53. The S. R. Jackson Company is preparing a cash receipts schedule for the second quarter of 2005. Sales on account for February and March 2005 are expected to be $50,000 and $60,000, respectively. Budgeted sales for the second quarter of 2005 are presented here.

The S. R. Jackson Company
Sales Budget
For the Quarter Ended June 30, 2005

	Apr	May	Jun	Total
Budgeted Cash Sales	$15,000	$20,000	$25,000	$ 60,000
Budgeted Sales on Account	30,000	40,000	50,000	120,000
Total Sales	$45,000	$60,000	$75,000	$180,000

Expected collection pattern for sales on account:

25 percent in the month of sale
50 percent in the month following the sale
25 percent in the second month following the sale
 0 percent uncollectible

Required: Prepare a cash receipts schedule for the second quarter of 2005.

LO 5: PREPARE A CASH RECEIPTS SCHEDULE FOR ONE QUARTER

9–54. The Hodson Company is preparing a cash receipts schedule for the third quarter of 2005. Sales on account for May and June 2005 are expected to be $100,000 and $120,000, respectively. Budgeted sales for the third quarter of 2005 are presented here.

The Hodson Company
Sales Budget
For the Quarter Ended September 30, 2005

	Jul	Aug	Sep	Total
Budgeted Cash Sales	$ 8,000	$ 9,000	$ 11,000	$ 28,000
Budgeted Sales on Account	80,000	90,000	110,000	280,000
Total Sales	$88,000	$99,000	$121,000	$308,000

Expected collection pattern for sales on account:

10 percent in the month of sale
60 percent in the month following the sale
30 percent in the second month following the sale
 0 percent uncollectible

Required: Prepare a cash receipts schedule for the third quarter of 2005.

LO 5: PREPARE A CASH RECEIPTS SCHEDULE FOR ONE QUARTER

9–55. The A. R. Oddo Company is preparing a cash receipts schedule for the fourth quarter of 2005. Sales on account for August and September 2005 are expected to be $200,000 and $220,000, respectively. Budgeted sales for the fourth quarter of 2005 are presented here.

The A. R. Oddo Company
Sales Budget
For the Quarter Ended December 31, 2005

	Oct	Nov	Dec	Total
Budgeted Cash Sales	$ 42,000	$ 46,000	$ 60,000	$148,000
Budgeted Sales on Account	210,000	230,000	300,000	740,000
Total Sales	$252,000	$276,000	$360,000	$888,000

Expected collection pattern for sales on account:

20 percent in the month of sale
70 percent in the month following the sale
10 percent in the second month following the sale
 0 percent uncollectible

Required: Prepare a cash receipts schedule for the fourth quarter of 2005.

LO 5: PREPARE A CASH RECEIPTS SCHEDULE FOR ONE QUARTER

9–56. The law firm of Hendricks & Hendricks is preparing a cash receipts schedule for the first quarter of 2005. Service revenue for November and December 2004 are expected to be $90,000 and $50,000, respectively. All billings are on account. There are no "cash sales." Budgeted service revenue for the first quarter of 2005 is presented here.

Hendricks & Hendricks
Service Revenue Budget
For the Quarter Ended March 31, 2005

	Jan	Feb	Mar	Total
Budgeted Service Revenue	$40,000	$50,000	$65,000	$155,000

Expected collection pattern:

30 percent in the month of sale
60 percent in the month following the sale
10 percent in the second month following the sale
 0 percent uncollectible

Required: Prepare a cash receipts schedule for the first quarter of 2005.

LO 5: PREPARE A CASH RECEIPTS SCHEDULE FOR ONE QUARTER

9–57. The medical practice of Healit & Quick is preparing a cash receipts schedule for the first quarter of 2005. Service revenue for November and December 2004 are expected to be $120,000 and $110,000, respectively. All billings are on account. There are no "cash sales." Budgeted service revenue for the first quarter of 2005 is presented here.

Healit & Quick
Service Revenue Budget
For the Quarter Ended March 31, 2005

	Jan	Feb	Mar	Total
Budgeted Service Revenue	$120,000	$130,000	$140,000	$155,000

Expected collection pattern:

20 percent in the month of sale
60 percent in the month following the sale
20 percent in the second month following the sale
 0 percent uncollectible

Required: Prepare a cash receipts schedule for the first quarter of 2005.

LO 5: PREPARE A CASH PAYMENTS SCHEDULE FOR ONE QUARTER

9–58. Marcy Steinmann and Company has prepared the following budgets for the first quarter of 2005:

Marcy Steinmann and Company
Selling and Administrative Expense Budget
For the Quarter Ended March 31, 2005

	Jan	Feb	Mar	Total
Salaries and Wages	$1,700	$2,200	$1,900	$ 5,800
Rent	300	300	300	900
Depreciation	200	200	200	600
Other	900	1.200	1,000	3,100
Total	$3,100	$3,900	$3,400	$10,400

Marcy Steinmann and Company
Purchases Budget
For the Quarter Ended March 31, 2005

	Jan	Feb	Mar	Total
Forecasted Unit Sales	50	60	70	180
+ Desired Ending Inventory	12	14	16	16
= Total Units Needed	62	74	86	196
− Beginning Inventory	(10)	(12)	(14)	(10)
= Units to Be Purchased	52	62	72	186
× Cost per Unit	$ 220	$ 220	$ 220	$ 220
= Cost of Purchases	$11,440	$13,640	$15,840	$40,920

Selling and administrative expenses are paid in the month incurred and purchases are paid in the month following the purchase. Purchases for December 2004 are $10,500. No equipment purchases or additional expenditures are made during the quarter.

Required: Prepare a cash payment schedule for the first quarter of 2005.

LO 5: PREPARE A CASH PAYMENTS SCHEDULE FOR ONE QUARTER

9–59. Jackson Sales Company has prepared the following budgets for the second quarter of 2005:

Jackson Sales Company
Selling and Administrative Expense Budget
For the Quarter Ended June 30, 2005

	Apr	May	Jun	Total
Salaries	$1,000	$1,200	$1,300	$3,500
Rent	200	200	200	600
Utilities	120	180	220	520
Depreciation	80	80	80	240
Other	500	600	650	1,750
Total	$1,900	$2,260	$2,450	$6,610

Jackson Sales Company
Purchases Budget
For the Quarter Ended June 30, 2005

	Apr	May	Jun	Total
Forecasted Unit Sales	70	80	90	240
+ Desired Ending Inventory	16	18	19	19
= Total Units Needed	86	98	109	259
− Beginning Inventory	(15)	(16)	(18)	(15)
= Units to Be Purchased	71	82	91	244
× Cost per Unit	$ 100	$ 100	$ 100	$ 100
= Cost of Purchases	$7,100	$8,200	$9,100	$24,400

Selling and administrative expenses are paid in the month incurred and purchases are paid in the month following the purchase. Purchases for March 2005 are $6,800. No equipment purchases or additional expenditures are made during the quarter.

Required: Prepare a cash payment schedule for the second quarter of 2005.

LO 5: PREPARE A CASH PAYMENTS SCHEDULE FOR ONE MONTH

9–60. The following budgeted information is available for the Top Coat Clothing Company for January 2005.

Salaries	$120,000
Rent	9,000
Utilities	1,200
Depreciation	3,200
Other Expenses	1,500
Purchases	380,000

Selling and administrative expenses are paid in the month incurred and purchases are paid in the month following the purchase. Purchases for December 2004 are $350,000. No equipment purchases or additional expenditures are made during the month.

Required: Prepare a cash payment schedule for January 2005.

LO 5: PREPARE A CASH PAYMENTS SCHEDULE FOR ONE MONTH

9–61. The following budgeted information is available for Jack's Feed Store in June 2005.

Salaries	$12,000
Rent	600
Electricity	140
Depreciation	800
Other Expenses	700
Purchases	80,000

Selling and administrative expenses are paid in the month incurred and purchases are paid in the month following the purchase. Purchases for May 2005 are $75,000. No equipment purchases or additional expenditures are made during the month.

Required: Prepare a cash payment schedule for June 2005.

LO 5: PREPARE A CASH BUDGET FOR ONE QUARTER

9–62. The following information is available for the Art Kriner Company for the first quarter of 2005:

	Jan	Feb	Mar
Budgeted Receipts from Credit Sales	$5,000	$5,500	$5,800
Budgeted Cash Sales	1,200	1,250	1,300
Budgeted Cash Payments	6,300	7,185	6,520

Beginning cash balance for January 2005 is expected to be $1,500. The company intends to maintain a cash balance of at least $1,000. The company has made arrangements to borrow from a local bank if necessary.

Required: Prepare a cash budget for the first quarter of 2005.

LO 5: PREPARE A CASH BUDGET FOR ONE QUARTER

9–63. The following information is available for the Dixon Company for the second quarter of 2005.

	Apr	May	Jun
Budgeted Receipts from Credit Sales	$500,000	$520,000	$550,000
Budgeted Cash Sales	100,000	105,000	112,000
Budgeted Cash Payments	670,000	615,000	627,000

Beginning cash balance for April 2005 is expected to be $90,000. The company intends to maintain a cash balance of at least $50,000. The company has made arrangements to borrow from a local bank if necessary.

Required: Prepare a cash budget for the second quarter of 2005.

LO 5: PREPARE A CASH BUDGET FOR ONE QUARTER

9–64. The following information is available for the Ortega Company for the first quarter of 2005:

	Jan	Feb	Mar
Budgeted Receipts from Credit Sales	$100,000	$110,000	$115,000
Budgeted Cash Sales	80,000	95,000	98,000
Budgeted Cash Payments	178,000	215,000	206,000

Beginning cash balance for January 2005 is expected to be $20,000. The company intends to maintain a cash balance of at least $15,000. The company has made arrangements to borrow from a local bank if necessary.

Required: Prepare a cash budget for the first quarter of 2005.

LO 5: PREPARE A CASH BUDGET FOR ONE MONTH

9–65. The following information is available for November 2005.

Budgeted Receipts from Credit Sales	$25,100
Budgeted Cash Sales	5,900
Budgeted Cash Payments	32,600

Beginning cash balance for November is expected to be $5,800. The company intends to maintain a cash balance of at least $5,000. The company has made arrangements to borrow from a local bank if necessary.

Required: Prepare a cash budget for November 2005.

LO 5: PREPARE A CASH BUDGET FOR ONE MONTH

9–66. The following information is available for October 2005.

Budgeted Receipts from Credit Sales	$300,000
Budgeted Cash Sales	80,000
Budgeted Cash Payments	410,000

Beginning cash balance for October is expected to be $60,000. The company intends to maintain a cash balance of at least $50,000. The company has made arrangements to borrow from a local bank if necessary.

Required: Prepare a cash budget for October 2005.

LO 5: PREPARE A CASH BUDGET FOR ONE MONTH

9–67. The following information is available for July 2005.

Budgeted Receipts from Credit Sales	$500,000
Budgeted Cash Sales	40,000
Budgeted Cash Payments	577,000

Beginning cash balance for July is expected to be $95,000. The company intends to maintain a cash balance of at least $75,000. The company has made arrangements to borrow from a local bank if necessary.

Required: Prepare a cash budget for July 2005.

LO 5: PREPARE A BUDGETED BALANCE SHEET AND BUDGETED STATEMENT OF CASH FLOWS FOR THREE MONTHS

9–68. The following information is available for the Perlmuter Printing Supply Company.

Perlmuter Printing Supply Company
Sales Budget
For the Quarter Ended September 30, 2004

	July	August	September
Budgeted Sales Dollars	$90,000	$80,000	$70,000

Perlmuter Printing Supply Company
Cost of Goods Sold Budget
For the Quarter Ended September 30, 2004

	July	August	September
Budgeted Cost of Goods Sold	$54,000	$48,000	$42,000

Perlmuter Printing Supply Company
Selling and Administrative Expense Budget
For the Quarter Ended September 30, 2004

	July	August	September
Salaries and Wages	$12,600	$12,000	$11,800
Rent	1,000	1,000	1,000
Depreciation	1,800	1,800	1,800
Other	3,800	3,000	2,900
Total	$19,200	$17,800	$17,500

Perlmuter Printing Supply Company
Budgeted Income Statement
For the Quarter Ended September 30, 2004

	July	August	September
Sales	$90,000	$80,000	$70,000
Cost of Goods Sold	54,000	48,000	42,000
Gross Profit	36,000	32,000	28,000
S&A Expense	19,200	17,800	17,500
Net Income	$16,800	$14,200	$10,500

Perlmuter Printing Supply Company
Purchases Budget
For the Quarter Ended September 30, 2004

	July	August	September
Cost of Purchases	$52,000	$46,000	$41,000

Perlmuter Printing Supply Company
Cash Receipts Schedule
For the Quarter Ended September 30, 2004

	July	August	September
Budgeted Receipts From			
Credit Sales	$78,000	$76,000	$68,000
Budgeted Cash Sales	9,000	8,000	7,000
Total Cash Receipts	$87,000	$84,000	$75,000

Perlmuter Printing Supply Company
Cash Payments Schedule
For the Quarter Ended September 30, 2004

	July	August	September
Purchases	$56,000	$52,000	$46,000
Selling and Admin. Expense:			
Salaries and Wages	$12,600	$12,000	$11,800
Rent	1,000	1,000	1,000
Other	3,800	3,000	2,900
Budgeted Cash Payments	$73,400	$68,000	$61,700

Perlmuter Printing Supply Company
Cash Budget
For the Quarter Ended September 30, 2004

	July	August	September
Beginning Cash Balance	$ 18,500	$ 32,100	$ 48,100
+ Cash Receipts	87,000	84,000	75,000
= Cash Available	$105,500	$116,100	$123,100
Cash Payments	(73,400)	(68,000)	(61,700)
= Balance before Borrowing	$ 32,100	$ 48,100	$ 61,400
+/– Borrowing/(Repayment)	-0-	-0-	-0-
= Ending Cash Balance	$ 32,100	$ 48,100	$ 61,400

Perlmuter Printing Supply Company
Balance Sheet
As of June 30, 2004

Assets:	
Current Assets	
Cash	$ 18,500
Accounts Receivable	20,000
Inventory	16,000
Total Current Assets	$ 54,500
Property, Plant, and Equipment	
Equipment	108,000
Less Accumulated Depreciation	(43,200)
Equipment, Net	$ 64,800
Total Assets	$119,300
Liabilities:	
Current Liabilities	
Accounts Payable	$ 56,000
Total Liabilities	$ 56,000
Stockholders' Equity:	
Paid-in Capital	
Common Stock	$ 1,000
Additional Paid-in Capital	10,000
Total Paid-in Capital	$ 11,000
Retained Earnings	$ 52,300
Total Stockholders' Equity	$ 63,300
Total Liabilities and Equity	$119,300

Required:

a. Prepare budgeted balance sheets for July, August, and September 2004.
b. Prepare budgeted statements of cash flows for July, August, and September 2004.

LO 5: DETERMINE MISSING BUDGET INFORMATION

9–69. Following is a partial performance report:

Description	Budget	Actual	Variance
Wages	$5,000	$5,200	$?
Store Rent	6,000	?	200 F
Utilities Expense	?	1,200	50 U

Required: Provide the missing information.

LO 5: DETERMINE BUDGET VARIANCES

9–70. Following is a partial performance report.

Description	Budget	Actual	Variance
Sales	$25,000	$22,000	$?
Cost of Goods Sold	20,000	17,600	?
Gross Profit	5,000	4,400	?

Required: Calculate the variances for this information and indicate whether they are favorable (F) or unfavorable (U).

LO 5: DETERMINE BUDGET VARIANCES

9–71. Following is a partial performance report.

Description	Budget	Actual	Variance
Rent Revenue	$15,000	$14,000	$?
Interest Expense	15,000	14,000	?

Required: Calculate the variances for this information and indicate whether they are favorable (F) or unfavorable (U).

LO 6: DISCUSS VARIANCES

9–72. Robin Wince owns a small chain of frame shops. All the frames and other merchandise the company sells is purchased by the company's central purchasing department. A partial performance report showing the direct costs for one of Robin's stores appears as follows:

	Budget	Actual	Variance
Sales	$200,000	$200,000	$ -0-
Cost of Goods Sold	120,000	110,000	10,000 F
S&A Expense	40,000	50,000	10,000 U
Income	$ 40,000	$ 40,000	$ -0-

Required: Robin is concerned even though the variance in income is zero. Because the total variance is zero, the store manager believes that there is no problem. Do you agree with the manager? Why?

LO 6: PREPARE A MEMO REGARDING VARIANCES

9–73. Matt Lehti owns the Zap Record Shop. He is in the process of examining the following performance report:

	Budget	Actual	Variance
Sales	$100,000	$120,000	$20,000 F
Cost of Goods Sold	60,000	72,000	12,000 U
Selling and Admin. Expense	10,000	9,000	1,000 F
Income	$ 30,000	$ 39,000	$ 9,000 F

Matt is very pleased that the company had favorable variances for sales and income. However, he finds the sizable unfavorable variance for cost of goods sold very disturbing. He is preparing himself for a serious discussion with the purchasing agent who is responsible for purchasing the merchandise sold.

Required: Assume that Matt Lehti has asked you for assistance in preparing for the meeting with the purchasing agent. Prepare a memo to Matt that provides him with any information you think would be helpful.

CHAPTER 10

Standard Costing

How do managers know which problems are the most pressing ones? How do they know how much time to spend solving such problems? Suppose, for example, that you are the production manager for Inline Skate Company. Your responsibilities include making sure that the plant produces high-quality skates at a relatively low cost. If the actual production cost for a pair of skates is $12.87, how would you know whether this amount is acceptable? In addition, how would you know which specific costs are too high, too low, or just right? You could focus on a selected cost area such as direct material, but you might be spending valuable time trying to control costs that are already under control.

standard costing The process of setting cost performance goals that benchmark acceptable performance and then using these cost goals to evaluate performance.

Fortunately, standard costing can help overcome some of the guesswork inherent to operating a business. **Standard costing** is the process of setting cost performance goals that benchmark desirable performance and then using these cost goals to evaluate performance. Under standard costing, employees work to establish performance goals that can be used as benchmarks for good performance. As these goals are being set, employees are planning how factory resources will be acquired and used. Then, once operations begin, employees strive to control costs so the goals can be met.

The goals also provide management with a basis for performance evaluation when actual results are compared to goals to help find areas of weakness.

If the Inline Skate Company used standard costing, you could evaluate the $12.87 cost per pair of skates by comparing it to the amount budgeted. In fact, standard costing would allow you to review each component of production cost. You would be able to detect cost overruns for direct material, direct labor, variable manufacturing overhead, or fixed manufacturing overhead. In short, standard costing provides managers with a means to quickly focus their attention on problem areas.

Learning Objectives

After completing your work on this chapter, you should be able to do the following:

1. Describe standard costing and indicate why standard costing is important.
2. Explain the concept of management by exception.
3. Contrast ideal and practical standards.
4. Identify and discuss the weaknesses of standard costing.
5. Compare standard costing, actual costing, and normal costing.
6. Determine standards for a manufacturing company.
7. Calculate standard cost variances for direct material, direct labor, variable manufacturing overhead, and fixed manufacturing overhead.
8. Describe the meaning of standard cost variances for direct material, direct labor, variable manufacturing overhead, and fixed manufacturing overhead.
9. Prepare journal entries to record standard costs and variances. (Appendix)

◆ WHY IS STANDARD COSTING USED?

standard A preestablished benchmark for desirable performance.

standard cost system A system in which cost standards are set after careful analysis and then used to evaluate actual performance.

In today's competitive environment, business success depends in large part on solid planning, as discussed in Chapter 9. Standard costing is often a key planning tool. When a company uses standard costing, it establishes performance standards for the coming year. A **standard** is a preestablished benchmark for desirable performance. A **standard cost system** is one in which a company, after careful analysis, sets cost standards and then uses them to evaluate actual performance.

Standard costing is used to bolster business success. In general, the use of standard costing encourages planning, establishes performance targets, and provides a basis for evaluating actual performance.

Planning is a critical part of any standard cost system. Managers and other employees work to gather information and investigate ways of achieving acceptable performance at the lowest cost. With this information, standards are established. For example, standards are created for the amount and cost of direct material, and for the number of direct labor hours and their cost. The process of planning provides benefits to the company because, once employees have established standards during the planning process, they know what needs to be done and how to do it most efficiently.

Once standards have been set, they can be used as performance targets. Managers and employees are encouraged to act so that actual results meet the expectations established by the standards. For example, if the production cost standard (the cost goal) for a pair of skates made by the Inline Skate Company is $13, employees are encouraged to make the skates for $13 or less. In an ideal situation, every employee would work to make the highest quality skates for less than the $13 standard cost.

variance The difference between actual performance and the standard.

To determine whether and where problems exist, managers compare actual results to the standards. A **variance** is the difference between actual performance and the standard. Variances can be used to help determine where managers should focus their attention.

unfavorable variance The difference between actual performance and standard performance when the actual performance falls below the standard.

Actual performance that falls below standard results in an **unfavorable variance.** Essentially, an unfavorable variance reflects a situation in which the cost of actual performance is higher than planned performance. For example, if the standard direct labor time to manufacture a desk is 12 minutes and it actually takes 15 minutes, the three-minute difference constitutes an unfavorable variance of three minutes. Because it is more costly to the company when three minutes of additional labor is used than was planned, an unfavorable variance is an indication that a problem may exist and management attention is needed.

favorable variance The difference between actual performance and standard performance when the actual performance exceeds the standard.

When actual performance exceeds the expectations established by the standard, a **favorable variance** results. In our desk example, if it actually takes 11 minutes to make the desk instead of the standard 12 minutes, the difference constitutes a favorable variance of one minute because cost to the company is reduced if labor time is one minute less than planned.

It might seem that a favorable variance indicates that management attention is not needed, but such is not always the case. Managers should review all variances, favorable and unfavorable, and use judgment and additional information to prioritize problem-solving efforts. For example, if a purchasing agent is able to buy direct material for less than the standard price, a favorable variance will occur. If the lower price is the result of purchasing substandard material, the "favorable" variance may not actually be to the company's benefit at all. Another reason to look into the cause of favorable variances is to learn how performance was improved. If the favorable variance is the result of improved performance, management may be able to learn how to make similar performance improvements in other areas of the company.

Items that have no variance should also be investigated. As discussed in Chapter 9, the absence of a variance should not be construed as meaning that everything is as it should be with that particular item. Managers must also remember that the cause of a variance may be the standard and not the performance. Standard setting is not an exact science. Standards must be reviewed often and changed as circumstances warrant.

It is most helpful if managers are able to review related standard cost variances together. For this purpose, a performance report is often prepared that summarizes variances for a particular operation of the company and shows where attention is needed. The process of focusing management attention on areas where actual performance deviates from the preestablished standards is called **management by exception.**

Under management by exception, managers first tend to problems associated with large variances. Then, once the large problems have been addressed, managers can turn to areas associated with lesser variances. Finally, as time permits, items where no variances exist are examined.

management by exception The process of focusing management attention on areas where actual performance deviates from the preestablished standards.

◆ STANDARDS—A CLOSER LOOK

Most companies set cost standards once each year. Even if variances occur, it is generally unwise to casually adjust standards during the year, because managers might be too quick to adjust them to eliminate an unfavorable variance instead of working to improve performance. Also, if standards are adjusted too often, performance becomes difficult to track. Performance that resulted in an unfavorable variance one month might result in a favorable variance the next month once the standard has been changed. Standards should be altered only if conditions change so significantly that the established standards lose their effectiveness as performance targets.

QUANTITY AND PRICE STANDARDS

Performance standards can be set for almost any business activity. For example, standards can be set for the number of product returns, or for the amount of employee turnover. In practice, however, standards are used most often to help control costs.

Two things can cause a cost to increase: the quantity used and the price paid. It is better to establish both a quantity standard and a separate price standard for each material used in production. For example, to say the direct material for product X should cost $3 per unit is not as helpful in controlling cost as saying that it should take 1.5 pounds of material at $2 per pound to make product X. Establishing a quantity and price standard provides performance targets for the amount of material used in production and a separate target for finding the material at the best purchase price.

Although it is also helpful to establish quantity and price standards for direct labor, we generally do not refer to labor in terms of *quantity* and *price*. Instead, we use the equivalent terms *hours* and *rate*. The quantity standard for labor is the number of hours, and the price standard is the rate.

IDEAL VERSUS PRACTICAL STANDARDS

During the planning process, managers and other employees work to set standards that will both help provide performance targets and provide a basis for performance evaluation. If we were setting a price standard for the purchase of gasoline, for example, we could set a cost goal of $0.50 per gallon, $5 per gallon, or any price in between. The object would be to select a standard that would challenge employees to find gasoline at the best price. If the standard is set at $0.50 per gallon, it is unlikely that employees will even try to achieve this impossible standard. On the other hand, if the standard is set at $5 per gallon, employees will be able to achieve the standard so easily that it will offer no incentive to find low-cost gasoline. Generally, it is best to select a standard that offers a challenging, yet achievable, performance goal.

Ideal Standards

ideal standard A standard that is attainable only under perfect conditions.

A standard that is attainable only under perfect conditions is called an **ideal standard.** Under ideal standards, there is no room for substandard performance of any kind. In a manufacturing setting, for instance, ideal standards assume that the plant operates in a perfect world with no machine downtime, no waste of direct material for any reason, and no employee rest breaks. In the real world, ideal standards are nearly impossible to achieve. Such standards may frustrate employees because, no matter how hard they try, they will never be able to meet them. In time, employees may throw up their hands and stop trying to meet the standards altogether.

Practical Standards

practical standard A standard that allows for normal, recurring inefficiencies.

A standard that allows for normal, recurring inefficiencies is called a **practical standard.** For example, in manufacturing, a practical standard for the quantity of direct material would allow for waste due to expected defects in the material. For labor, a practical standard would provide for employees working at a normal pace with adequate rest periods. When compared to ideal standards, practical standards are more realistic and less likely to result in unreasonable unfavorable variances. In addition, when practical standards are used, an unfavorable variance indicates that a true problem exists. Accordingly, most companies use practical standards.

SETTING STANDARDS

Often, standards are based on past performance. For example, if material Y was purchased for $4.45 per pound last year, it is likely it can be purchased for about $4.45 the next year; but using last year's actual amounts as next year's standards is overly simplistic. When setting standards, it is best to use historical information, and then incorporate any anticipated changes in efficiency or price.

It is usually best to use a team approach to establish each standard. Whether formal or informal, a team approach for gathering input from various knowledgeable employees will result in better, more appropriate standards. For example, when setting direct material standards for a manufacturer, a team approach would likely be better than a single employee setting the standards based solely on his or her own limited knowledge. The team might include accountants, production-line workers, production supervisors, purchasing agents, and others who are knowledgeable about the quality, use, sources, and prices of direct material. Then, the historical information provided by the accountants, information about usage and quality requirements provided by production personnel, and information about sourcing and pricing from the purchasing agent can be analyzed. Once the team has examined all this information, appropriate direct material standards can be set.

If reasonable standards are established, actual performance is accurately measured and compared to the standards, and a system to provide performance reports is put in place, standard costing can be a valuable management tool. A flowchart of how standard costing works is shown in Exhibit 10–1. Managers can then encourage employees

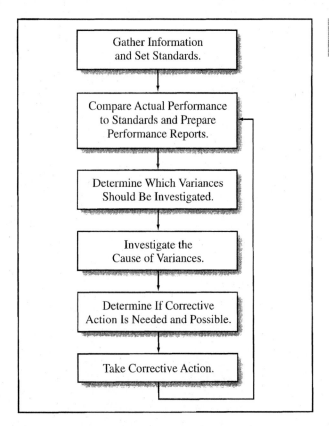

EXHIBIT 10–1   The Standard Costing Process

to strive to meet the performance goals established by the standards, and can use performance reports and management by exception to help direct their attention to trouble areas. Unfortunately, standard costing is not the answer to all management's problems. When managers rely too heavily on standard costing, serious problems occur.

PROBLEMS WITH STANDARD COSTING

To use standard costing as an effective management tool, managers must be aware of its drawbacks. The first problems may occur when standards are being set. Employees with relevent expertise are often consulted to help establish an appropriate standard. Most of these employees are keenly aware that the standard will be used later to evaluate their performance. With lax standards, employees will not have to work as hard to meet the goals set by the standard, and unfavorable variances will be less likely. With stringent standards, employees will have to work much harder to meet targeted goals. Accordingly, employees may be tempted to make sure that the standards adopted by the company are lax, resulting in suboptimal performance goals.

Another problem with standard costing stems from relying on historical information to set standards. If past performance was less than optimal, the new standards will call for performance that is less than optimal. The inefficiency of the past may be built into the new standards. Sometimes employees and lower-level managers deliberately manipulate actual performance so it appears that less stringent standards should be maintained. This way, employees are less likely to face the consequences of unfavorable performance variances in the future.

Still another serious problem associated with standard costing is that managers tend to manage everything "by the numbers." When a standard cost system is well established, managers often focus almost entirely on significant, unfavorable variances and overlook serious problems that do not give rise to unfavorable variances. For example, a manager may try desperately to reduce an unfavorable direct material variance while completely overlooking a significant product quality problem. Why? The product quality problem does not result in a variance; therefore, a manager whose attention is directed solely by management by exception would have no "exception" to direct him or her to the quality problem. Managers may get so engrossed in chasing down problems associated with unfavorable variances that they waste company time and resources as they try to rectify insignificant problems.

In addition, managers who use management by exception may spend so much time on unfavorable variances that they fail to recognize employees who are responsible for favorable variances. By failing to recognize employees who do a good job, managers lose the benefit of positive reinforcement as a management tool.

Yet another problem is that managers lose sight of the overall business operation as they focus on the multitude of details which have resulted in unfavorable variances. In time, managers focus so much on unfavorable variance details that they cannot see the forest for the trees. The overall performance of the company may suffer because managers are managing details while ignoring the big picture.

A summary of the problems associated with standard costing is presented in Exhibit 10–2. Take some time to become familiar with these problems.

WHO USES STANDARD COSTING?

Almost any business entity can use standard costing regardless of whether it is a for-profit or a not-for-profit organization. Although it is most often used by manufacturers, service and merchandising may also use standard costing. Whenever it is appropriate to establish standards of performance for purposes of planning and control, standard costing can be used. For example, a tire store might establish a standard for the amount of time it should take to change a set of tires. An oil change center might establish a standard for the amount of time it should take to change the oil and service an automobile. An airline catering company could develop standards for the quantity and price of each food item, the labor hours and labor rate to prepare each item, and a standard for the amount of overhead cost associated with each item it sells.

Problems with Standard Costing

1. Employees who help set standards may try to avoid unfavorable variances by setting lax standards.
2. Reliance on historical information may perpetuate past inefficiencies in current standards.
3. Managers that manage "by the numbers" may overlook significant problems that do not result in an unfavorable variance or waste time on insignificant unfavorable variances.
4. Managers may focus so much on unfavorable variances that they fail to recognize employees who are doing a good job.
5. Managers may focus so much on variances that they fail to see the big picture.

EXHIBIT 10–2   Summary of Standard Costing Problems

In a manufacturing environment, companies use a standard cost system to budget the cost of producing each individual unit of product. In effect, standard costing is like preparing a budget for a single unit of production. Managers estimate the cost of direct material, direct labor, variable manufacturing overhead, and fixed manufacturing overhead required to produce each item.

In Chapter 3 we discussed two types of cost systems. In an *actual cost system* we compute actual direct material, direct labor, and manufacturing overhead costs. In a *normal cost system* we compute actual direct material and actual direct labor costs, and use a predetermined application rate for manufacturing overhead. Standard costing goes one step further. In a standard cost system, estimated amounts are used for direct material, direct labor, and manufacturing overhead. Exhibit 10–3 compares the three cost systems.

EXHIBIT 10–3   Comparison of Actual, Normal, and Standard Cost Systems

Cost Classification	Actual Cost System	Normal Cost System	Standard Cost System
Direct Material	Actual	Actual	Estimated
Direct Labor	Actual	Actual	Estimated
Manufacturing Overhead	Actual	Estimated	Estimated

In the sections that follow, we discuss the details of how standard costing is used in manufacturing.

◆ BASIC STANDARD COSTING FOR A MANUFACTURER

When manufacturing companies use standard costing, standards are set for direct material, direct labor, variable manufacturing overhead, and fixed manufacturing overhead. We will walk through the most commonly used standards and variances using the Tree Top Mailbox Company as an example. Tree Top is a small company that makes a single product.

Tree Top Mailbox Company was founded by three college sophomores, Ali, Maria, and Bill. They started the company to earn spending money while they attended college. The trio had done some market research and determined that they could sell decorative wooden mailboxes for $10 each. They each planned to work about 60 hours per month for $10 per hour. Any remaining profits would be left in the company to be divided equally at the end of their venture.

The three entrepreneurs rented a garage to house the small company for $200 per month plus utilities. They purchased equipment—a table saw and drill press—for $900. The estimated useful life of the equipment is three years.

In October, Tree Top's first month of operation, the company was able to sell every mailbox produced. By the end of October, they had made and sold 300 boxes. As shown on the income statement in Exhibit 10–4, the company's profits for October totaled $305.

EXHIBIT 10–4 Tree Top's October 2004 Income Statement

Tree Top Mailbox Company
Income Statement
For the Month Ended October 31, 2004

Sales (300 mailboxes at $10 each)		$3,000
Less Expenses		
Direct Material	$ 600	
Direct Labor (180 hours at $10 per hour)	1,800	
Rent	200	
Utilities (all variable)	40	
Miscellaneous Variable Cost	30	
Depreciation	25	(2,695)
Net Income		$ 305

Discussion Questions

10-1. How did Ali, Maria, and Bill calculate the depreciation expense of $25 per month?

10-2. Can you tell from Exhibit 10–4 whether the three Tree Top employees met their business goals in the month of October? Why or why not?

Ali, Maria, and Bill were thrilled that their equity in the company had grown by $305 in the first month. They felt that information for October's business activity could be used to develop a standard cost system to help manage their company.

◆ SETTING DIRECT MATERIAL STANDARDS

As stated, setting direct material standards involves two important considerations: the quantity of material and the price paid. We now discuss each of these in some detail.

DIRECT MATERIAL QUANTITY STANDARD

direct material quantity standard The amount of direct material it should take to manufacture a single unit of product.

bill of materials A listing of the quantity and description of each item of direct material used to manufacture an individual product.

The amount of direct material it should take to make a single unit of product is called the **direct material quantity standard.** A bill of materials is often used to help establish direct material quantity standards. A **bill of materials** is a listing of the quantity and description of each item of direct material used to manufacture an individual product. The bill of material for the 7ULTRA-A CB radio made by *Cobra Electronics Corporation* includes just less than 300 items, as shown in Exhibit 10–5.

Each item of direct material, from the speaker to the smallest resistor, is listed. With input from engineering, production, and other personnel, a bill of materials can be prepared and direct material quantity standards can be set. For the Tree Top Mailbox Company, the bill of materials would be quite simple. Basically, it involves only one direct material—wood.

BILL OF MATERIAL FOR 7ULTRA-A

Item	Location / Remarks
COVER ASS'Y	
SPEAKER 8 OHM 0.3W 66MM P-250	
(+)TAPPING SCREW(BH)T3X6-2S (+)BH ZN-PLAT	SPK MTG:3
(+)TAPTITE SCREW(BH)T3X6 (+)BH BLK	UPPER.BOTTOM+ MAIN BODY:8
COVER UPPER ABS 94HB BLK	
COVER BOTTOM ABS 94HB BLK	
HOLDER(SPK)SPC 16X8XT1.2	SPK MTG:3
CUSHION 25X25XT5 RUBB.SP0.BLK STIC	
FELT &65XT0.3 FELT BLK	
FELT 10X110XT0.3 FELT STIC	
FELT 10X100XT0.3 FELT BLK	AIR VENT
ESCUTCHEON ASS'Y	
(+)MACHINE SCREW(FH)M2.6X4 (+)FH ZN-PLAT	
NUT M7 BSBM	
E.S.C ABS94 L153-S9001 BLK(7ULTRA-A)	
LENS ACRYL CLEAR	
KNOB(VOL.SQ) ABS 94HB BLK	95/08/18
KNOB(DOWN) ABS 94HB BLACK	95/08/18
KNOB(UP)ABS 94HB BLACK	
SPRING(COIL) SWP-3 &0.2	
FRONT BODY ASS'Y	
TRANSISTOR KTC2078(TO-220AB)	Q704
I.C KIA7217AP	IC401
P.C.B SUB 54X27X1.6	
JACK EARPHONE DHJ-3T	
CONNECTOR CH-239(A) SW-1229	
CONNECTOR SCN-16-4 PCB(R)	
MICA (FOR T.R 2SC2078)	
BUSHING(FOR T.R 2SC2078)	
VR10KB:15SK 161V	VR2
VR 50KA:RK16311116B153A	VR1
POWER CORD ASS'Y	
(+)MACHINE SCREW(BH)M3X10 (+)BH ZN-PLAT	TR:2
(+)TAPPING SCREW(BH)T3X6-2S (+)BH ZN-PLAT	M.P+MAIN BODY:4 HEAT SINK:1
NUT M3-1S SS41 ZN-PLAT	
WASHER SPRING M3 ZN-PLAT	TR:2
RIVET BLIND &3.2 ALB	NAME PLATE MTG:2
BODY MAIN EGI T1.0 US COATING	
HOLDER(ANT MTG)SPTE 29X35XT0.3 NI-PLAT	
CORD STOPPER P.P BLK	
ESD PROTECTOR CUP T0.05 (TRC-499)	
HEAT SINK ALP3 T2	IC MTG
HEAT SINK ALP3 T2	
SHIELD HOUSHING SPTE T0.3	
NAME PLATE ALP3 40X20XT0.4 (7ULTRA-A)	
MIC ASS'Y	
DISK CERAMIC 0.001UF DD330F102Z 50V	C959
MIC CONDENSER KUC4023-010010	
CURD CURLED 3CON 1SH 300MM BLK(KSK-23059)	
CONNECTOR PLUG SW-1461	
WIRE 1007 AWG 24 11/0.16 WHT	MIC(-)---SW
SW PUSH SPS-9522	
(-)SECURING SCREW M6X8 (P:1) ABS BLK	ACCESSORY
(+)TAPPING SCREW(PH)T3X8-2S (+)PH ZN-PLAT	ACCESSORY
(+)TAPPING SCREW(TH)T5X12-1S (+)TH ZN-PLAT	ACCESSORY
(+)WOOD SCREW (R+FH)2.7X18-1S (+)R+FH NI-PLAT	COVER MTG:3
WASHER 7X25X1.5T BLK RUBBER	ACCESSORY
WASHER(LOCK"B"TYPE) M3 "B"ZN-PLAT	ACCESSORY
ZN-PLAT	ACCESSORY
(+)PLUS SCREW(PH)3X10(+)PH ZN-PLAT	HOLDER MTG
COVER BOTTOM ABS 94HB BLK	
COVER UPPER(MIC)ABS 94HB BLK	
BRACKET (MIC)SPC 58X41XT1 CR-PLAT	
BRACKET(SET)SPC T1.5 BLK-SPRAY PICA	
HOLDER(MIC)PC BLK	
PLATE WEIGHT SPC 36X24XT3 ZN-PLAT	
KNOB(LEVER)ABS 94HB GRAY	
WIRE CLAMP (CORD)NYLON	
HOLDER(MIC) RUBB.(UL)BLK	
BOX MIC SW1S 222(W)X70(D)X52(H)	
POLYBAG P.P 100X100XT0.05	ACCESSORY
POLYBAG P.P 100X200XT0.05	
MAIN PCB AUTO ASS'Y	
FILM RESISTOR 100 1/ 8W 5% ST	R410.513.707.709
FILM RESISTOR 1K 1/ 8W 5% ST	R413.414.901
FILM RESISTOR 10K 1/ 8W 5% ST	R399.411.431. 502.508.515.964
FILM RESISTOR 100K 1/ 8W 5% ST	R404
FILM RESISTOR 1.2K 1/ 8W 5% ST	R518
FILM RESISTOR 150 1/ 8W 5% ST	R951-957
FILM RESISTOR 150K 1/ 8W 5% ST	R701
FILM RESISTOR 180 1/ 8W 5% ST	R962
FILM RESISTOR 1.8K 1/ 8W 5% ST	R420
FILM RESISTOR 22 1/ 8W 5% ST	R511
FILM RESISTOR 2.2K 1/ 8W 5% ST	R401.402.403.408.963
FILM RESISTOR 22K 1/ 8W 5% ST	R967
FILM RESISTOR 2.2 1/ 8W 5% ST	R711
FILM RESISTOR 270 1/ 8W 5% ST	R501
FILM RESISTOR 2.7K 1/ 8W 5% ST	R426.959
FILM RESISTOR 27K 1/ 8W 5% ST	R430
FILM RESISTOR 270K 1/ 8W 5% ST	R428.516
FILM RESISTOR 3.3K 1/ 8W 5% ST	R407.708
FILM RESISTOR 390 1/ 8W 5% ST	R510.702
FILM RESISTOR 3.9K 1/ 8W 5% ST	R406
FILM RESISTOR 47 1/ 8W 5% ST	R425.902
FILM RESISTOR 470 1/ 8W 5% ST	R512
FILM RESISTOR 4.7K 1/ 8W 5% ST	R503.703.704. 705.960
FILM RESISTOR 47K 1/ 8W 5% ST	R961
FILM RESISTOR 470K 1/ 8W 5% ST	R400
FILM RESISTOR 560 1/ 8W 5% ST	R504
FILM RESISTOR 5.6K 1/ 8W 5% ST	R405.409
FILM RESISTOR 68 1/ 8W 5% ST	R706
FILM RESISTOR 6.8K 1/ 8W 5% ST	R517
FILM RESISTOR 15K 1/ 8W 2% ST	R412
AXIAL CERAMIC 0.001UF UP050B102MK 50V	C404.426.427. 950.953.954
AXIAL CERAMIC 0.01UF EP050Y103MN 16V	C402.425.501. 504.508.518.520.
AXIAL CERAMIC 0.0022UF EP050X222MN 16V	C410
AXIAL CERAMIC 0.022UF RH050F 223Z 50V	C406.408.521.705.905
AXIAL CERAMIC 220PF UP050B221K 50V	C413.716
DIODE ZENER 1N5239B 9.1V 0.5W (DO-35)	D504
DIODE ZENER 1N5231B 5.1V 0.5W (DO-35)	D501
DIODE 1N4148(R.L)	D405.502.503.902.903
DIODE RECTIFIER 1N4004T/R 400V 1A (DO-41)	D404.701
COIL AXIAL 2.2UH:LAL03TB2R2M	RFC704
COIL AXIAL 6.8UH:LAL03TB6R8K	RFC509.706
COIL AXIAL 0.39UH:LAL02TBR39K	RFC701
MAIN PCB MANUAL ASSY	
METAL OXIDE RESISTOR15 2W 5% ST	R427
FILM RESISTOR 10 1/ 2W 5% ST MINI	R999
FILM RESISTOR 4.7K 1/ 2W 5% ST MINI	R712
RESISTOR SEMIFIXED 10KB RVM083H H 8DIA	RV1
RESISTOR SEMIFIXED 2K RVM083H	RV2
ELECT CAPACITOR 0.1UF 50V 20% 5X11	C403.956
ELECT CAPACITOR 10UF 16V 20% 5X11	C417.503.902
ELECT CAPACITOR 100UF 16V 20% 8X11	C424
ELECT CAPACITOR 10UF 16V 20% 4X7	C411
ELECT CAPACITOR 1000UF 16V 20% 12X16	C423
ELECT CAPACITOR 2.2UF 50V 20% 5X11	C707
ELECT CAPACITOR 220UF 16V 20% 10X12	C422.514
ELECT CAPACITOR 3.3UF 50V 20% 5X11	C416.421
ELECT CAPACITOR 33UF 16V 20% 5X11	C407.412.415
ELECT CAPACITOR 47UF 16V 20% 5X11	C430.515
ELECT CAPACITOR 470UF 16V 20% 10X12	C502.510
DISK CERAMIC 0.01UF HIK(B)F 103Z 50V	C721.722.723
DISK CERAMIC 0.022UF F 223Z 50V	C711.714
DISK CERAMIC 0.047UF X 473M 50V	C414.418
AXIAL CERAMIC 0.047UF SA105E473MAA 50V	C405
NPO100D 50V	
DISK CERAMIC 100PF NPO101K 50V	C712.718.999
DISK CERAMIC 12PF NPO120K 50V	C513.903
DISK CERAMIC 150PF SL 151K 50V	C715
DISK CERAMIC 270PF SL 271K 50V	C420
DISK CERAMIC 330PF SL 331K 50V	C717
DISK CERAMIC 39PF NPO390K 50V	C704
DISK CERAMIC 4PF NPO040D 50V	C706
DISK CERAMIC 470PF SL 471K 50V	C713
DISK CERAMIC 5PF NPO050D 50V	C506
DISK CERAMIC 82PF NPO820K 50V	C708
DIP TANTALUM 1UF 489D105X0025A125V	C957.958
DIP TRIMMER 20PF 6DIA CVN	CT1
TRANSISTOR KTC3194(O)	Q701.702
TRANSISTOR KTC3198(GR)	Q400.401.505.507
TRANSISTOR KTA1266(GR)	Q402.501.502. 503.506
TRANSISTOR KTC1006 (TO-92L)	Q703
I.C C5122A1P	IC501
DIODE GE 1N60	D402.403
CRYSTAL HC18U 10.240M 30PM	X1
FILTER CERAMIC LTU455HT	CF2
FILTER CERAMIC SK107M4-AC-20	CF1
TRASNFORMER CHOKE EI-19	CH1
TRANSFORMER POWER EI-24	T1
COIL RF CHOKE 0.8UH SPRING	RFC401
COIL SPRING 5X0.6X13.5T:R	RFC709
COIL SPRING 3.4X0.55X8.5T:R	RFC705
COIL RF CHOKE 10UH 10%	RFC707
COIL IFT 455KHZ-A	L902
COIL IFT 455KHZ-B	L903
COIL 27MHZ RX ANT	L901
COIL VCO	L501
COIL RF PRE AMP A TX27MHZ	L701.702
P.C.B MAIN 150 X121.5X1.6 94HB1/0	
MAIN PCB SMD ASS'Y	
F AMP MODULE ASS'Y	
CHIP RESISTOR 0 1/10W 5% T 2012	R200.219
CHIP RESISTOR 100 1/10W 5% T 2012	R203
CHIP RESISTOR 1K 1/10W 5% T 2012	R209
CHIP RESISTOR 10K 1/10W 5% T 2012	R207
CHIP RESISTOR 12K 1/10W 5% T 2012	R211
CHIP RESISTOR 15K 1/10W 5% T 2012	R218
CHIP RESISTOR 150K 1/10W 5% T 2012	R205
CHIP RESISTOR 1.8K 1/10W 5% T 2012	R206
CHIP RESISTOR 220 1/10W 5% T 2012	R212
CHIP RESISTOR 22K 1/10W 5% T 2012	R213
CHIP RESISTOR 3.3K 1/10W 5% T 2012	R210
CHIP RESISTOR 33K 1/10W 5% T 2012	R217
CHIP RESISTOR 3.9K 1/10W 5% T 2012	R202
CHIP RESISTOR 470 1/10W 5% T 2012	R204.208
CHIP RESISTOR 47K 1/10W 5% T 2012	R214.216
CHIP RESISTOR 560 1/10W 5% T 2012	R201
CHIP RESISTOR 82K 1/10W 5% T 2012	R215
ELECT CAPACITOR 1UF 50V 20% 4X7	C209
ELECT CAPACITOR 10UF 16V 20% 4X7	C204
CHIP CERAMIC 0.001UF CM21 X7R102K 50V AT	C206
CHIP CERAMIC 0.01UF CM21 X7R103K 50V AT	C201.203
CHIP CERAMIC 0.047UF CM21 X7R473K 50V AT	C202.205.207.208
TRANSISTOR KTA1504SY(SOT-23)	Q204
TRANSISTOR KTC3880SY(SOT-23)	Q201.202.203
DIODE GE 1N60	D201
P.C.B IF MODULE 44X16.88X1.6 94HB1/1	
VCO MODULE ASS'Y	
CHIP RESISTOR 0 1/10W 5% T 2012	R600.609
CHIP RESISTOR 10K 1/10W 5% T 2012	R606.607
CHIP RESISTOR 120K 1/10W 5% T 2012	R603
CHIP RESISTOR 22K 1/10W 5% T 2012	R608
CHIP RESISTOR 220K 1/10W 5% T 2012	R604
CHIP RESISTOR 2.7K 1/10W 5% T 2012	R605
CHIP RESISTOR 47 1/10W 5% T 2012	R601
CHIP RESISTOR 820 1/10W 5% T 2012	R602
CHIP CERAMIC 0.01UF CM21 X7R103K 50V AT	C601.610.611
CHIP CERAMIC 120PF CM21 CG 121J 50V AT	C608
CHIP CERAMIC 18PF CM21 CG 180J 50V AT	C602
CHIP CERAMIC 22PF CM21 CG 220J 50V AT	C603
CHIP CERAMIC 220PF CM21 CG 221J 50V AT	C607
CHIP CERAMIC 27PF CM21CG 270J 50V AT	C609
CHIP CERAMIC 33PF CM21 CG 330J 50V AT	C606
CHIP CERAMIC 47PF CM21 CG 470J 50V AT	C605
TRANSISTOR KTC3875SY	Q602
TRANSISTOR KTC3880SY(SOT-23)	Q601.603
DIODE VARICAP LV2209	D601
P.C.B VCO MODULE 30.7 X16.88X1.6 94HB1/1	
LOW PASS FILTER MODU	
CHIP CERAMIC 220PF CM21 CG 221J 50V AT	C801.805
CHIP CERAMIC 470PF CM21 CG 471J 50V AT	C802.803
COIL SPRING 3.4X0.55X6.5T:R	L802
COIL SPRING 3.4X0.55X7.5T:R	L803
COIL SPRING 3.4X0.55X8.5T:R	L804
P.C.B LPF MODULE 15.39X40.5 X1.6 94HB1/1	
4.5T SPRIN.COIL ASSY	L801
COIL SPRING 3.4X0.55X4.5T:R	
CORE 1108-KA-058 M9DTH3.7X6	
RF AMP H/H MODULE	
CHIP RESISTOR 0 1/10W 5% T 2012	
CHIP RESISTOR 100 1/10W 5% T 2012	R107
CHIP RESISTOR 10K 1/10W 5% T 2012	R106.108
CHIP RESISTOR 18 1/10W 5% T 2012	R104
CHIP RESISTOR 330 1/10W 5% T 2012	R103
CHIP RESISTOR 33K 1/10W 5% T 2012	R105
CHIP RESISTOR 470 1/10W 5% T 2012	R109.110
CHIP CERAMIC 0.01UF CM21 X7R103K 50V AT	C112
CHIP CERAMIC 150PF CM21 CG 151J 50V AT	C109
CHIP CERAMIC 220PF CM21 CG 221J 50V AT	C108
CHIP CERAMIC 33PF CM21 CG 330J 50V AT	C102
CHIP CERAMIC 47PF CM21 CG 470J 50V AT	C104
CHIP CERAMIC 680PF CM21 CG 681J 50V AT	C114
TRANSISTOR KTC3880SY (SOT-23)	Q102.103
DIODE SI CHIP KDS226 (SOT-23)	D101
P.C.B RF MODULE 39.25X16.88X1.6 94HB1/1	
6.5T SPRIN.COIL ASSY	L102.104
COIL SPRING 3.4X0.55X6.5T:R	
CORE 1108-KA-058 M9DTH3.7X6	
PACKING ASS'Y	
BOX TRAY SW1S 222(W)X127(D)X52(H)	
BOX INNER SW1S 224(W)X220(D)X54(H)	
BOX OUT DW1E 356(W)X238(D)X206(H)	
POLYBAG P.P 200X300XT0.05	SET:1 MANUAL:1
MANUAL OWNER'S MANUAL OWNER'S	
CARD REGISTRATION ARTPAPER 158X342	
CARD BOARD	
CB RULE	
SCHEMATIC DIAGRAM WOODFREEPAPER 420X297	
CARD INFORMATION WOODFREEPAPER 98.5X150	
LABEL CAUTION	
LABEL FCC POLYESTER 67X10XT0.05	
SUB PCB ASS'Y	
FILM RESISTOR 10K 1/ 8W 5% ST	R950
LED LAMP SLB55VR3 RED 3 V 60MW	LED1
LED DISPLAY UL-G233G-13 GRN	
SW TACT SAT-1102-2	SW3.4
SUB MATERIAL ASS'Y	
TUBE UL/CSA KEIT-30 AWG 12 (2&) CLEAR VINYL	
TUBE UL/CSA KEIT-30 AWG 2 (6.5&) CLEAR VINYL	
TUBE HIS 11M/M	
TUBE EMPIRE 1&	
PE SCOTCH 15M/M (0.015X20M)	
TAPE PACKING OPP (0.05X50M)	
TAPE PACKING O.P.P (0.05X25M) IVORY	
SOLDER BAR 63:37	
SOLDER ROSIN CO.WIRE60:40 0.04"-0.05"	
FLUX ROSIN	
THINNER FOR FLUX	
SILICON GREASE YG-6111 OR XG-6111	
STAVILIZER MATERIAL	
BOND #201	
COMPOUND #1200 500GR	

EXHIBIT 10-5 Bill of Materials for 7ULTRA-A CB Radio

To determine the direct material quantity standard for the Tree Top Mailbox Company using practical standards, Ali measured the wood included in a single mailbox. He determined that each mailbox was made of 16 feet of ¼ × 2 inch pine. Then he examined the scrap wood from the prior month's production and estimated that the amount of wood to make a single mailbox should be increased by 35 percent to allow for scrap due to knots and other expected defects in the wood. Accordingly, Tree Top adopted a practical direct material quantity standard of 21.6 feet (16 feet × 1.35% = 21.6 feet) per mailbox.

DIRECT MATERIAL PRICE STANDARD

direct material price standard The anticipated cost for each item of direct material used in the manufacture of a product.

In addition to the amount of direct material used, the price per measure of direct material will affect the total cost of direct material. The **direct material price standard** is the anticipated cost for each item of direct material used in the manufacture of a product. For the plastic used to make golf balls, the direct material price standard would be the budgeted cost per pound of plastic. For wire used in a CD player, the direct material price standard would be the budgeted cost per foot of wire. Notice that the direct material price standard reflects a price per measure of direct material (i.e., per foot of wire), *not* per unit of production (e.g., per CD player).

Because purchasing agents are generally knowledgeable about the price paid for direct material, they are likely to be key players in determining direct material price standards. Purchasing agents would also gather historical direct material price information, making necessary adjustments for any anticipated price changes.

As indicated, Tree Top uses wood that measures ¼ × 2 inches. The direct material price standard is expressed as an amount per foot of this wood. The Tree Top Mailbox Company has no purchasing agent, so Ali shopped around and found that high-quality pine wood could be purchased for $0.70 per 8-foot length. Also, Ali determined that no price increases were expected during the year. Accordingly, Tree Top established a standard price per foot of wood of $0.0875 ($0.70 ÷ 8 feet = $0.0875) per foot.

Although only a single direct material is used to make Tree Top's mailboxes, most products require the use of many different raw materials. Separate standards must be established for each direct material used in production. If production required the use of material A, material B, and material C, separate quantity and price standards must be prepared for each.

Once a manufacturer knows the direct material quantity standard and the direct material price standard, it can determine the standard cost for direct material per unit of production. For Tree Top, the standard cost for direct material of $1.89 is calculated by multiplying the standard quantity of 21.60 feet by the standard price of $0.0875, shown as follows:

$$\begin{array}{ccccc} \text{Standard} & & \text{Standard} & & \begin{array}{c}\text{Standard Direct}\\ \text{Material Cost}\end{array} \\ \text{Quantity} & \times & \text{Price} & = & \text{per Unit} \\ 21.60 \text{ feet} & \times & \$0.875 & = & \$1.89 \end{array}$$

◆ SETTING DIRECT LABOR STANDARDS

As with direct material, setting direct labor standards involves two important considerations: the number of direct labor hours and the wage rate per hour.

DIRECT LABOR EFFICIENCY STANDARD

direct labor efficiency standard The estimated number of direct labor hours required to produce a single unit of product.

The estimated number of direct labor hours required to produce a single unit of product is called the **direct labor efficiency standard.** When the direct labor force works efficiently, labor hours are kept to a minimum. Conversely, too many hours of direct labor relative to production would indicate labor inefficiency. The standard for the number of direct labor hours could be called the direct labor quantity standard, or the direct labor hours standard, but neither of these terms sounds quite right, which explains why this standard has come to be known as the direct labor efficiency standard.

Production supervisors and other production employees are often key players in establishing direct labor efficiency standards. Historical information about direct labor and production volumes are used to help establish an appropriate standard for the number of direct labor hours per unit of production. Also, information from industrial engineers, such as the results of time-and-motion studies, may be helpful in determining the amount of direct labor time it should take to efficiently produce a unit of product.

Tree Top's founders wanted to select a standard that would help encourage them to make as many mailboxes as possible, but allow them to work at a quick, yet reasonable pace. After reviewing their activities for October, the three agreed that the standard hours allowed for a single unit of production should be 0.6 hours (36 minutes). This time, then, became Tree Top's labor efficiency standard.

DIRECT LABOR RATE STANDARD

direct labor rate standard The planned hourly wage paid to production workers.

The **direct labor rate standard** is the planned hourly wage paid to production workers. The personnel manager is often a key player in determining the direct labor rate standard. Sometimes direct labor rates are established through collective bargaining or other employment agreements. Other times, a less formal procedure is used to set hourly pay rates. In either case, historical information coupled with information regarding anticipated pay rate changes establishes the direct labor rate standard. Often, companies compute an expected average hourly direct labor rate, which is used as the plant-wide direct labor rate standard. For Tree Top, Ali, Maria, and Bill agreed that, based on their original plan, the direct labor rate standard of $10 per hour should be used.

Once a company knows the direct labor efficiency standard and the direct labor rate standard, it can determine the standard labor cost per unit of production. In the case of Tree Top, based on the direct labor efficiency standard of 0.6 hours and the direct labor rate standard of $10 per direct labor hour, the standard labor cost to make a single mailbox is $6, shown as follows:

$$\begin{array}{ccccc} \text{Direct Labor} & & \text{Direct Labor} & & \text{Standard} \\ \text{Efficiency} & \times & \text{Rate Standard} & = & \text{Direct Labor} \\ \text{Standard} & & \text{(per hour)} & & \text{Cost per Unit} \\ 0.6\ \text{Hours} & \times & \$10\ \text{per Hour} & = & \$6 \end{array}$$

◆ SETTING VARIABLE MANUFACTURING OVERHEAD STANDARDS

Recall that manufacturing overhead includes all production costs that are not part of direct materials or direct labor. Manufacturing overhead includes costs of operating the factory such as rent, insurance, depreciation, supplies, taxes, raw materials handling, and so forth. Recall also that costs can be classified as either fixed or variable. Fixed costs are those that remain constant in total, even as activity changes. Variable costs, in contrast, increase in total as activity changes. Therefore, variable manufacturing overhead would include those manufacturing overhead costs that increase in total as production increases.

In Chapter 3, we saw that manufacturing overhead was often allocated to production based on direct labor hours, direct labor cost, machine hours, or some other allocation base. In this section, we illustrate how a standard cost system works when manufacturing overhead is allocated using direct labor hours as the allocation base. Although the specific calculations would be somewhat different, standard costing can be used for other allocation bases as well.

To set standards for variable manufacturing overhead, managers must first estimate variable manufacturing overhead costs. Once they estimate total variable manufacturing overhead, they can then determine a cost per direct labor hour, or per unit of some other allocation base.

For Tree Top Mailbox Company, variable manufacturing overhead cost includes utilities and miscellaneous variable cost, as shown on October's income statement presented in Exhibit 10–4. The miscellaneous variable cost includes the cost of indirect material such as glue, small nails, and wood stain. Based on October's results, Ali, Maria, and Bill estimated that variable manufacturing overhead cost would be about $63 to make 300 mailboxes. The $63 includes $33 for utilities and $30 for miscellaneous variable cost. Tree Top planned to allocate this variable overhead cost to production based on direct labor hours.

THE STANDARD VARIABLE MANUFACTURING OVERHEAD RATE

standard variable manufacturing overhead rate
The rate used to apply variable manufacturing overhead to units of manufactured product.

The rate used to apply variable manufacturing overhead to units of product is known as the **standard variable manufacturing overhead rate.** As stated, Ali, Maria, and Bill expected to work about 60 hours each, or a total of 180 direct labor hours per month. Based on the planned variable manufacturing overhead cost of $63 and 180 estimated direct labor hours, we compute a standard variable overhead rate of $0.35 by dividing the $63 budgeted variable manufacturing overhead by the 180 estimated direct labor hours, shown as follows:

Budgeted Variable Manufacturing Overhead	÷	Budgeted Direct Labor Hours	=	Standard Variable Manufacturing Overhead Rate
$63	÷	180 hours	=	$0.35 per hour

When the variable manufacturing overhead allocation is based on direct labor hours, once a manufacturer knows the direct labor efficiency standard and the standard variable manufacturing overhead rate per direct labor hour, it can determine the standard variable manufacturing overhead cost per unit. The standard variable manufacturing overhead cost to build a single unit of production is calculated by multiplying the direct labor efficiency standard (the estimated direct labor hours per unit) by the standard variable manufacturing overhead rate. For Tree Top, standard cost per unit for variable manufacturing overhead is $0.21, shown as follows:

Standard Direct Labor Hours Allowed	×	Standard Variable Manufacturing Overhead Rate	=	Standard Variable Mfg Overhead Cost per Unit
0.6 hours	×	$0.35 per hour	=	$0.21

◆ SETTING FIXED MANUFACTURING OVERHEAD STANDARDS

Unlike variable manufacturing overhead cost, which changes in total as production increases or decreases, fixed manufacturing overhead cost remains constant in total regardless of how many units are produced.

To set the fixed manufacturing overhead standards, manufacturers must first estimate the total cost of fixed manufacturing overhead. For Tree Top Mailbox Company, this amount consists of rent of $200 per month and monthly depreciation of $25 for the equipment used to make the mailboxes. Fixed manufacturing overhead then totals $225 per month ($200 + $25 = $225).

STANDARD FIXED MANUFACTURING OVERHEAD RATE

standard fixed manufacturing overhead rate
The rate used to apply fixed manufacturing overhead to units of manufactured product.

As with variable manufacturing overhead, fixed manufacturing overhead can be allocated to production based on units of production, direct labor hours, direct labor dollars, machine hours, or some other allocation base. The rate used to apply fixed manufacturing overhead to units of product is known as the **standard fixed manufacturing overhead rate.**

Our illustration assumes that Tree Top Mailbox Company allocates fixed manufacturing overhead to production based on direct labor hours. In such a case, we determine the standard fixed manufacturing overhead rate by dividing the total estimated fixed manufacturing overhead cost by the total estimated direct labor hours. In the case of Tree Top, the standard fixed manufacturing overhead rate of $1.25 per direct labor hour is calculated by dividing the budgeted fixed manufacturing overhead cost of $225 by the budgeted direct labor hours of 180 shown as follows:

Budgeted Fixed Mfg Overhead	÷	Budgeted Direct Labor Hours	=	Standard Fixed Mfg Overhead Rate
$225	÷	180 hours	=	$1.25

We calculate the standard fixed manufacturing overhead cost to build a single unit of product by multiplying the direct labor efficiency standard per unit by the standard fixed manufacturing overhead rate. For Tree Top, standard cost per unit for fixed manufacturing overhead is $0.75, shown as follows:

Standard Direct Labor Hours Allowed	×	Standard Fixed Mfg Overhead Rate	=	Standard Fixed Mfg Overhead Cost per Unit
0.6 hours	×	$1.25 per hour	=	$0.75

◆ TOTAL STANDARD COST PER UNIT

Once standards have been set for direct material, direct labor, variable manufacturing overhead, and fixed manufacturing overhead, the total standard cost per unit can be calculated. This amount reflects how much it *should* cost to produce a unit of product. The standard cost per unit represents a useful estimate that can be helpful for planning and setting selling prices. For Tree Top, the total standard cost per mailbox is $8.85, as shown in Exhibit 10–6.

EXHIBIT 10–6   Total Standard Cost per Mailbox Built

Standard Direct Material Cost per Mailbox	$1.89
Standard Direct Labor Cost per Mailbox	6.00
Standard Variable Manufacturing Overhead Cost per Mailbox	.21
Standard Fixed Manufacturing Overhead Cost per Mailbox	.75
Total Standard Cost per Mailbox	$8.85

As you might imagine, the *actual* cost of producing an item is almost never exactly the same as the *standard* cost. When actual cost exceeds standard cost, management should take steps to determine the cause of the variance, and, if necessary, take corrective action.

Actual total production cost that exceeds the standard may indicate that a general problem exists, but it provides almost no information that can help managers focus on the true cause of the problem. Managers need access to information they can use to isolate and address specific cost problems.

The next sections show how managers use standard costing to isolate specific problems for each production cost category.

◆ VARIANCE ANALYSIS

Standard costs can help control costs by serving as benchmarks to compare with actual production costs. To use standard costing as a control device, managers compare *standard costs* to *actual costs* to see whether a variance exists. Instead of calculating a single variance for total production cost, they make variances specific enough to isolate a particular production process problem. In this section we examine how we can calculate detailed standard cost variances for direct material, direct labor, variable manufacturing overhead, and fixed manufacturing overhead. We will walk through the calculations for each standard cost variance using Tree Top Mailbox Company as an example.

Unfortunately for Tree Top, November was not nearly as successful as October. The company produced and sold only 225 mailboxes in spite of demand for many more. The income statement for the month of November appears in Exhibit 10–7.

November's loss disturbed Ali, Maria, and Bill because they had spent nearly as much time at the shop as in October, but produced far fewer mailboxes. What changes should Tree Top make to get the company back on track? We can answer this question once we have calculated the variances and examined their causes.

To calculate standard cost variances, we use the standard costs discussed in the preceding sections, and compare them with Tree Top's actual performance. Actual performance data are obtained from various sources, including company reports and files. In our Tree Top Mailbox Company example, we have included the key details in November's income statement, presented in Exhibit 10–7.

Tree Top Mailbox Company
Income Statement
For the Month Ended November 30, 2004

Sales (225 mailboxes at $10 each)		$2,250
Less Expenses		
Direct Material (6,000 feet of wood)	$ 477	
Direct Labor (162 hours at $10.50 per hour)	1,701	
Rent	200	
Utilities (all variable)	50	
Miscellaneous Variable Costs	90	
Depreciation	25	(2,543)
Net Income		$ (293)

EXHIBIT 10–7 Tree Top's November 2004 Income Statement

DIRECT MATERIALS VARIANCES

Direct material variances can be used to answer three important questions:

1. Did the company use more or less direct material than it should have, based on the standards set?
2. Did the company pay more or less than it should have when the direct material was purchased from the supplier based on the standards set?
3. What was the cost impact of these quantity and price differences?

DIRECT MATERIAL QUANTITY VARIANCE

direct material quantity variance A measure of the over- or underconsumption of direct material for the number of units actually manufactured.

direct material usage variance Another name for the direct material quantity variance.

direct material efficiency variance Another name for the direct material quantity variance.

The **direct material quantity variance,** sometimes called the **direct material usage variance** or the **direct material efficiency variance,** is a measure of the overconsumption or underconsumption of direct material for the number of units actually manufactured. It informs management whether too much or too little direct material is used in the manufacturing process based on the standards. The direct material quantity variance is the difference between the standard quantity and the actual quantity of direct materials used. We follow three steps to calculate the direct material quantity variance. First, we calculate the standard quantity of direct material allowed for actual production. Second, we calculate the variance in units of direct material. Finally, we calculate the variance in dollars.

Step 1: Calculate the standard quantity of direct material allowed for actual production

The standard quantity of direct material allowed is the amount needed for actual production, according to the standard. It is the amount allowed for actual production. To calculate this amount, we determine how much direct material should have been used according to the standard to make the units actually produced.

Recall that Tree Top produced 225 mailboxes in November. To determine the quantity of the wood that *should* have been used to make 225 mailboxes, we multiply the direct material quantity standard (21.60 feet per unit) by the number of mailboxes produced (225). For Tree Top, the standard quantity of direct material allowed for the actual production of 225 mailboxes is 4,860 feet, shown as follows:

Standard Quantity per Unit	×	Number of Units Produced	=	Standard Quantity of Direct Material Allowed
21.60 feet	×	225 units	=	4,860 feet

We see from the calculations that 4,860 feet of wood is the standard direct material quantity allowed for the units produced—the direct material quantity that should have been used based on the number of units *actually* produced.

Step 2: Calculate the direct material quantity variance in units of direct material

We calculate the direct material quantity variance in units of direct material by subtracting the actual quantity of direct material used from the standard quantity of direct material allowed. For Tree Top Mailbox Company, we determine the direct material quantity variance in feet by comparing the quantity of wood it *should* have taken to make the 225 mailboxes (determined in step 1) to the quantity of wood it *actually* took to make the mailboxes (the actual quantity).

Discussion Question

10–3. If the actual amount of wood used was more than the standard quantity of wood, do you think the direct material quantity variance would be favorable or unfavorable? Explain your reasoning.

To use standard costing, a manufacturer must maintain a record of the quantity of direct material used in production. In the case of Tree Top, this information is found in the income statement as presented in Exhibit 10–7. A review of that income statement shows that the actual quantity of direct material Tree Top used to make the 225 mailboxes in November was 6,000 feet of wood. Often, the quantity of material used in production differs from the quantity of material purchased. For this calculation it is important to remember to use the quantity of material used, not the quantity purchased.

We calculate Tree Top's direct material quantity variance by finding the difference between the standard quantity of direct material allowed and the quantity of direct material used in production. In this case the variance is 1,140 unfavorable, shown as follows:

Standard Quantity Allowed for Production	–	Actual Quantity Used	=	Quantity Variance in Units of Direct Material (feet)
4,860 feet	–	6,000 feet	=	1,140 Unfavorable

We can see from the presentation that Ali, Maria, and Bill used 1,140 more feet of wood than the standard allowed to make the 225 mailboxes. Does this overuse of direct material really matter? Even if the direct material quantity variance in feet is 1,140 unfavorable, it *may* represent an insignificant dollar amount. To evaluate whether this variance is worthy of attention, we need to assign a dollar amount.

Step 3: Calculate the direct material quantity variance in dollars

To avoid contaminating the quantity variance with problems relating to the actual price paid for material, the dollar amount assigned to the direct material quantity variance is based on the standard direct material price, not the actual price. Tree Top's direct material quantity variance in dollars is $99.75. We calculated this amount by multiplying the direct material quantity variance (1,140 feet) by the direct material standard price of $0.0875, as follows:

Quantity Variance in Units of Direct Material (feet)	×	Standard Price per Unit of Direct Material (feet)	=	Quantity Variance in Dollars
1,140 Unfavorable	×	$0.0875	=	$99.75 Unfavorable

The direct materials quantity variance in dollars provides valuable information about the cost of using too much direct material to make the mailboxes. Now that a dollar amount has been assigned to the variance, we can evaluate its importance and devote the amount of management attention that is appropriate.

Discussion Questions ●

10–4. Based on Tree Top Mailbox Company's quantity variance, do you think that Ali, Maria, and Bill need to examine reasons for using so much wood? Explain your reasoning.

10–5. If the dollar amount of a variance is insignificant, does the variance information help Tree Top's management team determine where it should focus attention? Explain.

10–6. If there had been no variance, would this mean Tree Top used the appropriate amount of wood to build its mailboxes in November? Explain your reasoning.

We assume that only one direct material is used to make the mailboxes for Tree Top. In practice, most products require several different direct materials, ranging from one to thousands, and a manufacturer must compute a separate material quantity variance for each direct material used. The logic and computations, however, are similar to those presented here.

Once management calculates the direct material quantity variance it can assess the situation and, if necessary, take corrective action. Generally, a quantity variance should be discussed with the individuals who are responsible for the amount of direct material used. The focus of the discussion should be on finding and eliminating the cause of the variance. In many companies, the person responsible for direct material consumption is the production supervisor, who would attempt to determine the cause of the variance and take steps to eliminate it.

DIRECT MATERIAL PRICE VARIANCE

direct material price variance   A measure of the difference between the amount the company planned to pay for direct material purchased and the amount it actually paid for the direct material.

The **direct material price variance** is a measure of the difference between the amount the company *planned* to pay for direct material and the amount it *actually* paid. This variance provides an indication of whether the price paid to suppliers for direct material compares favorably to the standard price. To find the direct material price variance we use a two-step process. First, we determine the amount that should have been paid for the direct material. Second, we calculate the dollar amount of the direct material variance.

Step 1: Determine the amount that should have been paid for the direct material purchased according to the standard price

According to the detailed information on November's income statement, Tree Top Mailbox Company purchased 6,000 feet of wood. How much should the company have paid for the 6,000 feet of wood if it had been able to purchase it at the standard price? We determine this amount by multiplying the actual quantity of direct material purchased by the standard price. Often, the quantity of material purchased differs from the quantity of material used in production. For this calculation, we use the quantity of material purchased, not the quantity used in production shown as follows:

Actual Quantity Purchased	×	Standard Price per Unit of Direct Material (feet)	=	Quantity Purchased Priced at Standard
6,000 feet	×	$0.0875	=	$525

Our calculations show that, based on the standard price of $0.0875 per foot, the 6,000 feet of wood purchased should have cost $525.

Step 2: Calculate the dollar amount of the direct material price variance

We calculate the dollar amount of the direct material price variance by subtracting the actual cost of direct material from the standard cost of the direct material purchased (determined in step 1). According to the detailed information on November's income statement, Tree Top purchased the 6,000 feet of wood for $477. By comparing the standard cost of $525 to the actual cost of $477, we determine that the price variance is $48 favorable shown as follows:

Quantity Purchased Priced at Standard	−	Actual Direct Material Cost	=	Direct Material Price Variance
$525	−	$477	=	$48 Favorable

To review the calculations for the direct material price variance in dollars, we compare the amount the wood purchased *should* have cost, $525, to what the wood *actually* cost, $477, to determine the direct material price variance.

When a product requires the use of multiple direct materials, a manufacturer must compute separate material price variance for each direct material used. The logic and computations, however, are similar to those presented here.

Once management calculates the direct material price variance, it can assess the situation and, if necessary, take corrective action. In most manufacturing companies, direct material is purchased by purchasing agents working in the company's purchasing department. Therefore, direct material price variances are brought to the attention of the purchasing agent responsible for buying the particular direct material so that the price can be evaluated and corrective action taken when necessary.

In the case of Tree Top, the actual price paid for the wood was lower than the standard price, resulting in a favorable direct material price variance. It may seem that a favorable variance would not warrant investigation, but this is not always the case.

A significant favorable variance is worth examining for several reasons. First, repeated favorable variances may be an indication that the standard is too lax. Second, management should investigate the variance to see whether the techniques used to achieve the favorable variance can be used by other areas of the company to help reduce cost. Third, a favorable variance may have occurred because of a trade-off of some other value. For example, it might be achieved by purchasing direct material of a substandard quality.

Bill purchased the wood for Tree Top from the lumber company at a discounted price. The lumber company was able to offer the discount because another customer had refused the wood and the lumber company was overstocked. As it turned out, the wood had an unusually high number of knots and other blemishes. The substandard wood, then, may have caused the use of more direct material and direct labor than would have otherwise been required for production.

Discussion Questions

10–7. How might the purchase of wood at a discount affect the direct material quantity variance?

10–8. If there had been no variance, would this mean Tree Top paid what it should have for the wood used to build its mailboxes in November? Explain your reasoning.

DIRECT LABOR VARIANCES

Direct labor variances help managers answer three key questions:

1. Did it take more or fewer direct labor hours than it should have taken for the company to manufacture its products based on the standards set?

2. Was the company's hourly direct labor rate more or less than it should have been based on the standards set?

3. What was the cost impact of these differences in the number of direct labor hours and the hourly labor rate?

It may be helpful to consider some parallels between direct material and direct labor. Instead of using the terms *quantities* and *prices* as for direct material, we use *hours* and *rates* with direct labor. In reality, only the descriptive words change—the meanings stay the same. The "quantity" of direct material is similar to the "hours" of direct labor. Likewise, the "price" per measure of direct material is similar to the "rate" per hour of direct labor. Because of these similarities, the steps and calculations of standard cost variances for direct labor are comparable to direct material variances.

DIRECT LABOR EFFICIENCY VARIANCE

direct labor efficiency variance A measure of the difference between the planned number of direct labor hours and the actual number of direct labor hours for the units actually manufactured.

The **direct labor efficiency variance** is a measure of the over- or underconsumption of direct labor for the number of units actually manufactured. In other words, the direct labor efficiency variance informs management whether too much or too little direct labor is used in the manufacturing process based on the standards. This variance is comparable to the direct material quantity variance. Both are used to evaluate the quantity of something used. In the case of the direct material quantity variance, the focus is on the quantity of direct material used. In the case of the direct labor efficiency variance, the focus is on the quantity of direct labor hours used.

We use three steps to calculate this variance. First, we find the standard number of direct labor hours allowed for production. Second, we determine the variance in hours. Finally, we calculate the variance in dollars.

Step 1: Calculate the standard number of direct labor hours allowed for actual production

In this first step we determine the amount of direct labor time it *should* have taken to make all the units that were *actually* made during the period. According to the direct labor efficiency standard for Tree Top, it should have taken 0.6 hours (36 minutes) to make each mailbox. Because 225 mailboxes were made in November, the total amount of direct labor hours should have been 135 hours ($225 \times 0.6 = 135$).

Step 2: Calculate the direct labor efficiency variance in hours

We compute the direct labor efficiency variance in hours by subtracting the standard direct labor hours allowed from the actual number of direct labor hours worked. According to information taken from Tree Top's November income statement presented in Exhibit 10–7, the actual number of direct labor hours used in November was 162. By comparing the standard hours allowed for the 225 mailboxes, 135 hours, to the actual direct labor hours, 162 hours, we see that the direct labor efficiency variance in hours is 27 hours unfavorable shown as follows:

Standard Direct Labor Hours Allowed		Actual Direct Labor Hours		Direct Labor Efficiency Variance in Hours
135 hours	−	162 hours	=	27 hours Unfavorable

The variance between the standard and actual number of hours worked indicates that Tree Top's employees did not work very efficiently. If they had, they would have completed the 225 mailboxes in 135 hours, or maybe even less.

To grasp the true magnitude of the 27-hour unfavorable variance, we must assign a dollar amount.

Step 3: Calculate the direct labor efficiency variance in dollars

To avoid contaminating the efficiency variance with problems relating to the actual labor rate, we calculate the direct labor efficiency variance in dollars by multiplying the variance in hours by the standard direct labor rate, not the actual labor rate. In the case of Tree Top, we multiply the 27-hour unfavorable direct labor efficiency variance by the direct labor rate standard of $10, shown as follows:

Direct Labor Efficiency Variance in Hours		Direct Labor Rate Standard		Direct Labor Efficiency Variance in Dollars
27 hours	×	$10	=	$270 Unfavorable

Once management calculates the direct labor efficiency variance, it can assess the variance and, if necessary, take corrective action. The plant manager would probably ask the production supervisor or production-line employees to help determine why the unfavorable variance occurred. Once the cause of the problem is found, corrective action can be taken.

Tree Top determined that substandard wood caused the unfavorable direct labor efficiency variance. To make mailboxes of sufficient quality, Ali, Maria, and Bill needed extra time to cut the knots and other blemishes from the wood. The solution to the variance problem is to purchase only high-quality wood in the future.

DIRECT LABOR RATE VARIANCE

direct labor rate variance
A measure of the difference between the actual wage rate paid to employees and the direct labor rate standard.

The **direct labor rate variance** is a measure of the difference between the actual wage rate paid to employees and the direct labor rate standard. This variance shows the effect of unanticipated wage rate changes. The direct labor rate standard for Tree Top is $10 per hour. As you will note by looking at the November income statement in Exhibit 10–7, each of the three owners received a $0.50 raise during November. So, for Tree Top, the direct labor rate variance will indicate added cost caused by the pay raises. We use a two-step process to calculate the direct labor rate variance. First, we find the amount the company should have paid for direct labor for the hours worked. Second, we determine the dollar amount of the direct labor rate variance.

Step 1: Determine the amount that should have been paid for the actual direct labor hours worked according to the direct labor rate standard

In this step we determine how much the company should have paid for the direct labor hours actually worked, based on the direct labor rate standard. For Tree Top, the actual direct labor hours totaled 162 for November. By multiplying the 162 actual direct labor hours by the direct labor rate standard of $10, we determine that the company should have paid $1,620.00 shown as follows:

Actual Direct Labor Hours	×	Direct Labor Rate Standard	=	Actual Direct Labor Hours at the Standard Rate
162 hours	×	$10	=	$1,620

Once we determine what the company should have paid according to the standard, we can compare it to the amount actually paid to determine the direct labor rate variance.

Step 2: Calculate the dollar amount of the direct labor rate variance

We compute the dollar amount of the direct labor rate variance by subtracting the actual cost of direct labor from the standard cost of the direct labor actually worked. The direct labor rate variance compares the amount the actual direct labor hours should have cost to the actual cost. In the case of Tree Top, we find that the actual direct labor cost for November was $1,701, as shown on the November income statement in Exhibit 10–7. Tree Top's labor hours at standard should have cost $1,620. When we compare actual labor cost ($1,701) to standard cost ($1,620), we find an unfavorable direct labor rate variance of $81, calculated as follows:

Actual Direct Labor Hours at the Standard Rate	−	Actual Direct Labor Cost	=	Direct Labor Rate Variance
$1,620	−	$1,701	=	$81 Unfavorable

The calculated variance is unfavorable because the actual labor cost is higher than the cost based on the standard rate. This $81 unfavorable variance provides useful information to Ali, Maria, and Bill about the effect of their $0.50 per hour raise.

Discussion Questions ●

10–9. What effect did the $0.50 per hour pay raise have on November's profits?

10–10. In light of the financial problems that occurred in November, do you think Tree Top's owners should roll back the wage rate to $10 per hour? Explain your reasoning.

As with other variances, once management calculates the direct labor rate variance, it can assess the variance and, if necessary, take corrective action. Direct labor rate variances are caused by labor rate changes that are unanticipated. Generally, when labor rates are contractually set or a result of collective bargaining with labor unions, labor rate changes are not unexpected. Accordingly, these labor rates are factored into the labor rate standard. A labor rate variance can be caused by an unexpected rate change of some kind, or perhaps an unanticipated change in the makeup of the labor force. For example, if the company retains more experienced workers and has fewer new workers, an unfavorable rate variance is likely because new employees generally begin their employment at a lower hourly wage than experienced employees.

In the case of Tree Top Mailbox Company, the November income statement shows that Ali, Maria, and Bill gave themselves an unplanned $0.50 per hour raise. Although no corrective action will likely be taken, the trio now knows how the raise affected profits.

The direct labor variances reveal that Ali, Maria, and Bill had two important problems in November regarding direct labor cost. First, it took 27 extra hours to make the 225 mailboxes. The extra 27 hours increased labor cost by $270. Second, the hourly wage paid to Ali, Maria, and Bill was higher than the planned $10 standard wage rate. This higher wage rate increased labor cost by $81. The total effect of these two direct labor problems is $351 unfavorable.

MANUFACTURING OVERHEAD VARIANCES

Manufacturing overhead variances help managers answer two vital questions:

1. Did the company spend more or less on overhead items than it should have, based on the standards that were set?
2. Did the company utilize its production facility efficiently?

In this section we look at four different manufacturing overhead variances, two that deal with variable manufacturing overhead and two with fixed manufacturing overhead.

VARIABLE MANUFACTURING OVERHEAD EFFICIENCY VARIANCE

variable manufacturing overhead efficiency variance A measure of the variable manufacturing overhead cost attributable to the difference between the planned and actual direct labor hours worked.

The **variable manufacturing overhead efficiency variance** is a measure of the variable manufacturing overhead cost attributable to the difference between the planned and actual direct labor hours worked. Surprisingly, this variance relates more to the efficiency of direct labor than anything else. While production workers work in the factory, they consume electricity as they use lights and air conditioning and operate machinery. They also use supplies and other factory resources that all are part of manufacturing overhead. So, as workers work longer, they use more factory resources. How much more? The variable manufacturing overhead efficiency variance helps answer this question.

An unfavorable variable manufacturing overhead efficiency variance is a measure of the variable manufacturing overhead cost associated with the extra hours worked by direct labor. A direct relationship exists between the direct labor efficiency variance and the variable manufacturing overhead efficiency variance. Accordingly, if the direct labor efficiency variance is unfavorable, the variable manufacturing overhead efficiency variance will also be unfavorable. Likewise, if the direct labor efficiency variance is favorable, the variable manufacturing overhead efficiency variance will also be favorable.

The first two steps for calculating the variable manufacturing overhead efficiency variance are the same as those for determining the direct labor efficiency variance. These steps are to find the standard number of direct labor hours allowed for actual production and then to calculate the direct labor efficiency variance in hours.

Assuming the direct labor efficiency variance has been calculated, we review the information learned from those calculations before moving to the third step of the calculations, which is determining the variable manufacturing overhead efficiency variance in dollars.

Recall that our calculation showed that Tree Top used an extra 27 direct labor hours to make the 225 mailboxes in November. The extra 27 direct labor hours not only increased direct labor cost, but it also increased other costs. While Ali, Maria, and Bill worked the extra 27 hours, they consumed electricity, supplies, and other factory resources. In sum, the inefficiency of the workforce increased variable manufacturing overhead cost. Had they not worked the extra 27 hours, Tree Top's owners would have saved not only the labor cost, but also the factory resources they consumed as they worked the extra time.

Step 3: Calculate the variable manufacturing overhead efficiency variance in dollars

To calculate the variable manufacturing overhead efficiency variance in dollars, we multiply the direct labor efficiency variance in hours by the standard variable manufacturing overhead rate.

For Tree Top, the direct labor efficiency variance in hours we calculated earlier is 27 hours. We multiply this amount by the standard variable manufacturing overhead rate we calculated earlier of $0.35. This results in an unfavorable variable manufacturing overhead efficiency variance of $9.45 as shown as follows:

Direct Labor Efficiency Variance in Hours		Standard Variable Mfg Overhead Rate		Variable Mfg Overhead Efficiency Variance
27 hours	×	$0.35	=	$9.45 Unfavorable

Once management calculates the variable manufacturing overhead efficiency variance, it can assess the variance and take corrective action if necessary. Because the variable manufacturing overhead efficiency variance is based on direct labor efficiency, improving the direct labor efficiency variance will solve the variable manufacturing overhead efficiency variance problem.

Tree Top's variable manufacturing overhead efficiency variance is so small that it may warrant no management attention. Even so, as Ali, Maria, and Bill work to bring the direct labor efficiency variance under control, the variable manufacturing overhead variance will also improve.

Discussion Questions

10–11. If variable manufacturing overhead is allocated to production based on direct labor hours, why will an unfavorable variable manufacturing overhead efficiency variance always accompany an unfavorable direct labor efficiency variance?

10–12. If the direct labor efficiency variance is zero, will the variable manufacturing overhead efficiency variance also be zero? Explain your reasoning.

VARIABLE MANUFACTURING OVERHEAD SPENDING VARIANCE

variable manufacturing overhead spending variance The difference between how much was actually spent on variable manufacturing overhead and the amount that should have been spent based on the actual direct labor hours worked.

The **variable manufacturing overhead spending variance** is the difference between what was *actually* spent on variable manufacturing overhead and what *should* have been spent, based on the actual direct labor hours worked. The question this variance answers is, based on the actual number of direct labor hours worked, is variable manufacturing overhead cost in line? In the case of Tree Top, given that production took 162 direct labor hours, was variable manufacturing overhead more or less than it should have been for that many direct labor hours? To find the answer, we must first determine the standard variable manufacturing overhead for the actual number of hours worked and then calculate the overhead spending variance in dollars. Let's look at the first step in this process.

Step 1: Determine the standard variable manufacturing overhead for the actual number of hours worked

To determine the standard variable manufacturing overhead for the actual hours worked, we multiply the standard variable manufacturing overhead rate by the actual number of direct labor hours. This calculation shows us the amount that should have been spent for variable manufacturing overhead based on the actual labor hours worked. Based on Tree Top's standard variable manufacturing overhead rate of $0.35 per hour, the standard variable manufacturing overhead cost for the 162 actual direct labor hours is $56.70, shown as follows:

Actual Direct Labor Hours	×	Standard Variable Mfg Overhead Rate	=	Standard Variable Mfg Overhead for Actual Direct Labor Hours
162 hours	×	$0.35	=	$56.70

Now that we know how much Tree Top's variable manufacturing overhead should have been, we can compare it to the actual variable manufacturing overhead amount to determine the amount of the variance.

Step 2: Calculate the variable manufacturing overhead spending variance

We calculate the variable manufacturing overhead spending variance by comparing standard variable manufacturing overhead for the actual number of hours worked to the amount actually spent for variable manufacturing overhead. This calculation compares *actual* variable manufacturing overhead cost to what it *should* have been for the actual hours worked. In the case of Tree Top, the actual amount spent for variable manufacturing overhead in November was $140. By comparing this amount to the standard of $56.70, we determine that the variable manufacturing overhead spending variance is $83.30 unfavorable, shown as follows:

Standard Variable Mfg Overhead Cost for Actual Direct Labor Hours	−	Actual Variable Mfg Overhead Cost	=	Variable Mfg Overhead Spending Variance
$56.70	−	$140	=	$83.30 Unfavorable

Discussion Questions

10–13. What are some possible reasons why Tree Top Mailbox Company's variable manufacturing overhead spending was much higher than it should have been based on the standards?

10–14. If there had been no variance, would this mean Tree Top paid what it should have for variable manufacturing overhead in November? Explain your reasoning.

As managers assess the variable manufacturing overhead spending variance, they should keep in mind that it is a result of many different overhead expenditures. In practice, most companies break down the variable manufacturing overhead spending variance into separate variances for each variable manufacturing overhead item. For example, a manufacturer would have separate variance calculations for electricity, water, telephone, cleaning supplies, maintenance supplies, and so forth. The logic and calculations for each variance, however, would be similar to what we have presented here.

For Tree Top Mailbox Company, the trouble with variable manufacturing overhead cost is a combination of an unfavorable efficiency variance of $9.45 and an unfavorable spending variance of $83.30. Although the unfavorable efficiency variance will require little or no attention, the spending variance is sizeable and should be investigated. Each component of variable manufacturing overhead should be reviewed to see whether overhead spending can be reduced.

FIXED MANUFACTURING OVERHEAD BUDGET VARIANCE

The **fixed manufacturing overhead budget variance,** also called the **fixed manufacturing overhead spending variance,** is a measure of how actual total fixed manufacturing overhead compares to budgeted fixed manufacturing overhead. For example, if a com-

fixed manufacturing overhead budget variance The difference between the actual amount of total fixed manufacturing overhead cost and the budgeted fixed manufacturing overhead cost.

fixed manufacturing overhead spending variance Another name for the fixed manufacturing overhead budget variance.

pany expects fixed manufacturing overhead cost to be $200,000 per month, the budget variance indicates whether the actual fixed manufacturing overhead is more or less than the $200,000.

We take only one step to compute the fixed manufacturing overhead budget variance. The dollar amount is calculated simply by subtracting actual fixed manufacturing overhead cost from the budgeted fixed manufacturing overhead. For Tree Top, the fixed manufacturing overhead budget variance for November is zero, because actual fixed manufacturing overhead cost exactly equals the amount budgeted, shown as follows:

Budgeted Fixed Mfg Overhead Cost	−	Actual Fixed Mfg Overhead Cost	=	Fixed Mfg Overhead Budget Variance
$225	−	$225	=	$0

The company has only two fixed overhead items, rent and depreciation, so the fact that actual cost equaled budgeted cost is not surprising. If Tree Top purchased additional production equipment resulting in higher depreciation cost, an unfavorable variance could occur.

Fixed manufacturing overhead costs are generally associated with long-term commitments for specific factory resources. Examples of fixed overhead include the cost of depreciation on factory equipment, factory rent, insurance, and property taxes. Unlike other factory costs, fixed overhead is less likely to be affected by the routine decisions that managers and employees make daily. Therefore, the variation between the amount budgeted and the actual fixed factory overhead incurred is just as likely to be caused by a flawed budget as it is by spending decisions made during the budgeted period. For example, if a company budgets $50,000 for property taxes but the taxes are actually $51,000, the $1,000 variance that results is caused by a flawed budget, not by uncontrolled spending. Accordingly, fixed manufacturing overhead budget variances should be closely scrutinized to determine whether the required corrective action is to improve the budgeting process or to modify spending during the period.

Like variable manufacturing overhead, fixed manufacturing overhead comprises many different items. In practice, separate budget variances are calculated for each fixed manufacturing overhead item.

FIXED MANUFACTURING OVERHEAD VOLUME VARIANCE

fixed manufacturing overhead volume variance A measure of the utilization of plant capacity. This variance is caused by manufacturing more or less product during a particular production period than planned.

The last standard cost variance we discuss is the **fixed manufacturing overhead volume variance,** which measures utilization of plant capacity. This variance is caused by the manufacture of more or less product during a particular production period than planned. When a manufacturer invests in expensive production machinery, it does so in anticipation of producing a given amount of product. If the company expects to produce only a small amount of product, it invests in inexpensive, low-volume equipment. If, however, the company expects to produce a large volume of product, it usually acquires more costly, high-volume equipment. If expensive, high-volume equipment is purchased but actual production is low, then it is likely that the company spent too much on production capacity. The fixed manufacturing overhead volume variance focuses on this relationship between production capacity and the actual volume produced.

When Ali, Maria, and Bill formed their manufacturing company, they could have set up shop to produce a very small number of mailboxes using hand tools; or they could have chosen to invest heavily in a building and automated equipment, thereby greatly increasing their plant capacity. They chose to rent a small garage and invest a small amount in power tools that gave them a capacity to produce about 300 mailboxes per month. If they produce more than 300 mailboxes, that's great, but if they produce fewer, they are underutilizing their capacity to produce. In November, they produced only 225 mailboxes. Tree Top Mailbox Company, then, underutilized its capacity to produce by 75 mailboxes. Is this a big problem? To evaluate the magnitude of the problem we need to assign a dollar amount to the underutilization.

In the case of Tree Top Mailbox Company, the monthly fixed cost of $225 provides a capacity to produce 300 mailboxes. We follow three steps to calculate the fixed manufacturing overhead volume variance. First, we find the difference between expected and actual production. Second, we determine the standard number of direct labor hours associated with the production. Finally, we calculate the dollar amount of the fixed manufacturing overhead volume variance. We examine these steps in detail next.

Step 1: Calculate the difference between expected (budgeted) production and actual production

The budgeted production for Tree Top is 300 mailboxes per month. Tree Top's actual production was less than its budgeted production by 75 mailboxes, shown as follows:

Plant Production Capacity	−	Actual Number of Units Produced	=	Under- or Overproduction in Units
300 units	−	225 units	=	75 units under

Because Tree Top allocates fixed manufacturing overhead to production based on direct labor hours, we use the direct labor efficiency standard, with the standard fixed manufacturing overhead rate per direct labor hour, to calculate the dollar amount of the fixed manufacturing overhead volume variance.

Step 2: Determine the standard number of direct labor hours associated with the under- or overproduction

We determine the standard number of direct labor hours associated with the under- or overproduction by multiplying the under- or overproduction by the direct labor efficiency standard. In the case of Tree Top, the direct labor efficiency standard is 0.6 hours per unit. Accordingly, the standard direct labor hours associated with the underproduction of 75 mailboxes is 45 hours (75 units × 0.6 hours per unit), shown as follows:

Amount of Under or Overproduction	×	Direct Labor Efficiency Standard	=	Standard Direct Labor Hours for Under- or Overproduction
75 units	×	0.6 hours per unit	=	45 hours

Now that we know the number of standard hours associated with the over- or underproduction, we can assign a dollar amount based on the standard fixed manufacturing overhead rate per hour.

Step 3: Calculate the dollar amount of the fixed manufacturing overhead volume variance

We calculate the dollar amount of the fixed manufacturing volume variance by multiplying the standard number of direct labor hours associated with the under- or overproduction by the standard fixed manufacturing overhead rate per direct labor hour. In the case of Tree Top, the fixed manufacturing overhead volume variance is $56.25, calculated as follows:

Standard Direct Labor Hours for Under- or Overproduction	×	Standard Fixed Mfg Overhead Rate	=	Fixed Mfg Overhead Volume Variance
45 hours	×	$1.25	=	$56.25 Unfavorable

Once management calculates the fixed manufacturing overhead volume variance, it can attempt to determine what caused it. In the case of Tree Top, the variance resulted primarily from inefficiencies caused by substandard direct material. Surprisingly, however, fixed manufacturing overhead volume variances are often caused by marketing and sales activities, rather than by the production department. In general, production occurs in response to sales demand. If the product is selling poorly, production volume will be low because little product is needed to fulfill demand.

Conversely, if sales demand is high, production volume is likely to be high to meet demand.

◆ USING STANDARD COST VARIANCES TO MANAGE BY EXCEPTION

Once all the standard cost variances have been calculated, the accounting department prepares a performance report that lists each variance. Then managers can use management by exception to address the problems associated with the unfavorable variances, beginning with the largest. A performance report is presented in Exhibit 10–8 for Tree Top Mailbox Company.

EXHIBIT 10–8 Tree Top's November Performance Report

Tree Top Mailbox Company
Performance Report
For November 2004

Variance	Amount	Favorable/ Unfavorable
Direct material quantity variance	$ 99.75	Unfavorable
Direct material price variance	48.00	Favorable
Direct labor efficiency variance	270.00	Unfavorable
Direct labor rate variance	81.00	Unfavorable
Variable mfg overhead efficiency variance	9.45	Unfavorable
Variable mfg overhead spending variance	83.30	Unfavorable
Fixed mfg overhead budget variance	-0-	——
Fixed mfg overhead volume variance	56.25	Unfavorable
Total	$551.75	Unfavorable

As the Tree Top Mailbox Company example shows, sometimes relationships among standard cost variances can occur that help explain the cause of some variances. Also, managers must develop the skill to review the variances and then seek out their causes and possible remedies. Even though managers can use standard costing to spot pressing issues, they must be careful of its shortcomings. Standard costing is one management tool, but not the only tool.

Summary

In the process of operating businesses, managers must focus their valuable time on areas that need to be improved. One area that requires constant attention is controlling the costs of operations. A process designed to help managers focus on cost items that need attention is standard costing, which sets cost performance goals and then uses these goals to evaluate performance.

Differences between actual costs incurred and what the costs should have been, based on the standards, are called variances. A favorable variance results when actual cost is lower than cost based on standard. An unfavorable variance results when actual cost of actual performance is higher than cost based on standard. Using variances to direct management attention is called management by exception.

In establishing performance standards, managers can use either ideal standards, which can be attained only under perfect conditions, or practical standards, which allow for normal working conditions.

Although a standard costing system can be extremely helpful to managers, it has several potential problems. These include employees setting lax standards to avoid unfavorable variances, relying on historical information that may perpetuate past inefficiencies, and managing "by the numbers," thus overlooking significant problems that do not result in variances.

A standard cost system in a manufacturing environment uses estimates for the cost of direct materials, direct labor, and manufacturing overhead. This system is in contrast to both an actual cost system, which uses the actual cost for direct materials, direct labor, and manufacturing overhead, and a normal cost system, which uses actual costs for direct materials and direct labor, and estimates for manufacturing overhead.

The standards used in a manufacturing-type company generally include a direct material quantity standard, a direct material price standard, a direct labor efficiency standard, a direct labor rate standard, a standard variable manufacturing overhead rate, and a standard fixed manufacturing overhead rate.

To use standard costing as a control device, managers compare standard costs to actual costs to see what variance exist. Then they investigate variances, as appropriate, which is known as variance analysis. The variances most commonly used are the direct material quantity variance, the direct material price variance, the direct labor efficiency variance, the direct labor rate variance, the variable manufacturing overhead efficiency variance, the variable manufacturing overhead spending variance, the fixed manufacturing overhead budget variance, and the fixed manufacturing overhead volume variance.

Recording Product Cost Using Standard Costing

This appendix is intended to provide an overview of the accounting entries to record product costs using standard costing. To fully understand the material in this appendix, it is best if you have a basic understanding of debit and credit accounting procedures, including general journal entries and the use of T-accounts. If this is not the case, we suggest that you review Chapter 6 of our financial accounting text or the accounting procedures section of any introductory financial accounting text.

The recording process for standard costing involves ten basic types of transactions:

Transaction 1: Record the purchase of direct material and the direct material price variance.

Transaction 2: Record the use of direct material and the direct material quantity variance.

Transaction 3: Record the use of direct labor and the direct labor rate and efficiency variances.

Transaction 4: Record actual variable manufacturing overhead cost incurred.

Transaction 5: Record the application of variable manufacturing overhead to production.

Transaction 6: Close the variable manufacturing overhead accounts and record the variable overhead variances.

Transaction 7: Record actual fixed manufacturing overhead cost incurred.

Transaction 8: Record the application of fixed manufacturing overhead to production.

Transaction 9: Close the fixed manufacturing overhead accounts and record the fixed overhead variances.

Transaction 10: Close the standard cost variances to cost of goods sold.

To record these transactions we will use the following general ledger accounts:

1. Cash
2. Raw materials inventory
3. Work-in-process inventory
4. Direct materials price variance
5. Direct materials quantity variance
6. Direct labor efficiency variance
7. Direct labor rate variance
8. Variable manufacturing overhead efficiency variance
9. Variable manufacturing overhead spending variance
10. Fixed manufacturing overhead budget variance
11. Fixed manufacturing overhead volume variance
12. Variable manufacturing overhead incurred
13. Variable manufacturing overhead applied
14. Fixed manufacturing overhead incurred
15. Fixed manufacturing overhead applied
16. Accumulated depreciation
17. Accounts payable
18. Cost of goods sold

As we demonstrate the journal entries, we will analyze each transaction using the following four steps:

1. Determine if and when a transaction occurred, what accounts were affected, which account balances should increase, which should decrease, and by how much.
2. Determine which accounts we should debit and which we should credit.
3. Make the journal entry.
4. Review the entry to ensure it is in proper form and that the debits equal the credits.

The entries that follow are based on information from the Tree Top Mailbox Company example presented in this chapter.

Before we begin, it is important to know that when companies use standard costing, they maintain their direct materials, work-in-process, and finished goods inventories at standard cost. The standard cost variances account for the differences between the standard costs maintained in inventories and actual costs. Also keep in mind that when we record a standard cost variance, we need to credit the variance account if the variance is favorable and we need to debit the variance account if it is unfavorable.

Transaction 1: Record the purchase of direct material and the direct material price variance.

1. Let's assume that Tree Top purchased the 6,000 feet of wood on account for $477.00 on November 1, 2004. This transaction affects the raw materials inventory account, the accounts payable account and direct material price variance. Because Tree Top is using a standard cost system, we should increase the balance in the raw material inventory account by the 6,000 feet of wood priced at standard. At Tree Top's $0.0875 per foot standard direct material price, the standard cost of the 6,000 feet of wood is $525.00 (6,000 × $0875.00). Also, we should increase accounts payable by the $477.00 actual cost of the material. After all, that is how much Tree Top must pay for the wood. Finally, we should place the $48.00 favorable variance, the difference between the material's standard cost and its actual cost, in the direct material price variance account.

2. Because raw materials inventory is an asset account we increase it with a debit. Accounts payable is a liability account so we increase it with a credit. As we mentioned previously, if a variance is favorable, we should credit the variance account and if it is unfavorable, we should debit the variance account. Therefore, because it is a favorable variance, we credit the direct materials price variance account.

3. The general journal entry:

```
2004
Nov 1  Raw Materials Inventory                      525.00
            Accounts Payable                                   477.00
            Direct Material Price Variance                      48.00
         To record the purchase of raw material and
         The direct material price variance.
```

4. A final check of the entry reveals that we dated it correctly, made the debit part of the entry first, indented the credit account title, and the dollar amount of the debits equals that of the credits. The entry is fine.

Transaction 2: Record the use of direct material and the direct material quantity variance.

1. We will assume this transaction took place on November 2, 2004. The transaction affects the work-in-process inventory, raw materials inventory, and the direct material quantity variance accounts. We should decrease the balance of the raw materials inventory account based on the actual quantity of material used, priced at standard cost. Therefore we will decrease raw material inventory by 6,000 feet actually used in production multiplied by the standard cost of $.0875, or $525.00. When standard costing is used, we increase work-in-process inventory by the standard quantity of material allowed multiplied by the direct material price rate standard. In Tree Top's case, we would increase work-in-process inventory by $425.25, calculated as follows:

Number of Mailboxes Produced		Direct Material Quantity Standard		Direct Material Price Standard		Amount to Add to Work-in-Process
225	×	21.6 feet	×	$.0875	=	$425.25

Finally, we should place the $99.75 unfavorable variance in the direct material quantity variance account.

2. Because work-in-process materials inventory is an asset account, we increase it with a debit. Raw materials inventory is also an asset account so we decrease it with a credit. Because it is an unfavorable variance, we debit the direct materials quantity variance account.

3. The general journal entry:

```
2004
Nov 2  Work-in-Process Inventory                   425.25
         Direct Material Quantity Variance            99.75
            Raw Material Inventory                             525.00
         To record the use of raw material and
         the direct material quantity variance.
```

4. A final check of the entry reveals the entry is fine.

Transaction 3: Record the use of direct labor and the direct labor rate and efficiency variances.

1. We will assume this transaction took place on November 30, 2004. As we learned in Chapter 2, direct labor cost increases the work-in-process inventory account. When standard costing is used, we increase work-in-process inventory by the standard hours allowed multiplied by the direct labor rate standard. In Tree Top's case, we would increase work-in-process inventory by $1,350.00, calculated as follows:

Number of Mailboxes Produced		Direct Labor Efficiency Standard		Direct Labor Rate Standard		Amount to Add to Work-in-Process
225	×	0.6	×	$10	=	$1,350.00

We should decrease cash based on the actual amount actually paid to the labor force, or $1,701.00. The combination of the unfavorable efficiency variance of $270.00 and the unfavorable rate variance of $81.00 make up the difference between the amount recorded in work-in-process inventory and the amount paid out as wages.

2. Because work-in-process materials inventory is an asset account, we increase it with a debit. Cash is also an asset account so we decrease it with a credit. Because the variances are unfavorable, we debit both the direct labor efficiency variance and the direct labor rate variance accounts.

3. The general journal entry:

```
2004
Nov 30  Work-in-Process Inventory            1,350.00
        Direct Labor Efficiency Variance       270.00
        Direct Labor Rate Variance              81.00
            Cash                                           1,701.00
        To record direct labor cost and variances
```

4. A final check of the entry reveals the entry is fine.

Transaction 4: Record actual variable manufacturing overhead cost incurred.

1. Let's assume Tree Top's actual variable manufacturing overhead costs totaling $140.00 were paid in cash on November 30, 2004. This entry is relatively straightforward and one you should be familiar with if you studied the overhead entries we demonstrated in the appendix to Chapter 3. We should increase the variable manufacturing overhead incurred account for the actual cost of the manufacturing overhead and decrease cash for the amount paid.

2. We increase the variable manufacturing overhead incurred account with a debit and we decrease the cash account with a credit.

3. The general journal entry:

```
2004
Nov 30  Variable Manufacturing Overhead Incurred   140.00
            Cash                                              140.00
        To record actual variable manufacturing
        overhead cost for November.
```

4. A final check of the entry reveals that it is fine.

Transaction 5: Record the application of variable manufacturing overhead to production.

1. The manufacturing overhead cost allocated to production becomes part of work-in-process inventory so this transaction affects the work-in-process inventory account. Because Tree Top uses a standard cost system, the transaction also affects an account called variable manufacturing overhead applied. If you studied the overhead entries we covered in the appendix to Chapter 3, you will already be familiar with this entry. When we allocate manufacturing overhead to production in a standard cost system, we use a different account than the one we used when we recorded the actual overhead costs. By using two separate accounts, managers can keep track of both the actual overhead costs incurred and the amount applied to production. The amount of variable manufacturing overhead allocated to production is based on the variable manufacturing overhead standard rate. In other words, we allocate variable manufacturing overhead to production at

standard. In Tree Top's case, we would increase work-in-process inventory and variable manufacturing overhead applied $47.25, calculated as follows:

Number of Mailboxes × Produced	Direct Labor Efficiency × Standard	Standard Variable Manufacturing = Overhead Rate	Amount to Add to Work-in-Process
225 ×	.6 · ×	$0.35 =	$47.25

2. We increase the work-in-process inventory with a debit and the variable manufacturing overhead applied account with a credit.

3. The general journal entry:

> *2004*
> *Nov 30   Work-in-Process Inventory   47.25*
> *   Variable Manufacturing Overhead Applied   47.25*
> *   To record the allocation of variable manufacturing*
> *   overhead to production.*

4. A final check of the entry reveals the entry is fine.

Transaction 6: Close the variable manufacturing overhead accounts and record the variable overhead variances.

1. The difference between the $140.00 balance in the variable manufacturing overhead incurred account and the $47.25 balance in the variable manufacturing overhead applied account equals the combination of the $9.45 unfavorable variable overhead efficiency and the $83.30 unfavorable spending variances. These variance accounts are established when the variable manufacturing overhead incurred and the variable manufacturing overhead applied accounts are closed. Companies generally do this closing procedure only at year end. For demonstration purposes, we will assume that Tree Top has elected to close the overhead accounts to establish the variable overhead efficiency and spending variances at the end of November.

2. Because the variable manufacturing overhead incurred account has a debit balance, we close it with a credit, and because the variable manufacturing overhead applied account has a credit balance, we close it with a debit. As we previously mentioned, if the variance is favorable, we should credit the variance account. Conversely, if the variance is unfavorable, we should debit the variance account. For Tree Top, both the efficiency variance and the spending variance are unfavorable so the variance accounts will be debited.

3. The general journal entry:

> *2004*
> *Nov 30   Variable Manufacturing Overhead Applied   47.25*
> *   Variable Manufacturing Overhead Efficiency Variance   9.45*
> *   Variable Manufacturing Overhead Spending Variance   83.30*
> *   Variable Manufacturing Overhead Incurred   140.00*
> *   To close variable overhead accounts and record*
> *   the variable manufacturing variances*

4   A final check of the entries reveals that it is fine.

Transaction 7: Record actual fixed manufacturing overhead cost incurred.

1. Tree Top's actual fixed manufacturing overhead costs consist of $200.00 for rent and $25.00 for depreciation. We will assume the rent was paid on November 1 and the depreciation is recorded on November 30. We should increase the fixed manufacturing overhead incurred account for the actual cost of the manufacturing overhead. We should decrease cash for the $200.00 rent and increase accumulated depreciation for the $25.00 in depreciation.

2. We increase the fixed manufacturing overhead incurred account with a debit, and we decrease the cash account and increase the accumulated depreciation account with credits.

3. The general journal entries:

2004

Nov 1 Fixed Manufacturing Overhead Incurred 200.00
*   Cash 200.00*
*   To record rent for November*

*   30 Fixed Manufacturing Overhead Incurred 25.00*
*   Accumulated Depreciation 25.00*
*   To record depreciation for November*

4. A final check of the entries reveals that they are fine.

Transaction 8: Record the application of fixed manufacturing overhead to production.

1. As with variable manufacturing overhead, fixed manufacturing overhead cost allocated to production becomes part of work-in-process inventory. Because Tree Top uses a standard cost system, the transaction also affects an account called fixed manufacturing overhead applied. As was the case with variable manufacturing overhead, we allocate fixed manufacturing overhead to production at standard. In Tree Top's case, we would increase work-in-process inventory and variable manufacturing overhead applied by $168.75, calculated as follows:

Number of Mailboxes Produced	×	Direct Labor Efficiency Standard	×	Standard Fixed Manufacturing Overhead Rate	=	Amount to Add to Work-in-Process
225	×	.6	×	$1.25	=	$168.75

2. We increase the work-in-process inventory with a debit and the fixed manufacturing overhead applied account with a credit.
3. The general journal entry:

2004

Nov 30 Work-In-Process Inventory 168.75
*   Fixed Manufacturing Overhead Applied 168.75*
*   To record the allocation of fixed manufacturing*
*   overhead to production.*

4. A final check of the entry reveals the entry is fine.

Transaction 9: Close the fixed manufacturing overhead accounts and record the fixed overhead variances.

1. The difference between the $225.00 balance in the fixed manufacturing overhead incurred account and the $168.75 balance in the fixed manufacturing overhead applied account is equal to the combination of company's fixed manufacturing overhead budget variance and its fixed manufacturing overhead volume variance. In Tree Top's case, the company's fixed manufacturing overhead budget variance was zero, but its fixed manufacturing overhead volume variance totaled $56.25. As was the case with the variable manufacturing overhead variances, the fixed manufacturing overhead variance accounts are established when the fixed manufacturing overhead incurred and the fixed manufacturing overhead applied accounts are closed. For demonstration purposes, we will assume once more that Tree Top has elected to close the overhead accounts to establish the fixed overhead volume and budget variances at the end of November.
2. Because the fixed manufacturing overhead incurred account has a debit balance, we close it with a credit, and because the fixed manufacturing overhead applied account has a credit balance, we close it with a debit. As we previously mentioned, if the variance is favorable, we should credit the variance account. Conversely, if the variance is unfavorable, we should debit the variance account. For Tree Top, the fixed manufacturing overhead budget is zero, but the fixed manufacturing overhead volume variance is unfavorable so we will debit that variance account.
3. The general journal entry:

2004

Nov 30 Fixed Manufacturing Overhead Applied 168.75
*   Fixed Manufacturing Overhead Budget Variance ... 0.00*
*   Fixed Manufacturing Overhead Volume Variance ... 56.25*
*   Fixed Manufacturing Overhead Incurred 225.00*
*   To close fixed overhead accounts and record the*
*   fixed manufacturing variances*

4. A final check of the entries reveals that it is fine.

Transaction 10: Close the standard cost variances to cost of goods sold.

1. The variance accounts are monitored during the year but generally no accounting entries are made to dispense with the amounts until the end of the year. For demonstration purposes, we will assume that Tree Top has elected to close the variance accounts at the end of November.

   In most cases an accounting entry is made to close the standard cost variances to cost of goods sold. Because the amount of the variances is generally relatively small and most product cost ends up in cost of goods sold by year end, closing the variance accounts to cost of goods sold is adequate for most companies.

   At this point, Tree Top's variance accounts have the following balances:

	Debit Balance	Credit Balance
Direct Material Price Variance		$48.00
Direct Material Quantity Variance	$ 99.75	
Direct Labor Efficiency Variance	270.00	
Direct Labor Rate Variance	81.00	
Variable Manufacturing Overhead Efficiency Variance	9.45	
Variable Manufacturing Overhead Spending Variance	83.30	
Fixed Manufacturing Overhead Budget Variance	0.00	
Fixed Manufacturing Overhead Volume Variance	56.25	

2. To close Tree Top's variance accounts, if the variance account has a debit balance, we close the account with a credit and if the account has a credit balance, we will close it with a debit. Once this is done, we will enter an amount in the cost of goods sold account that will balance the entry.

3. The general journal entry:

   2004
Nov 30	*Cost of Goods Sold*	*551.75*	
	Direct Material Price Variance	*48.00*	
	Direct Material Quantity Variance		*99.75*
	Direct Labor Efficiency Variance		*270.00*
	Direct Labor Rate Variance		*81.00*
	Variable Manufacturing Overhead Efficiency Variance		*9.45*
	Variable Manufacturing Overhead Spending Variance		*83.30*
	Fixed Manufacturing Overhead Budget Variance		*0.00*
	Fixed Manufacturing Overhead Volume Variance		*56.25*
	To close standard cost variance accounts to cost of goods sold.		

4. A final check of the entries reveals that it is fine.

◆ APPENDIX SUMMARY

When a company uses standard costing, it maintains direct materials, work-in-process, and finished goods inventories at standard cost. The standard cost variances account for the difference between the standard cost maintained in inventory and actual costs. When we record a variance, we should credit the variance account if the variance is favorable and we should debit the variance account if it is unfavorable.

To record the purchase of raw material, we debit the raw materials inventory account for an amount equal to the actual quantity of material purchased multiplied by the standard price. We then credit accounts payable or cash for the actual purchase price of the material. The difference between the amount debited to raw material and the amount credited to accounts payable or cash is taken to the direct materials price variance account.

To record the use of direct material, we debit the work-in-process inventory account for an amount equal to the standard quantity of material allowed for production multiplied by the standard price. The amount we credited raw materials is equal to the actual quantity of material multiplied by the standard price. The difference between the amount debited to work-in-process inventory and the amount credited to raw materials inventory is taken to the direct material quantity variance account.

With respect to direct labor, we debit work-in-process inventory for an amount equal to the standard hours allowed for production multiplied by the standard direct labor rate. We credit cash or wages payable for the actual amount of wages paid to employees. The difference between the amount debited to work in process and the amount credited to cash is equal to the direct labor efficiency and rate variances.

With respect to variable manufacturing overhead, we debit the variable manufacturing overhead incurred account for the actual cost of variable manufacturing overhead. We debit work-in-process inventory and credit variable manufacturing overhead applied for an amount equal to the standard direct labor hours allowed for production multiplied by the standard variable overhead application rate. The difference between the balance of the variable manufacturing overhead incurred account and the variable manufacturing overhead applied account is equal to the variable overhead efficiency and spending variances. At year end, these variance accounts are established when the variable manufacturing overhead incurred and the variable manufacturing overhead applied accounts are closed.

With respect to fixed manufacturing overhead, we debit fixed manufacturing overhead incurred account the actual cost of fixed manufacturing overhead. We debit work-in-process inventory and credit fixed manufacturing overhead applied for an amount equal to the standard direct labor hours allowed for production multiplied by the standard fixed overhead application rate. The difference between the balance of the fixed manufacturing overhead incurred account and the fixed manufacturing overhead applied account is equal to the fixed overhead budget and volume spending variances. At year end, these variance accounts are established when the fixed manufacturing overhead incurred and the fixed manufacturing overhead applied accounts are closed.

Companies generally close the standard cost variance accounts to cost of goods sold at year end. Because the amount of the variances is generally relatively small and most product cost ends up in cost of goods sold by year end, closing the variance accounts to cost of goods sold is adequate for most companies.

Key Terms ●●●

- bill of materials, M–314
- direct labor efficiency standard, M–316
- direct labor efficiency variance, M–324
- direct labor rate standard, M–316
- direct labor rate variance, M–325
- direct material efficiency variance, M–320
- direct material price standard, M–315
- direct material price variance, M–322
- direct material quantity standard, M–314
- direct material quantity variance, M–320

- direct material usage variance, M–320
- favorable variance, M–309
- fixed manufacturing overhead budget variance, M–328
- fixed manufacturing overhead spending variance, M–328
- fixed manufacturing overhead volume variance, M–329
- ideal standard, M–310
- management by exception, M–310
- practical standard, M–311
- standard, M–309
- standard cost system, M–309

- standard costing, M–308
- standard fixed manufacturing overhead rate, M–318
- standard variable manufacturing overhead rate, M–317
- unfavorable variance, M–309
- variable manufacturing overhead efficiency variance, M–326
- variable manufacturing overhead spending variance, M–327
- variance, M–309

Review the Facts ●●

A. What is standard costing?
B. What is a standard?
C. What is a variance?
D. Describe management by exception.
E. How often do most companies set cost standards?
F. What are the two things that can cause cost to increase?
G. What is the difference between an ideal standard and a practical standard?
H. Briefly describe five problems with standard costing.
I. What is a bill of material?
J. What are the two direct material standards?
K. What are the two direct labor standards?
L. How can standard costs be used to control cost?
M. What is measured by the direct material quantity variance?
N. What is measured by the direct material price variance?
O. What is measured by the direct labor efficiency variance?
P. What is measured by the direct labor rate variance?
Q. What is measured by the variable manufacturing overhead efficiency variance?
R. What is measured by the variable manufacturing overhead spending variance?
S. What is measured by the fixed manufacturing overhead budget variance?
T. What is measured by the fixed manufacturing overhead volume variance?

Apply What You Have Learned ●●●●●●●●●●●●●●●●●●●●●●●●●●●●

LO 7: DETERMINE DIRECT MATERIAL VARIANCES

10–15. The Zhang Manufacturing Company purchased 4,000 pounds of direct material at $5.20 per pound. It used 2,700 pounds to make 5,000 finished units. The standard cost for direct material is $5 per pound and the quantity standard is 0.5 (one-half) pound per finished unit.

Required:

a. According to the appropriate standard, how much should the company have paid for the 4,000 pounds of direct material purchased?
b. Determine the direct material price variance based on the amount of direct material purchased.
c. According to the appropriate standard, how many pounds of direct material should have been used to make the 5,000 finished units?
d. Determine the direct material quantity variance in pounds of direct material.
e. Determine the direct material quantity variance in dollars.
f. Appendix: Prepare the following journal entries:

1. Record the purchase of direct material.
2. Record the use of direct material.

LO 7: DETERMINE DIRECT MATERIAL VARIANCES

10–16. The Carbonnell Manufacturing Company purchased 15,000 pounds of direct material at $1.30 per pound. It used 14,700 pounds to make 5,000 finished units. The standard cost for direct material is $1.35 per pound and the quantity standard is three pounds per finished unit.

Required:

    a. According to the appropriate standard, how much should the company have paid for the 15,000 pounds of direct material purchased?

    b. Determine the direct material price variance based on the amount of direct material purchased.

    c. According to the appropriate standard, how many pounds of direct material should have been used to make the 5,000 finished units?

    d. Determine the direct material quantity variance in pounds of direct material.

    e. Determine the direct material quantity variance in dollars.

    f. Appendix: Prepare the following journal entries:

        1. Record the purchase of direct material.

        2. Record the use of direct material.

LO 7: DETERMINE DIRECT MATERIAL VARIANCES

10–17. The Smithstone Company purchased 2,500 square feet of direct material at $6.30 per square foot. It used 2,055 square feet of material to make 500 finished units. The standard cost for direct material is $6.15 per square foot and the quantity standard is four square feet per finished unit.

Required:

    a. According to the appropriate standard, how much should the company have paid for the 2,500 square feet of direct material purchased?

    b. Determine the direct material price variance based on the amount of direct material purchased.

    c. According to the appropriate standard, how many square feet of direct material should have been used to make the 500 finished units?

    d. Determine the direct material quantity variance in square feet of direct material.

    e. Determine the direct material quantity variance in dollars.

    f. Appendix: Prepare the following journal entries:

        1. Record the purchase of direct material.

        2. Record the use of direct material.

LO 7: DETERMINE DIRECT MATERIAL VARIANCES

10–18. Econo Manufacturing purchased 20,000 square feet of direct material at $0.54 per square foot. It used 12,625 square feet to make 1,250 finished units. The standard cost for direct material is $0.55 per square foot and the quantity standard is 10 square feet per finished unit.

Required:

    a. According to the appropriate standard, how much should the company have paid for the 20,000 square feet of direct material purchased?

    b. Determine the direct material price variance based on the amount of direct material purchased.

    c. According to the appropriate standard, how many square feet of direct material should have been used to make the 1,250 finished units?

    d. Determine the direct material quantity variance in square feet of direct material.

    e. Determine the direct material quantity variance in dollars.

LO 7: DETERMINE DIRECT MATERIAL VARIANCES

10–19. The following information is presented for the Scout Manufacturing Company:

- Direct material price standard is $1.55 per gallon.
- Direct material quantity standard is 2.5 gallons per finished unit.
- Budgeted production is 1,000 finished units.
- 4,000 gallons of direct material were purchased for $6,000.

- 2,800 gallons of direct material were used in production.
- 1,100 finished units of product were produced.

Required:

    a. Determine the direct material price variance.

    b. Determine the direct material quantity variance in dollars.

LO 7: DETERMINE DIRECT MATERIAL VARIANCES

10–20. The following information is presented for the Flowvalve Manufacturing Company.

- Direct material price standard is $15 per pound.
- Direct material quantity standard is ¼ pound per finished unit.
- Budgeted production is 20,000 finished units.
- 6,000 pounds of direct material were purchased for $91,320.
- 4,650 pounds of direct material were used in production.
- 18,000 finished units of product were produced.

Required:

    a. Determine the direct material price variance.

    b. Determine the direct material quantity variance in dollars.

LO 7: DETERMINE DIRECT MATERIAL VARIANCES

10–21. The following information is presented for the Munter Manufacturing Company.

- Direct material price standard is $3.25 per pound.
- Direct material quantity standard is six pounds per finished unit.
- Budgeted production is 25,000 finished units.
- 175,000 pounds of direct material were purchased for $559,650.
- 155,200 pounds of direct material were used in production.
- 25,600 finished units of product were produced.

Required:

    a. Determine the direct material price variance.

    b. Determine the direct material quantity variance in dollars.

LO 7: DETERMINE DIRECT MATERIAL VARIANCES

10–22. Information from the Quincy Company is as follows:

Actual cost of 33,000 pounds of direct material purchased	$97,350
Direct material used in production	30,575 pounds
Actual production	2,980 units
Direct material price standard	$3 per pound
Direct material quantity standard per finished unit of production	10 pounds
Budgeted production	3,000 units

Required:

    a. Determine the direct material price variance.

    b. Determine the direct material quantity variance in dollars.

LO 7: DETERMINE DIRECT MATERIAL VARIANCES

10–23. Information from the Wayne Manufacturing is as follows:

Actual cost of 10,000 pounds of direct material purchased	$2,400
Direct material used in production	9,177 pounds
Actual production	980 units
Direct material price standard	$0.25 per pound
Direct material quantity standard per finished unit of production	9 pounds
Budgeted production	1,000 units

Required:

    a. Determine the direct material price variance.

    b. Determine the direct material quantity variance in dollars.

LO 7: DETERMINE DIRECT MATERIAL VARIANCES

10–24. Information from the Myco Manufacturing Company is as follows:

Actual cost of 120,000 feet of direct material purchased	$427,200
Direct material used in production	111,100 feet
Actual production	3,200 units
Direct material price standard	$3.50 per foot
Direct material quantity standard per finished unit of production	35 feet
Budgeted production	3,500 units

Required:

    a. Determine the direct material price variance.
    b. Determine the direct material quantity variance in dollars.

LO 7: DETERMINE DIRECT LABOR VARIANCES

10–25. The direct labor rate standard for Amy Manufacturing is $12 per direct labor hour. The direct labor efficiency standard is two hours per finished unit. Last month, the company completed 8,000 units of product using 16,350 direct labor hours at an actual cost of $194,565.

Required:

    a. According to the appropriate standard, how much should the company have paid for the 16,350 actual direct labor hours?
    b. Determine the direct labor rate variance.
    c. According to the appropriate standard, how many hours of direct labor should it have taken to produce the 8,000 units?
    d. Determine the direct labor efficiency variance in hours.
    e. Determine the direct labor efficiency variance in dollars.
    f. Appendix: Prepare a journal entry to record the direct labor and the direct labor rate and efficiency variances.

LO 7: DETERMINE DIRECT LABOR VARIANCES

10–26. The direct labor rate standard for Calspan Manufacturing is $18.50 per direct labor hour. The direct labor efficiency standard is six minutes or $\frac{1}{10}$ of an hour per finished unit. Last month, the company completed 105,650 units of product using 10,400 direct labor hours at an actual cost of $191,360.

Required:

    a. According to the appropriate standard, how much should the company have paid for the 10,400 actual direct labor hours?
    b. Determine the direct labor rate variance.
    c. According to the appropriate standard, how many hours of direct labor should it have taken to produce the 105,650 units?
    d. Determine the direct labor efficiency variance in hours.
    e. Determine the direct labor efficiency variance in dollars.
    f. Appendix: Prepare a journal entry to record the direct labor and the direct labor rate and efficiency variances.

LO 7: DETERMINE DIRECT LABOR VARIANCES

10–27. The direct labor rate standard for Key Largo Manufacturing is $10 per direct labor hour. The direct labor efficiency standard is three hours per finished unit. Last month, the company completed 2,800 units of product using 8,620 direct labor hours at an actual cost of $88,355.

Required:

    a. According to the appropriate standard, how much should the company have paid for the 8,620 actual direct labor hours?
    b. Determine the direct labor rate variance.
    c. According to the appropriate standard, how many hours of direct labor should it have taken to produce the 2,800 units?

d. Determine the direct labor efficiency variance in hours.

e. Determine the direct labor efficiency variance in dollars.

LO 7: DETERMINE DIRECT LABOR VARIANCES

10–28. The direct labor rate standard for Sakura Manufacturing is $15.25 per direct labor hour. The direct labor efficiency standard is 30 minutes or ½ hour per finished unit. Last month, the company completed 27,800 units of product using 14,050 direct labor hours at an actual cost of $215,246.

Required:

a. Determine the direct labor rate variance.

b. Determine the direct labor efficiency variance in dollars.

c. Appendix: Prepare a journal entry to record the direct labor and the direct labor rate and efficiency variances.

LO 7: DETERMINE DIRECT LABOR VARIANCES

10–29. The direct labor rate standard for Melissa Valdez Manufacturing is $10 per direct labor hour. The direct labor efficiency standard is 0.25 (one quarter) hour per finished unit. Last month, the company completed 38,000 units of product using 9,280 direct labor hours at an actual cost of $97,904.

Required:

a. Determine the direct labor rate variance.

b. Determine the direct labor efficiency variance in dollars.

c. Appendix: Prepare a journal entry to record the direct labor and the direct labor rate and efficiency variances.

LO 7: DETERMINE DIRECT LABOR VARIANCES

10–30. The following information is presented for the Marathon Manufacturing Company.

- Direct labor rate standard is $11.55.
- Direct labor efficiency standard is 2.5 hours per finished unit.
- Budgeted production is 1,200 finished units.
- Production required 2,910 direct labor hours at a cost of $33,174.
- 1,150 finished units of product were produced.

Required:

a. Determine the direct labor rate variance.

b. Determine the direct labor efficiency variance in dollars.

LO 7: DETERMINE DIRECT LABOR VARIANCES

10–31. The following information is presented for the Picas Manufacturing Company.

- Direct labor rate standard is $12.
- Direct labor efficiency standard is two hours per finished unit.
- Budgeted production is 2,200 finished units.
- Production required 4,560 direct labor hours at a cost of $54,036.
- 2,250 finished units of product were produced.

Required:

a. Determine the direct labor rate variance.

b. Determine the direct labor efficiency variance in dollars.

LO 7: DETERMINE DIRECT LABOR VARIANCES

10–32. The following information is presented for the Lew Green Manufacturing Company.

- Direct labor rate standard is $24.
- Direct labor efficiency standard is three hours per finished unit.
- Budgeted production is 775 finished units.
- Production required 2,375 direct labor hours at a cost of $57,475.
- 810 finished units of product were produced.

Required:

    a. Determine the direct labor rate variance.

    b. Determine the direct labor efficiency variance in dollars.

LO 7: DETERMINE DIRECT LABOR VARIANCES

10–33. Information from the Spin Manufacturing Company is presented as follows:

Actual number of direct labor hours	275
Actual direct labor cost	$4,620
Actual number of units produced	800 units
Direct labor rate standard	$16.10
Direct labor efficiency standard	.3 hours per unit
Budgeted production	850 units

Required:

    a. Determine the direct labor rate variance.

    b. Determine the direct labor efficiency variance in dollars.

LO 7: DETERMINE DIRECT LABOR VARIANCES

10–34. Information from the Popular Manufacturing Company is as follows:

Actual number of direct labor hours	1,275
Actual direct labor cost	$16,065
Actual number of units produced	1,255 units
Direct labor rate standard	$12
Direct labor efficiency standard	1 hour per unit
Budgeted production	1,200 units

Required:

    a. Determine the direct labor rate variance.

    b. Determine the direct labor efficiency variance in dollars.

LO 7: DETERMINE DIRECT LABOR VARIANCES

10–35. Information from the Electronic Manufacturing Company is as follows:

Actual number of direct labor hours	12,830
Actual direct labor cost	$292,524
Actual number of units produced	2,040 units
Direct labor rate standard	$23.10
Direct labor efficiency standard	6 hours per unit
Budgeted production	2,000 units

Required:

    a. Determine the direct labor rate variance.

    b. Determine the direct labor efficiency variance in dollars.

LO 7: DETERMINE DIRECT MATERIAL AND DIRECT LABOR VARIANCES

10–36. Information from the Atlantic Company is presented as follows:

Actual cost of 30,000 pounds of direct material purchased	$97,500
Direct material used in production	28,100 pounds
Actual number of direct labor hours	12,850
Actual direct labor cost	$165,765
Actual production	2,500 units
Direct material price standard	$3.30 per pound
Direct material quantity standard per finished unit of production	11 pounds
Direct labor rate standard	$13
Direct labor efficiency standard	5 hours per unit
Budgeted production	2,400 units

Required:

    a. Determine the direct material price variance.
    b. Determine the direct material quantity variance in dollars.
    c. Determine the direct labor rate variance.
    d. Determine the direct labor efficiency variance in dollars.

LO 7: DETERMINE DIRECT MATERIAL AND DIRECT LABOR VARIANCES

10–37. Information from the Progressive Company is presented as follows:

Actual cost of 9,000 pounds of direct material purchased	$2,200
Direct material used in production	7,800 pounds
Actual number of direct labor hours	980
Actual direct labor cost	$14,945
Actual production	240 units
Direct material price standard	$0.25 per pound
Direct material quantity standard per finished unit of production	30 pounds
Direct labor rate standard	$15
Direct labor efficiency standard	4 hours per unit
Budgeted production	250 units

Required:

    a. Determine the direct material price variance.
    b. Determine the direct material quantity variance in dollars.
    c. Determine the direct labor rate variance.
    d. Determine the direct labor efficiency variance in dollars.

LO 7: DETERMINE DIRECT MATERIAL AND DIRECT LABOR VARIANCES

10–38. Information from the Packard Company is presented as follows:

Actual cost of 1,000 pounds of direct material purchased	$10,280
Direct material used in production	830 pounds
Actual number of direct labor hours	1,220
Actual direct labor cost	$13,176
Actual production	400 units
Direct material price standard	$10 per pound
Direct material quantity standard per finished unit of production	2 pounds
Direct labor rate standard	$11
Direct labor efficiency standard	3 hours per unit
Budgeted production	450 units

Required:

    a. Determine the direct material price variance.
    b. Determine the direct material quantity variance in dollars.
    c. Determine the direct labor rate variance.
    d. Determine the direct labor efficiency variance in dollars.

LO 7: DETERMINE VARIABLE MANUFACTURING OVERHEAD VARIANCES

10–39. Billy Clifford Manufacturing applies variable manufacturing overhead to production on the basis of $15 per direct labor hour. The labor efficiency standard is five hours per finished unit. Last month the company produced 12,000 units and used 62,000 direct labor hours. Actual variable overhead cost incurred totaled $920,000.

Required:

    a. Determine the variable manufacturing overhead spending variance.
    b. According to the appropriate standard, how many direct labor hours should it have taken to produce the 12,000 units?
    c. Determine the direct labor efficiency variance in hours.
    d. Determine the variable manufacturing overhead efficiency variance in dollars.

LO 7: DETERMINE VARIABLE MANUFACTURING OVERHEAD VARIANCES

10–40. Clifford Knapp Manufacturing applies variable manufacturing overhead to production on the basis of $5 per direct labor hour. The labor efficiency standard is two hours per finished unit. Last month the company produced 11,000 units and used 22,400 direct labor hours. Actual variable overhead cost incurred totaled $111,700.

Required:

  a. Determine the variable manufacturing overhead spending variance.
  b. According to the appropriate standard, how many direct labor hours should it have taken to produce the 11,000 units?
  c. Determine the direct labor efficiency variance in hours.
  d. Determine the variable manufacturing overhead efficiency variance in dollars.

LO 7: DETERMINE VARIABLE MANUFACTURING OVERHEAD VARIANCES

10–41. Carlos Gonzalez Marine Manufacturing applies variable manufacturing overhead to production on the basis of $6 per direct labor hour. The labor efficiency standard is three hours per finished unit. Last month the company produced 15,000 units and used 45,650 direct labor hours. Actual variable overhead cost incurred totaled $277,700.

Required:

  a. Determine the variable manufacturing overhead spending variance.
  b. According to the appropriate standard, how many direct labor hours should it have taken to produce the 15,000 units?
  c. Determine the direct labor efficiency variance in hours.
  d. Determine the variable manufacturing overhead efficiency variance in dollars.
  e. Appendix: Prepare the following journal entries:

    1. Record the actual variable manufacturing overhead. (Use "various accounts" for the credit side of the entry.)
    2. Record the variable manufacturing overhead applied to production.
    3. Close the variable manufacturing overhead accounts and establish the variable overhead variance accounts.
    4. Close the variance accounts to cost of goods sold.

LO 7: DETERMINE VARIABLE MANUFACTURING OVERHEAD VARIANCES

10–42. Alpine Manufacturing applies variable manufacturing overhead to production on the basis of $13 per direct labor hour. The labor efficiency standard is four hours per finished unit. Last month the company produced 3,000 units and used 11,700 direct labor hours. Actual variable overhead cost incurred totaled $157,200.

Required:

  a. Determine the variable manufacturing overhead spending variance.
  b. Determine the variable manufacturing overhead efficiency variance in dollars.
  c. Appendix: Prepare the following journal entries:

    1. Record the actual variable manufacturing overhead. (Use "various accounts" for the credit side of the entry.)
    2. Record the variable manufacturing overhead applied to production.
    3. Close the variable manufacturing overhead accounts and establish the variable overhead variance accounts.
    4. Close the variance accounts to cost of goods sold.

LO 7: DETERMINE VARIABLE MANUFACTURING OVERHEAD VARIANCES

10–43. The Adler Manufacturing Company applies variable manufacturing overhead to production on the basis of $22 per direct labor hour. The labor efficiency standard is 0.5 hours per finished unit. Last month the company produced 14,500 units and used 7,300 direct labor hours. Actual variable overhead cost incurred totaled $162,000.

Required:

  a. Determine the variable manufacturing overhead spending variance.
  b. Determine the variable manufacturing overhead efficiency variance in dollars.

LO 7: DETERMINE VARIABLE MANUFACTURING OVERHEAD VARIANCES

10–44. The following information is presented for the Carol Green Manufacturing Company.
- Standard variable manufacturing overhead rate is $3.50 per direct labor hour.
- Direct labor efficiency standard is three hours per finished unit.
- Budgeted production is 810 finished units.
- Production required 2,370 direct labor hours.
- Variable manufacturing overhead cost was $8,500.
- 775 finished units of product were produced.

Required:
    a. Determine the variable manufacturing overhead spending variance.
    b. Determine the variable manufacturing overhead efficiency variance in dollars.

LO 7: DETERMINE VARIABLE MANUFACTURING OVERHEAD VARIANCES

10–45. The following information is presented for the Anne Reed Manufacturing Company.
- Standard variable manufacturing overhead rate is $7 per direct labor hour.
- Direct labor efficiency standard is six hours per finished unit.
- Budgeted production is 500 finished units.
- Production required 3,400 direct labor hours.
- Variable manufacturing overhead cost was $23,600.
- 550 finished units of product were produced.

Required:
    a. Determine the variable manufacturing overhead spending variance.
    b. Determine the variable manufacturing overhead efficiency variance in dollars.

LO 7: DETERMINE VARIABLE MANUFACTURING OVERHEAD VARIANCES

10–46. The following information is presented for the Willie Kemp Manufacturing Company.
- Standard variable manufacturing overhead rate is $2 per direct labor hour.
- Direct labor efficiency standard is four hours per finished unit.
- Budgeted production is 1,500 finished units.
- Production required 6,100 direct labor hours.
- Variable manufacturing overhead cost was $12,325.
- 1,550 finished units of product were produced.

Required:
    a. Determine the variable manufacturing overhead spending variance.
    b. Determine the variable manufacturing overhead efficiency variance in dollars.

LO 7: DETERMINE VARIABLE MANUFACTURING OVERHEAD VARIANCES

10–47. Information from the Systems Manufacturing Company is as follows:

Actual number of direct labor hours	12,000
Actual variable manufacturing overhead cost	$145,965
Actual number of units produced	2,440 units
Standard variable manufacturing overhead rate	$12.10 per direct labor hour
Direct labor efficiency standard	5 hours
Budgeted production	2,500 units

Required:
    a. Determine the variable manufacturing overhead spending variance.
    b. Determine the variable manufacturing overhead efficiency variance in dollars.

LO 7: DETERMINE VARIABLE MANUFACTURING OVERHEAD VARIANCES

10–48. Information from the Altos Manufacturing Company is as follows:

Actual number of direct labor hours	12,330
Actual variable manufacturing overhead cost	$74,490
Actual number of units produced	12,540 units
Standard variable manufacturing overhead rate	$6 per direct labor hour
Direct labor efficiency standard	1 hour
Budgeted production	12,000 units

Required:

a. Determine the variable manufacturing overhead spending variance.
b. Determine the variable manufacturing overhead efficiency variance in dollars.

LO 7: DETERMINE VARIABLE MANUFACTURING OVERHEAD VARIANCES

10–49. Information from the Aspen Manufacturing Company is as follows:

Actual number of direct labor hours	175,000
Actual variable manufacturing overhead cost	$2,400,000
Actual number of units produced	21,740 units
Standard variable manufacturing overhead rate	$14 per direct labor hour
Direct labor efficiency standard	8 hours
Budgeted production	20,000 units

Required:

a. Determine the variable manufacturing overhead spending variance.
b. Determine the variable manufacturing overhead efficiency variance in dollars.

LO 7: DETERMINE FIXED MANUFACTURING OVERHEAD VARIANCES

10–50. The Hill Manufacturing Company applies fixed manufacturing overhead at the rate of $5.50 per direct labor hour. Fixed manufacturing overhead is budgeted to be $330,000 per month. The direct labor efficiency standard is five hours per finished unit. Although budgeted production for the month was 12,000, the company only produced 11,800 units. Production required actual direct labor hours of 60,000 and actual fixed manufacturing overhead cost incurred was $325,000.

Required:

a. Determine the fixed overhead budget variance.
b. What is the difference between the planned number of units and the number of units actually produced?
c. Determine the fixed manufacturing overhead volume variance.
d. Appendix: Prepare the following journal entries:

1. Record the actual fixed manufacturing overhead. (Use "various accounts" for the credit side of the entry.)
2. Record the fixed manufacturing overhead applied to production.
3. Close the fixed manufacturing overhead accounts and establish the fixed overhead variance accounts.
4. Close the variance accounts to cost of goods sold.

LO 7: DETERMINE FIXED MANUFACTURING OVERHEAD VARIANCES

10–51. The Johnson Manufacturing Company applies fixed manufacturing overhead at the rate of $4.60 per direct labor hour. Fixed manufacturing overhead is budgeted to be $910,800 per month. The direct labor efficiency standard is three hours per finished unit. Although budgeted production for the month was 66,000, the company produced 67,800 units. Production required actual direct labor hours of 203,000 and actual fixed manufacturing overhead cost incurred was $920,000.

Required:

a. Determine the fixed manufacturing overhead budget variance.
b. What is the difference between the planned number of units and the number of units actually produced?
c. Determine the fixed manufacturing overhead volume variance.
d. Appendix: Prepare the following journal entries:

1. Record the actual fixed manufacturing overhead. (Use "various accounts" for the credit side of the entry.)
2. Record the fixed manufacturing overhead applied to production.
3. Close the fixed manufacturing overhead accounts and establish the fixed overhead variance accounts.
4. Close the variance accounts to cost of goods sold.

LO 7: DETERMINE FIXED MANUFACTURING OVERHEAD VARIANCES

10–52. The Quality Manufacturing Company applies fixed manufacturing overhead at the rate of $7 per direct labor hour. Fixed manufacturing overhead is budgeted to be $336,000 per month. The direct labor efficiency standard is three hours per finished unit. Although budgeted production for the month was 16,000, the company only produced 15,500 units. Production required actual direct labor hours of 60,000 and actual fixed manufacturing overhead cost incurred was $344,000.

Required:

a. Determine the fixed manufacturing overhead budget variance.
b. Did the company produce as many units as it had planned? What is the difference between the planned number of units and the number of units actually produced?
c. Determine the fixed manufacturing overhead volume variance.

LO 7: DETERMINE FIXED MANUFACTURING OVERHEAD VARIANCES

10–53. The following information is presented for the Oddo Manufacturing Company.

- Standard fixed manufacturing overhead rate is $2 per direct labor hour.
- Direct labor efficiency standard is four hours per finished unit.
- Budgeted production is 2,500 finished units.
- Budgeted fixed manufacturing overhead is $20,000.
- Actual fixed manufacturing overhead cost was $17,750.
- 2,150 finished units of product were produced.

Required:

a. Determine the fixed manufacturing overhead budget variance.
b. Determine the fixed manufacturing overhead volume variance in dollars.

LO 7: DETERMINE FIXED MANUFACTURING OVERHEAD VARIANCES

10–54. The following information is presented for the Alexander Manufacturing Company.

- Standard fixed manufacturing overhead rate is $6.50 per direct labor hour.
- Direct labor efficiency standard is two hours per finished unit.
- Budgeted production is 5,000 finished units.
- Budgeted fixed manufacturing overhead is $65,000.
- Actual fixed manufacturing overhead cost was $66,100.
- 5,150 finished units of product were produced.

Required:

a. Determine the fixed manufacturing overhead budget variance.
b. Determine the fixed manufacturing overhead volume variance in dollars.

LO 7: DETERMINE FIXED MANUFACTURING OVERHEAD VARIANCES

10–55. The following information is presented for the Adcox Manufacturing Company.

- Standard fixed manufacturing overhead rate is $9.50 per direct labor hour.
- Direct labor efficiency standard is nine hours per finished unit.
- Budgeted production is 9,000 finished units.
- Budgeted fixed manufacturing overhead is $769,500.
- Actual fixed manufacturing overhead cost was $755,360.
- 8,500 finished units of product were produced.

Required:

a. Determine the fixed manufacturing overhead budget variance.
b. Determine the fixed manufacturing overhead volume variance in dollars.

LO 7: DETERMINE FIXED MANUFACTURING OVERHEAD VARIANCES

10–56. Information from the Michael Manufacturing Company is as follows:

Actual number of direct labor hours	12,200
Actual fixed manufacturing overhead cost	$145,900
Actual number of units produced	2,400 units
Standard fixed manufacturing overhead rate	$12 per direct labor hour
Direct labor efficiency standard	5 hours
Budgeted production	2,500 units
Budgeted fixed manufacturing overhead	$150,000

Required:

  a. Determine the fixed manufacturing overhead budget variance.
  b. Determine the fixed manufacturing overhead volume variance in dollars.

LO 7: DETERMINE FIXED MANUFACTURING OVERHEAD VARIANCES

10–57. Information from the Jennings Manufacturing Company is as follows:

Actual number of direct labor hours	5,130
Actual fixed manufacturing overhead cost	$24,900
Actual number of units produced	5,400 units
Standard fixed manufacturing overhead rate	$5 per direct labor hour
Direct labor efficiency standard	1 hour
Budgeted production	5,000 units
Budgeted fixed manufacturing overhead	$25,000

Required:

  a. Determine the fixed manufacturing overhead budget variance.
  b. Determine the fixed manufacturing overhead volume variance in dollars.

LO 7: DETERMINE FIXED MANUFACTURING OVERHEAD VARIANCES

10–58. Information from the Cathy Manufacturing Company is as follows:

Actual number of direct labor hours	5,200
Actual fixed manufacturing overhead cost	$88,960
Actual number of units produced	2,700 units
Standard fixed manufacturing overhead rate	$15 per direct labor hour
Direct labor efficiency standard	2 hours
Budgeted production	3,000 units
Budgeted fixed manufacturing overhead	$90,000

Required:

  a. Determine the fixed manufacturing overhead budget variance.
  b. Determine the fixed manufacturing overhead volume variance in dollars.

LO 7: DETERMINE FIXED MANUFACTURING OVERHEAD VARIANCES

10–59. Todd Manufacturing Company's budgeted production is 200,000 units per month. Budgeted monthly fixed manufacturing overhead is $2,400,000 and is applied to production at a rate of $4 per direct labor hour. The direct labor efficiency standard is three direct labor hours per unit of production. Last month it took 520,000 actual direct labor hours to produce 175,000 units. Actual fixed manufacturing overhead for the month was $2,435,000.

Required:

  a. Determine the fixed manufacturing overhead budget variance.
  b. Determine the fixed manufacturing overhead volume variance.

LO 7: DETERMINE BUDGETED PRODUCTION AND FIXED MANUFACTURING OVERHEAD VARIANCES

10–60. The E. O. Mast Manufacturing Company applies fixed manufacturing overhead at the rate of $20 per direct labor hour. Fixed manufacturing overhead is budgeted to be $4,000,000 per month. The direct labor efficiency standard is two hours per finished unit. Last month the company produced 89,000 units using 180,000 direct labor hours and incurring fixed manufacturing overhead cost of $4,100,000.

Required:

   a. Determine the fixed manufacturing overhead budget variance.
   b. Did the company produce as many units as it had planned? What is the difference between the planned number of units and the number of units actually produced?
   c. Determine the fixed manufacturing overhead volume variance.

LO 7: DETERMINE BUDGETED PRODUCTION AND FIXED MANUFACTURING OVERHEAD VARIANCES

10–61. The Annie Manufacturing Company applies fixed manufacturing overhead at the rate of $10 per direct labor hour. Fixed manufacturing overhead is budgeted to be $418,000 per month. The direct labor efficiency standard is four hours per finished unit. Last month the company produced 9,800 units using 36,500 direct labor hours and incurring fixed manufacturing overhead cost of $410,000.

Required:

   a. Determine the fixed manufacturing overhead budget variance.
   b. Did the company produce as many units as it had planned? What is the difference between the planned number of units and the number of units actually produced?
   c. Determine the fixed manufacturing overhead volume variance.

LO 7: DETERMINE BUDGETED PRODUCTION AND FIXED MANUFACTURING OVERHEAD VARIANCES

10–62. The St. Hill Manufacturing Company applies fixed manufacturing overhead at the rate of $15 per direct labor hour. Fixed manufacturing overhead is budgeted to be $247,500 per month. The direct labor efficiency standard is six hours per finished unit. Last month the company produced 2,500 units using 15,500 direct labor hours and incurring fixed manufacturing overhead cost of $230,000.

Required:

   a. Determine the fixed manufacturing overhead budget variance.
   b. Did the company produce as many units as it had planned? What is the difference between the planned number of units and the number of units actually produced?
   c. Determine the fixed manufacturing overhead volume variance.

LO 7: DETERMINE BUDGETED FIXED FACTORY OVERHEAD AND FIXED MANUFACTURING OVERHEAD VARIANCES

10–63. Information from the South Manufacturing Company is as follows:

Actual number of direct labor hours	32,500
Actual fixed manufacturing overhead cost	$428,000
Actual number of units produced	8,000 units
Standard fixed manufacturing overhead rate	$12 per direct labor hour
Direct labor efficiency standard	4 hours
Budgeted production	9,000 units
Budgeted fixed manufacturing overhead	$?

Required:

   a. Determine the fixed manufacturing overhead budget variance.
   b. Determine the fixed manufacturing overhead volume variance in dollars.

LO 7: DETERMINE FIXED MANUFACTURING OVERHEAD VARIANCES

10–64. Information from the North Manufacturing Company is as follows:

Actual number of direct labor hours	13,000
Actual fixed manufacturing overhead cost	$50,000
Actual number of units produced	2,120 units
Standard fixed manufacturing overhead rate	$4 per direct labor hour
Direct labor efficiency standard	6 hours
Budgeted production	2,000 units
Budgeted fixed manufacturing overhead	$?

Required:

   a. Determine the fixed manufacturing overhead budget variance.
   b. Determine the fixed manufacturing overhead volume variance in dollars.

LO 7: DETERMINE FIXED MANUFACTURING OVERHEAD VARIANCES

10–65. Information from the West Manufacturing Company is as follows:

Actual number of direct labor hours	27,000
Actual fixed manufacturing overhead cost	$260,000
Actual number of units produced	3,250 units
Standard fixed manufacturing overhead rate	$9 per direct labor hour
Direct labor efficiency standard	8 hours
Budgeted production	3,500 units
Budgeted fixed manufacturing overhead	$?

Required:

   a. Determine the fixed manufacturing overhead budget variance.
   b. Determine the fixed manufacturing overhead volume variance in dollars.

LO 7: DETERMINE DIRECT MATERIAL, DIRECT LABOR, VARIABLE MANUFACTURING OVERHEAD AND FIXED MANUFACTURING OVERHEAD VARIANCES

10–66. Information from the Quintana Company is as follows:

Actual costs and amounts:	
Actual production	3,800 units
Actual cost of 23,000 pounds of direct material purchased	$89,700
Actual amount of direct material used	22,950 pounds
Actual direct labor cost	$23,205
Actual direct labor hours	1,950 hours
Actual variable overhead cost	$12,000
Actual fixed overhead cost	$18,000
Standards and other budgeted amounts:	
Budgeted production	4,000 units
Direct material price standard	$3.85 per pound
Direct material quantity standard	6 pounds per unit
Direct labor rate standard	$11 per hour
Direct labor efficiency standard per unit	0.5 hours
Standard variable manufacturing overhead rate	$5.50 per direct labor hour
Standard fixed manufacturing overhead rate	$10 per direct labor hour
Budgeted fixed manufacturing overhead	$20,000

Required: Determine the following variances:

   a. Direct material price variance
   b. Direct material quantity variance in dollars
   c. Direct labor rate variance
   d. Direct labor efficiency variance in dollars
   e. Variable manufacturing overhead spending variance

  f. Variable manufacturing overhead efficiency variance in dollars
  g. Fixed manufacturing overhead budget variance
  h. Fixed manufacturing overhead volume variance in dollars

LO 7: DETERMINE DIRECT MATERIAL, DIRECT LABOR, VARIABLE MANUFACTURING OVERHEAD AND FIXED MANUFACTURING OVERHEAD VARIANCES

10–67. Information from the Holzmann Company is as follows:

Actual costs and amounts:	
Actual production	6,300 units
Actual cost of 20,000 pounds of direct material purchased	$40,000
Actual amount of direct material used	19,100
Actual direct labor cost	$386,100
Actual direct labor hours	26,000 hours
Actual variable overhead cost	$165,000
Actual fixed overhead cost	$310,000
Standards and other budgeted amounts:	
Budgeted production	6,000 units
Direct material price standard	$2.10
Direct material quantity standard	3 pounds per unit
Direct labor rate standard	$15 per hour
Direct labor efficiency standard per unit	4 hours
Standard variable manufacturing overhead rate	$6.50 per direct labor hour
Standard fixed manufacturing overhead rate	$12.75 per direct labor hour
Budgeted fixed manufacturing overhead	$306,000

Required: Determine the following variances:

  a. Direct material price variance
  b. Direct material quantity variance in dollars
  c. Direct labor rate variance
  d. Direct labor efficiency variance in dollars
  e. Variable manufacturing overhead spending variance
  f. Variable manufacturing overhead efficiency variance in dollars
  g. Fixed manufacturing overhead budget variance
  h. Fixed manufacturing overhead volume variance in dollars

LO 7: DETERMINE DIRECT MATERIAL, DIRECT LABOR, VARIABLE MANUFACTURING OVERHEAD AND FIXED MANUFACTURING OVERHEAD VARIANCES

10–68. Information from the Collins Company is as follows:

Actual costs and amounts:	
Actual production	2,300 units
Actual cost of 16,000 pounds of direct material purchased	$19,360
Actual amount of direct material used	12,000
Actual direct labor cost	$46,410
Actual direct labor hours	4,750 hours
Actual variable overhead cost	$29,100
Actual fixed overhead cost	$50,125
Standards and other budgeted amounts:	
Budgeted production	3,000 units
Direct material price standard	$1.10
Direct material quantity standard	5 pounds per unit
Direct labor rate standard	$12 per hour
Direct labor efficiency standard per unit	2 hours
Standard variable manufacturing overhead rate	$6 per direct labor hour
Standard fixed manufacturing overhead rate	$8 per direct labor hour
Budgeted fixed manufacturing overhead	$48,000

Required: Determine the following variances:

    a. Direct material price variance

    b. Direct material quantity variance in dollars

    c. Direct labor rate variance

    d. Direct labor efficiency variance in dollars

    e. Variable manufacturing overhead spending variance

    f. Variable manufacturing overhead efficiency variance in dollars

    g. Fixed manufacturing overhead budget variance

    h. Fixed manufacturing overhead volume variance in dollars

CHAPTER 11

Evaluating Performance

Imagine for a moment that you open "The Right Step," a small shoe store in a local shopping center. After you're in business about six months, the store's success prompts you to open a second store in a shopping area across town. The second store also does very well, so you open a third, and in time, your shoe store chain grows to five stores.

For each store you open, you hire a store manager, because it is impossible to give each store your personal, hands-on management attention. Each store manager is responsible for the success of his or her location. You now oversee the managers at all of your stores, and one of your most important roles has become assessing the performance of these store managers.

As any business grows, the diversity of knowledge required to effectively manage combined with time constraints reduce the ability of a single manager to run the entire enterprise. When a manager can no longer manage the whole company single handedly, she or he must delegate management responsibility to subordinate managers. Evaluating the performance of these managers is the focus of this chapter.

Learning Objectives

After completing your work on this chapter, you should be able to do the following:

1. Describe centralized and decentralized management styles.
2. Describe the different types of business segments and the problems associated with determining segment costs.
3. Prepare a segment income statement.
4. Describe and calculate the return on investment.
5. Describe and calculate residual income and economic value added (EVA™).
6. Describe the balanced scorecard and the importance of nonfinancial performance measures.

◆ BUSINESS SEGMENTS

business segment A part of a company managed by a particular individual or a part of a company about which separate information is needed.

To help make businesses more manageable, their owners often divide them into parts. A **business segment** represents a part of a company managed by a particular individual, or a part of a company about which separate information is needed, perhaps to evaluate management performance or to help managers make better management decisions.

Companies can be segmented by geographic area or location, business function, product, product line, or department. A segment can be described as a department, a division, an area, a region, a product line, or some other designation. Examples of business segments include the Latin American Area of the **Dow Chemical Company,** an individual **Target** department store, a **Motorola** manufacturing plant, and the Department of Accounting at the **University of Miami.**

Obtaining detailed information about business segments is a vital part of the management decision process. Managers need information that relates to their business segment. Reports that provide information pertaining to a particular business segment are called **segment reports.** Segment reports should not be clouded by data that relate to other segments or by general information pertaining to the company as a whole. For example, if you were hired to be the manager of the **Hard Rock Cafe** in Orlando, Florida, and responsible for enhancing the restaurant's profits, you would benefit by having information about your particular restaurant. Although it might be somewhat helpful to know the overall profitability of the entire restaurant chain, specific information about the **Orlando Hard Rock** would be much more useful. You might want to know detailed sales information by product, by server, and by time of day. You would also want a comprehensive listing of your restaurant's expenses. Reports that include revenues and expenses for your restaurant only would help you to find opportunities to increase profits.

> **segment reports** Reports that provide information pertaining to a particular business segment.

Discussion Question

11–1. If you were the manager of the **Contemporary Hotel** at **Disney World,** what information would you want to help maximize the performance of the hotel?

SEGMENT INFORMATION

Depending on the needs of management and the availability of information, segment reports may be simple and include little detail, or they may be quite elaborate and include an abundance of detailed segment information. For example, it is possible for segment reports to consist simply of a listing of the segment's sales by product; or, segment reports may include sales, expenses, and other information. The extent of the information included in segment reports depends on management's need to know, balanced with the cost of providing the information.

◆ THE SEGMENT INCOME STATEMENT

> **segment income statement** An income statement prepared for a business segment.

An income statement prepared for a business segment is called a **segment income statement.** When preparing a segment income statement, companies use either the functional income statement or the contribution income statement format. Recall from our discussions in Chapter 6 that the functional income statement separates costs into product and period costs. The contribution income statement classifies costs by behavior, either variable or fixed. We know that a variable cost is one that changes in total based on some activity, whereas a fixed cost is one that remains unchanged regardless of the level of activity. To help you remember these two income statement formats, we compare them in Exhibit 11–1.

EXHIBIT 11–1 Functional and Contribution Income Statement Formats

Functional Format	Contribution Income Format
Sales	Sales
– Cost of Goods Sold (Product Cost)	– All Variable Costs (Product and Period)
= Gross Profit	= Contribution Margin
– Selling and Admin. Expense (Period Cost)	– All Fixed Costs (Product and Period)
= Net Income	= Net Income

> **segment margin** The amount of income that pertains to a particular segment.

To prepare a segment income statement, we gather revenue and expense information that pertains to the particular segment and then arrange it in the appropriate income statement format. The amount of income that pertains to a particular segment is called the **segment margin.** Because the contribution income statement format is particularly well suited for our work in this chapter, we use that format in all our remaining presentations. A segment income statement for the Miami office of the Quintana Company appears in Exhibit 11–2.

EXHIBIT 11–2   Segment Income Statement for the Miami Office

> *Quintana Company Miami Office*
> Segment Income Statement
> For the Year Ended December 31, 2004
>
> | | |
> |---|---:|
> | Sales | $1,200,000 |
> | Variable cost | 800,000 |
> | Contribution margin | 400,000 |
> | Fixed cost for Miami office | 300,000 |
> | Segment margin | $ 100,000 |

It is important that the segment income statement for the Miami office of the Quintana Company include all the appropriate information for the Miami office, and no more. Often, this is easier said than done. Generally, revenue can easily be traced to individual business segments; therefore, obtaining detailed revenue information by segment is not too difficult. Unfortunately, however, the same cannot always be said for cost information.

It is often difficult (if not impossible) to obtain cost information that includes all the costs for a particular segment and excludes costs associated with other segments. There are several reasons for this. First, it may be difficult to identify all the costs that relate to the segment. For example, say that the Norris Division of the NHL Company has three copiers. Certainly, the cost of these copiers should be included in any evaluation of the Norris Division. These three copiers, however, are just three of the 27 copiers owned by the NHL Company (the other 24 copiers are in other segments). The problem is that all 27 copiers were purchased by the central company purchasing department and Norris has no record of the cost of its three copiers.

Discussion Question

11–2. What are three other costs that relate directly to the Norris Division, but for which the division probably does not have information?

The second reason it may be difficult to identify costs to particular segments is that costs are often mixed together in the accounting process. An example of this might be advertising purchased by the NHL Company, which benefits not only the Norris Division, but also the five other divisions of the company. The exact amount that should be charged to the Norris Division is virtually impossible to determine accurately.

Discussion Question

11–3. What are three other costs that benefit the Norris Division but benefit at least one other division as well?

To help manage a business segment, we should include all the costs associated with the segment on cost reports prepared for it. It is equally important that costs that do not pertain to the segment be excluded from the segment's cost reports. In the case of variable costs, this is fairly straightforward. Variable costs can be traced directly to the business segments to which they pertain and then be included on the appropriate segment reports.

Fixed costs are more difficult to trace to individual business segments and therefore present more of a challenge. One problem with tracing fixed costs to business segments is that some fixed costs pertain to a single business segment whereas others ben-

direct fixed costs Fixed costs incurred to support a single business segment.

traceable fixed costs Another name for direct fixed costs.

common fixed costs Fixed costs incurred to support more than one business segment, or the company as a whole.

indirect fixed costs Another name for common fixed costs.

efit several segments or perhaps the company as a whole. Fixed costs that arise to support a single segment are called **direct fixed costs** or **traceable fixed costs.** These fixed costs can be traced to an individual business segment. Direct fixed costs should be included on the cost reports for the segment to which they pertain. Fixed costs that arise to support more than one segment or the company as a whole are called **common fixed costs** or **indirect fixed costs.**

This discussion of direct and indirect costs should not seem entirely new. It is a subject we covered in some depth in Chapter 2 when we discussed the concept of a cost object. As you recall, a cost object is any activity or item for which a separate cost measurement is desired. A cost that can be traced directly to a cost object is a direct cost, whereas a cost that is incurred to support multiple cost objects is an indirect cost. In our present discussion, the cost object is the business segment.

Because common fixed costs benefit several segments or the company in general, segment managers often have little control over them. A simple question can be asked to determine whether a cost is a common cost or a direct cost:

Would the cost continue if the segment were to disappear?

If the cost will continue even if the segment disappeared, the cost is a common fixed cost. If, on the other hand, the cost would disappear if the segment disappears, the cost is a direct fixed cost. There are very few, if any, common variable costs; thus, in virtually all instances, the common costs we must consider are fixed.

For many years there has been debate as to whether cost reports prepared for an individual segment should include some allocated amount of common fixed costs. Proponents of allocation maintain that common fixed costs benefit the entire company and therefore each segment should be charged for its "fair share" of the common cost. Further, they argue that it is impossible to determine true segment profitability if common costs are excluded. Opponents of allocation argue just the opposite. They maintain that because segment managers have little or no authority to control common fixed costs, these costs should not be included in segment reports. These folks believe it is unfair to charge a manager's department for costs that are out of his or her control. In addition, common fixed costs are generally distributed to various business segments based on an arbitrary allocation scheme and can make a segment appear to be unprofitable when, in fact, that segment is contributing to the overall profitability of the company. Managers may attempt to "control" the common fixed costs allocated to their segment by manipulating the allocation base.

Discussion Question

11–4. Let's say you are a segment manager at ***Motorola.*** How would you react to a charge made to your department for a portion of the cost of the fleet of corporate aircraft, even though you have never even seen one of the planes?

Both proponents and opponents of common fixed cost allocation to business segments feel strongly about their positions. There seems to be little question, however, that the practice of including common fixed costs in segment reports is losing popularity. This fact is not surprising when we consider that the main purpose of management accounting is to influence managers to act to benefit the company. It seems clear that including common fixed costs in segment reports can lead managers toward behavior that is counterproductive. Restricting a segment cost report to costs over which a manager has control makes it a more useful tool for supporting sound business decisions.

PITFALL OF ALLOCATING COMMON FIXED COSTS—A CLOSER LOOK

When a company allocates common fixed costs to segments, segment information may be misleading and result in disastrous business decisions. As an example, consider the segmented income statement for Flandro Feed Stores presented in Exhibit 11–3.

As you can see from Exhibit 11–3, the $60,000 common fixed cost has been allocated to the business segments based on relative sales volume, which means that

Flandro Feed Stores
Segment Income Statement
For the Year Ended December 31, 2005

	Company Total	North Store	South Store	Central Store
Sales	$500,000	$105,000	$225,000	$170,000
Variable cost	332,950	73,750	141,000	118,200
Contribution margin	167,050	31,250	84,000	51,800
Direct fixed cost	75,000	20,000	32,000	23,000
Segment margin	92,050	11,250	52,000	28,800
Common fixed cost	60,000	12,600*	27,000**	20,400***
Net income	$ 32,050	$ (1,350)	$ 25,000	$ 8,400

* $105,000 ÷ $500,000 = 21% × $60,000 = $12,600
** $225,000 ÷ $500,000 = 45% × $60,000 = $27,000
***$170,000 ÷ $500,000 = 34% × $60,000 = $20,400

EXHIBIT 11-3   Flandro Feed Stores Segment Income Statement

because the South Store provided 45 percent of the company's sales ($225,000 ÷ $500,000 = 45%), this store is allocated 45 percent of the common fixed cost ($60,000 × 45% = $27,000). Of the common fixed cost, 34 percent was allocated to the Central Store based on its percentage of sales, and 21 percent was allocated to the North Store. It appears that the North Store is unprofitable. Based on the information in Exhibit 11–3, it seems that profits could be increased if the unprofitable North Store is closed. By closing the North Store it appears that the $1,350 loss would be eliminated. Let's look at the results had the North Store been eliminated. The segment income statement for Flandro Feed Stores without the North Store is presented in Exhibit 11–4.

EXHIBIT 11-4   Flandro Feed Stores Segment Income Statement with North Store Eliminated

Flandro Feed Stores
Segment Income Statement
For the Year Ended December 31, 2002

	Company Total	South Store	Central Store
Sales	$395,000	$225,000	$170,000
Variable cost	259,200	141,000	118,200
Contribution margin	135,800	84,000	51,800
Direct fixed cost	55,000	32,000	23,000
Segment margin	80,800	52,000	28,800
Common fixed cost	60,000	34,200*	25,800**
Net income	$ 20,800	$ 17,800	$ 3,000

* $225,000 ÷ $395,000 = 57% (rounded) × $60,000 = $34,200
**$170,000 ÷ $395,000 = 43% (rounded) × $60,000 = $25,800

   As Exhibit 11–4 shows, when the North Store is eliminated, Flandro's net income actually declines from $32,050 to $20,800. On the surface this seems to make no sense, because the results in Exhibit 11–3 showed the North Store with a net loss for the year of $1,350. So, how did eliminating the North Store cause profits to drop by $11,250 ($32,050 − $20,800)? The answer lies in the practice of allocating common fixed cost.

Notice in Exhibit 11–4 that the common fixed cost of $60,000 did not change when the North Store was removed, because the common fixed cost is for items that are necessary to operate the company even if there are fewer stores. For example, even if the North Store closes, common costs for such items as accounting, finance, and the cost of operating the home office would continue. Therefore, the $60,000 common fixed cost would have to be distributed to the two remaining stores. Again, this is done based on relative sales values.

In truth, the North Store is contributing to Flandro's overall profitability. When the North Store is eliminated, so is its segment margin. It is not a coincidence that the $11,250 decline in profits without the North Store is exactly equal to the North Store's segment margin in Exhibit 11–3. If the North Store is eliminated, its segment margin disappears, but the common fixed cost remains and must be allocated to the remaining segments.

To avoid such misleading information and the poor decisions that can result, many companies have stopped the practice of allocating common fixed costs to segments. The segmented income statement for Flandro Feed Stores without the allocation of common fixed cost is shown in Exhibit 11–5.

EXHIBIT 11–5   Flandro Feed Stores Segment Income Statement Without Allocation of Common Fixed Cost

Flandro Feed Stores
Segment Income Statement
For the Year Ended December 31, 2005

	Company Total	North Store	South Store	Central Store
Sales	$500,000	$105,000	$225,000	$170,000
Variable cost	332,950	73,750	141,000	118,200
Contribution margin	167,050	31,250	84,000	51,800
Direct fixed cost	75,000	20,000	32,000	23,000
Segment margin	92,050	$ 11,250	$ 52,000	$ 28,800
Common fixed cost	60,000			
Net income	$ 32,050			

As shown in Exhibit 11–5, when common fixed costs are not allocated, the segment margin becomes the "bottom line" for each segment. This amount is a better indicator of segment profit performance because it considers only direct costs, costs over which the segment manager has control.

To provide useful information to help evaluate segment performance and to help segment managers make informed decisions, all direct costs that pertain to a particular segment must be included in the management reports for that segment. If a direct cost is excluded, it is unlikely that the segment manager will work to reduce that cost. For example, assume that a leased copy machine is used exclusively by the finance department of a major corporation. Assume further that the rent for the copy machine, plus the rent for all the other copy machines used by the company, is included in a monthly bill from the Acme Copy Machine Company. If the rent cost included on this single bill is not distributed (charged) to user departments, the cost for each department is understated by the amount of the rent. If this happens, the rent for the copy machine would be excluded from the information used to help evaluate the finance department's performance. Therefore, it is unlikely that the finance department manager would work to reduce the rental cost by switching to a less expensive copy machine. In fact, once the manager finds that the cost of the copy machine is not charged to the department, he or she might even upgrade to an overly elaborate copy machine knowing that the department will not be penalized for such an expenditure. Thus, it is important to include all costs associated with a business segment in the segment's cost reports.

ALLOCATING SERVICE DEPARTMENT COST

service department A business segment responsible for secondary (support) functions. Service departments provide service to the main business operations and to other service departments.

The main operation of a merchandiser is selling products. For a manufacturer, the main operation is manufacturing and selling products, and for a service business, the main operation is providing services to customers. In addition to any company's main business operation, however, secondary support operations also occur. Most companies, whether merchandisers, manufacturers, or service-type businesses, also have an accounting department, a personnel department, and other departments that provide support to the various functions of the company. Further, telephone service must be provided, and a facility (building) within which to operate. The business segments that handle these and other secondary operations are called **service departments.** These departments provide necessary services to the main business operations and other service departments.

Discussion Question

11–5. Besides the ones listed in the previous paragraph, what are three other service departments you think most companies have?

The cost of operating a service department can be substantial. This cost is allocated to the departments that use the services provided. In other words, if a particular department receives benefit from a service department, that department should be charged for the cost of the service.

Determining the amount of service department cost to charge various user departments is not an exact science. For some kinds of service cost, a direct correlation can be found between the amount of service provided to a department and the cost charged to that department. In these instances, the manager of the user department rarely disputes the charge. For other types of service cost, however, no direct cause and effect can be found. In that event, the cost charged to departments for services is based on an allocation method that may or may not be accurate or even fair. This allocation is much like that of common fixed cost to segments we discussed earlier. The allocation of service department cost when no correlation can be found between the service and the cost can actually cloud management's vision about the performance of a department.

As was the case with allocating fixed common cost to segments, certain managers believe that service department costs should be allocated, whereas others believe the practice should be stopped. As usual, both sides hold strongly to their views. Although some companies have stopped allocating service department cost, the majority of companies still maintain this practice. The responsibility of department managers is to be vigilant in making certain that the costs charged to their departments reasonably reflect the amount of service received. Examples of service departments and possible allocation bases are shown in Exhibit 11–6.

ACTIVITY-BASED SERVICE DEPARTMENT COST ALLOCATION

Activity-based costing is a topic we covered in Chapter 4 when we discussed alternative ways to allocate manufacturing overhead to units of product produced. Activity-based costing can also be a valuable tool for allocating service department cost to other departments. When possible, the allocation base used to allocate cost should be an activity that causes the cost. As stated in Chapter 4, an activity that causes cost to occur is called a cost driver. The two major benefits to using cost drivers to allocate service department cost are (1) this cost allocation method tends to be more fair and accurate, and (2) in attempting to control the cost allocated to their departments, managers will work to reduce the allocation base—the cost driver. Because the cost driver is also the cost cause, reducing the cost driver will actually reduce the amount paid by the company for goods and services. For example, when the cost driver used to allocate basic phone service is the number of phone lines, reducing the number of phone lines not

EXHIBIT 11–6   Representative Service Departments and Possible Allocation Bases

Service Department	Allocation Basis
Personnel Department	• Number of employees
Telephone	• Number of phones • Number of lines • Long-distance charges
Copy Machine or Copy Center	• Quantity of services used: • Number of single-sided copies • Number of double-sided copies • Number of bindings
Employee Cafeteria	• Number of employees • Number of meals served
Finance Department	• Amount of capital invested
Building Occupancy	• Square footage of building occupied
Computer Operations	• Computer mainframe time • Number of personal computers • Number of reports generated
Computer Programming	• Hours of programming
Office Services	• Square footage of office occupied • Number of offices
Engineering Department	• Number of engineering changes • Hours of engineering services
Maintenance	• Square footage of building occupied • Hours of maintenance
Aircraft Operations	• Number of passenger miles • Number of hours flown • Weight of load and distance flown

only reduces the allocation of phone cost, but it also reduces the amount the company spends for phone service. This reduction results in true cost savings for the company.

Discussion Question

11–6. Refer to the list of three service departments you made in response to Discussion Question 11–5. What is a possible allocation base for each of the departments you listed?

It is important to know about service department cost allocation for several reasons. First, as a department manager, you will need to know how to control service department costs allocated to your department. Second, you should be able to discriminate between costs that are arbitrarily allocated to your department and those that are equitable. Third, as a high-level manager, you should be able to recognize when an allocation method should be modified or replaced, because it does not result in information that provides incentives for managers to act in accordance with company goals.

Sometimes the allocation method can cause managers to do counterproductive things, especially when activity-based costing is not used to allocate costs. For example, consider what occurred in a major corporation when it changed the allocation base it used to distribute the cost of office space. Top managers felt that departments should not be charged for halls, elevator waiting areas, or other common areas but only for the office space dedicated entirely to the department's use. So, from a charge for all the square footage the departments occupied, the firm changed to a charge for only the square footage of the *enclosed* office space occupied by the departments. Some managers then recognized that their department's allocation for office space could be cut if they were to reduce the square footage used for enclosed offices. Accordingly, they removed the separating cubicle walls of several offices occupied by department secretaries and created for them work space in the new "common" area. The result was an increase in the amount of common space, and a marked decrease in the amount of square footage used for enclosed offices. Because the departments were only charged for enclosed office space, their office space cost allocation was reduced.

The change in allocation base worked to the detriment of the company as a whole, of course, because it incurred the cost of remodeling the office space even though the remodeling was completely unnecessary. Interestingly, only managers who had a working knowledge of how service department costs were allocated knew how to take advantage of the situation.

Discussion Question

11–7. Do you think the office space cost previously described should even be allocated? If not, explain your reasoning. If you answered yes, what would you suggest to the company to overcome the dysfunctional management behavior described?

Reducing the service cost allocated to a particular department is not a difficult task to accomplish. First, the department-level manager must determine what allocation base is being used. Second, the manager must reduce the amount of the allocation base consumed by the department. If the allocation base used is a cost driver, the actual cost involved will decrease. If the allocation base is arbitrary and unrelated to the actual cost, the amount allocated to the department will decrease, but the actual cost to the company will continue and simply be shifted to some other manager's department.

As an example of how to control service department cost allocation, assume that the cost of photocopies is allocated based on the number of copies made. A reduction in the number of copies made will reduce the copy cost allocated to the user department. Attempting to reduce the number of copies would include reviewing department procedures to ensure that only necessary copies are made. It might also include reviewing alternate imaging technology to find ways to reduce the need for photocopies. This same logic can be used to control the cost allocation for telephone use, which is often allocated to departments based on the number of phone lines used. To reduce the cost allocation, unnecessary telephones are eliminated.

In each of these two examples, because the allocation base is a cost driver, a reduction in the base would not only cause a reduction in the cost allocated to the department but would also cause a true reduction in cost to the company.

◆ APPROACHES TO SEGMENT MANAGEMENT

The strategy used to manage business segments varies from company to company. Some companies prefer that top management make all but the most routine decisions, whereas other companies prefer that lower-level managers make most or all of the decisions within their area. When almost all decisions are made by the top managers and little is left to the discretion of lower-level managers, the company is said to have a centralized management style. Conversely, if management decisions are made at the lowest possible management level, the company is said to have a decentralized management style. These management styles have both advantages and disadvantages.

CENTRALIZED MANAGEMENT

centralized management
A management style in which top managers make most management decisions.

When a **centralized management** style is used, top management makes most management decisions. Middle- and lower-level managers are responsible only for routine decisions and supervisory functions. This management style ensures that the wishes of top management are incorporated into each management decision. Top managers often have the most experience, which could lead to wise business decisions. A centralized management style has certain disadvantages:

1. Top managers must spend their valuable time making routine, low-level business decisions.
2. Top managers may not be intimately familiar with the various routine aspects of the business.
3. Lower-level employees have little opportunity to gain experience in decision making.

DECENTRALIZED MANAGEMENT

decentralized management A management style in which lower-level managers are responsible for decisions that relate to their segment of the company.

When a **decentralized management** style is used, lower-level managers are responsible for management decisions that relate to their segment of the business. When a highly decentralized management style is used, decisions are made at the lowest possible level in the organization.

A decentralized management style has several advantages. It helps spread the decision making responsibilities among the various management levels of the company and allows lower-level managers greater control over their business segments. Another benefit is that a decentralized management style provides an opportunity for lower-level managers to sharpen their decision making skills, thus providing the company with experienced managers to progress through the ranks to top management positions. Decentralization also means that decisions are made by the managers who are most familiar with the problems and opportunities occurring in the routine operations of the company. Top managers may be somewhat removed from the intimacies of the daily routine business operations and therefore would be hard pressed to make well-informed decisions. Another advantage is that it relieves top managers of the responsibility of routine decisions and allows them to focus on strategic decisions and the overall goals of the organization.

A disadvantage of decentralized management is that decisions may not entirely reflect the views of top managers. Also, decisions are made by managers who may be less experienced than the top managers.

Discussion Questions

11–8. If you were the chief executive officer of your company, would you prefer a centralized or decentralized management style? Why?
11–9. If you were a lower-level manager in your company, would you prefer a centralized or decentralized management style? Why?
11–10. What similarities do you see between our discussion here of centralized and decentralized management and our discussion in Chapter 9 of top-down and bottom-up budgeting?

◆ EVALUATING BUSINESS SEGMENTS

To evaluate the performance of business segments, we must first determine just what constitutes good performance. To establish whether a manager is doing a good job, for example, we must first have some idea of just what a "good job" means. To evaluate segment performance, a standard must be developed that establishes just what constitutes good performance.

The performance of a business segment can be evaluated based on a number of criteria. The most logical evaluation criteria match the scope of responsibility and authority afforded the segment's manager. That is, if a particular segment's manager has the responsibility and authority only to control costs, the segment performance should be evaluated based on criteria that focus on cost control. Conversely, if the segment manager has the responsibility to generate revenue and also to control costs, the segment's performance should be evaluated based on criteria that focus on profits. Segments may be categorized based on the criteria used for their evaluation. The most popular segment categories are revenue centers, cost centers, profit centers, and investment centers.

REVENUE CENTERS

revenue center A business segment in which the manager has responsibility and authority to act to increase revenues but has little or no control over costs and the amount invested in the segment.

A **revenue center** is a business segment whose manager has responsibility and authority to act to increase revenues but has little control over costs and the amount invested in the segment. The performance of a revenue center is evaluated based on the amount of revenue generated by the segment, and the manager is evaluated based on his or her ability to generate sales revenue.

An example of a business segment properly designated as a revenue center is a sales office whose segment manager has little or no control over costs. The results of the manager's actions would affect sales revenue but have minimal effect on cost.

COST CENTERS

cost center A business segment where the manager has responsibility and authority to act to decrease or at least control costs but has little or no control over the revenues generated or the amount invested in the segment.

A **cost center** is a business segment whose manager has responsibility and authority to decrease or at least control costs while keeping output high. Generally, cost center managers are not responsible for generating revenue, nor do they have control over the amount invested in the segment. The performance of a cost center is evaluated based on the amount of cost incurred by the segment, and the manager is evaluated based on his or her ability to control these costs.

Business segments that provide service to the company or customers but do not contribute directly to revenues are good candidates to be designated as cost centers. Examples of cost centers include the accounting department of a hospital, a repair department that handles warranty repair work, an assembly department, and an inspection facility in a manufacturing plant.

PROFIT CENTERS

profit center A business segment in which the manager has the responsibility and authority to act to increase revenue and decrease or at least control costs, but has little or no control over the amount invested in the segment.

A **profit center** is a business segment whose manager has the responsibility and authority to act to increase revenue and decrease or at least control costs but does not have control over the amount invested in the segment. The performance of a profit center is evaluated based on the amount of profits it generates. The manager of a profit center is evaluated based on his or her ability to increase revenue and control expenses, because profits are increased by increasing revenue and/or decreasing expenses.

Examples of profit centers include individual stores in a department store chain, a college bookstore, and a pathology testing center.

MEASURING PERFORMANCE OF REVENUE, COST, AND PROFIT CENTERS

The most commonly used method of evaluating the performance of revenue centers, cost centers, and profit centers is performance to budget. The sales goals established during the budgeting process can be used as a basis for evaluating the performance of revenue centers. If, for example, actual sales are higher than budgeted sales, this would be a favorable indication. If, on the other hand, actual sales are lower than budgeted sales, this would be an unfavorable indication. For a cost center, the goals established during the budgeting process for output and cost can be used as a basis for evaluating cost center performance. Actual production that exceeds budgeted production, for example, would be a favorable indication. Costs per unit of output that are lower than budgeted would also be a favorable indication. Obviously, favorable performance would be indicated by high output and low cost relative to output volume. For a profit center, the profit goals established during the budgeting process can be compared to actual profits to evaluate profit center performance. Favorable performance would be indicated by actual profits that meet or exceed budgeted profits.

It is often argued that having managers strive to meet budgeted performance targets is so simplistic that it leads to suboptimal performance. Managers may simply strive to meet the expectations established by the budget instead of trying to maximize sales. Another potential problem is that managers who are evaluated based on performance to budget can make themselves look good by negotiating relatively low budgeted sales and relatively high budgeted costs. Then when the actual sales are higher than budget, and the actual costs are lower than budgeted, the manager appears to have performed well. This information may seem familiar to you. Other chapters in the text included brief discussions of the problems associated with performance to budget as a way to measure managers' performance—a subject addressed in Chapter 9 when we presented the operating budget and again in Chapter 10 in the presentation of standard costing. Everything about the potential for counterproductive behavior inherent in the performance to budget evaluation technique applies to measuring the performance of revenue centers, cost centers, and profit centers.

If we move away from performance to budget as a means of evaluating revenue center managers, however, what do we put in its place? This topic has been a topic of debate for some time in management accounting circles. The answer, we suspect, is not to drop performance to budget as a performance measure entirely. Rather, it should be supplemented with other types of measures, some of which are presented near the end of this chapter. For now, just remember that a company runs a real risk of encouraging silly management behavior if it relies too heavily on performance to budget as a means of evaluating its managers.

INVESTMENT CENTERS

Does earning a profit of $100,000 constitute good performance? Before we can tell just how good it is, we should also consider the amount of investment required. Surely, almost any business segment can be profitable if there is an unlimited amount to invest in assets and technology. In business, the hope is to keep the profit high and the amount invested low.

investment center   A business segment that is evaluated based on the amount of profit generated relative to the amount invested in the segment.

An **investment center** is a business segment that is evaluated on the amount of profit generated relative to the amount invested in the segment. An investment center manager should strive to maximize profit while minimizing the amount of investment used to earn the profit. Reducing the investment in a given segment allows the freed-up funds to be used by other segments. If the funds are not needed by the company elsewhere, financing can be reduced.

If a segment manager has responsibility and authority for revenues, costs, and capital investment in the segment, it should probably be designated an investment center. Examples of business segments that might be designated investment centers are individual stores in a department store chain, a college bookstore, and a pathology testing center. Note that these examples are the same as those given for segments designated as profit centers in our earlier discussion, because the classification of a business segment as a revenue center, profit center, cost center, or investment center depends not only on the operation of the segment, but also, and as importantly, on the responsibility and authority afforded the segment's manager. If a manager's responsibility includes the generation of revenue, cost control, and control of the amount invested in the segment, then the business segment she or he manages should be designated an investment center.

As stated earlier, an investment center should be evaluated not only on the income generated by the segment, but also on the amount of investment required to earn the income. Obviously, the higher the net income, the better, and the lower the investment required to generate that net income, the better. To evaluate the performance of an investment center we must be able to quantify the relationship between income earned and the investment required. For example, if you are about to invest in a savings account, it might be beneficial to know that a $5,245 deposit will earn interest of $183.57 in one year's time. Without knowing the percentage interest rate of return, however, the amounts have little meaning when evaluating the performance of the savings account. In business, the percentage return on an amount invested is called the return on investment.

◆ RETURN ON INVESTMENT

In 1903, Pierre DuPont and two cousins, Alfred and Coleman, formed the E. I. DuPont de Nemours Powder Company by combining several gunpowder companies they had purchased from other DuPont family members. When the cousins purchased the companies, they paid for them by issuing bonds equal in value to the expected future earnings potential of the companies acquired to form the new business. Pierre and his cousins could realize a profit only when the income from the new company exceeded the projected income of the companies they had purchased. Therefore, if income did not increase, there would be only enough profits to pay the bonds, leaving no profit for the cousins. This transaction is an early example of a leveraged buyout.

Knowing only the amount of income was not enough to monitor the success of the new organization. Accordingly, Pierre DuPont devised the return on investment model to calculate the percentage return on the cousins' investment. The return on investment could be used to assess whether the returns of the individual segments of the DuPont Company exceeded the rate used to calculate the purchase price and interest payments on the bonds. Of course, the hope was that each of the segments of the DuPont Company would have a return on investment that exceeded the rate used to determine the purchase price. The company went on to become the ***DuPont Chemical Company*** we know today.

return on investment (ROI)   The percentage return generated by an investment in a business or a business segment.

Discussion Question

11-11. What similarities do you see between our discussion here of return on investment and our discussion in Chapter 8 of capital expenditures?

Since its inception, DuPont's return on investment model has been a popular method of evaluating investment centers. **Return on investment (ROI)** is the percentage return generated by an investment in a business or business segment. The ROI is calculated by dividing the amount of income by the amount invested. For example, assume that the Eastern Division of the Lisa Company generated a segment margin of $896,750 for 2005 and the amount invested in the division was $10,550,000. This information is interesting, but it is probably more meaningful to know the percentage return that the investment generated. The ROI for the Lisa Company is 8.5 percent, determined as follows:

$$\frac{\text{Segment income}}{\text{Investment in the segment}} = \text{Return on investment}$$

$$\frac{\$896,750}{\$10,550,000} = 8.5\%$$

After we determine the ROI for the division, the next question is, is the ROI adequate? If a company uses ROI as the measurement criterion for evaluating segment performance, it must establish a required rate for the ROI. The required rate of return that companies normally use is the weighted average cost of capital rate, as discussed in Chapter 8 concerning capital expenditures. Once established, the required ROI rate is used as a benchmark to evaluate the performance of the various investment centers in the company. A segment with an ROI that equals or exceeds the company's required rate will be viewed favorably, whereas a segment with an ROI that is lower than the required rate will be viewed as deficient. If we assume that the required rate for the ROI for the Lisa Company is 8 percent, then the Eastern Division's performance is certainly adequate.

Discussion Question

11-12. What similarities do you see between our discussion here of the ROI calculation and our discussion in Chapter 8 of the internal rate of return?

In evaluating segment performance, we can rank segments by their return on investment. For example, if the Western Division of the Lisa Company has income of $857,500 with an investment on $9,800,000, how does the performance of the Western Division compare to that of the Eastern Division? The return on investment of both divisions is presented as Exhibit 11–7.

EXHIBIT 11–7 Return on Investment for Both Divisions of Lisa Company

Eastern Division	**Western Division**
$\dfrac{\text{Segment Income}}{\text{Investment in the Segment}} = \text{ROI}$	$\dfrac{\text{Segment Income}}{\text{Investment in the Segment}} = \text{ROI}$
$\dfrac{\$896,750}{\$10,550,00} = 8.5\%$	$\dfrac{\$857,500}{\$9,800,000} = 8.75\%$

Based on the ROI, the performance of the Western Division is superior to that of the Eastern Division because its ROI is greater. In this case, the Western Division's manager may be rewarded because of that division's better performance. As you might imagine, the use of ROI tends to encourage competition among segment managers, who strive to enhance performance evaluation by choosing investments that will work to increase their segment's ROI.

For the ROI to increase, the ROI of any new investment must exceed the segment's current ROI. If a new investment promises an ROI that is equal to the segment's current ROI, the segment's ROI will remain unchanged. However, if the new investment's ROI is less than the segment's current ROI, the segment's ROI will decrease. For example, assume that the manager of the Eastern Division is contemplating a new investment in the hope of improving his or her performance evaluation. An investment opportunity is available that promises additional income of $123,750 and requires an additional investment of $1,500,000. The ROI for this new investment opportunity is 8.25 percent calculated as follows:

$$\frac{\text{New investment income}}{\text{Investment in the new project}} = \text{ROI}$$

$$\frac{\$123,750}{\$1,500,000} = 8.25\%$$

Based on the company's required rate of return of 8 percent, it seems that the project should be accepted. Will the manager of the Eastern Division accept the project because it exceeds the company's required ROI and would benefit the company as a whole? Unfortunately, the answer is probably no. The manager of the Eastern Division may not select this project because it would work to reduce the segment's current ROI, as shown in Exhibit 11–8.

Although the Eastern Division's ROI would still be well above the required ROI rate of eight percent, the new investment would reduce the division's ROI from 8.5 percent to approximately 8.47 percent.

When ROI is used as the segment performance measure, the evaluation is usually based not only on how the segment's ROI compares to the company's required rate, but also on how segment's ROI compares to the ROI of other segments. Therefore, managers will select only projects that will enhance their current ROI. Unfortunately, this often works to the detriment of the company as a whole, because projects that meet the company's required ROI rate are rejected simply because they will not increase the segment's ROI. Fortunately, another evaluation technique encourages managers to accept projects that have an ROI exceeding the company's required ROI rate. This evaluation technique is called residual income.

Eastern Division *Without* the New Investment Opportunity	Eastern Division *With* the New Investment Opportunity
$\dfrac{\text{Segment Income}}{\text{Investment in the Segment}} = \text{ROI}$	$\dfrac{\text{Segment Income}}{\text{Investment in the Segment}} = \text{ROI}$
$\dfrac{\$896,750}{\$10,550,00} = 8.5\%$	$\dfrac{\$896,750 + \$123,750}{\$10,550,000 + \$1,500,000} = 8.75\%$
	$\dfrac{\$1,020,500}{\$12,050,000} = 8.47\%$

EXHIBIT 11-8 Effect of New Project on Eastern Division's Segment ROI

◆ RESIDUAL INCOME AND ECONOMIC VALUE ADDED (EVA)

residual income The amount by which a segment's actual income exceeds the income needed to meet a company's required rate of return.

economic value added (EVA) Almost the same as residual income except that it is adjusted for certain accounting distortions.

Residual income is a technique used to evaluate investment centers by focusing on the amount by which a segment's actual income exceeds the income needed to meet the company's required rate of return. **Economic value added (EVA),** which is trademarked by the consulting firm of Stern, Stewart & Co., is similar to residual income except that Stern Stewart adjusted the calculation for certain distortions that stem from generally accepted accounting principles (GAAP). For example, EVA calculations require research and development (R&D) costs to be capitalized as an asset and amortized over the periods benefited, whereas R&D costs are treated as period expenses under GAAP. EVA has become very popular and many managers attribute significant improvements in company performance to its use in evaluating their managers. For our purposes, we will make no distinction between residual income and EVA.

To demonstrate residual income, let's take another look at the Lisa Company. Recall that the investment in the Eastern Division of the Lisa Company is $10,550,000 and that the company's required rate of return is 8 percent. With that said, the Eastern Division must earn $844,000 ($10,550,000 × 8%) just to equal the 8 percent required rate of return. This required earnings amount represents the dollar amount of earnings the segment must earn to equal the required rate of return for the company. Any earnings in excess of the required earnings (in this case, $844,000) will constitute the segment's residual income. For the Eastern Division, the $896,750 actual income exceeds the $844,000 required income by $52,750. Therefore, the residual income for the Eastern Division is $52,750, calculated as follows:

Actual Income	$ 896,750
Less Required Income ($10,550,000 × 8%)	$(844,000)
Equals Residual Income	$ 52,750

This is not to say that the Eastern Division only earned $52,750. Rather, the Eastern Division's income exceeded the company's required earnings by $52,750.

If the division's actual income were less than the income required to meet the company's required rate of return, the residual income amount would be a negative number. In our example, the positive residual income amount indicates that the segment's actual earnings exceed the company's required rate of return. In the unlikely event that residual income is zero, it would indicate that the actual income for the segment exactly equals the company's required rate of return.

Discussion Question •

11–13. What similarities do you see between our discussion here of the residual income calculation and our discussion in Chapter 8 of net present value?

We now calculate the residual income for the Western Division so we can evaluate the relative performance of the two divisions. Using the amounts previously presented for the Western Division, we calculate residual income as $73,500:

Actual Income	$ 857,500
Less Required Income ($9,800,000 × 8%)	$(784,000)
Equals Residual Income	$ 73,500

Notice that the residual income of the Western Division exceeds that of the Eastern Division. Accordingly, the performance of the Western Division would be viewed more favorably than that of the Eastern Division. In an attempt to improve the Eastern Division's relative performance, managers would strive to increase revenue, decrease expenses, or seek new, high-return investment opportunities.

When ROI is used to evaluate potential investment opportunities, managers invest only in projects with an anticipated return that exceeds the segment's current ROI. Projects that exceed the company's required rate of return but did not exceed the segment's current ROI would likely be rejected. Look again at the investment opportunity proposed for the Eastern Division. Recall that the project would require an investment of $1,500,000 with anticipated additional income of $123,750. Therefore, the total investment of the Eastern Division would increase to $12,050,000 ($10,550,000 + $1,500,000), while total segment income would increase to $1,020,500 ($896,750 + $123,750).

If residual income were used to evaluate segment performance, management of the Eastern Division would tend to accept the proposed project if it worked to increase residual income. Review the residual income for the Eastern Division both with and without the proposed investment opportunity. The data are presented in Exhibit 11–9.

EXHIBIT 11–9 Residual Income for Eastern Division With and Without Proposed Investment

Eastern Division *Without* the New Investment Opportunity		Eastern Division *With* the New Investment Opportunity	
Actual Income	$896,750	Actual Income	$1,020,000
Required Income		Required Income	
$10,550,000 × 8% =	$844,000	$12,050,000 × 8% =	$ 964,000
Residual Income	$ 52,750	Residual Income	$ 56,000

As you can see, the investment opportunity for the Eastern Division would increase residual income. Therefore, management of the Eastern Division would tend to favor the investment. Notice that the residual income method, unlike ROI, prompts managers to accept projects with return rates that exceed the company's required rate of return even if the project's rate of return falls short of the segment's current ROI.

◆ THE BALANCED SCORECARD AND NONFINANCIAL PERFORMANCE MEASURES

When you're driving a car, you can't focus just on your speedometer. You have to steer the car, watch the road, and pay attention to the traffic. As it is with driving your car, businesses cannot focus on just one measure of business performance. In the past, business in the United States has focused almost exclusively on financial amounts to measure success. Success has been gauged by how much revenue can be generated, how much costs can be reduced, or how much profit can be earned. Recently, however, many companies have begun to also consider nonfinancial performance measures in evaluating business performance. Managers are finding that a more strategic, balanced approach is necessary to drive corporate performance. Harvard professor Robert Kaplan and consultant David Norton have developed a management technique called the balanced scorecard. The balanced scorecard doesn't focus solely on financial objectives of the firm. Instead, the **balanced scorecard** is an integrated set of performance measures organized around four distinct perspectives—financial, customer, internal processes, and innovation and learning (see Exhibit 11–10). The balanced scorecard

balanced scorecard An integrated set of performance measures organized around four distinct perspectives—financial, customer, internal, and innovation and learning.

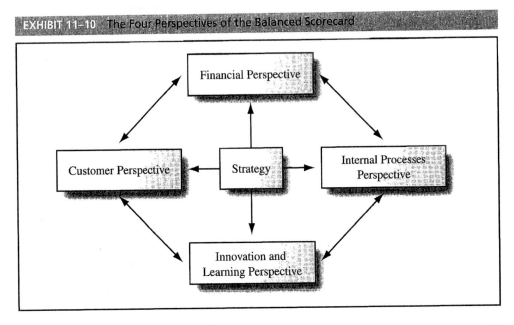

EXHIBIT 11–10 The Four Perspectives of the Balanced Scorecard

suggests these perspectives, but managers generally tailor them to suit their own business needs. In addition, managers create their own overall objectives and measures for each perspective. Then, based on the company's overall objectives, managers can create appropriate detailed departmental objectives and measures. Exhibit 11–11 shows examples of objectives and measures for the four balanced scorecard perspectives.

Although the balanced scorecard is often viewed as a performance measurement technique, Kaplan and Norton report that it can be much more:

> . . . innovating CEOs used the balance scorecard not only to clarify and communicate strategy, but also to manage strategy. They are using the measurement focus of the scorecard to accomplish critical management processes:
>
> 1. Clarify and translate vision and strategy
> 2. Communicate and link strategic objectives and measures
> 3. Plan, set targets, and align strategic initiatives
> 4. Enhance strategic feedback and learning[1]

To ensure that the balanced scorecard is not only a measurement and reporting tool but also a management technique that will effectively enhance a company's performance, it is important that each objective and each measure be closely aligned with the firm's overall goals and business strategy.

Setting objectives and a basis for measurement for each of the four scorecard perspectives allows managers and employees to focus on the success of each perspective and to avoid making the mistake of attending to one perspective while neglecting another. Attention to each of the four perspectives is critical to the success of all types of businesses. As we said at the beginning of this section, when you're driving a car, you can't just focus on your speedometer. When managing a business in today's competitive busi-

---

[1]From: Robert S. Kaplan and David P. Norton, *The Balanced Scorecard: Translating Strategy into Action.* Harvard Business School Press (Preface page ix, and page 10).

Perspective	Overall Objective	Examples of Measures
Financial	To succeed financially	• Operating income • ROI • EVA • Sales growth • Cost reductions
Customer	To achieve our vision of how we should appear to our customers	• Number of new customers • Customer retention • Depth of customer relationships • Market share • Time to fill orders • On-time deliveries • Customer complaints • Time to resolve complaints • Completeness of product-line offering • Customer satisfaction with products and services • Customer satisfaction with company employees
Internal	To excel at having superior business processes to satisfy our shareholders and customers	• Process quality measures • Lead time (time between when a customer places an order and when it is delivered) • Defect rates • Yield ratios of good items to items entering process • Waste, scrap and rework measures • Returns
Innovation and Learning	To sustain our ability to change and improve (Employee capabilities are a key ingredient to this objective.)	• Employee retention • Employee productivity • Average revenue per employee • Employee training • Reskilling (teaching employees new skills) • Information system capabilities (availability of useful information to employees) • Number of suggestions • Number of suggestions implemented

EXHIBIT 11–11 Examples of Objectives and Measures for the Four Balanced Scorecard Perspectives

ness environment, you can't focus solely on financial performance measures. In the following section we will discuss a few examples of nonfinancial measures in more detail.

EXAMPLES OF NONFINANCIAL PERFORMANCE MEASURES

Many managers are discovering that simply tracking the flow of dollars and cents does not ensure business success. Intense competition has prompted U.S. businesses to take a second look at nonfinancial performance measures in the hope that improved performance on these measures will ultimately lead to greater financial rewards.

Quality

To remain competitive, U.S. companies must produce the high-quality products their customers have come to expect. Thus, they have begun to monitor product quality in a number of ways. Production reports are no longer limited to data pertaining to numbers of units and unit cost. Information about the number of defective products and the amount of rework is now prepared and used as a basis for measuring segment success. Product quality is also monitored by tabulating the amount and nature of customer complaints. Product warranty repair costs and the number of repairs or service calls are also useful tools in evaluating product quality.

The trend in business today is to establish extremely high goals for quality. For **FedEx,** 100 percent on-time delivery is the goal. Imagine, not 90 percent or 95 percent, but 100 percent on-time delivery. This goal may seem impossible to achieve, but **FedEx** has mobilized the company to achieve high-quality performance in every aspect of the delivery process. From delivery truck maintenance to the package tracking system, quality is the hallmark of the company.

Discussion Question •

11-14. What, if any, are the potentially negative financial effects of focusing on quality?

Customer Satisfaction

In today's competitive business environment, customer satisfaction is often viewed as the most critical ingredient in achieving and maintaining success. But how can customer satisfaction be evaluated to measure segment performance? There are several ways. First, customer complaints can be monitored. At **IBM,** for example, detailed records are kept regarding each customer complaint. In addition to tracking the number of complaints, **IBM** records the nature and severity of each complaint and follows up every one to ensure that the customer's needs have been reasonably met.

To satisfy customers, you must first know what customers want. Surveys can be used to identify what is important to customers and to help determine whether they are satisfied with products and services. For example, buyers of **Infinity** automobiles are surveyed each time their cars are serviced. This survey accomplishes at least two important things. First, it provides information that can be used to evaluate the performance of the service facilities. Second, it can alert the company to an unhappy customer so that reasonable action can be taken to remedy that customer's complaint.

Discussion Question •

11-15. What, if any, are the potentially negative financial effects of focusing on customer satisfaction?

Employee Morale

An increasing number of companies are realizing that improving company morale will almost certainly increase profits. It stands to reason that employees who are happy with their jobs are more likely to work harder than those who are not. In addition, low morale leads to high turnover, which in turn substantially increases the cost of hiring and training employees. It follows, then, that managers should work to keep employee morale high. Measuring employee morale can be challenging, but some useful indicators of employee morale are the amount of absenteeism, the rate of employee turnover, and recruiting success rates.

Discussion Question •

11-16. What, if any, are the potentially negative financial effects of focusing on employee morale?

Employee Safety

In today's business world, it is critical that employees be provided with a safe work environment. **Dow Chemical Company,** for example, has invested a great deal of money in promoting safety in the workplace. Employees are routinely reminded of the importance of safety through company-provided posters, safety seminars, and safety awareness contests. The information **Dow** provides to its people is not limited to safety on the job, but also extends to automobile and home safety.

Dow Chemical is not alone in its campaign to promote safety. Many companies are using employee safety information to evaluate segment performance, and managers can be evaluated based on the number of safety seminars or other safety programs they hold per year.

Discussion Question •

11–17. What, if any, are the potentially negative financial effects of focusing on employee safety?

Efficiency

Efficiency has become one of the cornerstones of success for many companies. Efficiency is the measure of output achieved versus the amount of resources required. To increase production efficiency relative to material, companies are attempting to produce the maximum number of units with the minimum amount of wasted material. This efficiency can be measured by looking at the amount of material used and/or the amount of scrap material that remains per unit produced. For labor, efficiency can be measured by the relationship of production output to the direct labor required.

Many manufacturers are making major commitments to improve general plant efficiency. To be successful, these efforts must be supported by everyone from production-line workers to the chief executive officer. Typically, efficiency drives extend far beyond making minor changes and rallying the troops to work a little faster. Rather, they encompass major reorganizations of labor, new plant layouts, and innovative work flow philosophies, so it is vital that these efforts be supported by top management. Many of the concepts that contribute to increased plant efficiency are part of the just-in-time philosophy, which we'll look at next.

Discussion Question •

11–18. What, if any, are the potentially negative financial effects of focusing on efficiency?

◆ JUST-IN-TIME PHILOSOPHY

just-in-time (JIT) A philosophy that eliminates all unnecessary inventory and limits the use of company resources until they are absolutely needed to fulfill customer demand.

The **just-in-time (JIT)** philosophy involves eliminating all unnecessary inventory and limiting the use of company resources until they are absolutely needed to fulfill customer demand. Products are "pulled" through the system. That is, products are made in response to the *pull* from customer demand, rather than to the *push* to have inventory to fill orders that may or may not materialize.

Often, JIT is described too narrowly as a method of eliminating or greatly reducing inventory by delaying the purchase of raw material until it is needed for production. This view is greatly flawed and prompts many managers to reject the whole JIT idea. Limiting the use of company resources until they are needed for production cannot be achieved by simply adopting a mindset that purchases will be delayed until the last possible minute. Instead, the JIT philosophy focuses on delaying expenditures for inventory and reducing inventory levels to near zero by creating very efficient production processes that require only a minimal amount of inventory to successfully manufacture high-quality products.

One key component of JIT is that manufacturers must be able to depend on their suppliers for 100 percent on-time deliveries of 100 percent defect-free material. When JIT is implemented, manufacturers defer quality inspections to their suppliers and insist on parts and components that are free of defects. **Zero defects** is a term that is often used to describe the concept of products that are completely free of imperfections. In a JIT environment, zero defects becomes the norm.

zero defects Describes the concept of products that are completely free of imperfections.

For JIT to work, manufacturers must develop close relationships with suppliers who can provide absolutely on-time deliveries and absolutely consistent high quality. As part of the program to develop these close relationships, firms greatly reduce the number of their suppliers. By working with a core of carefully selected suppliers, the manufacturer is able to make substantial purchase commitments that help compensate suppliers for the added effort required to meet the manufacturer's demands. Also, the financial benefits they gain from receiving on-time deliveries of consistently high-quality products make it possible for manufacturers to justify paying a premium price for the goods they purchase.

In a JIT environment, setup times must be reduced to the lowest possible levels. As mentioned in Chapter 4, **setup time** is the time it takes to prepare manufacturing equipment for the production of a particular product. One major problem with long setup times is that while production equipment is being set up, it cannot be used to produce anything. The trouble does not end there, however. If setup time is substantial, fewer and longer production runs must be made to justify the substantial setup effort. It makes no sense to go through a long setup process to produce only a few units. The result of long production runs is higher inventory levels. This method is in direct conflict with the JIT philosophy. Conversely, if setup time is very short, running a short production run to produce fewer units of product is more feasible. With shorter production runs making fewer units, inventories can be reduced.

In JIT environments, setup time is now measured, and average setup times are used to evaluate the performance of segment managers. In factories using just-in-time production, setup time is reduced from hours or days to minutes.

Another focus of the JIT philosophy is reduced throughput time. **Throughput time** is the time between the entrance of a unit of production into the production process and the time it emerges as a finished product. It is an important measure of plant efficiency because the amount of money invested in work-in-process inventory can be lowered by reducing the time products are in the production process. In addition to reducing inventories, shorter throughput time frees production equipment so it can be used to make other products. Throughput time can thus be measured and used as a basis for evaluating performance.

Another hallmark of the JIT philosophy is reduction in lead time. **Lead time** is the time between the receipt of an order and the completion of a product ready for shipment. Decreasing setup and throughput times can greatly reduce lead time. Many manufacturers that have adopted JIT have reduced lead time from months or years to days or even hours. Lead time can be measured and used as a basis for evaluating plant performance.

In a further effort to increase efficiency, managers are working to reduce unscheduled downtime. **Unscheduled downtime** is the amount of time production equipment is out of service due to unscheduled repairs and maintenance. To keep this factor low, managers implement routine maintenance programs that not only keep unscheduled downtime to a minimum, but also keep machinery running at peak performance. Companies are now tracking unscheduled downtime and using the information to evaluate plant performance.

By now, you may be wondering just how these JIT production improvements can be achieved. They do not come cheaply or easily. A great deal of time and money must be spent to achieve the added efficiency that comes with a JIT production environment. Some key factors are improved plant layout and product flow, mechanized procedures for machine setup, convenient storage and labeling of machine parts used in the setup process, and a formal plant maintenance program.

The production plant layout should be designed so that raw materials enter the production process with little or no need to be transported to work stations. For example, when a new *Saturn* automobile is made, the truck that transports the seats to the factory is literally connected to the production building, and the seats are fed to the production line, in the proper order, through conveyors in the truck to conveyers in the factory. At *Saturn,* the days of buying an assortment of seats and storing them in a warehouse are gone. Gone, too, are the days when personnel picked through massive inventories of seats to find a particular color and style and transported the selected seats to the production line. By cooperating with a seat manufacturer and a transportation company, *Saturn* can depend on the seats not only arriving on time but being received in the correct order by color and style with zero defects. A backup plan for shipment delays is the responsibility of the supplier and transportation company.

In addition to facilitating efficient handling of raw material, a JIT environment should also strive to streamline the movement of material from one production process to the next. For example, the *Dunlop* golf ball factory in South Carolina has

---

setup time The time it takes to prepare manufacturing equipment for the production of particular products.

throughput time The time that passes from the time a unit of product enters the production process until it emerges as a finished product.

lead time The time that passes from the time an order is received until the product is complete and ready for shipment.

unscheduled downtime The amount of time production equipment is out of service due to unscheduled repairs and maintenance.

eliminated the use of hopper carts to transport golf balls from the painting process to the packaging process. This was achieved by changing the plant layout so that golf balls travel by conveyor from one process to the next. This production improvement saves time and eliminates the need for handling the golf balls between processes. An added feature of this change was the elimination of inspection stations between the painting department and the packaging department, as the golf balls were no longer subject to blemishes caused by rough treatment in the hopper carts. The production change worked to greatly increase plant efficiency and improve product quality.

Each manufacturing environment is unique. Managers and plant workers must cooperate to continually reinvent the production environment. Old production techniques and strategies must be set aside in favor of new standards of production excellence, efficiency, and product quality. Company management and production personnel must work together to achieve the world-class production excellence required in today's competitive business environment. It takes a team effort characterized by an innovative spirit and a willingness to invest in grand-scale changes.

Summary

As companies grow and the products and services they provide become more diversified, it becomes a virtual impossibility for one person to perform all management functions. More managers are required to operate and control the various facets of what we call management. A natural outgrowth of a company's evolution is the creation of business segments. A segment is any part of a company about which separate information is required to evaluate performance.

When a company is segmented, it will employ either a centralized management style or a decentralized management style. In a centralized company, upper management makes most of the important business decisions. In a decentralized company, lower-level managers are responsible for virtually all decisions that relate to their segment of the company.

Determining what costs should be charged to a particular business segment and the amount of those costs is sometimes very difficult. Some costs associated with operating a business segment are directly incurred by that segment. Others, however, are incurred to support more than one segment. These common costs must be allocated in some way to the segments receiving the benefit of the costs.

The four most commonly used designations of business segments are revenue centers, cost centers, profit centers, and investment centers. Revenue centers, cost centers, and profit centers are usually evaluated based on performance to budget. The performance of investment centers is most often evaluated using the return on investment (ROI), residual income, or economic value added (EVA).

Although performance to budget and either return on investment or residual income are still commonly used to evaluate business segment performance, other nonfinancial measures have become popular in recent years. The balanced scorecard is an integrated set of performance measures organized around four distinct perspectives—financial, customer, internal, and innovation and learning. Many companies are now emphasizing such elements as product quality, customer satisfaction, employee morale, safety in the workplace, and efficiency as ways to better measure and improve company performance.

Key Terms ●

- balanced scorecard, M–372
- business segment, M–356
- centralized management, M–364
- common fixed costs, M–359
- cost center, M–366
- decentralized management, M–365
- direct fixed costs, M–359
- economic value added (EVA), M–370

- indirect fixed costs, M–359
- investment center, M–367
- just-in-time (JIT), M–375
- lead time, M–376
- profit center, M–366
- residual income, M–370
- return on investment (ROI), M–368
- revenue center, M–366
- segment income statement, M–357

- segment margin, M–357
- segment reports, M–357
- service department, M–362
- setup time, M–376
- throughput time, M–376
- traceable fixed costs, M–359
- unscheduled downtime, M–376
- zero defects, M–375

Review the Facts ●

A. Describe a business segment.
B. What is the difference between direct fixed cost and common fixed cost?
C. What is a service department?
D. Why is it important to know about service department cost allocation?
E. Describe the difference between centralized and decentralized management.
F. Describe a revenue center.
G. Describe a cost center.
H. What is the difference between a profit center and an investment center?
I. Why is residual income sometimes preferred to return on investment?
J. Describe the balanced scorecard.
K. What are the four perspectives of the balanced scorecard?
L. List five nonfinancial performance measures.
M. What is meant by the just-in-time philosophy?
N. How can companies achieve the very low inventory levels embraced by the just-in-time philosophy?

Apply What You Have Learned ●

LO 2 & 3: PREPARE A SEGMENT INCOME STATEMENT WITH AND WITHOUT THE ALLOCATION OF COMMON FIXED COSTS TO SEGMENTS

11–19. The Almer Sales Company has two divisions. The following information is available for the year ended December 31, 2004:

The sales for Almer are $300,000 for the Eastern Division and $200,000 for the Western Division. Variable costs for the Eastern Division are $250,000, whereas variable costs for the Western Division are $170,000. Direct fixed costs of the Eastern Division are $20,000 and direct fixed costs of the Western Division are $15,000. The Almer Company allocates common fixed costs to segments based on relative sales. Common fixed costs for the company are $25,000.

Required:

a. Prepare a segment income statement for the company, which distributes common fixed costs to segments based on relative sales. Your answer should include a column for the total company and columns for each segment.
b. Do you think it is wise to evaluate the performance of a business segment based on income that includes an allocation for common fixed costs? Why or why not?
c. Prepare a segment income statement for the company, which does not distribute common fixed cost to segments. Your answer should include a column for the total company and columns for each segment.

LO 2 & 3: PREPARE A SEGMENT INCOME STATEMENT WITH AND WITHOUT THE ALLOCATION OF COMMON FIXED COSTS TO SEGMENTS

11–20. The Ted Green Sales Company has two divisions. The following information is available for the year ended December 31, 2004:

The sales for the company are $30,000 for the Northern Division, and $90,000 for the Southern Division. Variable costs for the Northern Division are $18,000, while variable costs for the Southern Division are $54,000. Direct fixed costs of the Northern Division are $5,000 and direct fixed costs of the Southern Division are $15,000. The company allocates common fixed costs to segments based on relative sales. Common fixed costs for the company are $10,000.

Required:

    a. Prepare a segment income statement for the company, which distributes common fixed costs to segments based on relative sales. Your answer should include a column for the total company and columns for each segment.

    b. Do you think it is wise to evaluate the performance of a business segment based on income that includes an allocation for common fixed costs? Why or why not?

    c. Prepare a segment income statement for the company, which does not distribute common fixed cost to segments. Your answer should include a column for the total company and columns for each segment.

LO 2 & 3: PREPARE A SEGMENT INCOME STATEMENT WITH AND WITHOUT THE ALLOCATION OF COMMON FIXED COSTS TO SEGMENTS

11–21. The Albert Pons Company has two divisions. The following information is available for the year ended December 31, 2004:

    The sales for the company are $200,000 for the Central Division, and $400,000 for the Southern Division. Variable costs for the Central Division are $150,000, whereas variable costs for the Southern Division are $300,000. Direct fixed costs of the Central Division are $19,000 and direct fixed costs of the Southern Division are $54,000. The company allocates common fixed costs to segments based on relative sales. Common fixed costs for the company are $27,000.

Required:

    a. Prepare a segment income statement for the company, which distributes common fixed costs to segments based on relative sales. Your answer should include a column for the total company and columns for each segment.

    b. Do you think it is wise to evaluate the performance of a business segment based on income that includes an allocation for common fixed costs? Why or why not?

    c. Prepare a segment income statement for the company, which does not distribute common fixed cost to segments. Your answer should include a column for the total company and columns for each segment.

LO 2 & 3: PREPARE A SEGMENT INCOME STATEMENT WITH AND WITHOUT THE ALLOCATION OF COMMON FIXED COSTS TO SEGMENTS

11–22. The Suzanne Elsea Company has three divisions. The following information is available for the year ended December 31, 2004:

    The sales for the company are $200,000 for the Central Division, and $400,000 for the Southern Division, and $600,000 for the Western Division. Variable costs for the Central Division are $150,000, variable costs for the Southern Division are $300,000, and variable costs for the Western Division are $450,000. Direct fixed costs of the Central Division are $20,000, direct fixed costs of the Southern Division are $54,000, and direct fixed costs of the Western Division are $100,000. The company allocates common fixed costs to segments based on relative sales. Common fixed costs for the company are $102,000.

Required:

    a. Prepare a segment income statement for the company which distributes common fixed costs to segments based on relative sales. Your answer should include a column for the total company and columns for each segment.

    b. Based on your answer for part a, which segment seems to have generated the least profit?

    c. Prepare a segment income statement for the company which does not distribute common fixed cost to segments. Your answer should include a column for the total company and columns for each segment.

    d. Based on your answer for part c, which segment seems to have generated the most profit?

LO 2 & 3: PREPARE A SEGMENT INCOME STATEMENT WITH AND WITHOUT THE ALLOCATION OF COMMON FIXED COSTS TO SEGMENTS

11–23. The Pitman Sales Company has three divisions. The following information is available for the year ended December 31, 2004:

The sales for the company are $100,000 for Division A, and $200,000 for Division B, and $300,000 for Division C. Variable costs for Division A are $50,000, variable costs for Division B are $100,000, and variable costs for Division C are $150,000. Direct fixed costs of Division A are $20,000, direct fixed costs of Division B are $30,000, and direct fixed costs of Division C are $60,000. The company allocates common fixed costs to segments based on relative sales. Common fixed costs for the company are $186,000.

Required:

    a. Prepare a segment income statement for the company, which distributes common fixed costs to segments based on relative sales. Your answer should include a column for the total company and columns for each segment.

    b. Based on your answer for part a, which segment seems to have generated the least profit?

    c. Prepare a segment income statement for the company, which does not distribute common fixed cost to segments. Your answer should include a column for the total company and columns for each segment.

    d. Based on your answer for part c, which segment seems to have generated the most profit?

LO 2 & 3: PREPARE A SEGMENT INCOME STATEMENT WITH AND WITHOUT THE ALLOCATION OF COMMON FIXED COSTS TO SEGMENTS

11–24. The Porter Sales Company has three divisions. The following information is available for the year ended December 31, 2004:

The sales for the company are $100,000 for Division 101, and $100,000 for Division 202, and $200,000 for Division 303. Variable costs for Division 101 are $50,000, variable costs for Division 202 are $60,000, and variable costs for Division 303 are $110,000. Direct fixed costs of Division 101 are $20,000, direct fixed costs of Division 202 are $30,000, and direct fixed costs of Division 303 are $50,000. The company allocates common fixed costs to segments based on relative sales. Common fixed costs for the company are $40,000.

Required:

    a. Prepare a segment income statement for the company, which distributes common fixed costs to segments based on relative sales. Your answer should include a column for the total company and columns for each segment.

    b. Based on your answer for part a, does it appear that one of the segments should be closed?

    c. Prepare a segment income statement for the company which does not distribute common fixed cost to segments. Your answer should include a column for the total company and columns for each segment.

    d. Based on your answer for part c, does it still seem that one of the segments should be closed?

LO 2: ANALYZE SEGMENT COST AND PREPARE A MEMO

11–25. The following segment income statement has been prepared for the Albertson Sales Company:

Albertson Sales Company
Segment Income Statement
For the Year Ended December 31, 2004

	Company Total	Medical Division	Industrial Division	Consumer Division
Sales	$750,000	$337,500	$157,500	$255,000
Variable cost	499,425	211,500	110,625	177,300
Contribution margin	250,575	126,000	46,875	77,700

Direct fixed cost	112,500	48,000	30,000	34,500
Segment margin	138,075	78,000	16,875	43,200
Common fixed cost	90,000	40,500[a]	18,900[b]	30,600[c]
Net income	$ 48,075	$37,500	$(2,025)	$12,600

[a]$337,500/$750,000 = 45\% \times $90,000 = $40,500$

[b]$157,500/$750,000 = 21\% \times $90,000 = $18,900$

[c]$255,000/$750,000 = 34\% \times $90,000 = $30,600$

The company President, Bob Albertson, is calling a management meeting to explore the idea of closing or selling the Industrial Division. Many managers are complaining that the division is "dragging the company down."

Assume that, in preparation for the meeting, Mr. Albertson has contacted you and asked that you explore the situation.

Required: Based on the information presented for the Albertson Sales Company, prepare a memo to Mr. Albertson which includes a brief summary of the problem and a proposed solution.

LO 2: IDENTIFY THE AREA OF RESPONSIBILITY ASSOCIATED WITH DIFFERENT TYPES OF BUSINESS SEGMENTS

11–26. Following are some popular segment classifications followed by three areas of management responsibility.

Segment Classification:
Revenue center   _____ _____ _____
Cost center   _____ _____ _____
Profit center   _____ _____ _____
Investment center _____ _____ _____

R = Revenue
C = Cost
I = Amount invested

Required: In the blank spaces provided, match the area or responsibility, revenue (R), cost (C), and amount invested (I) to the appropriate segment classification. Although not all the blank spaces will be used, some segment classifications will have more than one area of responsibility.

LO 4: DETERMINE RETURN ON INVESTMENT

11–27. The Chemical Division of CalChem Incorporated generated a segment margin of $220,680 for the year 2004 and the amount invested in the division was $1,226,000.

Required: Determine the return on investment for the Chemical Division.

LO 4: DETERMINE RETURN ON INVESTMENT

11–28. The Southern Division of the Benson Sales Company generated a segment margin of $790,020 for the year 2004 and the amount invested in the division was $4,158,000.

Required: Determine the return on investment for the Southern Division.

LO 4: DETERMINE RETURN ON INVESTMENT

11–29. The Automotive Division of the Bascom Company generated a segment margin of $1,916,800 for the year 2004 and the amount invested in the division was $11,980,000.

Required: Determine the return on investment for the Automotive Division.

LO 4: DETERMINE RETURN ON INVESTMENT

11–30. The Alcad Farm Products Company generated income of $558,620 for the year 2004 and the amount invested in the division was $3,286,000.

Required: Determine the return on investment for Alcad.

LO 2 & 4: DETERMINE AND INTERPRET RETURN ON INVESTMENT

11–31. The following information is available for the three divisions of the Pompano Company:

Amount invested in each division:	
Division A	$3,255,000
Division B	$2,145,000
Division C	$3,587,000

Segment margin of each division:	
Division A	$553,350
Division B	$407,550
Division C	$573,920

The required rate of return for the company is 16 percent.

Required:

a. Determine the return on investment for each division.
b. Rank the three divisions assuming they are considered profit centers.
c. Rank the three divisions assuming they are considered investment centers and performance is evaluated based on return on investment.
d. Why do the rankings for parts b and c differ?

LO 2 & 4: DETERMINE AND INTERPRET RETURN ON INVESTMENT

11–32. The following information is available for the three divisions of the Stevens Company:

Amount invested in each division:	
Division 101	$1,225,000
Division 202	$2,445,000
Division 303	$3,697,000

Segment margin of each division:	
Division 101	$198,450
Division 202	$371,640
Division 303	$569,338

The required rate of return for the company is 15 percent.

Required:

a. Determine the return on investment for each division.
b. Rank the three divisions assuming they are considered profit centers.
c. Rank the three divisions assuming they are considered investment centers and performance is evaluated based on return on investment.
d. Why do the rankings for parts b and c differ?

LO 2 & 4: DETERMINE AND INTERPRET RETURN ON INVESTMENT

11–33. The following information is available for the three divisions of the Reed Company:

Amount invested in each division:	
North Division	$7,225,000
South Division	$5,105,000
Central Division	$4,322,000

Segment margin of each division:	
North Division	$1,336,625
South Division	$ 898,480
Central Division	$ 816,858

The required rate of return for the company is 14 percent.

Required:

a. Determine the return on investment for each division.
b. Rank the three divisions assuming they are considered profit centers.
c. Rank the three divisions assuming they are considered investment centers.
d. Why do the rankings for parts b and c differ?

LO 5: DETERMINE RESIDUAL INCOME

11–34. The Eastern Division of the Key Largo Company generated a segment margin of $1,836,800 for the year 2004 and the amount invested in the division was $12,780,000. The company's required rate of return is 14 percent.

Required: Determine the residual income for the Eastern Division.

LO 5: DETERMINE RESIDUAL INCOME

11–35. Division A of the Emry Company generated a segment margin of $522,567 for the year 2004 and the amount invested in the division was $2,778,450. The company's required rate of return is 18 percent.

Required: Determine the residual income for Division A.

LO 5: DETERMINE RESIDUAL INCOME

11–36. Central Division of the Craft Company generated a segment margin of $244,765 for the year 2004 and the amount invested in the division was $1,335,500. The company's required rate of return is 17 percent.

Required: Determine the residual income for the Central Division.

LO 2, 4, & 5: DETERMINE AND INTERPRET RETURN ON INVESTMENT AND RESIDUAL INCOME

11–37. The following information is available for the three divisions of the Top Company:

Amount invested in each division:	
Division D	$7,555,000
Division E	$5,995,000
Division F	$3,082,000
Segment margin of each division:	
Division D	$1,133,250
Division E	$ 911,240
Division F	$ 493,120

The required rate of return for the company is 14 percent.

Required:

    a. Determine the return on investment for each division.
    b. Determine the residual income for each division.
    c. Rank the three divisions assuming they are considered profit centers.
    d. Rank the three divisions assuming they are considered investment centers and performance is evaluated based on return on investment.
    e. Rank the three divisions assuming they are considered investment centers and performance is evaluated based on residual income.
    f. Why do some of the rankings for parts c, d, and e differ?

LO 2, 4, & 5: DETERMINE AND INTERPRET RETURN ON INVESTMENT AND RESIDUAL INCOME

11–38. The following information is available for the three divisions of the Slick Company:

Amount invested in each division:	
Division 1	$1,155,000
Division 2	$3,988,000
Division 3	$3,080,000
Segment margin of each division:	
Division 1	$196,350
Division 2	$634,092
Division 3	$492,800

The required rate of return for the company is 15 percent.

Required:

a. Determine the return on investment for each division.
b. Determine the residual income for each division.
c. Rank the three divisions assuming they are considered profit centers.
d. Rank the three divisions assuming they are considered investment centers and performance is evaluated based on return on investment.
e. Rank the three divisions assuming they are considered investment centers and performance is evaluated based on residual income.
f. Why do some of the rankings for parts c, d, and e differ?

LO 2, 4, & 5: DETERMINE AND INTERPRET RETURN ON INVESTMENT AND RESIDUAL INCOME

11–39. The following information is available for the three divisions of the Kenyon Company:

Amount invested in each division:	
Division H	$5,188,000
Division I	$2,588,000
Division J	$6,386,000
Segment margin of each division:	
Division H	$ 933,840
Division I	$ 491,720
Division J	$1,136,708

The required rate of return for the company is 16 percent.

Required:

a. Determine the return on investment for each division.
b. Determine the residual income for each division.
c. Rank the three divisions assuming they are considered profit centers.
d. Rank the three divisions assuming they are considered investment centers and performance is evaluated based on return on investment.
e. Rank the three divisions assuming they are considered investment centers and performance is evaluated based on residual income.
f. Why do some of the rankings for parts c, d, and e differ?

LO 2 & 4: DETERMINE AND INTERPRET RETURN ON INVESTMENT

11–40. The following information is available for the three divisions of the Planet Company:

Amount invested in each division:	
Automotive Division	$1,235,000
Industrial Division	$2,005,000
Consumer Division	$6,022,000
Segment margin of each division:	
Automotive Division	$202,540
Industrial Division	$332,830
Consumer Division	$963,520

The required rate of return for the company is 14 percent. The company uses return on investment to evaluate segment performance.

The company is considering acquiring an automotive parts manufacturing company that is expected to provide income of $36,450. The acquisition would require an investment of $225,000. Although the prospective acquisition would fit nicely into the Automotive Division's operation, the Automotive Division's manager has voiced considerable reservations. He believes it would not be in the company's best interest to acquire the new segment.

The manager of the Industrial Division concurs with the Automotive Division manager. Oddly enough, the Consumer Division manager not only thinks the acquisition is a good idea, but has volunteered to accept it in her division.

Required:

    a. Determine the return on investment for each division.

    b. Do you feel that it is in the company's best interest to acquire the automotive parts manufacturer? Explain your answer.

    c. Why are the Automotive and Industrial Division managers reluctant to recommend the acquisition?

    d. Why would the Consumer Division manager volunteer to accept the proposed acquisition into her division?

LO 2 & 5: DETERMINE AND INTERPRET RESIDUAL INCOME

11–41. Refer to the information in problem 11–40.

Required: Explain how each of the managers' feelings about the acceptability of the proposed acquisition would differ if the company used residual income to evaluate segment performance instead of return on investment.

Glossary of Accounting Terms in Introduction to Management Accounting

accounting rate of return The rate of return for a capital project based on the anticipated increase in accounting operating income due to the project, relative to the amount of capital investment required. (p. M–223)

activity-based costing (ABC) A technique to allocate indirect cost to cost objects based on activities that cause the cost to occur. It is more accurate than traditional cost allocation. (p. M–99)

actual cost system System in which product cost reflects actual direct material cost, actual direct labor cost, and actual overhead cost. (p. M–72, M–97)

administrative cost All costs incurred by a company that are not product costs or selling costs. The cost of areas that provide support to the product and selling areas such as the cost of accounting, finance, employee relations, and executive functions. (p. M–20)

allocation base An amount associated with cost objects that can be used to proportionately distribute manufacturing overhead costs to each cost object. (p. M–71, M–97)

annuity A stream of equal periodic cash flows. (p. M–231)

balanced scorecard An integrated set of performance measures organized around four distinct perspectives—financial, customer, internal, and innovation and learning. (p. M–372)

bill of materials A listing of the quantity and description of each item of direct material used to manufacture an individual product. (p. M–314)

blended cost of capital Another name for the weighted average cost of capital. (p. M–210)

bottom-up budgeting A budget initially prepared by lower-level managers and employees. (p. M–265)

breakeven Occurs when a company generates neither a profit nor a loss. (p. M–153)

break-even point The sales required to achieve breakeven. This can be expressed either in sales dollars or in the number of units sold. (p. M–153)

budget performance report The evaluation instrument used to evaluate a manager's performance to budget. (p. M–286)

budgeted balance sheet A presentation of estimated assets, liabilities, and owners' equity at the end of the budgeted period. (p. M–261)

budgeted income statement Shows the expected revenues, expenses, and income for the period covered by the operating budget. (p. M–261)

budgeted statement of cash flows A statement of a company's expected sources and uses of cash during the period covered by the operating budget. (p. M–262)

business segment A part of a company managed by a particular individual or a part of a company about which separate information is needed. (p. M–356)

capital assets Long-lived expensive items such as land, buildings, machinery, and equipment. (p. M–207)

capital budget The budget that outlines how a company intends to allocate its scarce resources over a five-year, 10-year, or even longer time period. (p. M–207)

capital budgeting The planning and decision process for making investments in capital projects. (p. M–203)

capital investments Business expenditures to acquire expensive assets that will be used for more than one year. (p. M–203)

capital projects Another name for capital investments. (p. M–203)

cash budget Shows whether the expected amount of cash generated by operating activities will be sufficient to pay anticipated expenses during the period covered by the operating budget. (p. M–261)

cash payments schedule Presents the amount of cash a company expects to pay out during the budget period. (p. M–278)

cash receipts schedule Presents the amount of cash a company expects to collect during the budget period. (p. M–276)

centralized management A management style in which top managers make most management decisions. (p. M–364)

common cost Another name for indirect cost. (p. M–19)

common fixed costs Fixed costs incurred to support more than one business segment, or the company as a whole. (p. M–359)

compound interest Interest calculated on the original principal amount invested plus all previously earned interest. (p. M–228)

continual budgeting Another name for perpetual budgeting. (p. M–264)

contribution income statement An income statement that classifies cost by behavior (fixed cost and variable cost). (p. M–149)

contribution margin The amount remaining after all variable costs have been deducted from sales revenue. (p. M–150)

contribution margin ratio The contribution margin expressed as a percentage of sales. (p. M–151)

controller A company's chief accountant, who is responsible for the preparation of accounting reports for both external and internal decision makers. (p. M–7)

cost The resources forfeited to receive some goods or services. (p. M–18)

cost accounting A narrow application of management accounting dealing specifically with procedures designed to determine how much a particular item (usually a unit of manufactured product) costs. (p. M–4)

cost behavior The reaction of costs to changes in levels of activity. (p. M–117)

cost center A business segment where the manager has responsibility and authority to act to decrease or at least control costs but has little or no control over the revenues generated or the amount invested in the segment. (p. M–366)

cost driver An activity used as an allocation base for a particular cost that actually causes the cost to occur. (p. M–100)

cost object Any activity or item for which a separate cost measurement is desired. (p. M–18)

cost of capital The cost of obtaining financing from all available financing sources. (p. M–209)

cost of capital rate Another name for cost of capital. (p. M–209)

cost of debt capital The interest a company pays on all forms of borrowing. (p. M–210)

cost of equity capital   The percentage return required to satisfy equity investors. An important consideration is what equity investors give up when they invest in one company rather than another. (p. M–210)

cost of goods sold budget   Calculates the total cost of all the product a manufacturing or merchandising company estimates it will sell during the period covered by the budget. (p. M–261)

cost of services budget   Calculates the total cost of all the services a service-type business estimates it will provide during the period covered by the budget. (p. M–261)

cost pool   An accumulation of the costs associated with a specific cost object. (p. M–71, M–97)

cost–volume–profit (CVP) analysis   The analysis of the relationship between cost and volume and the effect of these relationships on profit. (p. M–153)

decentralized management   A management style in which lower-level managers are responsible for decisions that relate to their segment of the company. (p. M–365)

direct cost   A cost that can be easily traced to an individual cost object. (p. M–19)

direct fixed costs   Fixed costs incurred to support a single business segment. (p. M–359)

direct labor cost   The cost of all production labor that can be traced directly to a unit of manufactured product. (p. M–23)

direct labor efficiency standard   The estimated number of direct labor hours required to produce a single unit of product. (p. M–316)

direct labor efficiency variance   A measure of the difference between the planned number of direct labor hours and the actual number of direct labor hours for the units actually manufactured. (p. M–324)

direct labor hours   The time spent by production workers as they transform raw materials into units of finished products. (p. M–25)

direct labor rate standard   The planned hourly wage paid to production workers. (p. M–316)

direct labor rate variance   A measure of the difference between the actual wage rate paid to employees and the direct labor rate standard. (p. M–325)

direct material   The raw material that becomes a part of the final product and can be easily traced to the units produced. (p. M–25)

direct material efficiency variance   Another name for direct material quantity variance. (p. M–320)

direct material price standard   The anticipated cost for each item of direct material used in the manufacture of a product. (p. M–315)

direct material price variance   A measure of the difference between the amount the company planned to pay for direct material purchased and the amount it actually paid for the direct material. (p. M–322)

direct material quantity standard   The amount of direct material it should take to manufacture a single unit of product. (p. M–314)

direct material quantity variance   A measure of the over- or underconsumption of direct material for the number of units actually manufactured. (p. M–320)

direct material usage variance   Another name for the direct material quantity variance. (p. M–320)

direct materials cost   The cost of all raw materials that can be traced directly to a unit of manufactured product. (p. M–23)

discounting cash flows   Determining the present value of cash to be received in the future. (p. M–215)

economic value added (EVA)   Almost the same as residual income except that it is adjusted for certain accounting distortions. (p. M–370)

engineering approach   A method used to separate a mixed cost into its fixed and variable components using experts who are familiar with the technical aspects of the activity and associated cost. (p. M–124)

equivalent units   The number of units that would have been completed if all production efforts resulted in only completed units. (p. M–75)

factory burden   Another name for manufacturing overhead cost. (p. M–26)

factory overhead   Another name for manufacturing overhead cost. (p. M–26)

favorable variance   The difference between actual performance and standard performance when the actual performance exceeds the standard. (p. M–309)

financial accounting   The branch of accounting designed to provide information to external decision makers such as stockholders and creditors. (p. M–4)

financial calculator   A calculator that can provide an array of information regarding the time value of money including future and present values. (p. M–236)

finished goods inventory   Products that have been completed and are ready to sell. (p. M–24)

fixed costs   Costs that remain constant in total regardless of the level of activity. (p. M–118)

fixed manufacturing overhead budget variance   The difference between the actual amount of total fixed manufacturing overhead cost and the budgeted fixed manufacturing overhead cost. (p. M–328)

fixed manufacturing overhead spending variance   Another name for the fixed manufacturing overhead budget variance. (p. M–328)

fixed manufacturing overhead volume variance   A measure of the utilization of plant capacity. This variance is caused by manufacturing more or less product during a particular production period than planned. (p. M–329)

functional income statement   An income statement that classifies cost by function (product cost and period cost). (p. M–149)

future value   The value of a payment, or series of payments, at some future point in time calculated at some interest rate. (p. M–227)

high–low method   A method used to separate a mixed cost into its fixed and variable components using the mathematical differences between the highest and lowest levels of activity and cost. (p. M–130)

hurdle rate   Another name for cost of capital. (p. M–209)

hybrid firms   Companies that generate revenue from both providing services and selling products. (p. M–35)

ideal standard   A standard that is attainable only under perfect conditions. (p. M–310)

imposed budget   A budget in which upper management sets figures for operating activities that the rest of the company rarely, if ever, can negotiate. (p. M–265)

incremental budgeting   The process of using the prior year's budget or the company's actual results to build the new operating budget. (p. M–264)

indirect cost   A cost that supports more than one cost object. (p. M–19)

indirect fixed costs   Another name for common fixed costs. (p. M–359)

indirect labor   The labor incurred in support of multiple cost objects. (p. M–26)

indirect manufacturing cost   Another name for manufacturing overhead cost. (p, M–26)

indirect materials   Materials consumed in support of multiple cost objects. (p. M–26)

Industrial Revolution   A term used to describe the transition in the United States from an agricultural-based economy to a manufacturing-based economy. (p. M–8)

Institute of Management Accountants (IMA)   The leading professional organization devoted to management accounting. The IMA provides similar professional support to management accountants as the AICPA provides to financial accountants. (p. M–9)

internal rate of return (IRR)   The calculated expected percentage return promised by a proposed capital project. (p. M–220)

inventoriable costs   Another name for product cost. (p. M–19)

investment center   A business segment that is evaluated based on the amount of profit generated relative to the amount invested in the segment. (p. M–367)

job cost sheet   A document that tracks the cost of products and organizes and summarizes the cost information for each job. (p. M–64)

job order costing   A costing method that accumulates cost by a single unit or batch of units. (p. M–62)

just-in-time (JIT)   A philosophy that eliminates all unnecessary inventory and limits the use of company resources until they are absolutely needed to fulfill customer demand. (p. M–375)

labor time ticket   A document used to track the amount of time each employee works on a particular production job or a particular task in the factory. (p. M–68)

lead time   The time that passes from the time an order is received until the product is complete and ready for shipment. (p. M–376)

least-squares method   Another name for regression analysis. (p. M–132)

linear regression analysis   Another name for regression analysis. (p. M–133)

management accounting   The branch of accounting designed to provide information to internal economic decision makers (managers). (p. M–4)

management by exception   The process of focusing management attention on areas where actual performance deviates from the preestablished standards. (p. M–310)

managerial accounting   Another name for management accounting. (p. M–4)

manufacturing overhead   All activities involved in the manufacture of products besides direct materials or direct labor. (p. M–26)

manufacturing overhead allocation   The process of assigning or allotting an amount of manufacturing overhead cost to each unit of product produced based on some reasonable basis of distribution. (p. M–96)

manufacturing overhead cost   All costs associated with the operation of the manufacturing facility besides direct materials cost and direct labor cost. It is composed entirely of indirect manufacturing cost incurred to support multiple cost objects. (p. M–23)

master budget   Another name for operating budget. (p. M–256)

master operating budget   Another name for operating budget. (p. M–256)

materials requisition   A formal request for material to be transferred from the raw materials storage area to production. (p. M–67)

material stores   Another name for raw materials inventory. (p. M–24)

mission statement   A summary of the main goals of the organization. (p. M–205)

mixed cost   An individual cost that has both a fixed cost and a variable cost component. (p. M–123)

net cash flow   Cash inflow less cash outflow. (p. M–214)

net present value (NPV)   The present value of all cash inflows associated with a proposed capital project minus the present value of all cash outflows associated with the proposed capital project. (p. M–215)

normal cost system   System in which product cost reflects actual direct material cost, actual direct labor cost, and estimated overhead costs. (p. M–72, M–97)

operating budget   The budget that plans a company's routine day-to-day business activities for one to five years. (p. M–207)

operating budget   A budget for a specific period, usually one to five years, that establishes who is responsible for the day-to-day operation of a business during that time. (p. M–256)

opportunity cost   The benefit given up because one alternative is chosen over another. (p. M–187)

organizational goals   The core beliefs and values of the company. They outline why the organization exists and are a combination of financial and nonfinancial goals. (p. M–204)

outsourcing   Buying services, products, or components of products instead of producing them. (p. M–184)

overapplied manufacturing overhead   When more manufacturing overhead cost is applied to production than actual manufacturing costs incurred. (p. M–73)

overhead   In a manufacturing company, another name for manufacturing overhead cost; in a service type business, the indirect service cost. (p. M–26)

participative budget   A budget in which managers and employees at many levels of the company are involved in setting the performance standards and preparing the budget. (p. M–266)

payback period   A capital budgeting technique that measures the length of time a capital project must generate positive cash flows that equal the original investment in the project. (p. M–222)

performance to budget   A process of evaluating managers and employees based on how they perform against the budget. (p. M–285)

period costs   All costs incurred by a company that are not considered product cost. Includes selling and administrative cost. (p. M–19)

perpetual budgeting   The budgeting approach of updating the budget every month. (p. M–264)

practical standard   A standard that allows for normal, recurring inefficiencies. (p. M–311)

predetermined overhead application rate   An overhead allocation rate calculated using estimated annual manufacturing overhead cost and the annual estimated amount for the allocation base. (p. M–72, M–97)

present value   The amount future cash flows are worth today based on an appropriate interest rate (p. M–231)

process costing   A method of allocating manufacturing cost to products to determine an average cost per unit. (p. M–63)

product cost   The cost of the various products a company sells. (p. M–19)

production budget   Details the cost and number of units that must be produced by a manufacturer to meet the sales forecast and the desired ending inventory. (p. M–260)

profit center   A business segment in which the manager has the responsibility and authority to act to increase revenue and decrease or at least control costs, but has little or no control over the amount invested in the segment. (p. M–366)

profitability index   A method used to rank acceptable proposed capital projects. (p. M–219)

purchase order   A formal document used to order material from a vendor. (p. M–66)

purchase requisition A request form that lists the quantity and description of the materials needed. (p. M-65)

purchases budget Details the cost and number of units that must be purchased by a merchandiser to meet the sales forecast and the desired ending inventory. (p. M-260)

purchasing department A specialized department that purchases all the goods required by a company. (p. M-66)

qualitative factors Factors that cannot be measured by numbers—they must be described in words. (p. M-177)

quantitative factors Factors that can be measured by numbers. (p. M-177)

raw materials inventory Materials that have been purchased but have not yet entered the production process. (p. M-24)

real rate of return Another name for internal rate of return. (p. M-220)

receiving report A document that indicates the quantity of each item received. (p. M-66)

regression analysis A method used to separate a mixed cost into its fixed and variable components using complex mathematical formulas. (p. M-132)

relevant benefit A benefit (a revenue or cash inflow) that is pertinent to a particular decision. A future benefit that differs between alternatives. (p. M-177)

relevant cost A cost or outflow that is pertinent to a particular decision. A future cost that differs between alternatives. (p. M-177)

relevant costing The process of determining which dollar inflows and outflows pertain to a particular management decision. (p. M-177)

relevant information Information that is pertinent to a particular decision in that it has a bearing on which decision alternative is preferable. (p. M-177)

relevant net cash flows Future net cash flows that differ between or among the alternatives being considered. (p. M-214)

relevant range The range of activity within which cost behavior assumptions are valid. (p. M-121)

required rate of return Another name for cost of capital. (p. M-209)

residual income The amount by which a segment's actual income exceeds the income needed to meet a company's required rate of return. (p. M-370)

return on investment (ROI) The percentage return generated by an investment in a business or a business segment. (p. M-368)

revenue center A business segment in which the manager has responsibility and authority to act to increase revenues but has little or no control over costs and the amount invested in the segment. (p. M-366)

rolling budget Another name for perpetual budget. (p. M-264).

sales budget Details the expected sales revenue from a company's primary operating activities during a certain time period. (p. M-260)

sales forecast The prediction of sales for the period covered by the operating budget. (p. M-260, M-268)

scarce resources A term describing the limited amount of money a company has to invest in capital projects. (p. M-213)

scatter graph approach A method used to separate a mixed cost into its fixed and variable components by plotting historical activity and cost data to determine how a cost relates to various levels of activity. (p. M-124)

scientific management A management philosophy based on the notion that factories were run by machines—some mechanical and some human. Scientific management experts believed they could improve production efficiency by establishing standards of performance for workers. (p. M-8)

segment income statement An income statement prepared for a business segment. (p. M-357)

segment margin The amount of income that pertains to a particular segment. (p. M-357)

segment reports Reports that provide information pertaining to a particular business segment. (p. M-357)

selling and administrative expense budget Calculates all costs other than the cost of product or services required to support a company's forecasted sales. (p. M-261)

selling cost The cost of locating customers, attracting customers, convincing customers to buy, and the cost of necessary paperwork to document and record sales. (p. M-19)

sensitivity analysis A technique used to determine the effect on cost–volume–profit when changes are made in the selling price, cost structure (variable and/or fixed), and volume used in the CVP calculations. Also called "what if" analysis. (p. M-158)

service department A business segment responsible for secondary (support) functions. Service departments provide service to the main business operations and to other service departments. (p. M-362)

setup time The time it takes to prepare manufacturing equipment for the production of particular products. (p. M-376)

simple interest Interest calculated on the original principal amount invested only. (p. M-227)

special order An order that is outside a company's normal scope of business activity. (p. M-182)

standard A preestablished benchmark for desirable performance. (p. M-309)

standard cost system A system in which cost standards are set after careful analysis and then used to evaluate actual performance. (p. M-309)

standard costing The process of setting cost performance goals that benchmark acceptable performance and then using these cost goals to evaluate performance. (p. M-308)

standard fixed manufacturing overhead rate The rate used to apply fixed manufacturing overhead to units of manufactured product. (p. M-318)

standard variable manufacturing overhead rate The rate used to apply variable manufacturing overhead to units of manufactured product. (p. M-317)

strategic plan A long-range plan that sets forth the actions a company will take to attain its organizational goals. (p. M-205)

sunk costs A past cost that cannot be changed by current or future actions. (p. M-177)

throughput time The time that passes from the time a unit of product enters the production process until it emerges as a finished product. (p. M-376)

time-adjusted rate of return Another name for internal rate of return. (p. M-220)

time value of money The interest-earning potential of cash. (p. M-182)

time value of money The increase in the value of cash over time due to investment income. (p. M-215)

top-down budgeting A budget prepared by top managers in a company. (p. M-265)

traceable fixed costs Another name for direct fixed costs. (p. M-359)

treasurer The corporate officer who is responsible for cash and credit management and in charge of obtaining external financing and making investments for the company. (p. M-7)

underapplied manufacturing overhead When less manufacturing overhead cost is applied to production than actual manufacturing overhead costs incurred. (p. M-73)

unfavorable variance The difference between actual performance and standard performance when the actual performance falls below the standard. (p. M–309)

unscheduled downtime The amount of time production equipment is out of service due to unscheduled repairs and maintenance. (p. M–376)

value based management (VBM) A mechanism by which managers can make strategic and tactical decisions that serve to maximize the long-term value of an organization. (p. M–11)

variable costs Costs that change in total proportionately with changes in the level of activity. (p. M–118)

variable manufacturing overhead efficiency variance A measure of the variable manufacturing overhead cost attributable to the difference between the planned and actual direct labor hours worked. (p. M–326)

variable manufacturing overhead spending variance The difference between how much was actually spent on vari-able manufacturing overhead and the amount that should have been spent based on the actual direct labor hours worked. (p. M–327)

variance The difference between the amount budgeted and the actual amount. (p. M–286)

variance The difference between actual performance and the standard. (p. M–309)

weighted average cost of capital The combined cost of debt financing and equity financing. (p. M–210)

work-in-process inventory Products that have entered the production process but have not yet been completed. (p. M–24)

zero-based budgeting A process of budgeting in which managers start from scratch, or zero, when preparing a new budget. (p. M–265)

zero defects Describes the concept of products that are completely free of imperfections. (p. M–375)

Company Index: Management Accounting

Page numbers followed by *f* indicate figures.

Subject Index: Management Accounting

Page numbers followed by *f* indicate figures.